What they're saying about

The Complete Guide to Bed & Breakfasts, Inns & Guesthouses ...

... all necessary information about facilities, prices, pets, children, amenities, credit cards and the like. Like France's Michelin ...

— New York Times

Definitive and worth the room in your reference library.

— Los Angeles Times

... innovative and useful ...

—Washington Post

A must for the adventurous ... who still like the Hobbity creature comforts.

— St. Louis Post-Dispatch

What has long been overdue: a list of the basic information of where, how much and what facilities are offered at the inns and guesthouses.

— San Francisco Examiner

Standing out from the crowd for its thoroughness and helpful cross-indexing ...

—Chicago Sun Times

A quaint, charming and economical way to travel—all in one book.

— Waldenbooks (and USA Today)

Little descriptions provide all the essentials: romance, historical landmarks, golf/fishing, gourmet food, or, just as important, low prices. Take your pick!

— National Motorist

For those travelling by car, lodging is always a main concern ... The Complete Guide to Bed & Breakfasts, Inns & Guesthouses provides listings and descriptions of more than 2,500 inns.

— Minneapolis Star & Tribune

... the most complete compilation of bed and breakfast data ever published.

—Denver Post

Unique and delightful inns ...

— Detroit Free Press

THE COMPLETE GUIDE TO

BED &
BREAKFASTS,
INNS & GUESTHOUSES

IN THE UNITED STATES, CANADA, & WORLDWIDE

PAMELA LANIER

YAHOO! **Internet Life's Gold Star Sites:** **BEST BED & BREAKFAST GUIDE**

Pamela Lanier's www. TravelGuideS.com

"Cozy and charming, a bed-and-breakfast inn can be a refreshing change of pace from staying in a hotel. Whatever your destination, Pamela Lanier's site covers small inns around the world with a personal touch. Besides searching by geography, you can specify whether you're looking for a family place or a romantic getaway, select such amenities as historic locale or vegetarian food, and even limit your choice to B&Bs that you can book online. Most inn pages feature a photo and links to a map. Some even tell you which room is the best in the house, so you know what to ask for.**"**

Visit our websites: www.LanierBB.com
www.TravelGuideS.com
Email: lanier@TravelGuideS.com

Other Books By Pamela Lanier

Bed and Breakfast, Australia's Best
All-Suite Hotel Guide
Elegant Small Hotels
Elegant Hotels—Pacific Rim
Condo Vacations: The Complete Guide
Family Travel & Resorts
Golf Resorts: The Complete Guide
22 Days in Alaska
Cinnamon Mornings & Chocolate Dreams

The information in this book was supplied in large part by the inns themselves and is subject to change without notice. We strongly recommend that you call ahead to verify the information presented here before making final plans or reservations. The author and publisher make no representation that this book is absolutely accurate or complete. Errors and omissions, whether typographical, clerical, or otherwise, may sometimes occur herein. The inns in this directory are members of Bed and Breakfasts, Inns and Guesthouses International (BBIGI), one of the largest membership organizations serving independent lodgings worldwide.

The information about the properties in this publication is intended for personal use only. Any and all commercial use of the information in this publication is strictly prohibited.

For further information, please contact:
    The Complete Guide to Bed & Breakfasts,
        Inns and Guesthouses
    PO Box D
    Petaluma, CA 94953

© 2009 by Lanier Publishing Int., Ltd.
All rights reserved. Published 2006

2009 edition. First printing – 1982

ISBN 1-58008-969-0

Distributed to the book trade by:
    Ten Speed Press
    P.O. Box 7123
    Berkeley, CA 94707
    website: www.tenspeed.com   tel. 1-800-841-2665

Cover by Laura Lamar

Typeset by John Richards

Printed in Canada on recycled paper

Dedication

*One of the most basic human rights is to provide shelter
for one's self and family and to be able to provide refuge
and hospitality in its most ancient sense to others.
This book is dedicated to all those innkeepers who
give so much of themselves in providing a peaceful
refuge and take to heart, "Don't forget to show hospitality
to strangers, for some who have done this have
entertained angels without realizing it!"*

Dedicated to Bob Briggs

Acknowledgements

Corrine Rednour and George Lanier for your help, love, and support—thank you.

Edited by: The Editorial Staff at LanierBB: Shannon Holl, Valerie O'Brien, Megan Reed, Kelly McRae.

To my friends who were so generous with their time and skills:

Venetia Young, Carol McBride, Marianne Barth, Vincent Yu, Madelyn Furze, Rus Quon, Terry Lacey, John Garrett, Chris Manley, Mary Kreuger, Mr. Wiley, Adele Novelli, Mrs. Gieselman (the best English teacher ever), Mary Institute, Ingrid Head, Sumi Timberlake, Marvin Downey, Marguerite Tafoya, Peggy Dennis, Judy Jacobs, Derek Ng, Katherine Bertolucci, Margaret Callahan, Mary Ellen Callahan, Mariposa Valdés, Hal Hershey, Leslie Chan, Jane Foster, Carolyn Strange, Carrie Johnson, Sally Carpenter, Mary Flynn, Karen Aaronson, Fara Richardson, Gillian Pelham, Rachel Cullen, Byron Whitlock, Troy Arnold, Cliff Burdick, Chelsea Patocchi, Ruth Wilson, Janet Jenkins, Megan Cole, Miles Mattison, Stephen High, Lucius Bono, Rafe Magnuson, Staci Van Wyk, Melody Stewart, Russell Rottkamp, Steve Kelez, and Molly Craig.

Special thanks to Richard Paoli.

To the great folks in the Chambers of Commerce, State and Regional Departments of Tourism, I am most grateful.

To the innkeepers themselves who are so busy, yet found the time to fill out our forms and provide us with all sorts of wonderful information, I wish you all the greatest success.

Contents

INNS OF THE YEAR ❧ HONOR ROLL

2008   Devonfield Country Inn B&B, Lee, MA
2007   Tyee Lodge Oceanfront B&B, Newport, OR
2006   The Daughter's Inn, Napa, CA
2005   Amoré by the Sea B&B, Victoria, BC
2004   Cornerstone Victorian, Warrensburg, NY
2003   The Boothby Inn, Erie, PA
2002   Rosewood Inn, Bradford, NH
2001   Candlelite Inn, Bradford, NH
2000   Albergo Allegria, Windham, NY
1999   Black Friar Inn, Bar Harbor, ME
1998   Calico Inn, Sevierville, TN
1997   Legacy, Williamsburg, VA
1996   Chicago Pike Inn, Coldwater, MI
1995   Williamsburg Sampler, Williamsburg, VA
1994   Cap. Freeman, Brewster, MA
1993   Whalewalk Inn, Eastham, MA
1992   Lamplight Inn, Lake Luzerne, NY
1991   Kedron Valley Inn, S. Woodstock, VT
1990   The Veranda, Senoia, GA
1989   Wedgwood, New Hope, PA
1988   Seacrest Manor, Rockport, MA
1987   Governor's Inn, Ludlow, VT
1986   Carter House, Eureka, CA
1985   Joshua Grindle, Mendocino, CA

2009 INN OF THE YEAR
AMID SUMMER'S INN B&B
CEDAR CITY, UTAH

Amid Summer's Inn is a lovely turn of the century historic English Tudor home with romantic decor. Gary and Charlene have been interior designers for the past 35 years and use this experience to make each room highly individual. Gary's exquisite workmanship shows throughout the home with beautiful marble, stone, granite, and tile creations. Charlene's love for design shows as each individual room takes on a distinctive personality and flavor.

The numerous amenities begin with off-street parking and extend to a sumptuously decorated inn. The parlor features an original Rococo sofa and chairs dating from the 1800's. An inviting fireplace accents the arched ceiling that takes you back to days gone by while fresh flowers and chocolates add to the ambiance.

The Inn sits on a quiet, old-fashioned, tree-lined street, two doors from a gourmet restaurant and one and one half blocks from the Tony Award-Winning Utah Shakespearean Festival. It is centrally located between Bryce Canyon, Zion National Park, and Brian Head Ski Resort. A short stroll past the aromatic, award-winning flower garden takes you to Historic downtown shopping and other great places to dine.

Having owned a cake and candy store, Charlene enjoys making specialty candies in her spare time while she and Gary delight in creating new dishes for their guests.

Introduction

There was a time, and it wasn't so long ago, when bed and breakfast inns were a rarity in the United States. Travelers made do at a hotel or motel; there was no alternative. The few bed and breakfast inns were scattered across the rural areas of New England and California. They were little known to most travelers; often their only advertisement was by word of mouth.

But in a few short years that has changed, and changed in a way that could only be called dramatic. There has been an explosion in the number of bed and breakfast inns. Today, inns can be found in every state, and often in cities; they have become true alternatives to a chain motel room or the city hotel with its hundreds of cubicles.

This sudden increase in bed and breakfast inns started less than two decades ago when Americans, faced with higher costs for foreign travel, began to explore the backroads and hidden communities of their own country.

Other factors have influenced the growth and popularity of bed and breakfast inns. Among them, the desire to get away from the daily routine and sameness of city life; the desire to be pampered for a few days; and also the desire to stay in a place with time to make new friends among the other guests.

The restored older homes that have become bed and breakfast inns answer those desires. The setting most often is rural; the innkeepers provide the service—not a staff with name tags—and the parlor is a gathering place for the handful of guests. They are a home away from home.

The proliferation of these inns as an alternative lodging has created some confusion. It's been difficult to find—in one place—up-to-date and thorough information about the great variety of inns.

An effort to collect as much information about as many inns as possible in one book has been overdue. Now that has been remedied. You hold a copy of the result in your hands.

Richard Paoli,
Travel Editor
San Francisco Examiner

How to Use This Guide

Organization

This book is organized with the United States first, alphabetically by state, and within a state, alphabetically by city. The Commonwealth of Puerto Rico and US Virgin Islands are listed within the states. After the United States, Canada is listed alphabetically by province and then city. The Worldwide listings follow, organized by country and within the country by city. Our web site www.lanierbb.com can provide nearby cities and regions.

Three Types of Accommodations

Inn: Webster's defines an inn as a "house built for the lodging and entertainment of travelers." All the inns in this book fulfill this description. Many also provide meals, at least breakfast, although a few do not. Most of these inns have under 30 guestrooms.

Bed and Breakfast: Can be anything from a home with three or more rooms to, more typically, a large house or mansion with eight or nine guest accommodations where breakfast is served in the morning.

Guest House: Private homes welcoming travelers, some of which may be contacted directly but most of which are reserved through a reservation service organization.

Breakfasts

We define a **full breakfast** as one being along English lines, including eggs and/or meat as well as the usual breads, toast, juice, and coffee.

Continental plus is a breakfast of coffee, juice, and choice of several breads and pastry and possibly more.

Continental means coffee, juice, bread or pastry.

If there is a charge for breakfast, then we note it as (fee).

Meals

Some inns serve lunch and dinner or have a restaurant on the premises. Be sure to inquire when making your reservation.

Can We Get a Drink?

Those inns without a license will generally chill your bottles and provide you with set-ups upon request.

Prices

Price range is for double room, double occupancy in U.S. dollars, Canadian dollars, Euros (€), or international currency symbol (¤).

Appearing to the right of the price is a code indicating the type of food services available:

BB: Breakfast included in quoted rate

EP (European Plan): No meals

MAP (Modified American Plan): Includes breakfast and dinner

AP (American Plan): Includes all three meals

All prices are subject to change. Please be sure to confirm rates and services when you make your reservations.

Payment Methods

Not all establishments accept credit cards; however, if they do, it will be noted as Visa, MC, AmEx, Disc or Most CC. Some inns do accept personal checks. Inquire about the inn's policies.

Ratings

One of the beauties of bed & breakfast travel is the individual nature of each inn, and innkeepers thrive on their independence! Some inns are members of their local, state or national inn association (most of which have membership requirements), and/or are members of or are rated by AAA, Mobil and others. Each of these rating systems relies upon different inspection protocol, membership and evaluative criteria. We use *Rated* in the listings to designate inns which have informed us that they have been rated by or are affiliated with any of these groups. If ratings are important to you, we suggest that you call and inquire of the specific inn for details. We continue to find, however, that some very good inns remain unrated, simply because of their size or idiosyncratic nature.

Reservations

Reservations are essential at most inns, particularly during busy seasons, and are appreciated at other times. When you book, feel free to discuss your requirements and confirm prices, services and other details. We have found innkeepers to be delightfully helpful. Please tell your hosts that Pamela Lanier sent you!

Visit our web site — http://www.lanierbb.com

A deposit or advance payment is required at some inns.

Children, Pets, Smoking, and Handicap Equipped

Children, pets, smoking and physical handicaps present special considerations for many inns. Be sure to inquire when you book your room. Whether or not they can be accommodated is generally noted as follows:

	Yes	Limited	No
Children	C-yes	C-ltd	
Pets	P-yes	P-ltd	P-no
Smoking	S-yes	S-ltd	S-no
Handicap Equipped	H-yes	H-ltd	H-no

Bathrooms

Though shared baths are the norm in Europe, this is sometimes a touchy subject in the U.S.A. We list the number of private baths available directly next to the number of rooms. Bear in mind that those inns with shared baths generally have more than one.

When in accommodations with shared baths, be sure to straighten the bathroom as a courtesy to your fellow guests. If you come in late, please do so on tiptoe, mindful of the other patrons visiting the inn for a little R&R.

Manners

Please keep in mind when you go to an inn that innkeeping is a very hard job. It is amazing that innkeepers manage to maintain such a thoroughly cheerful and delightful presence despite long hours. Do feel free to ask your innkeepers for help or suggestions, but please don't expect them to be your personal servant. You may have to carry your own bags.

Sample Bed & Breakfast Listing

Price and included meals
Numbers of rooms and private baths
Payments accepted
Travel agent commission •
Limitations:
   Children (C), Pets (P)
   Smoking (S), Handicap Equipped (H)
Foreign languages spoken
Open all year unless noted

Name of inn
Street address and zip code
Phone numbers
Name of innkeeper

Name of city or town

Extra charge for
breakfast

Private bath

ANYPLACE —————————————————————————

Any Bed & Breakfast   75-95 B&B   Full breakfast (fee)
Any Street, ZIP code   8 rooms, 6 pb   Lunch, dinner
800-222-2222   Visa, MC •   sitting room
Fax: 444-444-4444   C-yes/S-ltd/P-no/H-ltd library, bicycles
555-555-5555   French, Spanish   antiques
Tom & Jane Innkeeper   Closed Feb–Apr

Large Victorian country house in historic village. Hiking, swimming and golf nearby. Old-fashioned comfort with modern conveniences.
✉ innkeeper@anyb&b.com ☯ www.anyb&b.com

Description given by the innkeeper about the
original characteristics of his establishment

Meals and drinks
Amenities

Addresses for e-mail and
web site

Note about International Phone Numbers: When dialing an international number the + sign indicates that you must dial 011 then the number listed. International properties that have a United States phone number will be displayed as 10 digit numbers and you will only need to enter 1 before calling.

Alabama

BIRMINGHAM

Cobb Lane B&B	89-119 BB	Elegant Full Hot Breakfast
1309 19th St S 35205	8 rooms, 8 pb	Cookies in the parlor,
205-918-9090	Visa, MC, AmEx, •	complimentary beverages in
Sheila & Ira Chaffin	C-ltd/S-no/P-no/H-ltd	guest refrigerator, take-out
		containers okay
		High speed wireless Internet,
		free parking, cable TV, air
		conditioned, trolley route, by
		26 restaurants

We invite you to get away from it all in a bygone era of Victorian comfort & genteel hospitality. Relax in our beautifully refurbished 1898 Natl Historic Registered Birmingham B&B and experience a restful night's sleep in one of our luxurious rooms.
✉ info@cobblanebandb.com ❂ www.cobblanebandb.com

FAIRHOPE

Bay Breeze Guest House	155-185 BB	Full breakfast
742 S Mobile St 36533	5 rooms, 5 pb	Snacks, complimentary wine
866-928-8976 251-928-8976	Most CC	Sitting room, library, bikes,
Bill & Becky Jones	C-ltd/S-no/P-ltd/H-ltd	suites, cable TV,
		accommodations for
		business travelers

On the shores of historic Mobile Bay with private pier and beach. Your hosts are lifelong area residents always available to cater to your needs, answer questions and make sure you enjoy our second decade providing the finest B&B service on Mobile Bay.

Church Street Inn	145-155 BB	Continental plus breakfast
51 S Church St 36533	3 rooms, 3 pb	Snacks
866-928-8976 251-928-8976	Most CC	Sitting room, bikes,
Bill & Becky Jones	C-ltd/S-no/P-no/H-no	fireplaces, cable TV

Listed on the National Register of Historic Places. Five generations of antiques. Park at the inn and walk to shops, restaurants, and municipal pier with a park and rose garden. Come enjoy our quaint, historic town!

Emma's Bay House	260-320 BB	Full breakfast
202 S Mobile St 36532	4 rooms, 4 pb	High speed Internet, fresh
251-990-0187	Most CC	cut flowers, balconies,
Betty Rejczyk	C-ltd/S-no/P-no/H-yes	seating areas, executive
		workspace, coffee, A/C.

Experience the relaxing atmosphere and superb amenities that set Emma's apart from other B&Bs. With its spectacular views and beautiful surroundings, Emma's is perfect for romantic getaways, corporate travel, special events and weddings.
✉ emmasbayhou1458@bellsouth.net ❂ www.emmasbayhouse.com

Montrose Hideaway B&B Retreat	150-325 BB	Brunch-style Breakfast
	6 rooms, 4 pb	Beverages and snacks
24437 Main St 36526	Most CC, •	available in the dining room
866-443-3299 251-625-4868	C-ltd/S-ltd/P-no/H-ltd	and self-service areas.
Greg & Mary McNair		TV/VCR, DSL, desks, self-
		service room, videos,
		gazebo, pond, hammock
		built for two, special events

Montrose Hideaway Bed-and-Breakfast Retreat is a unique inn located on Mobile Bay's Eastern Shore between Fairhope and Daphne. Experience casual elegance and relaxation at one of Coastal Living's 2006 favorites, a one of two Alabama Select Registry inns.
✉ gandmmcnair@earthlink.net ❂ www.montrosehideaway.com

Magnolia Springs B&B, Magnolia Springs, AL

MAGNOLIA SPRINGS

Magnolia Springs B&B	149-219 BB	Three Course Full Breakfast
14469 Oak St 36555	5 rooms, 5 pb	Well-stocked guest
800-965-7321 251-965-7321	Most CC	refrigerator is available 24
David Worthington	C-ltd/S-no/P-no/H-no	hours a day, hot tea, evening
		desserts
		Private bath with iron &
		hairdryer, Bedroom
		equipped with fresh flowers,
		cable TV, telephone

We guarantee your stay or your money back! Any B&B will promise you a wonderful stay, but when you stay with us, we will not only meet your expectations—we will exceed them! Your stay is risk free! ✉ info@magnoliasprings.com ○ www.magnoliasprings.com

MENTONE

Mountain Laurel Inn	105-165 BB	Full breakfast
624 Rd 948 35984	5 rooms, 5 pb	Homemade cookies, fruit
800-889-4244 256-634-4673	Visa, MC, Disc, *Rated*	drinks, tea, coffee, spiced
Sarah Wilcox	C-yes/S-no/P-no/H-no	apple cider, hot chocolate
		Sitting room, library,
		VCR/DVD, TV in room,
		hiking trails, hiking sticks,
		guest fridge, microwave

Peaceful getaway in Mentone, 7 acres on a bluff overlooking Little River. Stroll the grounds, hike to DeSoto Falls, relax on the porches. Beautiful rooms, privacy, full breakfast and many outdoor activities. Romantic setting.
✉ info@mountain-laurel-inn.com ○ www.mountain-laurel-inn.com

MONTGOMERY

Red Bluff Cottage	110-155 BB	Full breakfast
551 Clay St 36104	4 rooms, 4 pb	Wireless Internet, plush
888-551-2529 334-264-0056	Most CC, *Rated*	towels & robes, flowers, iron,
Barry & Bonnie Ponstein	C-yes/S-no/P-no/H-no	lighted parking, porches,
		gardens, gazebo

Award-winning B&B in the oldest historic neighborhood in Montgomery. This two-story raised cottage offers panoramic views of the river plain and state capitol. Family antiques and gazebo. ✉ info@redbluffcottage.com ○ www.redbluffcottage.com

TALLADEGA
River Rest, A Bed, Breakfast and Beyond	175-250 BB	Full breakfast
3883 Griffitt Bend Road 35160	5 rooms, 5 pb	High speed Internet, fire pit,
866-670-7378 256-268-0101	Most CC	hammock and hot tub
Richard & Ellen Mixon	S-ltd/P-no/H-ltd	

On Lake Logan Martin, white sandy beach, 6 decks, all king beds, HD direct TV in all rooms, 2 mile view of lake and hills, boat rides, spacious and private, most rooms with lake view, owners are very personable and great food! Y'all Come!
✉ richard@riverrestbedandbreakfast.com ◐ www.riverrestbedandbreakfast.com

Alaska

ANCHORAGE
A Loon's Nest	69-110 BB	Full breakfast
1455 Hillcrest Dr 99503	2 rooms, 2 pb	Continental breakfast in
800-786-9884 907-279-9884	Visa, MC	winter
John & Mary Ann Hanak	C-ltd/S-no/P-no/H-yes	Jacuzzi, den, library, TV & VCR

A Loon's Nest B&B is poised on a bluff overlooking Westchester Lagoon, a local park. One can appreciate views of the skyline of downtown Anchorage, and of the Alaska range with Mt. McKinley. ✉ ALoonsNest@webtv.net ◐ www.aloonsnest.com

A Rabbit Creek B&B and Antique Gallery	109-165 BB	Full breakfast
4540 Rabbit Creek Rd 99516	4 rooms, 4 pb	In-room refrigerator and
866-345-0733 907-345-7500	Visa, MC, AmEx, •	microwave.
Denise Knapp	C-ltd/S-no/P-no/H-yes	Hot tub on deck, library, art gallery and antiques (some for sale)

Voted "Best in Alaska" in Arrington's BnB Journal 2003 & 2004 Book of Lists. "Best Antiques" in 2005 Inn Traveler. Luxuriate in Honeymoon Hideaway, Asian, Safari or Antique rooms. Relax in ozonated hot tub overlooking Cook Inlet. Hiking trail to creek.
✉ rabbitcreek@alaska.net ◐ www.arabbitcreekbandb.com

Alaska's North Country Castle	159-249 BB	Full breakfast
14040 Joanne Court 99511	2 rooms, 2 pb	Fireplace, double Jacuzzi,
907-345-7296	Most CC, *Rated*, •	Alaskana library, 4 decks on
Cindy & Wray Kinard	C-ltd/S-ltd/P-no/H-no	3 levels, hairdryer, wireless
	Spanish and German with a slight Texas drawl	DSL, recycling

Luxury Bed & Breakfast next to wilds of Alaska! Earth Friendly Retreat on quiet, forested acreage. Sparkling treetop mountain & ocean views. Family & Romantic Getaway Suites, fireplace, double Jacuzzi, sunset deck. Gourmet breakfasts. Wildlife. Concierge.
✉ info@castlealaska.com ◐ www.castlealaska.com

Anchorage Jewel Lake B&B	40-250 BB	Full or continental breakfast
8125 Jewel Lake Rd 99502	5 rooms, 5 pb	Teas, wines, snacks & other
877-245-7321 907-245-7321	Most CC, •	munchies
Troy Roberts	C-yes/S-no/P-no/H-no	Large deck, fireplace, sitting room, guest kitchen, laundry facility

A wonderful alternative to a busy hotel. We are 3 miles from the Anchorage International Airport. Airline schedules to Anchorage usually mean late night arrivals and early departures, so take advantage of the extra sleep you will gain staying with us!
✉ info@jewellakebandb.com ◐ www.jewellakebandb.com

ANCHORAGE——————————————————————————

Anchorage Walkabout Town
1610 E St 99501
866-279-7808 907-279-7808
Sandra J. Stimson

95-115 BB
3 rooms, 2 pb
Most CC, *Rated*, •
C-yes/S-no/P-no/H-no
April-October

Full breakfast
Deck, cable TV, freezer, free
laundry, parking, 4 in a room

Downtown convenience with beautiful park and coastal trail. Hearty Alaskan breakfast of sourdough waffles, reindeer sausage.
✉ reservations@anchoragewalkabout.com ✆ www.anchoragewalkabout.com

---

Big Bear
3401 Richmond Ave 99508
907-277-8189
Carol Ross

105-125 BB
4 rooms, 4 pb
Visa, MC, Disc, •
C-yes/S-no/P-no/H-no

Full breakfast
Variety of complimentary
sodas, coffees, hot
chocolates & teas
Log home, antiques, Alaska
art, Native crafts, guest living
room, flower garden
w/waterfall & pond.

Log home with unique antiques, Alaska Native art & exceptional breakfasts—Alaskan cuisine and products, wild berry specialties. Old fashioned Alaska hospitality hosted by lifelong Alaskan and retired home economics teacher, Carol Ross.
✉ bigbearbb@alaska.net ✆ www.alaskabigbearbb.com

Chugach B&B
3901 Laron Ln 99504
866-333-4615 907-333-4615
Betty Husted

105-140 BB
3 rooms, 3 pb
Most CC, *Rated*, •
C-ltd/S-no/P-no/H-no
May 1 – September 30

Full or continental plus
Snacks, juice, sodas, fresh
hot popcorn, etc
Exercise & entertainment
room, lots of conveniences,
e-mail access in Chugach
Room

A stay at Chugach B&B, at the foot of the beautiful Chugach mountains, will be one of your most memorable Alaskan experiences. 15 minutes to airport & downtown. Walking distance to many sites.
✉ info@chugachbbalaska.com ✆ www.chugachbbalaska.com

Glacier Bear
4814 Malibu Rd 99517
907-243-8818
Cleveland & Belinda Zackery

70-120 BB
3 rooms, 3 pb
Visa, MC, *Rated*, •
C-ltd/S-ltd/P-no/H-no

Continental plus breakfast
Snacks
Hiking & biking trails,
restaurants nearby, sitting
room, 8 person spa

First class accommodations at reasonable rates. Luxurious contemporary home 1.2 miles from the airport & 3 miles to downtown. The rooms of this beautiful inn are decorated with a mix of Oriental and Victorian pieces.
✉ info@glacierbearbb.com ✆ www.glacierbearbb.com

Homestays at Homesteads
1711 South Creek, Eagle River
99503
907-272-8644
Sharon Kelly

85-135 BB
3 rooms, 1 pb
Cash, Checks, •
C-ltd/S-no/P-ltd/H-no

Full breakfast
Afternoon tea, snacks.
Relaxing or hiking for the
day? Kitchen privileges
available by request.
Take time to enjoy the semi-
wilderness – on the porch,
infront of the fire or skiing on
our trails.

Surrounded by wilderness, this secluded valley is 10 mi.toward Mt.McKinley (Denali) from Anchorage and 7 mi.from the highway. "Heaven Crest" accesses hiking/ski trails back valley to 2 glaciers, a year-round stream, and when visable, perfect views of Denai
✉ aaatours@ptialaska.net

BIG LAKE

Sunset View
Mile 2, S Big Lake Rd 99652
877-892-8885 907-892-8885
Kathy & Newell Glines

150-350 BB
11 rooms, 11 pb
Visa, MC, AmEx, •
C-yes/S-no/P-no/H-ltd

Full breakfast
Afternoon tea, snacks
Sitting room, Jacuzzis, suites,
fireplaces, TV, washer, dryer,
iron, computer and gym

Come visit our Lakefront Resort between Anchorage and Denali National Park, and you may wish you could stay forever. Everything you want is right here: your choice of lodging in either vacation homes or our Bed and Breakfast, The ultimate in luxury.
✉ glines@sunsetviewbb.com ◐ www.sunsetviewbb.com

COOPER LANDING

Alaskan Sourdough B&B and Wedding Chapel
18360 Bean Creek Rd 99572
907-595-1541
Willie & Lovie Johnson

140 BB
8 rooms, 8 pb
Visa, MC, AmEx,
Rated, •
C-yes/S-ltd/P-no/H-yes
Eskimo, French

Full breakfast
In-room tea, coffee, popcorn
& breakfast
Library, TV in rooms, sitting
room, bicycle

Relaxing & comfortable lodgings with warm Eskimo and Cajun hospitality on the quiet side of town, evoking the era of 1800's mining towns. Great sourdough pancakes. Surrounded by beautiful mountains and close to Kenai River.
✉ cooperlandingsourdough@yahoo.com ◐ www.alaskansourdoughbb.com

Kenai River Drifters Lodge
Mile 48.3 Sterling Hwy 99572
866-595-5959 907-595-5555
Bob Rima, Frank Williams

145-345 BB
12 rooms, 7 pb
Visa, MC, Disc, *Rated*,
•
C-yes/S-ltd/P-no/H-yes
Some Spanish & German

Continental breakfast
Fresh baked goods,
croissants, fresh fruit, bagels,
cereal, juices, brownies,
restaurants near by
Awesome Views, Sauna and
nightly campfire at rivers
edge, BBQ's, Guided Fishing
Rafting, Activities

Located at the Headwaters of the World Famous Kenai River, enjoy First Class Riverfront Cabins with incredible views of the Kenai River and Chugach Mountains. Known for the abundance of recreational opportunities, Cooper Landing is a destination for all.
✉ lodgemail@arctic.net ◐ www.drifterslodge.com

FAIRBANKS

2 Kings Country B&B
3714 Mitchell Ave 99709
907-479-2570
Sylvia King

79-139 BB
4 rooms, 2 pb
Visa, MC, Disc, *Rated*,
•
C-yes/S-ltd/P-no/H-no

Delicious hot breakfast
Accommodate business
travelers, WiFi, TV in all
rooms

Enjoy pioneer Alaskan hospitality. Experience garden setting, four quality, cozy and comfortable rooms, delicious hot breakfast, full kitchen for your convenience, TV/DVD/VCR, Wireless Internet. Laundry facilities, Private secure entrance.
✉ kingscountry@gci.net ◐ www.kingscountrybb.net

7 Gables Inn & Suites
4312 Birch Ln 99708
907-479-0751
Paul & Leicha Welton

50-200 BB
24 rooms, 24 pb
Visa, MC, AmEx,
Rated, •
C-yes/S-ltd/P-ltd/H-yes
Spanish, German

Full gourmet breakfast
Complimentary
refreshments
Sitting room, library, cable
TV/VCR, phones, Jacuzzis,
canoes

Luxury accommodations at affordable rates. Our rooms and suites have private baths with Jacuzzi tubs, cable TV/VCRs. A full gourmet breakfast is included in the room rates.
✉ gables7@alaska.net ◐ www.7gablesinn.com

FAIRBANKS

A-1 Yankovich Inn	85-99 BB	Full breakfast
2268 Yankovich Rd 99709	2 rooms	In the afternoon I offer
888-801-2861 907-479-2861	Visa, MC, •	snacks: pie, nut breads or
Jeanne Long	C-yes/S-no/P-no/H-ltd	cookies with tea. Dinner is
	some German & Spanish	available for $15
		Simmons Beautyrest
		mattress, clock radio,
		television, VCR, store
		luggage, wireless access

A-1 Yankovich Inn B&B, "your home away from home," is located in the hills above the University of Alaska, next to The Large Animal Research Farm. Minutes from downtown Fairbanks, airport, or train station.
✉ yankovich@alaska.net ◐ home.gci.net/~yankovich/

Fox Creek B&B	68-128 BB	Full breakfast
1.1 Mile Elliott 99712	2 rooms, 1 pb	Historical, Quiet, Secluded,
907-457-5494	Cash, Checks, *Rated*,	setting. Sitting room, deck,
Arna King-Fay & Jeff Fay	•	spacious rooms, family
	C-yes/S-ltd/P-yes/H-no	friendly facility.

Modern Alaskan-style home. Located in a quiet, secluded setting in historic Fox, Alaska. Just 12 miles from Fairbanks. Frequent northern lights, aurora and wildlife sightings. Lifelong Alaskan proprietors are your hosts.
✉ pam@foxcreekalaska.com ◐ www.foxcreekalaska.com

Pedro's Hide-A-Way	185-225 BB	Full breakfast
3303 Old Steese Hwy N 99710	2 rooms, 1 pb	Cereal, oatmeal, juice, fruits,
907-389-2204	C-yes/S-no/P-ltd/H-ltd	milk, coffee, teas, eggs,
Patty Gentry		bac/saus hashbrowns,
		yogurt, and much more
		Playground, garden area
		with an Arctic Spa. We have
		movies and gold pans to
		borrow!

Midnight Sun to Northern Lights, catch a glimpse at Pedro's Hide-A-Way! This Bed and Breakfast is a private, fully furnished log cabin available to you and your family for that vacation to Alaska or for a romantic weekend get away!
✉ patty.gentry@pedroshideaway.com ◐ www.pedroshideaway.com

GUSTAVUS

Blue Heron B&B at Glacier Bay	90-192 BB	Full gourmet breakfast in
Quarter Mile Dock Road	4 rooms, 4 pb	sunroom
99826	*Rated*	Tea, snacks, garden veggies
907-697-2337	C-yes/S-ltd/P-no/H-ltd	Sunroom, movie-library,
Deb Woodruff & Charlie Clements	Spanish & Japanese	suites, arctic gear,
	May–early September	binoculars, courtesy van,
		bikes, tour bookings, event
		plans

Blue Heron B&B at Glacier Bay is located in 10 acres of wildflowers with majestic mountain views. Choose between 2 Deluxe Kitchenette Cottages or 2 View Rooms in the Guesthouse. Enjoy the gourmet breakfasts, library, Alaskan videos, BBQ, bikes, garden and more. ✉ blueheron@gci.net ◐ www.blueheronbnb.net

HAINES

The Summer Inn B&B	75-120 BB	Full homemade breakfast
117 Second Ave 99827	5 rooms	Tea & cookies in the
907-766-2970	Visa, MC, •	afternoon
Lori Webster & Mary Ellen Summer	C-yes/S-no/P-no/H-no	Comfortable, spacious living room with Alaskan book collection

Charming, historic 5 bedroom house overlooking Lynn Canal. Celebrating our 22nd year of innkeeping in 2009! Walking distance to sites of Haines, Chilkat Valley Bald Eagle Preserve and Glacier Bay. ✉ innkeeper@summerinnbnb.com ◐ www.summerinnbnb.com

HOMER————————————————————————————————

A Stillpoint in Halibut Cove | 500 MAP | local, seasonal, health-
313 Shoreline Drive 99603 | 11 rooms, 2 pb | conscious
907-296-2283 | Visa, MC, • | Artistic vegetable gardens
Jan & Jim Thurston | S-no/P-no/H-ltd | promise healthy meals.
 | Spring, Summer and Fall | Seafood from our waters
 | | with fresh baked breads.
 | | Guided kayak/hiking,
 | | massage therapist, sauna,
 | | kayaks, meditation, yoga,
 | | retreats, weddings, Internet

Looking for the newest architectural award-winning wilderness lodge in Alaska? Then Stillpoint in Halibut Cove is the place for you! Across from Homer, a peaceful place for people to reconnect with themselves, nature, and a source beyond themselves.
📧 info@stillpointlodge.com 🌐 www.stillpointlodge.com

Beary Patch B&B | 89-210 BB | Full gourmet breakfast
664 Soundview Ave 99603 | 5 rooms, 4 pb | Home-made desserts served
907-235-2483 | Cash, Checks, • | in the evening
Raymond & Coletta Walker | C-ltd/S-no/P-no/H-no | Two common areas: one
 | | with games & media center,
 | | the other for quiet relaxation

The Beary Patch Bed & Breakfast, a gracious atmosphere in a spectacular setting, & offering an experience you will long remember. Guests keep returning for a touch of old world charm. 📧 bearypatch@ak.net 🌐 www.alaska-beary-patch.com

Tutka Bay Wilderness Lodge | 399-499 AP | Full breakfast
Kachemak Bay State Park | 6 rooms, 6 pb | Complimentary coffee, tea,
99603 | Visa, MC, *Rated*, • | soft drinks and snacks in
800-606-3909 907-235-3905 | C-ltd/S-ltd/P-no/H-no | rooms
Nelda & Jon Osgood | Mid-May to Mid- | Stunning vistas, nature trails,
 | September | modern bathrooms, fresh
 | | seafood, kayaking, sauna, hot
 | | tub

AAA 3-diamond rated Alaska Kenai Coast wilderness lodge. Only 30 minutes by boat from Homer, gateway to Katmai National Park. Wildlife, birding, hiking, sea kayaking, fishing for salmon and halibut, bears, whales, sea otters and eagles. Fresh seafood.
📧 tutkabaywildernesslodge@yahoo.com 🌐 www.tutkabaylodge.com

HYDER————————————————————————————————

Kathy's Korner B&B | 75-100 BB | Continental plus breakfast
505 Main St 99923 | 2 rooms | Internet, fax, copier, scanner,
250-636-2393 | Visa, MC | satellite TV, kitchen option,
Kathy & Ron Tschakert | C-ltd/S-ltd/P-no/H-no | vehicle rental and other
 | | amenities.

Our sunny deck is ideal for relaxing after a long day observing & photographing the wildlife, which abound in our valley. You may see both Black & Grizzly Bear strolling up & down the road. And if you are extremely blessed you may see one of our wolves.
📧 kathys_korner@hotmail.com

JUNEAU————————————————————————————————

A Cozy Log B&B | 120 BB | Full breakfast
8668 Dudley St 99801 | 2 rooms | Complimentary tea, snacks
907-789-2582 | Visa, MC, Disc, *Rated*, | & wine
Judy & Bruce Bowler | • | Guests services include
 | C-ltd/S-no/P-ltd/H-ltd | where to go and what to do,
 | | WiFi, bicycles, wood stove,
 | | cable TV/VCR

A top rated B&B in a civilized wilderness. Imagine sitting in a log home in Alaska, looking out on the forest, with a warm woodstove & local delights like blueberry pancakes for breakfast. 📧 cozylog@alaska.net 🌐 www.cozylog.net

JUNEAU

A Pearson's Pond Luxury Inn & Adventure Spa
4541 Sawa Circle 99801
907-789-3772
Steve & Diane Pearson

149-499 BB
7 rooms, 7 pb
Most CC, *Rated*, •
C-ltd/S-no/P-no/H-no

Continental plus; self-serve Afternoon tea, hospitality hour. Catering may be available for fee, advance notice required.
Hot tubs, fireplace, bicycles, kayak, boat, views, Internet, massage, gym, yoga, itinerary planning

Waterfront mini-eco-resort with hot tubs under Northern Lights, glacier views, wildlife, waterfall, garden gazebos, dock. Perfect for a 2 week honeymoon, adventure or business destination. Highest rated lodging in Alaska, AAA-4-Diamond & Select Registry.
✉ pearsonspond@gci.net ❂ www.pearsonspond.com

Alaska's Capital Inn
113 W 5th St 99801
888-588-6507 907-586-6507
Linda Wendeborn & Mark Thorson

99-339 BB
7 rooms, 7 pb
Most CC, *Rated*, •
C-ltd/S-no/P-no/H-ltd

Full breakfast
Afternoon treats, bottomless cookie jar and refreshments. Outdoor hot tub. Tour reservations. Wedding Commissioner. Planning and catering.
Champagne/flowers.

Experience turn-of-the-century elegance with contemporary comfort when you spend the night at this award-winning hillside mansion. Located in Juneau's historic district, everything is a short walk away. ✉ innkeeper@alaskacapitalinn.com ❂ www.alaskacapitalinn.com

---

Aurora View Inn on the Mountain
2917 Jackson Rd 99801
888-580-8439 907-586-3036
Gretta & Bob Wells

154 BB
2 rooms, 2 pb
Visa, MC, AmEx,
Rated, •
C-ltd/S-ltd/P-no/H-no

Continental plus breakfast
Snacks
Cable TV, DVD, robes, sauna room, gazebo, hot tub, trails, microwave

Enjoy full panoramic views of Juneau and the Gastineau channel in deluxe accommodations at the Aurora View Inn on the Mountain B&B.
✉ auroraview@gci.net ❂ www.auroraview.com

KETCHIKAN

Black Bear Inn
5528 North Tongass Highway
99901
907-225-4343
James & Nicole Church

100-225 BB
7 rooms, 7 pb
Visa, MC, AmEx,
Rated, •
C-yes/S-ltd/P-ltd/H-ltd

Continental plus breakfast
Snacks and drinks are always provided. Catered Meal Packages available for groups of 4 or more. Fireplaces, TVs w/ DVD/VCR players, refrigerators, free phone & wireless Internet, spa, laundry.

This affordable, elegant, waterfront Inn was designed for guest's privacy and relaxation. Completed in 2005 its unique furnishings, décor and amenities can only be matched by the finest of hotels. All of the Black Bear's rooms overlook the Tongass
✉ blackbearalaska@aol.com ❂ www.stayinalaska.com

Corner B&B
3870 Evergreen Ave 99901
907-225-2655
Carolyn & Win Wilsie

100-145 BB
1 rooms, 1 pb
Cash, Checks, *Rated*,
•
C-yes/S-ltd/P-no/H-ltd

Continental plus breakfast
Breakfast consists of fresh baked muffins, or Alaska size biscuits, fresh fruit, yogurt and juice.
Kitchen, Living room, private bathroom, queen beds, twin roll-away available. Two TV's, DVD/VCR.

Fully equipped, one bedroom apartment. Completely private. No stairs. Private phone. Two TVs, DVD/VCR. Clean and comfortable. One block to bus. Friendly hosts on site.
✉ cjwilsie@KPUNET.net ❂ www.cornerbnb.com

PALMER
─────────────────────────────

Alaska's Harvest B&B | 100-135 BB | Generous continental
2252 Love Dr 99645 | 5 rooms, 3 pb | breakfast
877-745-4263 907-745-4263 | Visa, MC, • | Snacks in rooms great for
Collette Hand | C-yes/S-no/P-no/H-no | day hikes or picnics
 | | Sat TV/VCR, DVD, Internet
 | | access, WiFi, phone,
 | | kitchenettes

*5200 sq ft home is 2 miles out of Palmer, on 15 acres with walking trails, barn with sheep &
moose who meander through our yard. Wholesome, smoke & alcohol-free. Alaskan decor,
great view of surrounding mountains.*
✉ harvest@mtaonline.net ◐ www.alaskasharvest.com

SEWARD
─────────────────────────────

Angels Rest on Resurrection | 89-259 EP | Cabins have kitchenette with
Bay, LLC | 8 rooms, 8 pb | stove, small fridge, toaster,
13730 Beach Drive, Lowell | Visa, MC | microwave, coffee maker,
Point 99664 | C-yes/S-no/P-no/H-yes | BBQ grill, etc.
866-904-7378 907-224-7378 | | Cabins are equipped for
Lynda & Paul Paquette | | comfort and relaxation with
 | | reading materials, AK DVDs,
 | | fishing poles, etc.

*Experience heavenly relaxation in these charming, modern cabins that sit on the beautiful
shores of Resurrection Bay, just south of Seward Alaska. Wildlife & scenery are amazing.
These cabins are among the nicest places to stay anywhere!*
✉ lanierbb@angelsrest.com ◐ www.angelsrest.com

Bears Den B&B | 135-185 BB | Continental breakfast
221 Bear Drive 99664 | 3 rooms, 3 pb | Coffee & tea
800- 232-7099 907-224-3788 | Visa, MC, Disc, • | TV with cable and remote
Richard & Shareen Adelmann | C-yes/S-ltd/P-no/H-ltd | control, VCR & DVD with a
& Family | April to October | selection of complimentary
 | | movies

*Comfort & relaxation await you at Bear's Den B&B and lodging.With three "dens" to
choose from, our goal is to provide the perfect lodging choice for your visit to Seward.Hon-
eymooners, business travelers and families will find what they need at Bear's Den.*
✉ bearsdenalaska@ak.net ◐ www.bearsdenalaska.com

Bell in the Woods | 75-159 BB | Full, lavish breakfast
13881 Bruno Rd 99664 | 6 rooms, 6 pb | Winter Only – Complete
888-729-5655 907-224-7271 | Visa, MC | dinner included in price
Brian & Leigh Ray | C-yes/S-ltd/P-no/H-no | along with light, continental
 | | breakfast.
 | | Internet, phone, laundry, fire
 | | pit, grill, private bathrooms.
 | | Kitchenettes available.

*Come enjoy one of the finest Bed and Breakfasts in the Seward area, and experience a
pleasant blend of refinement and rustic touches. Bell in the Woods has been serving guests
since 1997. The tradition of excellence continues. Come, be our guest.*
✉ info@bellinthewoods.net ◐ www.bellinthewoods.net

Brass Lantern B&B | 150 BB | Continental breakfast
331 2nd Ave 99664 | 2 rooms, 1 pb | Welcome basket, coffee, and
907-224-3419 907-224-3419 | Visa, MC, Disc | teas.
Maureen Lemme | C-yes/S-no/P-no/H-no | Kitchen, bath, comfortable
 | | sitting area, two cozy
 | | bedrooms and an upper
 | | deck with views of the bay

*Whether you're after holiday adventure or a quiet escape from the world, Brass Lantern
B&B is your haven. Rest, relax and retreat.*
✉ brasslanternbandb@yahoo.com ◐ www.brasslanternbandb.com

SEWARD

Harmony B&B
2411 Spruce St 99664
907-224-3661
Michael and Karen Vander Vegt

125 BB
3 rooms, 3 pb
Visa, MC, Disc
C-yes/S-no/P-no/H-no

Continental breakfast
Cable TV, WiFi, private baths, small deck and private entrances, on site washer & dryer.

Harmony B&B is peacefully nestled in the Forest Acres neighborhood, located 1 mile north of the harbor. Private rooms tastefully decorated with full baths & cable TV. A generous continental breakfast will get the day started deliciously!
✉ harmonybnb@arctic.net ◐ www.seward.net/~kevinc

Trail River Gardens B&B
Mi. 24.5 Seward Hwy. 99664
907-288-3192
Russ Burnard

102-128 BB
3 rooms, 3 pb
Visa, MC, •
C-yes/S-no/P-no/H-no

Full breakfast
Deck and common area

Trail River Gardens is a separate cottage from the host house, located just 50 feet from the banks of Trail River. There is a view of mountains in every direction.
✉ trailriver@hotmail.com ◐ www.trailriver.com

SITKA

Alaska Ocean View Bed & Breakfast Inn
1101 Edgecumbe Drive 99835
888-811-6870 907-747-8310
Carole and Bill Denkinger

99-249 BB
3 rooms, 3 pb
Most CC, *Rated*, •
C-ltd/S-no/P-no/H-ltd

Full and continental plus available
Snacks, popcorn, cookies, candy, nuts, chocolates, mints, snack mix, herbal, teas, coffee.
Concierge, library, luxurious robes, hot tub spa, fireplaces, free WiFi, free movies, guest computer

Western red cedar executive home in scenic setting. Walk to beach, wilderness trails, shopping, attractions and historic sites. Wonderful amenities in casual, relaxed setting, king/queen size beds.
✉ info@sitka-alaska-lodging.com ◐ www.sitka-alaska-lodging.com

SOLDOTNA

Longmere Lake Lodge
35955 Ryan Ln 99669
907-262-9799
Chuck & Leora Gibbons

120-290 BB
6 rooms, 6 pb
Visa, MC, AmEx, •
C-yes/S-no/P-no/H-no
June, July and August

Hearty breakfast
Sundays continental breakfast
Beautiful lakeside setting, fishing, seminar/business groups welcome

Picturesque lake setting, immaculate facilities, and warm service by longtime Alaskan hosts have given our lodge a strong reputation.
✉ bblodge@ptialaska.net ◐ www.longmerelakelodge.com

TALKEETNA

Grace & Bill's Freedom Hills B&B
22046 S Freedom Drive 99676
888-703-2455 907-733-2455
Bill & Grace Germain

120-140 BB
5 rooms, 3 pb
Visa, MC, •
C-yes/S-no/P-no/H-no
Filipino

Full & Continental
Kitchen, sun deck

Bed and breakfast in Talkeetna, AK with a great view of the Alaska range (Foraker, Hunter and Mt. McKinley). Enjoy accommodations at our B&B with spectacular view of Denali, clean and comfortable lodging, and a hearty full breakfast.
✉ gmgermain@att.net ◐ www.gbfreedomhillsbb.com

TALKEETNA

Talkeetna Roadhouse	21-140 EP	Full breakfast
13550 E. Main Street 99676	7 rooms	Breakfast, bakery, soups,
907-733-1351	Most CC, •	beer & wine. Famous
Trisha Costello	C-yes/S-no/P-ltd/H-ltd	cinnamon rolls, sourdough
		hotcakes, strong coffee.
		Private rooms, bunks and
		cabins. Coin-op laundry and
		complimentary wireless,
		coffee, tea and cocoa.

The Roadhouse, built between 1914–17, is one of the oldest establishments in "Beautiful Downtown Talkeetna." Our kitchen is open to the public and we've become famous for breakfast, hearty soups, homestyle baking, genuine frontier hospitality, cozy rooms.
✉ reservations@talkeetnaroadhouse.com 🌐 www.talkeetnaroadhouse.com

TOK

Cleft of the Rock	95-180 BB	Full breakfast
245 Sun Dog Trail 99780	8 rooms, 6 pb	Sitting room, suites, satellite
800-478-5646 907-883-4219	Most CC, *Rated*, •	TV, accommodates business
Bob & Betty Lou Buckwater	C-yes/S-no/P-yes/H-ltd	travelers

Warm, friendly, hospitality. Relax in our clean, comfortable cabins or guestrooms.
✉ bobbettylou@hotmail.com 🌐 www.cleftoftherock.net

VALDEZ

Downtown B&B Inn	45-100 BB	Continental plus breakfast
113 Galena Dr 99686	31 rooms, 21 pb	Afternoon tea
800-478-2791 907-835-2791	Most CC, •	Sitting room, cable TV,
Glen and Sharron Mills	C-yes/S-no/P-ltd/H-yes	accommodate business
	Spanish	travelers

Downtown B&B Inn offers travelers excellent accommodations year-round. Cozy and clean rooms, private bathrooms, and great continental breakfasts. Perfect location for those interested in fishing, sightseeing, and glacier tours in Prince William Sound.
✉ 1n2rs@gci.net 🌐 www.valdezdowntowninn.com

The Lake House	130-145 BB	Continental plus breakfast
Mile 6, Richardson Hwy 99686	5 rooms, 5 pb	Complimentary wine to
907-835-4752	Visa, MC, *Rated*, •	guests staying two or more
John Devens	C-yes/S-no/P-no/H-no	evenings
	Japanese	Sitting room, library,
	June through September	fireplaces, cable TV, wireless
		Internet, piano

This comfortable hideaway overlooking the sparkling blue waters of Robe Lake is located only 10 minutes from Valdez. The view is both grand and peaceful, the wildlife plentiful. Six rooms available for guests. Children welcome.
✉ jhdvns@aol.com 🌐 www.lakehousevaldez.net

WASILLA

Alaska's Lake Lucille B&B	79-155 BB	Summer & Weekends Full
235 West Lakeview Ave 99765	4 rooms, 2 pb	Breakfast
888-353-0352 907-357-0352	Visa, MC, •	Coffee pot with
Carol Smith	C-yes/S-no/P-no/H-no	complimentary coffee, tea &
	German	cakes; complimentary
		popcorn for evening snack
		Sitting room, meeting room
		for 12, lake and mountain
		views, crafting retreats

Stay at home with us at Lake Lucille B & B and let us provide you with the perfect romantic getaway. You're at home with country charm and a perfect location for crafting and scrapbooking retreats. We'll do all the work for you.
✉ Stay@alaskaslakelucillebnb.com 🌐 www.alaskaslakelucillebnb.com

WASILLA

Alaska's Snowed Inn B&B	109-149 BB	Gourmet Breakfast
495 S Begich Dr 99654	2 rooms, 2 pb	Enjoy complimentary sodas,
866-799-5169 907-376-7495	Visa, MC, •	juice, water, coffee, tea, hot
Charlotte Crockett	C-yes/S-ltd/P-ltd/H-no	chocolate, hot cider, and
	Some sign language	popcorn.
		Sitting room, balcony, fridge,
		microwave, lawn games,
		library, fine restaurants close
		to the Inn

The perfect place to stay on your way to and from Denali National Park. Just 40 minutes from Anchorage and a mile off the Parks Hwy. The Inn offers two large suites with private baths, a private entrance, and balcony. Located close to Palmer and Wasilla
✉ snowedinn@gci.net ◔ www.snowedinn-ak.com

Pioneer Ridge B&B Inn	99-159 BB	Full breakfast
2221 Yukon Cir 99654	6 rooms, 5 pb	Self-serve breakfast bar with
800-478-7472 907-376-7472	Most CC, *Rated*, •	fruit, cereal, etc.
Shannon & Leny Cullip	C-yes/S-no/P-ltd/H-ltd	Great room, 360 degree view
	Summer	room, sauna, WiFi Internet
		connection

Whether for a romantic getaway, family vacation, scrapbooking retreats or business meetings. Pioneer Ridge provides you with a home away from home in a setting of casual, Alaskan charm.
✉ info@pioneerridge.com ◔ www.pioneerridge.com

Shady Acres B&B	100-120 BB	Hot homestyle breakfast
1000 Easy St 99654	2 rooms, 2 pb	Wheelchair accessible,
800-360-3113 907-376-3113	Visa, MC, AmEx, •	telephones, roll-in showers
Fred & Marie Lambing	C-ltd/S-no/P-no/H-yes	

Located in Wasilla near Parks Highway and downtown. Surrounded by quiet, serene forest. Warm, cheerful, homey atmosphere, with indoor and outdoor entertainment space. Completely wheelchair-accessible.
✉ lambing@mtaonline.net ◔ www.shadyacresbnb.com

WRANGELL-ST. ELIAS NATIONAL PARK

Kennicott Glacier Lodge	159-259 BB	Continental plus breakfast
Lot 15, Millsite Subdivision	35 rooms, 10 pb	Full service restaurant,
99929	Most CC, •	breakfast buffet, lunch menu,
800-582-5128 907-258-2350	C-yes/S-no/P-no/H-yes	family-style dinner, beer,
Rich & Jody Kirkwood	May 22 – Sept 14, 2008	wine & snacks.
		Sitting room, library,
		panoramic front porch. We
		can book glacier hikes,
		flightseeing, rafting, etc.

Enjoy the awesome beauty of America's largest National Park from the comfort of our first-class wilderness lodge. The Kennicott Glacier Lodge, built in the style of the ghost town, has all the conveniences of a modern hotel, with 35 rooms and restaurant.
✉ info@KennicottLodge.com ◔ www.KennicottLodge.com

Arizona

BISBEE

Calumet & Arizona Guest House
608 Powell St 85603
520-432-4815
Joy & John Timbers

70-110 BB
8 rooms, 4 pb
Visa, MC
C-yes/S-ltd/P-yes/H-yes

Full breakfast
Guests select their full breakfast from our menu and it is cooked to order; there are many choices.
Living room, music room, dining room, patios, porches, library, information on the area

Grand Southwest home, built in 1906. Mission revival theme throughout beautiful house and gardens. The home was originally for the Secretary Treasurer of the Calumet & Arizona Mining Company. It later became their guesthouse. It is now an elegant B&B.
✉ info@calumetaz.com ✪ www.calumetaz.com

CAMP VERDE

Hacienda de la Mariposa
3875 Stagecoach Rd 86322
888-520-9095 928-567-1490
Michael & Donna Momeyer

195-225 BB
5 rooms, 5 pb
Most CC
C-ltd/S-ltd/P-no/H-no

Full breakfast
Complimentary beverages/wine
Sitting room, movie & book library, massage, pool, spa, TV, DVD, private entrances

Experience a magical blend of festive Old Mexico with comfort and luxury. A secluded five-acre oasis cradled by the beautiful Beaver Creek. Located in the heart of the Verde Valley, near Sedona.
✉ stay@lamariposa-az.com ✪ www.lamariposa-az.com

Luna Vista B&B
1062 E Reay Rd 86335
800-611-4788 928-567-4788

150-235 BB
4 rooms, 4 pb
Most CC, •
C-ltd/S-ltd/P-yes/H-ltd

Full breakfast & Sunday Brunch
Snacks, social hour refreshments, dinner available on request for added cost
Pool, spa, library/office, family room, private & common area patios

A secluded B&B oasis offering amenities of a luxury resort including pool, spa, steam room, exquisite meals, happy hour, gardens, creeks & trails with utmost in hospitality. Great location for weddings, reunions and retreats.
✉ info@LunaVistaBandB.com ✪ www.lunavistabandb.com

CAVE CREEK

Sleepy Hollow B&B
5522 E Tapekim Rd 85331
480-488-9402
Maureen Kuka

65-105 BB
3 rooms, 3 pb
Visa, MC, Disc
C-ltd/S-no/P-ltd/H-no

Continental breakfast weekdays -
Full, cooked breakfast on weekends
Southwest veranda, deck, living room, fireplace, TV

A stylish 2-story home with a Mexican tile roof and a full deck across the back with spectacular views of Black Mountain. Enjoy southwestern sunrises, sunsets, and crisp evening star gazing at its very best!
✉ innkeeper@sleepyhollowarizona.com ✪ www.sleepyhollowarizona.com

CAVE CREEK

Spur Cross B&B
38555 N School House Rd
85331
480-473-1038
Carolyn Johnstone

169-239 BB
4 rooms, 4 pb
Most CC, •
C-ltd/S-ltd/P-ltd/H-ltd

Full breakfast
Early a.m. continental,
specialty breakfasts
Jetted tubs, satellite
TV/VCRs, fridges,
microwaves, coffeemaker,
fireplace, outdoor hot tub

Spur Cross B&B offers affordable & unsurpassed luxury in the heart of beautiful Cave Creek, Arizona where a true western experience still exists.
✉ info@spurcrossbnb.com ❂ www.spurcrossbnb.com

CHINO VALLEY

Teapot Inn
989 W Center St 86323
877-636-7721 928-636-7727
Vera & Jim French

89-119 BB
5 rooms, 3 pb
Visa, MC, Disc
S-no

Full breakfast
Pillow top beds, cable
TV/VCR, wireless Internet,
plush robes, library, airport
shuttle

The Teapot Inn B&B is a refreshing alternative for the business traveler, vacationer or a romantic retreat, where you "Arrive as a Guest—Leave as a Friend." Just 15 miles north of Prescott. ✉ info@teapotinn.com ❂ www.teapotinn.com

CORNVILLE

J Bar T Ranch B&B
800-246-7584 928-634-4084
April & Jean Troxell

125-175 BB
4 rooms, 3 pb
C-yes/S-ltd/P-no/H-no

Breakfast fixings provided
Stocked refrigerators
Satellite TV, nature, beautiful
views, patio, exposed-beam
ceilings, Jacuzzi tubs,
swimming pool

Relax in our secluded, restful and quiet atmosphere, where the air is clean, the skies are blue and the sounds of nature are not forgotten. We are on Oak Creek, just 20 minutes from Sedona, Arizona.
❂ www.westerntravel.com/jt

ELGIN

Whispers Ranch Bed and Breakfast
1490 Hwy 83 85611
520-455-9246
Toni & Ross

85-140 BB
5 rooms, 4 pb
Visa, MC, Disc, *Rated*,
•
C-ltd/S-no/P-no/H-yes

Full breakfast
Special dietary needs
accommodated – vegetarian,
allergy-free & gluten-free
foods available
Classroom & Conference
Room, Internet Cafe, great for
corporate getaways!

Close to Tucson and Sierra Vista, worlds away from fast-paced city life. A beautiful Inn with exposed wood beams, loft sitting area and a stone fireplace is a serene sanctuary. At 5100 ft elevation and in a National Forest, the location is unique.
✉ ross@whispersranch.com ❂ www.whispersranch.com

FLAGSTAFF

Fall Inn to Nature
4555 S Lake Mary Rd 86001
888-920-0237 928-714-0237
Annette & Ron Fallaha

109-170 BB
3 rooms, 3 pb
Visa, MC, Disc, *Rated*
C-ltd/S-no/P-no/H-no

Full sit down served
breakfast
Cookies, chocolates on
arrival for 2-night stays,
dietary needs honored (if
needed)
In-room full body massages,
fruit/cheese tray, flowers,
WiFi, movies, robes, small
fridge

Rustic elegance with historic charm & hospitality, the "Best in the Southwest"! Get pampered in Georgette's Suite, the Southwest room, or large family suite (kids 8+ welcome). Amenities, private massages balcony, fireplace, Jacuzzi tub, in room sm. fridge
✉ info@fallinntonature.com ❂ www.fallinntonature.com

FLAGSTAFF

The Inn at 410
410 N Leroux St 86001
800-774-2008 928-774-0088
Gordon & Kim

175-300 BB
10 rooms, 10 pb
Visa, MC, *Rated*, •
C-ltd/S-ltd/P-no/H-ltd
Portuguese

Full breakfast
Cookies & iced tea or hot
homemade apple cider in
the afternoon with choice of
vodka or brandy
Sunny sitting room with
fireplace, quiet garden
gazebo, all rooms with
fireplaces & most with views

A top-10-rated Arizona bed & breakfast. Luxurious, romantic accommodations in historic downtown Flagstaff. Walk to restaurants & shops, or drive just 85 miles to the Grand Canyon. Featured in LA Times, NY Times, AAA, and Arizona Republic.
✉ info@inn410.com ◐ www.inn410.com

Starlight Pines B&B
3380 E Lockett Rd 86004
800-752-1912 928-527-1912
Richard, Michael, Mooshu,
Taz & Baxter

149-179 BB
4 rooms, 4 pb
Visa, MC, Disc, *Rated*,
•
C-ltd/S-no/P-no/H-ltd

Full Gourmet Breakfast
Guest ice box filled with
sodas/water water,
complimentary wine/bubbly
cider for special occasions!
Fireplaces, 14 foot ceilings,
views of Mt. Elden,
wraparound porch, Tiffany
decor throughout, WiFi!

Relax, Renew & Refresh! A top 10 AZ Inn! This Victorian style B&B boasts antique & Tiffany-filled rooms, private baths with vintage clawfoot tubs & a full gourmet breakfast. 3 Star Bed & Breakfast! Rand McNally Editor's Pick for 2006 & 2007.
✉ romance@starlightpinesbb.com ◐ www.starlightpinesbb.com

FOUNTAIN HILLS

Bedlam B&B
15253 N Skylark Cir 85268
480-837-9695
Pam Carlson

105-170 BB
4 rooms, 4 pb
Most CC, *Rated*, •
C-ltd/S-no/P-no/H-ltd
Some Spanish

Full breakfast
Porch swings, outdoor hot
tub upon request, swimming
pool, cable TV, high speed
Internet

Our home is built next to desert wilderness. A 5,000-ft. custom home on cul-de-sac acre. Designed for mountain views. ✉ pam.carlson@cox.net ◐ www.bedlambnb.com

GOLD CANYON

Sinelli's B&B
5746 & 5692 S. Estrella Rd.
85218
480-983-3650
Carl & Patricia Sinelli

95-120 BB
5 rooms, 5 pb
•
C-ltd/S-ltd/P-no/H-yes

Continental breakfast
Full breakfast available by
request, snacks,
complimentary wine
Lunch & dinner available,
sitting room

Casual Southwest living in the foothills of the Superstition Mountains. Short or long term stays available. Host able to teach popular poker games!
✉ sisu1941@msn.com

HEREFORD

Casa de San Pedro B&B
8933 S Yell Ln 85615
888-257-2050 520-366-1300
Karl Schmitt & Patrick Dome

160-160 BB
10 rooms, 10 pb
Most CC, *Rated*, •
C-ltd/S-no/P-no/H-yes

Full breakfast
Coffee, tea, famous pies and
other fresh baked goods. Use
our BBQs for your own
gathering or dinner
Great room, library with
PC/WiFi, birding software,
hiking trails, gazebo, full
gourmet breakfast

Casa de San Pedro B&B is located on 10 acres adjacent to the San Pedro Riparian Reserve and the San Pedro River. The perfect place for the eco-tourist/naturalist to explore and relax. Above all, it is quiet. 90 miles SE of Tucson, only inches from heaven.
✉ info@bedandbirds.com ◐ www.bedandbirds.com

JEROME

Mile High Inn
309 Main Street 86331
928-634-5094
Jet & Liz

85-120 BB
7 rooms, 3 pb
Most CC
C-ltd/S-no/P-ltd/H-ltd

Full breakfast
The Mile High Grill offers an
excellent variety of
homemade food.

The newly remodeled Mile High Inn offers affordable accommodations in the heart of this historic ghost town. Close to all of the activities in downtown Jerome. The Mile High Grill offers an excellent variety of homemade food.
✉ milehighgrill@yahoo.com ◑ www.jeromemilehighinn.com

NOGALES

**Hacienda Corona de
Guevavi**
348 S River Rd 85628
520-287-6503
Phil & Wendy Stover

189-249 BB
8 rooms, 8 pb
Visa, MC, Disc, •
C-ltd/S-no/P-ltd/H-yes
Spanish

Full breakfast
Complimentary beverage
and hors d'oeuvres
Fireplace, patio, living room,
game room, library, gardens,
pool, wireless Internet

Corona murals, birds singing in lush gardens, a sparkling mosaic tile swimming pool and delicious breakfasts all delight guests at historic Hacienda Corona. Central location between Tubac, Patagonia and Nogales makes exploring Santa Cruz County a breeze.
✉ stover@haciendacorona.com ◑ www.haciendacorona.com

PAGE

Canyon Colors B&B
225 S Navajo 86040
800-536-2530 928-645-5979
Beverly Jones

85-95 BB
2 rooms, 2 pb
Most CC
C-yes/S-no/P-no/H-yes

Full breakfast
Snacks, ice tea, hot chocolate
Pool, spa, video library,
fireplaces, AC, refrigerator,
whirlpool tub

Canyon Colors B&B is the oldest B&B in the southern Lake Powell region, continually serving guests since 1996. We enjoy a reputation for providing outstanding service.
✉ canyoncolors@webtv.net ◑ www.canyoncolors.com

PHOENIX

The Honey House
5150 N 36th St 85018
602-956-5646
Jeanette Irwin

89-109 BB
3 rooms, 3 pb
Visa, MC, AmEx,
Rated, •
C-yes/S-no/P-yes/H-no

Full breakfast
Sitting room, library, bikes,
hot tub, conference facility,
WiFi

Historic homesteaded property (1895). Lush acre has citrus grove, antique roses, and arbored gardens. Centrally located near museums, shopping and a golfer's paradise.
✉ honeyhous@aol.com ◑ www.travelguides.com/home/honeyhouse

Maricopa Manor B&B Inn
15 W Pasadena Ave 85013
800-292-6403 602-274-6302
Jeff Vadheim

129-239 BB
7 rooms, 7 pb
Most CC, *Rated*, •
C-yes/S-ltd/P-ltd/H-ltd
German, French,
Spanish
October-June

Breakfast in a basket
Sitting room, library,
seasonal pool with fountains,
hot tub

Charming, private, elegant urban setting. In the company of Phoenix's finest resorts, Maricopa Manor Bed & Breakfast Inn was noted by The New York Times, 11.26.04, "36 Hours in Phoenix," as a "pick" for Arizona visitors.
✉ res@maricopamanor.com ◑ www.maricopamanor.com

PRESCOTT————————————————————————————————

Blessing Retreat
2640 Glenshandra Dr 86305
928-771-1735
Linda Riley

85-105 BB
3 rooms, 3 pb
Visa, MC
C-yes/S-no/P-no/H-no

Full breakfast
afternoon tea and treats
massage therapist, laundry,
hot tub, prayer and
meditation room, library,
robes, & other comforts

Blessing Retreat is an elegant B&B providing every comfort for our guests. Located on 3 acres in the beautiful Williamson Valley recreational area of Prescott AZ. Especially appropriate for prayer retreats or writers retreats. Blue Ribbon baker on site!
✉ blessingretreat@gmail.com 🌐 blessingretreat.com

Gurley Street Lodge
909 West Gurley Street 86305
928-442-0200
Mark Winkler

129-159 BB
4 rooms, 4 pb
C-ltd/S-ltd/P-no/H-no

Full breakfast

A verdant, mountain retreat among towering pines and boulders. Easy mile walk to historic square, restaurants and shops. All rooms are spacious and tastefully decorated and furnished. Located in the slower west side of Prescott.
✉ info@gurleystreetlodge.com 🌐 www.gurleystreetlodge.com

Hotel Vendome
230 S Cortez St 86303
888-468-3583 928-776-0900
Frank & Kathie Langford

99-139 BB
21 rooms, 21 pb
Most CC, *Rated*, •
C-yes/S-no/P-no/H-ltd

Continental plus breakfast
Coffee, tea & hot chocolate
always available. Wine &
beer available in the bar.
Free wireless Internet in
lobby & bar, cable TV,
phones

Hotel Vendome is a charming, historic inn combining the warmth and comfort of a B & B with the privacy of a hotel. Conveniently located in the heart of downtown Prescott.
✉ vendomehotel@aol.com 🌐 www.vendomehotel.com

The Pleasant Street Inn
142 S Pleasant St 86303
877-226-7128 928-445-4774
Jeanne Watkins

130-185 BB
4 rooms, 4 pb
Visa, MC, Disc, *Rated*
C-ltd/S-no/P-no/H-ltd

Full breakfast
Soft drinks & bottled water
are complimentary
Cozy living room with
fireplace, lending library, CD
player, board games & hall
gift shop.

Named "One of Arizona's 10 best B & B's" by Phoenix Magazine, this stately 1906 Victorian home is in the Historic District and is the only B & B within easy walking distance (three blocks) to Courthouse Plaza's restaurants, shops and "Whiskey Row."
✉ info@pleasantbandb.com 🌐 www.pleasantbandb.com

Prescott Pines Inn
901 White Spar Rd 86303
800-541-5374 928-445-7270
Tony & Janet Fenner

100-320 BB
12 rooms, 12 pb
Most CC, *Rated*, •
C-yes/S-no/P-no/H-ltd

Full breakfast
Homemade cookies, coffee &
teas
BBQ, kitchenettes, library,
heating/ac, games, TV/DVD
library, WiFi.

Rated Prescott's best B&B for five years; 11 guestrooms in 3 guesthouses, and an A-frame chalet that sleeps up to 10, all on an acre with Ponderosa pines, Deodar cedars & gardens. Some rooms with fireplaces & kitchenettes.
✉ info@prescottpinesinn.com 🌐 www.prescottpinesinn.com

SEDONA

A Lodge at Sedona – A Luxury B&B Inn
125 Kallof Pl. 86336
800-619-4467 928-204-1942
Innkeeper

189-339 BB
14 rooms, 14 pb
Most CC, *Rated*, •
C-ltd/S-ltd/P-yes/H-yes
Spanish

Multi-course gourmet breakfast
Complimentary Sunset Snacks/hors d'oeuvres, cookies, fruit & beverages, spring water and Coffee 24/7
Guest lounges, fitness center & pool privileges, in-house massage, gift shop, WiFi Internet

"Romance and Intrigue, Comfort and Luxury, Beauty and Character, Escape and Adventure—The Lodge at Sedona—A Four Diamond AAA B&B Inn, has it all." AZ Daily News. A highly rated and recommended Sedona Luxury/B&B Inn located in the heart of Sedona.
✉ Info@LODGEatSEDONA.com ○ www.LODGEatSEDONA.com

A Sunset Chateau
665 S Sunset Dr 86336
888-988-3988 928-282-2644
Jean – Christophe Buillet

189-399 BB
23 rooms, 23 pb
Most CC, •
C-yes/S-ltd/P-no/H-yes
Spanish

Gourmet Breakfast
Pool, Jacuzzi, kiva fireplace, free concierge service, conference room, next to hiking.

A Sunset Chateau sits on a hilltop overlooking Sedona's famous red rock mountains. Spacious 600+ square foot suites start at only $199/Night. Amenities includes pool, Jacuzzi, stream, conference room, fireplaces, 2 person Jacuzzi tubs, kitchens, & more.
✉ information@asunsetchateau.com ○ www.asunsetchateau.com

A Territorial House
65 Piki Dr. 86336
800-801-2737 928-204-2737
Larry & Suzie Galisky

140-240 BB
4 rooms, 4 pb
Visa, MC, *Rated*, •
C-yes/S-ltd/P-no/H-no

Full Gourmet Breakfast
Afternoon tea, drinks & snacks
Sitting room, whirlpool tub, fireplace, deck, outdoor hot tub, wireless Internet, Satellite TV w/DVD

One of the "10 Best In The State" Phoenix Magazine June 2007 Old West Elegance combined with Old West Hospitality. Our Movie Character Theme Rooms give you a glimpse of YesterYear but with all of today's modern conveniences.
✉ info@territorialhouse.com ○ www.territorialhouse.com

Adobe Grand Villas
35 Hozoni Dr 86336
866-900-7616 928-203-7616
Stuart & Ilene Berman

399-760 BB
15 rooms, 15 pb
Most CC, *Rated*, •
C-yes/S-no/P-no/H-yes

Full breakfast
Complimentary beverages, afternoon hors d'oeuvres, fresh evening pastries, Personal Chef Service
Grand room, dining rooms, pool, spa, firepit, waterfall, balconies, fireplaces, whirlpool tubs

Bask in luxury at our private villas and be pampered in our "Mansion Style" master suites. Each guest accommodation includes a variety of premium amenities including fireplaces, private patios, tubs for two, walk in showers and breathtaking red rock views
✉ info@adobegrandvillas.com ○ www.adobegrandvillas.com

Adobe Hacienda B&B
10 Rojo Dr 86351
800-454-7191 928-284-2020
Pauline & Brad Staub

199-249 BB
5 rooms, 5 pb
Most CC, *Rated*, •
C-ltd/S-no/P-no/H-ltd

Traditional Southwest Breakfast
Afternoon snacks
Great room, fireplaces, Jacuzzis, cable, free WiFi, golf course packages, in-room massage available

Sedona's most authentic Southwest-style Bed & Breakfast. Five romantic guestrooms with Native American, festive Mexican, and Spanish Cowboy themes. Spectacular Red Rock and golf course views. Sedona's only B&B on a golf course.
✉ info@adobe-hacienda.com ○ www.adobe-hacienda.com

SEDONA ───────────────

Alma de Sedona Inn	189-305 BB	Full breakfast
50 Hozoni Dr 86336	12 rooms, 12 pb	Afternoon appetizers,
800-923-2282 928-282-2737	Visa, MC, *Rated*	luscious cookies, trail mix,
Lori Reinhold	C-ltd/S-no/P-no/H-yes	Raspberry Lemonade and
		Iced Tea
		Sitting room, fireplaces,
		swimming pool, cable TV,
		small meeting room, wireless
		Internet connection

Fodor's recommended and AAA 4-Diamond status because guests receive luxury, privacy, romance and impeccable service in the warmth of the Alma de Sedona Inn. Voted "Best Breakfast in the Southwest" by Arrington Travel. Wireless Internet in all rooms.
✉ innkeeper@almadesedona.com ◐ www.almadesedona.com

Apple Orchard Inn	125-215 BB	Full breakfast
656 Jordan Rd 86336	7 rooms, 7 pb	World-famous chocolate chip
800-663-6968 928-282-5328	•	cookies served in the
Peg Dohm	S-no/P-no/H-yes	afternoon
		Sitting room, cable TV with
		HBO, Jacuzzis, fridge,
		fireplaces, pool, hot tub

Nestled in the heart of "old" Sedona, the site of the historic Jordan Apple Farm, experience the Apple Orchard Inn's natural beauty surrounded by two acres of pinon pines, spruce, juniper trees, with spectacular views of Steamboat Rock & Wilson Mountain.
✉ info@appleorchardbb.com ◐ www.appleorchardbb.com

Boots & Saddles Romantic	225-305 BB	Gourmet Full Breakfast
B&B	6 rooms, 6 pb	Snacks, Chocolate Chip
2900 Hopi Dr 86336	Visa, MC, AmEx,	Cookies
800-201-1944 928-282-1944	*Rated*, •	Hot tubs for two, private
Irith & Sam Raz	C-ltd/S-no/P-no/H-yes	patios, fireplaces,
		refrigerators, cable TV/VCR,
		telescopes

Unique blend of the old west . . . casual elegance . . . . a romantic journey . . . spectacular views, in-room whirlpools & massages, fireplaces, private hot tubs. Voted Best Customer Service by inn-goers. Ranked #1 in Sedona by Guest Reviews.
✉ info@oldwestbb.com ◐ www.oldwestbb.com

Briar Patch Inn	205-395 BB	Full breakfast buffet
3190 N Highway 89 A 86336	19 rooms, 19 pb	Homemade cookies, tea,
888-809-3030 928-282-2342	Most CC, •	coffee
Rob Olson	C-yes/S-ltd/P-no/H-ltd	Sitting room, library, wireless
	Spanish	Internet in lodge, fireplaces,
		facials, massage, swimming
		hole

One of the most beautiful spots in Arizona. Cottages nestled on 9 spectacular acres on sparkling Oak Creek. Warm, generous hospitality. A real gem!
✉ stay@briarpatchinn.com ◐ www.briarpatchinn.com

Canyon Villa B&B Inn of	199-349 BB	Full breakfast
Sedona	11 rooms, 11 pb	Afternoon appetizers
40 Canyon Circle Dr 86351	Most CC, *Rated*, •	included daily at no
800-453-1166 928-284-1226	C-ltd/S-no/P-no/H-ltd	additional charge. Evening
Les & Peg Belch		coffee, tea, & fresh cookies.
		Sitting room, library,
		swimming pool, golf, hiking
		from premises, and full
		concierge service

Southwest-style inn faces the highlands desert, with unmatched bedside views of Sedona's red rocks. A luxury B&B providing exceptional guest service. All rooms have private patios or balconies.
✉ canvilla@sedona.net ◐ www.canyonvilla.com

SEDONA————————————————————————

The Canyon Wren – Cabins For Two 6425 N Hwy 89A 86336 800-437-9736 928-282-6900 Mike & Milena Pfeifer-Smith	155-175 BB 4 rooms, 4 pb Most CC S-no/P-no/H-ltd Slovenian	Continental plus breakfast Coffee, tea, hot chocolate always available Daily maid service in cabins, planning activities, in room massages available, CD and DVD library

Come and experience pause from the ordinary. Fodor's "best value in Oak Creek Canyon! In spectacular canyon with red rock views. Cozy red western cedar cabins have queen bed, full kitchen, fireplace, whirlpool bathtubs, decks, patios with gas grills.
✉ cnynwren@sedona.net ◐ canyonwrencabins.com

Casa Sedona B&B Inn 55 Hozoni Dr 86336 800-525-3756 928-282-2938 Paul & Connie Schwartz	149-309 BB 16 rooms, 16 pb Most CC, *Rated*, • C-ltd/S-ltd/P-no/H-ltd	Full Two-Course Breakfast Raspberry iced tea or hot spiced cider, coyote cookies, late afternoon appetizer buffet. Spa tubs, fireplaces, TV/VCR or Flat screen TV/DVD, CD players, refrigerator, iron, ironing board.

AAA 4-Diamond Inn featured on Travel Channel's "Best of the Best Hotels & Inns" series. Panoramic Red Rock views. Designed by Frank Lloyd Wright protege. Quiet, romantic, relaxing.
✉ casa@sedona.net ◐ www.casasedona.com

Cozy Cactus 80 Canyon Circle Dr 86351 800-788-2082 928-284-0082 Mark & Carrie Peterson	165-200 BB 5 rooms, 5 pb Most CC, *Rated* C-ltd/S-no/P-no/H-ltd	Full breakfast 2-bedroom & 1 bedroom suites, living rooms, fireplaces, kitchenettes, hiking, golfing.

Fantastic views from ranch-style facility on edge of national forest. Five comfortable rooms, 1 & 2 bedroom suites, with private baths, fireplaces, patios, birding and hiking trails outside the door.
✉ info@cozycactus.com ◐ www.cozycactus.com

El Portal Sedona 95 Portal Lane 86336 800-313-0017 928-203-9405 Steve & Connie Segner	179-499 EP 12 rooms, 12 pb Most CC, *Rated*, • C-ltd/S-ltd/P-yes/H-yes	Full breakfast option Wednesday night BBQ cookouts, Friday and Saturday nights a gourmet dinner is served Spa facilities, all guestrooms include television, radio, DVD, free Internet, and local phone calls

El Portal redefines the bed & breakfast experience. A private retreat of exceptional quality. Authentic 1910 adobe architecture, 1900–1930 furnishings, finest food & wines, and a fabulous location.
✉ info@innsedona.com ◐ www.elportalsedona.com

Grace's Secret Garden Bed and Breakfast 1240 Jacks Canyon Rd 86351 800-579-2340 928-284-2340 Grace Markuszewski	155-175 BB 3 rooms, 3 pb Most CC C-yes/S-ltd/P-ltd/H-ltd	Full breakfast Afternoon tea or coffee, with Grace's delightful home-baked cookies and cakes. Beautiful antiques, bath has a marble shower, private deck, refrigerator, TV, VCR.

In the great city of Sedona, you can enjoy yourself at Grace's Secret Garden Bed and Breakfast. Come and enjoy the quiet lifestyle, clean air, beautiful red rocks and miles of hiking trails.
✉ info@gracessecretgarden.com ◐ www.gracessecretgarden.com

SEDONA

Inn On Oak Creek
556 Hwy 179 86336
800-499-7896 928-282-7896
Jim Matykiewicz

200-295 BB
11 rooms, 11 pb
Most CC, *Rated*, •
C-ltd/S-no/P-no/H-yes

Full Gourmet Breakfast
Cookies and refreshments all
afternoon. Hors d'oueuvres
served from 5:00 to 6:00 pm.
Spa tubs, 1 suite, fireplaces,
TV/VCR, hairdryers, robes,
waterfront & views

Sedona's only AAA 4 diamond B&B on Oak Creek. Luxury, romance & culinary delights await you. A Select Registry Member & Mobil 3 Star rated.
✉ theinn@sedona.net ❂ InnOnOakCreek.com

Lantern Light Inn
3085 W Hwy 89A 86336
877-275-4973 928-282-3419
Ed & Kris Varjean

130-325 BB
4 rooms, 4 pb
•
C-ltd/S-ltd/P-no/H-no

Full on weekends, cont
weekdays
Private baths, TV,
refrigerator, some with
fireplace; guesthouse
sleeps 4

Rated one of "Arizona's 23 Best B&Bs and Homey Hideaways" by Phoenix Magazine. Charming oasis of greenery hidden in the trees facing Thunder Mountain, in the heart of Sedona.
✉ info@lanternlightinn.com ❂ www.lanternlightinn.com

Las Posadas of Sedona
26 Avenida De Piedras 86351
888-284-5288 928-284-5288
Jeff Dana

149-369 BB
20 rooms, 20 pb
Most CC, •
C-ltd/S-no/P-no/H-yes
Spanish

3 Course Gourmet Breakfast
Complimentary snacks &
hors d'oeuvres
Spacious suites with
fireplaces, Hot Tubs, Red
Rock Views, balcony or
patio, Free Internet Access.

Best value at Sedona's newest bed & breakfast suites. Select suites include private hot tubs or red rock views. Gourmet breakfast, appetizers, free Internet & WiFi, romantic fireplaces, plush mattresses, private balconies or patios. Simply unforgettable.
✉ gm@lasposadasofsedona.com ❂ www.lasposadasofsedona.com

Moestly Wood B&B
2085 Upper Red Rock Loop Rd
86336
888-334-4141 928-204-1461
Carol & Roger Moe

145-165 BB
2 rooms, 2 pb
Visa, MC
C-yes/S-ltd/P-no

Full breakfast
A selection of hot and cold
beverages available
throughout the day.
Sun deck, views, TV, phones,
free wireless Internet

Instead of staying at a Sedona hotel, consider our quaint Sedona bed and breakfast with clean and comfortable rooms. Your gracious hosts, Carol and Roger Moe, will enjoy making your stay a memorable one.
✉ moestlywood@sedona.net ❂ www.moestlywood.com

Rose Tree Inn
376 Cedar St 86336
888-282-2065 928-282-2065
Gary Dawson

95-149 EP
5 rooms, 5 pb
Visa, MC, *Rated*, •
C-ltd/S-yes/P-no/H-no

In-room coffee & tea,
kitchenettes
Patios, library, TV/VCR in
rooms, free WiFi

"Sedona's best kept secret . . . " is conveniently located near uptown Sedona. Five affordable, quiet rooms, two with fireplaces. Small, charming and cozy like a bed and breakfast, but with private kitchens. Free Internet access.
✉ info@rosetreeinn.com ❂ www.rosetreeinn.com

SEDONA

Sedona Cathedral Hideaway
866-973-3662 928-203-4180
Kathy & Larry Jaeckel

257-340 BB
2 rooms, 2 pb
Visa, MC, AmEx
C-ltd/S-ltd/P-no/H-ltd

Gourmet breakfast of your choosing
Afternoon or evening snack including homemade ice cream.Gourmet menu for you to choose from.
2 person shower, Jacuzzi, Spa, gourmet diet, sm. weddings, fridge, LCD TV/DVD, Sleep # bed, WiFi

Romantic, serene, red rock private, outdoor setting on 1 acre. Gourmet flexible menu. In-home Spa treatments. Green, WiFi & iPod jack. 2 luxury suites w/in-room 2 person jetted/Jacuzzi tub & separate shower room w/2 shower heads. Near golf & winery. Weddings.
✉ CathedralHideaway@wildblue.net ○ www.sedonacathedralhideaway.com/index.html

Sedona Views B&B
995 N Hwy 89A 86336
800-201-1944
Irith & Sam Raz

230-295 BB
6 rooms, 6 pb
Most CC
S-no/P-no/H-no

Full breakfast
Hot-tubs for two, great views, private entrances & patios, fireplaces, refrigerators, Internet

Nestled into a Red Rock wall adjacent the National Forest is the beautiful property of Sedona Views Bed and Breakfast. With the panoramic views of the rocks, the multitude of wildlife, it's hard to believe that you are only ¼ mile from Uptown Sedona.
✉ info@sedonaviewsbb.com ○ www.sedonaviewsbb.com

SIERRA VISTA

Birders Vista B&B
5147 S Kino Rd 85650
520-378-2493
Johnnie & Audrey Eskue

89-140 BB
4 rooms, 4 pb
Visa, MC, ●
C-yes/S-ltd/P-no/H-ltd

Full breakfast
A vegetarian, vegan or gluten-free menu is also available upon request. Library, garden with a pergola, large orchard, bird watching areas, sitting room with fireplace

A quiet retreat in the country with beautiful views of mountains only 10 minutes away from Ramsey Canyon and San Pedro Riparian Area. A stucco home located on 4 acres with butterfly and hummingbird gardens only 30 minutes from Bisbee or Tombstone.
✉ birdersvista@ssvecnet.com ○ www.birdersvista.com

SNOWFLAKE

Osmer D Heritage Inn
161 N Main St 85937
866-486-5947 928-536-3322
Dean & Sandra Porter

95-140 BB
11 rooms, 11 pb
Most CC, *Rated*, ●
C-ltd/S-ltd/P-ltd/H-yes
Spanish and French

Gourmet and Plentiful
Tea, chocolate, sweet breads, soft drinks, popcorn, dinners for additional fee
Parlor, patio, spa and exercise room, front porch, lawn swings, hammock, social hall for events

Step back in time and let us spoil you in this lovely restored 1890 Pioneer home. There are 11 rooms, all with tubs and showers. Enjoy the great breakfasts with fruit, sweet breads and gourmet dishes.
✉ mulcher85937@yahoo.com ○ www.heritage-inn.net

SONOITA

Rainbow's End B&B
3088 Hwy 83 85637
800-797-8274 520-455-0202
Jeff Chimene & Kay Aubrey-
Chimene

100-150 BB
5 rooms, 5 pb
Most CC, •
C-yes/S-no/P-yes/H-ltd

Self Serve Full Organic
Breakfast
Coffee, teas, fruit juices,
snacks available at all times.
Holistic body work and
massage for people and
animals with advanced
reservation, pet sitting.

Historic, 1920s ranch house located on a working equine therapy facility. Remodeled private guesthouse with porches and fireplace. Mountain-rimmed grassland views with breathtaking sunsets. Convenient to town and area attractions.
✉ lodging@grandadventuresranch.com 🌐 www.rainbowsendbandb.com

ST. DAVID

Down By The River B&B
2255 Efken Pl 85630
520-720-9441
Mike & Barb Hug

85-135 BB
4 rooms, 4 pb
Visa, MC
C-ltd/S-ltd/P-no/H-no

Full breakfast
BBQ, telescopes, pool table,
wireless Internet

Down By The River is a 15 acre property that borders the San Pedro River, within sight of the northern end of the world famous San Pedro National Riparian Area. Sit back on the porch in the evening and enjoy the peace & quiet.
✉ downbytheriverbb@hotmail.com 🌐 www.downbytheriverbandb.com

TEMPE

A Valley O' the Sun
866-941-1281 480-941-1281
Kathleen Kennedy Curtis

50-65 BB
2 rooms
Visa, MC, •
C-ltd/S-ltd/P-no/H-no

Continental plus breakfast
Full breakfast on weekends
Sitting room, close to nearby
attractions, cable TV, fax
available

A Valley O' the Sun B&B, established in 1983, is more than just a place to stay. Located in Tempe, near ASU, we are Arizona's only Irish Bed & Breakfast! Two night minimum stay.
✉ avots@att.net

TUBAC

Artist's Suite
7 Camino Otero 85646
800-255-2306
Trisha Ambrose

115-145 BB
1 rooms, 1 pb
Most CC, •
C-ltd/S-no/P-no/H-ltd
Canadian, French,
German and Spanish

Continental plus breakfast

The Artist's Suite is located at the Quilts Ltd. Gallery in the heart of Tubac. This custom decorated 3 room suite features pieces from the owner's private art collection, designer rugs and custom furnishings.
✉ daryen@gmail.com

TUCSON

A Sonoran Sunrise B&B
9970 E. Buckshot Circle 85701
866-780-5102 520-401-2112
Lynda Hendricks

110-145 BB
3 rooms, 3 pb
Visa, MC
S-no/P-ltd/H-no

Full breakfast

Sunrise in the Sonoran Desert is an experience to be treasured like no other. Enjoy your private time in the morning sipping coffee on one of the patios while listening to the coyotes & chirping birds, and viewing the colors of the sky over the mountains.
✉ lynda@asonoransunrise.com 🌐 www.asonoransunrise.com

TUCSON ──

Adobe Rose Inn
940 N Olsen Ave 85719
800-328-4122 520-318-4644
Marion & Jim Hook

90-205 BB
6 rooms, 6 pb
Visa, MC, AmEx,
Rated, •
C-ltd/S-no/P-no/H-no

Full breakfast
Swimming pool, Jacuzzi tub,
wireless Internet access,
cable TV, fireplaces, kitchen
amenities

Nestled in the Santa Catalina Mountains of Southern Arizona, Tucson offers enough diversions and appeal of the Southwestern lifestyle to tempt any vacationer or business group.
✉ innkeeper@aroseinn.com ◑ www.aroseinn.com

**Alta Vista Bed and
Breakfast**
11300 E Broadway Blvd. 85748
800-947-3037 520-647-3037
Gaila Smith

145 BB
2 rooms, 2 pb
Cash, Checks
C-ltd/S-no/P-no

Full breakfast
Beverages and homemade
goodies
Pool and whirlpool spa,
gardens, spa services,

Welcome to the serene desert oasis of Alta Vista Bed and Breakfast Inn of Tucson, Arizona. Our bed and breakfast is perched high upon a hill with panoramic views and guestroom offering a comfortable casual elegance for your getaway.
✉ altavistabandb@aol.com ◑ www.altavistabedandbreakfast.com/index.html

Bed and Bagels of Tucson
10402 E Glenn St 85749
520-603-1580
Sharon Arkin

85-150 BB
3 rooms, 1 pb
Cash, Checks
C-yes/S-ltd/P-yes/H-ltd
Spanish, German,
Hebrew

Choice of familiar or exotic
foods
Beverages, snacks, hot fudge
sundaes, baked goods
Pool/spa, bikes, in-room
phones, robes, TV/VCRs,
computer/DSL, fax, kitchen
& laundry available

Casually elegant pet/child/senior-friendly mountain view home. Gourmet breakfasts, homebaked treats, kitchen/laundry, DSL use. Pool/spa, safety fence. Birding aids. Near tennis, golf, hiking, dog park. $10/per night pet fee for each pet. Smoking on patio.
✉ sharon@bedandbagels.com ◑ www.bedandbagels.com

Casa de Angeles
4655 W Flying Diamond Dr
85742
520-744-1503
Karen & Jim Liessmann

150-170 BB
3 rooms, 3 pb
Visa, MC, Disc, *Rated*
C-ltd/S-ltd/P-no/H-no

Gourmet Breakfasts
Evening snack
First class accommodations,
private entrances, TV, DVD,
refrigerator in each room,
pool & spa

Welcome to Casa De Angeles! In English that means "House of Angels"! You will find "A Little Bit of Heaven" in this beautiful place in Tucson, Arizona. Come enjoy the homemade breakfasts prepared by your hosts and their hospitality.
✉ liessmann@casadeangeles.com ◑ www.casadeangeles.com

Casa Luna B&B
4210 N Saranac Dr 85718
888-482-7925 520-577-4943
Nancy & Stu Mellan

160-270 BB
4 rooms, 4 pb
Most CC, *Rated*
C-ltd/S-ltd/P-no/H-ltd
Spanish

Full breakfast
Kosher, vegan, other dietary
restrictions and requests
accommodated upon
request
Free WiFi, kitchen, fireplace,
pool, private patios &
entrances, hot tub, beautiful
foothills view

Experience the casual elegance of this intimate bed & breakfast, on 2.2 acres in the foothills of Tucson's Catalina Mountains. Enjoy stunning views of the mountains, sunrise & sunsets.
✉ info@Casa-Luna.com ◑ www.Casa-Luna.com

TUCSON

Casa Tierra Adobe B&B Inn
1155 W Calle Pima 85743
866-254-0006 520-578-3058
Dave Malmquist

135-285 BB
4 rooms, 4 pb
Most CC, *Rated*, •
C-yes/S-no/P-no/H-no
August 15-June 15

Full gourmet vegetarian
breakfast
Guests receive a welcoming
basket of fruit and snacks,
iced tea and chocolates upon
arrival.
Common room, books,
movies games, hot tub,
computer, WiFi, gym,
telescope, courtyard, Private
patios.

This rustically elegant home, Casa Tierra (Earth House), recalls haciendas of old Mexico. The all-adobe home features over fifty arches and includes entryways with vaulted brick ceilings and beautiful interior courtyards.
✉ info@casatierratucson.com 🌐 www.casatierratucson.com

Catalina Park Inn
309 E 1st St 85705
800-792-4885 520-792-4541
Mark Hall

139-189 BB
6 rooms, 6 pb
Most CC, *Rated*
C-ltd/S-ltd/P-no/H-ltd

Full breakfast
Afternoon tea & cookies
Sitting room, fireplace, lush
desert gardens, elegant
decor, many amenities, WiFi,
cable TV, robes

Stylish 1927 historic inn featuring six, beautifully decorated guestrooms and a full range of amenities. Enjoy our lush desert garden. 5 blocks to University of Arizona.
✉ info@catalinaparkinn.com 🌐 www.catalinaparkinn.com

Desert Dove B&B
1707 E Old Spanish Trl 85730
877-722-6879 520-722-6879
Harvey & Betty Ross

125-145 BB
2 rooms, 2 pb
Visa, MC, *Rated*
C-ltd/S-no/P-no/H-no

Full breakfast
Soft drinks, tea, coffee, and
afternoon snacks
Spa (including bathrobes),
phone, common area,
refrigerator & microwave;
coffee center open 24 hours

Welcome to the Old West, where here at Desert Dove you can relax, enjoy and reminisce. Our territorial adobe bed & breakfast is situated on four acres nestled in the foothills of the Rincon Mountains. Walking distance from the Saguaro National Park.
✉ info@desertdovebb.com 🌐 www.desertdovebb.com

El Presidio B&B
297 N Main Ave 85701
800-349-6151 520-623-6151
Patti Toci

120-150 BB
4 rooms, 4 pb
Rated, •
C-ltd/S-no/P-no/H-no

Full hot country breakfast
Complimentary in room
beverages and snacks
Phones, TV, WiFi, some
rooms with kitchenettes

Step back in time and experience the Southwestern charm of a desert oasis with the romance of a country inn. El Presidio B&B is a splendid example of American Territorial, blending the rich cultural heritage of Mexican and American building.
✉ elpresidio_bb@yahoo.com

Hacienda del Desierto
1770 E Rambling Trail 85747
800-982-1795 520-298-1764
David & Rosemary Brown

129-279 BB
4 rooms, 4 pb
Most CC, *Rated*, •
C-yes/S-ltd/P-no/H-no

Continental plus breakfast
Snack upon arrival
Books, spas, gardens, robes,
films, Dish network, wireless
high speed Internet,
computer, printer

Old Spanish style hacienda on 16 acres, next to National Park. A Romantic hideaway with mountain views. Enchanting courtyard gardens.
✉ oasis@tucson-bed-breakfast.com 🌐 www.tucson-bed-breakfast.com

TUCSON

The Historic Joestler Inn
1640 N Campbell Ave 85719
520-885-0883
Janos Siess

99-175 BB
6 rooms, 6 pb
Visa, MC, *Rated*, •
C-ltd/S-no/P-ltd/H-no

Full gourmet breakfast

The first B&B established in Tucson designed as a near perfect example of early "Santa Fe" style architecture. Our lush courtyard garden is shaded by citrus trees and enormous date palms and bursts with the color of bougainvillea.
✉ siessjanos@gmail.com ✺ thejoestlerhistoricinn.com

La Zarzuela, A Bed and Breakfast Inn
455 N Camino de Oeste 85745
888-848-8225 520-884-4824
Cliff Aberham & Lew Harper

275-325 BB
4 rooms, 4 pb
Visa, MC, Disc
P-no
Closed June–September

Full breakfast
Evening Beverages and appetizers served in our Great Room or on the Desert Terrace at sunset
Patios, pool, spa, concierge and travel planning services, daily maid service.

La Zarzuela is small enough to provide you the personal level of service we are committed to, yet large enough for the vacationer to meet new people, if you wish.
✉ stay@zarzuela-az.com ✺ www.zarzuela-az.com

Milagras Guesthouse
11185 W Calle Pima 85743
520-578-8577
Helen & Vivian

100 EP
1 rooms, 1 pb
Rated
C-ltd/S-ltd/P-ltd/H-ltd
Sept–May

Snacks, fresh fruit & beverages on arrival
Hot tub, fountains, hiking, nearby attractions

This Guest house offers 2 rooms with a private bath, 30 min west of Tucson. Romantic private, patios, outdoor fireplace, fountains, kitchenette, Direct TV, VCR, CDs and private phone. All rural in the lush Sonoran Desert.
✉ milagras@earthlink.net ✺ home.earthlink.net/~milagras

Mon Ami Bed & Breakfast
5902 E 9th St 85711-3223
520-444-0807
Patricia Sparks

85-140 BB
3 rooms, 3 pb
Visa, MC
C-yes/S-ltd/P-no/H-ltd

Full breakfast
Fine Dining! Your host, former owner of Penelope's Restaurant, is an award winning French Chef!
Private entrances, refrigerators, cable TV, WiFi, Jacuzzi, lap pool, enclosed patio, gardens, books

Mon Ami B&B, located in central Tucson, Arizona, boasts the best of both worlds. It i situated in a tranquil, residential neighborhood with acres of unspoiled desert landscape that frame unfettered views of the Catalina Mountains.
✉ monamibandb@cox.net ✺ www.monamibandb.com

Mountain Views
3160 N Bear Canyon Rd 85749
520-749-1387
Roy B. Kile

100 BB
2 rooms, 2 pb
Visa, MC, AmEx,
Rated, •
C-ltd/S-no/P-no/H-ltd

Full breakfast
Complimentary wine
Sitting room, swimming pool, cable TV, accommodate business travelers

Mountain Views B&B is nestled on 3.3 acres of secluded, vegetated desert on Tucson's far eastside, with beautiful panoramic mountain views.
✉ Rkile85749@aol.com ✺ www.mtviewsbb.com

Natural B&B
3150 E. Presidio Rd 85716
888-295-8500 520-881-4582
Marc Haberman

95 BB
3 rooms, 2 pb
Visa, MC
C-ltd/S-no/P-no

Full breakfast
Internet access, massage and infrared sauna, music systems, environ. friendly

At Tucson Natural B&B we offer all the comforts of home in a safe, healthy and personal environment. The friendliness, experience in holistic health and hospitality of Marc, your host, will make you feel welcome, and appreciate you as a guest.
✉ bleu5@cox.net ✺ www.tucson-natural-bnb.com

TUCSON—————————————————————————————————————

Peppertrees B&B
724 E University Blvd 85719
800-348-5763 520-622-7167
Ron & Jill McCormick

120-195 BB
6 rooms, 6 pb
Rated, •
C-ltd/S-no/P-no/H-no

Full gourmet breakfast

At the Peppertrees B&B Inn you will find the highest level of commitment to service and comfort. We place a great amount of emphasis on what we feel is important for someone when they are away from home.
✉ pepperinn@cox.net 🌐 www.peppertreesinn.com

Sam Hughes Inn
2020 East 7th Street 85719
520-861-2191
Susan Banner

85-135 BB
4 rooms, 4 pb
Most CC, *Rated*, •
S-no/P-no/H-ltd

Full breakfast
Game room, WiFi, guest PC,
shower robes, refrigerators,
individual heat/cool

If you are a tourist, visiting relatives, or have other business in the Tucson area, come sample the bounty that Tucson and the Sam Hughes Inn Bed and Breakfast have to offer.
✉ innkeeper@samhughesinn.com 🌐 www.samhughesinn.com

**Shoppe at Civano B&B
Suites**
5324 S. Civano Blvd 85747
520-207-2539
Alan Boertjens & Adele
Coronado

75-149 BB
3 rooms, 3 pb
Visa, MC, AmEx
C-yes/S-ltd/P-ltd/H-no

Continental breakfast
Evening treats and gourmet
Tassimo coffee and teas.
Pillow-top beds, wireless
Internet, mini fridge, pool,
tennis, yoga, pilates, facials,
massage, painting

Three exquisitely decorated rooms available in the neighborhood center of the environmentally planned Community of Civano. Also offering yoga & pilates classes, holistic skin care facials and waxing services, massage therapy, watercolor painting classes.
✉ ajb2@cox.net 🌐 www.shoppe-at-civano.com/SaC_BnB.htm

White Stallion Ranch
9251 W Twin Peaks Rd 85743
888-977-2624 520-297-0252
Russell True

242-515 BB
45 rooms, 45 pb
•
C-yes/S-yes/P-no/H-ltd
Sept. 1 – May 31

Full breakfast
Heated pool, hot tub, lighted
tennis, hiking, horseback
riding, petting zoo

This charming, informal ranch gives you a feeling of the Old West. Only here can you find 3,000 acres of wide-open space at the foot of ruggedly beautiful Tucson Mountains and Saguaro National Park.
✉ info@whitestallion.com 🌐 www.whitestallion.com

WILLIAMS—————————————————————————————————————

Grand Canyon B&B
1129 Stockmens 86046
888-635-2488 928-814-0516
Sheri & Del Terry

130-215 BB
4 rooms, 4 pb
Most CC
C-yes/S-no/P-no/H-no

Full breakfast

Grand Canyon B&B is a rustic wild west bed and breakfast with a woman's touch. The closest B&B to the Grand Canyon located at the base of Bill Williams Mountain.
✉ info@grandcanyonbandb.com 🌐 grandcanyonbandb.com

Grand Living B&B
701 Quarterhorse Rd 86046
800-210-5908 928-635-4171
Bill & Gloria Job

160-280 BB
7 rooms, 6 pb
Most CC, *Rated*
S-no/P-no/H-ltd

Full Gourmet Breakfast
Chocolates, wine upon
request.
Wireless Internet, books,
DVD/VHS, fridge, fireplaces,
TV, 2-person jetted tub,
outside sitting.

Our large log home offers country Victorian decor/artwork from all over the world, spacious guestrooms w/private bath & private entrance, hardwood floors, wireless Internet, big parking area, beautiful mountain scenery from a wrap around verandah
✉ job@grandlivingbnb.com 🌐 www.grandlivingbnb.com

Arkansas

ARKADELPHIA

Captain Henderson House B&B
349 N 10th St 71923
866-478-4661 870-230-5544
Vickie Jones

80-80 BB
7 rooms, 7 pb
Most CC
C-ltd/S-no/P-no/H-yes

Full breakfast
Assorted snacks & drinks
provided with baked goods
brought up each night
Dining room, conference
room, wireless Internet, in-
room phone & TV

This large 9,000 square foot home has been delicately restored; the detailed fretwork, pocket doors & elaborate paneling evoke just some of the charm you will encounter on your journey through the house.
✉ hendersonhouse@hsu.edu ✪ www.hsu.edu/Captain-Henderson-House

EUREKA SPRINGS

11 Singleton House
11 Singleton 72632
800-833-3394
Barb Gavron

95-150 BB
5 rooms, 5 pb
Most CC, *Rated*, •
C-yes/S-ltd/P-no/H-ltd
Spanish

Full gourmet breakfast daily
Guest ice-box, microwave,
complimentary ice tea,
lemonade, hot cocoa, herbal
teas, afternoon snack
B & B Internship Program,
free parking, historic walking
tour, small garden weddings,
early check-in

Quiet Historic District. Breakfast balcony overlooking award-winning garden. Some rooms with two beds. Suite sleeps five. Jacuzzi suite w/private balcony. Cottage at separate location. One block walk to shops or trolley. Seen on HGTV's If Walls Could Talk
✉ info@singletonhouse.com

1881 Crescent Cottage Inn
211 Spring St 72632
800-223-3246 479-253-6022
Ray & Elise Dilfield

109-149 BB
4 rooms, 4 pb
Visa, MC, Disc, *Rated*, •
S-no/P-no/H-no

Full breakfast
Complimentary soft drinks;
Fresh-baked cookies
Historic district, all rooms
have Jacuzzis, 2 rooms with
fireplaces

All the charm and elegance of National Historic Register Victorian home just a few minutes' stroll from downtown Eureka Springs' shops, galleries, restaurants, and night life.
✉ raphael@ipa.net ✪ www.1881crescentcottageinn.com

1884 Bridgeford House
263 Spring St 72632
888-567-2422 479-253-7853
Nadara (Sam) and Jeff
Feldman

115-179 BB
5 rooms, 5 pb
Visa, MC, Disc, *Rated*, •
C-ltd/S-ltd/P-no/H-no
Spanish

Full breakfast
In room treats
Some with fireplaces,
Jacuzzis, cable TV/VCR,
private entrances, decks

Southern hospitality combined with Victorian charm await you at our beautiful Queen Anne/Eastlake "Painted Lady" home! Nestled in the very heart of Eureka Springs. Listed on the National Register of Historic Places.
✉ innkeeper@bridgefordhouse.com ✪ www.bridgefordhouse.com

EUREKA SPRINGS————————————————————————————————

1908 Ridgeway House B&B	89-155 BB	Homemade breakfast
28 Ridgeway St 72632	5 rooms, 5 pb	Homemade evening dessert,
800-501-2503 479-253-6618	Most CC, •	coffee, teas
Gayla & Keith Hubbard	C-ltd/S-ltd/P-no/H-ltd	movie library, veranda and
		wireless Internet,
		reservations to shows,
		events

The Ridgeway House offers gracious Southern hospitality in Eureka Springs' quaint Historic District. The Ridgeway House is the ideal place for your getaway, whether an intimate weekend for two, a whole house reunion, a small meeting, or business retreat.
✉ rheureka@ipa.net ◐ www.ridgewayhouse.com

5 Ojo Inn B&B	95-225 BB	Full breakfast
5 Ojo St 72632	10 rooms, 10 pb	Complimentary in-room soft
800-656-6734 479-253-6734	Most CC, •	drinks & snacks
Richard & Jan Grinnell	C-ltd/S-ltd/P-yes/H-no	Hot tub, gazebo, Jacuzzis for
		two, fireplaces, weddings, off-
		street parking

Experience Victorian charm, exemplary Ozark hospitality and fabulous gourmet breakfasts. Situated on over an acre of wooded lot on the Historic Loop, and just a short stroll to downtown shopping, galleries & restaurants.
✉ innkeeper@5ojo.com ◐ www.5ojo.com

Arsenic & Old Lace	145-259 BB	Full gourmet breakfast
60 Hillside Ave 72632	5 rooms, 5 pb	Complimentary sodas, wine,
866-350-5454 479-253-5454	Visa, MC, Disc, *Rated*,	homemade cookies, snacks
Beverly & Doug Breitling	•	TV/VCRs, large video library,
	C-ltd/S-ltd/P-ltd/H-no	Jacuzzi tubs, fireplaces, spa
		showers

The premier Bed & Breakfast destination in Eureka Springs. Queen Anne style Victorian mansion with large wraparound veranda. Beautiful, private hillside setting in the Historic District. Escape to a time when life was slower and more romantic!
✉ ArsenicOldLaceBB@aol.com ◐ www.eurekaspringsromancebb.com

Candlestick Cottage Inn B&B	119-159 BB	Choice of Full or Cont. Breakfast
6 Douglas St 72632	5 rooms, 5 pb	Only Continental breakfast
800-835-5184 479-253-6813	Most CC, •	served Dec – Mar. Coffee/tea
Denise Coleman & Rita	C-ltd/S-ltd/P-ltd/H-no	in room, complimentary
Shepler		bottled water & soda.
		Restaurant & attraction
		reservations, light maid
		service, small weddings. On-
		site minister.

Nestled on a quiet wooded hillside one block from Historic Downtown shops, galleries & dining. Authentic Victorian Country setting in the Ozarks. Private baths, outside entrances, porches & off-street parking. Private lake front cottage also available.
✉ info@candlestickcottageinn.com ◐ www.candlestickcottageinn.com

Cliff Cottage Inn Luxury B&B	189-230 BB	Elf delivers full-gourmet breakfast
Heart of Historic Downtown 72632	8 rooms, 8 pb	Complimentary Champagne
800-799-7409 479-253-7409	Visa, MC, *Rated*, •	or wine, sodas, teas, coffee,
Sandra CH Smith	C-ltd/S-ltd/P-no/H-no	hot cocoa, cookie samplers
	French, Spanish,	for 2+ night stay
	German	Free video/book library;
		reservations to Passion Play,
		music show, carriage rides

Named one of top 6 "Most Romantic Inns in the South" by Romantic Destinations Magazine/Southern Bride. Only B&B in heart of Eureka's Historic Downtown. Off street parking. Elegant Jacuzzi suites, historic cottages. Gourmet breakfasts delivered to suites.
✉ cliffcottage@sbcglobal.net ◐ www.cliffcottage.com

EUREKA SPRINGS

Evening Shade Inn B&B
Highway 62 East 72632
800-992-1224 479-253-6264
Clark & Donna Hinson

135-190 BB
8 rooms, 8 pb
Most CC, *Rated*
C-ltd/S-no/P-no/H-no

Full Homemade Breakfast In Room
Homemade desserts in the evening
Jacuzzis, fireplaces, wireless Internet, cable TV, in-room phones, fax, gift shop, weddings

Evening Shade Inn is one of Eureka Springs, AK's finest B&Bs, featuring luxury suites and private honeymoon cottages perfect for any vacation or romantic getaway. Evening Shade Inn combines luxury, privacy, seclusion and convenience.
✉ eveningshadeinn@cox.net ◐ www.eveningshade.com

Green Tree Lodge
560 West Van Buren 72632
479-253-8807
Cindy Ellis

79-175 EP
6 rooms, 6 pb
Most CC
C-ltd/S-ltd/P-no/H-no

Coffee in rooms
Light maid service daily

Whether you are getting away to decompress for a few days or spend time with friends and family; Green Tree Lodge in Eureka Springs is the ideal location. We offer deluxe Jacuzzi cabins and suites perfect for any occasion.
✉ greentre@ipa.net ◐ www.eureka-springs-usa.com/greentree

Heartstone Inn & Cottages
35 Kings Hwy 72632
800-494-4921 479-253-8916
Rick & Cheri Rojek

95-169 BB
11 rooms, 11 pb
Most CC, *Rated*, •
C-ltd/S-ltd/P-no/H-no

Full gourmet breakfast
Complimentary beverages and homemade treats
Weddings, Jacuzzi suites, movies, massage therapy, golf privileges, gazebo, library, concierge

The definitive full service bed and breakfast in Eureka Springs, Arkansas. The Heartstone Inn is professionally operated and is renowned for providing the finest facilities and personalized service in Eureka Springs.
✉ info@heartstoneinn.com ◐ www.heartstoneinn.com

Inn at Rose Hall
56 Hillside Ave 72632
800-544-7734 479-253-8035
Zoie Kaye

129-179 BB
5 rooms, 5 pb
Visa, MC, Disc, *Rated*
S-no/P-no/H-no

Full breakfast
Coffee, tea, cold beverages & snacks
Outdoor stone courtyard, parlor, veranda, fireplace, Jacuzzi, weddings, wireless Internet

A luxurious bed and breakfast offering five exquisite suites, with private bath, Jacuzzi for two, fireplace, fresh flowers, designer linens, gourmet breakfast. Excellent wedding & getaway packages. ✉ innkeeper@innatrosehall.com ◐ www.innatrosehall.com

---

Land-O-Nod Victorian Inn
109 Huntsville Rd 72632
800-526-3263 479-253-6262
Pat Kearney

59-135 BB
40 rooms, 40 pb
Most CC, *Rated*
C-yes/S-ltd/P-no/H-yes
3/15 through 11/15

Continental breakfast
In-Room Coffee, Trolley Stop, Heated Pool, Free Local Calls, Cable Color TV, HBO, WiFi, New Rooms

Land-O-Nod
✉ landonod@sbcglobal.net ◐ www.landonod.com

Main Street Inn
217 N Main St 72632
479-253-5575
Judie Lockhart

65-165 BB
6 rooms, 6 pb
Visa, MC, AmEx
C-yes/S-ltd/P-yes/H-ltd

Full breakfast
Weddings, private off-street parking, double Jacuzzi's, furnished porches, gazebo, a garden swing

In the heart of the beautiful Eureka Springs historic district! Main Street Inn consists of 3 Victorian homes, which sit side by side. Whether you are looking for lodging at a B & B or the perfect location for your wedding ceremony we can meet your needs.
✉ bobjudie@arkansas.net ◐ www.angelsonmainstreet.com

EUREKA SPRINGS

Pond Mountain Lodge & Resort	89-170 BB	Full breakfast
218 Hwy 23 S 72632	8 rooms, 8 pb	Picnic lunch available, full
800-583-8043 479-253-5877	Visa, MC, *Rated*, •	kitchens, snack centers,
Kim Stryker	C-yes/S-no/P-yes/H-ltd	complimentary beverages
		Sitting room, library, hot
		tub/pool, fishing ponds,
		horseback riding, fireplace,
		TV/VCR

Mountain top breezes, panoramic views, casual elegance in cabins & suites with personal Jacuzzis; also includes fishing ponds, heated pool, riding stables, billiards and fireplace.
✉ innkeeper@pondmountainlodge.com ○ www.pondmountainlodge.com

Red Bud Manor	89-149 BB	Full breakfast
Kings Hwy 72632	3 rooms, 3 pb	Gourmet coffees and teas,
866-253-9649 479-253-9649	Most CC, •	small refrigerators stocked
Deborah Stroup	C-ltd/S-ltd/P-no/H-ltd	with complimentary
		beverages
		Porch, gardens, parlor,
		antiques, cable television,
		fresh flowers, coffee makers,
		Jacuzzi, weddings

Relax and pamper yourself at Red Bud Manor, one of Eureka's finest bed-and-breakfast inns. Built in 1891, Red Bud Manor is conveniently located on Eureka's Historic Loop within easy walking distance to the finest shops, spas and restaurants.
✉ redbudmanor@cox-internet.com ○ www.redbudmanorinn.com

Roger's Sunnyside Inn	85-150 BB	Full home-cooked breakfast
Ridgeway 72361	5 rooms, 5 pb	Evening dessert, soft drinks,
800-554-9499 479-253-6638	Most CC, •	tea, snacks
Draxie Rogers	C-yes/S-no/P-yes/H-no	Two parlors, formal dining
		room, Jacuzzi room, 1 suite
		ideal for families – sleeps 4.

Enjoy the beauty and history of this 1883 Victorian bed and breakfast inn, set in one of the most unique areas of the breathtaking Ozark Mountains. Sunnyside provides a range of settings- from total privacy to group meeting areas.
✉ draxierogers@yahoo.com ○ www.sunnysideinn.net/

Scandia B&B Inn	89-149 BB	Full breakfast
27 W. Van Buren 72632	7 rooms, 7 pb	Hot tub/spa, coffeemaker,
800-523-8922 479-253-8922	Most CC	fireplace/woodstove,
Bill and Libby Freeland	C-yes/S-no/P-yes/H-ltd	cable/satellite TV

Welcome to Scandia Inn Bed & Breakfast in Eureka Springs, Arkansas! Our charming 1940's era guest cottages combine privacy with the traditional services of a quality bed & breakfast inn.
✉ scandiainn@cox.net ○ www.scandiainn.com

HOT SPRINGS

Lookout Point	137-547 BB	Full breakfast
104 Lookout Circle 71913	13 rooms, 13 pb	Complimentary Innkeepers
866-525-6155 501-525-6155	Most CC, •	reception with delectable
Kristie & Ray Rosset	C-ltd/S-no/P-ltd/H-yes	desserts, cheese & crackers,
	limited Spanish	wine and tea.
		Sitting room & sunroom,
		book & video library,
		fireplaces, cable TV, WiFi,
		canoe, labyrinth, gardens.

An exceptional experience of peace & tranquility, pampering, and luxury in Hot Springs, Arkansas. This award-winning inn, on beautiful Lake Hamilton, in the Ouachita Mountains is designed for guest comfort, relaxation, and romance. Perfect for weddings.
✉ innkeeper@lookoutpointinn.com ○ www.lookoutpointinn.com

HOT SPRINGS

Overview B&B on Lake Hamilton
252 Overview Dr 71913
501-760-3142
Linda McKee

140-225 BB
4 rooms, 3 pb
Visa, MC, Disc, *Rated*
S-no/P-no/H-ltd

Full breakfast
Afternoon tea, snacks, water, soft drinks, coffee
Gathering room, library, fireplace, decks, billiard and home theater room

We have a million dollar view overlooking Lake Hamilton and the mountains—quiet, peaceful, relaxing. Great hearty breakfasts, fresh baked cookies/cakes to welcome you. Warm, inviting atmosphere. ✉ stay@overviewbnb.com 🌐 www.overviewbnb.com

Williams House Inn
420 Quapaw Ave 71901
800-756-4635 501-624-4275
Cathy Kuykendall

159-199 BB
9 rooms, 9 pb
Visa, MC, Disc, *Rated*,
•
C-ltd/S-ltd/P-no/H-yes

Full breakfast
Refreshment area with cookies, cocoa, cider & tea, in-room sodas, coffee & bottled water
Upstairs library and two spacious verandas, video library, WiFi access, garden sitting areas

Relax and Rejuvenate your spirit and body at Williams House Inn. This Victorian Inn envelopes you in comfort and elegance. Located within walking distance of historic down town Hot Springs. Weddings and special events customized to your taste.
✉ info@1890williamshouse.com 🌐 www.1890williamshouse.com

MOUNTAIN HOME

Mountain Memories B&B
45 Hwy 101 Cutoff 72653
870-492-2222
Linda McClellan

95-250 BB
3 rooms, 3 pb
Visa, MC
C-yes/S-no/P-no/H-no

Full breakfast
Drinks and snacks conveniently located in the den and game room.
Den w/fireplace, TV, board games; game room w/pool table, stereo; deck, gazebo, hiking trails, pool

Mountain Memories Bed & Breakfast is a luxury Inn located deep in the Arkansas Ozark Twin Lakes Country. Mountains surround this spacious 2-acre home. Just minutes from Lake Norfork & close to Bull Shoals & world-famous White River trout fishing area.
✉ mountainmemories@hotmail.com 🌐 www.mountainmemoriesbb.com

MOUNTAIN VIEW

Wildflower B&B On The Square
100 Washington St 72560
800-591-4879 870-269-4383
JR & Pam Rivera

65-135 BB
6 rooms, 7 pb
Most CC, *Rated*
C-ltd/S-no/P-no/H-ltd
Spanish

Full Hearty Buffet Breakfast
Homebaked afternoon snacks and beverages anytime, Guest pantry with refrigerator & microwave
Wraparound porch with rocking chairs, free WiFi, cable TV, CD players and luxurious linens.

Historic inn located on Court Square. All rooms have private baths, WiFi, cable TV, & are tastefully decorated. Full buffet breakfast w/PM snacks w/made from "scratch" baked goods. Wraparound porch w/rocking chairs, overlooks musicians playing on the sqr.
✉ wildflowerbb@yahoo.com 🌐 www.wildflowerbb.com

NORTH LITTLE ROCK

Baker House B&B
109 W 5th St 72114
501-372-9930
Scott & Sonja Miller

110-150 BB
5 rooms, 5 pb
Most CC
C-ltd/S-no/P-no/H-no

Full breakfast
Snack, coffee and cold drinks available 24 hours
Sitting Room, Antiques, Soaking tubs, Wireless Internet

Built in 1898–1899, the Baker House provides a beautiful Victorian experience for its guests, while at the same time providing all the comforts of the 21st century.
✉ innkeeper@bakerhousenlr.com 🌐 www.bakerhousenlr.com

California

AHWAHNEE————————————————————

Apple Blossom Inn 44606 Silver Spur Trail 93601 888-687-4281 559-642-2001 Candy 'Apple' Arthur	110-240 BB 5 rooms, 4 pb Most CC, • C-yes/S-ltd/P-ltd/H-ltd	Full breakfast Fruit, snacks and candy apples/treats when the apples are ripe. Picnic lunches available on request Sun deck and spa with gorgeous view of the Sierras, VCR's and video library, & organic apple orchard

The Apple Blossom Inn is located in Gold Country on historic Highway 49, the front yard of Yosemite National Park. Enjoy the serenity of your stay in the midst of our organic apple farm & gardens, while visiting the many recreational spots nearby.
✉ appleblossominn@sti.net ☼ www.appleblossombb.com

The Homestead 41110 Rd 600 93601 800-483-0495 559-683-0495 Cindy Brooks & Larry Ends	119-374 BB 6 rooms, 6 pb Most CC, *Rated*, • C-ltd/S-no/P-no/H-ltd Spanish	Continental breakfast Barbeque grill and picnic table available for guest use Free Internet access, toiletries, daily maid service, concierge services, in room massages available

Romantic private cottages with fully equipped kitchens on 160 wooded acres close to Yosemite, Gold Country, golf, hiking and restaurants. Equine layover available.
✉ homesteadcottages@sti.net ☼ www.homesteadcottages.com

Sierra Mountain Lodge Bed **& Breakfast** 45046 Fort Nip Trail 93601 800-811-7029 559-683-7673 John & Brenda Eppler	125-249 BB 6 rooms, 6 pb Visa, MC, • C-yes/S-ltd/P-no/H-ltd	Continental plus breakfast Breakfast includes, gourmet coffee, waffle bar, sausage, cold cereal, milk, OJ & a variety of teas Private kitchenettes, panoramic mountain views, wireless Internet, DVD & reading library, cable TV

A quiet country oasis with panoramic mountain views near the Southern Entrance to Yosemite. Choose a suite or a split-log family style cabin. All suites include private entry, bath, living room, kitchenette, continental plus breakfast & wireless Internet
✉ brenda@sierramountainlodge.com ☼ www.sierramountainlodge.com

ALAMEDA————————————————————

Webster House B&B Inn 1238 Versailles Ave 94501 510-523-9697 Andrew & Susan McCormack	125-175 BB 4 rooms, 4 pb AmEx, *Rated*, • C-yes/S-ltd/P-no/H-no	Full breakfast Restaurant, complimentary afternoon tea, dinner available Sitting room, library, suites, fireplace, conference, waterfall

Oldest house on Island in San Francisco Bay. 22nd City Historical Monument, built in New York and shipped around Cape Horn in 1854. Gothic Revival.
✉ WebsterHouse@netscape.net ☼ websterhouse2.home.comcast.net

Fensalden Inn, Albion, CA

ALBION————————————————————————————

Albion River Inn
3790 Hwy 1 N 95410
800-479-7944 707-937-1919
Pat Turrigiano

195-325 BB
22 rooms, 22 pb
Most CC, *Rated*
C-ltd/S-no/P-no/H-yes

Full breakfast
On site Restaurant is open
nightly serving our savory
coastal cuisine and award
winning wine list.
In-room wine, coffee, full
breakfast, robes, fireplaces,
cooking classes, wine
dinners, workshops.

Called "One of the West's Best Small Inns," by Sunset Magazine, our romantic oceanfront Inn and restaurant sits on ten dramatic clifftop acres overlooking the Pacific. Enjoy luxury, comfort, acclaimed cuisine and an award winning wine list.
✉ pat@albionriverinn.com ☍ www.albionriverinn.com

Fensalden Inn
33810 Navarro Ridge Rd 95410
800-959-3850 707-937-4042
Lyn Hamby

139-253 BB
8 rooms, 8 pb
Most CC, *Rated*, •
C-ltd/S-ltd/P-ltd/H-ltd

Full three course gourmet
breakfast
Wine & hors d'oeuvres at
5pm each evening in our
Great Room.
Sunporch w/board games &
jigsaw puzzle; office w/fax,
wireless Internet. Hairdryers
in room.

1850s Stagestop on several acres overlooking Pacific. Quiet romantic getaway, w/pampering atmosphere, antique appointed rooms w/fireplaces & private baths, gourmet breakfasts, evening hor d'oeuvres; 2 pigmy goats, 7 ducks, 2 pups & local wildlife & birds.
✉ inn@fensalden.com ☍ www.fensalden.com

APTOS————————————————————————————

Apple Lane Inn
6265 Soquel Dr 95003
800-649-8988 831-475-6868
Doug Groom or Bret Stoltz

120-200 BB
5 rooms, 5 pb
Most CC, *Rated*, •
C-yes/S-no/P-ltd/H-ltd

Full breakfast
Complimentary Bristol
Cream Sherry, tea, pistachios
& fruit bowl
Sitting room, library, suites,
fireplaces. Live music
Sunday morning by
arrangement

1870s Victorian Farmhouse on 2 country acres, just one mile from the beach. Five guest rooms decorated with museum quality antiques. Children & pets welcomed in the Wine Cellar Room. ✉ ali@cruzio.com ☍ www.applelaneinn.com

APTOS

Historic Sand Rock Farm	185-225 BB	Chef-prepared gourmet
901 Freedom Blvd 95003	5 rooms, 5 pb	breakfast
31-688-8005	Visa, MC	Wine reception & special
Cris Sheehan	C-yes/S-no/P-no/H-ltd	meals by arrangement
		Jacuzzis, down comforters,
		gardens, sitting areas

Historic, country estate featuring world-class Chef, Jacuzzi tubs, arts, antiques, down comforters, private baths, and gracious amenities on 10 wooded acres. Secluded between Santa Cruz and Monterey. ✉ reservations@sandrockfarm.com ○ www.sandrockfarm.com

ARROYO GRANDE

Abella Garden Inn B&B	219-325 BB	Buffet or continental, see
10 Oak St 93420	7 rooms, 7 pb	below.
00-563-7762 805-489-5926	Most CC, *Rated*, •	Busy Weekend: Breakfast
Gina Glass	C-ltd/S-no/P-no/H-no	buffet. Slower Periods:
	Spanish, Italian	Continental serve yourself.
	July, Aug. and Sept.	Snack basket, port
		Weddings & elopements in a
		Garden Oasis; Honeymoon/
		Anniversary Destination,
		Sitting room, fireplaces

5 minutes to San Luis Obispo, 2 miles to Pismo Beach, ½ mile from Historic Village of Arroyo Grande. Italian hospitality & luxury! Luscious garden oasis ideal for intimate weddings, in-room spa & fireplace, free WiFi Internet. ✉ info@abellagardeninn.com ○ www.abellagardeninn.com

AVALON

The Avalon Hotel on	195-545 BB	Continental plus breakfast
Catalina Island	15 rooms, 15 pb	In-room complimentary
24 Whittley Ave 90704	Visa, MC, AmEx	coffee, bottled water and
10-510-7070	C-yes/S-no/P-no/H-no	refreshments
Kathleen Gosselin		Rooftop deck, garden
		courtyard, koi pond,
		weddings, fridge, high speed
		Internet, wet bar, balcony

An environment of understated elegance, where luxurious bedding, unique artwork and hand-crafted hardwoods and tile combine to create an enchanting experience. Most of our rooms have breath-taking views of Avalon harbor. ✉ kate@theavalonhotel.com ○ www.theavalonhotel.com

BEN LOMOND

Fairview Manor	129-159 BB	Full breakfast
45 Fairview Ave 95005	5 rooms, 5 pb	Complimentary wine & hors
31-336-3355	Visa, MC, Disc, *Rated*,	d'oeuvres
Gael Glasson Abayon & Jack	•	Sitting room, bordered by
Hazelton	C-ltd/S-no/P-no/H-yes	river, weddings & meetings

Romantic country-style redwood home, majestic stone fireplace, 2.5 wooded acres in the Santa Cruz Mountains. Total privacy. Walk to town. A whole generation can identify with Santa Cruz, America's beach town. ✉ fairviewbandb@comcast.net ○ www.fairviewmanor.com

BERKELEY

The Brick Path B&B	155-190 BB	Continental plus breakfast
805 Marin Ave 94707	3 rooms, 3 pb	Free wireless Internet,
10-524-4277	Visa, MC	private telephone/answering
Wendy Sprague	C-yes/S-no/P-no	machine, refrigerator, coffee
		bar, cable TV/VCR

Immaculate and welcoming, The Brick Path B & B offers three unique and comfortable guestrooms in a lovely garden setting. Located in North Berkeley just one block from convenient Solano Ave. shopping, and approximately two miles from UC Berkeley. ✉ info@thebrickpath.com ○ www.thebrickpath.com

BERKELEY

Rose Garden Inn
2740 Telegraph Ave 94705
800-992-9005 510-549-2145
Kevin Allen

129-399 BB
40 rooms, 40 pb
Most CC, *Rated*, •
C-yes/S-ltd/P-no/H-ltd
Spanish

Full buffet breakfast
Afternoon tea, coffee, &
cookies
Free parking on a space-
available basis, cable TV,
free high speed Internet in
most rooms

*Experience . . . the charming comfort of our 40 guestrooms surrounded by flowerin
gardens, some with sweeping views and soothing fountains. Walking distance from U
Berkeley and among the finest of Bay Area highlights.*
✉ rosegardengm@aol.com ❸ www.rosegardeninn.com

BERRY CREEK

Lake Oroville
240 Sunday Dr 95916
800-455-LAKE 530-589-0700
Cheryl & Ronald Damberger

135-175 BB
6 rooms, 6 pb
Most CC, *Rated*, •
C-yes/S-ltd/P-yes/H-yes
French, Spanish

Full breakfast
Lunch & dinner available,
snacks
Sitting room, library,
Jacuzzis, fireplaces, cable
TV, accommodate business
travelers Pets Welcome

*Lake views, sunsets, stargazing. Secluded country setting, covered porches with privat
entrances. Enjoy a evening picnic meal while watching the beautiful sunsets over th
lake.A woodburning fireplace in the parlor, or a good book in the sunroom/library.*
✉ cheryl@lakeorovillebedandbreakfast.com ❸ www.lakeorovillebedandbreakfast.com

BIG BEAR

Alpenhorn B&B
601 Knight Ave 92315
888-829-6600 909-866-5700
Timothy & Linda Carpenter

202-312 BB
8 rooms, 8 pb
Visa, MC, AmEx,
Rated, •
C-ltd/S-ltd/P-no/H-yes

Four-course gourmet
breakfast
Wine with appetizers in the
evening, after dinner
liqueurs, chocolates
In-room spas for two,
fireplaces, TV/VCRs, private
balconies, extensive video
library, host weddings

*The perfect place for a garden wedding or romantic getaway. Relish a glass of wine whil
watching a sunset in our exquisite gardens, or sit by the fire and watch snow magicall
blanket the landscape. Enjoy modern elegance amidst tranquility.*
✉ linda@alpenhorn.com ❸ www.alpenhorn.com/welcome.html

BIG BEAR CITY

Gold Mountain Manor
1117 Anita 92314
800-509-2604 909-585-6997
Cathy Weil

139-309 BB
7 rooms, 7 pb
Visa, MC, *Rated*, •
C-ltd/S-ltd/P-ltd/H-no

Full Gourmet breakfast
Gooey chocolate chip
oatmeal cookies
Billiard table, parlor with
woodburning fireplace,
wraparound porch, library,
concierge service

*Historic log cabin B&B, secluded & romantic. Lots of special touches. Park-like setting
woodburning fireplaces, wraparound porch, candlelit breakfast, Jacuzzi tubs, spa trea
ments.*
✉ info@goldmountainmanor.com ❸ www.goldmountainmanor.com

BIG BEAR LAKE

Apples Bed and Breakfast Inn
2430 Moonridge Rd 92315
909-866-0903
Jim & Barbara McLean

156-266 BB
19 rooms, 19 pb
Most CC, *Rated*
C-ltd/S-no/P-no/H-yes

Full breakfast
Afternoon sparkling cider, herb cheese; evening coffee with dessert; free soft drinks, cookies
Jacuzzis, TVs, VCRs, gas fireplaces, outdoor hot tub, two meeting rooms, two in-room reclining chair

Apples Bed & Breakfast Inn, of Big Bear Lake in the Southern CA mountains is a Three Diamond AAA Awarded Bed and Breakfast set in the midst of an acre of pine trees, located one mile from the golf course, lake, as well as two major California ski resort
✉ host@applesbedandbreakfast.com ☏ www.applesbigbear.com

Eagle's Nest B&B
41675 Big Bear Blvd 92315
888-866-6465 909-866-6465
Mark & Vicki Tebo

110-165 BB
10 rooms, 10 pb
Most CC, *Rated*, •
C-ltd/S-ltd/P-ltd/H-no

Full breakfast
Snacks
Sitting room, spas, suites, fireplaces, cable TV

Full log B&B nestled in Ponderosa pines, mountain lodge decor with antiques and custom furnishings, full hearty breakfast.
✉ eaglesnestlodge@earthlink.net ☏ www.eaglesnestlodgebigbear.com

BISHOP

Joseph House Inn
376 W Yaney St 93514
760-872-3389
Hilde & Myriam Ruland

154-178 BB
5 rooms, 5 pb
Visa, MC, •
C-ltd/S-no/P-ltd/H-ltd
Spanish, German,
French

Full Gourmet Breakfast
Complimentary wine & small appetizer served in the living room with a cozy fire or in the gardens
Airport pick-up, corp. rates, group rates, corp retreats, TV/VCR/VCR, WiFi & in-house massages

Between the Eastern High Sierra and White Mtn ranges in the Owens Valley along Hwy 395, just 38 mi. south of Mammoth Lakes, 1 hr from Bristlecone Forest, Mono Lake and Bodie, 2 hrs from Yosemite Valley. Three acres of gardens. Weddings and events hosted.
✉ myriam@josephhouseinn.com ☏ josephhouseinn.com

BLUE LAKE

Worthington House Inn
521 First Ave 95525
707-668-1889
Rebecca Collins, Kimberly Owens & Terri Bayles

149-189 BB
5 rooms, 5 pb
Visa, MC
C-ltd/S-no/P-no/H-ltd

Full breakfast
Fresh ground coffee & select teas available all day
Gardens, library, cable TV & WiFi Internet, gift shop

Worthington House Inn offers beautifully appointed rooms, comfortable beds, large private baths & a delicious breakfast each morning with fresh coffee & select teas. Located in the Mad River Valley just minutes away from Arcata & Eureka.
✉ worthingtonhouseinn@suddenlink.net ☏ www.worthingtonhouseinn.com

CALISTOGA

Aurora Park Cottage
1807 Foothill Blvd 94515
877-942-7700 707-942-6733
Joe Hensley

205-305 BB
6 rooms, 6 pb
Visa, MC, AmEx, •
C-ltd/S-ltd/P-no/H-yes

Continental breakfast
Bottled water, biscotti, jelly bellies, coffee and tea.
Mini-fridge, coffee makers, cable TV, AC, plush towels, comfy robes and private decks

Free Champagne—Mention Lanier when you make your reservation and we'll have some chilled champagne and chocolates awaiting your arrival. Aurora Park Cottages is your private vacation retreat in Napa Valley wine country.
✉ innkeeper@aurorapark.com ☏ www.aurorapark.com

CALISTOGA————————————————————

Bear Flag Inn
2653 Foothill Blvd Hwy 128
94515
800-670-2860 707-942-5534
McNay Family

199-289 BB
5 rooms, 5 pb
Visa, MC, Disc, •
C-ltd/S-ltd/P-ltd/H-ltd

Full breakfast
Beverages and snacks
Parlor, pool, hot tub,
hammocks, pool table,
player piano, garden,
treadmill, TVs & Cable, WiFi

Featuring charming guestrooms, a full breakfast made with farm-fresh eggs produced here and wine & appetizers in the afternoon, Bear Flag Inn is your home away from home in Calistoga.
✉ 2mcnays@ap.net ○ www.bearflaginn.com

Brannan Cottage Inn
109 Wapoo Ave 94515
707-942-4200
Doug & Judy Cook

155-235 BB
6 rooms, 6 pb
Visa, MC, *Rated*, •
C-yes/S-no/P-yes/H-ltd
Spanish

Full breakfast
Friday evening wine &
appetizers with local
wineries, homemade
chocolate chip cookies every
night
A/C, fridge, queen bed, down
comforters, ceiling fans,
fireplaces in most rooms,
WiFi, private entry

Charming 1860 cottage-style Victorian, country furnishings, lovely grounds with gardens, lawns & a patio. It is walking distance to famous restaurants & spas & 15 wineries are within 2 miles. The inn is available for small meetings and special events.
✉ brannancottageinn@sbcglobal.net ○ www.brannancottageinn.com

Calistoga Wayside Inn
1523 Foothill Blvd 94515
800-845-3632 707-942-0645
Philippe Shepard

155-275 BB
3 rooms, 3 pb
Visa, MC, Disc, •
C-ltd/S-ltd/P-no/H-no
Spanish, French

Full breakfast
Tea, hot chocolate, afternoon
hors d'oeuvres
Fireplace, spa, spacious
living room, outdoor gardens
& patio, 4 blocks to town.
WiFi, satellite TV

Enjoy a taste of early California in this well-appointed circa-1928 Mediterranean style home. Conveniently located 4 easy blocks to Calistoga and close to Napa and Sonoma wineries. Relax in the peaceful grounds. All rooms with king beds and private baths.
✉ info@calistogawaysdeinn.com ○ www.calistogawaysideinn.com

Carlin Country Cottages
1623 Lake St 94515
800-734-4624 707-942-9102
George & Larry Costello

94-210 BB
15 rooms, 15 pb
C-ltd/S-no/P-no/H-no

Continental breakfast

Lose yourself in one of the private cottages that surround the quiet country garden and courtyard, read the morning paper or relax in the hot, spring-fed swimming pool and spa. Friendly Irish hospitality awaits you at Carlin Country Cottages.
✉ carlincottages@comcast.net ○ www.carlincottages.com

Chelsea Garden Inn
1443 2nd St 94515
800-942-1515 707-942-0948
Jennie Juarez-Ornbaun/Dave
& Susan DeVries

165-275 BB
5 rooms, 5 pb
Visa, MC, Disc, *Rated*,
•
C-yes/S-ltd/P-ltd/H-ltd

Full breakfast
Afternoon hors d'oeuvres
Spacious suites, fireplaces,
WiFi, TV/DVD, free movies,
guest computer, concierge,
pool, library

This charming Napa Valley B&B is conveniently located near wineries, spas, restaurants & other area activities. Spacious & private romantic suites with fireplaces, robes, cable TV w/DVD. Pool. Afternoon hors d'oeuvres, Free WiFi. AAA 3 diamonds, breakfast
✉ innkeeper@chelseagardeninn.com ○ www.chelseagardeninn.com

CALISTOGA

Cottage Grove Inn
1711 Lincoln Ave 94515
800-799-2284 707-942-8400
Donna Johnson

250-445 BB
16 rooms, 16 pb
Visa, MC, AmEx,
Rated, •
C-ltd/S-ltd/P-no/H-yes

Continental plus breakfast
Complimentary wine &
cheese reception each
evening, serving 6 different
Napa Valley Wines
Sunken Jacuzzi tub,
fireplace, DVD player, WiFi,
IPOD docks, flat screen TV's,
bikes, private porch

Romantic, private luxury cottages with serene comfort and elegance in the beautiful quaint town of Calistoga. Explore the wine country. Treat yourself to a spa visit. Walking distance to shops, restaurants and spas.
✉ cottage@sonic.net ✪ www.cottagegrove.com

The Craftsman Inn
1213 Foothill Blvd 94515
707-341-3035
Gillian & Nick Kite

166-299 BB
5 rooms, 5 pb
Most CC, •
C-ltd/S-no/P-no

Full gourmet champagne
breakfast
Bottled water,
complimentary wine,
nightcap decanter of Madeira
with homemade cookies
Flat screen TV/DVD, robes,
luxury toiletries, A/C, heat,
wireless Internet access,
CD/radio alarm

Our passion is to help our guests gain as much pleasure from their visit to this wonderful valley as we do from living here.
✉ info@thecraftsmaninn.com ✪ www.thecraftsmaninn.com

Fanny's
1206 Spring 94515
707-942-9491
Deanna Higgins

150-240 BB
2 rooms, 2 pb
C-ltd/S-no/P-no/H-no

Full country breakfast
Drinks and refreshments are
available throughout the day
A/C, alarm clocks in every
room, community room with
fireplace, board games,
parlor

A true wine country retreat. Fanny's Cozy B&B is tucked away in one of Calistoga's most peaceful neighborhoods and is centrally located with easy access for exploring both Napa and Sonoma valleys.
✉ info@fannysnapavalley.com ✪ www.fannysnapavalley.com

Foothill House
3037 Foothill Blvd 94515
800-942-6933 707-942-6933
Darla Anderson

185-325 BB
4 rooms, 4 pb
Most CC, *Rated*, •
C-ltd/S-no/P-no/H-no

Full breakfast
Complimentary wine &
cheese, sherry, 'Sweet
Dream' cookies
3 rooms & 1 cottage with
Jacuzzi tub, sitting room,
TV/VCR, movies, fireplace,
robes, slippers

Superior accommodations and attention await the guest of Foothill House. Your visit will be a special and memorable experience. Come be our guest for the finest in wine country hospitality and enjoy the comfort and luxury of Foothill House.
✉ info@foothillhouse.com ✪ www.foothillhouse.com

Garnett Creek Inn
1139 Lincoln Ave 94515
707-942-9797
Walter Marchant

155-325 BB
5 rooms, 5 pb
Most CC
C-ltd/S-no/P-no/H-yes

Continental breakfast
Breakfast in bed, handicap
accessible, off-street parking,
morning paper services,
gardens

On a tree-lined corner of Calistoga's historic main street, the Inn invites visitors to relax on its wide, covered porch or brick-lined gardens and watch California's wine world pass by. Or stroll to Calistoga's world-class spas and unique shops.
✉ info@garnettcreekinn.com ✪ www.garnettcreekinn.com

CALISTOGA————————————————

Hillcrest B&B
3225 Lake Co Hwy 94515
707-942-6334
Debbie O'Gorman

69-175 BB
3 rooms, 3 pb
Most CC, *Rated*, •
C-yes/S-ltd/P-yes/H-ltd

Continental breakfast
Complimentary wine is
available in the guest parlor,
help yourself anytime
Sitting room, library,
Jacuzzis, pool, movie
channel, fireplaces,
conference room

Secluded hilltop home with "million dollar view," furnished with antique silver, china, rugs
artwork, fireplaces, and ensuite Jacuzzis. Swimming, hiking and fishing on 50 secluded
acres. Pet friendly.

La Chaumiere
1301 Cedar St 94515
800-474-6800 707-942-5139
Ursula

175-250 BB
3 rooms, 3 pb
Visa, MC, *Rated*, •
C-ltd/S-no/P-no/H-no

Full Gourmet breakfast
Afternoon wine, cheese,
crackers
Living room area, hot tub,
courtyard, redwood tree
with tree house

Come away to Calistoga, in Napa Valley's Wine Country, where a night's stay at La
chaumiere awaits. On a quiet picturesque residential street, across from city park, ½ block
from downtown Calistoga. ✉ lachaumierebnb@yahoo.com 🔿 www.lachaumiere.com

Meadowlark Country House
601 Petrified Forest Rd 94515
800-942-5651 707-942-5651
Kurt & Richard

195-450 BB
10 rooms, 10 pb
Visa, MC, AmEx,
Rated, •
S-no/P-ltd/H-ltd
German

Full Gourmet Breakfast
TV, VCR, WiFi, in house
massage, gourmet breakfast
hot tub, sauna, sun decks,
Naturist pool. Dogs ok.

Elegant, relaxed B&B. Amenities of a luxury destination, ambience of a Napa Valley
retreat.
✉ info@meadowlarkinn.com 🔿 www.meadowlarkinn.com

Scarlett's Country Inn
3918 Silverado Trl 94515
707-942-6669
Scarlett Dwyer

155-225 BB
3 rooms, 3 pb
Most CC, *Rated*, •
C-yes/S-no/P-no/H-no
Spanish

Continental breakfast
Complimentary wine &
cheese
Sitting room, A/C, TVs,
microwaves & refrigerator,
coffeemakers, pool

Secluded French country farmhouse overlooking vineyards in famed Napa Valley. Break
fast served by woodland swimming pool.
✉ scarletts@aol.com 🔿 www.scarlettscountryinn.com

Trailside Inn
4201 Silverado Trl 94515
707-942-4106
Lani Gray

165-185 BB
3 rooms, 3 pb
Most CC, *Rated*, •
C-yes/S-ltd/P-yes/H-ltd

Continental plus breakfast
Complimentary wine
Mineral water, fireplace,
kitchens, library, A/C, spa,
private deck, pool

The Trailside Inn is a charming 1930s farmhouse centrally located in the beautiful Napa
Valley. Two suites sleep party of four. Family suite. Heated swimming pool, child and pet
friendly. TV and Hi speed Internet
✉ innkeeper@trailsideinn.com 🔿 www.trailsideinn.com

Wine Way Inn
1019 Foothill Blvd 94515
800-572-0679 707-942-0680
Gillian & Nick Kite

100-200 BB
6 rooms, 6 pb
Most CC, *Rated*
C-ltd/S-ltd/P-no/H-no
French, a little Dutch
and German

Full Gourmet Breakfast
Afternoon wine & cheese
Extensive decks, WiFi
throughout the property

Converted from a Craftsman-style family home in 1978, the Wine Way Inn is Calistoga's
oldest B&B. The loving care of the previous and current owners, have preserved the best of
the original while providing lodging with period charm and modern convenience.
✉ winewayinn@aol.com 🔿 www.winewayinn.com

CALISTOGA————————————————————————————

Zinfandel House	125-150 BB	Full breakfast
1253 Summit Dr 94515	3 rooms, 2 pb	Complimentary wine
707-942-0733	Visa, MC, *Rated*	Library, sitting room, hot tub,
Bette & George Starke	C-ltd/S-no/P-no/H-no	goose down comforters,
		music room and deck.

Beautiful home situated on wooded hillside, overlooking vineyards and mountains. Lovely breakfast served on outside deck or in dining room.
✉ bette@zinfandelhouse.com 🌐 www.zinfandelhouse.com

CAMBRIA————————————————————————————

The Blue Whale Inn	315-470 BB	Full breakfast
6736 Moonstone Beach Dr	7 rooms, 7 pb	Snacks, afternoon tea,
93428	Most CC, *Rated*	complimentary wine &
800-753-9000 805-927-4647	C-ltd/S-no/P-ltd/H-yes	cheese
Marguerite & Mary		Sitting room, library,
		fireplaces, cable TV,
		romantic mini suites

Gracious hospitality. Luxurious and romantic partial oceanview mini-suites & 1 full Suite with incredible ocean views. Gourmet breakfasts, wine, and hors d'oeuvres. AAA Four-Diamond Award.
✉ innkeeper@bluewhaleinn.com 🌐 www.bluewhaleinn.com

J. Patrick House	175-215 BB	Full breakfast
2990 Burton Dr 93428	8 rooms, 8 pb	Offering evening wine and
800-341-5258 805-927-3812	Visa, MC, *Rated*	hors d'oeuveres and killer
Ann & John	C-ltd/S-no/P-no/H-no	chocolate chip cookies
		Sitting room, library, in-room
		massage, games, CD Players

Award winning Inn on the California Central Coast. Authentic log home and carriage house nestled in the pines. Irish country comfort in accommodations with rooms uniquely appointed in "traditional" yet comfortable decor. Wood burning fireplaces.
✉ jph@jpatrickhouse.com 🌐 www.jpatrickhouse.com

Olallieberry Inn	135-225 BB	Full gourmet breakfast
2476 Main St 93428	9 rooms, 9 pb	Complimentary wine, hors
888-927-3222 805-927-3222	Visa, MC, AmEx,	d'oeuvres, cookies
Marjorie Ott	*Rated*, •	Gathering room, fireplaces,
	C-ltd/S-no/P-no/H-yes	antiques, special diets,
		massages, wireless Internet
		connection

1873 restored Greek Revival home, warm & inviting, nestled in the heart of the enchanting village of Cambria. Walk to antique shops, art galleries, gift shops, & fine restaurants.
✉ info@olallieberry.com 🌐 www.olallieberry.com

The Squibb House	125-185 BB	Breakfast delivered to your
4063 Burton Dr 93428	5 rooms, 5 pb	door
866-927-9600 805-927-9600	Visa, MC, AmEx, •	Afternoon cookies & tea,
Bruce Black	C-ltd/S-no/P-no/H-no	complimentary wine tasting
		Gardens, gazebo for small
		events, weddings, groups,
		retail store with Amish
		furniture & antiques

In the heart of Cambria, within steps of galleries, shops & restaurants, there is a place suspended in time. Relax in the main parlor, stroll the garden path or rock on the porch and watch the world go by from this beautifully restored inn.
✉ innkeeper@squibbhouse.net 🌐 www.squibbhouse.net

CAMBRIA——————————————————————————

White Water Inn	90-280 BB	Continental breakfast
6790 Moonstone Beach Dr	17 rooms, 17 pb	Fireplace, cable TV,
93428	Visa, MC, Disc, *Rated*	hairdryers, iron & board,
800-995-1715 805-927-1066	C-ltd/S-no/P-no/H-ltd	complimentary videos,
Ellen Lewis		sitting room, ocean views

One of the few independently owned inns in Cambria opposite the ocean. A calm, affable establishment in the Monterey Marine Wildlife Sanctuary, half way between San Francisco and Los Angeles.
✉ innkeeper@whitewaterinn.com ◔ www.whitewaterinn.com

CAPTIOLA——————————————————————————

Capitola Hotel	99-275 BB	Continental breakfast
210 Esplanade 95010	9 rooms, 9 pb	
888-395-9200 831-476-1278	Visa, MC, Disc	
Susan DaRoza	C-ltd/S-no/P-no/H-yes	

Just steps from the beach, our boutique hotel offers stylish and comfortable rooms with a Caribbean flair. Enjoy easy access to great shopping, dining and year-round outdoor activities.
✉ info@capitolahotel.com ◔ www.capitolahotel.com/index.html

CARDIFF BY THE SEA——————————————————————

Cardiff by the Sea Lodge	140-385 BB	Continental plus breakfast
142 Chesterfield 92007	17 rooms, 17 pb	Terrace, fireplaces, whirlpool
760-944-6474	Most CC, •	tubs, views
James & Jeanette Statser	C-yes/S-no/P-no/H-ltd	

Steps away from the blue Pacific Ocean and just minutes from all San Diego has to offer there is a place where lush gardens bloom year-round.
✉ innkeeper@cardifflodge.com ◔ www.cardifflodge.com

CARLSBAD——————————————————————————

Pelican Cove Inn	95-215 BB	Full breakfast
320 Walnut Ave 92008	10 rooms, 10 pb	Fireplaces, feather beds,
888-PEL-COVE 760-434-5995	Visa, MC, AmEx,	business accommodations,
Nancy & Kris Nayudu	*Rated*, •	TV, private entrances,
	C-yes/S-no/P-no/H-yes	Internet, beach equipment

Sun, blue skies, endless beaches, glorious sunsets, and the wide Pacific welcome you to Pelican Cove B&B Inn. We strive to make your stay memorable and enjoyable. Only steps from the ocean, fine restaurants and pleasant shops.
✉ PelicanCoveInn@pelican-cove.com ◔ www.pelican-cove.com

CARMEL——————————————————————————

Carmel Country Inn	275-425 BB	Expanded Continental
Dolores & 3rd Ave 93921	12 rooms, 12 pb	Breakfast
800-215-6343 831-625-3263	Visa, MC, AmEx,	In-room coffeemaker,
Amy Johnson	*Rated*, •	complimentary cream
	C-ltd/S-no/P-ltd/H-no	sherry
	Spanish	Fireplaces, Private Baths,
		Private Entrances, off street
		Parking, Wireless Internet,
		TV/DVD Players.

Carmel Country Inn Bed and Breakfast in Carmel, California offers a great blend of convenience, comfort, romance, and surrounding natural beauty near the beaches of beautiful Carmel by the Sea.
✉ info@carmelcountryinn.com ◔ www.carmelcountryinn.com

CARMEL————————————————————————————————————

The Colonial Terrace
San Antonio & 13th 93921
800-345-8220 831-624-2741

119-599 BB
26 rooms, 26 pb
Most CC, *Rated*, •
C-ltd/S-no/P-no/H-ltd
Spanish

Expanded Continental
Breakfast
Afternoon tea reception
offering fresh fruit & fresh-
baked cookies
All rooms have fireplaces,
many with ocean views,
Jacuzzi tubs, wet bars, some
with kitchenettes

Historic boutique hotel, one of Carmel's original hotels. Just steps from Carmel Beach, we offer rooms with fireplaces, ocean views, suites, and whirlpool tubs. Each room offers its own charm and personality.
✉ reservations@thecolonialterrace.com ◐ www.thecolonialterrace.com

The Crystal Terrace Inn
24815 Carpenter St 93921
800-600-4488 831-624-6400
Peter and Jackie Welling

79-450 BB
18 rooms, 18 pb
C-ltd/S-no/P-no/H-no

Continental plus breakfast
In-room coffee, afternoon
wine and champagne with
cheese, crackers and fruit
hour
Fireplaces, whirlpool tubs,
kitchens, private parking

One of Carmel's landmark inns, built in 1927, The Crystal Terrace has recently been totally remodeled and reflects the good taste and refined splendor of the best inns. Come enjoy distinctive lodging in a gentle paradise at our historic country inn
✉ reservations@carmelcrystalbayinn.com ◐ www.carmelcrystalterrace.com

Edgemere Cottages
San Antonio between 13th &
Santa Lucia St 93921
866-241-4575 831-624-4501
Gretchen Siegrist-Allen

120-250 BB
4 rooms, 4 pb
Visa, MC, •
C-ltd/S-no/P-yes/H-ltd
German, French,
Spanish, Italian, Dutch

Continental plus breakfast
Sitting room, fireplaces,
cable TV, accommodations
for business travelers, WiFi

Edgemere features quaint private cottages, continental breakfast, beautiful gardens, and is just a one block walk to Carmel Beach. The perfect setting for a romantic escape to the Monterey Peninsula.
✉ info@edgemerecottages.com ◐ www.edgemerecottages.com

Happy Landing Inn
Monte Verde bet. 5th & 6th
Ave 93921
800-297-6250 831-624-7917
Diane & Dawn

135-235 BB
7 rooms, 7 pb
Most CC, •
C-ltd/S-no/P-yes/H-ltd

Continental plus breakfast
Hot breakfast brought to
your room, weekend snacks
in the Great Room
Great room, gazebo &
gardens, TV, DVD/CD
players, WiFi, reading lamps,
hairdryers

Hansel & Gretel cottages in the heart of Carmel, like something from a Beatrix Potter book, one of Carmel's most romantic places to stay. All accommodations with private baths, 3 with fireplaces and 3 suites. Enjoy a warm breakfast brought to your room.
✉ info@carmelhappylanding.com ◐ www.carmelhappylanding.com

L'Auberge Carmel
831-624-8578
David Fink, Managing Partner

295-605 BB
20 rooms, 20 pb
Visa, MC, AmEx
S-no/P-no

European Breakfast
Intimate restaurant with a
4500 bottle, wine cellar on
premises.
Down bedding, luxurious
linens, LCD flat screen
television, soaking tubs,
twice-daily housekeeping

A European-style luxury hotel just four blocks from famous Carmel Beach and an easy stroll to the village's numerous art galleries, shops and restaurants. 20 thoughtfully appointed guestrooms offer sophistication and romantic allure.
✉ reservations@laubergecarmel.com ◐ www.laubergecarmel.com/index.php

CARMEL——————

Lamp Lighter Inn
SE Corner of Ocean Ave &
Camino Real 93921
831-624-7372   Bobby Richards

185-475 BB
11 rooms, 11 pb
Visa, MC, AmEx
C-yes/S-no/P-yes/H-no

Breakfast Basket
Fireplaces, TVs, phones,
private entrances

Charming inn with two cottages and four guestrooms, just steps to the beach. Couples, families and small groups will find accommodations at the Lamp Lighter Inn, some rooms with fireplaces, all have private baths. An enchanted setting with lush gardens.
✉ innkeeper@carmellamplighter.com ☉ www.carmellamplighter.com

Monte Verde Inn & Casa de Carmel
Monte Verde between Ocean
& 7th 93921
800-328-7707 831-624-6046
Bobby

185-350 BB
16 rooms, 16 pb
Visa, MC, AmEx, •
C-yes/S-no/P-yes/H-no

Breakfast basket
Sherry, coffeemaker, wine &
cheese, close by restaurants
TV, phone, refrigerator, hair
dryers, gardens and patios

Country-style inn, in the heart of downtown Carmel and 5 blocks to the ocean. Ideal for romantic getaways, honeymoons, families with children, vacations with friends, personal retreats & business travelers alike.
✉ innkeeper@carmelmonteverdeinn.com ☉ www.carmelmonteverdeinn.com

Sandpiper Inn
2408 Bay View Ave 93923
800-590-6433 831-624-6433
James Hartle

99-239 BB
17 rooms, 17 pb
Most CC, *Rated*, •
S-no/P-no/H-no

Continental plus breakfast
Afternoon tea & cookies
Library, wireless Internet,
fireside lounge, close to
tennis, golf, hiking

One-half block to Carmel Beach. European-style 1929 country inn, with some antiques and individual decor. Ocean views, gas-log fireplaces, 3 cottages, patio & garden areas. Mobil 2-star rating, 3 Diamonds AAA rating.
✉ sandpiperinn@yahoo.com ☉ www.sandpiper-inn.com/index_enter.htm

Sea View Inn
Camino Real @ 11th & 12th
93921
831-624-8778
Marshall & Diane Hydorn

110-185 BB
8 rooms, 6 pb
Most CC, *Rated*, •
C-ltd/S-no/P-no/H-no

Continental plus breakfast
Afternoon tea and coffee
Complimentary evening
wine, sitting room, library,
garden

When you arrive at the Sea View Inn you will be greeted by a friendly and knowledgeable staff, happy to advise you about the restaurants, shops, scenic and historic places that makes our Village such a special place.
✉ seaviewinncarmel@gmail.com ☉ www.seaviewinncarmel.com

Tally Ho Inn
Monte Verde at 6th St 93921
800-652-2632 831-624-2232
John Lloyd

189-339 BB
12 rooms, 12 pb
Most CC, *Rated*, •
C-yes/S-no/P-no/H-yes
Spanish

Continental plus breakfast
Afternoon tea, brandy
Floral garden, sun deck,
fireplaces, oceanviews, close
to beach

The Tally Ho features 12 rooms with private decks and ocean views. Rooms have fireplaces, 42" plasma TV's, Jacuzzi tubs, Bose Wave radios & refrigerators. Also featuring complimentary wireless Internet and during the week a full American breakfast buffet.
✉ jlloyd@pine-inn.com ☉ www.tallyho-inn.com

Tickle Pink Inn
155 Highland Dr. 93923
800-635-4774 831-624-1244

249-529 BB
35 rooms, 35 pb
Visa, MC, AmEx,
Rated, •
C-ltd/S-ltd/P-no/H-yes

Continental plus breakfast
Evening wine and cheese
reception, Limited room
service and wine list menu.
Limited room service menu,
breakfast delivered to your
room, daily newspaper,
movie library, robes.

Established and operated by the Gurries family, the Tickle Pink Inn at Carmel Highlands has graced this setting since 1956. With 35 rooms and suites, the Inn is intimate and private and offers the discriminating guest a variety of personalized services.
✉ kparker@ticklepinkinn.com ☉ www.ticklepinkinn.com

CARMEL

Tradewinds at Carmel
Mission St & Third Ave 93921
800-624-6665 831-624-2776
Yuriko Weathers

325-550 BB
28 rooms, 28 pb
Visa, MC, AmEx,
Rated, •
C-yes/S-no/P-ltd/H-yes
Spanish;Japanese

Continental Breakfast Buffet
Catering upon request, ask
our concierge about
restaurant reservations and
recommendations
Tropical design, exquisite
furnishings, romantic
atmosphere, fireplaces,
Kimono robes, spa slippers

Tradewinds Carmel is the luxury boutique hotel providing an elegant oasis just a short stroll from the Carmel Plaza, galleries and restaurants of Carmel-by-the-Sea. If you are looking for a romantic bed and breakfast, you've found it! Welcome.
info@tradewindscarmel.com www.tradewindscarmel.com

Vagabond's House Inn
4th & Dolores 93921
800-262-1262 831-624-7738
Julie Campbell

165-275 BB
13 rooms, 13 pb
Most CC, *Rated*, •
C-ltd/S-no/P-yes/H-no
French

Continental plus breakfast
Wine, snacks
Sitting room w/fireplace,
library, courtyard, 2 blocks
to downtown

Antique clocks and pictures, quilted bedspreads, fresh flowers, plants, shelves filled with old books. Sherry by the fireplace, breakfast served in your room.
innkeeper@vagabondshouseinn.com www.vagabondshouseinn.com

CARMEL VALLEY

Country Garden Inns
102 W. Carmel Valley Rd 93924
800-367-3336 831-659-5361
Dirk Oldenburg

119-215 BB
39 rooms, 39 pb
Visa, MC, AmEx, •
C-yes/S-no/P-no/H-no
German, Spanish

Buffet with waffle bar
Daily evening wine & cheese
hour.

#1 Rated B&B in Carmel Valley by Trip Advisor. Out of the reach of the coastal fog nestled in the Santa Lucia Mts and close to Carmel-by-the-Sea. Buffet style breakfast with waffle bar included. Walk to village with wine tasting, shopping, and dining.
concierge@countrygardeninns.com www.countrygardeninns.com

CASTRO VALLEY

Deer Crossing Inn
21600 Eden Canyon Rd 94552
510-537-4926
Cindi & Rick Hinds

130-295 BB
6 rooms, 6 pb
Visa, MC, *Rated*
C-ltd/S-no/P-no/H-ltd

Full breakfast
Afternoon social hour with
wine and food. Coffee and
tea available throughout the
day.
Outdoor deck, Gold Rush
themed dining room, water
beds, Jacuzzi tubs, TV/DVD,
fireplaces, privacy

PLAYBOY found us Secluded, Romantic & Sexy enough for a photo shoot July '07! Come and see San Francisco Bay Area's Most Romantic Gold Mine for Yourself! An Experience We Promise You Will Never Forget!
info@deercrossinginn.com www.deercrossinginn.com

CATHEYS VALLEY

Rancho Bernardo
2617 Old Hwy South 95306
877-930-1669 209-966-4511
Kathleen & Bernard Lozares

155-195 BB
2 rooms, 2 pb
Visa, MC, AmEx, *Rated*
C-ltd/S-no/P-no/H-ltd

Full country breakfast
Afternoon tea, cookies and
other snacks
Comp. wine for
honeymooners, fireplaces,
pool table, fax, videos,
TV/VCR

Secluded 120 acre cattle ranch with views of rolling hills, dotted with oak trees, Chinese rock walls, springs and grazing livestock on your way to or from magnificent Yosemite National Park.
kathleen@ranchobernardobnb.com www.ranchobernardobnb.com

CAYUCOS

Cayucos Sunset Inn
95 South Ocean Ave 93430
877-805-1076 805-995-2500
John & Lisa Mankins

189-359 BB
6 rooms, 6 pb
Visa, MC, AmEx, *Rated*
C-yes/S-no/P-no/H-ltd

Full breakfast
Evening hors d'oeuvres,
wine, sparkling water
Jacuzzi, library, fireplaces,
patio/balcony, spa
treatments

Escape to fine B&B lodgings built specifically for guests to relax and enjoy the calm beachside atmosphere, with 6 casually elegant rooms and suites. Enjoy views of the Pacific Ocean and Cayucos Pier, and spectacular sunsets. AAA 4 Diamond rated.
✉ info@cayucossunsetinn.com ✆ www.cayucossunsetinn.com

**On The Beach Bed &
Breakfast**
181 North Ocean Ave 93430
877-995-0800 805-995-3200
Patricia Weinsheimer

189-385 BB
14 rooms, 14 pb
Most CC
C-yes/S-no/P-no/H-ltd

Full breakfast
Afternoon wine, cheese and
other refreshments,
scrumptious evening
desserts
TV/DVD/VCR, fridge,
microwave, coffee pot, hair
dryer, iron; there's even an
electric towel warmer!

Select one of our oversized rooms with rich, luxurious appointments of hand-crafted woods, local artwork and beautiful fabrics. The surf will lull you to sleep & the views of the pier, beach, ocean & sunset out your window rival the most exclusive resorts
✉ info@californiaonthebeach.com ✆ www.californiaonthebeach.com

CHESTER

The Bidwell House
One Main St 96020
530-258-3338
Eva & Filip Laboda

85-175 BB
14 rooms, 12 pb
Visa, MC, *Rated*, •
C-ltd/S-no/P-no/H-yes

Three course gourmet
breakfast
Afternoon tea and
sandwiches, fresh fruit, giant
chocolate chip cookies
Sitting room, library, Jacuzzi
tubs in rooms, fireplaces

Historic Inn on the edge of Lassen National Park, beautiful Lake Almanor and next to the Feather River. Gourmet breakfast, a four-season paradise, world class dining, golfing, boating and shopping.
✉ reservation@bidwellhouse.com ✆ www.bidwellhouse.com

CHULA VISTA

**El Primero Boutique B&B
Hotel**
416 Third Ave 91910
619-425-4486
Pie & Sol Roque

110-140 BB
19 rooms, 19 pb
Most CC
C-yes/S-no/P-no/H-yes

Full breakfast
24 hour guest services,
friendly staff, courtyard,
kiosk, cable TV, WiFi, off
street parking

El Primero is Chula Vista's best-kept hotel secret. An historic, award winning B&B where guests wake up to a sumptuous, gourmet breakfast. Recipient of the city's first Historic Preservation Award and the Mayor's 2005 Beautification Award.
✉ pie@elprimerohotel.com ✆ www.elprimerohotel.com

CLOVERDALE

Old Crocker Inn
1126 Old Crocker Inn Rd 95425
800-716-2007 707-894-4000
Marcia & Tony Babb

155-245 BB
8 rooms, 8 pb
Visa, MC, •
C-yes/S-ltd/P-ltd/H-no

Full breakfast
Special events catered
Spa, pool, gas fireplace,
Jacuzzis, Internet access,
pullout sofa bed, cable
TV/DVD, bath amenities

Old Crocker Inn is a B&B set on an historic five-acre ranch above the Alexander Valley in Sonoma County, California. Relax in a quiet country setting, with all the amenities of a deluxe hotel.
✉ Innkeeper@oldcrockerinn.com ✆ www.oldcrockerinn.com

COARSEGOLD

Ravensbrook B&B
37621 Ravensbrook Way 93614
559-683-4792
Sherri A. Smith

90-160 BB
2 rooms, 2 pb
Visa, MC, *Rated*, •
C-ltd/S-ltd/P-ltd/H-ltd

Full breakfast
Tea, coffee & hot chocolate;
fresh fruit, biscotti, candy
Private deck, barbecue, spa,
Dish TV/VCR, videos, books,
games, DSL; casino shuttle
for extra fee

*Guest rooms are located on the first floor with a private dining room just for the guests.
Each room has a private bath & entrance, Dish TV/VCR & local phones. Video games,
books, snacks, microwave oven, refrigerator & laundry facilities available.*
✉ ravensbrookbandb@aol.com ♦ www.ravensbrook-yosemite.com

COLFAX

Rose Mountain Manor
233 Plutes Way 95713
866-444-Rose 530-346-0067
Barbara Bowers

95-169 BB
3 rooms, 3 pb
Visa, MC, Disc
C-ltd/S-ltd/P-no/H-no

Full breakfast
Early coffee & tea served to
your door, afternoon tea with
homemade scones served at
4:00
Walking path, electric
fireplaces, wood-burning
stove, TV, VCR/DVD player in
the parlour

*On five wooded acres in historic Colfax, CA, in California's Gold Country in the Sierra
Foothills, filled with charm and small town atmosphere. Rose Mountain Manor, a cozy,
secluded Victorian retreat, is easily accessed from Interstate 80.*
✉ innkeeper@rosemountainmanor.com ♦ www.rosemountainmanor.com

COLUMBIA

Columbia City Hotel
22768 Main St 95310
800-532-1479 209-532-1479
Dave Wood

125-145 BB
10 rooms, 10 pb
Most CC, *Rated*
C-yes/S-no/P-no/H-no

Continental breakfast
Dine in our Morgan
Restaurant or for more
casual fare, try out the
historic "What Cheer
Saloon"
Sitting room, full service
saloon, live theatre and ice
cream parlour

*A visit to the Columbia City and Fallon Hotels is a glimpse into one of the most fascinating
periods in our country's history, as well as one of California's finest restoration projects.
Discover the gold in California's Sierra Foothills!*
✉ esteiness@foreverresorts.com ♦ www.cityhotel.com

Columbia Fallon Hotel
11175 Washington St 95310
800-532-1479 209-532-1470
Tom Bender

65-130 BB
14 rooms, 14 pb
Most CC, *Rated*, •
C-yes/S-no/P-no/H-yes

Continental plus breakfast
Sitting room, rose garden,
live theater, gold panning
nearby, fishing

*Restored Victorian hotel, full of antiques in state-preserved Gold Rush town. Some of the
rooms have balconies where you can sit and enjoy the fresh air and watch the goings-on of
an authentic Gold Rush Era town. Elegant and intimate. Near Yosemite.*
✉ info@cityhotel.com ♦ www.cityhotel.com

CORONADO———————————————————————————————

Cherokee Lodge
964 D Ave 92118
877-743-6213 619-437-1967
Karen Johnson

135-175 BB
12 rooms, 12 pb
Most CC, •
C-yes/S-no/P-ltd/H-no

Continental breakfast
breakfast vouchers for
Continental breakfast at a
local diner coffee and tea in
rooms
WiFi , data ports,
washer/dryer, satellite TVs,
refrig, Free phone calls
within the US & most
countries, A/C

The Cherokee Lodge across the bay from downtown San Diego in the heart of Coronado Island and is located one block from downtown Coronado near numerous charming bistros & restaurants, & just four blocks from the beach & the historic Hotel Del Coronado.
✉ info@cherokeelodge.com ☯ www.CherokeeLodge.com

Coronado Village Inn
1017 Park Pl 92118
619-435-9318
Jauter & Ana Sainz

85-95 BB
15 rooms, 15 pb
Visa, MC, AmEx
C-yes/H-yes
Spanish

Self-serve continental
breakfast
Laundry, sitting room, cable
TV, maid service.

Located off Coronado's main street, Coronado Village Inn is a historic bed and breakfast decorated in old Spanish style. 1½ blocks to the ocean!
☯ www.coronadovillageinn.com

CROWLEY LAKE———————————————————————————

Rainbow Tarns B&B At Crowley Lake
505 Rainbow Tarns Rd 93546
888-588-6269 760-935-4556
Brock & Diane Thoman

110-155 BB
3 rooms, 3 pb
Cash, Checks, *Rated*
C-ltd/S-ltd/P-no/H-yes
Closed Dec 24–25,
Apr/Nov

Full country breakfast
Afternoon wine, snacks,
veggie meals by arrangement
Sitting room, library, 2 rooms
with Jacuzzis

Relax in the heart of High Sierra Mountains where the soothing sounds of flowing water and gentle breezes in the pines, the crystal clear sky and sparkling starry nights blend into an enchanting and memorable experience. Between Bishop and Mammoth Lakes.
✉ innkeeper@rainbowtarns.com ☯ www.rainbowtarns.com

DANA POINT————————————————————————————

The Blue Lantern Inn
34343 Blue Lantern St 92629
800-950-1236 949-611-1304
Lin McManon

190-600 BB
29 rooms, 29 pb
Most CC
C-yes/S-no/P-no/H-yes

Full breakfast
Afternoon wine, tea & hors
d' oeuvres, freshly-baked
cookies, drinks available
throughout the day
Meeting rooms, bikes,
Jacuzzi, fireplaces

Enjoy fabulous views of the Pacific from just about every window of this four diamond bed and breakfast inn—dramatically located on a bluff above the Dana Point Yacht Harbor.
✉ bluelanterninn@foursisters.com ☯ www.bluelanterninn.com

DESCANO———————————————————————————————

Golden Eagle Ranch
10460 Boulder Creek Rd 91916
619-659-9649
Lisa DeMars

125-180 BB
3 rooms, 2 pb
Visa, MC
S-no/P-no/H-no

Full breakfast
Large relaxing common
room with recliners, 65" TV,
80 DVD movies, surround
sound, WiFi, piano

Welcome to this cozy San Diego – Julian Bed & Breakfast Inn, home to abundant sunshine and a gentle breeze almost every day! A stone's throw from the Cuyamaca State Park. WiFi and DirecTV. Come for the comfy, country charm.
✉ Lisa@GoldenEagleGuestRanch.com ☯ goldeneagleguestranch.com/index.html

DESERT HOT SPRINGS

El Morocco Inn & Spa
66810 4th St 92240
800-288-9905 760-288-2527
Bruce Abney

169-229 BB
12 rooms, 12 pb
Most CC, *Rated*, •
S-ltd/P-no/H-ltd

Continental plus breakfast
You'll find complimentary
snacks and other beverages
always available in the
Kasbah Lounge.
Offering a range of Spa
Packages and Services
including Massages & Body
wraps & Concierge services!

For a "transporting experience"...the unique El Morocco Inn & Spa offers 12 sumptuous "guest chambers," each facing the Hot Mineral Springs swimming pool & fabric swathed spa in a sequestered courtyard setting. Great Spa treatments complete this escape!
✉ Info@elmoroccoinn.com ○ www.elmoroccoinn.com/index.htm

ELK

Elk Cove Inn & Spa
6300 S. Highway One 95432
800-275-2967 707-877-3321
Elaine Bryant

100-395 BB
15 rooms, 15 pb
Most CC, *Rated*, •
C-ltd/S-ltd/P-no/H-ltd
Spanish

Full gourmet breakfast
Direct beach access,
European-style day spa, free
WiFi, guest lounge with TV,
gazebo

Mendocino coast oceanfront, private stairs to the beach. 1883 former Lumber Baron's estate offers dramatic views, a Day Spa, and gazebo. 15 suites, cottages and charming rooms. Gourmet breakfast, welcome basket, complimentary cocktails & wine, free WiFi.
✉ innkeeper@elkcoveinn.com ○ www.elkcoveinn.com

Greenwood Pier Inn
5940 S. Hwy 1 95432
800-807-3423 707-877-9997

165-335 BB
12 rooms, 12 pb
Visa, MC, AmEx
C-ltd/S-no/P-yes/H-no

Full breakfast
Complete lunch and dinner
available from our restaurant
Fireplaces, great ocean
views, private decks, hot tub,
massage available

Rest—Reflect—Renew. From the decks, from the windows, you watch the whales, the seals, the gulls, the fog, and the sunset over the ocean. Walk the wide sandy beach in the state park just south of the inn.
✉ greenwoodpierinn@yahoo.com ○ www.greenwoodpierinn.com/inn/inn.html

Sandpiper House Inn
5520 S Hwy 1 95432
800-894-9016 707-877-3587
Jaci Schartz

150-275 BB
5 rooms, 5 pb
Most CC, *Rated*, •
C-ltd/S-no/P-no/H-no

Gourmet Breakfast
Wine & hors d'oeuvres in
the evening; complimentary
wine in your room
Antiques, fresh flowers,
gardens, fireplaces, fine
linens, down comforters,
feather pillows

Seaside country inn built in 1916. Rich redwood paneling in the living and dining rooms, lush perennial gardens that extend to the ocean bluff, stunning oceanviews, fireplaces in all of the rooms. ✉ sandpiperhouseinn@yahoo.com ○ www.sandpiperhouse.com

ENCINITAS

Inn at Moonlight Beach
105 N Vulcan Ave 92024
760-944-0318
Ann Dunham & Terry
Hunefeld

86-145 BB
4 rooms, 4 pb
Visa, MC, *Rated*
S-no/P-no/H-yes
Spanish

Continental plus breakfast
Fresh-ground Starbucks
coffee & delicious breakfast
of fresh baked pastries, fruit
& granola
Our sunny breakfast suite is
available to you through out
the day. Starbucks in your
suite.

The Inn is on a hillside overlooking Moonlight Beach and the Pacific Ocean in the quaint surfing beach community of Old Encinitas. Our 4 lovely suites offer plush linens, private bathrooms, wireless Internet, refrigerator and cable TV.
✉ annpdunham@gmail.com ○ www.innatmoonlightbeach.com

50   California

EUREKA————————————————————————————————

Carter House Inns
301 L St 95501
800-404-1390 707-444-8062
Mark & Christi Carter

195-195 BB
32 rooms, 32 pb
Most CC, •
C-yes/S-no/P-yes/H-yes
Spanish, French

Full breakfast
Wine, hors d'oeuvres,
cookies, tea, chocolate
truffles
Whirlpools, fireplaces, sitting
rooms, Jacuzzis, TV/VCR,
CD, stereo, gardens

4 Diamond Award Inn perched alongside Humboldt Bay in Victorian Eureka. Luxurious amenities, superior hospitality, spas, fireplaces, and antique furnishings. Wine Spectator Grand Award winning restaurant.
✉ reserve@carterhouse.com ○ www.carterhouse.com

The Ship's Inn B&B
821 D St 95501
877-443-7583 707-443-7583
Genie Wood

130-175 BB
3 rooms, 3 pb
Most CC
C-yes/S-ltd/P-ltd/H-no

Full breakfast
Internet access, WiFi, TV,
VCR, robes, dining room,
fireside common room,

Step back in time to those seafaring days in a cozy, relaxing atmosphere befitting Eureka's Victorian Seaport. Just blocks to charming Old Town and the new boardwalk.
✉ genie@shipsinn.net ○ www.shipsinn.net

FELTON————————————————————————————————

Felton Crest Inn
780 El Solya Heights Dr 95018-
9334
800-474-4011 831-335-4011
Hanna Peters

325-499 BB
4 rooms, 4 pb
Visa, MC, AmEx
C-ltd/S-ltd/P-no/H-ltd

Continental breakfast

A romantic getaway set in the majestic redwoods of the Santa Cruz Mtns. Enjoy all that the beautiful Monterey Bay and California's Central Coast have to offer. Uniquely located between San Francisco, Carmel and Pebble Beach, and the Santa Clara Valley.
✉ hannapeters@comcast.net ○ www.feltoncrestinn.com

FERNDALE————————————————————————————————

Gingerbread Mansion Inn
400 Berding St 95536
800-952-4136 707-786-4000
Robert & Juli, Sue & Vrice

155-305 BB
11 rooms, 11 pb
Visa, MC, AmEx,
Rated, •
C-ltd/S-no/P-no/H-ltd

Full breakfast
Afternoon English Tea
Four guest parlors (two with
fireplaces), English gardens,
offer bicycles and kayaks

Gingerbread Mansion Inn, built in 1899, has everything: elegance, quietude, charm, warm hospitality, comfort, attention to detail, antiques, romance and beautifully lush English gardens. ✉ innkeeper@gingerbread-mansion.com ○ gingerbread-mansion.com

Victorian Inn
400 Ocean Ave 95536
888-589-1808 707-786-4949
Lowell Daniels & Jenny Oaks

105-460 BB
13 rooms, 13 pb
Most CC, *Rated*, •
C-yes/S-no/P-no/H-ltd

Full breakfast
Lunch/dinner available,
snacks, restaurant, bar,
afternoon wine and cheese
Sitting room, suites, fireplace,
cable TV, wireless & cable
Internet access

The Victorian Inn stands as a monument to luxurious comfort and exquisite craftsmanship. It embodies the elegance and romance of the timber boom era on the North Coast.
✉ innkeeper@victorianvillageinn.com ○ www.victorianvillageinn.com

FISH CAMP————————————————————————————————

Narrow Gauge Inn
48571 Hwy 41 93623
888-644-9050 559-683-7720
Martha Vanaman

79-195 BB
26 rooms, 26 pb
Visa, MC, Disc, *Rated*,
•
C-yes/S-ltd/P-yes/H-no

Continental breakfast
Fine dining restaurant
(seasonal)
Seasonal pool & hot tub, gift
shop, nature trail

Celebrating the mountain atmosphere, the Narrow Gauge Inn is just 4 miles from Yosemite. Offering 26 charming rooms with balconies and mountain views, some pet-friendly. Seasonal restaurant. Weddings, reunions and events welcome.
✉ ngi@sti.net ○ www.narrowgaugeinn.com

FISH CAMP

Yosemite Big Creek Inn	129-249 BB	Buffet breakfast
1221 Hwy 41 93623	3 rooms, 3 pb	24-hour refreshment center
559-641-2828	Visa, MC, *Rated*	In-room massage available,
Pamela Salisbury	C-ltd/S-ltd/P-no/H-no	dedicated guest
		computer/printer, free
		wireless Internet & local
		phone

Yosemite Lodging at Big Creek Inn is the closest Bed & Breakfast lodging to the south gate of Yosemite National Park. A 3 guestroom inn ideally located just 2 miles from Yosemite in Fish Camp California.
✉ innkeeper@bigcreekinn.com ○ www.bigcreekinn.com

FORESTVILLE

Farmhouse Inn &	250-545 BB	Full breakfast
Restaurant	18 rooms, 18 pb	Michelin Star, Zagat
7871 River Rd 95436	Most CC, *Rated*	reviewed, 4 star restaurant.
800-464-6642 707-887-3300	C-ltd/S-no/P-no/H-yes	European style service,
Catherine & Joe Bartolomei		superb wine list. Th-Mon.
		Full concierge services,
		heated pool, spa services, WI
		access, beverage bar, fire pit
		& s'mores.

Northern California Wine Country Inn and Restaurant. Travel & Leisure Top 30 Inns, Michelin star, Zagat Best in Sonoma County, and Chronicle 100 Best restaurants. Luxury spa on site. Romantic getaway bed and breakfast central to Napa & Sonoma wineries.
✉ innkeep@farmhouseinn.com ○ www.farmhouseinn.com

FORT BRAGG

Country Inn	55-145 BB	Full gourmet breakfast
632 N Main St 95437	8 rooms, 8 pb	Fireplaces, sun deck, parlor,
800-831-5327 707-964-3737	Most CC, *Rated*, •	hot tub, Spa Treatments
Bruce & Cynthia Knauss	C-yes/S-no/P-no/H-yes	available, Skunk Train
		nearby

The Country Inn Bed and Breakfast, located in Fort Bragg on the Mendocino coast, invites you to "be our guests."
✉ cntryinn@mcn.org ○ www.beourguests.com

Glass Beach B&B Inn	105-175 BB	Full breakfast
726 N Main St 95437	10 rooms, 10 pb	Afternoon refreshments and
707-964-6774	Most CC, •	snacks, homemade cookies,
Nancy & Richard Fowler	C-yes/S-ltd/P-ltd/H-ltd	brownies, fudge
		WiFi, fireplaces, sitting room,
		cable TV, DVD/VCR,
		telephone and data port,
		fridges, microwave

Come relax in this 1920's Craftsman style home. Enjoy the peaceful scenery of Glass Beach, beautiful redwoods, botanical gardens, the Skunk Train, hiking trails and wonderful hospitality of our inn. A full breakfast to die for.
✉ glassbch@mcn.org ○ www.glassbeachinn.com

Weller House Inn	140-210 BB	Full breakfast
524 Stewart St 95437	10 rooms, 10 pb	Complimentary wine &
877-8-WELLER 707-964-4415	Most CC	cheese
Vivien LaMothe	C-ltd/S-no/P-no/H-ltd	Sitting room, library, cable,
	French, German, Danish,	Jacuzzi, fireplace,
		observation tower, hot tub,
		gardens, bike storage

Featured in New York Times and Sunset Magazine. This Victorian beauty built in 1886 includes a lavish breakfast served in a 900 square foot ballroom, and 2 rooms in water tower topped by 40 foot high, oceanview hot tub.
✉ innkeeper@wellerhouse.com ○ www.wellerhouse.com

GEORGETOWN

American River Inn
6600 Orleans St 95634
800-245-6566 530-333-4499
Will & Maria Collin

95-130 BB
13 rooms, 9 pb
Most CC, *Rated*, •

Full breakfast
Afternoon wine & hors
d'oeuvres
Pool, Jacuzzi, bicycles, bocce
ball

Historic Queen Anne-style bed & breakfast inn, complete with old fashioned hospitality and turn-of-the-century antique furnishings. Refurbished Summer '07 to exceptional beauty. Fantastic featherbeds. ✉ visitus@americanriverinn.com ◑ www.Americanriverinn.com

GEYSERVILLE

Hope-Merrill/Hope-Bosworth B&B
21253 Geyserville Ave 95441
800-825-4233 707-857-3356
Cosette & Ron Scheiber

149-289 BB
12 rooms, 12 pb
Most CC, *Rated*, •
C-ltd/S-no/P-no/H-ltd
Spanish

Full breakfast
Complimentary water; 24-
Hour coffee/tea/chocolate
machine; other beverages
available for purchase
Sitting room, library,
Jacuzzis, suites, swimming
pool, fireplace, cable TV in
some rooms

Facing each other are the Queen Anne Craftsman style Hope-Bosworth House and the strikingly restored Eastlake style Victorian Hope-Merrill House.
✉ moreinfo@hope-inns.com ◑ www.hope-inns.com

GROVELAND

All Seasons Groveland Inn
18656 Main St 95321
209-962-0232
Ann Schafer

129-169 BB
5 rooms, 5 pb
Visa, MC
C-yes/S-no/P-no/H-ltd

Continental plus breakfast
Fresh ground coffee stations;
a selection of herbal teas
Themed rooms, murals,
antiques, Jacuzzis,
fireplaces, picnic area by
creek (seasonal)

A work of art, located 26 miles from the west gate of Yosemite. Four rooms offer beautiful murals and world class amenities: elaborate bathrooms, Jacuzzi tubs, steam room & fireplaces. A Yosemite traveler's primary destination.
✉ askdranns@yahoo.com ◑ www.allseasonsgrovelandinn.com

Groveland Hotel at Yosemite National Park
18767 Main St 95321
800-273-3314 209-962-4000
Peggy & Grover Mosley

145-285 BB
17 rooms, 17 pb
Most CC, *Rated*, •
C-yes/S-no/P-yes/H-yes

Full Innkeeper's Breakfast
On-site gourmet dining, Wine
Spectator magazine's "Award
of Excellence" wine list, full
service bar
Conferences, weddings,
birthdays, anniversaries, spa
services, in-room extras

Beautiful, historic Gold Rush hotel. Gourmet dining inside or out in our courtyard, award winning wine list, 25 minutes to Yosemite. Golf, fishing, hiking, horses, spa services, winter sports nearby. Conference facility, weddings—lots to do and see!
✉ guestservices@groveland.com ◑ www.groveland.com

Hotel Charlotte
18736 Main St 95321
800-961-7799 209-962-6455
Victor Niebylski & Lynn
Upthagrove

108-159 BB
10 rooms, 10 pb
Visa, MC, AmEx, •
C-yes/S-no/P-ltd/H-ltd
Spanish, some Italian,
French, German

Pancake & Scrambled Buffet
Complimentary coffee, tea or
iced tea available almost any
time, restaurant and bar
onsite
Guest salon, cable TV, DSL &
WiFi Internet, piano, game
room, balcony, itinerary
planning

Hotel Charlotte is an historic B&B hotel on the way to Yosemite featuring a full service restaurant & bar. Yosemite National Park & Tuolumne River white water river rafting are popular local activities, as are wine tasting regions & Gold Rush towns.
✉ hotelcharlotte@aol.com ◑ www.HotelCharlotte.com

GUALALA ──────────────────────────────────

Whale Watch Inn by the Sea	180-300 BB	Full gourmet breakfast
35100 Hwy 1 95445	18 rooms, 18 pb	Complimentary wine at
800-942-5342 707-884-3667	Visa, MC, AmEx	check in. Saturday Wine &
Gretchen	C-ltd/S-ltd/P-no/H-ltd	Cheese gathering.
	Spanish and Japanese	Whirlpool tubs, beach
		access, fireplaces, decks,
		sauna

Whale Watch Inn is a getaway like no other, offering matchless luxury, privacy, and personal service in a dramatic contemporary setting. Inside your suite you will find designer comforts with richly upholstered couches and easy chairs, all with fireplaces
✉ info@whalewatchinn.com ● www.whalewatchinn.com

GUERNEVILLE ──────────────────────────────

Creekside Inn & Resort	98-270 BB	Full breakfast
16180 Neeley Rd 95446	28 rooms, 24 pb	Breakfast not available in
800-776-6586 707-869-3623	Visa, MC, AmEx, •	cottages, however, cottages
Lynn & Mark Crescione	C-yes/S-ltd/P-ltd/H-yes	have full kitchens
	Spanish	Library, sitting room,
		conference facilities, direct
		phone, pool, WiFi, HBO

A relaxed and friendly atmosphere best describes this bed & breakfast, situated in the redwoods near the Russian River. Guests may choose between 6 rooms in the B&B or one of the 22 cottages.
✉ stay@creeksideinn.com ● www.creeksideinn.com

Fern Grove Cottages	89-259 BB	Continental plus breakfast
16650 Hwy 116 95446	20 rooms, 20 pb	Sitting room, library, spa
888-243-2674 707-869-8105	Most CC, *Rated*	tubs, suites, pool, cable TV,
Mike & Margaret Kennett	C-yes/S-no/P-ltd/H-yes	wine tours and free wireless
		Internet

Comfortable cottages in the redwoods—many with living rooms, fireplaces. Some with spa tubs. Relax among beautiful gardens. Pool. Easy walk to town, river beaches. Warm hospitality. Great breakfast.
✉ innkeepers@ferngrove.com ● www.ferngrove.com

Sonoma Orchid Inn	139-245 BB	Full gourmet breakfast
12850 River Rd 95446	10 rooms, 10 pb	Homemade cookies,
888-877-4466 707-887-1033	Visa, MC, AmEx,	complimentary water, juice,
Brian Siewert & Dana Murphy	*Rated*, •	port & sherry
	C-yes/S-ltd/P-yes/H-ltd	Outdoor hot tub, great room
		with fireplace, library,
		satellite TV/Tivo, cable TV,
		DVD/VCR.

Historic Sonoma Orchid Inn is nestled along the Russian River offering comfort & charm, in the heart of Sonoma County's Wine Country. Easy access to wineries, the coast & San Francisco.
✉ innkeeper@sonomaorchidinn.com ● www.sonomaorchidinn.com

HALF MOON BAY ──────────────────────────────

Landis Shores Oceanfront Inn	285-345 BB	Full breakfast
211 Mirada Rd 94019	8 rooms, 8 pb	Appetizers, Premium Wines
650-726-6642	Most CC, *Rated*, •	Whirlpool Tub, Fireplace,
Ken & Ellen Landis	C-ltd/S-no/P-no/H-yes	TV/VCR, Fitness Room,
	Spanish	Private Deck, Wine List

Elegant oceanfront accommodations, private balconies, fireplaces, whirlpool tubs, TV/VCRs and more. Enjoy a gourmet breakfast each morning and premium wines and appetizers every afternoon.
✉ luxury@landisshores.com ● www.landisshores.com

HALF MOON BAY───────────────────────

Old Thyme Inn	155-325 BB	Gourmet full breakfast
779 Main St 94019	7 rooms, 7 pb	Complimentary afternoon
800-720-4277 650-726-1616	Most CC, *Rated*, •	hors d'oeuvres
Rick & Kathy Ellis	C-ltd/S-no/P-no/H-no	Library of videos and recent
	French	magazines, peaceful herb
		and flower garden

"A world away . . . but ever so close"—tucked in the seaside village of Half Moon Bay . . . the ideal garden retreat in which to relax and renew, or simply slow down and enjoy the charm and natural beauty of a small, coastal Northern California town.
✉ innkeeper@oldthymeinn.com 🌐 www.oldthymeinn.com

Pacific Victorian B&B	150-195 BB	Full breakfast
325 Alameda Ave 94019	4 rooms, 4 pb	Parlor, dining room, down
888-929-0906 650-712-3900	Most CC	comforters, fine linens,
Jeff & Lori Matthews	C-yes/S-ltd/P-no/H-yes	decks, whirlpool tubs, movie
		library, Internet

Elegantly decorated Victorian style Inn located in beautiful Miramar Beach, Half Moon Bay, California, within easy driving distance of San Francisco, California.
✉ pacificvictorian@msn.com 🌐 www.pacificvictorian.com

HEALDSBURG───────────────────────

Calderwood Inn	195-295 BB	Full gourmet breakfast
25 W Grant St 95448	6 rooms, 6 pb	Complimentary evening
800-600-5444 707-431-1110	Visa, MC, *Rated*, •	wine hour, port and late
Susan Moreno	C-ltd/S-ltd/P-no/H-no	night treats. Bottled water in
		guestrooms.
		On-site staff to book winery
		tours, limousine, dinner
		reservations, develop a wine
		tasting itinerary

Romantic 1902 Queen Anne Victorian surrounded by lush gardens, ancient trees, fountain and koi pond. Covered porch for relaxation or reading a good book. Lush landscaping. Walk to Plaza, restaurants, galleries, theaters, and wineries.
✉ innkeeper@calderwoodinn.com 🌐 www.calderwoodinn.com

Camellia Inn	129-269 BB	Full breakfast
211 North St 95448	9 rooms, 9 pb	Wine & Cheese tasting
800-727-8182 707-433-8182	Most CC, *Rated*, •	cocktail hour, hot beverages
Lucy Lewand	C-yes/S-ltd/P-no/H-ltd	& cookies at night, Chocolate
	Spanish	Covered Wednesdays
		Parlor, solarium, outdoor
		swimming pool, whirlpool
		tubs & fireplaces in deluxe
		rooms, free WiFi

A charming 1869 Italianate Victorian Inn in California's Sonoma Wine Country. Surrounded by 50 varieties of its signature camellias, the Inn blends an authentic vintage environment with modern and luxurious amenities for a memorable romantic getaway.
✉ info@camelliainn.com 🌐 www.camelliainn.com

Haydon Street Inn	175-395 BB	Full breakfast
321 Haydon St 95448	8 rooms, 8 pb	Homemade chocolate chip
800-528-3703 707-433-5228	Visa, MC, Disc	cookies available in the
John Harasty & Keren Colsten	S-no/P-no/H-no	afternoon, wine hour in the
		evening
		Comfortable public spaces,
		some rooms w/fireplaces,
		whirlpool tub, cable TV,
		patio and hammock.

Historic Wine Country Queen Anne home in this friendly Sonoma County town. Walk to historic town plaza with great restaurants, antique stores and wonderful boutiques.
✉ innkeeper@haydon.com 🌐 www.haydon.com

HEALDSBURG

Healdsburg Inn on the Plaza
112 Matheson St 95448
800-431-8663 707-433-6991
Jennifer Byrom

275-375 BB
12 rooms, 12 pb
Most CC, *Rated*
C-yes/S-no/P-no/H-yes

Full breakfast
Afternoon wine, tea & hors
d' oeuvres, freshly-baked
cookies, drinks available
throughout the day
Evening turndown, early
newspaper delivery to your
room, wireless Internet,
movies, books & games

This Four Sisters Inn blends the modern luxuries and sophisticated services of a boutique hotel with the traditional amenities and architecture of a B & B in the best location in town, right on the historic Healdsburg Plaza.
✉ healdsburginn@foursisters.com 🌐 www.healdsburginn.com

Holcomb House
401 Piper St 95448
707-433-9228
Lucille

165-195 BB
2 rooms, 2 pb
Visa, MC, AmEx
C-ltd/S-no/P-no/H-yes

self-serve
Jacuzzi, fireplace, cable TV,
accommodate business
travel, VCR, DVD, high speed
Internet.

California Craftsman bungalow built at the turn of the century. Furnished with antiques and a quilt collection that give character, charm and a homey atmosphere to the house.
✉ holcombh@comcast.net 🌐 www.holcombhouse.com

Irish Rose Inn
3232 Dry Creek Rd 95448
707-431-2801
Chris & Lanny Matson

160-200 BB
3 rooms, 3 pb
Visa, MC
C-ltd/S-no/P-no/H-no

Full breakfast

The Irish Rose is a wonderful Craftsman home located in the heart of Dry Creek Valley, Sonoma County, California.
✉ chris@theirishroseinn.com 🌐 www.theirishroseinn.com

Madrona Manor Wine
Country Inn & Restaurant
1001 Westside Rd 95448
800-258-4003 707-433-4231
Bill & Trudi Konrad

220-625 BB
21 rooms, 21 pb
C-ltd/S-no/P-no/H-ltd

Full breakfast
Restaurant
Heated pool, fireplaces,
balconies, A/C, terry robes, 8
acre gardens, meeting rooms,
weddings

Nestled in the hills above the Dry Creek Valley of Sonoma County, Madrona Manor is an exceptionally lovely Victorian estate surrounded by eight acres of wooded & landscaped grounds.
✉ info@madronamanor.com 🌐 www.madronamanor.com

Raford Inn of Healdsburg
10630 Wohler Rd 95448
800-887-9503 707-887-9573
Dane & Rita

150-250 BB
6 rooms, 6 pb
Visa, MC, AmEx,
Rated, •
C-ltd/S-no/P-no/H-ltd

Full breakfast
Complimentary evening
wine and cheese offering
Porch, vineyard views,
garden, patio, some
fireplaces, roses, in-room
massage.

Victorian farmhouse overlooks vineyards in the heart of the Russian River Valley of Sonoma County. Beautiful country setting is just 1½ hours from San Francisco, a 15 minute drive to Healdsburg Plaza.
✉ innkeeper@rafordinn.com 🌐 www.rafordinn.com

HOPE VALLEY

Sorensen's Resort
14255 Hwy 88 96120
800-423-9949 530-694-2203
John & Patty Brissenden

115-550 BB
35 rooms, 28 pb
Most CC, *Rated*, •
C-yes/S-no/P-ltd/H-ltd
Some Spanish

Sorensens Country Cafe
Snacks, restaurant, wine &
beer service
Library, hot springs nearby,
bikes & skis nearby, wood
burning stoves

Cozy creekside cabins nestled in the Alps of California. Close to Tahoe & Kirkwood, Hope Valley Outdoor Center. Hope Valley Resort features fly fishing, art and photo classes, history tours.
✉ info@sorensensresort.com ◑ www.sorensensresort.com

IDYLLWILD

Atipahato Lodge
25525 Hwy 243 92549
888-400-0071 951-659-2201
Sheila Weldon

80-190 BB
18 rooms, 18 pb
Most CC
C-yes/S-no/P-no/H-no

Continental breakfast on
weekends
All guestrooms have private
balconies, a kitchenette,
coffee maker, great forest
views.

Whether it be for a relaxing getaway, a family get-together or for a rugged wilderness adventure, rest assured that your visit to the Atipahato Lodge will be both enjoyable and memorable. We look forward to your visit!
✉ info@atipahatolodge.com ◑ www.atipahatolodge.com

Cedar Street Inn & Spa
25-870 Cedar St 92549
877-659-4789 951-659-4789
Herb Larson

89-160 EP
4 rooms, 4 pb
Visa, MC, Disc
C-ltd/S-no/P-ltd/H-no

Complimentary coffee, tea,
hot chocolate; very short
walk to four restaurants
Massage services, fireplaces,
meeting Solarium, officiant
for vow renewals

Comforts abound at the "Essence of Idyllwild" and the award winning Cedar Street Inn & Spa. Indulge in massage. Romance reigns in uniquely decorated themed rooms with fireplaces or rustic cabins.
✉ innkeeper@cedarstreetinn.com ◑ www.cedarstreetinn.com

The Lodge at Pine Cove
24900 Marion Ridge Dr 92349
866-563-4372 951-659-4463
Geary Boedeker

75-140 BB
5 rooms, 5 pb
Visa, MC, AmEx, *Rated*
C-ltd/S-no/P-no/H-no

Full breakfast
Assortment of coffee, teas,
hot chocolate
Small refrigerator, decks,
VCR & cable TV

The Lodge at Pine Cove is a 5-room B&B high in the San Jacinto Mountains at 6200 feet, just minutes from the beautiful mountain village of Idyllwild. Romantic packages. Wonderful private getaway.
✉ innkeeper@thelodgeatpinecove.com ◑ www.thelodgeatpinecove.com

Strawberry Creek Inn
26370 State Hwy 243 92549
800-262-8969 951-659-3202
Rodney Williams & Ian Scott

119-249 BB
10 rooms, 10 pb
Most CC, *Rated*
C-ltd/S-no/P-no/H-yes

Full breakfast
Sodas, bottled water, coffee,
tea, snacks, evening
appetizers on Friday &
Saturday
Library, fireplaces,
refrigerators, hammock,
wireless Internet, Aveda
amenities, organic
ingredients

Cool, clean mountain air, outdoor decks & gardens overlooking Strawberry Creek, hammocks. Member, Green Hotels Association. Featured in "Best Places to Kiss" & "Great Towns of Southern CA." Nine inn guestrooms, one private cottage.
✉ innkeeper@strawberrycreekinn.com ◑ www.strawberrycreekinn.com

INVERNESS

Bayshore Cottage
12372 Sir Francis Drake Blvd
94937
415-669-1148
Mr. & Mrs. Robert Cardwell

150-175 BB
1 rooms, 1 pb
Cash, Checks, *Rated*
S-no/P-no/H-no

Kitchen w/provisions for
breakfast
Provisioned w/fruit, hot/cold
cereal, pancake mix, yogurts,
eggs, bagels, English muffins,
beverages
Sitting room/library, hot tub,
cable TV, private deck, gas
barbecue. Inquire about
pets.

*A romantic, cozy cottage in a quiet secluded garden setting, looking toward Tomales Bay.
Located about ¾ of a mile south of the village of Inverness and 1 hour north of the Golden
Gate Bridge.*
◊ innformation.com/ca/bayshore

Dancing Coyote Beach
800-210-1692 415-669-7200
Janet Osborn

175-250 BB
3 rooms, 3 pb
Cash, Checks, *Rated*
C-ltd/S-ltd/P-ltd/H-no

Full breakfast
Fully equipped kitchens in
our cottages for self-service
dining
Fireplaces, views, decks,
parking, pet friendly,
beachfront property, outdoor
BBQ, outdoor showers

*You won't forget the time you spend at Dancing Coyote Beach. The graceful curve of the
shoreline, the sheltering pines and cedars, and relaxing by a fire crackling in the fireplace
will call you back again and again.*
✉ Theparsonage@hotmail.com ◊ www.dancingcoyotebeach.com

Inverness Valley Inn
13275 Sir Francis Drake Blvd
94937
800-416-0405 415-669-7250
Alden & Leslie Adkins

129-219 EP
19 rooms, 19 pb
Visa, MC, AmEx
C-yes/S-no/P-yes/H-yes
Dutch, German, Italian,
French

Kitchenettes stocked with
coffee, teas & spices.
Cable TV, thermostat-
controlled gas fireplace,
private patio, clock radio,
tennis courts, pool

*Located on 15 acres of natural beauty, 1½ hours from San Francisco, our refurbished A-
frame cottages each consist of four spacious units with high ceilings and plenty of light.
Some rooms and suites dog-friendly. Green "eco-friendly" inn.*
✉ info@Invernessvalleyinn.com ◊ www.invernessvalleyinn.com

Rosemary Cottages
75 Balboa Ave 94937
800-808-9338 415-663-9338
Suzanne Storch

156-365 BB
2 rooms, 2 pb
Visa, MC, AmEx,
Rated, ●
C-yes/S-ltd/P-ltd/H-ltd
Spanish, a little French

Continental plus breakfast
Complimentary tea, coffee
Kitchen, antiques, oriental
rugs, original art, fireplace,
decks, hot tub, gardens,
books, games

*Charming, romantic French country cottage nestled in secluded garden with dramatic
forest views. Close to beaches and hiking trails; families welcome.*
✉ innkeeper@rosemarybb.com ◊ www.rosemarybb.com

Ten Inverness Way
10 Inverness Way 94937
415-669-1648
Teri Mattson

162-202 BB
5 rooms, 5 pb
Visa, MC, Disc, *Rated*,
●
C-ltd/S-no/P-no/H-no
French, Spanish

Full breakfast
Wireless Internet & guest
computer

*A Pt. Reyes 1904 Craftsman Inn, steps from Tomales Bay, Ten Inverness Way is surrounded
by lush gardens, filled with the aroma of fresh home baking, and appointed with the finest
decor—pleasing to those with a quest for excellence.*
✉ inn@teninvernessway.com ◊ www.teninvernessway.com

INVERNESS

The Tree House B&B
73 Drake Summit 94937
800-977-8720 415-663-8720
Lisa Patsel

125-155 BB
3 rooms, 3 pb
Visa, MC, AmEx, •
C-yes/S-ltd/P-yes/H-no
Italian

Continental plus breakfast
Suites, fireplaces

The Treehouse offers a secluded, peaceful getaway nestled among the trees atop Inverness Ridge. Overlooking Point Reyes Station and Black Mountain, and adjacent to the National Seashore's hiking trails.
✉ treehousebnb@juno.com ❍ www.treehousebnb.com

JAMESTOWN

1859 Historic National Hotel & Restaurant
18183 Main St 95327
800-894-3446 209-984-3446
Stephen Willey

140-175 BB
9 rooms, 9 pb
Most CC, *Rated*, •
C-ltd/S-no/P-yes/H-no
Spanish

Breakfast buffet
Dining in our highly-acclaimed restaurant is a gourmet's delight; full-serve saloon & espresso bar
Historic saloon, concierge services, patio dining, balcony & a fun staff

Hotel c.1859 in heart of Gold Rush country. Our rooms are restored to the elegance of a romantic by-gone era. Enjoy our highly acclaimed restaurant with full bar on premises. Antique shopping, live theatre, golf, hiking & wine-tasting. Near Yosemite.
✉ info@national-hotel.com ❍ www.national-hotel.com

Victorian Gold B&B
10382 Willow St 95327
888-551-1852 209-984-3429
Ken and Anita Spencer

110-185 BB
8 rooms, 8 pb
Most CC, *Rated*
C-yes/S-ltd/P-yes/H-yes

Full breakfast
TV's, DVD players, AC, porches, large marble showers, clawfoot tubs, wireless Internet

The Victorian Gold is reminiscent of fine European Bed and Breakfast Hotels and offers eight unique rooms with private baths.
✉ innkeeper@victoriangoldbb.com ❍ www.victoriangoldbb.com

JAMUL

Jamul Haven
13518 Jamul Drive 91935
619-669-3100
William Roetzheim

199-329 BB
4 rooms, 4 pb
Visa, MC, •
C-ltd/S-no/P-ltd/H-ltd

Full breakfast
Pool, 2 spas, waterslide, waterfalls, gym, game room, pub, disco, pool pavilion, business center

Fully restored 1890 Victorian mansion in the mountains 25 minutes away from downtown San Diego. The six acre compound features a health spa, game room, gym, pub, disco, spas, pool, waterfalls, and much more.
✉ william@jamulhaven.com ❍ www.jamulhaven.com

JENNER

Jenner Inn Restaurant & Cottages
10400 Coast Hwy 1 95450
800-732-2377 707-865-2377
Diane & Julia

118-328 BB
23 rooms, 25 pb
Visa, MC, AmEx,
Rated, •
C-yes/S-no/P-ltd/H-yes
Spanish

Meatless breakfast
tea/coffee, cookies
Sitting room, fireside lounge, sauna, hot tubs & fireplaces

A unique country Inn on Sonoma's wine country coast. Panoramic waterviews from most rooms, suites and cottages. Fine dining, entertainment and many activities. Beautiful sunsets and romance abound.
✉ innkeeper@jennerinn.com ❍ www.jennerinn.com

JOSHUA TREE————————————————————————

The Desert Lily B&B	155-165 BB	3 course gourmet breakfast
8523 Star Ln 92252	3 rooms, 3 pb	Freshly baked homemade
877-887-7370 760-366-4676	Visa, MC, *Rated*, •	cookies, complimentary
Carrie Yeager	C-ltd/S-no/P-no/H-no	wine, beverages
	September – June	Private baths, private
		entrances, covered patio,
		private sitting room and
		library.

Intimate pueblo-style hideaway with panoramic views overlooking surreal Joshua Tree National Park's west gateway. Recommended in The Lonely Planet and Fodor guides.
✉ carrie@rosebudrubystar.com ☻ www.rosebudrubystar.com

JULIAN————————————————————————

Butterfield B&B	135-185 BB	Full breakfast
2284 Sunset Dr 92036	5 rooms, 5 pb	Complimentary coffees, tea,
800-379-4262 760-765-2179	Most CC, *Rated*, •	cider, cocoa, popcorn &
Ed & Dawn Glass	C-ltd/S-ltd/P-no/H-ltd	dessert in the afternoon;
		guest stocked fridge
		Sitting room, library, suites,
		fireplace, cable
		TV/VCR/DVD/CD, WiFi,
		piano, guitar, games

Relax on our three-acre, country garden setting in the quiet hills of Julian. Five unique rooms from country to formal decor. Famous gourmet breakfast. Just an hour from San Diego.
✉ info@butterfieldbandb.com ☻ www.butterfieldbandb.com

Eaglenest B&B	150-195 BB	Full breakfast
2609 D St 92036	4 rooms, 4 pb	Dessert snacks are fresh
888-345-6378 760-765-1252	Most CC	baked for your stay
Jim & Julie Degenfelder	C-yes/S-ltd/P-no	Pool, spa, fireplaces,
		A/C/heat, hot tubs,
		TV/VCR/CD

Eaglenest offers all the amenities of a four-star resort in the privacy and comfort of your own home in this mountain hamlet in San Diego County, a one block walk to local shopping, fine dining, attractions & entertainment in historic Julian.
✉ info@eaglenestbandb.com ☻ www.eaglenestbandb.com

Julian Gold Rush Hotel	155-215 BB	Full breakfast
2032 Main Street 92036	16 rooms, 16 pb	Sitting room, library
800-734-5854 760-765-0201	Visa, MC, AmEx,	
Steve & Gig Ballinger	*Rated*, •	
	C-yes/S-no/P-no/H-no	

The town's only designated landmark, capturing the charm and character of this 1800's Southern California mining town. In the heart of the Historic District, within walking distance of antique stores, gift shops, restaurants, museums and gold mines.
✉ bnb@julianhotel.com ☻ www.julianhotel.com

Orchard Hill Country Inn	195-450 BB	Full breakfast
2502 Washington St 92036	22 rooms, 22 pb	Complimentary afternoon
800-716-7242 760-765-1700	Visa, MC, AmEx,	hors d'oeuvres. A four-
Pat and Darrell Straube	*Rated*, •	course dinner is served on
	C-yes/S-no/P-no/H-yes	select evenings.
		Masseuse available, video
		library, conference facilities,
		weddings

Restful and romantic premier bed and breakfast with AAA Four Diamond attention to detail, caring staff and excellent dining. Gracious ambience, sweeping sunset views and seasonal gardens make us an unforgettable destination.
✉ information@orchardhill.com ☻ www.orchardhill.com

JULIAN ————————————————————————

Shadow Mountain Ranch B&B	135-150 BB	Full breakfast
2771 Frisius Rd 92036	6 rooms, 6 pb	Afternoon tea
760-765-0323	*Rated*	Sitting room, spas, swimming
Loretta & Jim Ketcherside	C-ltd/S-ltd/P-no/H-yes	pool, cable TV, lawn games, bus. trav., small weddings

Theme cottages. Full ranch breakfast, lap pool, mountain vistas, Jacuzzi tub. TV/VCR in each room. Quiet ranching area. Just an hour's drive from San Diego.
✉ jcketch@cableusa.com ◑ www.shadowmountainranch.net

Villa De Valor Hildreth House, circa 1898 B&B	165-210 BB	Full Gourmet Breakfast
2020 Third St 92036	3 rooms, 3 pb	Always something sweet in
877-96-VILLA 760-765-3865	Visa, MC, AmEx, •	the kitchen; old fashioned
Valorie Ashley	C-ltd/S-no/P-no/H-ltd	orange push-ups & ice cream sandwiches
		Parlor, aromatherapy sauna, massage, gardens, water pond, nostalgic video library, free WiFi, A/C

Located in the heart of Julian, CA, is your formal Victorian Bed & Breakfast home full of charm & ambience. Known in its heyday as the most elegant home in Julian. Historical Residence of Dr. H. L. Hildreth. 3 private, romantic suites.
✉ stay@villadevalor.com ◑ www.villadevalor.com

KENWOOD ————————————————————————

Birmingham B&B	160-295 BB	Full breakfast
8790 Sonoma Hwy 95452	5 rooms, 5 pb	Parlor, wrap-around porch,
800-819-1388 707-833-6996	Visa, MC, AmEx	vegetable & flower gardens
Nancy & Jerry Fischman	C-ltd/S-ltd/P-ltd/H-ltd	

Sit on the wraparound porch of this historic and gaze out at the beautiful vineyards and mountains of Sonoma Valley. The Inn is beautifully decorated in the Arts & Craft tradition, featuring Stickley furnishings and original works of art.
✉ info@birminghambb.com ◑ www.birminghambb.com

LA JOLLA ————————————————————————

Bed and Breakfast Inn at La Jolla	150-459 BB	Full Gourmet Candlelit Breakfast
7753 Draper Ave 92037	15 rooms, 15 pb	Complimentary fresh fruit,
888-988-8481 858-456-2066	Most CC, *Rated*, •	wine & cheese, sweets, fine
Jenna Moore	C-ltd/S-no/P-ltd/H-ltd	sherry, snacks & tea, bottled
	Spanish	water.
		Library/sitting room, complimentary beach towels, chairs & umbrellas, tennis rackets/ balls, concierge

Whether for business or a relaxing getaway at this historic & elegantly charming Inn, we have it all. A block from the beach in the heart of La Jolla by the Sea. So close, yet so far from it all, where romance makes memories & business becomes a pleasure.
✉ bedbreakfast@innlajolla.com ◑ www.innlajolla.com

Redwood Hollow Cottages	135-339 BB	Each unit has full kitchen
256 Prospect St 92037	7 rooms, 7 pb	Kitchens stocked with
858-459-8747	Most CC	oatmeal, teas, coffee,
Martin Lizerbram	C-yes/S-no/P-no/H-ltd	popcorn, hot chocolate and fresh fruit on arrival
		Free WiFi, private cottages, sleeper sofa, living room, fireplaces, beaches, maid service (fee)

A registered San Diego Historic Site with cottages and duplex homes in a garden setting. Cottages are family friendly, 4 with fireplaces, most with full kitchens. Close to everything La Jolla offers, down the street from Whispering Sands Beach access.
✉ lejolla@aol.com ◑ www.redwoodhollow-lajolla.com

LA SELVA BEACH

Flora Vista Inn
1258 San Andreas Rd 95076
877-753-5672 831-724-8663
Deanna & Ed

195-240 BB
5 rooms, 5 pb
Most CC
C-ltd/S-no/P-no/H-ltd

Full breakfast
Complimentary wine (or tea)
and cheese in the afternoon.
Box lunches available ($12
per person).
Clay tennis courts, TV,
wireless Internet, private
bathrooms, gas fireplaces

Located along the Pacific Coast Bike Route, between Santa Cruz and Monterey, the historic Flora Vista Inn is nestled among lush flower and strawberry fields, a short walk from spectacular beaches.
info@floravistainn.com www.floravistainn.com

LAGUNA BEACH

Casa Laguna Inn & Spa
2510 South Coast Hwy 92651
800-233-0449 949-494-2996
Francois Leclair & Paul Blank

150-650 BB
22 rooms, 22 pb
Most CC, •
C-yes/S-ltd/P-yes/H-no
Spanish

Full gourmet breakfast
Afternoon tea, snacks, wine
& cheese
A/C, luxurious bedding &
robes, DVD & CD players,
high speed Internet

Voted "Best in Orange County" nine consecutive years by the OC Register, Silver Medal Winner in the 2007 Inn-credible Breakfast Cook-off. Terraced on a hillside overlooking the Pacific Ocean, this historic Inn is a Sunset magazine featured "Romantic Stay."
innkeeper@casalaguna.com www.casalaguna.com

LAKE ARROWHEAD

Rose Gables
29024 Mammoth Dr 92352
866-201-4090 909-336-9892
Ray & Laurie Naud

125-195 BB
4 rooms, 4 pb
Visa, MC
C-ltd/S-no/P-no/H-no

Full breakfast
Fireplace, balcony,
refrigerator

Featured in "Best Places in Southern California." Perfect for a romantic getaway or just a quiet weekend away. With spacious rooms, fireplaces & private baths, it is the perfect spot for that special time together. Rose Gables, where memories are made . . .
rosegables@charter.net www.rosegables.com

LAKEPORT

Lakeport English Inn
675 N Main St 95453
707-263-4317
Karan & Hugh Mackey

155-221 BB
10 rooms, 10 pb
Visa, MC
C-ltd/S-no/P-no

Full breakfast
High Tea served Saturday
and Sunday between 12:00
and 2:30
Evening turndown service,
Italian Frette Sheets, plush
towels, hairdryers &
bathrobes

Lakeport English Inn is a delightful B&B, and no passports are needed here. Located in beautiful Lakeport, CA, with the best of Britain: scones with Devonshire cream and jam, English roses, darts, billiards, shopping and a library.
lakeportenglishinn@mchsi.com www.lakeportenglishinn.com

LEMON COVE

Plantation B&B
33038 Sierra Hwy 198 93244
800-240-1466 559-597-2555
Scott & Marie Munger

149-239 BB
7 rooms, 7 pb
Most CC, *Rated*, •
C-ltd/S-ltd/P-no/H-no

Gourmet breakfast
Complimentary beverages &
snacks
Hot tub, verandas,
courtyard, swimming pool,
fireplaces, landscaped
gardens

Nestled in the foothills of the Sierra Nevada Mountains, only 16 miles from Sequoia National Park. Seven romantic "Gone With The Wind" themed rooms and a Carriage House. Full, gourmet breakfast prepared by Chef Marie.
relax@plantationbnb.com www.theplantation.net

LITTLE RIVER

Inn at Schoolhouse Creek
7501 N Hwy 1 95456
800-731-5525 707-937-5525
Steven Musser & Maureen
Gilbert

156-399 BB
19 rooms, 19 pb
Most CC, •
C-yes/S-ltd/P-yes/H-yes
French

Full breakfast
Complimentary wine & hors
d'oeuvres
Oceanview hot tub, in-room
spa tubs, fireplaces, private
beach access, massage & spa
services

Experience true luxury on the Mendocino coast. Solitude. With 8+ acres of ocean view gardens, meadows, forest and a secluded beach cove, you will truly feel like you've gotten away from it all.
✉ innkeeper@schoolhousecreek.com ○ www.schoolhousecreek.com

LONG BEACH

Beachrunners' Inn
231 Kennebec Ave 90803
866-221-0001 562-856-0202
Pat Reed & Courtney Claverie

100-135 BB
5 rooms, 5 pb
Visa, MC, *Rated*
C-ltd/S-ltd/P-no/H-ltd

Continental plus breakfast
Snacks
Sitting room, library, spas,
cable TV, accommodations
for business travelers, hot
tub

Whether you're here on business or out for a weekend getaway, Beachrunners' Inn will provide guests with quality lodgings and all the comforts of home. Located in scenic Belmont Heights, we have easy access to Orange and Los Angeles Counties.
✉ reservations@beachrunnersinn.com ○ www.beachrunnersinn.com

Dockside Boat & Bed
Dock 5, Rainbow Harbor
90802
800-436-2574 562-436-3111
Kim Harris-Ryskamp & Kent
Ryskamp

200-300 BB
5 rooms, 5 pb
Most CC, *Rated*, •
C-yes/S-no/P-no/H-ltd

Continental plus breakfast
Complimentary light snacks
& water on-board
Complimentary high speed
wireless Internet, BBQ grill,
video/DVD library

Spend the night on a Yacht! Guests enjoy their very own private yacht at Rainbow Harbor. Beautiful views and steps away from fine dining, shopping and activities. Convenient to many major Southern California attractions.
✉ boatandbed@yahoo.com ○ www.boatandbed.com/longbeach.html

LOS OSOS

Julia's B&B by the Sea
2735 Nokomis Ct. 93412
805-528-1344
Julia Wright

85-95 BB
1 rooms, 1 pb
Most CC
C-ltd/S-no/P-no/H-ltd
German, French,
Spanish

Continental plus breakfast
Includes small fridge, range
top & microwave for guest
use
Spectacular view of the
ocean and Morro Rock Bay;
large deck with sitting area
and firepit

B&B by the Sea in the San Luis Obispo area. Charming bed and breakfast overlooking the ocean, perfect for short vacation, weekends or retreat. Close to Cambria, Hearst Castle, Paso Robles and Morro Bay.
✉ lmjuliawright@sbcglobal.net

LUCERNE

Kristalberg B&B
715 Pearl Ct 95458
707-245-7737
Mervin Myers

100-150 BB
3 rooms
Most CC, *Rated*, •
C-ltd/S-ltd/P-ltd/H-no
German, Spanish and
French

Full breakfast
Afternoon wine & cheese,
after dinner sherry

Kristalberg Bed & Breakfast offers spectacular views of Clear Lake from its mountain perch opposite Mount Konocti.
○ www.kristalbergbb.com

MALIBU CANYON

The Malibu Bella Vista	105-145 BB	Full breakfast
25786 Piuma Rd 91302	2 rooms, 2 pb	Please let us know if you
818-591-9255 818-591-9353	Visa, MC, AmEx	have any special dietary
Beth & Michael Kin	C-yes/S-no/P-ltd/H-no	needs
		Wood fireplace, A/C,
		TV/VCR/DVD, spa, private
		bath, massage

Located in Malibu Canyon, 5 miles from the Pacific Ocean. Nestled on the side of the Santa Monica Mountains with gorgeous views, thus the name Bella Vista. Children welcome. There are many amusement parks within a one(1) hour drive.
✉ michael_kin@netzero.net 🌐 www.malibubellavista.com

MAMMOTH LAKES

Cinnamon Bear Inn	89-198 BB	Full breakfast
113 Center St 93546	22 rooms, 22 pb	Snacks, complimentary wine
800-845-2873 760-934-2873	Most CC, *Rated*, •	Sitting room, Jacuzzis, suites,
Russ & Mary Ann Harrison	C-yes/S-no/P-no/H-ltd	fireplaces, cable TV, ski
		packages

"Who needs the Ritz?" We feature friendly folks, full breakfasts, free hors d'oeuvres & fabulous ski packages. Enjoy forest view rooms with private baths.
✉ cinnabear1@aol.com 🌐 www.cinnamonbearinn.com

MARIPOSA

Ace and Joyce's The	70-90 BB	Full breakfast
Ashworth House	5 rooms, 4 pb	"What to do, where to go"
4953 Ashworth Rd 95338	Visa, MC	information provided,
209-966-5504	C-ltd/S-ltd/P-no/H-no	spacious rooms & decks
Ace and Joyce		with outstanding views.

Close to Yosemite, reasonable rates, special weekly and monthly rates available, full breakfast served. Decks offer outstanding sunset views of surrounding mountains.
✉ yosjoyce@sti.net 🌐 www.yosemitelinks.com/ashworthhouse/index.html

Yosemite Bed and Breakfast	125-225 BB	Full breakfast
4501 Bridgeport Drive 95338	4 rooms, 4 pb	In room coffee & tea
888-528-9950 209-742-4018	Most CC, *Rated*, •	A/C, TV & DVD, wireless
Clay & Joy Black	C-ltd/S-ltd/P-ltd/H-ltd	Internet, free long distance
		telephone, small library,
		living room, gazebo

Yosemite B&B is hidden down a country lane, nestled in the oaks and pines. It is just five miles west of the historic gold mining town of Mariposa and 45 minutes from Yosemite National Park. Our two bedroom cottage has a full kitchen & living room.
✉ yosemitebedandbreakfast@gmail.com 🌐 yosemitebedandbreakfast.biz/index.html

MENDOCINO

Agate Cove Inn	159-329 BB	Full breakfast
11201 N Lansing St 95460	10 rooms, 10 pb	Complimentary sherry in
800-527-3111 707-937-0551	Visa, MC, *Rated*	room, homemade biscotti,
Laraine Galloway	C-yes/S-ltd/P-ltd/H-ltd	coffee, tea & hot chocolate
		Oceanviews, fireplace,
		private bath, TV/VCR/HBO,
		CD player, featherbed,
		private decks, hot tub

Perched on a bluff above the Pacific Ocean, Agate Cove Inn delivers a breathtaking view of the sea and rugged headlands. Our Farmhouse and cottages are set on two acres of beautiful coastal gardens, and 100-year-old cypress trees frame the property.
✉ info@agatecove.com 🌐 www.agatecove.com

Glendeven Inn, Mendocino, CA

MENDOCINO

Alegria Oceanfront Inn & Cottages
44781 Main St 95460
800-780-7905 707-937-5150
Elaine Wing & Eric Hillesland

159-299 BB
10 rooms, 10 pb
Visa, MC
C-yes/S-no/P-no/H-ltd

Full breakfast
Complimentary tea, coffee and hot chocolate
Coffeemaker, refrigerator, TV/VCR, microwave, hot tub, fireplace

Alegria is an ocean front B&B inn located in the village of Mendocino, CA. It features ocean view rooms and cottages, fireplaces, decks, a hot tub and a path to the beach. Interesting shops, galleries, fine restaurants, and the beach is just steps away.
✉ inn@oceanfrontmagic.com 🌐 www.oceanfrontmagic.com

Brewery Gulch Inn
9401 North Highway One
95460
800-578-4454 707-937-4752
Jo Ann Stickle

210-465 BB
10 rooms, 10 pb
Most CC, *Rated*, •
C-ltd/S-no/P-no/H-yes

Full gourmet breakfast
Wine hour with hors d'oeuvres; tea & coffee, fine food
Robes, toiletries, hairdryers, wine bar, concierge service, ocean views, fireplaces, Jacuzzi tubs

Set high on a bluff among natural landscaping overlooking Mendocino's Smuggler's Cove, each of Brewery Gulch Inn's 10 spacious & luxuriously appointed guestrooms are individually designed to capture views of the ocean.
✉ innkeeper@brewerygulchinn.com 🌐 www.brewerygulchinn.com

Dennen's Victorian Farmhouse
7001 N Hwy 1 Little River
95460
800-264-4723 707-937-0697
Fred Cox & Jo Bradley

135-270 BB
11 rooms, 11 pb
Visa, MC, AmEx,
Rated, •
C-ltd/S-no/P-no/H-ltd

Full breakfast delivered to room
Complimentary coffee and tea on request during the day and evening.
Spa tubs, wood fireplaces, feather beds, ocean access, in-room massage, free WiFi.
Concierge Services

Romantic Victorian home that inspired artist Thomas Kinkade. Private oceanview cottage. Featherbeds, fireplaces, spa tubs, ocean access, breakfast in bed. Free hi speed wireless Internet. AAA Three Diamond. Affordable luxury. Romance without pretense
✉ innkeeper@victorianfarmhouse.com 🌐 www.victorianfarmhouse.com

MENDOCINO

Glendeven Inn 8205 North Hwy One 95460 800-822-4536 707-937-0083 John & Mike	135-345 BB 10 rooms, 10 pb Most CC, *Rated* S-no/P-no/H-ltd German	Full in-room 3-course hot breakfast Wine & hors d'oeuvres included. Their Wine Bar[n] offers local fine wines, cheeses, and charcuterie. Sitting room, suites, wood fireplaces, llamas & chickens, fresh eggs, wine bar[n], full concierge.

Vogue Magazine's pick for Mendocino lodging, this 8-acre, luxury farmstead offers ocean-view suites, fireplaces, private balconies, gardens, pastured llamas, farm-fresh eggs, in-room breakfasts, a wine hour in Glendeven's Wine Bar[n], and free WiFi.
✉ innkeeper@glendeven.com ○ www.glendeven.com

Headlands Inn B&B Corner Howard & Albion 95460 800-354-4431 707-937-4431 Denise & Mitch	99-249 BB 7 rooms, 7 pb Most CC, *Rated* C-ltd/S-no/P-no/H-ltd	Full breakfast served in rooms Afternoon tea & cookies, complimentary juices, spring water & sherry always available in the parlor Robes, hairdryer, CD am/fm clock radio, bath amenities, bedside chocolate, SF newspaper w/breakfast

Relax on a featherbed in a romantic oceanview room, with a crackling fire and an exceptional full breakfast lovingly prepared & delivered to your room! Charming 1868 New England Victorian Salt Box located in the Historic Village of Mendocino.
✉ innkeeper@headlandsinn.com ○ www.headlandsinn.com

Joshua Grindle Inn 44800 Little Lake Rd 95460 800-GRINDLE 707-937-4143 Charles & Cindy Reinhart	189-359 BB 12 rooms, 12 pb Visa, MC, *Rated* C-ltd/S-no/P-no/H-no	Full gourmet breakfast Tea, snacks, soda & wine Oceanviews, fireplaces, whirlpool tubs, luxurious cotton robes

Experience the only AAA Four Diamond/Mobil 3 Stars B&B in Mendocino Village. Our welcoming home overlooks town. Park and forget about your car. Shops, restaurants and hiking trails are just a short stroll away. ✉ stay@joshgrin.com ○ www.joshgrin.com

Lighthouse Inn at Point Cabrillo 45300 Point Cabrillo Dr 95460 866-937-6124 707-937-6124 Jim Kimbrell	177-272 BB 6 rooms, 6 pb Visa, MC S-no/P-no/H-ltd	5 Course Gourmet Breakfast Wine & hors d'ouvres from 4-5:30 pm and private tour of the Point Cabrillo Lighthouse WiFi Internet access, coordinate and place reservations for guest adventures & dining

Beautifully restored, turn of the century, Head Lightkeepers House overlooking the Point Cabrillo Lighthouse and Light Station. The Inn is surrounded by a 300-acre Nature Preserve with breath-taking views of the coastal bluffs, headlands & Pacific Ocean.
✉ jimk@pointcabrillo.org ○ www.mendocinolighthouse.pointcabrillo.org/

MacCallum House Inn & Restaurant 45020 Albion St 95460 800-609-0492 707-937-0289 Jed & Megan Ayres & Noah Sheppard	175-425 BB 33 rooms, 33 pb Most CC, • C-yes/S-no/P-yes/H-ltd French and Spanish	Full breakfast Fine dining & full bar Gourmet breakfast, bar service, spa tubs, fireplaces, cottages, ocean views

An 1882 vintage Victorian with charming garden cottages, in the heart of Mendocino village. MacCallum House is a collection of the finest properties within the village of Mendocino. Each of our rooms offers a romantic and peaceful environment.
✉ info@maccallumhouse.com ○ www.maccallumhouse.com

MENDOCINO

Sea Gull Inn
44960 Albion St 95460
888-937-5204 707-937-5204
Jim & Ayla Douglas

75-185 BB
9 rooms, 9 pb
Visa, MC, AmEx
C-ltd/S-no/P-no/H-ltd
German

Organic breakfast
Choice of Coffee, tea or hot
chocolate
Fresh flowers, morning
newspaper on request,
garden and ocean views,
suites, wireless Internet

Sea Gull Inn is one of Mendocino's first bed and breakfast inns—located in the heart of town, the Sea Gull Inn is best known for its oceanviews, garden setting, distinctive guestrooms, and organic breakfast fare.
✉ seagull@mcn.org ◐ www.seagullbb.com

Sea Rock B&B Inn
11101 Lansing St 95460
800-906-0926 707-937-0926
Susie & Andy Plocher

179-385 BB
14 rooms, 14 pb
Most CC, *Rated*
C-ltd/S-ltd/P-no/H-no

Continental plus breakfast
Wine in room upon arrival,
tea, coffee
Ocean views, gardens, lawns,
fireplaces, king beds, some
whirlpools, robes,
sauna/massage, wireless

Elegant accommodations fully appointed with virtually every amenity imaginable. Stroll through colorful gardens, walk to town, curl up by the fire or relax on your deck and watch the sunset.
✉ innkeeper@searock.com ◐ www.searock.com

Seafoam Lodge
6751 N Coast Hwy One 95460
800-606-1827 707-937-1827
Kathy Smith

110-225 BB
24 rooms, 24 pb
Most CC
C-yes/S-no/P-yes/H-ltd

Continental breakfast
Ocean views, TV, VCR,
refrigerators, microwaves,
enclosed hot tub, decks

The Seafoam Lodge is located on a sweeping hillside, overlooking the Pacific Ocean. Panoramic ocean views and breathtaking sunsets await our guests from every room. Our comfortable guestrooms offer an affordable getaway you may wish to visit many times.
✉ seafoam@mcn.org ◐ www.seafoamlodge.com

Stanford Inn by the Sea- Big River Lodge
Hwy 1, Comptche-Ukiah Rd
95460
800-331-8884 707-937-5615
Joan & Jeff Stanford

195-470 BB
41 rooms, 41 pb
Most CC, *Rated*, ●
C-yes/S-yes/P-yes/H-yes
French, Spanish

Full breakfast
Wine, organic vegetables, full
bar and dinner service
Indoor pool, hot tub, decks,
nurseries, llamas, bicycles,
canoe rentals

Welcome to Mendocino's most celebrated Resort Lodge—a bed and breakfast hotel on the Mendocino Coast. A truly elegant country inn in a pastoral setting. All accommodations with ocean views, fireplaces, decks, antiques, four posters and TVs.
✉ stanford@stanfordinn.com ◐ www.stanfordinn.com

Whitegate Inn by the Sea
499 Howard St 95460
800-531-7282 707-937-4892
Richard & Susan Strom

159-319 BB
7 rooms, 7 pb
Visa, MC, AmEx,
Rated, ●
C-ltd/S-no/P-ltd/H-no
French, Spanish

Full Gourmet Breakfast
Complimentary wine & hors
d'oeuvres, homemade
cookies
Wedding planner, concierge
service, business center,
WiFi, Spa Services, E.M.T
Certified Baby-Sitter

Romantic and luxurious. All rooms are decorated in French and Victorian antiques. Gorgeous ocean and garden views. Featured in Sunset Magazine, Country Inns, Bon Appetit and Victorian Decorating.Perfect for Engagements, Weddings and Honeymoons.
✉ staff@whitegateinn.com ◐ www.whitegateinn.com/whitegate.php

MIDDLETOWN

Backyard Garden Oasis	119-159 BB	Full Country Breakfast
24019 Hilderbrand Dr 95461	4 rooms, 4 pb	Coffee and Tea in your own
707-987-0505	Most CC, *Rated*, •	Cottage
Greta Zeit	C-ltd/S-ltd/P-no/H-yes	Private cottage, king bed,
	Spanish	fireplace, A/C, fridge,
		skylight, wireless Internet,
		TV/VCR, phone, hot tub

Just 20 minutes from Calistoga, on the quiet side of the wine country, an AAA Three Diamond cottage in the mountains. Hot tub under the stars! King sized beds! Skylight! Great Breakfasts! Therapeutic Massage! Near Langtry Estate Winery, Harbin Hot Springs
✉ greta@backyardgardenoasis.com ◐ www.backyardgardenoasis.com

MILL CREEK

St. Bernard Lodge	89-149 BB	Full breakfast
Rt 5, Box 550 96061	7 rooms	Full restaurant and bar
530-258-3382	Most CC	service. Afternoon wine and
Jim Vondracek & Sharon	C-yes/S-no/P-no/H-no	hors d'oeuvres.
Roberts		Deck, stocked trout pond,
		Outdoor Hot Tub, indoor and
		outdoor games, robes and
		slippers, ice

Historical lodge with restaurant and seven rooms upstairs. Each room paneled with rustic knotty pine. Rooms overlook a broad meadow ringed with pine trees. Horse boarding available. Tavern area downstairs with pool table and T.V.
✉ stbernardlodge@citlink.net ◐ www.stbernardlodge.com

MILL VALLEY

Mill Valley Inn	169-419 BB	Continental breakfast
165 Throckmorton Ave 94941	25 rooms, 25 pb	All day tea service with
800-595-2100 415-389-6608	Most CC, *Rated*, •	choice of herbal, green and
Gary Sterman	C-yes/S-no/P-no/H-yes	black teas, evening wine
	French, Spanish	reception
		Fireplaces, cable TV, parking,
		voice mail, CD players,
		robes, Sun Terrace Lounge,
		business services

The Mill Valley Inn is tucked away in a redwood grove at the foot of Mt. Tamalpais, in downtown Mill Valley.
✉ millvalleyinn@jdvhospitality.com ◐ www.marinhotels.com/mill.html

MONTARA

Goose & Turrets B&B	145-190 BB	Four-Course Delicious
835 George St 94037	5 rooms, 5 pb	Breakfast
650-728-5451	Most CC, *Rated*, •	Complimentary afternoon
Raymond & Emily Hoche-	C-ltd/S-no/P-no/H-ltd	tea and treats available
Mong	French	Sitting room with woodstove,
		books, and music; fireplaces,
		quiet garden, local airport
		pickup, WiFi

A historic, classic B&B focusing on both B's: comfortable beds and four-course breakfasts. A slow-lane haven pampering fast-lane folks. Set in an acre of gardens.
✉ rhmgt@montara.com ◐ goose.montara.com

MONTE RIO

Rio Villa Beach Resort	110-199 BB	Continental breakfast
20292 Hwy 116 95446	11 rooms, 11 pb	Decks, gardens, river,
877-746-8455 707-865-1143	Most CC	fireplace
Ron Moore & Bruce Behrens	C-yes/S-ltd/P-no/H-ltd	

A cluster of green & white villa suites & studios surrounded by spacious decks, abundant gardens & lush lawns, sheltered by the redwoods. Located on the Russian River.
✉ innkeepers@riovilla.com ◐ www.riovilla.com

MONTEREY——————————————————

Jabberwock B&B
598 Laine St 93940
888-428-7253 831-372-4777
John Hickey & Dawn Perez

169-299 BB
7 rooms, 7 pb
Visa, MC, *Rated*, •
C-ltd/S-ltd/P-no/H-no

Full breakfast
5:00 hors d'oeuvres, sherry,
wine and other beverages
Sitting room, sun porch, 3
rooms with Jacuzzis, suite,
massage by arrangement,
bocce ball court

Once a convent, this charming Arts & Crafts style home sits just 4 blocks above Cannery Row & the Monterey Bay Aquarium. From the sunporch, overlook our gardens and enjoy fine Monterey Bay views. 3 rooms have Jacuzzis for two & 4 have fireplaces.
✉ innkeeper@jabberwockinn.com ◐ www.jabberwockinn.com

Old Monterey Inn
500 Martin St 93940
800-350-2344 831-375-8284
Patti Valletta

200-430 BB
10 rooms, 10 pb
Visa, MC, *Rated*, •
C-ltd/S-no/P-ltd/H-no
Spanish

Full gourmet breakfast
Tea, evening hors d'oeuvres,
wine, breakfast in bed
Sitting room, 5 double
whirlpool tubs, robes,
hairdryers, suites, library,
weddings, firelight spa

Classic English-style Tudor amid lush gardens. Exceptionally romantic. Service oriented inn with privacy valued. Breakfasts in bed are not to be missed.
✉ omi@oldmontereyinn.com ◐ www.oldmontereyinn.com

MOSS BEACH——————————————————

Seal Cove Inn
221 Cypress Ave 94038
800-995-9987 650-728-4114
Dana Kelley

215-350 BB
10 rooms, 10 pb
Most CC
C-yes/S-no/P-no/H-yes

Full breakfast
Afternoon wine, tea & hors
d' oeuvres, freshly-baked
cookies, drinks available
throughout the day
Executive board room for
small meetings up to 14, daily
housekeeping, robes,
fireplaces

Just 24 miles south of San Francisco, this serene hideaway is spectacularly set amongst a meadow of wildflowers and bordered by towering cypress trees.
✉ sealcoveinn@foursisters.com ◐ www.sealcoveinn.com

MOSS LANDING——————————————————

Captain's Inn at Moss Landing
8122 Moss Landing Rd 95039
831-633-5550
Capt. Yohn and Melanie Gideon

145-275 BB
10 rooms, 10 pb
Visa, MC, *Rated*
C-ltd/S-no/P-no/H-yes

Full breakfast
Fresh evening cookies,
snacks on Fri and Sat.,
Earlybird brown bag
breakfasts for early starters
Highspeed Internet, Fresh
flowers, fireplaces, cozy
robes, phone w/voice mail,
TV, feather pillows

Waterfront views with plush top beds, soaking tubs or romance showers, spa bath soaps, fresh flowers & glowing fireplaces. Snuggle & cuddle under comforters & quilts with feather pillows.
✉ res@captainsinn.com ◐ www.captainsinn.com

MOUNT SHASTA——————————————————

Mount Shasta Ranch B&B
1008 WA Barr Rd 96067
530-926-3870
Mary & Bill Larsen

70-125 BB
10 rooms, 4 pb
Most CC, *Rated*, •
C-yes/S-no/P-yes/H-no

Full breakfast
Afternoon tea, wine, snacks
Sitting room, library, ping-
pong, TV & phone in room

Affordable elegance in historical setting; Main Lodge, Cottage and Carriage House.
✉ mbenton1@snowcrest.net ◐ www.stayinshasta.com

MUIR BEACH

Pelican Inn
10 Pacific Way 94965
415-383-6000
Will Koza

207-291 BB
7 rooms, 7 pb
Visa, MC, *Rated*, •
C-yes/S-yes/P-no/H-ltd
Closed Christmas

Full English breakfast
Complimentary sherry,
dining room and bar. Lunch
and dinner available.
Sitting room, restaurant,
British pub, darts, close to
beach

A country inn capturing the spirit of 16th century England's West Country. 7 snug bedrooms, a cozy and hearty restaurant.
✉ innkeeper@pelicaninn.com 🜨 www.pelicaninn.com

MURPHYS

Dunbar House, 1880
271 Jones St 95247
800-692-6006 209-728-2897
Arline & Richard Taborek

190-280 BB
5 rooms, 5 pb
Most CC, *Rated*
S-no/P-no/H-no

Full country breakfast
Fresh baked cookies, comp.
appetizer plate & local bottle
of wine, port, sherry &
chocolates
Lovely gardens, sitting
rooms, library, gas-burning
stoves, clawfoot tubs, TVs,
DVD.

Intimate and authentically historic Italianate style bed & breakfast inn that offers guests a refreshing sense of ease, personal comfort, fine accommodations, hospitality, and unforgettable country cuisine. Walking distance to Main Street.
✉ innkeep@dunbarhouse.com 🜨 www.dunbarhouse.com

The Victoria Inn
402 Main St H 95247
209-728-8933
Michael Ninos

125-310 BB
15 rooms, 15 pb
Visa, MC, AmEx
C-ltd/S-no/P-no/H-ltd

Continental plus breakfast
Fireplaces, woodstoves,
clawfoot tubs or spas

Charming inn on historic Main Street in Murphys, CA. In the heart of Gold Country, Calaveras County. Fireplaces and wood stoves, clawfoot tubs or spas, eclectic furnishings. Four large suites, 11 guestrooms.
✉ victoria_inn@sbcglobal.net 🜨 www.victoriainn-murphys.com

NAPA

1801 Inn
1801 First St 94559
800-518-0146 707-224-3739
Darcy & Tom Tunt

265-425 BB
8 rooms, 8 pb
Most CC, *Rated*, •
C-ltd/S-no/P-no/H-yes
Spanish

Gourmet Breakfast
Wine, hors d'oeuvres, 24 hr
complimentary mini-bar
Private chef, full concierge
and in-room spa services,
flowering shade garden

A stylish B&B in the heart of downtown Napa. Luxurious Boutique Inn featuring resort-style accommodations. The inn caters to savvy travelers who demand excellence in an intimate setting.
✉ info@1801first.com 🜨 www.1801first.com

Beazley House
1910 First St 94559
800-559-1649 707-257-1649
Carol & Jim Beazley

199-339 BB
11 rooms, 11 pb
Visa, MC, *Rated*, •
C-ltd/S-ltd/P-ltd/H-ltd
Spanish

Full gourmet breakfast
Complimentary sherry
Spas, fireplaces, garden,
entertainment, sitting room,
library, winery & restaurant

Welcome to Beazley House! Elegant guestrooms have private baths and garden views. This luxury Napa Valley Bed and Breakfast includes whirlpool tubs, spa services, free wireless high speed Internet, and fireplaces with complete privacy in hide-away rooms.
✉ jim@beazleyhouse.com 🜨 www.beazleyhouse.com

NAPA—

Bel Abri
837 California Blvd 94559
877-561-6000 707-226-5825
Mary Alice Bashford

199-305 BB
15 rooms, 15 pb
Most CC
C-ltd/S-no/P-no/H-yes

Full breakfast
For a late night snack, we
have a mini refrigerator and
honor basket, evening wine
and cheese
Egyptian cotton linens,
vanities, plush robes,
CD/clock radio, cable TV,
wine tasting accommodations

Welcome to the Bel Abri, French for "Beautiful Shelter." This 15-room French Country Inn is located just off I-29 and First St in the revitalized town of Napa, nestled in the heart of the famous Napa Valley. ✉ info@belabri.net ◐ www.belabri.net

Blackbird Inn
1755 First St 94559
888-567-9811 707-226-2450
Edward Hansen

160-285 BB
8 rooms, 8 pb
Most CC
C-yes/S-no/P-no/H-yes

Full breakfast
Afternoon wine, tea & hors
d' oeuvres, freshly-baked
cookies, drinks available
throughout the day
Porch, fireplace, woodlands,
Jacuzzi, daily housekeeping,
private patio

Blackbird Inn offers the intimacy of a vintage hideaway, yet is an easy walk to many shops and restaurants. With its spacious front porch, huge stone fireplace and liberal use of fine woods, Blackbird Inn creates a warm, welcoming atmosphere.
✉ blackbirdinn@foursisters.com ◐ www.blackbirdinnnapa.com

Candlelight Inn
1045 Easum Dr 94558
800-624-0395 707-257-3717
Sam Neft

239-379 BB
10 rooms, 10 pb
Most CC, •
C-ltd/S-ltd/P-no/H-yes

3-course gourmet breakfast
Hors d'oeuvres & beverages
Concierge on staff, Jacuzzis,
heated swimming pool,
suites, fireplaces, cable TV

The Candlelight Inn is an elegant English Tudor, built in 1929 on a quiet, park-like, 1 acre setting on the banks of the Napa Creek.
✉ mail@candlelightinn.com ◐ www.candlelightinn.com

Cedar Gables Inn
486 Coombs St 94559
800-309-7969 707-224-7969
Ken & Susie Pope

209-339 BB
9 rooms, 9 pb
Most CC, *Rated*, •
S-no/P-no/H-no

3 Course Gourmet Breakfast
Chocolate Chip Cookies,
Evening wine&cheese in Old
English Tavern. Fruits, Sodas
and Teas 24hrs/day
Jacuzzi tubs, bath bombs,
Port, Chocolates, Robes,
blow dryer, WiFi, Concierge,
Large screen TV

Built in 1892, this 10,000 square foot Shakespearean mansion contains many intriguing rooms, winding staircases, an Old English Tavern and of course secret passageways. There are full bathrooms in all 9 rooms. Cooking classes are paired with Napa wines
✉ info@cedargablesinn.com ◐ www.cedargablesinn.com

The Cottages of Napa Valley
1012 Darms Ln 94558
866-900-7810 707-252-7810
Mike Smith & Mary Stevens

280-600 BB
8 rooms, 8 pb
Visa, MC, AmEx, •
C-ltd/S-ltd/P-no/H-no
Spanish

Continental breakfast
Breakfast basket with the
newspaper is delivered in
the morning to the front
porch of your cottage.
King bed, gas fireplace,
TV/DVD, Bose CD/radio,
heated floor tile in bathroom,
outdoor firepit.

Nothing can compare with the delight and comfort of your private cottage nestled in the trees and surrounded by understated elegance. With the charm that made this spot famous, you will feel right at home sitting on the patio with a cozy outdoor firepit.
✉ info@napacottages.com ◐ www.napacottages.com

NAPA

Hennessey House B&B
1727 Main St 94559
707-226-3774
Kevin and Lorri Walsh

139-329 BB
10 rooms, 10 pb
Most CC, •
C-ltd/S-no/P-no/H-no
Spanish

Full scrumptious breakfast
Complimentary wine &
cheese, afternoon tea
Patio and garden, parlor with
flat panel TV, WiFi, sauna.
Whirlpool tubs and
fireplaces in some room

Napa's 1889 Queen Anne Victorian B&B. "A Great Place to Relax." Walk to restaurants and shops. Share wine and conversation by the garden fountain.
✉ inn@hennesseyhouse.com ❻ www.hennesseyhouse.com

Hillview Country Inn
1205 Hillview Ln 94558
707-224-5004
Al & Susie Hasenpusch

175-275 BB
4 rooms, 4 pb
Most CC, *Rated*
C-ltd/S-ltd/P-no/H-no

Full breakfast
Cookies, candy, wine, bottled
water, soda, coffee
Living room, deck & lawn
area, cable TV

Spectacular 100-year-old estate. Each guest suite is distinctively decorated, with queen size bed, private bath, fruit and wine upon arrival, and a sweeping view of Napa Valley.
✉ info@hillviewinnnapa.com ❻ www.hillviewinnnapa.com

The Inn on First
1938 First St 94559
866-253-1331 707-253-1331
Jim Gunther & Jamie Cherry

125-385 BB
10 rooms, 10 pb
Most CC, •
C-ltd/S-no/P-yes/H-yes
Limited Spanish
6/1-10/31 & 11/ 1-5/31

Full Gourmet Breakfast
Sparkling wine, truffles,
homemade snacks, sodas,
and baked goods are waiting
for you upon arrival.
Whirlpool tubs, fireplaces in
all rooms; concierge service,
free Internet access & WiFi.

The Inn On First is the premier Napa Valley Bed and Breakfast experience. With Jacuzzi tubs and fireplaces in every room, sparkling wine, snacks, and chocolates upon arrival, and a great breakfast, you'll come to appreciate the magic of the Napa Valley.
✉ innkeeper@theinnonfirst.com ❻ www.theinnonfirst.com

Inn on Randolph
411 Randolph St 94559
800-670-6886 707-257-2886
Deborah Coffee

149-339 BB
10 rooms, 10 pb
Most CC
C-ltd/S-ltd/P-no/H-yes

Full breakfast
Sweet treats, coffee, tea
Parlor/library/game room;
grand piano, gardens with
patio, sundeck, gazebo,
fireplace, spa

Situated on one-half acre of landscaped grounds in historic "Old Town" Napa, you'll enjoy the serenity of a quiet residential neighborhood close to shops and restaurants.
✉ innonrandolph@aol.com ❻ www.innonrandolph.com

La Residence
4066 Howard Ln 94558
800-253-9203 707-253-0337
James DeLuca

275-475 BB
26 rooms, 26 pb
Most CC, *Rated*, •
C-yes/S-ltd/P-no/H-yes

Full breakfast
Complimentary wine and
cheese hour each evening.
Personal concierge, CD
players, DVD players,
hairdryers, Jacuzzi spa,
garden setting, pool

For the sophisticated traveler who enjoys elegant yet intimate style, La Residence is the only choice in Napa Valley. Two acres of landscaped grounds with ponds and fountains.
✉ graham@laresidence.com ❻ www.laresidence.com

NAPA——

McClelland-Priest B&B Inn
569 Randolph St 94559
800-290-6881 707-224-6875
Celeste Carducci

199-339 BB
6 rooms, 6 pb
Most CC, •
C-ltd/S-no/P-ltd/H-no

Gourmet breakfast
Evening hors d'oeuvres,
wine receptions
Spa, en-suite Jacuzzis &
fireplaces, evening
receptions, self-guided
winery tours, concierge
service

*Experience the Napa Valley from the stately elegance of the McClelland Priest B&B Inn.
Originally built in 1879 with a stained glass entry, ornate ceilings, spacious rooms, European ambience, modern comforts & luxury that sets this B&B apart from others.*
✉ celeste@historicinnstravel.com 🕭 www.historicinnstravel.com

The Napa Inn
1137 Warren St 94559
800-435-1144 707-257-1444
Brooke Boyer

120-295 BB
14 rooms, 14 pb
Most CC, *Rated*, •
C-ltd/S-no/P-ltd/H-yes
Spanish

Full breakfast
Afternoon port & sherry,
cheeses & desserts. Weekly
wine tasting with a featured
winery & appetizer
Fireplaces, whirlpool tubs,
balconies or patios. Wireless
Internet.

*A Romantic retreat in the heart of Napa. Two Victorians, adjacent to each other, make up
the Napa Inn. Luxury rooms and suites located on a tree-lined street just 3 blocks from the
town center. Enjoy a candlelight gourmet breakfast and afternoon delights.*
✉ info@napainn.com 🕭 www.napainn.com

Oak Knoll Inn
2200 E Oak Knoll Ave 94558
707-255-2200
Barbara Passino & John
Kuhlmann

350-750 BB
4 rooms, 4 pb
Visa, MC, *Rated*, •
C-ltd/S-ltd/P-no/H-ltd
Spanish

Full multi-course breakfast
Substantial evening wine
hour & hors d'oeuvres,
usually with small winery
representative, AM coffee
Complimentary wine, in-
room spa services,
swimming pool, free use of
nearby gym, concierge

*Romantic, elegant stone country inn surrounded by vineyards and panoramic views in the
Napa Valley. Spacious rooms with woodburning fireplaces. Napa's top rated inn has an
exceptional concierge service, nearby gym, great rooms, views and food.*
✉ oakknollinn@aol.com 🕭 www.oakknollinn.com

**Stahlecker House B&B
Country Inn & Gardens**
1042 Easum Dr 94558
800-799-1588 707-257-1588
Ron & Ethel Stahlecker

161-298 BB
4 rooms, 4 pb
Visa, MC, AmEx,
Rated, •
C-yes/S-no/P-no/H-ltd

Full Candlelight Breakfast
Coffee, sodas, lemonade, tea,
chocolate chip cookies
Creek, gardens, large
sundeck with lawn chairs,
WiFi, sitting room, spas,
library

*Stahlecker House is a AAA rated Inn (three diamonds). Secluded on one and a half acres
of lush manicured lawns and flowering gardens. A nostalgic gem in Napa Valley. Voted
"The Best Breakfast in the Southwest."*
✉ stahlbnb@aol.com 🕭 www.stahleckerhouse.com

NEVADA CITY

Emma Nevada House
528 E Broad St 95959
800-916-EMMA 530-265-4415
Andrew & Susan Howard

169-249 BB
6 rooms, 6 pb
Most CC, *Rated*
C-yes/S-no/P-no/H-ltd

Full breakfast
Afternoon tea, dessert, non-alcoholic beverage, and your favorite made-to-order espresso drink!
A/C, bath robes, fireplace, whirlpool tub, cable TV, business facilities, library, laundry, weddings

This charming home has been carefully restored and sparkles like a jewel from an abundance of antique windows, one of many marvelous architectural details. For the ultimate in gracious living and relaxation plan your next getaway at The Emma Nevada House.
✉ emmanevada@comcast.net ◐ www.emmanevadahouse.com

Piety Hill Cottages
523 Sacramento St 95959
800-443-2245 530-265-2245
Michael

95-180 BB
9 rooms, 9 pb
Visa, MC, AmEx, *Rated*
C-yes/S-ltd/P-no/H-ltd

Full or Continental breakfast
Gazebo & spa, free WiFi, cable TV & local phone, courtyard with BBQ, parking, walk to downtown

9 comfortable, casual, private cottages are perfect for singles, couples, families or business travelers. Our semi-gourmet hot or our delicious continental breakfast will be delivered to your cottage or outside in our beautiful, park-like courtyard.
✉ pietyhillcottages@comcast.net ◐ www.pietyhillcottages.com

The Red Castle Inn Historic Lodgings
109 Prospect St 95959
800-761-4766 530-265-5135
Conley & Mary Louise Weaver

120-180 BB
7 rooms, 7 pb
Visa, MC
C-ltd/S-no/P-no/H-no

Lavish five course buffet
Afternoon tea, sweets
Formal parlor, veranda, gardens, lit pathway into town

As one of the first Bed & Breakfast inns in California, the incomparable Red Castle Inn's singular sense of time & place has been acclaimed for more than four decades. A four story mansion offering seven guestrooms with private baths.
✉ stay@redcastleinn.com ◐ www.redcastleinn.com

NEWPORT BEACH

Little Inn by the Bay
2627 Newport Blvd 92663
800-438-4466 949-673-8800
Rahul & Gita

89-299 BB
18 rooms, 18 pb
Most CC
C-yes/S-no/P-no/H-yes
May to September

Deluxe Continental Breakfast
Mini-fridge, pantry, microwave and coffee maker available for guest use.
Beach equipment – bikes, beach chairs, boogie board, on-site parking, cable TV/HBO/VCR, newspapers

Thanks to its abundance of sun, surf, sand and shopping, everything you need for the perfect Newport Beach vacation can be found at the Little Inn By the Bay, one of the best Newport Beach hotels!
✉ reservations@littleinnbythebay.com ◐ www.littleinnbythebay.com

NIPOMO

Kaleidoscope Inn & Gardens
130 E Dana St 93444
866-504-5444 866-504-5444
Carolayne & Kevin Beauchamp

125-160 BB
5 rooms, 5 pb
Visa, MC, *Rated*, •
C-ltd/S-ltd/P-ltd/H-ltd

Full breakfast
Enjoy afternoon tea, hot cocoa, cookies and absolutely fabulous homemade fudge!
Garden, weddings, sitting room, library, wraparound veranda, gazebo

This extraordinary, beautifully restored Victorian bed & breakfast is located within an acre of breath-taking gardens. It is ocean-close, located midway between LA and San Francisco. Also adjacent to wineries and near fabulous Hearst Castle.
✉ info@kaleidoscopeinn.com ◐ www.kaleidoscopeinn.com

NIPTON———————————————————————————————————————

Hotel Nipton   79 BB   Full breakfast
107355 Nipton Rd 92364   5 rooms   Restaurant also serves
760-856-2335   Visa, MC, Disc   delicious lunch & dinner,
Jerry & Roxanne Freeman   C-yes/S-no/P-no/H-ltd   catering for groups also
                                                      available
                                                      Outdoor hot tubs, seclusion,
                                                      mountain biking, parlor

Hotel Nipton, a romantic adobe inn, was a favorite of 1920's silent film star Clara Bow.
Located in Mojave National Preserve.
✉ hotel@nipton.com ◯ www.nipton.com

OAKHURST———————————————————————————————————————

A Haven of Rest B&B   158-218 BB   Full breakfast
39681 Pine Ridge Rd 93644   2 rooms, 1 pb   Complimentary snacks,
559-642-2617   Visa, MC, Disc   assortment of coffee's & teas
Jody Telegan   C-yes/S-ltd/P-ltd/H-ltd Dish T.V., DVD and VCR with
                                                      extensive video library,
                                                      wireless Internet.Microwave
                                                      and refrigerator

15 miles from Yosemite 2 rm suite w/private bath & entrance, view of Sierra Mountains
and sm apple orchard. Service center in suite, private use of spa just outside your suite
Dish TV wireless Internet, your privacy guaranteed. Truly a Haven of Rest . . .
✉ jody@sti.net ◯ www.havenofrestbnb.com

Hounds Tooth Inn   95-225 BB   Full breakfast
42071 Hwy 41 93644   13 rooms, 13 pb   Afternoon wine, tea and
888-642-6610 559-642-6600   Most CC, *Rated*, •   coffee
Williams – Kiehlmeier   C-ltd/S-no/P-no/H-yes   Library, Jacuzzis and mini
                                                      suites available, rooms with
                                                      fireplaces, cable TV, sitting
                                                      room

12 room Victorian style inn located 12 miles from Yosemite's Southern entrance in
Oakhurst, 6 miles from Bass Lake. One luxury cottage available.
✉ robray@sti.net ◯ www.houndstoothinn.com

Pine Rose Inn   79-159 BB   Hot country breakfast
41703 Rd 222 93644   9 rooms, 9 pb   Complimentary wine, tea,
866-642-2800 559-642-2800   Visa, MC   coffee
Anita & Greg Griffin   C-yes/S-no/P-yes   Rose gardens, weddings,
                                                      Jacuzzis, fireplace

This quaint 9 room Inn, nestled within the Sierra Mountains, offers the peace and tranquil-
ty of the surrounding national forest.
✉ pineroseinn@sti.net ◯ www.pineroseinn.com

Vulture's View Bed and   120-165 BB   Continental plus breakfast
Breakfast   3 rooms, 3 pb   Wireless Internet, LCD TV,
39045 John West Rd 93644   Visa, MC   private outdoor spa,
559-683-8470   C-yes/S-no/P-yes/H-ltd   microwave, garden with
Judy Alexander   waterfall

Vulture's View Bed and Breakfast offers 3 spacious rooms and unobstructed, 180 degree
views of the 4,000 ft mountains surrounding the Oakhurst basin. Being off the beaten path
enhances our spectacular vistas of mountain sunsets and starlit evenings.
✉ jalex@sti.net ◯ www.yosemitevulturesviewbandb.com

OAKLAND

Acacia House B&B
Acacia Avenue at Ocean View
Drive 94618
510-610-2928
Brenda Reed

125-200 BB
2 rooms, 2 pb
Cash, Checks
C-ltd/S-no/P-no/H-no

Limited continental breakfast
Welcome fruit basket & wine,
mini refrigerator, suite has
microwave, toaster, coffee
maker
Wireless Internet, cable TV
with DVD/VHS & telephone
in the Acacia Suite

Acacia House, located in the Upper Rockridge residential district of Oakland, provides a peaceful & private base for the discerning guest traveling for personal or professional reasons.
✉ AcaciaHouseBB@aol.com ☀ www.acaciahousebb.com

OCCIDENTAL

Inn at Occidental
3657 Church St 95465
800-522-6324 707-874-1047
Jerry & Tina Wolsborn

259-679 BB
18 rooms, 18 pb
Visa, MC, AmEx,
Rated, •
C-ltd/S-no/P-ltd/H-yes

Full breakfast
Coffee, tea, cocoa, sweet
treats, wine & cheese
WiFi in Living room, library
with laptop & printer, full
concierge service

Gem nestled among giant redwoods, near vineyards/wineries, orchards, Russian River, ocean. Antiques, comfortable furnishings offer charm & elegance exceeded only by hospitality and a gracious staff.
✉ innkeeper@innatoccidental.com ☀ www.innatoccidental.com

OJAI

Emerald Iguana Inn
End of N Blanche St 93023
805-646-5277
Julia Whitman

159-359 BB
12 rooms, 12 pb
Most CC
S-ltd/P-no/H-ltd
Spanish, Indonesian,
French, Dutch

Continental breakfast
Snacks
Jacuzzis, swimming pool,
suites, clawfoot tub,
fireplace, cable TV

This property perfectly exemplifies the charm of the Ojai Valley. Exquisitely designed and decorated cottages and rooms in an extraordinarily beautiful and serene setting.
✉ innkeeper@blueiguanainn.com ☀ www.emeraldiguana.com

Inn Harmony
308 N Signal St 93023
888-640-6524
Deborah Clukey

185-305 BB
5 rooms, 5 pb
Visa, MC, AmEx
C-ltd/S-no/P-no/H-no

Full breakfast
Complimentary, soft drinks,
waters, afternoon tea or wine
with appetizers
Private garden, terrace,
patio, deep soaking tubs,
marble bathrooms

Luxury inn situated in the Vincent Mar Gardens in downtown Ojai, CA. Private garden terrace or patio, marble bathrooms, deep soaking tubs, are just a few of the amenities you will enjoy in this peaceful setting.
✉ info@innharmonyojai.com ☀ www.innharmonyojai.com

The Ojai Retreat
160 Besant Rd. 93023
805-646-2536
Ulrich, Clare & Teresa

75-215 BB
12 rooms, 10 pb
Visa, MC
C-ltd/S-no/P-no
German, French and
Swiss

Full breakfast
5 acres of lush gardens, small
library, living and meeting
room, yoga classes and
massage

With spectacular views from all guestrooms, the Ojai Retreat is a haven of beauty and tranquility. Nestled on a five-acre hilltop with lush gardens and walkways, the inn offers twelve completely renovated guestrooms.
✉ info@ojairetreat.org ☀ ojairetreat.org/

OROVILLE————————————————————

The Riverside B&B	95-165 BB	Full breakfast
45 Cabana Dr 95965	9 rooms, 9 pb	Private baths, cable TV,
530-533-1413	Visa, MC, *Rated*	spacious sitting area, wood
Larry Jendro	C-ltd/S-ltd/P-no/H-ltd	stove & king size bed

Romantic riverfront serenity in the heart of California's Gold Rush Country. Romantic rooms, some with Jacuzzis, wood stoves, sky lights and river views, all with private baths.
✉ riversidebnb@yahoo.com ○ www.riversidebandb.com

PACIFIC GROVE————————————————

Gosby House Inn	120-225 BB	Full breakfast
643 Lighthouse Ave 93950	22 rooms, 22 pb	Afternoon wine, tea & hors
800-527-8828 831-375-1287	Most CC, *Rated*, •	d' oeuvres, freshly-baked
Sharon Carey	C-yes/S-no/P-no/H-yes	cookies, drinks available
		throughout the day
		Morning newspaper
		delivery, evening turndown,
		bikes, daily housekeeping,
		fireplaces, patio

Located on the Monterey Peninsula, Gosby House Inn has been welcoming guests for over 100 years. This cheerful yellow and white Victorian mansion, with its carefully tended gardens and central patio, sets the standard for gracious innkeeping.
✉ gosbyhouseinn@foursisters.com ○ www.gosbyhouseinn.com

Green Gables Inn	135-300 BB	Full breakfast
301 Ocean View Blvd 93950	11 rooms, 8 pb	Afternoon wine, tea & hors
800-722-1774 831-375-2095	Most CC	d' oeuvres, freshly-baked
Honey Spence	C-yes/S-no/P-no/H-yes	cookies, drinks available
		throughout the day
		Fireplaces, spa tubs, daily
		housekeeping

Perhaps the most beautiful and famous inn located in California, the Green Gables Inn is a historic gem with panoramic views of the Monterey Bay. Every detail in this exquisite Queen Anne Victorian, built in 1888, has been meticulously restored.
✉ greengablesinn@foursisters.com ○ www.greengablesinnpg.com

Inn at 213 Seventeen Mile Drive	135-340 BB	Full breakfast
213 Seventeen Mile Dr 93950	16 rooms, 16 pb	Complimentary hors
800-526-5666 831-642-9514	Most CC	d'oeuvres, wine; fresh-
Dianna and Charlie Wareing	C-yes/S-no/P-yes/H-yes	brewed coffee, light snacks
		Garden, sitting & reading
		rooms, fireplace, spa

Set between Pebble Beach, Carmel, Monterey and close to the Big Sur coast. The area is renowned for its natural beauty, seasonal Monarch butterflies, grazing deer . . . along with the finest beaches, world class golf courses and Cannery Row.
✉ gerardastocking@yahoo.com ○ www.innat17.com

Martine Inn	179-469 BB	Gourmet Breakfast
255 Oceanview Blvd 93950	25 rooms, 25 pb	Wine, hors d'oeuvres, water,
800-852-5588 831-373-3388	Visa, MC, Disc, *Rated*,	soda, cookies, coffee, tea,
Don Martine	•	cocoa, fresh fruit
	C-yes/S-no/P-no/H-yes	Sitting room, game room,
	Spanish	conference room, hot tub,
		display of 6 vintage MG
		autos, turn down service

Steps from the sparkling blue waters of Monterey Bay, this lavish once private mansion, is now a meticulously restored resort, where every fixture & furnishing is an authentic antique. Breakfast is served on silver, crystal & lace. WiFi is throughout.
✉ don@martineinn.com ○ www.martineinn.com

PACIFIC GROVE

Old St. Angela Inn	150-275 BB	Full breakfast
321 Central Ave 93950	9 rooms, 9 pb	Complimentary wine, snacks
800-748-6306 831-372-3246	Visa, MC, Disc, *Rated*	& cookies
Jerry & Dianne McKneely	C-ltd/S-no/P-no/H-ltd	Solarium, garden with
		waterfall and outdoor firepit,
		rooms with fireplaces &
		Jacuzzi tubs

Intimate Cape Cod elegance overlooking Monterey Bay. Walking distance to ocean and beaches, Monterey Bay Aquarium, Cannery Row, and restaurants. Delicious breakfast.
✉ dianne@oldstangelainn.com ✪ www.oldstangelainn.com

Pacific Grove Inn	109-259 BB	Continental plus breakfast
581 Pine Ave 93950	16 rooms, 16 pb	Afternoon tea, snacks, soda
800-732-2825 831-375-2825	Most CC, *Rated*, •	machine
Jean Gilbertson	C-yes/S-no/P-no/H-yes	Fireplaces, TV/VCR, video
		library, phone, in-room
		fridge, heated towel racks

The Pacific Grove Inn is your home-away-from-home. Our personable Innkeepers are waiting to greet you. Come enjoy the ambience of a newly renovated Victorian home.
✉ info@pacificgrove-inn.com ✪ www.pacificgrove-inn.com

Seven Gables Inn	200-550 BB	Full breakfast
555 Ocean View Blvd 93950	25 rooms, 25 pb	Complimentary afternoon
831-372-4341	Visa, MC, AmEx,	wine & cheese served each
Ed Flatley and Susan Flatley	*Rated*, •	afternoon. Homemade
Wheelwright	C-ltd/S-no/P-no/H-ltd	cookies served each
	French, Spanish,	evening.
	German	Complimentary welcome
		treats in each room, evening
		turndown service, concierge
		services.

A truly romantic Inn on the very edge of Monterey Bay. All guestrooms have ocean views, private baths & are comfortably furnished with an eclectic collection of fine furnishings. Guest comfort & service is of utmost importance to us. See you soon!
✉ nborino@innsofmonterey.com ✪ www.pginns.com

PALM DESERT

The Inn at Deep Canyon	111-261 BB	Continental plus breakfast
74470 Abronia Trl 92260	32 rooms, 32 pb	In room coffee and tea
800-253-0004 760-346-8061	Most CC, *Rated*, •	Jacuzzi, pool, suites,
Linda Carter	C-yes/S-yes/P-yes/H-yes	fireplace, cable TV,
		accommodate business
		travel, wireless Internet

Charming hotel oasis in the desert. Quiet, secluded, heated pool, Jacuzzi, blocks from El Paseo.
✉ innkeeper@inn-adc.com ✪ www.inn-adc.com

The Mojave Resort	75-229 BB	Continental plus breakfast
73721 Shadow Mountain Dr	24 rooms, 24 pb	Private patios, pool, spa,
92260	Most CC	courtyard, health club
800-391-1104 760-346-6121	C-yes/S-no/P-no/H-ltd	privileges, meeting rooms
Sheila Weldon		

Experience the romance, glamour and sophistication of the desert of the 1940s in one of the newest luxury boutique Palm Desert hotels. Indulgent suites and guestrooms with creamy beds and all the special touches you expect.
✉ info@resortmojave.com ✪ www.resortmojave.com

PALM SPRINGS

Casa Cody Country Inn
175 S Cahuilla Rd 92262
800-231-2639 760-320-9346
Therese Hayes & Frank Tysen

79-429 BB
27 rooms, 27 pb
Most CC, *Rated*, •
C-ltd/S-ltd/P-ltd/H-yes
French, Dutch, German

Continental plus breakfast
Whirlpool spa, 2 swimming
pools, cable TV

A historic 1910 adobe two-bedroom house, once owned by Metropolitan Opera star Laurence Tibbett and frequented by Charlie Chaplin, is now open for our guests to stay in the heart of Palm Springs Village.   ✉ casacody@aol.com ◔ www.casacody.com

Rendezvous B&B
1420 N Indian Canyon Dr.
92262
800-485-2808 760-320-1178
Marty, Barb & Jake Cohen

160-240 BB
10 rooms, 10 pb
Most CC, •
S-ltd/P-no/H-ltd
Spanish

Full Gourmet Breakfast
Aside from our fabulous
breakfasts, we also include
appetizers and cocktails
each night of your stay
Flat-screen TVs, DVD and CD
players, wireless high speed
Internet, heated pool and hot
tub, massage

Where the romance of the '50s comes alive! This gorgeous oasis in the desert will cater to all your needs from a scrumptious breakfast, cocktail and appetizer hour, massage, and hundreds of great activities just around the corner.
✉ info@palmspringsrendezvous.com ◔ www.palmspringsrendezvous.com

Sakura Japanese Style B&B Inn
1677 N Via Miraleste 92262
800-200-0705 760-327-0705
George & Fumiko Cebra

90-125 BB
3 rooms, 3 pb
Most CC, •
C-yes/S-ltd/P-no/H-no
Japanese

Full breakfast
Breakfast can be served in
either American or Japanese
fashion, afternoon tea,
snacks
Jacuzzis, swimming pool,
cable TV, VCR, tennis courts
within walking distance, golf
courses

A distinct, quiet, relaxing, authentic Japanese experience, with beautiful Japanese artwork, antique kimonos, handmade futons, shiatsu massage, shoji windows, and Japanese garden.   ✉ info@sakurabandb.com

Sea Mountain Inn, Spa & Resort
877-928-2827 877-928-2827
Julie Dewe

199-999 BB
18 rooms, 18 pb
Most CC, *Rated*, •
S-yes/P-no/H-ltd
Spanish, French,
Japanese, Russian,
Italian

Full breakfast
Wine & cheese, coffee, tea,
iced tea, gourmet dining,
appetizers & sweets-rices -
margaritas spa bed
Pools, sauna, spa services, 24
hr. club, flat-screen plasma &
LCD TVs, wireless Internet
access spa

Nude Zen spa. An award-winning spa retreat in Southern California. Enjoy 24-hour whirlpool and contemplate the mountains above you. Relax in the sun and swim nude in fresh pool. The curative mineral waters have been used for centuries. Clothing optional.
✉ admin@seamountaininn.com ◔ www.nudespa.com

The Willows Historic Palm Springs Inn
412 W Tahquitz Canyon Way
92262
800-966-9597 760-320-0771
Kimberly Tucker, General
Manager

275-595 BB
8 rooms, 8 pb
Most CC, *Rated*, •
C-ltd/S-no/P-no/H-ltd

Full breakfast
Restaurant, afternoon tea,
snacks, evening wine & hors
d'oeuvres, poolside
beverages
Sitting room, library, pool,
hot tubs, gardens, waterfall,
mountain views, weddings &
events

Exquisite accommodations for discriminating guests in a historic home restored to recreate the ambience of Palm Springs in the 1930s.
✉ stay@thewillowspalmsprings.com ◔ www.thewillowspalmsprings.com

PASO ROBLES

Ann & George's B&B at Voladores Vineyard
1965 Niderer Road 93446
805-423-2760
Ann & George Perham

190-220 BB
2 rooms, 2 pb
Visa, MC, *Rated*
C-yes/S-no/P-no/H-ltd

Full Ranch Style Breakfast
A bottle of wine and a plate of fruit, cheese and crackers are provided in your room. Coffee maker and fresh flowers in room, wireless Internet, discounts for local wineries

Travel down a narrow country road to our secluded accommodations overlooking beautiful westside Paso Robles Wine Country, in Central California. Queen-sized beds in spacious private quarters overlooking Rancho de Voladores Vineyard. Enjoy incredible views
✉ ann@voladoresvineyard.com ○ www.voladoresvineyard.com/bb.htm

Asuncion Ridge Vineyards & Inn
805-461-0675
Philip Krumal

249-349 BB
3 rooms, 3 pb
Most CC
C-ltd/S-no/P-no/H-ltd

Champagne Breakfast Buffet
Guests are encouraged to enjoy a glass of locally crafted wine and cheese in one of 3 public rooms. Elegant suites, patios, private baths with soaking tubs, fine linens, stone fireplace, private decks

Asuncion Ridge Vineyards & Inn rests on 320 private oak studded acres with unobstructed ocean and forest views. Featuring luxury suites with fine linens, patios and large private baths with soaking tubs. mouth watering Chef prepared gourmet breakfasts.
✉ asuncionridge@hughes.net ○ www.asuncionridge.com

Canyon Villa
1455 Kiler Canyon Rd 93446
805-238-3362
Diane Babcock

240-280 BB
4 rooms, 4 pb
Visa, MC
C-ltd/S-no/P-no/H-ltd

Full breakfast
Complimentary hors d'oeuvres & wine served daily
Spa tubs, lush towels & robes, fireplaces, whirlpool tubs, turndown service

Nestled among the rolling hills and vineyards of Paso Robles wine country, the Canyon Villa will charm you with its Italian architecture, heavenly views, intimate setting and luxurious amenities.
✉ stay@thecanyonvilla.com ○ www.thecanyonvilla.com

Chanticleer Vineyard B&B
1250 Paint Horse Place 93447
805-226-0600
Carolyn Stewart-Snow

225-275 BB
3 rooms, 3 pb
Visa, MC
S-no/P-no/H-yes

Full breakfast
Wine with cheese and fruit plate in room on arrival
Full baths, luxury robes, iPod docking stations, fireplaces, morning kitchen, iron and ironing boards

A romantic B&B located on 20 acres in Paso Robles. Two rooms with luxury bath, fireplace, private deck and vineyard view. Walking distance to 8 wineries. Enjoy unpretentious comfort, thoughtful attention to detail with a touch of country charm.
✉ info@chanticleervineyardbb.com ○ www.chanticleervineyardbb.com

Creekside B&B
5325 Vineyard Dr 93446
805-227-6585
Nanci & Lauren Teran

240-270 BB
2 rooms, 2 pb
Visa, MC
C-ltd/S-ltd/P-no/H-ltd

Thur – Sun / Full Breakfast option
Complimentary local wine upon arrival
Porch, fireplace, kitchen

Our Inn is located midway between Los Angeles & San Francisco, in the heart of the beautiful & unique Central Coast's Wine Country near San Luis Obispo.
✉ nanci@thecreeksidebb.com ○ www.thecreeksidebb.com

PASO ROBLES───────────────────────────────────

Dunning Ranch Guest Suites
1945 Niderer Rd 93446
800-893-1847 800-893-1847
Jim & Angela Dunning

199-289 BB
2 rooms, 2 pb
Visa, MC, *Rated*
S-no/P-no/H-no

Continental breakfast
Complimentary wine tasting
at neighboring Estate winery.
Winery tours by
appointment too!
Large decks, outdoor BBQ,
porches, kitchenettes

Dunning Ranch Guest Suites are located on 40 acres with vineyards and an award-winning winery just steps away . . . The Inn features 2 luxurious, private guest suites. Suite#1 is a one bedroom Suite and Suite#2 is a 2 bedroom Suite. Wine tasting included.
✉ reservations@dunningranch.com ◐ www.dunningranch.com

High Ridge Manor
5458 High Ridge Rd 93446
805-226-2002
Cynthia Vaughn & James Roberts

195-345 BB
3 rooms, 3 pb
Visa, MC
S-ltd/P-no/H-no

Gourmet breakfast
Every day at 5:30pm hors
d'oeuvres and wine is
served in the billiard room.
Billiard room, wine cellar,
fireplaces, large whirlpool
tubs in room, private ent.,
private patios

High Ridge Manor offers magnificent views, tastefully appointed living quarters with over-sized whirlpool tubs in every room. Enjoy the best views in Paso Robles from every room. We offer gourmet meals and an elegant dining experience for all guests.
✉ highridgemanor@hotmail.com ◐ www.highridgemanor.net

Orchard Hill Farm
5415 Vineyard Dr 93446
805-239-9680
Deborah & Doug Thomsen

230-285 BB
3 rooms, 3 pb
Visa, MC, AmEx
C-ltd/S-ltd/P-no/H-no

Full gourmet breakfast
Assorted beverages, local
wines, fresh fruit, homemade
baked goods
Fresh flowers, robes,
featherbeds, down
comforters, fireplaces,
private decks, sitting areas

Wonderful setting on 36 pristine acres in the Paso Robles Wine Region. Beautiful gardens and views. Fresh flowers, antiques, comfy seating areas, beautiful interiors, comfy seating areas with fireplaces. Gourmet breakfasts and local wines included.
✉ orchardhillfarm@aol.com ◐ www.orchardhillbb.com

Wild Coyote B&B
3775 Adelaida Rd 93446
805-610-1311
Gianni Manucci

225-275 BB
5 rooms, 5 pb
Visa, MC, AmEx
S-ltd/P-no/H-no
Spanish (little)

Gourmet (Kati's special)
Complimentary bottle of
wine, tasting fee admission
and in room coffee bar
Artwork, patios, fireplace,
walking paths, winery tour &
private barrel tasting

Each room has been personally designed by the owner with New Mexico Adobe style, Hacienda interior décor, tribal artworks, comfy beds, private bathrooms & patios with a cozy fireplace to relax your body and soul.
✉ info@wildcoyote.biz ◐ www.wildcoyote.biz/bedandbreakfast.html

Winemaker's Porch at Frances James Vineyard
4665 Linne Rd 93446
805-237-2168
Marlowe & Corinne Evenson

175-250 BB
3 rooms, 3 pb
Most CC
C-ltd/S-no/P-no/H-ltd

Full breakfast
Complimentary wine
Sitting area, soaker tub,
fireplaces

The Winemakers Porch B&B sits on top of a knoll overlooking our Bordeaux vineyards. Our guests are invited to spend time sharing in our vineyard lifestyle. Luxury accommodations, complimentary bottle of wine, wireless Internet and gourmet breakfast.
✉ FJVineyard@aol.com ◐ www.francesjamesvineyard.com/bnb.html

PESCADERO

Pescadero Creek Inn B&B 393 Stage Rd 94060 888-307-1898 650-879-1898 Ken Donnelly	175-255 BB 4 rooms, 4 pb Visa, MC, *Rated*, • C-ltd/S-ltd/P-no/H-no	Full gourmet breakfast Afternoon wine & cheese from nearby Harley's Goat Farm Picnic baskets, bikes, comfortable down comforters, feather mattresses, antique claw foot tubs, fire

Enjoy a romantic escape to a century old farm with queen beds, period antiques and claw foot tubs. Near the coast, with secluded beaches, parks and miles of trails in redwoods. Join us for afternoon wine and cheese and a full organic breakfast.
✉ ken@pescaderocreekinn.com 🔗 www.pescaderocreekinn.com

PETALUMA

Howard's End 535 Howard 94952 707-778-6022 Aaron Crespi	80-155 BB 1 rooms, 1 pb Visa, MC, AmEx C-ltd/S-no/P-no/H-no	Fruit, coffee & orange juice

Howard's End in Petaluma was featured in Sunset Magazine highlighting the architecture and craftsmanship of the proprietor, Aaron Crespi. All of the furniture and cabinetry were designed and built by Mr. Crespi.
✉ thatcrespi@crespiland.com 🔗 www.crespiland.com/cottage.html

PLACERVILLE

Albert Shafsky House B&B 2942 Coloma St 95667 530-642-2776 Rita Timewell & Stephanie Carlson	135-185 BB 3 rooms, 3 pb Most CC C-ltd/S-ltd/P-no/H-ltd	Full hearty breakfast Wine & snacks at check-in between 4–7, cookies in the early afternoon, guest refrigerator Sitting room with library, games & satellite TV/VCR with movies, free high speed wireless Internet

Luxury in the heart of Gold Country. Queen Anne-style Victorian bed & breakfast, built in 1902, is close enough to stroll to town. Stay in Placerville & visit El Dorado wineries, Apple Hill, Coloma. 3 Diamond rated by AAA.
✉ stay@shafsky.com 🔗 www.shafsky.com

Blair Sugar Pine B&B 2985 Clay St 95667 530-626-9006 William & Kay Steffen	130-160 BB 3 rooms, 3 pb Most CC C-ltd/S-no/P-no/H-no	Full breakfast Evening refreshments Book & video libraries, WiFi, central A/C, feather beds, private baths, sitting room, chocolates

A unique turreted 1901 Queen Anne Victorian bed and breakfast located in historic downtown Placerville, featuring hillside gardens, original woodwork and a history of romance. Walk to shops, restaurants and more.
✉ stay@blairsugarpine.com 🔗 www.blairsugarpine.com

Fleming Jones Homestead B&B 3170 Newtown Rd 95667 530 344-0943 Mark & Robin Miller	135-250 BB 5 rooms, 5 pb Cash, Checks C-yes/S-ltd/P-yes/H-no some German, Spanish, Swedish	Full Multi-Course Gourmet Breakfast Welcome snacks Parlor, porch, private baths, WiFi

A little slice of heaven! This 1883 farmhouse & bunkhouse on 11 acres brings you back in time on this working miniature horse ranch & small vineyard with mountain views. Gourmet homemade breakfasts, thoughtful amenities. Dogs welcome!
✉ info@robinsnestranch.com 🔗 www.robinsnestranch.com/home/bb.php

POINT ARENA

Wharf Master's Inn
785 Port Rd 95468
800-932-4031 707-882-3171
Jay

85-255 BB
25 rooms, 25 pb
Most CC
C-yes/S-no/P-yes/H-yes

Expanded Continental
Breakfast
In-room two person Jacuzzi,
fireplaces, antiques,
panoramic ocean views,
balconies, feather beds

The Wharf Master's Inn is by far one of the most beautiful of all Mendocino & Point Arena hotels. Most rooms feature a two person, in-room Jacuzzi, panoramic ocean views, balconies, fireplaces & feather beds. A great romantic getaway.
info@wharfmasters.com www.wharfmasters.com

POINT REYES STATION

Marsh Cottage
415-669-7168
Wendy Schwartz

170-190 BB
1 rooms, 1 pb
Cash, Checks, *Rated*
C-yes/S-no/P-no/H-no

Full and continental plus
Complimentary coffee/tea
Kitchen, library/sitting area,
fireplace, porch, sun deck

Carefully appointed private cottage along Tomales Bay, near Inverness and Point Reyes National Seashore. Kitchen, fireplace, queen bed, deck overlooking the marsh and "Elephant" Mountain.
wenpaint@horizoncable.com www.marshcottage.com

**Old Point Reyes
Schoolhouse**
11559 Coast Route #1 94956
415-663-1166
Karen Gray

185-385 EP
4 rooms, 4 pb
Visa, MC
C-yes/S-no/P-yes/H-ltd

Kitchens, private baths,
fireplaces, laundry, pets,
BBQ, private gardens, WiFi,
conference buildin

Choose charming Jasmine Cottage, elegant Gray's Retreat, cozy Barn Loft, or beautiful Schoolhouse—or choose them all for your wedding, family reunion or retreat with generous conference building. Secluded on the edge of bustling Point Reyes Station.
PRSchool@sonic.net www.oldpointreyesschoolhouse.com

QUINCY

The Feather Bed
542 Jackson St 95971
800-696-8624 530-283-0102
Bob Janowski

120-175 BB
7 rooms, 7 pb
Most CC, *Rated*
C-yes/S-no/P-no/H-yes

Full breakfast
Afternoon tea, cookies &
fudge
Sitting room, porch,
Victorian garden, bikes,
fountain, fireplaces, A/C

Relax on the porch of this country Victorian inn. Enjoy the slower pace of a small mountain town. Savor fresh berry smoothies with a delicious breakfast. Experience the warmth & personal hospitality that are a tradition in Quincy and at The Feather Bed.
info@featherbed-inn.com www.featherbed-inn.com

The Sporting Inn
505 Main Street 95971
877-710-4300 530-283-4300
Claudia and Marvin Vickers

95-160 BB
8 rooms, 3 pb
Most CC
C-yes/S-no/P-yes/H-no

Full Country Style Breakfast
Snacks and soft drinks.
Wireless Internet access,
upstairs facility. Guide
service available. Boat and
trailer parking.

Located in Plumas County at the top of the Feather River Canyon in historic downtown Quincy California. Walking distance to the museum, theaters, shops, restaurants. Charming old-style hotel atmosphere, with full country breakfast. Fast Internet access.
thesportinginn@sbcglobal.net thesportinginn.com

REDDING

Shasta Cottage
13401 Calle de Lorena 96003
530-275-2670
Marian Pierce

79-89 BB
1 rooms, 1 pb
Visa, MC, Disc
C-yes/S-ltd/P-ltd/H-no

Continental breakfast
Patio, satellite TV, high speed
Internet connections, full
kitchen, washer/dryer

The cottage is located in the middle of about five acres of rolling hills that teem with wildlife. Deer, wild turkey, rabbits, squirrels and quail are frequent visitors.
questions@shastacottage.com www.shastacottage.com

REDDING

Tiffany House B&B	110-150 BB	Full breakfast
1510 Barbara Rd 96003	4 rooms, 4 pb	Complimentary
530-244-3225	Most CC, *Rated*, •	refreshments
Brady Stewart	C-yes/S-ltd/P-no/H-ltd	Sitting room, 1 room with
		spa, gazebo, swimming pool,
		parlor

Romantic Victorian within minutes of the Sacramento River, beautiful lakes, water sports, championship golf are all near by. Views of the Lassen mountain range. View of Calatrava Sundial Bridge from front yard.
✉ tiffanyhse@aol.com 🌐 www.tiffanyhousebb.com

REDWOOD CITY

Atherton Inn	139-249 BB	Full breakfast
201 W Selby Ln 94061	5 rooms, 5 pb	Cookies, cocoas, selection of
800-603-8105 650-474-2777	Visa, MC, AmEx,	teas, freshly squeezed
Tricia Young	*Rated*, •	orange juice, & large fruit
	S-ltd/P-no/H-no	bowl
	German	Free high speed Internet, TV,
		DVD, robes, hairdryer,
		phone, Euro down pillows,
		elevator

Warmth, luxury & hospitality abound in this newly built French style chateau. Conveniently located in the heart of the San Francisco Peninsula in a quiet residential neighborhood just one block from Atherton. We pamper you.
✉ athertoninn@gmail.com 🌐 www.athertoninn.com

RUTHERFORD

Rancho Caymus	155-450 BB	Continental breakfast
1140 Rutherford Rd 94573	26 rooms, 26 pb	Restaurant prix fixe menu on
800-845-1777 707-963-1777	Visa, MC, AmEx,	premises, dinner only
Otto Komes	*Rated*, •	Fireplaces, private balconies,
	C-ltd/S-no/P-no/H-ltd	wet bars, refrigerators

We invite you stay at our family's home away from home, the Rancho Caymus Inn. Our spacious hacienda-style inn has comfortable rooms with high-beamed ceilings.
✉ okomes@ranchcaymus.com 🌐 www.ranchocaymus.com

SACRAMENTO

Amber House B&B	169-279 BB	2 course gourmet breakfast
1315 22nd St 95816	10 rooms, 10 pb	Fresh cookies with beverage
800-755-6526 916-444-8085	Most CC, *Rated*, •	at turndown, coffee, tea &
Judith Bommer	C-ltd/S-no/P-no/H-no	sodas any time
	French, German	Italian marble, private baths,
		Jacuzzi bathtubs for two, free
		DSL, phones, cable TV,
		parking

Just 8 blocks from the State Capitol in Midtown, on a quiet street of historic homes, the Inn offers the perfect blend of elegance, comfort, and hospitality. The Inn is perfectly located, walking distance from downtown, restaurants, shops and galleries.
✉ info@amberhouse.com 🌐 www.amberhouse.com

SALINAS

Safari Bed & Breakfast	195-255 BB	Continental breakfast
900 River Road 93908	4 rooms, 4 pb	
800-228-7382 831-455-2447	Most CC	
	C-ltd/S-no/P-no/H-yes	

Listen to the lions and tigers roaring only yards from your canvas walled hotel suite. Each African tent style bungalow is creatively decorated and equipped with comfortable furniture and complete bathroom facilities. Wake to a continental breakfast.
✉ reservations@wildthingsinc.com 🌐 www.visionquestranch.com/html/b_b.html

SAN ANSELMO

San Anselmo Inn
339 San Anselmo Ave 94960
800-598-9771 415-455-5366
Peter and Julie McNair

99-199 BB
15 rooms, 13 pb
Visa, MC, AmEx
C-ltd/S-no/P-no/H-yes
German, French

Expanded Continental
breakfast
Visit us for Afternoon Tea
every Sunday from 3 –
5:30pm. Wine Bar open Wed
through Sat., 4–9 p.m.
Suites, WiFi, cable TV,
banquet room

This European style Inn provides privacy and comfort along with warm hospitality. Ou
B&B is the perfect base for exploring beautiful Marin County, San Francisco, the Napa
Sonoma wine countries, and Pt. Reyes National Seashore—all within a short drive.
✉ innkeepers@sananselmoinn.com ✪ www.sananselmoinn.com

SAN CLEMENTE

Casa Tropicana Boutique
Beachfront Inn
610 Avenida Victoria, at the
pier 92672
800-492-1245 949-492-1234
Rick and Sue Anderson

225-775 BB
8 rooms, 8 pb
Visa, MC, AmEx,
Rated, •
C-ltd/S-ltd/P-no/H-ltd
Spanglish

Extensive Buffet Breakfast
All rooms have mini fridges
with an assortment of snacks
and goodies-all
complimentary!
Rooms have fireplaces,
Jacuzzi tubs, flat screen tvs,
mini fridges and super comfy
beds.

Spanish-inspired architecture, ocean views, stylish comfortable decor, thoughtful amenitie
and at the pier, beach and sand in San Clemente, Orange County, CA.
✉ info@casatropicana.com ✪ www.casatropicana.com

SAN DIEGO

Bankers Hill Manor
2947 First Ave 92103
877-871-7602 619-293-0375
Linda & Terry Shoemaker

199-259 BB
3 rooms, 3 pb
Most CC
C-ltd/S-no/P-no

Full breakfast
Snacks, "Sunset Hour"
Tropical garden, living room,
dining room, Jacuzzi tub

Enjoy our centrally located Bed & Breakfast in the heart of beautiful San Diego. Experience
the unique luxury and space of the elegant Craftsman Manor. With over 4500 square feet
you can mingle or find a quiet space just for yourself.
✉ info@bankershillmanor.com ✪ www.bankershillmanor.com

Carole's B&B Inn
3227 Grim Ave 92104
800-975-5521 619-280-5258
C. Dugdale & M. O'Brien

119-259 BB
10 rooms, 5 pb
Most CC, *Rated*, •
C-ltd/S-ltd/P-no/H-no

Continental plus breakfast
Cheese
Sitting room, conference for
10, swimming pool, spa,
player piano, cable TV

Historical house built in 1904, tastefully redecorated/antiques. Centrally located near zoo
Balboa Park. Friendly, congenial atmosphere.
✉ carolesbnb@hotmail.com ✪ www.carolesbnb.com

Crones Cobblestone Cottage
1302 Washington Place 92103
619-295-4765
Joan Crone

150 BB
2 rooms, 1 pb
Cash, Checks
C-yes/S-no/P-ltd/H-yes

Continental breakfast
Living room, telephone, TV,
porch, garden

Crone's Cobblestone Cottage is a quiet and comfortable bed and breakfast retreat from the
world and an excellent home base for exploring San Diego. Ideal for business, travelers o
couples seeking a romantic hideaway.
✪ www.cobblestonebandb.com

SAN DIEGO———————————————————

Hillcrest House B&B	129-189 BB	Continental breakfast
3845 Front St 92103	5 rooms, 5 pb	Fresh baked specialties daily
619-990-2441	Visa, MC, *Rated*	Parlor with a fireplace,
Ann Callahan	S-no/P-no	playing cards, puzzles, a
		reading library, TV, wireless
		Internet access

Hillcrest House Bed & Breakfast is a wonderful and fun place to spend your next visit to the San Diego area. A conveniently located destination spot for everyone from business travelers and vacationers to honeymooners.
✉ hillcresthouse@cox.net ☽ www.hillcresthousebandb.com

Kasa Korbett	99-119 BB	Continental breakfast
1050 Front St 92103	4 rooms, 4 pb	
800-757-5272 619-291-3962	Visa, MC, AmEx, •	
Bob Korbett	C-yes/S-no/P-yes/H-no	

Newly-renovated 70 year-old Craftsman-style home. Lots of tourist attractions nearby. From Kasa Korbett, it's a short walk east to Hillcrest, with its neighboring nightclubs, restaurants and coffee houses. ✉ kasakorbett@yahoo.com ☽ www.kasakorbett.com

Keating House	115-165 BB	Full breakfast
2331 Second Ave 92101	9 rooms, 9 pb	Fruit bowl for snacks, coffee
800-995-8644 619-239-8585	Visa, MC, AmEx	& tea all day
Ben & Doug	C-ltd/S-ltd/P-no/H-ltd	Foyer, parlour and dining
	French, Spanish and a	room w/fireplaces, A/C,
	bit of Italian	gardens, porch, free WiFi

Historic Victorian: Keating House, four blocks from the entrance to Balboa Park. Convenient to downtown, convention center, zoo, museums, airport, trolley and the waterfront.
✉ benbaltic@yahoo.com ☽ www.keatinghouse.com

San Diego B&B	245 BB	Continental breakfast
3413 Bancroft St 92104	1 rooms, 1 pb	Water, tea & coffee
619-962-1691	Visa, MC	Private apartment with full
Breton & Karrie Buckley	C-ltd/S-no/P-no/H-no	kitchen, bath, living room,
		wireless Internet, plasma
		TV/home theater

Minutes from Balboa Park and downtown, the San Diego Bed and Breakfast is a sophisticated 700 square-foot luxury cottage that is the perfect honeymoon retreat and the business traveler's paradise. You will feel profoundly — and stylishly — at home.
✉ info@sdbb.us ☽ www.sdbb.us

SAN FRANCISCO———————————————

Albion House Inn	110-165 BB	3 Course American Breakfast
135 Gough St 94102	9 rooms, 9 pb	pastries and beverages and
800-400-8295 415-621-0896	Visa, MC, •	wine and cheese in front of
Albert	C-yes/S-no/P-no/H-no	the fireplace
	French, Spanish	Dining room, Grand Piano,
		TV/VCR, Internet
		connection, luxury robes,
		seasonal accommodations

Experience authentic San Franciscan hospitality at the Albion House Inn, a 9 room inn made of redwood trees. Three course American breakfast, dessert and beverages, wine and cheese is included.
✉ info@albionhouseinn.com ☽ www.AlbionHouseInn.com

Annie's Cottage	160-175 EP	Coffee, tea provided
1255 Vallejo 94109	1 rooms, 1 pb	Near wharf & downtown,
415-923-9990	Cash	phone/answering machine,
Annie Bone	S-no/P-no/H-no	TV/VCR, queen bed, high
		speed, wireless Internet

Guestroom with private entrance, private bath, sitting area, deck, refrigerator/microwave. Country hideaway in the middle of San Francisco. Furnished with antiques.
✉ annie@anniescottage.com ☽ anniescottage.com

SAN FRANCISCO——————————————————

Castillo Inn	65-90 BB	Continental breakfast
48 Henry St 94114	4 rooms	Wireless Internet for laptops.
800-865-5112 415-864-5111	Visa, MC, AmEx, •	Phone, voicemail,
Mario	C-ltd/S-no/P-no/H-no	refrigerator, microwave.
	Spanish	Parking at $10.00/night.

Gay accommodations mostly, though all are welcome. Clean, quiet and safe. Centrally located close to Castro & Market Streets. Ask for our winter rates discount (holidays and special events excluded). ✉ castilloinn@yahoo.com

Country Cottage	89-99 BB	Full breakfast
5 Dolores Ter 94110	4 rooms	Two sitting rooms, quiet
800-452-8249 415-899-0060	Visa, MC, AmEx,	garden patio, Internet WiFi in
Richard & Susan Kreibich	*Rated*, •	every room and parking
	C-ltd/S-ltd/P-no/H-no	available.
	Czech	

The Country Cottage B&B is a cozy country-style B&B in the heart of San Francisco. The four guestrooms are comfortably furnished with American country antiques and brass beds. Short walk to park, tennis courts, cafes & restaurants & bars. Free WiFi. ✉ reservations@bbsf.com

Hayes Valley Inn	76-112 BB	Continental breakfast
417 Gough St 94102	28 rooms	Free local calls and WiFi,
800-930-7999 415-431-9131	Visa, MC, AmEx	cable TV, vanities
Dawn Wiggins	S-no/P-ltd	

The Hayes Valley Inn is an inexpensive and friendly small hotel, nestled in the heart of San Francisco's charming Hayes Valley. It's a neighborhood known for its fine restaurants, boutique shops and art galleries. ✉ frontdesk@hayesvalleyinn.com ◑ www.hayesvalleyinn.com

The Inn at Union Square	189-399 BB	Extensive Continental
440 Post St 94102	30 rooms, 30 pb	Breakfast
800-288-4346 415-397-3510	Most CC, *Rated*, •	Wine & hors d'oeuvres
Norbert Mede	C-ltd/S-no/P-no/H-yes	Shoe shine, concierge &
	French, Spanish	room service, valet parking,
		high speed Internet, free
		health club pass

An elegant, cozy European-style hotel in the heart of San Francisco. A half-block from Union Square, close to the finest restaurants, best shopping & wonderful theater. Our location in unbeatable and our service impeccable! ✉ inn@unionsquare.com ◑ www.unionsquare.com

Inn on Castro	105-250 BB	Full breakfast
321 Castro St 94114	8 rooms, 7 pb	Complimentary brandy
415-861-0321	Most CC	Living room, contemporary
Jan de Gier	C-yes/S-no/P-no/H-yes	furnishings, fresh flowers
		throughout the inn, fireplace,
		library

An incomparable way to experience San Francisco's charm and hospitality from the heart of the City's gay and lesbian community.The Castro. The Inn on Castro is at Castro and Market on the residential side with views over the city and the Bay. ✉ Innkeeper@innoncastro.com ◑ www.innoncastro.com

The Inn San Francisco	105-255 BB	Full buffet breakfast
943 South Van Ness Ave 94110	21 rooms, 19 pb	Complimentary fruit, coffee,
800-359-0913 415-641-0188	Most CC, *Rated*, •	tea, sherry
Marty Neely	C-yes/S-no/P-no/H-no	Sun deck, English garden, hot
	Spanish, French,	tub, phones, TVs, parking,
	Cantonese, Mandarin	Whirlpool tubs, suites

Capturing the romantic spirit of the Victorian era, The Inn San Francisco invites you to be our guest and discover bed and breakfast comfort and hospitality with a warmth that is distinctly San Franciscan. Be welcomed as a friend. ✉ innkeeper@innsf.com ◑ www.innsf.com

SAN FRANCISCO

Moffatt House	73-148 BB	Continental plus breakfast
1401 7th Ave 94122	4 rooms, 3 pb	Fully equipped kitchen
415-661-6210	Visa, MC, AmEx, *Rated*	available in the suite for self-
Ruth Moffatt	C-yes/S-ltd/P-no/H-no	serve breakfast foods
	Spanish, French, Italian	Free wireless Internet,
		phone, TV and daily maid
		service, Jacuzzi tubs,
		balcony, suite

Moffatt House B&B in San Francisco has been a small family business, serving the Inner Sunset neighborhood for 25 years. Guests find the neighborhood a safe delight. Experience city life, the San Francisco way!
✉ moffattbb@sbcglobal.net ○ www.moffatthouse.com

Ocean Beach B&B	125-205 BB	Continental plus breakfast
611 42nd Ave 94121	2 rooms, 2 pb	Homemade cookies always
415-668-0193	Cash	available
Joanne	C-ltd/S-no/P-no/H-no	Board games, hairdryer, iron,
		microwave, fridge, library

Distinctive B&B accommodations with views of the Pacific Ocean located in a quiet, residential neighborhood just six blocks from Ocean Beach and three blocks from Golden Gate Park in San Francisco.   ✉ oceanbeachbb@aol.com ○ www.oceanbeachbb.com

The Parsonage	180-220 BB	Multi-course breakfast
198 Haight St 94102	5 rooms, 5 pb	In the evening guests are
888-763-7722 415-863-3699		welcomed home to a tray of
Joan Hull & John Phillips		chocolates and brandy!
		Marble bathrooms,
		fireplaces, 2 parlors, library,
		goose down comforters &
		imported linens

An 1883 Historical Landmark, Victorian home (formerly the McMorry-Lagan residence), The Parsonage's large, airy rooms are elegantly furnished with European & American antiques. Convenient to all San Francisco attractions.
✉ theparsonage@hotmail.com ○ www.theparsonage.com

Petite Auberge	139-269 BB	Continental plus breakfast
863 Bush St 94108	26 rooms, 26 pb	Evening wine & hors
800-365-3004 415-928-6000	Most CC, *Rated*, •	d'oeuvres
Eric Norman	C-yes/S-no/P-no	Parlor, garden patio,
		fireplaces in most
		guestrooms

With an ideal location, nestled between Nob Hill and Union Square, Petite Auberge is the perfect small hotel for a sightseeing trip to San Francisco or a special romantic getaway.
✉ petiteauberge@jdvhospitality.com ○ www.jdvhospitality.com/hotels/hotel/11

The Red Victorian B&B	89-229 BB	Continental breakfast
1665 Haight St 94117	18 rooms, 6 pb	Smoke-free and TV-free
415-864-1978	Most CC, *Rated*	
Rosie	C-yes/S-no	

Historic lodgings on world-famous Haight Street near Golden Gate Park. A Peaceful World Travelers hotel, a cozy gathering place for people, ideals and ideas for a better world.
✉ reservations@redvic.com ○ www.redvic.com

Stanyan Park Hotel	139-350 BB	Continental plus breakfast
750 Stanyan St 94117	36 rooms, 36 pb	Afternoon tea
415-751-1000	Most CC, *Rated*, •	Sitting room, bikes, suites
Norbert Mede	C-yes/S-no/P-no/H-yes	with kitchens, wireless
	Spanish, German	Internet, business center

The Stanyan Park Hotel is an elegant, thoroughly restored Victorian Hotel on the National Register of Historic Places that will take you back to a bygone era of style, grace and comfort. Awarded the AAA Three Diamond Rating.
✉ sales@stanyanpark.com ○ www.stanyanpark.com

88   California

SAN FRANCISCO────────────────────────────────

The Studio on Sixth
1387 Sixth Ave 94122
415-753-0495
Hope Mohr & Matt Zinn

80-140 BB
1 rooms, 1 pb
Most CC
C-yes/S-no/P-no/H-no

No meals included
Coffee houses, cafes &
excellent restaurants nearby
Garden, private entrance,
fully equipped kitchen, LCD
TV, telephone & wireless
Internet

Studio apartment that opens onto an ornamental garden. Private entrance, queen-size bed, fully-equipped kitchen, separate bath and vanity, LCD TV, private phone, and wireless Internet
✉ studioonsixth@gmail.com 🌐 www.studioonsixth.com

Washington Square Inn
1660 Stockton St 94133
800-388-0220 415-981-4220
Maria & Daniel Levin

179-329 BB
15 rooms, 15 pb
Most CC, *Rated*
C-ltd/S-no/P-no/H-yes
Portuguese, Spanish

Continental plus breakfast
Wine & hors d'oeuvres in
the evening, tea
Self parking, lobby, antiques,
fireplace, cable TV, robes,
courtyard, business services
in lobby

Delightfully situated in the very heart of San Francisco, the Washington Square Inn welcomes its guests with all the charm & comfort only a small European hotel can provide. Sixteen rooms feature European antiques, cable TV, soft robes and private baths.
✉ info@wsisf.com 🌐 www.wsisf.com

White Swan Inn
845 Bush St 94108
800-999-9570 415-775-1755
Eric Norman

189-309 BB
26 rooms, 26 pb
Most CC, *Rated*, •
C-yes/S-no/P-no/H-ltd

Continental plus breakfast
Complimentary wine & hors
d'oeuvres
Parlor, library, exercise
room, fireplace in each
guestroom, deck in back of
inn, garden patio

With crackling fireplaces in all 26 guestrooms and suites, the White Swan Inn is a romantic and atmospheric small hotel in the Nob Hill/Union Square area.
✉ whiteswan@jdvhospitality.com 🌐 www.whiteswaninnsf.com

SAN LUIS OBISPO────────────────────────────

Petit Soleil
1473 Monterey St 93401
800-676-1588 805-549-0321
John & Dianne Conner

159-299 BB
16 rooms, 16 pb
Most CC, *Rated*
C-yes/S-no/P-no/H-ltd
Spanish
April 15 – October 15

Full homemade breakfast
Complimentary wine & light
appetizer in the evening
Outdoor patio, garden,
getaway packages, wine
tasting, private baths,
wireless Internet, telephones

Find a touch of French village life at this delightfully renovated B&B. Individually themed rooms have whimsical art, custom furnishings, and CD players. Rates include wine pairings in the early evening and gourmet breakfasts.
✉ reservations@petitsoleilslo.com 🌐 www.petitsoleilslo.com

San Luis Creek Lodge
1941 Monterey St 93401
800-593-0333 805-541-1122
Patty Oxford

129-349 BB
25 rooms, 25 pb
Visa, MC, AmEx, *Rated*
C-ltd/S-no/P-no/H-ltd

Full breakfast
Refrigerator & microwave,
Starbucks coffee, lemonade
& lodge bars in the afternoon
Robes, free parking,
magazines, trolley, cable
TV/DVD library, WiFi, DSL,
desks, laundry, fitness room

The San Luis Creek Lodge is a charming, small San Luis Obispo bed and breakfast inn with the amenities of a small upscale hotel. No other hotels in San Luis Obispo have the combination of upscale amenities and high quality finishes in a newer building.
✉ info@sanluiscreeklodge.com 🌐 www.sanluiscreeklodge.com

AN RAFAEL————————————————————

erstle Park Inn 4 Grove St 94901 00-726-7611 415-721-7611 m Dowling	189-275 BB 12 rooms, 12 pb Most CC, *Rated*, • C-ltd/S-no/P-no/H-no	Full breakfast Complimentary evening wine & all day sodas & snacks Main parlor with a fireplace, limited open kitchen, 2½ acres of gardens, woods & orchard

*ll rooms have private baths, private patios or decks. All are furnished with rich fabrics
nd beautiful antiques. King suites with Jacuzzi tub.*
✉ innkeeper@gerstleparkinn.com ○ www.gerstleparkinn.com

anama Hotel Bayview St 94901 00-899-3993 415-457-3993 aniel Miller	100-195 BB 10 rooms, 10 pb Visa, MC, AmEx C-yes/S-no/P-ltd/H-ltd Spanish	Continental plus breakfast Full restaurant Historic dining room, tropical garden patio, room service

*landmark inn and restaurant for 60 years, between San Francisco and Wine Country.
he Panama is celebrated for its eccentric charm.*
✉ info@panamahotel.com ○ www.panamahotel.com

ANTA BARBARA————————————————————

White Jasmine Inn 327 Bath St 93101 05-966-0589 1arlies & John	154-309 BB 12 rooms, 12 pb Most CC, *Rated*, • C-ltd/S-ltd/P-no/H-no German, Spanish	Full breakfast Wine & hors d'oeuvres, home made cookies A privately usable Jacuzzi, wireless Internet access, fax, specialty items

*harming inn in prime residential downtown area and in the vicinity of beach. Inviting
icility. Delightful amenities. Lovely grounds. Cozy parlor. Accommodations range from
istefully playful to romantically elegant.*
✉ stay@whitejasmineinnsantabarbara.com ○ www.whitejasmineinnsantabarbara.com

ath Street Inn 720 Bath St 93101 00-341-2284 805-682-9680 1arie Christensen & Deborah entry	131-285 BB 12 rooms, 12 pb Visa, MC, *Rated*, • C-yes/S-no/P-no/H-ltd	Complete gourmet breakfast Afternoon refreshment of home baked cakes and cookies, tea and lemonade, evening wine & cheese Complimentary WiFi, video & book library, off street parking, upstairs & downstairs sitting rooms

*ocated close to the heart of old Santa Barbara, the Inn offers the traditional warmth &
ospitality of a European Bed & Breakfast.*
✉ innkeepers@bathstreetinn.com ○ www.bathstreetinn.com

asa Del Mar Inn 8 Bath St 93101 00-433-3097 805-963-4418 un Kim	129-329 BB 21 rooms, 21 pb Most CC, *Rated*, • C-yes/S-no/P-yes/H-yes Spanish	Continental plus breakfast buffet Evening wine & cheese buffet Sitting room, hot tub, Internet access, pet accommodations, guest kitchen, fireplaces, TV

*he Casa Del Mar Bed Breakfast Inn is the perfect accommodation destination of choice
or a California beach vacation. Mediterranean-style villa, quiet, charming. Courtyard Ja-
uzzi. Several units with fireplaces & kitchens.*
✉ yunkim@casadelmar.com ○ www.casadelmar.com

SANTA BARBARA———————————————————————————————

Cheshire Cat Inn
36 W Valerio St 93101
805-569-1610
Christine Dunstan

99-399 BB
17 rooms, 17 pb
Most CC, *Rated*, •
C-ltd/S-no/P-no/H-no

Continental plus breakfast
Wine & hors d'oeuvres
every afternoon
Hot tubs, balconies,
fireplaces, spa treatments,
outdoor Jacuzzi, gardens,
WiFi

New Low Winter Rates. Victorian elegance, uniquely decorated in Laura Ashley & Englis
antiques. Spa treatments, Jacuzzis, fireplaces, cottages with outdoor hot tubs.
✉ cheshire@cheshirecat.com ◐ www.cheshirecat.com

Harbor House Inn
104 Bath St 93101
888-474-6789 805-962-9745
Karen Traxler

109-325 BB
17 rooms, 17 pb
Visa, MC, AmEx,
Rated, •
C-ltd/S-no/P-no/H-ltd

Welcome breakfast basket 1s
day

The Harbor House Inn offers 17 upscale rooms and studios adorned with antique furnish
ings and collectibles. All of our rooms have a home away from home feeling which w
hope will add to the relaxation & comfort during your stay in beautiful Santa Barbara.
✉ info@harborhouseinn.com ◐ www.harborhouseinn.com

Old Yacht Club Inn
431 Corona Del Mar Dr 93103
800-676-1676 805-962-1277
Eilene Bruce & Vince Pettit

99-249 BB
14 rooms, 14 pb
Visa, MC, Disc, •
C-yes/S-no/P-ltd/H-ltd
Spanish

Full gourmet breakfast
Complimentary wine social,
sherry, coffee and tea,
homemade cookies
Complimentary bicycles,
beach chairs and beach
towels

Located 1 block from famous East Beach! Best location in the area! Santa Barbara's firs
and finest bed & breakfast. Our antique decorated Mission Craftsman Inn served as th
Santa Barbara Yacht Club in the roaring 1920s.
✉ info@oldyachtclubinn.com ◐ www.oldyachtclubinn.com

**The Orchid Inn at Santa
Barbara**
420 W Montecito St 93101
877-722-3657 805-965-2333
Jesper & Jill Sverdrup

165-385 BB
8 rooms, 8 pb
Visa, MC, •
C-ltd/S-no/P-no/H-ltd
Swedish, Spanish

Full hot breakfast
Evening wine & cheese
Full service spa, Jacuzzi
tubs, fireplaces, colorful
decor, sitting areas, business
accommodations

A stylish, contemporary bed and breakfast, two blocks from West Beach in Santa Barbar
The Orchid Inn offers a pleasurable escape to relax and feel at home in the charmin,
ambience.
✉ info@orchidinnatsb.com ◐ www.orchidinnatsb.com

**Prufrock's Garden Inn by
the Beach**
600 Linden Carpinteria 93013
8PR-UFR-OCKS 805-566-9696
Judy & Jim Halvorsen

99-399 BB
8 rooms, 7 pb
Visa, MC, Disc, *Rated*,
•
C-yes/S-no/P-no/H-yes
Spanish

Home-baked, fresh
ingredients
Drinks, desserts, fruits &
snacks are always available
'Best Beach in the West',
beach amenities, mountains,
Channel Islands, gardens,
fireplaces

Gracious personal hospitality in a traditional historic B&B Inn by 'one of the world's bes
beaches' (Nat'l Geographic Traveler). Reader's Favorite, LA Times; Most Romantic Ge
away, Santa Barbara Independent; featured in Land's End and Sunset Magazine.
✉ prufrocksgardeninn@yahoo.com ◐ www.prufrocks.com

SANTA BARBARA

Secret Garden Inn & Cottages 908 Bath St 93101 800-676-1622 805-687-2300 Dominique Hannaux	121-255 BB 11 rooms, 11 pb Most CC, • C-yes/S-no/P-yes/H-no French-Spanish	Full gourmet breakfast Wine & hors d'oeuvres at 5 PM Evening sweets, sitting room, garden, brick patio, bicycles

Guestrooms, suites & private cottages filled with charm, in a delightfully quiet and relaxing country setting. 4 rooms with private patio and outdoor hot tubs.
✉ garden@secretgarden.com   ○ www.secretgarden.com

Simpson House Inn 121 E Arrellaga 93101 800-676-1280 805-963-7067 Nicholas Davaz	255-615 BB 15 rooms, 15 pb Most CC, *Rated*, • C-ltd/S-ltd/P-no/H-yes Spanish	Gourmet vegetarian breakfast Wine, Mediterranean hors d'oeuvres buffet, hot/cold beverages, afternoon tea & dessert buffet Full concierge services, wireless Internet, private patios & decks, in-room massage, morning paper

Welcome to North America's only AAA Five-Diamond B&B. This beautiful Inn is located in a prestigious historic neighborhood of downtown Santa Barbara, and secluded in an acre of English gardens.
✉ info@simpsonhouseinn.com   ○ www.simpsonhouseinn.com

The Tiffany Country House 1323 De La Vina St 93101 800-999-5672 805-963-2283 Ian Martin Winn	220-550 BB 8 rooms, 8 pb Most CC, *Rated*, • C-ltd/S-no/P-no/H-no Spanish	Full breakfast Complimentary wine Spa tub in 5 rooms, fireplaces in 5 rooms, VCRs, in-room phones

Classic antiques & period furnishings welcome you throughout this lovely, restored 1898 Victorian. English Country-style decor.
✉ innkeeper@tiffanycountryhouse.com   ○ www.tiffanycountryhouse.com

The Upham Hotel 1404 De La Vina St 93101 800-727-0876 805-962-0058 Ian Martin Winn	220-550 BB 58 rooms, 58 pb Most CC, *Rated*, • C-yes/S-no/P-no/H-no Spanish/French	Continental plus breakfast Complimentary wine, coffee, tea, Louie's Restaurant Garden veranda, garden, valet laundry, phones, WiFi

A Victorian treasure in the heart of downtown Santa Barbara. Constructed of redwood with sweeping verandas, the 1871 landmark is surrounded by an acre of gardens and combines the intimacy of a B&B with the convenience of a full-service hotel.
✉ innkeeper@uphamhotel.com   ○ www.uphamhotel.com

Villa Rosa 15 Chapala St 93101 805-966-0851 Julia Finucan	129-319 BB 18 rooms, 18 pb Most CC, • C-ltd/S-no/P-no/H-ltd Spanish, French, German, Scandanavian	Continental plus breakfast Wine and hors Doeuvres served between 5pm to 7pm Sherry or Port Wine served between 9pm to 10pm

Let us pamper you in International style. Located just 84 steps from the beach. It exudes a warm, personal and sophisticated atmosphere. A cozy spa and pool are nestled in a walled-in courtyard for your privacy and relaxation.
✉ info@villarosainnsb.com   ○ www.villarosainnsb.com/html/home.html

SANTA CRUZ————————————————————————————————

Cliff Crest
407 Cliff St 95060
831-252-1057 831-427-2609
Adriana & Constantin
Gehriger

95-265 BB
6 rooms, 6 pb
Most CC, •
C-yes/S-no/P-no/H-yes
Spanish, German,
French, Swiss German

Full breakfast
Happy to accommodate
special dietary needs
Sitting room, large garden,
free parking

*Built in 1887 and perched on Beach Hill above the Santa Cruz Beach Boardwalk, this
historic Queen Anne Victorian overlooks the picturesque Santa Cruz Mountains & beaches.
The Inn features 6 guestrooms, each with private bath and several with fireplaces.*
✉ innkpr@CliffCrestInn.com ◑ www.CliffCrestInn.com

Pleasure Point Inn
2-3665 E Cliff Dr 95062
877-557-2567 831-475-4657
Tara & Ivy

250-295 BB
4 rooms, 4 pb
Visa, MC, *Rated*, •
C-ltd/S-ltd/P-no/H-yes

Expanded Continental
Breakfast
A welcome basket with
goodies
Fireplaces, whirlpool tubs, 4
suites, TV, private phones,
private baths, cable TV, iPod
dock, WiFi

*Pleasure Point Inn is an oceanfront B&B at the famous Pleasure Point Beach and offers
spectacular views of the Pacific Ocean. The Inn has a large roof-top deck where you can
soak in the hot tub.*
✉ Inquiries@PleasurePointInn.com ◑ www.PleasurePointInn.com

Seaway Inn
176 W Cliff Dr 95060
800-493-6220 831-471-9004
Stephanie Ausmus

110-350 BB
23 rooms, 23 pb
Most CC, •
C-yes/S-ltd/P-yes/H-no

Continental breakfast
Cookies, coffee, tea & apple
cider offered in the
afternoon.

*The Seaway Inn is a charming Santa Cruz hotel perched on a hillside overlooking the
gorgeous Monterey Bay. It has all the warmth and coziness of a classic beach hotel with a
full array of modern amenities.*
✉ info@seawayinn.com ◑ www.seawayinn.com

Valley View Vacation Rental
600 Hacienda Dr 95067
800-603-8105 650-321-5195
Tricia Young

195-325 BB
2 rooms, 2 pb
Visa, MC, AmEx
S-no/P-no/H-no
German, Spanish

Self-serve continental
breakfast
Entire house unhosted, with
2 bedrooms, 2 baths & spa
on secluded deck; one rate
for house! 4 adults

*An Entire Home All to Yourself! Overlooks 20,000 acres of redwoods. 10 minutes to Santa
Cruz beaches & ocean. 2 bedrooms, 2 baths, all amenities, granite kitchen, & hot spa on
the secluded deck.*
✉ tricia@valleyviewinn.com ◑ www.valleyviewinn.com

West Cliff Inn
174 West Cliff Drive 95060
800-979-0910 831-457-2200
Michael Hoppe

195-400 BB
9 rooms, 9 pb
Most CC
C-yes/S-no/P-no/H-yes

Full breakfast
Afternoon wine, tea & hors
d'oeuvres, freshly-baked
cookies, drinks available
throughout the day
Outdoor jetted hot tub, WiFi

*This distinctive inn is on a bluff across from Cowell's Beach and the famous Santa Cruz
Beach and Boardwalk. The stately, three-story Italianate Victorian with its spacious, wraparound porch was completely renovated and features a breezy, coastal decor.*
✉ westcliffinn@foursisters.com ◑ www.westcliffinn.com

SANTA MONICA

Channel Road Inn	230-450 BB	Full breakfast
214 West Channel Rd 94559	15 rooms, 15 pb	Afternoon wine, tea & hors
310-459-1920	Most CC	d' oeuvres, freshly-baked
Heather Suskin	C-yes/S-no/P-no/H-yes	cookies, drinks available
		throughout the day
		Evening turndown, early
		newspaper delivery to your
		room, wireless Internet,
		movies, books & games

With many rooms boasting fireplaces, jetted spa tubs and peeks of the ocean, this charming and finely crafted historic inn offers visitors to the Los Angeles area a relaxing haven by the sea.
✉ channelroadinn@foursisters.com ○ www.channelroadinn.com

SANTA ROSA

Melitta Station Inn &Spa	135-229 BB	Full 3 course gourmet
5850 Melita Rd 95409	6 rooms, 6 pb	breakfast
800-504-3099 707-538-7712	Most CC, *Rated*, •	English afternoon tea,
Jackie & Tim Thresh	C-ltd/S-ltd/P-no/H-ltd	snacks, tea/coffee, soft
	French, Dutch, Italian	drinks all complimentary
	(some)	Central air, ironing
		board/iron, free wireless
		broadband. Spa/massage
		room with 40 jet hot tub

English cottage hospitality at its best. The inn is cozily furnished with the owners' European antiques, and lies opposite Annadel State Park for biking. It is central to all Sonoma and Napa wineries. ✉ info@melittastationinn.com ○ www.melittastationinn.com

Safari West	120-255 BB	Continental breakfast
3115 Porter Creek Rd 95404	31 rooms, 31 pb	
800-616-2695 707-579-2551	Most CC	
Dan Hickman	C-yes/S-ltd/P-no/H-no	

Safari West . . . A night in the Sonoma Serengeti. The best way to visit is to spend the night, so you can hear the nightly serenade, the likes of which you've never heard outside of an African savannah.
✉ dhickman@safariwest.com ○ www.safariwest.com/cabins/

Vintners Inn	185-550 BB	Continental plus breakfast
4350 Barnes Rd 95403	44 rooms, 44 pb	John Ash & Co. restaurant,
800-421-2584 707-575-7350	Most CC, *Rated*, •	Front Room Bar & Lounge,
Percy Brandon	C-yes/S-no/P-no/H-yes	Vintners Inn Event Center,
	Spanish	Wedding Pavilion
		Wireless Internet, bell
		service, outdoor hot tub,
		walking trail, gym, massage
		room, bocce ball court

A European-styled estate in 92-acre vineyard. All king rooms offer patio/balcony with views of vineyards, gardens or courtyard & fountain. Award-winning John Ash & Co. Restaurant. Luscious grounds and Event Center. AAA Four Diamond rating.
✉ info@vintnersinn.com ○ www.vintnersinn.com

SANTA YNEZ

Edison Street Inn	200-350 BB	Full breakfast
1121 Edison Street 93460	5 rooms, 5 pb	Evening beverage & hors
805-693-0303	Visa, MC, AmEx	d'oeuvres
Larry Marino	S-no/P-no/H-yes	Fireplaces, balconies,
		Jacuzzi tubs, gazebo, porch,
		concierge service

Built in the style of an 1890's Victorian farmhouse, the Edison Street Inn is located in the historic Western township of Santa Ynez, and is situated in the rolling hills, ranches and world class vineyards and wineries of Santa Barbara County, CA
✉ edisonstreetinn@msn.com ○ www.edisonstreetinn.com

94   California

SANTA YNEZ

Santa Ynez Inn
3627 Sagunto St 93460
800-643-5774 805-688-5588
Rick Segovia

295-495 BB
20 rooms, 20 pb
Most CC
C-yes/S-no/P-no/H-yes

Continental plus breakfast
Enjoy wine, hors d'oeuvres,
evening desserts, and a full
gourmet breakfast in the
morning.
Whirlpool tub, balcony or
patios, concierge service,
fitness suite with sauna. Flat
screen HD TVs.

Discover Victorian grace and hospitality in the heart of Santa Barbara County wine country. Located just 3 miles from Los Olivos and Solvang, the Santa Ynez Inn offers lavish suites with fireplaces, Jacuzzi tubs and many amenities.
✉ rick@santaynezinn.com ☻ www.santaynezinn.com

SAUSALITO

Hotel Sausalito
16 El Portal 94965
888-442-0700 415-332-0700
Billy & Josephine Purdie

155-285 BB
16 rooms, 16 pb
Visa, MC, AmEx,
Rated, •
C-ltd/S-no/P-no/H-yes
Spanish, French

Continental breakfast
Downstairs cafe
Hairdryers, cable TV, DVD
players and High speed
Internet access in all rooms

The Hotel Sausalito has style, warmth and history. 16 luxurious rooms and suites feature custom-designed furnishings, hand crafted by local artisans. The hotel's décor conjures up images evocative of the French Riviera.
✉ info@hotelsausalito.com ☻ www.hotelsausalito.com

The Inn Above Tide
30 El Portal 94965
800-893-8433 415-332-9535
Mark Davis Flaherty

315-1,075 BB
29 rooms, 29 pb
Visa, MC, AmEx,
Rated, •
C-yes/S-no/P-no/H-yes
Spanish, French,
Chinese, Farsi, Arabic

Continental plus breakfast
Wine & cheese reception at
sunset
Most rooms have fireplaces
& private decks with
panoramic views of San
Francisco Bay & city skyline.

The Inn Above Tide is the only hotel in the entire Bay Area directly on the water. There is no better view of San Francisco. All 29 rooms and suites feature panoramic Bay views.
✉ stay@innabovetide.com ☻ www.innabovetide.com

SIERRA CITY

High Country Inn B&B
100 Greene Rd 96125
800-862-1530 530-862-1530
Bette & Bob Latta

110-150 BB
4 rooms, 4 pb
Most CC, *Rated*, •
C-ltd/S-no/P-no/H-no

Full breakfast
Snacks
Sitting room, library, suites,
fireplaces

Come away from the noise, the traffic, the crowds . . . Come to the High Country Inn. A unique Inn with outstanding ambience—spectacular views from each room, hearty gourmet breakfasts, private trout pond, and soothing sounds of the river.
✉ blatta@sccn.net ☻ www.hicountryinn.com

SOLEDAD

Inn at the Pinnacles
32025 Stonewall Canyon Rd
93960
831-678-2400
Jon & Jan Brosseau

200-290 BB
6 rooms, 6 pb
Visa, MC
C-ltd/S-no/P-no/H-yes
Weekends Only

Full breakfast
Wine & cheese
Sitting room, suites, gas
fireplaces, private patios, air-
jet tubs

Mediterranean-style country inn with surrounding vineyard and hillside views. Romantic setting. Four miles to the Pinnacles National Monument (west entrance); next to world-famous Chalone Winery.
✉ info@innatthepinnacles.com ☻ www.innatthepinnacles.com

OLVANG

olvang Gardens Lodge	119-249 BB	Continental plus breakfast
3 Alisal Rd 93463	24 rooms, 24 pb	Fireplaces, wireless Internet,
8-688-4404 805-688-4404	Most CC, •	Spa Cottage for massages,
aul & Diana Navratil	C-yes/S-no/P-no/H-yes	gardens, garden weddings,
	Czech and Spanish	family reunions

his Solvang B&B is in a quiet residential section, two blocks from shops, restaurants and ine tasting rooms. 24 unique rooms, marble bathrooms, fireplaces and antique furnish- gs. Surrounded by gardens and fountains. Close to Santa Ynez wineries.
✉ info@solvanggardens.com ○ www.solvanggardens.com

torybook Inn	195-325 BB	Full breakfast
9 1st St 93463	10 rooms, 10 pb	Tea and treats in the evening
0-786-7925 805-688-1703	Most CC, *Rated*	Sitting room with fireplace,
rigitte Guehr	C-yes/S-no/P-no/H-yes	conference & meeting
	Spanish	facilities, in-house catering

lassic European elegance nestled in the heart of Solvang. The Storybook Inn offers a treat into another world. Stay with us and discover the beautiful and unique Santa Ynez alley.
✉ info@solvangstorybook.com ○ www.solvangstorybook.com

ONOMA

Victorian Garden Inn	169-359 BB	Continental plus breakfast
6 E Napa St 95476	4 rooms, 3 pb	Breakfast served in the
0-543-5339 707-996-5339	Visa, MC, AmEx,	garden, the dining room, or
onna J. Lewis	*Rated*, •	in the room, afternoon tea or
	C-ltd/S-ltd/P-no/H-no	coffee and snacks.
	Spanish	Therapeutic hot tub, swimming pool, lush gardens, on-site massage services, free WiFi, iPod docks

et us spoil you at the Victorian Garden Inn, a bed and breakfast in Sonoma. Just a short alk from Sonoma's historic town plaza in Northern California's famed Wine Country, and rovides you with the best in Sonoma lodging.
✉ info@victoriangardeninn.com ○ www.victoriangardeninn.com

he Cooperage Inn	150-275 BB	Continental plus breakfast
1 First St W 95476	2 rooms, 2 pb	You may order a welcoming
07-996-7054	Most CC, •	bottle of champagne or
laudia Wagar	C-ltd/S-no/P-no/H-no	special flowers for birthdays & anniversaries. Perfect for wedding party dressup. The 2 suites combine into 1 large. Bike path. Bikes delivered

Velcome to The Cooperage Inn, a turn-of-the-century, historic bed & breakfast in Sonoma, n the heart of California's Wine Country.
✉ Innkeeper@TheCooperageInn.com ○ www.thecooperageinn.com

Cottage in the Vines	200-250 BB	Breakfast in a basket
8905 Carriger Road 95476	1 rooms, 1 pb	Stocked kitchen, & wine on
25-216-5881	Visa, MC	arrival. Gourmet snacks as
isa Leeb	C-ltd/S-no/P-no/H-no	well as a variety of beverages Wine tasting card that provides you with free wine tasting at over 20 Sonoma Valley wineries. WiFi

large one-bedroom guesthouse with a fully appointed kitchen, comfortable king-size bed nd even a Jacuzzi bathtub provide you with all the comforts of home. Enjoy the large eck with spectacular views, a bocce ball court, tennis court, and swimming pool
✉ lisainthevines@gmail.com ○ www.cottageinthevines.com

SONOMA————————————————————————————————

Hidden Oak
214 E Napa St 95476
877-996-9863 707-996-9863
Don & Valerie Patterson

195-245 BB
3 rooms, 3 pb
Most CC, •
C-ltd/S-ltd/P-no/H-no
April – November

Full breakfast
Complimentary cheese,
wine, tea and coffee
Bicycles, pool, guest
refrigerator, down
comforters, antique wood
furnishings, bathrobes

A touch of old Sonoma . . . Experience the warmth of this country home in the historic town of Sonoma in the Valley of the Moon. The Hidden Oak Inn is a tastefully restored California Craftsman Bungalow with beautifully decorated rooms.
✉ hoi@vom.com ✪ www.hiddenoakinn.com

The Inn at Sonoma
630 Broadway 95476
888-568-9818 707-939-1340
Rachel Retterer

165-300 BB
19 rooms, 19 pb
Most CC
C-yes/S-no/P-no/H-yes

Full breakfast
Afternoon wine, tea & hors
d' oeuvres, freshly-baked
cookies, drinks available
throughout the day
Hot tub, bikes, fireplace

Fall in love with the quiet pace, beautiful vistas and fabulous food and wine of the Sonoma Valley. Conveniently located just two blocks from the historic Sonoma Plaza, the Inn at Sonoma is the perfect destination for your Wine Country visit.
✉ innatsonoma@foursisters.com ✪ www.innatsonoma.com

Ramekins B&B
450 W Spain St 95476
707-933-0452
Marilyn & Leslie

135-250 BB
6 rooms, 6 pb
Most CC
C-ltd/S-no/P-ltd/H-yes

Continental plus breakfast
TV, phone with voice mail,
wireless Internet,
coffeemakers, hairdryers &
irons

Six luxuriously appointed rooms with private baths, one with a fireplace, tucked away on the 2nd floor of the popular culinary school featuring a gallery of incredible food-related art. Continental breakfast served each morning.
✉ inn@ramekins.com ✪ www.ramekins.com

Sonoma Chalet
18935 Fifth St W 95476
800-938-3129 707-938-3129
Joe Leese

110-225 BB
7 rooms, 5 pb
Most CC, *Rated*
C-ltd/S-no/P-no/H-ltd

Continental plus breakfast
Fireplaces, garden hot tub,
free bicycles, bathrobes,
toiletries

Sonoma Chalet offers cottages and B&B accommodations on three and a half very private acres. Just five minutes drive from Sonoma Plaza, this exceptional lodging includes fireplaces, garden hot tub, wooded groves and vineyards.
✉ sonomachalet@cs.com ✪ www.sonomachalet.com

Sonoma Hotel
110 W Spain St 95476
800-468-6016 707-996-2996
Tim Farfan & Craig Miller

110-248 BB
16 rooms, 16 pb
Most CC, *Rated*, •
C-yes/S-no/P-no/H-yes
Japanese, French,
Spanish

Continental breakfast
The Girl and The Fig
Restaurant & bar onsite.
A/C, TVs, phone with data
port

A wonderful vintage hotel (circa 1880) on Sonoma's historic plaza. Modern amenities have been added, including private baths, phones, TVs and A/C. Guests can walk to shops, historic sites and wineries.
✉ sonomahotel@aol.com ✪ www.sonomahotel.com

Sonoma Hotel, Sonoma, CA

SONORA

Barretta Gardens Inn	140-250 BB	Full breakfast
700 S Barretta St 95370	6 rooms, 6 pb	Afternoon refreshments
800-206-3333 209-532-6039	Visa, MC, *Rated*, •	All new beds, antiques,
Daniel & Astrid Stone	C-ltd/S-ltd/P-ltd/H-ltd	Jacuzzi tubs, business
	Swedish, German,	accommodations (i.e. fax),
	French, Italian	computers

This turn-of-the-century Victorian farmhouse offers ample space for solitude, a romantic getaway or small business meetings. We can arrange theatre tickets, restaurant reservations, golf and ski packages. We also feature brand new beds!
✉ barrettagardens@hotmail.com ❂ www.barrettagardens.com

Bradford Place Inn &	140-265 BB	Full cooked to order
Gardens	4 rooms, 4 pb	breakfast
56 W Bradford St 95370	Visa, MC, AmEx,	24 hour tea, hot chocolate
800-209-2315 209-536-6075	*Rated*, •	Complimentary wireless
Dottie Musser & John	C-ltd/S-ltd/P-no/H-no	Internet, FAX service, on-site
Eisemann		parking, mid-week rates for
		business guests

This stunning 1889 Victorian offers elegant nostalgia and white picket fences in historic downtown Sonora, California between Lake Tahoe and Yosemite. Exceptional service with breakfast cooked to order and served all morning.
✉ Innkeeper@bradfordplaceinn.com ❂ www.bradfordplaceinn.com

SOUTH LAKE TAHOE

Black Bear Inn	210-470 BB	Full breakfast
1202 Ski Run Blvd 96150	10 rooms, 8 pb	Evening wine & cheese
877-232-7466 530-544-4451	Most CC, •	Hot tub, fireplace, balcony
Kevin Chandler	C-ltd/S-no/P-no/H-yes	

A small luxury lodge with five guestrooms plus three cabins on a wooded acre in South Lake Tahoe. Close to the lake, restaurants, shopping, skiing, hiking, biking and boating.
✉ info@tahoeblackbear.com ❂ www.tahoeblackbear.com

SOUTH PASADENA

Arroyo Vista Inn
335 Monterey Rd 91030
888-9ARROYO 323-478-7300
Pat Wright

150-300 BB
10 rooms, 10 pb
Visa, MC, AmEx, *Rated*
C-ltd/S-ltd/P-yes/H-ltd
Spanish

Full Homemade Breakfast
Fresh-baked cookies and
gourmet candies, early
evening wine, cheese and tea
Events & weddings, bridal
showers, catering, wine
cellar, parking, wireless
Internet, reunions

Rooms with a view! This historical and newly restored 1910 Craftsman has 10 elegantly simple suites. Many have views; some have spa tubs; all are luxurious and calming.
✉ info@arroyovistainn.com ❸ www.arroyovistainn.com

SOUTH SAN FRANCISCO

Inn at Oyster Point
425 Marina Blvd 94080
800-642-2720 650-737-7633
Marla Catt

149-229 BB
30 rooms, 30 pb
Most CC
C-yes/S-ltd/P-ltd/H-yes

Continental breakfast
Dominic's Restaurant: lunch
& dinner available
Conference room, fireplaces,
cable TV, iron/board,
hairdryer, computer
workstation, Internet access

Spacious rooms with featherbeds, great views, a cozy fireplace, and a refreshment center help to relax and energize you. Your stay will delight your eye, soothe your mind and invigorate your palate.
✉ info@innatoysterpoint.com ❸ www.innatoysterpoint.com

ST. HELENA

Ambrose Bierce House
1515 Main St 94574
707-963-3003
John & Lisa Runnells

199-299 BB
4 rooms, 4 pb
Visa, MC, Disc, *Rated*,
•
C-ltd/S-no/P-no/H-no
Spanish

Full gourmet champagne
breakfast
Premium wines and cheeses
are served each evening
Hot tub, Jacuzzi tubs, canopy
beds, antiques, A/C, satellite
TV, warm hospitality

We invite you to experience the romantic charm and "warm and enthusiastic hospitality" of our 1872 Victorian bed and breakfast inn, right in the center of the finest wineries of Napa Valley . . .
✉ ambrose@napanet.net ❸ www.ambrosebiercehouse.com

The Ink House
1575 S. St Helena Hwy 94574
866-963-3890 707-963-3890
Kevin Outcalt

149-299 BB
6 rooms, 6 pb
Visa, MC, *Rated*, •
C-ltd/S-no/P-no/H-no

Full gourmet breakfast
Evening wine & appetizers
included, sherry & brandy
available
Parlor, VIP Winery pass,
game room, bicycles, glass
observatory, concierge
services, Internet access

Treat yourself to Victorian elegance in the midst of the Napa Valley's world famous wine growing region. Among the vineyards, and neighbors to some of the finest wineries and restaurants with a fabulous gourmet breakfast, luxurious rooms,& Internet access
✉ inkhousebb@aol.com ❸ www.inkhouse.com

Inn at Southbridge
1020 Main St. 94574
707-967-9400

300-420 BB
21 rooms, 21 pb
Most CC
C-yes/S-no/P-no

Continental breakfast
DVD/CD players, down
comforters, high speed
Internet, mini-fridge, coffee
makers, in-room safes

The Inn at Southbridge provides the perfect destination for lodging in Napa Valley. Within walking distance of wine tasting, fine dining, gourmet markets, galleries and boutiques, bicycling, hiking and romantic picnic settings.
✉ sbres@meadowood.com ❸ www.innatsouthbridge.com

ST. HELENA ───

Rose Garden Inn
1277 St. Helena Hwy S 94574
707-963-4417
Tom & Joanne "Joey"

170-210 BB
4 rooms, 4 pb
C-ltd/S-ltd/P-ltd/H-ltd

Full breakfast
Wireless Internet, pool

Turn of the century ranch foreman's home nestled on three acres amidst the world famous Myacama hills and vineyards.
✉ joey@rosegardeninn.org ◐ www.rosegardeninn.org

───

Rustridge Ranch
2910 Lower Chiles Valley 94574
800-788-0263 707-965-9353
Susan Meyer

150-300 BB
4 rooms, 4 pb
Most CC, •
C-ltd/S-no/P-ltd/H-ltd
Spanish

Full breakfast
Wine grown and produced
on the property and hors
d'ouevres
Tennis, sauna, pool,
vineyard, gardens, hiking
trails, outdoor museum,
winery, Internet access

Our comfortable western ranch-style guesthouse has sweeping views of vineyards, pastures, hillsides and ancient oak trees. It is located on a 442 acre working ranch, vineyard and winery in the secluded area of Napa Valley known as Chiles Valley.
✉ rustridge@rustridge.com ◐ www.rustridge.com/bnb.html

───

Shady Oaks Country Inn
399 Zinfandel Ln 94574
707-963-1190
John & Lisa Wild-Runnells

189-269 BB
5 rooms, 5 pb
Visa, MC, *Rated*, •
C-ltd/S-no/P-no/H-ltd
April 1st-November 1st

Gourmet champagne
breakfast
Premium wines and cheeses
are served each evening.
Fireplaces, Roman pillared
patio; innkeepers
knowledgeable concierges,
private entrance, TVs

Romantic and secluded on 2 acres, among finest wineries of Napa Valley. Elegant ambience, country comforts, antiques, fireplaces, port and fine linens in guestrooms. "Warm and gracious hospitality!"
✉ shdyoaks@napanet.net ◐ www.shadyoakscountryinn.com

───

Spanish Villa Inn
474 Glass Mtn. Rd 94574
707-963-7483
Roy & Barbara

207-275 BB
3 rooms, 3 pb
Visa, MC, •
C-ltd/S-no/P-no/H-no
Italian, Portuguese,
Spanish, French &
German
April-November

Continental plus breakfast
Lawn games, patios &
balconies, down beds,
Fireplace/TV room, Library

Experience Italy in Napa Valley with the splendor of a Tuscan, Mediterranean Villa. 1 mile from the Culinary Institute of America. We can accommodate your small group. All rooms have king beds, private baths, and balconies or patios.
✉ spanishvillainn@hotmail.com ◐ www.napavalleyspanishvilla.com

───

Sunny Acres
397 Main St 94574
707-963-2826
Lynn Hosburgh

179-124 BB
2 rooms, 2 pb

Full breakfast

Restored 1879 Victorian amidst 26 acres of vineyard, originally planted in 1859 by Dr. G.B.Crane. Easy walk to downtown St. Helena.
✉ sacres@napanet.net ◐ sunnyacresbandb.com

ST. HELENA───

The Wine Country Inn & Gardens
1152 Lodi Ln 94574
888-465-4608 707-963-7077
Jim Smith

260-700 BB
29 rooms, 29 pb
Visa, MC, *Rated*, •
C-ltd/S-no/P-no/H-ltd
Spanish

Full Buffet breakfast
Wine tasting & appetizers at afternoon social; complimentary evening restaurant shuttle service
Heated pool year round, balconies or patios, fireplaces, spa or hot tubs, daily tour to wineries

Built to resemble a converted winery, this Inn sits atop a landscaped knoll overlooking the vineyards of the Napa Valley. Casual, comfortable, "green luxury" is the hallmark of this renowned hostelry. Family built, owned and operated for over thirty years.
✉ jim@winecountryinn.com ◐ www.winecountryinn.com

Wine Country Villa
2000 Howell Mtn Rd 94574
866-963-9073 707-963-9073
Bill & Diane

125-300 EP
2 rooms, 2 pb
Visa, MC, AmEx,
Rated, •
C-yes/S-ltd/P-yes/H-no

Self-catered
Well equipped kitchen & dining area
Great room with fireplace, pool, spa, sauna, balconies, gardens, kitchen.

Wine Country Villa is set in a secluded and beautiful area with views of wooded hillsides, mountains and vineyards. Impeccably designed and appointed, it is an ideal retreat in the heart of the Napa Valley. ✉ info@winecountryvilla.com ◐ www.winecountryvilla.com

The Zinfandel Inn
800 Zinfandel Ln 94574
707-963-3512
Jerry Payton

225-349 BB
3 rooms, 3 pb
Visa, MC, *Rated*, •
C-ltd/S-no/P-no/H-no

Full breakfast
Complimentary wine truffles on arrival. World famous cookie jar
Sitting room, whirl pool tubs, suites, fireplaces, cable TV, phones, A/C, YVI lagoon style pool

English Tudor that looks like a castle in the vineyard. Located in the heart of Napa Valley. Two acres with a hot tub and beautiful lagoon pool. Acclaimed in Wine Spectator Magazine, Sunset Magazine, Food & Wine, and Best Places to Kiss. ◐ www.zinfandelinn.com

SUTTER CREEK───────────────────────────────────────

Foxes Inn of Sutter Creek
77 Main St 95685
800-987-3344 209-267-5882
Monique, Mike, & Morgan Graziadei

160-325 BB
7 rooms, 7 pb
Most CC, *Rated*
C-ltd/S-no/P-no/H-ltd

Choose from numerous entrees
coffee, tea and homemade cookies
Clawfoot tubs, library, fireplace, TV, VCR, music systems, cathedral ceilings, private entrances

Victorian Jewel in historic downtown Sutter Creek. Walking distance to shops, restaurants, wine tasting and theater. Select your gourmet breakfast from the menu, made-to-order and served to each room or in the lush gardens. Mobil 3-Star and AAA 4-Diamond.
✉ innkeeper@foxesinn.com ◐ www.foxesinn.com

The Hanford House Inn
61 Hanford St., Hwy. 49 95685
209-267-0747
Robert & Athena Gordon

115-249 BB
10 rooms, 10 pb
Most CC, *Rated*, •
C-yes/S-no/P-ltd/H-yes
Spanish

Full breakfast
Tea & cookies, snacks, champagne, wine & hors d'oeuvres
CD & VCR library, suites, fireplaces, Cable TV, guest pantry, conference room, Internet access

Peacefulness, serenity, casual elegance, featherbeds and modern amenities blended with warmth and hospitality provide your perfect escape. Nine spacious rooms blending the elegance of a gracious past with present day comforts. AAA 4 Diamond rating.
✉ robert@hanfordhouse.com ◐ www.hanfordhouse.com

SUTTER CREEK

Sutter Creek Inn	93-195 BB	Full breakfast
75 Main St 95685	17 rooms, 17 pb	Compl. refreshments
209-267-5606	Visa, MC, Disc, *Rated*,	large living room, piano,
Lindsay Way	•	library, A/C, gardens,
	C-ltd/S-ltd/P-no/H-ltd	massage, wood-burning
		fireplaces & swinging beds !

The Inn has been open and serving thousands of guests for over 35 years. Spacious grounds, patios, fireplaces, 17 rooms and cottages, and 4 of Jane Way's famous swinging beds. Eclectic style. Enjoy relaxed hospitality.
✉ info@suttercreekinn.com ○ www.suttercreekinn.com

TAHOE CITY

Cottage Inn at Lake Tahoe, Inc.	158-340 BB	Full breakfast
1690 W Lake Blvd 96145	15 rooms, 15 pb	Homemade cookies and
800-581-4073 530-581-4073	Visa, MC, *Rated*, •	coffee bar
Susanne Muhr	C-ltd/S-no/P-no/H-ltd	Private saunas, fireplaces,
	German	TVs/VCRs, fax machine

The Cottage Inn, 2 miles south of Tahoe City, features original knotty pine paneling throughout, with unique themes and charming Tahoe appeal.
✉ cottage@ltol.com ○ www.thecottageinn.com

Truckee River Ranch Lodge	85-200 BB	Continental breakfast
2285 River Rd, Hwy 89 Alpine	19 rooms, 19 pb	Fine dining restaurant &
Meadows Rd 96145	Visa, MC, AmEx, *Rated*	cocktail lounge
866-991-9912 530-583-4264	C-yes/S-no/P-ltd/H-yes	Antiques, down comforters
Bric Haley		or quilts, cable TV, Internet
		access, balconies

The perfect mountain location year-round! On the Truckee River near the north shore of Lake Tahoe, this "old Tahoe" lodge features 19 handsome rooms, and a dining room and bar cantilevered over the river in a beautiful location.
✉ info@riverranchlodge.com ○ www.riverranchlodge.com

TAHOE VISTA

Shore House at Lake Tahoe	190-310 BB	Full gourmet breakfast
7170 North Lake Blvd 96148	9 rooms, 9 pb	Afternoon appetizers & wine
800-207-5160 530-546-7270	Visa, MC, Disc, *Rated*,	All rooms gas fireplaces,
Marty & Barb Cohen	•	TVs, coffeemakers, iron,
	C-ltd/S-ltd/P-no/H-ltd	robes, hairdryers

Come experience a beautiful and romantic Lake Tahoe vacation getaway at the Shore House, located in Tahoe Vista, CA, on the North Shore. Central to all lake and mountain activities. Nine guestrooms with private baths, fireplaces, outdoor entrances.
✉ innkeeper@shorehouselaketahoe.com ○ www.shorehouselaketahoe.com

TEMPLETON

Carriage Vineyards B&B	140-235 BB	Full breakfast
4337 S El Pomar 93465	4 rooms, 4 pb	Snacks, complimentary soft
800-617-7911 805-227-6807	Visa, MC, Disc, •	drinks, estate olive oil tasting
Leigh Anne Farley	C-ltd/S-no/P-no/H-ltd	Sitting room, carriage house
		with 18 carriages, vineyards
		and olives, carriage rides,
		vineyard tours

100-acre ranch with 28 acres of wine grapes & 850 olive trees. Lovely rooms, great hospitality & delightful breakfasts. Peaceful & quiet.
✉ Stay@CarriageVineyards.com ○ www.carriagevineyards.com/bbhome.html

Country House Inn	150-170 BB	Delicious gourmet breakfast
91 S Main St 93465	5 rooms, 5 pb	Elegant lawns, flowers,
800-362-6032 805-434-1598	Visa, MC	terrycloth robes, fireplaces,
Dianne Garth	C-ltd/S-no/P-no/H-no	dining room, porch

Built in 1886 by the Founder of Templeton, the Inn is now a designated Historic Site. This old Victorian home has been lovingly restored and guests may look forward to sharing in the gracious living of a bygone era at Country House Inn.
✉ countryhouse@tcsn.net ○ thecountryhouseinn.com

TEMPLETON——————————————————————————————————

Hollyhock Farms	150-185 BB	Full breakfast
200 Hollyhock Ln 93465	2 rooms, 2 pb	The breakfasts are full,
805-239-4713	Visa, MC	gourmet meals designed for
Kim & Dick Rogers	C-ltd/S-no/P-ltd/H-no	wine lovers. We are flexible
		on dietary needs.
		Patio, wet-bar, farm tour, tour
		assistance for local wineries
		& sites, wireless Internet

A Paso Robles bed and breakfast in the midst of area wineries. The Cottage and Bungalow offer what few lodgings can . . . the charm, beauty and pleasant wonders of an organic farm. Removed from the traffic of town, quiet, a magnificent slice of rural life.
✉ hollyhock@tcsn.net ✆ www.hollyhock-farm.com

Venteux Vineyards Bed &	245 BB	Full breakfast
Breakfast	3 rooms, 3 pb	Venteux Vineyard wines,
1795 Las Tablas Road 93465	Visa, MC	artisan cheeses & hors
805-369-0126	C-ltd/S-no/P-no/H-ltd	d'oeuvres
Scott & Bobbi Stelzle		

In the very heart of the Paso Robles wine country, Venteux Vineyards is both an estate winery and a premium B&B. The Winemakers Residence features 2 luxurious guestrooms with private entrances and lavish baths and one barn apartment.
✉ bobbi@venteuxvineyards.com ✆ www.venteuxvineyards.com/rooms.html

TWAIN HARTE——————————————————————————————

McCaffrey House	145-200 BB	Full breakfast
23251 Hwy 108 95383	8 rooms, 8 pb	Complimentary wine &
888-586-0757 209-586-0757	Visa, MC, AmEx	sparkling cider in the early
Michael & Stephanie	C-yes/S-no/P-yes/H-no	evening; tea and cookies in
McCaffrey		the afternoon.
		Spa, concierge, business
		facilities, black iron fire
		stoves, individual
		thermostats, private patios

Four Diamond AAA/Select Registry B&B—Pure Elegance In a Wilderness Setting. An exquisite experience of comfort blended with fresh adventure, culinary excellence, and personal guest services.
✉ innkeeper@mccaffreyhouse.com ✆ www.mccaffreyhouse.com

UKIAH———————————————————————————————————

Vichy Hot Springs Resort	195-390 BB	Full buffet breakfast
2605 Vichy Springs Rd 95482	26 rooms, 26 pb	Warm carbonated Vichy
707-462-9515	Most CC, *Rated*, •	mineral baths, hot pool,
Gilbert & Marjorie Ashoff	C-yes/S-ltd/P-no/H-yes	Olympic size pool, hot stone
	Spanish	massage, facials

A historic hot springs country inn: quiet, elegant & charming. The warm, carbonated "Vichy" mineral baths are unique in North America. 700 private acres preserved for guests' enjoyment. Massage, facials, hot stone massage & yoga are offered.
✉ vichy@vichysprings.com ✆ www.vichysprings.com

VENICE——————————————————————————————————

Venice Beach House	145-235 BB	Continental plus breakfast
15 30th Ave 90291	9 rooms, 5 pb	Afternoon snack with tea
310-823-1966	Most CC, *Rated*	Sitting room, fireplace, steps
Brian Gannon	C-ltd/S-no/P-no/H-no	to beach, high speed
	Spanish	Internet, A/C

Historic beachfront getaway to Hollywood stars and Los Angeles celebrities, built when Abbot Kinney's Venice Beach merged European style with California tourism—now a romantic bed and breakfast with air conditioning in all rooms.
✉ reservations@venicebeachhouse.com ✆ www.venicebeachhouse.com

VENTURA

Bella Maggiore Inn	75-180 BB	Full breakfast
67 S California St 93001	24 rooms, 24 pb	Wine & cheese served
800-523-8479 805-652-0277	Most CC, *Rated*, •	between 5pm & 6pm daily
Thomas J. Wood	S-no/P-no/H-yes	Restaurant, free parking, TV,
		Internet, private baths, some
		rooms with decks, A/C, spas,
		fireplaces

The Bella Maggiore is an intimate Italian-style small hotel in the heart of downtown Ventura. Nona's Courtyard Cafe is on site. Complimentary evening appetizers and beverages and a full breakfast are included.
✉ bminn@pacbell.net

WATSONVILLE

Freedom Rose House B&B	125-225 BB	Full breakfast
2313 Freedom Blvd 95076	4 rooms, 3 pb	Proudly featuring locally
831-724-9169	Visa, MC, *Rated*	grown produce, please let us
Steve & Pam Dunlap	C-ltd/S-ltd/P-no/H-ltd	know of any diet restrictions
		Two large, comfortable
		public areas; 10,000+ volume
		cookbook library

The Freedom Rose House B&B is the perfect location for a Central Coast getaway. The 1880s-era Queen Anne Victorian has been completely restored to its original glory, combined with gracious hospitality it offers an ideal retreat for discerning guests.
✉ innkeeper@freedomrosehouse.com ♦ www.freedomrosehouse.com

WEAVERVILLE

Weaverville Hotel	99-190 EP	None
481 Main St 96093	7 rooms, 7 pb	Daily $5 Hotel Credits for
800-750-8853 530-623-2222	Visa, MC, •	each guest good at several
Jeanne and Brian Muir	C-ltd/S-no/P-no/H-ltd	nearby restaurants.
		Lounge, parlor/library,
		porch, on-site gift store.

Located in the midst of the Trinity Alps, in the historic downtown district of the old Gold Rush town of Weaverville, California. There is not a single stoplight in the entire county. This is truly God's country! ✉ stay@weavervillehotel.com ♦ www.weavervillehotel.com

WESTPORT

DeHaven Valley Inn	95-215 BB	Full Multi-Course Breakfast
39247 N Hwy 1 95488	9 rooms, 7 pb	Dinner on the weekends by
707-961-1660	Most CC, *Rated*, •	reservation only, beer and
David & Tammy Doriot	C-yes/S-ltd/P-ltd/H-ltd	wine may be purchased
		WiFi, hot tub, fireplaces,
		woodstoves, sitting room,
		games, DVDs, books

An 1875 farmhouse with cottages sits amid 20 acres of hills & meadows with a creek side path to the beach. Homey and serene, free from the hustle and bustle of Mendocino & Fort Bragg yet close enough for shopping, fine dining and theatre.
✉ dehavenvalleyinn@wildblue.net ♦ www.dehavenvalleyinn.com

Howard Creek Ranch	75-198 BB	Full Ranch Breakfast
40501 N Hwy 1 95488	12 rooms, 12 pb	Complimentary coffee, hot
707-964-6725	Most CC, *Rated*	cocoa & tea (inc. garden
Charles & Sally Grigg	C-ltd/S-ltd/P-ltd/H-ltd	fresh mint tea), kitchenettes
	German, Italian, Dutch,	& barbeques
	Spanish	Piano, hot tubs, sauna,
		gardens, library, solarium,
		swinging bridge, massage,
		onsite hiking/beach

Historic, rural farmhouse on 60 acres filled with collectibles, antiques & memorabilia. Unique health spa with privacy & dramatic views adjoining a wide beach. Refurbished historic carriage barn from virgin redwood milled by Inn owner. Onsite trails.
✉ howardcreekranch@mcn.org ♦ www.howardcreekranch.com

YOUNTVILLE——

Lavender B&B
2020 Webber Ave 94599
800-522-4140 707-944-1388
Gina Massolo

225-300 BB
8 rooms, 8 pb
Most CC, •
C-yes/S-no/P-no/H-yes
Sign language

Full breakfast
Afternoon wine, tea & hors
d' oeuvres, freshly-baked
cookies, drinks available
throughout the day
Porch, veranda, daily
housekeeping, patios,
fireplaces

Intimate and luxuriously cozy, Lavender, combines the warm colors of Provence with contemporary design elements to create a vibrant setting that blends old and new. A lovely heritage home is the centerpiece of the inn's four buildings.
✉ lavender@foursisters.com ❂ www.lavendernapa.com

Maison Fleurie
6529 Yount St 94599
800-788-0369 707-944-2056
Gina Massolo

130-300 BB
13 rooms, 13 pb
Most CC
C-yes/S-no/P-no/H-yes

Full breakfast
Afternoon wine, tea & hors
d' oeuvres, freshly-baked
cookies, drinks available
throughout the day
Concierge services, daily
housekeeping, private patio,
fireplace, robes, hot tub, pool

Napa Valley's Maison Fleurie, the "flowering house," is situated on half an acre of beautifully landscaped gardens—welcoming visitors to a Napa Valley inn reminiscent of southern France.
✉ maisonfleurie@foursisters.com ❂ www.maisonfleurienapa.com

Oleander House
7433 St Helena Hwy 94599
800-788-0357 707-944-8315
Kathleen Matthews

160-225 BB
5 rooms, 5 pb
Visa, MC, AmEx,
Rated, •
C-ltd/S-no/P-no/H-no
Spanish

Full breakfast
Complimentary soft drinks &
brandy
Sitting room, spa, patio, near
ballooning, tennis, golf,
dining, shops

Country French charm. Antiques. Spacious rooms with brass beds, private decks, fireplaces, central A/C, and Laura Ashley fabrics and wallpapers.
✉ Innkeeper@Oleander.com ❂ www.oleander.com

YUBA CITY——

The Harkey House
212 C St 95991
530-674-1942
Bob & Lee Jones

105-225 BB
4 rooms, 4 pb
Visa, MC, AmEx,
Rated, •
C-yes/S-ltd/P-yes/H-ltd

Fresh ground coffee, scones,
breads
In room coffee & teas,
afternoon tea, cookies,
popcorn
Concierge services, phones,
wireless Internet,
TV/CD/DVD, pool, spa,
library, horse shoes

An elegant and historic inn with intricacies not to be quickly unraveled. This B&B will charm newcomers with its beauty, while still engrossing those who know it well. Voted 'The Best Inn Yuba Sutter Area 2008'. Walking distance to restaurants & parks.
✉ lee@harkeyhouse.com ❂ www.harkeyhouse.com

Colorado

Snow Queen Victorian Lodge
124 E Cooper St 81611
970-925-8455
Norma Dolle Owner/"M"
Resident Manager

129-419 BB
10 rooms, 10 pb
Visa, MC, *Rated*, •
C-yes/S-no/P-no/H-no

Continental breakfast
Apres ski parties in winter
Parlor, fireplace, hot tub with
view of Aspen Mountain,
rooms with kitchens & decks

Historic 1886 Victorian B&B. Friendly, family run, affordable and just 2 blocks from downtown and ski lifts. Victorian rooms all have private baths, TV, phone and share outdoor hot tub with view of Aspen Mountain.
✉ sqlodge@rof.net ◑ www.snowqueenlodge.com

West Beaver Creek Lodge
220 W Beaver Creek Blvd
81620
888-795-1061 970-949-9073
Theresa & Robert Borg

159-369 BB
9 rooms, 9 pb
Most CC, *Rated*, •
C-yes/S-no/P-no/H-ltd

Full breakfast
Catering with prior
arrangement including
arrival night dinner,
rehearsal dinner, wedding
cakes
Sitting room, Jacuzzis, suites,
cable TV, wireless hi-speed
Internet, video library, pool
table

If you want to ski in world class Vail and Beaver Creek, and stay in the finest accommodations without paying those high rates, then West Beaver Creek Lodge in the heart of the Vail Valley is for you. Full service wedding ceremony & reception available.
✉ wbclodge@comcast.net ◑ www.wbclodge.com

Alps Boulder Canyon Inn
38619 Boulder Canyon Dr
80302
800-414-2577 303-444-5445
Jeannine & John Vanderhart

149-279 BB
12 rooms, 12 pb
Most CC, *Rated*, •
C-ltd/S-no/P-no/H-no
Spanish

Full breakfast
Afternoon tea, cookies
Two person Jacuzzis,
working fireplaces, TV's with
DirecTV/DVD/VCR/CD,
balconies, patio

A luxury Boulder, Colorado Bed and Breakfast Inn in scenic Boulder Canyon. Amenities include two person Jacuzzi tubs, fireplaces and mission furniture. Winner of many awards. Planning a romantic get-a-way?
✉ info@alpsinn.com ◑ www.alpsinn.com

Briar Rose B&B
2151 Arapahoe Ave 80302
888-786-8440 303-442-3007
Gary Hardin & Jessika Kimes

129-199 BB
10 rooms, 10 pb
Visa, MC, AmEx, •
C-ltd/S-ltd/P-no/H-no

Full, organic breakfast
Afternoon tea & cookies
A/C, fireplaces, high-speed
WiFi, guest computers

Bed and breakfast in the heart of Boulder offers organic breakfast, fine teas and ecologically conscious hospitality.
✉ briar_rose_bb@yahoo.com ◑ www.briarrosebb.com

BRECKENRIDGE

Allaire Timbers Inn
9511 Hwy 9 – S Main St 80424
800-624-4904 970-453-7530
Sue Carlson & Kendra Hall

145-390 BB
10 rooms, 10 pb
Most CC, *Rated*, •
C-ltd/S-no/P-no/H-yes

Full breakfast
Snacks, complimentary
wine, tea and coffee
Great Room with fireplace,
outdoor hot tub, sunroom,
free ski area shuttle, wireless
Internet

Looking for an accommodation away from the hustle and bustle? Want to find Brecken-ridge lodging that is romantic and intimate? You have found the most intimate way to experience Breckenridge at Allaire Timbers Inn, a distinctive Bed and Breakfast!
✉ allaire@colorado.net ❂ www.allairetimbers.com

CARBONDALE

Ambiance Inn B&B
66 N. 2nd Street 81623
800-350-1515 970-963-3597
Norma & Robert Morris

90-140 BB
4 rooms, 4 pb
Visa, MC
C-ltd/S-no/P-no/H-no

Full breakfast
Wireless Internet, air
conditioning

The Ambiance Inn is a contemporary chalet style home offering one suite and three rooms for the comfort of our guests. Our Inn is located conveniently within walking distance to the community's quaint shops and delightful restaurants.
✉ ambienceinn@aol.com ❂ www.ambienceinn.com

Van Horn House-Lions Ridge
0318 Lions Ridge Rd 81623
888-453-0395 970-963-3605
Susan & John Laatsch

85-95 BB
4 rooms, 3 pb
Visa, MC, AmEx, •
C-ltd/S-no/P-no/H-no

Full breakfast
Fluffy comforters, quilts or
robes, spectacular views, hot
tub & guest lounge

Comfort of a home away from home in the heart of the Roaring Fork Valley. Easy access to Aspen, Snowmass, Glenwood Springs, Carbondale, Redstone, the hiking and biking trails, ski slopes, fishing streams and hot springs of the White River National Forest.
✉ jlaatsch@aol.com ❂ www.vanhornhouse.com

CASCADE

America's Rocky Mountain Lodge & Cabins
4680 Hagerman Ave 80809
888-298-0348 719-684-2521
Brian & Debbie Reynolds

105-225 BB
6 rooms, 6 pb
Visa, MC, *Rated*
C-ltd/S-no/P-no/H-no

Gourmet 3-course breakfast
24-hour coffee, tea, cocoa &
cookies
Guest fridge, microwave,
outdoor hot tub, fireplaces,
tub for 2, cable TV/DVD,
wireless Internet

Nestled in the mountains at the entrance to Pikes Peak sits America's Rocky Mountain Lodge & Cabins, a rustic, elegant Colorado B&B & two private cabins with hot tubs, fireplaces & 3 course breakfasts. Romance & attractions packages. Family Reunions!
✉ info@rockymountainlodge.com ❂ www.rockymountainlodge.com

CEDAREDGE

Creek Side Bed & Breakfast
790 N Grand Mesa Dr 81413
970-856-7696
Terry & Carol Jarbo

90-100 BB
3 rooms, 1 pb
Cash, Checks
C-yes/S-ltd/P-no/H-yes

Full breakfast
Free wireless available upon
request, Gift baskets for
special occasions

Easy access along Scenic Byway Hwy 65. Breakfast is usually served on the deck which sets over the creek. When weather does not permit this it is served in the dinning room over looking the deck and creek.
✉ rivers3@surfbest.net ❂ creeksidebed-breakfast.com

COLORADO SPRINGS

Black Forest B&B Lodge & Cabins	75-350 BB	Continental plus breakfast
11170 Black Forest Rd 80908	7 rooms, 7 pb	Snacks, coffees, teas, cocoas
800-809-9901 719-495-4208	Most CC, *Rated*, •	Sitting room, library,
Susan Redden	C-yes/S-ltd/P-ltd/H-ltd	weddings, retreats, sauna,
	Some Spanish	fireplace, kitchen

Picture yourself in a massive log home built in the majestic Black Forest, the highest point east of the Rocky Mountains. Experience panoramic views with all the beauty of the Rockies, the towering Ponderosa pines, golden aspens & the fragrant meadows.
✉ blackforestbb@msn.com ◎ www.blackforestbb.com

The Cheyenne Canon Inn	105-235 BB	Full buffet breakfast
2030 W Cheyenne Blvd 80906	10 rooms, 10 pb	Wines, soda & appetizers,
800-633-0625 719-633-0625	Most CC, *Rated*, •	fresh baked sweets
Kevin & Izel Cooke	C-yes/S-ltd/P-no/H-no	Massage, Jacuzzi, fireplaces, library, guest computer with printer, special packages

An invitation to elegance . . . welcome to Colorado's finest historic bed & breakfast. Beautiful views & access to hiking, biking & driving tours. Mobil Four Stars.
✉ info@cheyennecanoninn.com ◎ www.cheyennecanoninn.com

Crescent Lily Inn	95-140 BB	Full breakfast
6 Boulder Crescent St 80903	5 rooms, 5 pb	Sitting room, suites, cable,
800-869-2721 719-442-2331	Most CC, •	fireplaces, jetted tubs,
Mark & Lin Medicus	C-ltd/S-ltd/P-no/H-ltd	conference room, wireless Internet access

Come enjoy the luxury of days gone enhanced with modern necessities, set in beautiful downtown Colorado Springs at this meticulously restored 100-year-old Queen Anne inn has beveled glass windows and an original tiled Van Briggle fireplace.
✉ info@crescentlilyinn.com ◎ www.crescentlilyinn.com

Holden House 1902 B&B Inn	145-160 BB	Full gourmet breakfast
1102 W Pikes Peak Ave 80904	5 rooms, 5 pb	Afternoon wine social & appetizers, freshly ground
888-565-3980 719-471-3980	Most CC, *Rated*, •	coffee, tea, bottomless
Sallie & Welling Clark	S-no/P-no/H-yes	cookie jar
		Living room w/fireplace, verandas, garden w/gazebo & fountains, refrigerators, snuggly robes, TV/DVD

Award-Winning Bed and Breakfast voted "Best" for Honeymoon/Anniversary and nearby attractions! Romantic and historic inn w/fireplaces and "tubs-for-two." Gourmet breakfast/afternoon wine social. Leisure/business packages. Centrally located. AAA inspected.
✉ mail@holdenhouse.com ◎ www.holdenhouse.com

Old Town GuestHouse	99-235 BB	Full breakfast
115 S 26th St 80904	8 rooms, 8 pb	Afternoon wine, beer & hors
888-375-4210 719-632-9194	Most CC, *Rated*	d'oeuvres, complimentary
Shirley & Don Wick	C-ltd/S-ltd/P-no/H-yes	soda, water, coffee, tea & hot chocolate
		Elevator, private hot tubs, steam showers, WiFi, game room, exercise room, conference facility.

Experience historic Old Town in urban luxury. Upscale amenities for adult leisure and business guests. Rooms have scenic views, private balconies, hot tubs or steam showers and private baths, of course. Private conference facility w/videoconferencing.
✉ Luxury@OldTown-GuestHouse.com ◎ www.oldtown-guesthouse.com

COLORADO SPRINGS

Our Hearts Inn Old	100-165 BB	Full breakfast
Colorado City	5 rooms, 5 pb	Coffee & tea service in each
2215 W Colorado Ave 80904	Most CC, *Rated*, •	room; biscotti, cookies,
800-533-7095 719-473-8684	C-yes/S-no/P-no/H-no	waters & sodas available
Andy & Pat Fejedelem		Jetted tub for 2, fireplaces,
		phones, hair dryers,
		irons/ironing boards,
		TV/VCR, free movies

Located in the Historic West Side of Colorado Springs, just 3 miles from Historic Manitou Springs. Cabins for getaways & families. Fireplaces, jetted tubs, TVs, A/C. Full breakfast to start a Rocky Mountain vacation day!
✉ hearts@inn-colorado-springs.com ◑ www.inn-colorado-springs.com

CORTEZ

Kelly Place Retreat & B&B	95-190 BB	Full country breakfast
14663 Road G 81321	11 rooms, 11 pb	Snacks, drinks, wine & beer
800-745-4885 970-565-3125	Visa, MC, Disc, •	available; lunch or dinner by
Jerene Waite & Marc Yaxley	C-yes/S-ltd/P-no/H-ltd	arrangement for groups of 8
		or more
		Conference room, lounge,
		courtyard, library, fireplace,
		hiking trails, sweat lodge

Comfortable adobe lodge & cabins on an archeological preserve near Mesa Verde National Park; bordering Canyons of Ancients National Monument, sw of Cortez. Ancient Anasazi ruins & kivas on-site. Hiking, biking, horse trips in sculpted red rock canyons.
✉ kelly@kellyplace.com ◑ www.kellyplace.com

CRESTED BUTTE

Cristiana Guesthaus	85-125 BB	Continental plus breakfast
621 Maroon Ave 81224	21 rooms, 21 pb	Complimentary hot
800-824-7899 970-349-5326	Most CC, •	beverages – teas, coffee, hot
Rosemary & Martin Catmur	C-ltd/S-no/P-no/H-no	chocolate and cider
		Sitting area with fireplace,
		outdoor hot tub with views,
		sauna, WiFi Internet access

Close to historic downtown. Relaxed, friendly atmosphere. Enjoy the hot tub, sauna, sun deck, and homebaked breakfast served in the cozy lobby.
✉ info@cristianaguesthaus.com ◑ www.cristianaguesthaus.com

Purple Mountain B&B and	84-199 BB	Full breakfast
Spa	5 rooms, 5 pb	Coffee, juice & teas
714 Gothic Ave 81224	Visa, MC, •	Hot tub, gardens, patio, spa
877-349-5888 970-349-5888	C-ltd/S-ltd/P-ltd/H-no	services
Chris Haver		

Crested Butte's historic Bed and Breakfast. The Purple Mountain B&B and Spa is located in town within walking distance of everything. Once Crested Butte's Mining Office we now have five cozy guestrooms, private bathrooms, and an outdoor hot tub . . .
✉ mail@purplemountainlodge.com ◑ www.purplemountainlodge.com

CRIPPLE CREEK

Carr Manor	80-350 BB	Continental breakfast
350 E Carr Ave 80813	15 rooms, 15 pb	Suites have cable TV, phone
719-689-3709	Most CC, *Rated*	& Internet access, small
Gary & Wini Ledford	C-ltd/S-no/P-no/H-ltd	fitness spa, art gallery and
		gift shop

The Carr Manor, a former 1890's school house, is delightfully appointed as a boutique hotel and operated in the home style of a bed & breakfast. The resort offers first-class accommodations, a conference center, ballroom, fitness & massage facilities.
✉ reservations@carrmanor.com ◑ www.carrmanor.com

CRIPPLE CREEK

Last Dollar Inn
315 E Carr Ave 80813
719-689-9113
Chip & Kathy Gregg

85-150 BB
6 rooms, 6 pb
Most CC
C-ltd/S-no/P-no/H-no

Full breakfast
Cookies, coffee cake and
daily fresh baked specials.
Complimentary soft drinks,
coffee and tea.
Sitting room, coffee room,
deck with mountain views
and walking distance from
historic Cripple Creek

Whether you choose the large new suite or a cozy little room, The Last Dollar Inn offers the peace & serenity that B&B travelers have grown to expect. Walk to local attractions and casinos.
✉ lastdollarinn@earthlink.net ◯ www.lastdollarinn.com

Whispering Pines B&B
127 Stratton Cir 80813
719-689-2316
Ed & Peggy Schillerberg

90-185 BB
5 rooms, 5 pb
Visa, MC, Disc
C-ltd/S-ltd/P-no/H-no

3-course breakfast
24-hour coffee/tea, soft
drinks
2 fireplace suites,
hydrotherapy air tubs,
indoor community room
w/satellite TV, microwave,
fridge

Nestled in the Rocky Mountains just one mile from the historic gold mining town of Cripple Creek, Colorado, sits the Victorian style Whispering Pines Bed & Breakfast, just one hour west of Colorado Springs and one hour north of Canon City.
✉ info@whisperingpinesbandb.net ◯ www.whisperingpinesbandb.net/

DENVER

Capitol Hill Mansion
1207 Pennsylvania St 80203
800-839-9329 303-839-5221
Carl S. Schmidt II

114-199 BB
8 rooms, 8 pb
Most CC, *Rated*
C-yes/S-no/P-no/H-ltd

Full breakfast
Complimentary wine,
snacks, refrigerator
Sitting room, hot tub, A/C,
cable TV, phones, wireless
Internet, fireplace,
heirlooms, original art

Downtown, walk to convention center, museums & restaurants from this nationally listed 1891 ruby sandstone mansion. Features high turrets, balconies and soaring chimneys.
✉ info@capitolhillmansion.com ◯ www.capitolhillmansion.com

Castle Marne B&B
1572 Race St 80206
800-92-MARNE 303-331-0621
The Peiker Family

90-270 BB
9 rooms, 9 pb
Most CC, *Rated*, •
C-ltd/S-no/P-no/H-no
Spanish, Hungarian

Full gourmet breakfast
Afternoon tea 4:30–6:00
Library, gift shop, game room
with pool table, computer,
fax, copier

Luxury urban inn. Minutes from convention center, business district, shopping, fine dining. National Historic landmark structure. 3 rooms with private balconies, hot tubs for 2.
✉ info@castlemarne.com ◯ www.castlemarne.com

Gregory Inn, LoDo
2500 Arapahoe St 80205
800-925-6570 303-295-6570
Stephen Gregory

129-259 BB
9 rooms, 9 pb
Visa, MC, AmEx
C-ltd/S-no/P-no/H-no

Full breakfast
Parlor, gathering room,
veranda, room service, big-
screen LCD projection TVs,
wireless Internet

Superior luxury hotel accommodations in a small, elegant Inn setting. Walking distance to Coors Field, Convention Center, Pavilions Shopping and LoDo—Denver's Lower downtown entertainment district.
✉ info@gregoryinn.com ◯ www.gregoryinn.com

DENVER

Holiday Chalet Victorian
1820 E Colfax Ave 80218
800-626-4497 303-437-8245
Crystal Sharp

94-160 BB
10 rooms, 10 pb
Most CC, *Rated*, •
C-yes/S-no/P-yes/H-no
Russian

Full breakfast
Full service tea room we also
offer lunch and dinner
selections by appointment!
Video Library, baby-sitting,
pet friendly including doggie
day care, beautiful
courtyard, WiFi

Nestled in Denver's historic Wyman district, we have offered warmth and comfort to travelers for over 52 years. Our luxury B&B is ideal for business travelers, vacationers and romantics. Full kitchens in every room. Pet-friendly. High speed Internet
✉ holidaychalet@aol.com ◑ www.holidaychalet.net

Queen Anne B&B Inn
2147 Tremont Pl 80205
800-432-4667 303-296-6666
Milan Doshi

115-215 BB
14 rooms, 14 pb
Most CC, *Rated*, •
C-ltd/S-no/P-no/H-ltd
Spanish

Made with local & organic
foods
Regional wines served in the
afternoon along with
appetizers
phone, A/C, jet tubs, garden,
bicycles, wireless Internet,
FREE parking

Award winning Victorian Inn, on National Register, faces quiet downtown park. Walk to mall, shops, museums, convention center/business district. Airport shuttle vans serve the inn. Selected for some 40 awards of excellence in its 21 years. GREEN HOTEL
✉ travel@queenannebnb.com ◑ www.queenannebnb.com

DILLON

Western Skies . . . A
Mountain B&B
5040 Montezuma Rd 80435
970-468-9445
Carole McCulloch

190-245 BB
3 rooms, 3 pb
Most CC
C-ltd/S-no/P-no/H-no

Full breakfast
Snacks provided in each
cabin
Phones with voice mail, CD
players, TV (cabins have
VCR/DVD player also)

Log cabins and riverfront lodge invite relaxation and romance at this secluded mountain hideaway, on 22 pine-forested acres. Come discover what Colorado living is really about.
✉ westernskies@wildblue.net ◑ www.westernskies-keystone-cabins.com

DIVIDE

Silver Wood B&B
463 County Rd 512 80814
800-753-5592 719-687-6784
Bess & Lawrence Oliver

85-99 BB
2 rooms, 2 pb
Visa, MC, Disc, •
C-yes/S-no/P-no/H-no
Limited German and
Spanish

Full breakfast
Snacks and refreshments.
Family room, suite, local
knowledge, WiFi, deck views,
satellite TV, ticket
arrangements.

Silver Wood Inn B&B is off the beaten path. Guests come here for the stillness, the great breakfasts, the views, the dark starry nights, the warm sunny days and the hosts. Royal Gorge, Cripple Creek and Breckenridge are easy day trips.
✉ innkeeper@silverwoodinn.com ◑ www.silverwoodinn.com

Stonehaven Inn
1815 Calcite Dr 80814
719-686-0833
Janis & Ferrel Minick

125 BB
4 rooms, 4 pb
Visa, MC
C-yes/S-no/P-no/H-no

Full breakfast
Homemade desserts, coffee
and tea.
Hot tub, WiFi, large porch,
beautiful private room for
meetings or any special
event.

Our unique B&B is built of 300 tons of Colorado river rock, and is situated on the western slope of Pikes Peak. Enjoy spectacular mountain views from our porch and listen to the sound of waterfalls or hike to a beautiful waterfall just minutes away.
✉ stonehaven.innkeeper@gmail.com ◑ www.stonehaveninnbnb.com

DOLORES

Lebanon Schoolhouse
24925 County Rd T 81323
877-882-4461 970-882-4461
Ken & Laura Hahn

95-125 BB
5 rooms, 5 pb
Visa, MC, Disc, •
C-yes/S-ltd/P-yes/H-no

Hearty gourmet fare
Appetizers, dinner by
request, licensed to serve
wine & beer
Weddings, retreats, large
common areas, TVs,
massage, guest kitchen,
laundry available, Internet

Historic 1907 Schoolhouse featuring luxurious appointments, spectacular views, quiet country setting & central to area attractions. Perfect for weddings, reunions & retreats, or romantic escapes. Families love the private kitchen and large common areas.
info@lebanonschoolhouse.com www.lebanonschoolhouse.com

DRAKE

River Forks Inn
1601 Big Thompson Canyon
80515
888-447-8817 970-669-6732
Bill Jones

59-150 BB
11 rooms, 4 pb
Visa, MC, Disc
C-yes/S-ltd/P-ltd/H-ltd

Full breakfast
Breakfast, lunch, and dinner
all available in our
restaurant.
Special events, weddings,
themed rooms, private
entrances, private deck, TV,
Free Wireless Internet.

Welcome to River Forks Inn. Founded in 1905, our wonderful inn is located along the banks of the Big Thompson in Drake, Colorado. Our lovely eleven-room inn and restaurant boasts wonderful views and wildlife. Live Entertainment Fri&Sat. WiFi Hotspot.
riverforksinn@riverforksinn.com www.riverforksinn.com

DURANGO

General Palmer Hotel
567 Main Ave. 81301
800-523-3358 970-247-4747
Paula Nelson

125-295 BB
39 rooms, 39 pb
Most CC
C-yes/S-no/P-no/H-no

Continental plus breakfast
Coffee, tea & cookies,
bedside chocolates
Meeting room, free local
calls, Internet access,
elevator, A/C, cable TV,
concierge service, lobby

The General Palmer Hotel, built in 1898, is a Victorian landmark in the Historic downtown district of Durango, Colorado. We have blended the comforts of modern living, with the elegance of a historical setting.
gphdurango@yahoo.com www.generalpalmer.com

Leland House B&B Suites & Rochester Hotel
721 E Second Ave 81301
800-664-1920 970-385-1920
Diane & Kirk Komick

119-229 BB
25 rooms, 25 pb
Most CC, *Rated*, •
C-yes/S-no/P-ltd/H-yes
Spanish, French,
Russian, Navajo

Full gourmet breakfast
Afternoon tea & homemade
cookies
Sitting room, conference
space for 75, catering
available, wireless Internet

Located in the historic district of downtown Durango, CO. Authentically restored late-Victorian 15 room Rochester hotel with the charm and luxury of the Old West; suites offered in the Leland House. Beautifully landscaped setting, flower-filled courtyard.
stay@rochesterhotel.com www.rochesterhotel.com

EMPIRE

The Peck House
83 Sunny Ave 80438
303-569-9870
Gary & Sally St. Clair

65-135 BB
10 rooms, 9 pb
Most CC, •
C-ltd/S-no/P-no/H-ltd
French

Continental breakfast
Restaurant, dinner available
Bar service, sitting room,
library, Jacuzzi

1862 Victorian Inn furnished in antiques. Near ski areas and historic districts. In Empire, 5 miles from Georgetown, this historic landmark is known for excellent food and dramatic mountain scenery. Gateway to Rocky Mtn. Natl. Park and Trail Ridge Road.
info@thepeckhouse.com www.thepeckhouse.com

ESTES PARK

Anniversary Inn	130-240 BB	Full gourmet breakfast
1060 Mary's Lake Rd 80517	5 rooms, 5 pb	Homemade cookies, tea,
970-586-6200	Visa, MC, Disc, *Rated*	sodas
Karin and Roger Steers	C-yes/S-no/P-no/H-no	Great room with moss rock fireplace, library, WiFi and TV/DVD in each room with jetted tubs

Charming turn-of-the-20th-century log home located one mile west of downtown Estes Park and only one mile from the entrance to Rocky Mountain National Park. Surrounded by ponderosa pines and spruce trees overlooking the Big Thompson River.
✉ steers12@msn.com ○ www.EstesInn.com

The Baldpate Inn	115-200 BB	Full gourmet breakfast
4900 S Hwy 7 80517	16 rooms, 6 pb	Award winning specialty
866-577-5397 970-586-6151	Visa, MC, Disc, *Rated*,	restaurant, features buffet
Lois Smith	•	with homemade soups,
	C-yes/S-no/P-no/H-no	salad, breads
	Late May through mid	next to Rocky Mountain
	Oct	National Park, free Wireless Internet, cozy Library with fireplace & TV, VCR

7 miles south of Estes Park, Colorado, this National Register property, the Baldpate Inn, is a classic mountain getaway, with superior B&B lodging, an award winning restaurant and fascinating museum.
✉ baldpateinn@aol.com ○ www.baldpateinn.com

Black Dog Inn B&B	125-250 BB	Full breakfast
650 S St Vrain Ave 80517	6 rooms, 6 pb	Tea, hot chocolate, ice tea,
866-786-0374 970-586-0374	Most CC	homemade cookies;
Carlos Albuquerque	C-ltd/S-ltd/P-ltd/H-no	candlelight dining for two WiFi, in-room massage available Weddings & Elopements

Romantic secluded getaway in the Rocky Mountains. Beautiful rooms with two person Jacuzzi.
✉ carlos@blackdoginn.com ○ www.Blackdoginn.com

Gilded Pine Meadows B&B	107-145 BB	Full Hearty Breakfast
861 Big Horn Dr 80517	3 rooms, 3 pb	Low fat, restricted, or
970-586-2124	Visa, MC, Disc	vegetarian diets by request
George and Caprissa Frawley	C-ltd/S-no/P-no/H-no	Friendly hosts, glassed-in porch, outdoor hot tub, enclosed gazebo, wildlife, WiFi, elopement

Gilded Pine Meadows Bed and Breakfast is a quiet and peaceful retreat. A Victorian cottage built by Estes Park pioneers in 1905. Beautiful and homey.
✉ info@gildedpinemeadows.com ○ www.gildedpinemeadows.com

Mountain Shadows Resort	139-169 BB	Continental breakfast
871 Riverside Dr 80517	8 rooms, 8 pb	Basket of coffee, tea,
888-577-0397 970-577-0397	Visa, MC, *Rated*, •	popcorn, cocoa and
Rob & Tina	C-ltd/S-ltd/P-yes/H-no	continental breakfast of muffins, juice, yogurt . . . 1st morn King bed, private hot tub, fireplace, cable TV, free WiFi, private deck

Mountain Shadows features luxury cabins, each with a private hot tub, in a romantic setting nestled in the heart of the Rocky Mountains. We are less then 1 mile from the main entrance to Rocky Mountain National Park and close to downtown Estes Park.
✉ info@mountainshadowsresort.net ○ www.mountainshadowsresort.net/

ESTES PARK

Taharaa Mountain Lodge, Inc.	155-345 BB	Full gourmet breakfast
3110 S St Vrain 80517	18 rooms, 18 pb	Happy hour of wine, beer &
800-597-0098 970-577-0098	Most CC, *Rated*, •	sodas daily
Ken & Diane Harlan	C-ltd/S-no/P-no/H-yes	Great Room, den, dining
		room, meeting room, spa
		with dry sauna, hot tub &
		massage room, Great Hall

Taharaa Mountain Lodge is a luxury lodge-style B&B offering unique accommodations: nine suites and nine lodge rooms, designed with the total comfort of our guests in mind. A Great Hall with panoramic views is available for weddings up to 200 guests.
✉ info@taharaa.com ◑ www.taharaa.com

Wildwood Inn	55-428 EP	Coffee in room
2801 Fall River Rd 80517	33 rooms, 33 pb	Full service day spa, library,
800-400-7804 970-586-7804	Visa, MC, *Rated*	hot tub room, video/DVD
Cindy Younglund-Liddell	C-yes/P-no/H-yes	library, in-room WiFi

Large family vacation homes, spacious river- or mountain-side suites, private deck rooms & hot tubs. Our upscale accommodations are surrounded by mountain peaks. Views of the Rocky Mountain National Park. We offer a full service day spa on site.
✉ info@esteswildwoodinn.com ◑ www.esteswildwoodinn.com

EVERGREEN

Bears Inn	145-220 BB	Full breakfast
27425 Spruce Ln 80439	11 rooms, 11 pb	Afternoon tea, snacks
800-863-1205 303-670-1205	Most CC, *Rated*, •	Sitting room, wireless
Vicki Bock	C-ltd/S-no/P-ltd/H-no	Internet, fax, spa

Nestled in the pine trees at 8,000 feet. Great snow-capped mountain views, 11 rooms, private baths, 1 two bedroom cabin, cable TV, outdoor spa and gas campfires.
✉ booknow@bearsinn.com ◑ www.bearsinn.com

Highland Haven Creekside Inn	130-370 BB	Full breakfast
4395 Independence Trail	17 rooms, 17 pb	Afternoon tea, snacks &
80439	Most CC, *Rated*	catering available
800-459-2406 303-674-3577	C-yes/S-no/P-no/H-no	Wireless Internet, romance
Gail Riley & Tom Statzell		trays, private hot tubs,
		Jacuzzi tubs, corporate
		facilities

Mountain hideaway with exquisite views of mountains, streams, towering pines and gardens. Stroll to quaint shops and fine dining on Main Street in Evergreen.
✉ info@highlandhaven.com ◑ www.highlandhaven.com

FRISCO

Frisco Lodge	39-399 BB	Full Gourmet Breakfast
321 Main St 80443	19 rooms, 13 pb	Afternoon snacks include
800-279-6000 970-668-0195	Most CC, *Rated*, •	homemade bread & soup in
Bruce Knoepfel	C-yes/S-no/P-no/H-no	the winter season
		Hot tub, Internet access, WiFi
		in rooms, ski & bike room,
		phones

Historic bed and breakfast lodge built in 1885. A unique inn, on Frisco's historic Main Street, features 1800s ambience. A Distinctive Mountain Lodge with Victorian Flair.
✉ info@friscolodge.com ◑ www.friscolodge.com

GOLDEN

The Dove Inn B&B	89-140 BB	Full breakfast
711 14th St 80401	8 rooms, 8 pb	Wireless Internet access,
888-278-2209 303-278-2209	Most CC, *Rated*	A/C, phones, cable TV,
Annette & Bill Lyttle	C-ltd/S-no/P-no/H-no	DVD/VCR, coffee makers,
		bottled water, clock radios

Built in 1868, the inn is nestled in the West Denver foothills. Walking distance to activities and shops in downtown Golden. Denver attractions and Rocky Mountains nearby. Full cooked breakfast. Private baths in all rooms. Whirlpool tubs & fireplaces.
✉ stay@doveinn.com ◑ www.doveinn.com

The Ice Palace Inn, Leadville, CO

HESPERUS

Blue Lake Ranch	135-375 BB	Regional gourmet breakfast
16000 Hwy 140 81326	16 rooms, 16 pb	Coffee & tea facilities,
888-258-3525 970-385-4537	Most CC, *Rated*, •	refrigerators, microwaves
Shirley & David Alford	C-yes/S-no/P-no/H-yes	Suites and casitas feature
	German, Spanish,	Jacuzzi tubs, fireplaces,
	Nepali, Arabic	private patios and more,
		WiFi, movie library

Southwest Colorado's award winning country inn, just minutes from Durango, Colorado and Mesa Verde National Park. Recently featured in Travel and Leisure's "30 Great Inns."
✉ bluelake@frontier.net ◷ www.bluelakeranch.com

LEADVILLE

The Ice Palace Inn	105-179 BB	Full breakfast
813 Spruce St 80461	5 rooms, 5 pb	Afternoon refreshments.
800-754-2840 719-486-8272	Most CC, *Rated*, •	Catering, Saturday night
Sherry Randall & Marcie	C-yes/S-no/P-no/H-no	dinners in the winter and
Stassi		special events in summer
		Parlor, game room, in-room
		air jetted tubs, video library,
		TV/VCR, sterno fireplaces

Located at the "Top of the Rockies" in historic Leadville is Colorado's most romantic Victorian inn. We serve the finest breakfast in town and the best fresh baked cookies in Colorado each afternoon. Come stay at the highest b & b in the United States!
✉ stay@icepalaceinn.com ◷ www.icepalaceinn.com

MANCOS

Abode at Willowtail Springs	219-359 BB	Full Kitchen
10451 County Rd 39 81328	3 rooms, 3 pb	Coffee, tea, organic juice,
800-698-0603 970-533-7592	Visa, MC, •	homemade bread, jam, fresh
Peggy & Lee Cloy	C-yes/S-no/P-no/H-no	fruit granola, eggs and fresh
		seasonings.
		Fully equipped kitchens,
		library, TV/VCR, gardens, hot
		tub, antiques, fishing, boats,
		computer, WiFi

An enchanted 60 acres, log cabins, antiques, fireplaces and kitchens. Set amid gardens and streams, facing bass lake and mountains. Comfortable, romantic, creative atmosphere. Minutes to Mesa Verde. ✉ bookings@willowtailsprings.com ◷ www.willowtailsprings.com

MANCOS────────────────────────────────

Flagstone Meadows Ranch	115-125 BB	Full breakfast
38080 Road K4 81328	8 rooms, 8 pb	Additional catered meals by
800-793-1137 970-533-9838	Visa, MC	arrangement
Harris Court	C-yes/S-no/P-no/H-no	Fireplaces, hot tub, deck, sauna, library, piano, wireless Internet, TV/DVD/VCR, bath amenities

Serenely set within the protective circle of the Four Sacred Mountains, the peaceful, unique warmth of our western lodge retreat, reminiscent of a more thoughtful, gentler time, begins to work its magic even before you step inside.
✉ info@flagstonemeadows.com ○ www.flagstonemeadows.com

Sundance Bear Lodge	105-195 BB	Full Breakfast
38890 Hwy 184 81328	5 rooms, 4 pb	Afternoon coffee/tea, soft
866-529-2480 970-533-1504	Most CC, •	drinks & snacks on the help
Susan & Bob Scott	C-yes/S-ltd/P-ltd/H-ltd	yourself buffet in the lodge Snacks, sitting room, hot tub, sauna, TV, computer & WiFi Internet access

Enjoy Mesa Verde & mountain views from decks or hot tub. 80+ acres plus canyon to explore. Bring family, dog, horses! Stay one day more in the Old West, it's worth it! Rest body & soul. Day trips galore on the San Juan Scenic Skyway, & in the 4 Corners.
✉ sue@sundancebear.com ○ www.SundanceBear.com

MANITOU SPRINGS────────────────────────────

Avenue Hotel, A Victorian B&B	79-145 BB	Full breakfast
711 Manitou Ave 80829	8 rooms, 8 pb	Snacks
800-294-1277 719-685-1277	Most CC, •	Massage therapy, wireless
Kevin Abney	C-ltd/S-ltd/P-no/H-no	Internet access, meeting space, guest computer, TV, VCR, DVD, phone

The Inn, established in 1984, was Manitou's first B&B. Some family suites, many antiques, large art collection. Walk to shops and restaurants in downtown historic district.
✉ info@avenuehotelbandb.com ○ www.avenuehotelbandb.com

Onaledge B&B	115-235 BB	Full breakfast
336 El Paso Blvd 80829	6 rooms, 6 pb	Complimentary afternoon
888-685-4515 719-685-4515	Visa, MC, Disc, *Rated*,	wine, tea & coffee
Brett Maddox	•	Jetted tub, fireplace, gardens,
	C-yes/S-ltd/P-no	beautiful views, snow-white mountains nearby, romance

This historic Arts & Crafts Bed and Breakfast offers lodging with the warmth and charm that Manitou Springs has become known for in Colorado. A luxurious Rocky Mountain retreat, ideal for a romantic weekend getaway or extended vacation.
✉ info@redcrags.com ○ www.onaledge.net

Red Crags Bed & Breakfast Inn	100-235 BB	Full breakfast
302 El Paso Blvd 80829	8 rooms, 8 pb	Afternoon coffee, tea, wine,
800-721-2248 719-685-4515	Visa, MC, Disc, *Rated*,	dessert
Brett R. Maddox	•	King beds, fireplaces, down
	C-ltd/S-no/P-no/H-no	comforters, robes, hot tub, cable TV, wireless Internet, sitting room

Historic 1880 Victorian mansion romantic hideaway. Lose yourself "Somewhere in Time." Antiques throughout, large common rooms, herb & flower gardens. King beds, private baths, fireplaces. A favorite of Teddy Roosevelt. AAA 3 Diamond, Mobil 3 Star.
✉ info@redcrags.com ○ www.redcrags.com

116   Colorado

MANITOU SPRINGS————————————————————

Rockledge Country Inn
328 El Paso Blvd 80829
888-685-4515 719-685-4515
Brett Maddox

160-325 BB
7 rooms, 7 pb
Visa, MC, Disc, *Rated*,
•
C-ltd/S-no/P-no/H-ltd

Full breakfast
Afternoon coffee, tea and
wine service with snacks,
wine & cheese on weekends,
romantic dinner
Whirlpools, fireplaces, robes,
luxury linens, bicycles,
concierge services

Rockledge Country Inn, a Manitou Springs Bed & Breakfast, provides a private and peaceful destination for the discriminating traveler, minutes from downtown Colorado Springs, Colorado College, U.S. Air Force Academy, and the Olympic Training Center.
✉ info@redcrags.com ◐ www.rockledgeinn.com

OURAY————————————————————————

China Clipper Inn
525 2nd St 81427
800-315-0565 970-325-0565
Earl Yarbrough

90-220 BB
13 rooms, 13 pb
Visa, MC, *Rated*, •
C-ltd/S-no/P-no/H-ltd

Delicious full breakfast
Sitting room, library, hot tub,
phones & data ports, free
wireless Internet, TV, A/C,
hairdryer

Elegant, romantic, comfortable inn centrally located in Switzerland of America. In-room tubs for two, fireplaces, garden hot tub. Pampering, utter relaxation guaranteed.
✉ china5@Q.com ◐ www.chinaclipperinn.com

St. Elmo Hotel
426 Main St 81427
866-243-1502 970-325-4951
DeeAnn Nathe

60-155 BB
9 rooms, 9 pb
Most CC, *Rated*, •
C-ltd/S-ltd/P-no/H-no

Breakfast buffet
Restaurant, complimentary
wine, coffee, tea
Piano, outdoor hot tub,
sauna, meeting room

Step back in time and relive the glory days of Colorado's colorful past at the St. Elmo. Ouray is a picturesque hamlet, surrounded by 14,000 foot peaks in the majestic San Juan Mountains of southwest Colorado.
✉ innkeeper@stelmohotel.com ◐ www.stelmohotel.com

Wiesbaden Hot Springs Spa & Lodgings
625 5th St 81427
888-846-5191 970-325-4347
Linda Wright-Minter

129-345 EP
17 rooms, 17 pb
Most CC
C-ltd/S-no/P-no/H-ltd

Complimentary coffee & tea
Hot springs Vaporcave,
outdoor pool, private
outdoor spa, massage & spa
treatments

A small, intimate natural hot springs spa and lodge known for its peaceful atmosphere, casual elegance and European flair. Located in a small mountain town; surrounded by the San Juan Mountains.
✉ lodge@wiesbadenhotsprings.com ◐ www.wiesbadenhotsprings.com

PAGOSA SPRINGS————————————————————

Elkwood Manor Luxury Bed & Breakfast
85 Easy St 81147
970-264-9166
Darlene & Daniel Gonzales

129-165 BB
4 rooms, 3 pb
Most CC, *Rated*
C-ltd/S-no/P-no/H-ltd

Gourmet Breakfast
Comp Wine & Appetizers
daily. Romantic Dinners
available. Box
lunches/picnic baskets also
available.
Candle light dinners, movies,
in-house massages, wireless
Internet, event & wedding
packages

Simple Elegance with a Country Feel Captures the character of Elkwood Manor. Luxury Suites with sitting rooms, fireplaces, private patios/decks & panoramic views. Comp Wine. Jacuzzi/Sauna on site. Free Wireless Internet; Anniv, B-day Honeymoon/Wedding Pk
✉ gonzada03@yahoo.com ◐ www.elkwoodmanor.com

PAONIA─────────────────────────────

Bross Hotel
312 Onarga Ave 81428
970-527-6776
Linda Lentz

115-125 BB
10 rooms, 10 pb
Visa, MC, *Rated*, •
C-ltd/S-no/P-no/H-no

Full breakfast
Snacks, lunch & dinner for groups
Sitting room, library, suites, cable TV, accommodate business travelers, hot tub

The Bross Hotel is a restored 1906 hotel furnished with antiques & handmade quilts. It provides easy access to Colorado's finest outdoor adventuring as well as cultural events and activities.
✉ brosshotel@paonia.com ❂ www.paonia-inn.com

PINE─────────────────────────────

Lower Lake Ranch
11883 S Elk Creek Rd 80470
303-838-6622
The Dunwody Family

135-165 BB
5 rooms, 5 pb
Visa, MC, Disc
C-ltd/S-ltd/P-ltd/H-ltd

Continental breakfast
Enjoy cool drinks in the summer and hot tea/coffee in the winter along with a fresh fruit basket
LLR offers seasonal outdoor activities from hiking, fly fishing, ice skating, bring your horse, etc.

Lower Lake Ranch began as a Guest Ranch in the late 1890's. Upon arriving, guests have been warmly greeted, made to feel right at home. The same beauty and hospitality of years past has been preserved for visitors today. Just 30 minutes from Denver.
✉ information@lowerlakeranch.com ❂ www.lowerlakeranch.com

RED FEATHER LAKES─────────────────

Red Feather Ranch B&B, LLC
3105 CR 69 80545
877-881-5215 970-881-3715
Carla & David McCandless

119-149 BB
5 rooms, 5 pb
Visa, MC
C-yes/S-ltd/P-yes/H-ltd

Full Country Breakfast
Homemade cookies, tea, cocoa, lemonade, sun tea, coffee, gluten free, homemade jellies, breads
Group retreats, weddings, hot tub, 3-stall barn for guest horses, electric blankets, in-room coffee

This beautiful Colorado mountain Bed and Breakfast caters to those seeking a romantic mountain getaway; an incredible riding vacation with their horse; an idyllic wedding experience; or an unforgettable private group retreat. Horse ranch facilities.
✉ info@redfeatherranch.com ❂ www.redfeatherranch.com

SALIDA─────────────────────────────

Century House Cottages
121 C Street 81201
800-922-0460 719-539-6988
Ruth Fisher

95-175 BB
2 rooms, 1 pb
Visa, MC
C-yes/S-ltd/P-no/H-no

Continental plus breakfast

Sweet 1908 cottage. Perfect downtown location, just 2 short blocks from the river and historic downtown offering restaurants, galleries, shops and entertainment. Ideal for couples or groups of up to 6. Three separate sleeping areas.
✉ srowe1023@yahoo.com ❂ www.centuryhousecottages.com

The Thomas House
307 E 1st St 81201
888-228-1410 719-539-7104
Tammy & Steve Office

75-149 BB
7 rooms, 7 pb
Most CC, *Rated*, •
C-yes/S-no/P-no/H-ltd

Full breakfast
Snacks, kitchenette stocked with soda, coffee, tea & pretzel jar
Sitting room, library, Jacuzzis, suites, cable TV, kitchenettes, guesthouses for long term stay

1880's railroad boarding-house decorated with family heirlooms, antiques & collectibles. Located in Salida's Historic Downtown.
✉ office@thomashouse.com ❂ www.thomashouse.com

118   Colorado

SOUTH FORK────────────────────────

Apple Dumpling B&B Inn
254 Beaver Creek Rd 81154
888-873-7583 719-873-9876
Bill & Robbie Meek

105-159 BB
7 rooms, 7 pb
Visa, MC, AmEx, •
C-ltd/S-no/P-no/H-no

Full 3-course breakfast
Bottled water, sodas,
homemade cookies, hot
chocolate, tea, house wine
Wireless Internet, fax,
satellite TV, DVD, sitting
room, 2 person whirlpool
tubs, concierge, fireplaces

Award winning Inn nestled beneath Beaver Mountain, just 200 yards from the Rio Grande National Forest, on 8 acres with beautiful mountain vistas from almost every room. Member of Distinctive Inns of Colorado.
✉ bill@appledumplingbandb.com ✆ www.appledumplingbandb.com

Arbor House Inn
31358 W US Hwy 160 81154
888-830-4642 719-873-5012
Keith & Laurie Bratton

120-165 BB
5 rooms, 5 pb
Visa, MC, AmEx, *Rated*
C-ltd/S-ltd/P-ltd/H-ltd

Full breakfast
Snacks, soft drinks, coffee &
tea, complimentary wine
Hot tub, riverside deck,
sitting room, fridge, satellite
TV, VCR/DVD, WiFi, fire pit,
fishing

Relax by the river in rustic mountain elegance. Five themed guestrooms. River, cliff, mountain and meadow views. Outdoor hot tub, private baths, honeymoon suite with in-room whirlpool tub and fireplace.
✉ info@arborhouseinnco.com ✆ www.arborhouseinnco.com

STEAMBOAT SPRINGS────────────────────────

The Alpine Rose B&B Inn
724 Grand St 80477
888-879-1528 970-879-1528
Merry Jo Riley

105-220 BB
6 rooms, 4 pb
Visa, MC, AmEx
C-ltd/S-no/P-no/H-ltd

Full breakfast
Snacks
Sitting room, library, Jacuzzi,
fireplace, cable TV,
accommodates business
travelers

Located in historic "Olde Town" Steamboat Springs, Colorado, the Alpine Rose offers the hospitality of a family Bed and Breakfast and all the comforts and conveniences that make for a special and unique mountain vacation.
✉ bnb@alpinerosesteamboat.com ✆ www.alpinerosesteamboat.com

Mariposa Lodge B&B
855 Grand St 80477
800-578-1467 970-879-1467
Cindy & Bob Maddox

129-179 BB
4 rooms, 4 pb
Visa, MC
C-ltd/S-no/P-no/H-no

Full breakfast

The Mariposa is a Southwestern-styled home with log beamed ceilings and Santa Fe style handcrafted doors nestled along the banks of Soda Creek in a quiet country-like setting. Only a few short blocks from downtown shopping and restaurants.
✉ mariposa@steamboatmariposa.com ✆ www.steamboatmariposa.com

STEAMBOAT SPRINGS────────────────────────

Steamboat Valley Guest House
215 12th St 80477
970-870-9017
George & Alice Lund

109-139 BB
1 rooms, 1 pb
Most CC
C-ltd/S-no/P-no/H-no

Continental plus breakfast
Hot Tub, sitting room, TV,
stationary bike

Our new mountain home features a 1 bedroom guest suite with queen bed, private bath and TV/Breakfast room. Extra room available with twin beds. Easy walk to Old Town restaurants, galleries and shops. Private hot tub and heated garage. Free bus to ski area
✉ galund@mac.com ✆ www.steamboatvalleyguesthouse.com

TRINIDAD—————————————————————————

Tarabino Inn	84-129 BB	Full breakfast
310 E 2nd St 81082	4 rooms, 2 pb	Tea, chocolates and cookies.
866-846-8808 719-846-2115	Most CC	Cotton robes & slippers,
Teresa Vila & Kevin Crosby	C-ltd/S-no/P-no/H-no	library, TV, VCR, telephone,
	Spanish	fine art gallery

Tarabino Inn Bed and Breakfast is one of the finest examples of the Historic Inns found in the Rocky Mountain region of Colorado. Visit Trinidad, Colorado and stay at Tarabino Inn B&B.
✉ host@tarabinoinn.com ◔ www.tarabinoinn.com

WALSENBURG—————————————————————

La Plaza Inn	59-90 BB	Continental breakfast
118 W 6th 81089	11 rooms, 11 pb	Afternoon tea, snacks, lunch
719-738-5700	Visa, MC, •	& dinner available,
Martie Henderson	C-yes/S-no/P-no/H-no	restaurant
		Sitting room, library, suites,
		cable TV, business traveler
		accommodations

Affordable elegance. Historic hotel built in 1907. Each room offers unique decor from king size luxury to large family suites. You'll love the ambience of La Plaza.

WINDSOR—————————————————————————

Porter House B&B Inn	95-165 BB	Full breakfast
530 Main St 80550	4 rooms, 4 pb	Afternoon Tea
888-686-5793 970-686-5793	Visa, MC, *Rated*, •	Library, bicycles, conference
Tom & Marni Schmittling	C-ltd/S-no/P-no/H-no	center for 30, outdoor hot
		tub, free wireless Internet
		access

Outstanding Colorado lodging in a romantic and historic 1898 Victorian Inn offering relaxation, comfort and a private courtyard. Cozy and inviting. Wonderful gourmet breakfasts. Fireplaces, Jacuzzi tub, TV's, free wireless Internet access.
✉ phbbinn@aol.com ◔ www.porterhouseinn.com

Connecticut

Bozrah House	99-150 BB	Full breakfast
347 Salem Tpke Rt 82 06334	3 rooms, 3 pb	Complimentary wine, tea,
888-488-7073 860-823-1551	Most CC	and coffee
Ed Hadley	C-ltd/S-ltd/P-no/H-no	Sitting room, bicycles, cable
		TV, accommodate business
		travelers, data port

Bozrah House B&B has three private accommodations. Each has a private bath and is distinctly furnished with treasures such as a pristine cherry sleigh bed. Enjoy a full candlelight breakfast.
✉ bozrahouse@aol.com ◐ www.bozrahouse.com

Fitch Claremont Vineyard	89-179 BB	Referred to as "the best
B&B	4 rooms, 4 pb	breakfast"
83 Fitchville Rd 06334	Most CC, *Rated*, •	A complimentary wine from
877-889-0266 860-889-0260	C-ltd/S-no/P-no/H-no	our vineyard
Nora & Warren Strong		Fireplace, library, dining
		room, & outdoor patio

We are a four room, 3 diamond Inn on the Old Fitch Farm Vineyard in SE CT. Minutes away from Foxwoods & Mohegan Sun Casinos and a short ride from Mystic coast and country, Mysticmore and all New England activities.
✉ innkeeper@fitchclaremonthouse.com ◐ www.fitchclaremonthouse.com

Chimney Crest Manor B&B	135-205 BB	Full breakfast .
5 Founders Dr 06010	5 rooms, 5 pb	Tea & cookies in Atrium
860-582-4219	Visa, MC, AmEx,	Suites with fireplace, kitchen
Dan & Cynthia Cimadamore	*Rated*, •	or thermospa, feather beds,
	C-ltd/S-no/P-no/H-no	down comforters, private spa
	February thru December	on premises

Tudor mansion with an unusual castle like atmosphere. Located 100 miles from New York and Boston. In the historic Federal Hill District. Chimney Crest Manor, built in 1930 is listed on the National Historic Register. In house spa with masseuse.
✉ Innkeeper@ChimneyCrestManor.com ◐ www.chimneycrest.com

3 Liberty Green B&B c.1734	120-220 BB	delicious home-made
3 Liberty St 06413	4 rooms, 4 pb	breakfast!
860-669-0111	Most CC, •	Spring water, coffee, teas, hot
Glenn Coutu	C-ltd/S-no/P-no/H-no	chocolate, cookies, cordials
		always available.
		2-person Jacuzzis,
		king/queen canopy beds,
		cable TV, DVD, hi-speed
		wireless, porch, parlor,
		massage

Indulge yourself in history & romance in a picturesque setting at this new CT B&B! Overlooking the picturesque Liberty Green, each guestroom has a double Jacuzzi & canopy bed! Walk to the beach, shops, restaurants, cafes, art galleries, spas & museums.
✉ info@3liberty.com ◐ www.3liberty.com/availability.html

DEEP RIVER

Riverwind Inn
209 Main St 06417
860-526-2014
Elaine & Leo Klevens

128-240 BB
8 rooms, 8 pb
Most CC, *Rated*
C-ltd/S-no/P-no/H-no

Full breakfast
Complimentary sherry,
snacks, beverages
4 common rooms, 3 with
fireplaces, one is a 12 foot
stone cooking fireplace

Immaculate rooms with period country antiques & reproductions. Candlelit country breakfast, in fireplaced dining rooms, begins the day; communal or private seating. Numerous common areas to relax by the fire or enjoy a book. Wireless Internet.
📧 innkeeper@riverwindinn.com 🌐 www.riverwindinn.com

EAST HADDAM

Bishopsgate Inn
7 Norwich Rd 06423
860-873-1677
The Kagel Family

120-205 BB
6 rooms, 6 pb
Visa, MC, Disc, *Rated*
C-ltd/S-no/P-ltd/H-no

Full breakfast
Dinner available
Sitting room, library,
fireplaces

Bishopsgate Inn is a Colonial house circa 1818, furnished with period antiques, and each floor of the Inn has a sitting area where guests often relax with a good book. Gracious hospitality and well appointed accommodations in a secluded setting.
📧 ctkagel@Bishopsgate.com 🌐 www.bishopsgate.com

GLASTONBURY

Butternut Farm
1654 Main St 06033
860-633-7197
Don Reid

95-120 BB
4 rooms, 4 pb
AmEx, *Rated*
C-yes/S-no/P-no/H-no

Full breakfast
Complimentary wine,
chocolates
Private entrances, living
room, TV/VCR, secluded
patio, full kitchen, fireplaces,
wireless Internet

Welcome to Butternut Farm Bed and Breakfast in beautiful Glastonbury, CT! This 18th-century jewel is furnished with period antiques. Attractive grounds with herb gardens and ancient trees, dairy goats and prize chickens. 10 minutes from Hartford.
🌐 www.butternutfarmbandb.com

The Connecticut River Valley Inn
2195 Main St 06033
860-633-7374
Wayne & Patricia Brubaker

175-250 BB
5 rooms, 5 pb
Most CC
C-ltd/S-no/P-ltd/H-no

Full breakfast

An Inn for All Seasons—An Inn for All Reasons. An oasis of calm during the long summer evenings; a spectacular vision of color in the autumn; frosty images glow in Winter; bursting of new growth in the Spring!
📧 frontdesk@ctrivervalleyinn.com 🌐 www.ctrivervalleyinn.com

GRANBY

Dutch Iris Inn
239 Salmon Brook St 06035
877-280-0743 860-844-0262
Bill & Nancy Ross

109-159 BB
6 rooms, 6 pb
Most CC, •
S-no/P-no/H-no

Full breakfast
Fresh coffee, tea, cold
beverages available all day
Digital cable TV in every
room, wireless Internet
access, daily local paper &
Sunday New York Times

Colonial elegance and gracious hospitality await you in this historic 1812 home set on 3 acres of landscaped grounds. Unwind and rejuvenate your senses! Winter, Spring, Summer, or Fall, there is always something special happening.
📧 info@dutchirisinn.com 🌐 www.dutchirisinn.com

122 **Connecticut**

GREENWICH——————————————————————————

Homestead Inn-Thomas Henkelmann
420 Field Point Rd 06830
203-869-7500
Theresa & Thomas Henkelmann

350-495 EP
18 rooms, 18 pb
Most CC, *Rated*, •
C-ltd/S-yes/P-no/H-yes
French, German,
Portuguese, Spanish,
Italian

A la carte
Thomas Henkelmann
restaurant on site,
exceptional, contemporary
European cuisine
Air conditioning, modem &
wireless Internet, cable TV &
VCR

Homestead Inn-Thomas Henkelmann is a four star luxury hotel and restaurant located in Greenwich, CT. A member of Relais and Chateaux, Relais Gourmands, Tradition et Qualite (Les Grandes Tables du Monde) and recipient of 4 stars from the New York Times.
✉ events@homesteadinn.com ○ www.homesteadinn.com

Stanton House Inn
76 Maple Ave 06830
203-869-2110
Tog & Doreen Pearson

149-239 BB
21 rooms, 21 pb
Most CC, *Rated*
C-ltd/S-no/P-ltd/H-ltd
Spring, Summer, Fall

Continental plus breakfast
Common room, dining room,
patio, pool, garden, fireplace,
balcony, whirlpool tub, A/C,
hair dryers

In this setting of cozy old world charm, The Stanton House Inn's twenty-one individually decorated bedrooms and suites offer modern comforts and amenities presented in an unpretentious and relaxed atmosphere. We offer a home away from home environment.
✉ shiinn@aol.com ○ www.shinngreenwich.com

GRISWOLD——————————————————————————

Homespun Farm B&B
306 Preston Rd 06351
888-889-6673 860-376-5178
Kate & Ron Bauer

145-175 BB
4 rooms, 3 pb
Visa, MC, •
C-yes/S-ltd/P-yes/H-no

Full breakfast
Snacks
Sitting room, library, Satellite
TV, conference, golf, hike, in-
room fireplaces

Homespun Farm B&B, a quintessential 1740 Colonial farmhouse listed on the National Register of Historic places, has beautifully kept grounds and rooms that will delight all travelers. Let us take you back in time with all the comforts of today!
✉ relax@homespunfarm.com ○ www.homespunfarm.com

IVORYTON——————————————————————————

The Copper Beech Inn
46 Main St 06442
888-809-2056 860-767-0330
Michael Audette

195-375 BB
22 rooms, 22 pb
Most CC, *Rated*
C-ltd/S-no/P-ltd/H-ltd

Full breakfast
Fine dining: French
contemporary/country
Down comforters/feather
pillows, pillow top and
memory foam mattress,
cable TV, XM Radio

Rediscover the art of relaxation at a magical country inn and restaurant just minutes from the scenic Connecticut River and the Long Island Sound shoreline. Period antiques, oriental rugs, and richly textured upholstery and fabrics.
✉ info@copperbeechinn.com ○ www.copperbeechinn.com

LAKEVILLE——————————————————————————

Wake Robin Inn
104-106 Rt 41 Sharon Rd 06039
860-435-2000
Michael Bryan Loftus

159-289 BB
38 rooms, 38 pb
Most CC
C-yes/S-no/P-no/H-no

Continental breakfast
Multiple parlors, decks, front
porches, A/C, 24-hr guest-use
PC, wireless Internet in main
Inn

Dramatic Georgian-Colonial Inn on 11 acres of rolling hills. 38 rooms with private baths, A/C, TV, multiple parlors, porches, decks. Michael Bryan's on-premises is a non-public Pub available for group booking for weddings, retreats and parties.
✉ info@wakerobininn.com ○ www.wakerobininn.com

LISBON

Branch Place B&B	125-145 BB	Full breakfast
34 Newent Rd 06351	2 rooms, 2 pb	Afternoon tea, snacks;
866-376-5885 860-376-5885	Visa, MC	Continental breakfast
Ethel & Thomas Bosse	S-no/P-no/H-no	available for early risers
		Sitting room, library,
		fireplaces, reading room,
		patio

Our B&B is a beautiful antique home, which was built by Revolutionary War Veteran Stephen Branch around 1790, and was featured on "Every Town Has a Story," WFSB, Hartford, Connecticut.
✉ branchplace@comcast.com ✆ www.thebranchplace.com

Lonesome Dove	129-179 BB	Full breakfast
332 S Burnham Hwy 06351	3 rooms, 3 pb	Gazebo, fresh flowers,
877-793-9880 860-859-9600	Visa, MC, AmEx	common room, movies,
Ruth MacDonald	C-ltd/S-no/P-no/H-no	special celebrations,
		fireplace

Peace & tranquility surround this contemporary, Cape-style home, sitting on three glorious acres. Relax in our glassed-in common room, watch a movie, or just sit & enjoy the fireplace. Three bedrooms feature queen beds, plush robes & fireplaces.
✉ macdore@sbcglobal.net ✆ www.lonesomedovebnb.com

MADISON

Tidewater Inn	115-245 BB	Full breakfast
949 Boston Post Rd 06443	9 rooms, 9 pb	Cold drinks, snacks, hot tea
203-245-8457	Most CC, *Rated*	& cocoa, coffee; late
Victoria Kolyvas	C-ltd/S-no/P-no/H-ltd	afternoon wine & cheese
	Greek	reception
		High speed Internet, beach
		passes, maps, brochures,
		hair dryers, irons, ironing
		boards, fax, copying

Enjoy elegant, romantic, luxury accommodations in beautiful Madison, CT. Close to beaches, Yale, Chamard Vineyard, Goodspeed Opera House, Essex & Chester villages—a wonderful alternative to a hotel or motel! Rooms with canopy bed, fireplace or Jacuzzi.
✉ escape@thetidewater.com ✆ www.TheTidewater.com

MANCHESTER

The Mansion Inn B&B	95-145 BB	Full breakfast
139 Hartford Rd 06040	5 rooms, 5 pb	Homebaked goods
860-646-0453	Most CC, *Rated*	Library, guest refrigerator
Bruce Hamstra	C-ltd/S-no/P-no/H-ltd	stocked with soda and
		bottled spring water

Read in bed by the fireside, on pillows slipped in hand embroidered linens; the library's books are all yours in a silk baron's mansion home. Historic District Award. Easy Interstate highway access.
✉ mansioninnkeeper@cox.net ✆ www.themansioninnct.com

MIDDLEBURY

Tucker Hill Inn	110-200 BB	Full breakfast
96 Tucker Hill Rd 06762	4 rooms, 4 pb	Tea & coffee served
203-758-8334	Visa, MC, *Rated*, ●	Sitting room, library, A/C,
Susan & Richard Cebelenski	C-yes/S-no/P-no/H-no	TV/DVD with free movies,
		small conf. facilities

Large Colonial-style inn near Village Green. Enjoy spacious period rooms and hearty breakfasts. Family suite available. Beautiful landscaped grounds.
✉ susan@tuckerhillinn.com ✆ www.tuckerhillinn.com

MYSTIC ───

The Adams House	95-175 BB	Full breakfast
382 Cow Hill Rd 06355	3 rooms, 3 pb	We serve a hearty breakfast
860-572-9551	Visa, MC	everyday
Gregory & Mary Lou Peck	C-ltd/S-no/P-no/H-no	Sitting room, fireplaces, garden cottage

We warmly welcome you to The Adams House in beautiful, historic Mystic. Each day, a delightful homemade breakfast is served at no extra charge. We have furnished our home with your comfort and convenience in mind. 2 room guest cottage available.
✉ adamshse@aol.com ◐ www.adamshouseofmystic.com

Harbour Inne & Cottage	55-300 BB	Continental breakfast
15 Edgemont St 06355	7 rooms, 7 pb	Kitchen privileges
860-572-9253	*Rated*, •	Sitting room, A/C, canoe &
Claude Falardeau	C-yes/S-yes/P-yes/H-no	boats, cable TV, fireplaces,
	French	hot tub, barbecues, picnic tables, kayak launch

Small inn, plus 3-room cottage on Mystic River. Walk to seaport and all attractions. Water front tables, canoeing, and boating.
✉ harbourinne@earthlink.net ◐ www.harbourinne-cottage.com

House of 1833 B&B	139-350 BB	5 course full gourmet
72 N Stonington Rd 06355	5 rooms, 5 pb	breakfast
800-FOR-1833 860-536-6325	Most CC, •	Fresh baked cookies and
Evan Nickles & Robert Bankel	C-yes/S-no/P-ltd/H-no	hospitality in our parlor in
	Greek, French	the afternoon
		Full size pool, clay tennis court (we have on site tennis rackets), massage, spa services nearby

Welcome to Mystic's celebrated Greek Revival Mansion and National Landmark house featuring 5 luxurious guest suites, 19th century furnishings, working wood-burning fireplaces, hot tubs, gourmet candlelight breakfast; comfort, romance, & convenience
✉ innkeeper@houseof1833.com ◐ www.houseof1833.com

Pequot Hotel B&B	95-175 BB	Full country breakfast
711 Cow Hill Rd 06355	3 rooms, 3 pb	Complimentary beverages,
860-572-0390	Visa, MC, *Rated*, •	picnic lunch available
Nancy Mitchell	C-ltd/S-no/P-no/H-no	2 sitting rooms, library, A/C, whirlpool tubs, wireless Internet access

Authentically restored 1840s stagecoach stop. Friendly, casual elegance amongst period antiques. Relaxing parlors, romantic fireplaces.
✉ pequothtl@aol.com ◐ www.pequothotelbandb.com

Steamboat Inn	125-300 BB	Continental plus breakfast
73 Steamboat Wharf 06355	11 rooms, 11 pb	Complimentary sherry, tea &
860-536-8300	Most CC, *Rated*, •	cookies
Kate Abel	C-ltd/S-no/P-no/H-ltd	Common Room, A/C, whirlpool tubs, fireplaces, water views

Steamboat Inn is the perfect escape for romantics. Our individually decorated and spacious guestrooms offer charming sitting areas, fireplaces, whirlpool tubs, and spectacular river views. ✉ kate@steamboatinnmystic.com ◐ www.steamboatinnmystic.com

The Whaler's Inn	109-159 BB	Continental plus breakfast
20 E Main St 06355	48 rooms, 48 pb	4 Star in-house Restaurant
800-243-2588 860-536-1506	Most CC, *Rated*, •	Sitting room, bicycles, suites,
Richard Przybysz	C-yes/S-no/P-no/H-ltd	fireplaces, data port phones, copy/fax available, cable TV

Enjoy all the charm and nearby attractions Mystic, CT offers as a guest at the Whaler's Inn. A phenomenal location, traditional architecture and decor with all the modern amenities a guest might desire. ✉ sales@whalersinnmystic.com ◐ www.whalersinnmystic.com

NEW HAVEN

Historic Mansion Inn
600 Chapel St 06511
888-512-6278 203-865-8324
Nick & Jacqueline

169-249 BB
7 rooms, 7 pb
Most CC, •
C-yes/S-no/P-ltd/H-ltd
French, Italian

Full breakfast
Study & Living Room
connected through 12' high
archway; mahogany double
doors

" The Place To Stay in New Haven"–The London Sunday Times, July 2007. The elegance
and style of a traditional B&B in downtown New Haven. Stately, high ceilings and just
across from the Park. Walk to fabulous, nearby restaurants and 4 blocks to Yale.
✉ innkeeper@thehistoricmansioninn.com ◐ www.thehistoricmansioninn.com

NEW MILFORD

The Homestead Inn
5 Elm St 06776
860-354-4080
Bill Greenman

85-145 BB
14 rooms, 14 pb
Visa, MC, AmEx, •
C-yes/S-no/P-ltd/H-ltd

Continental plus breakfast
Sitting room, front porch,
gardens, in village center,
wireless Internet access

A small 150 year old country inn, The Homestead Inn is located in a picturesque New
England town, next to village green, near shops, churches, restaurants, antiques, galleries,
hiking and crafts.
✉ reservations@homesteadct.com ◐ www.homesteadct.com

NIANTIC

Inn at Harbor Hill Marina
60 Grand St 06357
860-739-0331
Dave & Sue Labrie

135-255 BB
9 rooms, 9 pb
Visa, MC, AmEx,
Rated, •
C-ltd/S-no/P-no/H-no
French, Italian, Spanish

Classic Breakfast Buffet
Complimentary beverages
and snacks
Fireplaces, water views,
balconies, TVs, A/C, Wifi
Internet, kayaks, beach,
gardens, boat rides

Selected 2008–2009 "Best in New England." In Marina District, with panoramic views of the
harbor, our nine room, award-winning Inn features private baths, A/C, fireplaces, WiFi,
balconies and breakfast. Near Mystic, Mohegan Sun & Foxwoods
✉ info@innharborhill.com ◐ www.innharborhill.com

NORFOLK

Blackberry River Inn
538 Greenwoods Rd, Rt 44 W
06058
800-414-3636 860-542-5100
Jeanette Angel

169-289 BB
24 rooms, 15 pb
Most CC, *Rated*, •
C-yes/S-no/P-ltd/H-ltd
Spanish

Full country breakfast
Complimentary afternoon
tea served from 4:30 to 6:00
p.m.
Sitting room, library, pool,
Jacuzzi, 27 acres, lawns, 3
miles of hiking trails

A Colonial Inn built in 1763, the Blackberry River Inn lies nestled in the foothills of the
Berkshires, on 27 scenic rural acres. Listed on the National Register of Historic Places.
✉ bri@blackberryriverinn.com ◐ www.blackberryriverinn.com

Manor House
69 Maple Ave 06058
866-542-5690 860-542-5690
Michael Dinsmore & L. Keith
Mullins

130-255 BB
9 rooms, 9 pb
Visa, MC, •
C-ltd/S-no/P-no/H-no

Full breakfast
Complimentary tea, coffee,
cocoa & cookies
Whirlpools, wood & gas
fireplaces, private balconies,
piano, gazebo, gardens

Historic Victorian mansion furnished with genuine antiques, on 5 acres. Romantic, elegant
rooms. Deluxe room with gas fireplace, 2 person Jacuzzi.
✉ innkeeper@manorhouse-norfolk.com ◐ www.manorhouse-norfolk.com

NORFOLK

Mountain View Inn
67 Litchfield Rd 06058
866-792-7812 860-542-6991
Dean & Jean Marie Johnson

120-400 BB
7 rooms, 7 pb
Most CC, *Rated*, •
C-ltd/S-no/P-no/H-ltd
Closed January

Full breakfast
Join us for classical music
and a glass of sherry in the
main parlor.
Spa Service with Licensed
Massage Therapist available
by appointment

Lovingly restored, our 1900 Victorian Country-style Inn offers 7 large, unique guestrooms in the main house—all with private baths—your choice of double, queen, king or single bed accommodations. Our 2 BR guesthouse features a kitchen, fireplace . . .
✉ innkeepers@mvinn.com ⬥ www.mvinn.com

NORTH STONINGTON

Inn at Lower Farm
119 Mystic Rd 06359
866-535-9075 860-535-9075
Mary & Jon Wilska

110-185 BB
4 rooms, 4 pb
Visa, MC, AmEx, *Rated*
C-yes/S-no/P-ltd/H-no

Full breakfast
Afternoon tea with
homemade cookies and
stocked guest refrigerator
Wireless Internet, porch with
a swing & rocking chair,
library-sitting room,
hammock, recliner

Named a 2008 Editors' choice by "Yankee Magazine" Near Mystic, CT a AAA 3 diamond rated B&B in Southeastern CT near Stonington, New London, Westerly, RI, Foxwoods, and Mohegan Sun Casinos. A perfect respite in the heart of away from it all
✉ info@lowerfarm.com ⬥ www.lowerfarm.com

NORWALK

The Silvermine Tavern
194 Perry Ave 06850
888-693-9967 203-847-4558
Frank & Marsha Whitman

95-210 BB
11 rooms, 11 pb
Visa, MC, AmEx,
Rated, •
C-yes/S-yes/P-no/H-no

Continental breakfast
Lunch & dinner available in
restaurant, bar
Live Jazz, sitting room, new
suite, weddings and
conferences

Charming 225-year-old country inn only an hour from New York City. Decorated with hundreds of antiques. Live Dixieland jazz on Thursday through Saturday nights.
✉ innkeeper@silverminetavern.com ⬥ www.silverminetavern.com

NORWICH

Lathrop Manor Bed & Breakfast
380 Washington Street 06360
860-204-9448
Marco & Sheryl Middleton

150-300 BB
2 rooms, 2 pb
Visa, MC, AmEx
S-ltd/P-no/H-no

Full breakfast
Complimentary coffee, tea
and water anytime.
Beverages and hors
d'ouerves in the afternoon
Business center, library,
WiFi, in-room DVD with
access to DVD library and
massage for additional fee

Lathrop Manor is nestled in the heart of Norwichtown's Historic District and has a rich history and beautiful craftsmanship from the hand carved wooden beams to the wide board flooring throughout.
✉ innkeeper@lathropmanor.com ⬥ www.lathropmanor.com

OLD GREENWICH

Harbor House Inn
165 Shore Rd 06870
203-637-0145
Dawn Stuttig & Dolly Stuttig

149-300 BB
23 rooms, 23 pb
Visa, MC, AmEx, •
C-yes/S-no/P-no/H-no

Continental breakfast
Kitchen facilities, tea and
cookies
Sitting room, piano,
television, VCR, phone with
voice mail, air conditioning,
porch, weddings

Beautiful Inn, close to beach, walking distance to lovely New England town, train 1 mile away. 45 minutes to NYC! ✉ dawnstuttig@aol.com ⬥ www.hhinn.com

OLD MYSTIC

The Old Mystic Inn
52 Main St 06372
860-572-9422
Michael S. Cardillo, Jr.

135-215 BB
8 rooms, 8 pb
Visa, MC, AmEx,
Rated, •
S-ltd/P-no

Full country breakfast
Afternoon refreshments,
dinner packages October-
April
Hammock, gazebo, library,
Keeping Room, patio, parlor

Dating back to 1784, The Old Mystic Inn is located just minutes from Mystic Seaport and Aquarium. This charming Inn, formerly The Old Mystic Book Shop, has carried on that theme by naming each of the eight guestrooms after New England authors.
info@oldmysticinn.com www.oldmysticinn.com

OLD SAYBROOK

Deacon Timothy Pratt B&B
325 Main St 06475
800-640-1195 860-395-1229
Richard Dunn

145-200 BB
7 rooms, 7 pb
Visa, MC, AmEx,
Rated, •
C-ltd/S-no/P-no/H-no

Full wkends, expanded cont.
wkdays
Port wine, teas, coffee, hot
chocolate, cookies, spring
water always available
Beach passes, maps & lots of
advice provided; in-room
massage available, picnic
area, pretty grounds

Magnificent, award-winning B&B in Old Saybrook, a National Historic Register Inn. Elegant rooms with fireplaces, Jacuzzis, canopy beds. In historic district, on gas-lit Main Street. Walk to everything! Yankee Magazine's Editors Choice for 2006!
stay@pratthouse.net www.Pratthouse.net

POMFRET

Inn at Fox Hill Farm
760 Pomfret St 06258
860-928-5240
Polly & Nick LoPiccolo

215 BB
1 rooms, 1 pb
Visa, MC, •
C-ltd/S-no/P-no/H-no

Full breakfast
Complimentary snacks and
beverages, wine
Cottage suite, private patio
and deck, private
dining/kitchen area

You will feel at home as your hosts embrace you with warm hospitality. A beautiful view, convenient location, peaceful environment, and homey atmosphere make this perfect for your weekend retreat.
innkeepers@innatfoxhillfarm.com www.innatfoxhillfarm.com

POQUETANUCK VILLAGE

Captain Grant's 1754
109 Rt 2A 06365
800-982-1772 860-887-7589
Ted & Carol

89-179 BB
7 rooms, 7 pb
Most CC, •
C-ltd/S-no/P-ltd/H-ltd

Full breakfast
Dessert, wine, beer & soda
complimentary all day
3 common rooms, 3 story
deck, use of kitchenette
including fridge

Captain Grant's is a National Historic Inn located in a 1687 Colonial Village. We were featured on HGTV in 2002 and USA today in 2003. Our canopy beds and fireplaces are elegant and affordable. Let where you stay be as memorable as the places you visit.
stay@captaingrants.com www.captaingrants.com

RIDGEFIELD

Green Rocks Inn
415 Danbury Rd 06877
203-894-8944
Kim Wanamaker

150-250 BB
3 rooms, 1 pb
Visa, MC, AmEx
C-ltd/S-no/P-yes/H-ltd

Continental plus breakfast
Afternoon tea including
cappuccino and espresso
along with organic snacks,
TVs, wireless Internet, iPod
docking stations.

We are an eco-friendly B&B located in beautiful Ridgefield, CT. Our guestrooms feature all organic linens and towels, flat screen TV's, wireless Internet, ipod docking stations and much more. kim@greenrocksinn.com www.greenrocksinn.com

RIDGEFIELD ───────────────────────────────────────

West Lane Inn	170-425 BB	Plus A La Carte
22 West Ln 06877	17 rooms, 17 pb	Satellite TV/VCR, voice mail,
203-438-7323	Most CC, *Rated*, •	24 hour phone service &
Ms. Mayer & Debbie Prieger	C-yes/S-no/P-no/H-no	wireless DSL. DVD available
		upon request.

Situated in the historic district of Ridgefield the West Lane Inn combines the charm of an intimate country Inn with every convenience of a large hotel.
✉ west_lane_inn@sbcglobal.net ❂ www.westlaneinn.com

SALISBURY ───────────────────────────────────────

Barbara Ardizones B&B	155-195 BB	Fresh and seasonal
62 Main St 06068	3 rooms, 3 pb	Brandy, sherry, liquor
860-4353057	C-ltd/S-no/P-ltd/H-no	available in the library. Tea,
Barbara Ardizone		wine or mulled wine in the
		fall.
		Porch terrace, gardens,
		hammocks, lounges, lib
		books, TV/VCR, AC

My property, over an acre, is just outside town. The gardens are an escape from a busy life, with lounges & hammocks. There are 3 B&B rooms, each with private bath & AC for those warm summer months. The beds are all made up with down pillows & comforters.
✉ ardizone@sbcglobal.net ❂ www.barbaraardizone.com/bandb.htm

Earl Grey B&B	175-195 BB	Full gourmet breakfast
860-435-1007	2 rooms, 2 pb	Afternoon tea, snacks &
Patricia & Richard Boyle	Cash, Checks	complimentary wine
	C-ltd/S-no/P-no/H-ltd	Fireplaces, private baths,
	French, German, some	garden terraces, libraries
	Dutch, and a little	
	Japanese	

1850s era house with barn on a quiet, private hill, in and overlooking Salisbury village center. Two spacious rooms to choose from and a memorable full breakfast.
✉ richard.boyle@att.net

STONINGTON ───────────────────────────────────────

Another Second Penny Inn	99-249 BB	Five Course Full Breakfast
870 Pequot Trl 06378	3 rooms, 3 pb	Coffee, tea, hot chocolate,
860-535-1710	Most CC, *Rated*, •	homebaked cookies
Jim & Sandra Wright	C-ltd/S-ltd/P-ltd/H-no	Library, patio, five acres of
		gardens, fields & forest.

Consider: "If you have 2 pennies, with the first buy bread & with the second buy hyacinths for your soul." Our 1710 home offers 3 large guestrooms, private jetted baths, fireplaces, gardens, quiet country near Mystic. Voted Best Breakfast in New England.
✉ inn@secondpenny.com ❂ www.secondpenny.com

Inn at Stonington	150-445 BB	Continental plus breakfast
60 Water St 06378	18 rooms, 18 pb	Complimentary wine &
860-535-2000	Visa, MC, AmEx, •	cheese hour
William Griffin, Susan Irvine,	C-ltd/S-no/P-no/H-yes	Sitting room, library, bikes,
Anne Henson		suites, fireplaces, cable TV,
		accommodations for
		business travelers

Elegant hotel in the heart of the historic Stonington Borough. Stay in & enjoy your Jacuzzi tub, gas fireplace, & view of the Fisher's Island Sound. 400' deep water pier for yachts.
✉ manager@innatstonington.com ❂ www.innatstonington.com

STORRS

Fitch House B&B
563 Storrs Rd, Rt 195 06268
860-456-0922
Kay & Tony Holt

125-145 BB
3 rooms, 3 pb
Visa, MC
C-ltd/S-no/P-no/H-no

Full breakfast
A/C, cable TV, wireless or
dial-up Internet access,
nightly turndown service
with chocolates.

The Fitch House B&B offers elegant accommodations near the Univ. of Connecticut at Storrs. In the rolling hills of northeastern CT known as "The Quiet Corner." To stay at The Fitch House is to step back into a more gracious time with modern amenities.
✉ innkeeper@fitchhouse.com 🌐 www.fitchhouse.com

SUFFIELD

Lily House B&B
13 Bridge St 06078
860-668-7931
Bob & Lorraine Erickson

135-160 BB
3 rooms, 3 pb
Most CC
C-ltd/S-no/P-no/H-no

Full breakfast
Refrigerator stocked with
complimentary soda, bottled
water, snacks and other
beverages.
Common room with games,
books, convenience area, all
guestrooms have CD players

Set in the historic district of Suffield, this rambling old Victorian home offers a lovely place to stay as you journey through a quaint New England town. Close to fine and casual dining, parks, the "Walk of Homes" as well as Suffield Academy.
✉ lorraine@thelilyhouse.com 🌐 www.thelilyhouse.com

THOMPSON

The Cottage House
351 Route 193 06277
860-923-3886
Kelly

125-175 BB
6 rooms, 6 pb
Most CC
C-yes/S-ltd/P-no/H-ltd

Continental breakfast

Situated in the picturesque Quiet Corner of Connecticut, the Inn combines the grace of elegant luxury with the tranquility of beach house charm. Calming and comfortable, we're the perfect destination for a vacation retreat or a romantic getaway.
✉ mail@LTMcottagehouse.com 🌐 www.LTMcottagehouse.com

Lord Thompson Manor
Rt 200 06277
860-923-3886
Jackie & Andrew

180-215 BB
6 rooms, 3 pb
Visa, MC
C-yes/S-no/P-no/H-yes

Full breakfast
Afternoon tea, snacks, bar
service
Sitting room, suites,
fireplaces, cable TV,
accommodations for
business travelers

The stately elegance of Lord Thompson Manor, the serenity of the manicured grounds, luxury suites and outstanding service provide guests with the ultimate getaway or Weekend Wedding.
✉ mail@lordthompsonmanor.com 🌐 www.lordthompsonmanor.com

WALLINGFORD

The Wallingford Victorian B&B
245 N Main St 06492
877-269-4499 203-269-4492
Becky & Dave Barrett

109-169 BB
5 rooms, 5 pb
Most CC, *Rated*, •
C-ltd/S-ltd/P-ltd/H-no

Full breakfast
Guest kitchenette with
refrigerator, microwave,
coffee, tea and snacks
available 24 hours a day.
Games, movies, books. Free
wireless Internet access and
cable TV plus off street
parking.

Private rooms and suites in an 1891 Queen Anne Victorian offering midwestern hospitality and updated amenities. Enjoy a brass bed and whirlpool tub; or fireplace and private balcony. Watch cable TV or go on the Internet. Full breakfast served daily.
✉ innkeep@bedandbreakfastwallingford.com 🌐 www.bedandbreakfastwallingford.com

WESTBROOK───────────────────────

Angel's Watch Inn
902 Boston Post Rd 06498
860-399-8846
Bill & Peggy Millspaugh

135-195 BB
4 rooms, 4 pb
Most CC, *Rated*, •
C-ltd/S-no/P-no/H-ltd
A little Spanish

Continental plus breakfast
Beer, wine, sparkling cider,
bottled water, soda
Fireplaces, soaking tubs,
DVD/CD, radio, wireless
Internet, massage therapy,
manicure/pedicure

Stately Federal built in 1830. Comfortable elegance, romantic, private. Please, come . . . relax . . . and enjoy . . . Our sole purpose at Angels' Watch Inn is to give you your own private heaven.
✉ info@angelswatchinn.com 🌐 www.angelswatchinn.com

Captain Stannard House
138 S Main St 06498
860-399-4634
Mary & Jim Brewster

120-205 BB
9 rooms, 9 pb
Most CC
C-ltd/S-no/P-no/H-no

Full breakfast
Complimentary wine, beer,
soft drink and snacks
Billiards table, library, sitting
room, bicycles, walk to the
beach, formal dining room,
gardens

Connecticut Shoreline Inn offers 9 guestrooms, all with private bath, individually decorated. Large common areas. Full breakfast served at your candlelight table for two. A perfect romantic getaway.
✉ mary@stannardhouse.com 🌐 www.stannardhouse.com

Talcott House
161 Seaside Ave 06498
860-399-5020
Lucy Bingham & James M.
Fitzpatrick

195-225 BB
3 rooms, 3 pb
Most CC
C-ltd/S-no/P-no/H-yes
Mar.-Nov. but call ahead

Continental on weekdays
Afternoon tea and wine; full
breakfast on weekends
Sitting room, fireplaces,
cable TV, private veranda,
private bath, CD player,
ocean views

All rooms have beautiful ocean views that will take your breath away! Complete with private baths, fresh flowers, a grand piano, pure elegance, sunsets on the Atlantic, antiques, and ambience, you will never want to leave this place of luxury.
✉ lucretiawb@aol.com 🌐 www.talcotthouse.com

WETHERSFIELD───────────────────

Chester Bulkley House
184 Main St 06109
860-563-4236
Tom Aufiero

95-145 BB
5 rooms, 3 pb
Most CC, •
C-yes/S-no/P-no/H-no

Full breakfast
Afternoon tea
Fireplaces, ceiling fans, air
conditioning, fax, telephone

Nestled in the historic village of Old Wethersfield, Tom provides a warm and gracious New England welcome to the vacationer, traveler and business person.
✉ ChesterBulkley@aol.com 🌐 www.chesterbulkleyhouse.com

WOODSTOCK──────────────────────

B&B at Taylor's Corner
880 Route 171 06281
888-974-0490 860-974-0490
Brenda Van Damme

100-145 BB
3 rooms, 3 pb
Visa, MC, Disc, •
C-ltd/S-no/P-no/H-no

Full breakfast
Homemade cookies upon
arrival, complimentary fruit
& sodas
Wireless Internet, DirecTV,
XBox, private bathrooms &
fireplaces

A romantic Connecticut farmhouse (c.1795) offers 3 comfortable air-conditioned bed chambers with private baths and fireplaces. Surrounded by manicured gardens & towering trees. Listed on the National Register of Historic Places.
✉ info@taylorsbb.com 🌐 www.taylorsbb.com

Delaware

DOVER

State Street Inn	125-135 BB	Full breakfast
28 N. State St. 19901	4 rooms, 4 pb	Whirlpool tubs, exercise
302-734-2294	Most CC	room, parlor, family living
Mike & Yvonne Hall	C-ltd/S-no/P-no	room with TV

The State Street Inn offers charming guestrooms, each with private bath (two with whirlpool tubs). All four lovely guestrooms are beautifully decorated and furnished with antiques and reproductions. In-room amenities include cable TV and A/C.
✉ info@statestreetinn.com ○ www.statestreetinn.com

LEWES

The Inn at Canal Square	105-600 BB	European-Style Breakfast
122 Market St 19958	24 rooms, 24 pb	Seasonal fruit and cheese
888-644-1911 302-644-3377	Visa, MC, AmEx, *Rated*	tray
Ted Becker	C-yes/S-no/P-ltd/H-yes	fireplaces, cable TV, CD
		players, refrigerators, robes,
		business center, fitness
		room, free Internet

Nantucket-Style on the Delaware Coast. Located on the waterfront in the heart of Historic Lewes. Large rooms with private baths. Open year-round, with complimentary European-style breakfast. Ideal coastal escape and event destination.
✉ innatcanalsquare@verizon.net ○ www.theinnatcanalsquare.com

John Penrose Virden B&B	120-225 BB	Full breakfast
217 Second St 19958	3 rooms, 3 pb	Afternoon snack & beverage,
302-644-0217	Cash, Checks	fresh fruit & flowers in room
Ruth & Jim Edwards	C-ltd/S-no/P-no/H-ltd	Central heat, A/C, private
		parking, bikes, beach towels,
		chairs & umbrellas

The Virden House is a fourteen room 19th century Victorian located on the main street of Lewes, DE, within walking distance to many shops, fine restaurants & ½ mile to the beach.
✉ redwards@virdenhouse.com ○ www.virdenhouse.com

Lazy L at Willow Creek	110-215 BB	Full breakfast
16061 Willow Creek Rd 19958	6 rooms, 6 pb	We specialize in cooking
302-644-7220	Visa, MC, Disc, *Rated*	vegetarian or vegan
Joanne Cassidy	C-ltd/S-no/P-yes/H-ltd	breakfasts upon request;
		breakfast can be early
		Heated swimming pool, hot
		tub, pool table, screened
		porches, exercise area,
		extensive outdoor space,

This bed & breakfast is a great choice for a winter getaway or a summer vacation. Outside the resort town of Lewes, this 8 acre gem has it all. Very large guestrooms with large guest lounges & large game room. VERY Dog friendly, off leash play area.
✉ vacation@lazyl.net ○ www.lazyl.net

MILTON

Governor's B&B	80-135 BB	Full gourmet breakfast
327 Union St 19968	3 rooms, 3 pb	Sitting room, library,
866-684-4649 302-684-4649	Most CC	fireplaces, cable TV,
William & Deborah Post	C-ltd/S-ltd/P-no/H-no	refrigerator/microwave, A/C

Built in 1790, the inn is situated on two landscaped acres in the Milton Historic District. It was built by John Hazzard who piloted Washington across the Delaware. It is private and secluded.
✉ wdpost@aol.com

Governor's B&B, Milton, DE

REHOBOTH BEACH

BEDazzled, Bewitched &
Sea Witch
65 & 67 & 71 Lake Ave 19971
866-732-9482 302-226-9482
Inez L Conover

145-445 BB
17 rooms, 17 pb
Most CC, •
C-ltd/S-no/P-no/H-ltd

Continental plus breakfast
Tea, sweets & cordial bar,
catered parties
Jacuzzi, fireplace, movies,
Internet access, A/C

Cruise the beach, enjoy a gourmet brunch or take in the sophisticated nightlife. BEDazzled,
Bewitched & Sea Witch Inn & Spa are just steps from it all. Theme rooms, Jacuzzis,
weddings. Walk to Boardwalk.
✉ inez.conover@yahoo.com ◐ www.bewitchedbnb.com

Rehoboth Guest House
40 Maryland Ave 19971
800-564-0493 302-227-4117
Tom Napier-Collins

95-205 BB
14 rooms, 10 pb   .
Most CC
C-ltd/S-no/P-no/H-no

Continental breakfast
Complimentary wine &
cheese on Saturdays in
season
Porch, sun decks, outdoor
enclosed cedar showers,
wireless Internet

The Rehoboth Guest House is a charming gay-owned and operated Victorian beach house.
Located in the heart of Rehoboth Beach, Delaware, we're just steps from the boardwalk,
beach, and the Atlantic ocean.
✉ manager@rehobothguesthouse.com ◐ www.rehobothguesthouse.com

The Royal Rose Inn B&B
41 Baltimore Ave 19971
302-226-2535
Andy Dorosky

60-185 BB
7 rooms, 7 pb
Visa, MC, Disc
C-ltd/S-no/P-no/H-no

Buffet style breakfast
Tea & coffee
Sitting room, porch, sundeck
wireless Internet

Centrally located on Baltimore Avenue in the heart of Rehoboth Beach, the Inn is steps
away from shops, fine boutiques and the area's best restaurants and night life.
✉ innkeeper@royalroseinn.com ◐ www.royalroseinn.com

District of Columbia

WASHINGTON

Aaron Shipman House B&B	90-265 BB	Full breakfast served family
13th and Q Streets NW 20009	6 rooms, 6 pb	style
877-893-3233 413-582-9888	Most CC	Sitting room, gardens, library,
Kathy, Alan or Steve	C-yes/S-no/P-no/H-no	Victorian porch, piano,
	French, Spanish	antiques

A beautifully restored Victorian featuring original woodwork, stained glass, chandeliers, Victorian-style lattice porch, Art Nouveau and Victorian antiques.
✉ reservations@bedandbreakfastdc.com 🌐 www.aaronshipmanhouse.com

Adam's Inn	109-159 BB	Continental breakfast
1744 Lanier Place NW 20009	26 rooms, 15 pb	Tea, coffee
800-578-6807 202-745-3600	Most CC	Internet access, sitting
Anne Owens	C-yes/S-no/P-no/H-ltd	rooms, TV lounge, W/D,
	Spanish	guest kitchen, patio

Only 1 block from the Adams Morgan's restaurant district & 7 blocks from the Woodley Park Red Line Metro, the newly-renovated Adam's Inn is convenient to everything. Limited parking is available.
✉ adamsinn@adamsinn.com 🌐 adamsinn.com

Bloomingdale Inn	90-175 BB	Continental plus breakfast
2417 First St NW 20001	10 rooms, 1 pb	Coffee, tea served any time
202-319-0801	Most CC, •	A/C, parking, hairdryers,
Jim Wilson	C-ltd/S-no/P-no/H-ltd	telephones with free voice
	German	mail and T-1 computer
		access in all rooms

Our Inn offers our guests a home away from home, in close proximity to top tourist attractions, government offices, and the central business district. Walk to Children's Hospital & Washington Hospital Center. We have two beautiful cats that live with us.
✉ innkeeper@bloomingdaleinn.com 🌐 www.bloomingdaleinn.com

Carriage House on Capitol Hill	125-350 BB	Continental breakfast
3rd Street at South Carolina	5 rooms, 5 pb	
Ave SE 20003	Most CC	
877-893-3233 202-328-3510	C-ltd/S-no/P-no/H-no	
Kathy, Alan & Steve		

The Carriage House on Capitol Hill offers visitors to Washington DC exceptional convenience to the Smithsonian, National Monuments, and the Convention Center. We have 4 guestrooms, each with queen bed and private bath, or a self hosted 2 bedroom suite
✉ reservations@bedandbreakfastdc.com

Dupont at the Circle Inn	165-450 BB	Continental plus breakfast
1604 19th St NW 20009	9 rooms, 9 pb	Afternoon Sweets
202-332-5251	Most CC, *Rated*, •	Complimentary WiFi,
Anna, Breelyn, Melvin	C-ltd/S-no/P-no/H-no	afternoon refreshments
	German, Spanish, Greek	

Our charming Victorian inn is located in Dupont Circle just one block from the Metro. We offer modern conveniences such as WiFi. Our rooms are all unique and we are eager to welcome you.
✉ dupontatthecircle@comcast.net 🌐 www.dupontatthecircle.com

134   District of Columbia

WASHINGTON

Embassy Circle Guest House
2224 R St NW 20008
877-232-7744 202-232-7744
Laura & Raymond Saba

175-280 BB
11 rooms, 11 pb
Most CC
C-ltd/S-no/P-no/H-no
Arabic, French and
Spanish

Continental plus breakfast
Wine and light snacks every
evening from 5:30 – 7:00 PM
Phones with voicemail, free
WiFi/Internet in guestrooms
laptop in Dining Room

Embassy Circle Guest House, the newest DCInns B&B, is a stunning, historic Dupont Circle mansion. Located in an upscale DC neighborhood, Embassy Circle offers 10 spacious guestrooms, great food, great ambience, and warm personal hospitality.
✉ embassy@dcinns.com ☻ www.dcinns.com

Inn at Dupont Circle South
1312 19th St NW 20036
866-467-2100 202-467-6777
Robin Floyd

95-230 BB
8 rooms, 5 pb
Most CC, •
C-yes/S-no/P-no/H-no
Tagalog

Full buffet breakfast
Evening wine; snacks, tea,
bottled water
Featherbeds, down
comforters, wireless
connections, new flatscreen
TVs, gym passes

1886 Victorian with bay & Queen Anne windows, white marble & cherry pine hardwood floors, private rear garden, elegant rooms, sumptuous, full breakfast, complimentary wine Internet access.
✉ inn@theinnatdupontcircle.com ☻ thedupontcollection.com/dupontsouth.html

Kalorama Guest House
1854 Mintwood Place, NW
20009
800-974-6450 202-667-6369
Kurt Haraldson

115-185 BB
29 rooms, 15 pb
Most CC, •
C-ltd/S-no/P-no/H-no

Continental breakfast
Afternoon Sherry, cookies
and lemonade are served
Parlor with high speed
Internet access, morning
newspaper, iron, refrigerator
afternoon treats

An alternative to traditional hotels in DC—Victorian townhouses decorated in period furnishings. Antique-filled, spacious rooms. Parlor with Internet access, daily continental breakfast with morning newspapers served in our main home.
✉ info@kaloramaguesthouse.com ☻ www.kaloramaguesthouse.com/adams_location.shtml

Maison Orleans B&B
414 5th St SE 20003
202-544-3694
Bill Rouchell

140-180 BB
3 rooms, 3 pb
Cash, Checks
C-ltd/S-no/P-no/H-no

Continental plus breakfast
Sitting room, fireplaces,
accommodations for
business travelers, parking,
wireless Internet access

This turn-of-the-century Federal row house is located five blocks SE of the Nation's Capitol Library of Congress, and Supreme Court. Completely furnished with family pieces from the 30's and 40's.
✉ maisonorln@aol.com

Meridian Manor
16th and U. Street NW 20005
877-893-3233 202-328-3510
Kathy, Alan & Steve

115-275 BB
7 rooms, 5 pb
Most CC
C-yes/S-ltd/P-no/H-no
Russian

Continental plus breakfast

Meridian Manor B&B welcomes visitors with the charm and warmth of a private home. Centrally located in Washington's Dupont Circle neighborhood, just north of the circle proper at 16th Street and U. Streets. We are just 3 blocks to the Metro—5 minute walk.
✉ reservations@bedandbreakfastdc.com ☻ www.meridianmanordc.com

WASHINGTON——————————————————————————

Swann House	165-395 BB	Continental plus breakfast
1808 New Hampshire Ave NW	9 rooms, 9 pb	Afternoon refreshments &
20009	Most CC, *Rated*	evening cordials
202-265-4414	C-ltd/S-no/P-no/H-no	Parlour, Jacuzzis, swimming
Mary Ross & Rick Verkler		pool, suites, fireplace, cable
		TV, conference

Grand Richardson Romanesque mansion in Dupont Circle, D.C.'s most vibrant neighborhood. Eat at local outdoor cafes, walk to museums or relax by the pool or on our roof deck.
✉ stay@swannhouse.com ◯ www.swannhouse.com

Woodley Park Guest House	125-210 BB	Continental plus breakfast
2647 Woodley Rd NW 20008	18 rooms, 11 pb	Onsite parking available
866-667-0218 202-667-0218	Visa, MC, AmEx	$18.00 per day ($20.16 inc
Courtney Lodico	C-ltd/S-no/P-no/H-no	tax)
	French, Arabic, Spanish	

The first of the DCInns B&B's, the popular, 18-room Woodley Park Guest House has the best location in DC—just steps from the Woodley Park-Zoo Metro station and a short walk from Dupont Circle and Adams Morgan
✉ woodley@dcinns.com ◯ www.dcinns.com/woodley.html

Florida

AMELIA ISLAND

Elizabeth Pointe Lodge 98 S Fletcher Ave 32034 800-772-3359 904-277-4851 David & Susan Caples	225-425 BB 25 rooms, 25 pb Most CC, *Rated*, • C-yes/S-no/P-no/H-yes	Full breakfast Light lunch & dinner service available, complimentary wine hour, 24 hr room service Newspaper at the door daily, concierge services, complimentary DSL WiFi, beach equipment, bikes

Reminiscent of a turn-of-the-century lodge the Elizabeth Pointe Lodge is situated oceanfron on the small barrier island of Amelia. The Main House with 25 different rooms, the superior Ocean House with private decks and the cozy Miller Cottage.
✉ djcaples@lodgingresources.com ◒ www.elizabethpointelodge.com

Fairbanks House 227 S 7th St 32034 888 891-9882 904-277-0500 Bill & Theresa Hamilton	175-395 BB 12 rooms, 12 pb Most CC, *Rated*, • C-ltd/S-no/P-no/H-no	Full breakfast Complimentary social hour Sitting room, bicycles, pool, Jacuzzi, suites, conference facility

Island paradise. 8000 sq ft mansion with upscale accommodations nestled into Victorian seaside village. Romance packages 2–7 nights, retreats for "the girls." Twelve guestrooms. Smoke-free, including pool and grounds.
✉ email@fairbankshouse.com ◒ www.fairbankshouse.com

ANNA MARIA ISLAND

An Island Getaway at Palm Tree Villas 207 66th St 34217 888-778-7256 941-778-0910 Peggy Sawe	115-195 EP 6 rooms, 6 pb Most CC, *Rated*, • C-yes/S-ltd/P-no/H-ltd	Heated pool, full kitchens, king size beds with pillow- top mattresses, wireless broadband Internet

Top rated B&B and recommended by LIFE magazine. Warm hospitality awaits you in ou charming, old Florida style villas in lush tropical setting surrounding a delightful, heated pool. ✉ info@palmtreevillas.com ◒ www.palmtreevillas.com

Harrington House Beachfront B&B 5626 Gulf Dr 34217 888-828-5566 941-778-5444 Mark & Patti Davis	149-529 BB 18 rooms, 18 pb Visa, MC, Disc, *Rated*, • C-ltd/S-ltd/P-no/H-ltd	Full gourmet breakfast Complimentary chocolate chip cookies, and coffee/tea available all the time. Sitting room, bikes, kayaks, heated pool on the beach. In- room massages & Spa Servs. Reservation required

Come savor the intimate charm of Harrington House, one of Florida's most highly rated bed & breakfast inns located on a tranquil bit of paradise known as Anna Maria Island. Stunning sunsets, the soothing rhythm of waves on the beach, and warm hospitality.
✉ info@harringtonhouse.com ◒ www.harringtonhouse.com

APALACHICOLA

Bryant House B&B 101 6th St 32320 888-554-4376 850-653-3270 Brigitte Schroeder	87-250 BB 4 rooms, 4 pb Visa, MC, AmEx, *Rated*, • C-ltd/S-no/P-ltd/H-ltd German	Full German breakfast Complimentary wine Sitting room, DSL Internet access, cable TV/VCR, rose garden, fountain, fish pond

European hospitality in a quaint Victorian setting. Each room has its own special character, designed to fit your mood. Relax in a rocker on the wraparound porch or enjoy the quiet in the patio under the 150 year old magnolia tree.
✉ ken@bryanthouse.com ◒ www.bryanthouse.com

APALACHICOLA

Coombs House Inn	99-229 BB	Gourmet Breakfast
10 Sixth St 32320	23 rooms, 23 pb	Fresh fruit, yogurt, baked
88-244-8320 850-653-9199	Most CC, *Rated*, •	goods, gourmet coffee
Estella, Peggy & Marc	C-yes/S-ltd/P-ltd/H-yes	Beach chairs, towels,
		umbrellas & bicycles;
		weddings, meetings, family
		reunions, anniversaries

The Inn consists of The Mansion, Veranda Suites and The Villa, welcoming special guests who appreciate the charm and historical authenticity of another era, in an intimate atmosphere.
✉ lynnwilson2@aol.com 🌐 www.CoombsHouseInn.com

BIG PINE KEY

Barnacle B&B	125-205 BB	Full breakfast
557 Long Beach Dr 33043	4 rooms, 4 pb	Hot tub, bicycles,
00-465-9100 305-872-3298	Visa, MC, Disc	refrigerators, A/C, weddings
Tim & Jane Marquis	C-ltd/S-ltd/P-no/H-no	& receptions

Our intriguing Caribbean-style home "that nature designed." The Barnacle is located on the lush tropical island of Big Pine Key, FL, where peace, quiet and leisurely breezes prevail.
✉ barnacleb@bellsouth.net 🌐 www.thebarnacle.net

BOKEELIA

Bokeelia Tarpon Inn	159-325 BB	Full breakfast
8241 Main St 33922	5 rooms, 5 pb	H'ors d'oeuvres with wine,
866-827-7662 239-283-8961	Most CC, *Rated*	snacks & cold beverages are
Cynthia Welch	C-ltd/S-no/P-no/H-yes	available in the kitchen at
		any time
		Concierge services for tours
		and activities.

Steal away to this romantic Fort Meyers area bed and breakfast inn – an exquisite Pine Island Florida waterfront lodging near Sanibel and Boca Grande in charming Bokeelia. The Bokeelia Tarpon Inn is perfect for vacations and special occasions.
✉ info@tarponinn.com 🌐 www.tarponinn.com

CAPE CORAL-PINE ISLAND

Inn on the Bay	109-199 BB	Continental plus breakfast
12251 Shoreview Dr 33993	4 rooms, 4 pb	TV, A/C, refrigerator, views,
239-283-7510	Cash, Checks, •	porches, free use of canoes,
Tell us Lanier sent you	C-ltd/S-ltd/P-ltd/H-ltd	free local calls

Tropical island waterfront B&B, view manatee and dolphins from your porch, fantastic sunsets, free use of canoe, two 90' docks. Near Sanibel-JN Ding Darling Preserve.
✉ cmanatee2@msn.com 🌐 webbwiz.com/inn/

CAPTIVA ISLAND

Captiva Island Inn	99-700 BB	Full breakfast
11509 Andy Rosse Ln 33924	17 rooms, 17 pb	Lunch & dinner available,
800-454-9898 239-395-0882	Most CC, *Rated*, •	restaurant
Sandra Stilwell	C-yes/S-no/P-no/H-ltd	Bicycles, suites, cable TV,
		beach chairs, accommodate
		business travelers

Stay in the main inn or the surrounding cottages. Some have full kitchens and separate bedrooms. Our new 4-bedroom house is perfect for weddings. Pool and spa with gazebo on site.
✉ captivaislandinn@aol.com 🌐 www.captivaislandinn.com

DAYTONA BEACH

The Coquina Inn B&B	89-235 BB	Full breakfast
544 S Palmetto Ave 32114	4 rooms, 4 pb	Complimentary beverages
800-805-7533 386-254-4969	Most CC	and baked goodies
Steve & Rhonda	C-ltd/S-ltd/P-yes/H-no	Fresh flowers, bikes, cable
		TV, Internet access, guest
		phone, hot tub, off-street
		parking

Located in the beautiful oak-lined Daytona Beach Historic District, this handsome circa 1912 house boasts an exterior of Coquina rock blended from shells. Our personal attention and cozy setting invite you to a relaxing and romantic weekend getaway.
✉ coquinabnb@aol.com ☉ www.coquinainn.com

DELAND

Deland Country Inn	89-150 BB	Full breakfast
228 W Howry Ave 32720	5 rooms, 3 pb	Coffee & tea facilities, fridge,
866-403-8009 386-736-4244	Most CC	snacks
Mark Sutton	C-yes/S-no/P-ltd/H-ltd	We offer a variety of "extras"
		that can be arranged on
		request, cable TV, A/C,
		sitting room

The Deland Country Inn B&B Guest House is situated in downtown Deland, which is just off I-4 on the way to Daytona. Come stay in our traditional, British owned B&B, where you can enjoy a full cooked English style breakfast when you wake up.
✉ info@delandcountryinn.com ☉ www.delandcountryinn.sitesvp.com

FERNANDINA BEACH

The Amelia Island Williams House	175-275 BB	Full gourmet breakfast
103 S 9th St 32034	10 rooms, 10 pb	Baked goods, tea, wine,
800-414-9258 904-277-2328	Most CC, *Rated*, ●	appetizers
Deborah & Byron McCutchen	C-ltd/S-no/P-no/H-yes	Whirlpools, Jacuzzis, hot tub,
		bicycles, verandahs,
		balconies, paddle fans

"Top Inn of the Year," "Most Elegant Inn in U.S." These are just a few of the honors bestowed on The Amelia Island Williams House. Whirlpools, balconies, romance packages, wedding packages, specials.
✉ info@williamshouse.com ☉ www.williamshouse.com

FLAGLER BEACH

Island Cottage Oceanfront Villa Inn, Cafe' and Spa	199-450 BB	Full breakfast
2316 S Oceanshore Blvd 32136	9 rooms, 9 pb	Complimentary sparkling
87-ROMANCE-2 386-439-0092	Visa, MC, Disc, *Rated*, ●	spring water & in-room
Toni & Mark Treworgy		coffee & tea
	C-ltd/S-no/P-no/H-ltd	Heated pool, elegant spa,
	American Sign Language	fine dining restaurant
		Saturday evenings

One of Florida's top Honeymoon, Anniversary, Romantic Getaway and Elopement Destinations. Fireplaces, Jacuzzis for 2, king canopy beds, private decks, patios, heated swimming pool, private beach & ocean. Includes hot gourmet breakfast each morning.
☉ www.islandcottagevillas.com

GAINESVILLE

Magnolia Plantation	120-335 BB	Full breakfast
309 SE 7th St 32601	14 rooms, 14 pb	Complementary snacks &
800-201-2379 352-375-6653	Most CC, ●	beverages throughout day,
Joe & Cindy Montalto	C-yes/S-no/P-ltd/H-no	evening social hour with
		wine & snacks
		Library, sitting room,
		bicycles, 60-foot pond,
		gazebo, wireless Internet

Restored 1885 Victorian in downtown. Two miles from University of Florida. Beautifully landscaped gardens, pond, waterfalls and gazebo. 1, 2 and 3 bedroom cottages available.
✉ info@magnoliabnb.com ☉ www.magnoliabnb.com

GAINESVILLE

Sweetwater Branch Inn	90-245 BB	Full breakfast
625 E University Ave 32601	18 rooms, 18 pb	Wine and Cheese hour,
800-595-7760 352-373-6760	Visa, MC, AmEx, *Rated*	snacks, comp. wine. Dinner
Cornelia Holbrook	C-yes/S-no/P-ltd/H-ltd	available upon request.
	Spanish, Italian	Sitting rooms, airport/univ.
		transport

Enjoy a piece of the past; restored 1880s Victorian home with antiques, Florida gardens. Walk to historic district—fine dining, Hippodrome Theatre. 6 rooms with Jacuzzis. Many rooms with fireplaces.
✉ reserve@sweetwaterinn.com ◐ www.sweetwaterinn.com

GULFPORT

The Peninsula Inn & Spa	100-200 BB	Continental breakfast
2937 Beach Blvd S 33707	11 rooms, 11 pb	Fine dining restaurant, bar,
888-9000-INN 727-346-9800	Most CC, •	spa services on-site
Karen & Bob Chapman	C-yes/S-no/P-ltd/H-yes	Massage, facials, spa
		treatments on-site; pool,
		tennis, golf at nearby club

Elegant historic inn/spa, fine dining, cocktails. Perfect for short getaways, extended stays, business travel, intimate weddings, social/corporate events. Minutes from Tampa & St. Pete airports.
✉ kstjean377@aol.com ◐ www.innspa.net

Sea Breeze Manor B&B Inn	155-180 BB	Full breakfast
5701 Shore Blvd 33707	7 rooms, 7 pb	Beverages, snacks, wine and
888-343-4445 727-343-4445	Most CC, *Rated*	cheese, sherry, port
Lori Rosso	C-ltd/S-no/P-ltd/H-yes	Private balconies, bicycles,
		lounge chairs, beach towels,
		TV/VCR/CD in room

Waterfront B&B in charming artsy community. Private balconies and sitting areas in each suite give you a private resort feel. Park your car and walk to over 30 restaurants and shops on the waterfront. Indulge!
✉ rsvp@seabreezemanor.com ◐ www.seabreezemanor.com

HIGH SPRINGS

Grady House Historic Bed & Breakfast	105-275 BB	Full breakfast
420 NW 1st Avenue 32655	5 rooms, 5 pb	Complimentary beverages,
386-454-2206	Most CC	coffee, tea, soft drinks &
Paul & Lucie Regensdorf	C-ltd/S-no/P-no/H-no	home baked treats
		Wireless Internet and
		computer for guest's use,
		daily maid service, self-
		contained cottage available

Grady House will provide the setting for an idyllic retreat, complete with a perfect night's sleep and a memorable meal. We offer the warm hospitality and special touches to our guests that are too often forgotten in today's fast-paced world.
✉ gradyhouse@gradyhouse.com ◐ gradyhouse.com

HOLLYWOOD BEACH

Hollywood by the Sea B&B	149-279 BB	Great Omelets, Pancakes, &
301 Jackson St 33019	7 rooms, 7 pb	more
954-927-5301	Most CC	Special request with advance
Diana & Mike	C-yes/S-no/P-no/H-yes	notice.
	Spanish	Swimming pool, beach, WiFi,
		beach chairs/towels.
		Computer/fax/phone access,
		free local/USA calls

This unique, tropically elegant, "Vintage Florida" B&B is nestled on a barrier island directly on one of Florida's blue-ribbon, award-winning beaches. Our B&B offers a charming change from hotel chains where you are only a face. Here-you arrive home.
✉ thewesinhollywood@yahoo.com ◐ www.hollywoodbytheseabandb.com

INDIALANTIC

Windemere Inn by the Sea
815 S.Miramar Ave (A1A)
32903
800-224-6853 321-728-9334
Beth Fisher

149-390 BB
9 rooms, 9 pb
Visa, MC, *Rated*
C-ltd/S-no/P-no/H-ltd

Full gourmet breakfast
Afternoon "tea" with home
made pastries, tea and
sherry, guests enjoy a pantry
with drinks & snacks
Concierge services for dining
& recreation, cable TV,
wireless Internet, special
events & weddings

Windemere is a luxury ocean front B&B catering to both leisure & business travelers
Rooms are finely appointed with crisp linens, antiques & contemporary furnishings. Break
fast & "tea" are gourmet. TV available on request, wireless Internet access.
✉ stay@windemereinn.com ◐ www.windemereinn.com

INDIAN ROCKS BEACH

Laughing Lizard B&B
2211 Gulf Blvd 33785
727-595-7006
Bill Ockunzzi

130-170 BB
4 rooms, 4 pb
Visa, MC, Disc
S-no/P-no

Full breakfast
Coffee & snacks anytime.
Afternoon wine tasting at
5:30 p.m.
Hi-speed wireless Internet,
standard business services,
beach towels, chairs and
umbrellas available

This casual, eclectic B & B, 400' from the beach, is a contemporary throwback to Old
Florida's cottage-style architecture. In the quaint island community of Indian Rocks Beach
south of Clearwater Beach in the Tampa Bay area on Florida's West
✉ info@laughinglizardbandb.com ◐ www.laughinglizardbandb.com

INGLIS

Pine Lodge
649 Highway 40 West 34449
352-447-7463
Edwin & Lea Day

96-136 BB
9 rooms, 9 pb
Visa, MC, *Rated*
C-yes/S-ltd/P-ltd

Full country breakfast
People with dietary issues
are always considered
Cottages with kitchenettes,
swimming pool, cable TV

We invite you to come relax in a comfortable, warm & friendly atmosphere here at Pine
Lodge Bed & Breakfast. We offer 4 rooms, with private baths, 5 Cottages in the village
setting of Inglis in old Florida.British owned & operated
✉ pinelodgebb@aol.com ◐ www.pinelodgefla.com

JACKSONVILLE

House on Cherry Street
1844 Cherry St 32205
904-384-1999
Victoria & Robert Freeman

85-165 BB
4 rooms, 4 pb
Visa, MC, AmEx, *Rated*
C-ltd/S-no/P-no/H-no
Oct. 1st – March 30th

Continental Plus breakfast
Afternoon tea
Sitting room, color TV, A/C,
river porch, dock, fax,
organic garden

On the St. Johns River in historic district, a restored Colonial house filled with period
antiques, four poster beds, original art from Florida's finest artists. Have breakfast on the
river dock. Play croquet on the rolling lawn. Walk the labyrinth.
✉ houseoncherry@bellsouth.net ◐ www.houseoncherry.com

The Inn at Oak Street
2114 Oak St 32204
904-379-5525
Bob Eagle

120-180 BB
6 rooms, 6 pb
Most CC, *Rated*, •
C-ltd/S-no/P-no/H-no

Full gourmet breakfast
Evening wine hour, picnic
lunch, spa lunch, private
chef dining experience
Wireless Internet, coffee bar,
laptop area, spa, workout
room, bikes

Luxury 1902 B&B located in the historic Riverside district of Jacksonville. Spacious accom
modations in a luxurious and upscale atmosphere catering to business and leisure travel
ers. Spa services, wireless Internet and a full gourmet breakfast are offered.
✉ innatoakstreet@yahoo.com ◐ www.innatoakstreet.com

JACKSONVILLE

Riverdale Inn	109-189 BB	Full breakfast
1521 Riverside Ave 32204	10 rooms, 10 pb	Full service restaurant on
866-808-3400 904-354-5080	Most CC, •	premises for dinner and
Daniel Waln	C-ltd/S-ltd/P-ltd/H-ltd	special events plus Pub
		(Open Tues – Sat.)
		Pub on premise, free
		wireless high speed Internet,
		free local phone service, free
		on-site parking

The Riverdale Inn is a turn-of-the-century mansion located in the historic Five Points area of Riverside. A fine dining restaurant and full service pub is on the premises. The Inn welcomes special events for up to 50 people.
✉ info@riverdaleinn.com ◐ www.riverdaleinn.com

St. Johns House B&B	95-145 BB	Full breakfast
1718 Osceola St 32204	3 rooms, 3 pb	coffee and tea are provided
904-384-3724	Visa, MC, AmEx	in guestrooms; soft drinks
Joan Moore and Dan Schafer	C-yes/S-no/P-no/H-no	are available downstairs.
	Nov – May, closed March	Each room has a desk,
		reading chair & lighting,
		TV/DVD, iron, hairdryer &
		wireless Internet access

St. Johns House is geared to both business and leisure travelers. Its location is convenient to downtown, the sports complex and convention center. The surrounding historic district offers one of a kind shopping, dining and delightful walking venues.
✉ stjohnshousebb@aol.com ◐ www.stjohnshouse.com/stjohns.htm

JACKSONVILLE BEACH

Pelican Path B&B by the Sea	140-195 BB	Full breakfast
11 N 19th Ave 32250	4 rooms, 4 pb	Beverages placed in guest
888-749-1177 904-249-1177	Visa, MC, Disc, *Rated*,	refrigerator daily: bottled
Tom & Joan Hubbard	•	water, soft drinks, fruit juice
	S-no/P-no/H-no	Sitting room, bikes, cable,
	6 months	Jacuzzis, phones, TV/VCR,
		refrigerators, spa tubs

"Lieu de Loisir (A Place of Leisure)." Pelican Path enjoys a superb location—an oceanfront, residential neighborhood with easy access to beach, stores & restaurants.
✉ info@pelicanpath.com ◐ www.pelicanpath.com

KEY LARGO

Mullet Mansion	200-220 BB	Full breakfast
97920 Overseas Hwy 33037	2 rooms, 1 pb	Snacks, complimentary
305-852-9383	Cash, Checks, •	wine, afternoon tea
Suzy Roebling	C-ltd/S-ltd/P-no/H-ltd	Bicycles, Jacuzzi, suite,
		outdoor fireplace, cable TV,
		swim, paddle boat, wireless
		access

Your own mini-retreat. Gorgeous seaside sunsets and personalized service with any special requests. Our surroundings are private, soothing, and ideal for couples. We specialize in intimate Key Largo Weddings.
✉ mullet_mansion@yahoo.com ◐ www.mulletmansion.com

KEY WEST

Albury Court	119-299 BB	Continental breakfast
1030 Eaton St 33040	21 rooms, 21 pb	Flat LCD TVs, fireplaces,
877-299-9870 305-294-9870	Most CC, *Rated*	waterfall splash pool,
Julie Fondriest	S-ltd/P-no/H-yes	wireless Internet, Jacuzzi

Albury Court is a small compound of 5 historic buildings, in the "Old Town" area of Key West & 2 blocks from the harbor. Tailored for adults looking for a peaceful & romantic setting, in easy reach of Key West's best restaurants, nightlife & waterfront.
✉ albury@historickeywestinns.com
◐ www.historickeywestinns.com/properties/albury/albury_court.htm

KEY WEST ───────────

Andrews Inn & Garden Cottages
223 Eanes Ln 33040
888-263-7393 305-294-7730
Tom & Nancy Coward

140-365 BB
10 rooms, 10 pb
Most CC, *Rated*, •
C-ltd/S-ltd/P-ltd/H-no
Some French

Champagne Continental
Breakfast
Afternoon happy hour
Swimming pool, tropical
gardens, bikes, vaulted
ceilings, private baths, A/C,
Jacuzzis

Stroll down a shady lane off of Duval St., and you will find a lush tropical courtyard with a pool at its center and five charming rooms with private baths awaiting your arrival. We also have 3 cottage suites complete with their own Jacuzzis.
✉ info@andrewsinn.com ◐ www.andrewsinn.com

Atlantis House
1401 Atlantic Blvd 33040
800-615-9214 305-292-1532
Steven & Kayla Kessler

169-275 EP
2 rooms, 2 pb
Visa, MC, AmEx
C-ltd/S-ltd/P-no/H-no
Turkish, some Italian

Fresh lobster or Catch of the
Day Dinner caught by the
Host, Steve.
Hosts may assist in planning
activities, dining, sailing etc.

Atlantis House is an exotic retreat positioned on the Atlantic Ocean in tropical Key West and is the only guesthouse along the beaches. Featuring 2 romantic suites with private in room Jacuzzis, the Atlantis House offers special amenities for guests.
✉ atlanhouse@aol.com ◐ www.atlantishouse.com

Center Court Historic Inn & Cottages
1075 Duval St, C19 33040
800-797-8787 305-296-9292
Naomi Van Steelandt

98-588 EP
63 rooms, 63 pb
Visa, MC, Disc, *Rated*,
•
C-yes/S-ltd/P-yes/H-yes

Great restaurants all around
us!
Full Concierge services
including bikes/mopeds
delivered to your unit, in
room massage, etc.

Comfortable, luxurious, affordable and just steps from Duval Street, we offer lodging in many settings: guesthouses, historic inn rooms, villas, cottages and houses, all offering romantic Key West hideaways with private Jacuzzis, some with private pools.
✉ kwvacrentals@bellsouth.net ◐ www.vacationrentalskeywest.com

Chelsea House Pool & Gardens
709 Truman Ave 33040
800-845-8859 305-296-2211
Julie Fondriest

119-299 BB
33 rooms, 33 pb
Most CC, *Rated*, •
S-ltd/P-yes/H-ltd

Continental plus breakfast
Coffee bar
Ceiling fans, cable TV,
phones, refrigerators, room
safes, bath amenities

Beautifully restored Victorian mansion in the heart of Old Town Key West. Walking distance to everything. 33 unique rooms ranging from cozy to grand all with private bath.
✉ chelsea@historickeywestinns.com
◐ www.historickeywestinns.com/properties/chelsea/chelsea_house.htm

Conch House Heritage Inn
625 Truman Ave 33040
800-207-5806 305-293-0020
Sam Holland

108-248 BB
8 rooms, 8 pb
Most CC, *Rated*, •
C-ltd/S-ltd/P-no/H-yes
Spanish

Continental plus breakfast
Swimming pool, phone, TV,
A/C, parking, bikes,
refrigerators, gardens,
wireless Internet

The Conch House offers charming and romantic accommodations with traditional antique furnishings or tropical poolside cottages. Every luxurious amenity including breakfast and parking.
✉ info@conchhouse.com ◐ www.conchhouse.com

Curry Mansion Inn
511 Caroline St 33040
800-253-3466 305-294-5349
Edith Amsterdam

195-365 BB
28 rooms, 28 pb
Most CC, *Rated*, •
C-yes/S-no/P-ltd/H-yes
French, Spanish,
German, Italian

Full breakfast with omelets
Open bar cocktail party with
snacks and live music
Heated pool, hot tub, beach
pass, Internet access, parking

The Curry Mansion Inn . . . where the elegance of Key West's past is equaled only by the elegance of its presence.
✉ curryinn@aol.com ◐ www.currymansion.com

KEY WEST

Cypress House	179-575 BB	Continental plus breakfast
601 Caroline St 33040	22 rooms, 16 pb	Evening Happy Hour with
800-525-2488 305-294-6969	Most CC, *Rated*, •	self service full bar, snacks,
Dave Taylor	S-ltd/P-no/H-ltd	beer wine and soft drinks
	Spanish	Heated swimming pool, free
		high speed wireless Internet
		access, bicycle rentals on
		property

1888 Bahamian Conch mansion. Private, tropical. Large rooms with A/C, cable TV, phone, free wireless Internet access, refrigerator and ceiling fans. Walk to all historic sites, museums, Historic Seaport, shopping, restaurants and nightlife.
✉ CypressKW@aol.com 🌐 www.CypressHouseKW.com

Duval House	135-390 BB	Continental plus breakfast
815 Duval St 33040	28 rooms, 28 pb	3 suites with kitchenettes
800-223-8825 305-292-9491	Visa, MC, Disc, *Rated*,	Sitting room, sun deck, A/C,
Uwe Domogalla	•	in-room TV, gazebo in
	S-no/P-ltd/H-no	gardens, parking for $11/day
	German	

Duval House is a romantic tropical inn with century-old Victorian houses surrounding a large jungle-like garden and pool. "One of the 10 most affordable, romantic inns in the U.S.," Vacations Magazine.
✉ duvalhs@attglobal.net 🌐 www.duvalhousekeywest.com

Eden House	95-420 EP	Onsite cafe, cold drink at
1015 Fleming St 33040	39 rooms, 35 pb	check-in, restaurant,
800-533-KEYS 305-296-6868	Visa, MC, •	complimentary happy hour
Michael Eden	C-yes/S-ltd/P-no/H-ltd	Swimming pool, spa/hot tub,
		bicycles, family fun, photo
		gallery online, romance,
		suites, hammocks

Eden House in Key West, Florida offers the amenities of a hotel, with the intimacy of an inn or bed and breakfast. Relaxed but attentive in the style of a true Key West Florida guesthouse. Pool, Jacuzzi, lush grounds, a few blocks off Duval Street.
✉ elizabeth@edenhouse.com 🌐 www.edenhouse.com

The Grand Guest House	98-248 BB	Continental plus breakfast
1116 Grinnell St 33040	7 rooms, 7 pb	Full concierge, A/C, cable
888-947-2630 305-294-0590	Visa, MC, Disc, *Rated*	TV, in-room phone,
Jeffrey Daubman & Jim Brown	C-ltd/S-ltd/P-no/H-no	refrigerators, ceiling fans,
	December – May	free parking & WiFi.

Clean, crisp, affordable accommodations in the heart of Old Town Key West. Superior Small Lodging designation, member of the Key West Innkeepers Association, Frommer's Travel Guide "Find."
✉ grandguesthouse@bellsouth.net 🌐 www.GrandKeyWest.com

Heron House	169-399 BB	Continental plus breakfast
512 Simonton St 33040	23 rooms, 23 pb	Breakfast bar; weekend wine
800-294-1644 305-294-9227	Most CC, *Rated*, •	& cheese hour
Jeffrey Brannin	S-ltd/P-no/H-ltd	Orchid gardens, sun deck, in-
		room safes, pool, robes,
		concierge, phones, cable TV

Located in the heart of the historic district, offering all the intimacy and hospitality of a small southern guesthouse. From the moment guests step on the grounds they are surrounded by colorful orchids and lush, tropical plants. AAA 4 Diamond.
✉ heronkyw@aol.com 🌐 www.heronhouse.com

KEY WEST ────────────────────────────────

Island City House Hotel
411 William St 33040
800-634-8230 305-294-5702
Tasha & Gaines Dupree

150-420 BB
24 rooms, 24 pb
Visa, MC, AmEx,
Rated, •
C-yes/S-no/P-no/H-ltd

Continental plus breakfast
Widows Walk sun deck with
view; bikes, swimming pool,
garden

Choose from three unique houses: the Arch House, the Island City House, and the Cigar House, all share lush, tropical gardens with winding, brick pathways throughout.
✉ info@islandcityhouse.com ◐ www.islandcityhouse.com

Key Lime Inn
725 Truman Avenue 33040
800-549-4430 305-294-5229
Julie Fondriest

119-299 BB
37 rooms, 37 pb
Most CC
S-ltd/P-no/H-yes

Continental breakfast
Heated pool, free parking,
wireless Internet

Key Lime Inn is a 37-room historic hotel in the center of Key West's Old Town area—just two blocks from famous Duval Street. You can walk to restaurants and nightlife and enjoy the quaint houses in Key West's historic neighborhoods. ✉ keylime@historickeywestinns.com
◐ www.historickeywestinns.com/properties/keylime/key_lime_inn.htm

The Key West Bed & Breakfast
415 William St 33040
800-438-6155 305-296-7274
Jody Carlson

79-265 BB
8 rooms, 4 pb
Visa, MC, AmEx,
Rated, •
S-ltd/P-ltd/H-no

Continental plus breakfast
Sitting room, spa, library,
bicycles. Within walking
distance to Duval and the
docks.

This lovely 3-story Victorian is located on a quiet, tree-shaded street in the heart of Key West's "Old Town." Walk to the water and the sites and sounds that have made Key West infamous.
✉ relax@keywestbandb.com ◐ www.keywestbandb.com

Key West Harbor Inn
219 Elizabeth St 33040
800-608-6569 305-296-2978
Leonardo Welf

145-375 BB
11 rooms, 11 pb
Most CC, *Rated*, •
S-no/P-no/H-no
Spanish, Italian

Continental plus breakfast
Full open bar at happy hour
Bikes, indoor Jacuzzi, pool,
suites, cable, ceiling fans, CD
players, hairdryers

An elegant yet comfortable three story 1850 Victorian mansion in Old Town Key West. Enclosed gardens encompass the inn, Carriage House and Pool House to create your own private piece of paradise. Our friendly and thoughtful staff is here to help you.
✉ kwharborinn@yahoo.com ◐ www.keywestharborinn.com

Knowles House B&B
1004 Eaton St 33040
800-352-4414 305-296-8132
Les Vollmert & Paul Masse

129-279 BB
8 rooms, 8 pb
Visa, MC, Disc, *Rated*,
•
C-ltd/S-ltd/P-no/H-no

Continental plus breakfast
Complimentary wine
Jacuzzis, swimming pool,
cable TV

The Knowles House B&B is a charming, restored, and elegantly furnished, mid-1800s conch house centrally located in a handsome residential district of Key West.
✉ knowleshse@aol.com ◐ www.knowleshouse.com

La Mer Hotel & Dewey House
504 & 506 South St 33040
800-354-4455 305-296-6577
Carrie & Matthew Babich

169-465 BB
19 rooms, 19 pb
Most CC, *Rated*, •
S-no/P-no/H-yes
French, Spanish

Continental plus breakfast
Afternoon tea, cakes and
fruit
Library, dipping pool, access
to 3 pools, Jacuzzi, beach

Key West's only luxury oceanfront bed and breakfast emanates island elegance against the backdrop of a white sand beach and lush, tropical flora and fauna.
✉ info@southernmostresorts.com ◐ www.lamerhotel.com/la_mer.html

KEY WEST

La Pensione Inn
809 Truman Ave 33040
800-893-1193 305-292-9923
Freda Erwiin

118-368 BB
9 rooms, 9 pb
Most CC, *Rated*
S-no/P-no/H-yes
Spanish

Continental plus breakfast
Swimming pool, A/C, off-
street parking, bike rentals,
non-smoking rooms available

*La Pensione, a grand Classic Revival mansion, dates from Key West's Victorian Age. Sun
lovers enjoy the peaceful seclusion of the inn's sparkling pool and lounge deck. Key West's
legendary Duval Street is just steps away.*
✉ lapensione@aol.com ◐ www.lapensione.com

Lighthouse Court
902 Whitehead St 33040
877-294-9588 305-294-9588
Julie Fondreist

119-229 BB
40 rooms, 40 pb
Most CC
C-ltd/S-no/P-no/H-no

Continental breakfast
Large heated pool, pool bar,
fitness center, wireless
Internet, street parking

*An historic guest inn that is located next door to the Key West Lighthouse Museum and
across the street from the Ernest Hemingway Home and Museum. Just one block off Duval
Street, the location affords instant access to Key West's favorite attractions.*
✉ lighthouse@historickeywestinns.com
◐ www.historickeywestinns.com/properties/lighthouse/lighthouse_court.htm

Merlin Guesthouse
811 Simonton St 33040
800-642-4753 305-296-3336
Julia Fondriest

119-229 BB
20 rooms, 20 pb
Most CC
C-yes/S-no/P-ltd

Continental breakfast
Private courtyard with
splash pool, free wireless
Internet, street parking

*Merlin is a classic Key West guesthouse providing casual lodging at an ideal location. Just
one block from Duval Street, you will be steps away from Key West's best restaurants,
nightlife, shopping, and attractions.* ✉ merlin@historickeywestinns.com
◐ www.historickeywestinns.com/properties/merlin/merlin_guesthouse.htm

**The Mermaid & The
Alligator**
729 Truman Ave 33040
800-773-1894 305-294-1894
Dean Carlson & Paul Hayes

148-318 BB
9 rooms, 9 pb
Visa, MC, AmEx, ●
C-ltd/S-ltd/P-no/H-no

Full breakfast
Complimentary wine served
each evening, afternoon
lemonade, complimentary
bottled water and sodas.
Off-street parking, swimming
pool, tropical gardens, free
concierge services.

*An elegant circa 1904 Queen Anne house located in the center of Key West's Old Town,
offering the warm hospitality of a traditional Bed & Breakfast.*
✉ kwmermaid@aol.com ◐ www.kwmermaid.com

Nassau House
1016 Fleming St 33040
800-296 8513 305-296-8513
Bo & Lety Hall

139-249 BB
6 rooms, 6 pb
Visa, MC, AmEx,
Rated, ●
C-yes/S-ltd/P-no/H-yes
Spanish

Continental breakfast
Complimentary wine and
snacks for social hour
Library, bicycles, Jacuzzis,
suites, cable TV, wireless
Internet

*The Nassau House offers a casual, relaxed atmosphere to enjoy your Florida vacation. Not
your typical Key West Hotel, our rooms are individually decorated each with its own theme.*
✉ reservations@nassauhouse.com ◐ www.nassauhouse.com

Pilot House Guesthouse
414 Simonton St 33040
800-648-3780 305-294-8719
Scott Ferdinand

115-300 EP
14 rooms, 14 pb
Most CC, ●
S-ltd/P-no/H-ltd
December 20 – April 30

Fully equipped kitchens and
kitchenettes
Pool, spa, marble baths,
verandas, gardens, bicycles

*19th-century Victorian Guest House located in the heart of historic Old Town Key West. A
grand two-story mansion beautifully restored with all the comforts and conveniences.
Handicap accessible suites.*
✉ pilotkw@aol.com ◐ www.pilothousekeywest.com

KEY WEST

Simonton Court Inn
320 Simonton St 33040
800-944-2687 305-294-6386
Terry Sullivan

150-520 BB
30 rooms, 30 pb
Most CC
C-ltd/S-no/P-no/H-ltd

Continental plus breakfast
Pool, Jacuzzis, patios, air
conditioning, color cable
TV/VCR

Enter the serene setting of Simonton Court Historic Inn & Cottages, and be greeted b
fragrant tropical flowers blooming beneath gently swaying palms. One of the most beau
ful properties in Key West.
✉ simontoncourt@aol.com 🌐 www.simontoncourt.com

LAKE WALES

Chalet Suzanne Inn
3800 Chalet Suzanne Dr 33859
800-433-6011 863-676-6011
Hinshaw Family

169-229 BB
26 rooms, 26 pb
Most CC, *Rated*, •
C-yes/S-ltd/P-no/H-ltd

Full country breakfast
Serving Brunch 10:00 – 2:00
and Dinner 5:00 – 8:00. Cozy
lounge. Dining room closed
on Mondays.
Complimentary sherry in
room, fresh fruit & flowers;
pool, airstrip; spa services
available.

On National Register of Historic Places, a 26-room oasis for celebrants, travelers an
discriminating diners. Each delightfully different guestroom only steps from our sparklin
pool, museum, ceramic salon, airstrip, soup cannery and restaurant.
✉ info@chaletsuzanne.com 🌐 www.chaletsuzanne.com

LAKE WORTH

The Mango Inn
128 N Lakeside Dr 33460
888-626-4619 561-533-6900
Bill, Debbie Null, Judi Flyn

120-275 BB
10 rooms, 10 pb
Most CC, *Rated*, •
C-ltd/S-ltd/P-no/H-no

Continental/Full breakfast
Complimentary beverages &
sweets
Heated swimming pool,
fireplace, cable TV, VCR,
phone with data port,
hairdryer, iron, & robes.

Located in a quiet & secluded setting surrounded by lush tropical gardens. A heated poo
provides an area for quiet relaxation and refreshment. Our charming coastal hamlet is
stone's throw from golfing, scuba diving, snorkeling, fishing, and much more.
✉ info@mangoinn.com 🌐 www.mangoinn.com

LOXAHATCHEE

Southern Palm B&B
15130 Southern Palm Way
33470
561-790-1413
Cheri Reed

169-259 BB
7 rooms, 7 pb
Visa, MC, AmEx,
Rated, •
C-ltd/S-no/P-no/H-yes

Continental plus breakfast
Library, basketball court,
unique collection of animals,
wireless Internet

Tropical paradise with wildlife nestled on 20 acre wooded estate. Close to Palm Beach Pol
Equestrian Club, the equestrian showgrounds, Amphitheater, golf and Lion Country Safari.
✉ creed8559@aol.com 🌐 www.southernpalmbandb.com

MAITLAND

Thurston House
851 Lake Ave 32751
800-843-2721 407-539-1911
Carole Ballard

190-190 BB
3 rooms, 3 pb
Most CC, *Rated*, •
C-ltd/S-no/P-no/H-no

Continental or full available
Complimentary soda, water,
hot beverages and snacks
always available.
Screened porches, front &
back parlours, lake front,
walking paths

Beautiful 1885 Queen Anne Victorian farm house. Hidden away in a lake front 8 acre
setting, but moments from downtown Orlando, and Winter Park. Come experience the "ol
Florida." Suitable for business travel, with complimentary wireless Internet.
✉ thurstonbb@aol.com 🌐 www.thurstonhouse.com

MELBOURNE—————————————————————————————

Crane Creek Inn Waterfront B&B 907 E Melbourne Ave 32901 321-768-6416 Bob Shearer	100-199 BB 5 rooms, 5 pb Most CC, *Rated*, • S-ltd/P-yes/H-no	Full breakfast Complimentary teas, soft drinks, snacks, and water, cakes are also available Jacuzzis, swimming pool, suites, cable, hammock, hot tub

Enjoy our tropical paradise directly on the water. Built in 1925 with hardwood floors and a true "cracker style" architecture. Walk to downtown and fabulous restaurants and shops. Fish from our dock. Wireless Internet included.
✉ info@cranecreekinn.com 🌐 www.cranecreekinn.com

The Old Pineapple Inn 1736 Pineapple Ave 32935 888-776-9864 321-254-1347 Robert & Celeste Henry	110-175 BB 3 rooms, 3 pb Most CC C-ltd/S-no/P-no/H-ltd	Full breakfast Beverage fridge, snacks Porch, parlor, fireplace, antiques, high speed wireless Internet, pool

Nestled under live oak trees dripping with Spanish moss, The Old Pineapple Inn B&B is housed in the William H. Gleason House, listed on the National Register of Historic Places. Charm, comfort and companion-ability await you . . .
✉ innkeepers@oldpineappleinn.com 🌐 www.oldpineappleinn.com

MELBOURNE BEACH——————————————————————

Port d'Hiver 201 Ocean Ave 32951 866-621-7678 321-722-2727 Linda & Mike Rydson	200-525 BB 11 rooms, 11 pb Most CC C-ltd/S-no/P-no/H-yes	Full breakfast Afternoon light snack and beverage Full Concierge, AC, cable TV, high speed Internet, irons, hair dryer, makeup mirror, robes, pool

Welcome to Port d'Hiver (say port-DEE-vair), a luxury seaside B & B, located 200 feet from the Atlantic Ocean in Melbourne Beach, Florida. Our historic inn consists of 4 Key West-style buildings, connected by winding brick paths.
✉ info@portdhiver.com 🌐 portdhiver.com

MIAMI BEACH——————————————————————————

SoBeYou B&B 1018 Jefferson Ave. 33139 877-599-5247 305-534-5247 Susan Culligan	135-355 BB 10 rooms, 8 pb Visa, MC, AmEx, • C-yes/S-no/P-yes/H-yes Spanish	Full breakfast Free parking, cable LCD TV/DVD, pet friendly, pool panoramas, tropical garden views, library, WiFi

In the heart of South Beach lies a peaceful, private, intimate oasis with 10 luxurious, newly renovated poolside rooms. Beautiful sunny beaches, gyms, golf, tennis, stylish shops & exciting outdoor cafes & restaurants are all within walking distance.
✉ info@sobeyou.us 🌐 www.sobeyou.us

MOUNT DORA——————————————————————————

Captains' Inn 1507 N. Donnelly St. 32757 352-383-0650 Tamara Spieler	145-160 BB 4 rooms, 4 pb Visa, MC, Disc, *Rated*, • C-yes/S-ltd/P-yes/H-yes	Full breakfast Lunch & dinner available upon request by culinary chef Tamara Spieler bicycles, pool, billiards, horseshoes, croquet

The Captains' Inn bed & breakfast welcomes you home to an elegantly appointed stateroom that beckons you to relax. Your stateroom comes with all the extras, including cable television, DVD and wireless Internet.
✉ tnbcaptains@aol.com 🌐 captainsinnmountdora.com

MOUNT DORA————————————————————————————

Magnolia Inn	159-260 BB	Gourmet
347 E Third Ave 32757	6 rooms, 6 pb	Sodas, spring water, snacks,
800-776-2112 352-735-3800	Visa, MC, *Rated*, •	baked from scratch
Drew & Nice' Schultz	S-ltd/P-no/H-ltd	chocolate chip cookies &
	Jan – Dec	Scandinavian Almond Cake
		Gazebo with games, TV,
		stereo, Jacuzzi hot tub, patio
		hammock, swing, WiFi

A circa 1926 Mediterranean Estate. Six comfortable rooms with king/queen beds, TV/CD,
private baths, central A/C, full gourmet breakfast. Park and walk to town, enjoy peace and
tranquility at the Magnolia Inn and its one acre of tropical gardens.
✉ info@magnoliainn.net 🌐 www.Magnoliainn.net

NEW SMYRNA BEACH————————————————————————

Night Swan Intracoastal	110-200 BB	Full breakfast
B&B	15 rooms, 15 pb	Frozen yogurt
512 S Riverside Dr 32168	Most CC, *Rated*, •	Sitting Room, 4 suites,
800-465-4261 386-423-4940	C-yes/S-no/P-no/H-yes	playground nearby, 160 foot,
Chuck & Martha Nighswonger		2-story dock on the
		Intracoastal Waterway

Located in the Historic District on the Intracoastal Waterway, between Daytona Beach and
Kennedy Space Center; just one mile from the beach. Spacious 3-story home; full breakfast.
✉ info@NightSwan.com 🌐 www.NightSwan.com

OCALA————————————————————————————————

Heritage Country Inn	69-199 BB	Full breakfast
14343 W Hwy 40 34481	7 rooms, 7 pb	Candle light Steak Dinner
888-240-2233 352-489-0023	Most CC, *Rated*, •	cooked on a Stone, Classic or
Christa & Gerhard Gross	C-yes/S-ltd/P-no/H-yes	Shrimp Fondue
	German	Dining room, courtyard,
		gazebo, gas grill, sitting area,
		Jacuzzi tubs, satellite TV,
		fireplaces, DVD

Located in Ocala, the heart of central Florida's horse country, this delightful B&B is your
own private hideaway. Relax in the comfort and charm of one of our seven casually
elegant rooms, and enjoy the warmth and convenience of the Heritage Country Inn.
✉ info@heritagecountryinn.com 🌐 www.heritagecountryinn.com

ORANGE PARK—————————————————————————————

Club Continental Suites	95-200 BB	Continental plus breakfast
2143 Astor St 32073	22 rooms, 22 pb	Lunch & dinner (Tues – Fri)
800-877-6070 904-264-6070	Most CC, *Rated*, •	Sunday Brunch, bar,
Karrie Massee	C-yes/S-no/P-ltd/H-yes	restaurant, 7 tennis courts, 3
		pools

This romantic, intimate resort nestled on the banks of St Johns River features a Mediterra-
nean style mansion surrounded by Live Oaks draped in Spanish moss, manicured gardens
and gurgling fountains. Old World Florida still exists at the Club Continental.
✉ ccsinfo@bellsouth.net 🌐 www.clubcontinental.com

PENSACOLA————————————————————————————————

Springhill Guesthouse	115 BB	Continental breakfast
903 N Spring St 32501	3 rooms, 3 pb	Internet connection in each
800-475-1956 850-438-6887	Visa, MC, Disc, *Rated*,	suite, cable TV/VCR, laundry
Tara Smith	•	facilities, books, games and
	C-yes/S-no/P-no/H-no	videos.

Charming and comfortable, this Queen Anne style home in Historic North Hill is the place
to come home to. Conveniently located near downtown Pensacola and 10 minutes to the
beaches.
✉ springhillguest@att.net 🌐 www.springhillguesthouse.com

QUINCY

Allison House Inn
45 N Madison St 32351
888-904-2511 850-875-2511
Stuart & Eileen Johnson

80-155 BB
6 rooms, 6 pb
Visa, MC, Disc, *Rated*,
●
C-yes/S-no/P-ltd/H-yes

Continental plus breakfast
Full breakfast on weekends,
biscotti, sherry reception in
the afternoon
Bicycles, wireless Internet,
robes, hair dryers

In the heart of the historic district of Quincy, Florida. Filled with antiques from the British Isles, the Inn is mindful of an English country manor. Close to Tallahassee, beaches, taverns and more. An award winning Inn.
✉ innkeeper@tds.net 🌐 www.allisonhouseinn.com

McFarlin House
305 E King St 32351
877-370-4701 850-875-2526
Richard & Tina Fauble

90-200 BB
9 rooms, 9 pb
Rated
C-yes/S-no/P-no/H-ltd

Full breakfast
Snacks, dinner upon
request/notice
Sitting room, Jacuzzis,
fireplaces, cable TV,
corporate rates

Tobacco farmer John McFarlin built this Queen Anne Victorian, notable for its left-handed turret and grand wraparound porch, in 1895. Listed in the National Register.
✉ inquires@mcfarlinhouse.com 🌐 www.mcfarlinhouse.com

RUSKIN

Southern Comfort B&B Resort
2409 W Ravine Dr 33570
813-645-6361
Joe & Cathy Green

75-195 BB
6 rooms, 4 pb
Visa, MC
C-yes/S-no/P-yes/H-ltd

Full breakfast
Wireless Internet, weddings,
patio, pool, fireplace,
exercise room, hot tub,
tennis court

Welcome to our charming Southern Comfort Bed and Breakfast, located near Tampa and Sun City Center, FL. Our B&B is nestled between the Little Manatee River and Old Tampa Bay. Beautiful decor, gourmet breakfast, immaculate housekeeping and privacy.
✉ jgairplane@aol.com 🌐 www.southerncomfortbedandbreakfast.com

SANTA ROSA BEACH

Hibiscus Coffee & Guest House
85 Defuniak St 32459
850-231-2733
Cheri Peebles

140-300 BB
12 rooms, 12 pb
Visa, MC, AmEx
C-yes/S-ltd/P-ltd/H-yes

Full breakfast
Restaurant, sitting room,
library, bicycles, Jacuzzis,
suites, cable TV

Nestled among the trees, surrounded by herb & flower gardens, we are an old fashioned, romantic getaway, just up the street from the finest beaches in America.
✉ cheri@hibiscusflorida.com 🌐 www.hibiscusflorida.com

SARASOTA

Cypress – A B&B Inn
621 Gulfstream Ave. S 34236
941-955-4683
Vicki, Nina, & Robert

150-279 BB
5 rooms, 5 pb
Most CC
S-no/P-no/H-no

Full breakfast
Evening hors d'oeuvres &
inspired refreshments
served at sunset on Sarasota
Bay
Wireless Internet
connection, concierge
services, walking distance to
downtown & marina

Situated on historic grounds overlooking Sarasota Bay, The Cypress offers a unique lodging experience. This tropical oasis reflects the tone and demeanor of a bygone era, attracting the distant traveler, as well as those seeking a romantic getaway.
✉ thecypress@comcast.net

SARASOTA—————————————————————

La Palme Royale, A B&B Inn
624 South Palm Ave 34236
866-800-3921 941-284-8890
Timothy & Kristen Beury

150-285 BB
4 rooms, 4 pb
Visa, MC
C-yes/S-ltd/P-yes/H-no

Gourmet Continental
Friday afternoon cocktail
hour
All guestrooms have phones,
queen size bed, luxurious
linens, central A/C, Direct
TV, WiFi

*Situated in the luxurious downtown bay front district of Sarasota rests this 1924 historically
designated two-story Craftsman style home. Over looking the tranquil waters of Sarasota
Bay where your troubles are swept away.*
✉ reservations@lprsrq.com 🌐 www.lprsrq.com

SIESTA KEY—————————————————————

Turtle Beach Resort
9049 Midnight Pass Rd 34242
941-349-4554
Gail & David Rubinfeld

230-430 EP
20 rooms, 20 pb
Most CC
C-yes/S-no/P-yes/H-ltd

Discounted package at
Ophelia's Restaurant
Hot tubs in each room, comp
kayaks, bikes, boats, fishing
poles, etc., high speed
wireless Internet

*In 1991, we found a bay front property with cottages dating from the 1940s and transformed
it into an island paradise. With our private cottages, private hot tubs, and gourmet water
front dining next door, you'll have a vacation to remember forever!*
✉ info@turtlebeachresort.net 🌐 www.turtlebeachresort.com

ST. AUGUSTINE—————————————————————

44 Spanish Street
44 Spanish St 32084
800-521-0722 904-826-0650
Linda Larsen

115-219 BB
8 rooms, 8 pb
Most CC
C-yes/S-no/P-ltd/H-ltd

Full breakfast
Jacuzzi tubs, front and rear
2nd floor terraces, courtyard
dining room,

*44 Spanish Street allows you to relax at your own pace, or enjoy the privacy of your own
space, in our vintage brick courtyard or front and rear terraces on the 2nd floor. Steps
away are cafes, restaurants, shops, galleries, and historic sites.*
✉ 44spanishstreet@bellsouth.net 🌐 www.44spanishstreet.com

63 Orange St B&B
63 Orange St 32084
800-605-2063 904-824-6621
Jackie Kent

130-220 BB
5 rooms, 5 pb
Visa, MC, AmEx
C-yes/S-no/P-no/H-no

Full breakfast
Afternoon refreshments on
weekends. The Cookie jar is
always full.
We are always happy to
assist guests with
information about St.
Augustine

*Set among grand trees, in a quiet residential neighborhood, this grand 1884 home invites
you to enjoy a comfortable combination of charming, elegant Victorian antiques & 21st
century amenities.*
✉ jackie@63orangestreet.com 🌐 www.63orangestreet.com

Alexander Homestead B&B
14 Sevilla St 32084
888-292-4147 904-826-4147
Bonnie Alexander

169-229 BB
5 rooms, 5 pb
Most CC, *Rated*, •
C-ltd/S-ltd/P-no/H-no

Full breakfast
After dinner cordials and
complimentary sodas, beer
& wine available
Sitting room, Jacuzzis,
fireplaces, cable TV, luxury
linens, bath amenities, etc.

*1888 Victorian home restored to exquisite perfection. Five oversized Victorian bedchambers recreate the era when the passionate and the proper, the sensual and the sentimental,
the secret and the sensational, combined beautifully in everyday living.*
✉ bonnie@alexanderhomestead.com 🌐 www.alexanderhomestead.com

T. AUGUSTINE

t Journey's End	115-245 BB	Full breakfast
) Cedar St 32084	5 rooms, 5 pb	Complimentary afternoon
88-806-2351 904-829-0076	Most CC, •	snacks and beverages 24/7
>hn & Ellen Cook	C-yes/S-ltd/P-ltd/H-ltd	including beer, wine and
		soda.
		Paddle fans, wireless
		Internet, porches, side
		garden, common area, dining
		room, many extras offered.

ot your typical Victorian themed B&B. Journey to exotic destinations in rooms called
afari, Egypt, China, Key West . . . Built in 1890, the Inn was "reincarnated" in 1996, but still
as its original bones: hardwood floors, porches and more.
✉ contact@atjourneysend.com ◷ www.atjourneysend.com

ayfront Westcott House	119-279 BB	Full breakfast
16 Avenida Menendez 32084	15 rooms, 15 pb	Complimentary beer & wine
00-513-9814 904-824-4301	Most CC, *Rated*, •	happy hour and evening
yndsay, Janice & Robert	C-ltd/S-ltd/P-ltd/H-yes	dessert
>raubard	Hungarian, Russian,	Sitting room, games, library,
	Portuguese, German	bicycles

ayfront Westcott House, elegant, romantic, historic district inn, walking distance to attrac-
ons. Relax on porches, views of sailboats and dolphins, lighthouse. Weddings, reunions,
irls getaways, business retreat. Voted #1 bed and breakfast St. Augustine.
✉ info@westcotthouse.com ◷ www.westcotthouse.com

8eachfront B&B	129-289 BB	Full breakfast
)ne F St 32080	8 rooms, 8 pb	Cookies, coffee & teas
00-370-6036 904-461-8727	Most CC, *Rated*, •	Heated pool, outdoor Jacuzzi
_auren & Rich O'Brien	S-no/P-no/H-no	in gazebo, bicycles, robes,
		beach towels, beach
		furniture

)ceanfront on beautiful St. Augustine Beach and conveniently 10 minutes to the Historic
rea. Enjoy spectacular sunrises and stunning ocean views. Our guestrooms and suites,
ach unique, feature ocean views, dune views or garden views.
✉ info@beachfrontbandb.com ◷ www.beachfrontbandb.com

>arriage Way	119-269 BB	Full breakfast
0 Cuna St 32084	11 rooms, 11 pb	Complimentary wine,
00-908-9832 904-829-2467	Most CC, •	beverages & cookies, picnics
3ill Johnson & sons, Larry &	C-ltd/S-no/P-no/H-no	are available
ohn		Off-street parking, bicycles,
		romantic cottage closeby,
		WiFi, clawfoot tubs, antiques,
		common room

>arriage Way Bed & Breakfast is a traditional Victorian constructed between 1883 and
885 by Edward and Rosalie Masters. In the heart of the historic district and filled with
ntiques and reproductions, it boasts a casual and friendly atmosphere.
✉ bjohnson@carriageway.com ◷ www.Carriageway.com

>asablanca Inn on the Bay	129-349 BB	Full Two-Course Breakfast
4 Avenida Menendez 32084	23 rooms, 23 pb	A complimentary glass of
00-826-2626 904-829-0928	Most CC	house wine or beer at our
Vancy Cloud	C-ltd/S-ltd/P-ltd/H-ltd	Tini Martini Bar.
		Antiques, TV/DVD, Jacuzzi
		tubs, wireless Internet
		access, private sitting areas,
		sleep number beds

Twenty-three luxury suites and rooms in a bayfront location in historic St. Augustine,
>anoramic Matanzas Bay views, whirlpools, private porches and sundecks, antique fur-
1ishings, decorative fireplaces, private entries, and peaceful luxury.
✉ innkeeper@casablancainn.com ◷ www.casablancainn.com

ST. AUGUSTINE

Castle Garden
15 Shenandoah St 32084
904-829-3839
Bruce & Brian Kloeckner

89-229 BB
7 rooms, 7 pb
Most CC, *Rated*, •
C-ltd/S-no/P-ltd/H-no

Full breakfast
Complimentary bottle of
wine or champagne in
whirlpool rooms; picnic
lunches
Bicycles, fresh flowers, 3
bridal rooms with whirlpool

*St. Augustine's only Moorish Revival dwelling. Former Castle Warden Carriage House bui
in the 1800's. Restored gardens.*
✉ info@castlegarden.com ◐ www.castlegarden.com

Centennial House
26 Cordova St 32084
800-611-2880 904-810-2218
Lou & Beverlee Stines

139-260 BB
8 rooms, 8 pb
Visa, MC, *Rated*, •
C-ltd/S-ltd/P-no/H-yes
Summer and Winter

Full Elegant Breakfast
Early morning coffee/tea
Over-sized whirlpools,
fireplaces in larger rooms,
luxury baths

*Luxury in the Historic District. Featuring private, spacious baths, over-sized whirlpools, ga
fireplaces, cable TV/VCR, sound insulation, and individual room climate control. On th
horse-drawn carriage route.*
✉ innkeeper@centennialhouse.com ◐ www.centennialhouse.com

Inn on Charlotte Street
52 Charlotte St 32084
800-355-5508 904-829-3819
Lynne Fairfield

129-289 BB
8 rooms, 8 pb
Most CC
S-no/P-no/H-no

Full breakfast
Well-stocked guest
refrigerator
Cable TV, whirlpool tubs,
parlor, business services,
weddings

*The ideal location for discovering the city's wonderful restaurants, shops, and attractions
our Saint Augustine B&B puts the Florida city's 500 years of history right outside your doo.*
✉ innkeeper@innoncharlotte.com ◐ www.innoncharlotte.com

The Kenwood Inn
38 Marine St 32084
800-824-8151 904-824-2116
Pat & Ted Dobosz

105-250 BB
14 rooms, 14 pb
Visa, MC, Disc, *Rated*
C-ltd/S-no/P-no/H-no

Continental plus breakfast
Daily wine hour from 5pm-
7pm, complimentary coffee,
tea, lemonade, iced tea and
cookies all day
Several sitting rooms,
swimming pool, walled-in
courtyard, bicycles, wireless
Internet, free parking

*The Kenwood Inn is a traditional, old fashioned bed and breakfast inn located in the hear
of the historic district near the waterfront. Many amenities included such as a swimmin,
pool and secluded courtyard. Daily wine hour. Beverages and cookies.*
✉ info@thekenwoodinn.com ◐ www.thekenwoodinn.com

**Old City House Inn &
Restaurant**
115 Cordova St 32084
904-826-0113
James & Ilse Philcox

90-250 BB
7 rooms, 7 pb
Most CC, *Rated*
C-ltd/S-ltd/P-ltd/H-ltd
Spanish, Dutch, Czech,
Polish (limited)

Full breakfast
Complimentary wine &
cheese, award winning
restaurant on premises open
for snacks, lunch & dinner
Jacuzzis, decks, private
entrances & baths, cable TV,
WiFi, phones, softdrinks,
parking & bicycles

*The award winning Old City House Inn and Restaurant is located in the heart of St
Augustine's historic district. Step into the 1873 Old City House Inn and Restaurant & you
will be swept away by its historic relevance & distinctive legacy to St. Augustine*
✉ relax@oldcityhouse.com ◐ www.oldcityhouse.com

ST. AUGUSTINE
Our House of St. Augustine Cincinnati Ave 32084 904-347-6260 Dave Brezing	159-220 BB 5 rooms, 5 pb Most CC C-ltd/S-no/P-no/H-ltd Some French Oct. 1 to May 31	Full breakfast Complimentary bottled spring water is always available Free on-site parking and wireless Internet access, private baths & verandas, courtyard, kitchenettes

Make Our House your house for a weekend getaway, romantic retreat or cozy stay in the nation's oldest city. Three guestrooms have private baths, verandas and full breakfast in the dining room. Two Studios include in-room full breakfast & kitchenettes.
✉ ourhouse@ourhouseofstaugustine.com ◐ www.ourhouseofstaugustine.com

Southern Wind Inn 18 Cordova St 32084 800-781-3338 904-825-3623 Scott & Donna Forbes	99-239 BB 10 rooms, 10 pb Most CC, *Rated*, • C-ltd/S-no/P-no/H-no	Full breakfast Afternoon dessert, complimentary wine, iced tea Spacious verandas, large parlor, wraparound porch, cable TV & bicycles.

On the Carriage Trail through the historic district of St. Augustine, the Southern Wind Inn is an elegantly-columned 1916 masonry home offering exceptional B&B hospitality and a full breakfast each morning.
✉ innkeeper@southernwindinn.com ◐ www.southernwindinn.com

St. Francis Inn 279 St George St 32084 800-824-6062 904-824-6068 Joe & Margaret Finnegan	129-279 BB 17 rooms, 17 pb Most CC, *Rated*, • C-ltd/S-ltd/P-ltd/H-no American Sign Language	Full Southern Breakfast Iced tea, homemade cookies, coffee, social hour with complimentary wine & beer, evening desserts. Free on-site parking, swimming pool, bicycles, WiFi, DVD library, beach parking and amenities.

Antique filled rooms and suites, balconies, fireplaces, kitchenettes, whirlpool tubs, swimming pool, walk to everything, walled courtyard, parking. Built in 1791 and located in the Historic District, the inn is rich in old world charm and modern comforts.
✉ info@stfrancisinn.com ◐ www.stfrancisinn.com

Victorian House B&B 11 Cadiz St 32084 877-703-0432 904-824-5214 Marc & Jackie Rude	119-259 BB 10 rooms, 10 pb Most CC, *Rated*, • C-ltd/S-no/P-no/H-no	Full breakfast Wine, cordials, complimentary soda, tea, cookies & candies WiFi, Jacuzzi tubs, suites, cable TV, hairdryers, ceiling fans, sitting room

Our charming rooms have been lovingly restored and furnished in period antiques. The Victorian House, built in 1897, is located in the heart of the Historic District on the oldest Street in the U.S.
✉ victorianhouse@bellsouth.net ◐ www.victorianhousebnb.com

ST. AUGUSTINE BEACH
House of Sea and Sun B&B 2 B St 32080 904-461-1716 Patty Steder	139-225 BB 6 rooms, 6 pb Most CC C-ltd/S-no/P-no/H-ltd	Full breakfast Social Hour Beach equipment, private porches, patios, works of art, beautiful decor, wedding services, romance

Our goal at the House of Sea and Sun Oceanfront Bed and Breakfast on St. Augustine Beach is to make your stay as wonderful as possible. You may arrive as a stranger, but you'll leave as a friend.
✉ info@houseofseaandsun.com ◐ www.houseofseaandsun.com

ST. PETE BEACH

Inn on the Beach
1401 Gulf Way 33706
727-360-8844
Sheila McChesney

105-395 BB
17 rooms, 17 pb
S-ltd/P-no

Cont. Breakfast weekends
only
Coffee service daily
Full climate control, fully
equipped kitchens,
expanded cable TV, WiFi

You'll be right at home in our small, casually elegant Inn with twelve select rooms designed for your comfort and enjoyment. Feel your cares slipping away with the simple pleasures our beachfront location offers.
✉ info@innonbeach.com 🌐 www.innonbeach.com

ST. PETERSBURG

Beach Drive Inn B&B
532 Beach Dr NE 33701
727-822-2244
Roland Martino

149-275 BB
6 rooms, 6 pb
Most CC, •
C-ltd/S-ltd/P-ltd/H-no
Hebrew

Full breakfast
Wine & cheese welcome
nights, guest pantry and
vending area.
Mini-fridges, robes, rooftop
sun deck & garden, guest
terrace, free WiFi, and
bicycle

The "stay dreams are made of." Elegant B&B close to everything in downtown St. Petersburg. Our beautifully appointed rooms will take you away to a time when life seemed so much easier and most definitely more comfortable.
✉ info@beachdriveinn.com 🌐 www.beachdriveinn.com

Dickens House
335 8th Ave NE 33701
800-381-2022 727-822-8622
Ed Caldwell

109-235 BB
5 rooms, 5 pb
Visa, MC, AmEx
C-ltd/S-no/P-no/H-no

Full breakfast
Whirlpool tubs, TV, VCR,
refrigerators, laundry
service, WiFi, hair dryers,
irons & boards in room

Located in a National Historic District, this historic, award winning B&B in St. Petersburg offers craftsman bungalow style accommodations for modern business, vacation, and romance travelers. You'll love the exceptional breakfast cooked by owner/artist!
✉ info@dickenshouse.com 🌐 www.dickenshouse.com

Inn at the Bay B&B
126 4th Ave NE 33701
888-873-2122 727-822-1700
Dennis & Jewly Youschak

155-290 BB
11 rooms, 11 pb
Most CC, *Rated*, •
C-ltd/S-no/P-no/H-yes

Full gourmet breakfast
Complimentary drinks,
cookies, wine & cheese –
Friday & Saturday
Featherbeds, double
whirlpool tubs, phones &
high speed Internet in rooms

B&B restored in 2001, king and queen allergy-free featherbeds, private baths, double whirlpool tubs, in-room phones and high speed Internet, robes, hot, full breakfast, romance, vacation and business.
✉ info@innatthebay.com 🌐 www.innatthebay.com

La Veranda
111 5th Ave N 33701
800-484-8423x8417 727-824-9997
Nancy Mayer

89-250 BB
5 rooms, 5 pb
Most CC, *Rated*, •
C-yes/S-ltd/P-yes/H-ltd
German

Full breakfast
Bicycles, beach
chairs/towels, business
services, Internet access,
massages, library, VCR/cable
TV

Elegant restored 1910 mansion with multi-room suites all opening directly on to large verandas. Canopy beds, antiques, Oriental rugs & art fill our rooms with ambience & comfort.
✉ info@laverandabb.com 🌐 www.LaVerandabb.com

ST. PETERSBURG

Larelle House B&B
237 6th Ave NE 33701
888-439-8387 727-490-3575
Lawrence & Ellen Nist

139-209 BB
4 rooms, 4 pb
Visa, MC, Disc
C-ltd/S-no/P-ltd/H-no

Full breakfast
Evening wine & cheese in
the parlor, soft drinks and
homemade goodies available
in the dining room
Wireless Internet, nightly
turndown, garden spa,
complimentary bikes,
business services

The oldest Queen Anne Victorian home on Florida's west coast. A perfect location—nestled in the serenity of the historic Old Northeast residential district—yet less than two blocks away from the always happening St. Petersburg waterfront and downtown.
✉ info@larellehouse.com ○ www.larellehouse.com

Mansion House B&B and Spa
105 & 115 Fifth Ave NE 33701
800-274-7520 727-821-9391
Kathy & Peter Plautz

129-260 BB
12 rooms, 12 pb
Most CC, *Rated*, •
C-ltd/S-ltd/P-no/H-ltd
Oct-May; June-Sept

Full American breakfast
Complimentary soda, wine,
or water. Also, cookies,
muffins or seasonal treats
Swimming pool, Jacuzzi,
WiFi, 2 libraries, gardens,
free local calls, great robes,
off st. parking

12 luxury rooms, all private bathrooms, On-site spa Services available, waterfront/beach nearby, cable, pool, Jacuzzi tub, 10 common areas, courtyard garden, meeting/conf, phones/data ports, WiFi, robes, ceiling fans, weddings/receptions; reunions.
✉ mansion1@ix.netcom.com ○ www.mansionbandb.com

STARKE

Hampton Lake B&B
Hwy 301, 7 mi south of Starke
32091
800-480-4522 352-468-2703
Freeman & Paula Register

99-159 BB
6 rooms, 6 pb
Most CC, *Rated*, •
C-ltd/S-ltd/P-no/H-no

Full breakfast
Snacks, complimentary wine
Sitting room, bicycles, hot
tub, lake, fishing, boating,
porch, fireplace

Contemporary lakefront home on a cypress lake. Fish, swim, take a leisurely stroll through the open fields or enjoy a bike ride down country lanes. Relax and watch the sun set across the lake from the back porch.
✉ HamptonLBB@aol.com ○ www.hamptonlakebb.com

STUART

Inn on California B&B
405 SW California Ave 34994
772-781-2350
Ruth & Drew Campbell

100-150 BB
2 rooms, 2 pb
Visa, MC
C-yes/S-ltd/P-no/H-no

Continental plus breakfast
Guest refrigerator
Air conditioned, TV/DVD,
fax/copier, private entrance,
wake-up service, library,
massage available

A charming little Bed & Breakfast, located in the heart of historic downtown Stuart. Relax and reflect on your day! As you enter the front door, the friendly atmosphere is evident. You feel the warmth, as if it were to say "Welcome Home."
○ www.innoncalifornia.com

Inn Shepard's Park
601 SW Ocean Blvd 34994
772-781-4244
Marilyn Miller

95-200 BB
4 rooms, 2 pb
Most CC
C-ltd/S-ltd/P-ltd/H-no

Continental plus breakfast
Complimentary bottled
waters, sodas, and snacks
Beach gear, bicycles, and a
kayak for complimentary
use, concierge services
available

Key West-style B&B in the heart of historic downtown Stuart. Shops, restaurants and entertainment are within walking distance; championship golf and fishing are only a short drive away.
✉ marilyn@innshepard.com ○ www.innshepard.com

STUART

Manatee Pocket Inn
4931 SE Anchor Ave. 34997
772-286-6060
Greg & Candy Grudovich

90-130 BB
5 rooms, 5 pb
Most CC
C-ltd/S-ltd/P-no/H-yes

Full breakfast
Complimentary beverages
available all day
Sun deck, television, hi-
speed Internet, refrigerator,
microwave.

The Manatee Pocket Inn is located in the historic fishing village of Port Salerno, Martin County, Florida. The inn offers 5 guestrooms, each uniquely decorated, and all with private baths.
manateepocketinn@comcast.net www.manateepocketinn.com

VENICE

Banyan House B&B
519 S Harbor Dr 34285
941-484-1385
Chuck & Susan McCormick

139-189 BB
10 rooms, 10 pb
Visa, MC, *Rated*
C-ltd/S-no/P-no
Closed in December

Full breakfast
Sitting room, Jacuzzi,
bicycles, heated pool,
exercise room, pool table,
wireless Internet, gas grill

Historic Mediterranean-style home. Enormous Banyan tree shades courtyard, pool and spa. Sandy beaches nearby for sunning, swimming, fishing and shelling (prehistoric shark's teeth abound).
relax@banyanhouse.com www.banyanhouse.com

Horse & Chaise Inn
317 Ponce de Leon 34285
877-803-3515 941-488-2702
Lois Steketee

115-169 BB
9 rooms, 9 pb
Visa, MC, *Rated*
S-no/P-yes/H-yes
Oct 1 – July 4

Full breakfast
Snacks
Bicycles, beach chairs,
beach towels, fireplace

Come feel welcome in our 1926 home, an elegant depiction of historic Venice. Enjoy your stay in the Venice of yester-year.
innkeeper@horseandchaiseinn.com www.horseandchaiseinn.com

WEIRSDALE

Shamrock Thistle & Crown
12971 SE County Rd 42 32195
800-425-2763 352-821-1887
Brantley & Anne Overcash

95-220 BB
7 rooms, 7 pb
Most CC, *Rated*, •
C-ltd/S-ltd/P-no/H-ltd

Full breakfast
Complimentary Klondike
Bars, cookies, sodas, juice,
coffee, tea, hot chocolate,
apple cider
Whirlpool spas, fireplaces,
heated pool, porches, cable
TV, wireless Internet, coffee
makers

Where romance comes alive. Located in the rolling countryside 20 miles south of Ocala, the original structure, dating to 1887, is a historic landmark. Relax on one of the covered porches or enjoy a spectacular view from this hilltop setting.
shamrockbb@comcast.net www.shamrockbb.com

WEST PALM BEACH

Casa De Rosa
520 27th St 33407
888-665-8666 561-833-1920
Elaine & Frank Calendrillo

135-240 BB
4 rooms, 4 pb
Most CC, *Rated*, •
C-ltd/S-no/P-no/H-no
November1 thru April 31

Full Gourmet Breakfast
Afternoon snacks, wine, soft
drinks
Swimming pool, cable TV,
sitting room

Italy comes to Florida. An oasis in West Palm Beach. Wonderful gardens & pool area. 3 course gourmet breakfast is served daily in our dining room using the finest china. Totally Palm Beach.
elaine@casaderosa.com www.casaderosa.com

WEST PALM BEACH————————————————————————————

Grandview Gardens B&B
1608 Lake Ave 33401
561-833-9023
Peter Emmerich & Rick Rose

125-199 BB
5 rooms, 5 pb
Visa, MC, AmEx, •
C-yes/S-ltd/P-ltd/H-yes
German, Spanish and
French
Winter/Spring

European Continental Buffet
Innkeepers reception, small
snacks and drinks
Heated pool, sunbathing
terrace, tropical garden,
multi-lingual library, bicycles

Luxury B&B located in the historic neighborhood of downtown West Palm Beach, walking distance to City Place, the Palm Beach County Convention Center and the Kravis Performing Arts Center.
✉ grandviewinfo@grandview-gardens.com ○ www.grandview-gardens.com

Hibiscus House
501 30th St 33407
800-203-4927 561-863-5633
Raleigh Hill & Colin Rayner

89-210 BB
6 rooms, 6 pb
Most CC, *Rated*, •
C-ltd/S-no/P-yes/H-no

Full breakfast
Dining room
Gazebo, fishpond, tropical
gardens, pool

Hibiscus House was built in 1922 by Mayor David Dunkle during the Florida land boom, in the heart of Old Northwood · a National Register Historic District.
✉ info@hibiscushouse.com ○ www.hibiscushouse.com

**Hibiscus House Downtown
Bed & Breakfast**
213 S Rosemary Ave 33401
866-833-8171 561-833-8171
Missy Garrett

120-280 BB
9 rooms, 9 pb
Visa, MC, AmEx
C-yes/S-no/P-yes/H-yes

Full breakfast
Close to restaurants and
night life
TV/VCR, phone, high-speed
Internet access, porch

Hibiscus House Downtown is located in the very heart of Downtown West Palm beach-just 1 block from CityPlace and its fabulous shoppes, restaurants, & plazas. Our bed & breakfast guestrooms are individually furnished to provide an intimate, relaxed setting
✉ info@hibiscushousedowntown.com ○ www.hibiscushousedowntown.com

Knot So Fast
105 Lake Shore Drive 33403
561-329-2280
Brent & Debbie

150 BB
2 rooms, 1 pb
Most CC, •
C-yes/S-no/P-no/H-yes

Continental breakfast
Full 5 course dinner served
onboard for $30/person:
beef, seafood or chicken
Main Salon seating inside.
Sundeck seating with table
on deck. Breakfast seating in
galley.

Imagine staying aboard your very own private trawler yacht, with free Continental Breakfast out on the sundeck the next morning. Smell the salt air. Witness a beautiful sunset and the lights reflecting off the water.
✉ brentdeb@knotsofastcruises.com ○ www.knotsofastcruises.com

Georgia

AMERICUS————————————————————————————

Americus Garden Inn	99-149 BB	Full 3-course breakfast
504 Rees Pk 31709	8 rooms, 8 pb	Fruit, sodas, tea, coffee,
888-758-4749 229-931-0122	Most CC	bottled water, snacks
Mr. & Mrs. Kim and Susan	C-ltd/S-ltd/P-no/H-yes	Large common areas, 1.3
Egelseer		acre grounds with gazebo,
		personal & attentive service,
		wireless Internet

Americus Garden Inn Bed and Breakfast is a romantic, historic pre Civil War 1847 mansion with 8 spacious guestrooms each with king or queen beds, private in-room baths and full hot breakfast near Andersonville and Jimmy Carter National Historic Sites.
✉ info@americusgardeninn.com ◐ www.americusgardeninn.com

ATLANTA————————————————————————————

1890 King-Keith House B&B	110-210 BB	Full breakfast
889 Edgewood Ave NE 30307	6 rooms, 6 pb	Snacks & beverages
800-728-3879 404-688-7330	C-ltd/S-no/P-no/H-no	including wine in mini-
Windell & Jan Keith		kitchen (microwave &
		refrigerator) for all guests
		four porches (one screened),
		2 public parlors, WiFi &
		guest computer, Jacuzzi in
		Suite & Cottage

One of Atlanta's most photographed homes, this Victorian is loaded with period antiques, charm and romance. Close to downtown. Shops and restaurants nearby.
✉ kingkeith@mindspring.com ◐ www.kingkeith.com

Adele's Virginia Highland B&B	139-169 BB	Full breakfast
630 Orme Cir NE 30306	3 rooms, 3 pb	In-room complimentary
877-870-4485 404-892-2735	Most CC	snacks, bottled water, coffee,
Adele Northrup	C-ltd/S-no/P-no/H-no	tea.
		fireplace, screened porch
		with hammock, balcony,
		perennial gardens, cable
		TV/DVD, Internet

This Atlanta B&B is located in Virginia Highland, adjacent to Midtown and just two miles from Downtown Atlanta."The Highlands" is premier pedestrian neighborhood of restored 1920's craftsman bungalows, unique shops, restaurants, parks, and entertainment
✉ adele@virginiahighlandbb.com ◐ www.virginiahighlandbb.com

Beverly Hills Inn	129-249 BB	Continental plus breakfast
65 Sheridan Dr NE 30305	18 rooms, 18 pb	Sitting room, TV, library,
800-331-8520 404-233-8520	Most CC, *Rated*, ●	health club, walking distance
Mit Amin	C-yes/S-no/P-yes/H-no	to fine restaurants, business
		accommodation

The Beverly Hills Inn has an intriguing history dating back to 1929, when it opened as an apartment home for elderly single women seeking the convenience of a central location coupled with the prestige of living in the beautiful Garden Hills District.
✉ mit@beverlyhillsinn.com ◐ www.beverlyhillsinn.com

ATLANTA

Inman Park-Woodruff	115-140 BB	Continental plus breakfast
Cottage B&B	3 rooms, 3 pb	Snacks, custom breakfast,
100 Waverly Way NE 30307	Visa, MC, AmEx,	organic foods, and coffee
404-688-9498	*Rated*, •	maker. Breakfast features
Eleanor Matthews	C-ltd/S-no/P-no/H-no	Irish Soda Bread
		Exercise equipment or
		complimentary pass to local
		athletic club, Internet, A/C,
		cable TV, deck/patio

The Woodruff House has 12-foot ceilings, heart-of-pine floors, 18th and 19th century antiques, a private garden and safe parking. Deluxe, well-appointed rooms and private bathrooms. Stay includes Continental breakfast (customizable for special diets).
✉ info@inmanparkbandb.com ♦ www.inmanparkbandb.com

Laurel Hill B&B	115-170 BB	Full breakfast
1992 McLendon Ave 30307	5 rooms, 5 pb	High speed wireless Internet,
877-377-3212 404-377-3217	Most CC, *Rated*, •	terrycloth robes, hairdryers,
Dave Hinman	C-ltd/S-ltd/P-yes/H-no	bath products, irons and
	Weekends	ironing boards

Enjoy 1920's flavor—Two Tudor style homes close to Agnes Scott College, Emory University, City of Decatur, Downtown Atlanta, Georgia State University, Little 5 Points, & Virginia Highlands.
✉ reservations@laurelhillbandb.com ♦ www.laurelhillbandb.com

The Peach House	130-200 BB	Continental plus breakfast
88 Spruce Street 30307	4 rooms, 4 pb	Afternoon fruit, wine and
404-524-8899	Visa, MC	cheese served in the dining
Beverly Gibson	C-yes/S-no/P-ltd/H-no	room.
		Business services, front
		porch, piano parlor,
		courtyard, garden, half
		basketball court

The Peach House was built in 1906 in Atlanta's first suburb, historic Inman Park. Two renovations have restored the old manor to its original grandeur. The Peach House has something for everyone and the Innkeepers look forward to welcoming you.
✉ info@thepeachhousebb.com ♦ www.thepeachhousebb.com

Stonehurst Place	249-489 BB	Diets and allergies
923 Piedmont Ave NE 30309	4 rooms, 4 pb	considered
877-285-2246 404-881-0722	Most CC, •	Snacks, soft drinks,
Trenell Smith	C-ltd/S-no/P-ltd/H-no	complimentary wine, baked
		goods, chocolates
		First Class accommodations,
		furnishings, and breakfast in
		an updated National Historic
		Inn

Built in 1896, Stonehurst Place is a "green" lodging with a conscientious approach to luxurious surroundings in an environmentally-sound, quiet, National Historic Register home. Restored in 2007–2008. Great beds, breakfast, and amenities.
✉ Info@stonehurstplace.com ♦ www.stonehurstplace.com

Sugar Magnolia B&B	110-150 BB	Full breakfast
804 Edgewood Ave, NE 30307	4 rooms, 4 pb	Coffee, tea, soft drinks &
404-222-0226	Visa, MC, *Rated*, •	beer available any time
Debi Starnes & Jim Emshoff	C-ltd/S-no/P-no/H-no	Free WiFi, sitting/meeting
		room, business center, roof-
		top deck with waterfall
		garden

Sugar Magnolia is situated in the heart of the city of Atlanta, a B&B where excellence and comfort are mingled with the Southern charm of yesteryear and the exciting beat of the South's Olympic city.
✉ sugmagbb@aol.com ♦ www.sugarmagnoliabb.com

BRUNSWICK

Brunswick Manor	100-110 BB	Full gourmet breakfast
825 Egmont St 31520	4 rooms, 4 pb	Complimentary wine with
912-265-6889	Visa, MC, *Rated*, •	afternoon refreshments,
Claudia Tzucanow	C-ltd/S-ltd/P-ltd/H-ltd	wine, cheese and sherry in
	Some Spanish	rooms, early coffee
		Sitting room, library,
		verandah with antique
		wicker swing, terry cloth
		robes, extensive local info

Brunswick Manor B&B is located in the heart of Brunswick's historic Old Town facing one of the original town squares. Elegantly appointed with all the comforts & luxuries of a premier B&B. Enjoy the wrap-around verandah, arbored patio & inviting hot tub.
✉ brunswickmanor@bellsouth.net ◐ www.brunswickmanor.com

CLARKESVILLE

Glen-Ella Springs Inn	150-265 BB	Full breakfast
1789 Bear Gap Rd 30523	16 rooms, 16 pb	Dinner served each evening,
877-456-7527 706-754-7295	Most CC, *Rated*	by reservation. Wine sold by
Ed & Luci Kivett	C-yes/S-ltd/P-no/H-yes	the glass or bottle in dining
		room.
		Weddings & receptions,
		meeting/conference room,
		pool, herb & flower gardens,
		mountain creek, hiking

Wander down a gravel road & discover the peaceful setting of Glen-Ella Springs B&B Inn. Stroll around seventeen acres of meadows & gardens. Watch the birds, rock on the porches. Sit by the fireplace in the century-old inn. Savor the outstanding food!
✉ info@glenella.com ◐ www.glenella.com

CLAYTON

Beechwood Inn	189-209 BB	Full breakfast
220 Beechwood Dr 30525	8 rooms, 8 pb	Gourmet dinners & wine
866-782-2485 706-782-5485	Visa, MC, *Rated*, •	tastings by reservation
David & Gayle Darugh	C-ltd/S-no/P-no/H-ltd	Luxury linens, fireplaces,
		antiques, private patios &
		balconies, CD players,
		afternoon wine

Georgia's Premier Wine Country Inn. This romantic Inn offers the finest in historic accommodations for those visiting the Georgia Mountains. Selected as the "No. 1 Inn in North America for a Weekend Escape" by Inn Traveler Magazine.
✉ david-gayle@beechwoodinn.ws ◐ www.beechwoodinn.ws

COLUMBUS

Gates House B&B	105-165 BB	Full gourmet breakfast
737 Broadway 31902	7 rooms, 7 pb	Snacks, wine/tea/soft drinks
800-891-3187 706-324-6464	Visa, MC, AmEx, •	& fruit, luncheons, dinners,
Carolyn & Tom Gates	C-ltd/S-no/P-no/H-ltd	catering
		Jacuzzis, fireplaces, cable
		TV, cable modem, bicycles,
		fax, home theater room,
		porches with rockers

1873 Colonial Revival house furnished in Victorian antiques & spectacular window treatments. "Most comfortable beds in town." "Best Breakfast in Southeast" and "Best Decor and Interior Design" by Inn Traveler Magazine. Home Theater Room-big screen TV.
✉ info@gateshouse.com ◐ www.gateshouse.com

CUMBERLAND ISLAND

Greyfield Inn	395-575 BB	Full southern-style breakfast
888-357-7617 904-261-6408	11 rooms, 10 pb	Hors d'oeuvres during
The Ferguson Family	Visa, MC, Disc	nightly Cocktail Hour. All
	C-ltd/S-no/P-no/H-ltd	non-alcoholic beverages
		during your stay.
		Ferry Boat transportation,
		kayaks bikes, naturalist-led
		excursions, fishing & beach
		equipment

Turn-of-the-century mansion on pristine, tranquil Cumberland Island. Incredible beaches, marshes, wild horses and many species of birds. Victorian antiques, Tiffany lamps and Chippendale furniture. Large verandah with porch swings and rockers.
✉ seashore@greyfieldinn.com Ⓒ www.greyfieldinn.com

DAHLONEGA

Cavender Creek Cabins	125-200 EP	Fully equipped kitchens
200 Beaver Dam Road 30533	8 rooms, 8 pb	Hot tubs, fireplaces, A/C, TV,
866-373-6307 706-864-7221	Visa, MC, Disc	pool tables, games, special
Paul, Mary & Brian Hanson	C-yes/S-no/P-no/H-yes	events, reunions, catering by
		arrangement

The Cavender Creek Cabins complex is North Georgia's premier full service cabin resort. Cavender Creek's quality cabins are set in the breathtaking natural beauty of the mountains and blend a rustic setting with luxurious accommodations.
✉ phanson@alltel.net Ⓒ www.cavendercreek.com

Lily Creek Lodge	115-225 BB	Full breakfast
2608 Auraria Rd 30533	13 rooms, 13 pb	Homemade cookies, wine,
888-844-2694 706-864-6848	Visa, MC, AmEx,	hot chocolate, hot cider
Don & Sharon Bacek	*Rated*, •	Hot tub, pool, fireplace,
	C-yes/S-ltd/P-no/H-no	kitchen, TV/VCR/DVD,
	Some Spanish & French	games, gazebo, library,
		bocce, hammock, deck, WiFi

Romantic mountain bed and breakfast getaway in North Georgia wine country. The lodge is a fun and relaxing escape with secluded swimming pool & hot tub, bocce ball. Spa, winery & romance packages. 4 miles to historic Dahlonega shops & dining
✉ lilycreeklodge@windstream.net Ⓒ www.lilycreeklodge.com

Long Mountain Lodge	109-169 BB	Full breakfast
144 Bull Creek Rd 30533	6 rooms, 6 pb	Afternoon snacks
706-864-2337	Most CC	Satellite television,
Dianne Quigley	C-ltd/S-ltd/P-no/H-yes	fireplaces, wireless Internet
		access, bathrobes, whirlpool
		tubs, writing desks

Luxury guestrooms and suites on Long Mountain. Each room with breathtaking mountain views, beautiful rustic decor and gracious hospitality. Relax in the Library with a good book and enjoy gourmet breakfasts by former chef and owner, Dianne Quigley.
✉ innkeeper@longmountainlodge.com Ⓒ www.longmountainlodge.com

Mountain Laurel Creek Inn	149-195 BB	Full breakfast
& Spa	5 rooms, 5 pb	Local wines and beer offered
202 Talmer Grizzle Rd 30533	Most CC	in our pub, the Copper
706-867-8134	S-no/P-no/H-no	Penny Pub
Dennis Hoover		Sitting rooms, private
		balcony, spa tubs, gas
		fireplaces, Day spa,
		massages, facials, pub, WiFi

Featured in Dec. 08 issue of Southern Living Magazine as the place to stay in Dahlonega. Each room is a luxury treat, uniquely decorated with original artwork, fine linens, whirlpool tubs, fireplaces—your place for romance or a quiet mountain getaway
✉ info@mountainlaurelcreek.com Ⓒ www.mountainlaurelcreek.com

DAHLONEGA

Mountain Top Lodge at Dahlonega
447 Mtn Top Lodge Rd 30533
800-526-9754 706-864-5257
Paul Carmody

99-159 BB
13 rooms, 13 pb
Visa, MC
S-ltd/P-no/H-ltd

Full breakfast
Complimentary sherry & chocolate chip cookies
Private decks, fireplaces, Jacuzzi tubs, great room with satellite TV, library, game loft, Internet

Charming country B&B set on 14 acres in north Georgia mountain setting close to wineries, hiking and downtown Dahlonega. Second romantic getaway lodge with fireplaces, private decks and Jacuzzi tubs. Full southern style breakfast.
✉ mountaintop@windstream.net ◐ www.mountaintoplodge.net

Pura Vida USA
400 Blueberry Hill 30533
866-345-4900 706-865-7678
John Fernando

130-175 BB
24 rooms, 24 pb
Visa, MC, •
C-yes/S-no/P-ltd/H-yes
Closed Mon&Tues

Full breakfast
All of the cabins have a small refrigerator and its own coffee maker
Spa treatments, Jacuzzi, nature trails

Pura Vida USA is a B&B and Wellness Retreat Center located on 72 acres near the historic gold-rush town of Dahlonega, in the foothills of the Blue Ridge Mountains, just over an hour north of Atlanta. ✉ reception@puravidausa.com ◐ www.puravidausa.com

DARIEN

The Blue Heron Inn
1 Blue Heron Ln 31319
912-437-4304
Bill & Jan Chamberlain

95-140 BB
4 rooms, 4 pb
Most CC
C-ltd/S-no/P-ltd/H-ltd

Full breakfast
Home baked goods are provided as afternoon and evening snacks. Wine and cheese served each evening.
Decks, porches, Jacuzzi tubs, kitchenette, WiFi, fireplaces, meeting areas

Located on the edge of a large marsh and tidal creek, ideal for bird watchers and nature lovers. The Blue Heron Inn is perfect for those who want to experience the full beauty and activities of this tidewater community.
✉ blueheroninn@darientel.net ◐ www.blueheroninngacoast.com

ELLIJAY

Hearthstone Lodge
2755 Hwy 282 30705
800-695-0905 706-695-0920
Pat & Phil Cunniffe

179-199 BB
3 rooms, 3 pb
Most CC
S-no/P-no/H-no

Full 3 course breakfast
Light afternoon refreshments wine and cheese from 5-6pm, light dessert after dinner 8pm
Game room with pool table, spa with massages, steam room, outdoor hot tub, 500+ volume library

Experience gracious hospitality while enjoying privacy, seclusion and romance. Hearthstone offers three unique and distinctively different guest suites, each with a queen bed and private bath. On-site spa services.
✉ hearthstonelodge@alltel.net ◐ www.thehearthstonelodge.com

FORT OGLETHORPE

Captain's Quarters
13 Barnhardt Cir 30742
800-710-6816 706-858-0624
James & Julie Powell

120-168 BB
7 rooms, 7 pb
Most CC, *Rated*, •
C-ltd/S-no/P-no/H-ltd

Deluxe hot breakfast
Complimentary tea, coffee, soft drinks
Dining rm, parlor, library, original fireplaces, rocking chair porches, meeting/reception facilities

Fort Oglethorpe is 10 minutes from Chattanooga, this 1902 inn is located adjacent to Chickamauga Battlefield. Filled with beautiful antiques & Asian art, it offers a fine dining breakfast & luxurious linens for a truly romantic getaway.
✉ info@cqinn.com ◐ www.cqinn.com

HAMILTON

Magnolia Hall
127 Barnes Mill Rd 31811
877-813-4394 706-628-4566
Dale and Ken Smith

115-135 BB
5 rooms, 5 pb
Most CC, *Rated*, •
C-ltd/S-no/P-no/H-yes

Full breakfast
Snacks, complimentary
wine, candy
Sitting room, library, suites,
cable TV, horseshoe court,
independent thermostats,
walking trail

Magnolia Hall Bed & Breakfast is a beautifully restored 1880s Victorian home, situated on a lushly landscaped acre, 5 minutes from lovely Callaway Gardens
✉ kgsmag@juno.com ◐ www.magnoliahallbb.com

HELEN

Alpine Hilltop Haus B&B
362 Chattahoochee Strasse
30545
706-878-2388
Frankie Allen & Barbara
McNary

110-200 BB
5 rooms, 5 pb
Visa, MC, *Rated*
C-ltd/S-ltd/P-no/H-no

Full breakfast
Rooms with woodburning
fireplaces

Tree-covered, secluded, hilltop location. Short walk to Alpine Village center. Deck overlooking Chattahoochee River. Celebrate special occasions, i.e. anniversaries, birthdays and honeymoons.
✉ hilltop@hemc.net ◐ www.alpinehilltop.com

**Black Forest B&B and
Cabins**
8902 N Main St 30545
706-878-3995
Art & Lou Ann Connor

135-275 BB
12 rooms, 12 pb
Most CC
S-no/P-no/H-ltd

Full breakfast
Gourmet coffee, homemade
desserts
Waterfall weddings, gazebo,
deck w/view, patio with 20'
waterfall, koi pond,
concierge services

Truly a place where you can make memories that will last a lifetime! Black Forest Bed and Breakfast is located in picturesque Alpine Helen, at the foot of the Blue Ridge Mountains in North Georgia.
✉ blackforestbb@aol.com ◐ www.blackforest-bb.com

LOOKOUT MOUNTAIN

Chanticleer Inn
1300 Mockingbird Ln 30750
866-424-2684 706-820-2002
Rob & Audrey Hart

120-220 BB
17 rooms, 17 pb
Most CC, •
C-ltd/S-no/P-no/H-ltd

Full breakfast
Afternoon Cookies, Coffee,
Tea & Hot Chocolate
Large common room, in
ground pool, antiques,
fireplaces, whirlpool tubs,
high speed Internet

This historic, charming Inn was completely renovated in 2002. Luxurious rooms are simply decorated with king and queen beds, whirlpools, suites, fireplaces, antiques, and romantic packages. We are located directly across the street from Rock City Gardens.
✉ info@stayatchanticleer.com ◐ www.stayatchanticleer.com

MILLEDGEVILLE

Antebellum Inn
200 N Columbia St 31061
478-453-3993
Jane Lorenz

109-159 BB
5 rooms, 5 pb
Most CC
C-yes/S-ltd/P-ltd/H-yes

Gourmet breakfast served
Snacks, wine, afternoon tea
available
WiFi, hair dryers, iron &
board, cable TV/VCR,
movies, library, concierge
service

Located in the Historic District, we offer five elegant rooms, all of which have private baths. The Inn is one block from Georgia College & the State University Campus. A personal touch is given to guests with information on the city, tours & restaurants.
✉ Antebellum@alltel.net ◐ www.Antebelluminn.com

SAUTEE

Lucille's Mountain Top Inn
964 Rabun Rd 30571
866-245-4777 706-878-5055
Lucille and George Hlavenka

119-220 BB
9 rooms, 9 pb
Most CC, •
C-ltd/S-no/P-no/H-yes

Gourmet
Free 24-hour beverages,
evening dessert. Optional
candlelight in-room dinner,
and picnic lunches.
360 degree view of
mountains & valleys, spa,
meeting room. Business
retreats/weddings/
certificates

Lucille's Mountain Top Inn is located on a mountain top with over 5 private acres and a 360-degree view of the mountains. We are a new luxury B&B, perfect for romantic getaways and business retreats. On-site spa services available at the Mandala Spa.
✉ stay@lucillesmountaintopinn.com ☼ www.lucillesmountaintopinn.com

**The Stovall House Country
Inn and Restaurant**
1526 Hwy 255 N 30571
706-878-3355
Hamilton Schwartz

98 BB
5 rooms, 5 pb
Visa, MC, AmEx, *Rated*
C-yes/S-ltd/P-no/H-ltd

Continental plus breakfast
Restaurant
Sitting room, A/C, central
heating, historic register

Award-winning restoration of 1837 country farmhouse, on 28 serene acres with beautiful mountain views. One of the top 50 restaurants in Georgia.
✉ info@stovallhouse.com ☼ www.stovallhouse.com

SAVANNAH

118 West
118 W Gaston St 31401
912-234-8557
Andrea D. Walker

125-200 BB
1 rooms, 1 pb
Cash, Checks, *Rated*
C-ltd/S-no/P-ltd/H-yes

Continental breakfast
Fully equipped kitchen
Fireplace, digital satellite
cable TV with premium
movie channels, private
phone line

One bedroom garden apartment with living room, fully equipped kitchen & full size bath, located in an 1850 townhouse in Savannah's historic district.
✉ adwalker1@aol.com ☼ www.118west.com

**Amethyst Inn At Sarah's
Garden**
402 E Gaston St 31401
866-266-2714 912-898-0752
Jane & Rocky Reed

155-255 BB
8 rooms, 8 pb
Visa, MC, *Rated*, •
C-yes/S-no/P-ltd/H-no

Full breakfast
Afternoon social hour with
wine and lemonade &
appetizers
Sitting room, swimming pool,
suites, fireplace, cable TV

Beautiful 1888 Victorian home, recently restored to perfection. We are in the Historic District with 4 beautiful suites and 4 luxurious bedrooms with private baths. Beautifully decorated with all the modern conveniences.
✉ sarahsgarden900@bellsouth.net ☼ www.aiasg.com

Armstrong Inns
554 East Taylor St 31401
912-232-9175
William and Monique
Armstrong

225-460 BB
7 rooms, 5 pb
Most CC
C-yes/S-ltd/P-ltd/H-ltd
French

In-room full continental
breakfast
Greeting with in-room bottle
of wine, cheese and
refreshment. Pastry dish
replenished daily.
Wireless Internet, daily
housekeeping, private
chef/gourmet kitchens,
tourist info, fireplaces

Private luxury in the heart of Savannah. One of a kind and perfectly appointed, each Armstrong Inn offers the actual experience of living in a historic home in the heart of Savannah with all amenities of a luxury bed and breakfast.
✉ booking@armstronginns.com ☼ www.armstronginns.com

SAVANNAH────────────────────────────

Azalea Inn and Gardens 217 E Huntingdon St 31401 800-582-3823 912-236-2707 Teresa and Mike Jacobson	159-325 BB 9 rooms, 9 pb Most CC, • C-ltd/S-no/P-ltd/H-no	Full Southern gourmet breakfast Easy-living beverages, wine & cheese, plus home-baked evening desserts Free off-street parking, swimming pool, wireless Internet, comfy robes, cable TV, hair dryer, iron.

Lighthearted, laid-back southern leisure prevails at Azalea Inn and Gardens' mansion (c. 1889) near Forsyth Park. Off-street parking, WiFi, southern gourmet breakfast, wine & hors d'oeuvres, heritage gardens, balconies & pool. Tips to intimate Savannah.
✉ Azalea.Inn@comcast.net ○ www.azaleainn.com

Ballastone Inn 14 E Oglethorpe Ave 31401 800-822-4553 912-236-1484 Jim & Jennier Salandi	235-395 BB 16 rooms, 16 pb Visa, MC, AmEx, *Rated*, • C-ltd/S-ltd/P-no/H-ltd	Full Southern Breakfast Afternoon high tea, sterling silver old world china. Cocktail hour Gilchrist and Soames toiletries, round the clock staffing at your convenience and safety, elevator

The Ballastone Inn, a four-story Italianate Antebellum mansion built in 1838, combines old-fashioned elegance & charm. Only Inn in Savannah formal high tea daily, full service bar, fully staffed 24 hours a day for your service and safety. AAA four diamond
✉ inn@ballastone.com ○ www.ballastone.com

Catherine Ward House Inn 118 E Waldburg St 31401 800-327-4270 912-234-8564 Leslie Larson	159-329 BB 9 rooms, 9 pb Most CC, *Rated* C-ltd/S-ltd/P-ltd/H-ltd	Full breakfast Guests may bring their alcoholic beverage of choice, we happily supply glasses & endless ice Free faxes, WiFi, massages, common areas, private courtyard, balconies, Jacuzzi tub, fireplaces, TV

The Catherine Ward House is located on a quiet street in the Victorian District of Savannah, Georgia. This wonderful 19th century inn, under new ownership in April 2005, has had its rooms, its amenities, its policies, and its personality updated.
✉ contact@catherinewardhouseinn.com ○ www.catherinewardhouseinn.com

The Dresser Palmer House 211 E Gaston St 31401 800-671-0716 912-238-3294 Ron Jean	189-429 BB 15 rooms, 15 pb Most CC, *Rated*, • S-no/P-no/H-yes	Full Gourmet Southern Breakfast Evening Social from 5:30 to 7pm with complimentary wine, cheese, & hors d'oeuvres Complimentary off street parking for all of our guests, 24 hour concierge service, WiFi

Built in 1876, this Italianate Mansion provides a variety of spacious accommodations with king or queen beds with private baths and balcony, some with fireplaces.
✉ info@dresserpalmerhouse.com ○ www.dresserpalmerhouse.com

SAVANNAH

Foley House Inn
14 W Hull St 31401
800-647-3708 912-232-6622
Allisen & Grant Rogers

179-365 BB
19 rooms, 19 pb
Most CC, *Rated*
C-ltd/S-ltd/P-ltd/H-no

Full breakfast
Complimentary afternoon
refreshments, evening hors
d'oeuvre and wine, bedtime
port or sherry
Newspaper, fireplaces,
concierge services, personal
itineraries, complimentary
bottled water

Restored Antebellum mansion furnished with antiques & reproductions. Most rooms have original working fireplaces. Jacuzzis and private balconies in some rooms. Two lush and beautiful courtyards. Walking distance to all major attractions & restaurants.
✉ info@foleyinn.com 🕭 www.foleyinn.com

Green Palm Inn
548 E President St 31401
888-606-9510 912-447-8901
Diane McCray

129-219 BB
4 rooms, 4 pb
Most CC
C-ltd/S-no/P-no/H-no

Full gourmet breakfast
Afternoon dessert bar and
wine in the afternoon

Green Palm Inn, a family-owned 4-bedroom B&B in Savannah's historic district, exudes a calm, homey yet smart atmosphere attesting to the well-traveled innkeepers' devotion to guest pleasures. Recommended Fodor's and American Airlines.
✉ greenpalminn@aol.com 🕭 www.greenpalminn.com

Hamilton-Turner Inn
330 Abercorn St 31401
888-448-8849 912-233-1833
Jim & Gay Dunlop

189-369 BB
17 rooms, 17 pb
Most CC, *Rated*
C-ltd/S-no/P-ltd/H-yes
French

Full Gourmet Southern
Breakfast
Also included in rates:
Afternoon tea and sweets,
Evening wine and hor
d'oeuvres, Port and sweets
Wireless Internet, turndown,
whirlpool suites with sitting
room, fireplace, cable TV,
wheelchair lift

Experience gracious hospitality at the elegant Hamilton-Turner Inn. Nestled on picturesque Lafayette Square, this bed and breakfast is ideally situated in the center of Savannah's beautiful historic district for discovering all the secrets of Savannah
✉ innkeeper@hamilton-turnerinn.com 🕭 www.hamilton-turnerinn.com

Joan's on Jones B&B
17 W Jones St 31401
888-989-9806 912-234-3863
Joan & Gary Levy

160-185 BB
2 rooms, 2 pb
Cash, Checks, *Rated*
C-yes/S-no/P-yes/H-ltd
French

Continental breakfast
Complimentary wine
Heavenly firm mattress bed,
goose down pillows, high
count sheets, fresh flowers

An exquisite "jewel" in the restored 1883 Victorian townhouse that has graced Jones Street, in the heart of Savannah's National Historic Landmark District, for generations.
✉ joansonjones@comcast.net 🕭 joansonjones.home.comcast.net

The Presidents' Quarters
255 E President St 31412
800-233-1776 912-233-1600
Jane Sales / Fred Morris,
House Manager

209-325 BB
16 rooms, 16 pb
Most CC, *Rated*
C-yes/S-no/P-no/H-yes

Continental plus breakfast
Hot & cold beverages, wine
and hors d'oeuvres, fresh
cookies or southern pralines,
and cordials.
Fireplace, hair dryer, cable
TV, wet bars, room
thermostat, elevator,
parkside balcony &
courtyard.

Named one of the Best B&Bs & Inns in Savannah, "Luxury with a Legacy" prevails on preeminent Oglethorpe Square. The downtown historic Savannah inn features panoramic gardens, spacious rooms, free parking, elevator & sociable amenities.
✉ info@presidentsquarters.com 🕭 www.presidentsquarters.com

SAVANNAH

Savannah's B&B Inn
117 W Gordon St 31401
888-238-0518 912-238-0518
Jennifer McKenzie

129-219 BB
14 rooms, 14 pb
Visa, MC, Disc, *Rated*,
•
C-ltd/S-ltd/P-no/H-ltd

Full breakfast
Afternoon tea, weekend wine
& cheese reception, bedtime
warm chocolate chip cookies
and milk
Garden courtyards; walking
distance to historic
attractions & restaurants

A warm welcome awaits you at the Bed & Breakfast Inn in Savannah. Come on in and experience the charm of this wonderful city in our three restored 1853 Federal Row houses on Gordon Row. ✉ innkeeper@savannahbnb.com ○ www.savannahbnb.com

SENOIA

The Veranda Historic B&B Inn
252 Seavy St 30276
866-596-3905 770-599-3905
Rick & Laura Reynolds

125-155 BB
9 rooms, 9 pb
Most CC
C-ltd/S-no/P-no/H-yes

Full breakfast
Tea, snacks, soft drinks Food
for special events
Restaurant, wedding
facilities, receptions,
rehearsal dinners, TV room,
library, art gallery, gifts

Listed on the National Register for Historic Places, this historic Greek revival mansion inn was built in 1906 as the Holberg Hotel. Relax & enjoy the wraparound veranda porch with rocking chairs & porch swings or take a stroll through the grounds. ✉ reynolds2803@bellsouth.net ○ www.verandabandbinn.com

ST. MARYS

Emma's B&B
300 W Conyers St 31558
877-749-5974 912-882-4199
Angie & Jimmy Mock

119-189 BB
9 rooms, 9 pb
Most CC, •
C-ltd/S-no/P-ltd/H-no

Full breakfast
Sack lunches can be made
for your trip to Cumberland
Island.
Sitting room, formal living &
dining room and porches,
wireless Internet, luxury
linens/towels

Emma's Bed and Breakfast, the hidden jewel of St. Marys, is a beautiful escape to tranquility and relaxation. Offering the finest in lodging, hospitality and service, it is your Cumberland Island connection. ✉ reservations@emmasbedandbreakfast.com ○ www.emmasbedandbreakfast.com

Goodbread House
209 Osborne St 31558
877-205-1453 912-882-7490
Mardja Gray

99-139 BB
6 rooms, 6 pb
Visa, MC, AmEx, *Rated*
C-yes/S-no/P-yes/H-no

Full breakfast
Social hour with wine, sodas,
coffee or tea and homemade
dessert, afternoon tea &
luncheons
Spa treatments, healing,
retreats, golf, kayaking,
fishing, Ferry to the beach,
bikes

Victorian hideaway in quaint historic fishing village off I-95. Ferry to Cumberland Island National Seashore. Golf Cart Community. Healing and Spa Treatments. Personality Consultations. ✉ info@goodbreadhouse.com ○ www.goodbreadhouse.com

Spencer House Inn
200 Osborne St 31558
877-870-1872 912-882-1872
Mary & Mike Neff

125-235 BB
14 rooms, 14 pb
Most CC, *Rated*
C-yes/S-no/P-no/H-ltd

Full breakfast
Afternoon tea, sweets, baked
goods, picnic lunches
Living room, library,
expanded cable TV, DSL,
WiFi, business travel,
elevator

Gateway to Cumberland Island National Seashore. Verandahs with rockers, sunny common areas. Elevator for guests. Quiet, coastal historic village. Walk to restaurants, shops, museums and ferry. ✉ info@spencerhouseinn.com ○ www.spencerhouseinn.com

ST. SIMONS ISLAND

Beach B&B
907 Beachview Dr 31522
877-634-2800 912-634-2800
Joe McDonough

320-550 BB
7 rooms, 7 pb
Visa, MC, AmEx
C-ltd/S-no/P-yes/H-yes
German

Full breakfast
In Room beer, wine, sodas &
water, light snack items
Exercise pool, porches,
balconies, fireplace, wet bar,
Jacuzzi, weddings, events

*Beach B&B is a beautiful oceanfront Spanish-Mediterranean villa. Suites are furnished
with exquisite décor and detail. Guests can take advantage of our exercise pool and home
theatre, and it is within walking distance of the best restaurants.*
✉ reserve@beachbedandbreakfast.com ● www.beachbedandbreakfast.com

Village Inn & Pub
500 Mallory St 31522
888-635-6111 912-634-6056
Kristy Wilkes

160-245 BB
28 rooms, 28 pb
Most CC, *Rated*
C-yes/S-ltd/P-no/H-ltd

Continental breakfast
Intimate pub
Courtyard pool, meeting
space, private balconies,
iron/ironing boards, hair
dryers

*Nestled under the ancient live oak trees and between the parks and the historic oceanfront
Village and Lighthouse, you will find our unique Inn.*
✉ kristy@villageinnandpub.com ● www.villageinnandpub.com

STATESBORO

Historic Statesboro Inn
106 S. Main St 30458
800-846-9466 912-489-8628
Denman DuBose

95-175 BB
18 rooms, 18 pb
Visa, MC, Disc
C-yes/S-no/P-yes/H-yes

Full breakfast

*This country inn is a charming combination of two turn-of-the-century houses. The two
houses stand together on South Main Street in Statesboro's historic district, serving as a
symbol of the prosperity enjoyed by the founders of this old cotton community.*
✉ mandyatstatesboroinn@yahoo.com ● www.statesboroinn.com

THOMASVILLE

1884 Paxton House Inn
445 Remington Ave 31792
229-226-5197
Susie Sherrod

165-350 BB
9 rooms, 9 pb
Visa, MC, AmEx, *Rated*
C-ltd/S-no/P-no/H-no

Full gourmet
Afternoon and evening
refreshments
Phone/data ports, cable TV,
robes, hairdryer, iron, DVD,
pool/spa, computer

*AAA Four Diamond Award Inn, in beautiful historic Thomasville, Georgia. Designed for
adults, visited by royalty, perfect for leisure, romance or corporate guests. 30 minutes from
Tallahassee.*
✉ 1884@rose.net ● www.1884paxtonhouseinn.com

Dawson Street Inn
324 N Dawson St 31792
229-226-7515
Alice H. (Randy) Mitchell

145-155 BB
6 rooms, 6 pb
Most CC, ●
C-ltd/S-ltd/P-no/H-no

Full breakfast
Refreshments
Living room, pool, fireplaces

*1856 Colonial home on the Nat'l Register of Historic Places, 6 guestrooms with private
baths, 2 grand staircases, 12 foot ceilings, incredible woodwork, formal living room and
dining room, 10 fireplaces, formal grounds and beautiful swimming pool.*
✉ rdmitch@rose.net ● www.dawsonstinn.com

Tell your hosts Pamela Lanier sent you.

TYBEE ISLAND

Atlantis Inn	89-425 BB	In-season daily March – Oct.
20 Silver Ave 31328	16 rooms, 16 pb	We serve a continental plus
866-358-9233 912-786-6044	Most CC, •	breakfast on weekends
Natalie & Mel Gordon	C-yes/S-no/P-no/H-ltd	November-February
		WiFi, concierge service,
		TV/DVD, hot tubs & spa tubs
		in specialty suites, daily
		housekeeping

Our Charming, Romantic Inn was designed with themed rooms for that special get away; hot tubs and spa tubs are in our 5 honeymoon style suites. Or, choose a family style beach theme suite to escape to. Voted "Best Place to Stay" 06 & 07!
✉ atlantisinn@bellsouth.net 🌐 www.atlantisinntybee.com

The Outdoor Inn	110-170 BB	Continental breakfast
1102 Hwy 80 31328	4 rooms, 1 pb	Fully equipped kitchen
888-529-2542 912-844-9949	Most CC	Jacuzzi bath, balcony, great
Dale	C-yes/S-no/P-no/H-ltd	room, large screened porch,
		book selections, hot/cold
		outdoor showers

The view from the large screened porch of the Outdoor Inn looks South across miles of salt marsh and winding creeks. It's a great place to sit in the evenings and watch the egrets and herons that frequent the creek.
✉ seakayakga@aol.com 🌐 www.theoutdoorinn.com

Savannah Beach Inn	139-275 BB	Continental plus breakfast
21 Officers Row 31328	5 rooms, 5 pb	Wine reception
800-844-1398 912-786-0396	Most CC	Ocean view, fireplace, porch
Ann Last	C-ltd/S-ltd/P-no/H-no	

Close to Savannah with ocean views and near the Tybee Lighthouse, circa 1898. Savannah Beach Inn has five luxurious king and queen rooms with private baths, phone, and cable TV.
✉ ileader@telus.net 🌐 www.bbcanada.com/586.html

Tybee Island Inn	129-229 BB	Full breakfast
24 Van Horn 31328	5 rooms, 5 pb	Guest refrigerator is available
866-892-4667 912-786-9255	Most CC, •	to store perishables. Snacks
Cathy & Lloyd Kilday	C-ltd/S-no/P-no/H-no	or sweets are served in the
		afternoon.
		TV, king beds, large
		contemporary tubs/showers
		for 2, private porch or deck,
		wedding accommodations

Sleep your seashore fantasies in king and queen guestrooms inspired by the sea. Private baths with tubs for two, private decks or porch, A/C, cable TV. Tybee's NUMBER ONE bed and breakfast.
✉ info@tybeeislandinn.com 🌐 www.tybeeislandinn.com

VALDOSTA

Fairview Inn B&B	85-125 BB	Full breakfast
416 River St 31601	5 rooms, 5 pb	WiFi
229-244-6456	Visa, MC, AmEx	
Linda Green	C-yes/S-no/P-no/H-no	

Fairview Inn is located in the heart of Valdosta's oldest residential neighborhood, and immediately takes you back to the late 1800's when southern comfort and hospitality were a way of life.
✉ mystay@fairviewinn.info 🌐 www.fairviewinn.info

WASHINGTON ───────────────────────────────

Holly Court Inn
301 S Alexander Ave 30673
866-465-5928 706-678-3982
Philip & Margaret Rothman

120-185 BB
4 rooms, 4 pb
Most CC
C-yes/S-ltd/P-no/H-no

Full breakfast
24-hour complementary bar
with soft drinks and snacks
Fireplaces, parlor, dining
room, veranda, patio,
garden, library

The Holly Court Inn has been decorated with period antiques, all the better to immerse yourself in the flavor of the times. All of the rooms have modern amenities and guests are treated every morning to a delicious full breakfast.
✉ info@hollycourtinn.com ○ www.hollycourtinn.com

Southern Elegance B&B
115 W Robert Toombs Ave
30673
877-678-4775 706-678-4775
Jeanne Davis Blair

115-175 BB
4 rooms, 4 pb
Most CC
C-yes/S-ltd/H-yes

Country Breakfast
Complimentary champagne
(Honeymoon Suite), fruit
baskets, gourmet dinners
(weekends only)
Private garden, cable TV, CD
players, robes, fresh flowers

Experience the charm and romance of a bygone era in a beautifully restored Victorian Bed & Breakfast Inn located in historic Washington-Wilkes, Georgia.
✉ info@southernelegancebandb.com ○ www.southernelegancebandb.com

---

Washington Plantation
15 Lexington Ave 30673
877-405-9956 706-678-2006
Tom & Barbara Chase

150-220 BB
5 rooms, 5 pb
Visa, MC
C-ltd/S-ltd/P-no/H-ltd

Full breakfast
Wine & cheese in the
afternoon, goodies outside
your door by 7:00 am. Other
meals on request.
Fireplaces, telephones, WiFi
Internet, cable, robes &
slippers, coffeemakers, much
more

This fine old B&B inn began life in 1828 & grew into its present superb example of Greek Revival architecture. The 7 acres of grounds, planted with magnolias, oaks, dogwood, pecan, hickory, elm and crape myrtle, have served as a backdrop for history.
✉ info@washingtonplantation.com ○ www.washingtonplantation.com

Hawaii

BIG ISLAND, CAPTAIN COOK————————————————————

A Aloha Guest House
84-4780 Mamalahoa Hwy
96704
800-897-3188 808-328-8955
Johann Timmermann & Greg
Garriss

140-280 BB
5 rooms, 5 pb
Most CC, •
C-yes/S-ltd/P-yes/H-ltd
German

Mainly organic gourmet
breakfast
Jacuzzi, HDTV, high speed
Internet, WiFi, snorkel gear,
boogie boards, kayak rentals,
massage

*Located on the beautiful big island of Hawaii in the heart of South Kona Coffee Country.
Discover hospitality in comfortable, understated elegance. All accommodations feature
ocean and/or garden views. Kona coffee, gourmet breakfasts, hot tub access.*
✉ vacation@alohaguesthouse.com ◐ www.alohaguesthouse.com

Camp Aloha B&B
84-5210 Painted Church Rd
96704
808-328-2304
Joan & Casey McCarty

99 BB
1 rooms, 1 pb
Visa, MC
C-ltd/S-ltd/P-ltd/H-ltd

Continental breakfast
We offer made to order
breakfasts that you cook.
Kitchen is open to your use
24/7.
Pool, sun deck, hot tub,
fishponds, beautiful gardens,
and "wow" views.

*Life can be sweet in paradise on our five-acre tropical farm. About 20 miles south of Kailua-
Kona. Just minutes away by auto are world famous Kealakekua Bay with the Captain Cook
Monument and Place of Refuge on Honaunau Bay.* ✉ konajoan@yahoo.com

Diver Dan's B&B Hawaii
87-8133 Mamalahoa Hwy
96726
808-328-9546
Dan Ibbetson

145 BB
2 rooms, 2 pb
Cash
S-ltd/P-no/H-yes

Full breakfast
Coffee, island fruit juice
Great/Common Room, 60 ft
lap pool, ocean views,
kitchenette, king bed, snorkel
gear

*Mai! (come!) and be welcome at Diver Dan's B&B on the big island of Hawaii! We offer
great Pacific Ocean views and a great adventure! Our B&B is perched on top of a small
promontory in order to take full advantage of these magnificent ocean views.*
✉ diverdanbnb@hawaii.rr.com ◐ www.diverdansbnbhawaii.com

Hale Ho'ola B&B
85-4577 Mamalahoa Hwy
96704
877-628-9117 808-328-9117
Bob & Mary Dahlager

110-150 BB
3 rooms, 3 pb
Rated, •
C-yes/S-no/P-no/H-no

Full breakfast
Vegetarian, & special
requests, light snacks, coffee
& teas are always available
Sitting room, private lanai,
ocean views, beach towels,
mats, boogie boards, some
snorkel gear

*Hale Ho Ola is located on the Big Island of Hawaii amidst the unspoiled tropical country-
side of Old Hawaii. A two-story plantation-style home nestled on a ½ acre of tropical
gardens with panoramic ocean views. All guests suites are on the ground level.*
✉ tlc@hale-hoola.com ◐ www.hale-hoola.com

Ka 'awa Loa Plantation
82-5990 Napoo poo 96704
808-323-2686
Gregory Nunn & Michael
Martinage

125-195 BB
5 rooms, 4 pb
Most CC
C-ltd/S-no/P-no/H-ltd

Continental plus breakfast
Outdoor hot tub, outdoor
lava rock showers, 1,500
square-foot wrap-around
lanai, spectacular grounds

*A Guesthouse and start-up coffee farm in the heart of the Kona Coffee Belt. Nestled in
tropical surroundings 1,200 feet directly above Kealakekua Bay, our venue offers a wonderful spot to base your Big Island adventures.*
✉ info@kaawaloplantation.com ◐ www.kaawaloaplantation.com

BIG ISLAND, CAPTAIN COOK

Luana Inn	180-200 BB	Homemade high quality
82-5856 Napoopoo Road 96704	4 rooms, 4 pb	breakfast
877-841-8120 808-328-2612	Visa, MC, AmEx, •	Pool, hot tub, ample parking,
Ken Okagi & Erin Rene	C-ltd/S-no/P-no/H-ltd	wireless access, workstation, common room, BBQ and laundry facilities

Luana Inn offers total comfort in a gorgeous, secluded location within walking distance of Kealakekua Bay in beautiful South Kona on the Big Island of Hawaii. Join us for some of the most expansive, unobstructed ocean views anywhere on the Island.
✉ info@luanainn.com ◐ www.luanainn.com

Rainbow Plantation B&B	89-109 BB	Continental plus breakfast
81-6327 B Mamalahoa Hwy 96704	5 rooms, 5 pb	Coffee & tea, macadamia nuts all you can eat!
800-494-2829 808-323-2393	Most CC, •	Jungle Kitchen (open
Marianna & Reiner Schrepfer	German, French	Gazebo). High speed Internet access with your own laptop.

This private, natural, tropical island retreat is also a wildlife sanctuary for nature lovers on a coffee & macadamia nut farm above Kealakekua Bay. Private accommodations, open gazebo kitchen, BBQ, ocean views, great breakfasts. Wir sprechen Deutsch.
✉ reservations@rainbowplantation.com ◐ www.rainbowplantation.com

South Kona Hideaway	175-225 BB	Continental plus breakfast
83-5399 Middle Keei Rd 96704	2 rooms, 2 pb	Kona coffee is always available in your room, as well as
877-632-0999 808-328-0160	Most CC	tea, tropical juices & bottled water
Lou D'Angelo & Erik Hinshaw	C-yes/S-ltd/P-no/H-no	Private entrances, decks, refrigerator, microwave, WiFi, iPod docks, luxury linens

Escape to Hawaii in the heart of Kona coffee country. Relax on your private lanai & watch the sunset over Kealakekua Bay. Enjoy a breakfast of organic local fruit and freshly baked goods in the privacy of your own suite.
✉ info@southkonahideaway.com ◐ www.southkonahideaway.com

BIG ISLAND, HAWAII VOLCANOES NATIONAL PARK

Bamboo Orchid Cottage	139-189 BB	Tropical fruit, baked goods, cheese
11-3903 10th St 96718	4 rooms, 4 pb	Self-serve beverage bar
877-208-2199 808-985-9592	Visa, MC, AmEx, •	Great room, library, DVDs,
David Wood	C-yes/S-no/P-ltd/H-no	chess, outdoor hot tub, in room massage, guided hikes available.

Enjoy peaceful accommodations adjacent to Hawaii Volcanoes National Park. New Craftsman Cottage style home. Artisan beds with fine linens, private baths, cozy fireplaces & gourmet, tropical breakfast.
✉ BambooOrchidCottage@yahoo.com ◐ www.BambooOrchidCottage.com

BIG ISLAND, HILO

A Hawaiian Victorian Island Princess B&B	75-125 BB	Full breakfast
160 Kaiwiki Rd 96720	5 rooms, 3 pb	A convenient nook houses a self-serve coffee/tea station
866-953-8493 808-935-8493	Visa, MC, Disc	for refreshment at anytime of
Tom & Dianne Brookeman	C-ltd/S-no/P-yes/H-ltd	day or night.
		Grand Piano, Knowledgeable Staff, TV/DVD, Library, Guest Computer, Jacuzzi, Lovely Themed Rooms

In the Aloha Spirit, Tom & Dianne Brookman welcome you to VIP B&B, to their acre and a half of Hawaiian heaven. You will enjoy exploring all of what's wonderful on Big Island and the area surrounding Hilo.
✉ info@ahawaiianvipbandb.com ◐ www.ahawaiianvipbandb.com

BIG ISLAND, HILO————————————————————————

At the Beach with Friends	170-190 BB	Continental plus breakfast
369 Nene St 96720	3 rooms, 3 pb	Complimentary self service
808-934-8040	Visa, MC, AmEx, •	tea & coffee, snacks in the
Claudia Rohr & Scott Andrews	C-ltd/S-no/P-no/H-no	common room
		Beach, gardens, fish, sitting
		room, CD players, computer
		kiosk, WiFi, beach gear,
		maps, guide books

Big Island Bed and Breakfast in Hilo. Ocean view rooms. Beach access, swimming, snorkeling. Near to Hilo Airport, restaurants, shopping, farmer's market, waterfalls & historic Downtown Hilo. Close to Hawaii Volcano National Park, Akaka Falls, Mauna Kea
✉ beach@hilo.net ❂ www.bed-and-breakfast-hilo-hawaii.com

Emeraldview Guesthouse	180-220 BB	Full breakfast
272 Kaiulani St. 96720-2355	2 rooms, 2 pb	Private Entrance, Internet
808-961-5736	Visa, MC, *Rated*	access, private veranda,
Kenneth L. Richard	C-ltd/S-no/P-no/H-ltd	cable TV, outdoor Jacuzzi
	Japanese, Spanish,	spa
	Portuguese	

Enjoy a Hawaiian tropical breakfast from your room and beautiful views of waterfalls from your own private deck. Only a 15–20 minute walk from historic Hilo. We provide warm hospitality in this tropical paradise where no detail is overlooked.
✉ reservations@emeraldview.com ❂ www.emeraldview.com

Holmes' Sweet Home	80-95 BB	Hawaiian continental & fresh
107 Koula St 96720	2 rooms, 2 pb	fruits
808-961-9089	Visa, MC	
John & Charlotte Holmes	C-ltd/S-no/P-no/H-no	

Your private entrance from the lanai is through the sliding glass doors. Whether you choose the comfy and cozy Hawaiian Tropical Suite or the spacious Blue Ginger Suite, you will find each has a queen size bed and private bath.
✉ homswhom@hawaiiantel.net ❂ www.holmesbandb.com

Maureen's B&B	90-110 BB	Full breakfast
1896 Kalaniana'ole St 96720	4 rooms	Living room, Japanese tea
800-935-9018 808-935-9018	Most CC	room overlooks peaceful koi
Maureen Goto	C-ltd	ponds and a landscaped
		botanical garden.

Come visit! Return to "Old Hawaii." Enjoy our warm aloha and our generous breakfasts that always include tropical island fruits! Your vacation paradise located just steps from the beach and minutes from Hilo's finest downtown attractions!
✉ info@maureenbnb.com ❂ www.maureenbnb.com

Seascape Gardens B&B	105-160 BB	Full breakfast
2107 A Kaiwiki Rd 96720	2 rooms, 1 pb	Assorted drinks and local
808-961-3036	Cash, Checks, •	fruit kept in small refrigerator
Nancy K Molitor	C-yes/S-no/P-no/H-no	Use of barbecue and washer
	Spanish	and dryer if requested.

Coolly located just above Hilo with panoramic views of Hilo Bay to South Point and the active volcano. Plantation home was built in 1950's and has been extensively remodeled but the original charm remains. ✉ hilonancy@yahoo.com ❂ www.seascapegardens.com

Shipman House B&B	209-249 BB	Continental plus breakfast
131 Kaiulani St 96720	5 rooms, 5 pb	Snacks, tropical juices
800-627-8447 808-934-8002	Visa, MC, AmEx,	Historic house tour, library,
Barbara & Gary Andersen	*Rated*, •	grand piano, porch rocking
	C-ltd/S-no/P-no/H-ltd	chairs, free Internet wireless,
	Jan. 3 – Dec. 20	hula lesson

Near Volcanoes, museums, restaurants, gardens, snorkeling. Restored Victorian mansion on Reed's Island in Historic Hilo. Hawaiian koa wood antiques. Exotic flowers and estate-grown tropical fruits. Best breakfast around. Hula classes weekly. National Reg.
✉ innkeeper@hilo-hawaii.com ❂ www.hilo-hawaii.com

BIG ISLAND, HOLUALOA ——————————————————————————————

Holualoa Inn	270-360 BB	Full breakfast
76-5932 Mamalahoa Hwy	6 rooms, 6 pb	Ice tea and hot tea in the
96725	Most CC, •	afternoons, with homemade
800-392-1812 808-324-1121	C-ltd/S-no/P-no/H-no	cookies.
Cassandra Hazen		Pool, hot tub, covered
		outdoor Lanai, wireless
		Internet, 30 acres of tropical
		gardens

Get away from it all and experience another world. Kick off your flip flops and feel the grass between your toes as you gaze down on the bright blue ocean from this Kona B&B. Be at peace in your surroundings, experience aloha, experience Holualoa Inn.
✉ marketing@holualoainn.com ✪ www.holualoainn.com

The Orchid Inn	190-225 BB	Full breakfast
76-5893A Old Government Rd	2 rooms, 2 pb	
96725	Visa, MC, Disc, •	
808-324-0252	S-ltd/P-no/H-no	
Darrelyn M. Gravett		

The Orchid Inn reflects a style typical to a Hawaii of years past. This Kona Hawaii Bed & Breakfast is in the heart of the Kona coffee region surrounded by exotic coffee plantations with an occasional neighbor's house peeking through the trees.
✉ reservations@theorchidinn.com ✪ www.theorchidinn.com

BIG ISLAND, HONAUNAU ——————————————————————————————

A Dragonfly Ranch	100-300 BB	Healthy alternatives
84-5146 Keala O Keawe 96726	5 rooms, 5 pb	Organic Kona coffee, teas,
808-328-2159 808-328-9670	Visa, MC, AmEx, •	high protein grains, organic
Barbara Moore	C-yes/S-ltd/P-yes/H-no	fruit/nuts/seeds, sprouted
		breads
		Infrared sauna, labyrinth,
		soft laser, lomilomi massage,
		guided ocean tours (friendly
		wild dolphins)

Kona, Hawaii eco-tourism. Upscale tree house spa hosts romantic honeymoons, B&B families, workshops. Dolphins, snorkeling/diving, labyrinth, birding, yoga studio, lomilomi massage. New 2 bedroom private mini-spa with wheelchair access. Pets. Children.
✉ info@dragonflyranch.com ✪ www.dragonflyranch.com

Aaahhhà Paradise B&B	95-125 BB	Continental breakfast
83-5662 Old Government Rd	3 rooms, 3 pb	Coffee maker with comp.
96725	Visa, MC	organic 100% Kona coffee in
866-567-4375 808-938-3743	C-yes/S-ltd/P-no/H-no	each room.
Miles H. Mulcahy		High speed, wireless
		Internet, local calls, snorkel
		equipment/boogie boards,
		BBQ for guest use

Located on the Kona Coast of Hawaii's Big Island overlooking Honaunau and Kealakekua Bay. Just minutes away from beaches, restaurants and shopping areas.
✉ miles@aloha.net ✪ www.ahparadise.com

BIG ISLAND, HONOKAA ——————————————————————————————

Waianuhea B&B	195-400 BB	Full gourmet breakfast
45-3503 Kahana Dr 96727	5 rooms, 5 pb	Evening wine hour featuring
888-775-2577 808-775-1118	Most CC	new wine selections
Carol Salisbury & Reed Santos	C-ltd/S-ltd/P-no/H-yes	Daily maid service, nightly
		turndowns, Gilchrist/Soames
		bath products

Vacation on the Big Island of Hawaii! Getaway to a peaceful retreat in the tropical paradise that is the Hawaiian Islands.
✉ info@waianuhea.com ✪ www.waianuhea.com

BIG ISLAND, KAILUA KONA

Hale Maluhia Country Inn
76-770 Hualalai Rd 96740
800-559-6627 808-329-1123
Ken & Sue Smith cell: 808-896-8937

87-199 BB
5 rooms, 5 pb
Visa, MC, *Rated*, •
C-ltd/S-ltd/P-no/H-yes

Breakfast Buffet & Omelet bar
Island fresh fruits, fresh bread, omlette Bar, pastries, cereals, juice, teas & pure Kona coffee
Japanese spa w/massage jets, tropical gardens, BBQ area, beach accessories, library, swimfins, masks

A touch of aloha from old Hawai'i in this secluded, up-country, tropical Eden in the world's best climate. Featuring private baths, spa with massage jets, Koi ponds, stream, waterfalls, video library, wireless connection and a Breakfast Lover's Buffet.
✉ aloha@hawaii-inns.com ◐ www.hawaii-inns.com/hi/kna/hmh

Honu Kai B&B
808-329-8676
Wendi Wasson

140-175 BB
4 rooms, 4 pb
Visa, MC, •
C-ltd/S-no/P-no/H-ltd

Continental plus breakfast
Jacuzzi tub, concierge services, prearrange tours

E komo mai! Welcome! Hawaiian plantation style home with a Zen feel and luxurious amenities. Serene, peaceful, on 1.4 acres of tropical and old growth greenery. Perfect for small conferences, weddings or weekend getaways. Specializing in the Aloha spirit!
✉ honukaibnb@aol.com ◐ www.honukaibnb.com

Nancy's Hideaway B&B
75-1530 Uanani Pl 96740
866-325-3132 808-325-3132
Nancy Matthews

125-145 BB
2 rooms, 2 pb
Visa, MC
S-no/P-no/H-ltd

Continental breakfast
Wireless Internet, lanai (patio), phone (local calls free) and wet-bar

Enjoy all the Big Island has to offer with your own private cottage or studio tucked away on 3 acres in up-country Kona. Nancy's Hideaway offers privacy yet is conveniently located within minutes from Kailua-Kona. 3 night minimum stay.
✉ hideaway.kona@hawaiiantel.net ◐ www.nancyshideaway.com

BIG ISLAND, KAMUELA

Aaah The Views B&B Retreat
66-1773 Alaneo St 96743
808-885-3455
Erika & Derek Stuart

135-195 BB
3 rooms, 3 pb
Visa, MC, *Rated*, •
C-yes/S-no/P-no/H-no

Continental plus breakfast
Breakfasts of island fruits, fresh pastries, cereals, juices, local spreads/jams, honey, coffee, tea
On site massage, in room coffee and tea service, free wireless Internet for your laptop.

On the slopes of Mauna Kea, our peaceful, beautiful B&B offers cool, quiet nights with starry skies, sumptuous breakfasts beside the stream, spectacular views, & a restful, healing environment.
✉ erika@aaahtheviews.com ◐ www.aaahtheviews.com

BIG ISLAND, KAPOHO

Hale O Naia (House of the Dolphin)
14-5137 Alapai Point Rd 96778
808-965-5340
Sally Whitney

90-200 BB
3 rooms, 1 pb
C-ltd/S-no/P-no/H-ltd

Continental breakfast
New Jacuzzi hot tub, seclusion, beauty, sauna, sitting area, large Lanai, Kapoho Cove, swimming, TV

Lots of room to relax, read a book, write letters or just meditate on the sound of the soothing surf as it laps the back shore from Kapoho Cove. The house decor is tasteful and unique. The guestrooms and Master Suite, are all lavish and luxurious.
✉ dolphinwahine@yahoo.com ◐ www.hale-o-naia.com

BIG ISLAND, KEAAU

Ala Kai B&B
15-782 Paradise Ala Kai 96749
800-806-3646 808-966-7205
Mary Roblee and Pat Fay

100-175 BB
2 rooms, 2 pb
Visa, MC, *Rated*, •
C-ltd/S-no/P-no/H-no

Continental plus breakfast
TV, library, board games,
puzzles. Swimming pool,
coolers, beach chairs/towels
are available.

Ala Kai, in Hawaiian, means by the sea or road by the sea. Once you see our beautiful home, you will understand why we chose that name. Let the sounds of the ocean and palm trees lull you to sleep in one of our two beautiful guestrooms.
✉ info@alakaibb.com ○ alakaibb.com/index.htm

Art and Orchids
16-1504 39th Ave 96749
877-393-1894 808-982-8197
Jerry Gardner & Marklyn
Wilson

90-115 BB
3 rooms, 3 pb
Visa, MC, *Rated*, •
C-yes/S-no/P-no/H-ltd
German, Spanish

Continental plus breakfast
Coffee, tea, hot chocolate
Pool, hot tub, gazebo, beach
supplies, satellite TV/DVD,
library, kitchenette,
washer/dryer, WiFi

Wake to the sound of rain forest birds in our spacious home on the Big Island of Hawaii. Get away from it all in a quiet, relaxed setting. Enjoy walking through our grounds which include palm, bamboo, fruit, and native Ohia trees with hundreds of flowers.
✉ info@artandorchids.com ○ www.artandorchids.com

Kia'i Kai B&B
15-1825 Beach Rd 96749
888-542-4524 808-982-9256
John & Tory Mospens

105-165 BB
3 rooms, 3 pb
Visa, MC, *Rated*, •
C-yes/S-no/P-no/H-ltd

Full breakfast
Massage services, Jacuzzi,
swimming pool, suites, cable
TV, 2 night minimum, WiFi
Internet access

We invite you to join us at Kia'i Kai (key-ah-e-kye) where relaxation and the pure enjoyment of paradise are our goal. Whales seen in winter, dolphins and turtles seen all year. Full tropical breakfast with 100% Kona Coffee.
✉ innkeeper@hawaii-ocean-retreat.com ○ www.hawaii-ocean-retreat.com

BIG ISLAND, KEALAKEKUA

Kealakekua Bay B&B
800-328-8150 808-328-8150
Emily Peacock

140-220 BB
3 rooms, 3 pb
Visa, MC, AmEx

Continental breakfast

A luxurious Mediterranean-Polynesian-style villa overlooking the pristine Kealakekua Bay on the sunny south Kona coast of the Big Island of Hawaii.
✉ kbaybb@aloha.net ○ www.keala.com

BIG ISLAND, OCEAN VIEW

Bougainvillea B&B
Corner of Bougainvillea &
Kahili 96737
800-688-1763 808-929-7089
Martie Jean & Donald Nitsche

79-89 BB
4 rooms, 4 pb
Most CC, *Rated*, •
C-yes/S-yes/P-no/H-ltd

Full breakfast
Vegetarian and special diets
by request
Library, hottub, swimming
pool, satellite TV, BBQ, ping
pong, horseshoes, movies,
concierge

Nights and Breakfasts to Remember. Hosts Martie & Don, with 30 years in the travel industry, take extra care of their guests by offering a rewarding experience. Many amenities. Located midway between Kona & Hilo, 3 blocks off Hwy 11. Close to stores.
✉ peaceful@interpac.net ○ www.bougainvilleabedandbreakfast.com

BIG ISLAND, PAHOA

Coconut Cottage B&B
13-1139 Leliani Ave 96778
866-204-7444 808-965-0973
Jerry Cooksey & Todd Horton

110-160 BB
4 rooms, 4 pb
Visa, MC, AmEx
C-yes/S-ltd/P-ltd/H-ltd

Full gourmet breakfast
Lava Lounge activity room,
DVD library, books, games,
cds to borrow

Step back in time to vintage Hawaii when warm trade winds, the sweet smell of fresh plumeria leis and the distant sounds of naive ukuleles. Our B&B is surrounded by native flowers, waterfall, and genuine Bali bamboo hot tub with grass roof gazebo!
✉ info@coconutcottagehawaii.com ○ www.coconutcottagehawaii.com

Bougainvillea B&B, Ocean View, HI

BIG ISLAND, PAHOA————————————————————————

Lava Tree Tropic Inn	90-130 BB	Continental breakfast
14-3555 Puna Rd 96778	5 rooms, 2 pb	
808-965-7441	Visa, MC, *Rated*, •	
Irene Grunfeld	C-yes/S-no/P-no/H-yes	
	Hungarian, German,	
	Spanish, Italian	

Just 25 miles south of Hilo, in the lush Puna district of the Big Island of Hawaii, this tranquil haven is nestled in the heart of a magical rainforest, fragrant with scents of ginger, plumeria, and passionflower. The temperature is balmy year round.
✉ information@lavatreetropicinn.com 🌐 www.lavatreetropicinn.com

BIG ISLAND, SOUTH KOHALA————————————————————

Puako B&B	100-175 BB	Hawaiian continental
25 Puako Beach Dr 96743	4 rooms, 1 pb	breakfast
800-910-1331 808-882-1331	Visa, MC, AmEx	Fresh Island grown fruits,
Paul Andrade	C-ltd/S-no/P-no/H-ltd	local baked goods, island
		juices and most popular,
		100% Kona coffee
		King futon, queen bed,
		private baths and entrances,
		A/C, color TV, private
		Jacuzzi, maid service

Aloha and welcome to the Puako B&B on the Kohala Coast! Located on Puako Beach on the Island of Hawai'i, complete with luxury accommodations and an aloha with authenticity and style! Come visit us and see!
✉ puakobb@hawaii.rr.com 🌐 www.bigisland-bedbreakfast.com

BIG ISLAND, VOLCANO————————————————————————

A'alani Volcano Heart	100-125 BB	Continental breakfast
Hawaii	3 rooms, 3 pb	Coffee and tea available
470 Ulaino Rd 96713	Cash, Checks, *Rated*,	Kitchenette, sitting room
808-248-7725	•	with gas fireplace, honor fee
JoLoyce Kaia	C-ltd/S-no/P-no/H-no	laundry facilities

A vacation guesthouse near Volcano, on the Big Island of Hawaii. Explore Volcano National Park, exotic gardens, macadamia farms, Hilo's zoo & great restaurants! Relax in cool Volcano. Romantic and fun.
✉ joloyce@aol.com 🌐 ecoclub.com/hanamaui/volcano.html

178   Hawaii

BIG ISLAND, VOLCANO ─────────────────────────────

Aloha Junction
19-4037 Post Office Ln 96785
888-967-7286 808-967-7289
Robert & Susan Hughes

119 BB
4 rooms, 4 pb
Visa, MC, AmEx, •
C-yes/S-no/P-yes/H-no

Tropical breakfast
Vegetarian
Free Sauna, wireless Internet
& computer for all guests.

Situated just outside Hawaii Volcanoes National Park, in Volcano Village—on the Big Island of Hawaii—sits the Aloha Junction B&B. Spacious, affordable, with gracious hosts available onsite. Delicious, fresh breakfasts and four clean, comfortable rooms.
✉ alohajunction@hotmail.com 🌐 www.bnbvolcano.com

Aloha Place – Inn of Volcano
19-3820 Old Volcano Rd 96785
800-997-2292 808-967-7293
Joan Prescott-Lighter

140-165 BB
4 rooms, 4 pb
Visa, MC, •
C-yes/S-no/P-no/H-ltd
French, Hawaiian

All You Can Eat Island Style
In room mini-bar, hot
chocolate, Kona coffee
(regular and decaf) as well as
a selection of fine teas.
Private, secure entrances,
cableTV/VCR/DVD, Free
Internet, WiFi, housekeeping
and welcome candies.

Aloha Place- Inn of Volcano offers elegant, upcountry accommodations comprised of exquisitely appointed rooms. The expansive lanai is wonderful for afternoon reading or gathering with acquaintances.
✉ stay@alohaplace.com 🌐 www.alohaplace.com

Chalet Kilauea Collection
19-4178 Wright RD, BX 998
96785
800-937-7786 808-967-7786
David Warganich

65-289 BB
22 rooms, 16 pb
Visa, MC, Disc, *Rated*,
•
C-yes/S-ltd/P-no/H-no

Sumptuous Candle-lit
Continental
Afternoon Tea by fireside
from 3–5pm
Living room, library, Jacuzzi
tubs, fireplaces, wireless
Internet, flat LCD TV/DVD at
Inn at Volcano

The collection offers a selection of fine accommodations set immediately outside Hawaii's Volcanoes National Park. The collection is composed of 8 properties situated within Volcano Village and the Olaa rain forest reserve . . . peace and convenience!
✉ d.warganich@volcano-hawaii.com 🌐 www.volcano-hawaii.com

Guest House at Pali Uli
19-3870 Old Volcano Road
96785
800-997-2292 808-967-7293
Joan Prescott-Lighter

125-160 EP
4 rooms, 4 pb
Visa, MC, •
C-yes/S-no/P-no/H-ltd
French, Hawaiian

In room coffee/tea service,
hot chocolate and mini-bar.
Heat, cable TV/VCR/DVD,
videos, robes, hair dryer,
welcome chocolates, mini-
bar and refrigerator.

Come and experience true "Aloha" hospitality at its finest! No where else will you find such luxurious accommodations and ambience of old Hawaii.
✉ guesthouse@stayvolcano.com 🌐 www.stayvolcano.com

Kilauea Lodge
19-3948 Old Volcano Rd. 96785
808-967-7366
Lorna & Albert Jeyte

170-220 BB
14 rooms, 14 pb
Visa, MC, AmEx, *Rated*
C-yes/S-ltd/P-no/H-yes
German, Spanish

Full breakfast
Restaurant, bar, dinner
available 5pm–9pm,
Breakfast Daily
7:30am–10am, Sunday
Brunch 10am–2pm
Sitting room, hot tub, garden
gazebo, hot towel racks,
robes

Popular mountain lodge with full service restaurant. Nine rooms with fireplace. Hot tub, gazebos, gardens. One mile from spectacular Volcanoes National Park.
✉ stay@kilauealodge.com 🌐 www.kilauealodge.com

BIG ISLAND, VOLCANO——————————————————

My Island B&B
19-3896 Volcano Rd 96785
808-967-7216 808-967-7110
Gordon & Joann Morse & Kii Morse

85-165 BB
6 rooms, 4 pb
Visa, MC, Disc, •
C-yes/S-no/P-no/H-no

Continental breakfast
Inform host of special diets
Ponds, botanical garden

My Island B&B is a collection of historic bed and breakfast rooms, garden units, cottages and houses. Most are nestled in floral gardens, others in Volcano Village on the edge of Volcanoes National Park on the Big Island of Hawaii.
✉ myislandinn@hawaiiantel.net 🌐 www.myislandinnhawaii.com

Nancy's Volcano Cottages
19-4190 Iiwi Rd 96785
866-325-3132 808-325-3132
Nancy Matthews

99-109 BB
2 rooms, 2 pb
Visa, MC
C-yes/S-no/P-no/H-ltd

Continental breakfast
Breakfast included with first morning only.
Both cottages have dining area, lanai, laundry area, living room

Located in the rainforest, it's your home away from home offering privacy and convenience to area activities. Everything is here for you to enjoy your stay in this unique area of the Big Island.
✉ hideaway.kona@hawaiiantel.net 🌐 www.nancyshideaway.com

Volcano Country Cottages
19-3990 Old Volcano Rd 96785
888-446-3910 808-967-7960
Sandy & Garret Gooding

105-132 BB
4 rooms, 4 pb
Most CC, *Rated*, •
C-yes/S-ltd/P-no/H-no

Continental breakfast
Hot tub

Come share our little piece of paradise. Enjoy the privacy of your own cottage and the friendly advice of your hosts. We have several cottages, surely one will meet your needs. Check out the virtual tours on our web site.
✉ aloha@volcanocottages.com 🌐 www.volcanocottages.com

Volcano Guest House
11-3733 Ala Ohia St 96785
866-886-5226 808-967-7775
Bonnie Goodell & Alan Miller

115-130 BB
5 rooms, 5 pb
Visa, MC, *Rated*, •
C-yes/S-no/P-ltd/H-yes

Continental plus breakfast
Breakfast & snack materials available anytime
TV/VCR, telephone, wireless, hot tub spa, flashlights, umbrellas, library, nature trails

Handmade, housekeeping bed and breakfast cottages 5 minutes from Hawaii Volcanoes National Park. Six acres of forest with nature trails. Breakfast/snacks 24/7, line-dried linens, solar heating, recycling.
✉ innkeeper@volcanoguesthouse.com 🌐 www.volcanoguesthouse.com

---

Volcano Mist Cottage
11-3932 Ninth Street 96785
310-985-5560
Janet & Paul

245-295 BB
1 rooms, 1 pb
Visa, MC, •
C-ltd/S-no/P-no/H-no

Continental breakfast
Romantic fireplace, privacy, WiFi Internet access, Trek mountain bikes, in & outdoor showers, hottub

Volcano Mist Cottage is a handcrafted, eco-sensitive home on the summit of Kilauea. Our single cottage sanctuary is nestled in the rainforest adjacent to Hawai'i Volcanoes National Park, and offers absolute peace, privacy and romance in Volcano Village.
✉ relax@volcanomistcottage.com 🌐 www.volcanomistcottage.com

Volcano Rainforest Retreat
11-3832 Twelfth St 96785
800-550-8696 808-985-8696
Kathleen & Peter Golden

140-260 BB
4 rooms, 4 pb
Visa, MC
C-ltd/S-no/P-no/H-ltd

Continental plus breakfast
Retreat available for small groups, gathering place, bodywork, counseling

Wander the magical paths of this serene retreat, secluded in a lush native rain forest on the Big Island of Hawaii. Adjacent to Hawaii Volcanoes National Park.
✉ volrain@volcanoretreat.com 🌐 www.volcanoretreat.com

BIG ISLAND, VOLCANO

Volcano Teapot Cottage	195 BB	Continental breakfast
19-4041 Kilauea Rd 96785	2 rooms, 1 pb	
808-937-4976 808-967-7112	Visa, MC, AmEx	
Bill & Antoinette Bullough	S-no/P-no/H-no	

Fall under the spell of an enchanting turn-of-the century cottage in the heart of Volcano Village, Hawaii. Nestled on 3 acres of rainforest and surrounded by beautifully landscaped grounds, we invite you to experience the Hawaii of a bygone era.
✉ cottage@volcanoteapot.com 🌐 www.volcanoteapot.com

KAUAI, HANALEI

Bed Breakfast & Beach in Hanalei	125-175 BB	Continental plus breakfast
808-826-6111	3 rooms, 3 pb	Restaurants nearby,
	Cash, Checks, *Rated*,	supermarket and health food
	•	market nearby
	C-ltd/S-no/P-no/H-no	Sitting room, library, TV,
		coolers, snorkel equipment
		available

Elegance, peace & tranquility surrounded by lush mountains, tropical jungles, cascading waterfalls & most beautiful bay in the Hawaiian Island chain. 1 minute walk to Hanalei Bay.Can walk to quaint little surfing town. Very rural, country like.
✉ hanaleibay@aol.com 🌐 www.bestvacationinparadise.com/bandb.htm

River Estate	250-300 EP	Full gourmet kitchen.
5-6691 Kuhio Hwy 96714	2 rooms, 2 pb	Travel agency, activity
800 390-8444 808-826-5118	Most CC, •	bookings, area guide, local
Mark Barbanell	C-ltd/S-no/P-no/H-no	concierge.

River Estate is a secluded, romantic, air conditioned riverfront Kauai vacation rental which is 2 blocks from the beach on Kauai's north shore between Hanalei and Haena. It's situated in a lush botanical garden estate and central to the entire north shore
✉ info@riverestate.com 🌐 www.riverestate.com

KAUAI, KAPAA

Hale Lani B&B	125-185 BB	Island breakfast delivered
283 Aina Lani Pl 96746	4 rooms, 4 pb	daily
877-423-6434 808-823-6434	Most CC, •	Gift basket upon arrival filled
Ruth Johnson	C-yes/S-no/P-no/H-no	with Kauai treats
		Private hot tubs, beach and
		hiking equipment, on-site
		massage, stereo, TV, DVD,
		wireless Internet

One of Hawaii's 50 Best says Frommers, voted by inngoers "Best B & B to Recommend to Others" for 2006 by Arringtons, and recently featured in Inn Traveler Magazine, Hale Lani provides luxury accommodations in Kauai, complete with private hot tubs. Enjoy!
✉ innkeeper@halelani.com 🌐 www.halelani.com

KAUAI, KEKAHA

Ole Kamaole's Beach House	125-250 BB	Full "self-serve" breakfast
8663 Kaumaulii Hwy, Rt 50 96752	2 rooms, 2 pb	Bacon, eggs, waffles, bagels, coffee, juice & fresh fruit
800-528-2465 808-639-3614	Visa, MC, •	Full kitchen, cable TV,
Ole & Eileen Olson	C-ltd/S-ltd/P-no/H-no	wireless Internet, oceanfront,
	Some Hawaiian	whole property rental options

Beach house 80 feet from the ocean on Kauai's sunny Leeward side, at the foot of Mark Twain's "Grand Canyon of the Pacific," Waimea Canyon. Rain forest above, miles of empty beach below.
✉ OleHawaii@Hawaii.RR.com 🌐 www.OleHawaii.com

KAUAI, KOLOA

Hale Pohaku Beachside Cottages
2231 Pane Rd 96756
866-742-6462 808-742-8787
Summer Harrison

125-275 EP
11 rooms, 6 pb
Most CC, •
C-yes/S-no/P-no/H-ltd

Water, Hawaiian coffee & tea provided
Pool, boogie boards, beach chairs, weddings, full kitchens, washer & dryer, cribs, high chairs

Private vacation compound for two to 26, just a one minute walk from Poipu Beach. Our seclusion and amenities are perfect for family reunions, weddings, families traveling with kids, and travelers looking for a more Hawaiian experience than the condos.
✉ summer@aloha.net ✪ www.vacationrental-kauai.com

Poipu Plantation Resort
1792 Pe'e Rd 96756
800-634-0263 808-742-6757
Our friendly staff

125-210 BB
13 rooms, 13 pb
Visa, MC, *Rated*, •
C-ltd/S-ltd/P-no/H-ltd

Full breakfast
Full breakfast included for guests of the Inn. Kitchen w/o breakfast for vacation rental guests. Accommodations include A/C & many other features; beach towels & activity assistance in our office.

Poipu Beach Kauai from $125: four B&B Suites or nine Vacation Rental Suites with full kitchen. A/C with many features. Great for couples, honeymoons, families, commitment/wedding groups, reunions and just a great place to stay! Lots of Aloha shared here!
✉ plantation@poipubeach.com ✪ www.poipubeach.com

KAUAI, LAWAI

Hale Kua Guests on Kauai
4896 E Kua Rd 96765
800-440-4353 808-332-8570
Bill & Cathy Cowern

115-175 EP
5 rooms, 5 pb
•
C-yes/S-ltd/P-no/H-no

Fruit and nut trees available for the picking!
Units have kitchen, full bath, washer/dryer, TV, VCR, DVD, phone, queen bed

Aloha and welcome to the Hale Kua Guest Bed and Breakfast! Our secluded hillside retreat, located on Kauai's sunny south side, offers peace and serenity in one of our five choice accommodations. Looking for the perfect honeymoon spot? You've found it!
✉ treefarm@halekua.com ✪ www.halekua.com

Marjorie's Kauai Inn
3307-D Hailima Rd. 96765
800-717-8838 808-332-8838
Alexis & Mike

130-175 BB
3 rooms, 3 pb
Rated
S-no

Continental plus breakfast
High speed wireless Internet, DVD player and small library of films, coffee maker and microwave.

Marjorie's is perched above Kauai's Lawai Valley. Although the ambience is rural, you are five minutes from Old Koloa Town for shopping and ten minutes from world-famous Poipu Beach. "Do more than one fun thing in a day!"
✉ alexis@marjorieskauaiinn.com ✪ www.marjorieskauaiinn.com

KAUAI, PRINCEVILLE

Princeville Bed & Breakfast
3875 Kamehameha Rd 96722
800-826-6733 808-826-6733
Billie & Gary Sparks

135-300 BB
4 rooms, 4 pb
Visa, MC, AmEx,
Rated, •
S-no/P-no/H-no

Full breakfast
Many restaurants nearby
Located on 480 ft of Princeville golf course, tennis/health spa nearby, wireless Internet access

Enjoy views of the ocean, mountains, and the championship Makai Golf Course. Our luxury Kauai vacation rentals are perfect for your romantic Kauai wedding, honeymoon or next Hawaiian vacation.
✉ kauai@pixi.com ✪ www.Kauai-bandb.com

MAUI, HAIKU

Maui Dream Cottage
265 W Kuiaha Rd 96708
808-575-9079
Gregg Blue

110 EP
2 rooms
Visa, MC, *Rated*, •
C-yes/S-ltd/P-no/H-no
French, Spanish

Full kitchen
Full kitchen, washer-dryer,
phone, TV/VCR, cable and
high speed wireless Internet

Two acres of tropical fruits & flowers with ocean & mountain views. Full kitchens, washer/dryer & very private. Haiku itself is the old pineapple center of Maui. There are shops and an excellent restaurant within a minute from the house.
✉ gblue@aloha.net ❂ www.mauidreamcottage.com

MAUI, HANA

**Hana Maui Botanical
Gardens B&B Vacation
Rental**
470 Ulaino Road 96713
808-248-7725
JoLoyce Kaia

100-125 BB
2 rooms, 2 pb
Cash, Checks, *Rated*,
•
C-ltd/S-no/P-no/H-no

Continental breakfast
Coffee, tea, cocoa, juice,
muffins
Private kitchens, fresh fruit
picking, queen-size beds

Located in a tropical botanical garden—find the real Hawaii that few visitors see—there are two private studios available with kitchens, private baths and carports on the beautiful island of Maui. ✉ joloyce@aol.com ❂ www.ecoclub.com/hanamaui/hana.html

Hana Oceanfront Cottages
887-871-2055 808-248-7558
Dan & Sandi Simoni

250-275 EP
2 rooms, 2 pb
Visa, MC, Disc
S-no/P-no/H-no

Full Gourmet Kitchens
Fully appointed gourmet
kitchens are for guests to
create their own meals;
coffee and teas; Gas BBQ
Oceanfront lanais, gourmet
kitchens, gas BBQ grill,
beach chairs, umbrellas

In secluded and isolated Hana, Maui, Hawaii, these oceanfront vacation homes offer the finest in luxury vacation rentals. Many beach activities are right outside your door! Love is in the air . . . our inn is perfect for a romantic getaway for two!
✉ dansandi@maui.net ❂ www.myoceancottage.com

MAUI, KIHEI

Kai's B&B
80 E Welakahao Rd 96753
800-905-8424 x 24 808-874-6431
Rob & Patty Phillips

85-125 BB
4 rooms, 4 pb
Visa, MC, AmEx
S-no/P-no/H-no

Continental plus breakfast
for B&B
Bicycles, boogie boards,
umbrellas, beach chairs,
towels, snorkel gear

Situated in the heart of sunny Kihei, Maui, we are two blocks from the ocean and a short walk to sandy swimming beaches, dining, tennis, and shopping. We offer body-boards, bicycles beach chairs, towels, umbrellas, washer/dryer and snorkel gear as well!
✉ info@mauibb.com ❂ www.mauibb.com

MAUI, LAHAINA

Garden Gate
67 Kaniau Rd 96761
800-939-3217 808-661-8800
Jaime & Bill Mosley

119-229 BB
4 rooms, 4 pb
Visa, MC, *Rated*, •
C-yes/S-no/P-no/H-ltd
Spanish, little Japanese

Continental breakfast Mon-
Fri
TV, A/C, laundry,
irons/ironing boards,
refrigerator, coffeemakers,
wireless Internet, hairdryers

Garden Gate Bed and Breakfast is an elegant but affordable bed and breakfast centrally located close to Lahaina town and walking distance to Kaanapali beaches.
✉ info@gardengatebb.com ❂ www.gardengatebb.com

MAUI, LAHAINA

Lahaina Inn
127 Lahainaluna Rd 96761
800-669-3444 808-661-0577
Debbie

150-205 EP
12 rooms, 12 pb
Most CC, *Rated*, •
C-ltd/S-ltd/P-no/H-no

Tea, hot chocolate, & coffee
in morning
Antique fixtures, ceiling fan,
A/C, lanai, blow dryers,
beach towels, iron/board

Lahaina Inn is an elegant, 12 room B&B hotel in the heart of Lahaina Town. Each room is decorated with authentic antique furnishings, offering an atmosphere of charm and romance. ✉ inntown@lahainainn.com ◌ www.lahainainn.com

Penny's Place Inn Paradise
1440 Front St 96761
877-431-1235 808-661-1068
Penny & Keith Weigel

98-147 BB
4 rooms, 4 pb
Visa, MC, •
C-yes/S-no/P-no/H-no

Continental plus breakfast
Snacks, common kitchenette
w/toaster, refrigerator,
microwave, coffeemaker, ice
machine
Cable TV, laundry facilities,
on-site parking, small library,
Internet connection

Penny's Place Inn Paradise B&B is located on the island of Maui, on world famous Front Street in historic Old Lahaina Town. Just 150 feet from the water's edge, we offer ocean views of Lana'i, Moloka'i, and the leeward beaches of Lahaina.
✉ stay@pennysplace.net ◌ www.pennysplace.net

MAUI, MAKAWAO

Banyan B&B
3265 Baldwin Ave 96768
808-572-9021
Marty Herling

145-190 BB
7 rooms, 8 pb
Most CC
C-yes/S-ltd/P-no/H-yes

Continental breakfast
Coffee, tea, herbal tea, hot
cocoa, bananas, avocados,
other fruit from the property
when in season.
Wireless Internet, washer/
dryer, pool, Jacuzzi, swings
& hammocks, handicap
accessible room and pool

Cottages and suites in a centrally located shady, quiet retreat. Close, yet wonderfully removed from Maui's resort beachfront crowds. The Banyan B&B simply overflows with peace and Hawaii-ana including a swimming pool, Jacuzzi, yoga studio and gardens.
✉ info@bed-breakfast-maui.com ◌ www.bed-breakfast-maui.com

MAUI, PAIA

Blue Tile Beach House
459 Hana Hwy 96779
888-579-6446 808-579-6446
Angie & Paul Peters

90-250 BB
6 rooms, 6 pb
Visa, MC, AmEx,
Rated, •
C-yes/S-no/P-no/H-ltd

Continental breakfast
Grill available; kitchenettes
in the two oceanfront suites
Car rental discount available
upon booking.

The 4,800 sq. ft. house has a spacious main lobby with two spiral stairways leading to the two separate wings of the house. There are 6 bedrooms, all with private bathrooms. A beautiful grassy courtyard extends to the white sandy beach.
✉ info@beachvacationmaui.com ◌ www.beachvacationmaui.com

The Spyglass House
367 Hana Hwy 96779
800-475-6695 808-579-8608
Poni Brendan

110-180 BB
6 rooms, 4 pb
Most CC, *Rated*, •
C-yes/S-no/P-ltd/H-ltd
Espanol

Continental breakfast
Tea, coffee, juice, bagels,
frozen waffles & hot cereal,
full kitchen, barbecue
available
Living room, oceanfront
lanai, large lawn, parking,
kitchens, Jacuzzi, barbecue,
½ mile from town

Oceanfront Bed and Breakfast located ½ mile from surf town Paia. Three houses, 6 unique rooms, full kitch. 30 ft. from the water's edge. Enjoy white sand beaches, beautiful ocean views, as central as you can be on Maui to see the entire island.
✉ info@spyglassmaui.com ◌ www.spyglassmaui.com

184   Hawaii

OAHU, HONOLULU

Aloha Bed and Breakfast
909 Kahauloa Pl 96825
808-395-6694
Phyllis & Donald Young

75-100 BB
3 rooms
C-yes/S-no/P-no/H-no

Full breakfast
Will try to accommodate special dietary needs or preferences.
Wireless access, swimming pool w/ natural salt-to-chlorine, cable TV, large deck with patio sets.

Non-smoking B&B perched on Mariners Ridge in Hawaii Kai with wonderful views of water/mountains. Minutes to famed snorkeling beach, Hanauma Bay. Healthy breakfasts. Salt-filtered pool. Wireless access so bring your laptop computer.
✉ alohaphyllis@hawaii.rr.com ○ home.hawaii.rr.com/alohaphyllis/

Manoa Valley Inn
2001 Vancouver Dr 96822
808-947-6019
Theresa Wery

99-190 BB
7 rooms, 4 pb
Visa, MC, *Rated*, •
C-ltd/S-no/P-no/H-no

Continental plus breakfast
Tea, coffee, wine
Cable TV, large veranda for lounging

Historic Country Inn located in Honolulu. Peaceful, tropical setting with views of Waikiki city lights. Unique, tropical, heated salt water pool.
✉ manoavalleyinn@aloha.net ○ www.manoavalleyinn.com

OAHU, KAILUA

Hawaii's Hidden Hideaway B&B
1369 Mokolea Dr 96734
877-443-3299 808-262-6560
Janice

150-195 BB
3 rooms, 3 pb
Cash, Checks, •
C-yes/S-no/P-no/H-no

Continental plus breakfast
Snacks
Jacuzzi, cable TV/DVD player, WiFi, beach chairs/towels/mats, hairdryers, irons, laundry, telephone

Award Winning, "Most Romantic Hideaway" on Oahu, the fabulous landscaping and gardens make you feel that you are in another world. Ideal for honeymoons, special occasions, family vacations or business. Member: Better Business Bureau & Chamber of Commerce.
✉ hhhideaway@yahoo.com ○ www.ahawaiibnb.com

Kailua Hawaii Sheffield House
131 Kuulei Rd 96734
808-262-0721
Paul & Rachel Sheffield

90-125 BB
2 rooms, 2 pb
Visa, MC, •
C-yes/S-no/P-no/H-ltd

Breakfast provided 1st morning
Breakfast is sweet bread, fruit, juice, coffee and tea
Both rooms have WiFi, microwave, coffee maker, toaster & refrigerator

Looking for a tropical, paradise, Hawaii vacation near sandy Kailua Beach with warm ocean water—the island of Honolulu, Oahu? Think Sheffield House Bed and Breakfast for your accommodations for aloha, windsurfing, snorkeling, surfing, tours, or hiking.
✉ rachel@hawaiisheffieldhouse.com ○ www.hawaiisheffieldhouse.com

Papaya Paradise B&B
395 Auwinala Rd 96734
808-261-0316
Bob & Jeanette Martz

100-115 BB
2 rooms, 2 pb
Cash, Checks, *Rated*, •
C-ltd/S-no/P-no/H-no

Self catered
Hosts provide fresh brewed coffee/tea, cereals, milk, bagels, bread, etc. for guests' breakfast
Pool, TV, A/C, phone, Internet, free parking, beach accessories, library, refrigerator, micro, toasteroven

Hosted licensed home in residential beach community. Private entry & bath units, twenty miles from airport & Waikiki.½mile to Kailua Beach, 1 mile to Lanakai Beach. Furnished in rattan/wicker & opens onto pool & garden. Easy access to all attractions.
✉ rentme@hawaii.rr.com ○ kailuaoahuhawaii.com

Idaho

Paradise Valley Inn	99-150 BB	Full breakfast
300 Eagle Way 83805	6 rooms, 6 pb	Afternoon tea, cider, hot
888-447-4180 208-267-4180	Visa, MC, AmEx, *Rated*	chocolate and snack, catered
Kristyn Brunz	C-ltd/S-no/P-ltd/H-ltd	dinner can be arranged
		Library, hot tub (open 4/1 – 11/1), snowshoes, hiking or biking trails, massage, sitting areas

Experience one of the most dramatic vistas in North Idaho from every room. Large newer log B&B with elegant furnishings located on 18 wooded acres. Enjoy the romantic serenity and the unforgettable views. 3.5 miles away from highway noise, no neighbors!
✉ info@paradisevalleyinn.com ◎ www.paradisevalleyinn.com

Katie's Wild Rose Inn	115-235 BB	Full breakfast
7974 E Coeur'd Alene Lake Dr	3 rooms, 2 pb	Sitting room, Jacuzzis, suites,
83814	Visa, MC	fireplaces, Coeur d' Alene
800-371-4345 208-765-9474	C-ltd/S-no/P-no/H-ltd	lake view, game room
Karin & Gary Spence		

Overlooking beautiful Lake Coeur d'Alene is one reason Katie's Wild Rose Inn has become one of the most popular B&B and wedding facilities in North Idaho. Surrounded by pine trees, lilacs and wild rose bushes.
✉ stay@katieswildroseinn.com ◎ www.katieswildroseinn.com

Hearthstone Elegant Lodge	125-235 BB	Full breakfast
by the River	5 rooms, 5 pb	Afternoon tea, lunch &
3250 Hwy 12 Mile Post 64	Visa, MC, *Rated*, •	dinner available
83536	C-ltd/S-no/P-no/H-no	Spacious suites, guest
877-LODGE-4U 208-935-1492	German	library, meeting space,
Harty & Marjorie Schmaehl		quality amenities, Internet access

An elegant river lodge with fireplaces, Jacuzzis and river view balconies on the historic Lewis and Clark Trail. A twenty nine-acre pine forest setting. Extraordinary hideaway retreat. ✉ visit@hearthstone-lodge.com ◎ www.hearthstonelodge.com

Blue Heron Inn	109-199 BB	Full breakfast
4175 E Menan Lorenzo Hwy	7 rooms, 7 pb	Lunch bags available,
83442	Most CC, *Rated*, •	complimentary soft drinks,
866-745-9922 208-745-9922	C-ltd/S-no/P-ltd/H-yes	wine, and beer
Claudia & Dave Klingler		Conference Room, library, suites, fireplaces, hot tub

Relax and unwind at the Blue Heron Inn on the banks of the South Fork of the Snake River. Unmatched hospitality, beautiful views and delicious breakfasts will make your stay memorable. ✉ innkeeper@idahoblueheron.com ◎ www.idahoblueheron.com

Greyhouse Inn	65-150 BB	Full gourmet breakfast
1115 Hwy 93 S 83467	9 rooms, 7 pb	Lunch, dinner, afternoon tea
800-348-8097 208-756-3968	Most CC, •	upon request
Sharon & David Osgood	C-ltd/S-no/P-yes/H-no	Snacks, library, bikes, cable, hot tub, tours of Lewis & Clark

Victorian inn with guestrooms, also offers Lewis & Clark log cabins with log beds, private baths, large porch for viewing the beautiful mountains. Lemhi Shoshone and Trapper cabins: kitchenettes, queen beds and lofts with 2 twin beds, and great views.
✉ osgood@hughes.net ◎ www.greyhouseinn.com

Illinois

ALTON

Beall Mansion
407 E 12th St 62002-7230
866-843-2325 618-474-9100
Jim & Sandy Belote

119-358 BB
5 rooms, 5 pb
Most CC, •
C-ltd/S-no/P-no/H-no

Gourmet, Continental or
Area Cafe'
Delectable catering for
weddings & receptions,
meetings, and corporate
retreats.
Whirlpools for 2, fireplaces,
gourmet chocolates, plush
robes, expanded cable
TV/DVD/VCR, massage

Voted "Best Illinois Bed and Breakfast," Illinois Magazine Readers Poll. Whirlpools for two.
Fireplaces. Gourmet chocolates. Plush monogrammed robes. Need we say more? Located
25 minutes from the St. Louis Gateway Arch in historic Alton, Illinois.
✉ bepampered@beallmansion.com ◑ www.beallmansion.com

Jackson House
1821 Seminary St 62002
800-462-1426 618-462-1426
Hope Apple

120-165 BB
4 rooms, 4 pb
Visa, MC, *Rated*
C-ltd/S-no/P-ltd/H-ltd

Full breakfast
Complimentary wine
Sitting room, library,
Jacuzzis, cottages, fireplaces,
cable TV

In town, but with a relaxing, secluded atmosphere. Choose an elegant guestroom or one of
our cozy guesthouses—The Barn or The Cave.
◑ www.jacksonbb.com

BLOOMINGTON

Davis Rose Inn
1001 E Jefferson St 61701
309-829-6854
Chris & Rose Hotz

99-139 BB
3 rooms, 3 pb
Most CC
C-ltd/S-ltd/P-no/H-no

Full breakfast
Snacks, soda, bottled water,
cookies, coffee, tea, hot
chocolate . . . always
available for our guests
Wireless Internet, TV on
request only, 2 guest parlors,
bikes available

The Davis Rose Inn Bed & Breakfast is located in the Davis-Jefferson Historic District in
Bloomington, Illinois. The Inn has a total of 3 guestrooms, all furnished with period
antiques, queen sized beds, and loaded with charm. All rooms have private bath
✉ information@davisroseinn.com ◑ www.davisroseinn.com

Vrooman Mansion B&B
701 E Taylor St 61701
877-346-6488 309-828-8816
Pam & Dana Kowalewski

85-125 BB
5 rooms, 5 pb
Most CC, *Rated*
C-yes/S-ltd/P-no/H-no

Full breakfast
Wireless, common sitting
room with cable TV/VCR,
assorted video tapes, DSL,
library

Built in 1869, this B&B is nestled in a quiet neighborhood in Bloomington, 2 hours from
Chicago. Beautifully appointed rooms with antiques await you.
✉ information@vroomanmansion.com ◑ www.vroomanmansion.com

CHAMPAIGN

The Gold's B&B
2065 County Rd 525 E 61822
217-586-4345
Rita Gold

55 BB
3 rooms, 1 pb
Cash, Checks
C-yes/S-no/P-no/H-no

Continental plus breakfast
Cable TV, DVD

The Golds Bed & Breakfast is located west of Champaign just off Interstate 74. Country
charm & hospitality in an 1874 farmhouse. Handy to interstate & university attractions.
Furnished with antiques.
✉ ritagold59@gmail.com

CHICAGO————————————————————————————

China Doll Guest House	225-375 BB	Guest Prepared Bkfst
738 W Schubert Ave 60614	3 rooms, 3 pb	gourmet kitchens filled with
866-361-1819 773-525-4967	Visa, MC, *Rated*, •	dozens of breakfast foods
Jim & Yanan Haring	C-yes/S-ltd/P-yes/H-no	and your favorite beverages
	Mandarin	Sitting room, library,
		Jacuzzis, fireplaces, cable
		TV, office amenities,
		washer/dryer, housekeeping

Three private apartments especially designed for the business traveler, with superb personal comfort features. Complete office, in Lincoln Park.
✉ ChinaDollChicago@Yahoo.com 🌐 chinadollguesthouse.com

City Scene B&B	135-300 BB	Self-serve continental
2101 N Clifton Ave 60614	2 rooms, 2 pb	breakfast
800-549-1743 773-549-1743	Visa, MC	Full kitchen allows guest to
Mary Newman	C-ltd/S-no/P-no/H-no	prepare breakfast at leisure
		Sitting room with fireplace,
		bathroom with steam
		shower, TV/DVD/VCR, free
		high speed Internet access

Comfortable, private suite with one or two bedrooms, sitting room, kitchen and bath on a residential street, in the Sheffield Historic District. Close to dining, shopping, museums, parks, theatres and transportation.
✉ host@cityscenebb.com 🌐 www.cityscenebb.com

Gold Coast Guest House B&B	129-229 BB	Continental breakfast
113 West Elm St 60601	4 rooms, 4 pb	Afternoon tea, snacks
312-337-0361	Most CC, *Rated*, •	Comp. snack, sitting room,
Sally Baker	C-ltd/S-no/P-no/H-no	soaking tub, each unit has
		cable TV/CD/phone,
		computers, printers, DVD

This 1873 Victorian hides a contemporary secret inside . . . a 20 foot high window-wall lets the garden in while you enjoy breakfast.
✉ sally@bbchicago.com 🌐 www.bbchicago.com

Harvey House B&B	175-275 BB	Full Breakfast
708-848-6810	5 rooms, 5 pb	Deluxe robes, WiFi Internet
Beth Harvey	Most CC, *Rated*, •	access, color printer,
	C-ltd/S-no/P-no/H-no	fax/copier, TV/VCR, licensed
		massage therapist

Chicago Tribune Best Hotel List and Chicago Magazine Best Neighborhood Hotel, Brick Victorian B&B in Oak Park is 2 blocks walk to El & Metro trains for Chicago- 8 miles and airports. Fireplaces and Jacuzzis in suites, gourmet breakfast any time, WiFi
✉ harveyhousebb@gmail.com 🌐 www.harveyhousebb.com

The House of Two Urns	129-189 BB	Hot breakfast entree and
1239 N Greenview Ave 60642-3318	7 rooms, 5 pb	buffet
877-Two-Urns 773-235-1408	Visa, MC, Disc, •	Complimentary coffee/tea
Kapra Fleming and Miguel Lopez Lemus	C-yes/S-no/P-no/H-no	service all guests have
	German, Spanish, French	access to a shared or private
		kitchen(ette).
		Free WiFi, DISH TV, DVD
		movie library, local phone
		calls, computer w/Internet
		access, parking

Filled with antiques & original art, this urban inn is very convenient to shopping, sightseeing, superb restaurants & more. Offers 3 guestrooms, 1 suite or 3 apartments in Chicago's vibrant Wicker Park, very close to public transit and the expressway.
✉ info@twourns.com 🌐 www.twourns.com

CHICAGO —————————————————————————————————

Old Town Chicago Guest House 1442 N North Park Ave 60610 312-440-9268 Mike & Liz Serritella	185-275 BB 4 rooms, 4 pb Visa, MC, AmEx, *Rated*, • C-ltd/S-no/P-no/H-no	Continental plus breakfast Complimentary 24 hour breakfast & snacks Parking, WiFi, grand piano, videos, phonograph, washer & dryer, Life Fitness elliptical & bike

Downtown, spacious, elegant and new, this luxury lodging occupies the 3,250 square foot west wing of a 1999 Chicago city house. Four bedrooms each with en-suite bath, a private guest entrance and generous common areas make this an ideal vacation rental.
✉ mail@oldtownchicago.com ☉ www.oldtownchicago.com

Wicker Park Inn 1329 N Wicker Park Ave 60622 773-486-2743 Laura & Mikky Wright	129-189 BB 7 rooms, 7 pb Visa, MC, AmEx C-yes/S-no/P-no/H-no Spanish	Continental breakfast Microwave, fridge, iron/ironing board, wireless Internet, free parking

Located on a quiet, tree-lined street in Chicago's historic Wicker Park neighborhood, the B&B is near restaurants, vintage & boutique shops, art galleries, cafes, nightlife & all Chicago attraction. Just minutes from downtown via cab or nearby subway.
✉ wickerparkinn@sbcglobal.net ☉ www.wickerparkinn.com

CREAL SPRINGS —————————————————————————————

Oakridge Manor B&B 9049 Rt 166 62922 618-996-2237 Anna and Bob Bordenave	100-170 BB 4 rooms, 4 pb Visa, MC S-no/P-no/H-no	Full breakfast Snacks, sodas, fresh cookies SatTV, DVDs, Internet, swimming pool, pond, decks, patios, horse boarding, Dinners upon request

French country manor located on 98 acres in the center of the Shawnee National Forest area of Southern Illinois.
✉ innkeeper@oakridgemanor.com ☉ www.oakridgemanor.com

DU QUOIN —————————————————————————————————

Francie's Inn 104 S Line St 62832 877-877-2657 618-542-6686 Roland & Debra Scheller	80-105 BB 6 rooms, 6 pb Most CC, *Rated*, • C-ltd/S-no/P-ltd/H-no	Full breakfast Cable TV, hotel phone system, wireless Internet, complimentary snacks, beverages, rm. service avail.

The place for a getaway vacation, romantic escape or business retreat. Walking distance to restaurants and shops, or relax on one of our big decks.
✉ info@franciesinnonline.com ☉ www.franciesinn.com

EVANSTON ————————————————————————————————

Margarita European Inn 1566 Oak Ave 60201 847-869-2273 Michael Pure	79-179 BB 42 rooms, 22 pb Most CC, *Rated*, • C-yes/S-no/P-no/H-ltd Spanish	Continental breakfast Award winning Italian restaurant, Va Pensiero, serving dinner. Evening room service, high speed wireless Internet, English library, grand parlor

The Margarita European Inn offers 42 rooms, each individually appointed & furnished with antiques, providing a unique & memorable atmosphere. Experience the elegance & service of an era you thought only existed in memory. Restaurant;easy access to Chicago
✉ info@margaritainn.com ☉ www.margaritainn.com

GALENA—————

Aaron's Cottages & The Goldmoor Inn	215-345 BB	Full breakfast
9001 W. Sand Hill Rd 61036	17 rooms, 17 pb	Fine dining seven course
800-255-3925 815-777-3925	Most CC, *Rated*, ●	gourmet meal service at
Patricia Goldthorpe	C-ltd/S-no/P-ltd/H-yes	Goldmoor Dining.
		Complimentary room soft
		beverages.
		Massage services, mountain
		bikes, wireless Internet,
		weddings and receptions.

Galena, IL's most elegant inn. Luxury log cabins, cottages and suites with whirlpools, fireplaces and full breakfast included. Fine dining on premises. Romantic river view. Excellent wedding and reception location. Top rated since 1993. Great hospitality.
✉ goldmoor@galenalink.com ◐ www.goldmoor.com

Aldrich Guest House	100-150 BB	Full breakfast
900 3rd St 61036	5 rooms, 5 pb	Wine and cheese each
815-777-3323	Visa, MC	evening, pastries, cookies,
Fran & Brian Onak	C-ltd/S-no/P-no/H-no	soft drinks & water available
		all day.
		Library with TV/DVD, board
		games, sitting room,
		screened porch, lawn games.

1845 Greek Revival visited by Lincoln, Twain and Grant. The surrounding land was where Grant once trained his troops. One block from Grant's home. The ambience still remains in this quiet residential neighborhood.
✉ aldrich@aldrichguesthouse.com ◐ www.aldrichguesthouse.com

Annie Wiggins Guest House	95-235 BB	Full breakfast
1004 Park Ave 61036	7 rooms, 7 pb	Complimentary lemonade
815-777-0336	Most CC	Sitting room, library, suites,
Wendy & Bill Heiken	C-ltd/S-no/P-no/H-no	fireplace, porches, upright
		grand piano, refrigerator
		with ice

Romantic, historic mansion welcomes you to its whispers of the past. Shhh! Annie still thinks it's 1860. Seven guestrooms with queen size pillow top beds and private baths. Some with romantic soaking tubs for two or fireplaces.
✉ annie@anniewiggins.com ◐ www.anniewiggins.com

Belle Aire Mansion Guest House	90-185 BB	Full breakfast
11410 Rt 20 W 61036	5 rooms, 5 pb	Snacks, chocolate chip
815-777-0893	Visa, MC, Disc, ●	cookies in guestrooms, early
Jan & Lorraine Svec	C-yes/S-no/P-no/H-no	morning coffee buffet.
	Closed Christmas	Sitting room, Jacuzzis, suites,
	Day/Eve	fireplaces

A warm home with the friendliest Innkeepers you'll ever find. Located just minutes from Historic Galena on 11 beautiful acres. Innkeepers have been welcoming guests into their home for 20 years. Be prepared to be pampered!
✉ belleair@galenalink.com ◐ www.belleairemansion.com

Bernadine's Stillman Inn & Wedding Chapel	120-280 BB	Full breakfast
513 Bouthillier St 61036	7 rooms, 7 pb	Chocolate chip cookies, ice
866-777-0557 815-777-0557	Visa, MC, Disc, ●	cream bars, fruit and
Dave & Bernadine Anderson	C-ltd/S-ltd/P-no/H-ltd	popcorn
		Parlor with piano, Wedding
		Chapel, 2 acre garden filled
		courtyards, close to nature
		trail & Main St.

Romantic 1858 Victorian Mansion awarded "Best Innkeeper" and "Best Breakfast in the Midwest." Close to town and located in residential neighborhood with ample parking. Garden filled courtyards. Seven guestrooms with private baths.
✉ stillman@stillmaninn.com ◐ www.stillmaninn.com

GALENA

Captain Harris Guest House
713 S Bench St 61036
800-996-4799 815-777-4713
Frank & Anne McCaw

99-209 BB
5 rooms, 5 pb
Visa, MC, Disc
C-ltd/S-no/P-no/H-no

Full gourmet breakfast
Sitting room, library
Jacuzzis, suites, fireplaces,
cable TV, DVD, data ports

Historic home (c.1836) in the heart of Galena. Walk to all restaurants & attractions
Honeymoon cottage with whirlpool for that very special occasion.
✉ captainharris@mchsi.com ☻ www.captainharris.com

Cloran Mansion
1237 Franklin St 61036
866-234-0583 815-777-0583
Carmine & Cheryl Farruggia

99-225 BB
6 rooms, 6 pb
Most CC, *Rated*, •
C-ltd/S-ltd/P-ltd/H-yes

Full breakfast
Mini fridge with
complementary soda &
water in each room, cookies,
popcorn, candy, tea, coffee
Bicycles, screened gazebo,
video library, DVDs, wireless
Internet access, garaged
motorcycle parking

Romantic getaway in an 1880 Victorian Mansion. Relax by the warmth of the fireplace or in
one of the whirlpools built for two. A full country style breakfast awaits you in the morning
Simply the best!
✉ innkeeper@cloranmansion.com ☻ www.cloranmansion.com

Farmers' Guest House
334 Spring St 61036
888-459-1847 815-777-3456
Jess & Kathie Farlow

119-250 BB
9 rooms, 9 pb
Most CC, •
C-ltd/S-no/P-no/H-ltd

Full, hot breakfast
Snacks, beverages, wine &
cheese served at 6:00 pm
Sitting room, large common
areas, hot tub, Gift Shop in
B&B

Farmers' Guest House welcomes you with the delight and charm of a by-gone era plus the
conveniences of today. We attend to the little things . . . so you can enjoy your stay and
make our house your home.
✉ stay@galenabedandbreakfast.com ☻ www.farmersguesthouse.com

Park Avenue Guest House
208 Park Ave 61036
800-359-0743 815-777-1075
Sharon Fallbacher

95-145 BB
4 rooms, 4 pb
Visa, MC, Disc, *Rated*
C-ltd/S-no/P-no/H-no

Full breakfast
Early morning coffee,
Afternoon tea, snacks
Sitting room with TV, 2
parlours, gazebo, A/C,
fireplaces in rooms

Elegant yet comfortable, in quiet residential area. Short walk to beautiful Grant Park
Galena River and Main Street restaurants & shopping.
✉ parkave@galenalink.com ☻ www.galenaparkavenue.com

Pine Hollow Inn
4700 N Council Hill Rd 61036
815-777-1071
Larry & Sally Priske

110-160 BB
5 rooms, 5 pb
Visa, MC, Disc, *Rated*
C-ltd/S-ltd/P-no/H-no

Full breakfast
Hiking, whirlpool bath, quiet
seclusion, in room or stream
side massages, fireplace,
outdoor fire pit

A secluded country inn located on 120 acres, just 1 mile from downtown Galena. A
splendid location to view wildlife and nature at its very best. Relax in front of your own
cozy fireplace, or just kick back on the wrap-around porch. A peaceful getaway
✉ pine@pinehollowinn.com ☻ www.pinehollowinn.com

Pine Hollow Inn, Galena, IL

GALENA

Queen Anne Guest House	95-140 BB	award winning breakfast
200 Park Ave 61036	4 rooms, 4 pb	At parlor party, we serve
815-777-3849	Most CC	refreshments and appetizers
Mike & Anita Reese	C-yes/S-no/P-no/H-no	at 5 pm. A great way to know
		the other guests.
		Two parlors, library with
		books, games, cds and
		movies. A garden, fish pond
		and wireless Internet.

Located in a quiet neighborhood close to main Street, hiking/bike trail and Grant's Park and home. Our B&B has won numerous awards, including best breakfast in the Midwest. Come visit us in our historic, Victorian home and leave as a new friend.
✉ queenann@netexpress.net ❂ www.queenanneguesthouse.com

The Steamboat House B&B	105-155 BB	Full breakfast
605 S Prospect St 61036	5 rooms, 5 pb	Evening wine & cheese
800-717-2317 815-777-2317	Visa, MC, Disc	Walk to town location,
Charlene & Glen Carlson	C-ltd/S-no/P-no/H-no	private off-street parking,
		billiard room, parlors, high
		speed Internet

Grand mansion offering luxurious getaways, located only a block and a half away from downtown Galena. Heirloom antiques & historic photographs fill the parlors and five guestrooms of this premier Galena destination. Seasonal packages available.
✉ glenchar@thesteamboathouse.com ❂ www.thesteamboathouse.com

GRAFTON

Tara Point Inn & Cottages	168-216 BB	Continental breakfast
1 Tara Point Ln 62037	11 rooms, 11 pb	Complimentary snacks &
618-786-3555	Cash, Checks, ●	beverages
Alison Rohan & Sara Meyers	C-ltd/S-no/P-no/H-yes	Fireplaces, TV/VCR,
		whirlpool tubs

Enjoy the spectacular view of the Mississippi & Illinois Rivers. Watch wintering Bald Eagles. Cottages with fireplaces. Bike & antique along National Scenic Byway. Visit Lewis & Clark Interpretive Center.
✉ tarapoint@gtec.com ❂ www.tarapoint.com

Tell your hosts Pamela Lanier sent you.

HENRY

Mission Oak Inn	165 BB	Deluxe full breakfast
1108 County Rd 930E 61537	2 rooms, 2 pb	Dinners by reservation for
309-370-4083	Visa, MC, Disc, •	our guests
Denny & Jan Reed	C-ltd/S-no/P-no/H-no	Private porch, private
		entrance, private lake, 2-
		person whirlpool, DISH
		TV/DVD/CD, fireplace, WiFi

Mission Oak Inn offers a quiet, comfortable getaway from the stress of life. The inn is located on 120 acres, nestled next to the private 7-acre lake with abundant wildlife. This is a perfect romantic getaway.
✉ innkeepers@missionoakinn.com ❂ www.missionoakinn.com

KEWANEE

Aunt Daisy's B&B	99 BB	Full breakfast
223 W Central Blvd 61443	4 rooms, 4 pb	Snacks, complimentary
888-422-4148 309-853-3300	Most CC, *Rated*, •	dessert in evenings
Glen & Michele Schwarm	C-ltd/S-no/P-no/H-no	Library, suites

Elegant Victorian 1890 home. Many stained glass windows await the opportunity to charm you. Music parlor with a 1929 Aeolian player piano. All beds are king.
✉ auntdaisybb@verizon.net ❂ www.auntdaisy.net

MACOMB

Inselhaus B&B	90-145 BB	Gourmet breakfast
538 N Randolph St 61455	6 rooms, 6 pb	Inselhaus serves vegetarian,
309-833-5400	Most CC	vegan and other food upon
Dorothee Gossel	C-yes/S-ltd/P-ltd/H-no	request
	German	Porch, balcony, parlor, robes,
		hairdryers, TV/DVD,
		Internet, air conditioning

Inselhaus is one of Macomb's finest examples of houses built at the turn-of-the-century. Beautiful accommodations, private dining & special occasion facilities.
✉ info@inselhausbb.com ❂ www.inselhausbb.com

MAEYSTOWN

Corner George Inn	89-169 BB	Full breakfast
1101 Main St 62256	7 rooms, 7 pb	Wine cellar
618-458-6660	Most CC	Air conditioning, ballroom,
David & Marcia Braswell	C-ltd/S-no/P-no	sitting rooms

Located just 35 miles south of St. Louis, the inn was originally built as a hotel and saloon in 1884 by George Jacob and Sibilla Hoffmann. Today there are a total of 7 guestrooms, each with a private bath.
✉ cornrgeo@htc.net ❂ www.cornergeorgeinn.com

NAPERVILLE

Harrison House B&B	178-228 BB	Weekend full breakfast
26 N Eagle St 60540	5 rooms, 5 pb	Evening refreshments
630-420-1117	Most CC	A/C, DSL high-speed
N & L Harrison	C-ltd/S-no/P-no/H-no	Internet, phones, cable
		TV/VHS, CD players,
		whirlpool & claw foot tubs

Nestled in historic Naperville, Harrison House B&B (circa 1904) has been recently restored to reflect the elegance of the past, creating an atmosphere of quiet luxury.
✉ harrisonhousebb@aol.com ❂ www.harrisonhousebb.com

Tell your hosts Pamela Lanier sent you.

NEBO———————————————————————————

Harpole's Heartland Lodge	178-259 MAP	Full breakfast
Rt 1 Box 8A 62355	20 rooms, 20 pb	Lunch, banquet facilities
800-717-4868 217-734-2526	Most CC, *Rated*, •	Horseback riding, ATVs,
Gary Harpole	C-ltd/S-ltd/P-ltd/H-yes	sporting clays, fishing,
	January – September	hayrides, bonfire, hiking, etc.

An incredible sense of well-being invades your soul as you feel the stress drain out of your body & reality sink in—you'll be enveloped in luxury, with all of nature's beauty just outside the door.
✉ info@heartlandlodge.com 🌐 www.heartlandlodge.com

OREGON———————————————————————————

Pinehill Inn	99-195 BB	Both European and
400 Mix St 61061	6 rooms, 6 pb	American Plan
800-851-0131 815-732-2067	Most CC, *Rated*	Guest kitchen with food &
Chris & Ken Williams	C-ltd/S-no/P-no/H-no	beverages available 24/7
		Cable TV/VCRs, video
		library, Bose radios, fax
		service, A/C, porch, whole
		house WiFi

Gracefully nestled among century old pine trees, the Pinehill Inn Bed and Breakfast beckons you with light, color, space . . . the Rock River's most comforting oasis.
✉ info@pinehillbb.com 🌐 www.pinehillbb.com

OTTAWA———————————————————————————

Marcia's B&B	90-125 BB	Full breakfast
3003 N Illinois Rt 71 61350	2 rooms, 2 pb	Cottage has kitchenette,
815-488-5217 (cell) 815-434-5217	Cash, Checks	woodburning stove, Dish TV,
Marcia Nelson	C-ltd/S-no/P-ltd/H-no	VCR, CD, A/C

Stay in the country to relax or to find adventure. Guests will find comfortable rooms with reasonable rates. Independent cottage available. Overnight stabling or vacation with great riding trails.
✉ relax3003@yahoo.com

PAXTON———————————————————————————

Timber Creek B&B	99-199 BB	Full breakfast
1559 E State Route 9 60957	6 rooms, 6 pb	Snack & beverages in the
877-945-6569 217-379-2589	Visa, MC, *Rated*, •	evening, lunches or dinners
Tim & Beth Walder	C-yes/S-no/P-no/H-yes	can be catered for meetings
		Fireplaces, private sitting
		areas, Jacuzzi, upscale
		furnishings

Timber Creek is a sophisticated country retreat located at the end of a ¼ mile lighted, winding lane in a secluded meadow surrounded by trees and a stream. Six suites in the main inn, one separate cabin with full bed, kitchen and loft.
✉ info@timbercreekbb.com 🌐 www.timbercreekbb.com

PEORIA———————————————————————————

Randolph Terrace Historic B&B	105-145 BB	Formal Candlelight Breakfast
201 W Columbia Ter 61606	4 rooms, 4 pb	Tea, coffee, soda, hot
877-264-8266 309-688-7858	Most CC, *Rated*	chocolate, water
Kia & Mercedes Vega	C-ltd/S-no/P-no/H-ltd	Garage parking, robes,
	Spanish	hairdryers

Nestled in Peoria's historic Randolph-Roanoke district, this 1914 Georgian Revival home has been restored to turn-of-the-century elegance. The Randolph Terrace Historic Bed and Breakfast offers four guestrooms furnished with fine antiques.
✉ Kev@randolphterrace.com 🌐 www.randolphterrace.com

Tell your hosts Pamela Lanier sent you.

RICHMOND

The Richmond Inn
10314 East St 60071
866-330-2505 815-678-2505
David & Randi DelGatto

129-219 BB
4 rooms, 4 pb
Visa, MC, Disc, *Rated*
C-ltd/S-ltd/P-no/H-no
Spanish

Full Gourmet Breakfast
Sitting room, library,
Jacuzzis, suites, fireplaces,
cable TV, spa services,
quilting retreats

Relaxing retreat on 5 lush acres offers luxurious pampering at affordable prices, just an hour north of downtown Chicago. Three guestrooms and one suite. Specializing in quilting retreats ✉ randidelgatto@aim.com ◔ www.TheRichmondInn.com

ROCKFORD

River House B&B Getaway Retreat
11052 Ventura Blvd 61115
815-636-1884
Patty Michalsen

114-235 BB
8 rooms, 8 pb
Most CC, *Rated*
C-yes/S-ltd/P-no/H-ltd

Full gourmet or continental
Getaway Lodge Only:
Complimentary in room
snack basket, coffee maker,
mini-frig soft beverages
Jacuzzi, fireplace, satellite
TV, private porch &
entrance, group retreats,
weddings, scrapbooking

Two riverfront B&B homes offer both Jacuzzi & fireplace luxury suites for couples or child friendly lodging for family vacation travel; Check Availability or Reserve Online from website; Romantic Packages, Weddings, Murder Mystery, Scrapbooking, Retreats. ✉ innkeeper@riverhouse.ws ◔ www.riverhouse.ws/

ROSELLE

Lynfred Winery B&B
15 S Roselle Rd 60172
888-298-WINE 630-529-WINE
Lisa Klus

325-399 BB
4 rooms, 4 pb
Most CC, *Rated*
S-no/P-no/H-yes
Spanish

Full breakfast
Fresh fruit & cheese tray, a
premium wine tasting, a
private tour, fresh flowers &
gourmet breakfast.
Spa services, fireplaces,
winery, gift shop, balconies,
heated floors, whirlpool bath

At Lynfred Winery Bed & Breakfast, our friendly, professional team takes great pride in creating the ultimate escape: a historic hideaway where you can forget the pressures of everyday life. Immerse yourself in the beauty of nature and renew your spirits. ✉ wineinfo@lynfredwinery.com ◔ www.lynfredwinery.com

SHEFFIELD

Chestnut Street Inn
301 E Chestnut St 61361
800-537-1304 815-454-2419
Monika & Jeff Sudakov

95-175 BB
4 rooms, 4 pb
Visa, MC, Disc, *Rated*
C-ltd/S-no/P-no/H-no
French, Hungarian

Full breakfast
Snacks, baked goods; full
gourmet 4-course dinner
available upon request
Morning wake up tray,
laundry available, fax
capability, wireless Internet

Historic landmark offering gracious accommodations in the English tradition—relaxing, inviting, serene, sophisticated, lavishly elegant. Exquisite candlelight breakfasts. Full 4 course gourmet dinners. ✉ monikaandjeff@chestnut-inn.com ◔ www.chestnut-inn.com

SULLIVAN

Okaw Valley Orchard Inn
RR 2 Box 124 61951
217-728-4093
Mike & Jennifer Mitchell

89-115 BB
3 rooms, 3 pb
Visa, MC, Disc
C-ltd/S-no/P-no/H-no

Full breakfast
Complimentary beverages,
snacks, store
Wood stove or fireplace, decks
overlooking orchard, sitting
room, TV/DVD, DVD library,
hot tub, Internet

A simple and relaxing country atmosphere abounds at this barn style B&B, situated on a family run orchard. 3 large rooms decorated in country style with private baths and all of the comforts of home. ✉ jennifer@okawvalleyorchard.com ◔ www.okawvalleyorchardinn.com

The Mansion B&B, West Dundee, IL

WEST DUNDEE
The Mansion B&B	119-199 BB	Full breakfast/ weekend only
305 Oregon Ave 60118	4 rooms, 4 pb	Afternoon tea, snacks
847-426-7777	Most CC, •	Sitting room, library, bikes,
Steve Fang & Eda Tomasone	C-ltd/S-ltd/P-no/H-ltd	Jacuzzis, suites, fireplaces,
		cable, accommodate
		business travel, spa

*Experience the magnificence of an iron-ore baron's turn-of-the-century private estate, a
1907 mansion with original appointments of exquisite woodwork, lighting fixtures and
breathtaking leaded stained glass windows.*
✉ themansion@sbcglobal.net ☯ www.themansionbedandbreakfast.com

WHITE HALL
Greene Gables	85-125 BB	Full breakfast
503 Main St 62092	6 rooms, 4 pb	
217-374-6000	Most CC	
Jan & Terry Price	C-ltd/S-no/P-no/H-no	

*Greene Gables is an English Country Inn. We welcome you to stay at our Inn or book your
wedding, reunion, reception, luncheon, or just a week-end away.*
✉ greenegables@verizon.net

Indiana

ANGOLA

Angola's Tulip Tree Inn B&B
411 N Wayne St 46703
888-401-0002 260-668-7000
Katy & Mac Friedlander

100-135 BB
4 rooms, 2 pb
Most CC, •
C-ltd/S-no/P-no/H-no

Full Deluxe Breakfast
High tea available
Free wireless Internet
access, relax on our front
porch, rear sun deck, dish
satellite TV

Return to the peaceful 1890s at the beautiful Tulip Tree Inn Bed & Breakfast, a regal Queen Anne Victorian Mansion, recently renovated, but retaining its original craftsmanship.
✉ tuliptree@tuliptree.com ☼ www.tuliptree.com

AUBURN

Inn at Windmere
2077 Country Road 40 46706
260-925-3303
Paul & Susie Rexroth

80-145 BB
5 rooms, 3 pb
Visa, MC, Disc, *Rated*
C-yes/S-no/P-no/H-ltd

Full hot breakfast
Home made snacks &
beverages
Exercise equipment, wireless
Internet access, spa services
(extra charge), fireplaces,
bonfires

Peaceful, beautifully renovated farmhouse on 40 acres. Great for groups like scrapbooking weekend retreats or private getaways. Lots of places to get alone and relax indoors, rooms with fireplaces, and outdoors a wrap-around porch and gazebo.
✉ inn@innatwindmere.com ☼ www.innatwindmere.com

BLOOMINGTON

Grant Street Inn
310 N Grant St 47408
800-328-4350 812-334-2353
Paul Wagoner

139-289 BB
24 rooms, 24 pb
Most CC
C-ltd/S-no/P-no/H-ltd

Full breakfast buffet
Snacks, tea, coffee
Gathering parlor, books and
periodicals, party room
available, high speed
Internet access

Welcome to Grant Street Inn, a 24-room bed and breakfast inn located in the heart of charming Bloomington, Indiana. Just two blocks from Indiana University and four blocks from the courthouse square.
✉ gsi@grantstinn.com ☼ www.grantstinn.com

Wampler House B&B
4905 S Rogers St 47403
877-407-0969 812-824-2446
Diana Robinson

100-170 BB
8 rooms, 8 pb
Most CC
C-ltd/S-ltd/P-no/H-ltd

Full breakfast
Dessert in the evening, guest
bar has hot & cold drinks
High speed wireless Internet,
gas log fireplaces, cable
TV/VCR

At Wampler House guests will find a soft bed, pleasant surroundings steeped in history, friendly folks, and the privacy you crave. Ideal for a weekend getaway, honeymoon, anniversary or business trip.
✉ info@wamplerhouse.com ☼ www.wamplerhouse.com

BLUFFTON

Washington Street Inn	65-70 BB	Full breakfast
220 E Washington St 46714	4 rooms, 2 pb	Kitchenette with refrigerator
260-824-9070	Visa, MC, Disc	& drinks with iced mugs,
Kathy Gardner	C-yes/S-no/P-ltd/H-no	microwave, popcorn &
		evening snacks
		Air conditioning & TV in
		each room, sitting room filled
		with area interest reading &
		antiques

Step back in time in our 1896 Victorian home. Take your leisure, relax, enjoy a good night's sleep on down comforters, then savor coffee or choice of many teas and a scrumptious breakfast served with genuine Hoosier Hospitality.
✉ klgardner@adamswells.com ○ www.thewashingtonstreetinn.com

BRAZIL

McKinley House B&B	80 BB	Full breakfast
3273 E US Hwy 40 47834	3 rooms, 3 pb	Snacks are included, picnic
866-442-5308 812-442-5308	Cash, Checks	lunch & dinners available for
Tom & Julie Kinley	C-ltd/S-ltd/P-no/H-no	additional fee
		Accommodate business
		travelers, gatherings, murder
		mysteries, covered bridge
		and other festivals

On the National Road. In 1872 George Green McKinley, one of the contractors of the famed National Road, built a 14 room Italianate style house for his family. The house is built of red brick made on site from clay dug at nearby Croy Creek.
✉ mckinleybandb@aol.com

BREMEN

Scottish Bed & Breakfast	99-139 BB	Full breakfast
2180 Miami Trl 46506	4 rooms, 4 pb	Snacks & dessert in evening,
574-220-6672	Most CC	coffee all day
Brenda & Homer Miller	C-ltd/S-ltd/P-yes/H-ltd	Indoor/outdoor "Doggie
		Hotel," conference room,
		putting green, indoor pool,
		in-room massages (extra)

This B&B is nestled in the country in a tranquil, park-like setting. Features a indoor pool, putting green, exercise equipment and hot breakfast. All rooms have a queen or king select comfort bed and TV/DVD. Close to Notre Dame and Amish Country. Pets OK!
✉ info@scottishbb.com ○ www.scottishbb.com

BRISTOL

Bee Hive	75-90 BB	Full breakfast
51129 CR 35 46507	3 rooms, 1 pb	Complimentary
574-825-5023	Visa, MC, *Rated*	refreshments
Herb & Treva Swarm	C-yes/S-no/P-no/H-ltd	Sitting room, restaurant
		nearby, guest cottage
		available

Welcome to our cozy country B&B, built with rough-hewn timber and open beams. Snuggle under handmade quilts. Amish Heartland tours available.
✉ Beehivebb@yahoo.com ○ www.beehivebb.usclargo.com

CAMPBELLSBURG

James Wilkins House	55-75 BB	Full breakfast
225 W Oak St 47108	3 rooms	Afternoon tea, confections,
866-248-9198 812-755-4274	Visa, MC, *Rated*, ●	complimentary wine
Diane Callahan	C-yes/S-no/P-no/H-no	Sitting room, library, cable
		TV, games, puzzles, gazebo

Experience country hospitality in an elegant Victorian setting. Gourmet breakfast served by candlelight or in the gazebo.
✉ jwhbnb@jameswilkinshousebnb.com ○ www.jameswilkinshousebnb.com

CHESTERTON─────────────────────────

Gray Goose Inn
350 Indian Boundary Rd
46304
800-521-5127 219-926-5781
Tim Wilk

105-195 BB
8 rooms, 8 pb
Most CC, •
C-yes/S-no/P-yes/H-no

Full gourmet breakfast
Complimentary beverages,
tea, coffee, hot chocolate
snacks, microwave popcorn,
cookies, pastries.
Sitting & meeting rooms,
telephones in rooms, free
WiFi Internet, business
services

*Located in Indiana Dunes Country. English country house on private wooded lake. Charm
ing guestrooms, private baths, fireplaces, Jacuzzis, solarium, gourmet breakfast. Plenty o
jogging & hiking trails.*
graygoose@verizon.net www.graygooseinn.com

EVANSVILLE─────────────────────────

Cool Breeze B&B
1240 SE Second St 47713
812-422-9635
Katelin & David Hills

90-125 BB
3 rooms, 3 pb
Most CC, *Rated*, •
C-ltd/S-ltd/P-no/H-no

Full breakfast
Sitting room, library, off-
street parking, WiFi

*Historic 1906 home. American Eclectic style. A quiet, peaceful retreat ideal for a memora
ble romantic interlude & personal renewal. All rooms have queen beds, private baths,
phones & cable TV. Wireless Internet access.*
coolbreeze27@juno.com www.coolbreezebb.net

INDIANAPOLIS─────────────────────────

The DeWolf-Allerdice House
1224 N Park Ave 46202
317-822-4288 317-822-4299
Sandy & Cy Colvard

115-135 BB
4 rooms, 3 pb
Most CC
C-ltd/S-ltd/P-no/H-no

Gourmet breakfasts
Late afternoon refreshments
Catered dining events,
gardens, spa & sauna

*Welcome to our recently restored 1871 Italianate country estate that we named the DeWolf
Allerdice House, in honor of the original Victorian-era owners.*
innkeeper@dewolf-allerdicehouse.com www.dewolf-allerdicehouse.com

Old Northside Inn
1340 N Alabama St 46202
800-635-9127 317-635-9123
Emily & Joe Gillum

135-215 BB
7 rooms, 7 pb
Most CC
C-yes/S-no/P-no/H-ltd

Complete breakfast
A full snack bar including
bottled water, soda, tea,
coffee and more available 24
hours a day.
Wireless Internet, computer
access, faxes, music room
with piano, parlor, mini
kitchen area for use

*The mansion has been renovated in an elegant European turn-of-the-century motif to retain
its warm ambience, with the original maple slat flooring and incomparable hand-carved
cherry and mahogany woodwork.*
evg1234@hotmail.com www.oldnorthsideinn.com

Stone Soup Inn
1304 N Central Ave 46202
866-639-9550 317-639-9550
Jeneane Life & Jordan Rifkin

85-175 BB
7 rooms, 5 pb
Most CC, *Rated*
C-ltd/S-no/P-no/H-no
Japanese

Full breakfast on weekends
Continental breakfast
weekdays
Sitting room, library,
fireplaces, cable TV

*Historic inn built in 1901, filled with Mission-style antiques. Minutes from downtown India
napolis in the historic Old Northside neighborhood.*
stonesoupinn@iquest.net www.stonesoupinn.com

JEFFERSONVILLE

Old Bridge Inn	75-150 BB	Full breakfast
131 W Chestnut St 47130	5 rooms, 5 pb	Afternoon tea with 24-hour
866-284-3580 812-284-3580	Most CC, *Rated*	notice, snacks
Linda Williams	C-yes/S-no/P-ltd/H-no	Sitting rooms, Jacuzzis,
		fireplaces, accommodates
		business travelers

This historic home is located in Jeffersonville's historic district, within seconds of I-65 & Louisville, KY. Walk to shops, restaurants, & the Ohio River. Intimate weddings. Corporate rates available.
✉ innbridge@aol.com ○ www.oldbridgeinn.com

LAPORTE

Arbor Hill Inn & Guest	79-259 BB	Full hot breakfast
House	12 rooms, 12 pb	Lunch & dinner are served
263 W Johnson Rd 46350	Most CC, *Rated*, ●	with selections made 48
219-362-9200	C-yes/S-no/P-no/H-yes	hours in advance. Menus
L. Kobat, M. Wedow, K.		available on our website.
Demoret		Jacuzzi tubs, suites,
		fireplaces, cable TV, VCR,
		high speed Internet, coffee,
		irons, videos & games.

The Ultimate in Affordable Luxury! Historic 1910 A Greek Revival Home. Elegant, peaceful surroundings create a haven for business & leisure travelers. 9 luxury suites, executive amenities, great packages. Choose from the elegant Inn or themed Guesthouse.
✉ info@arborhillinn.com ○ www.arborhillinn.com

MARION

Burke Place B&B	75-95 BB	Full breakfast
722 W Fourth St 46952	4 rooms, 4 pb	Soft drinks, coffee/decaf, tea,
866-728-7228 765-664-7228	Visa, MC	fresh baked cookies & other
LeRoy Imler & John Lightle	C-ltd/S-no/P-no/H-no	snacks, other meals by
		arrangement
		Cable TV with remote,
		telephones, wireless
		Internet, fax, copier, lighted
		off-street parking

Burke Place is an urban B&B with a natural homelike warmth, friendly and relaxed atmosphere, where we cater to your personal considerations. Join us for a special get-away weekend or to relax after a weekday business or pleasure experience.
✉ limler@burkeplace.com ○ www.burkeplace.com

MICHIGAN CITY

Creekwood Inn	150-175 BB	Continental plus breakfast
Route 20-35 At I-94 46360	13 rooms, 13 pb	Dinner Wed-Sat. Business
800-400-1981 219-872-8357	Visa, MC, AmEx,	meetings & groups by
Peggie Wall & Pam Pawloski	*Rated*, ●	request.
	C-yes/S-no/P-no/H-yes	33 wooded acres, walking/ski
		trails, gardens, pond; two-
		story conservatory

Voted Best B&B in NW Indiana 2001, 2002, 2003, and 2004 and 2005 2006, 2007! Secluded 1930 English country manor with 13 rooms on 33 acres of woods & creeks. Fine dining in our historic parlor; unique meeting site.
✉ creekwd@adsnet.com ○ www.creekwoodinn.com

Tell your hosts Pamela Lanier sent you.

MICHIGAN CITY————————————————————

Duneland Beach Inn
3311 Pottawattamie Trl 46360
800-423-7729 219-874-7729
Hannah & Alexis

99-239 BB
8 rooms, 8 pb
Most CC
S-no/P-ltd/H-ltd

Full breakfast
Fine dining restaurant serves
dinner Tuesday-Sunday
(hours vary)
4 Jacuzzi suites, A/C,
fireplaces, access to private
beach on Lake Michigan

Experience the warmth of the friendly, neighborhood Duneland Beach Inn. Offering guests
a private beach, Jacuzzi suites, a full restaurant and a cozy bar. Nestled in a private
wooded community on Lake Michigan just one hour from Chicago.
✉ dunelandbeachinn@yahoo.com ✪ www.dunelandbeachinn.com

The Hutchinson Mansion
Inn
220 W 10th St 46360
219-879-1700
Mary DuVal

100-175 BB
10 rooms, 10 pb
Visa, MC, AmEx,
Rated, •
C-ltd/S-ltd/P-no/H-ltd

Full breakfast
Snacks
Sitting room, piano,
whirlpools, fax, tennis & golf
nearby

Elegant Victorian mansion distinguished by outstanding stained glass windows, notable
architectural details and magnificent antiques.
✪ www.hutchinsonmansioninn.com

Tryon Farm Guest House
1400 Tryon Rd 46360
219-879-3618
Claudia Geise

78-210 BB
5 rooms, 5 pb
Visa, MC
C-yes/S-ltd/P-yes/H-no

Full breakfast
Porch, parlors, tree house,
outdoor bathing spa,
massage

Tryon Farm Guest House is an 1896 Victorian farmhouse surrounded by 170 acres of
prairies, woods, meadows, and ponds. This award-winning B&B is situated in a unique
pastoral sanctuary just over an hour east of Chicago.
✉ tfgh@sbcglobal.net ✪ www.tryonfarmguesthouse.com

MIDDLEBURY————————————————————

Patchwork Quilt Country
Inn
11748 CR 2 46540
574-825-2417
John & Adrienne Cohoat

99-199 BB
15 rooms, 15 pb
Most CC, •
C-yes/S-no/P-no/H-ltd

Full country breakfast
Gift shop, nature trail,
game/fitness center, wireless
Internet

Quaint Country inn sits on 18 acres. Convenient to Shipshewana and Notre Dame. Gift
shop; tours available. All private baths. Wireless Internet. Weddings and catering available.
✉ stay@patchworkquiltinn.com ✪ www.patchworkquiltinn.com

NASHVILLE————————————————————

Story Inn
6404 S State Rd 135 47448
800-881-1183 812-988-2273
Rick Hofstetter

107-210 BB
13 rooms, 13 pb
Visa, MC, *Rated*, •
C-yes/S-no/P-ltd/H-yes
German, French

optional $7.50 per
person/morning
Breakfast and lunch served
until 2:30. Dinner by
reservation. Bar menu after
hours on weekends.
Restaurant, bar, sitting room,
larger units available for 2-6
persons.

Story Village is an 1850's rural town nestled in the hills of Brown County, IN, a place
known for covered bridges, clapboard churches, weather-beaten barns, & splendid fall
foliage.
✉ reservations@storyinn.com ✪ www.storyinn.com

ROCKPORT

Friendly Farms B&B	85-125 BB	Full or Cont. breakfast
2354 S 200 W 47635	5 rooms, 2 pb	Porch, horseback riding &
812-649-2668	C-yes/P-yes/H-yes	stables, indoor tennis club,
Joan Ramey		pond, canoe, kid friendly, A/C, antiques

Friendly Farms B&B is located adjacent to the fields of Ramey Riding Stables on Hwy 45. Choose from either the lodge or condo cottage; each adjacent to the fields of Ramey Riding Stables.
✉ jramey66@yahoo.com 🌐 www.rameycamps.com/site/bedandbreakfast.asp

SOUTH BEND

Innisfree B&B	95-155 BB	Full breakfast
702 W Colfax 46601	6 rooms, 4 pb	Afternoon tea
574-283-0740	Visa, MC, *Rated*	Fireplace, porch, foyer,
Cindy Lewis	C-yes/S-ltd/P-no/H-ltd	parlors, library

A Queen Anne styled historic home preserved with loving care, and we welcome you! Please join us and share the Celtic warmth and comfort of our home.
✉ innisfree.1@juno.com 🌐 www.innisfreebnb.com

Oliver Inn B&B	135-359 BB	Full breakfast
630 W Washington St 46601	10 rooms, 9 pb	Complimentary snacks in the
888-697-4466 574-232-4545	Most CC, *Rated*	Butlers' Pantry.
Tom & Alice Erlandson	C-yes/S-no/P-ltd/H-ltd	Library, fireplaces, cable TV/DVD, WiFi, A/C, sound machines, Dolphin Massagers, turn-down service

Magnificent 1886 Victorian mansion, one-acre estate with Carriage House and circa 1920 Playhouse. Jacuzzi, seven warming fireplaces, computerized baby grand piano, located right next to Tippecanoe Place Restaurant.
✉ oliver@michiana.org 🌐 www.oliverinn.com

SPEEDWAY

Speedway B&B	75-145 BB	Full breakfast
1829 Cunningham Rd 46224	6 rooms, 5 pb	Suite, fireplace, ponds, cable
800-975-3412 317-487-6531	Visa, MC, AmEx, *Rated*	TV, business traveler
Ann & Don Ninness	C-ltd/S-ltd/P-no/H-no	accommodations, wireless Internet, sitting room

Guests just keep coming back to visit this beautiful property tucked away in the little town of Speedway (located on the west side of Indianapolis) where visitors enjoy true Hoosier hospitality.
✉ Ann@centraloffice1.com 🌐 www.speedwaybandb.com

VALPARAISO

Inn at Aberdeen, Ltd.	103-198 BB	Full gourmet breakfast
3158 S State Rd 2 46385	11 rooms, 11 pb	Evening dessert, snacks &
866-761-3753 219-465-3753	Most CC, *Rated*	beverages
Bill, Val, Chris, Audrey & Mandy	C-yes/S-no/P-no/H-yes	Jacuzzi for 2, fireplace, balcony, cable TV/VCR, lazy ceiling fan, free wireless Internet

Travel back to the 1800s while enjoying your own Jacuzzi, balcony, cozy fire & truly regal service/amenities. 18-hole championship golf course.
✉ inn@innataberdeen.com 🌐 www.innataberdeen.com

VEVAY

Schenck Mansion B&B	90-200 BB	Full breakfast
206 W Turnpike St 47043	6 rooms, 5 pb	TV & VCR, private baths, air
877-594-2876 812-427-2787	Most CC	conditioning
Jerry & Lisa Fisher	C-ltd/S-no/P-no/H-ltd	

A unique, beautifully restored mansion of the 'second empire' located in southwestern Indiana's Switzerland County. Six, spacious & inviting rooms are complimented by a 4 story tower, copper-lined bath tubs, seven balconies & magnificent details.
✉ jlefisher@hotmail.com ○ www.schenckmansion.com

WATERLOO

Maple Leaf Inn	80-90 BB	Full breakfast
425 W Maple St 46793	4 rooms, 2 pb	Complimentary soft drinks,
877-402-5393 260-837-5323	Visa, MC	bottled water, juices and
Ken & Candi Surber	C-ltd/S-no/P-no	homemade goodies.
		Victorian Tea Room.
		Hot tub, nightly turn-down
		service, satellite TV, videos,
		CD player in each guestroom
		with CD's

Escape your hectic world; surround yourself with elegance and peace at the Maple Leaf Inn. The grand home, constructed in 1918, offers many places to relax and be refreshed. Each distinctly decorated room has its own personality.
✉ mapleleaf425@yahoo.com ○ www.mapleleafbnb.com

WINCHESTER

Winchester Guest House Inn	99-159 BB	Full breakfast
1529 S Main St 47394	8 rooms, 8 pb	Coffee, wide assortment of
866-816-8066 765-584-3015	Most CC, •	teas, evening snacks
Ted & Debra Davenport	C-yes/S-no/P-no/H-ltd	Indoor pool, hot tub, theater,
		conferences, golf, free DVD
		movies, massages, flowers,
		candies

Award winning B&B Resort & Conference Center. Indoor pool, spa, conference room, theater, billiards, table tennis, darts, golf, outdoor games, in-room free DVD movies, massage, fireplace rooms, all private baths. Your private country retreat.
✉ info@winchester-inn.com ○ www.winchester-inn.com

Iowa

BELLEVUE

Mont Rest	149-199 BB	Full breakfast
300 Spring St 52031	12 rooms, 12 pb	A gourmet dessert is
877-872-4220 563-872-4220	Most CC, *Rated*, •	included with your stay
Christine & Naomi	C-ltd/S-no/P-no/H-ltd	Murder Mystery, River
		Cruise, Winery Tour&
		Dinner, Golf, Ski, All Grown
		Up PJ Party, In-room Massage

Overlooking the majestic Mississippi River in Bellevue, Iowa, this Historic Inn is one of the most luxurious inns in the Midwest. The 12 guestrooms feature queen/king beds, beautiful views, fireplaces, and 2 person whirlpool tubs.
✉ innkeeper@montrest.com ◔ www.montrest.com

BURLINGTON

Schramm House B&B	95-225 BB	Full breakfast
616 Columbia Street 52601	6 rooms, 6 pb	
319-754-0373	Most CC	
Terry Arellano & Mitty Billups	C-ltd/S-ltd/P-no/H-ltd	

Historic Victoria home lovingly preserved four blocks from the banks of the Mississippi River. Contemporary interior design combined with old world charm. Appointed with fine art by regional artists. Quiet private parlor rooms to gather for wine tasting.
✉ info@schrammhouse.com ◔ www.schrammhouse.com

CEDAR RAPIDS

Belmont Hill Victorian	95-145 BB	Full breakfast
1525 Cherokee Dr NW 52405	5 rooms, 3 pb	Afternoon tea
319-366-1343	Visa, MC, AmEx	Suites, fireplace,
Ken & Shelley Sullens	C-ltd/S-no/P-no/H-ltd	accommodate business
		travelers, wooded grounds,
		gardens

Experience a unique level of pampering and privacy. Restored 1882 National Register home and carriage house. Immaculate accommodations, private baths. Lovely secluded grounds, terrace and gardens. ✉ shelley@belmonthill.com ◔ www.belmonthill.com

DES MOINES

Butler House on Grand	105-190 BB	Full breakfast
4507 Grand Ave 50312	7 rooms, 7 pb	Complimentary soft drinks,
866-455-4096 515-255-4096	Most CC, *Rated*	bottled water, microwave
Clark Smith & Lauren Kernan	C-ltd/S-no/P-no/H-no	popcorn, & sweets in galley
Smith		on each floor
		Jacuzzis, fireplaces, book
		and video library

Butler House on Grand is one of the top places to stay while visiting Des Moines. Come enjoy nostalgic elegance at its finest! Picked one of the 2006 Top Ten Most Romantic Inns.
✉ info@butlerhouseongrand.com ◔ www.butlerhouseongrand.com

DUBUQUE

The Hancock House	80-175 BB	Full breakfast
1105 Grove Ter 52001	9 rooms, 9 pb	Snacks, complimentary wine
563-557-8989	Most CC, *Rated*	& beer
Susan & Chuck Huntley	C-ltd/S-ltd/P-no/H-no	Sitting rooms, Jacuzzis,
		suites, fireplaces, cable,
		wireless Internet

Situated on the bluffs overlooking the city of Dubuque to the Mississippi River Valley. Furnished in Victorian period antiques offering a full breakfast and beverage center.
✉ chuckdbq@mchsi.com ◔ www.thehancockhouse.com

DUBUQUE————————————————————————————

The Mandolin Inn
199 Loras Blvd 52001
800-524-7996 563-556-0069
Amy Boynton

85-150 BB
8 rooms, 6 pb
Most CC, *Rated*
C-ltd/S-no/P-no/H-yes
Some Spanish & French

Gourmet breakfast
Welcome drink
Cable TV, wireless Internet
access, 2 sweet cats,
veranda, central air,
handicapped accessible

Beautifully restored 1908 Edwardian mansion dedicated to sharing elegance & comfort
Perfect for kindling romance or unwinding after business, as well as exploring the uppe
Mississippi River. Handicapped accessible. Wireless Internet access.
✉ innkeeper@mandolininn.com ○ www.mandolininn.com

The Redstone Inn & Suites
504 Bluff St 52001
888-582-1893 563-582-1894
Jerry & Kelly Lazore

75-195 BB
14 rooms, 14 pb
Most CC, •
C-yes/S-no/P-yes/H-no

Full breakfast
Afternoon tea, coffee &
snacks available in the parlor
Cable TV, free wireless
Internet, whirlpool suites,
laundry services, business
accommodations, fax

An elegant, intimate boutique hotel, a Queen Ann Victorian in the heart of Cable Car
Square. A historic lodging experience with the Mississippi River nearby. Wireless high
speed Internet, whirlpool suites, and private baths. Complimentary breakfast.
✉ info@theredstoneinn.com ○ www.theredstoneinn.com

The Richards House
1492 Locust St 52001
888-557-1492 563-557-1492
Michelle Stuart

40-115 BB
6 rooms, 4 pb
Most CC, *Rated*, •
C-yes/S-ltd/P-ltd/H-no

Full breakfast
Snacks, beverages
Sitting room, antiques,
concealed TVs, phones,
fireplaces

1883 Stick-style Victorian mansion with over 80 stained-glass windows. Seven varieties of
woodwork and period furnishings. Working fireplaces in guestrooms.
✉ innkeeper@therichardshouse.com ○ www.therichardshouse.com

GRINNELL————————————————————————————

Carriage House B&B
1133 Broad St 50112
641-236-7520
Ray & Dorothy Spriggs

60-80 BB
6 rooms, 6 pb
Visa, MC, *Rated*, •
C-ltd/S-no/P-no/H-no

Full breakfast
Afternoon tea available by
reservation and payment,
non-alcoholic beverages
Sitting room, library,
Jacuzzis, fireplaces,
accommodate business
travelers

Victorian home restored with your comfort in mind; gourmet breakfast; afternoon tea
available by reservation. Enjoy the wicker on the porch or read by the fire.
✉ irishbnb@iowatelecom.net ○ www.ia-bednbreakfast-inns.com/carriagehousegrinnell.htm

IOWA CITY————————————————————————————

A B&B Golden Haug
517 E. Washington 52240
319-354-4284
Nila Haug

105-200 BB
15 rooms, 15 pb
Most CC, •
C-ltd/S-no/P-no/H-ltd

Hearty gourmet breakfast
Bedside chocolates, in-room
mini bar
DSL & wireless Internet
access, massage therapist by
request, off street parking

Located in downtown Iowa City, this historic neighborhood home will provide the perfect
getaway to put your body and soul at ease. 15 guestrooms with private baths. Weekly and
monthly rates available. Unique accommodations with a whimsical touch.
✉ imahaug@goldenhaug.com ○ www.goldenhaug.com

KEOKUK

The Grand Anne B&B
116 Grand Ave 52632
319-795-6990 319-524-6310
Cretia & Rick Hesse

119-159 BB
5 rooms, 5 pb
Most CC
C-ltd/S-no/P-no/H-ltd

Full Gourmet Breakfast
Parlors, ballroom, billiards,
gardens, private bath,
TV/VCR, telephones,
refrigerators

Perched on a bluff overlooking the Mississippi River, the Grand Anne B&B redefines "affordable luxury." Designed by George F. Barber, the 22-room 1897 mansion is an elaborate example of Queen Anne style domestic architecture.
✉ grandannekeokuk@yahoo.com

MAQUOKETA

Squiers Manor
418 W Pleasant St 52060
563-652-6961
Virl & Kathy Banowetz

80-160 BB
8 rooms, 8 pb
Visa, MC, AmEx, *Rated*
C-yes/S-no/P-no/H-no

Full gourmet breakfast
Candlelight dessert
Sitting room, library, bridal
suite available, fireplaces,
whirlpool

Antique decor, crackling fireplaces and Victorian ambience provide for quiet times and intimate moments at Squiers Manor B&B. All of this and superior service, described recently by a guest as "definitive hospitality."
✉ innkeeper@squiersmanor.com ○ www.squiersmanor.com

MARENGO

Loy's Farm Bed & Breakfast
2077 KK Ave 52301
319-642-7787
Loy & Robert Walker

80 BB
3 rooms, 1 pb
Rated, •
C-yes/S-no/P-no/H-no

Full gourmet breakfast
Dinner available, snacks
Sitting room, library,
fireplaces, TV,
accommodations for
business travel

Contemporary 1976 farm home on a working 1550 acre farm. Hostess serves a gourmet farm breakfast, with lively conversation, farm tour, pheasant hunting. Relax and enjoy all this lovely country property has to offer.
✉ LBW20771@ia.net

MARION

Victorian Lace
300 E Main St 52302
888-377-5138 319-377-5138
James & Renee Condit

100-160 BB
2 rooms, 2 pb
Visa, MC, *Rated*, •
C-yes/S-ltd/P-no/H-ltd

Full breakfast
Asti wine or sparkling grape,
adult beverages & soda,
chocolates, meat & cheese
tray, cream puffs
Heated pool, garden. Great
place for weddings; minister
on site. New bicycles; close
to bike trails.

Close to Cedar Rapids and Marion—relax in a private whirlpool for two. Share a glass of wine or sparkling grape juice, chocolates, meat & cheese tray and an evening dessert. Wake up to a four-course candlelite breakfast. Queen-size beds. Free beer&wine.
✉ viclacebb@aol.com ○ www.victorian-lace-iowa.com

NEWTON

La Corsette Maison Inn
629 First Ave E 50208
641-792-6833
Anne Gerken

90-225 BB
7 rooms, 6 pb
Most CC, *Rated*, •
C-ltd/S-no/P-no/H-no

Full breakfast
Gourmet 6 course dinner,
restaurant
Whirlpools, fireplaces, sitting
room, WiFi, conferences,
meetings

Turn-of-the-century Mission-style mansion. Charming French bedchambers, beckoning hearths. Gourmet dining. 4½ star rating.
✉ lacorsettemaison@aol.com ○ www.lacorsette.com

La Corsette Mansion Inn, Newton, IA

ST. ANSGAR

Blue Belle Inn
513 West 4th St 50472
877-713-3113 641-713-3113
Sherrie Hansen

70-375 BB
10 rooms, 8 pb
Most CC, *Rated*
C-yes/S-no/P-no/H-yes
German (a little)

Full breakfast
Lunch, dinner, a wonderful
fondue feast, popcorn, hot
chocolate, coffee, soda
TV/VCR/DVD, movies,
wireless Internet,
kitchenette, library, piano,
conference rooms, spa
nearby

Romantic Victorian with gourmet dining, teahouse, fondue, stained glass, maple wood work, tin ceilings, queen/king beds, A/C, fireplaces, private Jacuzzis. Murder mysteries, weddings, cooking classes, wireless Internet, quaint shops. Handicap accessible.
✉ bluebelle@omnitelcom.com 🌐 www.BlueBelleInn.com

VINTON

The Lion & The Lamb
913 2nd Ave 52349
888-390-5262 319-472-5086
Rachel Waterbury

75-175 BB
6 rooms, 6 pb
Most CC, *Rated*, •
C-yes/S-no/P-no/H-no

Full breakfast
Five course Murder Mystery
Dinner
Free wireless Internet, many
attractions nearby, historic
town

1892 Victorian mansion with seven fireplaces. Each guestroom has a private bath, queen size bed, air conditioning, ceiling fan & TV. Murder Mystery Dinners are our specialty.
✉ request@lionlamb.com 🌐 www.lionlamb.com

Kansas

COUNCIL GROVE

The Cottage House
25 N Neosho 66846
800-727-7903 620-767-6828
Connie Essington

75-175 BB
28 rooms, 28 pb
Most CC, *Rated*, •
C-yes/S-yes/P-ltd/H-yes

Continental plus breakfast
Restaurant nearby
Sitting room, sauna room, 6
rooms with whirlpool tubs,
next to Neosho Riverwalk

Beautifully renovated Victorian hotel, with modern comforts & lovely antique furnishings—in historic "Birthplace of the Santa Fe Trail."
info@cottagehousehotel.com www.cottagehousehotel.com

LAKIN

Windy Heights B&B
507 Country Heights Rd 67860
620-355-7699
Chuck & Dianne Jaeger

60-65 BB
4 rooms, 4 pb
Visa, MC, AmEx
C-yes/S-no/P-yes/H-no

Full breakfast
Coffee, tea, continental
breakfast optional
Bikes, decks, cable TV, VCR
and movies

Relaxing, quiet, country atmosphere. Enjoy a challenging 9-hole golf course located across the backyard; the best pheasant and deer hunting in the state. Whether you choose to relax or explore—we're sure that you will enjoy your stay with us!
djaeger@pld.com www.windyheightsbandb.com

LEAVENWORTH

The Prairie Queen B&B
221 Arch St 66048
913-758-1959
Bob & Jan Topping

115-149 BB
3 rooms, 3 pb
Visa, MC, •
C-ltd/S-ltd/P-no/H-no

Full breakfast
Complimentary beverages
and snacks available
Guest sitting room with
fireplace, Wireless Internet

Elegance, romance & adventure abound at this 1868 Georgian Revival B&B. Enjoy wonderful food, history, or just relax during your stay. Plenty of shopping, museums, historic sites & restaurants.
info@prairiequeen.com www.prairiequeen.com

OSAWATOMIE

Enchanted Realm B&B
320 Main St 66064
913-755-3346 913-755-3346
Tami Pemberton & Sue Sifford

65-140 BB
5 rooms, 5 pb
Visa, MC
C-ltd/S-ltd/P-no/H-no

Family style
Beverages & snacks
available, "extras" offered for
a fee to make your stay even
more romantic
Massage, small meetings,
special events, catering,
small weddings, flowers,
chocolates, bubbly!!

A beautifully romantic, 3 story Victorian home built in 1904, with high ceilings, ornate molding, fireplaces, & much more. This B&B offers full family style breakfast, a large covered porch, "L" shaped yard, brick courtyard, garden & massage is available.
fluterby@iwon.com www.enchantedrealmbb.com

Kentucky

BELLEVUE

Christopher's B&B
604 Poplar St 41073
888-585-7085 859-491-9354
Brenda Guidugli

105-179 BB
3 rooms, 3 pb
Most CC, *Rated*, •
C-ltd/S-ltd/P-no/H-ltd

Continental plus during week
Snacks and water cooler.
WiFi, Suites, cable TV,
VCR/DVD player/movies,
Jacuzzi tubs, iron, ironing
board, hairdryer

Award-winning Christopher's B&B is named after the late 1800's Christian Church & the Patron Saint of Traveler's. Located near the Newport Aquarium and downtown Cincinnati and is easily accessible from many interstates.
✉ christophers@insightbb.com ❂ www.christophersbb.com

BEREA

Snug Hollow Farm
790 McSwain Branch 40336
606-723-4786
Barbara Napier

100-195 BB
4 rooms, 4 pb
Visa, MC
C-yes/S-ltd/P-no/H-ltd

Full breakfast
Goodies included; lunch &
dinner available upon
request
Massage, fishing, hiking,
sitting room, library,
fireplace, sunroom, porches,
forest

"50 Best Girlfriends Getaways of North America" National Geographic. 30 minutes from Berea, 1 hour from Lexington. Appalachia at its best! Unique & Secluded, 300 acres farmhouse, porches, restored cozy cabin, wildflowers, peaceful, comfortable, gardens
✉ info@snughollow.com ❂ www.snughollow.com

BLOOMFIELD

**Springhill Winery &
Plantation B&B**
3205 Springfield Rd 40008
502-252-9463
Eddie O'Daniel

115-140 BB
6 rooms, 4 pb
Visa, MC, Disc
C-yes/S-no/P-no/H-ltd

Full breakfast
Weekends: Full plantation
breakfast Midweek:
Continental Plus Wine tasting
available
Common sitting room, cable
TV/DVD/VCR, antiques,
family friendly, "Vintage
Wedding" accommodations

A stately, historic plantation, circa 1857, Springhill has become a destination to discover. Here, you'll experience the taste of Kentucky's award winning wines and the elegant southern charm of this Antebellum home set in the rolling hills & vineyards.
✉ springhillbnb@iglou.com ❂ www.springhillwinery.com

GEORGETOWN

Blackridge Hall
4055 Paris Pike 40324
800-768-9308 502-863-2069
Jim Black

109-229 BB
6 rooms, 6 pb
Most CC
C-ltd/S-no/P-no/H-no

Gourmet candlelight
breakfast
Elegant parlor, fireplace, tiled
sun room, formal dining
room, Jacuzzi

Built on a ridge with a view of the Lexington lights at night, the mansion has 10,000 sq. ft. of living space. Six guest suites and rooms are available, and all have names that indicate their decor. On 5 acres in the heart of horse country.
✉ JBlack@blackridgehall.com ❂ www.blackridgehall.com

GEORGETOWN

Bryan House	75-145 BB	Full breakfast
401 W Main St 40324	4 rooms, 4 pb	Homemade afternoon sweets
877-296-3051 502-863-1060	Most CC, •	Whirlpool tubs, dining room,
Janet & Stan Sekula	C-ltd/S-no/P-no/H-no	porches

Nestled in the heart of quaint Georgetown, Kentucky sits the stately 1891 Queen Anne home of a once prominent surgeon. Relax and enjoy a time when life was a bit slower paced in Scott County, Kentucky, and people enjoyed the finer amenities of life.
✉ bryanhouse@bellsouth.net ❂ www.bryanhousebnb.com

Jordan Farm B&B	100-125 BB	Continental Plus breakfast
4091 Newtown Pike 40324	4 rooms, 4 pb	Afternoon tea, snacks
502-863-1944	Cash, Checks, *Rated*	Near shops, restaurants,
Harold & Rebecca Jordan	C-ltd/S-no/P-no/H-yes	Jacuzzis, fridges

Jordan Farm offers a unique opportunity to stay on a beautiful 100-acre working Bluegrass thoroughbred farm. Perfect place for horse enthusiasts to stay.
✉ becky@beckyjordan.net ❂ www.jordanfarmbandb.com

Pineapple Inn	75-110 BB	Full breakfast
645 S Broadway 40324	4 rooms, 4 pb	Snacks, complimentary wine
502-868-5453	Visa, MC, *Rated*, •	Sitting room, bar service,
Muriel & Les	C-ltd/S-ltd/P-no/H-no	Heart of Bluegrass, horse country, spa available

Built in 1876—on historical register—gourmet breakfast in country French dining room. Four large private rooms/w baths, one with spa, each uniquely decorated with antiques.
❂ www.pineappleinnbedandbreakfast.com

HARRODSBURG

Aspen Hall Manor	105-155 BB	Full breakfast
558 Aspen Hall Dr 40330	4 rooms, 4 pb	Complimentary beverages &
888-485-8871 859-734-5050	Most CC	appetizers, lunch & dinner
Jill & Andrew Romero	C-yes/S-no/P-no/H-no	available
		Tea room, derby room, porch, private parties, weddings

Experience the southern elegance of an 1840 Greek Revival Manor House nestled in the quiet hills of Kentucky, in the historic town of Harrodsburg. Just thirty minutes from Lexington, less than one hour from Louisville.
✉ jill@aspenhallmanor.com ❂ www.aspenhallmanor.com

LEWISPORT

The River House	80-150 BB	Full breakfast
1510 Riverview Dr 42301	3 rooms, 3 pb	Balconies, walking path,
270-295-4199	Visa, MC	pool, exercise room, deck
Bernard Cox	C-ltd/S-no/P-no/H-ltd	

This unique Bed & Breakfast offers a relaxed atmosphere, beautiful grounds, & private quarters. Enjoy the magnificent evening sunsets over the Ohio River from one of four balconies including one that actually extends over the riverbank.
✉ theriverhouse@tds.net ❂ www.riverhousebnb.com

LEXINGTON

Gratz Park Inn	179-449 EP	Full breakfast
120 W 2nd St 40507	41 rooms, 41 pb	Jonathan at Gratz Park
800-752-4166 859-231-1777	Most CC, •	Restaurant
Zedtta Wellman	C-yes/S-no/P-yes/H-no	Fitness center, fine dining & banquet facilities, and a library with business center

Originally the first medical clinic west of the Allegheny Mountains, Gratz Park Inn has been restored to exemplify the Southern grace and charm for which Lexington is known.
✉ guestservices@gratzparkinn.com ❂ www.gratzparkinn.com

LOUISVILLE——————————————————————————

1853 Inn at Woodhaven
401 S Hubbards Ln 40207
888-895-1011 502-895-1011
Marsha Burton

95-225 BB
8 rooms, 8 pb
Most CC, *Rated*, •
C-ltd/S-no/P-ltd/H-ltd

Full breakfast
Coffee, tea and snacks in
each room, cookies and soft
drinks in common area
Sitting room, library,
whirlpool tubs, steam
showers, suites, fireplaces,
cable TV, WiFi

An elegant and comfortable Inn furnished with antiques. Located in a beautiful suburb 8
minutes from downtown Louisville, and close to all attractions including fine dining and
shopping. Features include gourmet breakfast, fine linens, beautiful gardens
✉ iwoodhavenb@aol.com ○ www.innatwoodhaven.com

Austin's Inn Place
915 South 1st St 40203
502-585-8855
Mary & Tom Austin

120-155 BB
8 rooms, 8 pb
Most CC
C-ltd/S-ltd/P-no/H-no

Full breakfast
Meeting rooms, game room,
library, parlor, wireless
Internet and gift shop.

Beyond B&B, Austin's Inn Place is a guest and gathering place in Old Louisville, Kentucky.
Featuring eight guestrooms, three dining rooms, parlor, game room, party room and bar all
just blocks from the center of downtown.
✉ austinsinnplace@bellsouth.net ○ www.austinsinnplace.com

Central Park
1353 S 4th St 40208
877-922-1505 502-638-1505
Nancy & Kevin Hopper

125-225 BB
6 rooms, 7 pb
Most CC, *Rated*, •
C-yes/S-ltd/P-no/H-no

Full breakfast
Complimentary afternoon &
evening beverages, snacks &
desserts
Formal parlor, porch &
garden, Jacuzzi, suites,
fireplaces, in-room phones,
high speed Internet

Located in the heart of the Old Louisville Historic District, we offer four elegant queen &
king guestrooms and one 2 bedroom suite and the Carriage House with kitchenette and all
rooms have private baths. Gourmet breakfast every morning.
✉ centralpar@win.net ○ www.centralparkbandb.com

Columbine Bed & Breakfast
1707 S Third St 40208
800-635-5010 502-635-5000
Rich May & Bob Goldstein

105-165 BB
6 rooms, 6 pb
Visa, MC, *Rated*, •
C-ltd/S-ltd/P-no/H-ltd
Italian

Gourmet breakfast
Snacks, bottled water, juices
& soft drinks
Marble fireplaces, library,
TV/VCR, telephones, garden,
screened porch

Magnificent historic mansion just minutes from Churchill Downs (Kentucky Derby), Louis-
ville International Airport, University of Louisville, and most major attractions.
✉ columbineinn@insightbb.com ○ www.thecolumbine.com

Dupont Mansion
1317 S Fourth St 40208
502-638-0045
Mary Pat White

129-239 BB
8 rooms, 8 pb
Visa, MC, AmEx, •
C-ltd/S-no/P-no/H-no

Full gourmet breakfast
Complimentary
refreshments
Library, gardens, fireplaces,
Jacuzzi, TV & dataports in
each room

Beautifully restored mansion, in historic Old Louisville, offers 15 foot ceilings, ornate
working fireplaces, a banquet style dining room, antique furnishings, crystal chandeliers &
formal gardens.
✉ info@dupontmansion.com ○ www.dupontmansion.com

LOUISVILLE

Inn at the Park
1332 S Fourth St 40208
502-638-0045
Gayle & Herb Warren

119-199 BB
8 rooms, 8 pb
Visa
C-ltd/S-no/P-no/H-no

Full breakfast
Complimentary refreshments
Sitting room, restful elegance, leisurely gourmet breakfasts, private balconies, beautiful gardens

Ideally located within the nation's largest collection of Victorian homes, the Inn at the Park offers an elegant setting with southern hospitality to delight the most discriminating traveler.
✉ info@oldlouisvilleinns.com 🌐 www.innatpark.com

Inn off the Alley
1325 Bardstown Rd 40204
502-451-0121
Gerry Harrah

105-145 BB
3 rooms, 3 pb
Visa, MC
C-yes/S-no/P-ltd/H-no

Stocked goodies in suite for bkfst.
Each room has cable TV, writing desk, separate phone line, radio/alarm clock, hair dryer, iron/board

Located on Bardstown Rd. in the heart of Louisville's Historic Highlands. Within walking distance you will find some of Louisville's finest restaurants, galleries and antique shops. Features 3 cozy, comfortable suites all professionally decorated.
✉ harrah@iglou.com

Pinecrest Cottage & Gardens
2806 Newburg Rd 40205
502-454-3800
Nancy Morris

110-165 EP
1 rooms, 1 pb
Visa, MC, AmEx
C-yes/S-ltd/P-no/H-ltd

Breakfast on own
Snacks
Fireplace, free Internet, tennis court, cable TV, swimming pool

Traditionally decorated, well-appointed guesthouse affording complete privacy. Free Wireless Internet
✉ pinecrest@insightbb.com 🌐 www.pinecrestcottageandgardens.com

---

Samuel Culbertson Mansion B&B
1432 S 3rd St 40208
866-522-5078 502-634-3100
Rudy Van Meter

109-179 BB
5 rooms, 5 pb
Most CC, •
C-ltd/S-ltd/P-ltd/H-no
German

Full breakfast
Complimentary snacks, lunch/dinner can be arranged
Sitting room, library, suites, fireplaces, cable TV, accom. bus. trav.

Louisville's most historic B&B, opulently furnished, southern gourmet breakfasts, close to downtown and Churchill Downs.
✉ inn@culbertsonmansion.com 🌐 www.culbertsonmansion.com

NEWPORT

Cincinnati's Weller Haus
319 Poplar St 41073
800-431-4287 859-431-6829
Leanne Saylor

125-199 BB
5 rooms, 5 pb
Most CC, *Rated*, •
C-yes/S-no/P-ltd/H-ltd

Full breakfast
Complimentary snacks & non-alcoholic beverages
Guest kitchen, patio & gardens, Jacuzzi tubs, high speed wireless Internet, 200+ movies, fireplaces

Choose from five uniquely decorated guestrooms to ensure your comfort; all with private bath, TV/VCR/DVD & phone. Need a romantic getaway? Our Jacuzzi suites may be what you're looking for at Weller Haus. Historic homes, English gardens and near downtown.
✉ wellerhaus@insightbb.com 🌐 www.wellerhaus.com

PETERSBURG─────────────────

First Farm Inn Kentucky
2510 Stevens Rd 41080
800-277-9527 859-586-0199
Jen Warner & Dana Kisor

108-162 BB
2 rooms, 2 pb
Visa, MC, Disc, •
C-ltd/S-ltd/P-ltd/H-ltd

Full homemade healthy
breakfast
Ask about special treats,
birthday cakes, etc.
Horseback riding, in-room
hot stone or conventional
massages, music room,
library, spa, fireplace

*First Farm Inn is an elegant, updated 1870s farmhouse on 20 acres just outside Cincinnati.
Horseback riding, spacious rooms, bountiful breakfast, in-room massages, outdoor hot tub,
ponds, boats, hammock, porch swing, rockers, cats, fireplaces, wireless*
✉ info@firstfarminn.com ○ www.firstfarminn.com

SPRINGFIELD─────────────────

**1851 Historic Maple Hill
Manor B&B**
2941 Perryville Rd Hwy 150
40069
800-886-7546 859-336-3075
Todd Allen & Tyler Horton

119-179 BB
7 rooms, 7 pb
Most CC, •
C-yes/S-no/P-ltd/H-no

Full Country "Gourmet"
Breakfast
Homemade desserts, 24-hour
beverage service, snacks,
Romance dinner ($65)
Antiques, luxury linens,
Jacuzzi, fireplace,
TV/VCR/DVD/CD, movie,
games, magazines,
newspapers

*Exceptional and elegant accommodations at a working Alpaca & Llama Farm. Voted #1 in
U.S. as the B&B with the "Most Historical Charm," "Kentucky's Best B&B," and "Best
Breakfast in the Southeast."*
✉ maplehillmanorbb@aol.com ○ www.maplehillmanor.com

VERSAILLES─────────────────

Storybook Inn
277 Rose Hill Ave 40383
877-279-2563 859-879-9993
C Elise Buckley

189-319 BB
4 rooms, 4 pb
Most CC, *Rated*
C-ltd/S-no/P-ltd/H-ltd
February thru December

Fresh, gourmet
Daily homemade goodies;
bottled water, soft drinks,
fruit, tea, coffee,
complimentary glass of wine
Hi-Speed Internet,
book/movie library, satellite
TV, DVD, massage, arrange
private horse farm tour

*"A delight to the senses! Elegant! Amazing! A real treasure!" are all descriptions used by
guests to describe A Storybook Inn. Upscale. Thick ultra comfortable mattresses and
bedding. Luscious breakfasts. Private, gorgeous surroundings near Lexington, KY.*
✉ stay@storybook-inn.com ○ www.storybook-inn.com

WILMORE─────────────────

The Potter's Inn
313 Walters Lane 40390
859-858-4348
Rudy & Pat Medlock

57-97 BB
4 rooms, 4 pb
Most CC
C-ltd/S-ltd/P-no/H-no

Full breakfast
Fresh fruit, tea, coffee, cocoa,
soda
Kitchenette & refrigerator for
guest use, floral gift and gift
baskets available for
purchase

*Artfully furnished each room has a private bath, queen sized bed, armoire, vanity and
comfortable boudoir chairs. The rooms are decorated in sumptuous colors and fabrics with
original art work & antiques that the Medlocks have collected in their travels.*
✉ thepottersinn@windstream.net ○ www.thepottersinn.com

Louisiana

BREAUX BRIDGE

Maison Des Amis	100-200 BB	Full Cajun breakfast
111 Washington St 70517	4 rooms, 4 pb	Complimentary beverages,
888-570-3043 337-507-3399	Most CC, *Rated*	muffins, candy,
Ellen Wicker	C-ltd/S-ltd/P-no/H-ltd	granola/oatmeal bars
	French	Laundry, tour information,
		dinner and swamp tour
		reservations, wireless
		Internet

Historic Creole/Caribbean residence, overlooks legendary Bayou Teche. Lush gardens, gazebo, glassed-in sun porch, private baths, antiques, original artwork. Full Cajun/Creole breakfast. Complimentary beverages, daily maid service, general tour information
✉ seeyou@maisondesamis.com 🌐 www.maisondesamis.com

GROSSE TETE

David's Country Cottages	95-125 BB	Deluxe continental breakfast
17985 S Sidney Rd 70740	3 rooms, 3 pb	Wine & cheese upon arrival;
225-648-2977	Most CC	dinner available. Cafe
Jeanie David	C-yes/S-ltd/P-ltd/H-no	serving Southern home style
		cooking on premises.
		Porches, rocking chairs,
		kitchens, TV, claw foot tubs.
		Fishing pond on property.

Imagine rocking on the front porch or strolling through the nature trail lined with hundred year-old oaks. Enjoy the peaceful surroundings of our lovely cottages in the country. 3 individual cabins. ✉ davidscc@eatel.net 🌐 www.davidscc.com

HAMMOND

Michabelle Inn &	75-125 BB	Full breakfast
Restaurant	7 rooms, 7 pb	Full service bar & restaurant,
1106 S Holly St 70403	Most CC, *Rated*	dinner package available
985-419-0550	C-ltd/S-ltd/P-ltd/H-ltd	Library, reception hall,
Chef Michel & Isabel Marcais	French, Portuguese	grounds

Louisiana's Number 1 Rated Country Inn by AAA, Michabelle is a Greek Revival Estate decorated in authentic French antiques, located in serene surroundings.
✉ michabelle@i-55.com 🌐 www.michabelle.com

KENNER

Seven Oaks Plantation	115-125 BB	Full breakfast
2600 Gay Lynn Dr 70065	2 rooms, 2 pb	Sitting room, library,
504-888-8649	Visa, MC	fireplaces, cable TV, porch
Kay & Henry Andressen	C-yes/S-ltd/P-no/H-no	swing

Luxury accommodations with antiques, gardens, and a pond. 10 minutes from airport, 20 minutes from French Quarter. Built from ruins of 7 oaks by world famous architect, A. Hays Town. ✉ hwkfa@bellsouth.net 🌐 www.7oaksplantation.com

LAFITTE

Victoria Inn & Gardens	120-250 BB	Full breakfast
4707 Jean Lafitte Blvd 70067	14 rooms, 14 pb	Onsite restaurant: open
800-689-4797 504-689-4757	Visa, MC, Disc, *Rated*,	Wednesday through Sunday
Dale & Roy Ross	•	6pm – 9:30pm
	C-yes/S-no/P-ltd/H-ltd	Swimming pool, Jacuzzi
	Spanish (with notice)	rooms, full concierge service
		for area tours & trips

Experience Cajun living near bayous once haunted by the pirate, Jean Lafitte. West Indies style plantation on 9 acres of gardens overlooking a lake.
✉ info@victoriainn.com 🌐 www.VictoriaInn.com

LAKE CHARLES

C.A.'s House	165-285 BB	Full breakfast
618 Ford St 70601	6 rooms, 5 pb	Snacks, coffee, refreshments
866-439-6672 337-439-6672	Most CC, *Rated*	Bikes, hot tub, kayaks,
Tanis Robinson	C-ltd/S-ltd/P-ltd/H-ltd	heated swimming pool
	Romanian	

C.A.'s House offers superb luxury accommodations. There are a range of rooms, from single rooms to luxury suites. Located in the heart of Lake Charles' Charpentier Historic District.

✉ waltersatt@aol.com ○ cas-house.com

NAPOLEONVILLE

Madewood Plantation	229-289 MAP	Full plantation breakfast
House	8 rooms, 8 pb	Lunch by reservation,
4250 Hwy 308 70390	Most CC, *Rated*, •	Vegetarian request or special
985-369-7151	C-ltd/S-ltd/P-ltd/H-ltd	food needs okay if requested
Keith & Millie Marshall	French	in advance
		Candlelit dinners, canopied
		beds, private baths, parlor,
		library, porches

A Greek Revival mansion turned country inn featuring wine & cheese, candlelit dinners with a house party atmosphere. Or choose a more romantic, private dinner, full breakfast, & antique canopied beds. Rated in top 54 inns by National Geographic Traveler.

✉ madewoodpl@aol.com ○ www.madewood.com

NATCHITOCHES

Casa Rio B&B	115-130 BB	Full breakfast
1326 Williams Ave 71457	2 rooms, 2 pb	Complimentary welcome
318-356-5698	Visa, MC, Disc	wine & cheese
Patricia & Terence Elliott	C-ltd/S-ltd/P-no/H-ltd	River deck & pier for fishing
	Spanish (limited)	

Enjoy the tranquil Cane River from our deck. Casually elegant home on two park-like acres, close to historic Front Street. Each suite has a private entrance and bath.

✉ pelliott@casariobandb.com ○ www.casariobandb.com

Chateau D'Terre	125-145 BB	Full breakfast
109 Jamar Dr 71457	2 rooms, 2 pb	Sitting room, Jacuzzi, cable
888-798-6566 318-354-7929	Visa, MC, AmEx	TV, wireless Internet access
Terrie & Lee McCallister	C-ltd/S-no/P-no/H-no	

A romantic French country style B&B Inn overlooking Sibley Lake in historic Natchitoches. Relax on the grand front porch, view the lake or explore the historic downtown area and visit lovely antique and craft shops.

✉ chateaudterre@hotmail.com ○ www.chateaudterre.com

The Good House	95-135 BB	Continental plus breakfast
314 Rue Poete St 71457	4 rooms, 4 pb	Complimentary soft drinks,
800-441-8343 318-527-1555	Visa, MC, AmEx	bottled water, English teas
Tod Working	C-ltd/S-no/P-no/H-no	and community coffee
		Landscaped garden,
		fountains, swimming pool,
		Jacuzzi tubs, reading nook,
		porch, fireplace

Built in 1930 by Professor Alvin Good and his wife, this cozy English cottage, embraced with ivy and nestled among enduring pecan trees, overlooks the ebb of Bayou Amulet.

✉ judgeporter@judgeporterhouse.com ○ www.goodhousebandb.com

NATCHITOCHES

Levy-East House
358 Jefferson St 71457
800-840-0662 318-352-0662
Judy & Avery East

125-200 BB
4 rooms, 4 pb
Visa, MC, AmEx,
Rated, •
S-no/P-no/H-no

Full gourmet breakfast
Champagne, cream sherry,
coffee/tea, chocolates
Sitting rooms, off-street
parking, front & back
galleries, ceiling fans

Enjoy luxurious leisure and elegant accommodations in this grand Antebellum home in the Historic District. Fine antiques, queen size beds with private Jacuzzi baths and gourmet breakfast.
✉ judy@levyeasthouse.com ◔ www.levyeasthouse.com

Queen Anne
125 Pine St 71457
800-441-8343 318-352-9206
Tod Working

125-135 BB
5 rooms, 5 pb
Most CC
C-ltd/S-no/P-no/H-no

Full breakfast
Complimentary wine, tea,
bottled water, soft drinks and
bedside chocolates
One and two person Jacuzzi
tubs, refrigerator, in room TV
with DVD and telephone

1905 two-story Victorian with a double wraparound porch. Five spacious bedrooms with queen and king beds, beautifully decorated, with private bath and Jacuzzi tubs. A full breakfast is served.
✉ judgeporter@judgeporterhouse.com ◔ www.queenannebandb.com

The Rusca House
124 Poete St 71457
866-531-0898
Bridget Williams

95-145 BB
4 rooms, 4 pb
Most CC
C-ltd/S-no/P-no

Full breakfast
Wine, refreshments, snacks
Private entrance, wireless
Internet, Jacuzzi tubs

Tasteful elegance and charm await you as you step back in time into a 1920's bungalow, which has been lovingly restored.
✉ bridget@ruscahouse.com ◔ ruscahouse.com

Samuel Guy House
309 Pine St 71457
800-984-1080 318-354-1080
Keri Fidelak

95-135 BB
5 rooms, 5 pb
Most CC
C-yes/S-no/P-no/H-no

Full breakfast
Cable TV, phones, coffee
makers, Jacuzzis,
bath/beauty supplies

Witness a piece of Louisiana history being brought back to life at the Samuel Guy House. Rooms are handsomely decorated with antique and reproduction period furniture, comfortable sitting areas, ceiling fans, spacious baths with Jacuzzi tub.
✉ willwill@cp-tel.net ◔ www.samuelguyhouse.com

The Steel Magnoila House
320 Jefferson St 71457
888-346-4095 318-238-2585
Christina & Dr. Richard

175-225 BB
4 rooms, 4 pb
Most CC
C-ltd/S-no/P-no/H-no

Full breakfast
Swimming pool, gardens,
wireless Internet, vine
covered arbor

From the unique architecture to its involvement in the Civil War, this home is truly a piece of Southern history. Known for the on-site filming of the award-winning classic "Steel Magnolias," there is something to be cherished by all who visit.
✉ steelhbb@cp-tel.net ◔ www.steelmagnoliahouse.com

Tante Huppe Inn
424 Jefferson St 71457
800-482-4276 318-352-5342
Robert "Bobby" DeBlieux

95-120 BB
3 rooms, 3 pb
Visa, MC, *Rated*
S-ltd/P-no/H-ltd

Continental breakfast
Grecian swimming pool,
galleries, patio

Located in the heart of the Natchitoches Landmark Historic District. Natchitoches is the oldest town in the Louisiana Purchase Territory, having been founded by the French in 1714.
◔ www.tantehuppe.com

NEW ORLEANS

1830 Dauphine House B&B
1830 Dauphine St 70116
504-940-0943
Karen Jeffries

65-125 BB
3 rooms, 3 pb
Visa, MC
C-ltd/S-no/P-no

Continental breakfast
Host lives on property;
laundry facilities available

Built in 1860, and one and a half blocks from the French Quarter near Bourbon and Esplanade, historic Dauphine House offers romantic rooms with private baths, hardwood floors and 12-foot ceilings.
✉ info@dauphinehouse.com ✪ www.dauphinehouse.com

1870 Banana Courtyard
1422 N Rampart St 70116
800-842-4748 504-947-4475
Mary Ramsey (aka the banana lady)

69-165 BB
12 rooms, 12 pb
Most CC, *Rated*
C-ltd/S-ltd/P-no/H-ltd
Y'at

Continental breakfast B&B only
Main B&B has free soft drinks, bottled water, granola bars, fruit, wine & beer when we're around
Phone, TV, A/C, hammock, porch swing, courtyard, rooms w/view or balcony, WiFi, business center

Ooh la la! In the 1800s, this B&B was bordello catering to society's elite. Great location, the French Quarter is ½ a block away, all the Quarter has to offer is in walking distance. A unique combination of amenities and accommodations in New Orleans
✉ bananacour@aol.com ✪ www.bananacourtyard.com

1896 O'Malley House
120 S. Pierce St 70119
866-226-1896 504-488-5896
Larry Watts & Brad Smith

99-200 BB
8 rooms, 8 pb
Visa, MC, AmEx, *Rated*
C-ltd/S-no/P-no/H-ltd

Full breakfast
Complimentary beer, wine, soft drinks and snacks.
Telephones with private voice mail, wireless DSL, color TV, Iron, hair dryers, fax service

The Colonial Revival residence is nestled in a neighborhood that boasts great food, music & culture. Recently renovated with hardwood floors & marble mantels, the rooms are beautifully decorated & include queen/king beds. Located near French Quarter.
✉ brad@1896omalleyhouse.com ✪ www.1896omalleyhouse.com

A Crescent City Guest House
612 Marigny St 70117
877-281-2680 504-944-8722
Matthew Harring

69-159 BB
4 rooms, 4 pb
Most CC
C-ltd/S-ltd/P-yes/H-no
September – May

Continental plus breakfast
Extended continental breakfast available 24 hours
Free off-street parking, wireless Internet, movies, patio & hot tub, maid service, tax included

Enjoy all of the excitement and charm that New Orleans has to offer. We are in the historic Faubourg Marigny, just three blocks from the French Quarter and the Riverfront Street Car Lines. Four guestrooms. Pets welcome, free off-street parking.
✉ ccgh@cox.net ✪ www.crescentcitygh.com

Aaron's Ingram Haus
1012 Elysian Fields 70117
504-949-3110
Scott Graves

89-165 EP
4 rooms, 4 pb
Most CC, •
C-ltd/S-ltd/P-no/H-no

Self catered breakfast
Self-catered kitchen with stove, fridge, coffee maker, microwave, toaster, etc.
A/C, free WiFi for your lap top, hairdryers, color cable TV, radio/alarm clocks.

Located only six blocks from world-famous Bourbon Street, within walking distance to most New Orleans attractions. The Frenchmen Street mecca of nightclubs, bars and a number of good and reasonably priced restaurants are within a few blocks of our door.
✉ ingramhaus@yahoo.com ✪ www.ingramhaus.com

NEW ORLEANS

Auld Sweet Olive B&B
2460 N Rampart St 70117
877-470-5323 504-947-4332
David Johnson/Dale Irvin

65-150 BB
6 rooms, 6 pb
Most CC
S-no/P-no/H-no
French

Continental plus breakfast
Fresh mint iced tea, snacks,
beverages
Library, laundry, irons,
spacious gardens, free WiFi

A gem in the Marigny! Airy & spacious, Sweet Olive offers visitors a relaxed and comfortable home base. Expertly handpainted wall finishes adorn each room. Unusual and classy, full of delight!
info@sweetolive.com ◎ www.sweetolive.com

Avenue Inn B&B
4125 St Charles Ave 70115
800-490-8542 504-269-2640
Joe & Bebe Rabhan

79-399 BB
17 rooms, 17 pb
Most CC, *Rated*, •
C-ltd/S-no/P-no/H-yes
Spanish

Continental plus breakfast
Afternoon tea, fruit & cheese
upon request, low carb and
special diet items available
Grand parlor & master dining
room, Creole porch, private
baths, voice mail, wireless
Internet access

1891 Grand Mansion on famed St. Charles Avenue streetcar line, minutes to the French Quarter. Enjoy the "Avenue" in a rocker on our veranda, rest in our restored guestrooms and drift back to the splendor of the past. Don't just visit New Orleans, live it!
stay@avenueinnbb.com ◎ www.avenueinnbb.com

Balcony Guest House
2483 Royal St 70117
800-395-2124 504-945-4425
Zak Rahman

89-129 BB
5 rooms, 5 pb
Visa, MC, AmEx
C-yes/S-no/P-yes/H-ltd

Full breakfast
A full hot breakfast
weekdays, hot brunch on
weekends
Balcony, parlor, laundry

Balcony Guest House, New Orleans is 'your bed and breakfast above' Schiro's Grocery and CafT . . . and conveniently located at 2483 Royal Street. Only 6 blocks down river from the French Quarter and 4 blocks from Frenchman Street.
contactus@balconyguesthouse.com ◎ www.balconyguesthouse.com

Burgundy B&B
2513 Burgundy St 70117
800-970-2513 504-942-1463
Carl Smith

90-150 BB
4 rooms, 4 pb
Most CC
C-ltd/S-ltd/P-ltd/H-ltd
German, French

Continental breakfast
Guest kitchen. Coffee
available throughout the day
on a self-serve basis.
Parlor, fireplaces, 12ft.
ceiling, courtyard, spa,
library, Cyber Cafe,
historical, porches, TV/DVD

We are a small and cozy gay owned and operated New Orleans Bed & Breakfast Inn, just a few blocks from the French Quarter. We can guide you to many local sites and attractions including restaurants, shopping, music clubs and more!
theburgundy@cox.net ◎ www.theburgundy.com

Bywater B&B
1026 Clouet St 70117
504-944-8438
Betty-Carol & Marti

65-125 BB
4 rooms, 1 pb
Visa, MC
C-ltd/S-no/P-ltd/H-no

Continental plus breakfast
Coffee and tea any time
Sitting room, library, cable
TV, VCR, covered porches,
patio

Completely renovated "double shotgun" house in National Historic District, full of contemporary Louisiana folk art, antiques, books, and music. Lovely brick patio with fishpond and porch swing.
bywaterbnb@juno.com ◎ www.bywaterbnb.com

NEW ORLEANS————————————————————————————————————

Columns Hotel
3811 St. Charles Ave 70115
800-445-9308 504-899-9308
Claire & Jacques Creppel

120-230 BB
20 rooms, 20 pb
Visa, MC, AmEx
C-ltd/S-no/P-no/H-ltd

Full breakfast
Restaurant and lounge on
premises.
Complimentary daily
newspaper, 24 hour front
desk staff, Garden District
location, in-room service

If you've ever yearned for grander, more romantic times . . . come to The Columns Hotel in the Garden District of New Orleans. The Columns Hotel, New Orleans' favorite historic hotel, welcomes you to experience a timeless and memorable stay in the South.
✉ columnshtl@aol.com ◐ thecolumns.com

Creole Gardens B&B
1415 Prytania St 70130
866-569-8700 504-569-8700
Miss Karen

89-299 BB
26 rooms, 26 pb
Most CC, *Rated*, •
C-yes/S-ltd/P-yes/H-ltd
French, Spanish, Cussin'
Cajun

Full Southern Breakfast
Full catering for weddings,
parties and meetings. Quiet
courtyard with fountain.
Lovely garden courtyard,
sitting room with grand
piano, Internet, cable TV

New Orleans hippest B&B. Located in the Lower Garden District, walking distance to fine dining, down home cooking, museums, and most attractions. Sumptuous full breakfast daily and a friendly southern staff eager to help you enjoy New Orleans.
✉ info@creolegardens.com ◐ www.creolegardens.com

Elysian Fields Inn
930 Elysian Fields Ave 70117
866-948-9420 504-948-9420
Leigh & Jim Crawford

109-269 BB
8 rooms, 8 pb
Most CC, *Rated*
C-yes/S-ltd/P-yes/H-yes

Full breakfast
Coffee & tea bar available all
day; bottled water
Flat screen TV, VCR/DVD
players, WiFi, daily
housekeeping, private Italian
marble bathrooms

Welcome to Elysian Fields Inn, the only AAA 4 Diamond-rated New Orleans B&B . . . a testament to our dedication to our guests. Historic 1850's Urban Inn. 8 tastefully decorated guestrooms each with flat-screen TV, DVD/VCR player and luxurious private baths.
✉ innkeeper@elysianfieldsinn.com ◐ www.elysianfieldsinn.com

The Elysian Guest House
1008 Elysian Fields Ave 70117
504-324-4311
Ted

85-135 BB
5 rooms, 5 pb
Most CC, •
C-yes/S-no/P-yes/H-no

Continental breakfast
Gardens, large hot tub,
antiques, privacy

Elysian Guest House is located only five short blocks to the French Quarter. New Orleans blocks are short, not like large city blocks. The Mighty Mississippi is also five blocks. House was built in the 1840s and is a Victoria Shotgun style home.
✉ info@elysianguesthouse.com ◐ elysianguesthouse.com

Fairchild House B&B
1518 Prytania St 70130
800-256-8096 504-524-0154
Beatriz Aprigliano-Ziegler

75-145 BB
9 rooms, 9 pb
Visa, MC, AmEx,
Rated, •
C-yes/S-no/P-no/H-no
Spanish, Portuguese

Continental plus breakfast
Sitting room, suites, cable TV,
off-street parking, courtyard
& garden

Classic, comfortable B&B located in the Lower Garden District, one block from streetcar line, 15 blocks to French Quarter.
✉ info@fairchildhouse.com ◐ www.fairchildhouse.com

NEW ORLEANS————————————————————————————

Garden District B&B	80-150 BB	Continental breakfast
2418 Magazine St 70130	4 rooms, 4 pb	Balconies, courtyard,
504-895-4302	Most CC	screened-in porch,
Raynell Dunham	C-yes/S-ltd/P-no/H-ltd	kitchenettes, cable TV,
	Spanish	Internet access

With a great location, you can shop, eat, drink & relax on Magazine St or take a quick streetcar ride to the French Quarter. Online Booking on our inn's web site. We now offer free Internet access and wireless access.
✉ info@gardendistrictbedandbreakfast.com ◐ www.gardendistrictbedandbreakfast.com

Gentry House B&B	100-175 BB	Continental breakfast
1031 St Ann St 70116	5 rooms, 5 pb	Kitchenettes stocked with
504-525-4433	C-yes/S-no/P-no/H-ltd	fruit, cereal, and other
Brian & Charlotte Furness		snacks.
		Family friendly, pet
		visitations in the courtyard,
		kitchenettes, romance, group
		accommodations

Enjoy New Orleans like a native. Start your days with sinfully flaky fresh croissants delivered to your door daily to enjoy en-suite or in the fountain-splashed courtyard. Stroll out to enjoy beautiful Jackson Square and enjoy the Mighty Mississippi!
✉ gentryhse@aol.com ◐ www.gentryhouse.com

Henry Howard House	87-450 BB	Continental breakfast
2041 Prytania St 70130	17 rooms, 17 pb	Sitting room, suites,
877-563-1411 504-561-8550	Most CC, *Rated*, •	balconies, phones with
Sherrie Fontana	C-yes/S-no/P-no/H-no	personal voicemail, Internet,
		cable TV, conference room

Welcome to the Henry Howard House! Experience the best of New Orleans and find out why the Henry Howard House is the place to be! Add a touch of style with our 1850s decor; the perfect place for a business presentation, corporate retreat, or wedding!
✉ info@henryhowardhouseinn.com ◐ www.hhhinn.com

Lafitte Guest House	99-399 BB	Continental plus breakfast
1003 Bourbon St 70116	14 rooms, 14 pb	Biscuits, juice, tea, and
800-331-7971 504-581-2678	Most CC, *Rated*, •	coffee.
Deems Brooks	C-ltd/S-no/P-ltd/H-ltd	Concierge services, wedding
	Some Spanish & French	rentals, parties, cooking
		school, and parking.

A luxury boutique hotel located in the residential area of Bourbon Street. Enjoy the sights and sounds of Bourbon Street as well as a retreat into your own personal French Quarter home.
✉ reservations@lafitteguesthouse.com ◐ www.lafitteguesthouse.com

Lagniappe Guest House	99-250 BB	Continental plus breakfast
1925 Peniston St 70115	5 rooms, 5 pb	Soda, juices, bottled water,
800-317-2120	Most CC, *Rated*, •	snacks
Helene & Ken Barnett	C-ltd/S-ltd/P-no/H-no	Sitting room, library,
		bicycles, tennis, cable TV, 2-
		bedroom corporate suite
		available.

A beautiful and comfortable bedroom, delicious breakfasts, a glass of wine on the veranda and hosts eager to help plan and guide you towards a memorable visit await you at Lagniappe B&B.
✉ info@lanyappe.com ◐ www.lanyappe.com

NEW ORLEANS——————————————————————

Maison Perrier	79-330 BB	Full breakfast
4117 Perrier St 70115	14 rooms, 14 pb	Snacks all day, wine, draft
888-610-1807 504-897-1807	Most CC, *Rated*, •	beer & cheese service on
Tom & Patricia Schoenbrun	C-yes/S-no/P-ltd/H-ltd	Friday & Saturday evenings
	Spanish, French	Professional & personal
		concierge service, licensed
		massage therapist on-site
		(appt. necessary)

Beautiful American Victorian, built in 1892, located in the Uptown/Garden district. Victorian charm, modern conveniences. Hot breakfast every morning. Minutes to the Quarter, all attractions. Free parking and free wireless Internet throughout the inn.
✉ innkeeper@maisonperrier.com ○ www.maisonperrier.com

Park View Guest House	80-150 BB	Continental breakfast
7004 St Charles Ave 70118	22 rooms, 19 pb	Sitting room, dining room
888-533-0746 504-861-7564	Most CC, •	overlooking Audubon Park,
	C-yes/S-no/P-no/H-no	cable TV, copying, fax,
		wireless Internet

A European style Grand Victorian guesthouse, the Park View is affordable, comfortable & conveniently located. Some of our guestrooms are furnished with simple to grand antiques.
✉ info@parkviewguesthouse.com ○ www.parkviewguesthouse.com

Rose Manor Inn	85-195 BB	Continental plus breakfast
7214 Pontchartrain Blvd 70124	9 rooms, 9 pb	Tea, coffee, soft drinks &
504-282-8200	Most CC, •	snacks
Peter & Ruby Verhoeven	C-ltd/S-no/P-no/H-ltd	Cable TV, refrigerator,
	Chinese, German	concierge services

All the elegance and decor of an English country house, situated only 10 minutes from the French Quarter, area attractions and convention center. Extremely comfortable, friendly atmosphere.
✉ roseinn@bellsouth.net ○ www.rosemanor.com

The Soniat House	240-625 BB	Continental breakfast
1133 Chartres St 70116	32 rooms, 32 pb	Wireless Internet, cable TV,
800-544-8808 504-522-0570	Most CC	daily newspapers, wake-up
Rodney & Frances Smith	C-ltd/S-no/P-no/H-ltd	service, antiques, bathrobes,
		individual A/C

Travel and Leisure named Soniat House "one of the best hotels in the world."
✉ stay@soniathouse.com ○ www.soniathouse.com

St. Charles Guest House	40-125 BB	Continental breakfast
1748 Prytania St 70130	36 rooms, 22 pb	Bakery
504-523-6556	Visa, MC, AmEx, *Rated*	Swimming pool, library,
	C-ltd/S-ltd/P-no/H-yes	ample reading material
	Spanish	(books/magazines)

Welcome to our lovely guesthouse. We offer comfortable accommodations at a reasonable price and are located near the French quarter in the historic Garden District.
✉ dhilton111@aol.com ○ www.stcharlesguesthouse.com

Sully Mansion B&B	110-250 BB	Continental plus breakfast
2631 Prytania St 70130	8 rooms, 8 pb	Full breakfast on weekends,
800-364-2414 504-891-0457	Most CC, *Rated*, •	complimentary home baked
Nancy & Guy Fournier	C-ltd/S-ltd/P-no/H-no	goods, honor bar
		Concierge services for
		restaurants, tours, outings,
		voice mail, WiFi, free
		parking, guest baskets

Built as a private home in 1890 the Sully Mansion is the only licensed bed and breakfast in the Garden District. Sully Mansion offers a unique combination of Southern hospitality, gracious accommodations and modern day conveniences. Come be our guest!
✉ sullym@bellsouth.net ○ www.sullymansion.com

NEW ORLEANS

Terrell House B&B
1441 Magazine St 70130
866-261-9687 504-247-0560
Linda O'Brien

140-350	Full breakfast
12 rooms, 12 pb	Cable television, wireless
Most CC	Internet, robes, coffee
C-ltd/S-ltd/P-ltd/H-ltd	makers, bottled water, and
	soft drinks

At the Terrell House in New Orleans, we invite you to be our guest and experience gracious Southern hospitality and immerse yourself in all New Orleans has to offer.
✉ lobrien@terrellhouse.com ❂ www.terrellhouse.com

Victorian House
914 N Rampart St 70116
866-408-5311 504-218-5661
Gregory App

105-230 BB	Continental breakfast
7 rooms, 7 pb	Wifi, central heat and air,
Visa, MC	house computer for those
C-yes/S-no/P-no	traveling sans laptop.

Experience, the unparalleled comfort and elegance of this newly-restored Victorian townhouse located in the heart of the French Quarter. We make you feel at home and are here make sure your stay in New Orleans is one you enjoy.
✉ info@victorianhousenola.com ❂ www.victorianhousenola.com

RAYNE

Maison D'Memoire B&B
Cottages
8450 Roberts Cove Rd 70578
866-580-2477 337-334-2477
Lyn & Ken Guidry

130-200 BB	Full breakfast
4 rooms, 4 pb	Some suites come with a
Most CC	chilled bottle of wine
C-yes/S-no/P-no/H-ltd	Porch, Jacuzzi, private lake,
	full kitchen, TV/VCR,
	coffeemaker

Recapture the precious memories of the past in our private, authentic Cajun cottages. Each guesthouse has its own pleasing personality. All cottages are at least 100 years old and are restored with love to their former glory.
✉ info@maisondmemoire.com ❂ www.maisondmemoire.com

SHREVEPORT

Fairfield Place
2221 Fairfield Ave 71104
866-432-2632 318-222-0048
Pat & Mark Faser

109-199 BB	Full gourmet breakfast
8 rooms, 8 pb	Bridal Luncheons, Tea
Most CC, *Rated*, •	Parties, Special Event
C-yes/S-ltd/P-yes/H-ltd	Catering, Homemade
	Goodies
	Sitting room, whirlpools,
	suites, one acre of
	gardens/grounds, weddings,
	phone, Internet, fax

Casually elegant inn in two lovely, adjoining homes built circa 1870. European and American antiques, gourmet breakfast, exquisite Victorian gardens. Large spacious rooms, king or queen beds and private baths. Ideal for business travelers and tourists.
✉ fairfieldplace@bellsouth.net ❂ www.fairfieldplace.com

ST. FRANCISVILLE

Barrow House Inn
9779 Royal St 70775
225-635-4791
Shirley Dittloff

115-160 BB	Unique Choice: Continental
8 rooms, 8 pb	or Full
Most CC, *Rated*, •	3 New Orleans-style egg
C-ltd/S-ltd/P-no/H-ltd	dishes ($5 fee)
	Over 500 DVDs, free WiFi &
	parking

You will discover antiques & ambience among two 200+ year-old houses in the heart of an unforgettable fairy-tale town, St. Francisville, Louisiana.
✉ website@topteninn.com ❂ www.topteninn.com

ST. FRANCISVILLE

Butler Greenwood
Plantation
8345 US Hwy 61 70775
225-635-6312
Anne Butler

135-185 BB
8 rooms, 8 pb
Visa, MC, AmEx,
Rated, •
C-yes/S-ltd/P-ltd/H-no
Some French

Continental breakfast
Swimming pool, pond,
extensive grounds and
gardens, in-room double
Jacuzzis, some fireplaces

8 private cottages, with plenty of historic charm, scattered across peaceful landscaped plantation grounds. All cottages have Jacuzzis, porch or deck. On National Register of Historic Places.
✉ butlergree@aol.com ❂ www.butlergreenwood.com

THIBODAUX

Naquin's B&B
1146 W Camellia Dr 70301
985-446-6977
Frank & Joyce Naquin

60-75 BB
4 rooms, 4 pb
•
C-yes/S-no/P-ltd/H-ltd
French

Full breakfast
Afternoon tea, snacks
Sitting room, cable TV,
accommodate business
travelers

Magic on the Bayou. Enjoy Cajun hospitality with a family of Acadian descent. Four bedrooms with private baths, 50 miles southwest of New Orleans.
✉ naquinsbb@hotmail.com ❂ www.naquinsbb.com

WEST MONROE

Rose Lee
318 Trenton St 71291
318-366-2412
Ken & Kathryn Huff

105-135 BB
5 rooms, 5 pb
Visa, MC, AmEx
C-ltd/S-ltd/P-ltd/H-no

Full breakfast
Dessert, fruit, beverages,
popcorn
Sitting room, cable TV,
kitchen & laundry facility,
accommodations for
business travel, phones

You might enjoy breakfast in the dining room or on the quaint balcony overlooking Antique Alley, a shoppers' paradise. A wonderful place to unwind & enjoy peaceful surroundings.
✉ roseleebnb@aol.com ❂ www.roseleebnb.com

Maine

ACADIA SCHOODIC───────────────────────────────

Acadia's Oceanside	118-198 BB	Full gourmet breakfast
Meadows Inn	15 rooms, 15 pb	Afternoon tea
Prospect Harbor, Rt 195 04669	Most CC	Sitting room, library,
207-963-5557	C-yes/S-no/P-yes/H-yes	fireplace, lawn games,
Sonja Sundaram, Ben Walter		flowers, private beach

Historic sea captain's home with magnificent oceanviews, on 200+ acres with private sand beach, Acadia National Park 5 minutes away, great hiking, biking, swimming, sea kayaking, canoeing.
✉ oceaninn@oceaninn.com ❂ www.oceaninn.com

ADDISON──────────────────────────────────────

Pleasant Bay B&B and	50-135 BB	Full breakfast
Llama Keep	4 rooms, 2 pb	Sitting room, family room
386 West Side Rd 04606	Visa, MC	w/TV, screened porch, deck,
207-483-4490	C-yes/S-no/P-no/H-ltd	trails, llama, deer
Leon Yeaton		

On a knoll, by the shores of Pleasant River, rests our 110 acre working llama and red deer farm. Enjoy the rise and fall of the tides, while gazing at the many shore birds and seals.
✉ pleasantbay@downeast.net ❂ www.pleasantbay.com/bandb.html

BAILEY ISLAND────────────────────────────────

Log Cabin, An Island Inn	159-309 BB	Full breakfast
5 Log Cabin Ln 04003	9 rooms, 9 pb	Dinner, bar
207-833-5546	Most CC, *Rated*	2 hot tubs, flowers,
Matt & Aimee York	C-ltd/S-no/P-no/H-yes	swimming pool
	April-October	

Nine luxurious rooms, all with private baths & private decks. All have spectacular ocean-views. Some with Jacuzzi tubs, some gas fireplace, some with kitchens. 2 with hot tub, heated pool open late spring to early fall.
✉ info@logcabin-maine.com ❂ www.logcabin-maine.com

BAR HARBOR───────────────────────────────────

Acadia Hotel	50-140 BB	Optional full brkfast plan
20 Mt Desert St 04609	11 rooms, 11 pb	avail.
888-876-2463 207-288-5721	Most CC, •	Cafe Bakery next door
Chris Coston	C-ltd/S-no/P-no/H-no	Location, some whirlpools,
	Inquire	cable TV, porch & balcony,
		A/C, private baths

Luxury on a budget. Newly renovated with A/C, TV, private baths, wireless. In downtown Bar Harbor, Maine near Acadia National Park.
✉ acadiahotel@aol.com ❂ www.acadiabarharbormaine.com

Anne's White Columns Inn	75-155 BB	Full breakfast
57 Mt Desert St 04609	10 rooms, 10 pb	Late afternoon wine, cheese
800-321-6379 207-288-5357	Most CC, *Rated*	and crackers
Anne & Robert Bahr	C-yes/S-no/P-no/H-no	Sitting room, cable TV,
	May-November	private baths, queen beds,
		covered porch, gardens

Anne's White Columns Inn, an impressive Georgian structure, is located in the Historical Corridor in downtown Bar Harbor.
✉ info@anneswhitecolumns.com ❂ www.anneswhitecolumns.com

BAR HARBOR────────────────────────────────

Atlantean Inn
11 Atlantic Ave 04609
800-722-6671 207-288-5703
Heidi Burnham & Gary Rich

120-255 BB
8 rooms, 8 pb
Visa, MC, AmEx
C-ltd/S-no/P-no/H-no
May 1-October 31

Full breakfast
Beverages & snacks are
always available in the well-
stocked butler's pantry
Beautiful gardens, fireplaces,
whirlpools, TV, WiFi

Tranquility in the heart of the village. Let each day in Bar Harbor begin with a fabulous full breakfast, and end relaxing with refreshments in the beautiful, peaceful gardens and grounds of Atlantean.
✉ atlantean1@verizon.net ☯ www.atlanteaninn.com

Aysgarth Station
20 Roberts Ave 04609
207-288-9655
Jane Holland & Steve Cornell

70-140 BB
6 rooms, 6 pb
Visa, MC, Disc, *Rated*
C-ltd/S-no/P-no/H-no

Full breakfast
Afternoon tea & snacks
Living room, dining room,
porch, 3rd floor sun deck

Aysgarth Station offers year round accommodations & extends New England hospitality & quiet comfort in a uniquely casual atmosphere, right in downtown Bar Harbor. Six guestrooms, only a short stroll to the waterfront harbor.
✉ innkeeper@aysgarth.com ☯ www.aysgarth.com

**Bar Harbor Castlemaine Inn
B&B**
39 Holland Ave 04609
800-338-4563 207-288-4563
Daniel & Diana Daigle

69-269 BB
17 rooms, 17 pb
Most CC, *Rated*
C-ltd/S-no/P-no/H-no
May thru October

Continental plus breakfast
Scones, muffins, breads and
coffee cake, as well as bagels,
fresh fruit, and a variety of
beverages
A/C, fridge, CATV/DVD/VCR,
Internet, fax, fireplace, decks.
Main St 3 blocks, ocean 2
blocks

The Inn is nestled on a quiet side street in Bar Harbor Village, surrounded by the magnificent Acadia National Park. AAA 3-Diamond and Mobil 3-Star rating. Well-appointed rooms, some with whirlpool and fireplace.
✉ info@castlemaineinn.com ☯ www.castlemaineinn.com

Bar Harbor Tides
119 West St. 04609
207-288-4968
Ray & Loretta Harris

275-425 BB
4 rooms, 4 pb
Visa, MC, Disc, *Rated*
C-ltd/S-no/P-no/H-no

Full breakfast
Sitting room, 2nd floor guest
living room with gas
fireplace

On the water, in-town Bar Harbor and near Acadia National Park. Very private. Sumptuous full breakfast on the verandah, with sweeping views of Frenchman's Bay.
✉ info@barharbortides.com ☯ www.barharbortides.com

Bass Cottage Inn
14 The Field 04609
866-782-9224 207-288-1234
Jeff & Teri Anderholm

185-365 BB
10 rooms, 10 pb
Visa, MC, AmEx
C-ltd/S-no/P-no/H-yes
Some Spanish, Italian,
German
Mid May – Late October

Full gourmet breakfast
Evening wine & hors
d'oeuvres – high season,
guest pantry snacks
Wireless Internet, early
coffee service, baby grand
piano, library, sunporch,
evening turndown

Bar Harbor's premier luxury inn, offering impeccable hospitality. The Bass Cottage Inn has been refurbished & reborn as a stylish ten-room inn that graciously blends old & new—without Victorian cliches.
✉ innkeeper@basscottage.com ☯ www.basscottage.com

BAR HARBOR————————————————————————

Cleftstone Manor
92 Eden St 04609
888-288-4951 207-288-8086
Robert & Anne Bahr

75-225 BB
16 rooms, 16 pb
Most CC
C-yes/S-no/P-no/H-no
Late April through Oct.

Full breakfast
Afternoon tea & fresh baked
cookies
Sitting rooms, library with
Internet access, cable TV,
phone, fireplaces

You are invited to stay with us at Cleftstone Manor on your next stay in Bar Harbor, Maine. Where better to experience the splendor of Eden than a stay at a mansion built in 1881. Cleftstone is the only mansion on the west side of Eden Street to survive.
✉ innkeeper@cleftstone.com ✪ www.cleftstone.com

Coach Stop Inn
715 State Hwy 3 04609
800-927-3097 207-288-9886
Jeff & Natalie Reynolds

125-155 BB
5 rooms, 5 pb
Visa, MC, *Rated*
C-ltd/S-ltd/P-no/H-ltd
Mid May – mid October

Full gourmet breakfast
Snacks, complimentary
wine, afternoon
refreshments
Suites, fireplaces, cable TV in
common room

Built in 1804 the Coach Stop is Bar Harbor's oldest inn, dating back to the presidency of Thomas Jefferson. Come see why "Down East" says Coach Stop Inn is "Where to Stay in Bar Harbor." Chef owned and operated and featured on "Emeril Live."
✉ info@coachstopinn.com ✪ www.coachstopinn.com

Graycote Inn
40 Holland Ave 04609
207-288-3044
Pat & Roger Samuel

95-185 BB
12 rooms, 12 pb
Most CC, *Rated*, •
C-ltd/S-no/P-no/H-no

Full breakfast
Early morning coffee tray
near room, and afternoon
refreshments
Fireplaces, sitting rooms,
balconies, free WiFi, garden,
walk to restaurants & shops

A Retreat from the Everyday. Open year-round. Green certified. Victorian with large rooms, some with fireplaces, sunrooms, or balconies. Large landscaped yard on quiet village street. Full hot breakfast. Walk to shops, galleries, restaurants. Free WiFi.
✉ innkeepers@graycoteinn.com ✪ www.graycoteinn.com

Hearthside B&B
7 High St 04609
207-288-4533
Susan & Barry Schwartz

80-175 BB
9 rooms, 9 pb
Visa, MC, Disc, *Rated*
C-ltd/S-no/P-no/H-no
May 1st to October 30th

Full breakfast
Afternoon tea & cookies
All rooms have A/C, 3 rooms
with fireplaces, 3 baths with
whirlpool jets. Free WiFi and
computer.

Small, gracious hostelry in quiet downtown location, elegant and comfortable, blend of antiques and traditional furniture. Rooms with private baths, some with fireplace, whirlpool tub or porch.
✉ bears@hearthsideinn.com ✪ www.hearthsideinn.com

Holbrook House
74 Mt Desert St 04609
800-860-7430 207-288-4970
Judy Sargent

110-200 BB
12 rooms, 12 pb
Visa, MC, *Rated*
C-ltd/S-no/P-no/H-no
May – October

Full breakfast
Afternoon refreshments
Sitting room, library,
enclosed bike storage, ample
parking, pool and hot tub

Relax amid the charm & ambience of Bar Harbor's Golden Years. Holbrook House is a lovely 1876 Victorian showplace on the historic corridor of Bar Harbor.
✉ info@holbrookhouse.com ✪ www.holbrookhouse.com

Holland Inn
35 Holland Ave 04609
207-288-4804
Evin & Tom Hulbert

55-165 BB
9 rooms, 9 pb
Visa, MC, *Rated*
C-ltd/S-ltd/P-no/H-ltd
May 1-Oct 31

Full gourmet breakfast
All private baths, A/C, cable
TV, sitting rooms, suites,
balcony and patios

A delightfully informal, non-Victorian bed and breakfast located within the historic village of Bar Harbor, Maine. Minutes from Acadia National Park and ferry to Nova Scotia.
✉ info@hollandinn.com ✪ www.hollandinn.com

BAR HARBOR————————————————————————————————————

The Inn at Bay Ledge
150 Sand Point Rd 04609
207-288-4204
Jack & Jeani Ochtera

100-475 BB
11 rooms, 11 pb
Visa, MC, *Rated*, •
C-ltd/S-no/P-no/H-ltd
May-Oct/June 15-Oct. 1

Full breakfast
Heated pool, fireplaces,
sauna, steam rooms,
Jacuzzis, meeting room

Atop an 80-foot cliff, towering pines and overlooking Frenchman Bay, sits the Inn at Bay Ledge. Literally clinging to the cliffs of Mount Desert Island with private Maine stone beach is one of the most breathtaking views that you could ever imagine.
✉ bayledge@downeast.net ❂ www.innatbayledge.com

Manor House Inn
106 West St 04609
800-437-0088 207-288-3759
Stacey & Ken Smith

82-250 BB
18 rooms, 18 pb
Most CC, *Rated*
C-ltd/S-no/P-no/H-no
Mid April thru late Oct.

Full Buffet Breakfast
Afternoon tea, refreshments
Sitting room, fireplaces,
gardens, whirlpool, gazebo

Welcome to Manor House Inn, Bar Harbor's Historic Victorian Inn. Conveniently located within 2 blocks, which is easy walking distance of village shops, restaurants and ocean activities. One mile from Acadia National Park.
✉ manor@me.acadia.net ❂ www.barharbormanorhouse.com

Mira Monte Inn
69 Mt Desert St 04609
800-553-5109 207-288-4263
Marian Burns

99-234 BB
17 rooms, 17 pb
Most CC, •
C-yes/S-no/P-no/H-yes
Mid-May. through Oct.

Full Breakfast Buffet
Complimentary late
afternoon innkeeper's social
Piano, sitting and meeting
rooms, fireplaces, balcony,
private phones, A/C,
televisions

Built in 1864 and named Mira Monte, "Behold the Mountains," for the beautiful surrounding peaks of Acadia National Park. Victorian estate complete with period furnishings and fireplaces. In-town location; within walking distance to the waterfront.
✉ mburns@miramonte.com ❂ www.miramonte.com

Moseley Cottage Inn
12 Atlantic Ave 04609
800-458-8644 207-288-5548
Pam and Scott Allen

68-230 BB
9 rooms, 9 pb
Visa, MC, Disc, *Rated*
C-yes/S-no/P-no/H-ltd
April-November

Homemade, bountiful
breakfasts
On-premises parking, parlor
with piano, front porch,
courtesy phone, computer,
WiFi

Beautiful 1894 Victorian Inn in a quiet location just a minute's walk to downtown Bar Harbor. Offering graciously decorated rooms, period furniture, working fireplaces & private porches. Enjoy your creative, homemade breakfast on our spacious grounds.
✉ pamskidog2@aol.com ❂ www.moseleycottage.net/

Primrose Inn-Historic Bar Harbor B&B
73 Mount Desert St 04609
877-TIME-4-BH 207-288-4031
Catherine & Jeff Shaw

99-249 BB
15 rooms, 15 pb
Most CC, *Rated*, •
C-ltd/S-no/P-no/H-ltd
May to October

Hearty full breakfast
Afternoon Tea featuring
freshly baked treats from the
Primrose kitchen
Wireless Internet access,
Daily newspapers delivered
to each room, Reserved
parking space

This romantic Bar Harbor Bed and Breakfast is perfectly located just a short stroll from Bar Harbor's Main Street and only a mile from magnificent Acadia National Park.
✉ relax@primroseinn.com ❂ www.primroseinn.com

Galen C. Moses House, Bath, ME

BAR HARBOR

Saltair Inn Waterfront B&B
121 West St 04609
207-288-2882
Matt & Kristi Losquadro

165-355 BB
4 rooms, 4 pb
Visa, MC, AmEx
C-ltd/S-no/P-no/H-ltd

Full breakfast
Afternoon refreshments;
complimentary coffee, tea,
sodas and water available 24
hours a day
Water views, fireplaces,
Jacuzzi, balcony, wireless
Internet access, TVs, CD
players, dining room

Come experience the magic of Bar Harbor at an elegant, waterfront Victorian Inn on the shores of Frenchman Bay. All rooms have elegant private baths en suite. Amenities include luxury linens, gas fireplaces, cable TV, CD players, and wireless Internet.
✉ relax@saltairinn.com ☏ www.saltairinn.com

BATH

Galen C. Moses House
1009 Washington St 04530
888-442-8771 207-442-8771
Jim Haught & Larry Kieft

119-259 BB
6 rooms, 5 pb
Most CC, *Rated*, •
C-ltd/S-no/P-yes/H-no

Full breakfast
Afternoon tea, wine
Turndown service, A/C, WiFi

Built in 1874, the Galen C. Moses House is reminiscent of the 19th century grand Victorian style. Selected for the National Register of Historic Homes.
✉ stay@galenmoses.com ☏ www.galenmoses.com

Inn at Bath
969 Washington St 04530
800-423-0964 207-443-4294
Elizabeth Knowlton

150-200 BB
8 rooms, 8 pb
Most CC
C-ltd/S-no/P-ltd/H-yes
Some Spanish

Full breakfast
Complimentary tea, coffee
Lovely living rooms, terrace
& porch; some rooms with
fireplaces and/or Jacuzzi

The Inn at Bath is a comfortably elegant B&B, full of color and light, situated in the midcoast region of Maine. Lovingly restored mid 1800's Greek Revival home surrounded by lovely gardens. Located in Bath's Historic District, walking distance to town.
✉ innkeeper@innatbath.com ☏ www.innatbath.com

BATH————————————————————

Kismet Inn Spa
44 Summer St 04530
207-443-3399
Shadi Towfighi

200-315 BB
5 rooms, 5 pb
Cash, Checks
S-no/P-no
Farsi, Azari and some
French

All organic, natural breakfast
Organic & natural dinner
menus, vegetarian non-
vegetarian, specialty brewed
tea, homemade yogurt
Complete in room spa
services, soaking tubs, yoga
& meditation, natural
bedding, library, classes.

Kismet Inn is located in the idyllic historic town of Bath, Maine across from the fountain of "The Spirit of the Sea" you will discover a small destination spot of extraordinary beauty. Exquisitely decorated with fine antiques, elegant Persian carpets
✉ stay@kismetinnmaine.com 🌐 www.kismetinnmaine.com

BELFAST————————————————————

Harbor View House of 1807
213 High St 04915
877-393-3811 207-338-3811
Mary Ellen & Ron Burrows &
Trish Jakielski

105-170 BB
6 rooms, 6 pb
Visa, MC
C-ltd/S-no/P-no/H-no
Some French, minimal
German

Full breakfast
Afternoon tea & sweets
Harborview deck, fireplaces,
cable & VCR

Historic home offers sweeping views of harbor. Spacious guestrooms with fireplaces & private baths provide many amenities. Enjoy hearty breakfast on view deck. Walk to downtown shops & dining.
✉ hosts@harborviewhouse.com 🌐 www.harborviewhouse.com

Jeweled Turret Inn
40 Pearl St 04915
800-696-2304 207-338-2304
Carl & Cathy Heffentrager

110-159 BB
7 rooms, 7 pb
Visa, MC, AmEx,
Rated, •
C-ltd/S-ltd/P-no/H-no

Full gourmet breakfast
Afternoon tea, cheese &
crackers, sherry
Sitting rooms, parlors,
antiques, tennis & pool
nearby

Our luxury Belfast, Maine Bed & Breakfast, is on The National Register of Historic Places. The Jeweled Turret Inn is centrally located on mid-coast Maine's Penobscot Bay, and is perfect for Maine vacations, a getaway or romantic honeymoon in New England
✉ info@jeweledturret.com 🌐 www.jeweledturret.com

BELGRADE————————————————————

Among the Lakes B&B
58 Smithfield Rd Rt 8 04917
207-465-4900
Polly Beatie & Sandy Famous

125-145 BB
5 rooms, 3 pb
Visa, MC
C-ltd/S-ltd/P-no/H-no
some French

Full hot breakfast
Library, parlor. Private dock
on Great Pond.

Charming and delightful B&B located in the heart of the beautiful Belgrade Lakes region. Quality accommodations in a quiet, peaceful historic home. Located on a large family property with private water and dock access on Great Pond.
✉ polly@amongthelakes.com 🌐 www.amongthelakes.com

BELGRADE LAKES————————————————————

Wings Hill Inn & Restaurant
9 Dry Point Dr 04918
866-495-2400 207-495-2400
Chris & Tracey Anderson

115-195 BB
6 rooms, 6 pb
Most CC, •
C-ltd/S-no/P-no/H-ltd
Some French & Spanish

Full breakfast
Complimentary afternoon
tea daily, award-winning
dinner menu available
Thursday through Sunday
Great Room with fieldstone
fireplace, lending library &
game collection; screened
lakeview porch

A lakeview inn, with unexpected touches and superb food. Featured in Down East Magazine in 2004, and named to Yankee Magazine's Editors' Choice list in 2005. Hiking, boating & renowned golf in the village; outlets & coastal points within an hour.
✉ wingshillinn@earthlink.net 🌐 www.wingshillinn.com

BETHEL——————————————————————————

The Chapman Inn
2 Church St 04217
877-359-1498 207-824-2657
Fred Nolte & Sandra Frye

33-129 BB
10 rooms, 6 pb
Most CC, *Rated*, •
C-yes/S-no/P-yes/H-no

Full breakfast
Sauna, fitness room,
bicycles, billiards, ping pong

The Chapman Inn is a delightfully quaint and charming inn located in the heart of Bethel's historic district, overlooking the town common. We include our world famous full gourmet breakfast, as well as warm, genuine hospitality with every stay.
✉ info@chapmaninn.com ✪ www.chapmaninn.com

The Sudbury Inn
151 Main St 04217
800-395-7837 207-824-2174
Bill & Nancy White

99-400 BB
18 rooms, 18 pb
Most CC, •
C-yes/S-no/P-ltd/H-no

Full breakfast
Fine and casual dining with
29 beers on tap
Sitting room, suites,
fireplaces, cable TV,
accommodate business
travelers, shuttle to ski area

Comfortable 18-room inn located 6.5 miles from Sunday River Ski Area. Lively pub with 29 beers on tap and great pub fare; more formal dining fireside featuring roasted duckling and rack of lamb.
✉ info@sudburyinn.com ✪ www.sudburyinn.com

BLUE HILL——————————————————————————

Barncastle B&B
125 South St 04676
207-374-2330
Isaac and Lori Robbins

125-175 BB
5 rooms, 5 pb
Most CC
C-yes/S-no/P-no/H-ltd
Mem. Day – Columbus
Day

Continental plus breakfast
Restaurant
Egyptian cotton sheets, flat
screen TV, mini-fridge, daily
maid service.

Built in the 1880's, Barncastle was the first of Blue Hill's grand summer cottages. A boutique hotel and restaurant, still welcoming summer visitors to Blue Hill more than 120 years later.
✉ info@barncastlehotel.com ✪ www.barncastlehotel.com

Captain Isaac Merrill Inn
Five Union St 04614
207-374-2555
Dan & Jane Hemmerly-Brown

95-175 BB
6 rooms, 6 pb
Most CC, *Rated*, •
C-ltd/S-no/P-ltd/H-no
Some: Spanish, French,
Japanese, Arabic

Full breakfast
Afternoon tea
Libraries, fireplaces, TV,
private baths

A charming retreat with romance and adventure from 1828, amidst original fireplaces, wide pine floors and four poster beds. Your hostess is the Captain's world-traveled, great, grand-daughter, "Florence Jane."
✉ captainmerrillinn@verizon.net ✪ www.captainmerrillinn.com

BOOTHBAY HARBOR——————————————————————

Admiral's Quarters Inn
71 Commercial St 04538
888-950-7724 207-633-3100
Jeff Teel

165-250 BB
7 rooms, 7 pb
Most CC, *Rated*
C-ltd/S-no/P-no/H-yes
April-Nov

Full breakfast
Complimentary coffee, tea,
juices and water anytime.
Sun room, parlor, panoramic
views of the harbor, Internet
and WiFi.Shared amenities at
Greenleaf Inn

A magnificent 1800's B&B that stands at the head of the Boothbay Harbor Peninsula. An oceanfront location with birds-eye views and the smell of the sea. Lobster boats, fishing, flying seagulls, sunrises, and sunsets are all part of the scenery.
✉ inns@greenleaflane.com ✪ www.greenleaflane.com

BOOTHBAY HARBOR

Atlantic Ark Inn	105-215 BB	Full gourmet breakfast
62 Atlantic Ave 04538	6 rooms, 6 pb	Complimentary afternoon
800-579-0112 207-633-5690	Visa, MC, AmEx, *Rated*	beverages, cheese buffet,
Donna	C-ltd/S-no/P-no/H-no	snacks & treats
	May-Oct.	Sitting room, wraparound
		porch, terraces, pillow top
		mattresses, turndown
		service, Jacuzzi WiFi, A/C

Quaint and intimate, this six guestroom inn offers lovely harbor views, balconies, Oriental rugs, mahogany furnishings, private baths, Jacuzzi, flowers, full breakfast and a short walk to town.
✉ donna@atlanticarkinn.com ◑ www.atlanticarkinn.com

Blue Heron Seaside Inn	145-265 BB	Full breakfast
65 Townsend Ave 04538	6 rooms, 6 pb	Complimentary tea & coffee
866-216-2300 207-633-7020	Visa, MC, *Rated*	in rooms, welcome beverage
Laura & Phil Chapman	C-ltd/S-no/P-no/H-ltd	on arrival
	May-December	Free use of kayaks from
		private dock, free wireless
		Internet, private waterfront
		decks off rooms

Fully restored 19th c. waterfront B&B. Luxury size A/C rooms, all with water views, furnished with antiques, all modern amenities and LCD HDTV. Panoramic two-bedroom suite available. Private boat dock with free boat use. Located in town with parking.
✉ info@blueheronseasideinn.com ◑ www.blueheronseasideinn.com

The Greenleaf Inn	165-250 BB	Full breakfast
65 Commercial St 04538	7 rooms, 7 pb	Coffee, tea, juices, soft drinks
888-950-7724 207-633-3100	Most CC	anytime
Jeff Teel	C-ltd/S-no/P-no/H-yes	Living room, porch,
		book/video library, games,
		hot tub, fitness room,
		Internet access, WiFi.

A spacious, restored New England cape style B&B nestled on a knoll overlooking scenic Boothbay Harbor, the Greenleaf Inn is your ultimate coastal lodging destination for vacations, honeymoons, anniversary gifts, and romantic getaways.
✉ inns@greenleaflane.com ◑ www.greenleaflane.com

Harbor House Inn	115-170 BB	Full breakfast
80 McKown St 04538	6 rooms, 6 pb	Snacks
800-856-1164 207-633-2941	Visa, MC	Sitting Room, Jacuzzi tubs,
Tom & Monica Churchill	C-yes/S-no/P-ltd/H-ltd	Harbor views, quiet relaxed
	May – October	setting, WiFi, TV/VCR

Experience Boothbay Harbor "the way Maine should be," relaxed, quiet & a great value. Each guestroom is spacious, uniquely designed & furnished with a Queen or King bed. The veranda provides the perfect place to view the harbor & enjoy breakfast.
✉ harborhse@ime.net ◑ www.harborhouse-me.com

The Harborage Inn	110-255 BB	Gourmet Full breakfast
75 Townsend Ave 04538	12 rooms, 12 pb	Waterfront lawn with seating,
800-565-3742 207-633-4640	Visa, MC, Disc, *Rated*	wraparound porches, Laura
Troy & Emery Chapman	C-ltd/S-no/P-no/H-no	Ashley rooms & suites
	April-late November	

All the modern amenities of a boutique hotel nestled on the Maine coast with the charm and attention to detail of a Bed and Breakfast.
✉ info@harborageinn.com ◑ www.harborageinn.com

BOOTHBAY HARBOR

Topside Inn	145-225 BB	Full breakfast
60 McKown St 04538	21 rooms, 21 pb	Snacks
888-633-5404 207-633-5404	Most CC	Sitting room, library, cable
Brian Lamb & Ed McDermott	C-ltd/S-no/P-no/H-ltd	TV
	early May – late October	

Prime hilltop location with panoramic views of the harbor, islands, lighthouses and ocean. Convenient walk to waterfront village restaurants and area attractions.
✉ info@topsideinn.com ◐ www.topsideinn.com

BRIDGTON

Noble House B&B	125-250 BB	Full Wicked-Good Breakfast
81 Highland Rd 04009	9 rooms, 9 pb	Famous Bottomless Cookie
888-237-4880 207-647-3733	Visa, MC, *Rated*, •	jar, Gourmet teas, Coffee,
Rick & Julie Whelchel	C-yes/S-no/P-no/H-ltd	Cocoa & soda
		Lake, park & beach,
		fireplaces, porches, grand
		piano, games, canoe &
		snowshoe, Free WiFi, Ski &
		Stay

Historic Victorian Inn above Highland Lake near the White Mountains, in Maine's Lakes & Mountains region. Jacuzzis, fireplaces & porches for your romantic getaway. Closest B&B to Shawnee Peak skiing.
✉ innkeepers@noblehousebb.com ◐ www.noblehousebb.com

BROOKLIN

DragonFlye Inn	100-125 BB	Continental organic breakfast
19 Naskeag Rd 04616	5 rooms, 5 pb	bicycles, wireless Internet
207-359-8080	Visa, MC, *Rated*	access, library,
Natasha & Joe Moore	C-yes/S-no/P-no/H-ltd	
	May 1 – October 15	

Welcome to DragonFlye Inn, an 1874 Victorian in historic Brooklin, Maine. Nestled between Mount Desert and Deer Isle, the inn offers a quiet retreat that is located at the tip of the Blue Hill Peninsula.
✉ dragonflyeinn@gmail.com ◐ www.dragonflyeinn.com

BROOKSVILLE

Oakland House Seaside	99-265 BB	Full breakfast
Resort	25 rooms, 22 pb	A gourmet "slow food"
435 Herrick Rd 04617	Visa, MC, *Rated*, •	dinner, catered events, wine,
800-359-7352 207-359-8521	C-yes/S-ltd/P-no/H-no	beer, beach lobster picnics.
Jim & Sally Littlefield	Japanese, Spanish,	common room with large
	Slovak depending upon	hearth, oceanside porch,
	staffing	firewood delivery, lake &
		ocean beach, hiking trails

A luxurious seaside inn, 15 family-sized cottages & restaurant with a spectacular vista of sea and islands. Dock, moorings, rowboats, lawn games, lake & ocean beaches. A casual romantic sophisticated coastal destination. Nearby shops to browse. Adventure!
✉ jim@oaklandhouse.com ◐ www.oaklandhouse.com

CAMDEN

Abigail's Inn	125-195 BB	Full breakfast
8 High St 04843	4 rooms, 4 pb	Tea, coffee, snacks, baked
800-292-2501 207-236-2501	Visa, MC, *Rated*, •	goods
Beth O'Connor & Kipp Wright	C-ltd/S-no/P-no/H-no	Two parlors with fireplaces,
		3 rooms with fireplaces,
		whirlpool tub, suites, cable
		TV, A/C, Internet

Let yourself be pampered—cozy rooms, delicious breakfasts, fireplaces, & great location. Come let us help you rest, relax & play. Park the car & enjoy yourself in beautiful Camden.
✉ innkeeper@abigailsinn.com ◐ www.abigailsinn.com

CAMDEN

Blue Harbor House
67 Elm St 04843
800-248-3196 207-236-3196
Annette & Terry Hazzard

125-185 BB
11 rooms, 11 pb
Most CC, *Rated*, •
S-no/P-no/H-no
Basic French

Full breakfast
Cocktail Hour! Enjoy a glass
of wine from our wine list
and choice of h'ors
d'oeuvres
Off street parking, daily
newspapers, Spa robes, A/C,
Gilchrist & Soames toiletries,
WiFi

Come to the Blue Harbor House whenever you need a place to relax and renew. The Inn is genuinely hospitable and refreshingly casual while Camden, Maine is an irresistible coastal village. Walk to the harbor and restaurants. Sumptuous breakfast. WiFi.
✉ info@blueharborhouse.com ◑ www.blueharborhouse.com

Camden Hartstone Inn
41 Elm St 04843
800-788-4823 207-236-4259
Mary Jo & Michael Salmon

105-275 BB
21 rooms, 21 pb
Visa, MC, *Rated*, •
C-ltd/S-no/P-ltd/H-no

Memorable full breakfast
Internationally recognized
cuisine makes dinner truly
memorable, afternoon tea
and cookies
WiFi, guest computer, spa,
gameroom, movie collection,
martini mixology classes

An enchanting hideaway in the heart of Camden village that Fodor's considers "An elegant and sophisticated retreat and culinary destination," this Mansard style Victorian built in 1835 offers a unique experience in pampered luxury.
✉ info@hartstoneinn.com ◑ www.hartstoneinn.com

Camden Windward House
6 High St 04843
877-492-9656 207-236-9656
Kristen & Jesse Bifulco

125-265 BB
8 rooms, 8 pb
Most CC, *Rated*, •
C-yes/S-no/P-no/H-ltd

Order from menu
Afternoon tea, bar service,
bar menu
Sitting room, library, Jacuzzi
suites, fireplaces, cable, WiFi
accommodate business
travelers, deck

Camden Windward House, listed on the National Registry of Historic Places, 1 block from Camden Village and Penobscot Bay Harbor. Warm hospitality and bountiful breakfasts await at this 1854 Greek revival. Walking distance to activities, shops and dining.
✉ bnb@windwardhouse.com ◑ www.windwardhouse.com

Captain Swift Inn
72 Elm St 04843
800-251-0865 207-236-8113
Norm & Linda Henthorn

119-245 BB
8 rooms, 8 pb
Visa, MC, *Rated*
C-yes/S-no/P-no/H-yes

Full breakfast
Gas logs in some rooms,
wireless Internet available,
all ensuite baths, suites with
whirlpool tubs

If you enjoy the warm atmosphere of yesteryear, or are a history or architecture buff, you'll appreciate the authenticity of the fully restored Federal period Captain Swift Inn. A short walk to downtown Camden & the harbor. Many outdoor activities nearby.
✉ innkeeper@swiftinn.com ◑ www.swiftinn.com

Inn at Sunrise Point
55 Sunrise Point Rd 04843
207-236-7716
Daina Hill

300-595 BB
10 rooms, 10 pb
Visa, MC, AmEx,
Rated, •
C-ltd/S-no/P-no/H-ltd
Chinese and Irish
April through November

Full gourmet breakfast
Tea, wine, hors d'oeuvres
Book & video library,
woodburning or gas
fireplaces in all rooms

The award-winning Inn at Sunrise Point invites you to discover a pampered haven for discriminating travelers. Luxury rooms & cottages with fireplaces & Jacuzzis.
✉ info@sunrisepoint.com ◑ www.sunrisepoint.com

CAMDEN—

Inns At Blackberry Common
82 Elms St 04843
800-388-6000 207-236-6060
Jim & Cyndi Ostrowski

99-269 BB
18 rooms, 18 pb
Visa, MC, Disc, *Rated*,
•
C-ltd/S-no/P-ltd/H-no

Full breakfast
Complimentary seasonal
afternoon refreshments;
gourmet dinner specials.
Three spacious parlors,
glorious perennial gardens,
fireplaces, whirlpools, A/C,
cable TV

Our Inns are an oasis set side by side amid splendid perennial gardens in the picture book village of Camden. Blackberry Inn, is a gracious 1849 "painted lady" Victorian Inn. The Elms B&B, is a stately 1806 Federal Colonial.
✉ innkeepers@blackberryinn.com ✆ www.innsatblackberrycommon.com

Lord Camden Inn
24 Main St 04843
800-336-4325 207-236-4325
Philip Woodland

89-289 BB
36 rooms, 36 pb
Visa, MC, AmEx,
Rated, •
C-yes/S-ltd/P-yes/H-yes

Full Buffet Style Breakfast
Private balconies, fitness
room, high speed wireless
Internet, free parking, in-
room spa service
Large, private balconies in
most rooms, new fitness
room, high speed wireless
Internet,

Luxury, historic Inn, fully restored & recently remodeled, 36 individually appointed rooms, oceanviews, large balconies, gas fireplaces, full breakfast, unsurpassed comfort, elegance & service. A stay worth remembering.
✉ info@lordcamdeninn.com ✆ www.lordcamdeninn.com

Swan House
49 Mountain St (Rt 52) 04843
800-207-8275 207-236-8275
Lyn & Ken Kohl

120-200 BB
6 rooms, 6 pb
Visa, MC, *Rated*
C-ltd/S-no/P-no/H-no

Full country breakfast
Sitting rooms, gazebo,
enclosed sunporch,
mountain hiking trail

Located in a quiet neighborhood, away from busy Route 1. Mountain hiking trail directly behind the inn. Short walk to Camden's—harbor, shops, & restaurants. Swan House is a traditional Bed & Breakfast that is family operated & owner occupied since 1993.
✉ hikeinn@swanhouse.com ✆ www.swanhouse.com

Timbercliffe Cottage B&B Inn
64 High St 04843
866-396-4753 207-236-4753
Karen & Dave Kallstrand

110-255 BB
6 rooms, 6 pb
Visa, MC, AmEx
C-ltd/S-no/P-no/H-no

Full breakfast
Cold beverages, coffee & tea
are available 24 hours.
Fireplaces, guest pantry,
garden, patio, parlor, library,
wireless Internet & parking.

A warm welcome awaits you at Timbercliffe Cottage B&B Inn. Nestled on a hillside in the shadow of Mt. Battie with a view of Penobscot Bay, this historic home wraps its arms around you and invites you to sit back and relax.
✉ innkeepers@timbercliffecottage.com ✆ www.timbercliffecottage.com

The Victorian by the Sea
33 Sea View Dr 04849
800-382-9817 207-236-3785
Jeanne & Robert Short

130-260 BB
7 rooms, 7 pb
Visa, MC, AmEx,
Rated, •
C-ltd/S-no/P-ltd/H-no

Full breakfast
Complimentary snacks &
beverages available 24 hours
a day in our Guests' Pantry
Large veranda with ocean
view; path to ocean; free
WiFi; parlor & sitting room,
books, games, TV

Romantic Inn with magnificent views of Penobscot Bay. Located just minutes north of Camden Harbor, but away from Route 1 traffic! Historic 1889 shingle-style Victorian-era cottage takes you back to a quieter time and place.
✉ inn@victorianbythesea.com ✆ www.victorianbythesea.com

CAMDEN

Whitehall Inn
52 High Street 04843
800-789-6565 207-236-3391
Greg & Sue Marquise

89-199 BB
45 rooms, 40 pb
Most CC, *Rated*, •
C-yes/S-no/P-no/H-yes
mid-May to late October

Full breakfast
Fine-dining restaurant & pub
fare
Restaurant, pub, Internet
access, WiFi, phones, private
baths, gardens, historic
neighborhood, gift

*The Whitehall Inn has been the first choice for discerning visitors coming to Camden,
Maine since 1901. The historic 45-room full service inn offers a romantic getaway on the
side of Mt. Battie, a short walk to Camden Harbor.*
✉ reservations@whitehall-inn.com ☯ www.whitehall-Inn.com

COREA

**Black Duck Inn on Corea
Harbor**
36 Crowley Island Rd 04624
207-963-2689
Barry Canner & Bob Travers

140-200 BB
6 rooms, 5 pb
Visa, MC, Disc, *Rated*,
•
C-ltd/S-no/P-no/H-no
Danish, some French
late May- mid Oct

Hearty, healthy, gourmet
Special diets: e.g. vegetarian,
non-wheat, catered with
advance notice
Sitting rooms, library,
bicycles, hiking trails –
kayaking services nearby

*Romantic settings, casual elegance, antiques and art. Overlooking working lobster harbor.
Village charm with rural atmosphere. Near national park and bird sanctuary.*
✉ info@blackduck.com ☯ www.blackduck.com

DAMARISCOTTA

Oak Gables B&B
36 Pleasant St 04543
800-335-7748 207-563-1476
Martha Scudder

95-150 BB
5 rooms, 1 pb
Visa, MC
C-yes/S-ltd/P-no/H-ltd

Full breakfast
Afternoon tea
Sitting room, swimming pool,
cable TV, rooms have A/C,
winterized cottage & more

*A beautiful inn, pristine setting with river frontage, views, hospitality and peaceful sur-
roundings. Charming rooms and guest cottage. Lovely studio apartment and river view
apartment. Heated pool.* ✉ martha@oakgablesbb.com ☯ www.oakgablesbb.com

DEER ISLE

Pilgrim's Inn
20 Main St 04627
888-778-7505 207-348-6615
Tina Oddleifson & Tony
Lawless

99-249 BB
15 rooms, 15 pb
Visa, MC, Disc, •
C-ltd/S-no/P-ltd/H-no
Mid May-Mid Oct

Full breakfast
On-site restaurant with
Tavern menu, homemade
cookies and beverages
throughout the day
3 acres of land, 500-foot
waterfront, library, TV in
common room, WiFi,
Adirondack chairs near
water

*For a respite from the cares and pace of your busy world, come to Pilgrim's Inn on Deer
Isle. Listed on the National Register of Historic Places and a member of the prestigious
Select Registry, Pilgrim's Inn is sure to please.*
✉ innkeeper@pilgrimsinn.com ☯ www.pilgrimsinn.com

DEXTER

The Brewster Inn
37 Zion's Hill Rd. 04930
207-924-3130
Mark & Judith Stephens

69-139 BB
10 rooms, 10 pb
Visa, MC, Disc
C-yes/S-no/P-no/H-yes

Full breakfast
We are happy to cater for
brunch, lunch or dinner
during your stay with a
minimum 72 hours notice
Cable TV, air conditioning,
fireplaces, whirlpool baths

*The Brewster Inn offers a warm, relaxing and friendly atmosphere. A former Governors
state mansion built in the late 1930's for then Governor Ralph Owen Brewster (later
Senator) and portrayed by Alan Alda in the award winning movie "The Aviator"*
✉ innkeeper@brewsterinn.com ☯ www.brewsterinn.com

DURHAM

The Royalsborough Inn at the Bagley House	139-179 BB	Full breakfast
1290 Royalsborough Rd 04222	7 rooms, 7 pb	Complimentary beverages, cookies, special event meals
800-765-1772 207-865-6566	Visa, MC, Disc, *Rated*, •	may be arranged
Marianne & Jim Roberts	C-yes/S-no/P-no/H-yes	Living room w/fireplace, library, snowshoeing, Alpaca Farm on property, therapeutic massage, WiFi

A country inn, six miles from L.L. Bean & other Freeport shopping. Convenient to major highways, Bates & Bowdoin colleges. The Inn offers a relaxing environment & sumptuous breakfast & has hosted many historical "firsts" in the town.
✉ royalsboro@suscom-maine.net ❂ www.royalsboroughinn.com

EAST BOOTHBAY

Five Gables Inn	140-235 BB	Full breakfast
107 Murray Hill Rd 04544	16 rooms, 16 pb	Tea and lemonade, along
800-451-5048 207-633-4551	Visa, MC, *Rated*, •	with homemade pastries and
Mike & De Kennedy	C-ltd/S-no/P-no/H-no	cookies, compliments of
	Mid-May to End of Oct	your hosts. Fireplaces, games, wraparound verandah, pool & boating nearby

The Five Gables Inn is a beautifully restored bed and breakfast inn in Maine, and the last of the turn-of-the-century summer hotels in the Boothbays perched on a garden-framed hillside overlooking picturesque Linekin Bay.
✉ info@fivegablesinn.com ❂ www.fivegablesinn.com

EASTPORT

The Milliken House	75-85 BB	Full gourmet breakfast
29 Washington St 04631	6 rooms, 6 pb	Complimentary wine, snacks
888-507-9370 207-853-2955	Visa, MC	Sitting room, library, family
Bill & Mary Williams	C-ltd/S-no/P-ltd/H-no	friendly facility, cable TV

Elegant accommodations in a large, gracious 1846 home furnished with ornately carved Victorian marble-topped furniture. Two blocks from historic waterfront district.
✉ millikenhouse@eastport-inn.com ❂ www.eastport-inn.com

Todd House	65-100 BB	Continental plus breakfast
1 Capen Ave 04631	6 rooms, 5 pb	BBQ deck with a view
207-853-2328	Checks	Library, fireplace, yard with
Ruth McInnis	C-yes/S-ltd/P-yes/H-yes	barbecue, picnic facilities

Step into the past in our Revolutionary War-era Cape Cod-style home with wide panorama of Passamaquoddy Bay, listed on the National Register of Historic Places. Children and pets welcome!

FREEPORT

Brewster House B&B	135-195 BB	Full breakfast
180 Main St 04032	7 rooms, 7 pb	Wireless Internet access,
800-865-0822 207-865-4121	Most CC, *Rated*	parlor with satellite TV, guest
Scott & Ruth Thomas	C-ltd/S-no/P-no/H-ltd	computer, suites, gardens, itinerary plans

Beautifully renovated 1888 Queen Anne Victorian home. Family suites, full-sized private bathrooms in all rooms, delicious full breakfast with fresh fruit and baked goods. Tastefully decorated with antiques.
✉ info@brewsterhouse.com ❂ www.brewsterhouse.com

FREEPORT

Captain Briggs House B&B
8 Maple Ave 04032
888-217-2477 207-865-1868
Charles and Beverly Tefer

100-230 BB
7 rooms, 7 pb
Visa, MC, Disc, *Rated*
C-yes/S-no/P-yes/H-no

Full breakfast
Early breakfast upon
request; special dietary
needs usually met with
advance notice
Common room w/cable TV,
small Refrigerator, VCR, and
free wireless Internet;

Historic 1853 Federal home with five beautiful guestrooms & a two-room suite. Located within easy walking distance to many fine shops & restaurants & situated on a large lot off a quiet, dead-end street. Hospitality, convenience & seclusion.
✉ info@captainbriggs.com ✆ www.captainbriggs.com

Kendall Tavern B&B
213 Main St 04032
800-341-9572 207-865-1338
Tim & Loree Rudolph

140-180 BB
7 rooms, 7 pb
Most CC, *Rated*, •
C-ltd/S-no/P-no/H-no

Full breakfast
Sweets in the evening
Fireplaces in library, parlor,
free wireless Internet access,
private baths

Kendall Tavern Inn is located at the north end of Freeport Village, just a short stroll from shops & restaurants & a perfect location from which to explore the coast of Maine. Great spot for a small wedding or company retreat.
✉ info@kendalltavern.com ✆ www.kendalltavern.com

FRYEBURG

Admiral Peary House
27 Elm St 04037
877-4ADMPRY 207-935-3365
Hilary Jones & Derrek
Schlottmann

139-199 BB
7 rooms, 7 pb
Most CC, *Rated*, •
C-ltd/S-no/P-no/H-no
French, German,
Spanish

Full gourmet breakfast
Complimentary beverages &
snacks 24 hours, afternoon
tea
Fireplaces, library, pool
table, A/C, free high-speed
Internet, WiFi in most
guestrooms

Quiet historic Inn 15 minutes from all North Conway activities, restaurants & shopping. Offers fireplaces, Jacuzzis, specials and packages, excellent breakfasts & more.
✉ innkeeper@admiralpearyhouse.com ✆ www.admiralpearyhouse.com

The Oxford House Inn
Rt 302 04037
800-261-7206 207-935-3442
Jonathan & Natalie Spak

119-179 BB
4 rooms, 4 pb
Most CC
C-yes/S-no/P-no/H-ltd

Full breakfast
Excellent restaurant on
premise featuring local
ingredients, full bar and wine
list.
Restaurant, bar, TV, wireless
Internet, A/C, game area,
back lawn panoramic views,
grand front porch

Maine B&B and country inn with restaurant located in western Maine Lakes and Mountains Region and the Mount Washington Valley. Mountain views, lodging with superb breakfasts, gourmet dining in a small hotel near the White Mountains.
✉ innkeeper@oxfordhouseinn.com ✆ www.oxfordhouseinn.com

Peace With-Inn
254 W Fryeburg Rd Rte 113 N
04037
877-935-7322 207-935-7363
The Link Family

115-185 BB
5 rooms, 5 pb
Most CC, •
C-ltd/S-no/P-no/H-no

Full Gourmet New England-
style
Complimentary
refreshments daily
Towel heaters, fine toiletries,
bottled water, fine linens,
European chocolate,
massage

c1750 New England farmhouse. Six guestrooms feature fine linens, fresh flowers, and antiques. Rates include afternoon refreshments and a full New England-style breakfast.
✉ info@peacewithinn.com ✆ www.peacewithinn.com

GEORGETOWN

Coveside B&B
6 Gotts Cove Ln 04548
800-232-5490 207-371-2807
Carolyn & Tom Church

135-200 BB
7 rooms, 7 pb
Most CC, *Rated*, •
C-ltd/S-no/P-no/H-ltd
French (limited)
May-Oct.

Full gourmet breakfast
Complimentary beer and soft
drinks, snacks
Screened porch, terrace,
canoe, bicycles, sitting
rooms

Stylish retreat on 5 waterfront acres, reminiscent of turn-of-the-century coastal cottages. All rooms overlook rocky Gotts cove and Sheepscot Bay; several have fireplaces, private balconies, and spa tub.
✉ innkeeper@covesidebandb.com ✪ www.CovesideBandB.com

The Mooring B&B
132 Seguinland Rd 04548
866-828-7343 207-371-2790
Penny & Paul Barabe

140-200 BB
5 rooms, 5 pb
Visa, MC, *Rated*
C-ltd/S-no/P-no/H-ltd
May through October

Full breakfast
Sitting room, library,
bicycles, fireplace, cable TV,
daily maid service, business
travelers welcome

A quiet, elegant setting on the coast of Maine. Five unique rooms, all with private baths, air conditioning and great ocean views. A wonderful location for that special family reunion, party or wonderful wedding.
✉ stay@themooringb-b.com ✪ www.themooringb-b.com

GORHAM

PineCrest B&B Inn
91 South St 04038
877-474-6322 207-839-5843
Matt & Amy Mattingly

99-159 BB
7 rooms, 7 pb
Most CC, *Rated*, •
C-yes/S-no/P-no/H-ltd

Full breakfast
Fine dining with Chef Mo
every Friday from June to
November, wine bar and
tastings every Friday
Luxury toiletries, fireplace,
wireless access, living
rooms, screened porch, patio
garden

A charming Victorian inn just minutes from Old Port, Portland, coastal beaches, the University of Southern Maine, Freeport Shops, family entertainment and more.
✉ Matt@pinecrestmaine.com ✪ www.pinecrestmaine.com

GOULDSBORO

Acadia View B&B
175 US 1 04607
866-963-7457 207-963-7457
Pat & Jim Close

135-165 BB
4 rooms, 4 pb
Visa, MC
C-ltd/S-no/P-no/H-ltd

Full breakfast
Ocean views with private
decks, great room, fireplace,
hammock, library, free
wireless Internet

We are located on a high ocean front bluff with breathtaking views of Frenchman's Bay, the mountains of Acadia National Park and the lights of Bar Harbor.
✉ acadiaview@wildmoo.net ✪ www.acadiaview.com

GREENVILLE

Blair Hill Inn at Moosehead Lake
351 Lily Bay Rd 04441
207-695-0224
Dan & Ruth McLaughlin

250-450 BB
8 rooms, 8 pb
Visa, MC, Disc, *Rated*,
•
C-ltd/S-no/P-no/H-no

Full Gourmet Breakfast
One of the top 10 restaurants
in Maine on premises – open
mid-June through mid-
October
Summer evening concerts,
beautiful gardens, Jacuzzi,
exercise room, library

A bed and breakfast inn overlooking Moosehead Lake, Greenville, Maine. The area's finest offers one of Maine's top 10 restaurants, exquisite lodging, renowned views. Stay with us once . . . and we'll stay with you forever. ✉ info@blairhill.com ✪ www.blairhill.com

HALLOWELL—————————————————————————————

Maple Hill Farm B&B Inn
11 Inn Rd 04347
800-622-2708 207-622-2708
Scott Cowger

85-205 BB
8 rooms, 8 pb
Most CC, *Rated*, •
C-ltd/S-no/P-no/H-yes

Full Country Menu Breakfast
Anytime tea & coffee,
homemade snacks; custom
catering provided for
prearranged groups & events
Full bar, A/C, sitting room, art
gallery, trails, whirlpools,
farm animals, wireless
Internet, cable

Maple Hill Farm B&B Inn & Conference Center near Augusta in Hallowell, Maine provides a unique combination of the peace & quiet of a country farm that is convenient to Maine's capital with all the services that today's travelers expect. Open year-round.
✉ stay@MapleBB.com ✪ www.MapleBB.com

HANCOCK—————————————————————————————

Crocker House Country Inn
967 Point Rd 04640
877-715-6017 207-422-6806
Elizabeth & Richard Malaby

85-165 BB
11 rooms, 11 pb
Most CC
C-yes/S-no/P-yes/H-ltd

Full Country Breakfast
Dinner with reservation
Moorings, kayak, bicycles,
separate sitting room,
pitched ceiling, multiple
beds available, romance

The Crocker House Country Inn, tucked away on the peninsula of Hancock Point, has fine cuisine and individually appointed guestrooms, each with a private bath.
✉ info@crockerhouse.com ✪ www.crockerhouse.com

HARRISON—————————————————————————————

Greenwood Manor Inn
52 Tolman Rd 04040
866-583-4445 207-583-4445
Rosie Weiser

120-220 BB
9 rooms, 9 pb
Visa, MC, AmEx
C-ltd/S-no/P-no/H-no

Full country breakfast
Fresh-baked afternoon
snacks
Fireplaces, suites, deck,
cable TV, canoes, bicycles,
snowshoes, gardens

Seven guestrooms, 2 suites, private baths, A/C, fireplaces. Luxury suite with whirlpool tub, wet bar, sitting room, fireplace. Situated on over 100 secluded acres with extensive lawn and gardens.
✉ info@greenwoodmanorinn.com ✪ www.greenwoodmanorinn.com

KENNEBUNK—————————————————————————————

Waldo Emerson Inn
108 Summer St 04043
877-521-8776 207-985-4250
John & Kathy Daamen

95-165 BB
4 rooms, 4 pb
Most CC, *Rated*, •
C-ltd/S-no/P-no/H-ltd
Dutch

3-course breakfast
Complimentary coffee, tea,
soft drinks, snacks, Poland
Springs Bottled water, Dutch
breakfasts
Handmade quilts, antiques,
private baths and fireplaces.
Complementary beach
parking passes & bikes

Waldo Emerson Inn is a Colonial style inn listed on the National Register of Historic Places. Antiques, romantic rooms with fireplaces, handmade quilts, bountiful breakfasts. Quilt shop for browsing.
✉ innkeeper@waldoemersoninn.com ✪ www.waldoemersoninn.com

KENNEBUNKPORT————————————————

1802 House Inn
15 Locke St 04046
800-932-5632 207-967-5632
Linda Van Goor & Jay Durepo

125-374 BB
6 rooms, 6 pb
Visa, MC, AmEx,
Rated, •
C-ltd/S-no/P-no/H-ltd

Three course gourmet
breakfast
Homemade cookies, coffee,
tea, lemonade, Comfort Food
Cook-Offs Fall and Winter
Concierge, Wedding & Event
Planning, Spa & Tee Times,
Dining Reservations and
Recommendations

Glorious golf, romantic, peaceful setting. Beautifully restored 1802 Colonial. Luxury rooms, period furnishings, whirlpool tubs, fireplaces, WiFi, cable TV. Gardens. Gourmet three-course breakfast daily. Weddings & honeymoons. Play & Stay golf packages.
✉ info@1802inn.com ❂ www.1802inn.com

Bufflehead Cove
Bufflehead Cove Ln 04046
207-967-3879
Harriet, Jim & Erin Gott

135-375 BB
6 rooms, 6 pb
Visa, MC, Disc, *Rated*
C-ltd/S-no/P-ltd/H-no
A little Spanish
May through November

Full breakfast
Herbal and regular teas, hot
chocolate, afternoon wine
and cheese
Whirlpool tubs, fireplaces,
turndowns, concierge
service, sitting room, dock,
boat access, area maps

Hidden away in the woods, on a bank of the Kennebunkport tidal river, Bufflehead Cove offers peace, privacy and pampering in a beautiful setting. Perfect service with all the amenities: turn downs, wine and cheese hour, delicious breakfasts, soft music.
✉ info@buffleheadcove.com ❂ www.buffleheadcove.com

Cabot Cove
7 South Maine St 04046
207-967-5424
Terri and Brian Kenny

185-725 BB
16 rooms, 16 pb
Visa, MC, AmEx, •
C-ltd/S-no/P-no/H-no
French
May 1st thru Oct 31st

Breakfast delivered to your
cottage
Full kitchen, TV/DVD, iPod
clock/radio, wireless
Internet, beach passes, use
of rowboats and kayaks

A magical enclave of 16 new and unique cottages all nestled in an idyllic tidal cove-side setting perfect for a romantic escape. Come stay with us for a night, or two, or more.
✉ info@cabotcovecottages.com ❂ www.cabotcovecottages.com

Cape Arundel Inn
208 Ocean Ave 04046
207-967-2125
Jack Nahil

125-385 BB
14 rooms, 14 pb
Most CC
C-ltd/S-no/P-no/H-ltd
Closed Jan & Feb

Continental plus breakfast
Full bar & dining room on
property
Ceiling fans, direct dial
telephones with data port,
fireplaces, TVs in most
rooms

Stately summer cottage built in 1895, on famed Ocean Avenue in Kennebunkport, Maine. Sweeping and incomparable views of the Atlantic.
✉ jack_nahil@capearundelinn.com ❂ www.capearundelinn.com

Captain Fairfield Inn
8 Pleasant St 04046
800-322-1928 207-967-4454
Leigh & Rob Blood

146-361 BB
9 rooms, 9 pb
Most CC, *Rated*
C-ltd/S-no/P-no/H-no

Full four-course gourmet
breakfast
Afternoon chocolate chip
cookies & a selection of
organic teas
WiFi, DVD library, beach
towels and passes, and much
more. Let us take care of all
the details . . .

Kennebunkport's Boutique Bed and Breakfast Inn. Romantic and historic, with luxurious amenities like flat panel TV/DVD, WiFi, fireplaces, hand-carved mahogany beds and designer bed and bath linens. Signature four-course breakfast & genuine hospitalit
✉ rlb@captainfairfield.com ❂ www.captainfairfield.com

KENNEBUNKPORT

Captain Jefferds Inn

5 Pearl St 04046	125-365 BB	3 Course gourmet breakfast
800-839-6844 207-967-2311	15 rooms, 15 pb	Afternoon tea with inn-baked
Sarah & Erik Lindblom	Most CC, *Rated*, •	goods, cheese and crackers,
	C-ltd/S-no/P-yes/H-no	lemonade or hot cider.
		Queen and king beds, feather
		beds, duvets, fine linens,
		WiFi, fireplaces, gardens,
		turn-down

Romantic, beautiful, peaceful, "a very special place". Historic residential district. Exceptional luxury amenities, fine linens, fireplaces, whirlpool spas, candlelight gourmet breakfast, afternoon tea.

✉ captjeff@captainjefferdsinn.com ☉ www.captainjefferdsinn.com

Captain Lord Mansion

6 Pleasant St 04046	199-499 BB	Full 3-course breakfast
800-522-3141 207-967-3141	16 rooms, 16 pb	Afternoon seasonal
Bev Davis & Rick Litchfield	Most CC, *Rated*, •	beverages & refreshments
	C-ltd/S-no/P-no/H-no	such as sweets, cheese,
		crackers and fresh fruit.
		On-premises spa, heated
		marble baths, double Jacuzzi
		tubs, K/Q 4 poster beds, gas
		fireplaces, A/C

An unforgettable romantic experience is your reward when you reserve one of the 16 large, beautifully appointed guestrooms at the Captain Lord Mansion.

✉ innkeeper@captainlord.com ☉ www.captainlord.com

English Meadows Inn

141 Port Rd 04043	125-341 BB	Full gourmet breakfast
800-272-0698 207-967-5766	10 rooms, 10 pb	Afternoon English Tea
Bruce & Valerie Jackson	Visa, MC, *Rated*, •	served on Thursday, Friday
	C-ltd/S-no/P-ltd/H-no	and Saturday by reservation
		only
		Library, garden with patio,
		beach parking pass,
		concierge, free wireless
		Internet, cottage available

The English Meadows Inn, a Bed & Breakfast Inn in the coastal village of Kennebunkport, Maine offers a unique English "Country House" experience offering different delights regardless of the season.

✉ innkeeper@englishmeadowsinn.com ☉ www.englishmeadowsinn.com

The Green Heron Inn

126 Ocean Ave 04046	135-325 BB	Gourmet three-course
201-967-3315	11 rooms, 11 pb	breakfast
Tony Kusuma & Dan Oswald	Visa, MC	Homemade sweets,
	C-yes/S-no/P-ltd/H-ltd	lemonade, iced tea, hot tea,
	Indonesian, Italian	coffee, hot chocolate
		Parlor, fireplace, porch,
		gardens, cards, movies,
		puzzles, morning newspaper,
		ocean nearby

Our Inn sits adjacent to a picturesque estuarine cove, near the mouth of the Kennebunk River. The water view provides a peaceful setting for your stay, less than a mile from Dock Square. Pets are $20 extra.

✉ innkeepers@greenheroninn.com ☉ www.greenheroninn.com

Harbor Inn

90 Ocean Ave 04046	125-210 BB	Full breakfast
207-967-2074	8 rooms, 8 pb	Parlor, fireplace, gardens,
Kathy & Barry Jones	Visa, MC, Disc	porch
	C-ltd/S-no/P-no/H-ltd	

Imagine yourself in another time and place, when the pace of life was slower and more gracious, a place where you feel comfortable and pampered. If you have such a desire and need to revitalize your spirit, then you deserve a vacation at the Harbor Inn.

✉ barry@covehouse.com ☉ www.harbor-inn.com

KENNEBUNKPORT

Kennebunkport Inn
One Dock Square 04046
800-248-2621 207-967-2621
Debra Lennon & Tom Nill

109-329 BB
49 rooms, 49 pb
Visa, MC, AmEx, *Rated*
C-yes/S-no/P-no/H-yes
French

Complimentary Deluxe
Continental
Pool, cable TV, restaurant,
golf, iPod docking stations,
fireplace, wireless Internet,
CD player

The Kennebunkport Inn offers a unique Maine lodging experience with beautiful guest-rooms located in a Victorian Mansion, Riverhouse or Wharfside buildings located right in Dock Square, the heart of all the shopping, dining and local attractions.
✉ stay@kennebunkportinn.com ◐ www.kennebunkportinn.com

The Maine Stay Inn
34 Maine St 04046
800-950-2117 207-967-2117
Judi & Walter Hauer

109-319 BB
17 rooms, 17 pb
Most CC, *Rated*, •
C-ltd/S-no/P-no/H-no

Full New England breakfast
Afternoon tea & sweets
Fireplaced sitting room,
charming wraparound
porch, spacious grounds,
Adirondack chairs

Distinguished Bed & Breakfast Inn located in Kennebunkport's Historic District. Choose the Victorian romance of a 19th century Inn room or the privacy of a romantic fireplace cottage suite. Walk to shops, restaurants and galleries. Beaches & harbor nearby.
✉ innkeeper@mainestayinn.com ◐ www.mainestayinn.com

Old Fort Inn
8 Old Fort Ave 04046
800-828-3678 207-967-5353
David & Sheila Aldrich

125-395 BB
16 rooms, 16 pb
Most CC, *Rated*, •
C-ltd/S-no/P-no/H-no
Mid April-Mid December

Buffet breakfast
Afternoon refreshments
Cable TV, phone in room,
WiFi, tennis, pool, Jacuzzis,
A/C, some fireplaces

A luxurious 16 guestroom resort in a secluded, charming setting. Yesterday's charm with today's conveniences. Within walking distance of the ocean. Private swimming pool and tennis court.
✉ info@oldfortinn.com ◐ www.oldfortinn.com

Shorelands Guest Resort
247 Western Ave, Rt 9 04046
800-99-BEACH 207-985-4460
Sonja Haag Ducharme &
Family

49-245 BB
28 rooms, 28 pb
Most CC, •
C-yes/S-ltd/P-yes/H-yes
French, German
April-October

Continental breakfast
Guest Cafe with coffee, tea
and cookies all day
Sitting room, library, bikes,
Jacuzzis, pool, suites, cable
TV, gas grills, maid service

A typical Maine country cottage resort, far from noise and congestion. Lawn and garden areas for relaxing, a short walk to a secluded, sandy beach.
✉ info@shorelands.com ◐ www.shorelands.com

The Tides Inn By-The-Sea
252 Goose Rocks Beach 04046
207-967-3757
M. Henriksen & K. Blomberg

145-325 BB
22 rooms, 22 pb
Most CC
C-yes/S-no/P-no/H-ltd
June-September

Continental breakfast
The Belvidere Victorian Bar
offers small plate comfort
cuisine & cocktails on the
oceanfront porch.
Fireplace, antique
furnishings, magnificent
ocean & beach views,
verandas & rocking chairs,
WiFi

Tides Inn By-The-Sea offers the simple charm of a turn-of-the-century Shingle-Style Inn, nestled across from the beautiful white sands of Goose Rocks Beach. The Belvidere Victori-an Bar offers the public libations & fine comfort dining.
✉ info@tidesinnbythesea.com ◐ www.tidesinnbythesea.com

KITTERY

Chickadee B&B
63 Haley Rd 03904
888-502-0876 207-439-0672
Walter & Brenda Lawrence

135 BB
4 rooms, 4 pb
Visa, MC
C-ltd/S-no/P-no/H-no

Full breakfast
Gardens, swimming pool,
front porch, private baths,
parlor, TV, library, games

The Chickadee B&B is a beautiful, Colonial home built in the late 1800's. It features four nicely appointed guestrooms, all with private baths, well kept grounds, perennial gardens, a swimming pool, and a gracious front porch for rocking or reading.
✉ chickadeebandb@comcast.net ○ www.chickadeebandb.net

Enchanted Nights B&B
Scenic Coastal Rte 103 03904
207-439-1489
Peter Lamardia & Nancy
Bogenberger

60-350 BB
8 rooms, 7 pb
Most CC, *Rated*, •
C-yes/S-ltd/P-yes/H-yes

Full or continental breakfast
Sitting room, family friendly
facility, bikes, tennis, sauna

A B&B in Kittery, Maine—one mile to Historic Portsmouth, New Hampshire. French Victorian & Country French ambience. Whimsical, colorful & fanciful, yet elegant.
✉ ceo@enchantednights.org ○ www.enchantednights.org

**Portsmouth Harbor Inn &
Spa**
6 Water St 03904
207-439-4040
Nat & Lynn Bowditch

110-225 BB
5 rooms, 5 pb
Visa, MC, *Rated*
C-ltd/S-no/P-no/H-ltd
Some French

Full gourmet breakfast
Homebaked cookies,
afternoon tea, port & sherry
Full day spa, massage, hot
tub, sitting room, games,
porch, patio, gardens

Comfortable brick Victorian with beautifully appointed rooms, water and city views, and luxurious day spa, featuring shopping and spa packages. Stroll to historic Portsmouth or Kittery and shop, catch a live performance, and dine. Recommended by NY Times
✉ info@innatportsmouth.com ○ www.innatportsmouth.com

LEWISTON

Ware Street Inn
52 Ware St 04240
877-783-8171 207-783-8171
Jan & Mike Barrett

110-210 BB
6 rooms, 6 pb
Most CC
C-ltd/S-no/P-no/H-no
French

Sumptuous buffet
Bedtime snacks, afternoon
tea, etc.
Turndown service,
hairdryer, cable TV/VCR,
WiFi, terrace, common living
room, den with computer

Refreshing oasis in the heart of the city. Comfort & gracious personal service abound in an inviting, unpretentious atmosphere, creating a feeling of warmth & welcome.
✉ info@warestreetinn.com ○ www.warestreetinn.com

MONHEGAN ISLAND

The Island Inn
1 Ocean Ave 04852
207-596-0371
Krista Lisajus

115-340 BB
32 rooms, 24 pb
Visa, MC
C-yes/S-no/P-no/H-no
French, Russian, Polish
Memorial Day–
Columbus Day

Full breakfast
Coffeehouse open daily –
pastries and light lunches;
Lunch and dinner available
for a fee
Sitting room, library,
property overlooking harbor
and ocean, suites, family
friendly, non-smoking

A turn-of-the-century summer hotel overlooking Monhegan Harbor, the ocean, and the setting sun. Relax in porch chairs or on lawn overlooking harbor. Cozy library and fireplaced sitting room. Your superb hostess, Krista, will be delighted to meet you!
✉ islandin@midcoast.com ○ www.islandinnmonhegan.com

NAPLES

Augustus Bove House	99-250 BB	Full breakfast
Corner of Rts 302 & 114 04055	7 rooms, 7 pb	Honeymoon/anniversary
888-806-6249 207-693-6365	Visa, MC, Disc, *Rated*,	tray, complimentary
Arlene & David Stetson	•	coffee/tea
	C-yes/S-ltd/P-yes/H-ltd	Sitting room, veranda, lawn

Recently restored, offers authentic Colonial accommodations in a relaxing atmosphere. Between 2 lakes, 20 minutes from mountain skiing. Let our staff pamper you, with impeccable service, at our beautiful mountainside Country inn!
✉ augbovehouse@roadrunner.com 🌐 www.NaplesMaine.com

Inn at Long Lake	105-260 BB	Full country breakfast
Lake House Rd 04055	16 rooms, 16 pb	Complimentary coffee, tea,
800-437-0328 207-693-6226	Visa, MC, *Rated*	cocoa and Chef's Inn-baked
Keith A. Neubert	C-ltd/S-no/P-no/H-no	cookies.
		Sitting room, library, Great
		Room with fieldstone
		fireplace.

As featured on The Oprah Show (1001 Ways to Be Romantic) We are Number 216. A Charming Victorian inn nestled by Long Lake, offering a cozy, relaxed atmosphere & Maine hospitality at its best! Rated one of the top 10 inns in country by INNovations magazine
✉ info@innatlonglake.com 🌐 www.innatlonglake.com

Lamb's Mill Inn	100-170 BB	Full breakfast
131 Lamb's Mill Road 04055	6 rooms, 6 pb	Refreshments available
207-693-6253	Visa, MC	WiFi, bath amenities, two
Laurel Tinkham, Sandy Long	C-ltd/S-ltd/P-no/H-ltd	dining rooms, off-street
		parking, gardens, common
		area, hot tubs, stoves

Lamb's Mill Inn is an inn for all seasons located on a country road in Naples, ME, a small picturesque village situated between Long Lake and Sebago Lake in the foothills of Maine's Western mountains. "Eew hike, ewe bike, ewe ski, ewe zzzzz"!
✉ Lambsmil@fairpoint.net 🌐 www.lambsmillinn.com

NEW HARBOR

Gosnold Arms	99-242 BB	Full breakfast
146 State Rt 32 04554	26 rooms, 26 pb	Sitting room, wharf, cable TV
207-677-3727	Visa, MC, *Rated*	available in some rooms &
The Phinney Family	C-yes/S-no/P-no/H-ltd	cottages
	Mid-May-Oct.	

Charming country inn & cottages, most with harbor or oceanviews. Located on the Pemaquid Peninsula of Maine, it is a true working harbor. The wharf is an ideal spot to view the activities of the harbor.
✉ info@gosnold.com 🌐 www.gosnold.com

NEWAGEN

Newagen Seaside Inn	135-285 BB	Full breakfast
60 Newagen Colony 04576	36 rooms, 36 pb	Onsite restaurant and pub
800-654-5242 207-633-5242	Visa, MC, AmEx	Weddings and events
Jason Schlosser	C-ltd/S-no/P-no/H-ltd	planned and hosted. Dock.

Commanding breathtaking views in all directions, the inn is home to 30 guestrooms, and six charming guest cottages are nestled in the Inn's 19 wooded acres. A classic seaside resort for nearly a century.
✉ innkeepers@newageninn.com 🌐 www.newagenseasideinn.com

NEWCASTLE

The Harbor View Inn at Newcastle 34 Main St 04553 207-563-2900 Joe McEntee	140-220 BB 3 rooms, 3 pb Visa, MC, • C-ltd/S-no/P-no	Full breakfast Wireless Internet, living room, deck, lawn, fireplace, library, dining room

The Harbor View Inn is a restored New England Cape, sitting on a knoll above Main Street in Newcastle.
✉ joe@theharborview.com ☯ www.theharborview.com

NOBLEBORO

Mill Pond Inn 50 Main St 04555 207-563-8014 Bobby & Sherry Whear	140 BB 6 rooms, 6 pb C-ltd/S-no/P-no	Full breakfast Iced tea on the lawn in the afternoon Dock with pier, hammocks for 2, complimentary canoes & bikes

On a pond, tucked away in the antique village of Damariscotta Mills, is the Mill Pond Inn. On more than one occasion, the Mill Pond Inn has been referred to as a "magical, mystical place." Six guestrooms with private baths.
✉ millpondinn@webtv.net ☯ www.millpondinn.com

NORTH HAVEN ISLAND

Our Place Inn & Cottages 704 Crabtree Pt 04853 207-867-4998 Marnelle Bubar	90-275 EP 5 rooms, 3 pb Visa, MC, AmEx C-yes/S-ltd/P-ltd/H-ltd	Main house sitting room with fireplace; cottages have own kitchen, bedroom

Our Place Inn is a renovated 19th century farmhouse with 3 self-contained cottages. A lighthouse cottage is under construction. We offer comfortable accommodations in an informal and relaxed setting.
✉ info@ourplaceinn.com ☯ www.ourplaceinn.com

NORTHEAST HARBOR

Maison Suisse Inn Main St & Kimball Ln 04662 800-624-7668 207-276-5223 The White Family & Friends	125-395 BB 16 rooms, 16 pb Visa, MC, AmEx C-yes/S-ltd/P-ltd/H-ltd Late Apr. – Early Nov.	Full or continental breakfast 24-hour afternoon tea and snacks; breakfast served @ restaurant across the street Sitting room, library, suites, fireplaces, cable TV, tennis, bike rentals, WiFi

Located minutes from Bar Harbor, in the timeless village of Northeast Harbor, this historic landmark shingle style inn offers inviting comfort in quiet elegance at Acadia's doorstep.
✉ maison@prexar.com ☯ maisonsuisse.com

OCEAN PARK

Nautilus By The Sea Guesthouse 2 Colby Ave 04063 800-981-7018 207-934-2021 Dick & Patte Kessler	65-175 BB 12 rooms, 10 pb Visa, MC, Disc C-yes/S-no/P-no/H-no May 16 to October 13	Continental breakfast Guest living room with cable TV/VCR and library, dunefront enclosed porch and open dunefront porch.

The Nautilus By The Sea directly on the ocean in historic Ocean Park, Maine has 12 rooms, suites, or apartments, with our continental plus breakfast served on the dunefront enclosed porch. We're 20 minutes from Portland's Jetport, 6 minutes from ME TPK.
✉ info@nautilusbythesea.com ☯ nautilusbythesea.com

Tell your hosts Pamela Lanier sent you.

OGUNQUIT

Admiral's Inn	69-199 BB	Continental breakfast
7 Main St 03907	45 rooms, 43 pb	Lounge
88-263-6318 207-646-7093	Most CC, *Rated*	Fire pit, Jacuzzi, swimming
Ken Holmes	C-yes/S-ltd/P-yes/H-ltd	pool, cable TV, wedding
	French	accommodations,
		group/reunion
		accommodations

Come experience Ogunquit with us! The Admiral's Inn is a resort located on spacious grounds in the center of the village. Stroll to the beach, the Marginal Way, Perkins Cove, The Ogunquit Playhouse and all of the village pleasures.
✉ admirals@gwi.net ○ www.theadmiralsinn.com

Beauport Inn on Clay Hill	130-195 BB	Full breakfast
99 Clay Hill 03907	5 rooms, 5 pb	All guestrooms have gas
00-646-8684 207-251-2941	Visa, MC	stove, tiled bath, cable TV,
George & Cathy Wilson	C-ltd/S-no	VCR, refrigerators, and high
		speed Internet

A spectacular newly-constructed stone English manor located on an 11-acre country setting, the Inn is nestled in between the Josiah River, Ogunquit's tennis courts, and rolling, forested hills. Ask about our apartment rental.
✉ gwilson6@maine.rr.com ○ www.beauportinn.com

Blue Shutters Inn	125-395 BB	Full breakfast buffet
6 Beachmere Pl 03907	14 rooms, 14 pb	Restaurant services, coffee
00-633-9550	Visa, MC, *Rated*	Cable TV, fireplaces, A/C,
Paul & Ewa Marino	C-yes/S-no/P-no/H-no	oceanview, lounging deck,
	Polish	"homey" living room, CD
		players

More than a Bed and Breakfast . . . Blue Shutters Inn has newly renovated, carriage house suites on a private path off the Marginal Way, centrally located to all of the attractions in Ogunquit.
✉ stay@blueshutters.com ○ www.blueshutters.com

Distant Sands B&B	95-165 BB	Full breakfast
32 Main St 03907	5 rooms, 4 pb	Wine & cheese, bottled
207-646-8686	Visa, MC, AmEx, *Rated*	water for guests
Robert Rush	C-ltd/S-no/P-no/H-no	Patio/deck oceanview,
	Closed Jan 15 to Apr 1.	gardens, cable TV, A/C,
		robes in room, beach towels
		available

Distant Sands Bed & Breakfast offers five beautifully appointed bedrooms in a restored 18th century farmhouse. The house abuts twenty-two acres of conservation land overlooking the Ogunquit River and the ocean in the distance.
✉ innkeeper@distantsands.com ○ www.distantsands.com

Gazebo Inn Ogunquit	69-279 BB	Full breakfast
72 Main St 03907	15 rooms, 15 pb	All day tea, coffee & sodas,
866-275-0648 207-646-3733	Visa, MC, AmEx, ●	snacks, wine weekends,
Scott Osgood	C-yes/S-no/P-yes/H-yes	dinner packages.
	Russian, German,	Pool, gym, pet friendly, on
	French	site spa, fireplaces, whirlpool
		tubs in room, balconies, walk
		to beach

An Ogunquit Maine Bed and Breakfast Inn on Main St in Ogunquit village. The trolley stops at our door, you can ride or walk to beaches, shops, restaurants & other attractions. Heated pool, 2 hot tubs , gym and spa, Suites with fire places, whirlpool tub
✉ contact@gazeboinnogt.com ○ www.gazeboinnogt.com

OGUNQUIT —————————————————————————————

Hartwell House Inn &	140-325 BB	Full gourmet breakfast
Conference Center	16 rooms, 16 pb	Afternoon tea and sweets
312 Shore Rd 03907	Most CC, *Rated*, •	daily.
800-235-8883 207-646-7210	C-ltd/S-no/P-no/H-yes	Conference and Function
Warren and Gilly Francis	Spanish	Center, golf privileges, A/C,
		Weekly Vacation Rentals.

Romantic country inn in Ogunquit. Open year-round, 1½ hours from Boston. Walk t
beach, village for fishing, whale watching, boutiques and lobster dining. Antiques, outle
nearby. 16 guestrooms/suites/studios. Dedicated conference center.
✉ innkeeper@hartwellhouseinn.com 🌐 www.hartwellhouseinn.com

The Leisure Inn	129-269 BB	Expanded Continental
73 School Street 03907	6 rooms, 6 pb	Breakfast
207-646-2737	Visa, MC	Wrap around sun porch,
Pam Batten	C-ltd/S-no/P-no/H-no	fireplace, free WiFi, cable TV
	Memorial day-	A/C, living room and patio
	Columbus d	

The Leisure Inn is a two minute walk to Ogunquit's finest restaurants, shops, bars, nigh
clubs and galleries. Clean and comfortable rooms with the finest amenities.
✉ Theleisureinn@aol.com 🌐 theleisureinn.com

The Morning Dove B&B	100-200 BB	Full breakfast
13 Bourne Ln 03907	6 rooms, 6 pb	Victorian front porch,
207-646-3891	Visa, MC	fireplaced gathering room,
Rob Leary	C-ltd/S-no/P-no/H-no	country gardens with pond,
		wireless Internet

A gracious Victorian bed & breakfast offering year round accommodations, in the heart o
Ogunquit. Set among country gardens, the Inn is perfect for an easy stroll to Perkin's Cove
the Marginal way, sandy beaches, & outstanding restaurants.
✉ themorningdove@maine.rr.com 🌐 www.themorningdove.com

Nellie Littlefield House	92-248 BB	Full breakfast buffet style
27 Shore Rd 03907	8 rooms, 8 pb	Afternoon refreshment
207-646-1692	Visa, MC, *Rated*	Outdoor heated pool, cable
Frank & Janet Araujo	C-ltd/S-no/P-no/H-ltd	TV, refrigerators, phone,
	Spanish, French	wireless Internet, in-house
		massages

Spectacular, 1889 three-story, grand Victorian house on Shore Road built by J.H. Littlefiel
for his wife, Nellie. An elegant house with ample piazza space, convenient to the beac
and the center of town.
✉ nlfh@gwi.net 🌐 www.nellielittlefieldhouse.com

Puffin Inn	69-209 BB	Full breakfast
433 Main St 03907	10 rooms, 10 pb	In-season afternoon
207-646-5496	Visa, MC, *Rated*	refreshments.
Mark Brunell / Steven Sousa	C-ltd/S-no/P-no/H-ltd	All rooms have a private
		bathroom, cable TV, A/C,
		sitting area, mini fridge,
		wireless Internet, iron

A charming historic Inn with spacious and comfortable rooms each with a sitting area an
private bathroom. Complimentary full breakfast each morning. Located on Route 1 step
away from town center. Walk to beaches, shopping, restaurants. Open year round.
✉ innkeeper@puffininn.com 🌐 www.puffininn.com

Tell your hosts Pamela Lanier sent you.

OGUNQUIT

Rockmere Lodge
150 Stearns Rd 03907
888-646-2985 207-646-2985
Andy Antoniuk, Bob Brown &
Doug Flint

105-225 BB
8 rooms, 8 pb
Visa, MC, Disc, *Rated*
C-ltd/S-ltd/P-no/H-no

Full breakfast
Beach towels, chairs &
umbrellas, CD/clock radio,
cable TV, VCR/DVD, movie
library, hairdryer, iron

Ogunquit's only oceanside B&B. Maine shingle-style cottage sitting on a knoll with a commanding view of the Atlantic. Midpoint on the Marginal Way between the town, main beach and Perkins Cove. Decorated with Victorian era antiques. Walk to everything.
✉ info@rockmere.com ❂ www.rockmere.com

The Terrace by the Sea
23 Wharf Ln 03907
207-646-3232
Sergio Becerra

49-242 BB
37 rooms, 37 pb
Visa, MC, *Rated*
C-ltd/S-ltd/P-no/H-no
Spanish
March 23 – December 09

Expanded continental
breakfast
Heated pool, tennis nearby,
balconies, full ocean view,
efficiency kitchens, wireless
Internet

The Terrace combines deluxe motel accommodations along with the elegance of a Colonial inn. Both offer spectacular ocean views in a peaceful, secluded setting at the end of Wharf Lane, across from the beach.
✉ tbts@gwi.net ❂ www.terracebythesea.com

The Trellis House
10 Beachmere Place 03907
800-681-7909 207-646-7909
Pat & Jerry Houlihan

95-225 BB
8 rooms, 8 pb
Visa, MC
C-ltd/S-no/P-no/H-no

Full breakfast
Afternoon beverages
Sitting room, porches,
oceanviews, trolley stop,
A/C, wireless Internet

A year-round inn close to all that is special to Ogunquit. Furnished with an eclectic blend of antiques, coupled with some oceanviews and quiet surroundings.
✉ info@trellishouse.com ❂ www.trellishouse.com

Yardarm Village Inn
406 Shore Rd 03907
888-927-3276 207-646-7006
Scott & Beverlee Drury

90-155 BB
10 rooms, 10 pb
Cash, Checks
C-yes/S-ltd/P-no/H-ltd
May – mid October

Continental breakfast
Beer, wine, cheese and
cracker shop
Hand-painted, Maine
blueberry dinnerware,
sailboat charter, Internet, gift
shop, waterfall & gardens

Charming New England Inn adjacent to Perkins Cove. Relax, enjoy ocean breezes from our veranda or find a spot near our bubbling waterfall. Sailing charters, beer/wine/cheese, handpainted Maine dinnerware and giftshop on premises.
✉ yardarm@maine.rr.com ❂ www.yardarmvillageinn.com

OLD ORCHARD BEACH

Atlantic Birches Inn
20 Portland Ave 04064
888-934-5295 207-934-5295
Ray & Heidi DeLeo

101-192 BB
10 rooms, 10 pb
Most CC, *Rated*, •
C-yes/S-no/P-no/H-ltd

Continental plus breakfast
Teas, coffee, cider, hot
chocolate
Sitting rooms, heated pool/
beach pool towels, TV, DVD
A/C, wrap around porch,
picnic table, gazebo

The Atlantic Birches Inn is an elegant yet casual bed and breakfast, in Old Orchard Beach. Two buildings, a Victorian Main House built in 1903 and a 1920's bungalow called The Cottage. Each building has 5 beautiful guestrooms available for your enjoyment
✉ Info@atlanticbirches.com ❂ www.atlanticbirches.com

ORLAND

Alamoosook Lakeside Inn
229 Soper Rd 04472
866-459-6393 207-469-6393
Gina Bushong

85-125 BB
6 rooms, 6 pb
Most CC, *Rated*, •
C-yes/S-no/P-no/H-yes

Full breakfast
We cater meetings,
weddings, parties and
retreats with seating for up to
150 people.
Fishing, skating, x-country
skiing, stone fireplace,
swimming, gardens, sun
porch, rec room

*Off a quiet dirt road, on the shore of Alamoosook Lake, deep in the heart of Downeast &
Acadia Maine, you'll find the Alamoosook Lakeside Inn — the perfect Maine inn to escape
from it all.*
✉ info@alamoosooklakesideinn.com 🌐 www.alamoosooklakesideinn.com

Orland House B&B
10 Narramissic River Dr 04472
207-469-1144
Cynthia & Alvion Kimball

85-115 BB
4 rooms, 4 pb
Visa, MC, AmEx,
Rated, •
C-ltd/S-no/P-no/H-no
Spanish and some
French

Full breakfast
Complimentary afternoon
tea, snacks, and wine
Sitting room, library, cable
TV, accommodate business
travelers, DSL, fax, private
porch on 4th room.

*1820s Greek Revival B&B with 20th century amenities. Located on the Narramissic River at
the head of Penobscot Bay, 30 minutes from Bangor, 50 minutes to Acadia National Park.*
✉ innkeeper@orlandhousebb.com 🌐 www.orlandhousebb.com

POLAND

Wolf Cove Inn
5 Jordan Shore Dr 04274
207-998-4976
Marie & Steven Struble

75-250 BB
10 rooms, 8 pb
Most CC, •
C-ltd/S-no/P-ltd/H-no

Full breakfast
Catered meals for group
gatherings
Sitting room, Jacuzzis,
fireplaces, cable TV, WiFi,
kayaks, accommodations for
business travelers

*Wolf Cove Inn is a romantic, elegant country inn with a spectacular lake view and a
beautiful, natural setting. The outside deck and terrace are the perfect setting for birdwatching, sunsets and quiet conversations.*
✉ info@wolfcoveinn.com 🌐 www.wolfcoveinn.com

PORTLAND

Celtic Cottage
1433 Westbrook Street 04102
207-329-7859 207-773-6072
Mary Kuebler

100-120 BB
3 rooms, 2 pb
Visa, MC
C-ltd/S-no/P-no/H-no

Hearty traditional breakfast
Complimentary passes to
Total Fitness Gym, down
comforter, free parking,
wireless Internet

*Explore the traditional ways of Celtic hospitality. Walk down the road to the Tate House
Museum built in 1755 by Captain Tate, mast agent to King George III. Take in a Sea Dogs
baseball game at Hadlock Field just 7 minutes from Celtic Cottage.*
✉ info@celticcottagemaine.com 🌐 www.celticcottagemaine.com

The Chadwick
140 Chadwick St 04102
800-774-2137 207-774-5141
Buddy Marcum

99-175 BB
4 rooms, 4 pb
Visa, MC, Disc, *Rated*
S-no/P-no/H-no

Full breakfast
Fresh baked cookies in the
afternoon upon your arrival
Sitting room, library,
fireplace, cable TV, wireless
Internet connection

*"Simple elegance" describes this Queen-Anne located in historic West End. Gourmet break-
fasts. Guestrooms tastefully decorated. All rooms offer Flat Screen DVD TV's . Only a short
walk to the Portland Harbor and Old Port Shops & Fine Dining.*
✉ info@thechadwick.com 🌐 thechadwick.com

PORTLAND

Inn at St. John	49-215 BB	Continental breakfast
939 Congress St 04102	39 rooms, 20 pb	Tea, lemonade, cookies
800-636-9127 207-773-6481	Most CC, *Rated*, •	(seasonal)
Paul Hood	C-yes/S-no/P-yes/H-no	Family friendly, cable TV, broadband & Internet connections, bike storage, free parking, A/C

Conveniently located off the West End of Downtown, Portland, ME, the Inn At St. John has been providing travelers with exemplary service for over 100 years, an enjoyable change from the ordinary hotel accommodation. Children and pets are welcome!
✉ theinn@maine.rr.com ○ www.innatstjohn.com

Morrill Mansion B&B	89-239 BB	Breakfast Buffet
249 Vaughan St 04102	7 rooms, 7 pb	Fresh fruit is available all
888-5morrill 207-774-6900	Visa, MC, Disc	day, and fresh baked treats
David Parker	C-ltd/S-no/P-no/H-no	can be found in the guest gathering room
		Private baths, TV with DVD players, AC, CD players, mini-fridges, off-street parking

Architectural details that make the Morrill Mansion B&B unique have been restored and modern amenities have been added to make your stay in Portland comfortable. Free off-street parking and Internet connection are included! We look forward to your visit.
✉ innkeeper@morrillmansion.com ○ www.morrillmansion.com

Percy Inn	89-209 BB	Continental plus breakfast
15 Pine St 04102	10 rooms, 10 pb	24 hour butler pantry with
888-41-PERCY 207-871-POET	Visa, MC, •	snacks & drinks
Dale Northrup, CTC	C-ltd/S-no/P-no/H-no	Parlor with 400 movies and CDs, pantry, bricked garden courtyard, sun deck

A stylish and intimate urban inn, situated in the heart of Portland's West End Historic District at Longfellow Square. Every room in this 1830 brick rowhouse has its own personality & sense of history, coupled with the comforts of today.
✉ innkeeper@percyinn.com ○ www.percyinn.com

Wild Iris Inn	79-150 BB	Continental plus breakfast
273 State St 04101	7 rooms, 5 pb	Afternoon snacks and tea at
800-600-1557 207-775-0224	Most CC	anytime
Diane Edwards	C-ltd/S-no/P-no/H-no	Sitting room with fireplace, cable, garden area, business office with high speed Internet, WiFi

A cozy seven room Bed and Breakfast conveniently located within walking distance of downtown Portland, and a short drive from area beaches and attractions. We are Portland's first certified green inn.
✉ diane@wildirisinn.com ○ www.wildirisinn.com

ROCKLAND

Berry Manor Inn	115-360 BB	Full breakfast
81 Talbot Ave 04841	12 rooms, 12 pb	24-hr guest pantry with
800-774-5692 207-596-7696	Visa, MC, AmEx,	homemade pies made by the
Cheryl Michaelsen & Michael	*Rated*, •	Berry Manor Inn Pie Moms
LaPosta	C-ltd/S-no/P-no/H-ltd	as seen on Food Network Many common areas for guests' use. Concierge services for boats, golf, restaurants and other needs.

Rockland's premier bed and breakfast inn and the only AAA 4-Diamond rated historic bed and breakfast inn in mid-coast Maine. Historic Victorian mansion with 12 luxury guest-rooms with fireplaces, private baths (many with whirlpool tubs). Green Certified.
✉ info@berrymanorinn.com ○ www.berrymanorinn.com

ROCKLAND ──────────────────────────────

Captain Lindsey House Inn
5 Lindsey St 04841
800-523-2145 207-596-7950
Capts. Ellen & Ken Barnes

136-211 BB
9 rooms, 9 pb
Most CC, *Rated*, •
C-yes/S-no/P-no/H-ltd
French

Full breakfast
Afternoon refreshments in
our private courtyard or in
front of the fire in the winter
Deck, private garden, library,
wireless Internet

*Nestled amongst the historic seaport buildings of downtown Rockland, the 9 room Captain
Lindsey House Inn, built in 1837 and one of Rockland's first Inns, offers a quiet, elegant but
comfortable & cozy retreat. One block from the harbor and ferry terminal*
✉ lindsey@midcoast.com ❂ www.lindseyhouse.com

Lakeshore Inn
184 Lakeview Dr 04841
866-540-8800 207-594-4209
Susan & Jim Rodiger

115-155 BB
4 rooms, 4 pb
Visa, MC, Disc, *Rated*,
•
C-ltd/S-ltd/P-no/H-no

Full breakfast
Coffee, tea, & soft drinks in
guest kitchen
Sun room with fireplace, TV,
DVD, VCR & movies,
enclosed outdoor hot tub

*Recently remodeled, the historic Lakeshore Inn has four guestrooms with queen beds,
private baths, hairdryers, fluffy robes, overlooking Lake Chickawaukie. Relax in our enclosed Jacuzzi hot tub. Enjoy a full breakfast in a tranquil, scenic setting.*
✉ info@lakeshorebb.com ❂ www.lakeshorebb.com

Lime Rock Inn
96 Limerock St 04841
800-546-3762 207-594-2257
P.J. Walter & Frank Isganitis

110-229 BB
8 rooms, 8 pb
Most CC, •
C-ltd/S-no/P-no/H-ltd

Full breakfast
seasonal fruit, homemade
breads, regional fruit jams
and, of course, plenty of
freshly brewed coffee
Wrap-around porch, gazebo,
two parlors, guest pantry,
some rooms with fireplaces

*All of the rooms at the Lime Rock Inn are decorated with care to create a home with
elegance and luxury, yet have charm and character to ensure comfort and hospitality.*
✉ info@limerockinn.com ❂ www.limerockinn.com

Old Granite Inn
546 Main St 04841
800-386-9036 207-594-9036
Edwin and Joan Hantz

90-185 BB
8 rooms, 7 pb
Most CC, •
C-yes/S-no/P-yes/H-ltd

Innovative full gourmet
breakfast
Sitting room, common areas,
garden, sunrise deck, guest
pantry, in-room TV option,
piano, book swap

*Comfortable historic inn overlooking a busy harbor filled with boats. We offer eight distinc-
tive rooms, seven with private bath, each furnished with luxurious linens, antiques and
contemporary accents. Greet each day with a full gourmet breakfast.*
✉ ogi@midcoast.com ❂ www.oldgraniteinn.com

ROCKPORT ──────────────────────────────

Island View Inn
908 Commercial Street 04856
207-594-5462
Dana Burton

79-229 EP
15 rooms, 15 pb
Visa, MC, AmEx
C-yes/S-no/P-no/H-yes
May- November

Coffee and tea in the
morning
Heated pool, large lobby
with fireplaces and cozy
seating area and cable TV

*Ocean front setting with oversize rooms and large decks. All rooms individually decorated
with a coastal theme. Beautiful landscaping and all rooms ocean view.*
✉ info@islandviewmaine.com ❂ www.islandviewinnmaine.com

ROCKPORT

Strawberry Hill Seaside Inn	79-199 EP	Coffee and tea in the
886 Commercial Street 04856	21 rooms, 21 pb	morning
800-589-4009 207-594-5462	Visa, MC, AmEx	Heated outdoor pool with
Dana Burton	C-yes/S-no/P-no/H-yes	deck, cable TV, large lobby
		with fireplaces and cozy
		seating area

Ocean front setting, beautiful landscaping and all rooms have a beautiful ocean view. We offer rooms with one king, one queen, or two full size beds. All rooms are individually decorated with a coastal theme.
✉ info@strawberryhillinn.com ○ www.strawberryhillseasideinn.com

SEARSPORT

Carriage House Inn	95-125 BB	Full breakfast
120 E Main St 04974	4 rooms, 4 pb	Coffee and teas in the
800-578-2167 207-548-2167	Visa, MC, Disc	afternoon
Marcia Markwardt	C-ltd/S-ltd/P-no/H-no	Historic, library, sitting areas,
		common rooms, gardens,
		antiques, parlor, den, formal
		dining room

Come stay in one of Maine's most photographed homes, & find your own refuge & inspiration! Listed on the National Register of Historic places, this 1874 Victorian sea captain's mansion was home to legendary Impressionist painter Waldo Pierce.
✉ info@carriagehouseinmaine.com ○ www.carriagehouseinmaine.com

Wildflower Inn	89-145 BB	Full breakfast
2 Black Rd S 04974	4 rooms, 4 pb	Various baked items such as
888-546-2112 207-548-2112	Visa, MC, AmEx	cookies & coffee cakes
Cathy Keating & Deb Bush	C-ltd/S-no/P-no/H-no	Wireless Internet access,
		lounge area with TV, books,
		games, A/C, gardens, pond
		and a porch

Welcome to the Wildflower Inn! You can unpack once & enjoy Mid-Coast Maine from Rockland to Bar Harbor. Relax in our parlors, walk around the grounds . . . make yourself at home! ✉ wildflowerinn@roadrunner.com ○ www.wildflowerinnme.com

SEBASCO ESTATES

Rock Gardens Inn	115-200 MAP	Full breakfast
Rt 217 04565	28 rooms, 25 pb	Rates include dinner. Weekly
207-389-1339	Cash, Checks	Lobster cookout, picnic
Ona Barnet	C-yes/S-no/P-no/H-ltd	lunches available
	June-Sept	Heated swimming pool,
		kayaks at Inn, golf, tennis and
		boating nearby, ten minutes
		from sandy beach

Enjoy a relaxing vacation in classic Maine style cottages on a private peninsula facing Casco Bay. Ocean front views, flower gardens, breakfast & dinner daily, lobster cookouts weekly. Art workshops are offered in June, early July, and September.
✉ info@rockgardensinn.com ○ www.rockgardensinn.com

SOUTHWEST HARBOR

The Birches B&B	105-150 BB	Full breakfast
46 Fernald Point Rd 04679	3 rooms, 3 pb	Dining room, living room,
207-244-5182	Cash, Checks	croquet court, garden, ocean
Richard Homer	C-yes/S-no/P-no/H-ltd	views

Three large airy rooms, private baths, ocean views, gardens, and the croquet court. We have 5 acres of grounds, no traffic noise, just 350 yards to the first tee at the golf course. Separate Old House available for rental.
✉ dick@thebirchesbnb.com ○ www.thebirchesbnb.com

SOUTHWEST HARBOR

The Claremont Hotel
22 Claremont Rd 04679
800-244-5036 207-244-5036
John W. Madiera

152-308 BB
45 rooms, 44 pb
Visa, MC
C-yes/S-no/P-no/H-ltd
May 24th – October 19th

Buffet Breakfast
Dinner and full bar available
daily
Cottages, tennis court,
croquet courts, dock,
moorings, bicycles, rowboat

*Classic Maine shorefront hotel providing summer refuge to visitors of Mt. Desert Island
since 1884. Located on Somes Sound, America's east coast fjord, and listed on the National
Register.* ✉ clmhotel@adelphia.net ✆ www.theclaremonthotel.com

Clark Point Inn
109 Clark Point Road 04679
207-244-9828
Jennifer & Mark

95-245 BB
5 rooms, 5 pb
Visa, MC, *Rated*
C-ltd/S-no/P-no/H-ltd

Unique 3 Course Gourmet
Breakfast
24 hr beverage buffet-Gran
Crema Espresso, Valrhona
Truffles, Homemade biscotti
tea sugars, comp drinks
Concierge service, private
parking, cedar porch,
rocking chairs, hammock,
picnic breakfast, afternoon
tea.

*An historic 1883 Colonial style Inn blending relaxed elegance, premier water views, Unique
Gourmet breakfasts & gracious hospitality. Spacious guestrooms offer private baths, fresh
flowers, luxury linens, homemade Valhrona Truffles & 24 hour beverage buffet*
✉ info@clarkpointinn.com ✆ www.clarkpointinn.com

Harbour Cottage Inn
9 Dirigo Rd 04679
888-843-3022 207-244-5738
Don Jalbert & Javier
Montesinos

149-285 BB
11 rooms, 11 pb
Visa, MC, *Rated*, •
C-yes/S-no/P-no/H-ltd
Spanish
April through October

Full and continental
breakfasts
Deck, pier, whirlpool, steam
showers, gas fireplace,
waterfront suites, bicycles

*Welcome to The Harbour Cottage Inn, a premier coastal Maine bed and breakfast inn
offering visitors to Acadia National Park an elegant yet casual and quiet retreat. Situated in
beautiful Southwest Harbor less than a mile from Acadia National Park.*
✉ info@harbourcottageinn.com ✆ www.harbourcottageinn.com

The Inn at Southwest
371 Main St 04679
207-244-3835
Sandy Johnson

105-185 BB
7 rooms, 7 pb
Visa, MC, *Rated*
C-ltd/S-no/P-no
May – November

Full breakfast
Afternoon coffee, tea &
cookies
Down-filled duvets, ceiling
fans, fine linens & towels, gas
log stoves, high speed
Internet access

*Overlooking the serene waters of Southwest Harbor, the Inn at Southwest combines Victori-
an charm & gracious hospitality. The inn is within walking distance of restaurants, shopping, and the marina.*
✉ reservations@innatsouthwest.com ✆ www.innatsouthwest.com

The Island House
36 Freeman Ridge Rd 04679
207-244-5180
Ann & Charles Bradford

85-185 BB
3 rooms, 3 pb
Cash, *Rated*
C-ltd/S-no/P-no

Full delicious breakfast
Breakfast for vegetarians;
varied menu to
accommodate guests
2 guestrooms in main home
as well as a 2 bedroom lost
apartment with private deck.
Internet access.

*The Island House has always offered old fashioned hospitality and a pleasant retreat for its
many guests. We continue that tradition in our newly built B&B located in a quiet wooded
setting nearby.*
✉ islandab@roadrunner.com ✆ www.islandhousebb.com

SOUTHWEST HARBOR

The Kingsleigh Inn 373 Main St 04679 207-244-5302 Dana & Greg Moos	130-305 BB 8 rooms, 8 pb Visa, MC, AmEx, *Rated* C-ltd/S-no/P-no/H-ltd May-October	4 course gourmet breakfast Afternoon homemade baked goods, in-room chocolate truffles & Port wine daily, robes, slippers & more Living Room w/fireplace (wood), wraparound porch w/harbor view, games & books

Overlooking picturesque Southwest Harbor, we offer a 4 course gourmet breakfast, some rooms have harbor views, private balconies, all have private baths, secluded 3-room turret suite w/fireplace. Enjoy soft robes, slippers, homemade chocolates, Port wine
✉ relax@kingsleighinn.com ✪ www.kingsleighinn.com

Penury Hall 374 Main St 04679 207-244-7102 Gretchen Strong	80-115 BB 3 rooms, 3 pb Visa, MC, *Rated* C-ltd/S-no/P-no/H-no	Full breakfast Complimentary wine, coffee, tea Sitting room, sauna, library, music, fine art, laundry, fridge

Comfortable rambling Maine home for us and our guests. Decor reflects hosts' interests in art, antiques, books, gardening, sailing.Shops and restaurants within walking distance and Acadia Nat'l Park only a mile away.
✉ tstrong@penuryhall.com ✪ www.penuryhall.com

SPRUCE HEAD

Craignair Inn 5 Third St 04859 800-320-9997 207-594-7644 Neva & Steve Joseph	75-174 BB 20 rooms, 14 pb Visa, MC, *Rated*, ● C-yes/S-no/P-yes/H-no Spring, Summer, Fall	Full or continental plus breakfast Restaurant, coffee, tea and full liquor license Library, flower garden, coastal activities, walking, hiking, ocean swimming

Charming Country Inn on the Coast of Maine, overlooking the Atlantic Ocean. Restaurant on premises, wonderful atmosphere. Quiet, peaceful, romantic. Fodor's Choice Award for 2008. Tasteful rooms, recently renovated with cable tv, telephone, some with a/c.
✉ innkeeper@craignair.com ✪ www.craignair.com

TENANTS HARBOR

East Wind Inn 21 Mechanic St 04860 800-241-VIEW 207-372-6366 Tim Watts & Joy Taylor	110-250 BB 22 rooms, 16 pb Visa, MC, AmEx, *Rated*, ● C-ltd/S-yes/P-ltd/H-ltd April-November	Full breakfast Restaurant on premises open 7 days a week, April to November Sitting room, entertainment, piano, conference room for 30

Our historic seaside inn is in a tiny, tranquil village on a rural peninsula—a peaceful base from which to enjoy Maine's scenic coast and the culturally rich Rockland area.
✉ info@eastwindinn.com ✪ www.eastwindinn.com

VINALHAVEN

Libby House Inn 8 Water St 04863 631-765-3756 207-863-4696 Phil Roberts	75-140 EP 6 rooms, 2 pb C-ltd/S-no/P-no/H-ltd May-October	None Served Library with fireplace, suites, enclosed front porch

Country Victorian house built in the grand style of the 1860s. Large common areas as well as large rooms many with couches. Friendly, quiet and an atmosphere of relaxed vacation, furnished in comfortable antiques.
✉ libbyhouse1869@yahoo.com ✪ www.libbyhouse1869.com

WALDOBORO

Blue Skye Farm	105-145 BB	Full breakfast
1708 Friendship Rd 04572	5 rooms, 4 pb	Lobster dinners by prior
207-832-0300	Visa, MC, •	arrangement
Jan Davidson	C-ltd/S-no/P-no/H-ltd	Picnic tables, hiking trails, outdoor grills, free wireless Internet

A restored 1770s house with extensive grounds and hundreds of acres of hiking trails, Blue Skye stylishly blends New England simplicity with old world grace. The privacy offered to its discerning guests makes it a favorite with artists & romantics alike
✉ jan@blueskyefarm.com ❂ www.blueskyefarm.com

Le Vatout B&B	85-120 BB	Full breakfast
218 Kalers Corner 04572	3 rooms, 1 pb	Porch, sauna, beautiful
207-832-5150	Visa, MC	gardens, walking paths,
Dominika Spetsmann	C-ltd/S-no/P-no/H-no	garage to store bikes, skis,
	German	etc., swing, tea house

Le Vatout is part of a sprawling farmhouse anchored in the granite landscape right where the Medomac River meets the ocean and the tide laps at the waterfall twice a day. Cozy, low-key and completely relaxed.
✉ dominika@levatout.com ❂ www.levatout.com

WALPOLE

Brannon Bunker Inn	90-180 BB	Continental plus breakfast
349 State Rt 129 04573	8 rooms, 6 pb	Kitchen facilities available
800-563-9225 207-563-5941	Most CC, *Rated*, •	Sitting room, porch, antique
Jeanne & Joe Hovance	C-yes/S-no/P-no/H-ltd	shop, 3 room suite for family

The Brannon-Bunker Inn's offers a welcoming spirit that calls to travelers and families to stay and experience the area's lilac-scented springs; maple-shaded summers; brilliantly colored autumns; or crisp, white winters.
✉ brbnkinn@lincoln.midcoast.com ❂ www.brannonbunkerinn.com

WATERFORD

Bear Mountain Inn	100-325 BB	Full breakfast
Route 35/37 04088	11 rooms, 9 pb	Cookies, homemade pies/ice
866-450-4253 207-583-4404	Visa, MC, *Rated*, •	cream snacks, popcorn, &
Jim Kerrigan	C-yes/S-ltd/P-ltd/H-ltd	soda, dinners for special events are offered Lake with beachfront, canoes, cable TV, indoor/outdoor fireplaces & hot tubs, great decks, BBQ grill

Bear Mountain Inn is a lakefront Bed & Breakfast located on 52 acres in Waterford, Maine. Country Inn features lakeview rooms, family suites & luxury romantic suites for a romantic getaway. Skiing, hiking, snowmobiling, canoeing, kayaking & more.
✉ innkeeper@bearmtninn.com ❂ www.bearmtninn.com

WESTBROOK

The Elms B&B	79-199 BB	Continental breakfast
102 Cumberland St 04101	7 rooms, 2 pb	Free parking, exercise room,
207-854-4060	Visa, MC	hot tub, sauna, WiFi, events,
Matt	C-yes/S-no/P-no/H-no	weddings, reunions

The Elms B&B, c 1882, just 10 minutes from the heart of down town Portland, ME, is a graceful historic home overlooking the Presumpscot River. With classic architecture, well-appointed rooms and amazing public spaces, it's a beautiful place to stay.
✉ innkeeper@elmsmaine.com ❂ www.elmsmaine.com

YORK————————————————————————————————————

Dockside Guest Quarters	140-298 BB	Continental plus breakfast
22 Harris Island Rd 03909	25 rooms, 25 pb	Lunch, dinner and cocktails
800-270-1977 207-363-2868	Visa, MC, Disc, *Rated*,	in adjacent restaurant.
Eric & Carol Lusty	•	Afternoon teas and treats
	C-yes/S-no/P-no/H-yes	daily in Maine House.
	April- November	Restaurant, lawn games, boat
		rentals, bikes, beach chairs,
		phones, A/C, cable TV,
		wireless Internet

Distinctive New England inn on 7 acre private peninsula bordering York Harbor on the Maine seacoast offering distinctive dining and lodging. Twenty-five rooms in 5 buildings, marina, restaurant, meeting facilities. ✉ eric@docksidegq.com 🌐 www.docksidegq.com

Morning Glory Inn	155-225 BB	Full breakfast
120 Seabury Rd 03909	3 rooms, 3 pb	Beaches and Harbors
207-363-2062	Most CC	nearby, Gardens, A/C,
Bonnie & Bill Alstrom	C-ltd/S-no/P-no/H-no	Individual Heat Control,
	Closed Winter	Cable TV/DVD, WiFi, Mini-fridges

Welcome to Morning Glory Inn! A boutique bed and breakfast nestled in picturesque coastal Maine. If you're looking for stylish, unique, alternative to hotel, motel and tradition-al bed and breakfast accommodations then we've got the place for you!
✉ morningglory@maine.rr.com 🌐 www.morninggloryinnmaine.com

YORK BEACH————————————————————————————————

The Candleshop Inn	80-185 BB	Full breakfast
44 Freeman St 03910	10 rooms, 3 pb	Full vegetarian breakfast-
888-363-4087 207-363-4087	Visa, MC, AmEx	vegan, lactose, gluten free
Barbara Sheff	C-yes/S-no/P-no/H-ltd	available. Fruit bowl, coffee,
	A little French	tea, water all day
		Deck, front porch,
		oceanviews, yoga, massage
		therapy, Reiki,
		Aromatherapy, retreats,
		Japanese garden

With its serene atmosphere and beautiful oceanviews, our 10 bedroom home is the perfect setting for replenishing the body, mind and spirit. We offer a free yoga class every morning followed by an all you can eat vegetarian breakfast. We welcome children.
✉ stay@candleshopinn.com 🌐 www.candleshopinn.com

YORK HARBOR————————————————————————————————

Inn at Tanglewood Hall	95-250 BB	Full Buffet Breakfast
611 York St 03911	6 rooms, 6 pb	Premium Tanglewood Brew,
207-351-1075	Visa, MC, AmEx	Select Gourmet Teas, Hot
Su & Andy Wetzel	C-ltd/S-no/P-no/H-ltd	Chocolate, and Special
		Treats available all day.
		Widescreen LCD Cable TV &
		DVD Players, Gas Fireplaces,
		Updated Private Baths, A/C,
		Luxurious Linens

Our romantic York Harbor Maine B&B Inn is set along estate-lined seacoast Route 1A amidst woodland gardens, just beyond the York Beach Lobster Cove ocean bend. Enjoy our casually elegant bed and breakfast nearby beaches, Ogunquit, Kennebunkport & Kittery.
✉ tanglewood@maine.rr.com 🌐 www.tanglewoodhall.com

York Harbor Inn, York Harbor, ME

YORK HARBOR

York Harbor Inn
Coastal Rt 1A 03911
800-343-3869 207-363-5119
Garry Dominguez

99-349 BB
54 rooms, 54 pb
Most CC, *Rated*, •
C-yes/S-no/P-no/H-ltd

Continental Plus Breakfast
Lunch, dinner, Sunday
brunch, fine dining and pub
menu
Hot tub, restaurant, pub,
A/C, CCTV, phone with data
port, many rooms with
fireplace, spas

Historic luxury oceanview Inn featured on "Great Country Inns." Dining recognized by Food & Wine Magazine. Ship's Cellar Pub with Martini Bar and fireplaces, hot tub. The place to stay in Southern Maine just one hour north of Boston. Open year round.
✉ info@yorkharborinn.com ◐ www.yorkharborinn.com

Maryland

ANNAPOLIS

1908-William Page Inn
8 Martin St 21401
800-364-4160 410-626-1506
Robert L. Zuchelli

190-295 BB
5 rooms, 3 pb
Visa, MC, *Rated*, •
C-ltd/S-no/P-no/H-no

Full breakfast
Complimentary soft drinks, juices, bottled water, tea & coffee served from wet bar in common room.
Porches, common room, & complimentary off-street parking, wireless Internet, concierge-style service

This 1908 historic district, 5-guest-room inn is furnished in antiques and family collectibles. Full breakfast, off-street parking and wireless Internet are provided at no additional cost.
✉ info@williampageinn.com ○ www.williampageinn.com

201 B&B
201 Prince George St 21401
410-268-8053
Graham W. Gardner

170-250 BB
4 rooms, 4 pb
Most CC
C-ltd/S-no/P-no/H-no

Full breakfast
Library, Jacuzzis, fireplaces, cable TV, accommodations for business travelers

Georgian mansion in premium location with parking and grounds. Spacious rooms with fine antiques. All bedrooms have attached baths, TV/VCR, A/C and refrigerator.
✉ bbat201@aol.com ○ www.201bb.com

Annapolis Inn
144 Prince George St 21401
410-295-5200
Joseph Lespier

259-479 BB
3 rooms, 3 pb
Visa, MC, AmEx, *Rated*
C-ltd/S-no/P-no/H-no
Spanish, Italian

Very elegant three-course breakfast
Afternoon tea, chocolates in rooms, soft drinks
A/C, heated Jacuzzi, towel warmers, heated marble floors, wireless Internet

The perfect Inn for the perfect getaway. Let us help create the ideal visit to fit your needs. Business, pleasure or vacation, our service is incomparable and our suites are spacious, elegant and luxurious. Pamper or surprise that special someone.
✉ info@annapolisinn.com ○ www.annapolisinn.com

Annapolitan B&B
1313 West St 21401
866-990-2330 410-990-1234
John & Joetta Holt

115-225 BB
7 rooms, 7 pb
Most CC
C-yes/S-no/P-no/H-yes

Full breakfast

If you're looking for a B & B in Annapolis, MD. You came to the right place. The Annapolitan B&B is centrally located and ready to host your special events.
✉ annapolitanbandb@yahoo.com ○ www.theannapolitan.com

The Barn on Howard's Cove
500 Wilson Rd 21401
410-266-6840
Mary Gutsche

150-150 BB
2 rooms, 2 pb
Cash, Checks, *Rated*, •

C-yes/S-no/P-no/H-no

Full breakfast
Snacks
Sitting room, near pool, tennis, dock, deep water docking available, canoes/kayak.

Charming restored 1850s horse barn overlooking a cove off the Severn River. A quiet waterfront location that is convenient to Annapolis, Baltimore, DC and the Eastern Shore. Surrounded with gardens and furnished with many antiques.
✉ gdgutsche@gmail.com ○ www.barnonhowardscovebandb.com

The Barn on Howard's Cove, Annapolis, MD

ANNAPOLIS

Chez Amis B&B
85 East St 21401
888-224-6455 410-263-6631
Don & Mickie Deline

165-215 BB
4 rooms, 4 pb
Visa, MC, AmEx, •
C-ltd/S-no/P-no/H-no

Full breakfast
Soft drinks, beer, wine,
peanuts, M&Ms, cookies,
and champagne or chocolate
cake (spec. occasions)
Sitting room,
European/country decor,
themed rooms, robes, TV,
A/C, antiques, over 200 DVDs
& tapes

*Former circa 1900 grocery store, transformed into a B&B in 1989. Perfect location for
enjoying historic area, harbor & Academy. Antiques and quilts decorate this charming
cozy, comfortable, and quaint bed and breakfast. Full breakfast and private baths.*
✉ stayatchezamis@verizon.net ○ www.chezamis.com

Flag House Inn
26 Randall St 21404
800-437-4825 410-280-2721
Charlotte & Bill Schmickle

190-350 BB
5 rooms, 5 pb
Visa, MC
C-ltd/S-no/P-no/H-no
Mid-February through
Dec

Full breakfast
Off street parking on site.
Swing on front porch.
Fireplace in guest sitting
room.

*1870 Victorian offering free off-street parking, king or twin beds in 4 guestrooms & a
room suite, each with private full bath and cable TV. Full hot breakfast in guest dining
room. Half-block to Waterfront's City Dock & USNA Visitor's Gate 1.*
✉ info@flaghouseinn.com ○ www.flaghouseinn.com

**Georgian House Bed &
Breakfast**
170 Duke of Gloucester 21401
800-557-2068 410-263-5618
Ann & Tom Berger

175-235 BB
4 rooms, 4 pb
Visa, MC, *Rated*
C-ltd/S-no/P-no/H-no

Full Gourmet Breakfast
We will seek to
accommodate dietary needs
or other restrictions if stated
in advance.
Suites, TV/VCR, outside
patio, antiques, gas fireplace,
sitting rooms, sofa/bed, claw
foot tubs

*Ann and Tom look forward to welcoming you to their home, The Georgian House. Annap-
olis is alive with treasures and images of the beginning of a new nation and is home to the
United States Naval Academy.* ✉ info@GeorgianHouse.com ○ www.GeorgianHouse.com

ANNAPOLIS

Gibson's Lodgings
110 Prince George St 21401
877-330-0057 410-268-5555
Beverly Snyder

119-259 BB
21 rooms, 17 pb
Most CC, •
C-ltd/S-ltd/P-no/H-yes

Continental plus breakfast
Free Parking in our
courtyard, Free WiFi, Air
Conditioning, Continental
Breakfast

The Location speaks for itself! In the heart of Annapolis, next to the City Dock and the Naval Academy. Walk to all the restaurants and historic sights. ALSO, FREE Parking and Continental Breakfast . . . are included.
✉ gibsonslodgings@starpower.net 🕐 www.gibsonslodgings.com

Meadow Gardens B&B
504 Wilson Rd 21401
410-224-2729
Wendy Mays

100-150 BB
3 rooms, 3 pb
Cash, Checks
C-yes/S-ltd/P-yes/H-ltd

Full breakfast
Self serve coffee, cocoa or
tea station
Swimming in creek or pool, 2
canoes, 2 kayaks, hammock,
dock, fishing, wireless
Internet, A/C

A sanctuary of peacefulness surrounded by 6.5 acres of lawn, gardens and woods. Located two miles from historic Annapolis offering the convenience of close proximity without the hassles of parking or city noise. Plenty of shopping, and great restaurants.
✉ wendymays@gmail.com 🕐 www.meadowgardenbandb.com

Scotlaur Inn
165 Main St 21401
410-268-5665
Ted & Beth Levitt

85-175 BB
10 rooms, 10 pb
Visa, MC, *Rated*, •
C-yes/S-no/P-ltd/H-no
Spanish

Full breakfast
Snacks, lunch and dinner
available in the restaurant
Accommodations for
business travelers, TV,
telephones, wireless Internet
access & air conditioning

The Scotlaur Inn offers ten beautifully decorated, old-fashioned guestrooms in the heart of Annapolis. The Scotlaur Inn and Chick & Ruth's Delly (where breakfast is served) have been a family owned business for 3 generations in the historic district.
✉ Info@ScotlaurInn.com 🕐 www.scotlaurinn.com

State House Inn
25 State Cir 21401
410-990-0024
Maureen Lucas

129-309 BB
7 rooms, 7 pb
Visa, MC, AmEx, •
C-ltd/S-no/P-ltd/H-ltd

Continental breakfast
Sitting room, Jacuzzis, cable
TV, suites, business traveler
accommodations, wireless
Internet

The State House Inn has all the amenities of a hotel and all the charm of a B&B. Conveniently located on State Circle in the heart of Historic Annapolis. Relax in spacious guestrooms with extraordinary views of downtown, including water views.
✉ statehouseinn@comcast.net 🕐 www.statehouseinn.com

BALTIMORE

1840s Carrollton Inn
50 Albemarle St 21202
877-385-1840 410-385-1840
Tim Kline & Miranda Winters

175-395 BB
13 rooms, 13 pb
Most CC, •
C-yes/S-no/P-no/H-yes

Full Gourmet Breakfast
Complimentary coffee and
tea service available
Plush robes, fresh flowers,
high-speed Internet access,
Flat Screen Cable Television
and fireplaces.

The Jewel of Jonestown! A block from Little Italy, 4 blocks from the Inner Harbor, boasting luxury rooms and suites with whirlpool tubs, fireplaces & decorator furnishings. Linger over coffee in a tranquil garden courtyard then explore Baltimore's sights.
✉ info@1840scarrolltoninn.com 🕐 www.1840scarrolltoninn.com

BALTIMORE————————————————————————————

Blue Door on Baltimore
2023 East Baltimore S 21231
410-732-0191
Roger & Cecelia

145-180 BB
3 rooms, 3 pb
Most CC
C-yes/S-no/P-no/H-no

3 Course grand breakfast
Continental + breakfast menu
on weekdays, afternoon tea,
welcome snack, soda &
bottled water
In-room satellite TV/music,
relaxing common areas,
Internet access

Located in the historic area of Butcher's Hill, and steps away from Patterson Park, you are
minutes away from all of Baltimore's business and entertainment venues.
✉ stay@bluedoor.com ◐ bluedoorbaltimore.com/site/

Celie's Waterfront Inn
1714 Thames St 21231
800-432-0184 410-522-2323

149-350 BB
9 rooms, 9 pb
Visa, MC, AmEx
C-ltd/S-no/P-no/H-no

Continental plus breakfast
Refrigerators, coffeemakers,
sodas, water
Free wireless Internet,
common area phone with
LD, satellite TV, A/C,
whirlpool tubs, fireplaces

The charm of Fells Point, the convenience to Baltimore and the romance of the area's most
renowned, historic B&B hotels make Celie's a local favorite. Couples, vacationers and
business travelers consider Celie's one of the Baltimore area's hidden gems.
✉ innkeeper@celieswaterfront.com ◐ www.celiesinn.com

Gramercy Mansion
1400 Greenspring Valley Rd
21153
800-553-3404 410-486-2405
Anne Pomykala & Cristin
Kline

150-375 BB
11 rooms, 11 pb
Most CC, •
C-yes/S-no/P-no/H-yes
Spanish

Full breakfast
In-room coffee, tea, juice,
soda, bottled water
Gardens, trails, tennis,
Jacuzzis, swimming pool,
suites, fireplaces, meeting
rooms, cable, Internet

A historic English Tudor Mansion crowns 45 acres of flower & herb gardens & woodland
trails. Peacefully secluded in scenic Greenspring Valley yet just fifteen minutes from down-
town Baltimore.
✉ info@gramercymansion.com ◐ www.gramercymansion.com

Phoenix Risin'
1429 Bolton St 21217
410-462-2692
Janice Orr

95-175 BB
3 rooms, 1 pb
Visa, MC
C-ltd/S-ltd/P-no/H-no

Full breakfast

When you enjoy a stay at Phoenix Risin' Bed & Breakfast is a place where guests can relax
their bodies and renew their souls. You can feel your rebirth begin. What's more, you can
be rejuvenated seven days a week, 365 days per year!
✉ jorrphoenixrisin@aol.com ◐ www.phoenixrisin.com

Scarborough Fair
1 E Montgomery St 21230
877-954-2747 410-837-0010
Barry Werner & Jeff Finlay

175-215 BB
6 rooms, 6 pb
Most CC
C-ltd/S-no/P-no/H-no

Full gourmet breakfast
Afternoon tea & sweets,
guest refrigerator with free
beverages
Free WiFi, free parking,
telephone, fireplaces,
whirlpool baths and gas
fireplaces in select rooms.

Within walking distance of Baltimore's Inner Harbor, Scarborough Fair has six beautifully
decorated rooms with private baths. Located in the Historic Federal Hill neighborhood with
bistros, art galleries, shops and the well known Cross Street Market.
✉ innkeeper@scarboroughfairbandb.com ◐ www.scarboroughfairbandb.com

BALTIMORE

Tair ar Ddeg	95-110 BB	Full and Continental
13 Elmwood Rd. 21210	1 rooms, 1 pb	Full breakfast on weekends
410-323-5279	Cash, Checks	and continental on weekdays
Richard & Kathleen	S-no/P-no/H-no	Cable TV, wireless Internet
		access, refrigerator, small
		desk, reading chair with
		good light.

Located in historic Roland Park, one of Baltimore's finest neighborhoods, Tair ar Ddeg B&B combines charm and ambience with a cozy room and modern conveniences in a historic setting and is convenient to both downtown Baltimore and outlying areas.
✉ tairarddeg@comcast.net ◑ www.tairarddeg.com

BOONSBORO

Stoney Creek Farm	225-250 BB	Full gourmet breakfast
19223 Manor Church Rd. 21713	4 rooms, 4 pb	Wine and cheese featured
301-432-6272	Most CC	each evening.
Denise Lawhead	S-no/P-no/H-yes	Fireplace, direct TV, and
		wireless Internet access.

Stoney Creek Farm awaits your arrival and welcomes you home to our historic bed and breakfast farmhouse situated on the rolling hills of beautiful Washington County, Maryland. ✉ innkeeper@stoneycreekfarm.com ◑ stoneycreekfarm.com

CHESAPEAKE CITY

Blue Max Inn •	100-250 BB	Full breakfast
300 Bohemia Ave 21915	10 rooms, 10 pb	Complimentary teas, coffee
877-725-8362 410-885-2781	Most CC, *Rated*, •	and snacks; chocolates on
Christine Mullen	C-ltd/S-ltd/P-no/H-yes	your pillow
		Sitting room, library, Jacuzzi,
		fireplace, cable TV/VCR,
		VHS library, conference, A/C,
		WiFi, parking

This elegant bed & breakfast is located in historic Chesapeake City, Maryland, along the shores of the famous Chesapeake and DE Canal. Built in 1854, The Blue Max Inn is a charming and romantic inn located in the heart of this historic town.
✉ innkeeper@bluemaxinn.com ◑ www.bluemaxinn.com

Ship Watch Inn	99-245 BB	Full gourmet breakfast
401 First St 21915	10 rooms, 10 pb	Complimentary bottled
877-335-5300 410-885-5300	Visa, MC, AmEx	water, juice & soda. Fresh
Gilda Martuscelli	C-ltd/S-ltd/P-no/H-yes	baked goods daily in
		addition to snacks & fruit.
		Foyer lounge, expansive
		outdoor decks, outdoor hot
		tub, picnic essentials,
		restaurant delivery

A stunning waterfront view can be enjoyed by all 10 guestrooms which are beautifully appointed in simple, elegant decor. A private bath accompanies each room and 6 feature whirlpool tubs with shower. ✉ innkeeper@shipwatchinn.com ◑ www.shipwatchinn.com

CHESTERTOWN

Great Oak Manor	165-310 BB	Breakfast includes a hot
10568 Cliff Rd 21620	12 rooms, 12 pb	entree
800-504-3098 410-778-5943	Most CC, *Rated*	Afternoon snack, evening
Cassandra Fedas	C-ltd/S-no/P-no/H-yes	port and sherry, Fresh fruit &
	Russian and Spanish	beverages all complimentary
		Conference rooms, massage,
		golf, bicycles, tennis, private
		beach, day/sunset cruises

Come for a romantic getaway to Great Oak where the only honking comes from the geese, where the closest highway is the duck flyway, and where the only traffic you see from your room are the boaters sailing the water of the Chesapeake Bay Waterfront.
✉ innkeeper@greatoak.com ◑ www.greatoak.com

CHESTERTOWN

The Inn at Mitchell House
8796 Maryland Pky 21620
410-778-6500
Jim & Tracy Stone

100-250 BB
7 rooms, 7 pb
Most CC, *Rated*
C-yes/S-ltd/P-no/H-no

Full breakfast
Complimentary beverages
Sitting rooms, fireplaces,
private beach, business
traveler accommodations

Take a step back in time in this 18th-century manor house in a quiet, rural setting. It is located between Chestertown and Rock Hall. Enjoy gardens, ponds and the Chesapeake Bay, a mere½mile away. This is nature lovers' paradise.
✉ innkeeper@innatmitchellhouse.com ◑ www.innatmitchellhouse.com

COLUMBIA

The Inn at Peralynna Manor
10605 Rt 108 21044
877-737-2596 410-715-4600
Cynthia & David Lynn

225-1,200 BB
18 rooms, 18 pb
Most CC, *Rated*
C-ltd/S-no/P-ltd/H-yes

Made to Order Breakfast
Beer/wine, soft drinks,
coffee/tea with fresh baked
cookies, pies, cakes and
evening hors d'oeuvres
WiFi, library, exercise
equipment, pool table,
theater TV, hot tub, in-room
spa services available

Peralynna Manor is a regal, 14,000 square foot, European-styled Country Manor located in Columbia, Maryland. Short & long-term rates, corporate & military discounts available. Romantic Getaways are our specialty! Host your next special event with us!
✉ peralynna@aol.com ◑ www.Peralynna.com

DEALE

Creekside B&B
6036 Parkers Creek Dr 20751
301-261-9438
Betty-Carol Sellen & Marti Burt

100-125 BB
3 rooms, 1 pb
C-ltd/S-no/P-no/H-no
Spanish

Continental plus breakfast
Use of living room, library,
canoes, decks, garden, pool,
hot tub

Creekside B&B is located in a small community on the western shore of Chesapeake Bay, 20 miles south of Annapolis. It is tastefully furnished in a blend of old oak & contemporary furniture.
✉ bcsellen@juno.com

DEEP CREEK LAKE

Carmel Cove Inn
Glendale Rd 21550
301-387-0067
Mary Bender

175-195 BB
10 rooms, 10 pb
Visa, MC, Disc, •
C-ltd/S-ltd/P-no/H-yes
Some French & German

Full breakfast
Snacks, complimentary guest
beverage bar with wine,
beer, soda and water
Huge English great room
with billiards, bikes, tennis,
hot tubs, skiing, fireplaces,
dock, canoe

Former Monastery is Deep Creek Lake's premier country inn. Tranquil wooded setting. Canoe, fish, swim from our dock. Jacuzzis, fireplaces, breakfast room service.
✉ innkeeper@carmelcoveinn.com ◑ www.carmelcoveinn.com

EASTON

Bishop's House B&B
214 Goldsborough St 21601
800-223-7290 410-820-7290
Diane Laird-Ippolito & John
Ippolito

185-195 BB
5 rooms, 5 pb
Most CC, *Rated*, •
S-no/P-no/H-no
Feb – Dec

Full sumptuous breakfast
Complimentary coffee,
selection of teas, hot
chocolate, sodas and snacks
Sitting rooms, bicycles,
fireplaces, whirlpools, wrap
around porch & courtyard
with fish pond

Enjoy a memorable visit to MD's Eastern Shore. Romantically furnished, in-town, centrally located for visiting all points of interest. Victorian ambience with 21st century comfort featuring working fireplaces, whirlpool tubs, WiFi, & sumptuous breakfasts!
✉ bishopshouse@skipjack.bluecrab.org ◑ www.bishopshouse.com

ASTON

Inn at 202 Dover	375-475 BB	Gourmet breakfast
202 East Dover St 21601	5 rooms, 5 pb	Restaurant at the Inn, open
866-450-7600 410-819-8007	Most CC	for dinner Thursday through
Ron & Shelby Mitchell	C-ltd/S-no/P-ltd/H-no	Monday
		All suites have steam
		showers and jetted tubs.

Built in circa 1874 this majestic Maryland B&B has been carefully restored. The Inn is located one block from downtown Easton in the heart of the Easton Historic District. The total experience is luxury and comfort in an inviting atmosphere.
✉ info@innat202dover.com ✪ www.innat202dover.com/index.html

John S. McDaniel House	189-189 BB	Full Gourmet Breakfast
14 N Aurora St 21601	5 rooms, 5 pb	Please inform us of any food
877-822-5702 410-822-3704	Visa, MC, AmEx, •	allergies or preferences. Full
Mary Lou & Fran Karwacki	C-yes/S-no/P-no/H-no	Snack Center in Main Dining
		Room.
		Central A/C, TV/VCR, cable,
		ceiling fans, down comforters
		& pillows, library, sitting
		room, porch

Come experience the tranquil charm of this historic Easton home offering the best of the old and new. We are within walking distance of most of Easton's historical sites.
✉ jsmcdanielhouse@netscape.net ✪ www.bnblist.com/md/mcdaniel/

ELKTON

Elk Forge B&B	89-239 BB	Full breakfast
807 Elk Mills Rd 21921	12 rooms, 12 pb	Beer, Wine, Champagne and
877-ELK-FORGE 410-392-9007	Most CC, *Rated*, •	various drinks for sale.
Harry & LeAnn Lendeman	C-yes/S-ltd/P-yes/H-yes	Evening desserts
		Chipping and Putting Green,
		Reading and Video Library,
		Conference/Game Room,
		Outdoor Hot Tub

Nestled on five acres of beautiful woods and gardens along the Big Elk Creek. The area is rich in history and natural beauty and is just 3 miles from I-95, and minutes from Newark and Wilmington, Delaware. Philadelphia and Baltimore are only an hour away.
✉ reservations@elkforge.com ✪ www.elkforge.com

ELLICOTT CITY

The Wayside Inn	159-219 BB	Full breakfast
4344 Columbia Rd 21042	6 rooms, 6 pb	Afternoon refreshments
410-461-4636	Most CC, *Rated*, •	served daily from 5 – 6 p.m,
Susan & David Balderson	C-yes/S-no/P-no/H-no	by prior request.
		Cable TV/VCR/movies,
		phones with dataport,
		concierge service, library,
		Free WiFi

History awaits you at the Wayside Inn. Located in historic Ellicott City, Maryland near Baltimore or Washington, D.C., the Wayside Inn is the perfect place to escape to the past.
✉ bnbboy@verizon.net ✪ www.waysideinnmd.com

GAITHERSBURG

The Gaithersburg Inn	150 BB	Full breakfast
104 Russell Ave 20877	2 rooms, 2 pb	Afternoon tea available
800-771-0282 301-330-1331	Visa, MC	Mini-fridge, cable TV,
Terry & Chris Kirtz	C-ltd/S-no/P-no/H-ltd	Internet access, handicap
		access, gazebo, parlor,
		fireplace

The Gaithersburg Inn is a historic 1892 Victorian home located in the Walker-Brookes Historic District adjacent to Olde Towne Gaithersburg. The house has been restored with great care to preserve the character and charm of the time period.
✉ info@gaithersburginn.com ✪ www.gaithersburginn.com

GRANTSVILLE

The Stonebow Inn
146 Casselman Rd 21536
800-272-4090 301-895-4250
Julyen Norman & Cathy Paine

150-200 BB
9 rooms, 9 pb
Most CC, *Rated*, •
C-ltd/S-no/P-ltd/H-ltd

Full gourmet breakfast
Complimentary coffee, tea, bottled water
Steam/dry sauna, porches, rocking chairs, gas fireplace

Nestled on the banks of the Casselman River in the mountains of western Maryland. Hiking, biking, fishing, skiing, scenic railway, Fallingwater, Deep Creek Lake, all in eas reach.
✉ info@stonebowinn.com ❂ www.stonebowinn.com

HAVRE DE GRACE

Spencer Silver Mansion
200 S Union Ave 21078
800-780-1485 410-939-1485
Carol Nemeth

80-160 BB
5 rooms, 3 pb
Most CC, *Rated*, •
C-yes/S-no/P-yes/H-yes

Full breakfast
Fireplace, Jacuzzi, massage therapy, parlors, WiFi

Built in 1896, the Spencer-Silver Mansion offers the perfect lodging while visiting histori Havre de Grace and the upper Chesapeake Bay region.
✉ spencersilver@erols.com ❂ www.spencersilvermansion.com

Vandiver Inn
301 S Union St 21078
800-245-1655 410-939-5200
John Muldoon

119-159 BB
18 rooms, 18 pb
Most CC, •
C-yes/S-no/P-no/H-ltd

Full breakfast
2 rooms private porch & entrance, gazebo, large front porch, phones in room, wedding and events

1886 Victorian mansion surrounded by historic sites, antiquing, museums, marinas. Dinne served on Friday & Saturday evenings. 2 blocks from Chesapeake Bay. Families ar welcome and all major credit cards are accepted.
✉ vandiverinn@comcast.net ❂ www.vandiverinn.com

MCHENRY

Lake Pointe Inn
174 Lake Pointe Dr 21541
800-523-5253 301-387-0111
Caroline McNiece

232-292 BB
10 rooms, 10 pb
Visa, MC, Disc, •
C-ltd/S-no/P-no/H-no

Full breakfast
Evening hors d'oeuvres & snacks such as cookies, fresh fruit and popcorn.
Hot tub, bicycles, kayaks, canoes, community tennis court

The Lake Pointe Inn, the oldest house on Deep Creek Lake in Western Maryland, is perched just 13' from water's edge & is located across from the Wisp Ski & Golf Resort.
✉ relax@deepcreekinns.com ❂ www.deepcreekinns.com

MONKTON

Slade's Inn
15820 Old York Rd 21111
877-329-6101 410-329-6101
Nancy Wallis & Philip Tagliaferri

200-300 BB
10 rooms, 10 pb
Visa, MC, AmEx
C-ltd/S-ltd/P-ltd/H-yes

Full breakfast

An upscale historical Victorian home recently renovated on 29 acres located in northern Baltimore county. All rooms include private shower spas or Jacuzzi tubs, fireplaces, high speed Internet, and climate control heating and cooling systems.
✉ info@sladesinn.com ❂ www.sladesinn.com

OXFORD

Combsberry B&B
4837 Evergreen Rd. 21654
410-226-5353
Cathy Magrogan

250-395 BB
6 rooms, 6 pb
Visa, MC, AmEx
C-ltd/S-no/P-ltd/H-no

Full breakfast
Sun room, spacious living room, formal gardens, boat dock, canoes, water views

Escape to Combsberry, a gracious combination of restored 18th century splendor with touches of luxury designed for unsurpassed comfort and privacy.
✉ combsberry@yahoo.com ❂ www.combsberry.net

OXFORD

Oxford Inn
504 Morris St 21654
410-226-5220
Dan & Lisa Zimbelman

110-175 BB
7 rooms, 7 pb
Most CC
C-yes/S-no/P-no/H-no

Full breakfast on weekends
Continental breakfast during
the week. Pope's Tavern
Restaurant.

Maryland's Eastern Shore's quaint bed and breakfast, The Oxford Inn, is located at the head of Town Creek in Oxford's Historic District.
✉ info@oxfordinn.net ◐ www.oxfordinn.net/

**Sandaway – Waterfront
Lodging**
103 West Strand Rd 21654
888-726-3292
Ben Gibson

149-350 BB
18 rooms, 18 pb
Visa, MC, AmEx,
Rated, •
C-ltd/S-no/P-no/H-ltd
April to November

Lite Breakfast
24 Hour Coffee and Tea,
Located in the Sandaway
Sitting Room
Non-smoking inn, private
beach, waterfront lawn

Chesapeake Bay Romantic B&B featuring waterfront rooms with porches, million dollar views, a private beach, and great sunsets. Just 7 miles to St. Michaels when you take the car ferry!
✉ info@sandaway.com ◐ www.sandaway.com

PRINCESS ANNE

Somerset House B&B
30556 Washington St 21853
410-651-4451
Deborah & Jay Parker

160 BB
6 rooms, 6 pb
Most CC, •
C-yes/S-ltd/P-ltd/H-no

Full breakfast
Afternoon refreshments &
gourmet dinner packages
available
Bocce or croquet on the
bowling lawn, gardens,
fireplaces

Located in the Princess Anne Historic District on the Eastern Shore of Maryland. You will enjoy the elegant and historic home, the extensive gardens, and the luxury of your own large well-appointed room, with private bath.
✉ info@somersethousemd.com ◐ www.somersethousemd.com

RIDGE

Bard's Field
15671 Pratt Rd 20680
301-872-5989
James & Audrey Pratt

BB
S-no/P-no/H-no

Continental plus breakfast
Sitting room, library

Sorry, we are currently closed due to illness! Need to get away? The modest 18th century manor house, Bard's Field, built about 1798, is typical of Tidewater Architecture. Located on the beautiful Rawley Bay overlooking the Potomac River.
✉ ajpratt@verizon.net

ROCK HALL

Inn at Huntingfield Creek
4928 Eastern Neck Rd 21661
410-639-7779
Joanne Rich

139-249 BB
8 rooms, 8 pb
Visa, MC, AmEx
C-ltd/S-ltd/P-ltd/H-ltd

Full breakfast
Tea table, cookies and soda
available at all times,
complimentary wine and
beer
Swimming pool, waterfront
dock, conference room,
library, great room

Elegant & historic 70 acre farm-estate. Beautiful telescoping farmhouse architecture. Ideal for country weddings or retreats. Well-appointed, comfortable rooms with fine linens and excellent beds designed to pamper. 1,100' waterfront & dock.
✉ huntingfieldcreek@verizon.net ◐ www.huntingfield.com

ROCK HALL ─────────────────────────

The Inn at Osprey Point
20786 Rock Hall Ave 21661
410-639-2194
Terry Nelson

75-270 BB
15 rooms, 13 pb
Most CC
C-yes/S-no/P-no/H-no

Continental breakfast
Fine dining Restaurant open
Wed.- Sun. from 5 p.m.,
Sunday Brunch 10:30 to 2:00
Full water views, weddings &
events, marina, pool,
gourmet restaurant, bar,
volleyball & bicycles

A luxurious northern Chesapeake Bay adventure destination located on 25 lush acres of waterfront solitude in the village of Rock Hall. On water's edge & delightfully secluded, we offer a wonderful full service destination.
✉ innkeeper@ospreypoint.com ☾ www.ospreypoint.com

Old Gratitude House B&B
5944 Lawton Ave 21661
866-846-0724 410-639-7448
Sandy & Hank Mayer

160-230 BB
5 rooms, 5 pb
Most CC
C-ltd/S-no/P-no/H-no

Full breakfast
Decks, kayaks, bikes

Sandy and Hank have created a relaxing, comfortable and elegant Bed & Breakfast that takes full advantage of the soothing water's edge, while also offering access to a variety of activities that will keep you busy.
✉ oldgratitudehouse@verizon.net ☾ www.oldgratitudehouse.com

ROYAL OAK ─────────────────────────

Royal Oak House B&B
25881 Royal Oak Rd 21662
410-745-3025
Hugo & Carol Rizzoli

-269 BB
2 rooms, 2 pb
Visa, MC, AmEx
C-ltd/S-no/P-no/H-no

Full breakfast
Afternoon tea, inn dinners,
special occasion brunches,
packed lunches
Concierge Services—Your
stay at Royal Oak House is all
about you. Tell us how we
can help!

A romantic country house, serene and elegant, minutes from the bustle of the charming town of St. Michaels on the Chesapeake Bay. Bicycle scenic back roads, stroll to the water and antiques shops, then enjoy sunset.
✉ hugo@royaloakhouse.org ☾ www.royaloakhouse.org

SCOTLAND ─────────────────────────

St. Michael's Manor B&B
50200 St Michael's Manor Wy
20687
301-872-4025
Joe & Nancy Dick

70-90 BB
4 rooms
C-ltd/S-no/P-no
Polish, French
3/1 – 10/23

Full breakfast
Complimentary wine
Sitting room, bicycles,
swimming pool, paddle
boats, canoes

Historic Federal period dwelling on Long Neck Creek. Furnished with quilts, antiques, collectibles. 10 acres with 3-acre vineyard.
✉ stmichaelsman@olg.com ☾ www.stmichaels-manor.com

SHARPSBURG ─────────────────────────

Antietam Overlook Farm
800-878-4241 301-432-4200
Mark Svrcek & Philip Graham-Bell

175-240 BB
5 rooms, 5 pb
Most CC, *Rated*, •
S-no/P-no/H-ltd

Full breakfast
Complimentary wine, sodas,
coffee, tea & snacks
After dinner drinks, sitting
room, library, large front
porch

Award-winning & extraordinary. Secluded 95-acre mountaintop 19th century Country Manor Inn with a four state view at Antietam National Battlefield. Located near Harpers Ferry & Shepardstown.
✉ Reservations@antietamoverlook.com ☾ www.antietamoverlook.com

Solomons Victorian Inn, Solomons, MD

SHARPSBURG

The Inn at Antietam	120-185 BB	Full Breakfast·
220 E Main St 21782	5 rooms, 5 pb	Sitting room, piano, bicycles,
877-835-6011 301-432-6601	Visa, MC, AmEx,	library
Charles Van Metre & Robert	*Rated*, •	
LeBlanc	C-ltd/S-ltd/P-no/H-no	
	Closed January	

Lovely 1908 Victorian, fully restored and furnished in antiques, on Antietam Battlefield in Civil War historic area. Featuring five suites.
✉ innatantietam@juno.com ♦ www.innatantietam.com

SHERWOOD

Lowes Wharf Marina Inn	95-199 BB	Continental breakfast
21651 Lowes Wharf Rd 21665	10 rooms, 10 pb	Dinner available, snacks,
888-484-9267 410-745-6684	Visa, MC, Disc	restaurant
Paul & Tracey Zelinske	C-yes/S-ltd/P-ltd/H-yes	Bar service, suites, cable TV;
		marina, ship and tackle
		store, pump out station

Country waterfront Inn located on the Chesapeake Bay proper. Featuring 10 guestrooms, all with waterviews, private bath, A/C-heat, coffee service, wireless Internet, refrigerator and satellite TV. Marina. Beach access. Restaurant and Tiki Bar onsite.
✉ info@loweswharf.com ♦ www.loweswharf.com

SOLOMONS

Solomons Victorian Inn	100-240 BB	Full breakfast
125 Charles St 20688	8 rooms, 8 pb	Hot & cold drinks,
410-326-4811	Visa, MC, AmEx, *Rated*	homemade cookies
Helen & Richard Bauer	C-ltd/S-no/P-no/H-ltd	3 rooms with whirlpool tubs,
		spa services, library

Let the Chesapeake romance you at this charming Queen Anne Victorian. Convenient to Washington, Baltimore and Richmond. The Inn has eight queen and king sized rooms, most with views, all with private bath. Larger rooms have whirlpool tubs and fireplaces.
✉ info@solomonsvictorianinn.com ♦ www.solomonsvictorianinn.com

ST. MICHAELS

Aida's Victoriana Inn
205 Cherry St 21663
888-316-1282 410-745-3368
Aida Khalil

129-369 BB
7 rooms, 7 pb
Visa, MC, •
C-ltd/S-no/P-ltd/H-no
Arabic, Spanish, German

Full breakfast
Friday welcome hour: drinks
and hors d'oeuvres. Also
complimentary non-
alcoholic beverages and
snack
Garden, views, fireplaces,
Direct TV & DVD in sun
room and in some of the
bedrooms

Aida's Victoriana Inn is located on the historic St. Michaels harbor. Situated next to the Chesapeake Bay Maritime Museum, we are in walking distance to all attractions. The inn is just 2 blocks from the main street, yet removed from the bustle of town.
✉ info@victorianainn.com ○ www.victorianainn.com

Five Gables Inn & Spa
209 N Talbot St 21663
877-466-0100 410-745-0100
Barbara Eveland

150-425 BB
20 rooms, 20 pb
Visa, MC, AmEx
S-no/P-yes/H-ltd

Continental plus breakfast
Afternoon refreshments,
bottled water
Whirlpools, fireplaces,
indoor pool, steam
room/spa, Aveda bath
products, conference center,
events

Rooms feature gas fireplaces, porches & whirlpools with fluffy robes & Aveda amenities. Enjoy the heated indoor pool, steam room & sauna with massage therapy & facials by appointment.
✉ info@fivegables.com ○ www.fivegables.com

George Brooks House B&B
24500 Rolles Range Rd 21663
866-218-1384 410-745-0999
Will Workman

120-240 BB
6 rooms, 6 pb
Visa, MC, *Rated*, •
C-ltd/S-no/P-ltd/H-no
Russian

Full breakfast
Guest refrigerator stocked
with sodas and bottled water
Massage by appointment,
outdoor hot tub, 7-speed
bikes, swimming pool, DVD
movie library

Restored Gothic Revival Victorian home built in 1908 was designated an Historic Site by Talbot County in 2001. This important county landmark was among two homes selected in 2003 by the State of Maryland for its prestigious "Preservation Award."
✉ georgebrookshouse@verizon.net ○ www.georgebrookshouse.com

Hambleton Inn B&B
202 Cherry St 21663
866-745-3350 410-745-3350
Sherry Manning

175-265 BB
5 rooms, 5 pb
C-ltd/S-ltd/P-no/H-no

Full Gourmet
Complimentary sherry &
port
Porches, water views,
antiques, wireless, Internet,
free parking

Nestled in the harbor of the historic district of St. Michaels, MD, the Hambleton Inn is an elegant, historic shipbuilder's home from another era. Located right on the water in one of the great sailing capitals, the Hambleton Inn is a treasure of the bay.
✉ innkeeper@hambletoninn.com ○ www.hambletoninn.com

Harris Cove Cottages
8080 Bozman Neavitt Rd 21663
410-745-9701
De & Jim Hammontree

330-370 EP
8 rooms, 8 pb
Cash, Checks, *Rated*
C-yes/S-no/P-no/H-no

Waterfront cottages, views,
A/C, rental boats, lounges,
gazebos, family friendly

Harris Cove Cottages has eight cottages. Six of these cottages are individual which form an echelon of sailors saluting our picturesque private driveway. The other two sit majestically as a centerpiece on two acres of bulkheaded waterfront property.
✉ bednboatgetaway@aol.com ○ www.bednboat.com/index.php

ST. MICHAELS

The Old Brick Inn
401 S Talbot St 21663
800-434-2143 410-745-3323

160-450 BB	Full Homemade Breakfast
20 rooms, 20 pb	snacks, cookies, teas, coffee
Visa, MC, AmEx,	Sitting room, outdoor pool,
Rated, •	hot tub, cable TV, Wireless
C-ltd/S-no/P-no/H-ltd	Internet

Located in the heart of St. Michaels, The Old Brick Inn is an elegant, historic (circa 1816) Inn, with the European charm of a Boutique Hotel and the comfort and personalized service found in only the finest B&Bs.
✉ innkeepers@oldbrickinn.com ✆ www.saintmichaelsmdbedandbreakfast.com

Parsonage Inn
210 N Talbot (Rt 33) 21663
800-394-5519 410-745-5519
Char & Bill Wilhelm

110-215 BB	Full gourmet breakfast
8 rooms, 8 pb	Afternoon tea at 4 pm
Visa, MC, *Rated*, •	Parlor with books & menus,
C-ltd/S-no/P-ltd/H-yes	special order wine & cheese
	or flower arrangements

*Welcome to the Parsonage Inn Bed and Breakfast, a unique brick Victorian in this National Historic District. Within walking distance of the maritime museum, shops and restaurants. Awarded ** by AAA and recommended by Mobil Travel Guide.*
✉ parsinn@verizon.net ✆ www.parsonage-inn.com

Wades Point Inn on the Bay
10090 Wades Point Rd 21663
888-923-3466 410-745-2500
The Feiler Family

152-260 BB	Full breakfast
26 rooms, 26 pb	Balconies, air conditioning,
Visa, MC, *Rated*	some kitchenettes
C-yes/S-no/P-no/H-yes	
March 15-Dec 15	

Grand Georgian style home on edge of Chesapeake Bay. Two thousand feet of gently curving shoreline wrap the Inn's private grounds, giving spectacular views to its rooms. Weddings/special events.
✉ wadesinn@wadespoint.com ✆ www.wadespoint.com

SYKESVILLE

Inn at Norwood
7514 Norwood Ave 21784
410-549-7868
Kelly Crum

135-225 BB	Full breakfast
6 rooms, 6 pb	Tea, coffee, homemade
Visa, MC, AmEx, *Rated*	cookies, snacks, soft drinks,
C-ltd/S-no/P-ltd/H-no	water
	Sitting room, library, movies,
	Jacuzzi tubs, fireplaces

The Inn at Norwood is a romantic Bed & Breakfast. We have six spectacular guestrooms, all newly renovated & decorated to reflect Maryland's colorful seasons. It is the perfect escape. ✉ innatnorwood@comcast.net ✆ www.innatnorwood.com

TANEYTOWN

Antrim 1844 Inc
30 Trevanion Rd 21787
800-678-8946 410-756-6812
Dorothy & Richard Mollett

160-400 BB	Full breakfast
39 rooms, 39 pb	Afternoon tea, six course
Most CC, *Rated*	dinner, full service bar
C-ltd/S-ltd/P-no/H-yes	Tennis, pool, fireplaces,
	cable TV, croquet, wireless
	Internet, bar, gardens

Antrim 1844's luxurious rooms & suites, nationally acclaimed fine dining restaurant & award-winning wine list have earned the Inn a place in connoisseurs' hearts.
✉ info@antrim1844.com ✆ www.antrim1844.com

TILGHMAN ISLAND

Black Walnut Point Inn
Black Walnut Rd 21671
410-886-2452
Brenda & Tom Ward

120-250 BB	Continental plus breakfast
7 rooms, 7 pb	Porches, wildlife preserve,
Visa, MC, *Rated*	outdoor pool & hot tub,
C-ltd/S-ltd/P-no/H-yes	fishing, boating, hammocks,
	private cottage

Located on 57 acres of a wildlife preserve on the southern tip of Tilghman Island, this inn with expansive waterfront views is a sanctuary. Watch the sun rise over the Choptank River and set over Chesapeake Bay and leave the cares of the world behind.
✉ mward@intercom.net ✆ www.blackwalnutpoint.com

TILGHMAN ISLAND

Chesapeake Wood Duck Inn
21490 Gibson Town Rd 21671
800-956-2070 410-886-2070
Kimberly & Jeffrey Bushey

139-249 BB
7 rooms, 7 pb
Visa, MC, AmEx,
Rated, •
C-ltd/S-no/P-no/H-no

Full, 3 course, gourmet
breakfast
Four-course, prix fix dinner
Saturday evenings
Sitting rooms, fireplace,
sunroom, 3 porches,
kayaking, restaurants &
wireless high speed Internet

*Enjoy Chesapeake Bay lodging on Tilghman Island. This romantic B&B getaway brims
with historic charm & gracious hospitality. The Inn offers a pristine waterfront setting,
gourmet cuisine, and a choice of six guestrooms & one cottage suite. AAA –Mobil*
✉ inn@woodduckinn.com ◎ www.woodduckinn.com

**Lazyjack Inn on Dogwood
Harbor**
5907 Tilghman Island Rd 21671
800-690-5080 410-886-2215
Captain Mike & Carol Richards

166-289 BB
4 rooms, 4 pb
Visa, MC, *Rated*, •
C-ltd/S-ltd/P-no/H-no

Three-course sit-down
breakfast
Afternoon refreshments,
turndown & chocolate mints
Saturday Dinners as
scheduled
Library, fireplaces,
reservation service, water
views, Jacuzzi/fireplace
suites free wireless DSL,

*Occasionally, rarely, you discover a sublime hospitality experience that changes your
whole notion of a getaway destination. Set against the backdrop of a quaint fisherman's
harbor, the Inn is comfortably elegant and renown for sumptuous, organic fare.*
✉ mikerichards@verizon.net ◎ www.lazyjackinn.com

VIENNA

The Tavern House
111 Water St 21869
410-376-3347
Harvey & Elise Altergott

85-95 BB
3 rooms
Rated, •
C-ltd/S-yes/P-no/H-no
Spanish, German

Full breakfast, with
conversation
Afternoon tea and
refreshments
Sitting room and a patio
under huge pecan trees;
tennis courts and boat ramp

*A restored Colonial tavern on the Nanticoke River, overlooking the river and marshes
beyond. Simple elegance; stark white lime plaster, original colors, and detailed woodwork.*
✉ altergott@shorecable.com ◎ tavernhouse.com

WHITEHAVEN

Whitehaven Hotel
2685 Whitehaven Rd 21856
877-809-8296 410-873-2000
Cindy Curran

110-150 BB
7 rooms, 7 pb
Visa, MC
S-ltd/P-ltd/H-ltd

Full breakfast
2 rooms with fireplaces,
kayaks, gift shop, porches,
piano room

*The Whitehaven Hotel is nestled on the shore of the Wicomico River, about 25 minutes
outside Salisbury. One of the last of its kind, saved from the wrecking ball through cooper-
ative efforts in 1995. Screened porch, working fireplaces.*
✉ dotinwhitehaven@aol.com ◎ www.whitehavenhotel.com

Massachusetts

AMHERST

Allen House Inn
599 Main St 01002
413-253-5000
Alan Zieminski & Ann King

75-195 BB
7 rooms, 7 pb
Visa, MC, *Rated*
C-ltd/S-no/P-no/H-no

Full breakfast
Afternoon tea, evening refreshments
Sitting room, library, veranda, gardens, A/C, wireless Internet, concierge service

Authentic 1886 stick-style Victorian on 3 acres. Seven spacious bed chambers, private baths, personal phones with modems, ceiling fans and central air conditioning. AAA 3-Diamonds rating. Historic Preservation Award from the Amherst Historical Commission.
allenhouse@webtv.net ✆ www.allenhouse.com

AQUINNAH

Duck Inn
10 Duck Pond Lane 02535
508-645-9018
Elise LeBovit

115-250 BB
5 rooms, 5 pb
Visa, MC
C-yes/S-ltd/P-ltd/H-no

Full organic breakfast

Located in the small town of Aquinnah (formerly Gayhead), the Duck Inn of Martha's Vineyard rests on 10 acres of ocean-view greenery. The inn is a 5 bedroom farmhouse built 200 years ago by a Native American whaler.
gayheadrealty@hotmail.com ✆ www.gayheadrealty.com/DuckInnofMarthasVineyard.html

BARNSTABLE

Ashley Manor
3660 Main St 02630
888-535-2246 508-362-8044
Vince Toreno & Patricia Martin

135-235 BB
6 rooms, 6 pb
Most CC, *Rated*, •
C-ltd/S-no/P-no/H-no

Full gourmet breakfast
Complimentary brandy, port and hazelnut sherry
Sitting room, A/C, tennis, garden, imported bedside chocolates

1699 mansion in the historic district. 6 guestrooms & suites with fireplaces and Jacuzzis, all with private baths. Walking distance to beach, village & harbor.
stay@ashleymanor.net ✆ www.ashleymanor.net

Beechwood Inn
2839 Main St (Rt 6A) 02630
800-609-6618 508-362-6618
Ken & Debbie Traugot

135-199 BB
6 rooms, 6 pb
Most CC, *Rated*, •
C-ltd/S-no/P-no/H-no

Full gourmet breakfast
Afternoon snacks & beverages
Parlor, veranda, garden, all rooms have A/C, WiFi, TV/VCR

Award winning romantic Victorian Inn along the historic "Old King's Highway." Six spacious guestrooms furnished with elegant antiques, some with fireplaces or views of Cape Cod Bay. Top rated by AAA and Mobil travel guides.
info@beechwoodinn.com ✆ www.beechwoodinn.com

Cape Cod's The Lamb and Lion Inn
2504 Main St (Route 6A) 02630
800-909-6923 508-362-6823
Alice Pitcher & Tom Dott

145-275 BB
10 rooms, 10 pb
Visa, MC, *Rated*, •
C-ltd/S-ltd/P-yes/H-no

Gourmet Continental Breakfast
All kinds of surprises—our breakfasts are some of the best on Cape Cod!
Heated pool, outdoor Jacuzzi, 11 fireplaces, sitting room, wireless Internet, lots of guest privacy!

An award-winning 1740's Inn on 4 acres in the historic district. 10 suites, 11 fireplaces, full-sized pool and year-round outdoor hot tub spa. Guest privacy is paramount! Voted "Best Mid-Cape B&B/Inn" Cape Cod Life Magazine, 2007-GOLD, 2008-SILVER
info@lambandlion.com ✆ www.lambandlion.com

BARNSTABLE

Honeysuckle Hill B&B	139-259 BB	4 Course Gourmet Breakfast
591 Rt 6A 02668	5 rooms, 4 pb	Chocolates, sherry, wines,
866-444-5522 508-362-8418	Visa, MC, AmEx, *Rated*	liqueurs, sodas, snacks, all
Freddy & Ruth Riley	C-ltd/S-no/P-no/H-ltd	day coffee & tea
	Portugese	A/C, screened porch, hot
		tub, near beaches, fresh
		flowers, concierge services,
		WiFi

Voted Best Mid-Cape B&B 2008. Gourmet breakfasts, close to beaches, island ferries and all Cape Cod attractions. Lovely English gardens with hot tub/spa. Enjoy WiFI, guest bicycles, gazebo, relaxing screened porch and many other 5 Star amenities.
✉ stay@honeysucklehill.com 🌐 www.honeysucklehill.com

BASS RIVER

Captain Isaiah's House	55-90 BB	Continental plus breakfast
33 Pleasant St 02664	6 rooms, 2 pb	Homebaked goodies
508-394-1739	Most CC, *Rated*	Sitting room, fireplaces, 2
Marge & Alden Fallows	C-ltd/S-no/P-no/H-no	studio apartments, whale
	mid June-mid Sept	watching nearby

Charming, restored old sea captain's house in historic Bass River area. Most rooms have fireplaces.
✉ info@captainisaiahs.com 🌐 www.captainisaiahs.com

BOSTON

198 Clarendon Square Inn	135-495 BB	Expanded Continental
198 W Brookline St 02118	3 rooms, 3 pb	Breakfast
617-536-2229	Most CC, *Rated*	Roof deck hot tub, grand
Stephen Gross	C-ltd/S-no/P-no/H-no	parlor and library, fireplaces,
	French, Portuguese	DVD, Internet access.

Internationally known for offering personal attention in a relaxed and sophisticated environment. Offering a unique and historic experience in Boston's center, you will enjoy Clarendon Square's style, history, and amenities with access to Boston's finest.
✉ stay@clarendonsquare.com 🌐 www.clarendonsquare.com

463 Beacon Street Guest House	79-169 EP	Complimentary coffee & tea
463 Beacon St 02115	20 rooms, 17 pb	in our lobby
617-536-1302	Visa, MC, Disc, •	Kitchenettes w/microwave &
	C-ltd/S-no/P-no/H-no	small refrigerator, cable TV,
		Direct-dial phones w/free
		local calls, A/C

We offer modestly priced accommodations in a warm, quite residential setting, minutes away from the heart of Boston.
✉ info@463beacon.com 🌐 www.463beacon.com

Abigayle's Bed and Breakfast	90-155 BB	Continental plus breakfast
Bay State Rd at Deerfield 02457	5 rooms, 5 pb	TV, private phones, desks,
888-486-6019 617-720-0522	Visa, MC, Disc, •	A/C
Marie Kemmler	C-yes/S-no/P-no/H-no	
	Chinese	

Elegant Victorian Boston 1896 Brownstone set on a quiet, tree-lined street. Near public transportation, restaurants and shops.
✉ info@bnbboston.com 🌐 www.bnbboston.com/boston-bnbs/b&bs_4c.htm

Adams B&B	119-179 BB	Continental breakfast
14 Edgerly Rd 02115	14 rooms, 10 pb	TV, living room, deck,
800-230-0105 617-536-4181	Visa, MC, AmEx	fireplace
Joe Haley	C-yes/S-no/P-no/H-no	

Like many of the finer hotels in Boston, we are centrally located in the Back Bay. We are an easy five minute walk to the Prudential/Hynes Convention Centers and the Back Bay/Fenway areas—yet unlike the finer Boston hotels, our rates are greatly less.
✉ info@adamsboston.com 🌐 www.adamsboston.com

BOSTON

Beacon Hill B&B

27 Brimmer St 02108	200-275 BB	Home-Cooked
617-523-7376	2 rooms, 2 pb	Vegetarian breakfast.
Susan Butterworth	*Rated*, •	Restaurants and
	C-yes/S-no/P-no/H-no	convenience stores one
	French	block away
		Garage nearby, elevator for
		luggage, A/C, flexible arrival
		time but must be confirmed.
		Leave luggage

Superb location in most exclusive, historically preserved downtown neighborhood. Private home in elegant 1869 Victorian townhouse overlooking river. Spacious rooms, private baths, homecooked breakfast. Price varies seasonally. ✉ bhillbb@gmail.com

Beacon Hill Hotel & Bistro

25 Charles St 02114	245-405 BB	Full breakfast
888-959-2442 617-723-7575	13 rooms, 13 pb	Breakfast, lunch and dinner
Peter Rait	Most CC	all available in the Bistro.
	C-ltd/S-no/P-no/H-yes	(Breakfast is included with
		room.)
		Plantation shutters, pedestal
		sinks, black & white
		photography, TFT DirecTV
		(movie channels), WiFi

The privileged location of The Beacon Hill Hotel makes it the perfect choice for travelers — business or leisure — who would like to make the gas-lit streets and brick sidewalks of Beacon Hill their own, without giving up the comforts they expect.
✉ stay@beaconhillhotel.com ○ www.beaconhillhotel.com

Bunker Hill B&B

80 Elm St 02129	135-180 BB	Full breakfast made to order
617-241-8067	2 rooms, 2 pb	Snacks & beverages at no
Christiane Wolff	Visa, MC	cost
	C-ltd/S-ltd/P-ltd/H-no	Library/video collection,
	German, some French	hairdryers, toiletries,
		bathrobes & slippers,
		laundry facilities, Internet

Quiet hideaway in downtown location just off the Freedom Trail, where the history of Boston began. 1885 Victorian, renovated in 2000. Antique decor with 21st century amenities. Your home away from home.
✉ crawolff@cs.com ○ www.bunkerhillbedandbreakfast.com

The Charles Street Inn

94 Charles St 02114	250-550 BB	European Deluxe
877-772-8900 617-314-8900	9 rooms, 9 pb	Continental
Sally Deane & Louise Venden	Most CC, *Rated*, •	Crackers, juice, bottled
	C-yes/S-no/P-yes/H-yes	water, Ferro Rocher
	German; Japanese	chocolates, fresh fruit
		CD/DVD/VCR library, in-
		room whirlpool tub,
		fireplace, fridge, cable TV,
		DSL & wireless Internet

Awards galore, loyal repeat guests, friendly personal attention. Unique amenities like marble fireplaces, antique furniture, private baths with Whirlpool tubs, and breakfast in bed. Watch our video and do 360 degree tour of all nine rooms on our web site.
✉ info@charlesstreetinn.com ○ www.CharlesStreetInn.com

The College Club

44 Commonwealth Ave 02116	105-275 BB	Continental breakfast
617-536-9510	11 rooms, 6 pb	Coffee and tea available all
Edith Toth, Gen. Mgr.	Visa, MC, *Rated*	day, snacks
	C-yes/S-no/P-no/H-ltd	Accommodations for
	Hungarian	business travelers

Our Victorian townhouse offers old-world charm & modern convenience. Recently redesigned rooms and decorated with antiques, listed on the National Register of Historic Places. The ideal launching point for your Boston Adventures!
✉ cclub.boston@verizon.net ○ www.thecollegeclubofboston.com

BOSTON

East Boston B&B
14 Crestway Rd. 02128
617-818-2800
Don & Joyce Mills

99-229 BB
4 rooms, 4 pb
Visa, MC, AmEx
C-yes/S-no/P-yes/H-ltd
French, German, Italian

Old Fashion breakfast
Dinner made to order. Fruit
& Veggies. Mills Coffee/Tea's
are made from our family
business.
Pick up!!! To and From Logan
Airport upon request.
Laundry service. Justice of
Peace on call.

Quiet Area for a good nights Old fashion home cooked breakfast made to order, 5 minutes from beach, downtown Boston. One minute from Logan Airport we provide pick up to and from Logan Airport as an extra feature for our guests.
✉ eastbostonbandb@aol.com

The Gryphon House
9 Bay State Rd 02215
877-375-9003 617-375-9003
Teresa Blagg

189-365 BB
8 rooms, 8 pb
Most CC, •
C-ltd/S-no/P-no/H-no

Continental plus breakfast
Fruit is always available in
the lobby, tea & coffee in
room
DVD library, iMac in lobby,
satellite TV, WiFi

The Gryphon House is located adjacent to Boston University, between Back Bay and Kenmore Square, near two major art museums and the home of the Boston Red Sox! We offer beautiful accommodations and gracious hospitality in a luxurious, historic brownstone.
✉ innkeeper@innboston.com ○ www.innboston.com

La Cappella Suites
290 North St 02113
888-523-9020 617-523-9020
Tricia Muse

95-215 BB
3 rooms, 3 pb
Visa, MC, AmEx
C-yes/S-no/P-no/H-no

Continental breakfast
Room rates include a
modest, complimentary, self-
serve Continental breakfast
in the individual suite
Cable TV and VCR,
complimentary local phone
service, wireless broadband
Internet access, balcony

Our Inn is located in historic Little Italy, steps from downtown shopping and historic sites, Quincy Market, TD Banknorth Garden, the Aquarium and restaurants. We offer value and convenience in an elegant setting. Great for tourists and business travelers
✉ TriciaMuse@aol.com ○ www.LaCappellaSuites.com

Oasis Guest House
22 Edgerly Rd 02115
800-230-0105 617-267-2262
Joe Haley

79-159 BB
30 rooms, 20 pb
Visa, MC, AmEx,
Rated, •
C-ltd/S-ltd/P-no/H-no

Continental breakfast
Complimentary coffee, juice,
fruit, and pastries available
every morning
Concierge, sitting room, fax
capabilities, hairdryers,
iron/board, TV, high speed
Internet

Two townhouses on a quiet residential street in the heart of Boston. Telephone, TV, central air, outdoor decks, parking, free wireless Internet.
✉ info@oasisgh.com ○ www.oasisgh.com

Taylor House
50 Burroughs St 02130
888-228-2956 617-983-9334
Dave Elliott & Daryl Bichel

129-245 BB
3 rooms, 3 pb
Most CC, *Rated*
C-ltd/S-no/P-ltd/H-no

Continental plus breakfast
Snacks, sodas, coffee station
TV/VCR in room, tape
library, common room,
wireless Internet, phones

Italianate Victorian home with spacious rooms, high ceilings, private baths, near public transportation, restaurants & shopping.
✉ Dave@taylorhouse.com ○ www.taylorhouse.com

BOSTON

The Victorian House
707 Bennington St 02128
617-818-2800
Don & Joyce Mills

99-225 BB
8 rooms, 4 pb
Visa, MC, AmEx
C-yes/S-no/P-yes/H-ltd
French, German

Old Fashion Home Made
Meals
Justice Of The Peace
available Murder Mystery
Guest weekends include
Murder Mystery and Dinner
Pick up to and from Logan
Airport upon request.
laundry service.

Victorian House is located 2 min. from Logan Airport, walking distance to Constitution Beach, restaurants & 5 min. to downtown Boston. Offers full breakfast daily, a mini-gym & common room. Features a honeymoon suite & all the charm of the Victorian era.
✉ eastbostonbandb@aol.com

BREWSTER

Brewster by the Sea
716 Main St 02631
800-892-3910 508-896-3910
Donna & Byron Cain

150-325 BB
8 rooms, 8 pb
Most CC, *Rated*, •
C-ltd/S-no/P-no/H-no

Full gourmet breakfast
Afternoon tea & cookies
Outdoor pool, whirlpool
tubs, outdoor Jacuzzi, A/C,
cable TV, HBO, phones

This beautiful, award-winning Inn offers the discriminating traveler exceptional hospitality, impeccable accommodations, abundant amenities & extraordinary attention to detail. A romantic, country inn.
✉ info@BrewsterByTheSea.com ❍ www.BrewsterByTheSea.com

Captain Freeman Inn
15 Breakwater Rd 02631
800-843-4664 508-896-7481
Donna & Peter Amadeo

155-235 BB
12 rooms, 12 pb
Visa, MC, *Rated*, •
C-ltd/S-no/P-no/H-no

Full breakfast
Afternoon tea, al fresco
dining
Sitting room, Jacuzzi,
bicycles, badminton, A/C,
swimming pool, croquet

Lovingly restored Victorian mansion. Queen canopy beds, romantic wraparound porch, fireplaces and whirlpool spas. Full breakfast, afternoon tea. In-ground pool, walk to beautiful Breakwater Beach.
✉ stay@captainfreemaninn.com ❍ www.captainfreemaninn.com

Isaiah Clark House
1187 Main St 02631
800-822-4001 508-896-2223
Philomena & Steve

145-195 BB
7 rooms, 7 pb
Visa, MC, AmEx, *Rated*
C-ltd/S-no/P-no/H-ltd
April 21-November 10

Full breakfast
Special diets, food allergies
Central Air Conditioning, 3
rooms with fireplaces, cable
TV, high speed WiFi. Queen
and King beds.

Experience the history and romance of old Cape Cod in Brewster, MA. A marvelous example of Colonial architecture circa 1785, the Isaiah Clark House is centrally located for easy access to area attractions. One of the few Historic Inns with Central A/C!
✉ innkeeper@isaiahclark.com ❍ www.isaiahclark.com

Old Sea Pines Inn
2553 Main St 02631
508-896-6114
Stephen & Michele Rowan

85-185 BB
24 rooms, 19 pb
Most CC, *Rated*, •
C-yes/S-no/P-no/H-yes
Italian, German
April-Dec. 22

Full breakfast
Complimentary beverage on
arrival, restaurant
Parlor with fireplace, deck,
Sunday dinner theatre
(summers only)

Early 1900s restored boarding school for young ladies located on Brewer Estate. One of the finest Inns on the New England seacoast, it comes complete with a spacious living room, completely restored formal dining room, and outdoor dining deck.
✉ info@oldseapinesinn.com ❍ www.oldseapinesinn.com

BRIMFIELD

Yankee Cricket B&B
106 Five Bridge Rd 01010-9703
413-245-0030
Bill & Sherry Simonic

110-150 BB
5 rooms, 1 pb
Most CC
C-yes/S-no/P-no/H-no

Full breakfast
Queen size & twin beds,
private & shared baths,
private entrance, sitting
room, dining room & deck

On a stone ridge overlooking the countryside, Yankee Cricket B&B offers guests a quiet woodlands retreat. Guests are warmly welcomed & offered the amenities of a new home with the coziness of an authentic 18th century inn.
✉ wsimonic@charter.net ✪ www.yankeecricket.com

BROOKLINE

Anthony's Town House
1085 Beacon St 02446
617-566-3972
Barbara & Viola Anthony

75-118 EP
14 rooms
Rated, ●
C-yes/S-no/P-no/H-no

Restaurant, stores nearby
Near major league sports,
historical sites, sitting room,
cable TV, A/C, WiFi

Turn-of-the-century restored Brownstone townhouse with spacious rooms in a Victorian atmosphere; family-operated for over 60 years. Subway at our doorstep, 10 minutes to downtown Boston. Listed on the National Register of Historic Places.
✉ info@anthonystownhouse.com ✪ www.anthonystownhouse.com

Beacon Inn
1087 & 1750 Beacon St 02446
888-575-0088 617-566-0088
Carmen Favuzza

79-229 BB
25 rooms, 25 pb
Most CC, *Rated*, ●
C-yes/S-no/P-no/H-no

Continental breakfast
All rooms include Internet,
A/C, telephone, and cable
TV.

The Beacon Inn, located in the Greater Boston area, consists of charming and inviting rooms at affordable rates.
✉ info@beaconinn.com ✪ www.beaconinn.com

The Beech Tree Inn
83 Longwood Ave 02446
800-544-9660 617-277-1620
Stacy Kaufman

119-179 BB
10 rooms, 8 pb
Visa, MC, AmEx
C-yes/S-no/P-yes/H-no
Japanese

Continental plus breakfast
Coffee, tea & cookies in the
afternoon
TV/VCR, A/C, hairdryers,
video library, dial-up &
wireless Internet

The Beech Tree Inn B&B, of Brookline, MA, once a Victorian-style private home, offers warmth and gracious hospitality at affordable prices. Its charming and casual bed and breakfast setting invites the busiest city slicker to come in and relax.
✉ info@thebeechtreeinn.com ✪ www.thebeechtreeinn.com

The Bertram Inn
92 Sewall Ave 02446
800-295-3822 617-566-2234
Astrid, Kristen, Luis, Stephen
& Courtney

109-329 BB
14 rooms, 14 pb
Most CC, *Rated*, ●
C-ltd/S-no/P-yes/H-no
Spanish, Italian

Full breakfast
Complimentary, cakes,
cookies, cheese and
crackers, snacks, coffee &
teas offered 24/7
Iron & board, WiFi Internet,
fax, TV with digital cable,
hairdryers in all rooms, A/C,
fireplaces

The Bertram Inn boasts classic Tudor detailing in the historic setting of Brookline, MA, within walking distance of shops, museums, restaurants, colleges, hospitals and public recreation. Enjoy all Boston has to offer, just minutes away.
✉ innkeeper@bertraminn.com ✪ www.bertraminn.com

BROOKLINE

Coolidge Corner Guest House	79-179 BB	Continental breakfast
17-19 Littell Rd 02146	9 rooms, 5 pb	Afternoon tea and snacks are
617-734-4041	Most CC	served and a kitchenette is
Shawn LaCount & Terri	C-yes/S-ltd/P-no/H-ltd	provided for guest use
Deletetsky		Cable TV, tennis courts, WiFi
		Internet, laundry, onsite
		parking, gardens, private
		bath, central ac

Welcome to the Coolidge Corner Guest House: "Bed and Bagel!" Our beautiful Victorian home, located just 10 minutes from downtown Boston, is a fresh and affordable alternative to typical inns, hotels and budget motels.
✉ info@bedandbagel.com ◐ www.bedandbagel.com

The Samuel Sewall Inn	109-349 BB	Full Breakfast Buffet
143 St Paul St 02446	14 rooms, 14 pb	Complimentary cakes,
888-713-2566 617-713-0123	Most CC, *Rated*, •	cookies, cheese & crackers,
Astrid, Kristen, Stephen	C-yes/S-no/P-no/H-yes	snacks, coffee & tea offered
	French, Spanish, Italian,	24/7
	Portuguese	Living room, patio, porch, fax
		available, wireless Internet,
		turndown service, concierge

Built in 1886 as a private residence, The Samuel Sewall Inn boasts beautiful Victorian accommodations in a restored Queen-Anne home, with luxurious amenities, friendly service, and modern conveniences. Just one block away from public transportation.
✉ innkeeper@samuelsewallinn.com ◐ www.samuelsewallinn.com

CAMBRIDGE

A B&B in Cambridge	85-325 BB	Crepes, waffles or pancakes,
1657 Cambridge St 02138	3 rooms	fruit
800-795-7122 617-868-7082	Visa, MC, AmEx,	Afternoon tea, snacks.
Doane Perry	*Rated*, •	Small library with antique
	C-ltd/S-no/P-no/H-no	rocker, nearby pool, cable
	French, German, Greek,	TV, Wifi, concierge [shop,
	Swahili	housing], voicemail

1897 Colonial Revival home, close to Harvard Square, affordable elegance near museums, theaters, restaurants. Fresh flowers, antiques, great beds. Crepes or pancakes, homemade bread and jam and afternoon tea. Wifi, voicemail, cable TV. Concierge service.
✉ DoanePerry@yahoo.com ◐ www.cambridgebnb.com

A Room at the Top	85-115 BB	Continental breakfast
51 Avon Hill St 02140	1 rooms	Milk, juice, coffee, tea
617-547-6136	Cash, Checks	We accept Pay Pal.
Joan Friebely	C-ltd/S-no/P-no/H-no	
	French	

The beauty of outdoors meets the comfort of the indoors in the 16'×25' space with windows all across the front, large skylights in the cathedral ceiling, and French doors to a private balcony in the trees. Separate entrance from the main house.
✉ jfriebely@rics.bwh.harvard.edu

Irving House at Harvard	95-375 BB	Continental plus breakfast
24 Irving St 02138	44 rooms, 29 pb	Afternoon tea with fruit,
877-547-4600 617-547-4600	Most CC, •	cookies, savory treats
Rachael Solem	C-yes/S-no/P-ltd/H-no	Sitting room, library, cribs,
	French, Spanish,	central A/C, fax, laundry,
	Russian, Bulgarian	conference room

Since 1945 Irving House has had affordable rates and the best proximity to Harvard Square. It's a large guesthouse that feels like home. Our staff is always ready to help you find your way around town, recommend a restaurant or call a taxi.
✉ reserve@irvinghouse.com ◐ www.irvinghouse.com

CAMBRIDGE

Isaac Harding House
288 Harvard St 02139
877-489-2888 617-876-2888
Lauren Summers

85-375 BB ·
14 rooms, 14 pb
Most CC, *Rated*
C-yes/S-no/P-no/H-yes
Bulgarian, Creole, Hindi,
Nepali

Hearty continental breakfast
Coffee, tea, cookies, goodies,
Thurs. wine, cheese
Free DSL access, free
parking, TV, phone, hair-
dryer, fax, museum passes

We are a beautiful restored and decorated Victorian house, with a spectacular rug collection, curious artifacts and original art. We are located in a safe residential neighborhood.
✉ reserve@harding-house.com ○ www.cambridgeinns.com/harding/

Parkside on Ellery
74 Elllery St 02138
617-492-5025
David

135-230 BB
3 rooms, 3 pb
Most CC
C-ltd/S-no/P-no/H-no

Continental breakfast
Internet access, cable TV,
clock radio, A/C, telephone
with voicemail, hair dryer,
iron

Excellent accommodations for the seasoned or casual traveler offer cleanliness, convenience and comfort. Steps from Harvard Square, minutes from Boston. Private entrances, baths, views, with arranged parking and all the requisite amenities.
✉ info@parksidebb.com ○ www.parksidebb.com

Prospect Place B&B
112 Prospect St 02139
800-769-5303 617-864-7500
Eric Huenneke

100-175 BB
4 rooms, 2 pb
Visa, MC
C-ltd/S-no/P-no/H-no

Full breakfast
Afternoon tea
Sitting room, business
traveler accommodations,
wireless Internet access

Nineteenth century charm at its best, with terrific & discreet modern updates. Gourmet quality full breakfast served on fine china & linens.
✉ info@prospectpl.com ○ www.prospectpl.com

CHATHAM

Captain's House Inn
369-377 Old Harbor Rd 02633
800-315-0728 508-945-0127
Jill & James Meyer

185-475 BB
16 rooms, 16 pb
Most CC, *Rated*, •
C-ltd/S-no/P-no/H-no

Full gourmet breakfast
Complimentary afternoon
cream tea, evening cookies,
morning coffee/tea service
Sitting room, bikes, lawn croquet, 3 new suites with fireplaces, concierge, laundry

Considered by many respected lodging critics as perhaps Cape Cod's finest inn, this Four Diamond sea captain's estate is the perfect choice for a romantic getaway or peaceful retreat. ✉ info@captainshouseinn.com ○ www.captainshouseinn.com

---

Carriage House Inn
407 Old Harbor Rd 02633
800-355-8868 508-945-4688
Paula & Tim Miller

129-269 BB
6 rooms, 6 pb
Visa, MC, *Rated*
C-ltd/S-no/P-no/H-no

Full breakfast
Snacks, guest fridge stocked
with cold beverages,
afternoon cookies
A/C, fireplaces, TVs,
DVD/CD players, coffee-
makers, hairdryers, Internet,
in room massage & facials

Welcome to the Carriage House Inn, a romantic, year-round B&B offering gracious hospitality and 6 beautifully appointed rooms in an ideal location. Spa packages available.
✉ info@thecarriagehouseinn.com ○ www.thecarriagehouseinn.com

**The Cranberry Inn of
Chatham**
359 Main St 02633
800-332-4667 508-945-9232
Kay & Bill DeFord

120-330 BB
18 rooms, 18 pb
Most CC, *Rated*
C-ltd/S-no/P-no/H-no

Full country breakfast
Afternoon tea
Hair dryers, telephone, cable
TV, air conditioning, WiFi, fire-
places, wet bars, mini-fridges

On the quiet outskirts of Chatham Village, The Cranberry Inn offers a memorable getaway in every season. Its stately presence on Main Street compliments neighboring cottages and shore homes. Lush gardens and a wide verandah make it all more inviting.
✉ info@cranberryinn.com ○ www.cranberryinn.com

CHATHAM

Old Harbor Inn
22 Old Harbor Rd 02633
800-942-4434 508-945-4434
Judy & Ray Braz

149-319 BB
8 rooms, 8 pb
Visa, MC, *Rated*, •
C-ltd/S-no/P-no/H-no

Full breakfast
Restaurants nearby, complimentary coffee and tea service, soft drinks & water also complimentary. Sitting room with fireplace, sun room, deck, A/C, Jacuzzi, wireless Internet access, fitness room

English country decor. King or queen beds. Full breakfast. Walk to seaside village attractions. The Old Harbor Inn is a Select Registry, Distinguished Inns of North America property. A highly-rated, award-winning Inn.
✉ info@chathamoldharborinn.com ◯ www.chathamoldharborinn.com

CHESTERFIELD

1886 House
202 East St 01012
800-893-2425+44 413-296-0223
Joe & Carol Lingg

95-130 BB
3 rooms, 2 pb
Visa, MC, Disc, •
C-yes/S-no/P-ltd/H-no
Spanish, Italian

Full breakfast
Complimentary tea and coffee, and nearby restaurants
Sitting room, library, robes, fireplaces, cable TV, central air conditioning , enclosed porch, WiFi

An authentic New England country farmhouse on 5 acres, in historic Chesterfield just off scenic routes 9 & 143. Cozy, intimate B&B. Beautiful fall colors; many outdoor activities to enjoy. Just 12 miles from Northampton & 8 miles from Look Park.
✉ innkeepers@1886house.com ◯ www.1886house.com

CONCORD

Colonel Roger Brown House
1694 Main St 01742
800-292-1369 978-369-9119
Mrs. Lauri Berlied

110-200 BB
5 rooms, 5 pb
Visa, MC, AmEx, •
C-ltd/S-no/P-ltd/H-no

Continental plus breakfast
Snacks, beverages
Desks with DSL Internet connections, voicemail, indiv. climate control, kitchenettes

Built in 1775, the house retains the architectural charm of hand-hewn beams and wainscot paneling with modern features such as high-speed DSL & cable TV. All of the suites are newly decorated with a mix of period, reproduction & contemporary furnishings.
✉ InnkeeperCRBH@aol.com ◯ www.colrogerbrown.com

Hawthorne Inn
462 Lexington Rd 01742
978-369-5610
Marilyn Mudry & Gregory Burch

115-315 BB
7 rooms, 7 pb
Most CC, *Rated*, •
C-yes/S-ltd/P-no/H-no

Continental plus breakfast
Welcome tray at check-in & evening tea, special wine-tray upgrade available
WiFi, DVD, telephone, bathrobes, hair dryer, iron, clock-radio, abundant toiletries

An intimate New England B & B, where history, literature & artistic whimsy intertwine, just 19 miles from Boston. The Hawthorne Inn is located close to the homes of Hawthorne, Alcott, Emerson, Thoreau's Walden Pond & Old North Bridge.
✉ inn@concordmass.com ◯ www.concordmass.com

North Bridge Inn
21 Monument St 01742
888-530-0007 978-371-0014
Heidi Senkler Godbout

165-250 BB
6 rooms, 6 pb
Visa, MC, AmEx
C-yes/S-ltd/P-yes/H-no

Full breakfast
Suites, kitchens, cable TV, wireless DSL, business accommodations

European-style B&B located in the heart of historic Concord, MA. Each of the Inn's 6 suites is newly renovated and redecorated in its own distinct style.
✉ info@northbridgeinn.com ◯ www.northbridgeinn.com

CUMMAQUID

Acworth Inn
4352 Old King's Hwy 02637
800-362-6363 508-362-3330
Lisa Callahan

105-229 BB
5 rooms, 5 pb
Visa, MC, AmEx,
Rated, •
C-ltd/S-no/P-no/H-no
German

Full breakfast
Tea & coffee all day,
specialty chocolates, most
rooms have refrigerators
Wireless Internet, robes,
concierge services, beach
towels/chairs, books/games,
on site Spa services

Cape Cod 19th century charm in the center of the historic district; especially noted for the hand painted furnishings; easy access to islands. Listed on the National Historic Register. Five romantic rooms, each with private bath and queen size beds.
✉ acworthinn@acworthinn.com ❂ www.acworthinn.com

DENNIS

Scargo Manor B&B
909 Main St, Rt 6A 02638
800-595-0034 508-385-5534
Debbie & Larry Bain

105-250 BB
6 rooms, 6 pb
Visa, MC, Disc
C-yes/S-no/P-no/H-no

gourmet breakfast
Restaurant next door and a 5
minute walk to fine dining.
Sitting room, library, bikes,
suites, fireplaces, cable TV,
lakefront, boats, WiFi

Elegant, comfortable lodging on Scargo Lake in historic restored sea captain's home. Directly on Scargo lake. Docks, small boats, bikes. Delectable full breakfast.
✉ info@scargomanor.com ❂ www.scargomanor.com

DENNISPORT

'By The Sea' Guests Bed & Breakfast and Suites
57 Chase Avenue & Inman
Road Extension 02639
800-447-9202 508-398-8685
Helen Kossifos

120-405 BB
17 rooms, 17 pb
Most CC, *Rated*, •
C-yes/S-no/P-no/H-ltd
Greek, German,
Portuguese, French
April 27- December 30

Full breakfast
Coffee, tea, homemade
treats, fresh fruit, Poland
Springs Water
HBO/cable TV, free high
speed Internet connections,
private beach, fully air
conditioned

Oceanfront B&B, AAA 3 Diamond property. Breakfast served overlooking private beach. Quaint villages, lighthouses, antique shops, museums, bicycle paths & golf courses all nearby.
✉ info@bytheseaguests.com ❂ www.bytheseaguests.com

An English Garden B&B
32 Inman Rd 02639
888-788-1908 508-398-2915
Anita Sangiolo

80-165 BB
11 rooms, 11 pb
Visa, MC, Disc, *Rated*,
•
C-ltd/S-no/P-no/H-yes
End of April-Oct.

Full breakfast included
Two living rooms, balconies
in every room, cable TV,
individual AC/Heat, free
guest computer & WiFi

Beautiful rooms & luxury suites with private baths, some with ocean views, 150 yards from sandy beach. Ocean temperature in summer—72 degrees! AAA triple Diamond rated, Yankee Magazine Editors Pick.
✉ engbb@comcast.net ❂ www.anenglishgardenbb.com

DUXBURY

Winsor House Inn
390 Washington St 02332
781-934-0991
David & Patricia O'Connell

140-210 BB
4 rooms, 4 pb
Most CC, *Rated*
C-yes/S-no/P-no/H-no

Full breakfast
Dinner daily at 4:30 pm (fee)
Fresh flowers, comforters,
reading materials

Charming 19th Century sea captain's home located in the quaint seaside village of Duxbury, 35 miles south of Boston, 10 miles from Plymouth.
✉ info@winsorhouseinn.com ❂ www.winsorhouseinn.com

EAST ORLEANS

Nauset House Inn
143 Beach Rd 02643
800-771-5508 508-255-2195
Cindy and John Vessella and
Diane Johnson

80-185 BB
14 rooms, 8 pb
Visa, MC, Disc, *Rated*
C-ltd/S-no/P-no/H-no
April-October

Full breakfast with choices
We serve Wine & hors
d'oeuvres in the late
afternoon in our commons
room. A great gathering
place.
Commons room,
conservatory, dining room

Nauset House Inn located on Cape Cod is an intimate 1810 farm house with a unique turn-of-the-century conservatory, just a short walk to Nauset beach. "This inn is the answer to those who want a home-away-from-home ambience with a hint of fantasy."
✉ info@nausethouseinn.com ✪ www.nausethouseinn.com

Ship's Knees Inn
186 Beach Rd 02643
888-744-7756 508-255-1312
Peter & Denise Butcher

90-350 BB
16 rooms, 14 pb
Visa, MC, Disc, *Rated*,
•
C-ltd/S-no/P-no/H-no

Continental breakfast
Sitting room, pool, tennis

The Ship's Knees Inn is a 180-year-old restored sea captain's home, only a three minute walk to beautiful Nauset Beach with rolling sand dunes. Pool and tennis on the premises.
✉ info@shipskneesinn.com ✪ www.shipskneesinn.com

EASTHAM

Inn at the Oaks
3085 County Rd, Rte 6 02642
877-255-1886 508-255-1886
Pam & Don Andersen

120-290 BB
10 rooms, 10 pb
Most CC, *Rated*, •
C-yes/S-no/P-ltd/H-ltd

Full breakfast
Dinner occ., afternoon tea &
dessert
Parlor & dining room with
fireplaces, billiard room, play
area, yard games, families
suites

The perfect spot for your Cape Cod family vacation. Welcoming families of all ages, we offer suites & amenities for children and adults, including a play area and spa services.
✉ stay@innattheoaks.com ✪ www.innattheoaks.com

EDGARTOWN

Ashley Inn
129 Main St 02568
800-477-9655 508-627-9655
Fred & Janet Hurley

150-325 BB
10 rooms, 10 pb
Most CC
C-ltd/S-no/P-no/H-no

Full breakfast
Afternoon tea & cookies
Flowers & chocolates in
room, antiques, fireplaces,
whirlpool tubs

Discover the essence of Martha's Vineyard at the award-winning Ashley Inn. As a welcomed guest, you'll enjoy the elegance of this historic Georgian home, the comfort of your chosen guestroom, and a fresh start on the day with a gourmet breakfast.
✉ relax@ashleyinn.net ✪ www.ashleyinn.net

Charlotte Inn
27 Summer St 02539
508-627-4751
Gerret & Paula Conover

295-950 BB
25 rooms, 25 pb
Visa, MC, AmEx
C-ltd/S-no/P-no/H-no

Full breakfast

In stately Edgartown, on the island of Martha's Vineyard, stands the Charlotte Inn. Within this venerable establishment's walls the proprietors have created a spirited revival of Edwardian-ear elegance.
✪ www.charlotteinn.net/

FAIRHAVEN

Fairhaven Harborside Inn & Spa	90-165 BB	Full breakfast
1 Main St 02719	6 rooms, 6 pb	Afternoon tea
508-990-7760	Cash, Checks	Sitting room, suite, views,
Sandra & Stephen Ledogar	C-ltd/S-no/P-no/H-ltd	accommodations for
		business travelers Internet
		access, fireplace, TV

Located directly on picturesque Fairhaven Harbor, the B&B offers 6 rooms that are just a short walk to Fairhaven center, bike paths & beaches. The inn is on the waterfront site where artist William Bradford's studio was located.
✉ fhis@comcast.net

FALMOUTH

Captain Tom Lawrence House Inn	105-220 BB	Full gourmet breakfast
75 Locust St 02540	7 rooms, 7 pb	Complimentary, afternoon,
800-266-8139 508-540-1445	Visa, MC, AmEx, *Rated*	home-baked snacks
Anne & Jim Cotter	C-yes/S-no/P-no/H-ltd	Sitting room, free WiFi, A/C,
		porch, cable TV and
		refrigerator in each room

Elegant, historic Cape Cod whaling captain's home. Close to sea beaches, numerous golf courses, restaurants, ferries to Martha's Vineyard & Nantucket. Private, fully furnished apartment available.
✉ CaptTomHouse@aol.com ○ www.CaptainTomLawrence.com

Mostly Hall	100-199 BB	Continental plus breakfast
27 Main St 02540	6 rooms, 6 pb	Lemonade & cookies in the
508-548-3786	Visa, MC, Disc	afternoon, hot cocoa or cider
Charlene & Rene Poirier	S-no/P-no/H-no	& warm brownies in cooler
	French	months
		Robes in room, TV/DVD
		players, sitting room, gazebo,
		porch, garden, wireless
		Internet, private bath

This 1849 plantation style home brings sophistication to a relaxed atmosphere. Corner guestrooms with in room private bath and comfortable sitting areas, robes in each room, afternoon treats and chocolates will make your stay unforgettable.
✉ stay@mostlyhall.com ○ www.mostlyhall.com

The Palmer House Inn	109-295 BB	Full Gourmet Breakfast
81 Palmer Ave 02540	17 rooms, 17 pb	Afternoon and evening
800-472-2632 508-548-1230	Most CC, *Rated*, ●	refreshments
Bill & Pat O'Connell	C-ltd/S-no/P-no/H-yes	Sitting rooms, porches,
		beautiful grounds, bicycles,
		turn-down service

Quiet elegance surrounds you in this romantic Victorian Inn, located in the Historic District. Beaches, shops, ferry shuttles and restaurants are only a short stroll away. Smoke free premises.
✉ innkeepers@palmerhouseinn.com ○ www.palmerhouseinn.com

Woods Hole Passage	95-195 BB	Full breakfast
186 Woods Hole Rd 02540	5 rooms, 5 pb	Tea and sweets in the
800-790-8976 508-548-9575	Most CC, *Rated*, ●	afternoon
Deb Pruitt	C-ltd/S-no/P-no/H-no	Bicycles, library, spacious
		grounds & gardens, outdoor
		shower, wireless Internet,
		going 'green'

Graceful 100 year-old carriage house and renovated barn providing a magical retreat year round. Walk to ocean, bay beaches, Spohr Gardens and Quisset Harbor. Swimming, boating, golf, tennis, shopping, museums, dining-all minutes from the Inn.
✉ inn@woodsholepassage.com ○ www.woodsholepassage.com

Windflower Inn, Great Barrington, MA

FLORENCE

The Knoll B&B	78-85 BB	Full breakfast
230 N Main St 01062	4 rooms	Living room with fireplace
413-584-8164	*Rated*	and cable TV, library, WiFi
Lee & Ed Lesko	C-ltd/S-no/P-no/H-no	

Large 1910 Tudor house in quiet rural setting, on 16 acres. Near 5 colleges: Smith, Amherst, Mt. Holyoke, University of Massachusetts and Hampshire.
✉ theknoll2@comcast.net ✆ www.theknollbedandbreakfast.com

GLOUCESTER

Lanes Cove House	100-150 BB	Continental plus breakfast
6 Andrews St 01930	3 rooms, 3 pb	Afternoon tea & coffee
978-282-4647	Most CC, •	Sitting room, kitchenette with
Anna Andella	C-ltd/S-no/P-no/H-no	2 night minimum
	April through December	

A lovely 1800s Victorian dollhouse on the ocean, quaint, cozy & comfortable, with stunning views of a fishing cove & sunsets. Peacefully located between downtown Gloucester & Rockport, close to Salem & Boston. Two night minimum, please.
✉ lanescove@comcast.net ✆ www.lanescovehouse.com

GREAT BARRINGTON

Christine's Bed & Breakfast	99-257 BB	Full hot breakfast
& Tearoom	3 rooms, 3 pb	Afternoon Tea with pastries
325 North Plain Rd 01236	Visa, MC, *Rated*	from pies to cobblers each
800-536-1186 413-274-6149	C-ltd/S-no/P-yes/H-no	day upon arrival.
Christine & Steve Kelsey		Turn down service, A/C,
		private baths, TV, phones,
		gardens, patio, fireplaces,
		wireless Internet

A Bed and Breakfast Carriage House Inn located in Great Barrington, Massachusetts.
✉ innkeepers@christinesinn.com ✆ www.christinesinn.com

Tell your hosts Pamela Lanier sent you.

GREAT BARRINGTON

Thornewood Inn	115-295 BB	Full breakfast
453 Stockbridge Rd 01230	15 rooms, 15 pb	Restaurant on site can cater
800-854-1008 413-528-3828	Visa, MC, AmEx,	private functions, reunions
Terry & David Thorne	*Rated*, •	etc., full bar.
	C-yes/S-no/P-ltd/H-no	In-house massage, Jacuzzis,
		pool, suites, fireplaces, hot
		tub, TV, WiFi, conference
		facilities, weddings

Exceptional turn of the century Dutch Colonial Inn set in the heart of the Berkshire Hills. Beautiful antique-appointed rooms, views, Jacuzzis, fireplaces, outdoor pool and in-house massage. Specializing in weddings. Near all attractions.
✉ info@thornewoodinn.com ❂ www.thornewood.com

Windflower Inn	100-250 BB	Full breakfast
Rt 23 01230	13 rooms, 13 pb	Afternoon tea, snacks
800-992-1993 413-528-2720	AmEx, *Rated*	Sitting room, library,
Claudia & John Ryan, Barbara	C-yes/S-no/P-no/H-ltd	swimming pool, high speed
Liebet		Internet throughout the
		building

Elegant, small country Inn. Beautiful rooms, some with fireplaces, all with private bath & A/C. Full breakfast with homemade breads, eggs & dairy from local farms, and afternoon tea. Ten acres of grounds & gardens. Family owned & operated for 28 years.
✉ wndflowr@windflowerinn.com ❂ www.windflowerinn.com

GREENFIELD

Brandt House Inn	95-249 BB	Cont. plus weekdays, full
29 Highland Ave 01301	9 rooms, 7 pb	weekends
800-235-3329 413-774-3329	Most CC, *Rated*, •	Afternoon tea,
John & Steve	C-ltd/S-ltd/P-ltd/H-no	complimentary wine, full
		breakfast on weekends,
		snacks
		Sitting room, library, tennis,
		Jacuzzis, cable, fireplaces,
		fax, phones

An elegant turn-of-the-century Colonial Revival mansion. Beautiful original woodwork and personally selected furnishings and decor. 9 guest suites, 7 with private baths.
✉ info@brandthouse.com ❂ www.brandthouse.com

HADLEY

Ivory Creek B&B Inn	159-199 BB	Full breakfast
31 Chmura Rd 01035	6 rooms, 6 pb	Guest kitchen available 24/7:
866-331-3115 413-587-3115	Visa, MC, AmEx,	coffee, tea, soda, juice; Hors
Tod & Judy Loebel	*Rated*, •	d'oeuvres 5pm and fresh
	C-yes/S-no/P-ltd/H-yes	cookies 8pm
		Multiple large comfortable
		common rooms, 11 fire-
		places, complimentary
		wireless Internet, spa, soft
		robes

Elegant but secluded, on 24 wooded acres with beautiful flower gardens and pond with waterfall. Hiking trails throughout the property. Within 5 miles of 5 colleges. Six spacious accommodations each with private bath and fireplace, luxurious beds/linens.
✉ pachaderm@aol.com ❂ www.ivorycreek.com

HYANNIS

Cape Cod Harbor House Inn	119-520 BB	Deluxe continental breakfast
119 Ocean St 02601	19 rooms, 19 pb	Fully-equipped kitchens
800-211-5551 508-771-1880	Most CC, *Rated*	Ocean views, Internet
Ken Komenda	C-yes/S-no/P-yes/H-no	access, DVD player w/free
	Mid April thru October	movies, online concierge,
		beach shuttle van

Eighteen mini-suites and the Harbor Suite, a honeymoon haven on scenic Hyannis Harbor. All have separate kitchens. Free WiFi. DVD players in rooms with free movies. Free breakfast. Walk to Kennedy Museum and Memorial. Free beach shuttle.
✉ stay@harborhouseinn.net 🕓 www.harborhouseinn.net

HYANNIS PORT

Marston Family B&B	-390 BB	Full Custom Breakfast
70 Marston Ave 02601	3 rooms, 1 pb	Please tell us your breakfast
508-775-3334	Cash, Checks	preferences before you arrive,
Marcus & Lynette Sherman	C-yes/S-ltd/P-yes/H-ltd	otherwise it's cook's choice.
	June 1- October 14	Free sailboat rides, sole use of
		bathroom & living room, wire-
		less net, TV, porch, crib, cot

Full 3 bedroom family suite for six persons, 6/24 to 9/5, $325/Day or $2200/wk. Rent 1, 2 or 3 rooms off season. Oldest house in Historic Hyannis Port, c.1786. Free WiFi. We host only one party at a time. ✉ marcus334@hotmail.com 🕓 www.catboat.com/b&b

Simmons Homestead Inn	130-320 BB	Full breakfast
288 Scudder Ave 02647	14 rooms, 14 pb	Complimentary evening
800-637-1649 508-778-4999	Cash, Checks, *Rated*,	wine
Bill Putman	•	Sitting rooms, porches, bikes,
	C-yes/S-ltd/P-yes/H-no	billiard room, sports car
		museum

Beautifully restored 1820 sea captain's home. Lovely grounds. Everything dedicated to just relaxing & fun. Collection of 60 red classic sports cars is reason enough to visit this unique inn. ✉ SimmonsHomestead@aol.com 🕓 www.SimmonsHomesteadinn.com

IPSWICH

The Inn at Castle Hill	175-385 BB	Continental plus breakfast
280 Argilla Rd 01938	10 rooms, 10 pb	Afternoon tea with our
978-412-2555	Most CC	selection of the finest quality
Diana Lannon	C-ltd/S-no/P-no	of loose leaf blended teas
		Plush terry robes, telephone,
		hair dryer, central A/C and
		heat, bicycles available on
		request

Step into a timeless place of understated elegance and serenity. The Inn at Castle Hill, centrally located on the spectacular 2,100-acre National Historic Landmark Crane Estate, welcomes you to experience its unique and elegant seaside charm.
✉ theinn@ttor.org 🕓 innatcastlehill.thetrustees.org

Ipswich B&B	115-150 BB	Full breakfast
2 East St 01938	7 rooms, 6 pb	Vegetarian & special diets on
866-IPSWICH 978-356-2431	Visa, MC, AmEx	request. We feature terrific
Margaret & Ray Morley	C-ltd/S-no/P-ltd/H-no	pancakes & our "special"
		French toast.
		A/C, private baths, TV,
		wireless DSL, free long
		distance in USA & Canada,
		40 seat restaurant

The Ipswich Bed and Breakfast is in the heart of Ipswich's historic district. We are within walking distance to town. The house, built by Robert Jordan in 1863, is a wonderful example of a Victorian home, with fine Italianate detail.
✉ ipswichinn@verizon.net 🕓 www.ipswichbedbreakfast.com

IPSWICH————————————————————————

Kaede B&B	95-165 BB	Full breakfast, rotating menu
16 N Main Street 01938	11 rooms, 9 pb	Please let us know of any
800-457-7799 978-356-8000	Visa, MC, AmEx,	food allergies or special
Jason Keough & Makiko	*Rated*, ●	dietary needs before arrival.
Tangeguchi Keough	C-ltd/S-ltd/P-no/H-no	Sitting room, suites,
	Japanese	fireplaces, cable TV,
		beaches, historic, Japanese
		twist on a traditional B&B

1845 Greek Revival/Federalist property in historic district. A combination of Japanese culture and New England tradition, we are more than a convenient location. Come enjoy Olde Ipswich and a slice of traditional Japanese culture at Kaede (Ka-eh-day).
✉ kaedebb@aol.com ◐ kaedebb.com

Rogers and Brown House B&B	149-189 BB	Chef's choice entree
83 County Rd 01938	3 rooms, 3 pb	Delicious entree, fruits,
800-585-0096 978-356-9600	Visa, MC	home baked breads,
Frank Wiedenmann &	C-ltd/S-no/P-no/H-no	chocolates, coffee, tea.
Johanne Cassia		Weight watchers, if
		requested.
		New Mattresses, A/C,
		wireless Internet, HDTV,
		gardens, shop. New bikes &
		helmets for guests available.

A warm welcome awaits you in our historic, NE home. A small, elegant B&B that offers comfort and relaxation. Ipswich is the perfect retreat year round. Enjoy a delicious breakfast by the crackling fire or kick back in an easy chair.
✉ oldeipswich@comcast.net ◐ www.oldeipswich.com/bb.html

LEE————————————————————————

Applegate Inn	150-385 BB	Full breakfast
279 W Park St 01238	11 rooms, 11 pb	Snacks, complimentary wine
800-691-9012 413-243-4451	Visa, MC, AmEx, *Rated*	and cheese
Gloria & Len Friedman	C-ltd/S-no/P-no/H-yes	Sitting room, library,
		bicycles, Jacuzzis, swimming
		pool, suites, fireplace

Applegate Inn a true a Bed and Breakfast, was built in the grand era of the 1920's. Privacy is all yours with our six acres of groomed trails & yard.
✉ LenandGloria@applegateinn.com ◐ www.applegateinn.com

Chambery Inn	89-289 BB	Deluxe Continental Breakfast
199 Main St 01238	9 rooms, 9 pb	Adjacent restaurant
800-537-4321 413-243-2221	Most CC, *Rated*	Adjacent bar, TV, spa, fire-
Joseph Toole	C-ltd/S-no/P-no/H-yes	place, refrigerator, Jacuzzi for
		two, wireless Internet access

Chambery Inn has French-inspired design and nine exceptional rooms. This nineteenth-century parochial school turned country inn possesses a unique character, a truly distinctive landmark in the beautiful Berkshire Hills.
✉ chamberyinn@toole.tc ◐ www.chamberyinn.com

Devonfield Country Inn B&B	160-375 BB	Full buffet and a hot entree
85 Stockbridge Rd 01238	10 rooms, 10 pb	Brandy, chocolates, bottled
800-664-0880 413-243-3298	Most CC, *Rated*, ●	water in rooms; guest pantry
Bruce & Ronnie Singer	C-ltd/S-no/P-ltd/H-ltd	with homemade cookies, tea,
	Spanish	coffee
		Heated pool, tennis, bicycles,
		lawn sports, archery range,
		exercise room, library, golf &
		ski area

A gracious English-style country house in the heart of the Berkshires sits on 32 acres only 2 miles from Main Street, Stockbridge, home of the Norman Rockwell Museum. Ideally situated for exploring the rolling tapestry of the Berkshire Hills.
✉ innkeeper@devonfield.com ◐ www.devonfield.com

LEE——————

Jonathan Foote 1778 House
One East St 01238
888-947-4001 413-243-4545
JoAnn Zarnoch

149-225 BB
5 rooms, 5 pb
Visa, MC
C-ltd/S-no/P-no/H-ltd

Full homemade breakfast
Homemade coffee cakes at
breakfast, homemade
cookies in the afternoon,
Lindt chocolates
Fireplaces, dinner
reservations, help with
directions to events and
attractions

Romantic 1778 farmhouse, full of history and charm, provides a country setting that is central to all Berkshire attractions. Fireplaces, antiques, and comfort abound.
✉ innkeeper@1778house.com ◐ www.1778house.com

LENOX——————

1897 Hampton Terrace B&B
91 Walker St 01240
800-203-0656 413-637-1773
Stan & Susan Rosen

175-345 BB
14 rooms, 14 pb
Most CC, •
C-ltd/S-ltd/P-no/H-yes

Full, hot, candlelit breakfast
Full BYOB bar set-up, in-
room Jacuzzis & fireplaces,
cable TV/VCR, free DSL

1897 in-town Lenox Gilded Age landmark home. An inn since 1937. After staying here, Traditional Home Magazine declared "enjoy Gilded Age glamour and relaxed elegance at one of the East Coast's premier getaway destinations" and "absolutely perfect."
✉ stan@hamptonterrace.com ◐ www.hamptonterrace.com

Birchwood Inn
7 Hubbard St 01240
800-524-1646 413-637-2600
Ellen G. Chenaux

150-310 BB
11 rooms, 11 pb
Most CC, *Rated*
C-ltd/S-ltd/P-yes/H-ltd
French, Spanish

Full award-winning breakfast
Afternoon tea, midnight
snack, guest pantry
Library, den, fireplaces,
cable TV, videos, wireless
Internet access, porch,
gardens, hammock

Birchwood Inn Bed and Breakfast, of Lenox, MA, has been welcoming friends, old and new, with warmth and congenial hospitality since 1767. The Inn is renowned for its romantic and comfortable country elegance and memorably decadent breakfasts.
✉ innkeeper@birchwood-inn.com ◐ www.birchwood-inn.com

The Cornell Inn
203 Main St 01240
800-637-0562 413-637-0562
Billie & Doug McLaughlin

70-400 BB
30 rooms, 30 pb
Visa, MC, Disc, *Rated*
C-ltd/S-no/P-no/H-yes

Full breakfast
Full service pub on premises
Koi pond, waterfall,
expansive decks, beautiful
gardens, wireless Internet

Our three, uniquely-styled guesthouses feature furnishings in Victorian, country and Colonial décor. Choose a cozy bedroom, a fully equipped suite with fireplace and kitchen or a room featuring a four-poster bed with fireplace and Jacuzzi.
✉ info@cornellinn.com ◐ www.cornellinn.com

Garden Gables Inn
135 Main St 01240
888-243-0193 413-637-0193
Dan & Brande Neyhard

154-498 BB
17 rooms, 17 pb
Most CC, *Rated*
C-ltd/S-no/P-no/H-ltd

Cooked to order full
breakfast
Complimentary sherry,
beverages & freshly baked
cookies & biscotti. Wine
tasting from owner's winery
Fireplaces, whirlpools,
porches, outdoor pool, spa
treatments, yoga classes,
wireless Internet

All the romantic charm of a Berkshire B&B but with four-star amenities! Guests of this historic Inn near Lenox Village & Tanglewood love the private baths/spa robes, spa room, pool, organic & locally sourced food and personal service. Green, eco-friendly.
✉ innkeeper@gardengablesinn.com ◐ www.gardengablesinn.com

LENOX

Kemble Inn	155-425 BB	Continental plus breakfast
2 Kemble St 01240	13 rooms, 13 pb	Conveniently located within
800-353-4113 413-637-4113	Visa, MC, AmEx	walking distance to the fine
Bosa Kosovic	C-ltd/S-no/P-no/H-yes	restaurants and shops in
		Lenox Village
		A/C, fireplaces, tennis

Elegant 1881 Georgian mansion, magnificent mountain views, spacious rooms with private baths, fireplaces, A/C, TV. Many have working marble fireplaces and Jacuzzis. Extended continental breakfast included.
✉ kemble@bcn.net ◐ www.kembleinn.com

Rookwood Inn	175-425 BB	Buffet style with one hot
11 Old Stockbridge Rd 01240	19 rooms, 19 pb	entree
800-223-9750 413-637-9750	Most CC, *Rated*	Afternoon refreshments
Amy Lindner-Lesser	C-yes/S-no/P-ltd/H-ltd	Sitting room, fireplaces, TV,
	Spanish	phones, clock/radios, robes,
		hairdryers, packages, free
		WiFi

Fairytale Queen Anne Victorian bed & breakfast . . . perfect for your dream getaway. Antique-filled guestrooms each with private bathroom; comfortable, yet elegant decor; delicious, heart healthy breakfasts. Walk to town, T'wood, & many cultural attractions.
✉ stay@rookwoodinn.com ◐ www.rookwoodinn.com

Stonover Farm B&B	325-575 BB	Cooked to order full
169 Under Mountain Rd 01240	5 rooms, 5 pb	breakfast
413-637-9100		Afternoon wine and cheese;
Tom & Suky Werman		We try our best to
		accommodate any dietary
		preferences.
		Greenhouse, library, patio,
		courtyard, pond, private
		phones w/voicemail,
		TV/DVD, Bose CD players,
		AC

Stonover Farm is a 110-year-old Berkshire "cottage" which served as farmhouse to the Stonover Estate, and which has been renovated extensively. Luxury accommodations include 3 suites & 2 self-contained cottages.
✉ stonoverfarm@aol.com ◐ www.stonoverfarm.com

Walker House	90-230 BB	Continental plus breakfast
64 Walker St 01240	8 rooms, 8 pb	Complimentary wine,
800-235-3098 413-637-1271	*Rated*	afternoon tea
Peggy & Richard Houdek	C-ltd/S-no/P-yes/H-ltd	Sitting room, piano,
	Spanish, French	computer with WiFi, library
		video theatre, opera & film
		weekends

Peggy & Richard Houdek invite you to share Walker House, their historic Berkshire residence. A landmark in classic American Federal architecture, now in its 3rd decade of welcoming guests. ✉ walkerhouse.inn@verizon.net ◐ walkerhouse.com

Whistler's Inn	90-300 BB	Full breakfast
5 Greenwood St 01240	15 rooms, 15 pb	Sip our complimentary
413-637-0975 413-637-0975	Most CC, *Rated*, •	sherry, port or afternoon
Lisa Mears	C-yes/S-no/P-no/H-no	teas. Daily snacks. Delights
	Spanish and Polish	du jour.
		TV/VCR, air conditioning,
		Internet access, gardens,
		music room, library, art
		gallery.

Featured on National TV , The Travel Channel. Celebrating our 35th year, Whistler's Inn is an 1820 English Tudor country manor house in the heart of New England's beautiful Berkshires. ✉ whistlersinn@hotmail.com ◐ www.whistlersinnlenox.com

Harborside House, Marblehead, MA

MARBLEHEAD

A Lady Winette Cottage B&B	125-150 BB	Nice Continental Breakfast
3 Corinthian Ln 01945	2 rooms	A/C, children over 5
781-631-8579	Cash, Checks	welcome, computer,
Susan M. Davies	C-ltd/S-no/P-no/H-no	conference rooms, laundry

A charming Victorian cottage nestled amongst gardens facing Marblehead Harbor. French doors open to your private deck overlooking the harbor. Enjoy breakfast on a large porch furnished with Cape Cod wicker overlooking the sailboats.
✉ Suziwinette@aol.com ◐ www.aladywinettecottage.com

Brimblecomb Hill	95-125 BB	Continental breakfast
33 Mechanic St 01945	3 rooms, 1 pb	Sitting room, fireplace,
781-631-3172	Visa, MC	garden, private entrances
Gene Arnould	C-ltd/S-no/P-no/H-ltd	

Enjoy the charm of this lovingly restored antique home which was featured in both "Better Homes and Gardens" and "Colonial Homes." Three clean, comfortable first floor guest-rooms with private or shared baths, two with private entrances.
✉ genearnould@verizon.net ◐ www.brimblecomb.com/home.html

Fox Pond B&B	90-250 BB	Continental plus breakfast
31 Arthur Ave 01945	3 rooms, 3 pb	Breakfast is served from
781-631-1630	Visa, MC	8:30–9:30am but coffee is
Ted Baker	C-ltd/S-no/P-no/H-ltd	available before breakfast for
		early risers.
		TV/AC, Internet access,
		washers and dryers, off-
		street parking, decks/brick
		patios, gardens, antique

Fox Pond is considered one of the North Shore's most romantic hideaways. The home features three large bedrooms with private marble baths, queen beds, TV and a/c. Located on a quiet cul-de-sac, guests can enjoy the peacefulness found in the gardens.
✉ foxpond@comcast.net ◐ www.foxpondbnb.com

MARBLEHEAD————————————————————————————

Harbor Light Inn
58 Washington St 01945
781-631-2186
Peter C. Conway

155-365 BB
20 rooms, 20 pb
Visa, MC, AmEx,
Rated, •
C-ltd/S-no/P-no/H-no

Continental plus breakfast
Afternoon refreshments, bar
& tavern for lunch & dinner
Sitting room, conference
room, double Jacuzzis,
courtyard, heated swimming
pool, WiFi, Tavern

Located in the heart of Old Town Marblehead, the Inn offers quick access to the harbor, shops and galleries, historic homes and a variety of restaurants. We look forward to making your stay in Marblehead memorable. Visit our new Tavern with quality menu.
✉ info@harborlightinn.com 🌎 www.harborlightinn.com

—————————————————————————————————————

Harborside House
23 Gregory St 01945
781-631-1032
Susan Livingston

85-100 BB
2 rooms
Checks, *Rated*, •
C-ltd/S-no/P-no/H-no
Un petit peu de Francais

Continental plus breakfast
Harbor Sweets candy,
homebaked cookies,
afternoon tea on request
Living room with fireplace,
deck, bicycles, cable
TV/VCR, WiFi, off-street
parking

This handsome 1850 home in the historic district overlooks picturesque Marblehead Harbor. Guests enjoy water views from its wood-paneled parlor, period dining room and summer breakfast porch. Two well-appointed guestrooms feature antique furnishings.
✉ stay@harborsidehouse.com 🌎 www.harborsidehouse.com

—————————————————————————————————————

**Notorious Annie's
Waterfront Inn**
115 Front St 01945
781-631-0558
Janet Sheehan

195-295 BB
2 rooms, 2 pb
Most CC
C-yes/S-no/P-no/H-no

Continental breakfast
Complimentary coffee and a
selection of teas are always
available.
Private decks, gardens,
private beach, kayaks, beach
towels, hot tub, mini fridge,
wireless Internet

A private cove with endless beats of waves upon a pebbled shore . . . ocean views, private decks and tubs to soak the world away while listening to the breeze.
✉ info@notoriousannies.com 🌎 www.notoriousannies.com

—————————————————————————————————————

Oceanwatch B&B
8 Fort Sewall Ln 01945
888-639-4034 781-639-8660
Diane & Paul Jolicoeur

165-300 BB
4 rooms, 4 pb
Visa, MC, AmEx, •
C-ltd/S-no/P-no/H-no
French

Continental breakfast
Sitting room, fireplaces,
cable TV, beach, ocean-front
park, deck

Victorian-era home in Old Marblehead, overlooking harbor entrance, next to pre-Revolutionary fort. Superb water views with private baths, TV, wireless Internet, and king-sized beds in all rooms. Walk to shops, restaurants and historic sites.
✉ oceanwatch@comcast.net 🌎 www.oceanwatchbandb.com

—————————————————————————————————————

Pheasant Hill Inn B&B
71 Bubier Rd 01945
888-202-1705 781-639-4799
Bill & Nancy Coolidge

95-185 BB
3 rooms, 3 pb
Visa, MC, AmEx,
Rated, •
C-ltd/S-ltd/P-no/H-no

Continental plus breakfast
Snacks
Sitting room, library, phones,
TV, A/C, suite with fireplace

Charming 1920 summer estate. Private all-suites getaway. Country-like setting & views to water. Memorable!
✉ information@pheasanthill.com 🌎 www.pheasanthill.com

MARBLEHEAD

The Seagull Inn
106 Harbor Ave 01945
781-631-1893
Skip & Ruth Sigler

140-250 BB
3 rooms, 3 pb
Visa, MC, *Rated*
C-yes/S-no/P-ltd/H-ltd

Continental plus breakfast
snacks, soft drinks, bottled
water, sherry, chocolates,
nuts
Sitting room, WiFi, bikes,
cable TV/DVD/VCR, video
library, kayaks, telephones,
refrigerators

On beautiful Marblehead Neck, just steps from the ocean & harbor, The Seagull Inn's guest suites offer seaside living at its best. Comfortable & private guest suites, expandable for families. Bicycles & kayaks free for guests. ✉ host@seagullinn.com ◐ www.seagullinn.com

MIDDLEBORO

On Cranberry Pond B&B
43 Fuller St 02346
508-946-0768
Jeannine, Ken & Tim Krushas

95-180 BB
6 rooms, 5 pb
Most CC, *Rated*, •
C-ltd/S-ltd/P-ltd/H-ltd

Gourmet Breakfast
Homemade snacks at night
with tea, coffee or Cranberry
Lemonade
nature trails, 3 bass fishing
ponds, birdwatching, deck,
kayaks, canoes, putting
green, stress-free

In the heart of the cranberry capital of the world. Gourmet Breakfast, homemade snacks, nature trails, birdwatching, fishing, canoeing, kayaking, putting green, Tweeter center, Foxboro stadium, Boston, Plymouth, WiFi, cable TV. DVDs, hairdryers, bathrobes. ✉ oncranberrypond@aol.com ◐ www.oncranberrypond.com

Rock Village B&B
109 Miller St 02346
508-947-3413
Doreen Sullivan

75-90 BB
3 rooms, 3 pb
Visa, MC, Disc
C-ltd/S-ltd/P-no/H-no

continental breakfast
Snacks, water and other
meals upon request
Wireless Internet, Toshiba
laptop, A/C, refrigerators,
seasonal pool, library, ping
pong, pool table

Rock Village B&B is noted for its historical significance to Rock Village. The Rock Mill employed over 90 people from village. The Atwoods legacy left behind the unique architecture, antique tiles, stained glassed windows, tiger oak bookcase ✉ rockvillagebb@comcast.net ◐ www.rockvillagebb.com

NANTUCKET

Brass Lantern Inn
11 N Water St 02554
800-377-6609 508-228-4064
Michelle Langlois

95-425 BB
16 rooms, 16 pb
Most CC, *Rated*, •
C-yes/S-no/P-yes/H-ltd
French

Continental plus breakfast
A wide selection of loose
teas & fresh-baked cookies
each afternoon, bottled
water in guestrooms
Telephones, TVs, A/C,
phones, robes, hairdryers,
irons, wireless Internet
access, concierge services

Welcome to Nantucket Island! Enjoy cobblestone streets, narrow lanes, rose-covered cottages and miles of sand beaches. The freshly-renovated Brass Lantern Inn is located in the Old Historic District, a 'walk to everything' location. Pet & family friendly. ✉ info@brasslanternnantucket.com ◐ www.brasslanternnantucket.com

NANTUCKET

The Carlisle House Inn
26 N. Water Street 02554
508-228-0720
Heather Sheldon

65-395 BB
13 rooms, 10 pb
Visa, MC, AmEx
C-ltd/S-no/P-no/H-no
some French, Spanish &
Italian

Expanded breakfast buffet
Complimentary weekend
wine and cheese parties in
summer & special weekends;
guest refrigerator
Free WiFi/Internet, guest
computer, working
fireplaces, hair dryers, some
HDTVs, A/C in all rooms

The island's premier guesthouse located only a short walk from beaches, restaurants and the town center. Fine rooms, canopied beds, fireplaces, a breakfast buffet and an award-winning garden combine to assure the best in New England hospitality.
✉ info@carlislehouse.com ◕ www.carlislehouse.com

Carriage House
5 Rays Ct 02554
508-228-0326
Haziel Jackson & Tomomi
Sato, Mom Jeanne

100-200 BB
7 rooms, 7 pb
Rated, •
C-yes/S-no/P-no/H-ltd
French, German,
Spanish, Japanese

Continental Plus breakfast
Guest refrigerator
Parlor, guest library of local
nature and history, patio,
beach towels, concierge
service

"Adorable" 1865 B&B on the prettiest, quietest, scallop-shelled country lane; "beautifully quiet, yet right in town." Personal attention for 2 generations. Seven guestrooms with antiques and vintage details. Children welcome!
◕ www.carriagehousenantucket.com

Century House
10 Cliff Rd 02554
508-228-0530
Gerry & Jean Heron

195-595 BB
18 rooms, 18 pb
Visa, MC, AmEx, *Rated*
C-yes/S-ltd/P-no/H-yes
French & German
May 15 – October 30

Gerry's Berry Buffet
Breakfast
Coffee (espresso &
cappuccino) & tea bar,
afternoon cookies &
lemonade
24 hr wireless Internet
access, elegant sitting room,
verandah, books &
newspapers, fresh flowers

Luxury inn bed and breakfast on Nantucket. Breezy, wrap-around veranda. Top cliff historic elite location quickly preferred for sophisticated traveler. Discover the Freedoms of Nantucket at the historic Century House B&B.
✉ centurybnb@aol.com ◕ www.centuryhouse.com

Cliff Lodge B&B
9 Cliff Rd 02554
508-228-9480
Sally Beck

145-475 BB
12 rooms, 12 pb
Visa, MC, AmEx
C-ltd/S-no/P-no/H-ltd

Continental breakfast
Afternoon snacks and tea
Fireplaces, art, dining room,
garden patio

Built in 1771 as a whaling master's home and situated on a gentle hill only a short walk from the ferry and the town, Cliff Lodge welcomes you to discover with heartwarming comfort, the unforgettable beauty and enchantment of this faraway island.
✉ info@clifflodgenantucket.com ◕ www.clifflodgenantucket.com

Cliffside Beach Club
46 Jefferson Ave 02554
800-932-9645 508-228-0618
Robert Currie

285-710 BB
27 rooms, 27 pb
AmEx
C-yes/S-no/P-no
French
May 21 to October 12

Continental breakfast
Private bar and café
Private beach, pool, sauna,
Internet, daily made service,
massage room, exercise
facility

With its breathtaking views of Nantucket Sound and the continued addition of amenities and services, Cliffside offers an intimate resort experience unparalleled by any other.
✉ ackbeach@aol.com ◕ www.cliffsidebeach.com

NANTUCKET

Cobblestone Inn
5 Ash St 02554
508-228-1987
Robin Hammer-Yankow

75-250 BB	Continental breakfast
5 rooms, 5 pb	Complimentary coffee, tea,
Visa, MC, *Rated*	soda, cookies
C-ltd/S-no/P-no/H-ltd	Suites, cable TV, antiques,
April – December	close to beaches, Kitchenette
	(Fully stocked with
	appliances and treats)

The Cobblestone Inn is a cozy, 18th century bed and breakfast. Built in 1725 and last renovated in 1997, the centuries blend as you walk the two blocks from Steamship Wharf to our quiet cobblestoned side street, in the heart of historic Nantucket Town.
✉ cobble@nantucket.net ◐ www.nantucket.net/lodging/cobblestoneinn

House of the Seven Gables
32 Cliff Rd 02554
508-228-4706
Sue Walton

100-250 BB	Continental breakfast
10 rooms, 8 pb	Coffee or tea, juice and fresh
Most CC	baked coffee cakes, muffins,
C-ltd/S-no/P-no/H-no	or Portuguese rolls
April-December	Sitting room, porches

A quiet Victorian in the Old Historic District. Walk to Main Street, beaches, museums and restaurants. A continental breakfast is served to your room each morning.
✉ info@houseofthesevengables.com ◐ www.houseofthesevengables.com

Island Reef Guest House
20 N Water St 02554
508-228-2156
Ernest Davis & Diane Metcalf

150-275 BB	Continental breakfast
12 rooms, 10 pb	Wireless Internet, cable TV,
Visa, MC, AmEx	garden & common room
C-yes/S-no/P-no/H-no	

Built in 1830, the Island Reef is a classic, Federal-style whaling captain's home. Ideally located on historic, cobblestoned North Water Street, the inn is just a short walk from Main Street, beaches, and Steamboat Wharf. ◐ www.islandreef.com

Jared Coffin House
29 Broad St 02554
800-248-2405 508-228-2400
Jim Storey

125-410 BB	Comp. expanded Grab & Go
52 rooms, 52 pb	Seasonal restaurant and
Most CC, •	lounge for dinner & take-out
C-yes/S-no/P-no/H-yes	Business center, telephones,
	TVs, weddings, banquets

Two historic buildings. Guestrooms with private baths, phone, TV (some have air conditioning). Seasonal restaurant and lounge. Downtown location. Walk from Ferry.
✉ jaredcoffinhouse@nironline.com ◐ www.jaredcoffinhouse.com

Martin House B&B
61 Centre St 02554
508-228-0678
Lee Sylva

155-395 BB	Continental plus breakfast
13 rooms, 10 pb	Complimentary sherry,
Visa, MC, AmEx, *Rated*	afternoon snacks and tea
C-ltd/S-no/P-no/H-no	Sitting room, fireplace,
	veranda, beach towels

Stately 1803 Mariner's home in Nantucket's historic district. Four poster canopy beds, 13 airy rooms. Our spacious accommodations blend the convenience and comforts of today with the romance and nostalgia of the past . . .
✉ info@martinhouseinn.net ◐ www.martinhouseinn.net

The Veranda House
3 Step Lane 02554
877-228-0695 508-228-0695
Scott Allan

129-639 BB	Continental plus breakfast
18 rooms, 18 pb	European style breakfast
Most CC, *Rated*	with gourmet bread basket,
C-ltd/S-no/P-no/H-yes	yogurt, granola, fresh fruit,
Mid- May through	afternoon cookies.
October	Harbor views, high-speed
	Internet, massage therapy on
	site, flat screen TV/DVD,
	turndown service

A retro-chic hotel with sweeping harbor views. Our Nantucket hotel is conveniently located in the heart of Old Nantucket Town. Walk out and explore the Island on foot or by bicycle. Allow our Concierge to arrange your activities and dining reservations.
✉ sherinn@comcast.net ◐ www.theverandahouse.com

NANTUCKET

The Wauwinet Inn	380-1,450 BB	Full breakfast
120 Wauwinet Rd 02584	33 rooms, 33 pb	Award-winning Topper's
800-426-8718 508-228-0145	Most CC	Restaurant
Bettina Landt	C-ltd/S-no/P-no/H-no	2 private beaches, private
	April thru October	Spa on premises,
		complimentary jitney to
		Nantucket Town

Experience The Wauwinet, Nantucket's premier waterfront resort. An idyllic blend of extraordinary service, superior food, gracious comfort and delightful surroundings has earned The Wauwinet critical acclaim.
✉ wauwinet@nironline.com ✆ www.wauwinet.com

The White House	150-305 BB	Voucher at local restaurant
48 Centre St 02554	4 rooms, 4 pb	No breakfast voucher for
508-228-9491	Visa, MC, AmEx	suite as it has a full kitchen
Sally Beck	C-yes/S-no/P-no/H-no	

Ideally located in the core district of Nantucket town just minutes from Main Street, Steamboat Wharf, shops, restaurants, galleries. Nicely appointed and meticulously clean.
✉ welcome@nantucketwhitehouse.com ✆ www.nantucketwhitehouse.com/main.html

NEW BEDFORD

The Orchard Street Manor	125-165 BB	Continental breakfast
139 Orchard St 02740	3 rooms, 3 pb	Formal parlor, chess &
508-984-3475	Visa, MC, AmEx	billiard room, library,
Al & Suzanne Saulniers	C-ltd/S-no/P-no/H-no	gathering room, fine dining
	French, Spanish	room, deck, guest fridge

Enjoy the luxury of New Bedford's whaling & textile past in a 1845 whaling captain's home, that was renovated/expanded in 1903 by a cotton baron to its current, graceful Georgian-Revival style. Eat lunch or dinner at nearby seafood or Portuguese eateries.
✉ theorchardstreetmanor@hotmail.com ✆ www.the-orchard-street-manor.com

NEW MARLBOROUGH

The Old Inn on the Green	206-365 BB	Continental breakfast
134 Hartsville New	11 rooms, 11 pb	Restaurant, tap room
Marlborough Rd 01230	Most CC, *Rated*	Antiques, porch, fireplace,
413-229-7924	C-yes/S-no/P-ltd/H-no	Jacuzzi, sitting rooms, A/C,
Peter Platt		pool, library, robes, TV/VCR

The Old Inn, once a stagecoach relay, offers authentically restored guestrooms, fine dining in intimate candlelit dining rooms and seasonal al fresco dining on the canopied garden terrace off the taproom.
✉ pplatt@oldinn.com ✆ www.oldinn.com

NEWBURYPORT

Clark Currier Inn	95-195 BB	Continental plus breakfast
45 Green St 01950	9 rooms, 9 pb	Afternoon tea
978-465-8363	Most CC, *Rated*	Parlor, fireplace, garden,
Bob Nolan	C-ltd/S-no/P-no/H-no	library, off street parking,
		small conference room
		available for business

Newburyport is famous for the number of buildings built in the Federal style, and the Clark Currier Inn is one of the city's finer examples. The building is actually two homes in one.
✉ ccinn1803@yahoo.com ✆ www.clarkcurrierinn.com

Essex Street Inn	115-260 BB	Continental breakfast
7 Essex St 01950	37 rooms, 37 pb	Wood fireplaces, whirlpool
978-465-3148	Most CC	tub, private decks, maid
Lori Guertin	C-yes/S-no/P-no/H-yes	service, coffee maker, hair
		dryer and TV.

The Essex Street Inn has 37 beautifully appointed rooms, each with their own modern conveniences. Whether you are indulging in a romantic getaway or coming for a peaceful rest, we trust you will find the Essex Street Inn to be an oasis from the ordinary.
✉ info@essexstreetinn.com ✆ www.essexstreetinn.com

NEWTON CENTRE

Park Lane B&B	75-110 BB	Continental plus breakfast
11 Park Lane 02459	3 rooms, 1 pb	Wireless Internet, GPS, bikes,
800-772-6759 617-964-1666	Most CC, *Rated*, •	cable TV, sell T cards & tour
Pat & Jim Pransky	C-yes/S-ltd/P-no/H-no	tickets, near T statn, sitting rm w/fireplace

A 10 minute walk to Newton Centre T Station (high speed light rail), in a quiet tree-lined neighborhood. ✉ pranpran1@gmail.com ◑ bostonbandb.com

NORTHAMPTON

Penrose Victorian Inn	115-165 BB	Full breakfast
133 Main St 01060	3 rooms, 3 pb	Fireplace, garden, antiques,
888-268-7711 413-268-3014	Visa, MC, Disc	parlor, music room, gazebo,
Nancy & Dick Zimmer	C-ltd/S-no/P-no/H-no	pool & high speed wireless Internet access.

The Penrose Bed & Breakfast Inn has a colorful fountain garden, antiques throughout, 7 fireplaces, rare chandeliers, lamps and welcoming candles in all the windows. Each spacious room comes with a large private Victorian accented bathroom.
✉ zimmer@penroseinn.com ◑ www.penroseinn.com

OAK BLUFFS

The Oak House	180-370 BB	Continental plus breakfast
75 Seaview Ave 02557	10 rooms, 10 pb	Afternoon tea
800-245-5979 508-693-4187	Most CC, *Rated*, •	Piano, sun porch, bicycles,
Betsi Convery-Luce	C-ltd/S-ltd/P-no/H-no	near town, ferry; Closest Inn
	Early May through Oct.	to the beach on Martha's Vineyard.

Romantic Victorian Inn on the beach, richly restored 1872 Governor's home. Oak paneling, wide porches, balconies, leaded windows, water views. Very cozy and attractive rooms and suites. ✉ Inns@vineyard.net ◑ www.vineyardinns.com/oakhouse.html

Tivoli Inn, On Martha's	85-265 BB	Continental breakfast
Vineyard	6 rooms, 3 pb	Teas & Poland spring water
125 Circuit Ave 02557	Visa, MC, Disc, •	available at all times
508-693-7928	C-yes/S-ltd/P-yes/H-no	Wireless Internet, cable TV,
Lisa & Lori Katsounakis		guest refrigerator and guest phone, lovely outdoor shower!

The Tivoli Inn is a Victorian gingerbread house with lots of charm and a clean and friendly atmosphere. Beautiful wraparound porch overlooking Hiawatha Park. Walk to shops, restaurants, nightlife, beach, biking trails, ferries, and public transportation.
✉ tivoli@capecod.net ◑ www.tivoliinn.com

ORLEANS

Morgan's Way	175-200 BB	Full gourmet breakfast
9 Morgan's Way 02653	Cash, Checks, *Rated*,	Guest refrigerators
508-255-0831		Sitting room, library, fresh
Page & Will McMahan	•	flowers, art collection, firm
	C-ltd/S-no/P-no/H-no	beds, heated pool, WiFi Internet

Romantic & elegant contemporary hideaway. Five acres of gardens & woodlands, heated pool; a birdwatcher's paradise. Art collection on site. Full, gourmet breakfast served. Romantic, poolside one bedroom cottage available for rental on a weekly basis.
✉ info@morganswaybandb.com ◑ www.morganswaybandb.com

PEABODY

Joan's B&B
RR 210 Lynn St 01960
978-532-0191
Joan Hetherington

75-90 BB
3 rooms, 1 pb
C-ltd/S-no/P-no/H-no
Closed March

Full breakfast
Afternoon tea, snacks
Sitting room, patio,
swimming pool, laundry, use
of whole house, e-mail for
availability

Located 10 minutes from historic Salem, 25 minutes from Boston, and 25 minutes from picturesque Gloucester and Rockport. All bedrooms have A/C. Wireless Internet access, pool, full breakfast.
✉ joanbandb@rcn.com

PETERSHAM

Winterwood at Petersham
19 N Main St 01366
978-724-8885
Jean & Robert Day

159-209 BB
6 rooms, 6 pb
Visa, MC, AmEx, •
C-yes/S-no/P-no/H-no

Continental plus breakfast
Sip a cooling cocktail on one
of our screened porches or
sip tea by the fire in the
library
Winterwood is available for
intimate weddings, birthday
and anniversary parties, full
liquor license

Winterwood is an elegant restored 1842 Greek Revival Mansion with 6 beautifully appointed guestrooms, most with fireplaces, all private baths, A/C, and breakfast. Winterwood is available for intimate weddings, cocktail receptions, and rehearsal dinners.
✉ winterwoodatpetersham@verizon.net ◑ www.winterwoodinn.net

PLYMOUTH

By the Sea B&B
22 Winslow St 02360
800-593-9688 508-830-9643
Roger & Brenda Silvieus

150-170 BB
3 rooms, 3 pb
C-ltd/S-ltd/P-no/H-ltd
April 1st thru Jan 2

Continental plus breakfast
All suites have private
entrances, ensuite baths, TV,
air conditioning &
refrigerators

At By the Sea B&B, the focus is on exquisite hospitality and accommodations to make your visit comfortable, relaxing and fun! On the harbor in historic Plymouth overlooking the Mayflower and steps away from Plymouth Rock. "The Jewel of Plymouth Harbor."
✉ bytheseabandb@aol.com ◑ www.bytheseabedandbreakfast.com

Jesse Harlow House
3 N Green St 02360
508-746-6877
Jay Shippole

135-275 BB
3 rooms, 3 pb
Most CC, •
C-ltd/S-no/P-ltd/H-ltd
May through November

Full breakfast
Guest refrigerator and 1-cup
coffee maker with comp.
beverages 24/7
Wireless Internet, cable TV,
back deck, garden, free
extras with longer stays

Recently voted Best B&B South Shore/Cape Cod Life. This downtown location is centrally located close to highways for day trips (most an hour or less)! Full three course gourmet breakfast and romance always on the menu . . .
✉ jay@jesseharlowhouse.com ◑ www.jesseharlowhouse.com

PROVINCETOWN

Aerie House & Beach Club
184 Bradford St 02657
800-487-1197 508-487-1197
Steve Tait & Dave Cook

35-310 BB
11 rooms, 8 pb
Most CC
C-yes/S-no/P-yes/H-ltd

Continental plus breakfast
All rooms are equipped with
a coffee maker and a supply
of coffee and tea.
TV/VCR/DVD/CD players,
DVD library, fireplace, gym,
hot tub, WiFi, laundry,
parking, sun deck, gifts

Offering a complete range of accommodations including rooms, suites, and efficiencies at either our Guesthouse perched atop Miller Hill, or our bayfront Beach Club, both located in Provincetown's charming East End gallery district.
✉ info@aeriehouse.com ◑ www.aeriehouse.com

PROVINCETOWN

Beaconlight Guesthouse
12 Winthrop 02657
800-696-9603 508-487-9603
Keith and Mark

80-410 BB
14 rooms, 12 pb
Most CC, •
C-yes/S-no/P-no

Continental plus breakfast

A Provincetown Tradition, the Beaconlight is centrally located in the favored West End of town, where everything is literally within a few minutes walk: health clubs, bike hire, restaurants, bars, clubs, shops, galleries, the beach and ocean.
✉ info@beaconlightguesthouse.com ✆ www.beaconlightguesthouse.com

---

The Brass Key Guesthouse
67 Bradford St 02657
800-842-9858 508-487-9005

140-485 BB
42 rooms, 42 pb
Visa, MC, Disc, •
S-ltd/P-no/H-yes

Continental plus breakfast
Poolside lemonade & iced
tea, cheese & crudities trays,
fine wines & beers each
afternoon
Courtyard, heated pool, in
ground spa, fireplaced
guestrooms & common
rooms, whirlpool tubs, decks

Provincetown's most unique guesthouse a half-block off Commercial Street, the Brass Key is a cozy retreat in the center of the action. Forty-two guestrooms in six 18th & 19th century houses and three cottages surrounding courtyard pool and in-ground spa.
✉ ken@brasskey.com ✆ www.brasskey.com

**Carpe Diem Guesthouse &
Spa**
12 Johnson St 02657
800-487-0132 508-487-4242
Rainer Horn, Jurgen Herzog,
Hans van Costenoble

95-425 BB
18 rooms, 18 pb
Most CC, *Rated*, •
S-ltd/P-no/H-no
German, French

Full German Style Breakfast
Wine & cheese hour from
5–6 pm, pastries, fruit, water,
coffee, tea, sherry & port
available all day
Guest office, WiFi, common
rooms/patios, parking, spa,
steam room, sauna, massage,
hot tub

Seize the day in our elegant Guesthouse & Spa Resort. Quiet location in center of town. Highest quality amenities, some rooms with fireplaces, whirlpool tubs, private patios. Famous homemade breakfast. On-site massage services, sauna and steam room.
✉ info@carpediemguesthouse.com ✆ www.carpediemguesthouse.com

**Crowne Pointe Historic Inn
& Spa**
82 Bradford Street 02657
877-276-9631 508-487-6767
David Sanford and Tom Walter

99-529 BB
40 rooms, 40 pb
Visa, MC, Disc, *Rated*,
•
S-ltd/P-no/H-ltd
Polish

Full breakfast
Afternoon tea, snacks &
wine. Our on site restaurant
will take care of all your
other dining needs.
Library, bikes, Jacuzzis, pool,
fireplaces, cable TV, full
service spa

Restored 1800's sea captain's mansion overlooking the harbor in the center of Provincetown. Unsurpassed hot buffet breakfast, spas, romantic in-room fireplaces & whirlpools.
✉ welcome@crownepointe.com ✆ www.crownepointe.com

Fairbanks Inn
90 Bradford St 02657
800-324-7265 508-487-0386
Alicia Mickenberg & Kathleen
Fitzgerald

105-279 BB
14 rooms, 12 pb
Visa, MC, AmEx, *Rated*
S-no/P-no/H-no

Expanded Continental
Afternoon snacks, guest
refrigerator
DVD library, microwave, sun
deck, parking, bike rack,
guest computer & WiFi

Highly recommended by guests and travel writers alike, The Fairbanks Inn is renowned for its unique blend of historic charm, guest amenities, and high standard of hospitality.
✉ alicia_kathy@fairbanksinn.com ✆ www.fairbanksinn.com

298   Massachusetts

PROVINCETOWN

Inn at the Moors
59 Provincelands Rd 02657
508-487-1342
Loretta O'Conner

99-225 BB
30 rooms, 30 pb
Visa, MC, AmEx
C-ltd/S-ltd/P-no/H-no
Mid-May through
October

Continental breakfast

All rooms face full view of the moor, a 180 degree view of the expansive salt marsh with sand dunes and Cape Cod on the horizon. This is one of the most captivating views in Provincetown and all of the Cape.
✉ info@innatthemoors.com ◷ www.innatthemoors.com

Snug Cottage
178 Bradford St 02657
800-432-2334 508-487-1616
James Mack & Peter Newton

95-250 BB
8 rooms, 8 pb
Most CC, *Rated*, •
C-ltd/S-no/P-no/H-no

Sumptuous breakfast buffet
Afternoon wine, soft drinks
& snacks
Car service to/from airport,
evening turn downs, high-
speed Internet & Aveda
luxury toiletries

Authentic Cape Cod Inn built in 1825 that surrounds you with history. We've preserved the best of the 19th century and added all the comfort and luxury you expect in a first class, modern Inn.
✉ info@snugcottage.com ◷ www.snugcottage.com

White Porch Inn
7 Johnston St 02657
508-487-0592
Thomas Shirk & Thomas
Bantle

120-315 BB
9 rooms, 9 pb
Visa, MC
C-ltd/S-no/P-no/H-ltd
German
April – December

Continental plus breakfast
Gas fireplaces in most
rooms, luxurious toiletries,
A/C, Flat Screen TV, DVD +
CD/radio

Provincetown's newest and award winning boutique guesthouse with a contemporary beach atmosphere on the Cape. Conveniently located just steps away from the fun of Commercial Street with its restaurants, shops, galleries, Johnson Street Beach, and more.
✉ info@whiteporchinn.com ◷ www.whiteporchinn.com

REHOBOTH

Gilbert's B&B
30 Spring St 02769
508-252-6416
Jeanne D. Gilbert

79-99 BB
5 rooms, 2 pb
Visa, MC, *Rated*, •
C-yes/S-no/P-no/H-no

Full breakfast
Afternoon tea
Sitting room, fireplaces,
accommodate business
travel

New England Cape was built in 1830s. Features original floors, windows and hardware. Gilbert's B&B has a fireplace, and hiking trails.
✉ JG@gilbertsbb.com ◷ www.gilbertsbb.com

ROCKPORT

Beach & King Street Inn
2 King St 01966
978-546-6601
Laurie Nugent & Tim
Giarrosso

119-249 BB
3 rooms, 4 pb
Visa, MC
C-ltd/S-no/P-no/H-ltd

Continental breakfast
Afternoon drinks and
homemade cookies
Wireless Internet access,
beach accessories, towels,
chairs, etc.

Sweeping ocean & beach views. Across from Rockport's Front Beach, an intimate Cape Ann B&B on the North Shore. Accommodations offer a picturesque setting with stunning ocean views and a 5-minute stroll to historic Bearskin Neck and the village.
✉ beachkingbb@hotmail.com ◷ www.beachkingbb.com

ROCKPORT

Captain's House
69 Marmion Way 01966
877-625-7678 978-546-3825
Gretchen and Tim Parker

130-195 BB
5 rooms, 5 pb
Visa, MC
C-yes/S-ltd/P-no/H-no
Early May to Early Nov

Continental plus breakfast
Living room, fireplace, sun
porch, wireless Internet,
cable TV

Set directly on a rocky shoreline, our guesthouse will give you that home-away-from-home feeling, with spacious living room with fireplace, comfortable furnishings & spectacular water views.
✉ info@captainshouse.com ◐ www.captainshouse.com

Emerson Inn by the Sea
1 Cathedral Ave 01966
800-964-5550 978-546-6321
Bruce & Michele Coates

99-379 BB
36 rooms, 36 pb
Most CC, *Rated*, •
C-yes/S-no/P-no/H-ltd

Full or continental plus
breakfast
Fine Dining Restaurant . . .
Wine Spectator Award of
Excellence. Hours/days of
service vary by season.
Sitting room, spa tubs,
heated swimming pool,
family friendly facility

The Emerson Inn By the Sea is a newly renovated, handsome white clapboard inn, which once welcomed Ralph Waldo Emerson into its peace and comfort. Also available are two seaside cottages.
✉ sbcoates@EmersonInnByTheSea.com ◐ www.EmersonInnByTheSea.com

---

Linden Tree Inn
26 King St 01966
800-865-2122 978-546-2494
Tobey & John Shepherd

110-235 BB
12 rooms, 12 pb
Most CC, *Rated*, •
C-yes/S-no/P-no/H-no

Full buffet breakfast
Assorted hot beverages
available throughout day and
evening, lemonade in
season, cookies
Sun room & living room for
guest use, living room has
large TV with DVD/VCR,
parking

Comfortable, romantic Inn with easy access to or from Boston by train. Short stroll to beaches, shops, galleries and restaurants. Lovely view of ocean and mill pond from cupola at top of house.
✉ lindentreeinn@gmail.com ◐ www.lindentreeinn.com

Sally Webster Inn
34 Mt Pleasant St 01966
877-546-9251 978-546-9251
John & Kathy Fitzgerald

80-140 BB
8 rooms, 8 pb
Visa, MC, *Rated*
C-ltd/S-no/P-no/H-no
Closed January

Full breakfast
Complimentary wine for
special occasions
Sitting room, TV/VCR,
wireless Internet access,
A/C, DVD movie loaner
library

Built in 1832, the Sally Webster Inn offers 8 guestrooms, all with private baths. Each room is decorated with period antiques, as is the rest of the house. Short walk to town center, beaches, and shops.
✉ sallywebsterinn@hotmail.com ◐ www.sallywebster.com

Seven South Street Inn
7 South St 01966
978-546-6708
Debbie & Nick Benn

89-189 BB
9 rooms, 9 pb
Visa, MC, AmEx, •
C-ltd/S-no/P-no/H-no

4-course gourmet served
breakfast
Afternoon tea, snacks
Sitting room, library,
bicycles, pool, cable TV,
business travel, private
baths, wireless Internet

Of all the inn's delights, our elegant four course breakfast is what guests talk about and remember most. Built in 1766, the Inn is ideally located to Rockport's enchanting village. An hour drive from Boston, Portsmouth, Lexington and Concord.
✉ theinn@sevensouth.net ◐ www.sevensouthstreetinn.com

ROCKPORT————————————————————————

The Tuck Inn B&B	86-146 BB	Continental plus breakfast
17 High St 01966	11 rooms, 11 pb	Snacks
800-789-7260 978-546-7260	Visa, MC, *Rated*	Sitting room, A/C, swimming
Liz & Scott Wood	C-yes/S-no/P-no/H-no	pool, bicycles, scenic walks, beach, multiple flower gardens

Cozy 1790 Colonial home in the quiet seaside village of Rockport. Hospitable & comfortable year' round lodging. Renowned home-baked breakfast. Antiques, quilts, gardens, pool, non-smoking. 2002 Editor's Pick Award—Yankee Magazine. AAA rated: 3 DIAMONDS!
✉ info@tuckinn.com ○ www.tuckinn.com

Yankee Clipper Inn	129-389 BB	Full breakfast
127 Granite St 01966	16 rooms, 16 pb	Dinner on Friday, Saturday &
800-545-3699 978-546-3407	Most CC, *Rated*, •	Sunday with reservations
Randy & Cathy Marks	C-yes/S-no/P-no/H-no	Swimming pool, oceanfront meeting & function room, concierge, wireless Internet access

The Yankee Clipper Inn is an oceanfront mansion and Cape in Rockport next to Gloucester, 40 miles from Boston. The Yankee Clipper is an ideal New England Vacation destination. Perfect for romantic getaways, honeymoons, and anniversaries.
✉ info@yankeeclipperinn.com ○ www.yankeeclipperinn.com

SALEM————————————————————————

The Salem Inn	119-350 BB	Hearty continental breakfast
7 Summer St 01970	40 rooms, 40 pb	Complimentary sherry
800-446-2995 978-741-0680	Most CC, *Rated*, •	Private garden, sitting room,
Richard & Diane Pabich	C-yes/S-no/P-ltd/H-no	A/C, canopy beds, fireplaces, Jacuzzi baths, kitchenettes, WiFi

Spacious, luxuriously appointed rooms in three elegantly restored historic homes. Located within easy walk of city's restaurants, attractions, museums and the waterfront.
✉ reservations@saleminnma.com ○ www.saleminnma.com

SANDWICH————————————————————————

1750 Inn at Sandwich Center	115-179 BB	Full breakfast
118 Tupper Rd 02563	5 rooms, 5 pb	Snacks
800-249-6949 508-888-6958	Visa, MC, AmEx, •	Central air, gazebo with
Jan & Charlie Preus	C-ltd/S-no/P-no/H-ltd	Jacuzzi, fireplaces, robes, 600 TC sheets, concierge, evening cordials

New England charm with a touch of southern hospitality, in the heart of Cape Cod's oldest seaside village. This inn, circa 1750, offers charming accommodations, beautiful public rooms, and spacious grounds.
✉ info@innatsandwich.com ○ www.innatsandwich.com

Aaron Burbank's Windfall House	85-145 BB	Full menu breakfast
108 Old Main St 02563	6 rooms, 4 pb	Afternoon tea
877-594-6325 508-888-3650	Most CC, •	Sitting room, library, suites,
Ted Diggle	C-yes/S-ltd/P-no/H-ltd	fireplaces, cable TV, accommodations for business travelers

A charming 1818 Colonial set in historic Sandwich Village. This gracious antique has retained many original features, such as wide-board floors and 3 fireplaces, one with a beehive oven.
✉ windfallhs@aol.com ○ www.windfallhouse.com

SANDWICH

Belfry Inne & Bistro	145-310 BB	Full breakfast
8 Jarves St 02563	21 rooms, 21 pb	Dinner (fee), afternoon tea
800-844-4542 508-888-8550	Visa, MC, AmEx, •	Restaurant, bar service,
Christopher Wilson	C-yes/S-no/P-no/H-no	Jacuzzi tubs, fireplaces,
		conference facilities

In a timeless Sandwich, Cape Cod setting, four architectural masterpieces, comprising The Belfry Inne & Bistro, each from a different time, grace Jarves and Main Streets. Fourteen suites, some featuring whirlpools, fireplace, A/C, TV, balconies.
✉ info@belfryinn.com ☎ www.belfryinn.com

Isaiah Jones Homestead	165-300 BB	Full gourmet breakfast
165 Main St 02563	7 rooms, 7 pb	Soft drinks, self serve coffee
800-526-1625 508-888-9115	Most CC, *Rated*	& tea always available,
Don & Katherine Sanderson	C-ltd/S-no/P-no/H-no	sherry or port available in
		the evening
		3 rooms with fireplace, 4
		rooms with glass front stove,
		4 with whirlpool tub, cable
		TV/DVD

An elegant Victorian B&B in historic Sandwich Village. The inn is furnished almost entirely with antiques. The curved staircase, beautiful woodwork, soft colors tell you you've found "the special place you've been looking for on Cape Cod."
✉ info@isaiahjones.com ☎ www.isaiahjones.com

SIASCONSET

The Summer House Inns &	275-2,000 BB	Continental plus breakfast
Cottages	34 rooms, 34 pb	Restaurant, lunch, dinner,
17 Ocean Ave 02564	Visa, MC, AmEx, •	bar room service
508-257-4577	C-yes/S-no/P-no/H-no	Sitting room, swimming pool,
Susan Manolis, General	April-Dec.	suites, fireplaces, Cable TV,
Manager		accommodate business
		travelers

Romantic cottages on a bluff overlooking the Atlantic, with Jacuzzis and two beautiful inns in Nantucket Town.
✉ reservations@thesummerhouse.com ☎ www.thesummerhouse.com

Wade Cottages	EP	Sitting room, suites, private
35 Shell St 02564	6 rooms, 6 pb	beach.
508-257-6308	Most CC	
Susanne & Wade Greene	C-yes/S-no/P-no/H-ltd	
	French	
	Late May-mid-October	

The Wade Cottages are a traditional Nantucket-style cluster of houses near the center of the historic village of Siasconset, on a bluff overlooking the open Atlantic. Weekly rentals only.
✉ seamail@wadecottages.com ☎ www.wadecottages.com

SOUTH EGREMONT

Weathervane Inn	115-300 BB	Full breakfast
17 Main St, Rt 23 01258	10 rooms, 10 pb	Afternoon tea, bar service
800-528-9580 413-528-9580	Visa, MC, AmEx, *Rated*	Sitting room, library, pool,
Maxine & Jeffrey Lome	C-yes/S-no/P-no/H-ltd	fireplaces, cable TV, yoga,
		massage

The Weathervane Inn, built in 1786, is centrally located to all Berkshire area attractions and features 10 guestrooms, each with private bath, and plenty of common rooms for game playing or watching the game, or just sitting by the fire.
✉ innkeeper@weathervaneinn.com ☎ www.weathervaneinn.com

SOUTH LEE

Historic Merrell Inn
1565 Pleasant St 01260
800-243-1794 413-243-1794
George Crockett

110-295 BB
10 rooms, 10 pb
Visa, MC, *Rated*, •
C-ltd/S-no/P-no/H-no

Full breakfast
Afternoon refreshments
Fireplace rooms, antiques,
telephones, A/C, secure
wireless Internet access

One of New England's most historic stage coach Inns, a few miles from Norman Rockwell Museum and Stockbridge. The only Inn included in the Historic American Buildings Survey. ✉ info@merrell-inn.com ☯ www.merrell-inn.com

SOUTH ORLEANS

A Little Inn on Pleasant Bay
654 S Orleans Rd 02662
888-332-3351 508-255-0780
Sandra, Pamela & Bernd

215-300 BB
9 rooms, 9 pb
Visa, MC, AmEx, •
C-ltd/S-no/P-no/H-no
German, French
May to September

European Breakfast Buffet
5:00 PM Sherry Hour
included
Two lounges, patios, A/C in
all rooms

Main house dates back to 1798 and may have been part of the Underground Railroad. Overlooking Pleasant Bay. Chatham and Orleans are minutes away. ✉ bernd@alittleinnonpleasantbay.com ☯ www.alittleinnonpleasantbay.com

SOUTH YARMOUTH

Captain Farris House
308 Old Main St 02664
800-350-9477 508-760-2818
Nancy & Michael

130-280 BB
10 rooms, 10 pb
Most CC, •
C-ltd/S-no/P-no/H-no

Full breakfast
Freshly baked goods every
afternoon, complimentary
sherry in the parlor.
Jacuzzi tubs, video library,
comp. popcorn and soft
drinks, robes, fresh flowers,
fireplaces

Tucked away on two acres in the historic Bass River Village of South Yarmouth. This architecturally significant Greek Revival style home has been restored to its former glory. World class antiques and exquisite window treatments adorn all the rooms. ✉ thecaptain@captainfarris.com ☯ www.captainfarris.com

STOCKBRIDGE

1862 Seasons on Main
47 Main St 01262
888-955-4747 413-298-5419
Joy Ziefer

135-330 BB
5 rooms, 5 pb
Visa, MC, AmEx, *Rated*
S-no/P-no/H-no

Full breakfast
Afternoon tea & snacks
Sitting room, cable TV,
fireplaces

An award winning Inn with unparalleled service, gourmet breakfasts, Frette linens, a business center & WiFi. Bike or walk to Stockbridge shops, restaurants, galleries, theater and museums. Just five minutes to Tanglewood. ✉ info@seasonsonmain.com ☯ www.seasonsonmain.com

Conroy's B&B
11 East Street, Rte 7 01262
888-298-4990 413-298-4990
Joanne & James B. Conroy

120-325 BB
9 rooms, 6 pb
Visa, MC, •
C-yes/S-no/P-no/H-ltd
A little Spanish
summer, fall

Full breakfast
Gardens, fireplaces, decks,
pool, hot tub

Conroy's B&B, an 1828 farmhouse in the Federal style, sits on three beautiful acres protected by a giant pine hedge. The wide lawn with mature maple trees, wonderful stone walls, old farm foundations and perennial gardens provides four season beauty. ✉ joanne@conroysinn.com ☯ www.conroysinn.com

STOCKBRIDGE

The Inn at Stockbridge	160-375 BB	Full candlelight breakfast
30 E St, Rt 7 N 01262	16 rooms, 16 pb	Complimentary wine &
888-466-7865 413-298-3337	Most CC, *Rated*, •	cheese, butlers pantry, tea
Alice & Len Schiller	C-ltd/S-no/P-no/H-ltd	Sitting room, library,
		antiques, phones, A/C, pool,
		fireplace, fitness room,
		massage room

Experience peaceful charm and elegance in a 1906 Georgian style mansion secluded on 12 acres. Sixteen well appointed guestrooms, many with a fireplace, double whirlpool and wonderful amenities. Let the cares of the world drift away
✉ innkeeper@stockbridgeinn.com 🌐 www.stockbridgeinn.com

STOW

Amerscot House	130-150 BB	Full breakfast
61 West Acton Rd 01775	4 rooms, 4 pb	Snacks and drinks available
978-897-0666	Most CC, *Rated*	in the Guests Sitting Room.
Viki Carter	C-yes/S-ltd/P-no/H-ltd	Conference facilities, copy
		and FAX machines, high
		speed wireless access

A beautiful, 18th century, Colonial home 27 miles outside Boston and close to historic Concord. The house has spacious living rooms for guests to enjoy as well as nearly 3 acres of gardens and woodlands. ✉ Viki@amerscot.com 🌐 www.amerscot.com

STURBRIDGE

Sturbridge Country Inn	119-199 BB	Continental breakfast
530 Main St 01566	15 rooms, 15 pb	Excellent 4 star restaurant
508-347-5503	Most CC, *Rated*, •	next door.Discounted Dinner
Pat Affenito	C-yes/S-ltd/P-no/H-yes	package available!
	spanish	Hot tubs, Colonial-style
		furnishings, heated pool and
		fireplaces.

Historic grand Greek Revival Inn where each room has a luxury bath with whirlpool area and fireplace. Walk to Old Sturbridge Village, antique shops and cafes.
✉ info@sturbridgecountryinn.com 🌐 www.sturbridgecountryinn.com

VINEYARD HAVEN

The Doctor's House	175-340 BB	Exceptional full country
60 Mt Aldworth Rd 02568	7 rooms, 7 pb	breakfast
866-507-6670 508-696-0859	Most CC, *Rated*, •	Iced tea and snacks,
Ms. Jilana Abrams	C-ltd/S-no/P-ltd/H-no	afternoon tea, bottled water,
	French	additional meals upon
		request
		Cable TV, sauna, bicycles,
		phone, fax, wireless Internet,
		assistance with island
		reservations

A warm, feel at home atmosphere tucked away on two quiet acres, amidst large colorful gardens. Short stroll to village and beach. All rooms with private baths and A/C. A full country breakfast (not buffet) is included too!
✉ info@doctorshouse.com 🌐 www.doctorshouse.com

Mansion House Inn, Health	99-516 BB	Full breakfast
Club & Spa	40 rooms, 40 pb	Zephrus Restaurant serves
9 Main St 02568	Most CC, *Rated*, •	island fresh, new American
800-332-4112 508-693-2200	C-yes/S-no/P-no/H-yes	cuisine
Susan & Sherm Goldstein		Complete use of Health Club,
		pool & outdoor cupola
		overlooking harbor; spa

Mansion House Inn, on Martha's Vineyard, is where your discovery of Island magic begins. Stroll to ferry & harbor, beach, restaurants & shops. Nearby golf, fishing, tennis & water sports. Affordable luxury.
✉ info@mvmansionhouse.com 🌐 www.mvmansionhouse.com

VINEYARD HAVEN

Thorncroft Inn	195-495 BB	Full breakfast
460 Main St 02568	14 rooms, 14 pb	Substantial continental
800-332-1236 508-693-3333	Most CC, *Rated*, •	breakfast delivered to room
Karl & Lynn Buder	S-no/P-no/H-yes	as alternative to breakfast in
	Portuguese	the dining room.
	End of May – Mid-	Renowned concierge
	October	services, elopements,
		Internet access

Romantic country inn. AAA Four Diamond Award every year since 1990. Mobil 3 stars. Fireplaces, central A/C, luxury suites with Jacuzzi or private hot tub.
✉ innkeeper@thorncroft.com ◯ www.thorncroft.com

WAREHAM

Mulberry B&B	60-100 BB	Full hearty New England
257 High St 02571	3 rooms	breakfast
866-295-0684 508-295-0684	Most CC, *Rated*, •	Afternoon tea, snacks
Frances A. Murphy	C-yes/S-no/P-no/H-no	Sitting room, library, bicycle
		routes with maps, restaurant
		discounts

Charming 1840s Cape Cod style home originally built by a blacksmith and once a general store operated by the B&B owner's grandfather. Close to Boston, historic Plymouth, cranberry harvesting and seaside activities.
✉ mulberry257@comcast.net

WELLFLEET

Inn at Duck Creeke	85-140 BB	Continental plus breakfast
70 Main St 02667	27 rooms, 19 pb	Much-reviewed Duck Creeke
508-349-9333	Most CC	Tavern with hip and homey
Bob Morrill & Judith Pihl	C-yes/S-no/P-no/H-ltd	food, lobster, charm,
	May-October	hospitality and some Jazz
		Hospitality, antique charm,
		family friendly. Near town
		galleries & beaches.
		Restaurant on property.

Enjoy Cape Cod charm. Step a bit back in time. The Inn sits on a knoll overlooking a creek and pond, near village, bay and beaches. Perfect place to relax and explore the seafaring and artist town. Savor sweet lobster and more at the town's oldest tavern
✉ info@innatduckcreeke.com ◯ www.innatduckcreeke.com

WEST BARNSTABLE

Bursley Manor	150-195 BB	Continental plus breakfast
651 Olde Kings Hwy, Rte 6A	5 rooms, 5 pb	Dining room, living room,
02668	Most CC, *Rated*	common room, fireplaces,
877-362-7788 508-362-7788	C-ltd/S-no/P-no/H-no	surrounding seaside
Sheila M. Bournival		community, TV/VCR

Bursley Manor is an old dairy farm, nestled among magnificent chestnut trees. Built in 1670, it's one of the oldest family properties in the quiet and peaceful village of West Barnstable on Cape Cod.
✉ sheilabournival@yahoo.com ◯ www.bursleymanor.com

The Maple Street Inn	135-225 BB	3-Course Gourmet Breakfast
208 Maple St 02668	3 rooms, 3 pb	Afternoon teas and sweets
800-959-0208 508-362-2980	Most CC	Private entrances, fireplaces,
Patricia Curran	C-ltd/S-no/P-no/H-ltd	private bath, feather bed,
		clawfoot soaking tub, A/C,
		cable TV, WiFi

Rest, relax, go antiquing, bike riding or visit nearby beaches. You're going to love the Maple Street Inn, a classic Cape Cod Bed and Breakfast. Private entrances, private bathrooms, and a wonderfully romantic atmosphere.
✉ innkeeper@capecodmaplestreetinn.com ◯ www.capecodmaplestreetinn.com

WEST BOYLSTON

The Rose Cottage	110 BB	Full breakfast
Rts 12 & 140 01583	5 rooms, 5 pb	Welcoming beverage
508-835-4034	*Rated*	Sitting room, suites,
Michael & Loretta Kittredge	C-yes/S-no/P-no/H-ltd	fireplaces, cable TV,
	Little Italian	accommodate business
		travelers

Gracious 1850 Gothic Revival cottage situated on 4 acres of lawn, overlooking Wachusett Reservoir. Only 10 minutes to Worcester.
✉ rosecottagebandb@aol.com

WEST FALMOUTH

Chapoquoit Inn	150-275 BB	Full breakfast
495 Rt 28A 02574	7 rooms, 7 pb	Tea, coffee & fresh fruit
800-842-8994 508-540-7232	Visa, MC, *Rated*	Bicycles, beach towels &
Kim & Tim McIntyre	C-ltd/S-ltd/P-no/H-ltd	beach chairs
	Conversational Japanese	
	& Spanish	

Make our home your home at Chapoquoit Inn, an elegant and romantic B&B located on over 3 acres in the heart of Historic West Falmouth Village. Experience the best of old Cape Cod at your doorstep!
✉ info@chapoquoit.com 🌐 www.chapoquoit.com

WEST HARWICH

Cape Cod Fiddlers Green Inn	95-175 BB	Full Irish breakfast
79 W. Main St. Route 28 02671	3 rooms, 3 pb	Central climate control,
508-432-9628	Most CC	private baths, garden tubs,
Eileen & Jack	S-ltd/P-ltd/H-no	cable televisions, A/C and
		refrigerators, pool

Fiddler's Green Inn is set on an acre, away from the hustle and bustle for the romantic. Four poster mahogany queen beds and central climate control, just beautiful! Private baths, color cable televisions and A/C all make your stay comfortable.
✉ capecodfiddlersgreen@msn.com 🌐 www.capecodfiddlersgreeninn.com

Tern Inn and Cottages	99-189 BB	Continental plus breakfast
91 Chase St 02671	8 rooms, 8 pb	Snacks
800-432-3718 508-432-3714	Visa, MC	Dining & function room,
David & Joan Bruce	C-yes/S-no/P-no/H-no	pool, cable TV, welcome
		business travelers, house
		phone, Internet access

Cape Cod as it should be! Guest rooms offer comfort at a very reasonable price. A unique property offering weekly family cottages or rooms at the Inn for a shorter visit. Queen beds, AC, color TV, private bath, and breakfast in our lovely dining room
✉ stay@theterninn.com 🌐 www.theterninn.com

WEST YARMOUTH

Inn at Lewis Bay	108-148 BB	Full breakfast
57 Maine Ave 02673	6 rooms, 6 pb	Afternoon refreshments at
800-962-6679 508-771-3433	Visa, MC, AmEx,	4:00
Janet & Dave Vaughn	*Rated*, •	Sitting room, views of the
	C-ltd/S-no/P-no/H-no	bay, beach chairs & towels

Lovely B&B just a block from the beach in a quiet seaside neighborhood. Enjoy full breakfast, afternoon refreshments and use of our beach chairs and towels. All rooms have private baths and A/C. ✉ stay@innatlewisbay.com 🌐 www.innatlewisbay.com

WESTFORD————————————————————————

Pine Needles B&B	100-130 BB	Full breakfast
148 Depot St 01886	3 rooms, 3 pb	BBQ Basket for small fee
978-399-0199	Visa, MC, •	Gas fireplace, A/C, cable TV,
Dave & Claire Davis	C-yes/S-no/P-no/H-no	sitting room, game room, fax
		& copy machines, access to
		the Internet

In the heart of historic Massachusetts, close to Boston, Concord & Lowell. A simple country inn providing all the comforts of home and gracious, New England hospitality.
✉ info@pineneedlesbb.com 🌐 www.pineneedlesbb.com

WILLIAMSTOWN————————————————————

House On Main Street	90-150 BB	Full breakfast
1120 Main St 01267	5 rooms, 2 pb	Dietary restrictions easily
888-750-6849 413-458-3031	Visa, MC, •	accommodated
Timothy & Donna	C-yes/S-no/P-no/H-ltd	Sitting room, fireplace in
		living room, cable TV, high
		speed Internet access

The charm of the Victorian era with the luxury of the 21st century. Nestled in a tree-lined setting, with the convenience of walking to the Clark Art Museum, Williams College, Williamstown Theatre Festival, shopping and dining.
✉ Relax@HouseOnMainStreet.com 🌐 www.HouseOnMainStreet.com

Steep Acres Farm B&B	70-160 BB	Full gourmet breakfast
520 White Oaks Rd 01267	4 rooms, 3 pb	Complimentary wine
413-458-3774	*Rated*	Sitting room, swimming, 1½
Mary & Marvin Gangemi	C-ltd/S-no/P-no/H-no	acre pond, fishing, hiking
		trails, boating

Country home on a high knoll—spectacular views of Berkshire Hills & Vermont's Green Mts. Furnished in country antiques.
✉ jmgangemi@adelphia.net

YARMOUTH PORT————————————————————

Colonial House Inn &	100-155 MAP	Continental plus breakfast
Restaurant	21 rooms, 21 pb	Full restaurant and bar
277 Main St, Rt 6A 02675	Most CC, *Rated*, •	available for Lunch & Dinner
800-999-3416 508-362-4348	C-yes/S-ltd/P-yes/H-yes	(Dinner included full menu
Malcolm J. Perna	Russian, German,	in room rate)
	French, Spanish,	Bar, indoor pool and Jacuzzi,
	Lithuanian	TV/VCR, free wireless/DSL,
		deck, garden, 24 hr Free
		Computer Center

On a street lined, with stately trees, stands the Colonial House Inn. Here the charm of old Cape Cod has been carefully preserved & the tradition of gracious dining & hospitality carried forward.
✉ info@colonialhousecapecod.com 🌐 www.colonialhousecapecod.com

Crook Jaw Inn	135-155 BB	Full breakfast
186 Main St 02675	5 rooms, 5 pb	Afternoon tea, snacks
800-625-6605 508-362-6111	Most CC, *Rated*	Sitting room, library,
Brian Howley	S-no/P-no/H-no	fireplaces, free WiFi, guest
		fridge, Jacuzzi, beach
		umbrellas & chairs

Originally built as a sea-captain's home, for many years, passengers in horse-drawn carriages came upon a welcomed stopover, Crockers Cottage, now the Crook' Jaw Inn.
✉ crookjawinn@aol.com 🌐 www.crookjawinn.com

YARMOUTH PORT

The Inn at Cape Cod	160-335 BB	Gourmet breakfast
4 Summer St 02675	9 rooms, 9 pb	Afternoon tea with home-
800-850-7301 508-375-0590	Most CC, *Rated*, •	baked cakes & cookies,
Michael & Helen Cassels	C-ltd/S-no/P-no/H-no	chocolates in rooms,
	French	refreshments always
		available
		Drawing room & library
		w/fireplaces, secure wireless
		Internet access, cable &
		DVD, concierge service

The Inn at Cape Cod is an award winning B&B located on historic route 6A in Yarmouth-port, MA. This elegant 1820 mansion is perfectly located in the Mid-Cape and is close to beaches and ferries. Gourmet breakfasts and tempting afternoon treats!
✉ stay@innatcapecod.com ✪ www.innatcapecod.com

Liberty Hill Inn	110-230 BB	Full gourmet breakfast
77 Main St, Rte 6A 02675	9 rooms, 9 pb	Afternoon tea and
800-821-3977 508-362-3976	Most CC, *Rated*, •	refreshments, sherry, port or
John Hunt & Kris Srihadi	C-ltd/S-no/P-no/H-yes	brandy for a night cap
	Indonesian	A/C, cable TV, wireless,
		whirlpools, fireplaces,
		concierge services 9am-9pm,
		Beach supplies

Gracious and elegant Greek Revival inn, c.1825. Nine luxuriously appointed guestrooms combine comfort and charm to create the ultimate romantic holiday. Cape Cod Travel Guide "Editors' Pick" 2006,#1 Trip Advisor Yarmouth, #3 Trip Advisor Massachusetts.
✉ libertyh@capecod.net ✪ www.libertyhillinn.com

Olde Captain's Inn	75-120 BB	Continental breakfast
101 Main St, Rt 6A 02675	5 rooms, 3 pb	Kitchen is fully equipped
888-407-7161 508-362-4496	Checks	with refrigerator, stove,
Sven Tilly & Betsy O'Connor	C-ltd/S-no/P-no/H-no	china, kitchen utensils &
		condiments.
		Maid, concierge service,
		cable TV, antiques,
		honeymooner and intimate
		rooms

Olde Captain's Inn is a charming 1812 sea captain's house located in the historic district of the village of Yarmouthport on Cape Cod. Within walking distance of many restaurants, craft and antique shops, and Cape Cod Bay.
✉ general@oldecaptainsinn.com ✪ www.oldecaptainsinn.com

One Centre Street Inn	145-235 BB	Full gourmet breakfast
1 Centre St 02675	5 rooms, 4 pb	Wireless network, cable
866-362-9951 508-362-9951	Most CC, *Rated*	TV/VCR, refrigerator, bottled
Mary Singleton, Judy Murphy	C-ltd/S-no/P-no/H-no	water, private concierge,
		three season porch

One Centre Street is a elegant 1824 parsonage with all the amenities of the present, but charm of the past. We are situated amongst stately Sea Captains homes and other historic parsonages. We are centrally located on Olde Kings Highway (Route 6A).
✉ sales@onecentrestreetinn.com ✪ www.onecentrestreetinn.com

Michigan

ALLEGAN───────────────────────

The Delano Inn Victorian B&B	99-209 BB	·Full breakfast
302 Cutler St 49010	6 rooms, 6 pb	Breakfast included in room
866-686-0240 269-686-0240	Most CC	rate every morning, gardens,
Scott and Karen Ehrich	C-ltd/S-no/P-no/H-ltd	refreshments, concierge
		service available

The DeLano Mansion in central Southwest Michigan is a short drive from Holland and Saugatuck. Offering luxury fireplace & whirlpool suites in a romantic Historic mansion. The Victorian gardens, fountain, and gazebo are ideal for weddings or romance.
✉ delanoinn@triton.net ♦ www.delanoinn.com

ALMA───────────────────────

Saravilla B&B	99-169 BB	Full breakfast
633 N State St 48801	7 rooms, 7 pb	Snacks & beverages
989-463-4078	Most CC, •	Fireplaces, pool table, ping
Linda & Jon Darrow	C-yes/S-ltd/P-no/H-no	pong table, hot tub, piano, air
		conditioning

Saravilla is a three story Dutch Colonial home built in 1894, and was originally a "summer cottage." Saravilla offers a delightful taste of the Bed and Breakfast experience for everyone.
✉ Ljdarrow@saravilla.com ♦ www.saravilla.com

ANN ARBOR───────────────────────

Ann Arbor B&B	169-229 BB	Full, hearty, hot breakfast
921 E. Huron 48104	9 rooms, 9 pb	Tea, coffee, pop, fruit, cereal
734-994-9100	Most CC	always available. 37 dinner
Pat Materka	C-ltd/S-no/P-no/H-no	restaurants within one mile.
		Private en suite bath, WiFi,
		DVD/TV, computer, hair
		dryer, iron, covered parking,
		hot tubs.

Join Pat & Bob Materka in a 1962 contemporary chalet with a large common area including a sunken living room with fireplace surrounded by an atrium dining area with a large deck overlooking the University of Michigan Central Campus.
✉ AnnArborBedAndBreakfast@GMail.com ♦ www.annarborbedandbreakfast.com

Vitosha Guest Haus	109-159 BB	Deluxe continental
1917 Washtenaw Ave 48104	10 rooms, 10 pb	Tea Service upon request
734-741-4969	Most CC, *Rated*, •	($10) w/pastry, fruit &
Kei J. Constantinov	C-yes/S-no/P-no/H-yes	chocolate (4pm). We cater
	Spanish	small events & conferences.
		Kosher, vegan & vegetarian
		menus upon request, daily
		room service, referrals to
		entertainment; taxis

Channel your inner gargoyle at Vitosha Guest Haus! Historic castlestone complex minutes from U.of M. classrooms. Ten rooms sleep 36, six fireplace rooms, en suite bathrooms, 22,000 sq. feet of historical significance with WiFi, pets on premises.
✉ info@a2vitosha.com ♦ www.a2vitosha.com

AUBURN HILLS

Cobblestone Manor
3151 University Dr 48326
800-370-7270 248-370-8000
Heather & Paul Crandall

179-349 BB
10 rooms, 10 pb
Most CC, •
C-ltd/S-no/P-no/H-yes

Full breakfast
Soft drinks, popcorn, fresh
cookies and mints always
available.
Whirlpool tubs, fireplaces,
high speed wireless Internet,
free workout facility nearby

*Voted "Best in Michigan" and "One of the Most Romantic Getaways in the Nation." Built in
1840, recently renovated with the modern amenities required by professional travelers.
Offers ten beautifully appointed guestrooms, onsite wedding chapel and gardens.*
✉ stay@cobblestonemanor.com ○ www.cobblestonemanor.com

AUTRAIN

Pinewood Lodge
10 miles west of Munising
49806
906-892-8300
Jerry & Jenny Krieg

145-175 BB
5 rooms, 5 pb
Visa, MC, Disc, *Rated*,
•
C-ltd/S-no/P-no/H-ltd

Full breakfast
Library, sitting room, sauna,
beach on Lake Superior,
gazebo, gardens. Best rooms
have fireplaces.

*An exquisite north woods log home surrounded by tall, Norway Pines. A few steps away
from the grandeur of the world's largest fresh water lake. Breakfast overlooking the beach,
Lake Superior & AuTrain Island.*
✉ pinewood@tds.net ○ www.pinewoodlodgebnb.com

BATTLE CREEK

Greencrest Manor
6174 Halbert Rd E 49017
269-962-8633
Tom & Kathy VanDaff

135-275 BB
8 rooms, 6 pb
Visa, MC, AmEx, *Rated*
C-ltd/S-no/P-no/H-no

Continental plus breakfast
Snacks
Sitting room, library, suites,
fireplaces, cable TV,
accommodations for
business travelers

*Words truly cannot describe this treasure of a typically "French" rural Manor. Its breathtak-
ing views around every corner, inside or out in the gardens, will persuade you to stay here
and relax.*
✉ klbvd@comcast.net ○ www.greencrestmanor.com

BELLAIRE

Applesauce Inn B&B
7296 S. M-88 49615
888-533-6448 231-533-6448
David & Wendy Keene

75-125 BB
3 rooms, 2 pb
Visa, MC, Disc
C-ltd/S-no/P-yes/H-ltd

Full breakfast
Evening dessert, 24 hour
beverages
Wraparound porch,
featherbeds, electric
fireplaces, Cable TV/VCR,
VHS, library, Internet Access

*At Applesauce Inn, we pride ourselves on casual comfort with all the amenities. Feather-
beds, fireplaces and interesting conversation are just the beginning! We may be small, but
we are big on hospitality!*
✉ info@applesauceinn.com ○ www.applesauceinn.com

BIG BAY

Big Bay Lighthouse
3 Lighthouse Rd 49808
906-345-9957
Jeff & Linda Gamble

125-190 BB
7 rooms, 7 pb
Rated, •
C-ltd/S-no/P-no/H-no

Full breakfast
Coffee, tea, hot chocolate all
day, evening snack of
cookies
Sitting room, library,
Jacuzzis, fireplaces, sauna

*Escape the ordinary. High on cliff overlooking Lake Superior, the Lighthouse beckons you
to experience a secluded retreat from modern life, with quiet nights and northern lights.*
✉ keepers@BigBayLighthouse.com ○ www.bigbaylighthouse.com

BROOKLYN

Dewey Lake Manor B&B
11811 Laird Rd 49230
800-815-5253 517-467-7122
Joe & Barb Phillips

79-139 BB
5 rooms, 5 pb
Visa, MC, *Rated*, •
C-ltd/S-ltd/P-ltd/H-no

Full breakfast
Picnic lunch (with prior
notice), snacks, tea, coffee,
(lemonade, cider in season)
always cookies
Sitting room, parlor with
piano, fireplace, bonfires,
paddle boats, canoe, grills,
massage available

Century-old historic home on Dewey Lake, a Southern Michigan getaway in the Irish Hills-sparkling lakes, hiking trails, gardens, country air, bird watching. This home, furnished with antiques, fireplaces and featherbeds, offers a "country retreat."
✉ deweylk@frontiernet.net ✪ www.deweylakemanor.com

CHARLEVOIX

Horton Creek Inn
5757 Boyne City Rd 49720
866-582-5373 231-582-5373
Dave & Jeannie Babbitt

125-200 BB
7 rooms, 5 pb
Visa, MC
C-ltd/S-no/P-no/H-ltd

Full breakfast
Soft drinks & waters
Lots of common space to
relax, visit or read, outdoor
pool & hot tub

Cedar log home on 60 acres of quiet pines in the north woods. Centrally located between Charlevoix, Petoskey and Boyne City. Gardens, trails, pool and hot tub for hours of relaxation. Five guestrooms and two-room suite for families or groups.
✉ jeannie@hortoncreekinnbb.com ✪ www.hortoncreekinnbb.com

CHELSEA

Chelsea House Victorian Inn
118 E Middle St 48118
877-618-4935 734-475-2244
James E Myles

115-210 BB
5 rooms, 5 pb
Visa, MC
C-yes/S-no/P-no/H-ltd

Full breakfast
Porch, Jacuzzi, fireplace,
weddings, business retreats,
private parties, baby
showers

This 1880's Queen Ann Victorian Inn is a full-service Bed and Breakfast with period decorated rooms, an intimate Carriage House suite, a large gathering space, and the finest hospitality imaginable.
✉ innkeeper@chelseahouseinn.com ✪ www.chelseahouseinn.com

CLARKSTON

Millpond Inn
155 N Main St 48346
800-867-4142 248-620-6520
Joan Kopietz

85-95 BB
5 rooms, 5 pb
Most CC, *Rated*
C-yes/S-no/P-ltd/H-ltd

Full breakfast
Snacks
Sitting room, cable TV, high
speed wireless Internet
access, accommodate
business travelers

A historic home in the village of Clarkston, where comfort, cleanliness and good food are paramount. Fresh flowers from the many gardens surrounding the Inn add a special touch to each room.
✉ millpondbb@email.com ✪ www.millpondinnbb.com

COLDWATER

Chicago Pike Inn & Spa
215 E Chicago St 49036
800-471-0501 517-279-8744
John & Nancy Krajny

100-195 BB
8 rooms, 8 pb
Visa, MC, AmEx, *Rated*
C-yes/S-no/P-no/H-yes

Full breakfast
Afternoon refreshments
Library, reception room,
some Jacuzzis, stained glass
windows, sitting areas, A/C,
wireless Internet

Welcome to Chicago Pike Inn & Spa Bed & Breakfast! "Lodging & Pampering in Victorian Elegance." A beautifully restored Victorian home right in the heart of the Coldwater historical district on Route 12 Heritage Trail. A great romantic getaway!
✉ john@chicagopikeinn.com ✪ www.chicagopikeinn.com

FENNVILLE

Heritage Manor Inn
2253 Blue Star Hwy 49408
888-543-4384 269-543-4384
Ross & Diane Hunter

90-180 BB
12 rooms, 12 pb
Most CC
C-yes/S-no/P-no/H-no

Full Buffet Breakfast
Stocked guest kitchen and
homemade cookies!
Heated indoor pool, Jacuzzi,
fireplaces, garden, volleyball
court, playset, wireless
Internet

Heritage Manor Inn offers a peaceful country setting for romantic getaways & family gatherings.
✉ rdhunter@heritagemanorinn.com 🌐 www.heritagemanorinn.com

J. Paules' Fenn Inn
2254 S 58th St 49408
877-561-2836 269-561-2836
Paulette Clouse

110-175 BB
5 rooms, 5 pb
Visa, MC, Disc
C-ltd/S-ltd/P-yes/H-ltd

Full breakfast
Wine & dessert in the
evenings.
Flower gardens, decks, fire
pit, picnic tables all on 2
acres, lots of outdoor places
to lounge

You don't have to go far to "Get-A-Way." Your Inn is awaiting you with 5 rooms, all with private baths, 3 with fireplaces, & 3 with Jacuzzi tubs, full breakfast. Stay three days & get a free bottle of Fenn Valley wine. Pets accepted. Non-smoking.
✉ jpaules@accn.org 🌐 www.jpaulesfenninn.com

Kingsley House B&B Inn
626 W Main St 49408
866-561-6425 269-561-6425
David Drees

115-215 BB
8 rooms, 8 pb
Most CC, *Rated*, •
C-ltd/S-no/P-no/H-ltd

Full gourmet breakfast
Seasonal snacks & beverages
in the afternoon
Wrap around porch, outdoor
movie theater, bicycles,
porch swing, hammock

Kingsley House B&B in the heart of Southwest Michigan is minutes from Saugatuck, Holland & South Haven. Offering romantic lodging with luxury Jacuzzis, fireplaces & gracious hospitality. The peaceful setting & friendly atmosphere make it an ideal getaway.
✉ romanticgetaways@kingsleyhouse.com 🌐 www.kingsleyhouse.com

FLINT

Avon House B&B
518 Avon St 48503
888-832-0627 810-232-6861
Arletta E. Minore

65 BB
3 rooms
Most CC
C-yes/S-no/P-no/H-no

Full breakfast
Sitting room, A/C, play yard,
extended stay rates, small
meetings, garden, wrap-
around porch

Enchanting Victorian home close to college and cultural center with art and entertainment. Driving distance to Birch Run Outlets and Frankenmuth. University of Michigan-Flint, Mott and Baker Colleges and Kettering University nearby.
✉ avonhsebed@aol.com 🌐 www.avonhousebandb.com

FRANKENMUTH

Frankenmuth Bender Haus
337 Trinklein St 48734
989-652-8897
Bev & Elden Bender

95-110 BB
4 rooms, 2 pb
Rated, •
C-ltd/S-no/P-no/H-no
German
April-November

Full breakfast
Sitting room, bicycles, cable
TV, central air conditioning
and tours available with
advance notice

Our traditional home is in the center of #1 tourist town. Our home is quiet and peaceful. Two blocks west of Main Street in the beautiful German town of Frankenmuth.
✉ benderjb@juno.com

GRANDVILLE

Prairieside Suites Luxury B&B	125-205 BB	Full or deluxe cont.-your
3180 Washington Ave SW	5 rooms, 5 pb	choice
49418	Most CC, •	An endless supply of cookies
616-538-9442	C-ltd/S-no/P-no/H-no	and baked goods, coffee, tea,
Cheri & Paul Antozak		homemade hot cocoa &
		microwave popcorn.
		Whirlpool Tubs for 2,
		Fireplaces, Massage
		Services, Packages, Room
		Services, Flowers, Quiet &
		Private

Voted "3rd Best Over All B&B in North America," "Best in the Midwest" & "Best of the Great Lakes"! Our Romantic Spa Rooms include: Whirlpool tub, Fireplace, King Bed, Private Bath, heated towel bar, AC/TV/VCR/cable, Ref/Micro. Massage services & packages ✉ cheri@prairieside.com ○ www.prairieside.com

HASTINGS

Adrounie House	70-140 BB	Full breakfast
126 S Broadway 49058	5 rooms, 5 pb	Parlor, fireplace in sitting
800-927-8505 269-945-0678	Most CC	room, two suites with
Don & April C. Tubbs	C-ltd/S-no/P-no/H-ltd	whirlpool, cable, A/C, WiFi
		high speed Internet

Whether you are traveling, house hunting, in the area for business, visiting friends, or just need to get away for the weekend, let us provide you with a Bed & Breakfast experience that will leave you refreshed. ○ www.adrounie.com

HOLLAND

The Inn at Old Orchard Road	110-120 BB	Full breakfast
1422 South Shore Dr 49423	3 rooms, 3 pb	Snacks, early morning coffee
616-335-2525	Visa, MC, Disc, *Rated*	& tea.
Elizabeth DeWaard	C-ltd/S-no/P-no/H-ltd	Cable TV, porch, patio,
		gazebo

Enjoy quiet solitude on a quaint front porch, a spacious patio, or a rustic gazebo at this 1906 Dutch farmhouse. Cozy guestrooms offer queen sized beds, private baths & "wake-up" coffee or tea. ✉ orchardroad@chartermi.net ○ www.theinnatoldorchardroad.com

Pigeon Creek Inn	200-295 BB	Full breakfast
13433 Bingham St 49424	3 rooms, 3 pb	Fireplace, TV, DVD, CD,
800-949-2275 616-836-4088	Most CC	balconies, large 2 person
Jack Wainer	C-ltd/S-no/P-no/H-ltd	(62"x66") whirlpool tubs,
		glass block showers

Contemporary luxury suites in a relaxed romantic atmosphere. Unlike most B&B's, the Pigeon Creek Inn is of new construction, specifically designed to be a weather-proof romantic getaway. 35 acre wooded setting. ✉ jack@pigeoncreekinn.com

JONESVILLE

Munro House B&B and Spa	139-219 BB	Made-to-order breakfast
202 Maumee St 49250	7 rooms, 7 pb	Complimentary soft drinks,
800-320-3792 517-849-9292	Most CC, *Rated*, •	cookies, snacks
Mike & Lori Venturini	C-yes/S-no/P-no/H-ltd	Massage & Day Spa services
		on-site

"The Most Comfortable Lodging in Southern Michigan." Events include Murder Mystery, Romance, Massage, & the original "Chef Night" cooking party. See our website for current events or call us to create something special for you on any day of the year. ✉ info@munrohouse.com ○ www.munrohouse.com

KALAMAZOO────────────────────────────

Hall House B&B
106 Thompson St 49006
888-761-2525 269-343-2500
David and Cathy Griffith

109-180 BB
5 rooms, 5 pb
Most CC, *Rated*
C-yes/S-no/P-no/H-no

Full breakfast on weekends
Deluxe Continental on
weekdays. Complimentary
beverages always available.
High speed wireless access,
DirecTV / VCRs in rooms, in
room phones, air
conditioning (during
summer).

Stately 1920s Georgian Colonial home minutes from downtown, Western Michigan University, and on the edge of the Kalamazoo College campus.
✉ innkeepers@hallhouse.com ✆ www.hallhouse.com

Kalamazoo House B&B
447 W South St 49007
866-310-0880 269-382-0880
Laurel & Terry Parrott

109-149 BB
9 rooms, 9 pb
Most CC
C-ltd/S-no/P-no/H-no

Full breakfast
Evening refreshments,
special diets accommodated
by request
Wireless Internet,
telephones, some whirlpool
tubs, spacious common
areas, cable TV, porches

Victorian elegance and modern convenience in downtown Kalamazoo, just steps from museums, theatres, fine dining and nightlife. Enjoy a delicious multi-course hot breakfast, evening refreshments and cookies & milk before bed at this highly rated B&B!
✉ thekalamazoohouse@msn.com ✆ www.thekalamazoohouse.com

LELAND──────────────────────────────

Whaleback Inn
1757 N Manitou Trail 49654
800-942-5322 231-256-9090
Scott & Tammie Koehler

89-269 BB
19 rooms, 19 pb
Visa, MC, *Rated*
C-yes/S-ltd/P-no/H-yes

Continental breakfast
24 hour Inglenook Room for
snacks and beverages.
Breakfast available Memorial
through Labor Day
Sitting room, hot tubs, sauna,
hiking, playground, lake,
swimming, basketball, WiFi
in all rooms

Relaxing getaway. Beautiful scenic area on Lake Leelanau. All 14 rooms, cottage and 4 cottage suite accommodations are new or recently remodeled, with private baths, WiFi, and ground floor entry.
✉ info@whalebackinn.com ✆ www.whalebackinn.com

LUDINGTON────────────────────────────

The Lamplighter B&B
602 E Ludington Ave 49431
800-301-9792 231-843-9792
Bill & Jane Carpenter

100-170 BB
5 rooms, 5 pb
Most CC, *Rated*
C-ltd/S-ltd/P-no/H-ltd

Full Gourmet Breakfast
You may enjoy your morning
coffee or tea and breakfast in
the dining room or the patio
Fireplaces, living room,
parlor, antiques, chandeliers,
Cable TV, Internet, Jacuzzi
tubs

The only 3 Diamond AAA rated B&B in the Ludington area. Located minutes from white, sandy beaches and Michigan's most beautiful State Park, The Lamplighter is the B&B of choice for travelers who want to step back in time without losing touch with today.
✉ lamplighter@ludington-michigan.com ✆ www.ludington-michigan.com

MACKINAC ISLAND

Bay View at Mackinac	95-425 BB	Full breakfast
906-847-3295	20 rooms, 20 pb	Afternoon & evening
Lisa Halleck	Most CC	refreshments
		Private baths, A/C, TV, VCR, free movie library, private telephones and outside porch veranda.

Warm comfortable days and cool starlit nights are the essence of the Bay View at Mackinac Island. From our standard room to the Bridal Suite, your Bay View accommodations share charming furnishings, elegant bedding ensembles and private baths.
✉ BayViewbnb@aol.com ✪ www.mackinacbayview.com

NEW BUFFALO

New Buffalo Inn & Spa	125-345 BB	Coupon to local restaurant
231 E Buffalo St 49117	12 rooms, 12 pb	cafe
800-469-7668 269-469-1000	Most CC, •	In-room Jacuzzis, outdoor
Lisa Werner & Gary Ramberg,	C-ltd/S-no/P-ltd/H-no	hot tub, fireplaces, on-site
Kurt & Tracy Hauseman	Swedish	spa services

Our mission is to create a peaceful, relaxing, private environment that will be spiritually rejuvenating for all of our guests. We also have five cottages to meet your needs, whether it's perks for your pets, or hot tub & fireplace with your honey! SPA!
✉ lisa@NewBuffaloInn.com ✪ www.newbuffaloinn.com

OMER

Rifle River B&B	50-75 BB	Continental breakfast
500 Center Ave 48749	4 rooms	
989-653-2543	C-yes/S-no/P-ltd/H-no	
Gerald & Judie Oboyle		

✉ judiea@surfmk.com

PENTWATER

Hexagon House	100-225 BB	Full breakfast
760 6th St 49449	5 rooms, 5 pb	Coffee, tea, lemonade,
231-869-4102	Visa, MC, *Rated*	cookies, brownies, nuts &
Tom & Amy Hamel	C-ltd/S-no/P-no	candies
		TV/DVD players, CD/radio, central air & heat, porches, Jacuzzi tub, electric fireplaces, massage

The Hexagon House B&B is the perfect romantic destination. Whether enjoying a quiet moment by the fireplace in our Victorian parlor or sharing wine under the stars on our spacious porches, hospitality and ambience will compliment your plans for romance.
✉ innkeepers@HexagonHouse.com ✪ www.hexagonhouse.com

PETOSKEY

Terrace Inn	69-189 BB	Deluxe Continental Breakfast
1549 Glendale 49770	37 rooms, 37 pb	Our restaurant offers an
800-530-9898 231-347-2410	Visa, MC, Disc, •	array of delicious entrees,
Mo Rave & Patty Rasmussen	C-ltd/S-no/P-no/H-no	home-made soups, specialty
	Jun-Aug Jan & Feb	salads & desserts
		coffee & tea gift shop wireless Internet restaurant wine and beer license massage by appt.

Our Historic Inn and restaurant was built in 1911 and has been in continuous operation since. Open year-round, the Inn offers 37 rooms from cozy cottage to whirlpool suites, a fantastic dining menu and friendly service!
✉ info@theterraceinn.com ✪ www.theterraceinn.com

PLYMOUTH

932 Penniman – A B&B	125-229 BB	Full breakfast
932 Penniman Ave 48170	5 rooms, 5 pb	Cookies, tea, popcorn, hot
888-548-4887 734-414-7444	Most CC, *Rated*, •	chocolate
Carey & Jon Gary	C-ltd/S-no/P-no/H-no	Library, whirlpool tubs,
		fireplaces, porches, wireless
		Internet, cable TV, accom.
		bus. travelers

Enjoy the informal elegance of this lovingly restored, 1903 Victorian home.
✉ innkeeper932@yahoo.com

SAUGATUCK

Bayside Inn	85-200 BB	Continental plus breakfast
618 Water St 49453	10 rooms, 10 pb	Snacks like popcorn and
269-857-4321	Most CC, *Rated*	cookies available in the
Kathy & Frank Wilson	C-yes/S-no/P-no/H-ltd	afternoon
		Converted boathouse,
		private bath & deck in
		rooms, cable TV, phones,
		wireless Internet access

*Bayside is a former boathouse, converted to a B&B, on the water near downtown Saug-
atuck. In-ground outdoor hot tub situated 4 feet from the water's edge. Six rooms and four
suites with private baths.*
✉ info@baysideinn.net ◐ www.baysideinn.net

Beachway Resort	55-275 BB	Coffee, fruit and doughnuts
106 Perryman St 49453	38 rooms, 38 pb	Snacks
269-857-3331	Most CC, *Rated*	Swimming pool, cable TV,
Frank & Kathy Wilson	C-yes/S-no/P-no/H-yes	VCR, video library, games,
	May-end of Oct.	sundeck

*The Beachway Resort is the closest hotel to Lake Michigan's award-winning Oval Beach.
Overlooking the harbor on the banks of the Kalamazoo River, just a 100-foot ferry ride to
downtown.*
✉ info@beachwayresort.com ◐ www.beachwayresort.com

Beechwood Manor Inn &	165-195 BB	Full breakfast
Cottage	3 rooms, 3 pb	Coffeemaker, coffees, teas,
736 Pleasant St 49453	Most CC	hot chocolate, refrigerator.
877-857-1587 269-857-1587	C-ltd/S-no/P-ltd/H-ltd	Antiques, fireplaces,
Gregg Smith & Sal Sapienza		veranda, A/C, wireless
		Internet access, parlor

*With our "ideal location," "gracious hospitality" and Innkeepers who have "perfected the
exact balance between being helpful and present and being discretely in the background,"
we invite you to come experience Beechwood Manor Inn*
✉ beechwoodmanor@comcast.net ◐ www.beechwoodmanorinn.com

Hidden Garden Cottages &	135-225 BB	Continental plus breakfast
Suites	4 rooms, 4 pb	Assorted snacks, teas,
247 Butler St 49453	Visa, MC, •	popcorn
888-857-8109 269-857-8109	S-no/P-no/H-ltd	Fireplaces, whirlpool tubs for
Daniel Indurante & Gary Kott		two, TVs with DVD/VCR,
		movies, mini-kitchens,
		wireless Internet

*Luxurious hideaways for two, perfect for guests seeking a more private bed & breakfast.
Elegantly furnished, steps away from shopping, dining, attractions. Perfect for honeymoons
or romantic getaways.*
✉ indakott@aol.com ◐ www.hiddengardencottages.com

SAUGATUCK————————————————————————————

The Kirby House
294 W Center St 49453
800-521-6473 269-857-2904
Jim Gowran

85-225 BB
8 rooms, 6 pb
Most CC, *Rated*
C-ltd/S-no/P-no/H-no

Full breakfast
Porch, gardens, fireplaces,
heated in-ground pool,
Jacuzzi, parlor, foyer, butler
pantry

The home is graced with quarter-sawn oak woodwork and panels, prismed windows, tall ceilings with gently curved moldings, a six sided tower, wrap-around front porch and beautiful gardens.
✉ jim@kirbyhouse.com ○ www.kirbyhouse.com

Maplewood Hotel
428 Butler St 49453
800-650-9790 269-857-1771
Catherine Simon

140-275 BB
15 rooms, 15 pb
Most CC, •
C-ltd/S-no/P-no/H-ltd

Full breakfast
Common room, fireplaces,
swimming pool, Jacuzzi tubs,
deck, parlor, lobby

On the quiet village green in the center of Saugatuck stands the Maplewood Hotel, a gleaming tribute to the 19th century. 15 guestrooms with exquisite furnishings & antiques. Suites offer Jacuzzi tubs & fireplaces or sitting area. Heated pool.
✉ info@maplewoodhotel.com ○ www.maplewoodhotel.com

Park House Inn
888 Holland St 49453
866-321-4535 269-857-4535
Melisa Raywood & Toni Trudell

130-205 BB
9 rooms, 9 pb
Most CC
C-ltd/S-no/P-ltd/H-yes

Full breakfast
Coffee, tea, soft drinks,
bottled water, snacks &
homemade cookies provided
for guests
Jacuzzi, hot tub, fireplace
suites, breakfast inside or
outside weather permitting

Stay with us and relive a bit of Saugatuck history. Built in 1857 by H. D. Moore, The Park House is one of Saugatuck's oldest residences. Special packages include romance getaways, spa weekends and much more . . .
✉ info@parkhouseinn.com ○ www.parkhouseinn.com

Sherwood Forest
938 Center St 49453
800-838-1246 269-857-1246
Susan & Keith Charak

110-205 BB
5 rooms, 5 pb
Visa, MC, Disc, *Rated*,
•
C-ltd/S-no/P-no/H-no
Atlantian

Full breakfast
Afternoon tea, snacks
Sitting room, bicycles, heated
pool, skiing, Jacuzzi, cottage

Surrounded by woods, this beautiful Victorian-style home offers fireplace-Jacuzzi suites, heated pool, bicycles, wraparound porch. ½block to Lake Michigan & spectacular sunsets.
✉ sf@sherwoodforestbandb.com ○ www.sherwoodforestbandb.com

Twin Gables Inn
900 Lake St 49453
800-231-2185 269-857-4346
Mike & Margaret Hull

99-266 BB
15 rooms, 15 pb
Most CC, •
C-ltd/S-no/P-ltd/H-yes

3 course gourmet breakfast
coffee, tea, popcorn, hot
cocoa, Chai Latte, hot cider,
chocolates, trail mix, cocktail
crackers
Hot tub, seasonal pool, A/C,
bikes, beach chairs,
umbrellas, library,
lg.common room, pond,
gardens

Slip into our charming and romantic Inn on the art Coast of Michigan. Choose one of our 15 beautiful rooms and enjoy a sumptuous breakfast overlooking the harbor. Beautiful ceremony & reception site for weddings & lrg.events 3 hrs. Chicago/Detroit
✉ relaxing@twingablesinn.com ○ www.twingablesinn.com

SOUTH HAVEN——————————————————————————————

A Country Place B&B
79 N Shore Dr N 49090
877-866-7801 269-637-5523
John & Cindy Malmstrom

98-155 BB
5 rooms, 5 pb
Visa, MC, Disc
C-ltd/S-no/P-no/H-yes
Feb – Nov

Full breakfast
Complimentary
refreshments all day, freshly
baked goodies for late
afternoon/evening snack
Fireplace, sitting room,
screened gazebo

Our 140 year old Greek Revival home is situated on 2 acres of woodland with Lake Michigan sandy beach access ½ block away. The focal point of the back lawn is a large screened gazebo where nature can be appreciated to the fullest.
✉ acountryplace@cybersol.com ✆ www.acountryplace.net

——

Carriage House at Harbor
118 Woodman St 49090
269-639-2161
Suzanne and David

125-260 BB
12 rooms, 12 pb
Most CC, *Rated*
S-no/P-no/H-yes

Lavish gourmet breakfast
Afternoon refreshments and
evening hors d'oeuvres.
Complimentary bottled
water and soft drinks.
Massages, Concierge
services. Complimentary
Water and Soft Drinks.
Refreshments/evening
appetizers

Harborside B&B, open year round, featuring gourmet food, superior service, designer rooms with cozy fireplaces & private baths. Our dining rooms, screened porch & decks overlook the harbor. Walk to town or across the street to the beach & amazing sunsets.
✉ suzanne@carriagehouseharbor.com ✆ www.carriagehouseharbor.com

——

Inn at the Park B&B
233 Dyckman Ave 49090
877-739-1776 269-639-1776
Carol Ann & Jerry Hall

120-260 BB
9 rooms, 9 pb
Visa, MC, Disc, *Rated*
S-no/P-no/H-yes

Full Gourmet breakfast
Evening hors d'oeuvres &
wine in the pub, freshly
baked cookies, coffee, tea,
bottled water, sodas
Parlor, day room and pub
with fireplaces, daily
newspapers & magazines,
books, videos

South Haven's Inn at the Park Bed & Breakfast has elegantly appointed guestrooms with cozy fireplaces and whirlpool tubs. Steps from downtown South Haven and Lake Michigan, the ideal place for South Haven getaways.
✉ info@innpark.com ✆ www.innpark.com

——

Sand Castle Inn
203 Dyckman Ave 49090
269-639-1110
Charles Kindred

135-295 BB
10 rooms, 10 pb
Most CC, *Rated*
C-ltd/S-no/P-no/H-yes

Full buffet style gourmet
breakfast
Light evening appetizers,
home baked goods, fresh
fruit, hot and cold beverages
always available.
Sitting rm, video library,
fireplaces, private balconies,
seasonal heated pool, priv.
bathrms, WiFi

Beautiful, restored, historic Lake Michigan Resort Hotel. 1 block to beach, 3 to downtown, shops, restaurants. Designer decorated. Fireplaces, private decks or balconies. Seasonal heated pool. Full gourmet buffet breakfast, light evening appetizers. WiFi.
✉ innkeeper@thesandcastleinn.com ✆ www.thesandcastleinn.com

SOUTH HAVEN

Yelton Manor B&B & The Manor Guest House 140 North Shore Dr 49090 269-637-5220 Elaine & Robert	145-295 BB 17 rooms, 17 pb Visa, MC, AmEx S-no/P-no/H-no April through December	Full breakfast Evening hors d'oeuvres Porches, parlors, books, Jacuzzis, fireplaces, wireless Internet, private baths, TV/DVDs

Fabulous lakeside Victorian mansion. Elegant fireplace and Jacuzzi rooms, lakeviews. Porches, parlors, antiques.
✉ elaine@yeltonmanor.com ◐ www.yeltonmanor.com

ST. JOSEPH

South Cliff Inn B&B 1900 Lakeshore Dr 49085 269-983-4881 Bill Swisher	89-229 BB 7 rooms, 7 pb Most CC, *Rated*, • C-ltd/S-no/P-no/H-no	Continental plus or full breakfast Sunday brunch, snacks Sitting room, library, formal gardens, fireplaces

South Cliff Inn is an English Country style B&B. The exterior is English Cottage style with decks overlooking Lake Michigan, lovely formal gardens & sunsets beyond compare.
✉ InnInfo@SouthCliffInn.com ◐ www.southcliffinn.com

STURGIS

Willow Glen Pond B&B 65984 M-66 49091 866-430-3334 269-651-3291 Nancy Stewart	99-169 BB 4 rooms, 4 pb Visa, MC C-yes/S-no/P-ltd/H-no	Full gourmet breakfast High tea &/or wine & savories are available at check-in, gourmet dinners, picnics for guests Beautiful weddings, event planning, outdoor spa, storage for guests' bicycles, motorcycles & boats.

Willow Glen Pond is an elegant, country destination with decided European flair in the heart of River Country & Old World, Amish settlements. Gourmet breakfasts, extensive gardens, antiques and luxurious surroundings are perfect for relaxing and romance.
✉ nancy@willowglenpond.com ◐ www.willowglenpond.com

SUTTONS BAY

Korner Kottage 503 N. St. Josephs Ave 49682 888-552-2632 231-271-2711 Linda & Jim Munro	106-170 BB 4 rooms, 4 pb Cash, Checks C-ltd/S-no/P-no/H-ltd	Full breakfast 24 hour coffee & tea service, snacks & homemade cookies Cable TV, refrigerator, ceiling fan, wireless Internet, guest phone & fax

At the Korner Kottage B&B, living the sweet life is not only possible, it's the rule. Come stay awhile. Feed your soul, inspire your heart. Rest your body. Revel in the romance for which this home was built, and steal away with your true love.
✉ info@kornerkottage.com ◐ www.kornerkottage.com

UNION PIER

Garden Grove Bed and Breakfast 9549 Union Pier Rd 49129 800-613-2872 269-469-6346 Jerry & Paula Welsh	99-289 BB 7 rooms, 7 pb Most CC, *Rated*, • C-ltd/S-no/P-no/H-no	Full delicious breakfast Tea, coffee, juices, bottled water, snacks Fireplace, CATV, VCR/DVD & libraries, mini-fridge, microwave, wet bar sinks, bicycles, beach chairs

A peaceful, romantic getaway, The Garden Grove B&B & Carriage House is a quiet cottage retreat, set among the tall pines, maples & tree sculptures near the sandy beaches of Lake Michigan.
✉ gardengrove@comcast.net ◐ gardengrove.net

UNION PIER

Sandpiper Inn
16136 Lakeview Ave 49129
800-351-2080 269-469-1146
Veronica Lynch & Jim Reilly

120-295 BB
9 rooms, 9 pb
Most CC, *Rated*
S-no/P-no/H-no

Full breakfast
Snacks Sun – Thursday; wine
& hors d'oeuvres
Friday/Saturday
Sitting room, library,
bicycles, Jacuzzis, fireplaces,
private beach with beach
towels provided

Elegant new home 20 feet from terraced stairs to private beach. Luxurious accommodations including screened verandahs, fireplaces, private baths, Jacuzzi tubs, queen size beds & spectacular views.
info@sandpiperinn.net www.sandpiperinn.net

WEST BLOOMFIELD

Wren's Nest
7405 W Maple Rd 48322
248-624-6874
Irene Scheel

65-115 BB
6 rooms, 3 pb
Visa, MC, AmEx
C-yes/S-no/P-ltd/H-no

Full breakfast
Tea Room
Fireplaces, living room, sun
porches, garden, goats

Historic Greek Revival home, c.1832. Charming bed and breakfast filled with treasured antiques such as her 1890s music box, cozy quilts, beautiful linens, fine Havilland china and more.
thewrensnestbb@sbcglobal.net www.thewrensnestbb.com

WHITEHALL

White Swan Inn
303 S Mears Ave 49461
888-948-7926 231-894-5169
Cathy & Ron Russell

109-179 BB
4 rooms, 4 pb
Most CC, •
C-ltd/S-no/P-ltd/H-no

Full breakfast
Coffee area, beverages &
homemade treats
Whirlpool suite, wraparound
screened porch, formal
dining room, off-street
parking

Award-winning B&B. Built circa 1884 for a sawmill owner, the White Swan Inn is a Queen Anne-style home surrounded by mature gardens. Located just a few minutes drive to the sugar-sand beaches of Lake Michigan. Halfway between Chicago & Mackinac Island.
info@whiteswaninn.com www.whiteswaninn.com

WILLIAMSTON

Topliff's Tara
251 Noble Rd 48895
517-655-8860
Sheryl & Don Topliff

85-140 BB
5 rooms, 3 pb
Visa, MC, Disc, *Rated*
C-ltd/S-no/P-no/H-no

Full breakfast
Snacks, fruit & non-alcoholic
beverages
Hiking, cross country ski
trails, hot tub, llamas

The B&B is located in the 1905 farmhouse on this 50-acre Grand Country estate. Guests may stroll through the many gardens, or visit the curious llamas at the fences.
info@topliffstara.com www.topliffstara.com

YPSILANTI

The Queen's Residence B&B
220 S. Huron St. 48197
734-340-2805
Marla & Joe Queen

125-145 BB
3 rooms, 3 pb
Visa, MC
C-ltd/S-no/P-no/H-no

Full breakfast
The Wild Turkey Tavern on
premises

Where memories are made. Located in downtown historic Ypsilanti, just minutes from Ann Arbor, The Queen's Residence is Southeastern Michigan's most elegant, yet affordable Bed & Breakfast.
innkeeper@queensresidence.com www.queensresidence.com

Minnesota

AFTON ───

Afton House Inn
3291 S St Croix Trl 55001
877-436-8883 651-436-8883
Gordy & Kathy Jarvis

79-285 BB
25 rooms, 25 pb
Visa, MC, AmEx,
Rated, •
C-yes/S-no/P-no/H-yes

Continental plus breakfast
Lunch & dinner at Catfish
Cafe 11:30am-10pm, fine
dining at the Inn's Wheel
Room or Pennington 5–10
Bar service, Jacuzzis,
fireplaces, cable TV, art
gallery, coffee & ice cream
shop; business travel

Historic country inn overlooking the marina & the scenic St. Croix River. Furnished with antique decor, private baths. Most rooms have gas fireplace & Jacuzzi for two. Views overlook Marina & St. Croix River. Fine dining & casual dining. Romantic getaway!
✉ kathy@aftonhouseinn.com ☉ www.aftonhouseinn.com

ANNANDALE ───

Thayer's Historic B&B
60 W Elm St – Hwy 55 55302
800-944-6595 320-274-8222
Sharon Gammell

145-245 BB
11 rooms, 11 pb
Visa, MC, AmEx, *Rated*
C-ltd/S-ltd/P-ltd/H-no

Full white linen breakfast
Happy to do vegan,
vegetarian, gluten & dairy
free, plus other special diets
with advance notice
Psychic readings, ghost
hunting, classes in
paranormal studies, 2
friendly cats, wedding
officiate

A top 10 USA haunted places to stay! This restored 1895 Old West Victorian is the home of psychic Sharon Gammell & offers murder mystery dinners, psychic readings and paranormal awareness development workshops & classes, ghost hunting and afternoon teas.
✉ slg@thayers.net ☉ www.thayers.net

COOK ───

Ludlow's Island Resort
8166 Ludlow Rd 55723
877-583-5697 218-666-5407
Mark & Sally Ludlow

200-300 EP
56 rooms, 56 pb
Most CC, *Rated*, •
C-yes/S-ltd/P-yes/H-no
May-October

Breakfast and dinner
available by request
Sitting room, library, tennis
court, sauna, family friendly
facility, wireless Internet

This private island is situated under a canopy of pine and birch on the water's edge. Explore the nearby wilderness. Ludlow's Island Resort is a luxury full-service resort for golf, fishing, honeymoons, family vacations and more.
✉ info@ludlowsresort.com ☉ www.ludlowsresort.com

DULUTH ───

A. Charles Weiss Inn
1615 E Superior St 55812
800-525-5243 218-724-7016
Timothy & Karla Edwards

110-160 BB
5 rooms, 5 pb
Visa, MC, Disc
C-ltd/S-no/P-no/H-no

Full breakfast
Complimentary wine
Sitting room, library,
Jacuzzis, suites, fireplaces,
cable TV

Historic 1895 Victorian Colonial with 5 fireplaces and whirlpool room. Located 3 blocks from Lake Superior, Lakewalk, quick access to Canal Park, skiing and 3 golf courses.
✉ acweissinn@duluthmn.com ☉ www.acweissinn.com

───

A. G. Thomson House, Duluth, MN

DULUTH

A. G. Thomson House
2617 E Third St 55812
877-807-8077 218-724-3464
Tim & Angie Allen

139-299 BB
7 rooms, 7 pb
Most CC, *Rated*
S-no/P-no/H-yes

Full gourmet breakfast
Complimentary evening
wine
Whirlpool & fireplace suites,
Lake Superior views, garden
walking trail, A/C, wireless
Internet

Voted one of the Top 15 Bed & Breakfast Inns in the U.S. for "Best Weekend Escape," "Best Breakfast in the Great Plains," and "Most Privacy." Spacious whirlpool and fireplace suites with private baths, Lake Superior views and sumptuous breakfast.
✉ info@thomsonhouse.biz ◐ www.thomsonhouse.biz

The Firelight Inn on Oregon Creek
2211 E Third St 55812
888-724-0273 218-724-0272
Jim & Joy Fischer

179-249 BB
5 rooms, 5 pb
Most CC, *Rated*
S-ltd/P-no/H-no

Full gourmet private
breakfast
Complimentary snacks, ice,
hot and cold beverages 24
hours a day
Jacuzzi whirlpool, fireplace,
TV/VCR/DVD, oversized
robes, hairdryer, A/C

Elegant bed and breakfast located in a historic neighborhood, minutes from Canal Park and Lake Superior. Romantic suites feature fireplaces, whirlpools, and breakfast delivered to your suite. Everything speaks luxury. Top rated B&B at Trip Advisor!
✉ info@firelightinn.com ◐ www.firelightinn.com

The Olcott House Bed & Breakfast Inn
2316 E 1st St 55812
800-715-1339 218-728-1339
David & Jerry

135-225 BB
6 rooms, 6 pb
Visa, MC, Disc, *Rated*
C-ltd/S-no/P-no/H-ltd

Full breakfast
Afternoon tea, snacks,
complimentary wine
Sitting room, library, suites,
fireplaces, TV/DVD, AC, CD
player, wireless, business
travelers

Recently renovated 1904 "Gone With the Wind" Georgian Colonial mansion set in the historic East End of Duluth, MN, port city. Six suites, carriage house. Honeymoon packages.
✉ info@olcotthouse.com ◐ www.olcotthouse.com

LANESBORO——————————————

Hillcrest Hide-Away B&B
404 Hillcrest St E 55949
800-697-9902 507-467-3079
Marvin & Carol Eggert

105-130 BB
4 rooms, 4 pb
Visa, MC, Disc
C-ltd/S-no/P-no/H-ltd

Full breakfast
Wake to the fragrance of
freshly baked bread outside
your door. Bottomless
cookie jar!
WiFi, Full A/C, concierge, off-
street parking, TV

*Freshly-baked bread appears outside your door, followed by a full breakfast each morning.
We boast large comfy rooms (some with extra sleeping space), private bathrooms, & peace
while being just 3 blocks from Root River Trail and Lanesboro's main street.*
✉ hillcresthideaway@yahoo.com ✆ www.hillcresthideaway.com

Mrs. B's Historic Inn
101 Parkway Ave N 55949
800-657-4710 507-467-2154
Terry & Meredith Neumann

124-165 BB
9 rooms, 9 pb
Visa, MC, Disc
C-ltd/S-no/P-no/H-ltd
Mid April thru October

Creative full breakfast
Afternoon refreshments &
homemade cookies.
Occasionally Truffles are
served during your visit
Lobby, fireplace, guest bar
for refreshments, bike
storage, garden patio seating
on the Root River

*Mrs B's Historic Lanesboro Inn in Minnesota's Bluff Country offers 9 unique rooms with
private baths in its 1872 limestone structure. A/C, WiFi, fireplaces, a sumptuous breakfast
prepared by the Inn's personal chef. In town, on the Root River Trail.*
✉ mrsbsinn@earthlink.net ✆ www.mrsbsinn.com

Stone Mill Suites
100 Beacon St E 55949
866-897-8663 507-467-8663
Colleen Lamon

100-180 BB
10 rooms, 10 pb
Visa, MC, Disc
C-yes/S-no/P-no/H-yes

Continental plus breakfast
Themed Suites, iron-claw
fireplaces, cable, mini micro-
fridges, double whirlpools, 1
blk to trail

*A Historic Inn at the Lanesboro Feed Mill. Unique lodging experience in 1885 limestone
building. 10 suites with themes that depict the history of the building and Lanesboro's
irresistible charm. Double whirlpool baths, lofts, iron-claw fireplaces.*
✉ stonemillsuites@hotmail.com ✆ www.stonemillsuites.com

MINNEAPOLIS——————————————

Elmwood House
1 E Elmwood Pl 55419
888-822-4558 612-822-4558
Robert Schlosser

75-105 BB
3 rooms, 1 pb
Most CC, *Rated*, •
C-yes/S-no/P-no/H-no

Continental plus breakfast
Sitting room, 2-bedroom suite
with private bath

*1887 Norman chateau, handsomely restored and listed on the National Register of Historic
Places. 3 miles from downtown, 10 miles from the Mall of America and the Minneapolis/St.
Paul airport.*
✉ innkeeper@elmwoodhouse.us ✆ www.elmwoodhouse.us

Evelo's B&B
2301 Bryant Ave S 55405
612-374-9656
David & Sheryl Evelo

95 BB
3 rooms
Most CC, *Rated*
C-ltd/S-no/P-no/H-no

Continental plus breakfast
An example is fresh fruit,
assorted fresh
breads/muffins, jam, juice,
yogurt, coffee & tea etc..
TV, refrigerator, coffeemaker,
air conditioning, phone,
maps, newspapers, Mpls.
info. and free WiFi.

*1897 Victorian with period furnishings. Located on the bus line, walk to Walker Art Center,
Minneapolis Art Institute, Children's Theater and downtown. Featured on WCCO TV news-
cast," Finding Minnesota," Chosen by City Pages as Best in the Twin Cities.*
✉ evelosbandb@comcast.net

MONTICELLO

Historic Rand House	115-175 BB	Full breakfast
1 Old Territorial Rd 55362	4 rooms, 4 pb	Afternoon tea, snacks,
888-295-0881 763-295-6037	Visa, MC, *Rated*, •	complimentary wine
Duffy & Merrill Busch	C-ltd/S-no/P-no/H-ltd	Sitting room, library,
		bicycles, tennis court,
		fireplaces

One of the last remaining great Victorian country estates established by one of Minneapolis' most prominent families. The Rand House offers more than 3 acres of lawns, ponds, fountains and gardens.
✉ info@randhouse.com ✪ www.randhouse.com

NEW ULM

Auf Deutsche Strasse B&B	109-169 BB	Full breakfast
404 S German St 56073	5 rooms, 5 pb	Complimentary glass of
866-226-9856 507-354-2005	Cash, Checks	wine. Hot Chocolate in the
Gary & Ramona Sonnenberg	C-ltd/S-no/P-no	winter months.
		Wireless Internet access, can
		accommodate small parties,
		showers, meetings

Comfort, Cuisine and Coffee—Relax and Rejuvenate in our comfortable and tastefully decorated rooms that feature queen and king sized pillow-top beds; some rooms have fireplaces and whirlpool tubs. Breakfast is four courses and our coffee is fresh ground.
✉ info@deutschestrasse.com ✪ www.deutschestrasse.com

RED WING

Golden Lantern Inn	99-235 BB	Full breakfast
721 East Ave 55066	5 rooms, 5 pb	Sitting room, library, Jacuzzi,
888-288-3315 651-388-3315	Most CC, •	suites, fireplace, cable TV,
Gary & Pat McKenna	C-ltd/S-no/P-no/H-no	VCR, DVD, massages
		arranged, packages

Elegance abounds at this wonderful Tudor Revival, formerly home to Red Wing Shoe presidents. A perfect choice for romantic getaways or business retreats, honeymoons, babymoons and weddings. Inn gets top scores for its food.
✉ info@goldenlantern.com ✪ www.goldenlantern.com

Moondance Inn	125-219 BB	Full breakfast
1105 W 4th St 55066	5 rooms, 5 pb	Complimentary wine &
866-388-8145 651-388-8145	Most CC	appetizers on weekends & a
Chris Brown Mahoney & Mike	C-ltd/S-ltd/P-no/H-no	tea & sweets service
Waulk		weekdays
		Wireless access, travel
		information, golf discounts,
		seasonal specials,
		wedding/event hosting

The Red Wing, MN. Moondance Inn is an architectural gem. Original woodwork, Tiffany and Steuben chandeliers, and a gilded ceiling are on display. All rooms feature private baths with whirlpools and fireplaces. Delicious full breakfasts are served daily.
✉ info@moondanceinn.com ✪ www.moondanceinn.com

Round Barn Farm B&B	159-249 BB	Full breakfast
28650 Wildwood Ln 55066	5 rooms, 5 pb	Complimentary drinks & ice
866-763-2276 651-385-9250	Most CC	Jacuzzis, fireplace, patio,
Robin & Elaine Kleffman	C-ltd/S-no/P-no/H-ltd	lounge

Come to the country! Come to where old fashioned American and European ambience meet in a 3-story, bracketed country manor farm home.
✉ info@roundbarnfarm.com ✪ www.roundbarnfarm.com

STILLWATER

Ann Bean Mansion
319 West Pine St 55082
877-837-4400 651-430-0355
Jeremy & Erin Drews

119-239 BB
5 rooms, 5 pb
Visa, MC, Disc
C-ltd/P-no/H-ltd

Multi-course gourmet
breakfast
Special diets accommodated
with prior notice
Wine/Beverage offered on
arrival, Fireplaces, Private
Whirlpool baths, parlor,
piano, WiFi

Grand historic Victorian mansion, noted for exceptionally large rooms, gourmet breakfasts (in bed if you wish) and outstanding hospitality! Celebrate an occasion, find retreat, enjoy a get-away...
✉ info@annbeanmansion.com ◐ www.annbeanmansion.com

Aurora Staples Inn
303 N 4th St 55082
800-580-3092 651-351-1187
Cathy & Jerry Helmberger

129-249 BB
5 rooms, 5 pb
Visa, MC, *Rated*
C-ltd/S-no/P-no/H-yes

Full 3 Course
Wine and hors d'oeuvres
during the check-in time; tray
with coffee/tea at 8 am, full
breakfast at 9
In-room massage, book filled
library with wood fireplace,
hold small weddings and
receptions

Queen Anne Victorian close to downtown shopping and restaurants. Wraparound front porch for relaxing, formal English Gardens with a fountain, View of St. Croix River.
✉ info@aurorastaplesinn.com ◐ www.aurorastaplesinn.com

James Mulvey Inn
622 W Churchill St 55082
800-820-8008 651-430-8008
Teary O'Hara

99-249 BB
7 rooms, 7 pb
Visa, MC, AmEx, *Rated*
C-ltd/S-no/P-no/H-ltd

Full breakfast
Welcome refreshments and
tea on weekends
Parlor, balconies, bicycles,
Jacuzzis, conference room,
fireplaces, wireless Internet,
picnic basket

This is an enchanting place. Built by a lumberman, James Mulvey in 1878, this Italianate residence graces the most visited historic river town in the upper Midwest.
✉ cynthia@jamesmulveyinn.com ◐ www.jamesmulveyinn.com

Lady Goodwood
704 S 1st St 55082
866-688-LADY(5239) 651-439-3771
Ron & Cynthia Hannig

109-189 BB
3 rooms, 3 pb
Visa, MC
C-ltd/S-no/P-no/H-no

Delicious four-course
breakfast
Business services, whirlpool
tubs, in-room CD players,
fireplace

Treat yourself to a restful, romantic stay at Lady Goodwood Bed and Breakfast, located just three blocks from beautiful and historic downtown Stillwater, Minnesota.
✉ info@ladygoodwood.com ◐ www.ladygoodwood.com

The Rivertown Inn
306 W Olive St 55082
651-430-2955
Lisa Lothson

175-325 BB
9 rooms, 9 pb
Most CC, *Rated*, •
C-ltd/S-no/P-no/H-ltd

Full breakfast
Complimentary wine & hors
d'oeuvres daily
Sitting areas, A/C, screen
porch, gazebo, whirlpool
baths

The Rivertown Inn's nine rooms are each named and decorated in the spirit of a 19th century poet. Veranda, patio, gazebo to enjoy beautiful gardens. Four blocks from downtown.
✉ rivertown@rivertowninn.com ◐ www.rivertowninn.com

VERGAS

Loghouse & Homestead
44854 Fredholm Rd 56587
800-342-2318 218-342-2318
Suzanne Tweten

115-235 BB
5 rooms, 5 pb
Visa, MC, Disc, *Rated*
C-yes/S-no/P-ltd/H-no
Spanish

Full breakfast
Welcome tray includes fruit, cheese, crackers, cake & nonalcoholic wine, Early a.m. tray & newspaper
Lakeside balconies, in-room whirlpools & fireplaces, canoes, row boats, hiking, games, snowshoes

Romantic, elegant lakeside retreat in restored 1889 log house and turn-of-the-century homestead, with in-room fireplaces and whirlpools. Private in room or shared breakfasts. Canoes, row boats, hammocks, snow shoes. Near Concordia College Language Camps.
✉ loghouse@tekstar.com ☎ www.loghousebb.com

WABASHA

The Historic Anderson House B&B
333 W Main St 55981
651-565-2500
Teresa & Mike Smith

69-195 BB
22 rooms, 21 pb
Most CC
C-yes/S-no/P-ltd/H-ltd

Full breakfast
Dining room is open to the public for lunch and dinner. Beverages, wine, and kid's menu available.
Restaurant, bar service, sitting room, meeting and banquet facilities. Spa services available

A true step back into yesterday. Established in 1856 it is considered to be the oldest continuously operated hotel in Minnesota. Enjoy views of the Mississippi River while having the purrrfect bed warmer spend the night.
✉ minncathouse@aol.com ☎ www.historicandersonhouse.com

WINONA

Windom Park
369 W Broadway 55987
866-737-1719 507-457-9515
Craig & Karen Groth

120-195 BB
6 rooms, 6 pb
Visa, MC, *Rated*
C-ltd/S-ltd/P-no/H-no
Polish

Full breakfast
Evening wine & cheese
Fireplaces, Jacuzzis, suites, cable TV, business facilities, free wireless Internet

Enjoy the quiet charm of our 1900 Colonial Revival home and take home a memory.
✉ ckgroth@hbci.com ☎ www.windompark.com

Mississippi

HERNANDO

Sassafras Inn
785 Hwy 51 S 38632
800-882-1897 662-429-5864
Eric & Teresa Hartung

110-245 BB
4 rooms, 4 pb
Visa, MC, AmEx
S-ltd/P-no/H-ltd

Full breakfast
Complimentary soft drinks &
bottled water
Indoor pool and Jacuzzi,
recreation room, movie
library & pool table, mini-
refrigerators

*Welcome to the Sassafras Inn, we look forward to answering any questions you may have
and providing you with a wonderful stay at our Bed & Breakfast.*
✉ sassyinn@memphis.to 🌐 www.memphis.to

JACKSON

Fairview Inn
734 Fairview St 39202
888-948-1908 601-948-3429
Peter & Tamar Sharp

144-314 BB
18 rooms, 18 pb
Most CC, *Rated*, •
C-yes/S-no/P-no/H-ltd
Spanish

Full Southern Breakfast
24 hour guest kitchen
stocked with coffee, snacks,
sodas, and a refrigerator to
store personal food.
High Speed wireless Internet,
sitting room, library, meeting
facilities, room service, cab
service.

*The Fairview Inn & Sophia's Restaurant welcomes you to enjoy its stately elegance. A
unique Bed & Breakfast experience awaits you in our 1908 Colonial Revival mansion, one
of the few architecturally designed homes of that period remaining.*
✉ peter.sharp@fairviewinn.com 🌐 www.fairviewinn.com

LAUREL

Wisteria B&B
706 N 5th Ave 39440
888-426-3805 601-426-3805
Peggy G. Schneider

100-125 BB
3 rooms, 3 pb
Most CC, *Rated*
C-yes/S-no/P-no/H-no

Gourmet breakfast
Soft drinks, bottled spring
water
Phone, wireless Internet,
cable TV, central air/heat,
fireplaces, private baths

*Located in the heart of the historic district on tree canopied Fifth Avenue, Wisteria Bed and
Breakfast was built in 1900 for one of Laurel's founders, Silas Gardiner. It is listed on the
National Register of Historic Places.*
✉ wist706@bellsouth.net 🌐 www.wisteriabedandbreakfast.com

LORMAN

Rosswood Plantation
2513 Red Lick Rd 39096
800-533-5889 601-437-4215
Jean & Walt Hylander

135 BB
4 rooms, 4 pb
Visa, MC, *Rated*, •
C-yes/S-ltd/P-no/H-ltd
March–October

Full breakfast
Sitting room, library, hot tub,
nature trails, swimming pool

*Authentic columned mansion on working plantation near Natchez, Vicksburg. Heirloom
antiques, canopied beds, Civil War history, slave quarters.*
✉ whylander@aol.com 🌐 www.rosswood.net

NATCHEZ———————————————————————

Antebellum Music Room B&B
804 Washington St. 39120
601-445-7466
Joe Stone

90-150 BB
3 rooms, 2 pb
Visa, MC, Disc, *Rated*,
•
C-yes/S-ltd/P-no/H-no

Full Southern Breakfast
Complimentary coffee & tea
throughout the day,
complimentary wine.
Wireless Internet, antique
shop, live piano music
offered, billiard room,
extensive porches.

A unique B&B situated in the Historic District, filled with antiques & history, offering a Master Bedroom & 2-bedroom Cottage. Guests enjoy private concerts in the Music Room, games in the Billiard Room & browsing a gallery of rare maps, prints & books.
✉ jstonehouse@bellsouth.net ◐ www.josephstonehouse.com

The Briars Inn & Gardens
31 Irving Ln 39120
800-634-1818 601-446-9654
Wendy Grandin

125-195 BB
15 rooms, 15 pb
Visa, MC, AmEx,
Rated, •
C-yes/S-ltd/P-no/H-yes

Plantation style breakfast
Honor bar, Thursday cocktail
receptions, popcorn daily
1812 Southern planter's
mansion, swimming pool,
large galleries, gardens
throughout 19 acres

Quintessential Southern Planter's mansion, site of the 1845 wedding of Jefferson Davis and Varina Howell. 19 acres of beautiful gardens with views of the Mississippi River. Voted Mississippi Tourism Association's "Best Secluded B&B"!
✉ thebriarsinn@bellsouth.net ◐ www.thebriarsinn.com

Burn Antebellum B&B Inn
712 N Union St 39120
800-654-8859 601-442-1344

130-180 BB
9 rooms, 9 pb
Visa, MC, AmEx,
Rated, •
C-ltd/S-no/P-ltd/H-no

Plantation style southern
breakfast
Wine, coffee, tea, nuts,
dinners by arrangement
Swimming pool, brick patios,
gardens, library, verandas,
group dinners/tours,
meetings

A spectacular Greek Revival (c.1834) home set on two exquisitely landscaped acres covered with camellias. Entry noted for graceful semi-spiral staircase.
✉ Book@TheBurnBnB.com ◐ www.theburnbnb.com

Devereux Shields House
709 N Union St 39120
888-304-5378 601-304-5378
Ron & Eleanor Fry

125-175 BB
8 rooms, 8 pb
Most CC, *Rated*, •
C-ltd/S-no/P-yes/H-ltd

Southern Plantation
Breakfast
Assorted hot and cold
refreshments.
TV, Heat/A/C, private baths,
WiFi, Pool and special diets
happily accommodated.

Escape to quiet times, comfort and history at The Devereaux Shields House c1893, a Queen Ann Victorian located in the beautiful Natchez historic district and just a few blocks from town center or stunning views of the Mississippi River.
✉ comfort@dshieldsusa.com ◐ www.dshieldsusa.com

Dunleith House & Gardens
84 Homochitto 39120
800-433-2445 601-446-8500
John Holyoak

135-280 BB
27 rooms, 27 pb
Most CC
C-ltd/S-no/P-no/H-ltd

Full breakfast
Castle Restaurant is on site.
Pool, luxurious bathrobes,
whirlpool tubs, fireplaces,
massage

The Dunleith Historic Inn features large, spacious rooms and is surrounded by 40 acres of landscaped gardens. Each room is exquisitely decorated with traditional and antique furnishings. Incomparable cuisine and catering. Perfect for the weekend getaway.
✉ dunleith@dunleith.com ◐ www.dunleith.com

NATCHEZ

Glenfield Plantation
6 Providence Rd 39120
601-442-1002
Marjorie & Lester Meng

100-150 BB
3 rooms, 3 pb
Visa, MC, •
C-yes/S-ltd/P-ltd/H-yes

Full breakfast
Complimentary wine
Sitting room, banquet
facilities, secure parking,
wireless Internet, 180
channel satellite TV

Family owned for 5 generations, circa 1778 Spanish & 1840 English Gothic architecture. On the National Register of Historic Places. Antiques throughout. Located one and a half miles from downtown Natchez.
✉ glenfieldbb@bellsouth.net ◔ www.glenfieldplantation.com

Linden B&B
1 Linden Pl 39120
800-2-LINDEN 601-445-5472
Jeanette Feltus

120-135 BB
6 rooms, 6 pb
Cash, Checks, *Rated*,
•
C-ltd/S-ltd/P-no/H-yes

Full breakfast
Early morning coffee
Sitting room, piano, banquet
facilities

Linden B&B is a traditional, Antebellum home furnished with family heirlooms. Surrounded by a park-like setting of mossy live oaks and lawns. Occupied by the same family since 1849.
✉ jfeltus@lindenbandb.com ◔ www.lindenbandb.com/index.html

Monmouth Plantation
36 Melrose Ave 39120
800-828-4531 601-442-5852
Ron & Lani Riches

195-325 BB
30 rooms, 30 pb
Most CC, *Rated*, •
C-ltd/S-no/P-no/H-no
French (on request)

Full breakfast
Dinner, bar
Sitting room, Jacuzzis, suites,
fireplaces, cable TV,
conference facility

26 wooded acres of landscaped grounds, with stocked fishing ponds, period buildings, and superbly renovated mansion house, a National Historic Landmark built in 1818.
✉ luxury@monmouthplantation.com ◔ www.monmouthplantation.com

POPLARVILLE

Jerine's Guest Cottage
107 Dauphine St 39470
601-795-4927 601-795-4546
Robert & Bettye Applewhite

85-100 BB
3 rooms, 1 pb
Visa, MC, AmEx, •
C-yes/S-ltd/P-no/H-ltd

Continental breakfast
Flat screen TV, WiFi Internet
access, living room, dining
room, full kitchen.

A special cottage with 3 bedrooms, large living room, kitchen & spacious yard. Located in a small town, nice shopping & near major malls on the Mississippi Gulf Coast.
✉ appleltd@datasync.com

PORT GIBSON

Oak Square B&B
1207 Church St 39150
800-729-0240 601-437-5300
William D. Lum

135-195 BB
7 rooms, 7 pb
Most CC, *Rated*, •
C-ltd/S-ltd/P-no/H-ltd

Full southern breakfast
Complimentary wine & tea
Victorian parlor, piano, TV,
courtyard, fountain, gazebo

Step back to an era of gracious living and Antebellum splendor in this luxurious 1850, Greek Revival mansion of the Old South. Overnight guests will be surrounded by a "Gone With the Wind" setting.
✉ oaksquarebandb@cs.com

VICKSBURG

Cedar Grove Mansion Inn
2200 Oak St 39180
800-862-1300 601-636-1000
Colleen Small

100-260 BB
34 rooms, 34 pb
Most CC, *Rated*, •
C-yes/S-ltd/P-ltd/H-yes

Full breakfast
Dinner (fee), sherry &
chocolates, soda (fee),
restaurant, bar service
Bikes, tennis court, pool,
suites

Experience Vicksburg in style. Cedar Grove Mansion offers a warm Southern welcome to all travelers to Vicksburg.
✉ Info@CedarGroveInn.com ◔ www.cedargroveinn.com

Missouri

ANNAPOLIS

Rachel's B&B
202 W Second St 63620
888-245-7771 573-598-4656
Sharon & Joe Cluck

90-145 BB
5 rooms, 5 pb
Most CC, •
C-ltd/S-ltd/P-no/H-yes

Full breakfast
Dinner by reservation,
drinks are in guestroom frig,
cookies, popcorn, hot drinks
in dining room
Elopements, weddings,
candlelight dinners, Jacuzzi
suites, hot tub, satellite TV,
massage

Enjoy the comfort and elegance of our romantic, country inn. Relax by the rivers, lakes, waterfalls, mountains and streams nearby. Enjoy the fragrant, quiet & secluded rose gardens. Romance specials, military discount and elopement packages available.
✉ info@rachelsbb.com 🌐 www.rachelsbb.com

BLUE EYE

White River Lodge
738 Ozark Hollow Rd 65611
800-544-0257 417-779-1556
Becky & Bill Babler

159-209 BB
5 rooms, 5 pb
Visa, MC
C-ltd/S-no/P-no

Full breakfast
During the afternoon there
are a variety of drinks and
snacks available
Great room with fireplace,
sun-room, patio, theater
room, fitness/game room,
WiFi, sauna, spa

This spacious log B&B near Branson has a spectacular Table Rock Lake view, luxurious amenities, attention to details and hospitality that will delight even the most discriminating guests.
✉ whiteriverlodge@platwls.com 🌐 www.whiteriverlodgebb.com

BRANSON

Crystal Cove
635 Compton Ridge Rd 65616
888-699-0444 417-338-2715
The Offutt Family

99-159 BB
6 rooms, 6 pb
Visa, MC, Disc
C-ltd/S-no/P-no/H-no

Full homemade Ozark
breakfast
Fireplace, king size bed with
designer linens, feather
beds, massage, candlelight
packages and more

Luxury log cabins and suites overlooking Table Rock Lake; close to the Branson Area. Serene setting perfect for romance, families & business travelers. Five minutes to Silver Dollar City.
✉ jennyoffutt@aol.com 🌐 www.crystalcovebranson.com

Gaines Landing B&B
521 W Atlantic St 65616
800-825-3145 417-334-2280
Daniel & Michele Williamson

110-145 BB
3 rooms, 3 pb
Visa, MC, *Rated*, •
C-yes/S-ltd/P-no/H-no

Full Country Breakfast Buffet
Coffee, popcorn, evening
snacks & goodies
Pool, full size private hot tub
in each suite, fireplace,
private patio

Romantic getaway B&B located in beautiful, historic downtown Branson, Missouri. Your luxurious, private hot tub is only minutes from the "strip," yet nestled in the quiet of secluded woods.
✉ Reservations@gaineslanding.com 🌐 www.tablerocklakebandb.com

Red Bud Cove B&B Suites, Branson, MO

BRANSON

Red Bud Cove B&B Suites	99-152 BB	Full breakfast
162 Lakewood Dr 65672	8 rooms, 8 pb	Packages, reunions, sitting
800-677-5525 417-334-7144	Visa, MC, Disc, *Rated*,	rooms, wireless Internet, hot
Carol & Rick Carpenter	•	tub, boat dock, picnic area.
	C-ltd/S-no/P-no/H-yes	

On beautiful Table Rock Lake only 15 minutes from Branson. Spacious lakefront suites, some with spa and fireplace.
✉ stay@redbudcove.com ◐ www.redbudcove.com

CARTHAGE

The Leggett House	90-115 BB	Full breakfast
1106 Grand 64836	5 rooms, 3 pb	Complimentary beverages &
417-358-0683	Visa, MC, Disc, *Rated*	snacks, please ask in
Don & Joy Sisco	C-ltd/S-ltd/P-no/H-ltd	advance about special
		dietary needs
		Reading nook, beautiful
		wood furnishings, canopy
		bed, antiques, fireplace,
		screened in porch, settee

Joseph Leggett commissioned local builder Joseph Prather to build his home at 1106 Grand, and it was completed in 1901. The Leggett House is now a wonderful Bed & Breakfast owned by Don and Joy Sisco.
✉ leggetthousebb@sbcglobal.net ◐ www.leggetthousebb.com

CHAMOIS

Old School on the Hill Bed and Breakfast	99-125 BB	Full breakfast
402 South Main Street 65024	2 rooms, 2 pb	Private coffee pot in each
573-291-3587 (cell) 573-763-5500	Visa, MC, Disc	room
Charlotte, Dawn and Becky Schaperclaus	C-ltd/S-no/P-ltd/H-no	WiFi, satellite TV

The Old School on the Hill Bed & Breakfast, a National Historic site erected in 1876, located in Chamois, offers two wonderful suites near the heart of Missouri wine country.
✉ relax@oldschoolonthehillbandb.com ◐ OldSchoolOnTheHillBandb.com/home

DEFIANCE

Das Gast Haus Nadler	112 BB	Full breakfast
125 Defiance Rd 63341	4 rooms	Complimentary wine
636-987-2200	Visa, MC, *Rated*	Sitting rooms, spa, bike trail
Dave & Jacquie Nadler	C-ltd/S-ltd/P-ltd/H-ltd	

Relax, refresh, enjoy this beautifully restored turn-of-the-century home . . . country luxury less than one hour from St. Louis.
✉ dghnadler@earthlink.net

EXCELSIOR SPRINGS

Inn on Crescent Lake	99-250 BB	Full breakfast
1261 St. Louis Ave 64024	10 rooms, 10 pb	Bar service available
866-630-5253 816-630-6745	Most CC, *Rated*, •	22 acres, swimming pool,
Edward & Irene Heege	C-ltd/S-ltd/P-no/H-ltd	paddle boats, hot tub, ponds, fishing, walking path, spa services

The Inn on Crescent Lake is a 1915 mansion on 22 acres surrounded by two ponds. Boats, swimming pool and walking path. Enjoy a relaxing and romantic getaway in a luxury suite or room.
✉ info@crescentlake.com ○ www.crescentlake.com

FULTON

Loganberry Inn	99-189 BB	Full gourmet breakfast
310 W 7th St 65251	6 rooms, 6 pb	Fireplace baskets, teas,
888-866-6661 573-642-9229	Most CC, *Rated*, •	fireside dinners
Carl & Cathy McGeorge	C-ltd/S-no/P-ltd/H-no	Sitting room, library, fireplace, cable TV/VCR/DVD, Starlit Spa, wedding gazebo

A "nationally recognized award-winning Inn," Loganberry Inn (c. 1899) is strolling distance to downtown Fulton & the historic district, featuring brick streets, unique antiques, art & specialty shops, an old-fashioned soda fountain & live jazz clubs.
✉ info@loganberryinn.com ○ www.loganberryinn.com

Romancing the Past B&B	129-169 BB	Full breakfast
830 Court St 65251	3 rooms, 3 pb	Tea, coffee, soda, and
573-592-1996	Visa, MC, AmEx, *Rated*	cookies.
Jim and Cate Dodson	C-ltd/S-ltd/P-no/H-ltd	Sitting room, outdoor hot tub, gardens, suites, fireplaces, cable TV, wireless Internet

Welcome to the historic Jameson home, now on the National Historic Register. Our beautiful B&B, a Missouri Top 10 Inn, offers quaint Victorian enchantments, while only being 3 blocks from the charming brick lined streets of our historic downtown district.
✉ romancingthepast@sbcglobal.net ○ www.romancingthepast.com

HANNIBAL

Garth Woodside Mansion	99-395 BB	Full breakfast
11069 New London Rd 63401	11 rooms, 11 pb	Cookies, cider, teas, coffee,
888-427-8409 573-221-2789	Visa, MC, AmEx,	cocoa, sherry
Col (Ret) John & Julie Rolsen	*Rated*, •	Library, tour planning, on
	C-ltd/S-ltd/P-no/H-no	site restaurant

Mark Twain was a frequent guest at this 36-acre estate. Most furnishings are original to the Victorian home. Elegance, privacy and hospitality galore.
✉ innkeeper@garthmansion.com ○ www.garthmansion.com

HERMANN

Angels B&B Inn

108 E Second St 65041
888-264-3553 573-486-5037
Larry and Lynda Salings

85-185 BB
7 rooms, 7 pb
Most CC, *Rated*
S-no/P-no/H-ltd
Ein bischen Deutsch, un
peu Francais
January – December

Full gourmet breakfast
Private blend coffee, teas,
herbals; picnics, dinners,
afternoon teas; romance
packages.
KATY trail 2 miles, AMTRAK
daily stops, in room
TV/HBO, in-room hairdryers,
warm homemade cookies

Your romantic, in-town Victorian lodging with 20th century amenities. Located in Missouri Wine Country's most scenic village. Slip away to a gentler era where grace and peace abound, wrapped in romance!
✉ lsalings@centurytel.net 🌐 www.angelsbbinn.com

Captain Wohlt Inn

123 E 3rd St 65041
573-486-3357
Mat & Kent Wilkins

75-185 BB
12 rooms, 12 pb
Most CC
C-ltd/S-ltd/P-no/H-yes

Full breakfast
Everyone loves Kent's
welcome cookies – they're to
die for!
Dining room, living room,
patio, deck, garden,
whirlpool tubs

The Captain Wohlt Inn, Hermann's Premier Historic Inn, is located in the heart of Hermann's beautiful Historic National Register District, offers old fashioned charm & comfort, as well as modern convenience.
✉ captainwohltinn@gmail.com 🌐 www.captainwohltbandb.com

Esther's Ausblick

236 W. 2nd St 65041
563-486-2170
Esther Heberle

75-180 BB
3 rooms, 3 pb
Cash, Checks
C-ltd/S-no/P-no/H-no

Full breakfast
Piano, entertainment center,
cozy gas fireplace, Victorian
antiques

Esther's Ausblick is situated in the city of Hermann overlooking the Missouri River within walking distance of the Historic District. The B&B has four large guestrooms, comfortable common areas, and lots of space to spread out.
✉ esther@esthersausblick.com 🌐 www.esthersausblick.com

Healing Stone B&B

78 Brown Rd 65041
573-486-5000
Phyllis Hannan

130-265 BB
4 rooms, 4 pb
Most CC
C-ltd/S-no/P-no/H-no
6 Months

Full breakfast
Wine and cheese tray can be
ordered
Bicycle rental, reiki,
reflexology

The Healing Stone Bed & Breakfast, located in Hermann, Missouri, is your sanctuary for a luxury bed and breakfast getaway, retreat, special occasion or a beautiful wedding destination. You will leave the Healing Stone Bed & Breakfast relaxed and refreshed
✉ phannan@healingstoneretreat.com 🌐 www.healingstoneretreat.com

Hermann Hill Vineyard & Inn

711 Wein Street 65041
573-486-4455
Peggy & Terry Hammer

166-351 BB
8 rooms, 8 pb
Visa, MC, Disc, *Rated*
C-ltd/S-no/P-no/H-yes

Full breakfast
Choice of four unique
breakfast entrees daily
served in your room or
kitchen, dinning room, and
deck
Movie library, cable,
Jacuzzis, fireplaces, WiFi,
towel warmers, DVD, VCR,
CD players, some hot tubs

Sited on a bluff overlooking the town, vineyard and river; upscale decor enhanced with antiques; lavishly appointed guestrooms; private and quiet.
✉ info@hermannhill.com 🌐 www.hermannhill.com

HERMANN

Nestle Inn
215 W 2nd St 65041
573-486-1111
Donna Nestle

135-188 BB	Full breakfast
4 rooms, 4 pb	Snacks
Visa, MC, AmEx,	River view, sitting room,
Rated, •	kings, Jacuzzis, suites,
C-yes/S-no/P-no/H-no	fireplaces, cable TV,
	accommodate business
	travel

Nestled cozily atop a bluff overlooking the scenic Missouri River, the Nestle Inn is the perfect getaway for romance and relaxation.
✉ harborhaus@yahoo.com ☉ www.nestleinn.com

The Stone Giraffe
1208 Hwy H 65041
573-486-5100
Sharon & Eddie

225-250 BB	Continental plus breakfast
5 rooms, 5 pb	Common rooms to
Cash, Checks	accommodate groups, porch
C-yes/S-no/P-no/H-no	with breathtaking views

The Stone Giraffe, "an uncommon guesthouse," built high on a hilltop overlooking Hermann, Missouri, is a stunning architectural showplace that uniquely blends the past and present.
✉ thestonegiraffe@yahoo.com ☉ www.thestonegiraffe.com

Stone Haus B&B
107 Bayer Rd 65041
573-486-9169
Linda & Larry Miskel

110-140 BB	Full breakfast
4 rooms, 4 pb	Evening snacks,
Most CC	complimentary soft drinks
C-ltd/S-ltd/P-no/H-no	Sitting rooms, fireplace,
	cable TV, Pick-up from train
	station

Located in historic Hermann & nestled in the rolling hills of Missouri wine country. The Stone Haus Bed & Breakfast was once a winery built in 1862. You will appreciate our home cooking, welcoming hospitality and beautiful surroundings.
✉ linar@ktis.net ☉ stonehausbandb.com

Wine Valley Inn
403 Market St 65041
573-486-0706
Gloria Birk & Pam Gillig

107-235 BB	Full breakfast
12 rooms, 12 pb	Conference room, Glory Be's
Most CC, *Rated*, •	Wine & Gift Shop located on
S-no/P-no/H-no	site

At the very center of historic Hermann Missouri, Wine Valley Inn, in the historic Begemann Building, offers beautifully appointed two-and-three room suites. Guests enjoy all the charm of yesteryear with all the comfort and convenience of today.
✉ winevalleyinn@centurytel.net ☉ www.wine-valley-inn.com

HOLLISTER

Cameron's Crag
738 Acacia Club Rd 65672
800-933-8529 417-334-4720
Kay & Glen Cameron

125-165 BB	Full hearty breakfast
4 rooms, 4 pb	Coffee, tea, hot chocolate
Visa, MC, Disc, *Rated*,	and microwave popcorn in
•	all guestrooms
C-ltd/S-ltd/P-no/H-ltd	Movie library, area maps &
	information available for
	most Branson shows and
	attractions

Just three miles from Branson! King beds, private hot tubs, and spectacular views. Suites in detached guesthouse also offer full kitchens and deluxe whirlpool tubs for two. Quiet & peaceful, yet easy access to area attractions. Full breakfast.
✉ kay@camerons-crag.com ☉ www.camerons-crag.com/rooms.html

INDEPENDENCE

Serendipity B&B
116 S Pleasant St 64050
800-203-4299 816-833-4719
Susan Walter

95 BB	Full breakfast
6 rooms, 6 pb	Library, suites
Most CC	
C-yes/S-no/P-yes/H-no	

Step back in time and enjoy the true romance of the Victorian era in our 1887 house, with total Victorian decor. Couples, families, children and pets welcome.
✉ serendipitybandb@sbcglobal.net ☉ www.serendipitybedandbreakfast.com

INDEPENDENCE

Woodstock Inn B&B
1212 W Lexington 64050
800-276-5202 816-833-2233
Todd & Patricia Justice

98-219 BB
11 rooms, 11 pb
Most CC, *Rated*, •
C-ltd/S-no/P-no/H-yes
Spanish

Full breakfast
Complimentary coffee, tea,
etc.
Spa tubs, fireplaces, TV/VCR,
CD players, coffee-makers,
Sprint PCS phones

The area's most award-winning Inn, The Woodstock Inn B&B was voted "Best B&B in Kansas City" '01 & '03. "Most Romantic Hideaway" '03. "Room of the Year" '03 and "Best B&B in the Midwest!" "04
✉ woodstock@independence-missouri.com ◐ www.independence-missouri.com

IRONTON

Plain and Fancy B&B
11178 Hwy 72 63650
888-546-1182 573-546-1182
Brenda & Tom Merello

110-195 BB
4 rooms, 4 pb
Most CC, *Rated*
C-ltd/S-ltd/P-yes/H-no

Full breakfast
Homemade cookies, soda &
bottled water
Front porch with chairs,
patio with firepit, swimming
pool, wedding gazebo & hot
tub.

A romantic Bed & Breakfast just 80 miles south of St. Louis in the heart of MO's Scenic Arcadia Valley, located conveniently near Johnson's Shut-ins, Elephant Rocks, Fort Davidson Civil War Site, Taum Sauk Mountain, The Ozark Trail & antique shopping.
✉ plainfancybb@hotmail.com ◐ www.plainfancybb.com

JACKSON

TLC Wellness B&B
203 Bellevue St 63755
573-243-7427
Gus & Trisha Wischmann

55-90 BB
4 rooms, 3 pb
Visa, MC, Disc
C-ltd/S-ltd/P-no/H-ltd

Full breakfast
Tea room
Gift shop, parlor, sitting
room, TV, telephones,
corporate rates, bay
windows, family heirlooms

Experience our type of hospitality—warm, relaxed and at home. Even though our 1905 Victorian house features turn-of-the-century quality, we think you will find our modern amenities comfortable.
✉ trybnb@yahoo.com

KANSAS CITY

Southmoreland on the Plaza
116 E 46th St 64112
816-531-7979
Mark Reichle & Nancy Miller
Reichle

109-250 BB
13 rooms, 13 pb
Visa, MC, AmEx, •
C-ltd/S-no/P-no/H-ltd
Closed December 24-25

Full breakfast
Complimentary wine and
hors d'oeuvres from
4:30–6:00
Living room, solarium,
fireplaces, decks, Jacuzzi,
gardens, pond, meeting
facilities

This Urban Inn sets a new standard for Bed and Breakfast hospitality and comfort. Twelve guestrooms in the main Inn and a luxury suite in the Carriage House offer private baths some with Jacuzzi tubs, telephones and off street parking.
✉ innkeeper@Southmoreland.com ◐ www.southmoreland.com

LAKE OZARK

Bass and Baskets
1117 Dogwood Rd 65049
573-964-5028
Ed & Debbie Franko

129-159 BB
4 rooms, 4 pb
Visa, MC
S-no/P-no/H-no

Full breakfast
TV/VCR, fireplace, deck,
Jacuzzi tubs

Come away to "Your Home at the Lake" at Bass and Baskets, where the decor will satisfy the inner fisherman in anyone! At this cozy lakeside B&B, you can sit quietly by the water, on the deck reading a book, or try any variety of water sports.
✉ stay@bassandbaskets.com ◐ www.bassandbaskets.com

MARTHASVILLE

Ashdon House
12027 Links Road 63357
636-463-2273
Melissa & Randy Messina

175-195 BB
2 rooms, 2 pb
Visa, MC, Disc
S-ltd/P-no/H-no

Full five-course gourmet
breakfast
Upon your arrival, enjoy our
Ashdon House Red Velvet
Punch, gourmet cheeses and
fruits.

The Ashdon House is a 19th century New England style home and Morgan Equestrian estate on 15 acres, set in the middle of Missouri wine country. The estate radiates country elegance, charm and hospitality.
✉ ashdonhouse@yahoo.com ✆ www.ashdonhouse.com

OSAGE BEACH

The Inn at Harbour Ridge
6334 Red Barn Rd 65065
877-744-6020 573-302-0411
Sue & Ron Westenhaver

99-199 BB
5 rooms, 5 pb
Visa, MC, *Rated*
C-ltd/S-ltd/P-ltd/H-no

Sinfully delicious breakfast
feast
Snacks & soda. 24/7 Flavia
coffee/tea service. Early
morning coffee trays
delivered to your door.
Private hot tubs, fireplaces,
paddleboat & swim dock on
quiet Lake cove.

Escape from the hustle and bustle of your hectic life to our award winning bed and breakfast! Located at the Lake of the Ozarks, we want to treat you to a very special B & B experience! ✉ info@harbourridgeinn.com ✆ www.harbourridgeinn.com

RHINELAND

Rendleman Home
173 Hwy 94 65069
573-236-4575
Doug

55-115 BB
4 rooms
Most CC
C-ltd/S-no/P-no/H-no
April-October

Full breakfast
Optional meal plan available
Bicycles, bonfires

The Rendleman Home Bed & Breakfast is a 1890's farm home at the 111 mile mark on the Katy Trail renovated as a welcome spot to rest and relax.
✉ webmaster@rendlemanhome.com ✆ www.rendlemanhome.com

ROCHEPORT

Amber House B&B
705 Third St 65279
573-698-2028
Steve & Mary Schlueter

139-249 BB
4 rooms, 4 pb
Visa, MC, Disc
C-ltd/S-no/P-no/H-no

Full gourmet breakfast
Complimentary beverages &
snacks always available in
Butler's pantry & 2nd floor
guest refrigerator
Electric fireplaces, TV/DVD,
free wi fi, luxury baths, in-
room climate control, sitting
areas

Located in the historic village of Rocheport, 2 blocks from the Katy Trail, Amber House combines Victorian elegance with fine furnishings, antiques, & modern amenities in 4 light-filled guestrooms, each with luxury bath.
✉ info@amberhousebb.com ✆ www.amberhousebb.com

**School House Bed &
Breakfast Inn**
504 Third St 65279
573-698-2022
Mike & Lisa Friedemann

135-260 BB
12 rooms, 12 pb
Visa, MC, Disc, *Rated*
C-ltd/S-no/P-no/H-ltd

Full breakfast
Freshly baked cookies at
check-in, tea, coffee, sodas
Central heat/air, ceiling fans,
private phones, WiFi,
TV/DVD player, library,
fireplaces

This wonderfully restored 3-story brick schoolhouse, listed on the National Register of Historic Places, serves as the perfect starting point for your relaxing bed and breakfast experience.
✉ innkeeper@schoolhousebb.com ✆ www.schoolhousebb.com

Virginia Rose, Springfield, MO

ROCHEPORT

Yates House
305 Second St 65279
573-698-2129
Conrad & Dixie Yates

149-289 BB
6 rooms, 6 pb
Visa, MC
C-ltd/S-no/P-no/H-no

Full Gourmet Breakfast
Dinner by reservation, fresh
cookies are made daily for
our guests, coffee & tea
available 24 hours
Gardens, locked bicycle
parking, gazebo, sun room,
jetted tubs

The Yates House Bed and Breakfast—luxury at its best! Each room is designed for your comfort. Luxurious sheets and bedding, robes, CATV, DVDs, wireless Internet access, CD players, beautiful gardens, antiques, cooking classes, dinner by reservation.
✉ yateshouse@socket.net ✇ www.yateshouse.com

SPRINGFIELD

Virginia Rose
317 E Glenwood St 65807
800-345-1412 417-883-0693
Jackie & Virginia Buck

70-120 BB
4 rooms, 4 pb
Visa, MC, Disc, *Rated*,
•
C-ltd/S-no/P-no/H-ltd

Full breakfast
Sitting room, accommodate
business travelers, large
parking area

Lovely country-Victorian hideaway, on tree-covered acre right in town. Private yet close to walking trail, antique and mall shopping and restaurants.

ST. CHARLES

Boone's Lick Trail Inn
1000 S Main St 63301
888-940-0002 636-947-7000
Venetia McEntire

125-325 BB
7 rooms, 7 pb
Most CC, *Rated*, •
C-yes/S-no/P-no/H-ltd

Full breakfast
In-room beverage service
Hiking/biking, sitting room,
conference, folk art,
rollaways available

Escape to restored 1840 Inn. Flower gardens, regional antiques, duck decoys, in historic river settlement. Duck hunting. Select Registry member.
✉ innkeeper@booneslick.com ✇ www.booneslick.com

ST. JOSEPH————————————————————————————————

Museum Hill B&B	120-160 BB	Full hearty gourmet
1102 Felix 64501	4 rooms, 4 pb	breakfast
816-387-9663	Visa, MC, AmEx, •	Fully stocked guest kitchen, a
John & Beth Courter	C-ltd/S-no/P-no/H-ltd	gourmet dinner may be
		ordered 24 hours in advance
		of arrival
		Sitting room, library,
		fireplaces, accommodations
		for business travelers, WiFi,
		Direct TV

Northwestern Missouri B & B with historic 1880s Victorian class. One suite, three guest-rooms, antiques, private baths, stained glass. In the heart of the Pony Express Region, near Lewis and Clark trail. Only 35 minutes from Kansas City Int'l Airport.
✉ museumhillbandb@yahoo.com ☾ www.museumhill.com

ST. LOUIS————————————————————————————————

Fleur-de-Lys Mansion –	150-295 BB	Full gourmet breakfast
Luxury Inn at the Park	4 rooms, 4 pb	Coffee, tea, soft drinks,
3500 Russell Blvd 63104	Most CC, *Rated*	bottled water, snacks,
888-693-3500 314-773-3500	S-no/P-no/H-no	complimentary cognac and
Jan & David Seifert		brandy
		Jacuzzis, hot tub, fireplaces,
		meeting room, spa services
		romantic dinners, carriage
		rides

Simply the best St. Louis has to offer! Award-winning historic inn recognized for intimate warmth, luxury and exceptional hospitality. Also very business-friendly. Five minutes from downtown St. Louis; 15 minutes from Clayton.
✉ seifert@thefleurdelys.com ☾ www.thefleurdelys.com

Napoleon's Retreat B&B	105-175 BB	Full breakfast
1815 Lafayette Ave 63104	5 rooms, 5 pb	Homemade cookies, tea, soft
800-700-9980 314-772-6979	Most CC, *Rated*	drinks
J. Archuleta & M. Lance	C-ltd/S-no/P-no/H-no	Sitting room, Jacuzzis, suites,
		fireplaces, cable TV, free
		wireless, refrigerators,
		phones

Stunning French Second Empire Victorian located in Lafayette Square, chosen as one of America's most beautiful neighborhoods. Just one mile from downtown. Beautifully ap-pointed rooms with private baths. Free wireless.
✉ napoleonsretreat@aol.com ☾ www.napoleonsretreat.com

Park Avenue Mansion	99-249 BB	Full breakfast
2007 Park Ave 63104	5 rooms, 5 pb	Hot coffee, tea, cocoa, cider
866-588-9004 314-588-9004	Most CC, •	and candies
Kathy Marks-Petetit & Mike	C-ltd/S-no/P-ltd/H-no	Cable TV/VCR, radio, clocks,
Petetit		robes, hair dryers, fine
		soaps, shampoos

Luxurious. Comfortable. Walk through original 14 foot doors to another century filled with elegance, charm & old world graciousness. Whether a business or leisure traveler, you won't want to leave.
✉ info@parkavenuemansion.com ☾ www.parkavenuemansion.com

STE. GENEVIEVE———————————————————————————————

The Inn St. Gemme Beauvais	89-179 BB	Full four course breakfast
78 N Main St 63670	9 rooms, 9 pb	Tea with dessert, hors
800-818-5744 573-883-5744	Most CC, *Rated*	d'oeuvres with wine
Janet Joggerst	C-yes/S-no/P-no/H-ltd	Special packages available, whirlpool tubs, fireplaces, gardens, TV/DVD, WiFi

Non-intrusive hospitality. All suites with private baths. Individual breakfast tables, waitress service, 8 entree choices! Janet Joggerst, the innkeeper at The Inn St. Gemme Beauvais, serves up a delicious and extremely satisfying breakfast.

✉ innstgemme@sbcglobal.net ◐ www.innstgemme.com

TRENTON———————————————————————————————

Hyde Mansion B&B Inn	65-110 BB	Continental breakfast
418 E 7th St 64683	6 rooms, 6 pb	Complimentary beverages,
660-359-1800 Cell 660-359-5631	Visa, MC, *Rated*	snacks
Robert & Carolyn Brown	C-ltd/S-no/P-no/H-no	Sitting room, library, baby grand piano, patio, screened porch

Inviting hideaway in rural America, 1949 mansion refurbished for your convenience. Popular with visiting executives, known for its unique rooms and friendly atmosphere.

✉ hydemansion@cebridge.net

WARRENSBURG———————————————————————————————

Cedarcroft Farm & Cottage	199-239 BB	Full breakfast
431 SE County Rd Y 64093	1 rooms, 1 pb	Complimentary evening
888-655-9830 660-747-5728	Visa, MC, *Rated*	snack, with cookies,
Sandra & Bill Wayne	S-ltd/P-no/H-no	chocolates, soft drinks, fruit, more
		Cottage, jetted tub, fireplace, dual-nozzle shower, dish LCD TV, DVD.

The Cottage on the Knoll at Cedarcroft Farm has all romantic amenities in a secluded meadow. Thermal jetted tub, fireplace, king bed, breakfast delivered to your door, complete privacy on 80-acre farm!

✉ romance@cedarcroft.com ◐ www.cedarcroft.com

Montana

ALBERTON

Ghost Rails Inn
702 Railroad Ave 59820
888-271-9317 406-722-4990
Thom Garrett & Grace Doyle

64-94 BB
9 rooms, 7 pb
Visa, MC, AmEx
C-yes/S-no/P-yes/H-no

Full breakfast
Homemade brownies, cakes,
other snacks; lemonade,
dinner, sack lunches with 48
hours prior notice
Under new ownership and
now open all year, we
specialize in Quilt Retreats
from Fall to Spring

This Alberton Montana B&B has 9 pretty rooms w/private baths. An easy day's drive from Seattle, just off I-90, its a great place for small reunions. The area is known for Milwaukee Railroad history, whitewater rafting, fly fishing, Hiawatha Bike Trail.
✉ info@ghostrailsinn.com ◐ www.ghostrailsinn.com

ANACONDA

Hickory House Inn
218 E Park 59711
866-563-5481 406-563-5481
MaryJane Rayfield

90-145 BB
5 rooms, 5 pb
Visa, MC, Disc
C-yes/S-ltd/P-ltd/H-yes

Full breakfast
We can accommodate
dietary restrictions, evening
tea available
Use of living room, reading
area, sunny porches, spa,
gardens

Hickory House Inn Bed and Breakfast prides itself on making sure our guests are comfortable and relaxed. Our rooms are quiet, well appointed and clean. MaryJane's breakfasts are 'legend'.
✉ hickoryhouseinn@msn.com ◐ hickoryhouseinn.com

BILLINGS

The Josephine
514 North 29th St 59101
800-552-5898 406-248-5898
Harvey & Linda Bybee

95-170 BB
5 rooms, 5 pb
Most CC
C-ltd/S-no/P-no/H-no

Full breakfast
Complimentary
snacks/beverages in evening
Cable TV, private phones,
wireless broadband, private
bathrooms, free guest pass to
gym

Lovely historic home within walking distance to downtown. Comfortably elegant, smoke-free, pet-free; a refreshing alternative that pampers business travelers with varied breakfast times, wireless Internet, 5 private bathrooms, cable TV, private phones.
✉ info@thejosephine.com ◐ www.thejosephine.com

BOZEMAN

Fox Hollow B&B
545 Mary Rd 59718
800-431-5010 406-582-8440
Nancy & Michael Dawson

99-169 BB
5 rooms, 5 pb
Most CC, *Rated*, ●
C-ltd/S-no/P-no/H-no

Full gourmet breakfast
Sitting room, high speed
wireless Internet access, hot
tub, art gallery, guest
computer

Luxury accommodation, panoramic mountain views, hospitality—uniquely Montana. Five guestrooms with private baths. Separate guesthouse with kitchen. Romantic honeymoon suite. AAA 3 Diamond, Mobil 3 Star, MTBBA.
✉ info@Bozeman-MT.com ◐ www.Bozeman-MT.com

BOZEMAN——————————————————————————————

Gallatin River Lodge
9105 Thorpe Rd 59718
888-387-0148 406-388-0148
Steve Gamble

150-400 BB
6 rooms, 6 pb
Visa, MC, AmEx,
Rated, •
C-yes/S-ltd/P-yes/H-yes

Full Breakfast
Fine dining restaurant for
lunch or dinner. Full bar,
Wine Spectator Award wine
list
Fly fishing guide service,
massage, conference and
wedding services, spa
nearby, library, trout pond

A fine country inn near Bozeman, MT, offering Jacuzzi suites, fine dining and fly fishing guide services, on a secluded ranch near the Gallatin River. Near Yellowstone National Park and Grand Teton Park, close to Big Sky Resort. Select Registry member.
✉ info@grlodge.com ☏ www.grlodge.com

Howlers Inn & Wolf Sanctuary
3185 Jackson Creek Rd 59715
888-HOWLERS 406-587-5229
Mary-Martha and Chris Bahn

105-195 BB
4 rooms, 4 pb
Visa, MC, AmEx, *Rated*
C-yes/S-no/P-no/H-no

Full breakfast
Sitting room, Jacuzzi,
fireplace, sauna, game room,
exercise facilities, home
theater, pool table

North America's only B&B and wolf sanctuary set on 42 acres in a beautiful alpine canyon. Dramatic log and stone home—each bedroom with full private bath and sweeping mountain views.
✉ howlersinn@Earthlink.net ☏ www.howlersinn.com

Lehrkind Mansion
719 N Wallace Ave 59715
800-992-6932 406-585-6932
Christopher Nixon, Jon
Gerster

139-189 BB
8 rooms, 8 pb
Most CC, *Rated*
C-ltd/S-no/P-ltd/H-no
German

Full breakfast
Afternoon tea
Sitting room, library, bikes,
large yard, mountain views,
fax, piano

An elegant, Queen Anne Victorian mansion furnished in 1890s antiques. Tea served in our music parlor accompanied by the 7 foot tall 1897 Regina music box!
✉ lehrkindmansion@imt.net ☏ www.bozemanbedandbreakfast.com

The Olive Branch Inn
202 Lindley Pl 59715
866-587-8403 406-587-8403
Antoinette Anthony

100-180 BB
5 rooms, 5 pb
Most CC, *Rated*
C-ltd/S-no/P-no/H-ltd

Organic continental and
offsite
Along with the offered
organic goods, enjoy a hot
breakfast from a nearby
locally owned cafe on us!
Flat screen TV, private
telephone, sitting room, free
high speed wireless Internet,
fax available

At The Olive Branch Inn, we are committed to encouraging, promoting, and supporting ecological consciousness. We are charter members of the "Green" Hotels Association and work with this association towards our mutual purpose and goals.
✉ info@theolivebranchinn.com ☏ www.theolivebranchinn.com

Silver Forest Inn
15325 Bridger Canyon Rd
59715
406-924-4222
Mike & Teresa

75-140 BB
6 rooms, 4 pb
Visa, MC, AmEx
C-yes/S-no/P-yes/H-no

Full breakfast
Hot tea & cocoa! There's an
honor bar with popcorn &
snacks!
Jacuzzi tub with Bridger
View Room, free WiFi in
common areas, sitting room,
fireplace

A beautiful historic 1932 log home nestled in the pines at the base of the Bridger Mountains. Perfect for vacations, romantic getaways, anniversaries, honeymoons, relaxation. Perfect for one to three day business or corporate retreats.
✉ silverforestinn@att.net ☏ www.silverforestinn.com

BOZEMAN

Voss Inn
319 S Willson Ave 59715
406-587-0982
Bruce & Frankee Muller

100-159 BB
6 rooms, 6 pb
Most CC, *Rated*, •
C-ltd/S-no/P-no/H-no
Spanish, Afrikaans

Full breakfast in parlor or in room
Afternoon tea; Friday night dinners by reservation
Gift shop, parlor, piano, telephones, fax, wireless Internet access, Victorian garden

The Voss Inn is a warm, elegant circa 1883 Victorian Italianate mansion beautifully restored and decorated with antiques, period wallpaper and furniture, surrounded by a lush English cottage garden. A gourmet breakfast is served privately or family style.
✉ vossinn@bresnan.net 🌐 www.bozeman-vossinn.com

COLUMBIA FALLS

Bad Rock Country B&B
480 Bad Rock Dr 59912
888-892-2829 406-892-2829
Serena & Mark Jackson

125-250 BB
8 rooms, 8 pb
Most CC, *Rated*, •
C-yes/S-no/P-no/H-yes

Full breakfast
Complimentary wine/snacks
Exercise room, library, small groups facility, game room and laundry facilities

Nestled among towering pines, Bad Rock, a Montana Bed and Breakfast Inn embraces ten private acres of rolling fields and evergreen groves twenty minutes from Glacier National Park, one of Mother Nature's great extravaganzas.
✉ stay@badrock.com 🌐 www.badrock.com

EMIGRANT

Paradise Gateway B&B
Guest Log Cabins
2644 Hwy 89 S 59027
800-541-4113 406-333-4063
Pete & Carol Reed

85-350 BB
7 rooms, 7 pb
Visa, MC, •
C-ltd/S-ltd/P-ltd/H-ltd
Norwegian

Full breakfast
Afternoon tea, snacks
Sitting room, library, cable TV, accommodates business travelers

Nestled in Paradise Valley, next to the North entrance to Yellowstone Park. Rimmed by majestic mountains, and the Yellowstone River is your front yard.
✉ paradisebandb@wispwest.net 🌐 paradisegateway.com

HAMILTON

Big Sky B&B
703 Mariah Ln 59840
800-953-3077 406-363-3077
Linda & Tim

102 BB
2 rooms, 2 pb
Most CC, *Rated*
C-ltd/S-no/P-no/H-no

Full breakfast
Beverages, snacks
Dining room, great room, refrigerator, high speed Internet

We're located on ten acres between the Bitterroot and Sapphire Mountains, under what seems to be an endless vibrant blue sky, overlooking the town of Hamilton, or just fifty miles south of Missoula Montana.
✉ stay@bigskybandb.com 🌐 www.bigskybandb.com

Deer Crossing B&B
396 Hayes Creek Rd 59840
800-763-2232 406-363-2232
Linda & Stu Dobbins

100-149 BB
6 rooms, 6 pb
Visa, MC, AmEx,
Rated, •
C-yes/S-no/P-yes/H-no

Full country breakfast
Fishing guide, shuttle, horseback riding, two creekside cabins, Dish TV, WiFi

Experience Old West charm and hospitality. 25 acres of tall pines and lush pastures. Incredible views. Hearty ranch breakfast served in our sunroom.
✉ info@deercrossingmontana.com 🌐 www.deercrossingmontana.com

342   Montana

HELENA

The Sleepy Senator
403 N Hoback St 59601
406-442-2046
Robert N. Clarkson

130-260 BB
2 rooms, 1 pb
Most CC, •
C-yes/S-no/P-ltd/H-no
Some Spanish

Optional full breakfast
Lunch, dinner, free snacks
Entertainment center,
computer with Internet,
DVD/VHS, local information,
sauna

Guests are saying: "Excellent!" "Comfortable digs!" "Love the sauna!" The Sleepy Senator Tourist House, just 3 blocks from the State Capitol, is a fully furnished 2 bedroom/3 bed, private townhouse with 'free' hot breakfast, snacks, & off-street parking.
✉ sleepysenator@mt.net ♦ www.clarksonstudio.com/sleepy/index.htm

HUSON

Running Horse Inn on the Ninemile
20250 Ninemile Rd 59846
406-626-0040
Janice Dersham

75-125 BB
3 rooms, 3 pb
Cash, Checks
C-ltd/S-no/P-no/H-no

Full breakfast
Afternoon refreshments
Great room with fireplace,
decks, 100 wooded acres to
explore

Nestled in the Ninemile Valley less than an hour from Missoula, the perfect retreat from your hectic daily life. Renew your spirit on 100 private acres in a beautiful mountain setting. Settle back with a book, or discover the richness of the outdoors.
✉ runninghorseinn@msn.com ♦ www.runninghorse-inn.com

KALISPELL

Emerald Sunrise B&B
115 Emerald Cove Rd 59901
406-212-4709 (cell) 406-755-4348
Tara Postovit

90-150 BB
2 rooms, 2 pb
Most CC
C-yes/S-no/P-no/H-no

Full breakfast
Hors' d' oeuvres and drinks
upon arrival
Wireless Internet, lakeside
Campfire & S'more-gasbord,
warm Montana river rock
fireplace

Emerald Sunrise Bed & Breakfast is a newly constructed Montana style waterfront home. Our B&B quarters are privately located on the lake level. Ashley Lake is a secluded, quiet sanctuary surrounded by state and national forests full of Montana wildlife.
✉ stay@emeraldsunrisebnb.com ♦ www.emeraldsunrisebnb.com

The Garrison Inn
2235 Ashley Lake Rd 59901
406-752-5103
Gene & Anne Marie Garrison

105-155 BB
3 rooms, 3 pb
Most CC
C-yes/S-ltd/P-yes/H-no

Full breakfast
Afternoon snack of cheese,
and beverages.
telescope, hiking trails, decks

Our log home is located 20 minutes from Kalispell and 2 miles before scenic Ashley Lake. Enjoy the spectacular views. All rooms are designed and furnished with your comfort in mind.
✉ TheInnKeepers@TheGarrisonInn.com ♦ www.TheGarrisonInn.com

The Master Suite
354 Browns Rd 59901
406-752-8512
Donna McKiernan

175-285 BB
1 rooms, 1 pb
Visa, MC
C-ltd/S-ltd/P-ltd/H-ltd

Full breakfast
Afternoon cocktails, hors
d'oeuvres
Special events up to 50,
concierge, bicycles, pets
allowed in luxury kennel,
wireless Internet

The Master Suite is a private luxury accommodation with million dollar views. Located on 15 acres in the gentle rolling hills overlooking the Flathead Valley in Kalispell, Montana.
✉ donnamck@usamontana.com ♦ www.mastersuitebedandbreakfast.com

MISSOULA

Blue Mountain B&B
6980 Deadman Gulch Rd
59804
877-251-4457 406-251-4457
Brady Anderson-Wood

105-155 BB
4 rooms, 4 pb
Visa, MC, AmEx, •
C-yes/S-ltd/P-no/H-no

Full breakfast
Complimentary beverages
and snacks
Garden, jetted tubs, views,
wildlife, patio, piano, library,
koi pond

Blue Mountain B&B is nestled on the mountainside among majestic Ponderosa Pines and meditative water gardens, creating a uniquely tranquil experience just minutes away from Missoula's business, sporting and cultural centers.
✉ stay@bluemountainbb.com ◉ www.missoula-bed-breakfast.com

RED LODGE

Inn on the Beartooth
6648 Hwy 212 S 59068
888-222-7686 406-446-1768
Debbie & Ron Van Horn

125-200 BB
6 rooms, 6 pb
Visa, MC
C-yes/S-no/P-no/H-no

Country Style Breakfast
Hot tubs, private deck, great
room, wood-burning stone
fireplace

Your Ideal Mountain Getaway, the Inn On The Beartooth is a newly built log lodge located at the base of the Beartooth Mountains. Rustic charm with all the modern conveniences.
✉ dnsenterprizes@yahoo.com

RONAN

Twin Creeks B&B
2295 Twin Creek Rd 59864
877-524-8946 406-676-8800
Chris & Judy

70-135 BB
7 rooms, 2 pb
Visa, MC
C-yes/S-no/P-no/H-no

Full breakfast
Home baked cookies, packed
lunch available
Direct TV in common rooms,
steam sauna, massage
available

Located in the beautiful Montana wilderness, we are a graceful retreat of magical proportions. Come share in our tranquil paradise, where it's easy to enjoy the Montana Experience. 7 rooms and outdoor tipis available.
✉ stay@twincreeksbb.com ◉ www.twincreeksbb.com

STEVENSVILLE

Bitteroot River B&B
501 South Ave 59870
406-777-5205
Tim & Shelley Hunter

99-129 BB
4 rooms, 4 pb
Visa, MC, Disc
C-ltd/S-ltd/P-no

Full breakfast
Fresh fruit, delicious egg
casseroles, French toast
made with banana bread,
fresh coffee and teas.
A/C, Internet, massage
therapy, fireplace, satellite
TV, CD player with CD's
included.

We offer a tranquil country-style setting with river front property, combined with the convenience of being located within a small town.
✉ timothymhunter@msn.com ◉ www.bitterrootriverbb.com

SUPERIOR

Forest Grove Lodge
1107 Mullan Rd E 59872
406-822-6637
Wil & Kelly Mitchell

130-155 BB
5 rooms, 5 pb
Visa, MC
C-ltd/S-ltd/P-no/H-no

Full breakfast
Dinner available ($25 per
person, with advanced
notice), snacks
Great room, wet bar, covered
deck

Nestled near the river in the Lolo National Forest, Forest Grove Lodge is surrounded by peaceful serenity. The Lodge offers five spacious bedrooms with private baths. Come, relax and enjoy a true Montana experience.
✉ info@forestgrovelodge.com ◉ www.forestgrovelodge.com

VICTOR ─────────────────────────────

Time After Time B&B
197 Pistol Ln 59875
888-642-3258 406-642-3258
Trish Hatfield

80-95 BB
3 rooms, 1 pb
Visa, MC
C-yes/S-no/P-no/H-ltd
April- November

Full breakfast
Light afternoon refreshments
Common area with piano,
gardens

Nestled amongst tourist friendly communities amid spectacular scenery, hiking, hunting, fly fishing, golfing, and biking, sits Time After Time. An enchanting little Bed & Breakfast you won't want to miss.
✉ timeaftertime@montana.com ❂ www.treasurestate.com/timeaftertime/

WEST GLACIER ─────────────────────────

Smoky Bear Ranch Lodge,
Cabins & Tipis
4761 Smoky Bear Lane 59936
800-555-3806 406-387-4249
Scott & Nancy Collard

70-250 BB
9 rooms, 9 pb
Visa, MC
C-ltd/S-ltd/P-no/H-ltd

Full breakfast
Lunch and Special Meals
Available (fee).
Satellite TV, refrigerator, hair
dryer, and large closets,
Tipis, Private Cabins, Day
Beds, Mt Views

Nestled along the western edge of the rugged Rocky Mountains of Glacier National Park, the remote North Fork of the Flathead River remains virtually unchanged and offers some of the purest, most vitalizing air and water in the United States.
✉ scott@smokybear.com ❂ www.smokybear.com

WHITEFISH ────────────────────────────

Good Medicine Lodge
537 Wisconsin Ave 59937
800-860-5488 406-862-5488
Betsy & Woody Cox

100-240 BB
9 rooms, 9 pb
Most CC, *Rated*, •
C-yes/S-no/P-no/H-yes
French

Gourmet full breakfast
Homemade Montana size
cookies are served with tea,
coffee and hot chocolate on
our guest bar.
Hot tub/guest
laundry/TV/Library (big
screen TV, DVD &
VHS)/common
areas/wireless DSL/ski boot
dryer

A classic Montana 3 suite and 6 guestroom bed and breakfast. Built of solid cedar; has balconies with stunning views, crackling fireplaces, outdoor spa, full breakfast, guest laundry and loads of western hospitality.
✉ info@goodmedicinelodge.com ❂ www.goodmedicinelodge.com

WOLF CREEK ───────────────────────────

Bungalow B&B
406-235-4276
Pat O'Connell Anderson

125-145 BB
4 rooms, 1 pb
Cash, Checks
C-ltd/S-ltd/P-no/H-no
April-December

Full breakfast
Complimentary coffee, tea,
soft drinks
Large yard for wildlife
watching, large great room

We have four gracious guestrooms, with additional twin beds available on the balcony. You will find a relaxing, peaceful mountain atmosphere near the Dearborn Rivers & The Lewis & Clark Trail.
✉ bungalow@montana.com

Nebraska

LINCOLN

Atwood House B&B	85-222 BB	Full breakfast
740 S 17th St 68508	4 rooms, 4 pb	Snacks, complimentary soft
800-884-6554 402-438-4567	Most CC, *Rated*	drinks
Ruth & Larry Stoll	C-ltd/S-no/P-no/H-no	Sitting room, library,
		Jacuzzis, suites, fireplace,
		cable TV

Experience the elegance of this 7,500+ sq ft 1894 Neoclassical Georgian Revival mansion. 3 suites with 2-person whirlpool (2 with fireplaces), flowers, Victorian furnishings & gourmet breakfasts. Ideal for romantic getaways or business travelers.

✉ Larry@atwoodhouse.com ◐ www.atwoodhouse.com

Nevada

BOULDER CITY

Milo's Inn at Boulder
534 Nevada Way 89005
702-294-4244
Karen & Stephen Gay, Milo
Hurst

169-199 BB
4 rooms, 4 pb
Visa, MC
C-ltd/S-no/P-ltd/H-ltd

Full breakfast
On-site cafe and wine bar
Off-street parking, satellite
TV, whirlpool tubs, wireless
Internet, concierge & on-call
spa service

Unique luxury in the heart of Boulder City, NV's historic Old Town. Waterfall and fireplace in private courtyard gardens. Queen beds, luxury linens, handcrafted furnishings, fireplaces in each of 4 rooms. Onsite cafe and wine bar. Weddings, events hosted.
✉ escape@milosinnatboulder.com ◐ www.milosinnatboulder.com

CARSON CITY

Deer Run Ranch B&B
5440 Eastlake Blvd 89704
800-378-5440 775-882-3643
David & Muffy Vhay

99-149 BB
2 rooms, 2 pb
Most CC, *Rated*
C-ltd/S-no/P-no/H-ltd

Full breakfast
Complimentary wine,
beverages
Snacks, refrigerator, sitting
room, library, TV, VCR,
private entry, wireless
broadband.

Western ambience in a unique architect-designed & built ranch house between Reno & Carson City overlooking Washoe Lake.

UNIONVILLE

Old Pioneer Garden
2805 Unionville Rd 89418
775-538-7585
Wilma "Mitzi" Jones

95 BB
11 rooms, 11 pb
Cash, Checks, *Rated*, •
C-yes/S-no/P-yes/H-yes

Full breakfast
Dinner is available for $12

The Old Pioneer Garden Country Inn is an oasis of Northern Nevada's high desert, dating back to 1861. The inn was built the same year that silver prospectors toured the area & established Unionville. AAA-rated.

VIRGINIA CITY

B Street House Bed and Breakfast
58 N. B St 89440
775-847-7231
Chris & Carolyn Eichin

109-139 BB
3 rooms, 3 pb
Visa, MC
C-ltd/S-no/P-no/H-no
Swiss German, German

Full gourmet breakfast
Afternoon tea with cookies
and snacks, teas, coffee &
cocoa in the parlor;
chocolates on arrival
Library, books about Nevada
& the West; cable TV/DVD,
free high-speed Internet,
parlor, mini-fridge

The B Street House B&B in the heart of Virginia City offers the elegance of the Old West. Your stay in this fully restored 1876 Henry Piper house will be an unforgettable one. There are three guestrooms with period furniture and a full gourmet breakfast.
✉ railwolf@comcast.net ◐ www.bstreethouse.com

Edith Palmer's Country Inn
416 South B St 89440
775-847-7070
Pat & Leisa Findley

95-140 BB
10 rooms, 10 pb
Visa, MC
C-yes/S-ltd/P-no/H-no

Continental plus breakfast
Restaurant nearby
Parlor, family suites, cable
TV, wireless Internet
available, weddings,
receptions, banquets

Victorian buildings date from 1863 and are surrounded by gardens & spectacular views. Enjoy period accommodations of the 1860s or stay in Marilyn's room named for Marilyn Monroe who stayed at the Inn during the filming of "The Misfits" in nearby Dayton
✉ info@edithpalmers.com ◐ www.edithpalmers.com

New Hampshire

The Darby Field Inn
185 Chase Hill Rd 03818
800-426-4147 603-447-2181
Marc & Maria Donaldson

140-290 BB
13 rooms, 13 pb
Visa, MC, AmEx,
Rated, •
C-ltd/S-no/P-no/H-no
Spanish

Full country breakfast
Classic country Inn dinner
menu & casual tavern menu
Spa services, heated
swimming pool (seasonal),
hiking, bird watching, old
time sleigh/carriage rides

Just 6 miles from North Conway, nestled in the White Mountains. Amenities: spa services, sleigh/carriage rides, award winning gardens, delicious food & friendly people. Local attractions include tax free shopping, Mt. Washington, Kancamaugus Highway.
✉ marc@darbyfield.com ☉ www.darbyfield.com

The Glynn House Inn
59 Highland St 03217
866-686-4362 603-968-3775
Pamela, Ingrid and Glenn
Heidenreich

149-299 BB
13 rooms, 13 pb
Visa, MC, *Rated*, •
C-yes/S-no/P-yes/H-no

Full gourmet breakfast
Afternoon refreshments,
wine & hors d'oeuvres
Pet friendly, central A/C,
individualized concierge
services, WiFi, fireplaces,
dbl. whirlpool tubs

Stay at "New Hampshire's Finest Small Inn"! The meticulously restored Glynn House provides the perfect setting for relaxation, romance and recreation. Elegant decor, scrumptious food and personalized service. Pet Friendly
✉ theglynnhouseinn@yahoo.com ☉ www.glynnhouse.com

Bedford Village Inn
2 Olde Bedford Wy 03110
800-852-1166 603-472-2001
Jack & Andrea Carnevale

190-350 BB
15 rooms, 15 pb
Most CC, *Rated*, •
C-ltd/S-no/P-no/H-yes
Spanish, Italian

Continental breakfast
Lunch, dinner, afternoon tea,
snacks, restaurant, wine &
cheese reception daily,
Sunday Brunch
Sitting room, free Internet,
Jacuzzis, suites, fireplaces,
cable HDTV, airport
transportation, valet

A multi-million dollar farm estate restoration. Elegant country dining and lodging in the middle of historical New England. The longest running four diamond property in NH; restaurant is also four diamond rated.
✉ guestservices@bedfordvillageinn.com ☉ www.bedfordvillageinn.com

Adair Country Inn & Restaurant
80 Guider Ln 03574
888-444-2600 603-444-2600
Brad and Ilja Chapman

195-375 BB
9 rooms, 9 pb
Most CC, *Rated*, •
C-ltd/S-no/P-no/H-no
ASL

Full scrumptious breakfast
Afternoon tea with
homemade sweets & cakes,
complimentary soft drinks,
cheese & crackers
In-room massage, activity rm
w/ pool table, large screen
TV, video library, snowshoes
& many trails

Casually elegant country home in a breathtaking setting, with views of the White Mountains. Romantic retreat on 200 acres surrounded by sweeping lawns, gardens, stone walls, woods, and wildlife.
✉ innkeeper@adairinn.com ☉ www.adairinn.com

BETHLEHEM

Bear Mountain Lodge
3249 Main St 03574
888-869-2189 603-869-2189
Carol & Michael Kerivan

165-340 BB
9 rooms, 9 pb
Most CC, *Rated*
C-ltd/S-no/P-no/H-yes

Homemade full breakfast
A guest pantry is stocked
with teas, hot chocolate,
cookies, sodas, snacks and
water.
Fireplaces, high speed
wireless Internet access,
steam showers and two
person Jacuzzi tubs

Grand lodge close to all of NH's White Mountain attractions. Nine rooms and suites with Jacuzzis & fireplaces. Private setting with panoramic views of Mt. Washington, great breakfasts and warm hospitality. Come see why guests say "it feels like home."
✉ info@bearmountainlodge.net ◐ www.bearmountainlodge.net

The Grande Victorian Cottage
53 Berkeley St 03574
603-869-5755
Frances & Steve Marszalkowski

115-135 BB
6 rooms, 6 pb
Cash, Checks, *Rated*
C-ltd/S-no/P-no/H-no
Memorial wkd – October

Full breakfast
Afternoon tea
Sitting room, porches,
gardens, antiques

Elegant B&B furnished in antiques, located off main street. Full breakfast/afternoon refreshments on our porch out by the garden. Centrally located to major attractions & recommended restaurants.
◐ www.GrandeVictorian.com

The Mulburn Inn at Bethlehem
2370 Main St 03574
800-457-9440 603-869-3389
Alecia Loveless

125-185 BB
7 rooms, 7 pb
Most CC, *Rated*, •
C-yes/S-no/P-yes/H-no

Full breakfast
Fresh coffee & hot tea
available 24 hours a day.
Library, ski & golf packages,
wrap around porches, hot
tub, wireless Internet

Sprawling 1913 summer cottage and family retreat known as the Ivy House, on the Woolworth Estate. Warm, fireside dining, hot country breakfast and rooms with fireplaces.
✉ info@mulburninn.com ◐ www.mulburninn.com

The Wayside Inn
3738 Main St, Rt 302 03574
800-448-9557 603-869-3364
Victor & Kathe Hofmann

108-148 BB
26 rooms, 26 pb
Most CC, *Rated*
C-yes/S-ltd/P-ltd/H-yes
French, German
May-Oct. & Dec.-March

Full breakfast
Dinner available; most
popular items are: Veal
Zurich, Wiener Schnitzel,
Crab Cakes, Rack of Lamb
Restaurant, common room
with fireplace and cable TV,
free wireless Internet access
in lobby and bar

The historic Wayside Inn is a favorite for family vacations, romantic getaways and group gatherings any time of the year. Enjoy golf, hiking, skiing or sightseeing in the White Mountains.
✉ info@thewaysideinn.com ◐ www.thewaysideinn.com

BRIDGEWATER

The Inn on Newfound Lake
1030 Mayhew Tpke, Rt 3A 03222
800-745-7990 603-744-9111
Larry Delangis & Phelps Boyce

105-355 BB
28 rooms, 24 pb
Most CC, •
C-ltd/S-no/P-no/H-no

Continental breakfast
Snacks, restaurant, bar
service
Fishing in lake, sitting room,
library, private beach, dock

The Inn has been refurbished and we invite guests to return to the times of relaxation and enjoyment. One of the few remaining true country inns. We have a 240-ft. private beach, private dock & boat moorings, on one of the cleanest lakes in the country.
✉ innonlake@metrocast.net ◐ www.newfoundlake.com

BRISTOL————————————————————————————————

Henry Whipple House
75 Summer St 03222
603-744-6157
Sandra Heaney

110-190 BB
8 rooms, 8 pb
Visa, MC, Disc
C-yes/S-no/P-no/H-ltd
Basic French and
Russian

Award winning full breakfast
Victorian, antiques,
fireplaces, cable TV, AC, bath
amenities, porch, deck and
Internet access

A grand old home set in the center of scenic New Hampshire. The house is typical of the Victorian era which can be seen in the architecture, oak woodwork, hardwood floors, chandeliers and stained glass windows which all add to the charm.
✉ info@thewhipplehouse.com ✆ www.thewhipplehouse.com

Pleasant View B&B
22 Hemp Hill Rd 03222
888-909-2700 603-744-5547
Heidi Milbrand

105-135 BB
7 rooms, 7 pb
Most CC
S-no/P-no/H-no

Full Country-Style Breakfast
The Inn is also available to
rent (up to 30 people) for
rehearsal dinners, baby or
bridal showers.
Great room, wood burning
stove, sitting rooms, a loft
with mountain views, patio,
honeymoon, romance

Nestled on a scenic rural road in New Hampshire's lakes region, Pleasant View Bed and Breakfast, a country Inn, provides a comfortable, cozy atmosphere for guests looking for a touch of home with spectacular mountain views.
✉ theinnwench@metrocast.net ✆ www.pleasantviewbandb.net

CAMPTON————————————————————————————————

Colonel Spencer Inn
3 Colonel Spencer Rd 03223
603-536-1755
Mary Jo & Scott Stephens

110-125 BB
6 rooms, 6 pb
Visa, MC
C-yes/S-no/P-ltd/H-no

Full country breakfast
Snacks & light drinks
Sitting room, cable TV, DVD,
VCR, library, wireless
Internet

Experience the charm of a cozy pre-Revolutionary home, now a bed and breakfast steeped rich in America's history. We are perfectly located between Plymouth and Campton in the surrounds of New Hampshire's spectacular White Mountains & Lakes Regions.
✉ innkeeper@colonelspencerbb.com ✆ www.colonelspencerbb.com

Mountain Fare Inn
Mad River Rd 03223
603-726-4283
Susan & Nick Preston

105-155 BB
10 rooms, 10 pb
Visa, MC, Disc, *Rated*
C-yes/S-no/P-ltd/H-ltd
A little French

Full breakfast
Afternoon tea & snacks
Sitting room, suites, fireplace,
cable TV, conference, sauna,
soccer field, family reunions

Lovely 1830's village farmhouse features the antiques, fabrics and feel of country cottage living. Picturesque gardens in the summer, foliage in the fall, and a true skier's lodge in the winter.
✉ mountainfareinn@verizon.net ✆ www.mountainfareinn.com

The Sunny Grange
1354 Rt 175 03223
877-726-5553 603-726-5555
Tami Anderson

119-300 BB
6 rooms, 6 pb
Most CC
C-ltd/S-no/P-no/H-no

Full breakfast
Beverages, snacks, wine,
evening treat
Hot tub, wireless Internet,
cable TV/VCR, fireplaces,
Jacuzzi tubs, garden,
hammock, A/C, bathrobes

At the Sunny Grange B&B, our guests are our top priority. We're happy to provide those extra touches to make your stay a special one.
✉ reservations@sunnygrange.com ✆ www.sunnygrange.com

CHOCORUA

The Brass Heart Inn 88 Philbrick Neighborhood Rd 03817 800-833-9509 603-323-7766 Don & Joanna Harte	80-260 BB 16 rooms, 10 pb Most CC C-yes/S-no/P-no/H-yes	Full breakfast Fine dining in our restaurant by reservation; summer/fall dining in the pub (no reservation needed). Cottages have microwave oven, coffeemaker, fridge.

We invite you to enjoy the peace and tranquility of our retreat that has delighted guests for over 100 years. Tucked away, yet close to all the Mt. Washington Valley has to offer!
✉ info@thebrassheartinn.com ○ www.thebrassheartinn.com

Riverbend Inn B&B 273 Chocora Mt. Highway 03817 800-628-6944 603-323-7440 Craig Cox & Jerry Weiss	100-250 BB 10 rooms, 6 pb Most CC C-ltd/S-ltd/P-no/H-no	Full breakfast Beverages Guest lounge area, library, fireplace, decks overlooking river, massage/yoga, wireless Internet

Chosen "Best Romantic B&B"-NH mag. Voted "Best Interior Design and Decor" and "Best Breakfast in New England"-Inn Traveler mag. Ten luxurious guestrooms on 15 wooded acres along the Chocorua River. Enjoy breakfast on the deck overlooking the river.
✉ info@riverbendinn.com ○ www.riverbendinn.com

CLAREMONT

Goddard Mansion B&B 25 Hillstead Rd 03743 800-736-0603 603-543-0603 Scott Raymond & Keith McAllister	100-170 BB 7 rooms, 3 pb Most CC, *Rated* C-yes/S-ltd/P-ltd/H-no	Continental plus breakfast Snacks Self serve tea, coffee, & hot cocoa anytime, sitting room, TV room, library, wireless Internet

Located in the Dartmouth-Lake Sunapee region of NH, The Goddard Mansion is a delightful, c. 1905, 18 room English Mansion. Acres of lawns and gardens, panoramic views, plenty of areas to sit and relax including a screened in porch, veranda, and tea house.
✉ info@goddardmansion.com ○ www.goddardmansion.com

DANBURY

Inn at Danbury 67 NH Route 104 03230 866-DANBURY 603-768-3318 Robert & Alexandra Graf	99-250 BB 14 rooms, 14 pb Visa, MC, Disc, *Rated*, • C-ltd/S-no/P-no/H-ltd Dutch, German and French	Full country breakfast Award winning German Restaurant serving Old World and New England comfort food in cozy Bistro WiFi, Personal trip planning, Massage, private parties, Ski & Stay, indoor pool, library, TV room

Family friendly Country Inn with award winning bistro serving German Old World and New England Favorites in the cozy barn style restaurant. 55 min. N of Manchester and 2 hours from Boston located in Central New Hampshire. 14 rooms with private baths.
✉ info@innatdanbury.com ○ www.innatdanbury.com

DOVER

Silver Fountain 103 Silver St 03820 888-548-6888 603-750-4200 B. Susan Chang	99-149 BB 9 rooms, 9 pb Most CC C-yes/S-no/P-no/H-yes Mandarin Chinese	Full breakfast We can accommodate dietary restrictions upon request. TV/DVD, robes, alarm clock w/CD, private bathroom, hairdryer, baby grand piano, wireless Internet

The Silver Fountain Inn is an elegant early 1870s Victorian that has maintained its original beauty and charm. Rooms range from $99-$149 and include private bath. The large sitting room has baby grand piano, ideal for intimate functions and gatherings.
✉ info@silverfountain.com ○ www.silverfountain.com

DURHAM

Three Chimneys Inn
17 Newmarket Rd 03824
888-399-9777 603-868-7800
Karen Meyer

99-239 BB
23 rooms, 23 pb
Most CC, *Rated*, •
C-yes/S-no/P-no/H-yes

Full breakfast
Snacks, afternoon social
hour, lunch and dinner
available in the restaurant,
bar service
Sitting room, library, cable,
Jacuzzis, fireplaces, high-
speed Internet

Discover a world of casual elegance at Three Chimneys Inn. This beautifully restored 1649 mansion and carriage house is situated on Valentine Hill overlooking her formal gardens, the Oyster River, and the Old Mill Falls.
✉ chimney3@threechimneysinn.com 🕙 www.threechimneysinn.com

EAST MADISON

Purity Spring Resort
HC 63 Box 40 Rt 153 03849
800-373-3754 603-367-8896

100-150 BB
10 rooms, 10 pb
Most CC
C-yes/S-ltd/P-no/H-ltd

Full Breakfast
Full service dining,
American Meal Plans &
other options
Fitness & Swim Center,
porches, gardens, lake,
canoes, sitting rooms
fireplaces, groups &
weddings

Choose from lodge rooms, private lakeside cottages or condominiums, the options will satisfy everyone. With a pristine private lake, family-friendly dining & stunning natural surroundings, Purity Spring Resort is the ideal, four-season destination.
✉ info@purityspring.com 🕙 www.purityspring.com

EATON

Inn at Crystal Lake & Pub
2356 Eaton Rd 03832
800-343-7336 603-447-2120
Bobby & Tim

109-239 BB
12 rooms, 12 pb
Most CC, *Rated*
C-ltd/S-no/P-ltd/H-ltd

Full breakfast
Full service dining and full
liquor service; Dining Room
and Pub, cookies
Cable TV/VCRs, CD/radios,
telephones, A/C

Comfortable guestrooms, luxury pampering, hearty breakfasts, central location, irresistible specials and award-winning packages. Now offering dinner and pub menus. Recommended by The Boston Globe and Ski Magazine.
✉ stay@innatcrystallake.com 🕙 www.innatcrystallake.com

ENFIELD

1793 Shaker Hill B&B
259 Shaker Hill Rd 03748
877-516-1370 603-632-4519
Nancy & Allen Smith

90-110 BB
4 rooms, 4 pb
Visa, MC
C-ltd/S-no/P-no/H-no

Full breakfast
Afternoon tea, snacks
Sitting room, accommodate
business travelers, locked
storage for your bike.

Newly renovated 1790s Colonial farmhouse. Gardens and wraparound porch, newly deco-rated rooms with down comforters and pillows. All private baths.
✉ info@shakerhill.com 🕙 www.shakerhill.com

Shaker Farm B&B
597 NH Rt 4A 03748
800-613-7664 603-632-7664
Joe & Cathy Gasparik

135 BB
6 rooms, 6 pb
Most CC
C-ltd/S-no/P-no/H-ltd

Hearty country breakfast
Period furniture, cable TV,
A/C, private baths, deck,
wireless Internet

You'll be delighted with the warmth and charm of the large and lovely rooms in the historic South Family Shaker Farm House. Genuine antique flavor and a warm and friendly atmosphere. A fireplace in the living room & a deck & screened in area for relaxing.
✉ jgasparik@aol.com 🕙 www.shakerfarm.com

EPPING

Plumercrest B&B	105-160 BB	Hearty Country Breakfast
22 Plumer Rd 03042-1707	4 rooms, 4 pb	Mike's handcrafted almond
877-777-1032 603-679-8308	Visa, MC, AmEx	biscotti, sodas, waters,
Michael & Maryanne Swegles	C-ltd/S-no/P-no/H-ltd	Senseo coffees and herbal
		teas, homemade truffles
		Wireless Internet, gazebo,
		business travelers, wooden
		architecture, beautiful
		location, antiques

Situated on a crest rising above Plumer Road, Plumercrest is a fine example of Victorian Italianate architecture. Welcome to the Plumercrest Bed and Breakfast! This stately mansion reveals the grandeur of the Victorian era . . . come on in and see!
✉ info@plumercrest.com ⟳ www.plumercrest.com

FRANCONIA

Franconia Inn	105-235 BB	Full breakfast
1300 Easton Rd 03580	35 rooms, 34 pb	Restaurant, full bar
800-473-5299 603-823-5542	Visa, MC, AmEx,	Lounge with movies, library,
Richard (Alec) Morris	*Rated*, •	bicycles, heated pool, 4 clay
	C-yes/S-yes/P-no/H-no	tennis courts, horse back
	Mem. Day—April 1st	riding, soaring

Since 1863, The Franconia Inn has welcomed guests with the tranquil appeal of country life, in an elegant setting that is both unpretentious and inviting.
✉ info@franconiainn.com ⟳ www.franconiainn.com

Historic Lovetts Inn	135-245 BB	Full country breakfast
Rt 18 03580	18 rooms, 18 pb	Afternoon tea each day at
800-356-3802 603-823-7761	Visa, MC, Disc	3:00 pm, dinner available.
Janet & Jim Freitas	C-yes/S-no/P-yes/H-ltd	Casual and fine dining
		Sitting rooms, outdoor pool,
		walking/biking/cross
		country ski trails, alpine
		skiing, pet friendly

Built in 1784 and listed on the National Register of Historic Places. "Where the Art of Fine Dining Remains a Cherished Tradition," Lovetts Inn offers a variety of accommodations in either the historic inn or intimate cottages, most with fireplaces.
✉ innkeepers@lovettsinn.com ⟳ www.lovettsinn.com

Horse and Hound Inn	105-165 BB	Full breakfast
205 Wells Rd 03580	8 rooms, 8 pb	Dining room serves dinner
800-450-5501 603-823-5501	Most CC, •	Wednesday through
Bill Steele & Jim Cantlon	C-yes/S-yes/P-yes/H-no	Saturday nights by
	summer, fall, winter	reservation
		Stone fireplaces, patio, large
		back lawn, lounge with TV,
		VCR in living room

1830 farmhouse renovated in 1946 to create an old-fashioned New England B&B. Relaxing atmosphere in a wooded setting, situated on 8.5 private acres.
✉ info@horseandhoundnh.com ⟳ www.horseandhoundnh.com

FRANKLIN

The Maria Atwood Inn	127-127 BB	Full breakfast
71 Hill Rd, Rt#3A 03235	7 rooms, 7 pb	Complimentary snacks,
603-934-3666	Most CC, *Rated*, •	beverages, fruit & cookies
Sandi & Fred Hoffmeister	C-yes/S-no/P-no/H-no	Library, garden, free wireless
		Internet access, free long
		distance phone calls
		anywhere in US & CAN

Surrounded by lush green trees and shrubbery lies the Maria Atwood Inn. The allure and mystique of this large Colonial home takes you back into a different time. A relaxed, friendly atmosphere refreshes traveler's physical & mental being as well.
✉ info@atwoodinn.com ⟳ www.atwoodinn.com

GILFORD

The Inn at Smith Cove
19 Roberts Rd 03249
603-293-1111
Bob & Maria Ruggiero

90-180 EP
12 rooms, 12 pb
Most CC, *Rated*
C-yes/S-no/P-no/H-no

No meals included.
Sitting room, Jacuzzis,
private beach, gazebo, boat
slips, antiques

Circa 1898 Victorian Country Inn on Lake Winnepesaukee. Close to Gunstock Ski Area, outlet shopping, golf courses, health club, fishing, hiking. We now have wireless Internet access.
🌐 www.innatsmithcove.com

GLEN

The Bernerhof Inn
Rt 302 03838
800-548-8007 603-383-9132
George & June Phillips

99-219 BB
9 rooms, 9 pb
Most CC, *Rated*, •
C-ltd/S-no/P-no/H-no

Full breakfast
Dinner available in
restaurant & pub, box
lunches or ski snacks on
request
Sitting room, free WiFi,
CyBear lounge, gardens,
cooking school, outdoor
pool, cable TV, phone

Warm, friendly Victorian Inn, circa 1880. Individually appointed rooms with Jacuzzi, fireplace and suites. Romantic escape packages. Host of "A Taste of the Mountains Cooking School." Pamper yourself, you deserve it!
✉ stay@bernerhofinn.com 🌐 www.bernerhofinn.com

The Covered Bridge House
404 SR 302 03838
800-232-9109 603-383-9109
Dan & Nancy Wanek

89-139 BB
5 rooms, 5 pb
Visa, MC, Disc, *Rated*
C-yes/S-no/P-no/H-no

Full Country Breakfast
River swimming & tubing,
garden, hot tub; living room,
A/C, gift shop, family suite

Feel at home in our cozy bed and breakfast by the Saco River next to our own restored 1850's Covered Bridge. We offer five guestrooms individually decorated in traditional Colonial decor with antique furnishings.
✉ info@coveredbridgehouse.com 🌐 www.coveredbridgehouse.com

GREENFIELD

Greenfield Inn
749 Forest Rd 03047
800-678-4144 603-547-6327
Vic & Barbara

59-159 BB
9 rooms, 7 pb
Visa, MC, *Rated*, •
C-yes/S-no/P-no/H-no

Full breakfast
Jacuzzis, hayloft suite,
phones, hot tub, hideaway
suite

Welcome to a four season, southern New Hampshire, Mountain Country mansion. Sleep in Victorian splendor. Breakfast is a party with crystal, china and Mozart. 90 minutes from Boston.
✉ innkeeper@greenfieldinn.com 🌐 www.greenfieldinn.com

HAMPSTEAD

Stillmeadow at Hampstead
545 Main St 03841
603-329-8381
Margaret & Willie Mitchell

135-165 BB
3 rooms, 3 pb
Cash, Checks
C-ltd/S-no/P-no/H-no
Scottish!

Full breakfast, local produce
Fantastic breakfasts using
local farm produce. Baked
treats.
Guests Victorian parlor with
woodstove, patio, individual
parking spaces

Under new ownership. Southern New Hampshire's premier B&B. Beautiful historic 1850 Colonial "Italianate" Style house set in two acres of gardens with many original features combined with the highest levels of modern comfort and amenities.
✉ margaret.mitchell@still-meadow.com

HAMPTON BEACH

D.W.'s Oceanside Inn	169-270 BB	Choice of breakfast items off
365 Ocean Blvd 03842	9 rooms, 9 pb	menu
866-OCEANSIDE 603-926-3542	Most CC, *Rated*, •	Self-service bar on back
Duane (Skip) & Deb	S-no/P-no/H-no	deck, sitting room, library,
Windemiller	Late May to Columbus	beach chairs & towels. WiFi
	Day	available.

D.W's Oceanside Inn is a small elegant lodging overlooking the Atlantic Ocean and miles of beautiful sandy beaches along New Hampshire's 18 mile coastline in Hampton Beach. Named 2005 "Innkeepers of the Year" by the NH Lodging & Restaurant Assoc.
✉ info@oceansideinn.com ◗ www.oceansideinn.com

HANCOCK

Hancock Inn	125-290 BB	Delicious full breakfast
33 Main St 03449	14 rooms, 14 pb	Restaurant, dinner available
800-525-1789 603-525-3318	Most CC, *Rated*, •	Sitting room, library,
Robert Short	C-yes/S-no/P-ltd/H-yes	Jacuzzis, suites, fireplace,
		cable TV, bar

Since 1789, the 1st year of Washington's Presidency, the Hancock Inn has been in continuous operation, hosting thousands of visitors, from cattle drovers & rum runners, aristocracy & a U.S. President. Listed on the National Register of Historic Places.
✉ innkeeper@hancockinn.com ◗ www.hancockinn.com

HANOVER

The Trumbull House	120-300 BB	Sumptuous Breakfast
40 Etna Rd 03755	6 rooms, 6 pb	Swimming pond, meadows,
800-651-5141 603-643-2370	Most CC, •	sugar maple grove,
Hilary Pridgen	C-ltd/S-no/P-ltd/H-no	basketball half-court, trails,
		Internet access, TV/VCR

Hanover's first and finest Bed & Breakfast offers luxury country lodgings just four miles east of Dartmouth College & three miles from the Dartmouth-Hitchcock Medical Center.
✉ trumbullhouse@gmail.com ◗ www.trumbullhouse.com

HART'S LOCATION

The Notchland Inn	195-365 BB	Full country breakfast with
Route 302 03812	16 rooms, 16 pb	choices
800-866-6131 603-374-6131	Visa, MC, Disc, *Rated*,	Dinner, restaurant, bar
Ed Butler & Les Schoof	•	beverages, wines & beer
	C-ltd/S-no/P-ltd/H-ltd	Sitting room, library, piano,
		Jacuzzis, suites, fireplaces,
		conferences, hot tub,
		cottages

Comfortably elegant 1860s mansion on 100 forested acres. 8 spacious rooms, 5 suites, & 3 cottages, all but 1 with wood burning fireplaces. Pets and families will find the cottages most appealing.
✉ innkeepers@notchland.com ◗ www.notchland.com

HAVERHILL

Gibson House B&B	135-175 BB	Full breakfast
341 Dartmouth College Hwy	8 rooms, 8 pb	Afternoon tea
03765	Most CC, *Rated*, •	Sitting rooms, porches,
800-989-2150 603-989-3125	C-yes/S-no/P-ltd/H-no	formal gardens, library,
Marty Cohen & Susie Klein	German	tennis courts, fireplaces
	May – October	

1850s Stagecoach Inn beautifully redone by owner. Antiques throughout, murals, 50 foot porches with sunset views of Connecticut River Valley, overlooking gardens, lily pond, wildflower meadow. Weddings, conferences, workshops, retreats hosted.
✉ gibsonhousebb@charter.net ◗ www.gibsonhousebb.com

HEBRON

Six Chimneys & A Dream
5 S. Mayhew Turnpike 03241
603-744-5848
Juli Pruden

80-160 BB
6 rooms, 3 pb
Visa, MC, AmEx
C-yes/S-no/P-no/H-no
Spanish

Full breakfast

Built in 1791 as a stagecoach inn at Newfound Lake, Six Chimneys & A Dream retains all historical charm with modern comfort. Easy access to all the Lakes and White Mountains regions of New Hampshire have to offer.
✉ 6chimneys@metrocast.net ❂ www.sixchimneys.com

HOLDERNESS

Inn on Golden Pond
1080 US Route 3 03245
603-968-7269
Bill & Bonnie Webb

165-210 BB
8 rooms, 8 pb
Most CC, *Rated*, •
C-ltd/S-no/P-no/H-no

Full breakfast
A/C, sitting room, suites, game room, porch and fireplace, free Internet and WiFi.

Located on 50 wooded acres across the street from Squam Lake, setting for "On Golden Pond." Eight spacious rooms and a friendly yet professional atmosphere. Innkeepers have owned/operated for 25 years.
✉ innkeepers@innongoldenpond.com ❂ www.innongoldenpond.com

Squam Lake Inn
28 Shepard Hill Rd 03245
800-839-6205 603-968-4417
Rae Andrews & Cindy Foster

155-180 BB
8 rooms, 8 pb
Visa, MC, AmEx
C-ltd/S-no/P-no/H-ltd

Full breakfast
Squam Lake Inn Cafe is open from 5/30–10/15, Tu-Sat, 11–2. Lobster rolls, sandwiches & salads!
Fireplace, lobby, library, Internet, deck, covered porch and accommodations for small events.

Squam Lake Inn is an eight room, century old Victorian Farmhouse just steps from Squam Lake on Shepard Hill Road in the quaint village of Holderness.
✉ stay@squamlakeinn.com ❂ www.squamlakeinn.com

INTERVALE

The Old Field House
Rt. 16A 03845
603-356-5478
Rod & Linea Hopwood

120-195 BB
20 rooms, 20 pb
Most CC
C-yes/S-no/P-no/H-no

Breakfast Buffet

The Old Field House is a quiet country lodge with the personalized atmosphere of a small inn, but the amenities of a larger New Hampshire hotels. Both families and couples will appreciate our wide variety of lodging options.
✉ frontdesk@oldfieldhouse.com ❂ www.oldfieldhouse.com

JACKSON

Carter Notch Inn
163 Carter Notch Rd 03846
800-794-9434 603-383-9630
Sally Carter & Dick Green

99-250 BB
8 rooms, 8 pb
Visa, MC, Disc, *Rated*, •
C-ltd/S-no/P-no/H-no

Full breakfast
Afternoon tea & cookies, complimentary wine & beer
Sitting room with log fire, outdoor hot tub, guest Internet/Wifi, Jacuzzis, swimming pool, cable TV

Beautifully located on a quiet country road overlooking the Wildcat River & golf course, with panoramic mountain views. Wraparound front porch, impeccably clean rooms. Honeymoon suites with Jacuzzis & balconies, a lounge with fireplace & great breakfasts!
✉ info@carternotchinn.com ❂ www.carternotchinn.com

JACKSON—————————————

Inn at Ellis River
17 Harriman Rd 03846
800-233-8309 603-383-9339
Lyn Norris-Baker & Frank
Baker

119-299 BB
21 rooms, 21 pb
Most CC, *Rated*, •
C-ltd/S-no/P-no/H-ltd

Full gourmet country
breakfast
Afternoon refreshments,
dinner by two day advance
reservation
Atrium with hot tub, sauna,
heated pool, pub, cable TV

An enchanting country Inn offering romance & relaxation, nestled by the Ellis River in the heart of the White Mountains. Let the serenity of the Inn & its surroundings create unforgettable memories.   ✉ stay@innatellisriver.com ❂ www.innatellisriver.com

Inn at Jackson
12 Thorn Hill Rd 03846
800-289-8600 603-383-4321
Don & Joyce Bilger

119-259 BB
14 rooms, 14 pb
Most CC, *Rated*, •
C-ltd/S-no/P-no/H-ltd

Full 3-course country breakfast
Afternoon snacks & refreshments, arrival refreshments
available by request
Wireless Internet, fireplaces,
A/C, TV, DVD, hot tub, massage available

The inn maintains 14 spacious guestrooms, many with fireplaces and cozy seating areas. The inn's recently redesigned common rooms provide a romantic setting for our delicious breakfasts and afternoon refreshments. Enjoy mountain views from our hot tub.
✉ info@innatjackson.com ❂ www.innatjackson.com

Inn at Thorn Hill
Thorn Hill Rd 03846
800-289-8990 603-383-4242
Jim & Ibby Cooper

169-440 BB
25 rooms, 25 pb
Most CC
C-ltd/S-no/P-no/H-yes

Full breakfast
3 dining rooms, 3,000 bottle
wine list, lounge featuring
New England cuisine,
Afternoon Tea
Fireplaces, Jacuzzis, spa
services, gardens, views,
antiques, weddings, Wine
Dinners

The Inn at Thorn Hill & Spa is one of the most outstanding—and most romantic—historic country inns in the eastern United States. Located in the classic New England village of Jackson in the heart of New Hampshire's White Mountains.
✉ stay@innatthornhill.com ❂ www.innatthornhill.com

Nestlenook Estate and Resort
Dinsmore Rd 03846
800-659-9443 603-383-9443
Robert Cyr

139-339 BB
7 rooms, 7 pb
Visa, MC, Disc, *Rated*,
•
C-ltd/S-no/P-no/H-no

Continental breakfast
Social hour with wine &
snacks
Sitting room, bikes, pool,
skating, snowshoeing,
Austrian sleigh rides, boats,
horseback rides

Experience the romance of Victorian elegance on our 65-acre estate. One of the most authentic, luxurious Victorian experiences in New England. 7 guestrooms with private 2-person Jacuzzi bathroom and period antiques.
✉ info@nestlenookfarm.com ❂ www.nestlenookfarm.com/NestlenookFarm

The Wentworth
1 Carter Notch Rd 03846
800-637-0013 603-383-9700
Fritz & Ellie Koeppel

119-319 MAP
41 rooms, 41 pb
Most CC
C-yes/S-no/P-no/H-yes
French, Spanish,
German, Swiss

Full breakfast
Meal Plan rates include a four
course dinner and breakfast,
Bed & Breakfast rates available
Cable TV, central heat & fully
air conditioned, 18 hole golf
course, pool, tennis and skiing

The Wentworth is an elegant country inn offering unique lodging and fine dining year round. Enjoy your stay in the heart of the White Mountains of New Hampshire, an exceptional location for a memorable wedding day or corporate retreat.
✉ reservations@thewentworth.com ❂ www.thewentworth.com

JACKSON

Whitney's Inn
357 Black Mountain Road
03846
800-289-8600 603-383-8916
Don Bilger

109-249 BB
26 rooms, 26 pb
Visa, MC, AmEx
C-yes/S-no/P-ltd/H-ltd

Full breakfast
Whitney's provides two
onsite dining options, the
Birches Restaurant and the
Shovel Handle Pub.
Cable HD television, DVD
players, CD players, pool,
fireplaces, and wireless
Internet.

Whitney's Inn has been welcoming families and couples since the 1840s. With its charming guestrooms, excellent dining, two pubs and neighbor Black Mountain it is the perfect place for a getaway.
info@whitneysinn.com www.whitneysinn.com

JACKSON VILLAGE

Wildcat Inn & Tavern
Main St 03846
800-228-4245 603-383-4245
Stewart Dunlop

59-259 EP
11 rooms, 11 pb
Visa, MC, AmEx
C-yes/S-no/P-ltd/H-no

Restaurant, tavern on site
Sitting areas, special events,
weddings, garden

Nestled in the heart of Jackson Village the Wildcat Inn & Tavern has welcomed guests to dine by candlelight, relax by a crackling fire, dance in our tavern and snuggle in our cozy beds for almost 100 years.
sleep@wildcattavern.com www.wildcattavern.com

JAFFREY

Benjamin Prescott Inn
Rt 124E 03452
888-950-6637 603-532-6637
Charlie & Sue Lyle

90-180 BB
10 rooms, 10 pb
Visa, MC, AmEx,
Rated, •
C-ltd/S-no/P-no/H-no
American Sign Language

Full breakfast
Complimentary tea and
baked goodies
Sitting room, A/C, satellite TV
in common rms & suite, free
Wireless Internet throughout

Relax..indulge..in this historic 1853 Inn. Let it slow your pace as it invites you to hike Mt. Monadnock, visit galleries and gourmet restaurants, country fairs along with summer theatre, concerts and weekly lecture series. 2 hours from Boston.
innkeeper@benjaminprescottinn.com www.benjaminprescottinn.com

JEFFERSON

Applebrook B&B
Route 115A 03583
800-545-6504 603-586-7713
Joy & Tom McCorkhill

90-220 BB
9 rooms, 9 pb
Most CC, *Rated*
C-yes/S-no/P-yes/H-no

Full breakfast
Home cooked dinners
offered to groups of ten or
more
Family and pet friendly, hot
tub rooms available, family
suites, cable TV, HDTV

A casual, comfortable, put-your-feet-up kind of place. The spacious sunny living room has beautiful sunset views of Mt. Washington. Family and pet friendly. We are a Yankee Magazine Editors' Choice.
info@applebrook.com www.applebrook.com

KEENE

Colony House
104 West Street 03431
603-352-0215
Joslin Kimball Frank

120-135 BB
3 rooms, 3 pb
Cash, Checks
C-ltd/S-no/P-no/H-no

Continental plus breakfast
Guest pantry provides a
refrigerator, microwave,
electric teapot and other
conveniences.
Wireless Internet & satellite
TV, books, magazines, board
games, robes, luxury linens

The Colony House is listed on the National Historic Register and sits as a cornerstone of Keene's downtown historical district. It is located within easy walking distance of the theatre, shops, colleges, restaurants & parks.
jkimball.frank@verizon.net www.colonyhouse104.com

LINCOLN

The Red Sleigh Inn B&B	75-195 BB	Full Country Breakfast
191 Pollard Rd 03251	6 rooms, 4 pb	Complimentary tea and
603-745-8517	Visa, MC, *Rated*	coffee served
Bill & Loretta Deppe	C-ltd/S-no/P-no/H-no	Television in the Sitting room, library, summer gardens, activity planning, sun porch with mt. views

Enjoy the warm relaxed atmosphere of this family-run B&B close to town in the heart of the beautiful White Mts. Six guestrooms decorated with antiques afford panoramic views of the surrounding mountains. Hearty full country breakfast included.
✉ redsleigh@adelphia.net ◑ www.redsleighinn.com

LONDONDERRY

Tiffany Gardens B&B	110-145 BB	Special Breakfasts
15 King John Dr 03053	2 rooms, 2 pb	Free snacks, coffee, tea,
603-432-0418	Most CC	soda, cheese, crackers &
Jim & Kathy McMahon	C-ltd/S-no/P-no/H-no	chocolates, special vegan breakfast by request Robes, hair dryer, mini-fridge, cable TV, DVD player, high-speed wireless Internet and fresh flowers

Romantic retreat for the avid gardener who loves flowers, plants & wildlife and tranquility. Relax and stroll in the 1 acre fully landscaped garden with 8 water features, 300+ flowering trees and shrubs. 5 min. from Tupelo Music Hall, 45 min from Boston.
✉ info@tiffanygardens.com ◑ www.tiffanygardens.com

LYME

Breakfast On The Connecticut	125-274 BB	Full breakfast
651 River Rd 03768	15 rooms, 15 pb	In-room bottled water, coffee,
888-353-4440 603-353-4444	Visa, MC	tea in common room,
Donna & John Andersen	C-yes/S-no/P-ltd/H-yes	complimentary sodas Sunroom, gazebo protected spa, TV/VCR, phones, individual climate control, canoes, kayaks, bicycles

High on a knoll overlooking the scenic Connecticut River and the hills of Vermont, discover the comforts of Breakfast On The Connecticut, with its beautiful views and surroundings, whatever the season.
✉ breakfast.connecticut@valley.net ◑ www.breakfastonthect.com

MANCHESTER

Ash Street Inn	149-199 BB	Full breakfast
118 Ash St 03104	5 rooms, 5 pb	Afternoon tea available
603-668-9908	Visa, MC, AmEx	(reservations required)
Darlene & Eric Johnston	C-ltd/S-no/P-no/H-no	Complimentary wireless access, cable TV, phone, off street parking, comp. airport pickup/drop off

The perfect alternative to Manchester NH hotels. Try the Ash Street Inn on your next trip and see for yourself the difference between Bed and Breakfast Inns and hotels.
✉ innkeeper@ashstreetinn.com ◑ www.ashstreetinn.com

MEREDITH

Meredith Inn B&B	134-209 BB	Full breakfast
2 Waukewan St 03253	8 rooms, 8 pb	Living room with fireplace,
603-279-0000	Visa, MC, Disc, *Rated*,	books, games, in-room
Janet Carpenter	●	whirlpool tubs & fireplace
	C-ltd/S-no/P-no/H-ltd	

The Meredith Inn is an 8 room Victorian bed & breakfast with private baths, cable TV, A/C, phones, whirlpool tubs & fireplaces. Full country breakfast. Smoke-free property.
✉ inn1897@metocast.net ◑ www.meredithinn.com

NEW LONDON———————————————————————————

Inn at Pleasant Lake	135-215 BB	Full breakfast
853 Pleasant St 03257	10 rooms, 10 pb	Afternoon tea, bar service,
800-626-4907 603-526-6271	Visa, MC, Disc, *Rated*	restaurant
Linda & Brian MacKenzie	C-yes/S-no/P-no/H-ltd	Sitting room, lake, a wonderful environment for business retreats & weddings

Ten well-appointed guestrooms. Full breakfast and afternoon tea included. Panoramic views of Mt. Kearsarge and Pleasant Lake. Reservations required for five course, pre-fix dinner—available Wednesday-Sunday.
✉ info@innatpleasantlake.com ◔ www.innatpleasantlake.com

New London Inn	129-225 BB	Continental plus breakfast
353 Main St 03257	23 rooms, 23 pb	New Tavern Menu. Fine
800-526-2791 603-526-2791	Most CC, *Rated*	dining in one of New
Bridget LeRoy & Eric Johnson	C-ltd/S-no/P-ltd/H-ltd	Hampshire's hottest
	French	restaurants (NH Magazine, Nov. 2005) 100% Egyptian cotton sheets, WiFi, TV/DVDs, bath amenities, turndown service.

The New London Inn offers 23 individually decorated rooms, all with private bath. Relax in our casually elegant common areas, complete with a library of books & games and two crackling fireplaces. Walk to restaurants, shops, Colby-Sawyer college, or hike.
✉ newlondoninn@excite.com ◔ .www.newlondoninn.us

NORTH CONWAY———————————————————————

1785 Inn & Restaurant	69-259 BB	Full country breakfast
3582 White Mountain Hwy 03860	17 rooms, 12 pb	Full-service restaurant, lounge/pub, room service
800-421-1785 603-356-9025	Most CC, *Rated*, •	2 sitting rooms, A/C,
Becky & Charlie Mallar	C-yes/S-ltd/P-no/H-ltd French	swimming pool, skiing, honeymoon/romance pkgs

Historic inn overlooking famous view of the White Mountains with award-winning restaurant. Fine dining, friendly service, fabulous views, outstanding wine list in a romantic Colonial atmosphere.
✉ the1785inn@aol.com ◔ www.the1785inn.com

Brookhill B&B	219-409 BB	Full breakfast
26 Balcony Seat View 03860	2 rooms, 1 pb	Homemade cookies, snacks,
888-356-3061 603-356-3061	Visa, MC	juices, coffee, tea, and sodas
Susan & Rod Forsman	C-ltd/S-no/P-no/H-no Spanish	available in the suite's kitchen Wood fireplace, 1 or 2 bedroom multi-room suite, private entrance, first floor, views, ski from door

Brookhill B&B is one of North Conway and Jackson NH's most unique and luxurious lodgings with a private-entrance one or two bedroom suite, a magnificent view of Mt. Washington, and a long list of luxury, upscale amenities.
✉ brookhillbb@roadrunner.com ◔ www.brookhillbb.com

The Buttonwood Inn	99-299 BB	Full breakfast
64 Mount Surprise Rd 03860	10 rooms, 10 pb	Afternoon tea baked treats.
800-258-2625 603-356-2625	Visa, MC, AmEx,	Large common rooms with
Bill & Paula Petrone	*Rated*, •	fireplaces, heated pool, Hot
	C-ltd/S-no/P-no/H-ltd French, German, Italian	Tub, TV/DVDs, Free WiFi, Fridge

1820s farmhouse on 6 secluded acres of fields and forests. Ten newly renovated guestrooms, all with private baths. Two miles from North Conway. Heated swimming pool and hot tub. Award winning gardens with mountain views.
✉ innkeeper@buttonwoodinn.com ◔ www.buttonwoodinn.com

NORTH CONWAY

Cabernet Inn
3552 White Mountain Hwy
03860
800-866-4704 603-356-4704
Jessica & Bruce Zarenko

95-235 BB
11 rooms, 11 pb
Most CC, *Rated*, •
C-ltd/S-no/P-no/H-yes

Full Country Breakfast
Afternoon refreshments, we
try to accommodate dietary
restrictions with advance
notice
Two common living rooms
with woodburning fireplaces,
outside deck & patio

*Enjoy the warmth and elegance of this romantic 1842 country inn set among towering
pines, just a stroll away from breathtaking views of Mt. Washington. Unforgettably romantic
and exquisitely maintained. Simply . . . elegant!*
✉ info@cabernetinn.com 🌐 www.cabernetinn.com

Cranmore Inn
80 Kearsarge 03860
800-526-5502 603-356-5502
Bob Prendergast

65-235 BB
18 rooms, 18 pb
Visa, MC, *Rated*, •
C-yes/S-ltd/P-ltd/H-no
Spanish

Full breakfast
Afternoon tea
Sitting room, library,
swimming pool, suites, cable
TV

*The Cranmore Inn is an authentic country inn, continuously operated since 1863. Antique
furnishings and country prints lend charm to comfortably modern queen beds & facilities.*
✉ info@cranmoreinn.com 🌐 www.cranmoreinn.com

Cranmore Mountain Lodge
859 Kearsarge Rd. 03860
800-356-3596 603-356-2044
Frederique & Thierry Procyk

74-255 BB
20 rooms, 20 pb
Visa, MC, AmEx
C-yes/S-no/P-ltd/H-ltd
French

Cooked-to-order Country
Breakfast
Refreshments between 5 pm
and 6 pm (Friday & Saturday
only). Full gluten free
breakfast available
Heated Pool, Hot Tub, tennis,
pond stocked with trout,
BBQ grills, picnic table, child
& pet friendly

*Family friendly & historic B&B on 8 quiet acres off the beaten path, with year round hot
tub, heated pool, tennis court, pond stocked with trout and many other amenities. Offering
20 beautiful rooms and suites, all with private baths and free WiFi.*
✉ thelodge@north-conway.com 🌐 www.cranmoremountainlodge.com

Kearsarge Inn
42 Seavey St 03860
800-637-0087 603-356-8700
Stewart M. Dunlop

79-259 BB
15 rooms, 15 pb
Visa, MC, AmEx,
Rated, •
C-yes/S-no/P-yes/H-ltd

Continental breakfast
Our restaurant on property
is Decades Steakhouse &
Martini Bar is open year
round for dinner
Common sitting area, gas
fireplaces, A/C, Jacuzzi tubs,
luxury accommodations,
great farmers porch

*Nestled in the heart of North Conway village, the Kearsarge Inn is a romantic B&B within
walking distance of sightseeing, shopping, fine dining, and a variety of outdoor activities.*
✉ innkeeper@kearsargeinn.com 🌐 www.kearsargeinn.com

Locust Hill B&B
267 Kearsarge Rd 03860
603-356-6135
Cynthia & Conrad Briggs

65-90 BB
1 rooms, 1 pb
Visa, MC, *Rated*, •
C-yes/S-no/P-no/H-no

Full country breakfast
Sitting room, library,
swimming pool, suites, cable
TV

*A B&B in the British tradition. Vacation accommodations in a private home. Close to the
village, but in a residential area, with pleasant grounds, gardens, and swimming pool.
Skiing is just minutes away.*
✉ innkeeper@locusthillnh.com 🌐 www.locusthillnh.com

NORTH CONWAY

Nereledge Inn
94 River Rd 03860
888-356-2831 603-356-2831
Laura Glassover

78-234 BB
11 rooms, 5 pb
Most CC
C-yes/S-no/P-no/H-no

Full breakfast
Evening snack, coffee, tea,
hot chocolate, popcorn
always available; guest fridge
Spacious common areas,
fireplaces & woodstoves,
pantry w/fridge, microwave,
books & magazines

An old-fashioned 1787 inn off Main Street in the village of North Conway. Hearty country breakfasts. Close to skiing, climbing, hiking & biking. Walk to river for fly-fishing, swimming & canoeing. Yankee Magazine Editor's Choice for 2005.
info@nereledgeinn.com www.nereledgeinn.com

Old Red Inn & Cottages
2406 White Mountain Hwy
03860
800-338-1356 603-356-2642
Richard & Susan Lefave

88-198 BB
17 rooms, 15 pb
Visa, MC, Disc, *Rated*
C-yes/S-ltd/P-ltd/H-no
French

Full breakfast
Living room with fireplace,
meeting facilities, WiFi,
seasonal pool. Some cottages
have kitchenettes.

A romantic get-a-way for two, or a family vacation trip, North Conway's Old Red Inn & Cottages puts you right in the middle of the Mount Washington Valley. You can walk to town for dining, a train ride, outlet-shopping or just plain relaxing.
OldRedInn@RoadRunner.com www.oldredinn.com

Red Elephant Inn B&B
28 Locust Ln 03860
800-642-0749 603-356-3548
Tana & Nelson Hall

110-225 BB
8 rooms, 8 pb
Most CC, *Rated*
C-ltd/S-no/P-no/H-no
French

Full breakfast
Coffee/tea,
fruit/cookies/chocolates;
special dietary needs
accommodated with notice
Den w/ LCD TV, library,
outdoor pool,
fireplaces/stoves, cable
TV/DVD/VCR, Jacuzzi tubs,
WiFi

A four-season historic bed and breakfast inn tucked away on a quiet wooded lane just off the main route through the Village of North Conway, nestled in the Mount Washington Valley in the heart of the White Mountains of New Hampshire. Private baths and ac.
info@redelephantinn.com www.redelephantinn.com

Riverside Inn B&B
372 Route 16A 03860
866-949-0044 603-356-0044
Kenneth & Chris Lydecker

109-225 BB
6 rooms, 6 pb
Most CC
C-ltd/S-ltd/P-no/H-ltd

Full Country breakfast
Afternoon tea with home-
baked cookies
Gas fireplaces, spa tubs,
library, four seasons of
activity and entertainment.

Newly renovated rooms & suites, romantic fireplaces, spa tubs, private baths, directly on the beautiful East Branch Saco River, central location, near everything, quiet-off the beaten path, small inn with attentive personal service, full country breakfast
info2@riverside-inn-bed-breakfast.com www.riverside-inn-bed-breakfast.com

Spruce Moose Lodge & Cottages
207 Seavey St 03860
800-600-6239 603-356-6239
Nellie & Leon Filip

89-299 BB
11 rooms, 11 pb
Visa, MC
C-ltd/S-no/P-ltd/H-no

Full country breakfast
Breakfast not included for
cottages
Groups, cottages, Great
Room, private baths,
complimentary toiletries,
dog friendly

A four-seasons haven for White Mountains travelers almost since its granite foundation was laid more than 150 years ago. Lodge rooms, bungalows, cottages, and Victorian house lodgings available. Dog friendly!
mainmoose@sprucemooselodge.com www.sprucemooselodge.com

NORTH CONWAY

Wildflowers Inn	90-275 BB	Full breakfast cooked to
3486 White Mountain Hwy	9 rooms, 9 pb	order
03860	Most CC	Homemade cookies,
866-945-3357 603-356-7567	C-yes/S-ltd/P-no/H-yes	brownies, pastries
Bob & Emily Koch	Chinese & Taiwanese	Fireplaces, HDTV-50" in
		common area, Jacuzzi suites,
		hot tub, spectacular views of
		Mt Washington

Wildflowers Inn Bed & Breakfast commands the finest views of Mt Washington. We offer a warm & comfortable home for you to relax and enjoy. A four season Inn that is earning a reputation for fine hospitality and service.
✉ info@wildflowersinn.com ✪ www.wildflowersinn.com

NORTH WOODSTOCK

Wilderness Inn B&B	70-175 BB	Full gourmet breakfast
57 S Main St 03262	8 rooms, 8 pb	Afternoon tea, hot cider,
888-777-7813 603-745-3890	Most CC, *Rated*, •	cocoa, lemonade
Michael & Rosanna Yarnell	C-yes/S-no/P-no/H-no	Sunporch, central AC,
	French & Italian	fireplace in living room,
		fireplace & Jacuzzis in some
		rooms, cable TV, Wifi

"The quintessential country inn" circa 1912, located in a quaint New England town. The inn has seven family suites and a "honeymoon" cottage. All private baths. Gourmet breakfast.
✉ info@thewildernessinn.com ✪ www.thewildernessinn.com

Woodstock Inn Station &	63-199 BB	Full breakfast
Brewery	33 rooms, 31 pb	Fireplaces, Jacuzzi, cable TV,
135 Main St 03262	Most CC, *Rated*	A/C, in-room phone, indoor
800-321-3985 603-745-3951	C-yes/S-yes/P-no/H-ltd	pool and exercise room
Scott & Peggy Rice		available

One of the most visited country inns in the White Mountains. 33 rooms with cable TV, A/C, and in-room phone; some with Jacuzzis and gas fireplaces. Two restaurants, entertainment and brew pub on premises.
✉ relax@woodstockinnnh.com ✪ www.woodstockinnnh.com

PLYMOUTH

Bridgewater Mountain B&B	110-160 BB	Full breakfast
984 Bridgewater Hill Rd 3264	2 rooms, 2 pb	Please ask us about other
603-968-3966	Visa, MC	personal services.
Virginia K. Slayton	C-ltd/S-no/P-no/H-no	
	April 15 – October 31	

Gracious & friendly this high country B&B is surrounded by beautiful mountain views, organic gardens, stone walls & ancient maples, a perfect spot for rest & renewal as well as convenient access to lakes, the White Mountains, and areas schools and camps.
✉ vslayton@bridgewatermountain.com ✪ www.bridgewatermountain.com

Federal House Inn –	135-189 BB	Full breakfast
Historic B&B	5 rooms, 5 pb	Complimentary hospitality
27 Rt 25 03264	MC, AmEx, Disc, •	bar, tea & cookies, wine &
866-536-4644 603-536-4644	C-ltd/S-no/P-no/H-no	cheese daily
Frank & Andrea Morese		Gathering room, library,
		wireless Internet, heated spa,
		robes, plush towels, pillow
		top mattresses

An elegant 1835 Brick Federal Colonial Bed & Breakfast Inn. Nestled at the base of Tenney Mountain, just minutes from Plymouth State University and Holderness School.
✉ stay@federalhouseinnNH.com ✪ www.federalhouseinnnh.com

PORTSMOUTH

Inn at Strawbery Banke
314 Court St 03801
800-428-3933 603-436-7242
Sarah Glover O'Donnell

115-170 BB
7 rooms, 7 pb
Most CC, *Rated*
C-ltd/S-no/P-no/H-ltd

Full breakfast
Sitting rooms, outdoor
garden, all guestrooms have
A/C, parking

*This historic, Colonial inn charms travelers with its beautiful rooms and outdoor garden.
Located in the heart of old Portsmouth.*
✉ sallyjaggard@hotmail.com ○ innatstrawberybanke.com

Martin Hill Inn
404 Islington St 03801
603-436-2287
Margot Doering

105-210 BB
7 rooms, 7 pb
Visa, MC
C-ltd/S-no/P-no/H-no
Spanish

Full breakfast
Dietary needs and
preferences are happily
accommodated, including
vegan & gluten free
selections.
Dinner reservations, spa
appointments, gift baskets &
flowers arranged on request.

*Providing a special retreat to the seacoast of NH for over 30 years, the Inn features 7
unique rooms with private baths. Walk 10 minutes to downtown Portsmouth's restaurants,
boutiques & waterfront. A full gourmet breakfast & lovely gardens await you.*
✉ reservations@martinhillinn.com ○ www.martinhillinn.com

Sise Inn
40 Court St 03801
877-747-3466 603-433-1200
Diane Hodun

119-279 BB
34 rooms, 34 pb
Most CC, *Rated*, •
C-yes/S-no/P-no/H-yes

Expanded continental
breakfast
All day coffee, tea and spring
water, plus fresh baked
cookies every afternoon
Round-the-clock staffing, oak-
paneled elevator, free
parking, new WiFi,
TV/DVD/VCR

*Much larger and more accommodating than a typical Portsmouth Bed and Breakfast, each
of the Sise Inn's 34 guestrooms and suites is uniquely decorated with period furnishings
and reproductions. Each room and suite includes a private bath and amenities.*
✉ info@siseinn.com ○ www.siseinn.com

SANBORNTON

**Ferry Point House on Lake
Winnisquam**
100 Lower Bay Rd 03269
603-524-0087
Eric and Andrea Damato

120-165 BB
9 rooms, 9 pb
Cash, Checks, *Rated*
C-ltd/S-no/P-no/H-no
Jan 1-Dec 31

Country gourmet
Beverage and snack at check-
in
Jacuzzi, gazebo, porch,
fireplace, dining room

*Gracious country Victorian situated on picturesque Lake Winnisquam. Built in 1800's,
offers country gourmet breakfasts.*
✉ info@ferrypointhouse.com ○ www.ferrypointhouse.com

SHELBURNE

Mt. Washington B&B
421 State Rt 2 03581
877-466-2399 603-466-2669
Mary Ann Mayer

90-180 BB
7 rooms, 7 pb
Visa, MC, •
C-yes/S-no/P-no/H-no

Hearty Hot Breakfast
Complimentary home baked
goodies, soda, tea, hot
chocolate
Sitting room, movie library,
games, puzzles

*Come be pampered at this Romantic 1800's Federal Farmhouse nestled in the White
Mountains with views of Mts. Washington, Madison, Adams and the Androscoggin River. 7
guestrooms, all have private baths, 2 with Whirlpool tubs. Getaway from it all!*
✉ mtwashbb@yahoo.com ○ www.mtwashingtonbb.com

SILVER LAKE

Lake View Cottage	125-195 BB	Full candlelight breakfast
24 Rosewood Ln 03875	5 rooms, 5 pb	Afternoon refreshments, 24
800-982-0418 603-367-9182	Most CC, •	hour coffee, tea, cocoa
Becky Knowles	C-ltd/S-no/P-no/H-no	Library, Jacuzzis, fireplaces, sitting area, boats, dock, fishing, romance, concierge

This restored lakeside Victorian Inn offers spectacular views, romantic getaways, swimming, boating, snowmobiling from our door and many lake and mountain activities.
✉ info@lakeviewcottage.com 🌐 www.lakeviewcottage.com

SNOWVILLE

Snowvillage Inn	129-269 BB	Full country breakfast
136 Stewart Road 03832	18 rooms, 18 pb	Our menu features authentic
800-447-4345 603-447-2818	Most CC	New England Regional
Karen & Bern Galat	C-yes/S-no/P-yes/H-no	Cuisine with a focus on seafood
		Award-winning gardens, multi-level dining room, living room with fireplace, 3 season porch

Snowvillage is a country inn situated six miles southeast of Conway, New Hampshire with spectacular views of Mt. Washington and the Presidential Range of the White Mountains.
✉ info@snowvillageinn.com 🌐 www.snowvillageinn.com

SUGAR HILL

Sugar Hill Inn	95-350 BB	Full Country breakfast
116 Route 117 03586	14 rooms, 14 pb	Dining Thursday-Sunday,
800-548-4748 603-823-5621	Most CC, *Rated*, •	Pub,
Steven Allen	C-yes/S-no/P-no/H-no	swimming pool, Spa, gardens, tavern, restaurant

Incredible lodging, food & hospitality with some of the finest mountain views in New Hampshire. Cottages, pool and whirlpool bath, privacy, activity packages.
✉ info@SugarHillInn.com 🌐 www.sugarhillinn.com

Sunset Hill House – A Grand Inn	139-399 BB	Full breakfast
231 Sunset Hill Rd 03586	30 rooms, 30 pb	Tea, coffee all day, afternoon
800-786-4455 603-823-5522	Most CC, *Rated*, •	homebaked cookies
Lon & Nancy Henderson	C-yes/S-no/P-ltd/H-yes	On-site heated pool, golf,
	German, French	Nordic ski, snowshoe, fireplaced parlors, fine dining, tavern, groups

For views, food, & ambience, guests & press agree that Sunset Hill House has "New England's most spectacular mountain views," (Yankee Magazine) & "NH's most spectacular Meal," (NH Magazine). Award winning full service inn in the heart of the Mountains.
✉ innkeeper@sunsethillhouse.com 🌐 www.sunsethillhouse.com

SUNAPEE

Dexter's Inn & Tennis Club	125-185 BB	Full breakfast
258 Stagecoach Rd 03782	21 rooms, 21 pb	Afternoon refreshments
800-232-5571 603-763-5571	Most CC, *Rated*, •	Tennis, swimming,
John Augustine & Penny Berrier	C-yes/S-no/P-ltd/H-ltd	volleyball, basketball, game
	German, French	room, kids playroom, library

A warm & welcoming, family-friendly, country inn with magnificent views and idyllic grounds. Tennis, swimming, game room, library on-site. Minutes to golf, skiing, shopping, the mountains and lakes.
✉ dexters@tds.net 🌐 www.dextersnh.com

SWANZEY

Bridges Inn at Whitcomb House
27 Main St 03446
603-357-6624
Susan & David Schuster

90-150 BB
5 rooms, 5 pb
Visa, MC, *Rated*, •
C-yes/S-no/P-ltd/H-ltd
Spanish

Full breakfast
Snacks, chocolates in room,
coffee & tea anytime
Cable TV; wireless Internet;
accommodate business
travelers; seasonal hot tub;
A/C in guestrooms

Idyllic 1792 inn located in a quaint village in beautiful southwestern New Hampshire near the six covered bridges for which the inn is named. Five rooms, each with private bath, are set aside for guests. Visit Cheshire County's six covered bridges.
✉ innkeeper@bridgesinn.net ○ www.bridgesinn.com

Inn of the Tartan Fox
350 Old Homestead Hwy
03446
877-836-4319 603-357-9308
Wayne & Meg

85-135 BB
4 rooms, 4 pb
Visa, MC, AmEx
C-ltd/S-no/P-no/H-yes

Four Course Gourmet
Breakfast
Picnic lunches on request,
gluten free, vegetarian meals
with prior notice.
Library, gardens, A/C,
fireplaces, gift shop, wireless
Internet, student discounts,
corporate rates.

1832 Manorhouse with Celtic styled rooms. Antiques, private baths, heated marble floors, fireplaces, gift shop. One fully accessible room. Scrumptious gourmet breakfast. 3 miles to Main St. Keene.
✉ info@tartanfox.com ○ www.tartanfox.com

TAMWORTH

Highland House
Cleveland Hill Rd 03886
603-323-7982
N. Dale Bragdon

85-170 BB
4 rooms, 2 pb
Cash, Checks
C-ltd/S-no/P-ltd/H-no

Cont. or Full available on
request

Welcome to Highland House Bed and Breakfast and N. Dale Bragdon Event Planning and Catering set on a hill above picturesque Tamworth, New Hampshire, where seasons set a magical stage for recreation, arts, and entertainment.
✉ highlandhouse@gmail.com ○ www.highlandhousetamworth.com

WALPOLE

Inn at Valley Farms B&B & Cottages
633 Wentworth Rd 03608
877-327-2855 603-756-2855
Jacqueline Caserta

175-220 BB
6 rooms, 6 pb
Visa, MC
C-ltd/S-no/P-no/H-ltd

Three course decadent
breakfast
Homemade cookies, coffee,
selection of tea & soft drinks
always available
Working organic farm,
renown chocolate, beautiful
sun room, game room, full
library, walking trails

Gracious 1774 Colonial home on tranquil 100-acre organic farm. Elegant rooms with three-course gourmet breakfast, 3-bedroom self-sufficient cottages or farmhouse perfect for families. Beautiful grounds w/ extensive gardens, fine dining and more nearby.
✉ info@innatvalleyfarms.com ○ www.innatvalleyfarms.com

WENTWORTH

Hilltop Acres B&B
East Side & Buffalo Rd 03282
603-764-5896
Marie Kauk

100-125 BB
6 rooms, 6 pb
Visa, MC, •
C-yes/S-no/P-yes/H-no
May-October

Continental plus breakfast
Gardens, fireplace, sitting
room, cottages

A country retreat with private baths, flower gardens, a sitting room with a fireplace, cable TV, housekeeping cottages.
✉ info@hilltopacres.net ○ www.hilltopacres.net

WEST CHESTERFIELD————————————————————

Chesterfield Inn	175-345 BB	Full breakfast
20 Cross Road 03446	15 rooms, 15 pb	Full country breakfast is
800-365-5515 603-256-3211	Most CC, *Rated*, •	included. Dinner is served
Phil & Judy Hueber	C-yes/S-no/P-yes/H-no	nightly in our candlelit
		dining room.
		TV, phones, wireless
		Internet, mini fridge in room,
		air conditioning, breakfast in
		bed.

Come and relax awhile at this elegant yet comfortable renovated New Hampshire Farm-house with its cathedral ceilings and rambling views of the Connecticut River Valley. Privacy, and delicious cuisine are yours at one of the best Inns in New England!
✉ chstinn@sover.net ○ www.chesterfieldinn.com

WILTON CENTER————————————————————————

Stepping Stones B&B	75-85 BB	Full breakfast
6 Bennington Battle Tr 03086	3 rooms, 3 pb	Complimentary tea, wine,
888-654-9048 603-654-9048	Checks, *Rated*, •	coffee, chocolates, fruit &
Ann Carlsmith	C-yes/S-ltd/P-ltd/H-no	cookies
		Stereo, cable TV, DVD,
		looms, library, sitting room,
		game room, breakfast room,
		gardens

Landscape designer's sanctuary for visitors who seek country tranquility, in a warm and welcoming atmosphere. Set in Monadnock hills, near picture-book village. Summer theater and music. Dogs welcome! Wireless access.
✉ acarlsmith@steppingstonesbb.com ○ www.steppingstonesbb.com

New Jersey

ASBURY

Berry Preserve B&B
215 Turkey Hill Rd 08802
908-479-6242
Diann & Steve Berry

70-135 BB
3 rooms, 2 pb
Visa, MC, AmEx
C-ltd/S-no/P-no/H-no
April – December

Full breakfast
Afternoon refreshments
A/C, cable TV, reading chairs
& lights, vintage films & VCR,
hairdryers, wireless Internet
access

Unwind at the Berry Preserve B&B, a tranquil ten-acre woodland retreat, with genial hosts Steve and Diann Berry. Experience a world of arts and crafts in this unique contemporary lodging with all the comforts of home and easy access to major highways.
✉ berrypreserve@comcast.net ◐ www.berrypreserve.com

ATLANTIC HIGHLANDS

Blue Bay Inn
51 First Ave 07716
732-708-9600
Bob Hilton

169-399 BB
27 rooms, 27 pb
Visa, MC, AmEx
C-yes/S-no/P-no/H-yes

Continental breakfast
5 Star restaurant on site.

The Blue Bay Inn is the only boutique hotel on the Jersey shore. Its oversized luxurious rooms, deluxe suites and extended stay fully furnished apartments are havens of enlightened comfort.
✉ info@bluebayinn.com ◐ www.bluebayinn.com

AVON BY THE SEA

Atlantic View Inn
20 Woodland Ave 07717
877-367-6522 732-774-8505
Debbie & Chris Solomita

150-335 BB
12 rooms, 12 pb
Visa, MC, Disc, *Rated*
C-ltd/S-no/P-no/H-no

Full breakfast
Early continental, afternoon
refreshments, cookies,
complimentary bottled
water, snacks, juices
Sitting room, fireplaces, all
rooms have TV/VCR, beach
badges, chairs, towels,
umbrellas, bicycles

This warm & comfortable B&B was built over a century ago as a grand summer cottage overlooking the ocean. The charm of an English seashore home is captured in furnishings of mahogany, antiques, traditional wicker & hand-painted pieces.
✉ avibb@optonline.net ◐ www.atlanticviewinn.com

Avon Manor & Cottages
109 Sylvania Ave 07717
732-776-7770
Greg Dietrich

65-285 BB
9 rooms, 9 pb
Most CC, *Rated*, •
C-ltd/S-no/P-ltd/H-ltd
Italian

Full breakfast
Tea & snacks,
complimentary wine, lunch
Golf lesson, beach badges,
chairs & towels, putting
green, tandem bicycle,
Family Cottage

Central NJ, Spring Lake area, steps from the finest beach & boardwalk on the coast of N.J. Extensive breakfast menu, specials, Jacuzzi & fireplace suites. Romantic & golf packages on our web site. Large Cottage rental also available.
✉ gregmav@aol.com ◐ www.avonmanor.com

Cashelmara Inn, Avon by the Sea, NJ

AVON BY THE SEA

Cashelmara Inn
22 Lakeside Ave 07717
732-776-8727
Mary Wiernasz, Martin
Mulligan

100-375 BB
14 rooms, 14 pb
Visa, MC, Disc, *Rated*
C-ltd/S-no/P-no/H-no
Spanish in am

Full country breakfast to
order
Tea & goodie table, ice
machine, soda/bottled water
on the honor system
Beach chairs, badges and
towels, maid service,
wireless Internet

*Our grand staircase, museum quality antiques & golden retriever warmly welcome you.
Waterviews, many from bed, are complimented by designer fabrics & fireplaces. In-season
free beach badges, towels, chairs and umbrellas with $15 set up service.*
✉ cashelmara5@aol.com ✪ www.cashelmara.com

BARNEGAT LIGHT

**Sand Castle Bed and
Breakfast**
710 Bayview Ave 08006
800-253-0353 609-494-6555
Nancy Gallimore

175-425 BB
7 rooms, 7 pb
Visa, MC, *Rated*
C-ltd/S-no/P-no/H-no

Full breakfast
Complimentary tea, coffee
and soft drinks
Fireplace, Jacuzzi, parlor,
rooftop deck, pool, exercise
room

*The Sand Castle Bed and Breakfast is the premiere accommodation on Long Beach Island
for adult couples and singles. Each of five bayfront guestrooms and two luxury suites offer
fireplace, private bath, some with Jacuzzi, and a romantic, quiet setting.*
✉ info@sandcastlelbi.com ✪ www.sandcastleLBI.com

BEACH HAVEN

Island Guest House B&B
207 3rd St 08008
877-LBI-STAY 609-709-5791
Joanne & Mark Spulock

125-399 BB
15 rooms, 12 pb
Visa, MC, *Rated*
C-yes/S-no/P-no/H-no

Full breakfast
Afternoon tea time and
specialty treats from the
kitchen
Outdoor garden, bicycle for
two, WiFi, beach
chairs/badges, cafe kitchen,
A/C, balconies, Jacuzzis.

*The Island Guest House has been Voted the Best Bed & Breakfast on Long Beach Island. It
is a turn-of-the-century historic inn, located oceanside in the heart of Beach Haven, New
Jersey. Come and experience the restfulness of a European style guesthouse.*
✉ islandguesthouse@comcast.net ✪ www.lbinet.com/islandguesthouse

BEACH HAVEN

Julia's of Savannah	175-350 BB	Full breakfast
209 Centre St 08008	9 rooms, 9 pb	Afternoon Tea
609-492-5004	Visa, MC	Beach chairs, towels,
Tom & Angela Williams	C-ltd/S-no/P-no/H-yes	bicycles and off-street
	Feb to 1st weekend Dec	parking

Long Beach Island, NJ's premier bed and breakfast, providing guests with exquisite decor and gracious hospitality. Nine comfortable, relaxing rooms, some with whirlpool tubs, private verandahs and working fireplaces.
✉ juliasofsavannah@netscape.net ○ www.juliasoflbi.com

Victoria Guest House	165-295 BB	Buffet breakfast
126 Amber St 08008	14 rooms, 14 pb	If you have a dietary
609-492-4154	Visa, MC	restriction, let us know.
Marilyn, Leonard, John &	S-ltd/P-no/H-ltd	Wednesday evening wine
Judy Miller	May thru September	and cheese. Afternoon tea
		Bikes, beach chairs & towels,
		heated pool, bottled water,
		beach badges, wireless
		Internet, A/C, TV w DVD

Situated four houses from the ocean. We offer spacious guestrooms, attractively decorated with cheerful exposure. Linger on our wraparound porches or take a cooling dip in our heated pool.
✉ victoria_guest_house@msn.com ○ www.lbivictoria.com

Williams Cottage Inn	195-425 BB	Full breakfast
506 South Atlantic Ave 08008	8 rooms, 8 pb	Gourmet Coffee & tea,
609-492-7272	Visa, MC, Disc	afternoon refreshments
Amy & Hans Herberg	S-no/P-no/H-yes	TV, DVD player, WiFi,
	Norwegian	individual climate control,
		complimentary use of
		bicycles and tennis rackets

This 120 year old beach front Victorian mansion has been lovingly restored, lavishly decorated and richly appointed with the finest designer amenities to make it the most luxurious B&B Inn ever to grace the Jersey Shore.
✉ innkeeper@williamscottageinn.com ○ www.williamscottageinn.com

BELMAR

The Inn at the Shore	125-145 BB	Full breakfast
301 Fourth Ave 07719	11 rooms, 4 pb	Tea, snacks, refrigerator,
732-681-3762	Visa, MC, AmEx,	microwave, coffee & tea
Tom & Rosemary Volker	*Rated*, ●	available in guest pantry
	C-yes/S-ltd/P-no/H-no	Jacuzzi, fireplaces,
		aquarium, phones, TV/VCR,
		wireless Internet patio & gas
		grill, A/C, Health Spa

Let us pamper you at our family-friendly, Victorian country seashore inn, while you rock away & enjoy sea & lake breezes on a wraparound porch.
✉ tomvolker@optonline.net ○ www.theinnattheshore.com

BLAIRSTOWN

Alexander Adams	135-245 BB	on weekends
Homestead	3 rooms, 3 pb	Continental Plus breakfast
31A Auble Rd 07825	Most CC	served during the week.
908-459-4018	C-ltd/S-no/P-no/H-ltd	Sitting room, swimming pool,
Edie & Alan Sauck		suites, fireplaces, cable TV

Let us give you a little getaway that rejuvenates you. Relax and enjoy time in our private cottage or one of our delightful suites. Conveniently located near Hope, NJ just one hour from NYC and 30 minutes from the Shawnee and Camel Back ski resorts.
✉ info@alexanderadamshomestead.com ○ www.alexanderadamshomestead.com

CAPE MAY

The Abbey B&B Inn
34 Gurney St @ Colombia Ave
08204
866-884-8800 609-884-4506
Jay & Marianne Schatz

95-200 BB
7 rooms, 7 pb
Visa, MC, Disc, *Rated*
C-ltd/S-ltd/P-no/H-no
Easter-Dec.

Full buffet breakfast dining
room
Complimentary wine, snacks
at teatime.
2 parlors, library, piano,
harp, off-street parking,
wireless Internet, beach
chairs, beach passes.

Elegantly restored Gothic Revival villa with period antiques. Genuine merriment in a warm unobstrusive atmosphere. A/C available in season. Onsite Parking. One block from Atlantic Ocean in the heart of the historic district.
✉ theabbey@verizon.net 🕒 www.abbeybedandbreakfast.com

Angel of the Sea
5 Trenton Ave 08204
800-848-3369 609-884-3369
Lorie Whissell

95-315 BB
27 rooms, 27 pb
Most CC, *Rated*, •
C-ltd/S-no/P-no/H-no

Full breakfast
Early morning coffee service,
afternoon tea & sweets,
evening wine and cheese
Off-street parking, beach
chairs, towels/umbrellas,
complimentary bikes,
concierge, cable TV, WiFi.

Cape May's most luxurious B&B Victorian mansion. Fabulous oceanviews, ½ block from the beach. Rooms have private baths, ceiling fans, clawfoot tubs, cable TV and WiFi.
✉ info@angelofthesea.com 🕒 www.angelofthesea.com

Bayberry Inn
223 Perry St 08204
877-923-9232 609-884-9232
Andy & Toby Fontaine

120-295 BB
5 rooms, 5 pb
Most CC
C-ltd/S-no/P-no/H-ltd

Full, 3 Course Breakfast
Specialties include gourmet
delights; afternoon tea
complete with homemade
treats
Guest refrigerator, fireplaces,
beach chairs & towels, on
site parking, dinner
reservations, WiFi

Enjoy Cape May's ambience and the serenity of a by-gone era in the historic district. Unwind at our relaxing, romantic seaside B&B inn. Hospitality, Victorian charm and only two blocks from the beach, one block from shopping, dining and theater.
✉ bayberryinnkeeper@sisna.com 🕒 www.bayberryinncapemay.com

Beauclaire's B&B
23 Ocean St 07675
609-898-1222
Sandy Finnegan

95-255 BB
6 rooms, 6 pb
Most CC, *Rated*
C-ltd/S-no/P-no/H-no

Full gourmet breakfast
Afternoon refreshments &
snacks
½ block to beach, off-street
parking, beach chairs,
Internet access

Beauclaire's is a renowned Victorian style Bed & Breakfast open all year & located in the historic district in Cape May. Just a half block from the beach & two blocks from the center of town.
✉ innkeeper@beauclaires.com 🕒 www.beauclaires.com

Bedford Inn
805 Stockton Ave 08204
866-215-9507 609-884-4158
Archie & Stephanie Kirk

120-265 BB
10 rooms, 10 pb
Visa, MC, *Rated*, •
S-no/P-no/H-ltd

Full buffet breakfast
Afternoon refreshments, hot
beverage service 24 hours
Dining room, parlor, 3
porches, limited on-site
parking, private baths, A/C,
TV/VCR/DVD, hairdryer

Bedford Inn is an elegant 1883 Italianate seaside inn that has an unusual double staircase, and lovely antique-filled rooms and suites. A full, memorable, breakfast and afternoon refreshments are served daily.
✉ info@bedfordinn.com 🕒 www.bedfordinn.com

CAPE MAY————

Carroll Villa Hotel
19 Jackson St 08204
877-275-8452 609-884-9619
Mark Kulkowitz & Pam Huber

110-289 BB
21 rooms, 21 pb
Most CC, *Rated*, •
C-yes/S-no/P-no/H-no

Full breakfast
Great lunch & dinner served
on our European front porch,
skylit, dining room or Garden
terrace
Wireless Internet, happy
hour daily

National landmark hotel with critically acclaimed restaurant, located in historic Cape May. We are a small family run business with 21 rooms, all with private bath & shower.
✉ manager@carrollvilla.com ✆ www.carrollvilla.com

Cliveden Inn & Cottage
709 Columbia Ave 08204
800-884-2420 609-884-4516
Susan & Al DeRosa

130-190 BB
10 rooms, 10 pb
Checks, *Rated*
C-ltd/S-ltd/P-no/H-no

Full breakfast buffet
Afternoon tea, snacks
Library, veranda, rocking
chairs, Victorian cottage
available

Fine accommodations, delicious breakfasts and gracious hospitality have made the Cliveden one of the popular inns of Cape May.
✆ www.clivedeninn.com

The Dormer House
800 Columbia Ave 08204
800-884-5052 609-884-7446
Lucille & Dennis Doherty

99-250 BB
14 rooms, 14 pb
Most CC, *Rated*
C-ltd/S-no/P-no/H-ltd

Full breakfast
Afternoon Tea & Treats
Sitting room, glass enclosed
breakfast porch, bikes,
Jacuzzi room, comp. beach
chairs/towels

One of the great summer houses of the 1890s. Enjoy your full breakfast and tea all year long on our sun porch. An inn for all seasons. "Come for the tea, stay for the night."
✉ dormerhouse@gmail.com ✆ www.dormerhouse.com

Fairthorne B&B
111-115 Ocean St 08204
800-438-8742 609-884-8791
Ed & Diane Hutchinson

230-280 BB
10 rooms, 10 pb
Most CC, *Rated*, •
C-ltd/S-no/P-no/H-no

Full breakfast
Afternoon tea and guest area
with soda, water, ice, coffee
and tea
Public library across street,
bicycles, sitting room, near
ocean

Voted "Best in the East" B&B by Inn goers. "The Discerning Traveler" chose us as one of the East's most delightful and delicious destinations—Romantic Hideaways 2002.
✉ fairthornebnb@aol.com ✆ www.fairthorne.com

Gingerbread House
28 Gurney St 08204
609-884-0211
Fred & Joan Echevarria

110-298 BB
6 rooms, 3 pb
Visa, MC, *Rated*
C-ltd/S-ltd/P-no/H-no
April – December

Full breakfast
Afternoon tea with baked
goods and refreshments
Wicker-filled porch, parlor
with fireplace, Victorian
antiques, A/C, LCD flat panel
TVs, WiFi

The Gingerbread House is a meticulous and comfortable 1869 inn. It is a woodworkers masterpiece using the innkeepers woodworking talents. It is conveniently located½block from the beach, in the heart of Cape May's historic district.
✉ info@gingerbreadinn.com ✆ www.gingerbreadinn.com

The Humphrey Hughes House
29 Ocean St 08204
800-582-3634 609-884-4428
Lorraine & Terry Schmidt

135-350 BB
10 rooms, 10 pb
Visa, MC, AmEx, *Rated*
S-no/P-no/H-no
Mid-April-Oct.

Full breakfast
Afternoon tea & treats
Library, veranda, beach,
tags, rocking chairs,
Victorian cottage

Enjoy a full breakfast on our large, wraparound verandah. Cozy Victorian cottage. Center of Historic District.
✉ thehumphreyhughes@comcast.net ✆ www.humphreyhugheshouse.com

CAPE MAY

John F. Craig House
609 Columbia Ave 08204
877-544-0314 609-884-0100
Chip & Barbara Masemore

145-265 BB
8 rooms, 8 pb
Most CC
C-ltd/S-no/P-no/H-no

Full breakfast
Afternoon tea, snacks
A/C in all rooms, some
fireplaces in rooms, cable
TV/VCR, refrigerators

Welcome to our whimsical yet romantic Bed and Breakfast, an Inn located in the center of Historic Cape May, New Jersey . . . designed for your comfort and our informality. Our inn is rated #8 on Travel Channel's list of Best Beach Communities.
✉ chipbarbara@comcast.net ◐ www.johnfcraig.com

John Wesley Inn & Carriage House
30 Gurney St 08204
800-616-5122 609-884-1012
Bonnie & Lance Pontin

150-325 BB
8 rooms, 8 pb
Most CC, *Rated*, ●
C-ltd/S-ltd/P-no/H-no

Full gourmet breakfast
Each afternoon a variety of
seasonal appropriate (hot or
cold) refreshments are
served.
½ block to beach, 2 blocks to
mall, on-site parking,
Internet, TV, iPod, Safes, A/C,
sunroom/wet bar

"Where Antiques and Amenities Harmonize!" Completely renovated. Centrally located in the Cape May Historic District of Stockton Row, ½block from beach and 2 blocks from the walking mall. Park your car On-Site and forget about it. Walk to fine dining
✉ info@johnwesleyinn.com ◐ www.johnwesleyinn.com

Leith Hall Historic Seashore Inn
22 Ocean St 08204
877-884-1400 609-884-1934
Susan & Elan Zingman-Leith

105-320 BB
8 rooms, 8 pb
Visa, MC, Disc, *Rated*
C-ltd/S-no/P-no/H-no
French, Yiddish

Full breakfast
Afternoon English tea with
cakes & cookies. Iced tea
and lemonade with cakes &
cookies in summer.
Ocean views, whirlpools,
fireplaces, cable
TV/VCRs/DVDs, A/C, large
porch, wireless Internet,
library

Elegantly restored 1880s home in the heart of the Victorian district. Only half block from the beach, with ocean views and a large wraparound porch with rocking chairs.
✉ stay@leithhall.com ◐ www.leithhall.com

The Mainstay Inn
635 Columbia Ave 08204
609-884-8690
Diane Clark

195-360 BB
12 rooms, 12 pb
Visa, MC, *Rated*
C-ltd/S-no/P-no/H-yes
April-Janurary 1st

Full breakfast (Sept-June)
4–5 p.m. daily: hot/iced tea,
home made sweets, fresh
fruit & tea sandwiches or
cheese spreads.
12 A/C rooms, piano, 3 sitting
rooms

An elegant Victorian Inn within a lovely garden setting. The Inn and adjacent Cottage feature wide rocker-lined verandas and large rooms, which are lavishly and comfortably furnished.
✉ mainstayinn@comcast.net ◐ www.mainstayinn.com

CAPE MAY————————————————————————————————

The Mission Inn
1117 New Jersey Ave 08204
800-800-8380 609-884-8380
Susan Babineau-Roberts

205-350 BB
8 rooms, 8 pb
Visa, MC, AmEx, *Rated*
C-ltd/S-no/P-no/H-no

Full gourmet breakfast
Home baked cookies, tea,
hot cocoa, lemonade,
afternoon refreshments with
appetizers & hors d'oeuvres
Maid service, beach towels,
chairs umbrellas, bikes,
wireless, parking 2 sitting
rms, concierge service

Cape May's California Spanish Mission-style Inn. King beds, 2-person Jacuzzis, 2-person spa showers, fireplaces, iPod radios, central A/C & heat, TV/DVD, 3-course gourmet breakfast, parking, beach chairs, towels, umbrellas, bicycles, refreshments.
✉ info@missioninn.net ◐ www.missioninn.net

Mooring B&B
801 Stockton Ave 08204
609-884-5425
Leslie Valenza & Vince Casale

150-275 BB
11 rooms, 11 pb
Visa, MC, •
C-ltd/S-no/P-no/H-no
French
Mid-April to Mid-Nov

Full & Continental breakfast
avail
Afternoon tea
On-site parking, guest
kitchen, WiFi access, outside
showers, beach towels

Victorian mansard structure furnished in original period antiques with contemporary upgrades. One block to ocean and easy walking distance to fine restaurants and shopping.
✉ leslie@themooring.com ◐ www.themooring.com

Peter Shields Inn
1301 Beach Dr 08204
609-884-9090
Bridget & Jill

99-395 BB
9 rooms, 9 pb
Visa, MC, Disc, •
C-ltd/S-ltd/P-no/H-no

Full breakfast
Dinner, wine & cheese daily,
snacks, restaurant,
hospitality suite
Sitting room, fireplaces,
cable TV, library, beach
chairs & umbrella

Oceanfront 1907 Georgian revival mansion is an architectural masterpiece in Cape May, New Jersey. The Inn has 9 well appointed guestrooms all with private baths, most of which have Jacuzzis and fireplaces.
✉ petershieldsinn@comcast.net ◐ www.petershieldsinn.com

Poor Richard's Inn of Cape May
17 Jackson St 08204
609-884-3536
Harriett Sosson

120-180 BB
8 rooms, 8 pb
Most CC, *Rated*
C-ltd/S-ltd/P-no/H-no
Valentines-New Year's

Continental breakfast
Sitting room, Oriental rock
garden, near beach

Classic gingerbread guesthouse offers accommodations with eclectic Victorian and country decor.
✉ harriettsosson@verizon.net ◐ www.poorrichardsinn.com

The Queen Victoria B&B
102 Ocean St 08204
609-884-8702
Anna Marie & Doug McMain

110-495 BB
32 rooms, 32 pb
Visa, MC, Disc, *Rated*
C-ltd/S-no/P-no/H-ltd

Full buffet breakfast
Afternoon tea with sweets
and savory, in the English
fashion, complimentary
beverages
Bicycles, beach chairs,
evening turndown, wireless
Internet, TV/DVD &
refrigerator in all rooms.

Renowned historic Cape May B&B open all year with thirty-two antique-filled rooms & luxury suites, all with private bath, many with whirlpool tub and fireplaces.
✉ stay@queenvictoria.com ◐ www.queenvictoria.com

CAPE MAY

Rhythm of the Sea
1123 Beach Ave 08204-2628
800-498-6888 609-884-7788
Robyn & Wolfgang Wendt

205-375 BB
9 rooms, 9 pb
Most CC, *Rated*
C-ltd/S-no/P-no/H-no
German

Full breakfast
Beverage service daily,
dinner by prior arrangement
Gathering rooms, parking,
bikes, beach towels, beach
chairs, concierge

With the ocean as the front yard, fragrant breezes and a wealth of seaside activities, Rhythm of the Sea is an ideal location for a Cape May getaway. Savor sumptuous meals, relaxed and peaceful privacy and 'gemuetlichkeit.'
✉ stay@rhythmofthesea.com 🌐 www.rhythmofthesea.com

Saltwood House B&B
28 Jackson St 08204
800-830-8232 609-884-6754
Don Schweikert

170-330 BB
4 rooms, 4 pb
Visa, MC, AmEx, *Rated*
C-ltd/S-ltd/P-no/H-no
April-December

Full breakfast
Home-baked cookies all the
time, use of microwave, in-
room refrigerator, coffee/tea
makers
Sitting room, suites, cable TV,
DVD players & DVD library,
parking, WiFi, guest laptop

Ideally located mid-block on Cape May's oldest street, this meticulously restored and authentically furnished 1906 Inn captures the essence of a historic, private residence.
✉ saltwoodhouse@aol.com 🌐 www.saltwoodhouse.com

Southern Mansion
720 Washington St 08204
800-381-3888 609-884-7171
Barbara Wilde

150-470 BB
25 rooms, 25 pb
Most CC, *Rated*
C-ltd/S-no/P-no/H-ltd
Spanish

Full breakfast
Afternoon tea, lunch or
dinner for fee
Concierge, wedding facilities,
corporate retreats, fireplaces

"Only place to stay in Cape May" –NY Times. Luxurious, meticulously restored 1863 Mansion. Includes huge romantic rooms and suites, original antiques, hardwood floors, gourmet food and luxurious amenities.
✉ sales@southernmansion.com 🌐 www.southernmansion.com

Victorian Lace Inn
901 Stockton Ave 08204
609-884-1772
Carrie & Andy O'Sullivan

99-295 BB
8 rooms, 8 pb
Rated
C-yes/S-no/P-no/H-no

Full breakfast
Kitchenettes in each suite
Spa, Jacuzzis, library,
wireless Internet, fax service,
beach towels & chairs,
fireplaces

Beautiful all-suite Colonial Revival inn, with oceanviews and fireplaces. The Cottage has a fireplace and Jacuzzi. The Victorian Lace Inn is a classic, cedar-sided B&B by the sea.
✉ innkeeper@VictorianLaceInn.com 🌐 www.victorianlaceinn.com

Wilbraham Mansion
133 Myrtle Ave 08204
609-884-2046
Doug Carnes

110-280 BB
10 rooms, 10 pb
Visa, MC
C-ltd/S-ltd/P-no/H-no

Full breakfast
Afternoon tea
Indoor heated pool (20 X 40),
bicycles, 2 dining rooms, 2
parlors, TV room

Experience today's comforts & yesterday's Victorian elegance in one of Cape May's oldest & finest homes overlooking Wilbraham Park.
✉ dcarnes@shippersadvocate.com 🌐 www.wilbrahammansion.com

CAPE MAY

The Windward House	100-250 BB	Full breakfast
24 Jackson St 08204	9 rooms, 9 pb	Afternoon tea, sherry
609-884-3368	Visa, MC, Disc, *Rated*	Sitting room, library,
Sandy & Owen Miller	C-ltd/S-no/P-no/H-no	fireplace, sunporch, A/C, TV, beach chairs, refrigerators, wireless Internet

Windward House contains some of Cape May's finest collections and antiques. The beach and mall are½block away and most of Cape May's restaurants and tour sites are within walking distance. ✉ info@windwardhouseinn.com ◐ www.windwardhouseinn.com

CLINTON

Riverside Victorian	85-130 BB	Full breakfast
66 Leigh St 08809	6 rooms, 4 pb	Afternoon refreshments
908-238-0400	Most CC	TV/VCR, A/C, telephone &
Monita & Owen McElroy	C-ltd/S-no/P-no/H-ltd	in-room high-speed Internet service, fireplace, fridge, fax machine

Step back in time and enjoy Victorian splendor in an inviting, friendly atmosphere. Whether your stay is business related or simply to get away for awhile, you will find a warm welcome waiting for you here!
✉ mail@riversidevictorian.com ◐ www.riversidevictorian.com

FLEMINGTON

Main Street Manor	130-215 BB	Full breakfast
194 Main St 08822	5 rooms, 5 pb	Afternoon tea, 24 hour coffee
908-782-4928	Most CC, *Rated*	& tea, baked goodies &
Donna & Ken Arold	C-ltd/S-no/P-no/H-no	seasonal fruits, complimentary wine & cordials
		Personal service, many books, board games, cards, DVD library.

Relish the tranquility of this 1901 Victorian Manor House, nestled in the heart of Flemington's historic district. Fireplaces, featherbeds and an elegant candlelight breakfast are a few of the indulgences awaiting your arrival.
✉ innkeeper@mainstreetmanor.com ◐ www.mainstreetmanor.com

Silver Maple Organic Farm B&B	75-175 BB	full homemade country breakfast
483 Sergeantsville Rd 08822	5 rooms, 5 pb	complimentary soft drinks,
908-237-2192	Most CC, *Rated*, •	coffee/tea , waters, fruits and
Steven Noll	C-yes/S-no/P-yes/H-ltd	snacks 24/7.
		Robes, A/C, down comforters, rec room, living room, fireplace, gardens, pool, deck, hot tub, tennis

Historic Country Farmhouse / minutes to New Hope, Lambertville, Frenchtown, Doylestown & Flemington / We embrace diversity / Kid & Pet Friendly / Pool, Hot-tub, Tennis / Full Country Breakfast / Rural Country Setting/ Extra Comfortable Rooms and Rates!
✉ silvermaplebandb@gmail.com ◐ www.silvermaplebandb.com

FORKED RIVER

Inn at Rviers Edge Marina	100-250 BB	Full breakfast
223 E Lacey Rd 08731	3 rooms, 3 pb	
609-971-0025	Visa, MC	
Robert Royle & Patricia Chritian	C-ltd/S-no/P-no/H-no	

Welcome to our romantic riverside getaway, nestled upon the shores of the Forked River. The perfect environment to rekindle romance, celebrate birthdays, anniversary or that special weekend getaway. The Inn is Forked River's only B&B with its own marina.
✉ innatriversedge@verizon.net ◐ www.innatriversedge.com

FRENCHTOWN——————

Widow McCrea House	100-300 BB	Gourmet Candlelit 3 Course
53 Kingwood Ave 08825	6 rooms, 6 pb	Complimentary bottle of
908-996-4999	Visa, MC, *Rated*	wine en suite upon arrival,
Burt Patalano, Lynn Marad	C-ltd/S-no/P-ltd/H-yes	evening cordials, afternoon
		tea by request.
		Private cottage with Garden
		and Fountains, Parlor,
		Fireplaces, Jacuzzis, cable
		TV/DVD/CD, free WiFi.

Charming 1878 Victorian Inn features spacious suites with fireplaces/Jacuzzis. English cottage with private gardens, statuary and fountains. Six elegant guestrooms. Fine antiques, queen size featherbeds, private baths, candlelight breakfast.
✉ widowmccrea@sprintmail.com ☙ www.widowmccrea.com

HIGHLANDS——————

Sandy Hook Cottage B&B	159-299 BB	Full breakfast
36 Route 36 07732	4 rooms, 2 pb	Hot & cold buffet breakfast,
732-708-1923	Most CC, *Rated*, •	fresh baked cookies, cakes,
Eddy Sousa & Nick	C-ltd/S-no/P-no/H-ltd	fruit, iced tea & evening wine
Evangelista	Spanish	& cheese
	April – October	Outdoor Jacuzzi, cable TV,
		wireless Internet, in-room
		refrigerator, fireplace,
		sunporch, deck/lounge

Seaside cottage overlooking Sandy Hook and the Atlantic Ocean, just 35 minutes from NYC via ferry. Ocean views, magnificent beaches, just minutes to Red Bank, Ocean Grove & Asbury Park.
✉ info@sandyhookcottage.com ☙ www.sandyhookcottage.com

SeaScape Manor	145-245 BB	Full breakfast
3 Grand Tour 07732	4 rooms, 4 pb	Complimentary wine
732-291-8467	Visa, MC, AmEx	Panoramic ocean views,
Sherry Ruby, Gloria Miller,	C-ltd/S-no/P-ltd/H-ltd	sitting room, library, bikes,
Robert Adamec		ocean swimming

Secluded manor nestled in the tree covered hills, overlooking the blue Atlantic and Sandy Hook National Recreation area. Escape to elegance. 45 minutes from NYC.
✉ seascape25@comcast.net ☙ www.seascapemanorbb.com

LAMBERTVILLE——————

BridgeStreet House	100-250 BB	Continental plus breakfast
75 Bridge St 08530	5 rooms, 5 pb	Snacks, beverages,
800-897-2503 609-397-2503	Visa, MC, AmEx	Cable color TV, A/C,
Dolores Holmes	C-ltd/S-ltd/P-no/H-no	bathrobes, fine English soaps

Our beautiful bed & breakfast is a pre-Victorian Federal style row home situated in the heart of historic Lambertville, NJ.
✉ bridgestinn@comcast.net ☙ www.bridgestreethouse.com

Chimney Hill Estate Inn	194-419 BB	Full country breakfast
207 Goat Hill Rd 08530	12 rooms, 12 pb	Our Butler Pantry always has
800-211-4667 609-397-1516	Visa, MC, AmEx,	a great selection of teas,
Terry Anderson	*Rated*, •	cookies and snacks, sherry
	C-ltd/S-no/P-no/H-no	and iced tea.
		Intimate weddings and
		elopements, fireplaces,
		Jacuzzis, couple massages,
		gardens and alpacas.

Romantic, elegant 1820 Fieldstone Estate Property, very upscale and private. Estate consists of eight county acres of gardens, fields & woods and Alpacas. Located in Lambertville, the mecca of art & dining. Nearby Bucks County and New Hope, PA.
✉ info@chimneyhillinn.com ☙ www.chimneyhillinn.com

LAMBERTVILLE

York Street House
42 York St 08530
888-398-3199 609-397-3007
Laurie & Mark Weinstein

125-275 BB
6 rooms, 6 pb
Most CC, •
C-ltd/S-no/P-no/H-no

Full breakfast
Complimentary hot and cold
beverages, homemade
cookies
Common rooms, fireplaces,
gardens, cable TV, Jacuzzi
tubs, free high speed Internet
access

Quiet, elegant Georgian Colonial Revival Inn. Fireplaces, canopies, Jacuzzi tubs, Waterford chandelier, and complimentary beverages. Full gourmet breakfast every morning.
✉ innkeeper@yorkstreethouse.com 🌐 www.yorkstreethouse.com

MEDFORD

The Iris Inn at Medford
45 S Main St 08055
609-654-7528
Edie Wagner

85-175 BB
9 rooms, 9 pb
Most CC, *Rated*
C-yes/S-no/P-no/H-no

Full breakfast
Sitting room, suites, cable TV,
business traveler
accommodations, wireless
Internet

The Iris Inn is a beautifully preserved 1904 doctor's residence featuring original chestnut woodwork, stained glass windows, chandeliers and pocket doors.
✉ theirisinn@msn.com 🌐 www.theirisinn.com

NEW EGYPT

Dancer Farm B&B Inn
19 Archertown Rd 08533
866-DANCER6 609-752-0303
Diana Lee Black

135-310 BB
10 rooms, 10 pb
Most CC, *Rated*
C-yes/S-no/P-no/H-ltd

Full breakfast
Afternoon coffee, tea and
snack
Sitting room, library,
bicycles, suites, fireplaces,
cable TV, accommodations
for business travelers

Warmth and comfort, with that "welcome home" attitude, envelopes you as you are shown to your guestroom or suite. Leave any thought of schedule behind as your agenda now includes only "rest and relaxation!"
✉ innkeeper@dancerfarm.com 🌐 www.dancerfarm.com

378   New Jersey

NEWTON————————————————————————————

The Wooden Duck B&B
140 Goodale Rd 07860
973-300-0395
Beth & Karl Krummel

125-299 BB
9 rooms, 9 pb
Most CC, *Rated*
S-no/P-no/H-yes

Full breakfast
Snacks and beverages
available 24/7
Game room, living room,
outdoor swimming pool,
hiking, fireplaces, satellite
TV, free wireless Internet

Country estate on 10 wooded acres adjacent to a beautiful State Park. Outdoor activities year-round. Full country breakfast served in dining room. Perfect romantic getaway, yet all amenities required by business travelers including wireless Internet.
✉ woodenduckinn@earthlink.net ✪ www.woodenduckinn.com

NORTH WILDWOOD————————————————————————

Candlelight Inn
2310 Central Ave 08260
800-992-2632 609-522-6200
Bill & Nancy Moncrief

110-265 BB
10 rooms, 10 pb
Visa, MC, AmEx, •
C-ltd/S-no/P-no/H-no

Full breakfast
Afternoon refreshments
including wine. Soft drinks
and bottled water are
complimentary
WiFi, hot tub, TV/DVD
(DVDs free), CD player &
fireplaces in all rooms, 3
suites, whirlpool tubs

Seashore Queen Anne Victorian B&B with genuine antiques, fireplaces, wide veranda. Getaway specials & murder mystery parties available. Close to the beach & boardwalk.
✉ info@candlelight-inn.com ✪ www.candlelight-inn.com

Summer Nites 50's Theme B&B
2110 Atlantic Ave 08260
866-ROC-1950 609-846-1955
Sheila & Rick Brown

105-275 BB
8 rooms, 8 pb
Most CC, *Rated*, •
S-ltd/P-no/H-yes

Full breakfast
Afternoon refreshments of
root beer floats, milkshakes
& soft pretzels
Wrap-around porch, game
room, Jacuzzi, Internet
access, pool table, bicycles,
beach towels

Summer Nites, located in beautiful North Wildwood, NJ has all of the modern amenities, while retaining and capturing the excitement and uniqueness of the early days of Rock-and-Roll. Choose from the Elvis Suite, Marilyn Room, 60's Suite and 5 more rooms.
✉ info@summernites.com ✪ www.summernites.com

OCEAN CITY————————————————————————————

Brown's Nostalgia B&B
1001 Wesley Ave 08226
866-223-0400 609-398-6364
Harmon & Marjorie Brown

113-180 BB
8 rooms, 8 pb
C-ltd/S-no/P-no/H-ltd

Full breakfast
Afternoon snacks and drinks
Fireplaces, Jacuzzis, decks,
porch, powder room,
parking, exercise room, hot
tub, bikes, beach tags

A 1900s inn offering lodging accommodations in the center of Ocean City, New Jersey, just walking distance from the beach and boardwalk.
✉ brownsnj@comcast.net ✪ www.brownsnostalgia.com

Inn the Gardens B&B
48 Wesley Rd 08226
609-399-0800
Jennifer Torres

99-169 BB
7 rooms, 7 pb
Visa, MC
C-yes/S-no/P-no/H-ltd
Spanish

Continental plus breakfast
Afternoon beverages
Porches, balconies, outdoor
enclosed shower, garden
patio, beach tags, WiFi
access

Beautiful balconies to enjoy those ocean breezes. Located in the quiet north end of the island. Spacious side yard & backyard with a beautiful patio & gardens. Old fashion charm and modern conveniences make you feel right at home.
✉ innthegardens@aol.com ✪ www.innthegardens.com

SPRING LAKE

Ashling Cottage
106 Sussex Ave 07762
888-ASHLING 732-449-3553
Joanie & Bill Mahon

109-295 BB
11 rooms, 9 pb
Visa, MC, *Rated*
C-ltd/S-no/P-no/H-no

Full breakfast
Continental breakfast on any discounted day.
Complimentary bottled water, soda, iced tea
Beach passes, chairs & umbrellas, bikes, lrg screen TV/VCR, health & fitness ctr passes

One block to ocean. Recommended by Travel & Leisure Mag. Rated "One Of The Top Six Beach Houses In NJ"—NJ Life Mag. Also, convenient: Lake (½ blck)—Town (2 blcks), Wonderful dining—5 min walk.
✉ beautifuldream@ashlingcottage.com ❂ www.AshlingCottage.com

Chateau Inn & Suites
500 Warren Ave 07762
877-974-5253 732-974-2000
Scott Smith

89-359 EP
37 rooms, 37 pb
Most CC, *Rated*, •
C-yes/S-no/P-no/H-ltd

Gourmet Continental Breakfast
Gourmet coffee bar with herbal teas and flavored syrups, afternoon cookies, ice tea and lemonade
Spa & Fitness Center Passes, WiFi Internet, bicycles, DVD movie rentals, beach and tennis passes

The historic Chateau Inn and Suites offers elegance and romance unmatched at the Jersey Shore. Enhancements include Fireplaces, Jacuzzis, balconies overlooking "The Lake" and just a short walk to Spring Lake's prestigious beaches, shopping and boardwalk.
✉ info@chateauinn.com ❂ www.chateauinn.com

Spring Lake Inn
104 Salem Ave 07762
732-449-2010
Barbara & Andy Seaman

99-599 BB
16 rooms, 16 pb
Most CC, *Rated*, •
C-yes/S-no/P-no/H-ltd
Spanish

Great breakfast
Jersey fresh fruit, candy, smoked salmon, bagels
Wireless Internet, cable TV, beach badges, fireplaces, ocean views

Circa 1888 Victorian with 80-foot porch, fireplaces, parlor, ocean views, digital cable, the heart of an intimate hotel and the soul of a B&B. One short block to the ocean & boardwalk. Quiet. Great breakfast!
✉ springlakeinn@aol.com ❂ www.springlakeinn.com

Victoria House
214 Monmouth Ave 07762
888-249-6252 732-974-1882
Lynne & Alan Kaplan

99-399 BB
8 rooms, 8 pb
Most CC, *Rated*, •
C-ltd/S-no/P-no/H-no

Full gourmet breakfast
Afternoon tea, evening cordials & chocolates
TV/VCR, movies, A/C, bikes, beach passes & chairs & towels, health club passes

A romantic getaway to refresh, renew & relax. Come visit our lovingly restored Queen Anne Victorian home and lose yourself. We're open all year round. Named as "One of Top Ten Inns in New Jersey," by American Dreams.
✉ info@victoriahouse.net ❂ www.victoriahouse.net

Villa Park House
417 Ocean Rd 07762
732-449-3642
Matthew & Dara Schmid

100-425 BB
8 rooms, 7 pb
Visa, MC, AmEx, *Rated*
C-yes/S-no/P-no/H-no

Full breakfast
Parlor, porch, weddings, A/C, refrigerator, bikes, also:
beach badges, chairs, towels & umbrellas

A grand Victorian era home that has been a welcome retreat for visitors since 1896. We have been the choice for many wanting to relax & rejuvenate near the Atlantic Ocean.
✉ info@villaparkhouse.com ❂ www.villaparkhouse.com

Whistling Swan Inn, Stanhope, NJ

SPRING LAKE

White Lilac Inn	139-359 BB	Full breakfast
414 Central Ave 07762	9 rooms, 9 pb	Afternoon refreshments,
732-449-0211	Most CC, •	early bird coffee
Mari Kennelly	C-ltd/S-no/P-no/H-no	Beach badges, bicycles, parking, A/C, cable TV/VCR, fireplaces, whirlpool

A Romantic, Victorian Inn with southern charm and triple-tiered porches awaits your arrival. Enjoy the warm hospitality, relax by the fireplace, start your day with our delicious breakfasts.
✉ Mari@whitelilac.com 🌐 www.Whitelilac.com

STANHOPE

Whistling Swan Inn	105-249 BB	Full breakfast buffet
110 Main St 07874	9 rooms, 9 pb	Complimentary sherry,
888-507-2337 973-347-6369	Most CC, *Rated*, •	snacks, juices, sodas, home
Liz Armstrong	C-ltd/S-ltd/P-no/H-no	made cookies
		Sitting rooms, fireplace, Jacuzzi (suites), TV/VCR/DVD, high speed Internet

Voted Top Ten B&B in the US by the Inn Traveler magazine! We cordially welcome you to the Whistling Swan Inn, an elegantly restored 1905 Victorian home. Take a step back in time & experience true Victorian ambience.
✉ info@whistlingswaninn.com 🌐 www.whistlingswaninn.com

STOCKTON

Woolverton Inn	145-425 BB	Full country breakfast
6 Woolverton Rd 08559	13 rooms, 13 pb	Snacks
888-264-6648 609-397-0802	Visa, MC, AmEx,	Sitting room, suites,
C. McGavin, M. Lovette,	*Rated*, •	fireplaces, Jacuzzis, gardens,
M. Smith	C-ltd/S-no/P-no/H-ltd	meeting facilities
	Some Spanish and German	

A 1792 stone manor house on 10 acres of lawns and gardens, surrounded by 400 acres of rolling farmland. So close to everything, but a world away. Elegant hearty breakfasts.
✉ sheep@woolvertoninn.com 🌐 www.woolvertoninn.com

VENTNOR––

Carisbrooke Inn	79-375 BB	Homemade multi-course
105 S Little Rock Ave 08406	9 rooms, 9 pb	breakfast
609-822-6392	Most CC, *Rated*, •	Evening wine & homemade
John Battista	C-ltd/S-no/P-no/H-ltd	specialties
	Italian	Wireless Internet, fireplace,
		beach chairs, tags,
		umbrellas/towels, A/C,
		computer, parking, meeting
		room

Enjoy Atlantic City's #1 customer rated accommodations. Nestled in historic Ventnor, steps from the beach, this 1918 Inn is within blocks of the Atlantic City Boardwalk & Casinos. Enjoy personalized service & creatively prepared breakfasts.
✉ info@carisbrookeinn.com ◐ www.carisbrookeinn.com

Come Wright Inn B&B	85-325 BB	Four course gourmet
5003 Ventnor Ave 08406	6 rooms, 5 pb	breakfast
609-822-1927 609-822-1927	Visa, MC, Disc, *Rated*	Coffee & tea available for
Stephen & Dianne Wright	C-ltd/S-ltd/P-no/H-ltd	early risers. Afternoon tea is
		served Victorian style with
		desserts
		Weddings, off-street parking,
		near bike rentals, DVD/VHS
		library, wireless Internet,
		free beach badge

A Victorian B&B located 1½ blocks from the beach & boardwalk & one mile from Atlantic City's casinos. Our four-story seashore Inn offers a peaceful haven. A four course gourmet breakfast & Afternoon Tea will make your tastebuds happy.
✉ comewrightinn@aol.com ◐ www.comewrightinn.com

WILDWOOD––

Holly Beach Hotel B&B	99-255 BB	Full breakfast
137 E Spicer Ave 08260	18 rooms, 18 pb	Occasional evening desserts,
800-961-7758 609-522-9033	Visa, MC	24 hour beverages available
Cynthia & Robert Buziak	C-ltd/S-no/P-no/H-ltd	Porch, whirlpools, outdoor
		hot tub, refrigerators, cable
		TV, wireless Internet

We invite you to experience the warmth and charm of years past in our 3 story Georgian style hotel, built in 1914. Located in a quiet neighborhood, yet within walking distance to everything.
✉ cynthia@hollybeach.com ◐ www.hollybeach.com

The Sea Gypsy B&B	95-175 BB	Full breakfast
209 E Magnolia Ave 08260	10 rooms, 10 pb	Old fashioned candy
609-522-0690	Most CC	cupboard with candy,
Todd & Natalie Kieninger,	C-yes/S-no/P-no/H-no	cookies, popcorn & goodies,
Anna Grimm		wine & other drinks
		Sitting room, bicycle, Jacuzzi,
		suites, TV/DVD/VCR,
		VHS/DVD library, maid
		service, verandah, shuttle

The Sea Gypsy B&B is a quiet B&B get-away in the heart of Wildwood on the Jersey seaside. A charmingly restored 1903 Victorian with a turret, sun deck, wide porches and a hot tub. Bring the entire family for seaside fun, adventure and comfort.
✉ info@theseagypsy.com ◐ www.theseagypsy.com

New Mexico

Casa Del Rio
19946 Hwy 84 87510
800-920-1495 505-753-2035
Eileen Sopanen de Vigil

109-149 BB
4 rooms, 4 pb
Visa, MC, *Rated*, •
C-ltd/S-ltd/P-ltd/H-no
Spanish

Full breakfast
Wakeup tray to room, in-room refrigerators
Hand-carved furniture, handmade crafts, viga and latilla ceilings, fireplaces, and patios

A small hacienda amidst Georgia O'Keeffe's red cliffs reflects the peaceful beauty of New Mexico. For an enchanted getaway come stay with us and enjoy the best hiking, birding and biking. We are in the heart of it all midway between Santa Fe and Taos.
✉ casadelrio@newmexico.com ○ www.casadelrio.net

Adobe Garden at Los Ranchos B&B
641 Chavez Rd NW 87107
505-345-1954
Lee & Tricia Smith

115-135 BB
6 rooms, 6 pb
Visa, MC
C-yes/S-no/P-no/H-no

Full breakfast

At Adobe Garden, you are steeped in the richness of Colonial Spanish architecture and the private, semi-rural village of Los Ranchos de Albuquerque. Wake up to the warmth of New Mexico sunshine and a sumptuous breakfast prepared to perfection.
✉ adobegarden@spinn.net ○ www.adobegarden.com

Adobe Nido B&B
1124 Major Ave NW 87107
866-435-6436 505-344-1310
Rol & Sarah Dolk

119-234 BB
3 rooms, 3 pb
Most CC, *Rated*
C-ltd/S-ltd/P-no/H-no

Full breakfast
Sauna, suites, fireplaces, jetted tubs in rooms

Our oasis in the city offers southwest adobe living. Close to Old Town/Downtown. Great base for day trips in central NM area. 1 hour from Santa Fe. Suite available, sauna, jetted tubs for two. Day spa in neighborhood. Must call to confirm res. request.
✉ info@adobenido.com ○ www.adobenido.com

Anderson's Victorian House
11600 Modesto Ave NE 87122
505-856-6211
Judy Anderson

85-95 BB
2 rooms, 2 pb
Visa, MC
C-yes/S-no/P-no/H-no

Full breakfast
Afternoon tea, dessert, fruit, non-alcoholic beverage, wine/cheese
Cable, washer/dryer, computer, TV, BBQ grill

Situated near the base of the Sandia Mountains, Anderson's Victorian House offers the best of Albuquerque. Far enough away from the city to ensure quiet, yet close enough for quick access to the local attractions.
✉ judybandb@comcast.net

Bottger Mansion of Old Town
110 San Felipe NW 87104
800-758-3639 505-243-3639
Steve & Kathy Hiatt

115-179 BB
8 rooms, 8 pb
Most CC, *Rated*
C-ltd/S-no/P-no/H-no
March – October

Sumptuous gourmet breakfast
Tea, coffee, iced lemonade & homemade treats
Parlor with fireplace, shaded courtyard, cable TV with VCR, private baths & telephones

Enjoy the comfort & romance of the Bottger Mansion of Old Town, a Victorian bed and breakfast½block from the plaza in historic Old Town. Walk to fine dining, galleries, museums, or relax in our beautiful courtyard or parlor.
✉ info@bottger.com ○ www.bottger.com

ALBUQUERQUE

Casita Chamisa B&B
850 Chamisal Rd NW 87107
505-897-4644
Arnold Sargeant

105-125 BB
3 rooms, 2 pb
Visa, MC, AmEx
C-yes/S-no/P-yes/H-no

Continental plus breakfast
Sitting room, patio, decks,
indoor pool, hot tub

Albuquerque's first B&B. Two bedroom country guesthouse and 19th century adobe house with two large bedrooms each with a fireplace and private bath. Archaeological site, indoor heated swimming pool, TV's and high speed Internet.
✉ chamisainn@aol.com ◑ www.casitachamisa.com

Hacienda Antigua Inn
6708 Tierra Dr NW 87107
800-201-2986 505-345-5399
Bob Thompson

129-209 BB
8 rooms, 8 pb
Visa, MC, AmEx,
Rated, •
C-yes/S-ltd/P-yes/H-ltd

Full breakfast
Snacks
Sitting room, hot tubs, swimming pool, great for small reunions, fireplaces, spa

Walk through the massive carved gates of Hacienda Antigua and step back in time. The gentle courtyard, with its big cottonwood and abundance of flowers, is the heart of this 215 year old adobe hacienda. AAA 3 Diamonds, Mobil 3 Stars.
✉ info@haciendantigua.com ◑ www.haciendantigua.com

Heritage-Spy House Bed & Breakfast
207 & 209 High St. NE 87102
888-342-0223 505-842-0223
Steve & Kara Grant

89-209 BB
9 rooms, 7 pb
Most CC
C-ltd/S-no/P-no/H-ltd

Full Gourmet Breakfast
Afternoon tea, homemade
snacks & fresh fruit provided
Cable TV, telephones, central
heat/air, free wireless
Internet

1907 Historic Dutch Colonial style home offering beautifully decorated rooms and gourmet breakfast, in Albuquerque's Historic Huning Highland neighborhood, near downtown restaurants and other attractions. Weddings and special events welcome as well.
✉ info@albuquerquebedandbreakfasts.com ◑ www.albuquerquebedandbreakfasts.com

---

Los Poblanos Inn
4803 Rio Grande Blvd NW
87107
866-344-9297 505-344-9297
Armin & Penny Rembe

155-450 BB
8 rooms, 8 pb
Visa, MC, AmEx, •
C-yes/S-ltd/P-no/H-ltd
Spanish, French, Italian

Gourmet full organic
breakfast
Baked goods and treats in
the kitchen at 5:00 p.m. daily
Personal room phones,
Cable TV in library &
wireless Internet in most
rooms

Listed in both the National & NM Register of Historic Places, Los Poblanos is set amidst 25 lush acres. Exquisitely decorated rooms, gourmet organic breakfasts.
✉ info@lospoblanos.com ◑ www.lospoblanos.com

The Mauger Estate B&B
701 Roma Ave NW 87102
800-719-9189 505-242-8755
Tammy Ross

99-204 BB
8 rooms, 8 pb
Most CC, *Rated*, •
C-yes/S-no/P-ltd/H-no

Full breakfast
Snacks, complimentary
wine, sweets
Sitting room, family friendly
facility, satellite TV, free hi-
speed wireless Internet, free
parking

The Mauger Estate B&B (pronounced Major) is a wonderfully intimate, restored Queen Anne residence, where high ceilings and rich woodwork offer an old-fashioned and rewarding experience. It is Albuquerque's most centrally located bed and breakfast.
✉ maugerbb@aol.com ◑ www.maugerbb.com

Old Town B&B
707 17th St NW 87104
888-900-9144 505-764-9144
Nancy Hoffman

85-120 BB
2 rooms, 2 pb
Cash, Checks, *Rated*,
•
C-yes/S-no/P-no/H-no

Full breakfast
Refreshment in room
Garden patio, kiva fireplace

Old Town B&B provides the comforts of home in a quiet, secluded garden setting, with a wealth of interesting activities just minutes away from its doorstep.
✉ nvrhoffman@gmail.com ◑ www.inn-new-mexico.com

ALBUQUERQUE

Petroglyphs! Guest House	85-140 BB	Full breakfast
8032 Petroglyph Av NW 87120	2 rooms, 1 pb	
505-480-3870	Most CC	
Carol Nordengren	C-yes/S-no/P-ltd/H-ltd	

The only lodging adjacent to Petroglyph National Monument, yet it's a quick 10 minutes to "Old Town" and museums. There are 20,000+ petroglyphs and 7200 acres right out the front door. Great views, hiking, birding and rock art.
✉ innkeeper@PetroglyphsGH.com ✪ www.PetroglyphsGH.com

ALGODONES

Hacienda Vargas B&B Inn	89-189 BB	Full country breakfast
1431 Hwy 313 El Camino Real	7 rooms, 7 pb	Evening snacks, hot tea
87001	Visa, MC, AmEx,	Sitting room, library, golf
800-261-0006 505-867-9115	*Rated*, •	course nearby, private
Cynthia & Richard Spence	C-ltd/S-ltd/P-ltd/H-ltd	Jacuzzis, phone access
	Spanish	

Conveniently located between Albuquerque and Santa Fe, NM. Southwest Hacienda in a historic 17th c. setting. All 7 rooms and suites have private baths, private entrances, most with fireplaces and some with Jacuzzis. On-site wedding chapel.
✉ stay@haciendavargas.com ✪ www.haciendavargas.com

ARTESIA

Heritage Inn B&B	94-109 BB	Continental
209 W Main 88210	11 rooms, 11 pb	Business traveler
866-207-0222 575-748-2552	Most CC, *Rated*	accommodations, use of
Sue Kehoe	C-yes/S-no/P-ltd/H-yes	health club, wireless
		Internet, cable TV, deck

In SE New Mexico, crossroads to adventure, located downtown, convenient to shops and restaurants. 2nd story property, quiet, very clean and comfortable. Preferred by business and leisure travelers, "a gem in the desert."
✉ innkeeper@artesiaheritageinn.com ✪ www.artesiaheritageinn.com

BERNALILLO

La Hacienda Grande	89-129 BB	Full breakfast
21 Barros Rd 87004	6 rooms, 6 pb	Snacks, New Mexico wine
800-353-1887 505-867-1887	Most CC, *Rated*, •	available in the evenings
Troy & Melody Scott	C-ltd/S-ltd/P-yes/H-ltd	Weddings, retreats, Jacuzzi
		tub for 2 (1 room), business
		travelers

250 year-old authentic adobe hacienda with two-foot thick walls; wood ceilings, fireplaces, private baths, air cooled. Midway between Santa Fe and Albuquerque.
✉ lhg@swcp.com ✪ www.lahaciendagrande.com

CEDAR CREST

Elaine's, A B&B	99-149 BB	Full breakfast
72 Snowline Rd-SL Estates	5 rooms, 5 pb	Tea, coffee, hot chocolate,
87008	Most CC	drinks
800-821-3092 505-281-2467	C-ltd/S-no/P-no/H-no	Fireplace, European
Elaine O'Neil		antiques, Jacuzzi tubs in
		some rooms and outside,
		wireless Internet

Charm, elegance, and gracious hospitality in a beautiful three-story log home, nestled in the evergreen forests. Breathtaking alpine views make this a perfect location for a romantic rendezvous. High speed Internet keeps the business traveler connected.
✉ elaine@elainesbnb.com ✪ www.elainesbnb.com

CHAMA

The Parlor Car B&B	79-159 BB	Full breakfast
311 Terrace Ave 87520	3 rooms, 3 pb	Box lunches on request,
888-849-7800 505-756-1946	Most CC, *Rated*, •	snacks, welcome basket
Wendy & Bonsall Johnson	C-yes/S-no/P-no/H-no	Sitting room, library, Jacuzzi
		in 1 room, cable TV

Luxuriate in cool, clean mountain air in an historic Victorian banker's home. Guests are treated to the luxury enjoyed by the socially elite of the early 20th century at economy pricing.
Ⓞ www.parlorcar.com

CHIMAYO

Casa Escondida Bed &	99-159 BB	Full, hot, sit-down breakfast
Breakfast	8 rooms, 8 pb	Snacks, teas, coffees,
64 County Rd 0100 87522	Visa, MC, •	lemonade
800-643-7201 505-351-4805	C-yes/S-no/P-yes/H-ltd	Outdoor hot tub, fireplaces,
Belinda Bowling		private decks & patios,
		woodburning stove

Secluded mountain B&B on 6 acres, in the historic village of Chimayo, just 35 minutes north of Santa Fe. Ideal central location for splendid day trips & ski outings throughout northern NM. Four of 8 rooms are pet-friendly.
✉ info@casaescondida.com Ⓞ www.casaescondida.com

CORRALES

Casa de Koshare Bed &	104-145 BB	Full breakfast
Breakfast	3 rooms, 3 pb	coffee, tea and snacks
122 Ashley Lane 87048	Visa, MC	Wireless Internet, fax,
505-898-4500	C-ltd/S-ltd/P-no/H-ltd	satellite TV, VCR & DVD,
John & Marie Beemer		outdoor chapel, a labyrinth
		(meditation path)

Welcome to our beautiful Albuquerque bed and breakfast located in the Village of Corrales with its charming shops, vineyards and mountain vistas. Whether you are visiting for fun, or business our goal is you "Arrive a guest and leave a friend."
✉ info@casadekoshare.com Ⓞ www.casadekoshare.com

Chocolate Turtle B&B	78-140 BB	Full breakfast
1098 W Meadowlark Ln 87048	4 rooms, 4 pb	Chocolate turtles in each
877-298-1800 505-898-1800	Visa, MC, AmEx, *Rated*	room, complimentary snacks
Dallas & Nancy Renner	C-ltd/S-no/P-no/H-ltd	and cookies available
		Great Room, Portal & Patio,
		TV in Great Room, WiFi, CD
		players in guestrooms

Classic adobe style home with 4 colorful guestrooms in picturesque Corrales, a historic farming community in the Rio Grande river valley of New Mexico. Country-like setting, incredible mountain views, horses, and golf. Weddings, meetings. AAA 3 Diamonds.
✉ Innkeeper@chocolateturtlebb.com Ⓞ www.chocolateturtlebb.com

---

Tell your hosts Pamela Lanier sent you.

CORRALES

Nora Dixon Place B&B
312 Dixon Rd 87048
888-667-2349 505-898-3662
Norris & Cynthia C. Tidwell

104-124 BB
3 rooms, 3 pb
Most CC, *Rated*, •
C-yes/S-no/P-ltd/H-ltd

Full breakfast
Fresh ground coffee, brewed
teas, and milk
Sitting room, suites,
fireplaces, conference
facilities, TV, phones

Quiet New Mexico Territorial Style B&B, facing Sandia Mountain in Corrales. Located on the northside of Albuquerque where historic sites are easily visited on day excursions.
✉ noradixon@comcast.net ❂ www.noradixon.com

EDGEWOOD

**Lazy K Ranch Bed &
Breakfast**
27 Autumnwood Ct 87015
877-281-2072 505-281-2072
Lisa & Andrew Kwas

99-250 BB
4 rooms, 4 pb
Cash, Checks
C-ltd/S-no/P-no/H-no

Full breakfast
Wine or tea with
refreshments, snacks are
always available
Game room, pool table,
parlor, fireplace, Jacuzzi,
garden, deck, patio, private
log cabin

Come and enjoy the peaceful hospitality of mountain living. Just minutes from Albuquerque and Santa Fe along the historic Turquoise Trail. Four bedrooms all with private bathrooms, some with Jacuzzi tubs. Romantic getaway with gorgeous views.
✉ lazykranchbandb@yahoo.com ❂ www.geocities.com/lazykranchbandb

ESPANOLA

Inn at the Delta
243 N Paseo De Onate 87532
800-995-8599 505-753-9466
Emery & Dolores Maez

110-165 BB
10 rooms, 10 pb
Most CC, *Rated*
C-yes/S-no/P-ltd/H-ltd
Spanish

Continental plus breakfast
Wireless Internet, in-room
massage therapy, whirlpools
tubs, kiva fireplaces

Featuring hand made Mexican tile floors, the authentic Adobe structure is considered to be one of the most beautiful structures in Northern New Mexico. The Inn is centrally located between eight northern New Mexico Pueblos.
✉ emery.maez@gmail.com ❂ www.innatthedelta.biz

FARMINGTON

Casa Blanca B&B Inn
505 E La Plata St 87401
800-550-6503 505-327-6503
David and Shirley Alford

135-175 BB
8 rooms, 8 pb
Most CC, *Rated*, •
C-yes/S-no/P-no/H-yes
Spanish

Full gourmet breakfast
Lunch & dinner available.
Coffee, tea and snacks in
rooms.
Sitting room, library,
Jacuzzis, suites, fireplaces,
cable TV, wireless, accom.
business traveler

Beautiful Mediterranean-style home built and handcrafted by the original owner's father in the 1950s; has made a perfect transition to a bed & breakfast inn. AAA three diamond rating.
✉ info@casablancanm.com ❂ www.casablancanm.com

GILA

Casitas de Gila Guesthouses
50 Casita Flats Rd 88038
877-923-4827 575-535-4455
Becky & Michael O'Connor

130-210 BB
5 rooms, 5 pb
Most CC
C-ltd/S-ltd/P-no/H-yes

Continental plus breakfast
Stocked kitchen
Hot tub, art gallery,
fireplaces, free WiFi, full
kitchens, spotting scope,
library of books

Southwestern guesthouses & art gallery on 226 acres overlooking Bear Creek and the Gila Wilderness, near Silver City, New Mexico. Our Stress-Free Zone was selected by Sunset Magazine in 2007 as a "Top 10 Hidden Getaway." Explore by day, relax at night!
✉ info@casitasdegila.com ❂ www.casitasdegila.com

JEMEZ SPRINGS

Desert Willow	149-169 BB	Full breakfast
15975 Hwy 4 87025	1 rooms, 1 pb	Deck overlooking river, fully
575-829-3410	Most CC, *Rated*, •	equipped kitchen, 2
Leone Wilson	C-yes/S-no/P-yes/H-ltd	bedroom cottage with
		fireplace

Tucked into a quiet, mountain canyon with sheer cliffs rising from the river along New Mexico's Jemez Mountain Trail, the Dragonfly Cottage at the Desert Willow B&B in Jemez Springs, New Mexico is a nature-lovers' delight!
✉ wilsons@desertwillowbandb.com ♻ www.desertwillowbandb.com

LAS CRUCES

A Lodge on the Desert	55-95 BB	Continental breakfast
215 South Weinrich Road	6 rooms, 6 pb	Beverages and snacks
88005	Cash, Checks	available 24 hours
575-523-9605	C-ltd/S-no/P-ltd/H-ltd	Outdoor kitchen, patios,
Laverne Tromble		garden, antiques, weight
		room, library, laundry,
		balcony, Reunions/weddings

Romantic, Secluded Bed and Breakfast. A Lodge on the Desert sits high atop the West Mesa. 200 mile views. Sparkling night lights. Sunrise over Organ Mountains. Weddings. Parties. Monthly rates encourage extended stays. Bridal Suite. Antiques, Fountains
✉ laverne@alodgeonthedesert.com ♻ www.alodgeonthedesert.com

DreamCatcher Inn B&B de	105-135 BB	Full breakfast
Las Cruces	3 rooms, 3 pb	Coffee & tea are provided for
10201 Starfly Rd 88011	Most CC	all to enjoy, popcorn, guest
866-298-1935 575-522-3035	C-ltd/S-no/P-ltd/H-yes	kitchen
Ken & Anita McLeod		TV, DVD/VCR, small sound
		system, phone, high-speed
		Internet connection in each
		room

Minutes from the lights, hustle, and bustle of Las Cruces, NM. Close to fine dining, shopping, NM State University, NASA. Three guestrooms, on 10 acres, for those who love to hike and enjoy the peace and tranquility of the beautiful High Desert.
✉ dreamcatcherinn@yahoo.com ♻ www.dreamcatcherinn.com

Hilltop Hacienda B&B	95-135 BB	Full breakfast
2600 Westmoreland Ave 88012	3 rooms, 3 pb	We will accommodate your
877-829-7142 575-382-3556	Most CC, *Rated*, •	special diet needs as best we
Teddi Peters	C-ltd/S-ltd/P-ltd/H-yes	can.
	Spanish, Portuguese	Sitting room, library,
		fireplace, cable TV, 20 acres
		of peace & quiet

Lodging in Las Cruces includes a secluded, romantic B&B with breathtaking sunrises and sunsets, atop 20 beautiful acres with 360 degree views of mountains, Las Cruces, and Mesilla Valley.
✉ thehilltophacienda@yahoo.com

NAVAJO DAM

D's B&B	90 BB	Full breakfast
#10 CR 4265 87419	6 rooms	Glass of wine
505-632-0044	Visa, MC	shared bath, themed
Chuck Pearson	C-ltd/S-no/P-ltd/H-yes	guestrooms, quiet, relaxing
		escape, pet accommodations

A friendly B&B next to some of the world's finest trout fishing with six, uniquely appointed guestrooms. The rooms are themed around the region's flora, just footsteps away from the San Juan River.
✉ host_chuck_pearson@hughs.net ♻ www.dsbandb.com

NOGAL

Evergreen Manor
389 State Hwy 37 88341
575-336-1231
David & Bonnie Lambert

79-179 BB
4 rooms, 4 pb
Most CC
C-ltd/S-no/P-ltd/H-no

Full breakfast
Afternoon tea, non-alcoholic
beverage included. Sunday
brunch, picnic baskets and
dinner available.
Turndown service, ceiling
fans, fridge, hot tub, board
games, library, washer/dryer

*Peaceful charm, elegance and gracious hospitality in an iconic Walton country home,
nestled in the evergreen forests. Refresh your spirit, pamper yourself or rendezvous for
romance in exquisite rooms with gourmet breakfasts. Art & activities 15 mins away.*
✉ info@evergreenruidoso.com ✪ www.evergreenruidoso.com

PLACITAS

Blue Horse B&B
300 Camino de las Huertas
87043
877-258-4677 505-771-9055
Tom & Cathy Hansen

99-129 BB
3 rooms, 3 pb
Visa, MC
C-ltd/S-no/P-ltd/H-no

Full breakfast
Complimentary beverages
and snacks
Fireplaces, inviting
courtyard, whirlpool jetted
tub, surrounded by
mountains, unique
furnishings

*Nestled in the beautiful high desert foothills of Albuquerque's Sandia Mountain. Relax in
comfortable Southwestern rooms amidst glorious mountains, mesas, sunsets and stars.*
✉ info@bluehorsebandb.com ✪ www.bluehorsebandb.com

RUIDOSO

Ruidoso Skies
110/110A Main Rd 88355
800-950-2510 575-257-2510
Judy Wilkie

169-169 EP
4 rooms, 4 pb
Visa, MC
C-ltd/S-no/P-no/H-no

Spurs/Lace, Sleepy Hollow,
Wild Rose/Little Adobe are
self-service cabins
Hot tubs, whirlpool tubs,
fireplaces, private patios,
gazebo, BBQ grills, kitchens,
TV, Washer Dryer

*Ruidoso Skies Located in Ruidoso's scenic "Upper Canyon" has two special lodges for
couples and two family cabins. Family cabins are 2bed/2bath & fold-down sofa. Family
cabins sleep 6. Family cabins have washer/dryers and private hot tubs.*
✉ ruidososkies@yahoo.com ✪ www.ruidososkies.com

SANTA FE

Alexander's Inn B&B
529 E Palace Ave 87501
888-321-5123 505-986-1431
Regan

165-275 EP
4 rooms, 4 pb
Visa, MC, AmEx,
Rated, •
C-yes/S-no/P-yes/H-no
French

Each arriving guest is
welcomed with a basket of
wine, chips, salsa,
homemade cookies & fruits
Award-winning spa,
concierge services, WiFi,
robes, green hotel.

*Our traditional Santa Fe casitas, featuring kiva fireplaces, New Mexican furnishings and
décor, full kitchens and patios, are perfect for the discerning traveler, a family get together
or a romantic holiday.*
✉ alexinn@osogrande.com ✪ www.alexanders-inn.com

Aliento B&B
31 Bonanza Creek Rd 87508
505-473-2776
Ruth Dobbins

95-135 BB
5 rooms, 5 pb
Most CC
C-ltd/S-no/P-ltd
German, French,
Spanish

Serve Yourself Breakfast
Wireless high speed Internet,
phones in each room

*This beautiful ten acre property with its gracious New Mexico style adobe hacienda gives
you plenty of room to breathe. Enjoy the relaxed atmosphere in traditional eclectic Santa
Fe style as captured in our one hundred year old hacienda.*
✉ info@alientobnb.com ✪ www.alientobnb.com

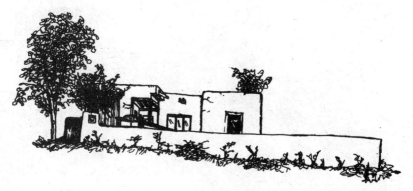

Casa de La Cuma B&B, Santa Fe, NM

SANTA FE———

Bobcat Inn
442 Old Las Vegas Hwy 87505
505-988-9239
Amy & John Bobrick

95-149 BB
7 rooms, 7 pb
Visa, MC
C-yes/S-no/P-no/H-yes
Closed mid-January

Full breakfast
High tea available (summer),
homemade cookies & hot
chocolate (winter)
Fireplace, great room,
gardens, massage,
complimentary wireless
Internet access

Nature lovers dream with old world ambience. Located in the foothills of Santa Fe. Beautiful gardens, stunning views of the mesa, gourmet breakfast.
✉ res@nm-inn.com ❂ www.nm-inn.com

Casa De La Cuma B&B
105 Paseo de la Cuma 87501
877-741-7928 505-216-7516
Colleen Davidson

145-275 BB
7 rooms, 7 pb
Most CC, *Rated*, •
C-ltd/S-no/P-no/H-no
Spanish (limited)

Full breakfast
Full Breakfast includes hot
entree, fresh fruits, coffee,
teas and seasonal juices,
homemade snack
Outdoor hot tub, some
fireplaces, TV, DVD/CD
players, library, Internet
access

Casual comfort in the heart of Santa Fe. Warm and serene adobe home with original artwork and furniture. 4 blocks to the historic Plaza, shopping, restaurants, galleries, library and museums.
✉ info@casacuma.com ❂ www.casacuma.com

Don Gaspar Inn
623 Don Gaspar Ave 87501
888-986-8664 505-986-8664
Shirley & David Alford

115-355 BB
10 rooms, 10 pb
Most CC, *Rated*, •
C-yes/S-no/P-no/H-yes

Gourmet Southwestern
Buffet
Private gardens and
courtyards

Three historic homes in the heart of Santa Fe, just a short walk to the Plaza. Selected as a "Top 10 Romantic Inns for 2003" and Travel & Leisure's "Top Lodging Secret in Santa Fe."
✉ info@dongaspar.com ❂ www.dongaspar.com

Dunshee's B&B and Casita
986 Acequia Madre 87505
505-982-0988
Susan Dunshee

140-162 BB
2 rooms, 2 pb
Visa, MC, *Rated*
C-yes/S-no/P-no/H-no

Continental plus breakfast
Continental plus in casita,
full breakfast in suite,
homemade cookies
Sitting room, refrigerator, TV,
private patio & gardens

Romantic hideaway in adobe compound in historic zone. Choice of 2-room suite or 2-bedroom guesthouse furnished with antiques.
✉ sdunshee@aol.com ❂ www.dunshees.com

Dunshee's B&B and Casita, Santa Fe, NM

SANTA FE

El Farolito
514 Galisteo St 87501
888-634-8782 505-988-1631
Walt Wyss & Wayne Mainus

150-250 BB
8 rooms, 8 pb
Most CC, *Rated*, •
C-yes/S-no/P-no/H-no

Continental plus breakfast
Sitting room, A/C, family
friendly facility, private
entrances, fireplaces

In the city's historic district, just a short walk to the Plaza, El Farolito offers 8 romantic casitas. All accommodations feature patios, authentic Southwestern decor & art.
✉ innkeeper@farolito.com ◐ www.farolito.com

El Paradero B&B
220 W Manhattan Ave 87501
866-558-0918 505-988-1177
Sue Jett & Paul Elliott

95-180 BB
15 rooms, 15 pb
Visa, MC, AmEx, *Rated*
C-ltd/S-no/P-ltd/H-ltd

Full Gourmet Breakfast
Afternoon Tea Time
Open courtyard w/garden,
common rooms, central
cooling in rooms, guest
computer with Internet
access

Experience old Santa Fe charm in this 200 year-old adobe farmhouse bed & breakfast. Located in the historic downtown district just a few minutes walk from the Plaza, museums, shops & restaurants.
✉ info@elparadero.com ◐ www.elparadero.com

Four Kachinas Inn
512 Webber St 87501
800-397-2564 505-982-2550
Wayne Mainus & Walt Wyss

110-215 BB
5 rooms, 5 pb
Most CC, *Rated*, •
C-yes/S-no/P-no/H-yes
Spanish (limited)

Continental plus breakfast
Afternoon tea
Sitting room

Only 4 blocks from historic Plaza. Furnished with handcrafted furniture, Navajo rugs & Indian art. Serving breakfast and award winning baked goods.
✉ info@fourkachinas.com ◐ www.fourkachinas.com

Guadalupe Inn
604 Agua Fria St. 87501
505-989-7422
Dolores Myers & Henrietta
Quintana

145-195 BB
12 rooms, 12 pb
Most CC, *Rated*, •
C-yes/S-no/P-no/H-yes
Spanish and ASL

Full breakfast
Breakfast burritos, huevos
rancheros, eggs (almost any
style), pancakes or French
toast.
A/C, satellite TV, telephone,
some whirlpool baths,
DSL/wireless

Located in the oldest district of Santa Fe, the historic Guadalupe District. Visit our historic downtown plaza . . . a nice six-block stroll from our B&B.
✉ office@guadalupeinn.com ◐ www.guadalupeinn.com

SANTA FE————————————————————————————————

Hacienda Nicholas B&B
320 E Marcy St 87501
888-284-3170 505-992-8385
Carolyn Lee

125-240 BB
7 rooms, 7 pb
Visa, MC, AmEx,
Rated, •
C-yes/S-no/P-yes/H-yes
French

Full breakfast with local
cuisine
Afternoon tea and nightly
wine & cheese hour
Award-winning spa, garden,
outdoor kiva fireplace,
wireless Internet, cable TV,
A/C

*Unwind in the peace and tranquility afforded by extra thick adobe walls and the heavenly
scent of a luscious rose garden. We are now operating as a "Green Inn" and find new ways
every day to operate in a more eco-friendly fashion.*
✉ info@haciendanicholas.com ◐ www.haciendanicholas.com

Inn On the Paseo
630 Paseo De Peralta 87501
800-457-9045 505-984-8200
Inn on the Paseo Reservations

89-239 BB
18 rooms, 18 pb
Most CC, *Rated*, •
C-yes/S-no/P-no/H-ltd

Continental breakfast
Private entrances, antiques,
large accommodations,
Jacuzzi tub, fireplace, A/C,
wireless Internet

*Inn on the Paseo, discover our Southwestern charm and hospitality conveniently located in
the Historic District of Santa Fe, you will find yourself within walking distance to the Plaza,
Canyon Road, shops, galleries and gourmet restaurants.*
✉ stay@innonthepaseo.com ◐ www.innonthepaseo.com

Las Palomas B&B
460 W San Francisco St 87501
877-982-5560 505-982-5560

99-286 BB
53 rooms, 53 pb
Most CC, *Rated*, •
C-yes/S-no/P-yes/H-yes

Deluxe Continental Breakfast
Breakfast & coffee bar
Wireless Internet access, hot
tub & sauna, fitness center,
kids play area

*Nestled amongst a secluded tree covered compound just 3 short blocks from Santa Fe's
Historic Plaza. The historic casitas of Las Palomas built of traditional adobe bricks have
been maintained to preserve the authentic feel of Santa Fe.*
✉ stay@laspalomas.com ◐ www.laspalomas.com

Madeleine B&B Inn
106 Faithway St 87501
888-877-7622 505-982-3465
Carolyn Lee

120-250 BB
7 rooms, 7 pb
Visa, MC, Disc, •
C-ltd/S-ltd/P-no/H-no

Full breakfast
Afternoon tea & dessert,
Nightly wine & cheese hour
Award-winning onsite spa,
luxuriously soft robes,
privileges at El Gancho
Health and Tennis Club

*This elegant 1886 Victorian, in secluded garden setting near the Plaza & Convention
Center, offers full breakfasts & an evening wine & cheese hour. Our Indonesian-inspired
spa, staffed with master-level therapists, offers the ultimate in spa treatments.*
✉ info@madeleineinn.com ◐ www.madeleineinn.com

Two Casitas
511 Douglas 87504
866-832-0589 505-984-2270
Wendy Kapp

95-360 EP
20 rooms, 20 pb
Visa, MC, *Rated*, •
C-yes/S-no/P-ltd/H-ltd

Coffee, tea, full kitchens;
breakfast not included
Kitchens, free parking,
fireplaces, cable TV/VCR,
iron, patios, phone, A/C

*Vacation rental homes, varying in size from quaint studios for a perfect romantic getaway
to spacious three bedroom, three bath houses for the whole family. Walking distance to the
Plaza, the town's historic center.*
✉ santafe@twocasitas.com ◐ www.twocasitas.com

SANTA FE──────────────────────────────────

Water Street Inn	150-250 BB	Continental plus breakfast
427 W Water St 87501	11 rooms, 11 pb	Evening appetizers,
800-646-6752 505-984-1193	Most CC, *Rated*	complimentary wine,
Mindy Mills	C-yes/S-no/P-yes/H-ltd	turndown service
	Spanish	Sitting room, hot tub, suites,
		fireplaces, flat screen cable
		TV with DVD, wireless
		Internet

Award winning adobe inn two blocks from the Plaza. Superior amenities, convenience, and a fun, relaxed atmosphere. Walking distance to museums, shops, galleries and fine restaurants, we offer authentic southwest accommodations.
✉ info@waterstreetinn.com ○ www.waterstreetinn.com

SILVER CITY──────────────────────────────

The Inn on Broadway	95-160 BB	Full breakfast
411 W Broadway 88061	4 rooms, 4 pb	Sodas, snacks, guest
866-207-7075 575-388-5485	Most CC	refrigerator
Sandra Hicks	C-ltd/S-ltd/P-no/H-ltd	Library, shady veranda, walk
		to restaurants

The Inn on Broadway is located in Silver City's Historic District. Walk to restaurants, art galleries and shops. Relax on our shady veranda overlooking the garden or in our cozy library. Enjoy a delicious, homemade breakfast after a restful night's sleep.
✉ info@innonbroadwayweb.com ○ www.innonbroadwayweb.com

TAOS───────────────────────────────────

Abbe de Touchstone Inn,	145-350 BB	Full Gourmet Breakfast
Spa & Gallery	10 rooms, 10 pb	Destination Spa Package
110 Mabel Dodge Ln 87571	Visa, MC, *Rated*, •	includes breakfast, lunch,
800-758-0192 575-758-0192	C-ltd/S-no/P-no/H-no	and supper. Meals available
Bren Price	Spanish	for seminars, wedding
		Free wireless Internet, full
		service spa – packages;
		concierge bookings

Destination Spa and Gallery, romantic 10 rooms—historic significance to Taos. Adobe dates circa 1800. Original art, mountain views, labyrinth. Fireplaces, fountains, gardens, wireless Internet, weddings, workshops & meeting space.
✉ touchstoneinn@gmail.com ○ www.touchstoneinn.com

Adobe & Pines Inn	98-195 BB	Full gourmet breakfast
4107 Road 68 87557	8 rooms, 8 pb	Private entrance/baths,
800-723-8267 505-751-0947	Visa, MC, •	fireplaces, whirlpools,
Katherine & Louis Costabel	C-yes/S-ltd/P-yes/H-no	TV/VCR/DVD/CD players,
		video/CD library, spa service

Historic adobe hacienda transformed into one of the most charming/luxurious hideaways in the Southwest, says Frommers, Fodors, HGTV, many more. Private entrances/baths, fireplaces, whirlpools, gardens, full breakfasts, Cable TV/VCR/DVD, video/CD library.
✉ mail@adobepines.com ○ www.adobepines.com

Adobe and Stars	95-190 BB	Full breakfast
584 State Hwy 150 87571	8 rooms, 8 pb	Get acquainted hour with
800-211-7076 575-776-2776	Most CC, *Rated*, •	beverage & snacks
Judy Salathiel	C-yes/S-no/P-yes/H-yes	Beautiful common area, hot
	Spanish	tub under the stars, Jacuzzi,
		robes, hairdryers, fireplaces

Southwestern pueblo adobe style Inn with kiva fireplaces, beamed ceilings, hot tub under the stars, Jacuzzi tubs, 360 degree mountain views, full breakfasts, skiing, mountain biking and hiking access.
✉ jsalathiel@yahoo.com ○ www.TaosAdobe.com

TAOS————————————————————————

Casa Benavides B&B
137 Kit Carson Rd 87571
800-552-1772 505-758-1772
Barbara & Tom McCarthy

89-300 BB
39 rooms, 39 pb
Most CC
C-yes/S-no/P-no/H-yes

Full breakfast
Afternoon tea with home
baked goodies
Hot tub, wood burning
fireplaces, A/C and, or
ceiling fans, cable TV, VCR's,
covered portals

Casa Benavides Bed and Breakfast is for the Taos traveler who wants luxury lodging, not just overnight accommodations, while visiting Northern New Mexico. Listed on the State and National Historic Taos Registry.
✉ casabena@newmex.com 🜨 www.taos-casabenavides.com

Country Inn of Taos
720 Karavas Rd & Upper
Ranchitos Rd 87571
800-866-6548 505-758-4900
Yolanda Deveaux & Judd Platt

145-165 BB
8 rooms, 8 pb
Visa, MC
C-ltd/S-no/P-no/H-no

Full breakfast
Kiva fireplaces, patios, art,
garden

Enjoy an extraordinary vacation at our historic Taos bed and breakfast hacienda, nestled among beautiful gardens and towering trees on 22 acres in Taos, New Mexico.
✉ info@taos-countryinn.com 🜨 www.taos-countryinn.com

Hacienda Del Sol
109 Mabel Dodge Ln 87571
866-333-4459 575-758-0287
Donna & Sparky

135-325 BB
11 rooms, 11 pb
Most CC, *Rated*, •
C-yes/S-no/P-no/H-ltd
German, French

Full breakfast
Complimentary snacks
Library, fireplaces, gallery,
outdoor hot tub, robes,
gardens, health club access,
computer w/WiFi

200-yr-old adobe hideaway purchased by Taos' legendary art patroness Mabel Dodge for her Indian husband, Tony. Adjoins vast Indian lands, close to Taos Plaza. Tranquility, mountain views. "One of the US's top 10 romantic inns," USA Today.
✉ sunhouse@newmex.com 🜨 www.taoshaciendadelsol.com

The Historic Taos Inn
125 Paseo del Pueblo Norte
87571
800-TAOS-INN 575-758-2233
Carolyn Haddock & Doug
Smith

75-275 EP
44 rooms, 44 pb
Most CC, *Rated*, •
C-yes/S-ltd/P-no/H-ltd

Award winning Doc Martins
Restrnt. on site. Adobe Bar
features Margaritas and a
New Mex bistro menu.
Greenhouse Jacuzzi, Fine
Dining, Live Music, Kiva
Fireplaces, Art Shows,
Internet, Wellness Packages

Founded on a rich legacy of excellence. Our guests are eager to sample the atmosphere of old Taos yet expect modern amenities. The Historic Taos Inn has everything a visitor to Taos wants under one roof. Southwestern rooms, bar and fine dining.
✉ marketing@taosinn.com 🜨 www.taosinn.com

Inger Jirby's Casitas
207 Ledoux St 87571
866-758-7333 575-758-7333
Inger Jirby

175-300 EP
2 rooms, 2 pb
Visa, MC, AmEx,
Rated, •
C-yes/S-no/P-no/H-ltd

Casitas have full kitchens,
washer/ dryers, full
entertainment centers and
WII games. Fireplaces too

Enjoy a true Taos experience. The magical guesthouses are beautifully furnished and equipped with all the comforts of home. Southwest furnishings, fabulous flagstone floors, bright, interesting décor, beautiful spiral staircases, kiva fireplaces.
✉ jirby@newmex.com 🜨 www.jirby.com/pages/casitas_home.html

TAOS

Inn on La Loma Plaza
800-530-3040 505-751-0178
Jerry & Peggy Davis

150-425 BB
10 rooms, 10 pb
Most CC, *Rated*
C-yes/S-no/P-yes/H-ltd

Full breakfast
Private entrances, baths,
sitting areas, fireplaces,
patios, phones, cable TV, CD,
radio, kitchenettes

A historic Taos landmark, an intimate and luxurious setting 2 blocks from downtown Taos. Each room has its own distinctive ambience created by a combination of handcrafted furniture, antiques and southwestern fabrics.
✉ laloma@vacationtaos.com ◐ www.taos-bed-breakfast.com

La Dona Luz Inn
206 Des Georges Lane 87571
888-758-9060 575-758-9000
Paul Castillo

89-229 BB
5 rooms, 5 pb
Most CC, •
C-yes/S-ltd/P-yes/H-ltd

Continental breakfast
Rooftop priv. hot tub, wood
burning adobe fireplaces,
Jacuzzi baths, patios

"The Essence of Old Taos." Delight in the ambience of this quaint & colorful adobe inn, with rooms richly decorated in the Taos tradition. Fine art work & Indian & Spanish antiques are displayed throughout the house. It is the closest B&B to the plaza.
✉ info@ladonaluz.com ◐ www.stayintaos.com

La Posada de Taos
309 Juanita Ln 87571
800-645-4803 575-758-8164
Brad Malone

124-219 BB
6 rooms, 6 pb
Most CC, *Rated*, •
C-ltd/S-ltd/P-yes/H-yes

Full Gourmet Breakfast
Afternoon Tea, snack service
Sitting room, patios, sun
room, portals, fireplaces,
courtyards

La Posada de Taos is a historic adobe inn just two blocks west of 400-year old Taos Plaza. You'll enjoy nothing less than excellence each morning when breakfast is served. Our focus is your comfort, so come and join us any time of year.
✉ laposada@laposadadetaos.com ◐ www.laposadadetaos.com

Mabel Dodge Luhan House
240 Morada Ln 87571-6468
800-846-2235 575-751-9683
Maria Fortin

98-300 BB
19 rooms, 19 pb
Visa, MC, AmEx
C-ltd/S-no/P-no/H-ltd

Full gourmet breakfast
Private baths, fireplaces,
kitchen facilities, cottages,
views, patios, classes &
workshops

Charming, elegant, historic 1920s adobe inn and conference center, once the home of a wealthy patron of the arts and creative sanctuary for many artists. Panoramic view. Quiet patios and a tree-lined acequia. Many art and creativity workshops offered.
✉ mabel@mabeldodgeluhan.com ◐ www.mabeldodgeluhan.com

Orinda B&B
461 Valverde 87571
800-847-1837 505-758-8581
John & Cathryn Ellsworth

104-169 BB
5 rooms, 5 pb
Visa, MC, AmEx, *Rated*
C-ltd/S-no/P-ltd/H-no

Full breakfast
Afternoon tea & snacks
Sitting room, library, spa
services, suites, fireplaces

Orinda B&B is a 70+ year old adobe hacienda combining unequalled mountain views in a country setting. We're a short 10-minute walk to center of town with its famed plaza, excellent restaurants, galleries and museums.
✉ orinda@newmex.com ◐ www.orindabb.com

TAOS SKI VALLEY

Austing Haus
1282 State Hwy 150 87525
800-748-2932 575-776-2649
Paul Austing

79-195 BB
23 rooms, 23 pb
Visa, MC, *Rated*, •
C-yes/S-ltd/P-no/H-ltd
Closed April 10 – May 10

Hot buffet breakfast
Sitting room, hot
tub/exercise room,
fireplaces, cable TV, hi speed
Internet, free ski shuttle.

A mountain inn nestled in the southern Rockies of northern New Mexico, specializing in romantic getaways and weddings. Owner is an award winning chef. Charming fireplace rooms are available.
✉ austing@taosnet.com ◐ www.austinghaus.net

TAOS SKI VALLEY

Columbine Inn &	69-185 BB	Continental plus breakfast
Conference Center	20 rooms, 20 pb	Sitting room, hot tub, board
1288 Hwy 150 87525	Most CC, •	games, frequent stay
888-884-5723 575-776-5723	C-yes/S-no/P-ltd/H-no	program, free ski shuttle, free
Susie & Paul Geilenfeldt	May-Oct, Nov-April	WiFi

Authentic alpine Inn, in the heart of the Taos Mountains. Come to the mountains & let us be your home away from home. Friendly, fun & convenient. Ski school & packages; conference center for 75.
✉ psgeilen@taosnet.com ● www.columbineinntaos.com

THOREAU

Zuni Mountain Lodge B&B	115 MAP	Full breakfast
40 Perch Dr 87323	8 rooms, 8 pb	Afternoon tea, snacks,
505-862-7616	Cash, Checks, *Rated*	complimentary wine
Richard Morrow & Robert	C-yes/S-ltd/P-ltd/H-ltd	Sitting room, suites, lounge,
McCuen	French, German,	game room, library, video
	Spanish	library

Comfortable rooms provide places for meditation and relaxation, or planning a day of touring. Delicious meals and the finest blend of wilderness, "roughing it," & home. American B&B Association 3 Crowns, AAA 3 Diamonds ratings.
✉ zuniml@cnetco.com ● www.zuniml.com

New York

ADAMS BASIN

Adams Basin Inn
425 Washington St 14410
888-352-3999 585-352-3999
Pat Haines

115-145 BB
4 rooms, 4 pb
Visa, MC, *Rated*
C-ltd/S-no/P-no/H-no

Gourmet and freshly baked
pastries
Tea or coffee served upon
arrival; bottled water, sodas
available in guest refrigerator
Common area of parlor,
tavern and porch are open to
guests; available for
weddings and showers

Nestled next to the historic towpath of the Erie Canal, Adams Basin Inn is a delight to lovers of antiques, exceptional food and relaxation.
✉ hainespat@hotmail.com 🌐 www.adamsbasininn.com

ALFRED STATION

Country Cabin Manor B&B
1289 SR 244 14803
607-587-8504
Judy Burdick

94-149 BB
4 rooms, 4 pb
Visa, MC, Disc
C-ltd/S-no/P-no/H-ltd

Full breakfast
Tea, soft drinks, bottled
water, hot chocolate
Deck, pond, fishing,
whirlpool tub, dining room,
fireplace, sitting room, high
speed Internet, fax

Located ¾ mile from Alfred, NY, in the scenic foothills of the Allegheny Mountains. Quiet, romantic getaway, year round vacation spot, many recreational activities in the area.
✉ jaburdalburd@juno.com 🌐 www.countrycabinmanor.com

AMSTERDAM

Amsterdam Castle
49 Florida Ave 12010
518-843-5201
Susan and Manfred Phemister

100-150 BB
3 rooms, 2 pb
Visa, MC
C-ltd/S-ltd/P-ltd/H-yes

Continental plus breakfast

A 36,000 square foot former National Guard Armory converted into a unique private residence. Featured on HGTV's Rezoned. Men love the military history and women love to feel like a princess.
✉ events@amsterdamcastle.com 🌐 www.amsterdamcastle.com

**Halcyon Farm Bed &
Breakfast**
157 Lang Rd 12010
800-470-2170 518-842-7718
June & John Leonard

100-160 BB
5 rooms, 5 pb
Visa, MC, Disc, *Rated*
C-ltd/S-ltd/P-no/H-no

Full gourmet breakfast
Iced or hot tea; homemade
baked goods served
Air conditioning, fireplaces,
guest living room and library,
TV with DVD player, piano

Halcyon Farm B&B is a peaceful country retreat just 40 minutes from Saratoga & Cooperstown and 5 miles from I-90. The elegant Federal brick home was restored in 2001 and is updated with modern amenities. 3 Diamond AAA.
✉ june@halcyonfarm.com

AQUEBOGUE

Dreamer's Cove Inn
15 Bay Ave 11951
631-722-3212
Michelle Logan

175-450 EP
18 rooms, 18 pb
Most CC
C-yes/S-no/P-ltd/H-no

Private beach, boat docks,
wireless Internet, A/C, cable
TV, full kitchens, water-view
decks, BBQ

Enjoy your own private beach on the Peconic Bay on Long Island's North Fork. Beach front and water-view rooms available with private decks and full kitchens. Near the vineyards, Tanger outlet shopping, Splish Splash and the Hamptons. Boat docks available.
✉ info@dreamerscoveinn.com 🌐 www.DreamersCoveInn.com

Adams Basin Inn, Adams Basin, NY

AUBURN

10 Fitch
10 Fitch Ave. 13021
315-255-0934
Cheryl Barber

180-355 BB
3 rooms, 3 pb
Most CC
C-ltd/S-ltd/P-no/H-ltd

Full breakfast
Complimentary snacks,
beverages, bottled water
Fireplaces, library, sun room,
garden, A/C, antiques,
Jacuzzi hot tub, balcony,
breakfast in suite,

*A luxurious romantic inn conveniently located between the wineries and Skaneateles, NY.
Professionally decorated and adorned with Mac-Kenzie Childs home furnishings, antiques,
original artwork, designer fabrics and decadent silk draperies.*
✉ innkeeper@10fitch.com ☉ www.10fitch.com

AVON

White Oak B&B
277 Genesee St 14414
585-226-6735
Barbara B. Herman

105-115 BB
3 rooms, 3 pb
Visa, MC
C-yes/S-no/P-no/H-no

Full breakfast
On request: vegetarian, non-
dairy, low cholesterol, or low
carb
Cable TV/DVD, sitting room,
library, accommodate
business travelers, all rooms
with A/C

*An 1860 Second Empire Victorian home set in a country village, affording convenient
access to Western New York attractions and activities. Period furnishings, lovingly chosen,
will welcome you in every room.*   ✉ avon-bnb@frontiernet.net ☉ www.whiteoakbandb.com

BAINBRIDGE

Berry Hill Gardens
242 Ward-Loomis Rd 13733
800-497-8745 607-967-8745
Jean Fowler

115-185 BB
8 rooms, 8 pb
Most CC
C-yes/S-ltd/P-no/H-no
Spanish, German, Italian,
French

A full, healthy-living
breakfast
Coffee, tea; guest
convenience kitchen
Ceiling fans, bathrobes, eco-
friendly, library

*A country B&B situated high on a hilltop overlooking miles of rural beauty in Central New
York. Museums, golf, fishing, hunting, artisans & fascinating history. Five comfortable
guestrooms in the Inn and three rooms in our lodge with over 300 acres to roam.*
✉ info@berryhillgardens.com ☉ www.berryhillgardens.com

Tell your hosts Pamela Lanier sent you.

400   New York

BALLSTON SPA

Lewis House
38 E High St 12020
518-884-9857
Preston Lewis

100-250 BB
3 rooms, 3 pb
Visa, MC, AmEx
C-yes/S-ltd/P-no/H-no

Full breakfast
Afternoon tea, evening
dessert, coffee
Fireplace, living room, dining
room, games, books, videos

Victorian and romantic ambience can be found in the historic Saratoga district. Enjoy comfortable accommodations in one of the three guestrooms where you will be able to sleep in tranquility while being able to enjoy all that Saratoga, NY has to offer.
✉ info@lewishouse.com ❁ www.lewishouse.com

BLOOMING GROVE

Dominion House
50 Old Dominion 10914
845-496-1826
Joe & Kathy Spear

105-199 BB
4 rooms, 2 pb
Most CC
C-yes/S-no/P-no/H-ltd

Full breakfast
Specialties of the house are
caramel sticky buns, Peach
French Toast and scones.
Snacks 24 hours.
Large parlor, slate top pool
table, hot tub, swimming
pool, library, business
accommodations

"A Taste of Elegant Country Living!" Built in 1880 by Benjamin H. Strong, a local farmer whose family settled in Orange County in the seventeen hundreds. Situated on 4.5 acres, at the end of a country lane in central Orange County.
✉ kathy@thedominionhouse.com ❁ www.thedominionhouse.com

BLUE MOUNTAIN LAKE

The Hedges
Hedges Rd 12812
518-352-7325
Patricia Benton

205-320 MAP
31 rooms, 31 pb
Cash, Checks, *Rated*
C-ltd/S-no/P-no/H-yes
May through October

"Made to order" breakfast
Beverages, iced tea,
lemonade, coffee, during
day. Evening snack.Full bar
service at Dinner.
Canoes, Kayaks, sand beach,
tennis court, library,
game/common room,
housekeeping service. WiFi

On the shores of Blue Mountain Lake, in the heart of America's largest State Park, The Hedges offers the relaxation & recreation of an historic Adirondack Great Camp.
✉ thehedges@frontiernet.net ❁ www.thehedges.com

BOLTON LANDING

Boathouse Bed & Breakfast Inc
44 Sagamore Rd 12814
518-644-2554
Joe & Patti Silipigno

150-395 BB
7 rooms, 7 pb
Visa, MC, AmEx, *Rated*
C-ltd/S-ltd/P-no/H-no

Full breakfast
Some rooms have
whirlpools, fireplaces and
microwaves

Historic bed and breakfast located directly on Lake George, open year round. This famous and unique B&B has been featured in Motor Boat and Sailing, The Great and the Gracious, and Unique Homes.Also featured on PBS "Rustic Living" 2008
✉ Stay@boathousebb.com ❁ www.boathousebb.com

BOUCKVILLE

Ye Olde Landmark Tavern
US Route 20 & Canal Rd 13310
315-893-1810
Stephen Hengst

125-140 BB
5 rooms, 5 pb
Most CC
C-yes/S-no/P-no/H-no
April-December

Continental breakfast
Dinner, restaurant, bar
service
Suites, cable TV, private
baths, traditional early
America decor, canopy bed,
wireless Internet

Historic cobblestone building on National Register, in antique center of New York State. Near Colgate University, Hamilton College.
✉ yeoldelandmark@yahoo.com ❁ www.yeoldelandmark.com

BRANCHPORT

Gone With the Wind on Keuka Lake
14905 West Lake Rd 14418
607-868-4603
Linda & Robert Lewis

85-155 BB
10 rooms, 8 pb
Most CC
C-ltd/S-no/P-no/H-ltd

Full breakfast
Fruit, home-baked Rhett's
Rhubarb coffee cake, one of
Aunt Pitti Pat's many flavors
of pancakes
Private cove, gazebo, canopy
of trees, Log Lodge, retreats,
reunions

Stately stone mansion above Keuka Lake, serving guests since 1989. Walk the many trails on 14 acres or swim in the waters of the private cove. Chat around the breakfast table. Toss your troubles to the wind.
✉ gwwkeukalake@hotmail.com ◔ www.gonewiththewindonkeukalake.com

BROCKPORT

The Victorian
320 Main St 14420
585-637-7519
Sharon M. Kehoe

84-150 BB
5 rooms, 5 pb
•
C-yes/S-no/P-no/H-ltd
Spanish

Full breakfast
Afternoon tea
Sitting room, library,
fireplace, fax, cable TV,
wireless Internet access, in-
room phone, phone card

Late 19th-century Queen Anne home, with pleasing blend of antiques & modern furnishings. Short walk from historic Erie Canal.
✉ sk320@aol.com ◔ www.victorianbandb.com

BRONX

The Bronx Guesthouse
East 233 St 10466
718-881-7022
Chef Denisey

75-160 BB
4 rooms
Most CC, •
C-ltd/S-no/P-yes

Self-serve Continental
Satellite TV, board games, fax
machine, Internet

The Guest House offers an eclectic and peaceful retreat. Built at the turn of the century, the house retains much of the old world flavor. Explore the proximity of local attractions.
✉ reservations@bronxguesthouse.com ◔ www.bronxguesthouse.com

BUFFALO

Beau Fleuve B&B Inn
242 Linwood Ave 14209
800-278-0245 716-882-6116
Ramona & Rik Whitaker

130-160 BB
4 rooms, 4 pb
Most CC, *Rated*, •
C-ltd/S-no/P-no/H-no
Some Spanish
Closed January

Full breakfast
Always-available
complimentary snacks,
cookies, soft drinks, juices,
tea, hot chocolate, cider.
In-room coffeemaker, robes,
hair dryer, bath amenities;
guest fridge, microwave,
parlor; WiFi, A/C.

Forget hotels! Enjoy the serene and comfortable elegance of Buffalo's finest B&B, where your hosts have provided gracious hospitality, delectable candlelight breakfasts, and complimentary concierge services for 18 years in this beautiful 1882 property.
✉ beaufleuve@verizon.net ◔ www.beaufleuve.com

CANANDAIGUA

1795 Acorn Inn
4508 Rt 64 S 14424
866-665-3747 585-229-2834
Sheryl Mordini

166-275 BB
5 rooms, 5 pb
Most CC, *Rated*, •
C-ltd/S-no/P-no/H-no
German

Full gourmet breakfast
Complimentary hot & cold
beverages & snacks
Common room w/large
fireplace, library, outdoor
hot tub, small
weddings/reunions, family
gatherings

Thoroughly renovated & beautifully appointed with fine furnishings & antiques, the 1795 Acorn Inn offers the simple elegance of the past seamlessly integrated with modern comfort & luxury. AAA Four Diamond rated for eleven consecutive years.
✉ acorninn@rochester.rr.com ◔ www.acorninnbb.com

CANANDAIGUA

ChambTry Cottage B&B	119-169 BB	Full breakfast
6104 Monks Rd 14424	4 rooms, 4 pb	Tea, coffee, cookies, snacks
585-393-1405	Visa, MC, *Rated*	Sitting room, library,
Terry & Zora Molkenthin	C-ltd/S-no/P-no/H-no	video/DVD library, garden
	Czech	seating areas

ChambTry Cottage is a fully renovated, 100 year-old farmhouse. The decor is Old World or French country. All four guestrooms feature private bath, TV/VCRs, CD players, alarm clocks, some fireplaces.
✉ euroctge@frontiernet.net 🌐 www.chamberycottage.com

Morgan Samuels Inn	119-295 BB	Full breakfast
2920 Smith Rd 14424	6 rooms, 6 pb	Dinner with advance
585-394-9232	Visa, MC, Disc, *Rated*,	reservations, afternoon tea
Brad Smith	•	available on request
	C-ltd/S-no/P-no/H-no	Library, tennis court,
		Jacuzzis, suites, fireplaces,
		balconies

Sense the value, as you Travel the 1900', tree-lined drive to a secluded 1810 English mansion, See and experience "the difference between ordinary and legendary."Afternoon tea, beverages, and appetizers.The cuisine is considered among the best in No America
✉ morsambb@aol.com 🌐 www.morgansamuelsinn.com

CANDOR

The Edge of Thyme, A B&B	90-145 BB	Full breakfast
Inn	5 rooms, 3 pb	High tea by appointment
6 Main St 13743	Most CC, •	Sitting rooms w/fireplaces,
800-722-7365 607-659-5155	C-yes/S-no/P-no/H-no	AC, piano, indoor games,
Frank & Eva Mae Musgrave		lawn games, gift shop,
		wireless available

Featured in Historic Inns of the Northeast. Visit a turn-of-the-century Georgian home. Enjoy leaded glass windowed porch, marble fireplaces, period sitting rooms, gardens & pergola.
✉ innthyme@twcny.rr.com 🌐 www.edgeofthyme.com

CANTON

Ostrander's B&B	80-90 BB	Full breakfast
1675 State Hwy 68 13617	4 rooms, 4 pb	Evening dessert, beverages,
877-707-2126 315-386-2126	Visa, MC, AmEx,	in-room fridge
Al & Rita Ostrander	*Rated*, •	Sitting room, free wireless
	C-ltd/S-no/P-no/H-no	Internet, cable TV, VCR, DVD,
		phones, A/C, cottages with
		full kitchen

Whether you arrive for business or for pleasure, we offer the perfect combination of convenience & quiet comfort. Visit the sheep barn, play with border collie dogs or shop in our gift shop.
✉ info@ostranders.com 🌐 www.ostranders.com

CAZENOVIA

Brae Loch Inn	115-170 BB	Continental breakfast
5 Albany St 13035	12 rooms, 12 pb	Dinner available seven
315-655-3431	Most CC, *Rated*, •	nights a week, fine dining or
James & Valerie Barr	C-yes/S-no/P-ltd/H-no	casual pub menu, Brunch on
	Spanish	Sunday
		Fireplaces, gift shop, lounge
		with pool table, full bar,
		dinners nightly

Family owned & operated since 1946. As close to a Scottish Inn as you will find this far west of Edinburgh! Serving exquisite fine dining and casual pub menu nightly. Specializing in warm, comfortable accommodations.
✉ braeloch1@aol.com 🌐 www.braelochinn.com

CAZENOVIA

Brewster Inn	70-235 BB	Continental breakfast
6 Ledyard Ave 13035	17 rooms, 17 pb	Restaurant
315-655-9232	Most CC, *Rated*	Jacuzzis, fireplaces, TV, air
Richard Hubbard	C-ltd/S-no/P-no/H-yes	conditioning, massage

The Inn's elegance is richly enhanced by exquisite woodwork, including solid mahogany and antique quartered oak. Today, The Brewster Inn is a truly fine country inn catering to discerning diners and travelers.
C www.thebrewsterinn.com

CENTERPORT

Centerport Harbor	199-239 BB	Full breakfast
129 Centershore Rd 11721	1 rooms, 1 pb	In-room tea kettle,
631-754-1730	Visa, MC, *Rated*, •	coffeemaker, and beverages
Jean & Jim Vavrina	C-yes/S-ltd/P-no/H-ltd	available. Lower rate without
		breakfast.
		Cable TV, waterfront, private
		beach, private balcony,
		private full bath

The perfect venue for a romantic getaway, a relaxing vacation, or a change of pace for the business traveler from hotels/motels. Overlooking scenic harbor, private beach & dock. Gourmet breakfast served in room/private balcony.
✉ centerport.hrbr.bnb@lycos.com

CHAUTAUQUA

Spencer Hotel	165-250 BB	Full breakfast
25 Palestine Ave 14722	24 rooms, 24 pb	Tea, catered dinner buffets &
800-398-1306 716-357-3785	Visa, MC, *Rated*, •	picnic lunches during the
Helen Edgington	C-yes/S-no/P-no/H-yes	summer months
		Spa services, enrichment
		workshops, special events

The literary-themed, four-season boutique resort in the heart of the historic Chautauqua Institution begins its second century with refreshed spa services and enrichment workshops, and adding further modern amenities in an historic venue.
✉ stay@thespencer.com C www.thespencer.com

CHERRY CREEK

Cherry Creek Inn B&B	85-150 BB	Full breakfast
1022 West Rd 14723	4 rooms, 4 pb	Refreshment refrigerator
716-296-5105	Visa, MC	(accessible 24/7) stocked
Sharon Howe Sweeting	C-yes/S-no/P-no/H-no	with numerous drinks and
		goodies
		Library, WiFi, hot tub,
		gardens, lawn games

Luxurious accommodations on 31 acres in Amish country. Experience Chautauqua County through literary pursuits, indoor & outdoor games, antiquing, birding, hiking and snow sports. Library, hot tub and WiFi.
✉ innkeeper@cherrycreekinn.net C www.cherrycreekinn.net

CHERRY VALLEY

42 Montgomery	150-175 BB	Full gourmet breakfast
42 Montgomery St 13320	5 rooms, 3 pb	
607-264-9974	Visa, MC	
Melanie	C-yes/S-no/P-no/H-no	

Relax on the wide front porch with a glass of wine, or join lively conversation in the parlor. Spacious, inviting and quiet suites with large reading chairs and queen size beds offer perfect nights sleep on scented linens. Close to attractions, shopping.
✉ melanie@42montgomery.com C www.42montgomery.com/pgs/main20.html

CHERRY VALLEY───────────────────────

Limestone Mansion	95-195 BB	Full Country Breakfast
33 Main St 13320	14 rooms, 5 pb	
607-264-3741	Visa, MC	
Wolfgang & Loretta Welter	C-ltd/S-ltd/P-no/H-no	
	Mid May – Mid October	

Wake up to a full country breakfast in our restored, charming turn of the century Victorian mansion with spacious rooms, beautiful woodwork and period antiques that allows you to step back in time to the hospitality and comfort of a bygone era.
🌐 www.limestonemansion.com

CHESTERTOWN───────────────────────

The Fern Lodge	350-525 BB	Full breakfast
46 Fiddlehead Bay Road 12817	4 rooms, 4 pb	A small menu of in-room
518-494-7238	Visa, MC, AmEx,	options available.
Sharon Taylor	*Rated*, •	Pool table, wine cellar, game
	S-no/P-no/H-no	table, nine-person theatre,
		sauna, exercise equipment,
		WiFi & bicycle

In the midst of the Adirondack Mountains, overlooking Friends Lake, there stands a wondrous Guesthouse where luxurious Adirondack lodging, indulgent baths and unforgettable breakfasts join in an atmosphere of rustic elegance and lakeside living.
✉ sharon@thefernlodge.com 🌐 www.thefernlodge.com

Friends Lake Inn	299-479 MAP	Full country breakfast
963 Friends Lake Rd 12817	17 rooms, 17 pb	Full dinner service available,
518-494-4751	Most CC, *Rated*, •	full wine bar
John & Trudy Phillips	C-ltd/S-no/P-no/H-yes	Library, swimming,
		Adirondack suites with view,
		outdoor sauna, massages,
		hiking, snowshoeing

Fully restored 19th century Inn with lakeviews and 4 rooms with working fireplaces. Award-winning restaurant & wine list, x-country skiing, snowshoeing, private beach canoes & kayaks on Friends Lake.
✉ trudy@friendslake.com 🌐 www.friendslake.com

CITY ISLAND───────────────────────

Le Refuge Inn B&B	135 BB	Continental breakfast
586 City Island Ave 10464	7 rooms	French dining room offering
718-885-2478	*Rated*	lunch and dinner by
Pierre Saint-Denis	C-ltd/S-no/P-ltd/H-ltd	reservation, also Sunday
	French, Spanish	brunch
		Ideal for weddings, private
		parties, romantic dinners,
		weekend escapes, salon,
		piano, porches

Beautifully restored 19th century sea captain's house. A romantic seven room Victorian inn, overlooking the 300-year-old harbor on City Island.
🌐 LeRefugeInn.com

CLARENCE───────────────────────

Asa Ransom House	110-330 BB	Full Breakfast
10529 Main St, Rt 5 14031	10 rooms, 10 pb	Bar, Snacks, Dinner (except
800-841-2340 716-759-2315	Visa, MC, Disc, *Rated*,	Mon.), Lunch on Weds., High
Robert & Abigail Lenz	•	Tea on Tue., Thur., Sat.
	C-yes/S-no/P-ltd/H-yes	Fireplaces, cable TV, free
	Closed January	Internet, refrigerators,
		porches, balconies,
		whirlpool tub, pets limited

Village inn with herb garden, regional dishes, homemade breads & desserts, gift shop. Awarded #1 B&B in Buffalo News. Top three in food, service, hospitality, and historic charm in Bee Readers Survey.
✉ innfo@asaransom.com 🌐 www.asaransom.com

CLAVERACK

1805 House
775 Snydertown Rd 12513
518-929-5923
Tom & Maria Elena Benton

125-188 BB
3 rooms, 3 pb
Most CC, •
C-yes/S-no/P-yes/H-ltd
Spanish

Full breakfast
Pond, dining room

Set on over 100 acres of natural beauty, our historic eyebrow Colonial home offers a quiet, pastoral getaway conveniently situated between the Berkshire and Catskill Mountains.
✉ 1805house@gmail.com ✪ www.1805house.com

CLINTON

The Artful Lodger
7 East Park Row 13323
888-563-4377 315-853-3672
Susan and Tim Sweetland

99-169 BB
5 rooms, 5 pb
Most CC, *Rated*
C-yes/S-no/P-no/H-yes

Full breakfast
Coffee, tea, cocoa, snacks
and soft drinks
Free WiFi, art gallery, sitting
room w/ tv, private baths,
guest fridge, book exchange,
copier/fax

This 1835 Federal Style residence has been transformed by the architect / innkeeper into an elegant 5-room inn, showcasing the work of regional artists. With each changing season, the Artful Lodger offers a changing palette of activities.
✉ artful@dreamscape.com ✪ www.artfullodger.net

COLD SPRING

The Pig Hill Inn
73 Main St 10516
845-265-9247
Kyle Gibbs

150-250 BB
9 rooms, 9 pb
Most CC
C-ltd/S-no/P-no/H-yes
Czech, Slovak, Russian

Full breakfast
Tea & pastries, wine & beer
cash bar
Conservatory, terraced
garden, luxurious four-poster
beds, privacy, romance,
trolley services nearby

At The Pig Hill Inn, we have raised self-indulgence to a fine art. Experience our warm hospitality and relax from the pressures of your everyday routine. Enjoy privacy and romance for a weekend escape or stay for a whole week.
✉ pighillinn@aol.com ✪ www.pighillinn.com

COLD SPRING HARBOR

Swan View Manor
45 Harbor Road 11724
631-367-2070
Lisa Aloisio

132-225 BB
18 rooms, 18 pb
Most CC
C-ltd/S-no/P-no/H-no

Continental breakfast
Complimentary coffee, soft
drinks, fruit & snacks.
Formal afternoon tea
available upon request.
Sitting room with fireplace,
A/C, cable TV, phone,
wireless Internet,
refreshments.

At the Swan View, the comfort & enjoyment of your stay is of the utmost importance to us. This bed & breakfast, nestled on the North Shore of Long Island in Cold Spring Harbor, a town that is truly enchanting. ✉ info@swanview.com ✪ www.swanview.com

COOPERSTOWN

The Cooper Inn
15 Chestnut St 13326
800-348-6222 x2 607-547-2567
John D. Irvin

115-260 BB
15 rooms, 15 pb
Visa, MC, AmEx,
Rated, •
C-yes/S-no/P-no/H-no

Continental breakfast
Special breakfast price &
comp bottle of wine at
nearby Otesaga Resort
Free WiFi, cable TV, heat,
A/C, pool & fitness ctr at
nearby Otesaga Hotel,
reduced golf green fees

The Cooper Inn contains 15 rooms, each with modern amenities including phone, free wireless Internet access, cable television, central heat, air conditioning, and private bath. Use of Otesaga Hotel facilities during their season.
✉ Reservation1@Otesaga.com ✪ www.CooperInn.com

COOPERSTOWN ────────────────────────────

Diastole B&B	159-239 BB	Cooked to order breakfast
276 Van Yahres Rd 13326	4 rooms, 4 pb	Sitting room with fireplace,
607-547-2665	Visa, MC, *Rated*, •	hot tub, WiFi, refrigerator,
Brigitte Priem	C-ltd/S-no/P-no/H-no	microwave, hiking trails
	April 1-October 31	

Great accommodations five minutes from the Baseball Hall of Fame, fifteen minutes from Dreams Park and Glimmerglass Opera. All rooms have view of the lake.
✉ diastole@hughes.net 🌐 www.diastolebb.com

The Inn at Cooperstown	105-525 BB	Continental plus breakfast
16 Chestnut St 13326	18 rooms, 18 pb	Coffee, tea, and other hot
607-547-5756	Visa, MC, AmEx, •	drinks available; iced tea &
Marc & Sherrie Kingsley	C-yes/S-no/P-no/H-ltd	lemonade served on the
		porch in the summer
		Guestrooms have A/C,
		CD/clock radio, hairdryer,
		iron/ironing board, wireless
		Internet access

Beautifully restored Victorian inn providing genuine hospitality and spotless, comfortable guestrooms. The only Select Registry property in Cooperstown, the inn is just a short walk from the National Baseball Hall of Fame, shopping and fine dining.
✉ info@innatcooperstown.com 🌐 www.innatcooperstown.com

COOPERSTOWN ────────────────────────────

Landmark Inn	105-285 BB	Full Homestyle Breakfast
64 Chestnut St 13326	11 rooms, 11 pb	High-speed Internet, video
866-384-3466 607-547-7225	Visa, MC, AmEx, •	library, refrigerators, A/C,
Gary Sherer	C-yes/S-no/P-no/H-yes	cable TV, VCRs, telephones

A charming 19th century B&B in the heart of historic Cooperstown. Situated on two acres in the center of the village offering a convenient, comfortable home for guests.
✉ info@landmarkinncooperstown.com 🌐 www.landmarkinncooperstown.com

Main Street B&B	109-169 BB	Full breakfast
202 Main St 13326	3 rooms, 3 pb	Family friendly facility, sitting
800-867-9755 607-547-9755	C-yes/S-ltd/P-no/H-no	room, TV, A/C, ponds
Ron & Susan Streek		

A Victorian B&B within walking distance to Baseball Hall of Fame and the highlights of Cooperstown. Lovely front porch for relaxation.
✉ rms202@stny.rr.com 🌐 www.mainstreetbandb.info

Nelson Avenue Pines	109-194 BB	French countryside breakfast
20 Nelson Ave 13326	3 rooms, 3 pb	Coffee, tea, cocoa, biscotti,
607-547-7118	Cash, Checks	cookies, cereal
Penney Silvis Gentile	C-yes/S-no/P-no/H-no	Sitting room, family suite,
		porch with lake view. Across
		the street from golf course,
		tennis courts.

A warm welcome awaits you at our country French B&B. Come and relax and capture the charm of the past in our recently renovated 1870's Victorian home decorated in country French and antiques. Walking distance to the Baseball Hall of Fame.
✉ napines@stny.rr.com 🌐 www.nelsonavenuepines.com./

Overlook B&B	139-159 BB	Continental plus breakfast
8 Pine Blvd 13326	3 rooms, 3 pb	Warm hospitality, TV/VCR in
607-547-2019	Cash, Checks	common area, living room,
Jack & Gayle Smith	C-yes/S-no/P-no/H-no	off-street parking

Overlook B&B rises in Victorian splendor on stately Pine Boulevard. Accommodations are offered in light and spacious rooms, all with private baths. A short stroll from the Baseball Hall of Fame, The Farmers' Museum, Fenimore House and Main Street.
✉ information@OverlookBB.com 🌐 www.overlookbb.com

COOPERSTOWN

Rose & Thistle B&B
132 Chestnut St 13326
607-547-5345
Patti D'Esposito

125-200 BB
4 rooms, 4 pb
Most CC
S-ltd/P-no/H-no

Full breakfast
Snacks, cookies, cakes,
chips, pretzels, coffee and
tea are available
Parlor, porch, Internet
access, A/C, TV

An enchanting experience awaits at this turn-of-the-century Victorian B&B. Old world charm & new world luxury combines to let you experience "Bed & Breakfast in an elegant tradition." ✉ stay@rosenthistle.com 🌐 www.rosenthistle.com

Tunnicliff Inn
34-36 Pioneer St 13326
607-547-9611
Tom

75-225 BB
17 rooms, 17 pb
Visa, MC, Disc
C-yes/S-no/P-no/H-no

Hot buffet breakfast
"The Pit" restaurant on
premises.
A/C, digital cable TV, movie
library, wireless Internet

A 17 room Inn located in the center of Downtown Cooperstown. Restaurant & Tavern known as the "Pit" on the premises. We have banquet facilities for rehearsal dinners, birthdays and anniversaries. ✉ tunnicliffinn@stny.rr.com

Whisperin' Pines Chalet
RD 3, Box 248, Rt 11 13326
888-547-5650 607-547-5640
Chris and Erin Doucas

125-180 BB
5 rooms, 5 pb
Visa, MC, Disc
C-yes/S-no/P-no/H-ltd

Full breakfast
Common area with big
screen TV. Large deck,
private walking trail, creek
with 2 waterfalls

Whisperin' Pines Chalet invites you to enjoy European charm in a country setting. A large Swiss style chalet, that has grown from a small summer camp to a luxurious bed and breakfast out of pure love of hospitality.
✉ whisperinpines@att.net 🌐 www.wpchalet.com

The White House Inn
46 Chestnut St 13326
607-547-5054
Marjorie & Ed Landers

95-195 BB
7 rooms, 7 pb
Most CC
C-yes/S-no/P-no/H-yes

Full gourmet breakfast
All guestrooms have cable
TV, telephone, Internet
access and private baths. In-
ground pool in yard

The White House Inn provides the comforts of home, the elegance of fine lodgings, gracious hospitality, and the convenience of parking on-site and walking to local attractions. Enjoy the seclusion of our private garden with inground pool.
✉ reserve@thewhitehouseinn.com 🌐 www.thewhitehouseinn.com

CORINTH

Agape Farm LLC
4839 Rt 9 N 12822-1709
518-654-7777
Fred & Sigrid Koch

120-150 BB
3 rooms, 3 pb
Visa, MC, Disc, *Rated*
C-yes/S-no/P-no/H-yes

Full breakfast
Snacks
Gardens, trout stream, farm
animals, dogs, cats, family
friendly facility

Nestled in the Adirondacks, Agape Farm is a country farmhouse on 33 scenic acres. Enjoy true country hospitality, relax on the charming wraparound porch, enjoy fellowship in the inviting living room, or sing around the piano. Children welcome.
✉ agapefarmbnb@adelphia.net 🌐 www.geocities.com/agapefarm/

CORNWALL

Cromwell Manor Inn
174 Angola Rd 12518
845-534-7136
Jack Trowell & Cynthia Krom

165-380 BB
12 rooms, 12 pb
Visa, MC, AmEx,
Rated, •
C-ltd/S-no/P-no/H-yes

Full breakfast
Chocolate chip cookies, 24
continental breakfast
available, picnic baskets.
Fireplaces, in-room massage,
spa options, patio/fountain,
wireless Internet, computers.

Top 10 Inn of NY, "Highly recommended"...USA Today. "A fantastic B&B!"...CBS Early Show. This stunning 1820 Greek Revival Mansion is set on 7 lush acres with scenic Hudson Valley views.
✉ cmi@hvc.rr.com 🌐 www.cromwellmanor.com

CROTON ON HUDSON

Alexander Hamilton House	125-350 BB	Full gourmet breakfast
49 Van Wyck St 10520	8 rooms, 8 pb	Chocolate chip cookies
914-271-6737	Most CC, *Rated*, •	Sitting room, two person
Barbara Notarius & Cyd Klein	C-yes/S-no/P-no/H-no	whirlpool tubs, swimming
	French	pool, suites, fireplaces, cable
		TV, DSL, Wifi

We are a romantic Victorian Inn close to all the attractions of the lower Hudson Valley, 48 minutes from the heart of NYC. River view, village setting, with pool.
✉ alexhous@bestweb.net ✆ www.alexanderhamiltonhouse.com

DE BRUCE

De Bruce Country Inn on	110-125 MAP	Full breakfast
the Willowemoc	14 rooms, 14 pb	Dinner from menu included,
982 De Bruce Rd 12758	*Rated*, •	bar
845-439-3900	C-yes/S-ltd/P-yes/H-no	Library, sauna, pool, private
	French	forest preserve, trout pond,
		art gallery, lake & mountain
		views

In the Catskill Forest Preserve, with its trails, wildlife, & famous trout stream, our turn-of-the-century inn offers superb dining overlooking the valley.
✆ www.debrucecountryinn.com

DOVER PLAINS

Old Drovers Inn	139-315 BB	Continental plus breakfast
Old Route 22 12522	7 rooms, 7 pb	On site restaurant with fine
845-832-9311	Most CC	dining
Emily & Rayn	C-yes/S-no/P-yes/H-yes	Fireplaces, sitting rooms,
		meetings, weddings,
		reunions, restaurant

Old Drover's Inn, an historic upstate New York B&B offers guests a tranquil and heart-warming experience. A refuge for road-weary travelers in the Hudson Valley for over 250 years.
✉ shoshi@olddroversinn.com ✆ www.olddroversinn.com

DRYDEN

Candlelight Inn	95-165 BB	Full breakfast
49 W Main St 13053	5 rooms, 5 pb	Air conditioning, fireplace,
800-579-4629 607-844-4321	Most CC	in-ground heated pool, in-
Doris Nitsios	C-yes/S-no/P-ltd/H-no	room TVs

Relax in antique filled and cozy rooms in our circa 1828 Federal home. Surround yourself in style and comfort. Five charming rooms with private baths, TVs, and air conditioning.
✉ Innkeeper@CandlelightInnNY.com ✆ www.candlelightinnny.com

DUNDEE

1819 Red Brick Inn	95-125 BB	Full breakfast
2081 Rt 230 14837	5 rooms, 5 pb	Complimentary beverages,
607-243-8844	Visa, MC, Disc	home baked refreshments
Wendy and Robert	C-ltd/S-no/P-no/H-ltd	Dining rooms, parlor,
Greenslade		fireplace, sun porch, pond

We invite you to spend a relaxing interlude in our beautifully restored, 1819 Federal style home, located in a tranquil country setting in the heart of the Finger Lakes.
✉ redbrickinn@frontiernet.net ✆ www.the1819redbrickinn.com

Tell your hosts Pamela Lanier sent you.

DUNDEE

Sunrise Landing B&B
4986 Apple Rd Ext 14837
866-670-5253 607-243-7548
Robert & Barbara Schiesser

150-215 BB
3 rooms, 3 pb
Most CC
C-ltd/S-no/P-no/H-no

Full breakfast
Refrigerator with complimentary non-alcoholic beverages in your room.
Large dock and waterfront, paddle boat and canoe, piano, A/C

Venture off to a quieter spot and discover Sunrise Landing B&B, pristine lodging accommodations nestled peacefully on a wooded hillside on the west shore of Seneca Lake.
✉ relax@sunriselandingbb.com 🌐 www.sunriselandingbb.com

EAST CHATHAM

The Inn at Silver Maple Farm
1871 Rt 295 12060
518-781-3600
Ross & Nancy Audino

100-295 BB
11 rooms, 11 pb
Most CC, *Rated*
C-yes/S-no/P-no/H-yes

Full breakfast
Afternoon tea, cookies, beverages, light snacks
Great Room, cable TV, A/C, hairdryers, irons, wireless Internet, in-room phones

Lovely accommodations in a beautifully converted post-and-beam barn, nestled in the foothills of the Berkshires. Shaker-inspired furnishings; gourmet breakfast in the Great Room.
✉ info@silvermaplefarm.com 🌐 www.silvermaplefarm.com

EAST HAMPTON

The 1770 House
143 Main St 11937
631-324-1770
Demi Reichart

295-1,495 BB
7 rooms, 7 pb
Visa, MC, AmEx
C-ltd/S-no/P-no/H-ltd

Full & Continental
Restaurant, Tavern & seasonal garden dining
Hand pressed Frette linens, plasma TVs, gas fireplaces, parlor & garden

Historic Colonial inn offers seven guestrooms with private baths, antiques and modern indulgences, and separate 2 bedroom Carriage House with loft. On site restaurant with downstairs tavern. Wine Spectator Award of Excellence, 2007.
✉ innkeeper@1770house.com 🌐 www.1770house.com

Bend in the Road Guest House
58 Spring Close Hwy 11937
631-324-4592
Carolyn & Frank Bistrian

100-265 BB
2 rooms, 2 pb
Cash, Checks
C-yes/S-no/P-yes/H-no

Continental plus breakfast
Breakfast served end of June thru Labor Day, otherwise it is self-catered.
Antiques, TVs, DVD players, refrigerators, AC, living room, fireplace, pool, garden, hammock

Our quiet rambling farmhouse sits on a twenty-two acre farm with a driving range for golfers, and encircled by a private jogging path perfect for running your dogs, far from roads and traffic.
✉ frankbist@aol.com 🌐 www.bendintheroadguesthouse.com

Getaway House
4 Neighborhood House Dr 11937
631-324-4622
Johnny Kelman

100-375 BB
4 rooms, 2 pb
Visa, MC, AmEx, •
C-ltd/S-no/P-no/H-ltd

Continental breakfast
Large pool, central air conditioning, bicycles, beach passes, fireplace

A charming bed and breakfast nestled in a wooded setting, yet close to the village and ocean beaches. Central air conditioning and 20 x 40' swimming pool. Continental breakfast served on the patio.
✉ windsigh@earthlink.net 🌐 www.getawayhouse.com

EAST HAMPTON

Mill House Inn	295-1,195 BB	Best full breakfast on the
31 N Main St 11937	10 rooms, 10 pb	East End
631-324-9766	Most CC, •	Homemade cookies around
Sylvia & Gary Muller	C-yes/S-no/P-yes/H-ltd	the clock & afternoon
	Spanish, German	beverages
		Full Concierge Services, A/C,
		gas fireplaces, whirlpool
		baths, high speed wireless
		Internet

A gracious Bed & Breakfast Inn in the heart of historic East Hampton Village. Beautifully appointed rooms & spectacular dog-friendly suites. Walk to superb beaches restaurants antiques galleries theatres & shops. Enjoy the best breakfast in the Hamptons!
✉ innkeeper@millhouseinn.com 🌐 www.millhouseinn.com

EAST MARION

Arbor View House	195-295 BB	Full breakfast
8900 Main Rd 11939	4 rooms, 4 pb	High Tea, afternoon snacks
800-963-8777 631-477-8440	Most CC, *Rated*, •	Fireplace, library, decks, spa
Wilfred Joseph & Veda Daley	C-yes/S-no/P-no/H-ltd	services, massages, Jacuzzis,
Joseph		flower garden

Arbor View House is an historic Victorian B&B in the Long Island, New York wine country. Romance, spa services, private Jacuzzi baths and full breakfasts in an elegant setting. Come join us.
✉ wjoseph@earthlink.net 🌐 www.arborviewhouse.com

Quintessentials B&B & Spa	225-325 BB	Full breakfast
8985 Main Rd 11939	5 rooms, 5 pb	Seasonal Goodies including
800-444-9112 631-477-9400	Most CC	Afternoon Refreshments,
Sylvia Daley	C-ltd/S-no/P-no/H-no	Snacks & Fruit Basket.
	German, Portuguese,	Full-service spa on premises,
	Spanish	steam room, Meditation
		garden, gazebo, whirlpool,
		fireplaces, DVD/books

Quintessentials B&B and Spa is a romantic inn on the North Fork in Long Island Wine Country, featuring a full-service Spa, deluxe rooms with fireplaces, private sundecks, whirlpool baths, near fine beaches & 33 wineries & just 90 miles from New York City.
✉ innkeeper@quintessentialsinc.com 🌐 www.QuintessentialsInc.com

EAST QUOGUE

The George Inn	275-375 BB	Full breakfast
25 Josiah Foster Path 11942	4 rooms, 4 pb	Afternoon tea, wine and
631-653-6509	Most CC	cheese, dessert, fruit,
Virginia Alpi	C-ltd/S-no/P-no/H-no	beverages.
		AC, TV/DVD/CD, business
		accom., fireplace, whirlpool
		tubs, library, wireless
		Internet access.

We feature four guestrooms each with luxurious amenities, including private baths with whirlpool tubs, fresh white towels, flowers and bath scents. Three rooms have separate shower facilities in addition to the whirlpool tubs.
✉ valpiint@optonline.net 🌐 theginn.com

ELLICOTTVILLE

Jefferson Inn of Ellicottville	79-209 BB	Full breakfast
3 Jefferson St 14731	7 rooms, 7 pb	Sitting room, parlor, suites,
800-577-8451 716-699-5869	Most CC, *Rated*, •	fireplace, cable TV, wireless
Jean Kirsch	C-yes/S-no/P-yes/H-yes	Internet, afternoon sweets

Charming 1800's Victorian Inn located in the center of Ellicottville just steps from shops, spas and restaurants. Rock in a chair on the wrap around porch or soak in the outdoor hot tub. Enjoy local golf, antiquing, hiking, skiing, and Amish country.
✉ info@thejeffersoninn.com 🌐 www.thejeffersoninn.com

FAIRPORT

Clematis Inn
2513 Penfield Rd 14450
585-388-9442
Theda Ann Burnham

135-145 BB
3 rooms, 2 pb
Cash, Checks
C-yes/S-no/P-yes/H-no

Vegetarian fare, no refined
sugar
Attention given to special
diets, afternoon tea
Sitting room, library,
sunroom, terry cloth robes,
hairdryers

A 1900 Historic National Folk House is the perfect lodging for your comfort, when you visit Upstate New York. The warm hospitality of The Clematis Inn will make your stay most Innjoyable.
clematis@rochester.rr.com www.clematisinn.com

FLEISCHMANNS

Breezy Hill Inn
835 Breezy Hill Rd 12430
845 254-5615
Michelle and Alan Sidrane

125-280 BB
4 rooms, 4 pb
Visa, MC
C-ltd/S-no/P-no/H-yes
French, Portuguese,

Full breakfast
We accommodate food
allergies and offer a gluten
free breakfast, if requested
recreation room w/pool
table, byob bar, exercise and
steam rooms, porch, den,
Internet, Flatscreen DirecTV

Located 2 hours from NYC in the heart of the Catskills, minutes from skiing, hiking, antiquing and swimming, Breezy Hill Inn, a newly restored Victorian Catskills bed and breakfast provides restful getaways, gourmet breakfasts and luxury in the country.
info@breezyhillinn.com www.breezyhillinn.com

River Run B&B Inn
882 Main St 12430
845-254-4884
Melissa & Ben Fenton

79-185 BB
9 rooms, 5 pb
Visa, MC
C-yes/S-ltd/P-ltd/H-no

Continental plus breakfast
Fireplace, sitting room,
library, stained glass,
beautiful grounds, labyrinth,
piano

Award winning New York Catskills Bed and Breakfast Inn accommodations. Our Inn is set on a lovely acre of land, which gently slopes down to a stream. Enjoy hiking trails, superb skiing, antiquing, auction, fishing, golf and tennis.
info@riverrunbedandbreakfast.com www.riverrunbedandbreakfast.com

FORESTBURGH

Inn at Lake Joseph
162 St Joseph Rd 12777
845-791-9506
Ivan & Ru Weinger

125-385 BB
15 rooms, 15 pb
Visa, MC, AmEx, *Rated*
C-ltd/S-ltd/P-ltd/H-no
Spanish and Portuguese

Full breakfast
All day help yourself lunch
or snack bar
Pool, fishing, boating,
kayaking, tennis, bicycles,
cross country skiing,
tobogganing

High in the Catskill Mountains, just two hours from New York City, exists a romantic, 140-year-old country estate on a 250 acre private lake, within thousands of acres of forest and wildlife preserve.
inn2@lakejoseph.com www.lakejoseph.com

GENEVA

Bragdon House
527 South Main St 14456
315-781-6320
Diana & Jennifer Wenz

120-175 BB
3 rooms, 3 pb
Visa, MC, AmEx, *Rated*
C-ltd/S-no/P-no/H-ltd

Full breakfast
Free High Speed Wireless
Internet, Veranda, Parlor,
Fireplaces, AC, Cable
TV/DVD , Lakeviews,
Romance

This delightfully decorated bed & breakfast offers beautiful guestrooms with king & queen size beds, decorative fireplaces, and a veranda overlooking the shore of Seneca Lake. We are centrally located within the Finger Lakes Wine Trails.
bragdonhousebb@yahoo.com www.bragdonhousebb.com

Greenville Arms 1889 Inn, Greenville, NY

GREENPORT

The Bartlett House Inn
503 Front St 11944
631-477-0371
Jack & Diane Gilmore

150-280 BB
10 rooms, 10 pb
Visa, MC, *Rated*
C-ltd/S-ltd/P-no/H-no

European Breakfast
Fireplace, conferences,
wireless Internet, porch,
gardens

Stately Colonial Revival home featuring 10 guestrooms, all with private bath & furnished with one of a kind pieces. Located near North Fork wineries, beaches, Greenport Village & Shelter Island. A special place to get away from it all and feel pampered.
✉ info@bartletthouseinn.com ◐ www.bartletthouseinn.com

Stirling House
104 Bay Avenue 11944
800-551-0654 631-477-0654
Clayton Sauer

175-295 BB
3 rooms, 3 pb
Most CC, *Rated*, •
C-ltd/S-ltd/P-no/H-ltd
French

Full breakfast
Afternoon tea, gourmet
snacks, lemonade, assorted
beverages, guest fridge.
Wraparound porch,
expansive waterviews,
breakfast/sitting room, WiFi,
iPod docking station

Your 1880's-era Victorian "home-away-from-home." Relax & enjoy Greenport & our beautiful environs with our unobstructed water views from our front porch and rooms. The highest concentration of lighthouses in the US. Beach passes available. Immaculate.
✉ info@stirlinghousebandb.com ◐ www.thestirlinghouse.com

GREENVILLE

Greenville Arms 1889 Inn
Rt 32 South St 12083
888-665-0044 518-966-5219
Kim & Mark LaPolla

115-235 BB
16 rooms, 15 pb
Visa, MC, Disc, *Rated*,
•
C-ltd/S-no/P-ltd/H-ltd
Spanish

Full breakfast from menu
Gourmet chocolate shop on
site, Afternoon Tea, dinner
by reservation on most
nights
Wireless Internet access, art
workshops, quilt art
workshops, secluded 50'
pool, living/sitting room

Historic 1889 Victorian Inn welcoming guests for 50 years. Gardens, outdoor pool, chocolate shop and an atmosphere of warmth and charm invite guests to relax. A delicious breakfast completes a memorable stay.
✉ stay@greenvillearms.com ◐ www.greenvillearms.com

GREENWICH

Country Life B&B
67 Tabor Rd 12834
518-692-7203
Richard & Wendy Duvall

95-180 BB
4 rooms, 4 pb
Cash, *Rated*, •
C-yes/S-no/P-no/H-ltd
Spanish, German,
French

Full breakfast
Candy dish and sherry in
room, coffee & tea maker in
parlor
Patio, library, swimming
hole, sunsets, sitting room,
hammock, porch swing &
picnic table, birding

A unique experience awaits you around Saratoga Springs. Our 1829 farmhouse B&B is situated in Washington County within the towns and villages of the Battenkill Valley on 118 acres of woodlands, meadows, waterfalls and a swimming hole
✉ stay@countrylifebb.com ♺ www.countrylifebb.com

HADLEY

Saratoga Rose Inn & Restaurant
4136 Rockwell St 12835
800-942-5025 518-696-2861
Claude & Richard

135-220 BB
6 rooms, 6 pb
Most CC, •
C-ltd/S-no/P-no/H-ltd
French

Full gourmet breakfast
Fine dining restaurant 3½
stars Albany Times Union,
wine dinners, beer dinners,
ghost dinners
Library, garden, all rooms
w/fireplaces, TVs, AC,
private baths, 4 with private
hot tubs, free WiFi

Romantic Queen Anne Victorian mansion & carriage house. Six unique suites each with private bath, A/C, fireplace. Four suites with private hot tubs, two on decks, two ensuite. Full breakfast. Fine dining restaurant with extensive wine list & full bar.
✉ info@saratogarose.com ♺ www.saratogarose.com

HAGUE

Ruah B&B
9221 Lake Shore Dr 12836
800-224-7549 518-543-8816
Judy & Peter Foster

120-225 BB
4 rooms, 4 pb
Most CC
C-ltd/S-no/P-no/H-no

Full breakfast
Sitting rooms, mountain
views, fireplace, balcony,
lounge

Ruah B&B has large, bright common rooms with massive windows that bring "The Queen of the Lakes" and the surrounding Adirondack Mountains into every room.
✉ ruahbb@aol.com ♺ www.ruahbb.com

HAMLIN

The Country Corner
317 Redman Rd 14464
585-964-9935
Linda DeRue

100 BB
3 rooms, 1 pb
Cash, Checks
C-ltd/S-no/P-no/H-no

Continental breakfast
Complimentary beverages &
snacks
Wrap-around porch, sun
room, sitting room, air
conditioning

If you love the country and history and are looking for a relaxing getaway, this is the place for you. Country Corner in Hamlin, NY is convenient to the Rochester area, near Brockport; very close to Hamlin Beach State Park, a short drive to Niagara Falls.
✉ jderue1@rochester.rr.com ♺ thecountrycorner.com

HAMMONDSPORT

Amity Rose Inn
8264 Main St 14840
800-982-8818 607-569-3402
Ellen & Frank Laufersweiler

115-150 BB
4 rooms, 4 pb
Most CC, *Rated*
C-ltd/S-ltd/P-no/H-ltd
Mid April thru Nov

Full breakfast
Afternoon refreshments and
homemade baked
cookies/brownies, etc.
Spacious sitting room with
fireplace, TV room, outside
balcony, porches & patio

A 1900 country house. 2 rooms have 6 foot whirlpool soaking tubs, one a 2 room suite. Nice, large living room with fireplace. Dinner boat nearby.
✉ amityroseinfo@yahoo.com ♺ www.amityrose.com

HAMMONDSPORT

Park Inn Hotel
37-39 Sheather St 14840
607-569-9387

99-109 BB
5 rooms, 5 pb
Visa, MC, Disc
C-ltd

Full breakfast
Restaurant & tavern
Private dining/conference
room, A/C, sitting room,
phone, TV

The Park Inn is an authentic village inn, situated on Hamondsport's charming Village Square, that has been providing food, drink & lodging to travelers for more than a century.
🌐 www.parkinnhotel.biz

HERKIMER

Bellinger Rose B&B
611 W German St 13350
866-867-2197 315-867-2197
Chris & Leon Frost

125-155 BB
4 rooms, 4 pb
Most CC, •
C-yes/S-ltd/P-no/H-no

Breakfast Menu
Tea, coffee, soft drinks,
snacks
Hot tub, on-site massage
therapy, heat/AC control,
TV/DVD, robes and bath
amenities, Jacuzzi tubs

Our quiet, romantic surroundings afford a Victorian experience unlike all others, complete with on-site massage services. Escape from the hectic world of the city. Relax by the fire, or enjoy our stone patio complete with fountains, waterfalls & pond.
✉ bellingerrose@hotmail.com 🌐 www.bellingerrose.com

Portobello Inn
5989 State Route 5 13350
315-823-8612
Roland S. Randall

110-150 BB
5 rooms, 5 pb
Most CC
C-ltd/S-no/P-no/H-no

Full breakfast
Coffee, tea, juices, soft
drinks, homebaked cookies,
desserts & snacks
Fireplaces, wireless Internet,
fax, antique shop, library,
country club use – golf,
tennis & pool

Enjoy a gracious B&B experience! Classic Italianate inn overlooking the Mohawk River Valley & the Erie Canal since the 1840s. From our wraparound porch & Victorian veranda, enjoy views reminiscent of the Tuscan hills of Italy.
✉ stay@portobelloinn.com 🌐 www.portobelloinn.com

HIGH FALLS

Captain Schoonmaker's B&B
913 State Rte 213 12440
845-687-7946
Judy & Bill Klock

140-195 BB
5 rooms, 5 pb
Most CC, *Rated*, •
C-ltd/S-no/P-no/H-no

Fireside Gourmet Breakfast
Coffee, tea & yummy
homemade cookies always
available!
3 Common rooms with
fireplaces, trout stream,
waterfalls, gardens, fireside
dining, wireless Internet

Fall asleep to the sound of the stream and waterfall. Hear the rooster softly crowing while you snuggle under your down comforter. The scent of the wood burning fireplaces, luscious breakfasts, and country air will keep you returning to this country B & B!
✉ schoonmkr1@aol.com 🌐 www.captainschoonmakers.com

Whispering Pines B&B
60 Cedar Hill Rd 12440
845-687-2419
Celia & HD Seupel

110-169 BB
4 rooms, 4 pb
Visa, MC, Disc, *Rated*
C-ltd/S-no/P-no/H-no
German, French

Full buffet breakfast
Afternoon tea
Sitting room, library, baby-
sitting available, VCR, 2
rooms with Jacuzzis

Light filled B&B on 50 acres of woods. Historic sightseeing, crafts, woodland-walking, fine dining, antiquing, biking; enjoy the quiet.
✉ CSeupel@cs.com 🌐 www.whisperingpinesbb.com

Tell your hosts Pamela Lanier sent you.

HILLSDALE

The Bell House
9315 State Rt 22 12529
518-325-3841
Marilyn Simon

145-205 BB
5 rooms, 4 pb
Visa, MC, AmEx
C-ltd/S-no/P-no/H-no
Spanish

Full breakfast
Dinner on request,
refreshments available
Sitting room, library,
swimming pool, Jacuzzi,
bikes, fireplaces, cable TV

Gracious country lodging in an 1830s home filled with American antiques. In-ground swimming pool in a garden setting. Gourmet breakfast in dining room or on wraparound porch.
info@bellhousebb.com www.bellhousebb.com

Swiss Hutte Country Inn & Restaurant
Rte 23 12529
518-325-3333
Gert & Cindy Alper

100-210 BB
14 rooms, 14 pb
Visa, MC, *Rated*
C-yes/S-no/P-yes/H-yes
German

Full breakfast
Full service restaurant, bar
service, outdoor patio dining
Fridge, cable TV, in-room
phones, parlor, tennis,
swimming pool, skiing,
hiking

Swiss Hutte is just what you would expect from a country inn with a Swiss Innkeeper. It's clean, charming, friendly, comfortable and it features an outstanding kitchen. Nestled in a hidden, wooded valley in the Berkshires.
8057@msn.com www.swisshutte.com

HONEOYE

Greenwoods B&B Inn
8136 Quayle Rd 14471
800-914-3559 585-229-2111
Lisa & Mike Ligon

129-169 BB
5 rooms, 5 pb
Most CC, *Rated*, •
C-ltd/S-no/P-no/H-ltd
April thru November

Full breakfast
Gourmet picnic basket by
prior arrangement
Sitting room, library,
Jacuzzis, suites, fireplaces,
cable TV

Greenwoods is a country inn displaying influences from the "Great Camps" of yesterday. A hilltop setting provides panoramic lake and valley views from a rustic log home. Experience a peaceful retreat, the best of yesterday the tasteful comforts of today!
innkeeper@greenwoodsinn.com www.greenwoodsinn.com

HUNTER

The Fairlawn Inn
7872 Main St 12442
518-263-5025
Chuck Tomajko

129-279 BB
9 rooms, 9 pb
Most CC, •
C-ltd/S-no/P-ltd/H-ltd

Full breakfast
Snack basket, cookie jar,
complimentary soft drinks,
water & juices
TV with cable, telephones,
A/C, four common area
rooms, pool table &
fireplaces

Beautifully restored country home in the Catskills. In the shadow of Hunter Mountain, a four season resort area. Three story corner turret, wraparound porches, sumptuous breakfast. Concierge services—many things to do within walking distance.
finn1@hvc.rr.com www.fairlawninn.com

Washington Irving Inn
6629 Rt 23A 12442
518-589-5560
The Jozic Family

140-190 BB
15 rooms, 15 pb
Visa, MC, AmEx,
Rated, •
C-yes/S-no/P-no/H-no

Full breakfast
Victorian tea on Saturday &
Sunday, restaurant on
premises, cocktail lounge
Outdoor pool, TV/VCR,
whirlpool baths, garden

The inn's distinctive architectural charm and informal atmosphere make everyone feel welcome. Suitable for romantic getaways, family outings/reunions, weddings, group and corporate retreats.
washingtonirvinginn@verizon.net www.washingtonirving.com

The Fairlawn Inn, Hunter, NY

HYDE PARK

Costello's Guest House
21 Main St 12538-1307
845-229-2559
Patsy Newman Costello

65-85 EP
2 rooms
Rated
C-ltd/S-no/P-no/H-no

We don't serve breakfast,
however, there are several
restaurants nearby.
Near Roosevelt
Home/Library, Culinary
Institute, Vassar, Marist, &
Vanderbilts. Wireless
Internet.

Federal style home built in the mid-1850's. Located in the Historic District of the Village of Hyde Park. Comfortable, A/C guestrooms.
✉ Patsyc97@AOL.com

Le Petit Chateau Inn
39 W Dorsey Lane 12538
845-437-4688
Valerie Hail

165-280 BB
4 rooms, 4 pb
Visa, MC, AmEx
C-yes/S-no/P-ltd/H-no

Full breakfast
A welcome gift of
refreshments and cheese
from France
Sitting rooms, small
conference room, Internet
access, Restaurant
Reservations, Private Chef
Events

Small, European style inn located½mile from the renowned Culinary Institute of America. Every room is named after a French wine region. Full gourmet breakfast prepared by CIA chefs.
✉ info@lepetitchateauinn.com 🌐 www.lepetitchateauinn.com

The Willows
53 Travis Rd 12538
845-471-6115
Lisa & Lee Fraitag

140-165 BB
2 rooms, 2 pb
Visa, MC
C-ltd/S-ltd/P-no/H-no

Full breakfast
Snacks, soda, water
WiFi, refrigerators in rooms,
freezer, fireplace and cable
TV in living room.

Country farmhouse from 1765 where you will be indulged by a Culinary Institute of America graduate. Recently featured on the FoodNetwork's "Tyler's Ultimate" show.
✉ stay@willowsbnb.com 🌐 www.willowsbnb.com

Tell your hosts Pamela Lanier sent you.

ITHACA————————————————————————————

A Slice of Home B&B	70-200 BB	Full breakfast
607-589-6073	5 rooms, 5 pb	Drinks, snacks available
Beatrice Fulmer	Visa, MC, *Rated*	Sitting room, hot tubs, suites,
	C-ltd/S-ltd/P-ltd/H-no	cable TV, wireless Internet,
	Some German	accommodations for
		business travel

We specialize in self-tour planning, hiking, winery tours, huge, delicious breakfasts. All rooms have private baths, A/C, TV, use of hot tub. An 18 hole golf course is within walking distance!
✉ info@sliceofhome.com 🌐 www.sliceofhome.com

The Hound & Hare	110-250 BB	Full gourmet breakfast
1031 Hanshaw Rd 14850	4 rooms, 4 pb	Afternoon tea, snacks
800-652-2821 607-257-2821	Most CC, *Rated*	Sitting room, library,
Zetta Sprole	C-yes/S-no/P-no/H-no	bicycles, Jacuzzi, cable,
		suites, fireplaces, whirlpool
		tubs, WiFi

White brick Colonial built on land given to my forebears by General George Washington for service in Revolutionary War. Four tastefully decorated guestrooms with heirlooms and antiques, with fresh flowers for your pleasure.
✉ info@houndandhare.com 🌐 www.houndandhare.com

Log Country Inn B&B of	70-250 BB	Full breakfast
Ithaca	13 rooms, 9 pb	Afternoon tea in winter,
800-274-4771 607-589-4771	Most CC, *Rated*, ●	vegetarian and vegan
Slawomir & Wanda Grunberg	C-yes/S-ltd/P-yes/H-ltd	breakfast available on
	Polish, Russian	request
		Sitting room, library, sauna,
		fireplace, Jacuzzi, computer,
		Internet access in some
		rooms

Enjoy Wanda's blintzes and Russian pancakes. Rest in cozy rooms furnished with custom made furniture. Family friendly and pets are welcome too. Historic, sulfur spring water, walking trails on the property as well as ponds and 100 acres of woods
✉ wanda@logtv.com 🌐 www.logtv.com/inn

JAY————————————————————————————

Book & Blanket B&B	80-100 BB	Full breakfast
12914 State Route 9N 12941	3 rooms, 1 pb	Afternoon tea – request
518-946-8323	AmEx	Sitting room, library,
Kathy, Fred, Sam & Zoe the	C-yes/S-no/P-no/H-no	fireplace, porch swing,
Basset Hound		piano—Village Green and
		Covered Bridge short walk.

1850s Greek Revival near Lake Placid. Picturesque Adirondack hamlet with village green, covered bridge and swimming hole. Bedrooms honor famous authors.
✉ bookinnjay@aol.com 🌐 www.bookandblanket.com

KEENE————————————————————————————

The Bark Eater Inn	55-295 BB	Full country breakfast
Alstead Hill Rd 12942	17 rooms, 10 pb	Trail lunches by request
800-232-1607 518-576-2221	Most CC	Fireplace, three spacious
Joe-Pete Wilson	C-yes/S-ltd/P-ltd/H-ltd	common rooms, antiques,
		horseback riding and skiing
		on premises

Originally a stagecoach stopover, the inn is an old farm nestled in the famous Adirondack Mountains, minutes from the Olympic village of Lake Placid.
✉ info@barkeater.com 🌐 www.barkeater.com

KEENE VALLEY

Trail's End Inn
62 Trail's End Way 12943
800-281-9860 518-576-9860
David Griffiths & Susan
Lindtelgen

100-230 BB
12 rooms, 8 pb
Most CC, •
C-ltd/S-no/P-ltd/H-no

Full breakfast
Snacks, lunch
Sitting room, library,
Jacuzzis, suites, fireplaces,
cable TV, WiFi high speed
Internet

Secluded 1902 lodge & cottages in the Adirondack mountains; clawfoot tubs, patchwork quilts, wood floors, fireplaces. Hike, bike, ski, visit Lake Placid Olympic sites. Weddings and groups hosted.
✉ innkeeper@trailsendinn.com ✺ www.trailsendinn.com

LAKE CLEAR

Hohmeyer's Lake Clear Lodge
6319 SR 30 12945
877-6ADKALPS 518-891-1489
Cathy & Ernest Hohmeyer

189-399 MAP
15 rooms, 15 pb
Most CC
C-yes/S-no/P-ltd/H-no
German, Spanish

Full breakfast
Gourmet European cuisine
w/ Adirondack local
ingredients included in pkg.
Vegan & Vegetarian options
Specialty suites some with
Jacuzzi, fireplace and
kitchen. Sunset lake-views.
Sleigh Rides, massage.

Imagine one of the last original Adirondack lodges awarded 2008 Nat Geo "Stay List" for "sense of place." Immerse yourself in a 25 acre Great Camp style destination experience with handcrafted lodgings, and original Adirondack Alps culinary magic.
✉ info@lodgeonlakeclear.com ✺ www.lodgeonlakeclear.com

LAKE LUZERNE

Lamplight Inn B&B
231 Lake Ave 12846
800-262-4668 518-696-5294
Gene & Linda Merlino

125-239 BB
15 rooms, 15 pb
Visa, MC, AmEx,
Rated, •
C-ltd/S-ltd/P-no/H-yes

Full breakfast menu
Complimentary tea & coffee
available any time. Cookies
at check in time. Wine &
beer licensed.
Guest sitting room with
games, coffee & tea, Service
bar for Wine. Special
romance packages for rms

Pamela Laniers' 1992 "Inn of the Year." Still going strong. Between Lake George & Saratoga Springs. Romantic 1890 Victorian & Carriage House, fireplace bedrooms. Suites with Jacuzzi/fireplace. TVs, phones. Full breakfast menu. Romance packages.
✉ stay@lamplightinn.com ✺ www.lamplightinn.com

LAKE PLACID

Brook's Sunshine Cottage B&B & Apt. Suites
6 Maple St 12946
518-523-3661
Bernadine & Joe Brooks

70-550 BB
10 rooms, 6 pb
Visa, MC
C-ltd/S-no/P-no/H-ltd

Continental breakfast buffet
Kitchenette
Two living rooms
w/fireplaces, deck, gas grills,
lounge chairs, off-street
parking

Charming European Style Bed & Breakfast, located on quiet Maple Street, bordering Hillcrest Avenue Park. Entire, century old, traditional house with spacious areas for relaxation, reading, or game playing is available for groups.
✉ brooks@brookssunshine.com ✺ www.brookssunshine.com

Paradox Lodge
2169 Saranac Ave 12946
877-743-9078 518-523-9078
Chef Moses & Nan
LaFountaine

140-245 BB
8 rooms, 8 pb
Visa, MC
C-ltd/S-no/P-no/H-no

Full breakfast
Restaurant and full bar
WiFi, A/C, fireplace, Jacuzzi,
kayaks, canoe, restaurant

Paradox Lodge was built in 1899 on Paradox Bay in Lake Placid, NY. Paradox Lodge provides a quiet and comfortable atmosphere for guests. Featured in Rachel Ray's Tasty Travels on the Food Network; if that doesn't say good food, we don't know what does!
✉ paradoxlodge@roadrunner.com ✺ www.paradoxlodge.com

LAKE PLACID

South Meadow Farm Lodge	115-170 BB	Full breakfast
Rt 73 (Cascade Rd) 12946	7 rooms, 6 pb	Family style dinner for
800-523-9369 518-523-9369	Most CC, •	parties of 6 adults or more
Tony & Nancy Corwin	C-yes/S-no/P-no/H-ltd	and trail lunch are optional
		Free x-country skiing and
		mountain biking; beautiful,
		peaceful views

Come hike, bike or cross country ski out our back door. Your stay includes a full breakfast served family style. Our 7 room lodge sits down in a meadow with fantastic mountain views. Smoke free. Be sure to visit our Maple sugar house.
✉ ncorwin@southmeadow.com ○ www.southmeadow.com

LEW BEACH

Beaverkill Valley Inn	105-340 BB	Full breakfast
7 Barnhart Rd 12753	20 rooms, 20 pb	Afternoon Tea, lunch &
845-439-4844	Most CC	dinner available
Chris Jurgens	C-yes/S-ltd/P-no/H-yes	Game room, lounge & bar,
		sundeck, tennis courts,
		casting pond, ice skating,
		skiing, hiking, fishing

What do people enjoy here? It's the year-round access to outdoor activities & a chance to relax & reconnect with nature, take a break from the city or to enjoy a romantic getaway.
✉ innkeeper@beaverkillvalleyinn.com ○ www.beaverkillvalleyinn.com

LITTLE FALLS

Canal Side Inn	99-135 BB	Full breakfast
395 S Ann St 13365	3 rooms, 3 pb	French and American
315-823-1170	Visa, MC, AmEx, *Rated*	cuisine served nightly at 5
James and Carol Aufmuth	C-yes/S-no/P-ltd/H-ltd	pm. Wine Spectator Award.
	French	AAA three diamond award.
	Closed February	Cocktail lounge, dining room,
		wireless Internet, bicycle
		storage, workout space
		available

Welcome to the Canal Side Inn, serving traditional French & American cuisine with gracious overnight guest suites. The Inn is located a short walk from the scenic Erie Canal in Historic Canal Place District.
✉ innkeeper@canalsideinn.com ○ www.canalsideinn.com

LIVERPOOL

Ancestor's Inn at the Bassett	95-125 BB	Full breakfast
House	4 rooms, 4 pb	Complimentary beverages
215 Sycamore St 13088	Most CC	and snacks
888-866-8591 315-461-1226	C-yes/S-ltd/P-no/H-no	In-Room cable TV/VCR, high-
Mary & Dan Weidman		speed Internet access,
		movies, books, central A/C,
		hairdryer, alarm clock

Located in the village of Liverpool, NY, in the historic Bassett House. Decorated in the high Victorian style and has all of today's comforts. Walk to the beautiful Onondaga Lake Park and local restaurants. Reasonable rates.
✉ innkeeper@ancestorsinn.com ○ www.ancestorsinn.com

Tell your hosts Pamela Lanier sent you.

LIVINGSTON MANOR

The Guest House
408 Debruce Rd 12758
845-439-4000
Shaun & Andrea Plunket

144-245 BB
6 rooms, 6 pb
Most CC, *Rated*, •
C-yes/S-ltd/P-yes/H-no
French, German, Italian,
Hungarian

All essentials provided in
cottage
Tea, coffee & fruit provided,
evening drinks offered in
hosts house
Jacuzzis, BBQ, fly fishing,
hiking, heated pool in
summer, practice tennis
court, pets welcome

Rustic luxury on this 40-acre Catskill estate. All rooms with private bath or Jacuzzi. Full breakfast, hiking & fly fishing on the property. 6 cottages available. First class dining and antique stores are just minutes away.
✉ andrea@theguesthouse.com ◐ www.theguesthouse.com

Lanza's – A Country Inn
839 Shandelee Rd 12758
845-439-5070
Richard & Mary Lanza

99-139 BB
9 rooms, 9 pb
Visa, MC, AmEx, *Rated*
C-ltd/S-no/P-no/H-no

Full breakfast
Dinner available, afternoon
tea, snacks, complimentary
wine, restaurant
Bar service, sitting room

The personal attention & service you receive at Lanza's sets it apart. This is coupled with clean, comfortable rooms & great food. Cozy pub & restaurant for dining; catering available.
✉ info@lanzascountryinn.com ◐ www.lanzascountryinn.com

LOCKPORT

Hambleton House
130 Pine St 14094
716-439-9507
Hambleton Family

70-105 BB
3 rooms, 3 pb
Visa, MC, •
C-ltd/S-ltd/P-no/H-no

Continental plus breakfast
Private baths, AC, wrap
around porch for smoking.
off street parking, bicycle
storage, Internet access

Gracious, historic 1850s home in the city of Lockport. Offers 3 spacious guestrooms with private baths, A/C, glistening hardwood floors, high ceilings, wraparound porch. A short walk to the 35 Lock on the Erie Barge canal. Close to many highlights.
✉ hambletbb@aol.com ◐ www.niagarabedandbreakfast.com

Maplehurst B&B
4427 Ridge Rd 14094
716-434-3502
Mark & Peggy Herbst

65-85 BB
4 rooms, 3 pb
Most CC, *Rated*, •
C-ltd/S-ltd/P-no/H-no
Some German

Full breakfast
Afternoon tea, snacks
Sitting room, cable TV,
accommodate business
travelers

Historic, spacious, antique-filled country bed & breakfast located minutes from world famous scenic and historic sites. Large, comfortable guestrooms tastefully decorated.
✉ maplehurstmkh@earthlink.net ◐ www.maplehurst.us/index.html

MARGARETVILLE

**Margaretville Mountain Inn
& Village Suites**
1478 Margaretville Mtn Rd
12455
845-586-3933
Carol & Peter Molnar

75-300 BB
8 rooms, 8 pb
Visa, MC, AmEx
C-yes/S-no/P-no/H-no

Full breakfast
Fully equipped kitchen with
suite
Jacuzzi spa room, living
room, fireplace, parlor, free
WiFi, in room HD-TV,
weddings, special events

Our Historic Queen Anne Victorian was built atop Margaretville Mountain in 1886 to take full advantage of the spectacular view of Catskill Mountain State Park.
✉ MMIBNB@catskill.net ◐ www.margaretvilleinn.com

MARIAVILLE

Mariaville Lake B&B
176 Batter St 12137
518-864-5252
Rick & Lorrie Runnels

105-195 BB
5 rooms, 5 pb
Visa, MC, Disc
C-yes/S-no/P-no/H-no

Full breakfast
We welcome vegetarians! We try to use local and organic fare whenever possible. Hiking nearby, dock, canoe, kayaks, swimming, antiques, deli within walking distance.

Mariaville Lake Bed & Breakfast in Schenectady County is a federal style home situated on picturesque Mariaville Lake.It's the perfect place to land after your busy day. We offer rest or activity and a beautiful, peaceful setting.
✉ innkeeper@mariavillelakebb.com ◐ www.mariavillelakebb.com

MIDDLE GROVE

Meadow Hill B&B
359 LeRoux Rd 12850
518-584-1626
Christina Putnam

125-175 BB
3 rooms, 3 pb
Visa, MC
C-ltd/P-no/H-no
May – October

Full breakfast
Drinks & snacks
Cable TV, wireless Internet, A/C, sun porch

Meadow Hill Bed & Breakfast is situated on a beautiful 14-acre hillside meadow just seven miles west of Saratoga Springs, NY. Three guestrooms with private baths and air conditioning.
✉ tina.putnam@gmail.com ◐ www.meadowhillbb.com

MILLER PLACE

Miller Place Ark B&B
179 N Country Rd 11764
631-474-1898
Lorraine & Bob Opitz

115-160 BB
3 rooms, 3 pb
Visa, MC
C-ltd/S-no/P-no/H-no

Continental Weekdays
Full breakfast is served on weekends and holidays, Continental on weekdays, complimentary beverages
Pond, hammock, fireplace, living room, pool, wireless high-speed Internet

Nestled in the historic hamlet of Miller Place, The Miller Place Ark recalls a simpler time.
✉ mpark@buoy.com ◐ www.millerplaceark.com

MILLERTON

Simmons' Way Village Inn
53 Main St 12546
518-789-6235
Jay & Martha Reynolds

189-225 BB
9 rooms, 9 pb
Most CC
C-yes/S-no/P-no/H-no

Full breakfast
Martha's Restaurant
Porches, fireplaces, draped canopy beds, sitting areas

Graceful retreat in grand Victorian elegance and civility. Near CT border in the Berkshire Foothills. Antiques, fireplaces, porches and historic candlelit silver service highlight memorable accommodations and international cuisine.
✉ info@simmonsway.com ◐ www.simmonsway.com

MILTON

Buttermilk Falls Inn & Spa
220 North Rd 12547
877-746-6772 845-795-1310
Lindsay Pugnali

225-650 BB
15 rooms, 15 pb
Visa, MC, AmEx
C-ltd/S-no/P-ltd/H-ltd
German, Spanish

Full breakfast
Gourmet afternoon tea served daily
Spa, fireplaces, private baths, whirlpools, hiking, cable, wireless Internet, living & dining rooms

70-acre Hudson River Estate: Escape & indulge! 75 miles from NYC. Ideal for romantic getaways & weddings. Exquisite gardens, flowering terraces, wildflower fields, winding brooks, trails, ponds, waterfalls. Spa, fireplaces, private baths, whirlpools.
✉ info@buttermilkfallsinn.com ◐ www.buttermilkfallsinn.com

MONTGOMERY

Academy House Inn & Spa	85-225 BB	Full breakfast
136 Clinton St 12549	8 rooms, 6 pb	Delicious afternoon tea and
845-457-5770	Most CC, *Rated*	light snack served.
F Edward Devitt II	C-ltd/S-no/P-no/H-no	Full service gourmet
	Espanol	breakfast, special event &
		wedding hosting, spa on
		premises

The Academy House Inn & Spa is a hidden gem of the Hudson Valley. The destination to relax and unwind in, with deluxe accommodations, soothing spa treatments and delicious gourmet breakfasts. ✉ edevitt@hotmail.com ◑ www.academyhouseinn.com

Borland House	105-175 BB	Full breakfast
130 Clinton St 12549	5 rooms, 3 pb	Tea & baked goods are
845-457-1513	Visa, MC, *Rated*	always available in the
Bill & Carol Freeman	C-yes/S-no/P-ltd/H-no	dining room for guests to
	French	help themselves.
		Internet, TV/DVD, fireplace,
		sitting rooms, porch, library,
		luxury linens, guest
		refrigerator,

This gracious Greek Revival home offers a romantic escape from your routine. So kick off your shoes, share some wine, relax in one of our cozy reading nooks, browse in our antique shop, and sleep in comfort before waking up to a sumptuous breakfast.
✉ carolfreeman@hvc.rr.com ◑ www.theborlandhouse.com

MUMFORD

Genesee Country Inn B&B	120-195 BB	Full country breakfast
948 George St 14511	10 rooms, 10 pb	Coffee, tea, snacks, and
800-697-8297 585-538-2500	Visa, MC, Disc, *Rated*,	cookies; guest pantry
Deborah & Richard	•	A/C, phones, fax, wireless
Stankevich	C-ltd/S-no/P-no/H-ltd	Internet, TV/VCR, library,
		deck by pond, gazebo, sun
		room, meeting room

The Genesee Country Inn was built in 1833. This historic stone mill inn has 10 guestrooms with private baths located on Spring Creek. Ponds, waterfall, patio decks and gazebo are situated on 8 acres. We're at the beginning of the Finger Lakes.
✉ stay@geneseecountryinn.com ◑ www.geneseecountryinn.com

NAPLES

Monier Manor	160-190 BB	Full breakfast
154 N Main St 14512	4 rooms, 4 pb	Sitting room, library,
585-374-6719	Visa, MC, Disc, *Rated*,	fireplaces, in-room massage,
Bruce & Donna Scott	•	parlor, dining room, library
	C-ltd/S-no/P-no/H-no	

1840's Manor Home. 4 bedroom luxury accommodations including fireplaces, private baths, outdoor spa & fabulous breakfasts in a village known as "America's Switzerland."
✉ monierma@rochester.rr.com ◑ www.moniermanor.com

Vagabond Inn	125-255 BB	Full breakfast
3300 Sliter Rd 14512	6 rooms, 6 pb	Large variety of teas, hot
877-554-6271 585-554-6271	Most CC, *Rated*, •	chocolate, hot cider,
Patti Fitzgerald Coles	S-ltd/P-ltd/H-yes	Starbuck's fresh ground
		coffee, juices, sweets
		In house massage,
		manicures, pedicures, two
		sitting rooms, pool with
		Japanese gardens, private
		spas

The Elegant Escape voted the "Most Romantic Inn" known for its panoramic views with individual hot tub spas/fireplaces/pool. 100 acre estate nestled within Hi Tor State Park's 16K acres offers total seclusion in the heart of Finger Lakes Wine Country
✉ vagabondinn@frontiernet.net ◑ www.thevagabondinn.com

NEW BERLIN

Sunrise Farm B&B	70-95 BB	Full breakfast
331 County Hwy 17 13411	2 rooms, 1 pb	Complimentary wine
607-847-9380	C-yes/S-no/P-ltd/H-no	Well-behaved dogs accepted,
Janet Schmelzer		A/C

Quiet farm on a hill in the rural community of Pittsfield. Swimming and hiking at nearby State Parks. Short drive to Cooperstown.Dog-friendly. Small enough for hosts to be flexible.
✉ jluddite@frontiernet.net

NEW PALTZ

Moondance Ridge	209-299 BB	Healthy and Creative
55 Shivertown Rd 12561	5 rooms, 5 pb	Breakfast
800-641-5618 845-255-4161	Visa, MC, AmEx	Complimentary beverages,
Kathy Drew	S-no/P-ltd/H-yes	healthy snacks and
		homemade baked goods
		throughout the day
		Luxury suites with
		whirlpools, fireplaces, WiFi,
		DVD, central A/C, spa
		services, sauna

You are always welcome at the Moondance Ridge B&B of New Paltz! Five luxury suites feature fireplaces, whirlpools, cable TV and WiFi. Enjoy creative and healthy breakfasts in the dining room overlooking our certified backyard wildlife habitat.
✉ innkeeper@moondanceridge.com ○ www.moondanceridge.com

Mountain Meadows B&B	145-155 BB	Full breakfast
542 Albany Post Rd 12561	4 rooms, 4 pb	Afternoon refreshments,
845-255-6144	Visa, MC, Disc	delicious home-baked goods
Corinne D'Andrea & Art	C-yes/S-no/P-ltd/H-ltd	daily
Rifenbary		Recreation room with pool
		table, guest kitchen, large in-
		ground pool, hot tub, lawn
		games, A/C

Beautiful grounds and panoramic views of the Shawangunk Mountains provide the backdrop for our contemporary B&B. An ideal place for nature lovers who enjoy casual and comfortable living.
✉ mtnmead542@aol.com ○ www.mountainmeadowsbnb.com

NEW YORK CITY

102 Brownstone Boutique	200-275 EP	Coffee & tea, candy, popcorn
Hotel	6 rooms, 6 pb	Private suites, full kitchen,
102 W 118th St Ste 1 10026	Visa, MC, AmEx,	Jacuzzi, local
212-662-4223	*Rated*, ●	phones/answering machine,
Lizette Lanoue	C-ltd/S-no/P-no/H-no	cable TV, DVD, WiFi
	Spanish and a little	
	French	

102 Brownstone offers just the place for you to visit New York but experience it like a true native! Private quarters & amenities make you feel right at home. Please contact your host for current rates!
✉ Stay@102brownstone.com ○ www.102brownstone.com

1291 Bed & Breakfast	39-450 BB	24 hour self service
337 W 55th St 10019	31 rooms, 9 pb	Coffee, tea, milk, toast,
212-397-9686	Visa, MC	peanut butter, jelly
Roland Solenthaler	C-ltd/S-no/P-ltd/H-no	Lounge with big screen TV,
	German, French, Italian,	Internet access, phone with
	Spanish, Swiss german	free local calls, bike/scooter
		rentals

A young, highly professional and motivated team greets you at 1291 Bed & Breakfast. We are located on 55th Street between 8th and 9th Avenues, right in the heart of Manhattan. Times Square and Central Park are in walking distance.
✉ 1291@1291.com ○ www.1291.com

NEW YORK CITY────────────────────

36 Riverside Wyman House
36 Riverside Dr 10023
212-799-8281
Pamela & Ron Wyman

279-389 BB
6 rooms, 6 pb
Rated, •
C-ltd/S-no/P-no/H-no

Breakfast Basket
Complimentary "get started"
breakfast basket for first
morning only.
Luxury, outstanding
attention to detail, sleep
sofas, kitchenette, Cable TV,
WiFi, maid service

Located on sunny Riverside Park, Wyman House has been lauded by hundreds of happy travelers for its gracious hospitality. You'll find the finest accommodations with the utmost attention to detail.
✉ pam@wymanhouse.com ◔ www.wymanhouse.com

Chelsea Inn
46 W 17th St 10011
800-640-6469 212-645-8989
Harry Chernoff

109-279 BB
32 rooms, 10 pb
Most CC, •
C-yes/S-ltd/P-no/H-no
Spanish, Polish, Italian

Continental breakfast
Voucher for breakfast at
Nana's Treats, the charming
coffee shop downstairs
Refrigerator, coffeemaker,
hot plate – silverware &
plates upon request

Chelsea Inn is a four story walk-up (no elevator) which offers a choice of suites or single rooms, private or shared baths—all with refrigerator, coffee maker and sink. The rooms are generously large and suites are huge.
✉ reservations@chelseainn.com ◔ www.chelseainn.com

Chelsea Pines Inn
317 W 14th St 10014
888-546-2700 212-929-1023
Jay Lesiger & Al Ridolfo

150-299 BB
26 rooms, 21 pb
Most CC, •
C-ltd/S-no/P-no/H-ltd

Continental plus breakfast
Coffee & cookies all day
Outdoor patio, greenhouse,
all rooms have A/C, color TV
with HBO, phone and fridge

One of the most popular gay & lesbian Inns in the city, but everyone is welcome here. Chelsea Pines is charmingly decorated with original vintage film posters from the Golden Age of Hollywood.
✉ cpiny@aol.com ◔ www.chelseapinesinn.com

East Village B&B
244 E 7th St, Apt. #5-6 10009
212-260-1865
Betty-Carol Sellen

150-175 BB
3 rooms
C-ltd/S-no/P-ltd/H-no

Self-serve continental
breakfast
Coffee, tea available anytime
Hairdryers, alarm clocks,
New York guidebooks, TV,
video player & stereo

Newly renovated apartment in a period building. Contemporary furniture & art. Two bedrooms are suitable for two & one for a single only. Living room & dining area available to guests. There are two shared bathrooms.
✉ evbandb@juno.com

The Inn on 23rd
131 W 23rd St 10011
877-387-2323 212-463-0330
Annette Fisherman

229-399 BB
14 rooms, 14 pb
Most CC, *Rated*
C-yes/S-no/P-no/H-ltd
Spanish, German

Continental plus breakfast
Complimentary wine and
cheese in the afternoon
Sitting room, library, cable,
suites, fax, copier,
hairdryers, iron, A/C,
newspapers. Internet-email.

A sumptuous B&B in the heart of New York City. Enjoy the conveniences of a first class Manhattan hotel, in a setting one might expect in Martha's Vineyard or Vermont.
✉ reservations@innon23rd.com ◔ www.innon23rd.com

NEW YORK CITY————————————————————————

Ivy Terrace B&B	200-325 BB	Continental plus breakfast
230 E 58th St #1A 10022	5 rooms, 5 pb	Restaurant downstairs,
516-662-6862	Most CC, •	afternoon tea
Vinessa & Sue	C-yes/S-no/P-ltd/H-no	Cable TV, local telephone,
		extra jack for laptop hookup

Private, elegantly furnished apartments in the heart of New York's Eastside. Enjoy your own terrace as well as a full kitchen and private bath.
info@ivyterrace.com www.ivyterrace.com

Rooms to Let	190-250 BB	Continental Breakfast offered
83 Horatio St 10014	4 rooms, 1 pb	
212-675-5481	C-ltd/S-no/P-no/H-no	
Marjorie Colt		

Greek Revival residence, c.1840, retains much of its original feeling. In historic Greenwich Village, moments away from the trendy Meatpacking District with designer shops and fashionable clubs. A calm, quiet retreat from the action found all around.
margecolt@aol.com www.roomstolet.net

Stay the Night	75-205 EP	Jacuzzis, fireplace
18 E 93rd St 10128	4 rooms, 4 pb	
212-722-8300	Visa, MC	
Nick Hankin	C-yes/S-no/P-no	

Fully renovated and very secure, on a tree-lined block between 5th and Madison Avenues two minutes from Central Park. Four suites with ensuite baths, two guestrooms, and a 1 bedroom apartment with full kitchen and bath with Jacuzzi.
nick@staythenight.com www.staythenight.com

Sugar Hill Harlem Inn	150-275 BB	Continental breakfast
460 W 141st St 10031	10 rooms, 10 pb	Any food can be ordered.
212.234.5432	Visa, MC, AmEx	There is an in house chef.
Jeremy Archer	C-yes/S-no/P-yes/H-ltd	A/C, laundry, WiFi,
		computers, fireplace, garden,
		function room for weddings,
		baby showers

Sugar Hill, forever known as home to many Harlem Renaissance artists and for its rich cultural history, is now home to the new Sugar Hill Harlem Inn, the only B&B in NYC to use renewable energy. A fully renovated Victorian townhouse built in 1906.
info@sugarhillharleminn.com www.sugarhillharleminn.com

Tony's Place	90-205 EP
133 W 119th St 10026	7 rooms
888-224-8262 212-864-3301	Most CC, •
Tony Ndogo	S-no/P-no/H-no

Tony's Place is the place to stay when you are looking to be part of Manhattan and its culture. You will be carried away by the Victorian ambience.
tony.ndogo@verizon.net tonysplacebnb.homestead.com/Home.html

NEWBURGH————————————————————————

Goldsmith Denniston B&B	165 BB	Full breakfast
227 Montgomery Street 12550	4 rooms, 4 pb	Private baths, air
845-562-8076	Most CC	conditioning, patio, lawn for
Nancy Billman	C-ltd/S-no	badminton or croquet,
		library

Denniston House is an elegant Bed and Breakfast in the heart of the historic district of Newburgh, New York — the gateway to the Hudson Valley. Denniston House offers comfort, elegance and good food in a setting convenient to the many area attractions
dennistonbb227@aol.com www.dennistonbb.com

NIAGARA FALLS

Butler House B&B
751 Park Pl 14301
866-706-8199 716-284-9846
Mike & Marcia Yoder

89-139 BB
4 rooms, 4 pb
Visa, MC, Disc
C-ltd/S-no/P-no/H-no

Homemade Breakfasts
A/C, cable TV, clock radio,
hairdryers and ironing
boards, wireless Internet

Snuggled amongst the beautiful trees and homes, on a quiet two way street in the heart of Niagara Falls. Within walking distance to the Majestic Niagara Falls, Seneca Niagara Casino and Canada.
✉ butlerhousebb@yahoo.com 🌐 www.butlerhousebb.com

The Red Coach Inn
2 Buffalo Ave 14303
800-282-1459 716-282-1459
Tom Reese

99-199 BB
31 rooms, 31 pb
Visa, MC, Disc, *Rated*,
•
C-ltd/S-no/P-no/H-ltd

Continental plus breakfast
Restaurant for lunch, dinner
or snacks
Restaurant, bar service,
sitting room, library,
Jacuzzis, suites, kitchenettes

Affordable luxury! Modeled after the Old Bell Inn, in Finedon, England, The Red Coach Inn has been welcoming guests to Niagara Falls since 1923.
✉ innkeeper@redcoach.com 🌐 www.redcoach.com

NORTH RIVER

Garnet Hill Lodge
13th Lake Rd 12856
800-497-4207 518-251-2444
Mary & Joe Fahy

99-150 BB
26 rooms, 26 pb
Most CC
C-yes/S-no/P-yes/H-yes

Full breakfast
The Log House Restaurant
Free WiFi, whirlpool bath
tubs, A/C, Direct TV, decks

Walking into The Log House at Garnet Hill Lodge you're greeted by the spaciousness of a great hotel, the warmth of a rustic Adirondack mountain lodge, and the friendly charm of your favorite country inn. ✉ mary_fahy@msn.com 🌐 www.garnet-hill.com

OLIVEREA

Slide Mt. Forest House
805 Oliverea Rd 12410
845-254-4269 845-254-5365
Ralph Combe, Jr.

85-225 BB
19 rooms, 15 pb
Cash, Checks, *Rated*
C-yes/S-no/P-no/H-no
German

Full breakfast
Lunch & dinner available
(fee)
Restaurant, bar, pool, sitting
room, hiking, tennis courts,
fishing, wireless Internet

Fresh air, nature and a touch of Old World charm await you at our German/American Catskill Mountains Inn.
✉ slide_mtn@yahoo.com 🌐 www.slidemountain-inn.com

PALENVILLE

The Clark House
3292 Rt 23A 12463
518-678-5649
Michael & Christine Clark

105-225 BB
5 rooms, 5 pb
Visa, MC, AmEx
C-ltd/S-no/P-no/H-no

Full breakfast
10 person hot tub, sitting
room, fireplace, conference,
on-site caterer, weddings,
Jacuzzis, WiFi

Magnificent Victorian guesthouse located in the heart of the Catskill Mountains—only 2 hours north of NYC. Easily accessible by bus. Hiking trails and skiing are minutes away. Two deluxe suites with fireplace and whirlpool available.
✉ theclarkhousebb@yahoo.com 🌐 www.catskillsbb.com

PENN YAN

Finton's Landing On Keuka Lake
661 E Lake Rd 14527
315-536-3146
Doug & Arianne Tepper

179 BB
4 rooms, 4 pb
Visa, MC, Disc, *Rated*
C-ltd/S-no/P-no/H-no
Dutch
Weekends, May to
Harvest

Full two-course breakfast
Wraparound porch, 165'
beach, hammock, gazebo,
canoe, paddleboat, swim,
Wireless Internet Access

Waterfront Victorian, private baths & A/C, 165' secluded beach on Keuka Lake, wireless wide-area Internet access, romantic porch, fireplace, canoe, paddleboat. Garage space for your bicycles! Bring your kayak! Bring your laptop—wireless access.
✉ tepperd@eznet.net 🌐 home.eznet.net/~tepperd

PENN YAN

Fox Inn
158 Main St 14527
800-901-7997 315-536-3101
Cliff & Michele Orr

109-214 BB
6 rooms, 6 pb
Visa, MC, AmEx,
Rated, •
C-yes/S-ltd/P-no/H-no

Full breakfast
Bar service
Sitting room, library, Jacuzzis
for two, fireplaces, cable
TV/VCR, Suite available, A/C,
business

1820 Greek Revival Inn furnished with Empire furnishings, marble fireplaces, sun porch, parlor with billiards table and formal rose gardens.
✉ info@foxinnbandb.com ✪ www.foxinnbandb.com

Trimmer House B&B
145 E Main St 14527
800-968-8735 315-536-0522
Gary Smith

99-349 BB
7 rooms, 7 pb
Visa, MC, AmEx, *Rated*
C-ltd/S-ltd/P-no/H-ltd
Chinese

Full breakfast
Snacks
Sitting room, library,
Jacuzzis, suites, fireplaces,
cable TV, wireless Internet

1891 Queen Anne Victorian. Romantic atmosphere in the heart of New York wine country. Let us pamper you in our luxurious surroundings. Close to wineries, shops and restaurants. Adjacent Guesthouse.
✉ innkeeper@trimmerhouse.com ✪ www.trimmerhouse.com

Tudor Hall B&B on Keuka Lake
762 E Bluff Dr 14527
315-536-9962
Priscilla & Don Erickson

165-205 BB
3 rooms, 3 pb
Visa, MC
C-ltd/S-no/P-no/H-no
spring, summer and fall

Full breakfast
Complimentary chocolates
Sitting rooms, library, bikes,
spa, suites, fireplaces, cable
TV, private beach, wireless
network

Elegant English Tudor house with terraced gardens & private beach on Keuka Lake, in the heart of NY State's Finger Lakes wine region. Fall asleep to the sound of water lapping outside your window.
✉ tudorhall@hotmail.com ✪ www.p-port.com/tudorhallbb

Wagener Estate B&B
351 Elm St 14527
315-536-4591
Cathy Wenzel

119-169 BB
5 rooms, 5 pb
Visa, MC, AmEx
C-ltd/S-no/P-no/H-no

Full candlelight breakfast
Victorian Tea Luncheon
available, for private parties.
Guest rooms have queen
beds, private in rm. bath, TV,
VCR, A/C and wireless
Internet access.

Ambience in Finger Lakes Wine Country. Our 1700's National and State Historic Register home sits on top a knoll on 5 pastoral acres. Furnished with period antiques. On the wine trail, a short walk to village shops, restaurants and lakeside parks.
✉ wagener-estate@wagenerestate.com ✪ www.wagenerestate.com

PIERMONT

RiverView B&B
845-353-0778
Alida Whelehan

145-210 BB
5 rooms, 5 pb
Most CC, •
C-yes/S-ltd/P-yes/H-ltd
Some Dutch

Full breakfast
Prepared to your
specifications at the Nyack
Location and help yourself at
the Piermont Location.
Sitting room, laundry
facilities, pool, wireless
Internet access, water views,
walk to town.

RiverView Bed and breakfast, South Nyack, charming, historic, 1835 private home, 2 secluded acres with pool on the Hudson River. Other property in Piermont, on tidal waterway, walking distance to town, bus from NYC. Short & long term corporate rentals.
✉ reservations@riverviewbnb.com ✪ www.riverviewbnb.com

PINE CITY

Rufus Tanner House
60 Sagetown Rd 14871
800-360-9259 607-732-0213
Donna & Rick Powell

90-150 BB
4 rooms, 4 pb
Visa, MC, *Rated*
C-ltd/S-no/P-yes/H-no

Full breakfast
Snacks, soda, tea, candy
Sunroom, Jacuzzi, fireplaces,
A/C, TV/CD player, ceiling
fans, aromatherapy, outdoor
hot tub, robes

Located in the Finger Lakes region of New York between Corning and Elmira, Rufus Tanner House bed & breakfast caters to wandering romantics, sightseers and business travelers.
✉ rthouse@stny.rr.com ✪ www.rufustanner.com

PINE ISLAND

Cider Mill Inn B&B
207 Glenwood Rd 10969
845-258-3044
Robert Lipinsky

150-250 BB
3 rooms, 3 pb
Most CC
C-ltd/S-no/P-no/H-no

Full breakfast
All rooms with private bath.
Outdoor hot tub available all
year and pool during
summer months.

The Cider Mill Inn is a country retreat in the heart of the Hudson Valley. A beautifully restored 1865 Victorian farmhouse offering a tranquil setting for a special getaway.
✉ info@cidermillinn.com ✪ www.cidermillinn.com

PORT JEFFERSON

Golden Pineapple B&B
201 Liberty Ave 11777
631-331-0706
Tom & Jennifer Simko

135-210 BB
3 rooms, 3 pb
Visa, MC, *Rated*
C-ltd/S-no/P-no/H-no

Full breakfast
Evening cordials and
chocolates
On site catering,
acupuncture, massage,
central A/C, cable TV, high
speed Internet

A quiet retreat where guests can relax and unwind. Steps away, the quaint harborside village of Port Jefferson beckons visitors with a vast array of unique shops, delectable restaurants and a plethora of interesting historical & recreational activities.
✉ info1@goldenpineapplebandb.com ✪ www.goldenpineapplebandb.com

The White House on High Street
651 High St 11777
866-474-0003 631-474-0003
Marge Riggio

175-260 BB
3 rooms, 3 pb
Most CC
C-ltd/S-ltd/P-no/H-no

Gourmet breakfast
Self-serve snack bar with
snacks, teas, cookies, fresh
fruit
Swimming pool, hot tub,
Jacuzzis, game room

A truly elegant bed and breakfast set in the picturesque village of Port Jefferson on Long Island's exclusive north shore. The inn is a perfect retreat for the vacationer and business traveler alike.
✉ info@whitehousebb-portjefferson.com

PRATTSBURGH

Feather Tick 'N Thyme
7661 Tuttle Rd 14873
607-522-4113
Maureen & John Kunak

100-125 BB
4 rooms, 2 pb
Visa, MC, *Rated*
C-ltd/S-ltd/P-no/H-no

Full breakfast
Complimentary wine,
welcome basket of coupons,
snacks, refreshments readily
available
Sitting room, refrigerator for
guest use, arcade, campsite,
lawn games, gift shop

An "unforgettable stop in thyme." Country Victorian offers romantic getaway, luxurious furnishings, antiques, quiescent sleep, gracious hospitality, hiking, biking, campfires and lawn games.
✉ info@bbnyfingerlakes.com ✪ www.bbnyfingerlakes.com

PURLING

Bavarian Manor Country Inn	79-199 BB	Full breakfast
866 Mountain Ave 12470	18 rooms, 18 pb	Restaurant, dinner available,
518-622-3261	Visa, MC, Disc	bar service
Suzanne & Stanley	C-yes/S-no/P-yes/H-no	Jacuzzis, fireplaces, cable
Oldakowski	German, Polish	TV, massage sessions, WiFi
		Internet

Nestled on 100 acres in the Catskill Mountains, this 4-story Victorian Inn overlooking a private lake has been welcoming guests since 1865 with its friendly, relaxed, casual atmosphere. Eighteen guestrooms with private baths.
✉ innkeeper@bavarianmanor.com 🌐 www.bavarianmanor.com

RED HOOK

The Grand Dutchess	150-195 BB	Full breakfast
7571 Old Post Rd 12571	5 rooms, 5 pb	Hot & cold drinks always
845-758-5818	Visa, MC, AmEx	available
Elizabeth Pagano & Harold	C-ltd/S-no/P-no/H-no	Parlors, porches, great room,
Gruber		dining room, living room,
		private baths

The Grand Dutchess boasts the perfect setting for your leisurely or romantic getaway, meetings, corporate retreats, & other gatherings. A breathtaking backdrop of the magnificent Hudson River Valley, relaxing atmosphere & attention to detail.
✉ dutchessinnkeeper@earthlink.net 🌐 www.granddutchess.com

Red Hook Inn	135-285 BB	Full breakfast
7460 S Broadway 12571	8 rooms, 8 pb	Prix Fixe Dining/advance
87 REDHOOK 1 845-758-8445	Visa, MC	reservations required
Patricia Holden	C-yes/S-no/P-no/H-no	Sitting room, Jacuzzis, suites,
	Arabic, French, Spanish,	fireplaces, cable TV, outdoor
	Greek	whirlpool tub, Rolls Royce &
		Chauffeur

Beautiful Federal Era Inn, built in 1842. Rooms are light, airy & comfortable, all with private baths, some with whirlpool baths & fireplaces.
✉ redhookinn@aol.com 🌐 www.theredhookinn.com

RHINEBECK

Olde Rhinebeck Inn c.1745	195-275 BB	Full gourmet country
340 Wurtemburg Rd 12572	4 rooms, 4 pb	breakfast
845-871-1745	Visa, MC	Coffee station, guest fridge
Jonna Paolella	C-ltd/S-no/P-no/H-no	stocked with complimentary
		beverages.
		Sitting room, Jacuzzi, suites,
		satellite TV, Country
		Atmosphere, Unique
		Antiques, Private entrances

Chosen as one of the top 10 inns in North America by Forbes.com, Olde Rhinebeck Inn is ideally located to enjoy the highlights of the Hudson River Valley. Authentic, Elegant, Rustic, Intimate. This lovely little inn is a genuine find, see for yourself!
✉ innkeeper@rhinebeckinn.com 🌐 www.rhinebeckinn.com

Primrose Hill B&B	150-175 BB	Full breakfast
567 Ackert Hook Rd 12572	2 rooms, 2 pb	Snacks, beverages
845-698-0370	Most CC	Cable TV, CD/DVD players,
Dave & Karen O'Riley	C-ltd/S-ltd/P-no/H-no	large selection of movies,
		wireless Internet service

Primrose Hill B&B is located on a private 3 acre setting in the scenic Primrose Hill area of Rhinebeck. Picture yourself spending a leisurely getaway in one of two beautifully appointed guestrooms. Wake up pampered to a hearty country breakfast.
✉ doriley@hvc.rr.com 🌐 www.primrosehillbb.com

RHINEBECK

Stone Church Road B&B
339 Stone Church Rd 12572
845-758-2427
Richard and Marsha DeBlasi

95-125 BB
4 rooms, 2 pb
Most CC
C-yes/S-ltd/P-no/H-no

Full breakfast
Fresh fruit, soft drinks,
bottled water, candy,
homemade cookies
Sitting room, library, satellite
TV, nature trail, outdoor
games, patios, board games,
private entrance

Lovely country setting 10 minutes north of the center of Rhinebeck; convenient to area attractions. Four comfortable rooms with scenic views. A common room with a variety of games and satellite TV. Private guest entrances. Flexible breakfast time.
✉ stay@stonechurchroadbedandbreakfast.com ○ www.stonechurchroadbedandbreakfast.com

Veranda House
6487 Montgomery St 12572
877-985-6800 845-876-4133
Yvonne Sarn

150-215 BB
5 rooms, 5 pb
Visa, MC, AmEx
C-ltd/S-no/P-no/H-no

Full gourmet breakfast
Breakfast on terrace
Sitting room, library, central
A/C, concierge service,
veranda with wicker, in room
phones

Charming 1842 Federal house located in the scenic town of Rhinebeck, NY, in the heart of the Hudson Valley. Restaurants, fairs, antiques. Gourmet breakfasts.
○ www.verandahouse.com

ROCHESTER

428 Mount Vernon
428 Mt Vernon Ave 14620
800-836-3159 585-271-0792
Philip & Claire Lanzatella

125-140 BB
7 rooms, 7 pb
Most CC, *Rated*, •
C-ltd/S-ltd/P-no/H-ltd

Full breakfast from menu
Afternoon tea
Cable TV, off street parking,
nightly turn down service,
wireless Internet, A/C

Elegant estate home on two wooded acres at the entrance to historic Highland Park. All seven antique-filled rooms have phones, cable TV, WiFi, and private baths.
✉ planzat1@rochester.rr.com ○ www.428mtvernon.com

A B&B at Dartmouth House
215 Dartmouth St 14607
800-724-6298 585-271-7872
Ellie & Bill Klein

129-179 BB
4 rooms, 4 pb
Most CC, *Rated*
C-ltd/S-no/P-no/H-no

Full breakfasts by candlelight
Bottomless cookie jar filled
with home-baked cookies,
complimentary beverages
available at all times
High speed wireless, grand
piano, AC, movies, guest
computer/printer, TV/VCRs,
parking, porches, priv. yard

Welcome to A B&B at Dartmouth House-a quiet, spacious Tudor in Rochester's cultural Park-East Ave. district. Hosts are well-traveled and love people. Located in an architecturally fabulous residential neighborhood near downtown. Walk to museums, restaurants
✉ stay@dartmouthhouse.com ○ www.dartmouthhouse.com

A B&B at the Edward Harris House
35 Argyle St 14607
800-419-1213 585-473-9752
Susan Alvarez

139-189 BB
5 rooms, 5 pb
Visa, MC, AmEx,
Rated, •
C-ltd/S-no/P-no/H-no
Spanish, a little
Portuguese

Full breakfast
A complimentary welcome
package. Catered picnics &
meals available on request.
Pls contact the Inn.
Sitting room, library, suites,
fireplaces, cable TV, wireless
Internet, AC

The most convenient B&B in Rochester, this 1896 mansion is listed on the Nat'l Register of Historic Places. In the heart of the Arts & Cultural District. One block to Park & East Avenues' shops, cafes, fine dining, galleries & museums.
✉ innkeeper@edwardharrishouse.com ○ www.edwardharrishouse.com

ROCK CITY FALLS

The Mansion of Saratoga	125-399 BB	Served every morning from
801 Rte 29 12863	10 rooms, 10 pb	8:30–10am
888-996-9977 518-885-1607	Visa, MC, AmEx, •	Innkeepers reception every
Lori Wodicka	C-ltd/S-no/P-no/H-ltd	evening from 5–7pm. Coffee,
	Closed in January only.	tea, water & fruit available
		24/7.
		Public phone in hallway,
		cable TV, free wireless
		Internet, 4-acres w/pond,
		ducks, waterfalls, fountain.

Step back in time & experience the romance of the 19th Century. Built in 1866, the historic Mansion is a luxurious villa located 7mi from the action of Saratoga Springs & 25 minutes from spectacular Lake George.
✉ infodesk@themansionsaratoga.com ◗ themansionsaratoga.com

ROME

Maplecrest B&B	85 BB	Full gourmet breakfast
6480 Williams Rd 13440	3 rooms, 3 pb	Beverage on arrival
315-337-0070	•	Refrigerator use, central A/C,
Diane Saladino	C-ltd/S-no/P-no/H-no	sitting room, grill, picnic
		facilities, free WI-Wf

Modern split-level home. Close to historic locations. Adirondack foliage, lakes and skiing. Near Griffins Business Park.
✉ czarnina1@verizon.net

S WORCESTER

Charlotte Valley Historic Inn	110-175 BB	Full breakfast
Charlotte Valley Rd 12197	5 rooms, 3 pb	Afternoon tea, snacks
607-397-8164	Cash, Checks, *Rated*	Sitting room, tennis court,
Lawrence & Joanne	C-yes/S-no/P-no/H-ltd	suite, fireplaces, cable TV
Kosciusko		

Elegance in the country. An historic Stagecoach Stop built in 1832. Fine period antiques—experience history in idyllic Charlotte Valley, where the sidewalk ends.
✉ charlottevalley@yahoo.com ◗ www.cooperstownchamber.org/cvinn

SALISBURY MILLS

Caldwell House B&B	160-245 BB	Full 3 course breakfast
25 Orrs Mills Rd 12577	5 rooms, 5 pb	Complimentary sodas,
800-210-5565 845-496-2954	Visa, MC, AmEx, •	homemade baked goods and
Gene Sheridan	C-ltd/S-ltd/P-no/H-no	coffee 24 hours a day
	Spanish, Italian	Front porch, sitting room, 2
		fireplaces, TV/VCR, room
		phones, Jacuzzi, air
		conditioning, gift shop

Winner 2008 B & B of Distinction NYS Hospitality Assn. 2008 Best B&B in Hudson Valley. Elegant and romantic 1803 Colonial on 3 landscaped acres furnished with antiques, fine linens and fresh flowers. Near West Point, Storm King Art Center & outlets.
✉ info@caldwellhouse.com ◗ www.caldwellhouse.com

SARANAC LAKE

Sunday Pond B&B	85 BB	Hearty Adirondack Breakfast
5544 State Rte 30 12983	4 rooms, 4 pb	Trail lunches and complete
518-891-1531	Most CC	dinner menus are available
Lesley & Dick Lyon	C-yes/S-no/P-no/H-no	for guests
		Great room w/fireplace,
		stereo/ DVD; laundry
		services, activity planning,
		picnic area w/gas grill

Adirondack style lodging in a peaceful forest setting. Enjoy Summer, Winter, Spring and Fall with us, in the heart of the Northern Adirondacks. Experience the scent of balsam, the haunting cry of the loon and the tranquility of nature in comfort.
✉ info@sundaypond.com ◗ www.sundaypond.com

SARATOGA SPRINGS

Batcheller Mansion Inn	145-435 BB	Continental Mon-Fri, off
20 Circular St 12866	9 rooms, 9 pb	season
800-616-7012 518-584-7012	Visa, MC, AmEx	Wireless Internet, TV, phone,
J. Michael Taylor	C-ltd/S-no/P-no/H-no	refrigerator, robes, irons &
		boards, concierge services

A Saratoga Springs New York Bed and Breakfast Inn, The Batcheller Mansion Inn has a notable history. Built in 1873 by George Sherman Batcheller, it sits majestically on the corner of Circular Street and Whitney Place.
✉ mail@batchellermansioninn.com ◐ www.batchellermansioninn.com

Chestnut Tree Inn	BB	Continental plus breakfast
9 Whitney Pl 12866	7 rooms, 7 pb	Afternoon tea, lemonade,
866-427-0838 518-587-8681	Visa, MC	complimentary wine, snacks
Cathleen & Bruce DeLuke	C-ltd/S-no/P-no/H-no	Sitting room, antiques, porch,
	May through October	spas, A/C

Restored turn-of-the-century guesthouse. Walk to racetrack & downtown. Furnished with antiques; large wraparound porch furnished with wicker. All rooms have private baths and air-conditioning.
◐ www.chestnuttreeinn.net

Fox 'n' Hound B&B	157-400 BB	Gourmet Breakfast
142 Lake Ave 12866	5 rooms, 5 pb	Beverages & snacks in the
866-369-1913 518-584-5959	Visa, MC	afternoon
Marlena Sacca	C-ltd/S-ltd/P-no/H-no	Sitting room with fireplace,
		music room with piano and
		games, swimming pool

Fox 'n' Hound B&B is a 1904 Breezee Victorian masterpiece built for prominent Saratoga banker, J. Wagman. In walking distance to most of Saratoga's attractions, it offers old world elegance with modern amenities, comfort, privacy and European hospitality.
✉ innkeeper@foxnhoundbandb.com ◐ www.foxnhoundbandb.com

Saratoga Arms	195-625 BB	Full breakfast
497 Broadway 12866	31 rooms, 31 pb	There are many restaurants
518-584-1775	Most CC, *Rated*	within walking distance from
Noel & Kathleen Smith	C-ltd/S-no/P-no/H-yes	the inn.
		Private bath, TV, telephone,
		voice mail, data ports, air
		conditioning

In the heart of historic downtown district, near shopping, restaurants, and museums. Award winning, 31 room, concierge hotel. Ideal for meetings, business and leisure travelers. Famous horse racing takes place just steps from our beautiful inn. Join us!
✉ ASmith@SaratogaArms.com ◐ www.SaratogaArms.com

Westchester House B&B	140-470 BB	Continental Plus breakfast
102 Lincoln Ave 12866	7 rooms, 7 pb	Complimentary beverages,
888-302-1717 518-587-7613	Most CC, *Rated*, ●	snacks
Bob & Stephanie Melvin	C-ltd/S-ltd/P-no/H-no	Fireplace, guest fridge, in-
	French, German	room phones w/voice mail,
	April thru November	data ports, WiFi

Gracious, Queen Anne Victorian Inn surrounded by old fashioned gardens. Elegant bedrooms combine old world ambience with modern comforts. Walk to all Saratoga Springs' attractions. Wireless Internet available.
✉ innkeeper@westchesterhousebandb.com ◐ www.westchesterhousebandb.com

SCHROON LAKE

Silver Spruce Inn	100-150 BB	Full breakfast
2005 Rt 9 12870	8 rooms, 8 pb	Porch, dining room, parlor,
518-532-7031	Visa, MC	perennial gardens, gazebo
Phyliss Rogers	C-ltd/S-no/P-no/H-ltd	

The Silver Spruce Inn is a spacious Adirondack country home, rich in local history with large, very nicely appointed and tastefully decorated guestrooms.
✉ info@silverspruce.com ◐ www.silverspruce.com

SHARON SPRINGS

Clausen Farms B&B Inn Rt 20 13459 518-573-2527 518-284-2527 Tim & Kathy Spofford	105-175 BB 13 rooms, 13 pb Most CC C-yes/S-no/P-no/H-ltd May through October	Full breakfast Afternoon and evening refreshments

The ninety mile views from Clausen Farms over the Mohawk Valley into the Adirondacks and the Green Mountains of Vermont are just as beautiful today as they were in 1890 when Henry Clausen, Jr. purchased the property.
✉ spoft@aol.com ✆ www.clausenfarmsbandb.com

Edgefield B&B 153 Washington St 13459 518-284-3339 Daniel M. Wood	135-205 BB 5 rooms, 5 pb Cash, Checks, • C-yes/S-no/P-no/H-no May – November	Full breakfast Afternoon tea, complimentary evening refreshments Living room, veranda, fireplace, friendly host & cat

A well-appointed Edwardian home in historic village near Cooperstown & Glimmerglass Opera. Comfortable, elegant English country-house decor, antiques. Five guestrooms (queen or twin), private baths.
✉ info@edgefieldbb.com ✆ www.edgefieldbb.com

SILVER CREEK

Pinewoods Cottage B&B 11634 York Rd 14136 716-934-4173 Estelle M. Crino	85-150 BB 4 rooms, 4 pb Visa, MC C-yes/S-ltd/P-no/H-ltd Closed from 12/15-4/15	Full breakfast Snacks, 3 course Victorian tea in Lavender and Lace room. Sitting room, fireplaces, DirecTV

Surrounded by woodlands and walking trails. Beautifully appointed bedrooms with private baths, queen beds, A/C. An eclectic atmosphere of antiques and family history. Gourmet breakfast daily.
✉ emcrino@gmail.com ✆ crinopinewoodscottage.com

SILVER SPRINGS

Little Bit of Heaven 21 S Main St 14550 585-493-2434 Donald Kemp	75-98 BB 4 rooms, 4 pb Visa, MC, Disc C-yes/S-no/P-no/H-no	Four Course Breakfast Snacks A/C, ceiling fans, cable TV/VCR, sitting room, enclosed porches, formal dining room, turndown service

The elegant & charming Little Bit of Heaven Bed and Breakfast is a beautiful 1893 Victorian home, located only 7 miles from the Castile entrance to Letchworth State Park and close to Houghton College, Geneseo University, and Swain Ski Area.
✉ kempdl@yahoo.com ✆ www.littlebitofheaven.net

SKANEATELES

1899 Lady of the Lake 2 W Lake St 13152 888-685-7997 315-685-7997 Sandra Rademacher	132-175 BB 3 rooms, 3 pb Most CC C-ltd/S-no/P-yes/H-no	Gourmet breakfast Complimentary bottled water, soda & beer Sitting room, porch, library, cable TV & DVD in guestrooms, complimentary Internet access

An elegant 19th century Queen Anne Victorian located in the heart of this historic village, on the shore of Skaneateles Lake.
✉ sandra@ladyofthelake.net ✆ www.ladyofthelake.net

A Butler's Manor, Southampton, NY

SKANEATELES

Benjamin Porter House
10 State St 13152
315-685-3191
Katherine Burke

225-275 BB
3 rooms, 3 pb
Most CC, •
C-ltd/S-no/P-ltd/H-yes

Full breakfast
Requests encouraged,
afternoon tea
Patio, fountain, garden, pond,
fireplaces

The Benjamin Porter House is located in the heart of Skaneateles, a minute walk from the lake, shopping, restaurants, and all the charms a small village has to offer. The home is surrounded by tall maple trees, a stream and a pond.
✉ info@benjaminporterhouse.com ○ www.benjaminporterhouse.com

SOUTHAMPTON

A Butler's Manor
244 N Main St 11968
631-283-8550
Chris & Kim Allen

160-599 BB
5 rooms, 5 pb
Visa, MC, AmEx,
Rated, •
C-ltd/S-no/P-no/H-no
French
March – December

Full breakfast
Complimentary homemade
cookies and sherry in the
rooms
Shuttle service to and from
the village beaches; rose
garden, patio, pool, library

An elegant Colonial house, A Butler's Manor takes its name from Christopher's profession. A proper British butler, his personal service along with Kim's attention to detail will make your stay an experience in hospitality you won't soon forget.
✉ innkeepers@abutlersmanor.com ○ www.abutlersmanor.com

SOUTHOLD

Acorn Hollow B&B
2110 Oaklawn Ave 11971
631-765-1234
Robert & Mary Ann Skoblicki

175-265 BB
3 rooms, 3 pb
Visa, MC, AmEx
C-ltd/S-no/P-no/H-no

Full breakfast
Refreshments on arrival,
afternoon tea, shared guest
refrigerator with
complimentary bottled water
Concierge service; free
wireless Internet; beach
passes, chairs & towels

Located in the midst of the beautiful Long Island (North Fork) Wine Region in NY. Close to beaches. Our high quality accommodations and intimate setting lend themselves to rest, relaxation & romance all year. Private baths, whirlpool tubs & fireplaces.
✉ acrnhllw@optonline.net ○ www.acornhollowbandb.com

ST. JOHNSVILLE

Inn by the Mill
1679 Mill Rd 13452
866-568-2388 518-568-2388
Ron and Judith Hezel

150-375 BB
5 rooms, 5 pb
Visa, MC, AmEx, *Rated*
C-ltd/S-no/P-no/H-ltd
5/1-11/1; winter breaks

Deluxe Continental Breakfast
Unlimited 24/7
complimentary ice cream,
gourmet desserts
Sitting room, library,
fireplaces, bicycles, waterfall,
gardens, hot tub, smoke-free,
WiFi, AC

Welcome to Inn by the Mill, a romantic upscale bed & breakfast, located in upstate-central New York! Historical 1835 stone grist mill, miller's home, flower and water gardens, elegant rooms & private baths. Your vacation will be flawless. Free ice cream!
✉ stay@innbythemill.com ✪ www.innbythemill.com

STONE RIDGE

Baker's B&B
24 Old Kings Hwy 12484
888-623-5513 845-687-9795
Doug Baker & Linda Delgado
Baker

108-178 BB
5 rooms, 5 pb
Visa, MC
C-ltd/S-no/P-no/H-no
Spanish

Gourmet breakfast
Sitting room, suites,
fireplaces, sun room

Built in 1780, this stone farmhouse sits on 14 acres in the beautiful Mid-Hudson Region of New York State with spectacular views of the Shawangunk Mountains, streams and the open fields of a 500 acre farm. Celebrating our 30th year!
✉ bakersbandb@aol.com ✪ www.bakersbandb.com

The Inn at Stone Ridge
3805 Main St 12484
845-687-0736
Dan & Suzanne Hauspurg

195-395 BB
11 rooms, 9 pb
Most CC, *Rated*
C-ltd/S-no/P-no/H-ltd

Full breakfast
Restaurant & bar
Some fireplaces, Jacuzzis,
fine dining, vacation rental

18th century Dutch Colonial mansion set on 150 acres in rural Ulster County, NY, where the Hudson meets the Catskill Mountains. Available as a large private house, by suite or by room. Full service restaurant & bar. Only 95 mi. from NYC.
✉ info@innatstoneridge.com ✪ www.innatstoneridge.com

Victorian Knoll B&B
30 Peak Farm Rd 12484
866-262-0100 845-687-9639
Patti & Tom Habersaat

150-200 BB
3 rooms, 3 pb
Visa, MC
C-ltd/S-no/P-no/H-ltd

Full breakfast
Afternoon tea
Verandah, pond, gazebo,
gardens, Jacuzzi, parlor,
dining area

Victorian Knoll offers you access to a vast array of excellent dining, historical, cultural & natural entertainment adventures. Let the charm of a bygone era embrace you today & throughout the year.
✉ info@victorianknoll.com ✪ www.victorianknoll.com

SYRACUSE

Bed & Breakfast Wellington
707 Danforth St 13208
800-724-5006 315-474-3641
Wendy Wilber & Ray Borg

125-160 BB
5 rooms, 4 pb
Most CC, •
C-yes/S-no/P-no/H-no

Full breakfast on weekends
Continental plus weekdays,
afternoon tea, special diets
accommodated
Scent-free fluffy towels,
robes, TV/VCRs, phone, free
WiFi, central air conditioning

1914 Arts & Crafts style home currently on the National & New York State Register of Historic properties. 2006 Finalist, NYS Hospitality & Tourism Association "Bed & Breakfast of Distinction." Help Us Celebrate Our 20th Year of Premier Service.
✉ innkeepers@bbwellington.com ✪ www.bbwellington.com

TRUMANSBURG

Halsey House B&B
2057 Trumansburg Rd 14886
800-387-5590 607-387-5428
KC Christopher & Mitch
Clarke

189-279 BB
5 rooms, 5 pb
Visa, MC
C-ltd/S-ltd/P-no/H-ltd

Full breakfast
Game room, library,
TV/DVD/VCR, A/C, wireless
Internet access, plush
bathrobes

A Federal style historic mansion located in the Finger Lakes region of New York. Stunning scenery, expansive lakes, gorges, waterfalls and scenic wine trails surround us. A perfect romantic, restful getaway featuring luxury and comfort.
✉ kc@halseyhouse.com ◐ www.halseyhouse.com

Juniper Hill B&B
16 Elm St 14886
888-809-1367 607-387-3044
Bruce Digenti & David
Kuranda

155-299 BB
4 rooms, 4 pb
Visa, MC, Disc, *Rated*
C-ltd/S-no/P-no/H-no

Full gourmet breakfast
Snack Buffet: assorted chips,
popcorn, pretzels, fruit, tea,
cocoa, cold drinks, cookies
Wireless Internet, luxury
pillow top mattresses, plush
robes/slippers, inroom flat
screen tv/dvd Lib

Juniper Hill B&B and American Impressionist Art Gallery is nestled on nearly four acres and is within easy walking distance to the Main Street of Trumansburg, NY. Juniper Hill B&B offers quiet privacy yet convenient access to Ithaca shops and fine dining.
✉ info@AtJuniperHill.com ◐ www.AtJuniperHill.com

UNADILLA

Westwood Guest Cottage
286 Fred Braun Rd 13849
212-579-9685
Lisa Moskowitz & Doren Slade

165-185 EP
1 rooms, 1 pb
Visa, MC, AmEx,
Rated, •
C-yes/S-ltd/P-yes/H-no
Spanish
May – November

Full kitchen and outside grill
Living room, monitor/VCR
with tapes, linens, picnic
area, 20'x40' pool, canoe

Private 2-bedroom hideaway with fully equipped kitchen, nestled on 11 acres of woods. Near Oneonta & Cooperstown. Charming antiques, patio, grill, pool and phone. Relax and explore. $25 pet fee for entire stay.
✉ westwoodguestcottage@nyc.rr.com ◐ www.westwoodguestcottage.com

UTICA

Adam Bowman Manor
197 Riverside Dr 13502
877-724-7268 315-724-7266
Marion & Barry Goodwin

85-95 BB
4 rooms, 2 pb
Visa, MC, *Rated*, •
C-yes/S-no/P-no/H-yes
Some Italian & German

Full Country Breakfast
Sitting room, A/C, fountain,
quaint gazebo, lush
landscaping

Nestled in the foothills of the Adirondacks beside the Erie Canal, this historic 1823 brick Federal Manor offers the elegance once enjoyed by the Duke & Duchess of Windsor.
✉ bargood@yahoo.com

The Pratt Smith House
10497 Cosby Manor Rd 13502
315-732-8483
Anne & Alan Frederick

75 BB
2 rooms, 2 pb
Rated
C-yes/S-no/P-no/H-no

Full breakfast
Cable TV, sitting room

1815 brick Colonial, wide plank floors, antiques; set on 22 acres in a woodsy residential area convenient to city, area attractions, NY's thruway.
✉ alannem@roadrunner.com

UTICA

Rosemont Inn B&B
1423 Genesee St 13501
866-353-4907 315-790-9315
Rita & Bob Sleys

109-209 BB
7 rooms, 7 pb
Most CC, *Rated*
C-ltd/S-no/P-no/H-no
Italian, Spanish

Full breakfast
Cold & hot drinks and
snacks can be found in the
main hall. Afternoon tea
available.
Double parlor, library,
wireless Internet access

The Inn is a wonderful place to relax and unwind. Rosemont Inn offers travelers the warmth and security of returning to a homelike atmosphere after a long day's journey.
✉ stay@rosemontinnbb.com ◐ www.rosemontinnbb.com

WARRENSBURG

Cornerstone Victorian B&B
3921 Main St 12885
518-623-3308
Doug & Louise Goettsche

99-199 BB
5 rooms, 5 pb
Most CC, •
C-ltd/S-no/P-no/H-no
German

Five-course Gourmet
Breakfast
Homemade dessert daily, 24-
hour beverage pantry
Sitting rooms, WiFi, cable TV,
fireplace, wraparound porch,
small library

Awarded Arrington's #1 "Best B&B Breakfast," Lanier's "Inn of the Year, 2004." Grand Victorian with gleaming woodwork & perennial gardens. Delightful rooms, some with Jacuzzi or fireplace. Near Lake George, Saratoga Springs & Gore Mountain Ski Area.
✉ stay@cornerstonevictorian.com ◐ www.cornerstonevictorian.com

Country Road Lodge
115 Hickory Hill Rd 12885
518-623-2207
Steve & Sandi Parisi

102-112 BB
4 rooms, 4 pb
Cash, Checks, •
C-ltd/S-no/P-no/H-no

Full breakfast
Lemonade, iced/hot teas,
and coffee available at all
times. Fresh muffins (chef's
choice) at 7 AM.
Scenic sitting room with
Franklin stove, books,
screened gazebo, perennial
garden paths. Free WiFi.

A cedar-shingled cottage at the end of a country road. Idyllic setting on the Hudson River in the Adirondack foothills, near Lake George. Sociable hosts. No traffic or TV. Common room with comfortable seating, Franklin stove. Perennial gardens, birds.
✉ mail@countryroadlodge.com ◐ www.countryroadlodge.com

The Glen Lodge B&B
1123 Route 28 12885
800-867-2335 518-494-4984
Aimee & Douglas Azaert

118-129 BB
8 rooms, 8 pb
Visa, MC
C-yes/S-no/P-no/H-yes

Full breakfast
Sauna, large porches, quiet
sitting room, stone fireplace
and air conditioning.

Take in the beauty and nature of the Adirondack Mountains of Upstate New York, at The Glen Lodge & Market. From the beautiful stone fireplace to the Adirondack styled cedar wood furniture, we invite you to indulge yourself in total relaxation and comfort.
✉ info@TheGlenLodge.com ◐ www.theglenlodge.com

Seasons B&B
3822 Main St 12885
518-623-3832
Eileen M. Frasier

125-199 BB
5 rooms, 3 pb
Visa, MC, •
C-ltd/S-no/P-no/H-no

Full breakfast
Afternoon tea/coffee with
sweets, evening beverages
available
Personal robes, hairdryers,
cable TV, A/C; massage
therapist available, WiFi

Italian-villa style residence, c.1830, with comfortable, unique accommodations. The house is situated at the top of a small hill & mostly surrounded by a dense landscape of trees & evergreens. A four season location with many year round events.
✉ eileen@seasons-bandb.com ◐ www.seasons-bandb.com

WARWICK

Brass Rose Inn
29 Main St 10990
845-986-5603
Alice Lerro

95-160 BB
4 rooms, 4 pb
Visa, MC, Disc
C-yes/S-no/P-no

Full breakfast
Rooms have A/C, cable TV,
coffee makers. In room
massages are available.
Wireless Internet.

Brass Rose Inn, a restored one hundred-year-old brick building, is located on Main Street in the Historic Village of Warwick. The Inn is surrounded by many quaint shops, wineries & great restaurants. ✉ brassroseinn@aol.com ✹ www.brassroseinn.com

Peach Grove Inn
205 Route 17A 10990
845-986-7411
John & Lucy Mastropierro

140-225 BB
6 rooms, 6 pb
Visa, MC, AmEx
C-ltd/S-no/P-no/H-ltd

Full breakfast
Afternoon tea
Fireplaces, whirlpool tubs,
central AC, some rooms with
TV/VCR/DVD

The Peach Grove Inn is one of the most majestic lodgings in the lower Hudson Valley, with richly appointed antiques, spacious private rooms and baths, Jacuzzis, and more. ✉ peachgrv@warwick.net ✹ www.peachgroveinn.net

Warwick Valley
24 Maple Ave 10990
888-280-1671 845-987-7255
Loretta Breedveld

120-185 BB
6 rooms, 6 pb
Most CC, •
C-ltd/S-ltd/P-no/H-no

Full breakfast
Sitting room, bicycles,
fireplace, TV, covered porch,
DSL, copier, video & book
library

Begin discovering the Hudson Valley along the historic tree-lined district of Warwick in upstate New York. The Warwick Valley B&B Inn provides guests with the comfort and warmth of an elegant home setting with hospitality at its finest! ✉ loretta@warwick.net ✹ www.wvbedandbreakfast.com

WATERLOO

Through the Grapevine B&B
108 Virginia St 13165
866-272-1270 315-539-8620
Michael & Joan Smith

100-110 BB
2 rooms, 2 pb
Most CC
C-yes/S-ltd/P-no/H-no

Full breakfast
Sitting room, spas, fireplaces

Our charming 1870 Italianate is your own private retreat, offering a gourmet breakfast and fresh home-roasted and ground coffee. We are convenient to Finger Lakes, wineries and fine restaurants. ✉ thegrapevine4@aol.com ✹ www.throughthegrapevinebnb.com

WEST WINFIELD

The Old Stone House
588 State route 51 13491
315-822-6748
Susan Huxtable

120-185 BB
3 rooms, 1 pb
Cash, Checks
C-ltd/S-no/P-no/H-ltd
May – October

Full breakfast
Freshly brewed gourmet
coffee, muffins or coffee
cake, afternoon tea.
A music room, living room,
dining room, and screened-
in-verandah are available

Enjoy the quiet pastoral, rural setting of the historic Old Stone House Bed and Breakfast (1830), a beautiful Georgian three story quarried limestone home adjacent to the Chepachet Mill Pond. ✉ oldstonehousebb@aol.com ✹ www.theoldstonehousebb.com

Southern Comfort
658 Forks Road 13491
315-822-6991
Pamela Andela

100-185 BB
3 rooms, 1 pb
Visa, MC, Disc
C-ltd/S-no/P-no/H-no

5 course southern breakfast
A/C, wireless Internet.
Massage and hairstylist
available.

Southern hospitality mixed with Victorian charm is what you'll receive when you stay at the Southern Comfort B&B. ✉ Pva956@cs.com ✹ www.southerncomfort-bed-and-breakfast.com

WESTFIELD

The William Seward Inn	98-235 BB	Full breakfast
6645 S. Portage Rd. 394 14787	12 rooms, 12 pb	Fine dining restaurant with
800-338-4151 716-326-4151	Most CC, *Rated*, •	casual atmosphere
Jane and Charles Breeding	C-ltd/S-no/P-yes/H-yes	in room massage, whirlpool,
		fireplaces, restaurant,
		library, wireless Internet
		access in all rooms

Located in the heart of Chautauqua County, NY, minutes from Chautauqua Institution. This finely restored 1837 country inn is a destination for many travelers seeking tranquility and relaxation with fine dining and luxury accommodations.
✉ innkeeper@williamsewardinn.com ◐ www.williamsewardinn.com

WESTHAMPTON BEACH

1880 Seafield House B&B	150-250 BB	Full breakfast
2 Seafield Ln 11978	3 rooms, 3 pb	Complimentary sherry and
800-346-3290 631-288-1559	Most CC, *Rated*, •	muffins
Elsie Collins	C-yes/S-no/P-no/H-no	Sitting room, piano, tennis
		court, library, pool

Built back in 1880, this Victorian home is conveniently located in the village of Westhampton Beach, on Long Island, near some of the finest shops and restaurants. This exquisite bed and breakfast features two guest suites complete with private baths.
✉ elsie.collins@verizon.net ◐ www.1880seafieldhouse.com

WESTPORT

The Inn on the Library Lawn	80-210 EP	TV/VCR in room, Free
1234 Stevenson Rd 12993	10 rooms, 10 pb	wireless high speed Internet
888-577-7748 518-962-8666	Most CC, *Rated*	access, Cafe and Bookstore
Anthony & Alexandra	S-ltd/P-no/H-no	on site.
Wheeler		

Elegant Victorian inn with period decor & furnishings. Lake Champlain views. Walk to restaurants, marina, beach, golf, theater & shopping.
✉ innmail@hotmail.com ◐ www.theinnonthelibrarylawn.com

WINDHAM

Albergo Allegria	83-299 BB	Full gourmet breakfast
#43 Rt 296 12496	22 rooms, 22 pb	Complimentary guest pantry
518-734-5560	Visa, MC, *Rated*, •	(24 hrs)
Lenore & Vito Radelich	C-yes/S-no/P-no/H-yes	Sitting room, fireplaces,
	Croatian, Italian	cable TV/VCR, videos, bikes
		& tennis (fee)

Highly awarded 1892 Victorian mansion nestled in the northern Catskill Mountains. Set on 2 acres of manicured lawns & country gardens. Voted 2000 Inn of the Year!
✉ mail@albergousa.com ◐ www.AlbergoUSA.com

WOODSTOCK

Enchanted Manor of	165-325 BB	Full breakfast
Woodstock	4 rooms, 4 pb	Tea, wine, fruit, vegan and
23 Rowe Rd 12401	Visa, MC, Disc, •	vegetarian available
845-679-9012	C-ltd/S-no/P-ltd/H-no	Heated pool, outdoor hot
Claudia & Rolan		tub, massage therapy, gym,
		steam room, Jacuzzi tubs

Elegant yet comfortable home with beautiful furnishings, on eight storybook acres. Extraordinary 6-level deck overlooking pond; cascading waterfall; serenity and peace.
✉ enchantedmanor@aol.com ◐ www.enchantedmanorinn.com

Tell your hosts Pamela Lanier sent you.

WOODSTOCK

Twin Gables of Woodstock
73 Tinker St 12498
845-679-9479
Henrique Tischler

89-140 BB
9 rooms, 3 pb
Most CC, *Rated*
C-ltd/S-no/P-no/H-no

Continental breakfast
Parlor to sit, relax, and
socialize; front patio to enjoy
a beautiful day

Twin Gables Guest Home is a Woodstock landmark, known for its relaxed, friendly atmosphere and charming ambience. Woodstock attracts visitors from all over the world. Come explore this "most famous small town in the world."
✉ info@twingableswoodstockny.com ◑ www.twingableswoodstockny.com

---

The Wild Rose Inn
66 Rock City Rd 12498
845-679-8783
Ms. Marti Ladd

175-275 BB
5 rooms, 5 pb
Visa, MC
C-yes/S-no/P-no/H-no

Continental plus breakfast
Complimentary brandy and
truffles in each room
Jacuzzis, suites, cable TV,
accommodate business
travel, garden, free WiFi,
swimming pool

Award-winning gingerbread mansion in the heart of town. Elegant accommodations with superior amenities for a romantic get-away.
✉ wildrosebb@aol.com ◑ www.thewildroseinn.com

**The Woodstock Inn on the
Millstream**
48 Tannery Brook Rd 12498
800-420-4707 845-679-8211
Karen Pignataro

129-245 BB
18 rooms, 18 pb
Visa, MC, AmEx, *Rated*
C-yes/S-no/P-no/H-ltd
Italian, French

Bountiful Continental
Breakfast
HBO, A/C, stream, private
pond for recreational use,
continental breakfast, free
WiFi

Your retreat in the heart of Woodstock. Relax by the stream or amidst our exquisite gardens, sunny lawns and towering pines, then stroll into the lively village of Woodstock for shopping, dining, and galleries.
✉ info@woodstock-inn-ny.com ◑ www.woodstock-inn-ny.com

YOUNGSTOWN

Cameo Inn
3881 Lower River Rd 14174
716-745-3034
Greg & Carolyn Fisher

85-180 BB
4 rooms, 2 pb
Visa, MC, *Rated*, •
C-ltd/S-ltd/P-no/H-no

Full breakfast
Library, piano, great room,
cable TV in suites, VCR/DVD,
in-room clock radios,
wireless Internet

Choose our secluded English manor house on three acres along the Niagara river for that quiet getaway you deserve! On the Seaway Trail, close to all attractions, minutes north of Niagara Falls. Offering suites, fireplaces, piano, great room and a library.
✉ info@cameoinn.com ◑ www.cameoinn.com

North Carolina

Inn at the Bryant House
214 N Poplar St 28315
800-453-4019 910-944-3300
Ashley & Matt Baker & Shir

99-139 BB
8 rooms, 6 pb
Most CC
C-ltd/S-no/P-no/H-ltd

Full breakfast
Social hour with tea,
lemonade and homemade
snacks
Fax and other business
services, weddings, sitting,
dining & living rooms,
antiques, bath amenities

Many activities and points of interest in the Pinehurst area will add pleasure to your stay at the Inn at the Bryant House. Full gourmet breakfast each morning. We look forward to your visit with us.
✉ innatbryanthouse@yahoo.com 🜚 www.innatbryanthouse.com

B&B Country Garden Inn
1041 Kelly Rd 27523
800-251-3171 919-303-8003
Bud & Beth McKinney

100-150 BB
3 rooms, 3 pb
Most CC
C-yes/S-no/P-no/H-no

Full breakfast
Afternoon tea, snacks
Sitting room, Jacuzzis, suites,
cable, gazebo, fishing

Our secluded, cozy inn is perfect for a romantic weekend getaway, on eight plus acres of ponds and gardens in the North Carolina countryside. Convenient to Research Triangle Park and the Triangle area. Wine tastings, weddings, retreats and events hosted.
✉ inn@budnbeth.com 🜚 www.bnbcountrygardeninn.com

1889 WhiteGate Inn & Cottage
173 E Chestnut St 28801
800-485-3045 828-253-2553
Ralph Coffey & Frank Salvo

125-419 BB
11 rooms, 11 pb
Visa, MC, AmEx, *Rated*
C-ltd/S-ltd/P-ltd/H-yes

Full 3-course gourmet
breakfast
Evening refreshments
Award-winning gardens,
parlor, fireplaces, games, koi
pond, solarium

Circa 1889 shingle-style house, surrounded by beautifully landscaped grounds with a greenhouse/conservatory filled with orchids & tropical plants.
✉ innkeeper@whitegate.net 🜚 www.whitegate.net

1899 Black Walnut B&B
288 Montford Ave 28801
800-381-3878 828-254-3878
Peter & Lori White

195-285 BB
8 rooms, 8 pb
Visa, MC, AmEx, *Rated*
C-ltd/S-no/P-yes/H-yes

Full gourmet breakfast
Afternoon tea at 5:30, wine,
cheese, hors d'oeuvres,
pastries, complimentary
guest beverages
Living room, koi ponds,
terrace & porch, reading &
movie library, VCR en-suite

Historic property, beautifully restored. Featured in "1000 Places to See Before You Die." Interiors are luxurious, with 8 guestrooms with king or queen beds, fireplaces, private baths en suite, newly renovated carriage house.
✉ info@blackwalnut.com 🜚 www.blackwalnut.com

ASHEVILLE

A Hill House B&B Inn	120-260 BB	Full breakfast
120 Hillside St 28801	9 rooms, 9 pb	Afternoon tea, snacks,
800-379-0002 828-232-0345	Most CC, *Rated*, •	sweets on pillow
Bill & Terry Erickson	C-ltd/S-no/P-no/H-no	Sitting room, Jacuzzi, suites,
	German	fireplace, cable TV, WiFi,
		wrap around porch, fitness
		studio

Hill House Bed and Breakfast in Asheville is renowned for its comfortable, casual feel. As such, we enjoy taking care of our guests and strive to provide those special touches — from exceptionally restful beds to delightful breakfasts.
✉ info@hillhousebb.com 🌐 www.hillhousebb.com

Albemarle Inn	130-370 BB	Full gourmet breakfast
86 Edgemont Rd 28801	11 rooms, 11 pb	Afternoon refreshments
800-621-7435 828-255-0027	Visa, MC, AmEx,	Concierge, Wireless Internet,
Cathy & Larry Sklar	*Rated*, •	In-room massages, sitting
	C-ltd/S-no/P-no/H-no	room, sun porch, veranda,
		English garden

AAA four-diamond rated. Elegant 1907 Greek Revival mansion on landscaped grounds in the residential Grove Park section of Asheville. Features exquisite carved oak staircase & spacious guestrooms with luxurious linens, robes and amenities.
✉ info@albemarleinn.com 🌐 www.albemarleinn.com

Applewood Manor Inn B&B	150-225 BB	Full breakfast
62 Cumberland Circle 28801-1718	6 rooms, 6 pb	Afternoon complimentary
800-442-2197 828-254-2244	Most CC, *Rated*	refreshments from 5–6 pm
Nancy & Larry Merrill	C-ltd/S-ltd/P-ltd/H-no	Sitting room, suites,
	Spanish	fireplaces, fresh flowers,
		chocolates, balconies, arbor
		with swing

Welcome to Applewood Manor Inn B&B! Your new hosts Larry and Nancy Merrill will make your trip to Asheville, cozy and comfortable. Their beautiful Inn will bring you the comforts of home and hospitality fit for royalty!
✉ innkeeper@applewoodmanor.com 🌐 www.applewoodmanor.com

At Cumberland Falls B&B	145-260 BB	Three course candlelit
254 Cumberland Ave 28801	6 rooms, 6 pb	gourmet
888-743-2557 828-253-4085	Visa, MC, Disc, *Rated*,	Afternoon tea, snacks,
Patti & Gary Wiles	•	complimentary wine and
	C-ltd/S-no/P-no/H-no	cheese on Saturday by
	Spanish	request.
		Jacuzzis, fireplaces, cable,
		corporate travelers,
		concierge services, free WiFi

We are a turn-of-the-century home located in Historic Asheville. Our home features waterfalls and magnificent gardens, Jacuzzis and fireplaces. Totally renovated property insures your comfort. Concierge services complete with printed directions.
✉ fallsinn@aol.com 🌐 www.cumberlandfalls.com/trackhomepage.php?ListingSite=travelguides

Bent Creek Lodge	135-185 BB	Full breakfast
10 Parkway Crescent 28704	10 rooms, 10 pb	Afternoon snacks, dinner by
877-231-6574 828-654-9040	Visa, MC, Disc, •	reservation for groups of 6 or
Doug & Jodee Sellers	C-ltd/S-no/P-no/H-yes	more
		Walking trails, pool table,
		gardens, concierge service,
		two sitting rooms with
		satellite TV, lodge

Stay in the heart of the mountains you came to see in this elegantly, rustic lodge, only yards from the Blue Ridge Parkway and 10 miles from downtown Asheville. Enjoy the mountain views, the fireplace, the scrumptious breakfast, & hiking trails on site.
✉ bentcreek@ioa.com 🌐 www.bentcreeknc.com

Chestnut Street Inn, Asheville, NC

ASHEVILLE

Biltmore Village Inn
119 Dodge St 28803
866-274-8779 828-274-8707
Aaron Hazelton

220-325 BB
6 rooms, 6 pb
Most CC, *Rated*, •
C-ltd/S-no/P-ltd/H-ltd
Spanish

Full breakfast
Afternoon refreshments
Wireless Internet, concierge

Built by Vanderbilt's lawyer, this Victorian mansion is a landmark on the National Register. Closest Bed & Breakfast to the Biltmore Estate with mountain views, large rooms, private baths Jacuzzi tubs, fireplaces, wireless, DVD players, flat screen tvs.
✉ info@biltmorevillageinn.com 🌐 www.biltmorevillageinn.com

Bridle Path Inn
30 Lookout Rd 28804
828-252-0035
Carol & Fred Halton

105-150 BB
8 rooms, 8 pb
Visa, MC, AmEx
C-yes/S-ltd/P-no/H-yes

Full breakfast
Dinner by great cooks, picnic
baskets
Sitting room, verandah,
hiking trails

The Inn is comfortable, quaint & secluded on a hill overlooking downtown Asheville. Enjoy an elegant, full breakfast in front of the fireplace in winter or in summer on the wide verandah . . . savoring the moment . . . while viewing the surrounding mountains.
✉ Innkeeper@BridlePathInn.com 🌐 www.BridlePathInn.com

Chestnut Street Inn
176 E Chestnut St 28801
800-894-2955 828-285-0705
LaDonna and Joe Lasko

129-249 BB
8 rooms, 8 pb
Visa, MC, AmEx, *Rated*
C-ltd/S-no/P-no/H-no

Full breakfast
Wine & Cheese Fri.& Sat.
night 5–7 Soda, Hot Tea,
Coco & beer always
available. Afternoon sweet
Wireless Internet service,
XM radio, satellite TV,
Jacuzzi tubs, fireplaces, large
front porch

The Chestnut Street Inn is an easy walk or drive to downtown Asheville. This 1905 Colonial Revival home is an architectural delight featuring the original staircase with a "courting bench," ornate mantels, high ceilings, and large porches.
✉ innkeeper@chestnutstreetinn.com 🌐 www.chestnutstreetinn.com

ASHEVILLE

Corner Oak Manor
53 Saint Dunstans Rd 28803
888-633-3525 828-253-3525
Karen & Andy Spradley

135-195 BB
4 rooms, 4 pb
Most CC, *Rated*, •
C-ltd/S-no/P-no/H-no

Full breakfast
Snacks
Sitting room, A/C, fireplace,
cottage has TV & fireplace

Elegant & comfortable; full gourmet breakfast; queen size beds; outdoor deck; flowers/chocolates. 1920 English Tudor located near the Historic Biltmore House & Gardens.
✉ corneroak@aol.com 🌐 www.corneroakmanor.com

The Lion and The Rose
276 Montford Ave 28801
800-546-6988 828-255-7673
Jim & Linda Palmer

140-225 BB
5 rooms, 5 pb
Most CC, *Rated*
C-ltd/S-no/P-no/H-no

Full breakfast
Tea/coffee, snacks, soft
drinks & bottled
water—available 24 hours a
day.
Antiques & art, large sloping
lawn, two parlors, fireplaces,
Jacuzzi, cable, DVD players

Beautiful Georgian Mansion, leaded/stained glass & antiques throughout. Sumptuous gourmet breakfast, morning coffee/tea delivered to your door. In Montford Historic District. Walking distance to downtown Asheville.
✉ info@lion-rose.com 🌐 www.lion-rose.com

North Lodge on Oakland
84 Oakland Rd 28801
800-282-3602
Greg Adkins

120-180 BB
6 rooms, 6 pb
Visa, MC
C-ltd/S-no/P-no/H-no

Gourmet three-course
breakfast
Guest refrigerator with
complimentary bottled
waters and sodas, snack
pantry & freshly baked
cookies
Gardens with lighted gazebo
& fountain, in-room
massages available,
concierge assistance

Visiting Asheville? Looking for relaxation and convenience? Come to North Lodge and enjoy the peace and serenity of this 1904 house, nestled on an acre of gardens and featuring six tastefully appointed guestrooms.
✉ stay@northlodge.com 🌐 www.northlodge.com

Oakland Cottage B&B
74 Oakland Rd 28801
866-858-0863 828-994-2627
Mary & Byron Bridges, Jim
Reid, Dusty Pappas

100-150 BB
5 rooms, 5 pb
Most CC
C-yes/S-no/P-ltd/H-no

Full breakfast
WiFi, guest laundry, DVD
library, books & games, crib
& high chair available.

Oakland Cottage a Bed & Breakfast is an Arts & Crafts style historic home, circa 1910. This 5,000 square ft "cottage" has been naturally broken into private & roomy suites. The open common areas & porches create a warm welcoming & spacious feel.
✉ info@VacationInAsheville.com 🌐 www.oaklandcottage.com

Old Reynolds Mansion
100 Reynolds Heights 28804
800-709-0496 828-254-0496
Helen Faber

90-155 BB
12 rooms, 12 pb
Most CC, *Rated*
C-ltd/S-ltd/P-no/H-no
Weekends only

Full breakfast
Snacks, beverage,
complimentary wine
Sitting room, verandahs,
pool, A/C, televisions,
refrigerator, telephone

A restored 1850 Antebellum mansion. Wide verandahs, mountain views, woodburning fireplaces, huge old swimming pool.
✉ innkeeper@oldreynoldsmansion.com 🌐 www.oldreynoldsmansion.com

ASHEVILLE

Pinecrest B&B
249 Cumberland Ave 28801
888-811-3053 828-281-4275
Janna & James Martin & Stacy
Shelley

130-210 BB
5 rooms, 5 pb
Visa, MC, Disc, *Rated*,
•
C-ltd/S-no/P-no/H-no

Full gourmet breakfast
Afternoon tea, snacks,
complimentary wine
Sitting room, library,
fireplaces, TV, sunroom, fine
linens, lush robes, welcome
business travelers

Turn-of-the-century residence with European elegance. A parlor with fireplace, sunroom, and five beautifully appointed guestrooms. Stone patio and landscaped gardens for outdoor enjoyment & relaxation.
✉ innkeeper@pinecrestbb.com ◑ www.pinecrestbb.com

Princess Anne Hotel
301 E Chestnut St 28801
866-552-0986 828-258-0986
Howard Stafford

129-289 BB
16 rooms, 16 pb
Visa, MC, AmEx
C-ltd/S-ltd/P-no/H-ltd

Full breakfast
Coffee and tea/afternoon
wine & hors d'oeuvres
Veranda, parlor, fireplace,
living room, TV, library,
Internet, computer station,
off street parking

Built in 1922 and recently renovated, the Princess Anne Hotel is an historic boutique inn located just minutes to attractions such as the Blue Ridge Parkway, the Biltmore Estate, and downtown Asheville.
✉ info@princessannehotel.com ◑ www.princessannehotel.com

Richmond Hill Inn
87 Richmond Hill Dr 28806
800-545-9238 828-252-7313
Susie Zimmerman

205-615 BB
37 rooms, 37 pb
Visa, MC, AmEx,
Rated, •
C-yes/S-ltd/P-no/H-yes

Full gourmet breakfast
Gourmet restaurant,
afternoon tea
Library, garden rooms, turndown, phone, TV, conference
facilities

Historic 1889 Victorian inn, magnificently renovated, with gracious service and fine dining. Elegant setting for meetings & weddings. AAA Four Diamond, Mobil Four Star, Wine Spectator Award of Excellence.
✉ reservations@richmondhillinn.com ◑ www.richmondhillinn.com

Wright Inn & Carriage House
235 Pearson Dr 28801
800-552-5724 828-251-0789
Barbara & Bob Gilmore

105-235 BB
11 rooms, 11 pb
Most CC, *Rated*, •
C-ltd/S-no/P-no/H-no

Full breakfast
Snacks, complimentary
beverages around the clock,
Friday and Saturday
afternoon social hour
Sitting room, 3 Zone central
A/C, whirlpools, fireplaces,
TVs, wireless Internet,
phones

The Wright Inn & Carriage House represents one of the finest examples of Queen Anne architecture found in the Historic Montford District.
✉ info@wrightinn.com ◑ www.wrightinn.com

BALSAM

Balsam Mountain Inn
68 Seven Springs Dr 28707
800-224-9498 828-456-9498
Kim and Sharon Shailer

145-229 BB
50 rooms, 50 pb
Visa, MC, Disc, *Rated*,
•
C-ltd/S-ltd/P-no/H-yes
French

Full breakfast
Restaurant
Game room, porches, 26
acres, springs,
rhododendron forest

Rest, read, ramble, romp and revel in the easy going hospitality of our Southern mountains. Magical enchantment awaits at our historic inn. Library, mountain views.
✉ balsaminn@earthlink.net ◑ www.balsaminn.com

BANNER ELK

Blueberry Villa and Banner Elk Winery 60 Deer Run Ln 28604 828-898-9099 828-260-1790 Dede Walton & Dick Wolfe	189-289 BB 8 rooms, 8 pb Most CC C-ltd/S-ltd/P-no/H-yes	Full breakfast Complimentary wine tasting at our own Banner Elk Winery Daily Maid Service

Inn, vineyard & winery on 7 acres in the heart of Carolina High Country. Eight distinctive bedrooms with private baths & Jacuzzis. Terrace overlooks private trout pond. Intimate weddings, family retreats, corporate gatherings hosted. On-site catering.
✉ info@blueberryvilla.com ✪ www.blueberryvilla.com

The Inn at Elk River 875 Main Street West 28604 828-898-9669 Sherry & Fred Bowman	95-175 BB 8 rooms, 8 pb C-ltd/S-no/P-ltd/H-no	Full breakfast Evening social hour with fresh baked, homemade goodies, or wine and cheeses. Great room, fireplace, meeting rooms

A Colonial Williamsburg style Inn nestled in the mountains of NC. 8 quaint rooms with either Queen or King beds, 4 with woodburning fireplaces and all have balconies with views of the Elk River Valley. All stays come with our famous full country breakfast
✉ elkriverinn@skybest.com ✪ www.elkriverinn.com

Mountainside Lodge B&B 1709 Broadstone Rd 28604 877-687-4333 828-963-4006 Don & Debbie Jones	120-175 BB 4 rooms, 4 pb Visa, MC C-ltd/S-ltd/P-no/H-ltd	Full breakfast Afternoon appetizers, evening homemade desserts, sodas, ice tea, lemonade, bottled water, and coffees Rock or swing on our 800 square ft. front wrap porch, reading room

The utmost in southern hospitality with spectacular mountain views and serenity awaits you at our rustic and elegant B&B located in historic Valle Crucis.
✉ dondebj@nc.rr.com ✪ www.mountainsidelodgebb.com

BEAUFORT

Anchorage House B&B 211 Turner St 28516 800-934-9968 252-728-9908 Angela Mooring	67-200 BB 6 rooms, 6 pb Most CC, *Rated*, • C-yes/S-no/P-yes/H-ltd	Full breakfast Breakfast in bed ($30), picnic lunch ($9) Wireless Internet, bicycles, key-less entry, late check-ins, some pet friendly rooms.

Historic B&B one and a half blocks from downtown Beaufort and 5 minute drive to area beaches. Walk to the ferries to the horse islands and lighthouse. Open year around and accept government, military, state rates. Lodging includes a full breakfast.
✉ anchoragehouse@ec.rr.com ✪ www.anchoragehouse.net

Captains' Quarters Bed & Biscuit 315 Ann St 28516 800-659-7111 252-728-7711 Ms. Ruby & Captain Dick Collins	80-130 BB 3 rooms, 3 pb Most CC, *Rated* C-ltd/S-ltd/P-no/H-ltd	Full English Style Breakfast "Toast the Sunset" complimentary beverages, Ms. Ruby's famous "Riz" biscuits with breakfast Parlor & formal dining room, fireplaces, ceiling fans, WiFi & fax, courtesy airport shuttle

Our Historic Victorian "Home of Hospitality with Quiet Elegance" located in the heart of the historic district is furnished with family heirlooms & antiques. The wrap-around front Veranda faces South West into the prevailing summer breeze.
✉ captqtrs@coastalnet.com ✪ www.captainsquartersbedandbiscuit.com

BEAUFORT

Pecan Tree Inn	100-190 BB	Continental plus breakfast
116 Queen St 28516	7 rooms, 7 pb	Cold drinks
800-728-7871 252-728-6733	Most CC, *Rated*, •	Jacuzzis, bikes, beach
David & Allison DuBuisson	C-ltd/S-no/P-no/H-ltd	equipment, patio seating,
		large garden, wireless
		Internet

Romantic, antique-filled 1866 Victorian home in the heart of Beaufort's Historic District. A warm & comfortable lodging from which to discover Beaufort, the gem of the southern Outer Banks.
✉ innkeeper@pecantree.com ◐ www.pecantree.com

BELHAVEN

Belhaven Water Street B&B	85-115 BB	Full breakfast
567 E Water St 27810	3 rooms, 3 pb	Complimentary soft drinks &
866-338-2825 252-943-2825	Visa, MC, *Rated*	bottled water are available at
Karen & Andrew Fisher	C-ltd/S-no/P-no/H-yes	anytime in the butler's
		pantry. BYOB
		Front porch with harbor
		view, fireplaces, Jacuzzi,
		wireless Internet. Marina
		Pick Possible!

100-year-old home offers three guestrooms, all with private baths, view of harbor, & working fireplaces. The Belhaven Room features a Jacuzzi. The spacious living room has a cozy fireplace, baby grand piano, books, games, and TV. Butler's Pantry w/drinks
✉ ahfisher@embarqmail.com ◐ www.belhavenwaterstreetbandb.com

BLACK MOUNTAIN

Red Rocker Inn	105-210 BB	Full breakfast buffet
136 N Dougherty St 28711	17 rooms, 17 pb	Afternoon Tea, Coffee, and
888-669-5991 828-669-5991	Most CC	Baked Goods; Dinner
Doug & Jenny Bowman	C-ltd/S-no/P-no/H-no	available as well.
	Closed January	Sitting room, gardens, large
	weekdays	porch, suites, fireplaces,
		antiques, elegant
		accommodations, A/C, safes

Named the Best B&B in Asheville and all of Western North Carolina 6 years in a row. Voted by the readers of Southern Living Magazine as one of the top three inns in the South. Recommended by The New York Times. Exceptional lodging and Southern dining!
✉ info@redrockerinn.com ◐ www.redrockerinn.com

BLOWING ROCK

Blowing Rock Victorian Inn	119-255 BB	Full breakfast
242 Ransom Dr 28605	5 rooms, 5 pb	Evening social
828-295-0034	Visa, MC, •	Jacuzzis, fireplaces, cable
Scott Seaman	C-ltd/S-ltd/P-yes/H-no	TV, sunroom

Elegantly restored Victorian home nestled in the heart of Blowing Rock, NC. The "Romantic Inn" of Blowing Rock. Whirlpools, fireplaces, decks, balconies & porches.
✉ info@blowingrockvictorianinn.com ◐ www.blowingrockvictorianinn.com

BREVARD

The Inn at Brevard	99-260 BB	Full breakfast
315 E Main St 28712	15 rooms, 15 pb	Dinner on Thursday, Friday,
828-884-2105	Visa, MC, *Rated*	Saturday, & Sunday by
Faye & Howard Yager	C-yes/S-ltd/P-yes/H-ltd	reservation. Fine wines, full
	French	bar.
		Sitting rooms; access to
		private camping, hiking,
		fishing, waterfalls.

The Inn at Brevard, beautifully located in the Heart of Brevard. Antiques, shopping, dining, & more are just minutes away! Come join us & experience the magic of the mountains!!!
✉ brevard@theinnatbrevard.com ◐ www.theinnatbrevard.com

448   North Carolina

BREVARD

The Red House
266 W Probart St 28712
828-884-9349
Daniel & Tracie Trusler

99-175 BB
5 rooms, 5 pb
Most CC, •
C-yes/S-no/P-ltd/H-no

Full English Breakfast
Special dietary requirements
met with advance notice
Porches, air-conditioned,
ample parking, private
cottage, pet rooms, secure
bike or boat lock up

The newly renovated Red House Inn provides comfortable accommodations in downtown Brevard. A short walk from shopping and dining opportunities. Easy driving distance to Brevard Music Center, Pisgah National Forest and Dupont State Forest.
✉ info@brevardbedandbreakfast.com 🌐 www.brevardbedandbreakfast.com

BRYSON CITY

Folkestone Inn
101 Folkestone Rd 28713
888-812-3385 828-488-2730
Steve & Eva Clayton

109-163 BB
10 rooms, 10 pb
Most CC, *Rated*, •
C-ltd/S-no/P-no/H-no
Spanish

Full Bountiful Breakfast
Complimentary snacks, soft
drinks, water
Sitting room, library, game
room, porch, rocking chairs,
balconies, beautiful grounds,
A/C, WiFi

An old-fashioned bed & breakfast at the Deep Creek entrance to the Great Smoky Mountains National Park just two miles north of Bryson City, a sleepy mountain town.
✉ innkeeper@folkestone.com 🌐 www.folkestone.com

Fryemont Inn
245 Fryemont St 28713
800-845-4879 828-488-2159
Monica & George Brown

125-270 MAP
46 rooms, 46 pb
Visa, MC, Disc, *Rated*
C-yes/S-no/P-ltd/H-no

Full breakfast and dinner
menu.
Bar Menu offered in Fireside
Bar
Full service fireside bar,
billiards, fireplaces, rocking
chair porch, swimming pool,
patio

A mountain tradition in lodging and fine dining since 1923. Full country breakfast & excellent four course dinner. Casual elegance and rustic beauty, overlooking Great Smoky Mountains National Park.
✉ fryemont@dnet.net 🌐 www.fryemontinn.com

BURNSVILLE

Terrell House B&B
109 Robertson St. 28714
888-682-4505 828-682-4505
Mike & Laura Hoskins

90-100 BB
6 rooms, 6 pb
Most CC
C-ltd/S-no/P-no/H-no
French

Full breakfast
Parlor, formal dining room,
large back porch, gazebo,
gardens, nearby attractions

The Terrell House is a restored, early 1900's Colonial, built as a girl's dormitory for the Stanley McCormick School. The bed and breakfast inn has six lovely guestrooms, each with private bath, sitting area, and queen or twin beds.
✉ terrellhouse@hotmail.com 🌐 www.terrellhousebandb.com

CANDLER

Owl's Nest Inn at Engadine
2630 Smokey Park Hwy 28715
800-665-8868 828-665-8325
Gerda Angevine

145-250 BB
11 rooms, 11 pb
Most CC, *Rated*, •
C-yes/S-no/P-yes/H-no
German

Full breakfast for Inn guests
Afternoon tea, snacks,
complimentary wine,
breakfast for cabin guests $10
per person
Sitting room, Jacuzzis, suites,
fireplaces, cable TV,
accommodations for
business travelers

Historic Victorian Inn built in 1885; mountain views; fireplaces; Jacuzzi suite; situated on 12 acres of beautiful rolling hills, yet just 15 minutes from downtown Asheville and the Biltmore Estate.
✉ info@engadineinn.com 🌐 www.engadineinn.com

CAPE CARTERET

Harborlight Guest House
332 Live Oak Dr 28584
800-624-VIEW 252-393-6868
Bob Pickens & Debbie Mugno

165-315 BB
6 rooms, 6 pb
Visa, MC, AmEx,
Rated, •
C-ltd/S-no/P-no/H-yes

Full breakfast
Snacks, in-suite breakfast,
coffee service
Fireplaces, Jacuzzis,
TV/VCR, refrigerator

Romantic coastal inn located on the central NC coast. Luxury suites feature two-person whirlpools, fireplaces, waterviews, & in-suite breakfast. Recently named a top undiscovered inn in America!
info@harborlightnc.com www.harborlightnc.com

CHAPEL HILL

Inn at Bingham
Mebane Oaks Rd 27514
800-566-5583 919-563-5583
Francois & Christina

150-195 BB
4 rooms, 4 pb
Most CC, *Rated*, •
C-yes/S-ltd/P-no/H-no
French, Spanish

Full breakfast
Snacks, complimentary wine
and cheese
Sitting room, library, small
meetings, wedding facilities

This 208-year-old b&b inn is tucked away on 10 acres under large pecan trees. Just west of Chapel Hill and the University of North Carolina. Once was the homestead for the headmaster of the Bingham School.
fdeprez@mebtel.net www.chapel-hill-inn.com

CHARLOTTE

The Duke Mansion
400 Hermitage Rd 28207
888-202-1009 704-714-4400
The Lynnwood Foundation

179-279 BB
20 rooms, 20 pb
Visa, MC, *Rated*
C-yes/S-no/P-no/H-yes

Gourmet, made-to-order
breakfast
Dinner, beverages, snacks
Sitting room, library, cable
TV/VCR, voice mail, wireless
Internet

Dedicated to offering fine cuisine, beautiful amenities, relaxing atmosphere and remarkable service. With an emphasis on Southern charm, our historic home is a welcome alternative to large, impersonal corporate campuses or hotels.
 www.dukemansion.com

CHIMNEY ROCK

The Wicklow Inn
307 Main St, Hwy 64/74A
28720
877-625-4038 828-625-4038
Sharon Lloyd

120-145 BB
5 rooms, 5 pb
Visa, MC, *Rated*
C-ltd/S-no/P-no/H-ltd

Full breakfast
Dining alcove with a mini
fridge
Sitting room, cable TV, claw-
footed tub, mini fridge, sofa
sleeper, views of river and
Chimney Rock

Small, cozy bed and breakfast on banks of Rocky Broad River in Blue Ridge Mountains. Rustic furniture. 2 blocks from Chimney Rock Park. 45 minutes from Biltmore Estate.
wicklowinn@earthlink.net www.thewicklowinn.com

CULLOWHEE

The River Lodge B&B
619 Roy Tritt Rd 28723
877-384-4400 828-293-5431
Cathy Sgambato

125-240 BB
6 rooms, 6 pb
Visa, MC, *Rated*
C-ltd/S-no/P-no/H-no

Full breakfast
Afternoon tea, snacks &
complimentary wines
Greatroom, 1923 antique
Brunswick Billiard table,
giant fireplace, games,
gardens and acreage, cozy

On a bend in the Tuckasegee River sits this elegant Smoky Mountain Bed and Breakfast Lodge built with 100 year old hand-hewn logs taken from old barns and cabins in the Smoky Mountains region. A Comfy Bed, A Memorable experience.
cathy@riverlodge-bb.com www.riverlodge-bb.com

DAVIDSON

Davidson Village Inn	125-175 BB	Continental plus breakfast
117 Depot St 28036	18 rooms, 18 pb	Afternoon tea & fresh baked
800-892-0796 704-892-8044	Most CC, *Rated*, •	goodies; our kitchen is
Gordon & Rebecca Clark	C-yes/S-no/P-no/H-yes	stocked with a wide variety
		of drinks & snacks
		Conference/banquet room,
		library, sitting room,
		concierge services

"Where Old World Charm Meets New World Comforts!" Amidst the gently rolling hills of the Carolina Piedmont lies the village of Davidson. Remember a time when small towns offered a slower pace and a friendly welcome to all visitors? Davidson still does.
✉ reservations@davidsoninn.com ◐ www.davidsoninn.com

DILLSBORO

The Chalet Inn	96-188 BB	Full breakfast
285 Lone Oak Dr 28789	6 rooms, 6 pb	Snacks, complementary
800-789-8024 828-586-0251	Most CC, *Rated*, •	imported beer or wine
George & Hanneke Ware	C-ltd/S-no/P-no/H-ltd	Fireplaces, Jacuzzi for 2,
	German, Dutch, French	private balconies, A/C, WiFi,
	3rd Fri in Mar-New Years	pool/sauna/tennis privileges,
		TV/Rec Room

Views of the Smoky Mountains, private flower-bedecked balconies, babbling brook and bountiful breakfast beckon you to this romantic inn, in Western NC between Dillsboro, Bryson City and Cherokee. Closest B&B to the Great Smoky Mountains National Park.
✉ paradisefound@thechaletinn.com ◐ www.chaletinn.com

The Dillsboro Inn	90-225 BB	Continental breakfast
146 N River Rd 28725	7 rooms, 7 pb	Suites, waterfall, campfire,
866-586-3898 828-586-3898	Visa, MC, •	fireplaces, river views, trout
T. J. Walker	C-ltd/S-ltd/P-ltd/H-ltd	fishing

On white water river next to waterfall and riverfront park, within walking distance of Dillsboro's craft shops, restaurants, and the Great Smokey Mountain Railroad. Seven riverfront suites with porches overlooking the waterfront. Nightly campfires.
✉ info@dillsboroinn.com ◐ www.dillsboroinn.com

DUCK

Advice 5 Cents B&B	155-265 BB	Continental plus breakfast
111 Scarborough 27949	4 rooms, 4 pb	Neighborhood pool, tennis,
800-238-4235 252-255-1050	Visa, MC	beach access. Cable TV,
Donna Black & Nancy	C-ltd/S-no/P-no/H-no	wireless Internet. On-site
Caviness	March-November	massage therapy.

Advice 5¢ is located in the heart of Duck, just a short walk from the village and situated between the waters of the Atlantic and the Currituck Sound. The traditionally-styled Outer Banks home offers guestrooms with private baths and decks.
✉ advice5cents@charter.net ◐ www.advice5.com

DURHAM

The Blooming Garden Inn	110-225 BB	Full gourmet breakfast
513 Holloway St 27701	5 rooms, 5 pb	Complimentary wine, tea,
888-687-0801 919-687-0801	Most CC, *Rated*, •	snacks
Frank & Dolly Pokrass	C-yes/S-no/P-no/H-no	Library, antiques, 2-person
		Jacuzzi suites, smoke-free,
		modem connections, free
		WiFi, cable TV

Vibrant colors and floral gardens transform this restored, gated Victorian inn into a cozy, memorable retreat, in downtown historic Durham. Smoke-free. Smaller events arranged. Very personable hosts. Close to the new Durham Performing Arts Center.
✉ bloominggardeninn@msn.com ◐ www.bloominggardeninn.com

DURHAM

Carol's Garden Inn
2412 S Alston Ave 27713
877-922-6777 919-680-6777
Carol & Steve Barden

85-100 BB
2 rooms, 2 pb
Most CC, *Rated*
C-yes/S-no/P-no/H-no

Full breakfast
Afternoon refreshments,
complimentary soft drinks,
teas
High speed Internet, free
wireless Internet, dialout,
sitting room, walking path

Whether on a business trip, vacation, romantic weekend getaway or just driving through, you will have a pleasant and relaxing stay.
✉ carol@CarolsGardenInn.com 🌐 www.CarolsGardenInn.com

EDENTON

Captain's Quarters Inn
202 W Queen St 27932
800-482-8945 252-482-8945
Don & Diane Pariseau

110-135 BB
8 rooms, 8 pb
Visa, MC, *Rated*
C-ltd/S-no/P-no/H-yes

Full breakfast
Welcome refreshments;
afternoon beverages &
snacks; Gourmet dinners
offered with or without wine
Jacuzzi, parlor, dining room,
porch, living room, wine list,
wireless Internet

Our inn is located in the historic district of "The South's prettiest town," Edenton, North Carolina. We offer Wine & Dine and Sailing & Golfing Packages. Coming soon—Captain Cook Package, which includes a cooking demonstration with chef Diane.
✉ innkeeper1@captainsquartersinn.com 🌐 www.captainsquartersinn.com

Granville Queen Inn
108 S Granville St 27932
252-482-5296
David & Dora

95-135 BB
7 rooms, 7 pb
Most CC
C-ltd/S-no/P-no/H-yes

Varied breakfast choices
Coffee, tea, and hot
chocolate always available
Fireplaces, private balconies,
cable TV, VCRs, and
telephones

From the moment you step in the door at the Granville Queen Inn, it will be our pleasure to see that your visit is a memorable escape from the daily routine. 1907 neoclassical manor offering 7 guestrooms with private bath.
✉ stay@granvillequeen.com 🌐 www.granvillequeen.com

Trestle House Inn
632 Soundside Rd 27932
800-645-8466 252-482-2282
Peter Bogus

67-134 BB
5 rooms, 5 pb
Most CC, *Rated*
C-yes/S-no/P-no/H-yes

Full Gourmet breakfast
Complimentary wine or soft
drink upon arrival
Private bathrooms, A/C,
ceiling fans and free wireless
Internet

The Inn is surrounded on 3 sides by water in historic Edenton, North Carolina. The Trestle House Inn B&B is a waterfront retreat, originally built in 1972. Located on 5 acres, from the viewing deck guests may see a vast array of wildlife and birds.
✉ peter@trestlehouseinn.com 🌐 www.trestlehouseinn.com

FRANKLIN

Buttonwood Inn
50 Admiral Dr 28734
888-368-8985 828-369-8985
Liz Oehser

89-109 BB
3 rooms, 3 pb
Visa, MC, Disc, *Rated*
C-yes/S-no/P-no/H-ltd

Full breakfast
Sitting room, king bed,
loveseat, decorative
fireplace, and private
bathroom, Amish decor

Completely surrounded by tall pines, small and cozy Buttonwood will appeal to the person who prefers simplicity and natural rustic beauty.
✉ info@buttonwoodbb.com 🌐 www.buttonwoodbb.com

FUQUAY VARINA

Fuquay Mineral Spring Inn
333 S Main St 27526
866-552-3782 919-552-3782
John & Patty Byrne

110-195 BB
5 rooms, 5 pb
Most CC, *Rated*
C-ltd/S-ltd/P-no/H-ltd
Some Spanish and
French

Full breakfast
Tea, wine, beer, coffee, soda,
espresso, and juice
Sitting room, library, and
garden; all rooms have cable
TV, Wireless Internet and
Bose radios

The Fuquay Mineral Spring Inn and Garden is an Historic Landmark Inn and Garden located in the heart of the Fuquay Springs Historic District across from the Fuquay Mineral Spring Park. Chefs offer cooking classes on most Wednesday evenings at the Inn.
✉ jbyrne@fuquayinn.com 🌐 www.fuquayinn.com

GRANITE FALLS

Thistle House B&B
25 Hillside Ave 28630
828-313-3989
Phyllis Esler

110-125 BB
4 rooms, 4 pb
Most CC
C-ltd/S-no/P-ltd/H-ltd

Full breakfast

A peaceful place of beauty and relaxation nestled in the quaint and quiet little town of Granite Falls. A place to stay for a night, a weekend or a week.
✉ manager@thistlehousebb.com 🌐 www.thistlehousebb.com

HERTFORD

1812 on the Perquimans
385 Old Neck Rd 27944
252-426-1812
Peter & Nancy Rascoe

80-85 EP
4 rooms, 4 pb
Visa, MC
C-yes/S-ltd/P-no/H-yes

Full breakfast avail for $5.
Afternoon tea, dessert, fruit
Canoe, bicycles

Beautiful home located near historic Hertford and the Perquimans River. 30–50 mile historic country road bike tour nearby.

HIGHLANDS

4½ Street Inn
55 4½ St 28741
888-799-4464 828-526-4464
Helene & Rick Siegel

115-165 BB
10 rooms, 10 pb
Visa, MC
C-ltd/S-no/P-no/H-yes
March – December

Gourmet breakfasts
Homemade cookies, wine,
appetizers, drinks
Hot tub, bicycles, parlor with
books, music, games,
birdwatching, gardens

A perfect combination of romantic country charm and understated elegance, the 4½ Street Inn offers a secluded sanctuary walking distance to town.
✉ relax@4andahalfstinn.com 🌐 www.4andahalfstinn.com

The Chandler Inn
790 N 4th St 28741
888-378-6300 828-526-5992
Randy & Letty Power

98-205 BB
14 rooms, 14 pb
Visa, MC, Disc, *Rated*,
●
C-ltd/S-no/P-no/H-yes
Spanish

Gourmet Breakfast
Breakfast includes
homemade souffles, muffins, coffee,
juice, tea, fruit & cereal
Tennis court, fireplaces,
cable TV, outside decks &
swings, courtyard & private
entrance, free WiFi

Romantic Country Inn! Bed and Breakfast with air-conditioning, fireplaces, private baths, private entrances, non-smoking, free WiFi.
✉ thechandlerinnc@yahoo.com 🌐 www.thechandlerinn.com

HIGHLANDS

Colonial Pines Inn B&B
541 Hickory St 28741
866-526-2060 828-526-2060
Chris & Donna Alley

67-160 BB
7 rooms, 7 pb
Visa, MC, AmEx
C-ltd/S-no/P-no/H-no

Full breakfast
Cider, hot chocolate, tea,
sherry, cookies, snacks
Free wireless Internet, suites,
kitchens, fireplaces, grand
piano, cable TV, videos,
library.

Perched on a 2-acre hillside in-town with a soothing mountain view from a breezy wrap-around veranda. Moderately priced rooms, spacious suites, private cottages. Sumptuous breakfasts, afternoon refreshments, & berry gardens.
✉ sleeptight@colonialpinesinn.com 🌐 www.colonialpinesinn.com

Fire Mountain Inn
800-775-4446 828-526-4446
Hiram Wilkinson & Mathew
Gillen

205-385 BB
15 rooms, 15 pb
Visa, MC, AmEx, •
C-yes/S-no/P-yes/H-ltd

Full country breakfast
Breakfast not included in
rates for cabins, lunch &
dinner available by advance
order
Guests receive a guide to
dining & all activities in the
area

One of the most unique & spectacular mountaintop hideaways in America. On hundreds of acres with long range mountain views, just outside the upscale mountain village of Highlands, NC.
✉ reservations@firemt.com 🌐 www.firemt.com

Main Street Inn
270 Main St 28741
800-213-9142 828-526-2590
Gary Garner

135-245 BB
18 rooms, 18 pb
Most CC, *Rated*
C-ltd/S-no/P-ltd/H-no

Full breakfast
Afternoon tea, wine bar and
dinner service
Piano and tapas bar,
fireplaces, cable TV, Air
conditioned rooms, Wireless
Internet, Off street parking

Rated as #2 top inn in the US, The Main Street Inn has been welcoming guests for over 135 years. An 1881 Federal Farmhouse renovated in 1998, Inn offers 20 charming & cozy rooms with private baths, piano bar with appetizer menu, private off street parking.
✉ info@mainstreet-inn.com 🌐 www.mainstreet-inn.com

HOT SPRINGS

Mountain Magnolia Inn
204 Lawson St 28743
800-914-9306 828-622-3543
Pete & Karen Nagle

88-268 BB
10 rooms, 10 pb
Cash, Checks
C-yes/S-no/P-yes

Full breakfast
Dinner is served nightly in-
season, complimentary tea,
coffee, soda
Beer & wine, massage, a
variety of packages,
concierge service

An 1868 Victorian Inn located outside Asheville in the quaint town of Hot Springs. Featured in This Old House and HGTV. Offering lodging, dining nightly, weddings and special packages.
✉ innkeepers@mountainmagnoliainn.com 🌐 www.mountainmagnoliainn.com

KITTY HAWK

Cypress Moon Inn
1206 Harbor Ct 27949
877-905-5060 252-261-5060
Greg and Linda Hamby

135-210 BB
3 rooms, 3 pb
Visa, MC
C-ltd/S-no/P-no/H-no

Full breakfast
Sitting room, porches,
kayaks, windsurfing, sailing
& surfing lessons, satellite
TV, room fridges

The Cypress Moon Inn rests on the shore of The Albemarle Sound, in the village of Kitty Hawk, NC. There are three guestrooms all with a spectacular view over the Sound. The beach is just one mile away.
✉ cypressmooninn@mindspring.com 🌐 www.cypressmooninn.com

LAKE LURE

The Chalet Club
532 Washburn Rd 28746
800-336-3309 828-625-9315
Bob & Anne Washburn

138-330 BB
12 rooms, 12 pb
Visa, MC, *Rated*, •
C-yes/S-ltd/P-no/H-ltd
Spring through Fall

Full breakfast
Free soft drinks
Library, spacious cottages,
satellite TV, wireless Internet,
firewood

The Chalet Club is a secluded mountainside retreat, offering the opportunity to recreate in a spectacular setting and relax in the tranquility of a variety of accommodations. A B&B plan with numerous activities included—or a rate for Lodging available.
✉ chaletclub@msn.com ✪ www.chaletclub.com

Linne 'Ardan at Lake Lure
294 Tryon Bay Cir 28746
828-625-8182
Linda and Aaron White

140-250 BB
3 rooms, 3 pb
Visa, MC, Disc
C-ltd/S-no/P-no/H-ltd

Gourmet Full breakfast
Laird's High Tea
($45/couple). Beverages,
hors d'oeuvres, aperitifs and
after dinner deserts.
Parlor, gathering room,
antiques, robes and slippers,
reading library, verandas,
package tours

Step back into time and experience the ancient hospitality of the Highland Scots as is known far and wide. A 100,000 welcomes to Linne 'Ardan, an award winning B&B located on a ridge overlooking Lake Lure in the Western North Carolina mountains.
✉ the_laird@linneardan.com ✪ www.lakelurebedandbreakfast.com

LAKE TOXAWAY

Earthshine Mountain Lodge
1600 Golden Rd 28747
828-862-4207
Marion Boatwright

170-220 BB
13 rooms, 13 pb
Visa, MC, Disc, *Rated*,
•
C-yes/S-no/P-no/H-yes

Full country breakfast
Lunch and dinner included,
appetizers, fresh fruit &
beverages
High ropes, zipline course,
children & family activities,
baby sitting

Earthshine—the storybook, grandmother's farm, family vacation you've always dreamed about. Surrounded by 83 gorgeous acres, our 1½ story log lodge overlooks the beautiful Blue Ridge Mountains.
✉ earthshine@citcom.net ✪ www.earthshinemtnlodge.com

LEICESTER

Wildberry Lodge B&B
135 Potato Branch Rd 28748
866-863-2525 828-683-2525
Ken & Glenda Cahill

149-399 BB
5 rooms, 5 pb
Most CC
C-ltd/S-no/P-no/H-ltd

Full breakfast
Afternoon tea, fruit, non-
alcoholic beverages, snacks,
Dinner by reservation with
Your Personal Chef
Library, satellite TV
DVD/VCR, pool table, decks,
dry heat sauna

Experience the casual sophistication of Wildberry Lodge. Constructed of handcrafted red pine logs, nestled in the Newfound Mountains, 15 miles from Asheville, NC.
✉ innkeepers@wildberrylodge.com ✪ www.wildberrylodge.com?ref=lanierbb.com

LITTLE SWITZERLAND

Big Lynn Lodge
10860 Hwy 226-A 28749
800-654-5232 828-765-4257
Dene Armstrong

115-162 MAP
40 rooms, 40 pb
Visa, MC, Disc, *Rated*,
•
C-ltd/S-ltd/P-no/H-ltd
German
April 15-Oct.

Full breakfast
Fruit
Sitting room, library, player
piano lounge, TV, billiards,
shuffleboard, high speed
Internet

Come to the Big Lynn Lodge where the air is always fresh and cool, the views are spectacular, and the food is simply delicious. No matter what your taste, we have the right accommodations for you.
✉ info@biglynnlodge.com ✪ www.biglynnlodge.com

LITTLE SWITZERLAND

Switzerland Inn
86 High Ridge Rd 28749
800-654-4026 828-765-2153
Gary & Jackie Jensen

55-190 BB
20 rooms, 20 pb
Visa, MC, AmEx
C-yes/P-ltd

Full breakfast
Restaurant
Swimming pool (in season),
tennis courts, shuffle-board,
fireplace, weddings, WiFi

Since 1910 the Switzerland Inn has offered a unique experience to the traveler seeking something out of the ordinary. Tucked away in the mountains of Western North Carolina, on the Blue Ridge Parkway, it is one of the finest Inns in the Southeast.
✉ info@switzerlandinn.com ◐ www.switzerlandinn.com

MAGGIE VALLEY

Brooksong B&B
252 Living Waters Ln 28751
866-926-5409 828-926-5409
Betty & Cletis Wagahoff

135-160 BB
5 rooms, 5 pb
Visa, MC
C-ltd/S-no/P-no/H-yes

Full breakfast
WiFi, fireplaces, refrigerators,
jetted tubs, separate showers
and cable TV

Nestled in the heart of the Great Smoky Mountains on the banks of Jonathan Creek in the scenic little town of Maggie Valley, North Carolina is Brooksong, a Victorian bed and breakfast.
✉ info@brooksong.com ◐ www.brooksong.com

MANTEO

Cameron House Inn
300 Budleigh St 27954
800-279-8178 252-473-6596
Beth Storie & Michael
McOwen

130-220 BB
6 rooms, 6 pb
Visa, MC, AmEx, •
C-ltd/S-no/P-no/H-ltd
French

Continental breakfast
Snacks, stocked fridge with
soft drinks & water, home
made cookies and cakes and
other goodies
Bicycles, outdoor fireplace,
huge front porch swing,
sitting room, library

Arts and Crafts style Inn that invites you to rest, relax and enjoy the simple pleasures of Roanoke Island. Centrally located on the Outer Banks of North Carolina, with many attractions and activities within an hour's drive.
✉ innkeepers@cameronhouseinn.com ◐ www.cameronhouseinn.com

The White Doe Inn B&B
319 Sir Walter Raleigh St 27954
800-473-6091 252-473-9851
Bebe & Bob Woody

175-325 BB
8 rooms, 8 pb
Visa, MC, *Rated*
C-ltd/S-no/P-no/H-ltd

Full Four-Course Served
Breakfast
Gourmet teas, coffees,
cappuccino, espresso,
desserts and sherry
available afternoons &
evenings
Parlor, library, gardens,
bicycles, whirlpools, bedside
fireplaces, in-room spa
services, weddings

A beautiful Victorian Inn providing spacious, comfortable surroundings with turn-of-the-century antiques. Amenities include fireplaces, private baths, 2-person whirlpools, four-course breakfast, spa services, balconies, gardens and concierge service.
✉ whitedoe@whitedoeinn.com ◐ www.whitedoeinn.com

MARS HILL

B&B at Ponder Cove
1067 Ponder Creek Rd 28754
866-689-7304 828-689-7304
Martha Abraham

175-205 BB
4 rooms, 4 pb
Visa, MC
C-ltd/S-no/P-yes/H-no

Gourmet with a down home
twist
Double whirlpools,
fireplaces, WiFi, VCRs, Direct
TV, luxurious robes

Dog-friendly B&B & newly restored 1938 Bungalow offer country chic luxury on 91 private acres with pasture & mountain vistas. Whirlpools, fireplaces, king beds. Gourmet breakfasts offered in B & B. Bungalow, sleeps 4 with full kitchen & outdoor hot tub.
✉ martha@pondercove.com ◐ www.pondercove.com

MARS HILL

Bald Mountain House
85 Woodfern Lane 28754
866-680-9329 828-680-9329
Monica & Tony Martin

105-175 EP
3 rooms, 3 pb
Most CC
C-ltd/S-no/P-no/H-no
Spanish

Voucher for breakfast,
restaurant style Italian
espresso & cappuccino,
guest beverages
Candlelight fireplaces,
satellite TV/DVD, books,
games and DVDs, wireless
Internet, pool, tennis

The Bald Mountain House is situated in the heart of the Great Smoky Mountains near Asheville, NC. The unspoiled natural beauty of the Cherokee and Pisgah National Forests surround you with ever-changing mountain views.
✉ baldmountainhouse@yahoo.com 🌐 www.baldmountainhouse.com

MOUNT AIRY

Maxwell House B&B
618 N Main St 27030
336-786-2174
Twyla & Roger Sickmiller

129-169 BB
4 rooms, 4 pb
Visa, MC, AmEx,
Rated, •
C-ltd/S-no/P-ltd/H-ltd

Four Course Gourmet
Breakfast
Afternoon and evening
refreshments are always
available
Large porch, library, piano
room, gift shop, spa
treatments by appointment

Welcome to the Maxwell House Bed & Breakfast at the Historic Merritt House, a beautiful brick and granite Victorian home built in 1901. Nestled in the foothills of the Blue Ridge Mountains, in Downtown "Mayberry," and in the Wine Country of NC.
✉ maxwellhousebb@hotmail.com

Sobotta Manor B&B
347 W Pine St 27030
336-786-2777
Thurman & Robin Hester

129-149 BB
4 rooms, 4 pb
Most CC, •
C-ltd/S-no/P-ltd/H-ltd

Full gourmet breakfast
Coffee, soda and snacks

North Carolina welcomes you to visit and fall in love with Mount Airy or Mayberry, as it is known to many, with grace and hospitality we are located in the heart of Yadkin Valley wine country and just 15 miles from the Blue Ridge Parkway.
✉ sobottamanor@aol.com 🌐 www.sobottamanor.com

The Thompson House
804 E Pine St 27030
866-719-0711 336-719-0711
Mark Smith

105-145 BB
3 rooms, 3 pb
Visa, MC, *Rated*
C-yes/S-ltd/P-ltd/H-no

Full breakfast
Complimentary soft drinks
and snacks are available
Cable TV and Internet access
in each room, pet friendly
with innkeeper permission

The Thompson House B&B Harmony Hills is a two-story Victorian located in the Flat Rock area of Mt. Airy. Outside the house, the wraparound porch has plenty of rocking chairs. There is also a small outdoor balcony upstairs. Child and pet friendly.
✉ markcsmith@embarqmail.com

NAGS HEAD

The First Colony Inn
6715 S Croatan Hwy 27959
800-368-9390 252-441-2343
Tom Matthews

79-299 BB
26 rooms, 26 pb
Visa, MC, AmEx, *Rated*
C-yes/S-no/P-no/H-yes

Continental breakfast
Full Continental Breakfast
served with at least one hot
item. Manager's Social each
afternoon
Library, verandas, pool,
croquet, ocean, fishing,
weddings, beach, computer,
Internet, weddings

Elegant 26-room inn with Southern hospitality, verandahs along all 4 sides; English antiques, wonderful big beds. Walkway to our private gazebo on the dune; ocean view & sound views on third floor.
✉ innkeeper@firstcolonyinn.com 🌐 www.firstcolonyinn.com

NAGS HEAD————————————————————————————————

Nags Head Beach Inn
303 East Admiral St 27959
800-421-8466 252-441-8466
Ken & Lisa Muglia

75-190 BB
8 rooms, 8 pb
Most CC
S-no/P-no/H-no
Spring, Summer, Fall

Continental plus breakfast
Great restaurants nearby
Lobby, Jacuzzi tub, pool,
individual temp control, TV,
125 yds to beach, bikes,
beach chairs

Welcome to Nags Head Beach Inn, located in the heart of Nags Head, North Carolina! 125 yards from the beach. Walk to restaurants and shopping, take a ride on the bike path, or just grab a chair and umbrella and relax. Great Shingle Style Inn.
✉ nagsheadbeachinn@aol.com ◐ www.nagsheadbeachinn.com

NEW BERN————————————————————————————————

The Aerie B&B
509 Pollock St 28562
800-849-5553 252-636-5553
Michael & Marty Gunhus

119-169 BB
7 rooms, 7 pb
Most CC, *Rated*, •
C-ltd/S-no/P-no/H-no

Full gourmet breakfast
Evening social hour with
wine & hors d'oeuvres
Massage by appointment,
Whirlpool baths in 3 suites,
spa shower tower in 2 rooms.

Relax and share the warmth and charm of this turn-of-the-century Victorian home, one block from the Tyron Palace in the heart of the historic district.
✉ info@aeriebedandbreakfast.com ◐ www.aeriebedandbreakfast.com

Harmony House Inn
215 Pollock St 28560
800-636-3113 252-636-3810
Ed & Sooki Kirkpatrick

109-175 BB
10 rooms, 10 pb
Visa, MC, Disc, *Rated*,
•
C-yes/S-no/P-no/H-ltd
Korean

Full homemade breakfast
Wine & cheese hour from
6PM to 7PM, sodas available
throughout guests' stay
Two-person Jacuzzis in some
suites, parlor, games, porch
with swings & rocking chairs

Comfortable yet elegant. Unusually spacious c.1850 home. Rockers/swings on porch. In historic district near Tryon Palace, Fireman's Museum, Historic Trolley Tour, antique shops, and restaurants. Most of our guests park and walk throughout their stay.
✉ stay@harmonyhouseinn.com ◐ www.harmonyhouseinn.com

Meadows Inn B&B
212 Pollock St 28560
877-551-1776 252-634-1776
John & Betty Foy

122-166 BB
8 rooms, 7 pb
Visa, MC, AmEx, *Rated*
C-yes/S-no/P-no/H-no

Full breakfast
Hot and cold beverages,
homemade cookies, snacks
Spacious gathering room
with a large screen TV,
TV/VCRs in all rooms, free
WiFi Internet Access

Nestled peacefully in the heart of the downtown historic district, this c 1847 Antebellum inn has been welcoming guests since 1980. Accommodations to suit the business or family traveler. Perfect for that romantic getaway you have been planning.
✉ meadowsinnbnb@earthlink.net ◐ www.meadowsinn-nc.com

Sail Inn
714 Pollock St 28562
866-731-6036 252-259-8507
Michael McMillan & Karen
Snyder

75-120 BB
3 rooms, 2 pb
Most CC
C-ltd/S-ltd/P-no/H-no

"Continental Plus" breakfast
24/7: Complementary hot
coffee, or tea, chilled sodas,
or water, fresh fruit too.
Cable TV, DVDs, free WiFi,
iPod station, iron w/ironing
board, hairdryer, coffee
maker, games, books

"A simple inn reflecting a quieter time." Sail on in to the Sail Inn, where we strive to provide an intimate personal setting for our overnight guests in a quaint, historic home.
✉ sailinn@yahoo.com ◐ www.sailinn.biz

OCRACOKE

Castle on Silver Lake
Silver Lake Rd 27960
800-471-8848 252-928-3505
Castle Innkeeper

139-269 BB
11 rooms, 11 pb
Visa, MC, AmEx
C-ltd/S-no/P-no/H-no
Closed January

Full breakfast
AC, Cable TV/VCR/CD,
Whirlpool Tubs, Private
Entrances, Library,
Fireplaces, Business
Accommodation

Relax in comfortable, non-smoking rooms in this three-story inn. The rooms are tastefully decorated with antiques and each room has its own private bathroom. The Castle, located on Ocracoke Island, North Carolina offers elegant amenities and so much more!
✉ innkeeper@thecastlebb.com ♦ www.thecastlebb.com

Thurston House Inn
685 Hwy 12 27960
252-928-6037
Donna Boor

95-155 BB
8 rooms, 8 pb
Visa, MC, Disc, •
C-ltd/S-no/P-no/H-ltd

Southern Buffet Breakfast
Sitting room, cable TV, hot
tub

Covered porches with swing and rockers, private grounds with lush native plants and graying cedar shake buildings set the scene for a perfect island retreat.
✉ stay@thurstonhouseinn.com ♦ www.thurstonhouseinn.com

PILOT MOUNTAIN

Pilot Knob Inn
361 New Pilot Knob Ln 27041
336-325-2502
Will & Jennifer Allen

99-249 BB
12 rooms, 12 pb
Visa, MC, *Rated*, •
S-no/P-no/H-yes

Full breakfast
6 acre lake-fishing, boating
hiking & biking on property,
sauna, whirlpools for two,
hottubs, fireplace

Cabins with whirlpool tubs for two, a lake with boats & fishing, honeymoon suites, hiking, mountain areas, local wineries & full breakfast located near the Yadkin Valley Wine Trail & Blue Ridge Parkway.
✉ info@pilotknobinn.com ♦ www.pilotknobinn.com

PISGAH FOREST

The Pines Country Inn
1780 Hart Rd 28768
828-877-3131
Mary McEntire

55-75 BB
18 rooms, 18 pb
Rated
C-yes/S-no/P-no/H-yes
May 15 thru Oct. 31

Full country breakfast
Sitting room, piano,
children's play yard, great
biking & hiking

Quiet, homey country inn. Fantastic view. Accommodations in the Inn or the 4 cabins and cottages.

PITTSBORO

Rosemary House B&B
76 West St 27312
888-643-2017 919-542-5515
Karen Pullen

89-179 BB
5 rooms, 5 pb
Visa, MC, Disc
C-yes/S-no/P-no/H-no

Vegetarian
Cookie jar, complimentary
drinks, hot chocolate &
Afternoon English Tea
Wireless high-speed Internet,
cable TV, rocking chairs on
huge porch

Welcome to our gracious 1912 Colonial Revival Bed & Breakfast, listed on the National Register of Historic Places. Comfortable accommodations, personal service, delicious breakfasts.
✉ karen@rosemary-bb.com ♦ www.rosemary-bb.com

RALEIGH

The Oakwood Inn B&B
411 N Bloodworth St 27604
800-267-9712 919-832-9712
Doris & Gary Jurkiewicz

144-254 BB
6 rooms, 6 pb
Most CC, *Rated*, •
C-ltd/S-no/P-no/H-no

Full breakfast
Complimentary wine,
snacks, soda, evening sweets
Sitting room, piano, parlor,
porch, massage therapist

Victorian retreat nestled in the heart of Raleigh's Historic Oakwood District. Six guestrooms, each with private bath, remote control fireplaces, cable TV, free WiFi.
✉ innkeepers@oakwoodinnbb.com ♦ www.oakwoodinnbb.com

RIDGECREST

Inn On Mill Creek
3895 Mill Creek Rd 28770
877.735.2964 828.668.1115
Dave & Brigette Walters

149-199 BB
7 rooms, 7 pb
Visa, MC, Disc, *Rated*
C-yes/S-no/P-yes/H-ltd

Full breakfast
Baked goods, fresh fruit and
juice from our orchards
Hiking & biking trails, paddle
boat on the lake, organic fruit
orchard, Jacuzzi tubs,
fireplaces

*This Asheville/Black Mountain area B&B and orchard on 7 acres is literally surrounded by
North Carolina's Pisgah National Forest, centrally located between the Biltmore Estate in
Asheville, Mount Mitchell, and Chimney Rock/Lake Lure.*
✉ info@innonmillcreek.com 🌐 www.innonmillcreek.com

SAPPHIRE

Woodlands Inn of Sapphire
19259 Rosman Hwy 28774
828-966-4709
Lisa Groff, John & Mary K
Crandall

75-135 BB
14 rooms, 14 pb
Most CC
C-yes/S-no/P-yes/H-no

Full breakfast
Sitting room, Jacuzzis, suites,
fireplaces, cable TV, pet
friendly

*"Our Secret in the Heart of the Blue Ridge Mountains" Old fashioned mountain hospitality
with accommodations that are pleasant for a romantic getaway, or just the simple enjoyment of natural beauty and peaceful serenity.*
✉ woodlandsinn@citcom.net 🌐 www.woodlandsinn.net

SEAGROVE

The Duck Smith House
465 North Broad Street 27341
888-869-9018 336-873-7099
Sisters, Barbara & Suzanne
Murphy & Daisy Mae

135-135 BB
4 rooms, 4 pb
Most CC, *Rated*
C-yes/S-no/P-no/H-ltd

We serve a complete
breakfast
Beverage with cheese tray,
Seagrove is a dry city so feel
free to bring in wine, etc.
Small in-room TV, large
common room TV, natural
scenery, wrap around porch
with wicker furniture

*Escape, relax and recharge with the Duck Smith House Bed & Breakfast. Nothing but the
best while you are our guests! We serve a complete breakfast which may include Stuffed
French Toast, which is Barbara's signature dish, or another breakfast favorite!*
✉ scmdaisy@aol.com 🌐 www.ducksmithhouse.com

SYLVA

Galvladi Mountain Inn
1498 Branch Falls Tr 28779
877-631-0125 828-631-0125
Dave Stubbs & Terry Matre

300-400 BB
5 rooms, 5 pb
Visa, MC, Disc
C-yes/S-no/P-no/H-no
April 1- November 1

Full meal Plan
Hors D'ourves in the evening
before dinner
Library, exercise room,
solarium, porch and terrace

*Perched atop 250 acres of protected Great Smoky Mountains forestland, The Galvladi
Mountain Inn is situated just 45 minutes west of Asheville, N.C.. The Inn sports 5 luxurious
rooms, inviting common areas, including an elegant Great Room.*
✉ info@galvladi.com 🌐 www.galvladi.com

Mountain Brook Cottages
208 Mountain Brook Rd #18
28779
800-258-4052 828-586-4329
Gus, Michele, Maqelle
McMahon

90-159 EP
12 rooms, 12 pb
Cash, •
C-yes/S-yes/P-no/H-ltd
Some French

Breakfast beverage setups
only
Jacuzzis, fireplaces, front
porch swings, one & two
bedroom cottages

*Quaint c.1930s cottages with fireplaces & porch swings. Nestled on a brook-filled, wooded
mountainside in Smokies. Near Dillsboro, Franklin, Cherokee, Asheville.*
✉ mcmahon@mountainbrook.com 🌐 www.mountainbrook.com

TROY

The Blair House B&B
105 Blair St 27371
866-572-2100 910-572-2100
Claudia Bulthuis

75-120 BB
4 rooms, 4 pb
Visa, MC
C-yes/S-ltd/P-no/H-yes

Full breakfast
Complimentary refreshment
center

Still family owned, The Blair House (1893) invites you to visit the heart of NC. Shop Seagrove potteries or hike the Uwharries then relax in a spacious suite.
✉ innkeeper@blairhousebb.com 🌐 www.blairhousebb.com

VALLE CRUCIS

The Baird House
1451 Watauga River Rd 28679
800-297-1342 828-297-4055
Tom & Deede Hinson

129-179 BB
7 rooms, 7 pb
Visa, MC, •
C-ltd/S-ltd/P-no/H-ltd

Full breakfast
Colas, coffee, hot tea,
homemade chocolate chip
cookies
Sitting room, Jacuzzis,
fireplaces, cable TV with
DVD & VCR players, wireless
Internet

The Baird House was built in 1790, it is the oldest house in the county and is a restored Colonial farmhouse on 12 private acres. During each unique season of the year our guests relish the spectacular beauty of the Watauga River.
✉ bairdhouse@charter.net 🌐 www.bairdhouse.com

Lazy Bear Lodge
315 Lazy Bear Tr 28692
828-963-9201
Anne Winkelman

145-160 BB
5 rooms, 5 pb
Visa, MC
C-ltd/S-no/P-no/H-yes

Full breakfast
The restaurant is sometimes
open for Saturday night
dining for overnight guests.
Gas fireplaces, sitting areas,
porches, TV, CD/radio, fans,
jetted/claw footed tub & Spa
room

Overlooking historic Valle Crucis in the North Carolina High Country, minutes from the Blue Ridge Parkway, Boone and Blowing Rock, Lazy Bear Lodge is a mountain retreat built from the ground up and beautifully furnished with guest's comfort in mind.
✉ mawinkelman@skybest.com 🌐 www.lazy-bear-lodge.com

The Mast Farm Inn
2543 Broadstone Rd 28691
888-963-5857 828-963-5857
Sandra Deschamps Siano &
Danielle Deschamps

89-429 BB
14 rooms, 14 pb
Most CC, •
C-yes/S-no/P-no/H-yes
French & Spanish

Full gourmet breakfast
Restaurant featuring fresh,
organic regional cuisine;
espresso & wine bar in the
inn
A large wraparound porch,
spacious grounds, organic
gardens, pond and creek

The Mast Farm Inn has been welcoming guests since the 1800s; while we have added modern amenities, the hospitality remains the same: attentive and sincere. Eight spacious guestrooms and six romantic getaway cottages offered. Come make yourself at home.
✉ henri-deschamps@mastfarminn.com 🌐 www.mastfarminn.com

WARRENTON

Ivy Bed and Breakfast
331 N Main St 27589
800-919-9886 252-257-9300
Jerry & Ellen Roth

90-120 BB
4 rooms, 3 pb
Most CC, *Rated*, •
C-yes/S-ltd/P-ltd/H-no

3-course, candlelit breakfast
A guest refrigerator with soft
drinks & bottled water
provided, coffee and tea
available 24 hours
Sitting room, working
fireplaces in dining room &
parlor, wireless high speed
Internet access

An elegant 1903 Victorian home furnished with beautiful antiques, in historic Warrenton, North Carolina, a short drive from Raleigh, NC & Richmond, VA. Relax by the fireplace on those cool mornings or rock on the wraparound front porch.
✉ info@ivybedandbreakfast.com 🌐 www.ivybedandbreakfast.com

Andon-Reid Inn, Waynesville, NC

WASHINGTON

Moss House
129 Van Norden St 27889
252-975-3967
Rebecca & Scott Sipprell

110-240 BB
4 rooms, 4 pb
Visa, MC, AmEx,
Rated, •
C-ltd/S-ltd/P-no/H-no
January 1-Dec. 31

Full breakfast with elegance
Living room, sitting area, in
room TV's , fax, wireless
Internet, all private baths,
central A/C

Washington NC's premier Bed and Breakfast, located in the historic district, one block from the Pamlico River. Walking distance to local gourmet restaurants and shops. Original artwork and antiques in a comfortable, coastal style.
✉ info@themosshouse.com ◑ www.themosshouse.com

WAYNESVILLE

Andon-Reid Inn
92 Daisey Ave 28786
800-293-6190 828-452-3089
Ron and Rachel Reid

129-179 BB
5 rooms, 5 pb
Most CC, *Rated*
C-ltd/S-no/P-no/H-no

Our special four-course
breakfast
Complimentary
refreshments available all
day & evening along with
freshly baked pastries.
Delicious!
Garden room, reading,
TV/DVD, lower level
recreational center, sauna,
pool table, fitness, WiFi

The beauty of the mountains, the quaint town of Waynesville, the comfort & relaxation of the romantic, historical Andon-Reid Inn is yours, and just a phone call away. Unwind and relax. Plan your special event with us and let us pamper you.
✉ info@andonreidinn.com ◑ www.andonreidinn.com

Brookside Mountain Mist Inn
142 Country Club Dr 28786
877-452-6880 828-452-6880
Carolyn Gendreau & Dina Giunta

129-169 BB
5 rooms, 5 pb
Visa, MC, AmEx, •
C-ltd/S-ltd/P-no/H-ltd

Full breakfast
We will accommodate
special dietary needs
In-room massages, video
library, lending library

Overlooking the Balsam Mountain Ridge, this one-story luxury inn provides the peacefulness and elegance you deserve. Enjoy the quaint town of Waynesville with its assortment of shoppes, cafes and restaurants along with golf right across the street.
✉ info@brooksidemountainmistbb.com ◑ www.brooksidemountainmistbb.com

WAYNESVILLE

Can't Find It Inn
879 Mountain Side Dr 28786
828-734-1088 828-452-4186
Pat Puckett

135-150 BB
2 rooms, 2 pb
Visa, MC
S-ltd/P-no/H-no

Full breakfast
Snacks and soft drinks
Satellite TV, VHS/DVD, CD
players, coffee makers and
fridge, luxurious bath robes,
wireless Internet

A secluded two suite B&B specializing in romance and privacy. No crowds, no community meals, no children. Enjoy life the way it was meant to be.
✉ cantfinditinn@hotmail.com ✆ www.cantfinditinn.com

Inn at Iris Meadows
304 Love Lane 28786
888-466-4747 828-456-3877
Becky and George Fain

225-300 BB
7 rooms, 7 pb
Most CC
S-no/P-ltd/H-no

Full breakfast
Mid-afternoon refreshments
with coffee or tea.
Fluffy robes, hairdryers,
irons and ironing boards,
TV/VCR's, phone, and clock
radios.

Located in the heart of the Great Smoky Mountains, the inn is nestled amidst five rolling acres overlooking the picturesque town of Waynesville.
✉ info@irismeadows.com ✆ www.irismeadows.com

Old Stone Inn Mountain Lodge & Restaurant
109 Dolan Rd 28786
800-432-8499 828-456-3333
David Gardner

110-175 BB
18 rooms, 18 pb
Most CC, •
C-yes/S-ltd/P-yes/H-no

Full, hot breakfast included
Award-winning, fine dining
restaurant with full-service
bar open six nights a week.
Guest sitting room with
fireplace and full-service bar.
Wireless Internet.

Tucked away on 6½ wooded acres yet within walking distance of downtown Waynesville, this rustic mountain lodge offers 18 comfortable guestrooms and unsurpassed dining. Tranquil and secluded yet close to everything!
✉ reservations@oldstoneinn.com ✆ www.oldstoneinn.com

The Swag Country Inn
2300 Swag Rd 28785
800-789-7672 828-926-0430
Deener Matthews

430-750
15 rooms, 15 pb
Most CC, *Rated*, •
C-ltd/S-ltd/P-no/H-yes
April 29 – November 18

Full breakfast
All 3 meals included in rate
Library, piano, sauna,
racquetball, hiking, croquet,
badminton, pond

Tucked, snuggled, positioned, located and sitting spectacularly atop a 5000' mountain ridge, this log & rock lodge offers the ultimate high country wilderness experience.
✉ letters@theswag.com ✆ www.theswag.com

The Windover Inn
117 Old Hickory St 28786
866-452-4411 828-452-4411
Glenn & Jennifer Duerr

105-175 BB
8 rooms, 8 pb
Most CC
C-ltd/S-ltd/P-no/H-no

Full breakfast
Freshly baked cookies, Fri.
and Sat. PM munchy food,
complimentary bottled
water, organic coffees
Refrig. every flr, AM coffee
on every flr, teas, hot choc.,
in suite brkfst, TV/DVD
player, firepit

Rejuvenate your spirit in our North Carolina luxury accommodations. Nestled in the quaint historic town of Waynesville, between the Blue Ridge Mountains of western North Carolina and the Smoky Mountains, we're just 30 minutes from Asheville!
✉ relax@windoverinn.com ✆ www.windoverinn.com

WEAVERVILLE

Inn on Main Street
88 S Main St 28787
877-873-6074 828-645-4935
Dan & Nancy Ward

125-165 BB
7 rooms, 7 pb
Most CC, *Rated*, •
S-no/P-no/H-no
Spanish, some German
& French

Full breakfast
Complimentary evening
refreshments, plus snacks,
soft drinks always; picnic
lunches sold
Porches & parlor, fireplaces,
cable TV/DVD/VCR,
whirlpool tubs, Biltmore
tickets, rafting

A romantic eco-friendly getaway near Asheville and the Biltmore Estate in quiet, artsy Weaverville. Walk to cafes, live music, galleries and a scenic mountain lake. Antiques, crafts, golf, rafting, hiking, skiing & the Blue Ridge Parkway nearby.
✉ relax@innonmain.com ✪ www.innonmain.com

WILLIAMSTON

Big Mill B&B
1607 Big Mill Rd 27892
252-792-8787
Chloe G. Tuttle

69-135 BB
4 rooms, 4 pb
Most CC
C-ltd/S-ltd/P-no/H-ltd
Some Spanish
May 1-October 15

Continental plus breakfast
Breakfast served in the
room; candlelight catered
gourmet dinners and picnic
lunches available
Bicycles, fireplace, cable TV
in rooms, DVD, wireless
Internet, coin laundry, phone
every room, iron

Featured in Our State magazine and the site of a recent Playboy photo shoot, this coastal Carolina countryside B&B is a favorite of romantics and those who seek privacy. Just minutes from major highways, it is the perfect stopover to the Outer Banks
✉ info@bigmill.com ✪ www.bigmill.com

WILMINGTON

C.W. Worth House B&B
412 S 3rd St 28401
800-340-8559 910-762-8562
Margi & Doug Erickson

140-180 BB
7 rooms, 7 pb
Visa, MC, Disc, *Rated*,
•
C-ltd/S-ltd/P-no/H-no

Full breakfast
Complimentary beverages
and snacks available.
3 sitting rooms, wireless
Internet, porches, gardens,
decorative fireplaces, 1 room
with whirlpool

The C. W. Worth House Victorian Bed & Breakfast, located in the Historic District, is known for its striking Queen Anne architecture, romantic atmosphere, and gardens. Your hosts greet you warmly and make you feel at home.
✉ relax@worthhouse.com ✪ www.worthhouse.com

Graystone Inn
100 S Third St 28401
888-763-4773 910-763-2000
Rich & Marcia Moore

169-379 BB
9 rooms, 9 pb
Visa, MC, AmEx,
Rated, •
C-ltd/S-no/P-no/H-no
German, Italian

Full & continental plus
breakfast
Complimentary wine and
snacks
WiFi, sitting room, piano,
robes, library, fitness center,
phones with voice mail

Recently named "One of America's Top 10 Most Romantic Inns" by American Historic Inns. The Graystone Inn is an AAA Four Diamond property and member of Select Registry.
✉ contactus@graystoneinn.com ✪ www.graystoneinn.com

Rosehill Inn B&B
114 S Third St 28401
800-815-0250 910-815-0250
Tricia & Bob Milton

139-199 BB
6 rooms, 6 pb
Most CC, *Rated*, •
C-ltd/S-no/P-no/H-no

Full breakfast
Sitting room, library,
premium cable TV in rooms,
some VCRs, luxurious
bathrooms, wireless Internet

Romantic lodging at its best! Beautifully restored 1848 Victorian Neo-classical home, in the heart of Wilmington's historic district, near Cape Fear River, beaches, shopping, dining and entertainment. Six guestrooms with period antiques, private baths.
✉ rosehill@rosehill.com ✪ www.rosehill.com

WILMINGTON

The Verandas	169-269 BB	Full breakfast
202 Nun St 28401	8 rooms, 8 pb	Complimentary wine, beer,
910-251-2212	Visa, MC, AmEx,	sherry, sodas, snacks,
Dennis Madsen, Charles	*Rated*, •	homemade cookies
Pennington	C-ltd/S-no/P-no/H-no	Sitting room, cable TV, piano,
	American Sign Language	wireless Internet

Grand, affordable luxury on a quiet street two blocks from riverwalk, restaurants, shopping. Large corner rooms with private baths, phone, TV & wireless Internet. The Verandas is for traveling executives as well as a comfortable weekend retreat.
✉ verandas4@aol.com 🌐 www.verandas.com

WILSON

Whitehead Inn & Executive	90-149 BB	3 Course full breakfast
Suites	11 rooms, 11 pb	Friday &Saturday evening
600 Nash St NE 27893	Most CC, *Rated*	wine service.
252-243-4447	C-ltd/S-ltd/P-no/H-yes	4 elegantly appointed parlors
Jim & Mary Powell		& verandas, cable TV, WiFi,
		Internet on guest computer,
		golf

Selected as one of "best places to stay in the South," the Whitehead Inn is an elegant and romantic respite. AAA Three Diamonds. 12 rooms in four historic homes under majestic trees. Near Barton College, antique shops & 4 golf courses. Minutes from I-95.
✉ reservations1@whiteheadinn.com 🌐 www.whiteheadinn.com

WINSTON-SALEM

Augustus T. Zevely Inn	90-235 BB	Continental plus-wkdy, full-
803 S Main St 27101	12 rooms, 12 pb	wknds
800-928-9299 336-748-9299	Visa, MC, AmEx,	Evening wine & cheese,
Linda Anderson	*Rated*, •	freshly baked cookies
	C-ltd/S-ltd/P-ltd/H-no	nightly, coffee & tea during
		day, bottled water in room
		Fax & copier, restaurant
		reservations, on site parking,
		late check-in/check-out, pet
		accommodations

Circa 1844 Moravian-style inn restored to museum quality. Only lodging in historic Old Salem. Rooms individually furnished in Lexington Old Salem and Bob Timberlake collection. Heated outdoor covered porch. Featured in Country Living. AAA & Mobile rated.
✉ reservations@winston-salem-inn.com 🌐 www.winston-salem-inn.com

Ohio

ALEXANDRIA

WillowBrooke Bed 'n Breakfast
4459 Morse Rd 43001
800-772-6372 740-924-6161
Sandra Gilson

115-185 BB
5 rooms, 5 pb
Visa, MC, Disc
C-ltd/S-no/P-no/H-ltd

Full breakfast
Balconies, fireplaces,
outdoor hot tub, Internet
access, sauna, satellite TV,
Jacuzzi suites

Secluded, elegant English Tudor Manor House with separate Guest House in 34 acres of woods. Large luxurious suites with candlelight, fireplaces, featherbeds & Jacuzzi tubs add to the romantic atmosphere.
✉ wilbrk@aol.com 🌐 www.willowbrooke.com

BALTIC

Mel & Mary's Cottages
2972 Township Rd 190 43804
330-893-2695
Leon & Karen Troyer

99-160 EP
8 rooms, 8 pb
Visa, MC, Disc
C-yes/S-no/P-no/H-ltd
Pennsylvania Dutch

Fireplaces, satellite TV,
campfire, suites

A quiet and peaceful country setting in the heart of Amish Country with cottages, suites, family houses, and a ½ acre pond.
✉ mmcottages@wifi7.com 🌐 www.melandmaryscottages.com

BARNESVILLE

Georgian Pillars
128 E Walnut St 43713
888-425-3741 740-425-3741
Janet Thompson

80-110 BB
4 rooms
Visa, MC
C-yes/S-no/P-no/H-no

Full breakfast
Fireplace, 2 Victorian
Parlors, business friendly
Internet, tv's in rooms

The Georgian Pillars is a 1900 Georgian Revival Home, with lavish oak woodwork and stained glass windows, that has been lovingly decorated in the teal and mauve hues of the Victorian era. We have four spacious rooms, 2 shared baths, business friendly.
✉ bruce.thompson2@comcast.net 🌐 www.georgianpillars.8m.com

BERLIN

Coblentz Country Cabin
5130 TR 359 44610
877-99-SLEEP 330-893-1300
Elvin Coblentz

65-249 BB
6 rooms, 6 pb
Visa, MC, Disc
C-yes/S-no/P-no/H-no

Kitchenette
Fireplace, Jacuzzi, A/C, heat,
cable TV/VCR, Internet

Welcome to Coblentz Country Cabins, beautiful country lodging nestled on a wooded hillside in the heart of Ohio's Amish Country, the largest Amish settlement in the world.
✉ ecoblentz@valkyrie.net 🌐 www.amishcountrylodging.com

Donna's Premier Lodging
East St 44610
800-320-3338 330-893-3068
Johannes & Donna Marie Schlabach

149-369 BB
23 rooms, 23 pb
Visa, MC, Disc, *Rated*
C-ltd/S-ltd/P-no/H-ltd

Please inquire about
breakfast
Fresh fruit and pastry platter
along with sparkling apple
cider.
Pamper your sweetie with a
relaxing in room massage.
Ask about our other
sweetheart packages.

Welcome to Donna's Premier Lodging located in Berlin, Ohio! Experience a romantic, luxurious stay in one of our beautifully appointed honeymoon and anniversary cottages, cedar log cabins, chalets, bridal suites or villas, and enjoy all of our amenities.
✉ info@donnasb-b.com 🌐 www.donnasofberlin.com

BERLIN

Graystone Cottages
5572 N Market St 44610
877-231-2912 330-231-4495
Mark & Dorothy Yoder

79-179 BB
4 rooms, 4 pb
Visa, MC
C-yes/S-no/P-no/H-yes

Pasties, fresh fruit, juice, coffee
½ block from all the best Amish Country shopping, Jacuzzis, kitchenettes

Graystone Cottages is located in the center of Berlin, the most popular town in Holmes County, OH. In the midst of horse-drawn Amish buggies and local gift shops, the bed and breakfast offers a very quiet, private, and warm environment.
✉ dorothy@graystone-cottages.com ❂ www.graystone-cottages.com

BURTON

Red Maple Inn
14707 S Cheshire St 44021
888-646-2753 440-834-8334
Gina N. Holk

119-200 BB
18 rooms, 18 pb
Most CC, *Rated*, •
C-yes/S-yes/P-no/H-yes

Deluxe Continental Breakfast
Wine & cheese, light appetizers, in-room chocolates
Music in room, sitting room, library, Jacuzzis, bikes

Overlooking peaceful Amish country. Relax, refresh, & recharge in our 17 rooms and 1 suite with Jacuzzis, balconies, fireplaces, library, all with great staff. Fitness center and conference room. Near antique & Amish craft shops, 7 golf courses, and more.
✉ info@redmapleinn.com ❂ www.redmapleinn.com

CEDARVILLE

Hearthstone Inn & Suites
10 S Main St 45314
877 644-6466 937-766-3000
Stuart & Ruth Zaharek

109-169 BB
20 rooms, 20 pb
Visa, MC, AmEx, *Rated*
C-yes/S-no/P-ltd/H-yes

Deluxe Continental Breakfast
Dine locally in nearby Yellow Springs, a delightful village with eclectic shops! 10 minutes away.
Game room w/free video library, bicycle rentals, wireless Internet

Delightful country inn offering 20 great guestrooms & Jacuzzi king suites. Ideal for romantic getaways, antiquing, biking, hiking & relaxing in the Dayton/Springfield area! All non-smoking.
✉ hearthstoneinn@juno.com ❂ www.HearthstoneInn.com

CHARM

Guggisberg Swiss Inn/Amish Country Riding Stables
5025 State Rt #557 44617
877-467-9477 330-893-3600
Eric & Julia Guggisberg

79-220 BB
24 rooms, 24 pb
Visa, MC, Disc, *Rated*
C-ltd/S-no/P-no/H-yes

Continental breakfast
Complimentary wiener roast/country picnic Sunday evenings weather permitting (June – October)
Horseback riding stable on premises, horse-drawn sleigh rides in winter, wireless Internet

The Guggisberg Swiss Inn is family owned and operated. We invite you to join us at this unique lodging facility, in one of the largest and friendliest Amish communities in the world. Live entertainment most weekends April through October. Packages.
✉ innkeeper@guggisbergswissinn.com ❂ www.guggisbergswissinn.com

CLEVELAND

Brownstone Inn Downtown
3649 Prospect Ave 44115
216-426-1753
Mr. Robin Yates

75-95 BB
4 rooms, 4 pb
Most CC, *Rated*, •
C-ltd/S-no/P-ltd/H-no

Full breakfast
Snacks, kitchenette for guests to use
Sitting rooms, fireplaces, cable TV, business services

Brownstone Inn Downtown staff is here to provide unique adventures for any occasion (almost). Beautiful townhouse located minutes from all cultural, educational and musical activities.
✉ ryates1@mindspring.com ❂ www.brownstoneinndowntown.com

CLEVELAND

Clifford House	100-155 BB	Full breakfast
1810 W 28th St 44113	4 rooms, 2 pb	In room refrigerator:
216-589-0121	Most CC, •	assorted soda & water,
James Miner	C-ltd/S-ltd/P-ltd/H-no	cookie jars, lots of books &
		some movies
		Central A/C, coffee maker,
		hair dryer, high speed WiFi,
		cable TV

Comfortable and homey is the key to this owner occupied grand, eclectic and charming 1868 Queen Anne home. Two suites with private baths, include an extended stay apartment and a soaring third floor space. Two additional cozy rooms share a large bath.
✉ jminer@cliffordhouse.com ❂ www.cliffordhouse.com

Glendennis B&B	120-168 BB	Full organic breakfast
2808 Bridge Ave 44113	1 rooms, 1 pb	Sitting room, library,
216-589-0663	Most CC, •	business traveler
David & Emily Dennis	C-yes/S-ltd/P-ltd/H-no	accommodations, garage
	French	parking

Cleveland's urban oasis is an 1862 brick home in the historic Ohio City neighborhood. Enjoy privacy and comfort, full organic breakfast, and walk to world-class restaurants.
✉ glendennis@sbcglobal.net ❂ glendennis.com

J. Palen House	125-175 BB	Full breakfast
2708 Bridge Ave 44113	4 rooms, 4 pb	Evening "goodie" tray,
216-664-0813	Visa, MC, AmEx	coffee, tea & snacks
Scott West	C-ltd/S-ltd/P-no/H-no	Wifi, cable TV, private
		courtyard and laundry
		facilities

This 1880's restored Victorian in the historic Ohio City District, is anything but ordinary. The beautifully decorated rooms incorporating playful antiques, spa baths, WiFi and a delicious 3 course breakfast make this a retreat for business or pleasure.
✉ jpalenhouse@aol.com ❂ www.jpalenhouse.com

Stone Gables B&B	110-190 BB	Elegant gourmet full
3806 Franklin Blvd 44113	5 rooms, 5 pb	breakfast
877-215-4326 216-961-4654	Most CC	Vegetarian meals on request,
Richard Turnbull & James	C-yes/S-no/P-ltd/H-no	tea, coffee, snacks always
Hauer	Spanish	available.
		Deck, gardens, library, sitting
		room, parlor, piano, high
		speed Internet, WiFi,
		massage schedulable.

Stone Gables Bed & Breakfast is in Ohio City, a historic neighborhood near the west side of Cleveland, only 1 mile to downtown. Our 5 elegant rooms are designed with your comfort in mind. Romantic whirlpool tub rooms, cozy suites all with private baths.
✉ stonegablesbnb@yahoo.com ❂ www.stonegables.net

COLUMBUS

German Village Guesthouse	145-245 BB	Deluxe continental
748 Jaeger St 43206	5 rooms, 5 pb	Refrigerator stocked with
866-587-2738 614-437-9712	Most CC, •	milk, juices and snacks that
John Pribble	C-yes/S-no/P-no/H-no	you may enjoy at any time
		Indoor/outdoor fireplaces,
		gardens, parking, WiFi,
		Internet phones, cable TV,
		DVD players & library

More boutique hotel than traditional bed and breakfast, the German Village Guesthouse offers 3 spacious & contemporary guestrooms, all with fantastic private baths, and 2 luxuriously appointed suites, in an historic urban neighborhood setting.
✉ info@gvguesthouse.com ❂ www.gvguesthouse.com

COLUMBUS

Harrison House
313 W 5th Ave 43201
800-827-4203 614-421-2202
Lynn Varney

129 BB
4 rooms, 4 pb
Most CC, *Rated*
C-yes/S-no/P-ltd/H-no

Full breakfast
Vegetarian and special diets
meal planning. Please advise
in advance.
Guest parlor, free parking,
cable TV, free WiFi

Take a step back in time, relax & enjoy its original cut glass windows, magnificent wood-work, elegant lace curtains & picturesque landscaping.
✉ lynn@harrisonhouse-columbus.com ◐ www.harrisonhouse-columbus.com

House of the Seven Goebels
4975 Hayden Run Rd 43221
614-761-9595
Pat & Frank Goebel

100 BB
2 rooms, 2 pb
Visa, MC, AmEx
C-ltd/S-no/P-no/H-no

Full & Continental breakfast
Cool water, fruit
Music room, parlor,
woodburning fireplace,
Oriental rugs

From the pineapple hospitality sign above the front walk, to the warmth of the music room and parlor, The House of the Seven Goebels beckons to those that enjoy and appreciate the past.
✉ fgoebel@columbus.rr.com

Juergen's B&B
525 S 4th St 43206
614-224-6858
Rosemarie Keidel

65-75 BB
2 rooms
Visa, MC, *Rated*
C-ltd/S-no/P-no/H-no
German

Full breakfast
German bakery & restaurant
on the premises, afternoon
cake & coffee
Perfect location near many
attractions, parking, 7 day
cancellation policy by mail

Comfortable lodgings with shared bath close to downtown, historic German Village, parks, dining, gardens. Bakery on premises.

Short North B&B
50 E. Lincoln St 43215
800-516-9664 614-299-5050
Sandy Davis

129-149 BB
7 rooms, 7 pb
Most CC
C-ltd/S-no/P-no/H-no

Full breakfast
Cable TV, wireless Internet,
private parking, small
business retreats

Urban delight in the Short North Arts District. Minutes from Downtown Columbus, Ohio State University and the Columbus Convention Center. We're just steps away from the best galleries, restaurants, specialty shops, clubs and pubs that the city offers.
✉ 50-lincoln@excite.com ◐ www.columbus-bed-breakfast.com

DAYTON

Inn Port Bed & Breakfast and Suites
22, 137-139 Brown St 45402
937-224-7678
Leslie & Jeff Gonya

69-139 BB
6 rooms, 4 pb
Most CC, •
C-ltd/S-no/P-ltd/H-no

Continental plus breakfast
Complimentary soda &
water, a bottle of "2 Pups"
homemade wine available
on request
High speed Internet, satellite
TV, CD player in each
guestroom, guest kitchen

Within walking distance of many of the tastes, sights and sounds of downtown Dayton, Inn Port is your lodging oasis in the heart of the historic Oregon District. Ideal for a romantic getaway, girls' night out or a visit to the University of Dayton.
✉ innport@sbcglobal.net ◐ www.innport.com/guesthouse/guesthouse.html

Tell your hosts Pamela Lanier sent you.

DELAWARE

Welcome Home Inn
6640 Home Rd 43015
800-381-0364 740-881-6588
Forrest & Brenda Williams

99-135 BB
5 rooms, 5 pb
Most CC
C-yes/S-no/P-no/H-ltd

Full Breakfast
Snacks in rooms & Inn Home
Bakery goods for order
Sitting room, porch,
accommodate business
travelers, antiques, grand
piano, walking trail thru
woods

*A Southern farmhouse style home located on six wooded acres. Wraparound wicker filled
porch. Oak antiques. Grand piano in large dining room.*
✉ info@welcomehomeinn.com ◐ www.welcomehomeinn.com

DELLROY

Whispering Pines B&B
1268 Magnolia Rd SW 44620
866-452-5388 330-735-2824
Bill & Linda Horn

185-235 BB
9 rooms, 9 pb
Most CC, *Rated*, •
C-ltd/S-ltd/P-no/H-yes

Full breakfast
Afternoon home-made
chocolate chip cookies, tea &
coffee.
2-person whirlpool tubs,
fireplace, balcony, lakeviews,
great food, romance, in-room
massage

*Your dream place on the lake, nestled on 7 rolling acres with a perfect view of beautiful
Atwood Lake. Relax in a 2-person whirlpool-tub, sip wine on your balcony and wake up to
a delicious breakfast.*
✉ whisperingpines@atwoodlake.com ◐ www.atwoodlake.com

DOVER

**Olde World B&B and Tea
Room**
2982 State Rt 516 NW 44622
800-447-1273 330-343-1333
Jonna Cronebaugh

70-140 BB
5 rooms, 5 pb
Most CC, *Rated*, •
S-no/P-yes/H-ltd

Full gourmet breakfast
"Dinner by Moonlight" &
"Olde World Supper"
packages available with
advance order.
TV, CD, robes, A/C, private
bath, hot tub, massages,
golfing

*Our Victorian Italianate farmhouse features guestrooms with "olde world" culture. Enjoy
delicious local food & genuine comfort and hospitality. Stroll our beautiful gardens and
take in the peaceful scenery. Ask about our special seasonal packages!*
✉ info@oldeworldbb.com ◐ www.oldeworldbb.com

DUNDEE

Yeowza Resorts B&B
8480 Possum Hollow Rd, NW
44624
888-493-6992 330-852-3270
James Wallick

85-225 BB
10 rooms, 10 pb
Most CC
C-yes/S-ltd/P-ltd/H-yes

Full Brkfast Sat, Sun; Cont.
wkdys
Romantic candlelight
dinners, Picnic Basket
lunches
Private Hot Tubs; wireless
Internet; trails; lake
w/paddleboats, canoes,
fishing; banquets/wedding

*Come away to a secluded Log Cabin paradise nestled in the heart of Amish Country.
Weekend Getaways, Dream Weddings, Honeymoons . . . A quiet place for leisurely afternoons in the sun or romantic moonlit strolls along the shore of our illuminated lake.*
✉ info@yeowzaresorts.com ◐ www.yeowzaresorts.com

FINDLAY

Lambs Ear B&B	69-99 BB	Full breakfast
St Rt 568 45840	4 rooms, 3 pb	Lunch, dinner upon request
419-424-5810	Visa, MC, *Rated*	Sitting room, whirlpool tubs,
Lorena Oman	C-ltd/S-no/P-yes/H-no	fireplaces, accom. bus.
		travelers, banquet room
		avail., catering

1915 homestead with original 1850's barn. Antique and country decor, 2 fireplaces, walking trails, pond with canoe, whirlpool tubs. Close to shopping, 5 golf courses, many parks, and antique shops.
✉ lambsear@turbosurf.net ◐ www.lambsear.com

FRANKLIN FURNACE

RiverView Inn B&B	99-129 BB	Full breakfast
91 Riverview Dr 45629	4 rooms, 4 pb	Packaged snacks, soft drinks,
888-388-8439 740-355-4004	Most CC, *Rated*	iced teas, bottled water
George & Bobbie Sich	C-yes/S-no/P-no/H-ltd	Exercise room, outdoor hot
		tub, whirlpool tub, satellite
		TVs, wireless Internet,
		business center.

The Riverview Bed & Breakfast Inn is a modern, spacious California-style home with a large elevated wraparound deck, outdoor hot tub, and upstairs balcony. All rooms have wall-to-wall carpeting, satellite TV, and private baths.
✉ riverviewbb@roadrunner.com ◐ www.riverhost.com

FREDERICKTOWN

Heartland Country Resort	180-240 BB	Full breakfast
3020 Township Rd. 190 43019	4 rooms, 4 pb	Afternoon tea, snacks, lunch
800-230-7030 419-768-9300	Most CC, *Rated*, ●	and dinner available
Dorene Henschen	C-yes/S-ltd/P-yes/H-ltd	Sitting room, screened
		porch, Jacuzzis, fireplaces,
		luxury suites, trails and stalls
		for horses

Hospitality, adventure, and romance await you at this luxury horse ranch northeast of Columbus, Ohio. Scenic woods, hills, pastures, and recreation or relaxation, on over 100-acres. Family friendly, large groups welcome.
✉ heartbb@bright.net ◐ www.heartlandcountryresort.com

FREDRICKSBURG

Gilead's Balm Manor	100-175 BB	Full breakfast
8690 CR 201 44627	6 rooms, 6 pb	Snacks, complimentary
888-612-3436 330-695-3881	Most CC, *Rated*, ●	sparkling juice
Harry & Cheryl Welch	C-ltd/S-ltd/P-no/H-ltd	Jacuzzis, fireplaces, satellite
		TV, free videos, small lake,
		paddleboat

European elegance in Amish Country. 6 luxurious rooms, 12 ft ceiling, waterfalls Jacuzzi, fireplaces, kitchenette, private bath, A/C, satellite TV, VCR, CD player.
✉ info@gileadsbalmmanor.com ◐ www.gileadsbalmmanor.com

GLENMONT

Annie's Place at Nature's	150-175 BB	Continental plus breakfast
Retreat	3 rooms, 2 pb	Enjoy fresh Amish baked pie
12061 TR 252 44628	Visa, MC	and a loaf of bread from our
330-231-0108 330-377-4783	C-yes/S-ltd/P-ltd/H-no	local Amish Bakery in
Bob & Karen Hunter	Every season	addition to breakfast
		Hot tub, satellite dish,
		fireplace, trails, hay rides,
		horse rental available, catch
		& release pond.

This Civil War era farmhouse has 3 bedrooms and 2 baths and can sleep up to 6 people. Kitchen, reading room, fireplace, gazebo with hot-tub. Reservations are for the whole house, not individual rooms. Special arrangements possible for more than 6 persons.
✉ info@naturesretreat.net ◐ www.naturesretreat.net

HOCKING HILLS

Glenlaurel Inn
14940 Mount Olive Rd 43149
800-809-REST (7378) 740-385-4070
Greg & Kelley Leonard

149-339 BB
19 rooms, 19 pb
Most CC, *Rated*, •
S-no/P-no/H-yes

Gourmet breakfast
We offer a dining experience like no other . . . we serve fine cuisine with a Scottish flair
Hot tubs, secret gardens, fireplaces, conference facility, weddings, walking trails, gift shop & spa

Welcome to the Glenlaurel Inn, a Scottish Country Inn with wooded cottages and crofts, labeled the "premier romantic getaway in the Midwest" and conveniently located just one hour southeast of Columbus, Ohio in the Hocking Hills.
✉ info@glenlaurel.com ◐ www.glenlaurel.com

KINSMAN

Dream Horse Guesthouse
9532 SR 7 44428
330-876-0428
Allan and Catherine Kaulback

65-150 BB
4 rooms, 4 pb
Visa, MC, Disc
C-yes/S-no/P-yes/H-no

Full breakfast
Horse stalls, dog & cat areas, horse lessons & trail riding, kitchen, massage, Jacuzzi, garden

Pet/horse/family friendly! Come to a majestic, historic timber frame barn B&B in Lake Pymatuning resort area of northeast Ohio. Massage, horseback lessons & trail riding by appt. Endless activities, calendar of events for arts, museums. Area eagle nests!
✉ kinsmanbarncats@embarqmail.com ◐ www.dreamhorseguesthouse.com

LEBANON

Hardy's Bed and Breakfast Suites
212 Wright Ave 45036
877-932-3266 513-932-3266
Phyllis & Al Hardy

155-185 BB
10 rooms, 9 pb
Visa, MC
C-ltd/S-ltd/P-no/H-ltd

Full breakfast
Fresh baked desserts in your room when you arrive, tea & coffee in room
Suites, massage therapy, parlor with fireplace, flower gardens and porches

Enjoy our four beautifully furnished Victorian homes and gardens, all at one location in the Floraville District of Historic Lebanon, OH. Experience one of eight private suites for your romantic special occasion or relaxing getaway.
✉ hardys@go-concepts.com ◐ www.hardysproperties.com/hardy%27s_haven.html

LOGAN

A Georgian Manner B&B
29055 Evans Rd 43138
800-606-1840 740-380-9567
B.J. King

105-249 BB
5 rooms, 3 pb
Visa, MC, •
S-no/P-no/H-yes

European Breakfast
Coffee, tea, snacks, sodas
Jaccuzzi Suites, fireplace, canoe, Lake Logan, kitchen, Wedding Pavilion, hiking, Wedding Ceremony

A Georgian Manner Bed & Breakfast B&B Inn is in the Hocking Hills on Lake Logan, Logan, Ohio. Outdoor wedding chapel is our specialty. The Ohio Honeymoon Suite/Jacuzzi is perfect for romantic getaways, elopements, honeymoons, anniversaries, ladies night out
✉ ageorgianmanner@hocking.net ◐ www.georgianmanner.com

Inn & Spa at Cedar Falls
21190 State Rt 374 43138
800-65-FALLS 740-385-7489
Ellen Grinsfelder & Terry Lingo

125-289 BB
26 rooms, 26 pb
Visa, MC, AmEx, •
C-ltd/S-no/P-yes/H-yes
Closed Christmas

Full breakfast
Lunch & dinner available, Restaurant on premises.
Spa, gift shop, bar service, sitting room, business retreats welcome

Log cabins, secluded cottages and antique furnished rooms. Three cabins with whirlpool tubs; 12 cottages with whirlpool tubs. Gourmet meals prepared from the inn's organic garden. Gift shop, spa & restaurant.
✉ info@innatcedarfalls.com ◐ www.innatcedarfalls.com

LONDON

Alexandra's B&B
117 N Main St 43140
740-852-5993
Ron & Susan Brown

85-179 BB
8 rooms, 7 pb
Visa, MC, AmEx,
Rated, •
C-ltd/S-no/P-no/H-ltd

Full breakfast
Porches, Jacuzzi, wedding
accommodations, company
retreats, family reunions . . .
you name it!

Walking into Alexandra's Bed and Breakfast may give the feeling of stepping back in time, but amongst the beautiful antiques you will find all the necessities of modern life.
✉ info@alexandrasbb.com ◐ www.alexandrasbb.com

MIAMISBURG

English Manor
505 E Linden Ave 45342
937-866-2288
Julie & Larry Chmiel

89-125 BB
5 rooms, 3 pb
Most CC, *Rated*
C-ltd/S-no/P-ltd/H-no

Full breakfast
Teas, luncheons and dinners
for groups with advance
reservations
Wireless available
throughout the property.

A Tudor style mansion. Tranquility in a setting of elegance, hand-rubbed wood, leaded glass windows & antique furnishings. Step back in time.
✉ englishmanorohio@yahoo.com ◐ www.englishmanorohio.com

MILLERSBURG

The Barn Inn
6838 CR 203 44654
877-674-7600 330-674-7600
Paul & Loretta Coblentz

99-219 BB
11 rooms, 11 pb
Most CC, •
C-ltd/S-ltd/P-no/H-yes

Full Country Breakfast
Coffees, tea, baked items,
popcorn
Fireplaces, satellite TV,
double size Jacuzzis, suites,
recliners, DVD/VCR, WiFi

Your Lodging Choice—Enjoy generous hospitality and a great country breakfast in a beautifully restored barn in Ohio Amish country where you'll witness rural Amish life of a by-gone-era. Standard-VIP rooms, private baths, Jacuzzis, fireplaces, WiFI . . .
✉ reservations@thebarninn.com ◐ www.thebarninn.com

Fields of Home Guest House
7278 CR 201 44654
330-674-7152
Mervin & Ruth Yoder

65-145 BB
7 rooms, 7 pb
Visa, MC, Disc, *Rated*
C-yes/S-no/P-no/H-ltd
Limited German

Continental plus breakfast
Snacks, complimentary
sodas
Suites, fireplaces, hot tubs,
whirlpool baths,
kitchenettes,
accommodations for
business travelers

Our log cabin B&B invites you to relax and enjoy the peace and quiet of rural Amish Country. Enjoy perennial gardens, fish pond and paddle boat. We offer such amenities as fireplaces, kitchenettes, whirlpool bathtubs, and two-person hot tubs.
◐ www.fieldsofhome.com

Garden Gate Get-a-Way
6041 Township Rd 310 44654
330-674-7608
Herb & Carol Steffey

105-185 BB
5 rooms, 5 pb
Visa, MC, Disc, *Rated*
C-ltd/S-no/P-no/H-ltd
Closed Sunday

Homemade Breakfast Buffet
Homemade evening snack,
coffee, tea, hot chocolate,
popcorn, in-room bottled
water.
Common room with
refrigerator, microwave,
video library, books &
magazines; Games & Card
too.

Named One of the Top 10 Bed and Breakfasts in the United States. Our Berlin Township bed & breakfast is in Holmes County Ohio Amish Country. Best noted for perennial gardens & evening campfire.
✉ info@garden-gate.com ◐ www.garden-gate.com

MILLERSBURG

Holmes With A View	118-245 BB	Continental breakfast
3672 TR 154 44654	6 rooms, 6 pb	Whirlpool tub, gas fireplace,
877-831-2736 330-893-2390	Most CC	kitchen, wireless Internet
Paul & Miriam Grossi	C-ltd/S-no/P-no/H-yes	

Our charming hillside suites offer magnificent views of the rolling Amish farmland of Holmes County, Ohio. The secluded location permits privacy, and yet is central to the neighboring communities of Charm, Berlin and Millersburg.
✉ pagrossi@juno.com ○ www.holmeswithaview.com

The Inn at Honey Run	104-290 BB	Continental breakfast
6920 Country Rd #203 44654	43 rooms, 43 pb	Lunch & dinner available
800-468-6639 330-674-0011	Most CC	Game & reading room,
Phil Jenkins	C-ltd/S-no/P-no	fireplaces, deck gardens,
		concierge

Nestled on 60 acres in the heart of the Ohio Amish Country, the Inn at Honey Run is a serene oasis of nature and wildlife, comfort and privacy, fine dining and warm hospitality.
✉ info@innathoneyrun.com ○ www.innathoneyrun.com

Orchard Guest House	190-300 BB	Continental breakfast
7029 CR 203 44654	3 rooms, 3 pb	Family/game room,
866-674-2768 330-674-2768	Visa, MC	VCR/DVD, rollaway beds
Dave & Mariam Schlabach	C-yes/S-no/P-no/H-no	available, complete privacy,
		linens provided

Our B&B offers a quiet and relaxing stay, whether you are looking for a quiet place for your honeymoon/anniversary, or for a family gathering or retreat for your group of up to 10 persons. Just 4 miles from Berlin on a country road.
✉ hrorchard@valkyrie.net ○ www.orchardathoneyrun.com/orchard_house.htm

MOUNT VERNON

The Chaney Manor B&B Inn	125-150 BB	Full breakfast OR discount
7864 Newark Rd 43050	3 rooms, 3 pb	without
740-392-2304	Visa, MC, Disc, •	Dinners with advance
Freda & Norman Chaney	C-ltd/S-no/P-ltd/H-ltd	reservations, snacks.
	French and German	Romantic stays: heart cakes,
	(limited)	candies!
		Deep seated 2 person
		Jacuzzi, therapeutic
		massage, warm stones for
		self-therapy.

Winner of 3 awards for North America!! One of the most unusual, romantic, historic Inns in Ohio. Huge suites, gourmet meals, Roman Jacuzzi room, massage. Six acres with gardens, pond, covered dock and bridge. Honeymoons, reunions, meetings, etc.
✉ chaney@ecr.net

Locust Grove Ranch B&B	129-159 BB	Full Country Breakfast
12480 Dunham Rd 43050	4 rooms, 4 pb	Evening dessert included
740-392-6443	Visa, MC	Pool, fireplaces, library,
Cindy & Marwood Hallett	C-ltd/S-no/P-ltd/H-no	piano, deck, massages, free
		phone, wireless high-speed,
		horse arena & boarding

A newly built ranch and Arabian horse breeding farm where guests may enjoy the peaceful atmosphere of 75 quiet, rural acres, with luxurious guestrooms with private baths, an extensive library, outside decks & pool, herb garden & orchard.
✉ cindy@locustgroveranch.com ○ www.locustgroveranch.com

474 Ohio

MOUNT VERNON

Russell-Cooper House
115 E. Gambier St 43050
740-397-8638
Tom Dvorak

75-100 BB
6 rooms, 6 pb
Visa, MC, AmEx
C-ltd/S-no/P-no/H-ltd

Gourmet Candlelit Breakfast
Elegant Ballroom available
for business and social
luncheons, dinners & parties
Carved cherry mantle
fireplace, library, common
room, sun room, outdoor hot
tub, WiFi

Nestled in the heart of Mount Vernon, Ohio, America's Hometown, is this remarkable high Victorian mansion, Circa 1830. It is home to the fifth generation family and a National Award Winning Bed and Breakfast.
✉ innkeeper@russell-cooper.com 🌐 www.russell-cooper.com

NAPOLEON

The Augusta Rose B&B
345 W Main St 43545
877-590-1960 419-592-5852
Ed & Mary Hoeffel

80-85 BB
4 rooms, 4 pb
Visa, MC, AmEx, •
C-yes/S-no/P-no/H-no

Full breakfast
Snacks, soda and ice water
are available in the sitting
room.
2 sitting rooms—one with TV,
recreational assistance.
Wireless Internet access

Stately Victorian with wraparound porch, located one block from scenic Maumee River. Tranquil small town.
✉ innkeepers@augustarose.com 🌐 www.augustarose.com

NEW CONCORD

Friendship House B&B
62 W Main St 43762
877-968-5501 740-826-7397
Dan & Diane Troendly

75-85 BB
5 rooms, 5 pb
Visa, MC, *Rated*
C-ltd/S-no/P-no/H-no

Continental plus breakfast
Snacks
Sitting room, cable TV,
accommodate business
travelers

Relax in the comfort of our 1830s landmark home, lovingly furnished with antiques. Located across the street from Muskingum College and is within walking distance to restaurants, the S Bridge, and all college locations. We can recommend a favorite museum.
✉ info@bedandbreakfastohio.com 🌐 www.bedandbreakfastohio.com

NORWALK

Georgian Manor Inn
123 W Main St 44857
800-668-1644 419-663-8132
Judy & Gene Denney

110-200 BB
4 rooms, 4 pb
Visa, MC, AmEx,
Rated, •
C-ltd/S-no/P-no/H-no
Closed Christmas

Full breakfast
Soft drinks, snacks, 5
minutes from great casual,
family-owned restaurant
5 public rooms including
large library, sun porch,
gardens, 2 porches, 2 patios,
walk to day spa

AAA 4 Diamond rated, stately mansion on historic West Main St., 1.4 acres with gardens, near Lake Erie and Sandusky vacation hot spots. Plush surroundings & elegant accommodations with 4 guestrooms & 5 public rooms. Spa, dining, shopping & golf nearby.
✉ GeorgianManor@neo.rr.com 🌐 www.georgianmanorinn.com

OBERLIN

1830 Hallauer House B&B
14945 Hallauer Rd 44074
877-774-3406 440-774-3400
Joe & Sue Woodward

125-185 BB
3 rooms, 3 pb
Visa, MC, Disc
S-no/P-no/H-no

Full breakfast
Mini-fridge stocked with
snacks and beverages
Music room, AC, in-room frig,
wireless net, in-ground
heated pool, gardens, sauna,
whirlpool tub, TV

Greek Revival home on 2 acres offers 3 bedrooms, 1 of which is a suite that will sleep 7, each with private bath, satellite TV, air conditioning, and refrigerators. Secluded, pool, gardens, music room, full breakfast. Near Oberlin College campus.
✉ hallauerhouse@verizon.net 🌐 www.hallauerhousebnb.com

OBERLIN

Ivy Tree Inn & Garden	84-120 BB	Full breakfast
Oberlin	4 rooms, 4 pb	Afternoon tea, catered small
195 S Professor St 44074	Visa, MC, •	meeting/events
440-774-4510	C-ltd/S-no/P-no/H-no	Sitting room, cable TV,
Ron Kelly & Steve Coughlin		garden tours, small meetings

Oberlins's First B&B, est. 16 yrs. 1850's Historic Home. Award winning inn & garden with designer guestrooms, private baths and gorgeous gardens. 2 blocks to Oberlin College. "Best Scenic View in Oberlin."
✉ conorr12@yahoo.com

PAINESVILLE

Fitzgerald's Irish B&B	95-150 BB	Full breakfast on weekends
47 Mentor Ave 44077	4 rooms, 4 pb	Beverages and continental
440-639-0845	Visa, MC, Disc, *Rated*	breakfast on weekdays
Debra & Tom Fitzgerald	C-ltd/S-no/P-no/H-no	Sitting room, satellite TV room

Irish hospitality awaits you in our 16-room French Tudor, which will charm you with its unique castle-like architecture. 3 miles from Lake Erie beaches, 15 mins from 25+ wineries & 30 minutes from Cleveland.
✉ fitzbb@gmail.com ◐ www.fitzgeraldbb.com

POLAND

Inn At The Green	75 BB	Continental plus breakfast
500 S Main St 44514	4 rooms, 4 pb	Complimentary wine
330-757-4688	Visa, MC, *Rated*, •	Oriental rugs, deck, patio,
Ginny & Steve Meloy	C-yes/S-no/P-no/H-no	antiques, garden, sitting room, fireplaces

Authentically restored Victorian townhouse in preserved Western Reserve Village near Youngstown. Convenient to Turnpike and I-80. Just outside door, historic Main Street; just inside, comfort and elegance.
◐ www.innatthegreen.com

PORT CLINTON

Sunnyside Tower B&B Inn	79-189 BB	Full breakfast
3612 NW Catawba Rd 43452	10 rooms, 5 pb	Sitting room, tennis court,
888-831-1263 419-797-9315	Most CC, *Rated*, •	spas, fireplaces, cable TV,
John & Diana Davenport	C-yes/S-ltd/P-ltd/H-yes	accommodate business travelers

Historic 1879 Victorian Farmhouse on 20+ acres on Catawsa Island near Put-In-Bay and Cedar Point. Romantic and comfortable surroundings. ½ mile from the ferry to Lake Erie Islands.
✉ ssidetowr@cros.net ◐ www.sunnysidetower.com

RAVENNA

Rocking Horse Inn	80-120 BB	Continental plus breakfast
248 W Riddle Ave 44266	4 rooms, 2 pb	Afternoon tea & snacks,
800-457-0439 330-297-5720	C-yes/S-no/P-no/H-no	coffee, tea, sodas, hot
Robert Walker		chocolate available anytime, complimentary wine Spas, satellite TV, DVD players, BBQ grill, games, Internet, fax, laundry facilities, library

Welcome to the Rocking Horse Inn, a Victorian mansion first built in 1867, it took nearly a decade to complete. Extensive porches filled with white wicker furniture and decorated with seasonal decoration. The Inn is overflowing with Victorian antiques.
✉ rockhorsen@aol.com

SAGAMORE HILLS

Inn at Brandywine Falls
8230 Brandywine Rd 44067
888-306-3381 330-467-1812
George & Katie Hoy

139-325 BB
6 rooms, 6 pb
Most CC, *Rated*, •
C-ltd/S-ltd/P-ltd/H-yes

Full Candlelight Breakfast
Library, sitting room,
fireplaces, Jacuzzi

Built in 1848, the Inn at Brandywine Falls is an impeccable country place, part of the tapestry of 33,000 acres of parkland and Cuyahoga Valley National Park, adjacent to the Brandywine waterfall. Six rooms, all with well-appointed private baths.
✉ brandywinefallsinn@windstream.net ◑ www.innatbrandywinefalls.com

SANDUSKY

Wagner's 1844 Inn
230 E Washington St 44870
419-626-1726
Barbara Wagner

70-125 BB
3 rooms, 3 pb
Visa, MC, Disc
C-ltd/S-no/P-yes/H-ltd

Continental plus breakfast
Complimentary chocolates
Billiard room with TV, air
conditioning, screened in
porch, patio, fireplaces.

Step back into history with a quiet retreat from the hustle and bustle of today's world at Wagner's 1844 Inn in Sandusky, Ohio. Elegantly restored Victorian home. Listed on National Register of Historic Places. Near Lake Erie attractions.
✉ wagnersinn@sanduskyohio.com ◑ www.lrbcg.com/wagnersinn

SUGARCREEK

Breitenbach B&B
307 Dover Rd 44681
800-843-9463 330-343-3603
Deanna Bear

75-85 BB
4 rooms, 4 pb
Visa, MC
C-ltd/S-no/P-no/H-no

Full breakfast
Complimentary wine
Fireplaces, cable TV

A beautiful, comfortable home located in the heart of Ohio's Amish Country. We serve our own Breitenbach wine in the evening, and a full country breakfast in the morning.
✉ amishwine@tusco.net ◑ www.breitenbachwine.com/bed_fr.htm

TOLEDO

Mansion View Inn B&B
2035 Collingwood Ave 43620
419-244-5676
Don & Brenda Spurlin

129-149 BB
4 rooms, 4 pb
Visa, MC
S-no/P-no/H-no

Enjoy a full gourmet
breakfast
Historic mansion &
neighborhood, walking tours,
gourmet breakfast, Art,
antique shopping, WiFi, TV

Enjoy splendor in a historic 1887 eighteen room Victorian Mansion with four beautiful bed & breakfast rooms. Mansion View can also host special events. It is situated near the Toledo Museum of Art, the Convention Center, dining and shopping.
✉ innkeeper@mansionviewtoledo.com ◑ www.mansionviewtoledo.com

WESTERVILLE

Westerville Inn
5 S West St 43081
877-816-5247 614-882-3910
Brenda & Terry Winebrenner

105-125 BB
3 rooms, 3 pb
Visa, MC, Disc, •
C-yes/S-ltd/P-ltd/H-ltd
Sign

Full breakfast
Homemade cookies under
the pie plate, coffee, tea, hot
chocolate & other beverages
upon request.
Wireless Internet, fax/copier
available, garden, fish pond,
information on local
attractions

Originally a two room cabin, built to house a widow & her 11 children, the Inn was renovated in the 1920s and sits on a half-acre surrounded by a white picket fence. Conveniently close to historic uptown Westerville for shopping & fun.
✉ info@westervilleinn.com ◑ www.westervilleinn.com

Oklahoma

ARDMORE ────────────────────────────────

Shiloh Morning Inn	159-299 BB	Three Course Breakfast
2179 Ponderosa Rd 73401	9 rooms, 9 pb	Weekend wine and cheese,
888-554-7674 580-223-9500	Most CC, *Rated*, •	dinner baskets by
Linda Humphrey	S-no/P-no/H-yes	reservation on Friday &
		Saturday evenings.
		Walking trails throughout
		property, TV/VCR (with over
		300 movies), mini-fridge,
		whirlpool tubs

An oasis to leave cares behind as you enjoy the rural Oklahoma countryside. Romantic, secluded getaway; soak in a private hot tub, stroll on 73 acres of gated privacy, & enjoy life as it was meant to be.
✉ innkeepers@ShilohMorning.com ☼ www.ShilohMorning.com

BROKEN BOW ────────────────────────────────

Lago Vista B&B	200-250 BB	Full breakfast
Hwy 259A 74728	4 rooms, 4 pb	Girls Gone Wine and Beer
580-494-7378	Most CC	served each evening. Snacks
Chandra Rickey	S-ltd/P-yes/H-no	and non alcoholic beverages
		during entire stay
		Jacuzzi tub, bath amenities,
		fireplace, wireless Internet,
		balconies, Satellite TV, game
		room, views

A Tuscan style house where all 4 guestrooms have balconies with views of Broken Bow Lake. Each room has a fireplace, Jacuzzi tub, walk-in shower and luxury bed linens. While visiting Lago Vista enjoy Beavers Bend State Park and Broken Bow Lake.
✉ lagovistabedandbreakfast@yahoo.com ☼ www.lagovistabedandbreakfast.com

EDMOND ────────────────────────────────

Aaron's Gate Country	249-339 BB	Self-cooked breakfast
Getaway	4 rooms, 4 pb	Drinks, popcorn, famous
73044	Most CC	Maple Walnut Cookies
877-540-1300 405-282-0613	S-no/P-no/H-no	Full kitchens, grill, fireplaces,
Gary & Martha Hall		Jacuzzis, hot tubs

Private honeymoon cottages for two. Exclusive retreat for magical romance. Jacuzzis for two, fireplaces, full entertainment centers, European spa showers, and screened porches with hot tubs for two.
✉ innkeeper@arcadianinn.com ☼ www.aaronsgate.com/aarons-gate-about

Arcadian Inn B&B	159-249 BB	Full breakfast
328 E First 73034	8 rooms, 8 pb	Dinner by reservation,
800-299-6347 405-348-6347	Most CC, *Rated*, •	complimentary sodas, water
Martha & Gary Hall	S-no/P-no/H-no	& snacks
		Sitting room, hot tubs,
		Fireplace, wireless Internet

Luxurious, romantic setting, sumptuous homemade breakfast. Intimate getaway for couples, perfect for the business traveler. Specializing in preferential treatment.
✉ innkeeper@arcadianinn.com ☼ www.arcadianinn.com

NORMAN

Montford Inn
322 W Tonhawa 73069
800-321-8969 405-321-2200
William & Ginger Murray,
Phyllis & Ron Murray

99-239 BB
16 rooms, 16 pb
Most CC, *Rated*, •
C-yes/S-no/P-no/H-yes

Full breakfast
Early evening wine, soft
drinks & snacks
Fireplaces, 2 outdoor/private
hot tubs, six cottages with 2-
person whirlpools

*Nestled in the heart of Norman, OK, the Montford Inn B&B invites you to experience the
comfort of being at home, yet be a part of something special. Urban 16-room inn with 6
cottage suites. Restaurants, shops, parks, University of Oklahoma nearby.*
✉ innkeeper@montfordinn.com ◐ www.montfordinn.com

OKLAHOMA CITY

**Grandison Inn at Maney
Park**
1200 N Shartel Ave 73103
888-799-4667 405-232-8778
Claudia & Bob Wright

99-199 BB
8 rooms, 8 pb
Most CC
C-ltd/S-no/P-ltd/H-ltd

Full Breakfast on weekends
In-room dinners, picnic
baskets, snacks & stocked
refrigerator
Airport pickup, romantic
amenities & packages
available

*Each bedroom has its own personality & story, decorated with handsome antiques. Rooms
are complete with private bath including luxurious Jacuzzi tubs & an abundance of
romantic amenities!*
✉ grandison@coxinet.net ◐ www.grandisoninn.com

SULPHUR

Echo Canyon Resort
549 Lawton Ave 73086
580-421-5076
Carol Ann & Joe Van Horn

119-249 MAP
13 rooms, 13 pb
Most CC
C-ltd/S-ltd/P-no/H-ltd

3 course gourmet breakfast
Gourmet Dinner included in
rates
Spa, massages, Jacuzzis,
sitting rooms, private
balconies, robes & bath
sheets, 50 movie channels

*A unique spa resort, on twenty seven private gated acres, with five star dining. Romantic
luxury destination.*
✉ ecmanor@brightok.net ◐ www.echocanyonresort.com

Oregon

ARCH CAPE——————————————————————————————————

Arch Cape House	119-299 BB	2 Course Gourmet Breakfast
31970 E Ocean Rd 97102	9 rooms, 9 pb	Gardens, Jacuzzi, living
800-436-2848 503-436-2800	Visa, MC, •	room, oceanview deck, WiFi,
Cynthia & Stephen Malkowski	C-ltd/S-no/P-ltd/H-yes	2 minute walk to beach,
		spa/sauna room

The setting of Arch Cape is between a forest and the sea, creating a feeling of tranquility and peacefulness. The beach is a 2 minute walk from the inn, and six of the rooms have an ocean view.
✉ info@archcapeinn.com ✆ www.archcapehouse.com

ASHLAND——————————————————————————————————

A Midsummer's Dream	150-230 BB	Full breakfast
496 Beach St 97520	5 rooms, 5 pb	All suites have fireplaces &
877-376-8800 541-552-0605	Visa, MC, Disc	spa tubs; finest linens, towels
Lisa Beach	C-ltd/S-no/P-no/H-yes	& robes

Ashland's newest romantic inn housed in a 1901 Victorian, just 8/10 of a mile from downtown Ashland and the Shakespeare Festival.
✉ info@amidsummer.com ✆ www.amidsummer.com

Arden Forest Inn	135-225 BB	2 course family-style
261 W Hersey St 97520	5 rooms, 5 pb	breakfast
800-460-3912 541-488-1496	Visa, MC	Complimentary coffee, tea,
William Faiia & Corbet	S-no	iced refreshments
Unmack		Library, art, guest kitchen,
		high-speed Internet, garden,
		fountains, gazebo, heated
		pool, sundeck

Providing a sanctuary for theatre lovers, this unique Ashland, Oregon bed and breakfast is situated on an acre of lush, park-like gardens and offers over 15 years of hospitality excellence.
✉ info@afinn.com ✆ www.afinn.com

Chanticleer Inn	165-195 BB	Full breakfast
120 Gresham St 97520	6 rooms, 6 pb	Cookies, sherry and port
800-898-1950 541-482-1919	Cash, Checks, *Rated*	Living room with fire place,
Ellen & Howie	C-ltd/S-no/P-no/H-ltd	NY Times, AC & TV-DVD in
	Spanish, French and	each room, WiFi, gardens,
	Japanese	koi pond & hammock

Elegant newly renovated 1920 Craftsman in Ashland's historic neighborhood a short stroll to the Oregon Shakespeare Festival, restaurants, galleries, and Lithia Park. The Chanticleer Inn B&B offers comfortable quiet rooms, full gourmet breakfasts and more.
✉ comfy@ashlandbnb.com ✆ www.ashlandbnb.com

Country Willows B&B Inn	115-255 BB	Full breakfast
1313 Clay St 97520	9 rooms, 9 pb	Complimentary cookies and
800-WILLOWS 541-488-1590	Most CC, *Rated*	refreshments; selection of
Chuck & Debbie Young	C-ltd/S-no/P-no/H-yes	whole-leaf teas
		Porches, heated pool,
		Jacuzzi, wireless, lawns &
		gardens, barn-style suites,
		fireplaces, hiking

The ultimate resort-style Oregon B&B inn, snuggled against a rolling hillside on a lush five acres of farmland. Surrounded by magnificent southern Oregon Siskiyou and Cascade Mountain ranges. Nine unique rooms and suites furnished with antiques. Pool.
✉ innkeeper@countrywillowsinn.com ✆ www.countrywillowsinn.com

ASHLAND

DeLaunay House
185 N Pioneer 97520
541-621-5409
Deborah DeLaunay

135-250 BB
4 rooms, 4 pb
Visa, MC
C-ltd/S-no/P-no/H-no

Basket of goodies upon arrival
Complimentary coffee, tea, hot cocoa, popcorn, cereal bars, oatmeal in basket upon arrival.
Patio, porch, dining area, spa services, wireless Internet, AC, cable TV

Renovated in 2002, the DeLaunay House is now a luxury guest home featuring original artworks, collectables, heirloom antiques with handpainted accents & handknotted rugs. Experience lush velvets, quality bedding, & all the attention to detail.
✉ info@delaunayhouse.com ✪ www.delaunayhouse.com

Hersey House & Bungalow
451 N Main St 97520
888-343-7739 541-482-4563
Lorraine Peterson

95-225 BB
6 rooms, 6 pb
Visa, MC, Disc, •
C-ltd/S-no/P-ltd/H-no

Full Gourmet Breakfast
Cookies, afternoon beverage and Harry & David truffles each evening.
WiFi, deck, gardens

A beautifully preserved Craftsman home surrounded by lush gardens within walking distance of downtown theaters. Five guestrooms with king/queen beds & private baths or a fully equipped cottage. A delightful gourmet breakfast is served each morning.
✉ innkeeper@herseyhouse.com ✪ www.herseyhouse.com

The Iris Inn
59 Manzanita St 97520
800-460-7650 541-488-2286
Vicki & Greg Capp

95-175 BB
5 rooms, 5 pb
Visa, MC, *Rated*, •
C-ltd/S-no/P-no/H-ltd
Spanish, Italian, French

Elegant full breakfasts
Lemonade & sun tea for hot summer days. Wine at 5 p.m.; sherry, port & chocolates after theater.
Mountain views, cottage garden, WiFi, custom amenities, robes, nightly turndown, great reading light

Our tradition of 27 years of excellence continues! On a quiet street near theaters & town, relax in the garden or enjoy a winter escape. View rooms & delectable breakfasts! AAA 3 diamond inn. WiFi.
✉ innkeeper@irisinnbb.com ✪ www.irisinnbb.com

Lithia Springs Resort & Gardens
2165 W Jackson Rd 97520
800-482-7128 541-482-7128
Kay Spring

149-299 EP
25 rooms, 25 pb
Most CC, *Rated*, •
C-yes/S-no/P-ltd/H-yes
Spanish

Breakfast available for extra cost. Complimentary wine & cheese available between 5 – 6 pm
Hotspring fed, in-room whirlpool tubs, gardens, themed rooms, $20 pet cleaning fee

Enjoy luxurious suites and cottages with 2 person, in-room whirlpools fed from our natural hot springs. Full Breakfast served each morning. Hors d'oeuvres and wine tasting each afternoon.
✉ kay@lithiaspringsresort.com ✪ www.ashlandinn.com

McCall House
153 Oak St 97520
800-808-9749 541-482-9296
Nola O'Hara

100-245 BB
10 rooms, 10 pb
Most CC, *Rated*, •
C-ltd/S-no/P-no/H-ltd

Full sumptuous breakfast
Afternoon treats
High speed Internet access, guest phones, off-street parking, fireplaces

Just one block from the acclaimed Oregon Shakespeare Festival, our lovingly restored Italianate mansion offers luxurious accommodations in Victorian-inspired suites and guestrooms.
✉ mccall@mccallhouse.com ✪ www.mccallhouse.com

ASHLAND

Oak Street Cottages
171 Oak St 97520
541-488-3778
Constance Dean

210-280 EP
4 rooms, 4 pb
Visa, MC
C-yes/S-no/P-ltd/H-yes

Each cottage has a self-contained kitchen
Some with Jacuzzis, fireplaces, living room, dining room, phones, TV, VCR, patio, BBQ

Gather your family and friends for your very own "Ashland Experience." Our four cottages sleep 6, 8 or 11, and children are welcome. Let Oak Street Cottages be your family's "home away from home." Stay 6 nights, 7th night is free! We specialize in groups.
✉ constance@oakstreetcottages.com ◐ www.oakstreetcottages.com

Pelton House B&B
228 B Street 97520
866-488-7003 541-488-7003

75-195 BB
5 rooms, 5 pb
Visa, MC, *Rated*
C-ltd/S-no/P-no

Full breakfast
Afternoon tea, dessert, non-alcoholic beverages included; optional lunch and dinner available

In Ashland's Railroad District near the Shakespeare theater, the historic Pelton House Bed & Breakfast has all the amenities. AAA rated, wireless Internet, a scrumptious breakfast, exquisite bathrooms, turn-down service and wonderful hospitality
✉ info@peltonhouse.com ◐ www.peltonhouse.com

Romeo Inn
295 Idaho St 97520
800-915-8899 541-488-0884
Don & Deana Politis

105-215 BB
6 rooms, 6 pb
Visa, MC, *Rated*, •
C-ltd/S-no/P-no/H-ltd

Full breakfast
Complimentary refreshments, iced tea, soft drinks, homemade cookies & snacks
Swimming pool, Jacuzzi, king beds, fireplaces, private entrances, in room spa tub, wireless Internet

Romeo Inn is an elegant Cape Cod in a quiet residential area just 8 blocks from the Oregon Shakespeare Festival, away from the hustle & bustle of downtown affording guests the opportunity to relax & unwind. King beds, pool, fireplaces, spa, WiFi & more!
✉ innkeeper@romeoinn.com ◐ www.romeoinn.com

The Winchester Inn, Restaurant & Wine Bar
35 South Second St 97520
800-972-4991 541-488-1113
Michael & Laurie Gibbs

135-295 BB
19 rooms, 19 pb
Most CC, *Rated*
C-yes/S-no/P-no/H-ltd
German, some Spanish

Two course gourmet breakfast
Full service restaurant & wine bar
Garden, gazebo, jetted tubs, fireplaces, balcony, antiques, afternoon pastry treats delivered to room

Victorian hideaway complete with lush gardens & fine dining. This enchanting Inn is within walking distance of the Oregon Shakespeare Festival, Lithia Park, restaurants & shopping.
✉ innkeeper@thewinchesterinn.com ◐ www.winchesterinn.com

ASTORIA

Astoria Inn
3391 Irving Ave 97103
800-718-8153 503-325-8153
Mickey Cox

85-100 BB
4 rooms, 4 pb
Visa, MC, •
S-ltd/P-no/H-no

Hearty breakfasts
Fresh baked cookies
Veranda overlooks the Columbia River, sitting room, cable TV

Often mentioned as the best location in Astoria, the inn's new make-you-smile colors on the outside make you feel welcome and relaxed inside. A happy place with good food for happy times.
◐ www.astoriainnbb.com

ASTORIA————————————————————————————————

Britta's Inn B&B
1237 Kensington Ave. 97103
503-325-4940
Rona & Skip Davis

120-150 BB
2 rooms, 2 pb
Cash, Checks, *Rated*
C-ltd/S-no/P-no/H-ltd

Full breakfast
Organic food. Dietary needs
catered. Complimentary
bottled water, chocolates,
tea, cookies, fruit.
WiFi, Sat.TV, DVDs, robes,
hair dryer, toiletries, etc.
Special occasion gift baskets
arranged.

Lovingly restored over the past several years, the Inn is registered in the National Historic Districts, and is an Historic Landmark. Centrally located in Astoria, on the N.W. Oregon coast, this rare beauty captures early 1900's "Arts and Crafts" design.
✉ Innkeeper@BrittasInn.com ◐ www.brittasinn.com

Franklin Street Station B&B
1140 Franklin St 97103
800-448-1098 503-325-4314
Rebecca Greenway

85-140 BB
7 rooms, 5 pb
Visa, MC, *Rated*
C-yes/S-no/P-no/H-no

Full breakfast
Coffee & tea in all rooms, 2
sittings for breakfast
Wireless Internet in all
rooms. In room breakfast
when requested.

1900 Victorian home on the Oregon Coast, in Astoria Oregon. Columbia River views. All queen beds and private baths, fireplaces, balconies. Quiet, comfortable. Walking distance to historic downtown Astoria. "A Warm Welcome Awaits You."
✉ franklinststationbb@yahoo.com ◐ www.astoriaoregonbb.com

Grandview B&B
1574 Grand Ave 97103
800-488-3250 503-325-5555
Charleen Maxwell

66-188 BB
9 rooms, 7 pb
Most CC, *Rated*, •
C-ltd/P-no

Full breakfast
Snacks
Sitting room, canopy beds,
books, games, binoculars,
liquor not permitted

Light, airy, cheerful Victorian close to superb Maritime Museum, Lightship, churches, golf, clam-digging, fishing, beaches and rivers.
✉ grandviewbedandbreakfast@go.com ◐ www.pacifier.com/~grndview

Rose River Inn B&B
1510 Franklin Ave 97103
888-876-0028 503-325-7175
David & Pam Armstrong

85-160 BB
5 rooms, 5 pb
Visa, MC
C-ltd/S-no/P-no/H-no

Full breakfast
Breakfast is served at 9:00
a.m.
Sitting room, suites,
fireplaces, cable TV, DVD,
sauna and wireless Internet

Historic bed and breakfast in Astoria, Oregon on the Columbia River. The Rose River Inn is a beautiful 1912 Craftsman style home in a National Historic district of Astoria, Oregon, the oldest American city west of the Rockies.
✉ roseriverinn@charter.net ◐ www.roseriverinn.com

AURORA————————————————————————————————

Anna Becke House B&B
14892 Bobs Ave 97002
866-383-2662 503-678-6979
Terri Roberts

130-130 BB
3 rooms, 3 pb
Visa, MC, Disc
S-no/P-no/H-no

Full gourmet breakfast
"Serve yourself" afternoon &
evening refreshment guest
lounge
Cable TV, DVDs, wireless
Internet and guest robes.

Spend a night in a classic craftsman bungalow that could be right out of the pages of your favorite decorating magazine! And just a short stroll from its quiet historic neighborhood to the heart of Oregon's Antiques Capital.
✉ info@annabeckehouse.com ◐ www.annabeckehouse.com

BEND

Cricketwood Country B&B	105-145 BB	Full breakfast
63520 Cricketwood Rd 97701	4 rooms, 4 pb	Cookies, drinks, snacks,
877-330-0747 541-330-0747	Most CC, *Rated*	guest refrigerator
Jim & Tracy Duncan	C-ltd/S-no/P-ltd/H-no	Outdoor spa, 2-person spa
		tubs, in-room satellite
		TV/VCR/DVD, videos/DVDs,
		fireplaces, fax, Internet

Individualized breakfasts served at the time you choose in your room or with other guests. Warm cookies, beverages, in-room TV/VCR/DVD, media library, spas, fireplaces and more! One of Time Magazine's "Best Places to Stay." Separate pet friendly cottage.
✉ innkeeper@cricketwood.com ◑ www.cricketwood.com

Lara House Lodge B&B	169-289 BB	Multi-course gourmet
640 NW Congress St 97701	6 rooms, 6 pb	breakfast
800-766-4064 541-388-4064	Most CC, •	Pacific Northwest wines and
Amy Morgan & Ginger Reed	S-no/P-no/H-ltd	specialty hors d' ouevres are
		served daily from 5–6pm
		Sun room, cozy fireplace, 2
		outdoor porches, downtown
		location

Lara House Lodge is a magnificent 1910 Craftsman conveniently located in downtown Bend's historic district, across the street from beautiful Drake Park. Enjoy our luxurious furnishings, exquisite bedding, and gourmet breakfasts.
✉ larahousebandb@bendbroadband.com ◑ www.larahouse.com

The Sather House B&B	119-169 BB	Full breakfast
7 NW Tumalo Ave 97701	4 rooms, 4 pb	Cable TV, Wireless Internet
888-388-1065 541-388-1065	Most CC, *Rated*, •	Connection, Living Room,
Robbie Giamboi	C-ltd/S-ltd/P-no/H-ltd	Fireplace, Board Games.

This carefully restored stately Craftsman style Bed and Breakfast home is located in a neighborhood of older historical homes. Walking distance to Downtown, Drake Park & Deschutes River.
✉ satherhouse@aol.com ◑ www.satherhouse.com

BRIGHTWOOD

Brightwood Guesthouse	135-150 BB	Full 5-course breakfast
64725 E Barlow Trail Rd 97011	1 rooms, 1 pb	Snacks, beverages,
888-503-5783 503-622-5783	Cash, Checks, *Rated*,	complimentary wine or
Jeff & Bonnie Rames	•	bubbly when notified of
	C-ltd/S-ltd/P-no/H-ltd	special occasion
		Living room, library, washer
		& dryer, TV/VCR, games,
		flowers, art supplies

Peaceful, private, romantic cabin of your own in the forest of Mt Hood. Lovely water garden, pretty territorial views from each window, fantastic breakfasts. Everything provided for your comfort and convenience.
✉ brightwoodbnb@hotmail.com ◑ www.Mounthoodbnb.com

BROOKINGS

A Beachfront B&B by	109-139 BB	Continental plus breakfast
Lowden's	2 rooms, 2 pb	Coffee, tea, popcorn, milk,
14626 Wollam Rd 97415	Visa, MC	hot chocolate, orange juice,
800-453-4768 541-469-7045	C-yes/S-no/P-no/H-no	water, jams & peanut butter
Gary & Barbara Lowden		Ambience fireplace with
		remote control; free WiFi; 2
		night and 5 night discounts

Ocean and river frontage with easy beach access. Incredible view from your private luxury suite. Fireplace, TV/VCR/DVD, fridge, microwave, toaster, coffeemaker. Near redwood forest. No smoking/pets.
✉ glowden@charter.net ◑ www.beachfrontbb.com

Lobenhaus B&B and Vineyard, Carlton, OR

BROOKINGS

Country Retreat B&B
16980 Coho Dr 97415
800-856-8604 541-469-8884
Evelyn

130-147 BB
2 rooms, 2 pb
Most CC, •
C-ltd/S-no/P-ltd/H-ltd

Full Country Breakfast
Afternoon tea, coffee, hot
chocolate, cookies
Cable TV/DVD/VCR, free
wireless Internet, Jacuzzi on
veranda, billiard room,
fireplace in room

Two separate, large luxury rooms with private baths & private entrances with huge windows. Free high-speed Internet, Billiard Room, veranda-Jacuzzi, fireplace in room. Small weddings. 3 miles on N-Bank Chetco River Rd.
✉ info@countryretreatbnb.com ✆ www.countryretreatbnb.com

Holmes Sea Cove B&B
17350 Holmes Dr 97415
888-290-0312 541-469-3025
Lorene Holmes

150 BB
2 rooms, 2 pb
Visa, MC
C-yes/S-no/P-no

Continental plus breakfast
Hot tub/spa with ocean view,
gazebo, scenic trail, semi-
private beach

Overlooking the beautiful Oregon coast with a scenic trail to a semi-private beach. Holmes Sea Cove B&B is a place of peace and privacy. Cottage and 2 room suite available. 3 night minimum stay on the Pacific Suite.
✆ www.harborside.com/~holmes/

CARLTON

**Lobenhaus B&B and
Vineyard**
6975 NE Abbey Rd 97111
888-339-3375 503-864-9173
Joe & Shari Lobenstein

145-180 BB
6 rooms, 6 pb
Visa, MC, Disc
C-ltd/S-no/P-no/H-ltd

Full Oregon Bounty
Breakfast
Refreshments and snacks
provided at check in. Wine
for purchase. Guest
refrigerator in dining area
Wireless Internet, fireplace,
satellite big screen HD TV
DVD – large common areas,
expansive grounds

Nestled in a peaceful wooded setting on 27 acres, our unique tri-level lodge has 6 beautifully appointed guestrooms, each with a private bathroom. View the woods and spring fed creek from your window or open your door to step onto the expansive deck.
✉ innkeeper@lobenhaus.com ✆ www.lobenhaus.com

CENTRAL POINT

The Willows	150-225 BB	Full breakfast
3347 Old Stage Rd 97502	5 rooms, 5 pb	Afternoon tea/snacks during
866-665-3020 541-665-3020	Visa, MC, AmEx,	summer season
Joe & Sandra Dowling	*Rated*, •	In-room TV and DVD/VCR,
	C-ltd/S-no/P-ltd/H-no	telephone/data port, WiFi,
		A/C, in-ground pool, tennis,
		croquet

Experience the modern yet historic accommodations at this authentic Rogue Valley Orchard Mansion. The upscale bed and breakfast resort is listed in the National Register and has a wonderful history. Each room is appointed with elegant furnishings and art.
✉ scu73@aol.com 🌐 thewillowsbedandbreakfast.com

CHRISTMAS VALLEY

Outback B&B	95 BB	Full breakfast
92946 Christmas Valley Hwy	2 rooms, 2 pb	Soft drinks, tea, coffee,
97641	•	popcorn, baked items
541-420-5229	C-ltd/S-ltd/P-ltd/H-no	17'4" deck, walking trails
Dave & Betty Hickerson		

B&B built in 2002 in Central Oregon's High Desert, close to many historical sites. Private rooms each with their own baths. 100+ acres to wander & see nature.
✉ twohicks@starband.net 🌐 www.outbackbedandbreakfast.com

COOS BAY

Old Tower House B&B	115-165 BB	Continental & Gourmet
476 Newmark Ave 97420	4 rooms, 4 pb	Tea & coffee available upon
541-888-6058	Visa, MC, •	request.
Thomas & Stephanie Kramer	C-ltd/S-no/P-no/H-no	TV/DVD/VCR, video library,
		antiques, sun porch

Historic home in Coos Bay filled with history, antiques, and ambience. Gourmet breakfasts served in the main house.
✉ oldtowerhouse@yahoo.com 🌐 www.oldtowerhouse.com

CORBETT

Brickhaven B&B	100-125 BB	Full breakfast
38717 E Historical Columbia	3 rooms, 2 pb	coffee and tea always
River Hwy 97019	Visa, MC	available
503-695-5126	C-ltd/S-no/P-no/H-no	Steinway Grand Piano, a
Ed & Phyllis Thiemann		video library and stereo
		sound

Brickhaven Bed & Breakfast is a beautiful, serene hide-away in the hills overlooking the Columbia River Gorge. Breathtaking views of the river and its gorge welcome you to this quiet retreat.
✉ Brickhvn@comcast.net 🌐 www.brickhaven.com

CORVALLIS

The Hanson Country Inn	125-165 BB	Full breakfast
795 SW Hanson St 97333	4 rooms, 4 pb	Sitting rooms, private decks,
541-752-2919	Most CC	garden area, library, Internet
Patricia Covey	C-ltd/S-no/P-ltd/H-ltd	access

Charming country home with splendid architectural details. Brimming with cozy warmth, unique charm and elegant ambience. A truly wonderful experience that you will want to enjoy again and again!
✉ contact@hcinn.com 🌐 www.hcinn.com

CORVALLIS

Harrison House
2310 NW Harrison Blvd 97330
800-233-6248 541-752-6248
Hilarie Phelps & Allen
Goodman

99-145 BB
5 rooms, 5 pb
Most CC, *Rated*
C-yes/S-no/P-no/H-no

Full breakfast
Willamette Valley wines,
afternoon tea, cold sodas,
spring water & snacks
Sunroom/library, in-room
WiFi, phones, TV with DVD,
local truffles, hazelnuts &
spring water

Gracious hospitality & comfort in a beautifully furnished, historic Dutch Colonial home. 4 rooms with private baths & a lovely detached Cottage Suite. Walk to OSU, restaurants, and shopping. Seasonal breakfasts, local wines, & all business amenities.
✉ stay@corvallis-lodging.com ◐ www.corvallis-lodging.com

DAYTON

Wine Country Farm
6855 Breyman Orchards Rd
97114
800-261-3446 503-864-3446
Joan Davenport

150-225 BB
9 rooms, 9 pb
Visa, MC, *Rated*, •
C-ltd/S-no/P-no/H-ltd
Spanish

Full country breakfast
Homebaked cookies,
complimentary wine
Sitting rooms, library,
Jacuzzi, sauna, suites,
fireplaces, movie library,
massage therapist

Spectacular views from a historic French style eclectic farmhouse surrounded by its own vineyards. Wonderful country farm breakfast. Complimentary wine from our own tasting room. We're a destination in 1000 Places To See Before You Die by Patricia Schultz
✉ jld@winecountryfarm.com ◐ www.winecountryfarm.com

DEPOE BAY

Harbor Lights
235 SE Bay View Ave 97341
800-228-0448 541-765-2322
Melanie Richardson

129-179 BB
13 rooms, 13 pb
Most CC, *Rated*, •
C-ltd/S-no/P-ltd/H-yes

Cooked to Order Breakfast
Now serving full dinners on
selected evenings. (At menu
price)
Harbor View Rooms,
Wireless Internet, cable TV
with dvd/vcr player, off
street parking

Harbor Lights Inn overlooks "The World's Smallest Harbor" in Depoe Bay, Oregon, which offers a unique setting on Oregon's Central Coast. Easy access to fishing, beach combing, agate hunting whalewatching, hiking, shopping and restaurants.
✉ harborlights@cablespeed.com ◐ www.theharborlightsinn.com

Pana-Sea-Ah B&B
4028 Lincoln Ave 97341
866-829-3368 541-764-3368
Mary & Robert Hauser

119-199 BB
4 rooms, 4 pb
Visa, MC, •
S-no/P-ltd/H-yes

Full breakfast
Wine, cider, hot chocolate,
coffee, tea, cookies, brownies
Great room, views, hot tub
on the deck overlooking the
ocean, Internet access, WiFi,
TV/DVD library

Pana-Sea-Ah B&B on the Oregon Coast was custom built in 1999 with your quiet comfort in mind. Our large 3200 sq. ft. home is just steps from the beach.
✉ innkeeper@panaseah.com ◐ panaseah.com

EUGENE

C'est La Vie Inn
1006 Taylor St 97402
866-302-3014 541-302-3014
Anne-Marie Lizet

105-250 BB
5 rooms, 5 pb
Visa, MC, AmEx, *Rated*
C-ltd/S-ltd/P-ltd/H-no
French

Full breakfast
Coffee, tea, cold beverages &
beer, cookies in the butler's
pantry, wine available to purchase
Flat screen TV with CD player
& DVD, WiFi, computer, library, robes, organic lavender
bath products

*All of the guest offerings, from the cozy Gauguin room to the opulent Casablanca suite, are
uniquely decorated, and all have private baths. Elegant features include plush bathrobes,
individual cooling/heating controls, cable TV/DVD, and free WiFi.*
contact@cestlavieinn.com www.cestlavieinn.com

Lorane Valley B&B
86621 Lorane Hwy 97405
541-686-0241
Esther & George Ralph

125-145 BB
1 rooms, 1 pb
Visa, MC, AmEx
C-yes/S-ltd/P-no

Full breakfast
Fresh cut flowers, book
loans, videos, Jacuzzis

*Three and a half miles from the hustle and bustle of Eugene is a haven of tranquility. Our
corner of the world is a beautiful, two level cedar home set on 15 acres overlooking the
Lorane Valley.* LoraneValleyBandB@att.net www.loranevalleyBandB.com

FLORENCE

Edwin K B&B
1155 Bay St 97439
800-833-9465 541-997-8360
Marv & Laurie VandeStreek

125-175 BB
7 rooms, 7 pb
Visa, MC, Disc, *Rated*
C-ltd/S-no/P-no/H-no

Elegant five-course breakfast
Espresso drinks, sherry, tea,
and cookies
Living room with fireplace,
Jacuzzi tubs, hairdryers,
private courtyard

*Built in 1914, nestled on the rugged coastline of Oregon, the Edwin K defines the tradition
of fine accommodations.* info@edwink.com www.edwink.com

FOSSIL

**Wilson Ranches Retreat
B&B**
16555 Butte Creek Rd 97830
866-763-2227 541-763-2227
Phil & Nancy Wilson

75-95 BB
7 rooms, 2 pb
Visa, MC, AmEx
C-yes/S-ltd/P-no/H-ltd

Full 'cowboy' breakfast
Fully equipped kitchen
Satellite television, business
traveler accommodations

*Welcome to the Wilson Ranches Retreat Bed and Breakfast in North Central Oregon. A
9,000 acre working cattle ranch takes you off the beaten track to our rustic hideout.*
npwilson@wilsonranchesretreat.com www.wilsonranchesretreat.com

GLIDE

**Steelhead Run B&B & Fine
Art Gallery**
23049 N Umpqua Hwy 97443
800-348-0563 541-496-0563
George & Nancy Acosta

75-135 BB
6 rooms, 6 pb
Most CC, *Rated*, •
C-yes/S-ltd/P-ltd/H-ltd
February 10 – January 2

Continental plus breakfast
Special diets prepared with
arrangements

*The B&B is on a bluff overlooking the North Umpqua River. Five acres of beautiful
waterfront property with easy access to the river. Voted People #1 Choice. The place to stay
in Southern Oregon.* steelhead@steelheadrun.com www.steelheadrun.com

GOLD BEACH

Endicott Gardens
95768 Jerry's Flat Rd 97444
866-212-1220 541-247-6513
Patrick & Beverly Endicott

80-210 BB
4 rooms, 4 pb
C-ltd/S-ltd/H-ltd

Full or Continental plus
breakfast
Seasonal fruit, coffee and tea
Fireplace, gardens, pond,
decks overlooking the
gardens

*Spectacular grounds with several fruit trees, flowers, shrubs and exotic plants. The home
features four guestrooms in a separate wing, each with private bath.*
www.endicottgardens.com

GOLD BEACH

Tu Tu' Tun Lodge
96550 N Bank Rogue 97444
800-864-6357 541-247-6664
Dirk & Laurie Van Zante

125-550 EP
20 rooms, 20 pb
Visa, MC, *Rated*, •
C-ltd/S-ltd/P-no/H-ltd
May—October

Meal plans: breakfast only,
$18, b'fast & dinner, $57.50,
lunch $15, outside guests by
reservation
Library, sitting room,
swimming pool, games, 2
outdoor hot tubs

Secluded lodge nestled on banks of the Rogue River, with country inn hospitality, gourmet meals, white water excursions, guided fishing. Two houses, two suites, and sixteen rooms available.
✉ tututunlodge@charter.net ○ www.tututun.com

GOLD HILL

Rogue River Guest House
41 Rogue River Hwy 97525
877-ROGUEBB 541-855-4485
Joan Ogilvie & Doug Rowley

120-170 BB
2 rooms, 2 pb
Cash, Checks, •
C-yes/S-no/P-ltd/H-no

Full breakfast
Lunch, dinner by request;
complimentary wine
Jacuzzi suite available with
spectacular oceanview

A completely refurbished 1890's farmhouse along the Rogue River in Southern Oregon, halfway between Medford and Grants Pass. Comfortable surroundings with all the amenities.
○ www.rogueriverguesthouse.com

GRANTS PASS

Flery Manor B&B
2000 Jumpoff Joe Cr Rd 97526
541-476-3591
Marla & John Vidrinskas

110-220 BB
5 rooms, 4 pb
Visa, MC, *Rated*, •
C-ltd/S-no/P-no/H-no
Lithuanian, Russian

Full 3 course gourmet
breakfast
Afternoon tea, snacks, wine
Sitting room, library,
fireplace, piano, gazebo with
waterfall, stream, pond, free
WiFi

"Elegant, romantic, secluded." Suites include fireplace, Jacuzzi, and private balcony. There is a library, parlor with piano, and a huge balcony with extraordinary views. Outdoors you may enjoy ponds, waterfall, streams, and a gazebo.
✉ flery@flerymanor.com ○ www.flerymanor.com

The Lodge at Riverside
955 S.E. 7th St 97526
877-955-0600 541-955-0600
Tamara Larson

135-325 BB
32 rooms, 32 pb
Most CC, *Rated*, •
C-yes/S-no/P-no/H-yes

Expanded Continental
Breakfast
Evening wine and cheese
reception and bedtime milk
and cookies.
Outdoor pool and spa,
fireplaces, Jacuzzis, meeting
rooms, restaurant, catering
and special events

Let the scenic Rogue River become your backyard as you catch your breath in richly decorated, oversized rooms. Experience the best of Grants Pass, Oregon—for quiet pleasures, whirlwind vacations or corporate meetings.
✉ tamara@thelodgeatriverside.com ○ www.thelodgeatriverside.com

Weasku Inn
5560 Rogue River Hwy 97527
800-4-WEASKU 541-471-8000
Erik R. Johnson

195-325 BB
17 rooms, 17 pb
Most CC, *Rated*, •
C-yes/S-ltd/P-no/H-yes

Deluxe Continental breakfast
Evening wine & cheese
reception. Catering services
available.
Sitting room, fireplaces,
cable TV, wireless Internet,
conference facility & outdoor
deck

A cozy riverfront inn built around a colorful, historic fishing lodge. Decorated with locally hand-crafted furniture, one of a kind lamps, hand-quilted bed covers, chairs & fishing memorabilia.
✉ reservations@weasku.com ○ www.weasku.com

HOOD RIVER

Hood River BnB
918 Oak St 97031
541-387-2997
Jane & Jim Nichols

85-135 BB
4 rooms, 2 pb
Visa, MC
C-ltd/S-no/P-ltd/H-yes
French

Full breakfast
Tea, snacks & cookies, all in
a great home
Sitting rooms, guest-use
computer with Internet
access, library, deck,
hammock, grill, picnic table

Just 3 blocks from downtown Hood River, OR, our B&B is ideal for those who want a comfortable place to relax & call home during your stay in the Gorge or at Mount Hood. Large, comfortable rooms with local fruit and good breakfasts.
✉ jane@hoodriverbnb.com 🌐 www.hoodriverbnb.com

Inn At The Gorge
1113 Eugene St. 97031
877-852-2385 541-386-4429
Frank & Michele Bouche

129-159 BB
5 rooms, 5 pb
Visa, MC
C-yes/S-no/P-no/H-ltd

Full breakfast
Wraparound porch,
backyard terrace, free
wireless Internet service,
DVDs, off-street parking

Built in 1908, this Queen Anne style home has operated as a Bed and Breakfast since 1987. We are located within walking distance to downtown shops and restaurants.
✉ stay@innatthegorge.com 🌐 www.innatthegorge.com

Villa Columbia Bed and Breakfast
902 Oak Street 97031
800-708-6217 541-386-6670
Boba & VJ Jovanovic

139-169 BB
5 rooms, 5 pb
Visa, MC
C-ltd/S-no/P-no/H-ltd

Three-course gourmet
breakfast
Complimentary beverages
and handcrafted pastries are
available throughout the day.
AC/heat, fireplace, private
bathrooms, Jacuzzi, plush
robes, towels, hair dryer.
Private parking

The comfortable elegance of the house is accentuated by the wonderful river views that fill each window and allow you to view the Columbia River Gorge from our Bed and Breakfast.
✉ info@villacolumbia.com 🌐 www.villacolumbia.com

JACKSONVILLE

Bybee's Historic Inn
883 Old Stage Rd 97530
877-292-3374 541-899-0106
Vikki Lynn & Tina Marie

145-175 BB
5 rooms, 5 pb
Visa, MC
C-ltd/S-no/P-no/H-yes

Full gourmet breakfast
Afternoon snack
Covered porch, koi pond,
gazebo, library, phone, TV,
broad band Internet

Our Classic Revival Victorian era home is situated on 3+ acres, centrally located just one mile from the Britt Gardens in Jacksonville, Oregon, 15 miles from Ashland and 6 miles from Medford.
✉ innkeepers@bybeeshistoricinn.com 🌐 www.bybeeshistoricinn.com

Jacksonville Inn
175 E California St 97530
800-321-9344 541-899-1900
Jerry & Linda Evans

159-450 BB
12 rooms, 12 pb
Most CC, *Rated*, •
C-yes/S-no/P-ltd/H-yes
Greek, Danish, Italian,
Spanish

Full breakfast
Restaurant, lounge, wine
tasting; lunch & dinner
additional; gourmet catering
on and off premises
Luxurious cottages with
many amenities available; a
connoisseur's wine shop
with over 2,000 wines.

The Inn offers its guests elegance in a historic setting, with gourmet dining, a connoisseur's wine cellar, luxurious hotel accommodations, and 4 honeymoon cottages that are "suites extraordinaire."
✉ jvinn@mind.net 🌐 www.jacksonvilleinn.com

JACKSONVILLE

Jacksonville's Magnolia Inn
245 N 5th St 97530
866-899-0255 541-899-0255
Robert & Susan Roos

90-160 BB
9 rooms, 9 pb
Most CC, *Rated*, •
C-ltd/S-no/P-no/H-ltd

Continental breakfast from
bakeries
Gourmet coffees, teas,
European pastries, oatmeal,
fruit
TV/VCR/extended cable,
high-speed Internet, guest
kitchen, outdoor veranda

*Featured in Sunset Magazine and AAA's Via magazine. Located across from the museum,
just two short blocks to town. Park your car and walk to award winning restaurants.
Comfortable elegance in the heart of Jacksonville.*
✉ maginn@charter.net ◉ www.magnolia-inn.com

McCully House Inn
240 E California St 97530
800-367-1942 541-899-1942

135-325 BB
4 rooms, 4 pb
Visa, MC, AmEx
C-ltd/S-no/P-no

Deluxe Continental Breakfast
Sitting room, many amenities
available

*Combining history & elegance with impeccable taste, the McCully House captures the
essence of 19th century Oregon. Listed among the top 10 romantic inns in the United States
by Vacations Magazine, guests say it is an experience to remember & return to.*
✉ ryan@mccullycountryhouseinn.com ◉ mccullyhouseinn.com

TouVelle House B&B
455 N Oregon St 97530
800-846-8422 541-899-8938
Gary Renninger Balfour

149-195 BB
6 rooms, 6 pb
Visa, MC, Disc, *Rated*
C-ltd/S-no/P-no/H-no
German

Gourmet three-course
breakfast
Tea & hot beverages
Beautiful gardens, swimming
pool, sauna, spacious
verandas, high speed
wireless Internet, fridge, AC

*TouVelle House Bed & Breakfast is ready to welcome you with a gentle, serene environ-
ment where you can relax knowing that all of your needs have already been anticipated.*
✉ info@touvellehouse.com ◉ www.touvellehouse.com

KLAMATH FALLS

Crystalwood Lodge
38625 Westside Rd 97601
866-381-2322 541-381-2322
Elizabeth Parrish & Peggy
O'Neal

77-197 BB
7 rooms, 7 pb
Visa, MC, •
C-yes/S-no/P-yes/H-no

Full breakfast
To go lunches upon request,
comfort food dinners,
prepared and stored,
available around the clock
Great Room, deck, porches,
snowshoes, outdoor spa,
boats, canoes, pet-friendly,
WiFi, meadows, woods

*Just outside Crater Lake National Park, pet friendly Crystalwood Lodge features informal
excellence, comfortable rooms, full breakfasts, and superb wines and micro-brews . . . the
place to base your all-seasons adventures in the Southern Oregon Cascades.*
✉ reservations@crystalwoodlodge.com ◉ www.crystalwoodlodge.com

LA GRANDE

Stange Manor Inn
1612 Walnut St 97850
888-286-9463 541-963-2400
Ron & Carolyn Jensen

110-145 BB
4 rooms, 4 pb
Visa, MC, *Rated*
C-ltd/S-no/P-no/H-no

Full breakfast
Breakfast always includes
bottomless juice, coffee
cakes, muffins, fresh fruit and
a main course
Living room, TV/VCR/DVD,
fireplace, books and
periodicals, and brochures
on points of interest

*Capturing the romance and elegance of a former era, Stange Manor is a lovingly preserved
Georgian Colonial mansion, which beckons even the casual traveler to bask in its comfort
and hospitality.*
✉ innkeeper@stangemanor.com ◉ www.stangemanor.com

LA PINE

DiamondStone Guest Lodges
16693 Sprague Loop 97739
866-626-9887 541-536-6263
Doug & Gloria Watt

99-350 BB
10 rooms, 10 pb
Most CC, *Rated*, •
C-yes/S-ltd/P-yes/H-no

Full breakfast
Coffee, tea, complimentary
beverages – beer, wine,
juices.
Western art, hot tub, outdoor
BBQ, free movie library.

DiamondStone manages several luxurious, comfy, rural Vacation Rentals. DS B&B offers private baths, TV/DVD/VCRs/phones, outdoor spa. Featured in "Northwest Best Places" it is at the heart of the recreational mecca that is Central Oregon—golf, fish, ski!
✉ diamond@diamondstone.com ○ www.diamondstone.com

LAFAYETTE

Kelty Estate B&B
675 3rd St 97127
503-560-1512
Nicci Stokes

129-179 BB
5 rooms, 5 pb
Most CC
C-ltd/S-ltd/P-ltd/H-ltd

Full breakfast

The Kelty Estate is a historic B&B in the heart of Oregon's wine country, one hour from Portland and the coast. As a guest of the Kelty, you are welcome to book our limousine to chauffeur you around the lush landscape or your own private wine tour.
✉ keltyestate@gmail.com ○ www.keltyestatebb.com

LINCOLN CITY

Brey House Oceanview Inn
3725 NW Keel Ave 97367
877-994-7123 541-994-7123
Milt & Shirley Brey

99-159 BB
5 rooms, 5 pb
Most CC, *Rated*, •
C-yes/S-no/P-no/H-no

Full breakfast
Homemade desert for
breakfast
Sitting room, hot tub,
oceanview deck, landscaped
yard, beach walking,
fireplaces, Internet

The ocean awaits you just across the street. We are located within the city limits of Lincoln City. Short walk to restaurants, shopping and casino.
✉ sbrey@wcn.net ○ www.breyhouse.com

O'Dysius Hotel
120 NW Inlet Ct 97367
800-869-8069 541-994-4121
Cind Taylor

159-365 BB
30 rooms, 30 pb
Most CC, •
S-no/P-yes/H-yes

European Continental
Breakfast
Coffee, fruit in lobby, evening
social with wine and nibbles.
Library, fireplace lounge,
TV/VCR, telephones,
whirlpool tubs, parking,
elevators, interior corridor

A place on the Oregon coast where guests can expect the amenities and services that only an award winning hotel can provide. Romantically nostalgic, overlooking the Pacific Ocean. It's all here for you. Come stay, enjoy, relax.
✉ stay@odysius.com ○ www.odysius.com

MANZANITA

Spindrift Inn
114 Laneda Ave. 97130
503-368-1001
Corinna Otto

60-130 EP
14 rooms, 14 pb
Most CC, •
C-yes/S-no/P-ltd/H-yes
German

Library, movies, high speed
wireless access. Some rooms
have kitchenettes.

Built in 1946, Spindrift Inn retains its quaint charm and cozy appeal. Affordable rooms open onto a private inner flower garden, where you can enjoy a book away from the bustle outside.
✉ info@spindrift-inn.com ○ www.spindrift-inn.com

MANZANITA

Zen Garden B&B
8910 Glenesslin Lane 97130
503-368-6697
Mrs. Smigel

100-160 BB
2 rooms, 2 pb
Cash, Checks
S-no/P-no/H-no
Czech, Italian, German,
Russian.

Full breakfast
Breakfast is a delicious, hot
dish served with assorted
fresh fruit, coffee or tea and
orange juice
Suite, private entrance, patio,
private living room, fridge,
microwave, big screen TV,
VCR, romance

Zen Garden B&B provides deluxe accommodations only a few feet from level access to the legendary Manzanita seven mile beach. This lovely beach is only a short walk from your room.
csmigel@nehalemtel.net www.neahkahnie.net/zengarden

MCMINNVILLE

A Tuscan Estate
809 NE Evans 97128
800-441-2214 503-434-9016
Jacques & Liz Rolland

130-250 BB
5 rooms, 5 pb
Most CC
C-ltd/S-no/P-no/H-no
French, Spanish

Full breakfast
Afternoon coffee, tea & fresh
baked cookies, private
dinners
Sitting parlor, morning coffee
room, fireplace

1928 historic estate, 5 blocks from historic downtown. Close to Linfield College, Delphian School, antique shopping & wineries. 45 minutes to coast, 50 minutes to Mt. Hood ski resorts.
innkeeper@a-tuscanestate.com www.a-tuscanestate.com

Baker Street B&B Inn
129 SE Baker St 97128
800-870-5575 503-472-5575
Cheryl Hockaday & Lou
Driever

119-250 BB
5 rooms, 5 pb
Most CC, *Rated*
C-ltd/S-ltd/P-ltd/H-no

Three breakfast options
One block from city park,
jetted tub, clawfoot tubs with
showers, cottages

In the heart of Wine Country, Baker Street Inn is a downtown B&B with 3 guestrooms and 2 private cottages, near Linfield College and historic downtown. Three breakfast options. Midway between the Coast and Portland. Ask about La Nouveau Chateau!
cheryl@bakerstreetinn.com www.bakerstreetinn.com

Mattey House
10221 NE Mattey Ln 97128
877-434-5058 503-434-5058
Jack & Denise Seed

125-165 BB
4 rooms, 4 pb
Visa, MC, AmEx
C-ltd/S-no/P-no/H-no
German, French, some
Italian

Full breakfast
Tea, lemonade, cookies in
the afternoon. Local wines
available by the glass
Sitting room, parlor, porch
swing, vineyard, orchard,
indoor & outdoor games

An 1892 Queen Anne Victorian surrounded by stately cedars and overlooking the vineyard, the Mattey House offers a secluded setting in the heart of the Oregon wine country. Centrally located for all wineries, restaurants and local attractions.
mattey@matteyhouse.com www.matteyhouse.com

Steiger Haus
360 SE Wilson St 97128
503-472-0821
Dale & Susan DuRette

95-150 BB
5 rooms, 5 pb
Visa, MC, Disc, *Rated*
C-ltd/S-no/P-no/H-ltd

Full seasonal breakfast
Early continental breakfast
baskets, cheese and fruit
plates, seasonal picnics
Sitting room, movies &
games, English garden, WiFi,
honor bar, regional wine list,
wine tours

In the heart of Oregon Wine Country. Unique architecture in a park-like town setting. Walking distance to gourmet restaurants. Charm and hospitality plus!
reservations@steigerhaus.com www.steigerhaus.com

MCMINNVILLE

Youngberg Hill Vineyards & Inn
10660 SW Youngberg Hill Rd 97128
888-657-8668 503-472-2727
Nicolette Bailey

150-290 BB
7 rooms, 7 pb
Visa, MC, *Rated*, •
C-ltd/S-no/P-no/H-ltd

Full breakfast
Cheese & cracker plates
Library, lounging salon,
dining rooms, spa, wine
tastings, tours

A premier Oregon wine country inn atop a mountain with commanding views over the valleys below, Youngberg Hill Inn is one of Wine Spectator's favorite locations.
✉ info@youngberghill.com ◐ www.youngberghill.com

MEDFORD

Under the Greenwood Tree
3045 Bellinger Ln 97501
541-776-0000
Joseph & Barbara Lilley

120-140 BB
4 rooms, 4 pb
Most CC
C-ltd/S-no/P-yes/H-no

Full breakfast
Complimentary tea & treats
Pond, gazebo, garden,
llamas, weddings, hammocks

This Country B&B Inn is set on 10 quiet and peaceful acres of idyllic grounds. It is surrounded by gracious Oregon gardens and interesting antique farm buildings dating to the Civil War Era.
✉ utgtree@qwest.net ◐ www.greenwoodtree.com

MERLIN

Rogue Glen Lodge
10526 Galice Rd 97532
541-474-1888
Barbara Moore

125-155 BB
4 rooms, 4 pb
Most CC
C-yes/S-ltd/P-yes/H-no

Full breakfast
river access, wireless
satellite Internet access,
indoor or outdoor dining,
free long distance calls

Offering comfortable lodging and hospitality on the Scenic Section of the Rogue River. When the river calls to you, for rafting, fishing, hiking, or relaxing, come stay at the Rogue Glen Lodge. Just 15 miles from Grants Pass in southern Oregon.
✉ stay@rogueglen.com ◐ www.rogueglen.com

NEWBERG

University House of Newberg B&B
401 N. Meridian St 97132
866-538-8438 503-538-8438
Leigh Wellikoff

150-250 BB
3 rooms, 2 pb
Visa, MC
C-ltd/S-no/P-no/H-no

Continental breakfast
Tea, popcorn, chocolate,
crackers, juice, other snacks.
Hot tub, massage therapy
available, full business
center with WiFi, concierge
service, etc.

University House provides the quintessential Oregon wine country experience. We offer the intimate charm of a beautifully restored 1906 home furnished with the warmth of stunning family antiques. There are no other guests in the house during your stay.
✉ hostess@universityhousenewberg.com ◐ www.universityhousenewberg.com

NEWPORT

Ocean House, An Oceanfront Inn
4920 NW Woody Way 97365
866-495-3888 541-265-3888
Charmaine & Lex

135-250 BB
8 rooms, 8 pb
Most CC, *Rated*, •
S-no/P-no/H-yes

Full breakfast
All rooms with ocean views
& fireplace, 4 rooms with
whirlpool, oceanfront
gardens, WiFi

Unforgettable in any season, Ocean House offers gracious lodging for adult travelers. Spectacular views of the ocean and the incomparable Oregon coastline can be seen from every room as well as the Great Room, dining area and the spacious decks.
✉ reservations@oceanhouse.com ◐ www.oceanhouse.com

NEWPORT

Tyee Lodge Oceanfront B&B
4925 NW Woody Way 97365
888-553-8933 541-265-8953
Charmaine & Lex

99-210 BB
6 rooms, 6 pb
Most CC, *Rated*, •
C-ltd/S-no/P-no/H-ltd

Full Course Breakfast
Complimentary hot and cold
beverages, wines, fresh
baked cookies, popcorn;
accommodate special diets
Private trail to beach,
outdoor firepit, sitting room,
wireless, TV on request,

*Come and enjoy our natural setting along the bluffs of peaceful Agate Beach in Newport.
Our park-like setting is unequaled on the Oregon Coast. Sit by your window or by the fire
and watch the waves. All 6 rooms have gas fireplaces.*
✉ reservations@tyeelodge.com ❂ www.tyeelodge.com

OTIS

Lake House B&B
2165 NE East Devils Lake R
97368
888-996-8938 541-996-8938
Mary Sell

95-150 BB
3 rooms, 3 pb
Visa, MC, Disc
C-yes/S-ltd/P-no/H-no

Full breakfast
Fireplace, sitting room,
private hot tub, rowboat or
canoe, dock, fishing

*Cedar home and guest cabin located on a 680-acre freshwater lake, only two miles from
the Pacific coastline & downtown Lincoln City. Very quiet area, large rooms, private
entrance.* ✉ lakehousebnb@charter.net ❂ www.lakehousebb.com

PACIFIC CITY

The Craftsman B&B
35255 4th St 97135
503-965-4574
Michael Rech

110-150 BB
4 rooms, 4 pb
Most CC
C-ltd/S-ltd/P-no/H-no

Full breakfast
Baked goodies upon arrival
and throughout the day.
Miele Nespresso coffee
machine. Wine list.
game table, hot tub, sun
deck, DVD library, fireplace,
reading inglenook, WiFi,
fisherman's sink

*The Craftsman B&B welcomes you to experience the beautiful Oregon Coast in style, grace
and comfort. Everything in town is within walking distance. Park your car, relax and
unplug. No lace, no doilies!* ✉ innkeeper@craftsmanbb.com ❂ www.craftsmanbb.com

PARKDALE

Old Parkdale Inn
4932 Baseline Rd 97041
877-687-4669 541-352-5551
Mary & Steve Pellegrini

120-145 BB
3 rooms, 3 pb
Visa, MC
C-ltd/S-no/P-ltd/H-no

Hearty Northwest breakfast
Complimentary drinks in
room. Wine, beer, snacks
plates, picnic baskets, fondue
available
Fireplaces, books, puzzles,
games, laundry, gardens,
pond, WiFi, guest computer,
full kitchens

*A romantic and artistically decorated Bed and Breakfast Inn located in the Upper Hood
River Valley, Parkdale, Oregon. Each of our 3 guestrooms, all with private baths, are
unique with an artist's theme. Monet, Gauguin and O'Keefe prints adorn the walls.*
✉ parkdale@hoodriverlodging.com ❂ www.hoodriverlodging.com

PORTLAND

72nd Avenue Studios
3415 NE 72nd Ave 97213
503-288-8501
Peggy Sullivan

65-75 EP
2 rooms, 2 pb
Cash, Checks
C-yes/S-no/P-no/H-no
Spanish
Spring through
December

NONE
Coffee, tea and self-service
dishes
Private entry courtyard and
kitchen

*The 72nd Avenue Studios, located in an old-fashioned neighborhood in NE Portland, offers
two studio apartments for guest lodgings, and a lovely site for private events in the
backyard gardens.* ✉ studios_72nd_Ave@hotmail.com ❂ www.72ndavenuestudios.com

PORTLAND

A Painted Lady Inn
503-335-0070
Jody Runge

109-179 BB
5 rooms, 3 pb
Most CC
C-ltd/P-no/H-yes

Full breakfast
Delightful garden patio and
covered front porch with
swing

Located in vibrant, hip Northeast Portland, A Painted Lady Bed and Breakfast Inn offers a calm oasis in the heart of the city. Just steps from wonderful shops and fine restaurants, A Painted Lady will be your Portland home-away-from-home.
✉ jrunge15@comcast.net ✪ www.apaintedladyinn.com

Bluebird Guesthouse
3517 SE Division St 97202
503-238-4333
Chris Moehling

50-90 BB
7 rooms, 2 pb
Visa, MC
C-ltd/S-no/P-no/H-ltd

Simple Continental Breakfast
A full kitchen guests can use
to prepare meals
In-room A/C & heat controls.
Complementary: WiFi,
Internet computer, local
phone, maps.

Charming, friendly & reasonably priced, the Bluebird Guesthouse is located in the heart of Southeast Portland. We're on Division Street—minutes to all of the city's attractions and a short walk to some of the best restaurants, cafes, shops & nightlife.
✪ www.bluebirdguesthouse.com

Britannia at Terwilliger Vista
515 SW Westwood Dr 97201
888-244-0602 503-244-0602
Carl & Irene

105-200 BB
5 rooms, 5 pb
Visa, MC, *Rated*, •
C-ltd/S-no/P-no/H-ltd

Full or continental breakfast
Complimentary wine, sodas
& water
Sitting room, library, suites,
fireplaces, cable TV, wireless
Internet

An elegant Georgian Colonial located in the West Hills of Portland. Situated on over a ½ acre of gardens, manicured lawns, and mature trees. This inn features blonde Honduran mahogany woodwork and Waterford crystal chandeliers throughout.
✉ terwilligervista@gmail.com ✪ www.terwilligervista.com

Georgian House B&B
1828 NE Siskiyou 97212
888-282-2250 503-281-2250
Willie Jean & Dick Canning

90-120 BB
4 rooms, 2 pb
Visa, MC, *Rated*
C-ltd/S-ltd/P-no/H-no
Inquire

Full breakfast
Afternoon tea, restaurant
Sitting room, library, tennis
court, TV, VCR, phones in
rooms, A/C

You'll enjoy 4 delightful rooms; 2 are suites. Close to area attractions on historic & quiet street. Trees & foliage are prefect for walks. Easy parking, close to mass transit. Innkeepers are Portland natives. Est. 1987. Lots of parking & bus & light rail.
✉ webmaster@thegeorgianhouse.com ✪ www.thegeorgianhouse.com

Lion & the Rose Victorian B&B
1810 NE 15th Ave 97212
800-955-1647 503-287-9245
Steven Unger

124-189 BB
6 rooms, 6 pb
Most CC, *Rated*
C-ltd/S-no/P-no/H-no

Full breakfast
Complimentary beverages,
light refreshments
Telephones w/free local &
long distance, cable TV, data
ports, high-speed wireless
Internet access

Exceptional B&B on the National Register of Historic Places, this majestic 1906 Queen Anne Victorian mansion takes you to another time. Six unique guestrooms, with private baths, emanate Victorian charm. ✉ innkeeper@lionrose.com ✪ www.lionrose.com

ROSEBURG

Hokanson's Guest House
848 SE Jackson 97470
541-672-2632
John & Victoria Hokanson

65-114 BB
3 rooms, 3 pb
C-ltd/S-no/P-no

Full 3-course breakfast
Weddings & small group
meetings

1882 Gothic Revival Victorian. Features antique furnishings and your choice of full 3-course or continental breakfast, in the midst of downtown Roseburg. Recapture romance, celebrate a special event or house your out of town guest in style.
✉ Jbhokanson@yahoo.com ✪ www.hokansonsguesthouse.com

496   Oregon

SEASIDE

10th Avenue Inn B&B
125 10th Avenue 97138
800-745-2378 503-738-0643
Jack & Lesle Palmeri

109-169 BB
3 rooms, 3 pb
Most CC, *Rated*, •
C-ltd/S-no/P-no/H-no
Un poquito Espanol

Hearty full breakfast
Complimentary early coffee
& evening tea served upon
request. Specialty gift
baskets also available.
Steinway & Sons grand
piano, cozy parlour fireplace
w/oceanview, books, games,
puzzles, conversation

Light cascades into this former home of a circuit court judge, circa 1908. Casual elegance combined with a view of the Pacific Ocean. Three guestrooms with king-sized beds, ensuite baths. A small cottage next door is perfect for small groups or families.
✉ stay@10aveinn.com ◔ www.10aveinn.com

Gilbert Inn B&B
341 Beach Dr 97138
800-410-9770 503-738-9770
Gilbert Inn LLC

99-170 BB
10 rooms, 10 pb
Most CC, *Rated*
S-no/P-no/H-no

Full breakfast
Fruit & baked cookies,
coffee, tea & sherry
Sitting room, games, books,
DVD movies

Seaside's only Queen Anne Victorian, the Gilbert Inn is in beautiful condition after 120 years. Country French furniture and antiques are part of the atmosphere that invites you to enjoy and relax. The Gilbert Inn is an oasis in Seaside, Oregon.
✉ gilbertinn@seasurf.net ◔ www.gilbertinn.com

SISTERS

Blue Spruce B&B
444 S Spruce St 97759
888-328-9644 541-549-9644
Sandy Affonso

129-189 BB
5 rooms, 5 pb
Visa, MC, *Rated*
C-ltd/S-no/P-no/H-no

Full breakfast
Snacks
Sitting room, bicycles,
fireplaces, cable TV, spa
tubs, towel warmers

Comfortable king beds, large spa tubs, & towel warmers provide luxury in a rustic setting. Generous breakfasts. Full cookie jar. Deer in backyard. Walk to shops & restaurants.
✉ innkeeper@blue-Spruce.biz ◔ www.blue-spruce.biz

SOUTH BEACH

Stone Crest Cellar Bed & Breakfast
9556 South Coast Hwy. 97366
541-867-6621
Judy & Craig Joubert

135-190 BB
2 rooms, 2 pb
Most CC
C-ltd/S-ltd/P-no/H-ltd

Full breakfast
Evening wine & appetizers
Ocean views, private baths,
sitting room, deck

You will feel like royalty with the wonderful amenities and services you will receive at this most spectacular castle-like Bed & Breakfast. Located just minutes from the Oregon Coast town of Newport.
✉ jjoubert@stonecrestbb.com ◔ www.stonecrestbb.com

ST. HELENS

Nob Hill Riverview B&B
285 S 2nd St 97051
503-396-5555
Matthew & Tana Phemester

110-210 BB
3 rooms, 3 pb
Most CC, *Rated*, •
C-ltd/S-no/P-no/H-ltd
Some Spanish

Full Hot Organic Gourmet
Breakfast
In the late afternoon guests
can enjoy a complimentary
Afternoon Tea and
appetizers upon request.
Gathering rooms, wood-
burning fireplace, sunroom
filled with flowers, TV,
business accommodations

Nob Hill Riverview Bed and Breakfast loves to pamper our guests! The home is newly restored, fresh and beautiful. Listed on historical places. A true 1900 Arts and Craft home. Beautiful views of the river from most rooms. Upscale and luxury.
✉ stay@nobhillbb.com ◔ www.nobhillbb.com

STEAMBOAT

Steamboat Inn	170-290 EP	Evening dinner available,
42705 N Umpqua Hwy 97447	19 rooms, 19 pb	aperitif and hors d'oeuvres
800-840-8825 541-498-2230	Visa, MC, *Rated*, •	Library, fireplaces, decks,
Sharon & Jim Van Loan	C-yes/S-no/P-ltd/H-yes	A/C, fly-fishing guides,
	March through	
	December	

Commanding a breathtaking view of the North Umpqua River, the Steamboat Inn is nestled among the towering firs of the Umpqua National Forest. We are about two hours by car from airports at Eugene and Medford.
✉ patricialee@hughes.net ❂ www.thesteamboatinn.com

WALDPORT

Cliff House B&B	110-225 BB	Full breakfast
1450 SW Adahi Rd 97394	4 rooms, 4 pb	Afternoon tea, coffee, fresh
541-563-2506	Visa, MC, *Rated*	lemonade, cookies
Sharon Robinson	C-ltd/S-no/P-no/H-no	Sitting room, hot tubs, decks,
	Dutch	ocean gazing, wireless
		Internet

Cliff House Bed and Breakfast, a luxuriously restored historic home, overlooks the Pacific Ocean and Alsea Bay on the Central Oregon Coast. Experience a renaissance of elegance and old world charm transposed into the 21st century.
✉ innkeeper@cliffhouseoregon.com ❂ www.cliffhouseoregon.com

WHEELER

Old Wheeler Hotel	65-145 BB	Continental plus breakfast
495 Hwy 101 97147	7 rooms, 7 pb	Complimentary snacks &
877-653-4683 503-368-6000	Most CC, *Rated*, •	beverages anytime
Winston Laszlo & Maranne	C-ltd/S-no/P-no/H-ltd	Sitting room, common room,
Doyle-Laszlo	Rudimentary French	Cable TV with DVD, free
	and Spanish	WiFi, bath amenities,
		morning paper

Charming, historic refuge in the heart of the north Oregon coast. Stunning views from every room. Shopping and dining just steps away! Fishing, boating, kayaking, and scenic train excursions.
✉ info@oldwheelerhotel.com ❂ www.oldwheelerhotel.com

Wheeler On The Bay Lodge	80-155 EP	Complimentary tea, coffee,
580 Marine Dr 97147	10 rooms, 10 pb	cocoa
800-469-3204 503-368-5858	Visa, MC, *Rated*, •	Spa, fireplace, TV, DVD/VHS
Pat Scribner	C-yes/S-ltd/P-ltd/H-ltd	movies, massage, fridge,
		micro, coffee maker,
		telephones, kayaks

Two hours west of Portland is a rare find on Oregon Coast. Wheeler on the Bay Lodge on Nehalem Bay Estuary has water & Neahkahnie Mt. views. Services include spas, massages, movies, kayaks, private boat dock. Charter boat, fishing or crabbing.
✉ WheelerLodge@nehalemtel.net ❂ www.wheeleronthebay.com

YACHATS

Ambrosia Gardens B&B	110-125 BB	Full breakfast
95435 Hwy 101 S 97498	4 rooms, 4 pb	Complimentary tea & soft
541-547-3013	Cash, Checks	drinks
Mary Coello	C-ltd/S-no/P-ltd/H-no	Porch, gardens, ponds,
		Jacuzzi, living room, WiFi,
		ocean-garden-forest views

South of Yachats, bordering Siuslaw National Forest, across from Sea Rose Beach is a haven of natural beauty called Ambrosia Gardens. Set on 2.75 acres with extensive gardens along the central Oregon coast. Outside Jacuzzi. Full breakfast. Antiques. WiFi
✉ Mary@ambrosia-gardens.com ❂ www.ambrosia-gardens.com

498   Oregon

YACHATS————————————————————————————

New England House	159-179 BB	Full 5 course breakfast
227 Shell St 97498	1 rooms, 1 pb	Fresh pastry daily with tea &
541-547-4799	Visa, MC, Disc, •	coffee, refrigerator stocked
Lily & Lee Banks	C-ltd/S-no/P-no/H-no	with ice, bottled water, cold
	Indonesian	beverages
		Library, fireplace, views, free
		WiFi, TV/VCR/DVD, phone,
		microwave, toaster oven,
		daily maid service

You are the Only guest! 5 course Full breakfast & Afternoon Tea. Oceanview suite with woodburning fireplace, king size bed, sundeck overlooking the ocean & village across the Bay. Easy access to sandy beach a few yards away. Romantic getaway.
✉ lily@newenglandhouse.com ◐ www.newenglandhouse.com

SeaQuest Inn	170-350 BB	Full breakfast
95354 Highway 101 97498	7 rooms, 7 pb	Daily home-baked goodies,
800-341-4878 541-547-3782	Visa, MC, *Rated*	coffee, tea, hot cocoa, hot
Kelley & Gabe Essoe	C-ltd/S-no/P-no/H-ltd	cider
		Jacuzzi tubs, private deck,
		ocean views, great room,
		sitting room, 2 ponds, sandy
		beach, vast lawn

As our most welcomed guest—indulgent comfort, ocean views, the crashing surf, and your own warm, inviting Jacuzzi tub are only the beginning pleasures that await your arrival at the oceanfront SeaQuest Inn Bed and Breakfast in Yachats, Oregon.
✉ kelley@essoe.com ◐ www.seaquestinn.com

Pennsylvania

AARONSBURG

The Aaronsburg Inn
100 E Aaron's Square 16820
814-349-8626
Jack & Jane Van Heyst

99-199 BB
7 rooms, 7 pb
Most CC
C-yes/S-ltd/P-ltd/H-ltd

Continental+ or Full
Coffee & tea with home
baked snacks
Pool, private baths, down
bedding, turndown service,
library, WiFi, business
services, guest kitchen

Casual elegance with a cosmopolitan flair in historic Aaronsburg. Close to Penn State, Bucknell, Woodward. Conveniently located for football, antiquing, fishing, fine dining & romantic getaways.
✉ jandj89@verizon.net ○ www.aaronsburginn.com

ABBOTTSTOWN

The Altland House
Rt 30 Center Square 17301
717-259-9535
Sonja McMillion

105-175 BB
10 rooms, 10 pb
Most CC, *Rated*, •
C-yes/S-no/P-yes/H-no

Continental plus breakfast
Restaurant, bar service
Jacuzzis, suites, cable TV

A country inn with exquisite cuisine and gracious hospitality in a cozy historic atmosphere.
✉ sonja_mcmillion@altlandhouse.com ○ www.altlandhouse.com

ADAMSTOWN

Living Spring Farm B&B
Route 568 19501
888-329-1275 610-775-8525
Debra Cazille

105-179 BB
4 rooms, 4 pb
Visa, MC
C-ltd/S-no/P-ltd/H-ltd

Full breakfast
Snacks, wine, teas & coffee
Sitting room, fireplace, cable
TV, robes & hair dryers in
rooms, WiFi

Charming 200 year-old stone farmhouse on 32 acres. This "gentlemen's farm" offers quiet and relaxation, far from the hustle & bustle. 3 guestrooms in the main house and a Private Cottage.
✉ DebCaz@worldnet.att.net ○ www.livingspringfarm.com

ATHENS

Failte Inn & Antique Shop
State Rd 1043 Sheshequin
18810
570-358-3899
Sarah & James True

80-120 BB
5 rooms, 5 pb
Most CC, *Rated*
C-yes/S-ltd/P-no/H-ltd

Full hot breakfast,
Continental before 8:00 am,
complimentary wine/brandy
in pub
Bar, sitting room, library,
suites, frplc, cable, accom.
bus. travelers, outdoor spa &
water garden

Revisit yesterday's elegant Victorian era. Large, beautiful guestrooms with luxurious amenities. Gourmet breakfasts on endless wraparound verandas. English style pub dating from Prohibition days.
✉ thefailteinn@webtv.net ○ www.failteinn.com

BANGOR

Belle Reve B&B
7757 Martin's Creek/ Belvidere
Rd 18013
888-549-8608 610-498-2026
Shirley & Thomas Creo

110-225 BB
6 rooms, 3 pb
Visa, MC, AmEx
C-ltd/S-no/P-no/H-no

Full & Continental Plus
breakfast
Afternoon tea, snacks
Sitting room, cable TV,
accommodations for
business travelers, riverside
gazebo, WiFi

Belle Reve, our "beautiful dream," is located on the Delaware River, the boundary between Pennsylvania and New Jersey, making attractions in both states easily accessible.
✉ reservations@bellereveriverside.com ○ www.bellereveriverside.com

500   Pennsylvania

BARTO

Landhaven B&B
1194 Huffs Church Rd 19504
610-845-3257
Ed & Donna Land

95-150 BB
5 rooms, 5 pb
C-ltd/S-no/P-no/H-yes

Full Country Breakfast
TV, fax & telephones
available in the common
seating area; library

Converted 1871 General Store offering quaint comfortable rooms with specialty baths and showers for each room. Homemade country-style breakfasts. Calming country views. On-site concerts, antique shop. Many packages available, or create your own!
✉ info@landhavenbandb.com ◊ www.landhavenbandb.com

BETHLEHEM

The Sayre Mansion
250 Wyandotte St 18015
877-345-9019 610-882-2100
Carrie Ohlandt

150-295 BB
18 rooms, 18 pb
Most CC
C-yes/S-no/P-ltd/H-yes

Full breakfast
Parlors, fireplace, air
conditioning, private baths,
telephones, wireless Internet
access, cable TV

Meticulously restored, this bed and breakfast Inn offers luxury and comfort in 18 guest-rooms each preserving the architectural details of the mansion.
✉ innkeeper@sayremansion.com ◊ www.sayremansion.com

BIRD IN HAND

Bird-in-Hand Village Inn & Suites
2695 Old Philadelphia Pike
17505
800-914-2473
Jim & John Smucker

79-224 BB
24 rooms, 24 pb
Most CC, *Rated*
C-ltd/S-ltd/P-no/H-ltd
February-December

Continental plus breakfast
Evening snacks
Sitting room, 2-hour Dutch
Country bus tour, suites
w/hot tub, fireplace,
refrigerator, meeting room

Beautifully restored historic inn located in Pennsylvania Dutch Country. Victorian-style architecture and furnishings in a rural setting. Complimentary tour of PA Dutch country.
✉ lodging@bird-in-hand.com
◊ www.bird-in-hand.com/index.php/places_to_stay/stay_overview/village_inn_suites

Greystone Manor Victorian Inn
2658 Old Philadelphia Pike
17505
717-393-4233
Angela Skiadas

59-189 BB
10 rooms, 10 pb
Most CC, *Rated*, •
C-yes/S-no/P-yes/H-yes
Greek

Full breakfast
Snacks and beverages,
poolside menu, catering
menu, family reunion
dinners avail., pig roasts
avail.
Pool and hot tub, sitting
rooms, pantry, numerous
patios and balconies, picnic
area, dining room

1845 Victorian Mansion in the heart of the Amish country. Centrally located only 5 minutes away from all the shopping, food, and entertainment. Perched atop a hill on 2 beautiful acres, award winning gardens, pool, Jacuzzi, & surrounded by 3 Amish farms.
✉ angela@greystonemanor.com ◊ www.greystonemanor.com

Mill Creek Homestead B&B
2578 Old Philadelphia Pike
17505
717-291-6419
Bob and Lori Kepiro

79-99 BB
4 rooms, 4 pb
Visa, MC, Disc, •
S-no/P-no/H-no .

Continental breakfast
Guest microwave, toaster
oven and refrigerator with
pay-as-you use soda etc
complim. tea, coffee,
TV room with cable
tv/vcr/dvd Formal Living Rm
Dining Rm Swimming pool
Jacuzzi (April to Dec)

The sight of our Historic 1790 Inn from the outside is just a prelude of what's inside! Located in the heart of the picturesque Amish farming community, guests will enjoy warm Christian hospitality for the perfect getaway to relax and "recharge!"
✉ lkepiro@comcast.net

BLOOMSBURG

The Inn at Turkey Hill
991 Central Rd 17815
570-387-1500
Andrew Pruden

109-225 BB
23 rooms, 23 pb
Most CC
C-yes/S-ltd/P-yes/H-ltd

Continental breakfast
Dinner every evening
Cozy tavern, whirlpools &
fireplaces, duck pond &
gazebo

The Inn at Turkey Hill is a moment's drive from Interstate 80 in Bloomsburg, an oasis along the highway, a world of peaceful strolls by the pond, personal wake-up calls, gourmet cuisine and beautifully appointed guestrooms.
✉ andrew@innatturkeyhill.com ◐ www.innatturkeyhill.com

BLUE BALL

Blue Ball B&B
1075 Main St 17506
800-720-9827 717-355-9994
Frank & Jeanne Warsheski

75-145 BB
6 rooms, 6 pb
Visa, MC, Disc
C-yes/S-no/P-ltd/H-yes

Full breakfast
Fireplace, Jacuzzi, large
common sitting area with TV

The Blue Ball Bed and Breakfast is located in the heart of romantic Amish Country. You are minutes away from Sight and Sound, American Music Theatre, Amish woodcrafts and Amish quilt shops, museums, antiques, and shopping while enjoying the countryside.
✉ pudone@ptd.net ◐ www.blueballbandb.com

BOILING SPRINGS

Gelinas Manor Victorian B&B
219 Front St 17007
866-297-2588 717-258-6584
Lee & Kity Gelinas

69-129 BB
4 rooms, 3 pb
Most CC, •
C-yes/S-no/P-no/H-no

Full breakfast
Coffee, cocoa, tea 24/7
Sitting room, library, suites,
A/C, email & fax services

Guests will find the highest levels of service, comfort, ambience, and elegance in this circa 1870 home in an historic village. Fly fishing, car shows, Appalachian trail nearby. Midway between Hershey & Gettysburg.
✉ Lee@gelinasManor.com ◐ www.GelinasManor.com

CANADENSIS

Brookview Manor
2960 RR 447 18325
800-585-7974 570-595-2451
Gaile & Marty Horowitz

130-225 BB
10 rooms, 10 pb
Most CC, *Rated*
C-ltd/S-no/P-no/H-no

Full gourmet breakfast
Casual to gourmet dinner by
award winning chef,
reservations required in our
restaurant
Sitting room, TV/DVD,
library, lawn games, hiking,
Jacuzzi, fireplaces, enclosed
wrap around porch

We invite you to recapture the art of relaxation in an enchanting country Inn. We are nestled in the heart of the Poconos across from the Brodhead Creek. Hike, golf, ski, antiquing and gambling nearby. Romantic accommodations with Jacuzzis and fireplaces
✉ innkeepers@TheBrookviewManor.com ◐ www.thebrookviewmanor.com

CARLISLE

Pheasant Field
150 Hickorytown Rd 17015
877-258-0717 717-258-0717
Dee Fegan & Chuck DeMarco

119-209 BB
7 rooms, 7 pb
Most CC, *Rated*, •
C-ltd/S-no/P-ltd/H-yes

Full breakfast
Snacks, soft drinks available
anytime
Sitting room, tennis court,
horse boarding available,
labyrinth on-site, VCR/DVD
movies

Lovely 200 year-old brick farmhouse in a country setting. History, antiques, fly fishing, car shows. Appalachian trail nearby. Labyrinth on-site for quiet meditation. Extended-stay apartment available.
✉ stay@pheasantfield.com ◐ www.pheasantfield.com

CASHTOWN

Cashtown Inn	140-175 BB	Full breakfast on weekends
1325 Old Route 30 17310	7 rooms, 7 pb	Continental breakfast during
800-367-1797 717-334-9722	Most CC, *Rated*	the week, restaurant – lunch
Jack & Maria Paladino	C-ltd/S-ltd/P-no/H-ltd	and dinner, bar service
		Sitting room, library, suites,
		cable TV, accommodations
		for business travelers

Civil War landmark; antiques, artwork, country decor. Relax on the porches or fireside in the Tavern. Delectable food, gracious hosts and history that comes alive!
✉ cashtowninn@earthlink.net 🌐 www.cashtowninn.com

CHADDS FORD

Fairville Inn	160-295 BB	Full and Continental
506 Kennett Pike, Rt 52 19317	15 rooms, 15 pb	Breakfasts
877-285-7772 610-388-5900	Most CC	Afternoon tea with cheese,
Rick & Laura Carro	C-ltd/S-ltd/P-no/H-yes	fruit, and inn-baked goods.
		Satellite TV, telephone, and
		wireless Internet in each
		room. Most rooms have a
		fireplace and deck.

Elegant accommodations in Chadds Ford, PA. Located in the heart of Brandywine Valley minutes from Longwood Gardens, Winterthur and the Brandywine River (Wyeth) Museum. Enjoy the elegance of our individually decorated rooms and the comforts of our kitchen.
✉ info@fairvilleinn.com 🌐 www.fairvilleinn.com

Hamanassett B&B &	160-450 BB	Full breakfast
Carriage House	8 rooms, 8 pb	Complimentary snacks, soft
725 Darlington Rd 19017	Visa, MC, AmEx, *Rated*	drinks, bottled water, fresh
877-836-1212 610-459-3000	C-ltd/S-ltd/P-ltd/H-no	baked cookies.
Glenn & Ashley Mon		All business services, in
		room massage. Free high
		speed wireless

Historic elegance in the Brandywine Valley. Experience exceptional personal service & Southern hospitality at our English country Bed & Breakfast in the beautiful Brandywine Valley. Child and dog friendly carriage house. Member of Select Registry.
✉ ashley@hamanassett.com 🌐 www.hamanassett.com

CHURCHTOWN

Inn at Twin Linden	125-265 BB	Full breakfast
2092 Main St 17555	8 rooms, 8 pb	Complimentary snacks,
866-445-7614 717-445-7619	Most CC, *Rated*, •	coffee & tea available 24/7,
Sue & Norm Kuestner	C-ltd/S-no/P-no/H-ltd	Saturday evening fine dining
		by reservation
		Jacuzzi tub, fireplace, cable,
		VHS/DVD, free WiFi, private
		dining tables, business
		meeting space

Elegant accommodations in historic estate for discriminating inn-goers. Private baths and dining tables, Jacuzzis, fireplaces, renowned gourmet cuisine.
✉ info@innattwinlinden.com 🌐 www.innattwinlinden.com

CLEARFIELD

Christopher Kratzer House	65-90 BB	Full breakfast
101 E Cherry St 16830	3 rooms, 2 pb	Fine dining restaurants
888-252-2632 814-765-5024	Visa, MC, Disc, *Rated*,	around the corner.
Bruce & Ginny Baggett	•	Snacks, sitting room, library,
	C-yes/S-ltd/P-yes/H-no	attic flea market for
		browsing, A/C

1828 historic house overlooking river & park. Two suites with private bath (1 suite may be divided into adjoining rooms, with shared bath).
✉ bbaggett@pennswoods.net

CLIFFORD

Fern Hall	125-200 BB	Full breakfast
RD 1, Crystal Lake 18413	7 rooms, 4 pb	Dinner is available Friday
570-222-3676	Visa, MC, AmEx	and Saturday night. Lunch
Diane Wiseman	C-yes/S-no/P-no/H-ltd	available when golf course is
		open.
		Bar service, sitting room,
		library, cable TV,
		accom.bus.travel, golf
		course.

Former Summer estate of James Johnson, founder of Johnson & Johnson pharmaceutical Co. Fern Hall is home to our restaurant, Bed & Breakfast, and the Clubhouse of Scottish Glen, a scenic nine-hole daily fee golf course.
✉ fernhallinn@gmail.com ○ www.fernhallinn.com

COLUMBIA

The Columbian	100-125 BB	Full breakfast
360 Chestnut St 17512	5 rooms, 5 pb	Complimentary beverages &
800-422-5869 717-684-5869	Most CC, *Rated*	snacks
Karen Umlauf	C-yes/S-ltd/P-no/H-no	Sitting room, A/C, TVs,
		wireless Internet, fireplaces,
		porches, patio, hot tub, spa

Restored turn-of-the-century circa 1897 mansion. Includes wraparound sun porches, stained-glass window, & tiered staircase. Decorated with antiques in Victorian or Country style.
✉ inn@columbianinn.com ○ www.columbianinn.com

EAGLES MERE

Crestmont Inn	110-240 BB	Full country breakfast
Crestmont Dr 17731	15 rooms, 15 pb	Dinner, restaurant, bar
800-522-8767 570-525-3519	Visa, MC, *Rated*, ●	service
Fred & Elna Mulford	C-yes/S-no/P-no/H-no	Commons room, coffee & tea
		room, bicycles, tennis court,
		private whirlpool, lake
		access, cable TV

A hidden treasure nestled in the Endless Mountains in "the town that time forgot, Eagles Mere, Pennsylvania."
✉ crestmnt@epix.net ○ www.crestmont-inn.com

Eagles Mere Inn	169-269 MAP	Full Country breakfast
Corner of Mary & Sullivan Ave	19 rooms, 19 pb	Gourmet dinner included,
17731	Visa, MC, Disc, *Rated*,	excellent wine list
800-426-3273 570-525-3273	●	Pub
Matt Gale	C-yes/S-no/P-no/H-yes	

Ultimate stress relief! Guests enjoy warm hospitality, gourmet meals included in rates, outstanding wines and peaceful relaxation.
✉ relax@eaglesmereinn.com ○ www.eaglesmereinn.com

EAST BERLIN

Bechtel Victorian Mansion	115-175 BB	Full breakfast
400 West King St 17316	6 rooms, 6 pb	Complimentary tea
800-331-1108 717-259-7760	Visa, MC, AmEx,	Sitting room, TV with VCR
Carol & Richard Carlson	*Rated*, ●	and DVD, movies, A/C,
	C-yes/S-ltd/P-no/H-no	meeting room, garden

1897 Victorian mansion with 6 guestrooms. All rooms have private bath & A/C. Beautifully decorated in country Victorian style, furnished with period antiques, accented with porcelain dolls, teddy bears & toys.
✉ bechtelvictbb@aol.com

EAST EARL

A Suite Escape
417 Fairview Street 17519
877-273-7227 717-445-5649
Joanne Martin

139-169 BB
2 rooms, 2 pb
Most CC
C-yes/S-no/P-no/H-ltd

Full breakfast
Breakfast is in your room or
on your patio
Hot Tub, flat screen TV's,
fireplaces

*Come and escape the hustle and bustle of everyday life and enjoy the heart of PA Dutch
Country. Enjoy our beautiful view and private suites, creating the perfect getaway for the
romantic or family vacation. Soak in our hot tub under the stars.*
✉ sjmartin@dejazzd.com 🌐 www.asuiteescape.com/index.htm

EAST STROUDSBURG

Cranberry Manor B&B
114 Cherry Lane Rd 18301
570-620-2246
Ric and Sharon Anderson

125-170 BB
5 rooms, 5 pb
Most CC
C-ltd/S-no/P-no/H-ltd

Candlelight breakfast
Butler's pantry; snacks,
beverages
Library with TV, CD stereo,
VCR; porches, pool table,
fireplaces, A/C, wireless
Internet access.

*A former summer boarding home situated on 14 acres at the edge of the Tannersville
Cranberry Bog. An all-season inn with a rural mountain locale and urban convenience.
Come let Cranberry Manor be your quiet mountain getaway where your pleasure is ours.*
✉ cranberrymanor@enter.net 🌐 www.cranberrymanor.com

EASTON

The Lafayette Inn
525 W Monroe St 18042
800-509-6990 610-253-4500
Paul & Laura Di Liello

125-225 BB
18 rooms, 18 pb
Most CC, *Rated*
C-yes/S-no/P-ltd/H-yes
Italian

Full breakfast
Complimentary snacks,
sodas, coffee, teas
Sitting room, whirlpools,
suites, fireplaces, cable TV,
DVDs, fax, dataports, WiFi

*Our 18 antique filled rooms and landscaped grounds offer distinctive accommodations in
Pennsylvania's historic Lehigh Valley. Romantic suite getaways; family-friendly guestrooms.*
✉ info@lafayetteinn.com 🌐 www.lafayetteinn.com

ELIZABETHTOWN

Conewago Manor Inn
2048 Zeager Rd 17022
717-361-0826
Keith & Laura Murphy

165-200 BB
9 rooms, 9 pb
Visa, MC, *Rated*
C-ltd/S-no/P-no/H-no

Full breakfast
Snacks & soft drinks
Sunroom, library, workout
room, fireplaces, TV with
VCR, special service upon
request

*A romantic bed and breakfast on Conewago Creek near Hershey, Harrisburg and Lancaster
County. Elegant Victorian rooms with whirlpool baths, fireplaces, most with balconies.
Perfect for wedding receptions, small business meetings and getaways.*
✉ cminn@earthlink.net 🌐 www.conewagomanorinn.com

West Ridge Guest House
1285 West Ridge Rd 17022
877-367-7783 717-367-7783
Zanna Towns

90-165 BB
9 rooms, 9 pb
Most CC, *Rated*
C-ltd/S-ltd/P-no/H-ltd

Full breakfast
Full breakfast is served every
morning from 7 – 9 am to
accommodate even the early
riser.
Whirlpools, exercise room,
gazebo, decks, fireplaces,
videos, pool, tennis, high
speed wireless

*A beautiful county estate . Each of our nine rooms is individually decorated. All our rooms
have TV/VCR, phone, A/C. Some rooms with decks, fireplaces and whirlpool tubs. Conveniently located between Hershey, Harrisburg & Lancaster Dutch Country area.*
✉ wridgeroad@aol.com 🌐 www.westridgebandb.com

ELYSBURG

Plum Pudding Inn
201 N Market St 17824
888-785-7586 570-672-1999
Liz & Fred

85-135 BB
6 rooms, 6 pb
Most CC, *Rated*
C-yes/S-ltd/P-ltd/H-ltd

Full breakfast
Afternoon tea, snacks
Sitting room, library,
swimming pool, fireplaces,
cable TV, airport service,
wireless Internet

Located in the Susquehanna Valley. We offer more than just a room, we offer a romantic atmosphere with old fashioned hospitality and service with a smile! All rooms are themed.
Liz@plumpuddinginn.com ✆ www.PlumPuddingInn.com

EPHRATA

Historic Smithton Inn
900 W Main St 17522
877-755-4590 717-733-6094
Dorothy Graybill

95-165 BB
7 rooms, 7 pb
Visa, MC, *Rated*, •
C-ltd/S-no/P-ltd/H-ltd

Full breakfast
Complimentary tea, snacks
Sitting room, fireplaces,
some whirlpool baths,
gardens, some canopy beds

A 1763 historic village inn in picturesque Lancaster County, home of the PA Dutch people. Amish, Mennonite, Bretheren, etc.
Smithtoninn@dejazzed.com ✆ www.historicsmithtoninn.com

The Hurst House
154 East Farmersville Road
17522
800-603-9227 717-355-5151
Rich & Bert Hurst

135-175 BB
5 rooms, 5 pb
Visa, MC
C-ltd/S-no/P-no/H-yes

Full breakfast
Wireless Internet, fireplaces,
A/C, exercise room,
accommodating business
meetings & parties

We invite you to The Hurst House B&B, in Ephrata, Lancaster County, PA. An elegant Victorian Mansion located on top of the Katza Buckle overlooking hundreds of beautiful Amish & Old Order Mennonite farms in the heart of the Pennsylvania Dutch Country.
TheHurstHouse@gmail.com ✆ www.hursthousebandb.com

Kimmell House B&B
851 S State St 17522
800-861-3385 717-738-3555
Dave & Bonnie Harvey

95-135 BB
4 rooms, 4 pb
Visa, MC, Disc
C-ltd/S-no/P-no/H-no

Full breakfast
Afternoon tea
Fireplace, patio and garden

Kimmell House B&B is a charming Georgian sandstone built in 1795 located in Ephrata, PA. The B&B offers four rooms and is conveniently located within minutes of historic areas, antique markets, shopping outlets, fine restaurants and wineries.
info@kimmellhouse.com ✆ www.kimmellhouse.com

Twin Pine Manor B&B
1934 W Main St 17522
888-266-0099 717-733-8400
Norm Kurtz

99-225 BB
8 rooms, 8 pb
Most CC
C-ltd/S-ltd/P-no/H-ltd
April to Mid-December

Full breakfast
Exercise room with sauna,
CD players, cable TV,
Jacuzzis, sitting room

Twin Pine Manor is a spacious 15 room mansion with 8 guestrooms with private baths. Six rooms have Jacuzzis (for 2) and fireplaces. Located in the heart of Pennsylvania Dutch Country, we offer a countryside retreat setting for bed & breakfast guests.
twinpinemanor@hotmail.com ✆ www.twinpinemanor.com

ERIE

The Boothby Inn LLC
311 West 6th Street 16507
866-BOOTHBY 814-456-1888
Wally & Gloria Knox

130-170 BB
4 rooms, 4 pb
Most CC, *Rated*
S-no/P-no/H-no

Full breakfast
Guest kitchen with snacks
TV, phone, dataport,
conference facilities

Experience the finest accommodations downtown Erie has to offer. Catering to the business traveler and vacationer, the Inn boasts warm and sophisticated hospitality.
info@theboothbyinn.com ✆ www.theboothbyinn.com

ERWINNA————————————————————————————

Golden Pheasant Inn	155-235 BB	Continental plus breakfast
763 River Rd 18920	8 rooms, 8 pb	Dinner (Tuesday-Sunday),
800-830-4474 610-294-9595	Visa, MC, *Rated*, •	wine in room
Barbara & Michael Faure	C-ltd/S-ltd/P-ltd/H-ltd	Restaurant, bar, canoes,
	French, Spanish, Italian	Delaware Canal & River,
		hiking/biking

1857 fieldstone inn situated between river and canal. The rooms are furnished with an incredible blend of antiques. "A bite of France in Bucks County."
✉ barbara@goldenpheasant.com ○ www.goldenpheasant.com

FAIRFIELD————————————————————————————

The Historic Fairfield Inn	130-225 BB	Continental breakfast
15 W Main St 17320	5 rooms, 5 pb	Fine dining restaurant &
717-642-5410	Visa, MC	tavern, casual lunch fare,
Joan & Sal Chandon	C-yes/S-no/P-no/H-no	Sunday brunch
		Dinner theatre, conference
		facilities, banquet setup,
		wedding parties, wireless
		Internet

A tradition of exceptional service, fine cuisine, & luxury accommodations since 1786. Guestrooms and suites with private baths, A/C, cable TV, wireless Internet. On-site tavern and restaurant.
✉ innkeeper@thefairfieldinn.com ○ www.thefairfieldinn.com

FARMINGTON————————————————————————————

Quiet House B&B with	169-189 BB	Full Hot Breakfast
Cottages	7 rooms, 7 pb	Restaurant, complimentary
US Rte 381 South 15437	Most CC	wine
800-784-8187 724-329-4606	C-ltd/S-ltd/P-no/H-no	Bicycles, tennis court,
Marty & Judy		fireplaces, chapel,
		accommodations for
		business travelers

Pre-Civil War Georgian farmhouse plus 3 cottages and one loft for a romantic getaway. Full of country charm and memories that will refresh your days. A place to reflect on life's priorities.
✉ quiethouse@quiethousebnb.com ○ www.quiethousebnb.com

FAYETTEVILLE————————————————————————————

Angelic Inn Dolls & Gifts	109-189 BB	Full breakfast
1090 Ragged Edge Inn 17222	10 rooms, 10 pb	Refreshments available in
888-900-5880 717-261-1195	Most CC, *Rated*	the butler's pantry
Kay Mitchell	C-yes/S-ltd/P-ltd/H-ltd	A/C, TV/VCR, Murder
		Mystery Weekends, wrap-
		around porch, fireplaces,
		whirlpools, special events

Travel the same route that General Lee and his men took into Gettysburg and stay in this country Victorian Mansion. The Inn features Honeymoon Suites with fireplaces and whirlpool tubs for your wedding night, anniversary or birthday.
✉ rei@gettysburginns.com ○ www.gettysburginns.com

FLEETWOOD————————————————————————————

Golden Oaks Golf Club B&B	80-115 EP	Tee times and greens fees
10 Stonehedge Dr. 19522	3 rooms, 2 pb	arranged, cable TV.
610-944-6000	Visa, MC, AmEx	Restaurant on premises.
Marina Heffner	C-yes/S-ltd/P-no/H-no	

Intimate and charming, a renovated 1850's farm house beautifully decorated and the perfect setting for your overnight accommodations. Stay and play at Golden Oaks!
✉ lou@goldenoaksgolfclub.com ○ www.goldenoaksgolfclub.com/specials/stay-and-play.html

FRANKLIN

The Lamberton House	70-130 BB	Full breakfast
1331 Otter St 16323	5 rooms, 5 pb	Evening dinners are
866-632-7908 814-432-7908	Visa, MC, AmEx	available at an additional
Mary & Jim Nicklin	C-yes/S-no/P-no/H-no	charge- advance
		reservations required.
		Library, drawing room,
		wireless Internet

Restored 1874 Queen Anne Victorian mansion, a delightful refuge from the stress of modern life. Five gracious guest bedrooms with a full breakfast provided each morning. Located mid-way between Pittsburgh and Erie, PA. Event facilities for up to 40.
✉ info@lambertonhouse.com ✪ lambertonhouse.com

GETTYSBURG

A Sentimental Journey B&B	89-110 BB	Continental breakfast
431 Baltimore St 17325	5 rooms, 4 pb	Cable TV, AC, porch, living
717-337-0779 717-642-5188	Most CC	room, antiques
Barbara & Steve Shultz	S-no/P-no	

Nostalgic guestrooms in Gettysburg's historic district. Low rates plus discounts for weeknights, multiple nights or off-season. All rooms are unique and you are within walking distance to everything.
✉ aceshigh@embarqmail.com ✪ www.asentimentaljourneybb.com

Baladerry Inn at Gettysburg	135-240 BB	Full breakfast
40 Hospital Rd 17325	10 rooms, 10 pb	Snacks, coffee & tea
800-220-0025 717-337-1342	Most CC, *Rated*, •	Sitting room, library, tennis,
Suzanne Lonky	C-ltd/S-no/P-no/H-no	fireplace, conferences, in-room phones

Private, quiet, historic and spacious country location at the edge of the Gettysburg National Historic Park.
✉ innkeeper@baladerryinn.com ✪ www.baladerryinn.com

Battlefield Bed & Breakfast	125-250 BB	Delicious full hot breakfast
2264 Emmitsburg Rd 17325	8 rooms, 8 pb	Afternoon cookies,
888-766-3897 717-334-8804	Most CC, *Rated*, •	lemonade, coffee, and tea
Florence Tarbox	C-yes/S-no/P-yes/H-yes	Daily Civil War history programs, WiFi, TV, fireplaces, romance packages, row boat, petting zoo

The only bed and breakfast in an original Civil War stone home nestled on 30 private acres of the Gettysburg Battlefield. Our peaceful farm has a beautiful lotus pond, petting zoo, & nature trails.
✉ battlefieldbedandbreakfast@gmail.com ✪ www.gettysburgbattlefield.com

The Brafferton Inn	95-199 BB	Full country breakfast
44 York St 17325	18 rooms, 18 pb	Complimentary coffee, tea &
866-337-3423 717-337-3423	Most CC	snacks
Joan, Brian, AmyBeth Hodges	C-ltd/S-no/P-no/H-no	Victorian inspired rooms, queen four poster beds, sitting areas, gas fireplaces, TV, kitchenette

Stone and clapboard inn circa 1786 near the center square of Gettysburg. The rooms have stenciled designs and antiques. The Brafferton Inn is a special place, filled with a wonderful mix of history, culture and art.
✉ innkeepers@brafferton.com ✪ www.brafferton.com

GETTYSBURG

Brickhouse Inn
452 Baltimore St 17325
800-864-3464 717-338-9337
Tessa Bardo & Brian Duncan

115-179 BB
14 rooms, 14 pb
Visa, MC, Disc, *Rated*,
•
C-ltd/S-ltd/P-no/H-ltd

Full breakfast
Lemonade, mulled cider,
homemade sweets, cookies
Sitting rooms, beautiful
garden, easy walk to
restaurants, museums, shops
and battlefield

1898 brick Victorian & adjacent c.1830 bullet-scarred historic Welty House, nestled in the historic district. Walk to battlefields, great restaurants, antique and gift shops.
✉ stay@brickhouseinn.com ❂ www.brickhouseinn.com

The Doubleday Inn
104 Doubleday Ave 17325
717-334-9119
Todd & Christine Thomas

129-159 BB
9 rooms, 9 pb
Visa, MC, Disc, •
C-ltd/S-ltd/P-no/H-no

Full hot breakfast
Afternoon tea and snacks
WiFi throughout, extensive
gardens with outdoor
seating, historian discussions
on selected evenings.

Experience the ONLY B&B located directly on the Gettysburg Battlefield! Enjoy our unique historic atmosphere featuring splendid views, friendly hosts, cozy antiques and a sizeable collection of Civil War memorabilia. Simply paradise for history lovers!
✉ info@doubledayinn.com ❂ www.doubledayinn.com

James Gettys Hotel
27 Chambersburg St 17325
888-900-5275 717-337-1334
Stephanie Stephan

140-250 BB
12 rooms, 12 pb
Most CC, *Rated*
C-yes/S-no/P-no/H-yes
French

Continental breakfast
Fresh ground coffee &
imported British teas,
homemade cookies and
fresh chocolates during
turndown.
Suites, wireless Internet
service, cable TV,
telephones, kitchenettes, and
all conveniences of home.

This fully renovated circa 1804 historic hotel in downtown Gettysburg offers twelve tastefully appointed suites with living rooms, kitchenettes, bedroom and private bath. Gracious amenities, warm hospitality and exceptional service.
✉ info@jamesgettyshotel.com ❂ www.jamesgettyshotel.com

Keystone Inn
231 Hanover St 17325
717-337-3888
Doris Martin

105-179 BB
7 rooms, 7 pb
Visa, MC, *Rated*
C-yes/S-ltd/P-no/H-ltd

Full breakfast from menu
Sodas, coffee, tea
Sitting room, library, suite
with TV, microwave & fridge,
tennis nearby

A wonderful late Victorian. Great house near the historic battlefields. Lovely flower gardens. Comfort is our priority. Country breakfasts.
✉ dmartin@supernet.com ❂ www.keystoneinnbb.com

Lightner Farmhouse
2350 Baltimore Pike 17325
717-337-9508
Dennis & Eileen Hoover

110-189 BB
7 rooms, 7 pb
Visa, MC, Disc, *Rated*
C-yes/S-no/P-no/H-ltd

Full breakfast
Snacks & beverages
Sitting room, library, suites,
cable TV, porch, nature trail,
assistance with tours or
reservations

Historic house built in 1862, served as Union Hospital during Gettysburg battle. Nineteen acres of landscape with nature and history trail. Conveniently located three miles south of Gettysburg on 26 quiet acres.
✉ innkeepers@lightnerfarmhouse.com ❂ www.lightnerfarmhouse.com

GETTYSBURG

Passages Inn Gettysburg	110-155 BB	Full breakfast
267 Baltimore St 17325	3 rooms, 3 pb	Dietary restrictions happily ac-
717-334-7010	Visa, MC	commodated.
Paulette Lee & Gary Froseth	C-ltd/S-no/P-no/H-no	Guest parlor, reading materi-
	French	als, games, complimentary
		beverages, WiFi.

A B&B "with an international accent," centrally located in downtown historic Gettysburg in a renovated pre-Civil War home. Decor reflects the innkeepers' travel, work and interests. ✉ innkeeper@passagesinngettysburg.com ☾ www.passagesinngettysburg.com

Quite The Stir B&B	145 BB	Continental plus breakfast
Bungalow	2 rooms, 1 pb	High speed Internet, antique
500 W Middle St 17325	Most CC	books
717-549-3631	C-ltd/S-no/P-no/H-no	
Macks & Company		

Quite The Stir invites you to step back in time to the 1940s and the WWII era. A cozy bungalow located 4 blocks from downtown Lincoln Square in the historic west side of Gettysburg, 1 block from the historic Gettysburg Civil War Battlefield! ✉ innkeeper@quitethestir.com ☾ www.quitethestir.com

Slocum House Inn	90-100 BB	Full breakfast
200 Blue Berry Rd 17324	3 rooms, 3 pb	Complimentary beverages
717-528-7390	Cash, Checks	Swimming pool, gardens,
Carol Schafer	C-ltd/S-no/P-no/H-ltd	pond, satellite TV, VCR, library

Romantic country inn on 25 rustic acres. Beautifully restored c1759 home is a treat for travelers who want a unique country experience. Although the home was originally constructed as a settler's log cabin, it has been expanded over the years. ✉ schafer1@embarqmail.com ☾ www.slocumhouseinn.com

GLEN MILLS

Sweetwater Farm	135-295 BB	Full breakfast
50 Sweetwater Rd 19342	14 rooms, 14 pb	Billiard room, library,
800-793-3892 610-459-4711	Most CC	swimming pool, fitness
Sean & Farrell Kramer	C-ltd/S-no/P-ltd/H-ltd	center, massage

1734 stone mansion on 50 manicured acres. Seven elegantly decorated rooms in the main house with fireplaces & canopied beds. There are 7 cottages—5 of which are child and pet friendly. ✉ info@sweetwaterfarmbb.com ☾ www.sweetwaterfarmbb.com

GORDONVILLE

After Eight B&B	109-300 BB	Full breakfast
2942 Lincoln Hwy E 17529	10 rooms, 10 pb	Coffee, tea, fruit, fruit drinks,
888-314-3664 717-687-3664	Most CC, *Rated*	sodas, water and snacks
Robert & June Hall	C-ltd/S-ltd/P-no/H-ltd	throughout the day.
		Sitting room, antique decor,
		game table, guest Internet,
		WiFi, gardens, fountains,
		gazebo

Renovated Colonial brick home from 1818, in the center of the Pennsylvania Dutch, Amish heartland. Elegantly decorated and antique filled guestrooms with modern amenities and private baths. ✉ bob@aftereightbnb.com ☾ www.aftereightbnb.com

HANOVER

Beechmont Inn	104-169 BB	Full breakfast
315 Broadway 17331	7 rooms, 7 pb	Help yourself cookie jar with
800-553-7009 717-632-3013	Most CC, *Rated*, •	homemade cookies, soft
Kathryn & Thomas White	C-ltd/S-no/P-no/H-yes	drinks, bottled water
		Wireless Internet, guest
		computer station, library, in-
		room telephones, fax, copier,
		guest fridge

Centuries of charm greet you. Sumptuous breakfasts and warm hospitality are our hallmarks. Whether on holiday or business, enjoy gardens, patios and porches, creating treasured memories of your stay. ✉ innkeeper@thebeechmont.com ☾ www.thebeechmont.com

HERSHEY───

1825 Inn Bed & Breakfast	114-239 BB	Full breakfast
409 S Lingle Ave 17078	8 rooms, 8 pb	Evening snacks with coffee
877-738-8282 717-838-8282	Most CC	and tea
Will McQueen	C-ltd/S-no/P-no/H-no	Gardens, porch, parlor,
		gazebo

Our historical Inn offers you the tranquility and comfort of the country along with our lovely gardens and inviting surroundings. However, we are near all the Hershey city conveniences.
✉ info@1825inn.com ◐ www.1825inn.com

───

Berry Patch	125-229 BB	Full breakfast
115 Moore Rd 17046	7 rooms, 7 pb	Garden, veranda, Jacuzzi,
888-246-8826 717-865-7219	Cash	fireplace, patio, cable TV,
Bunny Yinger	S-no/P-no/H-ltd	VCR, gourmet gifts

The Berry Patch Bed and Breakfast is pleased to offer a variety of Lebanon, PA accommodations. We invite our guests to choose one of the beautifully decorated guestrooms from our Pennsylvania Dutch Country Inn.
✉ bunny@berrypatchbnb.com ◐ www.berrypatchbnb.com

HOLICONG───

Ash Mill Farm	140-295 BB	Full breakfast
5358 York Rd 18928	7 rooms, 7 pb	Sodas & bottled water
215-794-5373	Most CC, •	Television in all rooms, air
David Topel	S-no/P-no/H-no	conditioning, king and queen
	Spanish, Danish	beds, wireless Internet,
		fireplace

Elegant 1790 grand manor house and 11 acre working sheep farm, with a romantic, nature walk. Named in June 2000 Travel & Leisure's top 12 U.S. Bed & Breakfasts. A Bucks County landmark ideal for weddings, retreats or that perfect weekend getaway.
✉ info@ashmillfarm.com ◐ www.ashmillfarm.com

HONESDALE───

Double W Ranch B&B	130-175 BB	Full Country Breakfast
RR 2 Box 1540 18431	10 rooms, 10 pb	Our inn is located on a fruit
877-540-7262 570-226-3118	Most CC	farm.
	C-yes/S-ltd/P-no/H-ltd	Big screen TV (satellite),
		horses, large living room,
		beautiful scenery, reunions
		and weddings.

Nestled in a lovely secluded spot at the highest point of the Northern range of the Pocono Mountains, you will find our couple hundred acre horse ranch and fruit farm. Enjoy our restful and magnificent scenery, in a friendly and informal atmosphere.
✉ doublew@ptd.net ◐ www.doublewranchbnb.com

HONEY BROOK───

1865 Waynebrook Inn	89-279 BB	Full breakfast
4690 Horseshoe Pike 19344	20 rooms, 20 pb	Flat screen cable TV,
610-273-2444	Most CC	complimentary high speed
	C-yes/S-no/P-no/H-ltd	Internet, Jacuzzi tubs

Come experience the rich history and refined hospitality of the Waynebrook Inn, Est. 1865. Our charming hotel has been splendidly refurbished and is nestled in the midst of beautiful Amish farm country near Lancaster in historic Chester County.
✉ Stay@WayneBrookInn.com ◐ www.waynebrookinn.com

HUMMELSTOWN

The Inn at Westwynd Farm	60-174 BB	Full breakfast
1620 Sand Beach Rd 17036	7 rooms, 6 pb	Afternoon tea, snacks,
877-937-8996 717-533-6764	Most CC, •	complimentary wine
Carolyn Troxell	C-ltd/S-no/P-no/H-yes	Sitting room, library, Jacuzzis, fireplaces, cable TV, accommodations for business travelers

An unforgettable bed & breakfast experience amidst rolling hills, horses & pastures. Enjoy lovely country views, gourmet breakfasts and comforting amenities accented by antiques, fireplaces, and luxurious linens.
✉ innkeeper@westwyndfarminn.com ◐ www.westwyndfarminn.com

HUNTINGDON

The Inn at Solvang	100-135 BB	Full 3-course breakfast
301A Stonecreek Rd (Rte 26) 16652	5 rooms, 5 pb	Sitting room, library, deck, cable TV, music room, 3rd
888-814-3035 814-643-3035	Visa, MC, AmEx, *Rated*	floor terrace, conference
Stephanie Lane	C-ltd/S-no/P-no/H-yes	facilities

The Inn at Solvang is a gracious, secluded, southern Colonial style house noted for exceptional gourmet breakfasts. Unwind, enjoy a stroll through our woods, fish our private trout stream at Stone Creek, or play 18 holes at Standing Stone Golf Course.
✉ innkeeper@solvang.com ◐ www.solvang.com

HUNTINGTON MILLS

Hart's Content B&B	85-95 BB	Full breakfast
12 Daro Rd 18622	3 rooms, 3 pb	Pool, pond (with canoe and
570-864-2499	Cash, Checks	rowboat), 27 wooded acres,
Gerry & Ken Hart	C-yes/S-no/P-no/H-no	wildlife, fishing, wireless Internet available

Harts' Content, located near Ricketts Glen, nestled on 27 wooded acres. Consider us, a quiet getaway that abounds with wild beauty. Enjoy a fabulous and creative breakfast. Swim in the pool, relax with a bottle of wine in pond house, or wander the woods.
✉ kahart@epix.net

INTERCOURSE

Carriage Corner	68-99 BB	Full breakfast
3705 E Newport Rd 17534	5 rooms, 5 pb	Afternoon tea available, use
800-209-3059 717-768-3059	Visa, MC, *Rated*, •	of guest refrigerator
Gordon & Gwen Schuit	C-ltd/S-no/P-no/H-no	Common room, central A/C, library, cable TV, gazebo, outdoor deck, bathrobes

Located in the hub of the Amish farmland and tourist area; relaxing country atmosphere. Dinner with an Amish family can be arranged. The B&B is a unique blend of hospitality, laughter and kindness.
✉ gschuit@comcast.net ◐ www.carriagecornerbandb.com

The Inn & Spa at Intercourse Village	159-399 BB	5 Course Gourmet Candlelit
3542 Old Philadelphia Pike 17534	9 rooms, 9 pb	Fruit, pretzels, sodas, coffee, tea
800-664-0949 717-768-2626	Most CC, *Rated*	Separate sitting room,
Ruthann Thomas	S-no/P-no/H-no	Jacuzzi's, Grand Suites, gas burning fireplaces, cable TV, WiFi

AAA 4 Diamond Award. A romantic Inn & Spa for couples in the Historic Village of Intercourse. K/Q beds, private in-suite baths, gas burning fireplaces, Grand Honeymoon suites with Jacuzzi for two.
✉ innkeeper@inn-spa.com ◐ www.amishcountryinns.com/inn/index.htm

JIM THORPE

The Inn at Jim Thorpe	105-389 BB	Continental plus breakfast
24 Broadway 18229	45 rooms, 45 pb	Snacks, lunch & dinner
800-329-2599 570-325-2599	Most CC, *Rated*, •	available, restaurant, bar
David Drury	C-yes/S-no/P-no/H-yes	Sitting room, game room,
		suites, whirlpools, fireplaces

Nestled in the folds of several dramatic mountains, Jim Thorpe is one of the country's most scenic and historic towns. Our historic hotel is one of our town's landmark treasures.
✉ reservations@innjt.com ◐ www.innjt.com

LANCASTER

Apple Bin Inn	129-259 BB	Full country breakfast
2835 Willow Street Pike 17584	5 rooms, 5 pb	Complimentary soft drinks &
800-338-4296 717-464-5881	Most CC	snacks
Steve & Jamie Shane	C-yes/S-no/P-no	Swimming pool, library, TV
		+DVD/VCR, gazebo, private
		cottage w/fireplace, wireless
		Internet access.

In the heart of Lancaster County & PA Dutch Country, our inn features 5 delightful guestrooms and scrumptious breakfasts! Just minutes from "Sight & Sound" theatres, Strasburg Railroad, outlet malls, antique & craft shopping, and all Amish attractions!
✉ stay@AppleBinInn.com ◐ www.AppleBinInn.com

Australian Walkabout Inn	139-289 BB	Full breakfast
837 Village Rd 17602	5 rooms, 5 pb	Complimentary beverages
888-WALKABT 717-464-0707	Visa, MC, *Rated*	In-room whirlpools/hot tub,
Lynne & Bob Griffin	C-ltd/S-no/P-no/H-no	fireplaces, TV/DVD, mini
		fridge, bathrobes

Built in 1925 by a famous local master cabinet maker, featuring superior construction methods such as native chestnut pocket doors and inlaid flooring. Large front porch with inviting swing. Luxury suites, cozy rooms, cottages, all with private baths.
✉ stay@walkaboutinn.com ◐ www.walkaboutinn.com

E.J. Bowman House	120-190 BB	Full . . . fresh fruit, pastry,
2672 Lititz Pike, Rt 501 17601	5 rooms, 5 pb	entree
877-519-1776 717-519-0808	Most CC	Refreshments upon arrival,
Chef Alice & MurphEy	C-ltd/S-no/P-no/H-no	hot & cold beverages &
	Polish, Spanish	homemade goodies available
	Closed Christmas	at all times
		Large parlor, music, dining
		rooms, sitting gardens+pond,
		library w/ many CDs/DVDs,
		paperback xchange

This elegant circa 1860 Italianate Victorian mansion & developing landscape have been restored to offer the traveler & business person a perfect, restful & secure retreat with modern accommodations.
✉ alice.ey@ejbowmanhouse.com ◐ www.ejbowmanhouse.com

Equestrian Estates B&B	89-189 BB	Full breakfast
221 Shultz Rd 17603	6 rooms, 6 pb	Tea, Coffee, and Snacks
717-464-2164	Cash, Checks	anytime
Linda & David Stoltzfus	C-yes/S-ltd/P-no/H-no	Cable TV, DVD players,
	Pennsylvania Dutch	Wireless Internet, porch,
		horses and stables, Mini
		horse cart rides on
		weekends

Come to Amish Country and step back into time. Spend a romantic honeymoon, or anniversary or just a special getaway with your special someone in Lancaster County, Pennsylvania in our beautifully restored, historic brick farm house and carriage house.
✉ linda@equestrianbnb.com ◐ www.equestrianbnb.com

LANCASTER

Flowers & Thyme B&B
238 Strasburg Pike 17602
717-393-1460
Don & Ruth Harnish

95-169 BB
3 rooms, 3 pb
Visa, MC, *Rated*
C-ltd/S-no/P-no/H-no

Full breakfast
An evening meal with an
Amish family may be
arranged with advance
reservations
Three common area rooms
for conversation, reading,
watching TV, or playing
board games.

In a rural area 1 mile from Rt. 30. Enjoy our country setting soaking in the peacefulness of our surroundings. Choice of rooms with a fireplace, 2 person Jacuzzi or a canopy bed. Close to outlets, Sight & Sound/AMT theaters, and craft and gift shops.
✉ stay@flowersandthyme.com ○ www.flowersandthyme.com

Hollinger House
2336 Hollinger Rd 17602
717-464-3050
Cindy & David Mott

110-325 BB
6 rooms, 6 pb
Most CC
C-yes/S-ltd/P-ltd/H-no

Full country breakfast
Evening dessert offered,
snack station, coffee station,
free soda
1 Guest House, cable TV, 5½
acres, balconies & porches, 6
guestrooms with private
baths, parking

A three story, 1870 Adams-period mansion with double balconies set on 5½ acres. Original hardwood floors, columns, high ceilings and fireplace. Modern conveniences, A/C, private baths, Cable TV, wireless Internet. One guesthouse sleeps seven or more.
✉ majestic@hollingerhousebnb.com ○ www.hollingerhousebnb.com

King's Cottage B&B
1049 E King St 17602
800-747-8717 717-397-1017
Janis Kutterer, Ann Willets

150-325 BB
8 rooms, 8 pb
Visa, MC, AmEx
C-ltd/S-no/P-no/H-ltd

Full Gourmet Breakfast
Afternoon refreshments
Massage room, hot tub,
sunroom, piano, guest
kitchen, water garden, patio

A Top 10 Most Romantic Inn, in the heart of PA Dutch Country. An elegant B&B with whirlpools, fireplaces and gourmet breakfast. Near Amish farms, antique & quilt shops, outlets & historic sites.
✉ info@kingscottagebb.com ○ www.kingscottagebb.com

Pheasant Run Farm B&B
200 Marticville Rd 17603
717-872-0991
Bob & Vivian Abel

125-175 BB
4 rooms, 4 pb
Visa, MC, AmEx
C-ltd/S-no/P-no/H-no

Full breakfast
Coffee & tea
Reception room, rose
gardens, porch

Pheasant Fun Farm is a beautifully converted barn B&B in picturesque Lancaster County. The bed and breakfast features four rooms with private baths and combines today's modern luxuries with the barn's original architectural features.
✉ vivianbob@earthlink.net ○ www.pheasantrunfarmbb.com

Silverstone Inn & Suites
62 Bowman Rd 17602
877-290-6987 717-290-6987
Toni & Lorin Wortel

149-289 BB
8 rooms, 8 pb
Most CC, *Rated*, •
C-ltd/S-ltd/P-no/H-ltd
Dutch

Full breakfast
Bar snacks & complimentary
drinks
Events, marble bathrooms,
flat-screen TV/DVD, WiFi,
individual heat/AC, unique
decor, gardens

Welcome to Silverstone Inn and Suites B&B! A romantic and award-winning historic limestone house c. 1750, nestled quietly in the heart of the Amish area of Lancaster County, PA, on its own 10 acre maple syrup and sheep farm. Eight rooms and suites.
✉ toni@theplacetostay.com ○ www.silverstoneinn.com

Shearer Elegance B&B, Linfield, PA

LEWISBURG

Pineapple Inn
439 Market St 17837
570-524-6200
Charles & Deborah North

125-165 BB
6 rooms, 6 pb
Most CC, *Rated*
C-yes/S-no/P-no/H-no
German

Full country breakfast
Complimentary tea, snacks
A/C, pool nearby, piano, tea
room, sitting room, tennis,
wonderful restaurants,
wireless Internet

The beautifully restored 1857 Federal Victorian home rests in the Historic District. Just blocks from Bucknell University. Susquehanna University and Penn State University are a short but scenic drive form the inn. Beautiful architecture, great antiquing.

✉ pineappleinn@dejazzd.com ✪ www.pineappleinnbnb.com

LIGONIER

Campbell House B&B
305 E Main St 15658
888-238-9812 724-238-9812
Patti Campbell

89-150 BB
6 rooms, 6 pb
Most CC
C-ltd/S-no/P-no/H-no

Full breakfast
Complimentary snacks &
beverages
House phone, fax, computer
for guest use, highspeed
wireless Internet.

Charming accommodations, with a Victorian & eclectic flavor, await those who long for a smoke-free, peaceful retreat, a romantic interlude, or are visiting the Laurel Highlands.

✉ innkeeper@campbellhousebnb.com ✪ www.campbellhousebnb.com

LINFIELD

Shearer Elegance B&B
1154 Main St 19468
800-861-0308 610-495-7429
Shirley & Malcolm Shearer

109-165 BB
7 rooms, 7 pb
Most CC, *Rated*, •
C-ltd/S-no/P-no/H-ltd

Full breakfast
Sitting room, private baths,
Jacuzzi tubs, massage
therapy

22 room Victorian with 3 acres of gardens in summer, and 35 decorated Christmas trees in winter. After more than 10 years serving travelers and vacationers in the suburban Philadelphia area, Shearer Elegance Bed & Breakfast is bigger and better than ever.

✉ contact@shearerelegance.com ✪ www.shearerelegance.com

LITITZ

The Alden House
62 E Main St 17543
800-584-0753 717-627-3363
John & Lynndell Eccleston

99-139 BB
7 rooms, 7 pb
Visa, MC, AmEx, *Rated*
C-ltd/S-no/P-no/H-no

Full breakfast
Dinner with Amish arranged
Sitting room, suites with
fireplace, porches, antiques,
free wireless Internet access

Enjoy a gourmet breakfast by candlelight in our circa 1850 brick Federal style home, in historic Lititz. Relax on our porches and walk to museums, shops, local attractions, and fine dining.
✉ inn@aldenhouse.com ○ www.aldenhouse.com

Speedwell Forge B&B
465 Speedwell Forge Road
17543
877-378-1760 717-626-1760
Dawn Darlington

125-225 BB
5 rooms, 5 pb
Most CC, •
C-ltd/S-no/P-no/H-no

Full breakfast
Dessert
whirlpool tubs, fireplaces,
private bath, antique
furnishings, sitting areas and
more!

Built in 1760 on 120 acres, and listed on the National Register of Historic Places. We offer 3 elegant guestrooms and 2 cottages, all with private baths, central air, and wireless Internet. Many rooms include a fireplace, whirlpool tub, and kitchenette.
✉ stay.1@speedwellforge.com ○ www.speedwellforge.com

LOCK HAVEN

Carriage House B&B
439 W Main St 17745
570-748-5799
Sharon Best

79-104 BB
4 rooms, 3 pb
Visa, MC
C-yes/S-no/P-no/H-no

Full breakfast
Snacks
Sitting room, library,
fireplaces, cable TV,
accommodates business
travelers, central air

Historic brick inn furnished with antiques & collectibles. Tea & treats upon arrival. Two grand fireplaces & one guestroom with private balcony.
✉ carriagehouse@carriagebanb.com ○ www.carriagebandb.com

MACUNGIE

Stone House Inn & Spa
165 East Main St 18062
610-967-0343
Jan & Fran

85-160 BB
4 rooms, 4 pb
Most CC
C-ltd/S-no/P-no/H-ltd

Full breakfast
Snacks, cookies, assorted
beverages, coffee
Ceiling fans & A/C, flat
screen cable TV, Internet
access, plush linens & robes,
common rooms, spa

This small town inn, surrounded by towering sycamore trees, is a wonderful alternative to the typical hotel stay, offering warm hospitality, charm & the very best amenities in the casual, comfortable elegance of a painstakingly restored stone farmhouse.
✉ stonehse@ptd.net ○ www.stonehouseinnandspa.com

MANHEIM

Rose Manor
124 S Linden St 17545
800-666-4932 717-664-4932
Susan

99-140 BB
5 rooms, 5 pb
Visa, MC, *Rated*, •
C-ltd/S-no/P-no/H-no

Full breakfast
Complimentary sherry
Picnic baskets, sitting room,
gardens

Lancaster County 1905 manor house. Comfortable, elegant English manor house decor & cooking reflect herbal theme. Surrounded by rose & herb gardens. Full breakfast included.
✉ rosemanor@paonline.com ○ www.rosemanor.net

MARIETTA

B.F. Hiestand House B&B
722 E Market St 17547
877-560-8415 717-426-8415
Pam & Dallas Fritz

165-275 BB
6 rooms, 6 pb
Most CC
C-yes/S-no/P-yes/H-ltd

Full breakfast
Snacks, afternoon tea
Sitting room, suites, cable TV,
hot tub, veranda, fireplaces,
A/C

Historic 1887 High Queen Anne Victorian. Experience the elegance of a bygone era. Enjoy breakfast in our charming dining room. Exquisite parlors with 12-foot ceilings, pocket doors and fireplaces.
✉ info@bfhiestandhouse.com ○ www.bfhiestandhouse.com

Lavender Patch
190 Longenecker Ave 17547
717-426-4533
Marian & Chet Miller

115-125 BB
3 rooms, 3 pb
Visa, MC
C-yes/S-no/P-no/H-ltd

Full breakfast
Afternoon tea
WiFi, pool, gazebo &
gardens, cable TV & VCR

Welcome to the charming Lavender Patch Bed and Breakfast in Marietta, Lancaster County, Pennsylvania. With an eye for detail, this lovely home features 3 rooms, delicious breakfast, afternoon tea, pool, hand painted decorative walls and gardens.
✉ lavpatch@desupernet.net ○ www.lavenderpatch.com

Vogt Farm
1225 Colebrook Rd 17547
800-854-0399 717-653-4810
Keith & Kathy Vogt

105-160 BB
4 rooms, 4 pb
Visa, MC, *Rated*, •
C-ltd/S-no/P-no/H-no

Full breakfast
Snacks & beverages 24 hours
Sitting room, suites,
fireplaces, cable TV, accom.
bus. travelers

We welcome you to our Lancaster County bed and breakfast and our beautiful farm, with the cows grazing in the meadow. Vogt Farm was built by Mennonites in the mid-1800s. You will find us friendly and accommodating.
✉ stay@vogtfarmbnb.com ○ www.vogtfarmbnb.com

MCCLURE

Mountain Dale Farm
330 Hassinger Way 17841
570-658-3536
Ken & Sally Hassinger

70-90 EP
15 rooms, 13 pb
Visa, MC
C-yes/S-ltd/P-ltd/H-no

Meals may be provided if
schedule permits, but only
with prior arrangements.
Extra charge for meals.
Kitchen available for guest
use; individual cabins offer
privacy

If you're looking for a wholesome, family-oriented environment for overnight lodging, an extended vacation, family reunion or other special event then you've come to the right place. Scenic rolling country, animals, fishing, hiking.
✉ mountaindale@mountaindale.net ○ www.mountaindale.net

MCCONNELLSBURG

Crampton Manor B&B
270 Country Lane 17233
717-491-2813
Linda & Michael Crampton

75-135 BB
5 rooms, 4 pb
Cash, Checks
C-ltd/S-no/P-no/H-no

Full breakfast
Please advise us in advance
of any dietary restrictions
Wireless high speed Internet,
porch, private entrance,
cathedral ceiling, TV,
kitchen, fireplace

Crampton Manor B&B is a private, mountain retreat located on 100 breathtaking acres. Comprised of The Main House, The Hayloft and The Carriage House. All of our accommodations offer heat and A/C with ceiling fans and free high speed wireless Internet.
✉ cramptonmanor@embarqmail.com ○ www.cramptonmanor.com

MECHANICSBURG

Kanaga House
6940 Carlisle Pike 17050
877-952-6242 717-766-8654
Dave & Mary Jane Kretzing

95-175 BB
6 rooms, 6 pb
Most CC, *Rated*
C-yes/S-no/P-no/H-ltd

Full Breakfast
Snacks
Spacious common areas,
fireplaces, phones, cable TV,
weddings, wireless Internet

Kanaga House is an elegant B&B on US 11 in the center of the Carlisle, Gettysburg, Hershey, Lancaster vacation region. We offer beautiful landscaped grounds, large gazebo with tables, downstairs common rooms with fireplaces and breakfast at your time.
✉ stay@kanagahouse.com ✆ www.kanagahouse.com

MERCERSBURG

The Mercersburg Inn
405 S Main St 17236
717-328-5231
Lisa & Jim McCoy

140-450 BB
17 rooms, 17 pb
Visa, MC, Disc, *Rated*,
•
C-ltd/S-no/P-no/H-no
Russian

Full breakfast – 3 course
gourmet
Afternoon tea/scones,
weekends, evening
refreshments
Byron's Dining Room on
premise; fine dining Thurs-
Sun, full bar, fireplaces

A stately, 20,000 sq ft Georgian mansion on 5 acres of terraced lawns. Once the private residence of Ione & Harry Byron, the home is now a 17 guestroom country inn.
✉ innkeepers@mercersburginn.com ✆ www.mercersburginn.com

MILFORD

Laurel Villa Country Inn
2nd & E Ann St 18337
570-296-9940
Janice Halsted & Carl
Muhlhauser

110-165 BB
10 rooms, 10 pb
Visa, MC, Disc
C-yes/S-ltd/P-ltd/H-no
Hungarian, German,

Continental plus breakfast
Full bar, dinner served Wed-
Sun, Wine & Spirit Tastings
monthly. Menu items include
seafood, veal, duck
Private gardens with Koi
pond, rockers on front porch,
sitting room, suites, fireplace,
cable TV,

Country inn on quiet side street. Candlelight dining; cozy sitting room with fireplace. Extensive gardens in a park-like setting, with koi pond & benches for relaxing.
✉ info@laurelvilla.com ✆ www.laurelvilla.com

MOUNT JOY

Hillside Farm
607 Eby Chiques Rd 17552
888-249-3406 717-653-6697
Gary Lintner

90-250 BB
5 rooms, 5 pb
Most CC, *Rated*, •
C-ltd/S-no/P-no/H-no

Full breakfast
Afternoon & evening snacks
Sitting room, book library,
baby grand piano, A/C, 6-
person spa, balcony

A quiet, secluded, bed & breakfast, farm stay located in the heart of Lancaster, Pennsylvania Amish Country. Overlooks Chickies Creek with dam & waterfall; entirely surrounded by working farms.
✉ innkeeper@hillsidefarmbandb.com ✆ www.hillsidefarmbandb.com

NEW BERLIN

The Inn at New Berlin
321 Market St 17855
800-797-2350 570-966-0321
Bob & Nancy Schanck

139-219 BB
11 rooms, 11 pb
Most CC, *Rated*, •
C-ltd/S-no/P-no/H-ltd
Closed 2 weeks in Jan.

Full breakfast
Gabriel's Restaurant, Wine
Spectator Award List, tavern,
dinner served Weds. – Sun.,
weekend lunches
Massages, Carriage House
Spa, Gabriel's Gifts, porch,
gardens, deck, sitting areas,
fireplaces

Uptown experience in a rural setting—experience the wooded hills and rolling farmlands of Central Pennsylvania. Wine Spectator acclaimed fine dining. Relax with a Swedish Massage. Luxurious base for indulging in a clutch of quiet pleasures.
✉ visit@innatnewberlin.com ✆ www.innatnewberlin.com

NEW HOLLAND

Richmond House	95-115 BB	Full breakfast
371 E Main St 17557	5 rooms, 5 pb	Guest refrigerator &
866-279-7599 717-355-0450	Visa, MC	microwave
Dolores & Tim Walter	C-ltd/S-no/P-no	Central A/C, high-speed
		wireless Internet, each room
		has its own TV

A country cottage located in the heart of PA Dutch Country with easy access to all the attractions. We provide you with a warm, spacious room, a private bath, full-breakfast and enough country/colonial charm to brighten your stay with us.
✉ richmondhousebnb@comcast.net ✪ www.richmondhousebnb.com

NEW HOPE

1870 Wedgwood Bed	95-325 BB	Continental plus breakfast in
Breakfast Inn of New Hope,	10 rooms, 10 pb	bed
PA	Visa, MC, AmEx,	The Guest Pantry 24/7.
111 W Bridge St 18938	*Rated*, •	Hot/cold drinks, just-baked
215-862-2570	C-yes/S-ltd/P-yes/H-yes	cookies, hard candies and
Carl & Nadine Glassman	French, Hebrew, Dutch,	fruit . . . Saturday Tea
	Italian	Victorian gazebo, dbl
		Jacuzzis, in-rm massage,
		frplcs, brkfst-in-bed, Snack
		baskets, Chocolates

Bucks County New Hope Victorian manse. Two-person Jacuzzi tubs, frplcs, fresh flowers, gingerbread porches.1989 "Inn Of The Year"! On 2 private, park-like acres in New Hope. Open year round. Walk to vibrant village center . . . steps from Inn. WiFi, Brkfst bed.
✉ stay@wedgwoodinn.com ✪ www.WedgwoodInn.com

Cookie's Pineapple Hill Inn	94-249 BB	Full breakfast
1324 River Rd 18938	9 rooms, 9 pb	Afternoon tea, snacks,
888-866-8404 215-862-1790	Most CC, *Rated*, •	evening sherry
Kathryn & Charles "Cookie"	C-ltd/S-no/P-no/H-no	Sitting room, library, pool,
Triolo		cable TV, fireplaces,
		telephones, wireless Internet

Enjoy the charm of a beautifully restored, Colonial manor house built in 1790. Set on almost 6 acres, this Bucks County B&B rests between New Hope's center and Washington Crossing Park.
✉ innkeeper@pineapplehill.com ✪ www.pineapplehill.com

Fox and Hound B&B of New	95-195 BB	Full breakfast
Hope	8 rooms, 8 pb	Afternoon refreshments
246 W Bridge St 18938	Visa, MC, Disc, *Rated*	A/C, cable TV, some with
215-862-5082	C-ltd/S-no/P-no/H-no	fireplace, private patio,
Lisa Menz	French, Spanish,	balcony or sundeck, wireless
	German	Internet, parking

Elegant 1840 stone farmhouse. Short walk to New Hope & Lambertville, near all Bucks County attractions. All rooms with private bath, A/C, some with fireplace, patio, balcony or sundeck. Reduced midweek rates. Wireless Internet.
✉ innkeeper@foxhoundinn.com ✪ foxhoundinn.com

The Inn at Bowman's Hill	295-555 BB	Gourmet 3 course a la carte
518 Lurgan Rd 18938	6 rooms, 6 pb	Bottled water, soft drinks,
215-862-8090	Most CC, *Rated*	afternoon tea sandwiches &
Mike Amery	C-ltd/S-no/P-no/H-yes	refreshments, cheeseboard
	Norwegian, Swedish	in suite
	Danish	In-room massage, heated
		whirlpools, pool, hot tub,
		newspapers, in-room
		tea/coffee making

AAA Four-Diamond, Condé Nast Johansens. 2-person heated whirlpool tubs, heated pool, hot tub, fireplaces, King-size featherbeds, gourmet breakfast. An award-winning romantic getaway on a 5-acre estate. Private, luxurious and memorable!
✉ info@theinnatbowmanshill.com ✪ www.theinnatbowmanshill.com

NEW HOPE

Inn at Stoney Hill
105 Stoney Hill Rd 18938
866-590-9100 215-862-5769
Judy L. Lawson

99-249 BB
8 rooms, 8 pb
Visa, MC
C-ltd/S-ltd/P-no/H-no

Full breakfast
Complimentary snacks and
beverages available upon
arrival.
Sitting room, gardens, A/C,
cable TV, fluffy white
bathrobes, Jacuzzis

Comfortable rooms with private baths, Some rooms with Jacuzzi Tubs and private patios, Gourmet full breakfast, Quiet, with views of Gardens and woods, located ¾ of a mile from downtown New Hope, in Bucks County, PA
✉ info@innatstoneyhill.com ○ www.innatstoneyhill.com

NEW OXFORD

Chestnut Hall B&B
104 Lincoln Way 17350
888-886-5660 717-624-8988
Steve & Tina McNaughton

99-150 BB
4 rooms, 4 pb
Visa, MC
C-ltd/S-no/P-no/H-no

Full breakfast
Snacks and beverages
Private bath, plush robes,
cable TV, individually
controlled A/C, electric
controlled fireplace

Chestnut Hall is embodied in Victorian style at its finest. Preserved woodwork, wooden inlaid floors and a chestnut square box staircase will lead you to your private room on the second floor. Each room has been preserved to allow you to enjoy yesteryear.
✉ chestnuthallbb@yahoo.com ○ www.chestnuthallbb.com

NEW TRIPOLI

Dockside B&B
6089 Herring Ct 18066
610-698-2448
Robert & Donna Herring

120-195 BB
4 rooms, 4 pb
Visa, MC
C-ltd/S-no/P-no/H-ltd

Full breakfast
Snacks, fruit, soda, bottled
water
Deck, waterfront, Jacuzzis,
compact refrigerators,
Internet access, A/C, fresh
flowers

Every effort has been made for our guests to enjoy a quiet, comfortable, and memorable stay. Take a stroll around our 6 acre waterfront property, or just rest in the gentle breeze and enjoy the view from our three level deck.
✉ herringr@ptd.net ○ www.docksidebed.com

NORTH EAST

Grape Arbor B&B
51 E Main St 16428
866-725-0048 814-725-0048
Dave & Peggy Hauser

90-160 BB
8 rooms, 8 pb
Visa, MC, Disc
C-ltd/S-ltd/P-no/H-ltd

Full breakfast
Daily hors d'oeuvres, free
beverages & treats
Library with games, videos,
outside patio & porch

Two historic neighboring 1830s brick mansions. Elegant rooms and suites with private baths, antiques, some with Jacuzzi or private entrance. Four-course breakfast and many special touches.
✉ grapearborbandb@aol.com ○ www.grapearborbandb.com

Light on the Lake B&B
11934 Seitzinger Rd 16428
814-725-9115
Marcia & Dennis Groce

BB
2 rooms, 2 pb
C-ltd/S-ltd/P-no/H-no

Full breakfast

Located on one of Lake Erie's best beaches and only a short walk to the marina, Light on the Lake B&B is a modern home and offers two guestrooms with a choice of a light or hearty breakfast that is served each morning.
✉ marcia&dennis@lightonthelake.com ○ www.lightonthelake.com

OAKMONT

Doone's Inn at Oakmont
300 Rt 909 15139
412-828-0410
Lorna "Doone" Irvin

165-300 BB
9 rooms, 9 pb
Most CC, *Rated*
C-ltd/S-ltd/P-no/H-yes

Full breakfast
Sitting room, fireplace, cable
TV, bath tubs, fitness center,
WiFi, Putting Green

Eight luxurious rooms with private bathrooms plus our new suite, complete breakfast, all amenities of finer hotels and full fitness center. Massage therapy and personal trainer available by appointment.
✉ lornairvin@comcast.net ◑ doonesinnatoakmont.com

ORRTANNA

Hickory Bridge Farm
96 Hickory Bridge Rd 17353
717-642-5261
Robert & Mary Lynn Martin

85-165 BB
9 rooms, 8 pb
Visa, MC, Disc, *Rated*
C-ltd/S-yes/P-no/H-no

Full breakfast
Dinner available Friday-
Sunday
Sitting room, fireplaces,
bicycles, fishing, 8 miles from
Gettysburg

Relax in the country by enjoying a cozy cottage by the stream, a hearty breakfast at the farmhouse, and dining in restored PA barn on weekends. Historic and romantic setting.
✉ marylynn@hickorybridgefarm.com ◑ www.hickorybridgefarm.com

PARADISE

**Beiler's Bed & Breakfast
Suites**
3153 Lincoln Hwy E 17562
800-915-3994 717-687-8612
Elam & Barbie Beiler

95-150 BB
8 rooms, 8 pb
Visa, MC, Disc, *Rated*,
●
C-yes/S-no/P-no/H-no
Pennsylvania Dutch

Full breakfast
Enjoy coffee, tea, hot
chocolate & fresh spring
water available at all times in
our sun porch
Gorgeous 2 level brick patio
with therapeutic hot tub,
gardens, birds, cafe tables,
BBQ, WiFi

A young family of Amish background who have owned and operated Beiler's Bed & Breakfast since 1993, we've renovated this turn of the century Colonial style home with private baths and private entrances so that you can enjoy your stay in comfort.
✉ barbiebeiler@comcast.net ◑ www.beilersbnb.com

Frogtown Acres B&B
44 Frogtown Rd 17562
888-649-2333 717-768-7684
Joe & Gloria

99-115 BB
4 rooms, 4 pb
Visa, MC
C-ltd/S-ltd/P-no/H-yes
Pennsylvania Dutch

Full breakfast
Sitting room, fireplace,
conference facility. Amish
farm visit.

Peaceful, romantic and unique getaway in Amish country. Our Inn is located in our beautifully remodeled carriage house. This is truly our little piece of Paradise.
✉ thefrogs@frogtownacres.com ◑ www.frogtownacres.com

PERRYOPOLIS

The Inn at Lenora's
301 Liberty 15473
724-736-2509
Bob, Lenora & Owen Palonder

100-185 BB
12 rooms, 12 pb
Visa, MC, AmEx,
Rated, ●
C-yes/S-ltd/P-no/H-yes

Full breakfast
The Inn at Lenora's also has
won Pennsylvania's top 20
restaurants
Cable TV, phone with
modem port, individual heat
& A/C controls, custom-
made wood furnishings

A relaxing retreat for city dwellers, a sanctuary for nature lovers, & impressive landmarks for history buffs. Guests enjoy a memorable gourmet dining experience in the relaxed ambience of Lenora's—one of the top 20 restaurants in PA.
✉ dine@lenoras.com ◑ www.lenoras.com

PHILADELPHIA

The Gables B&B
4520 Chester Ave 19143
215-662-1918
Warren Cederholm & Don
Caskey

125-185 BB
10 rooms, 8 pb
Most CC, •
C-ltd/S-no/P-no/H-no

Full breakfast
Snacks
Sitting room, fireplaces,
cable TV, business travelers,
private phones, WiFi,
computer station

One of Pennsylvania's finest, restored Victorian mansions. Winner of the Historic Preservation Award. Near University of PA, Drexel University, hospitals and museums, 12 minutes to center city Philadelphia by easy public transportation. Free Parking.
✉ gablesbb@aol.com ✆ www.gablesbb.com

Lippincott House
2023–2025 Locust Street 19103
215-523-9251
Mary Beth Hallman

175-225 BB
4 rooms, 4 pb
Most CC
C-yes/S-no/P-ltd/H-no

Full breakfast
Complimentary soft drinks
and cheese are served
between 5pm – 7pm

Lippincott House lies in the heart of Philadelphia, one block from Rittenhouse Square. This exquisite grand mansion, constructed in 1897, combines 19th century grace with 21st century comfort.
✉ reservations@lippincotthouse.com ✆ www.lippincotthouse.com/default.htm

---

Morris House Hotel
225 S 8th St 19106
215-922-2446
Gabriela Buresova

179-349 BB
15 rooms, 15 pb
Visa, MC, AmEx
C-yes/S-no/P-no/H-no

Continental breakfast
An Afternoon Tea
A/C, CD, clock radio,
TV/DVD, wireless Internet,
garden, sitting room, library,
suites, antiques

This registered national historic landmark has been renovated into a luxury boutique hotel which offers the coziness of a bed and breakfast, in an 18th century setting, combined with the luxuries of today. ✉ info@morrishousehotel.com ✆ www.morrishousehotel.com

---

Silverstone B&B
8840 Stenton Ave 19118
800-347-6858 215-242-3333
Yolanta Roman

95-150 BB
6 rooms, 6 pb
Visa, MC, *Rated*
C-yes/S-no/P-no/H-ltd
Polish, French

Full breakfast
Afternoon tea, wine
Cable TV/VCR in rooms,
wireless Internet, swimming
pool, fitness center

This stunning Victorian Gothic B&B is located in historic Chestnut Hill, full of history, just minutes from the Philadelphia Metro area.
✉ yolanta@silverstonestay.com ✆ www.silverstonestay.com

Thomas Bond House
129 S 2nd St 19106
800-845-2663 215-923-8523
Dan Weese

115-190 BB
12 rooms, 12 pb
Most CC, *Rated*, •
C-yes/S-no/P-no/H-no

Full breakfast
Full breakfast weekends,
continental plus weekdays,
evening wine & cheese, fresh
baked cookies
Hairdryer, TV, phone, fireplace, whirlpool, local calls,
free WiFi

Circa 1769, listed in National Register. Individually decorated rooms. Only lodging in Independence National Historical Park. One of top 25 historic inns, AAA & Mobile rated.
✉ info@thomasbondhousebandb.com ✆ www.thomasbondhousebandb.com

PHOENIXVILLE

Morning Star B&B
610 Valley Forge Rd 19460
866-261-3289 610-935-7473
Rebekah Ray

105-150 BB
4 rooms, 2 pb
Visa, MC, •
C-ltd/S-no/P-ltd/H-no

Full breakfast
Afternoon Tea
Sitting Room, library, spas,
suites, billiards table, parlor,
pet and family friendly,
romance, TV

Our B&B is in a historic home, built first in the 1820's by a Quaker family active in the Underground Railroad. Very few changes have been made since the renovation in 1890s. Fresh eggs are served at breakfast, produced by our own free range chickens!
✉ p-e-s-t-o@excite.com ✆ www.morningstarbandb.net

PITTSBURGH

Morning Glory Inn	145-450 BB	Full breakfast
2119 Sarah St 15203	6 rooms, 6 pb	Wine
412-431-1707	Most CC, •	Sitting room, library, bicycles,
Nancy Eshelman	C-yes/S-ltd/P-ltd/H-yes	suites, fireplaces, conferences

Tucked away in the city's South Side, Pittsburg, PA's most eclectic, diverse and dynamic neighborhood, is a delightful discovery: an 1862 Italianate style Victorian brick townhouse since 1996 a downtown Pittsburgh B&B, the Morning Glory Inn.
✉ nancy@gloryinn.com 🌐 www.gloryinn.com

The Priory Hotel	134-210 BB	Continental plus breakfast
614 Pressley St 15212	24 rooms, 24 pb	Complimentary wine, snacks
866-377-4679 412-231-3338	Most CC, *Rated*, •	Honor bar, cable TV,
John Graf	C-yes/S-no/P-no/H-ltd	accommodations for
		business travelers, WiFi

A European style hotel in Pittsburgh with 24 guestrooms, carefully restored to Victorian elegance. Offers the modern amenities of a larger facility and the personality and personal service that only a small boutique hotel can offer.
✉ info@thepriory.com 🌐 www.thepriory.com

POINT PLEASANT

Tattersall Inn	140-195 BB	Full breakfast
37 River Rd, Rt 32 18950	6 rooms, 6 pb	Afternoon tea & light snack,
800-297-4988 215-297-8233	Visa, MC, *Rated*	complimentary glass of wine
John & Lori Gleason	C-ltd/S-no/P-no/H-no	1750s Common Room, walk-
		in fireplace, multiple
		porches, gardens, private
		bath, A/C, TV

Beautiful, historic c. 1753 manor home. Porches, fireplaces, antiques, breakfast, tea, private baths. Centrally located in Bucks County by the Delaware River, within 7–8 miles to New Hope, Lambertville, Frenchtown, Peddlar's Village and Doylestown.
✉ info@tattersallinn.com 🌐 www.tattersallinn.com

READING

B&B on the Park	BB	Continental plus breakfast
1246 Hill Rd 19602	5 rooms, 4 pb	Antiques, parlor,
610-374-4440	Most CC	chandeliers, porch, cable TV
George & Cindy Heminitz	C-ltd/S-no/P-no/H-ltd	& A/C

We would like to invite you to come to Reading, PA, to relax in our gracious hospitality with Victorian style at Bed & Breakfast on the Park.
✉ info@parkbandb.com 🌐 www.parkbandb.com

REINHOLDS

Brownstone Colonial Inn	89-119 BB	Full breakfast
590 Galen Hall Rd 17569	4 rooms, 4 pb	Wireless Internet, TV,
877-464-9862 717-484-4460	Most CC	fishpond and gardens
Brenda Miller	C-ltd/S-no/P-no/H-ltd	

Built by early German Mennonite settlers, this 210-year-old sandstone farmhouse is situated on seven-acres amid Mennonite farmland and countryside. Located to many tourist attractions, yet far enough away in the country to give you the respite you crave.
✉ info@brownstonecolonialinn.com 🌐 www.brownstonecolonialinn.com

RONKS

Candlelight Inn B&B	89-179 BB	Full breakfast
2574 Lincoln Hwy E 17572	7 rooms, 7 pb	Afternoon tea & snacks
800-77-CANDL 717-299-6005	Visa, MC, Disc, *Rated*,	Sitting room, antiques,
Tim & Heidi Soberick	•	oriental rugs, Victorian style,
	C-ltd/S-no/P-no/H-no	Jacuzzi, fireplaces, A/C,
	French, Italian	suites, romantic

The Candlelight Inn Bed & Breakfast, an Amish Country B&B, is centrally located in Lancaster County, PA making it the perfect destination. This large Georgian B&B is enclosed by farmland and offers a gracious, romantic, and relaxing retreat.
✉ candleinn@aol.com 🌐 www.candleinn.com

RONKS

Olde Homestead Suites
3515 B West Newport Rd 17572
717-768-3300
Merlin & Mary Lou Yutzy

99-199 BB
9 rooms, 9 pb
Visa, MC, Disc
C-yes/S-no/P-no/H-ltd

Full breakfast
Sunday-Continental breakfast
Patio, common room,
DVD/VHS players, Jacuzzi
tubs, massage therapy

Olde Homestead Suites features 8 suites and one private cottage with private baths, some with king beds, Jacuzzi, waterfall shower/tubs and fireplaces in the heart of Dutch Country Pennsylvania.
✉ innkeeper@oldehomesteadsuites.com ✆ www.oldehomesteadsuites.com

SHAWNEE ON DELAWARE

The Gatehouse Country Inn B&B
Corner of River Rd & Waring Dr 18356
570-420-4553
Cindy and Gordon Way

155-205 BB
4 rooms, 4 pb
Visa, MC, •
C-ltd/S-ltd/P-no/H-no

Full breakfast
We will attempt to
accommodate your dietary
needs if you let us know in
advance.
Pool/game room, great room,
courtyard, grounds, antique
shop

Originally a 1900's carriage house, barn, stable, hayloft and icehouse, The Gatehouse Country Inn was renovated into an elegant summer home by the famous musician and bandleader, Fred Waring. Featuring 4 individually decorated rooms each w/ private bath.
✉ gatehousekeeper@aol.com ✆ www.gatehousecountryinn.com

Santosha on the Ridge
Mosier's Knob Road 18356
570-476-0203
Leslie Underhill

135-185 BB
3 rooms, 3 pb
Visa, MC, AmEx
C-ltd/S-no/P-no/H-no

Organic
Afternoon cookies or
pastries with hot tea, coffee
or juice
Indoor yoga studio with
classes, massage available,
all rooms have A/C, TV/DVD
player, robes

Located 72 miles west of Manhattan, nestled in the heart of the Pocono Mountains, Santosha on the Ridge is a secluded sanctuary where you can relax and rejuvenate your mind, body and spirit.
✉ info@santoshaontheridge.com ✆ www.santoshaontheridge.com

Stony Brook Inn
5 River Rd 18356
888-424-5240 570-424-1100
Rose Ann Whitesell & Pete Ferguson

100-160 BB
4 rooms, 4 pb
Visa, MC, Disc
S-no/P-no/H-no

Full country breakfast
Afternoon tea, snacks,
complimentary beverages
WiFi, cable TV, large living
room with stone fireplace,
large screened in porch,
heated swimming pool

Built in 1853, we offer 4 rooms highlighted with antiques. All rooms are A/C and have private baths. A full country breakfast is served in our cheery dining room or screened-in porch.
✉ sbinn@ptd.net ✆ www.stonybrookinn.com

SHIPPENSBURG

Dykeman House
6 W Dykeman Rd 17257
717-530-1919
John and Rachelle Davidson

99-129 BB
4 rooms, 4 pb
Most CC, *Rated*
C-ltd/S-no/P-no

Full country breakfast
Complimentary beverage,
cheese and cracker snack
provided in the late
afternoon
Balcony, yards

The Dykeman House today sits on approximately 4 acres of what once was a 450 acre estate established in 1740. The land next to and surrounding the house contains numerous springs, and has been known as Indian Springs and today as Dykeman Spring.
✉ innkeeper@dykemanhouse.com ✆ www.dykemanhouse.com

SHIPPENSBURG

McLean House	60-69 BB	Full breakfast
80 W King St 17257	4 rooms, 2 pb	Evening snacks and
800-610-0330 717-530-1390	*Rated*	beverages by request
Bob & Jan Rose	C-yes/S-ltd/P-no/H-no	Double parlors with TV and
		board games, screened
		porches; bordering creek,
		Historic District

The McLean House (c 1798) is in the Historic District of Shippensburg. Guests say: "warm, comfortable, restful," "elegant but very affordable," "family friendly" Several restaurants within 2 blocks. 10 minute walk to university. AAA—3 diamonds.
✉ jrose@pa.net ◔ mcleanhousebandb.com.

SMOKETOWN

Homestead Lodging	51-81 BB	Continental breakfast
184 Eastbrook Rd 17576	5 rooms, 5 pb	Microwave available and
717-393-6927	Visa, MC, Disc, •	refrigerators in rooms with
Bob & Lori Kepiro	C-ltd/S-no/P-no/H-no	"pay as you use" sodas,
		water, juices, snacks
		Wireless Internet, AC, cable
		TV, refrigerator, hair dryers,
		clock radio, iron/board avail.

Christian family owned B&B where you can rest, relax & recharge. Bob & Lori provide personal attention, warm hospitality & knowledge of the area. Centrally located in heart of Amish farms & country. ✉ lkepiro@comcast.net ◔ www.homesteadlodging.net

SOMERSET

Glades Pike Inn	65-125 BB	Full breakfast
2684 Glades Pike 15501	5 rooms, 5 pb	Complimentary wine on
800-762-5942 814-443-4978	Most CC	weekends
Janet L. Jones	C-ltd/S-no/P-no/H-no	Swimming pool

Welcoming guests since 1842 when it was built as a stagecoach stop, on a 200-acre dairy farm in the center of Laurel Highlands. Close to skiing, golf, state parks, Falling Water. Five guestrooms offer period architecture with modern conveniences.
✉ fwmjj@sprynet.com ◔ www.gladespike.com

Quill Haven Country Inn	95-120 BB	Full breakfast
1519 N Center Ave 15501	4 rooms, 4 pb	Coffee, tea, hot chocolate,
866-528-8855 814-443-4514	Most CC, *Rated*, •	soda, complimentary glass of
Carol & Rowland Miller	C-ltd/S-ltd/P-no/H-no	wine, cookies, bottled water
		Cable TV/VCR, movies, A/C,
		common room w/fireplace,
		off-street parking, outdoor
		deck & hot tub, WiFi

Experience the informal, yet elegant atmosphere of this 1918 Gentleman's farmhouse, built in the style of the Arts and Crafts Period and furnished with antiques and fine reproductions. Private baths, full breakfast, wireless Internet, outdoor hot tub.
✉ quill@quillhaven.com ◔ www.quillhaven.com

SOUTH STERLING

The French Manor	165-340 BB	Full Gourmet Breakfast
50 Huntingdon Drive 18460	15 rooms, 15 pb	Afternoon Tea, Gourmet
877-720-6090 570-676-3244	Most CC, *Rated*, •	French Cuisine during
The Logan Family	S-no/P-no/H-ltd	dinner, fine selection of
		wines and cocktails
		Hiking trails, massage
		therapy, afternoon tea, room
		service, 4-diamond
		restaurant, spa services

The French Manor is an enchanting stone chateau with an intimate, elegant ambience. Plan a perfect romantic getaway at this mountaintop castle. The French Manor's guest-rooms are designed to emphasize both privacy and luxury while maintaining intimacy.
✉ info@thefrenchmanor.com ◔ www.thefrenchmanor.com

STARLIGHT

The Inn at Starlight Lake
289 Starlight Lake Road 18461
800-248-2519 570-798-2519
Sari & Jimmy Schwartz

100-255 BB
23 rooms, 19 pb
Visa, MC, •
C-yes/S-no/P-ltd/H-ltd

Delicious breakfast
Full service restaurant and
bar offering breakfast, lunch,
dinner, selection of wines &
cocktails
Lake front, swimming, tennis
boating, bicycles, hiking,
fishing, cross country skiing,
snowshoeing

Surrounded by rolling hills, wood and lakes, the Inn is a perfect country retreat. Enjoy recreation from swimming to skiing, romantic rooms, excellent food & spirits and congenial atmosphere.
✉ info@innatstarlightlake.com ◑ www.innatstarlightlake.com

STRASBURG

The Limestone Inn
33 E Main St 17579
800-278-8392 717-687-8392
Denise & Richard Waller &
daughters

89-129 BB
6 rooms, 5 pb
Most CC, *Rated*
C-ltd/S-no/P-no/H-no

Full gourmet breakfast
Tea, coffee, snacks, cold
drinks
Sitting rooms, library, bicycle
storage, patio

The Limestone Inn B&B (circa 1786) is listed in the National Register of Historic Places and is situated in the heart of Lancaster's Amish country.
✉ limestoneinn@yahoo.com ◑ www.thelimestoneinn.com

Strasburg Village Inn
1 W Main St 17579
717-687-0900
Angela Skiadas

69-169 BB
10 rooms, 10 pb
Most CC, *Rated*, •
C-yes/S-no/P-no/H-no

Continental plus breakfast
Lunch & dinner available in
our restaurant on site,
restaurants nearby
Sitting room, suites with
jetted tubs, canopy beds

1788 National historic landmark with rooms set in Colonial Williamsburg-style complete with period pieces, antiques, private baths, tv, breakfast included. Great location for tourist activities and must sees and todo's. ½mile from Sight and sound
✉ skiadasang@aol.com ◑ www.strasburg.com/index.html?id=38&volume=Inn

SUNBURY

River View Inn B&B
103 Chestnut St 17801
866-592-4800 570-286-4800
Linda & Gary DeGroat

98-129 BB
6 rooms, 6 pb
Most CC
C-yes/S-ltd/P-yes/H-no

Full breakfast
Winter Weekdays -
Continental breakfast
Wireless Internet access, gas
fireplaces, hot tub, full
kitchen access

Come and experience a casual Victorian stay in historic Sunbury, PA. The River View Inn features elegant Victorian decor, six well appointed bedrooms and a great view of the Susquehanna River and the Shikellamy State Park overlook.
✉ reservations@riverview-inn.com ◑ www.riverview-inn.com

UNION DALE

Stone Bridge Inn
Lyon St 18470
570-679-9200

90-195 BB
13 rooms, 13 pb
Most CC
C-yes/S-no/P-no/H-ltd

Continental breakfast
Casual, fine dining restaurant
on premises; Tavern menu
also available with lighter
fare.
Indoor pool, hot tub, Internet
access. Massages and
manicures available with
appointment.

We will remind you of a quaint, alpine hide-away. Here, vacationing is synonymous with relaxation. Fine dining and pleasantly inviting accommodations are yours on 200 scenic acres of forests and pastureland overlooking the rolling mountains.
✉ sbinn@nep.net ◑ www.stone-bridge-inn.com

UNIONTOWN

Inne at Watson's Choice
234 Balsinger Rd 15401
888-820-5380 724-437-4999
Nancy & Bill Ross

105-200 BB
12 rooms, 12 pb
Visa, MC, Disc, *Rated*,
•
C-ltd/S-no/P-no/H-yes
French

Four course breakfast
Continental breakfast served
at 7:00 a.m. for early tours at
Frank Lloyd Wright homes
Sitting room, library,
accommodate business
travelers

Restored circa 1800 Western Pennsylvania farmhouse offering charm & ambience of yester-year and just a short drive to Frank Lloyd Wright's "Fallingwater" and "Kentuck Knob" located in the Laurel Highlands of southwestern Pennsylvania.
✉ innkeeper@watsonschoice.com ○ www.watsonschoice.com

VALLEY FORGE

Great Valley House of Valley Forge
1475 Swedesford Rd 19355
610-644-6759
Pattye Benson

94-129 BB
3 rooms, 3 pb
Most CC, *Rated*
C-yes/S-no/P-ltd/H-no
Limited French

Full Gourmet Breakfast
Swimming pool, free wireless
Internet, cable TV, guest
refrigerator & microwave,
sitting room

Built before the Revolutionary War, the 300-yr. old Great Valley House retains original fireplaces, antiques & random-width wood floors. As you enjoy breakfast, there may be a fire in the old kitchen walk-in fireplace.
✉ stay@greatvalleyhouse.com ○ www.greatvalleyhouse.com

WASHINGTON CROSSING

Inn to the Woods
150 Glenwood Dr 18977
215-493-1974
David Gerard & Brady Barr

149-265 BB
7 rooms, 7 pb
Visa, MC, AmEx, •
S-no/P-no/H-no

Gourmet country breakfast
Evening refreshments &
sweets
Woodland setting with
hammocks, stone terrace &
fish pond, concierge
services, on-site massage

Enter the tranquility and beauty of the woods. Nestled in the center of Bucks County, our Inn features 7 uniquely appointed guestrooms with fireplaces & luxurious private baths. Open 7 days a week.
✉ Innkeeper@inn-bucks.com ○ www.inn-bucks.com

WELLSBORO

Kaltenbach's
743 Stonyfork Rd & Kelsey St
16901
800-722-4954 570-724-4954
Lee Kaltenbach

90-150 BB
10 rooms, 10 pb
Visa, MC, *Rated*, •
C-yes/S-no/P-no/H-no
Spanish

Full breakfast
Afternoon tea, snacks, wine
Lunch/dinner by
reservation, sitting room,
library, tennis court,
Jacuzzis, free Internet access

Featuring antique quilts made by the owner's grandmother 80 years ago. Nearby rails to trails, hiking and biking through the canyon.
○ www.kaltenbachsinn.com

WYALUSING

Wyalusing Hotel
111 Main St 18853
570-746-1204
Chris & Jeannie Woodruff

60-90 BB
10 rooms, 10 pb
Most CC
C-yes/S-no/P-yes/H-ltd

Continental breakfast
100 Seat dining room. 100
country bar room.
Direct dial telephones,
Internet access, cable TV,
climate control, sitting room,
deck, private baths

The Wyalusing Hotel enjoys a wide reputation for fine food & warm hospitality. A friendly atmosphere awaits you at Wyalusing Hotel, located along the shores of the Susquehanna River, amidst some of Pennsylvania's most beautiful mountain scenery.
✉ cjwood@ptd.net ○ www.wyalusinghotel.com

Puerto Rico

CAYEY

Jajome Terrace Guesthouse & Restaurant
Carretera 15 KM 18.6 00736
787-738-4016
Sara Cano

107-124 BB
10 rooms, 10 pb
Visa, MC, AmEx
C-yes/S-no/P-no/H-yes
Spanish

Continental breakfast
Private balcony, A/C, deck.
No TV, no phones, no
swimming pool – come and
relax!We now have WiFi

Located in the beautiful mountains of Cayey Puerto Rico, above sea level 2,800 feet, Jajome Terrace is the ideal place to escape the city and enjoy a meal in peaceful surroundings.
✉ reservation@jajometerrace.com 🌐 www.jajometerrace.com

CEIBA

Ceiba Country Inn
Carr 977 KM 1.2 00735
888-560-2816 787-885-0471
Sue Newbauer & Dick Bray

85-95 BB
9 rooms, 9 pb
Most CC, *Rated*, •
C-yes/S-ltd/P-no/H-yes

Continental plus breakfast
Bar service, library, family
friendly facility and daily
maid service.

Pastoral setting with a view of the sea. Centrally located for trips to the rainforest, beaches, outer islands and San Juan.
✉ prinn@juno.com

RINCON

Blue Boy Inn
556 Black Eagle Street 00677
787-823-2593
Marc Tremblay

135-205 BB
8 rooms, 8 pb
Visa, MC, •
C-ltd/S-ltd/P-ltd/H-yes
French and Spanish

Gourmet Breakfast
High speed Internet and
wireless, daily maid service,
2 BBQ areas and many
outside sitting areas.

Welcome to Rincon, a wonderful and relaxed beach town in the west of Puerto Rico called 'la Porta del Sol.' Spectacular sunsets, a variety of outdoor activities, and an ample selection of restaurants will make your stay unforgettable.
✉ info@blueboyinn.com 🌐 www.blueboyinn.com

Tres Sirenas Ocean Front
26 Sea Beach St 00677
787-823-0558
Harry & Lisa Rodriguez

175-300 BB
4 rooms, 4 pb
Visa, MC
C-yes/S-no/P-ltd/H-no
Spanish

Full gourmet breakfast
Pool, Jacuzzi, cable TV, A/C
& fans, beach towels, lounge
chairs, in room spa services.

Tres Sirenas Beach House offers tropical elegance, right at water's edge of the most fabulous beach in Puerto Rico.
✉ lisamasters@mac.com 🌐 www.tressirenas.com

SAN JUAN

El Canario by the Sea Hotel
4 Condado Ave 00907
800-533-2649 787-722-8640
Mathilda Jean Baptiste

90-144 BB
25 rooms, 25 pb
Most CC, *Rated*, •
C-yes/S-no/P-no/H-no
Spanish

Continental breakfast
Pastries, fruit, cereal, coffee,
tea & juice
A/C, private bath, cable TV,
telephone, in-room safe,
inner garden courtyard

Comfortable & affordable. Friendly staff, informal atmosphere & central location make this B&B a favorite with business & holiday travelers alike. 20 steps to beach.
✉ canariopr@aol.com 🌐 www.canariohotels.com/sea.htm

SAN JUAN ─────────────────────────────

El Canario Inn
1317 Ashford Ave 00907
800-533-2649 787-722-3861
Marcos Santana

105-149 BB
25 rooms, 25 pb
Most CC, *Rated*, •
C-yes/S-no/P-no/H-no
Spanish

Continental breakfast
Fruit, pastries, cereal, coffee,
tea & juice
Patios, A/C rooms, TV,
phone, private bathroom,
Bermuda ceiling fans

El Canario Inn is San Juan's most historic & unique B&B. Near beach, casinos, boutiques & restaurants. Relaxing patios are filled with tropical foliage & the melody of coquis.
✉ canariopr@aol.com ◑ www.canariohotels.com/inn.htm

Hosteria Del Mar Beach Inn
#1 Tapia St Ocean Park 00911
877-727-3302 787-727-3302
Elsie Herger, Mercedes Mulet

69-264 BB
24 rooms, 24 pb
Rated, •
C-yes/S-ltd/P-yes/H-yes
Spanish

Continental plus breakfast
Restaurant
Cable TV, A/C

Cozy beach Inn by the sea. Rooms with wonderful views of the Atlantic. One or two bedroom apartment, offering breakfast, lunch and dinner in a tropical gazebo on the beach. Weddings and events hosted.
✉ hosteria@caribe.net ◑ www.hosteriadelmarpr.com

Tres Palmas Inn
2212 Park Blvd 00913
888-290-2076 787-727-4617
Manuael Peredo

81-175 BB
18 rooms, 18 pb
Visa, MC, AmEx,
Rated, •
C-yes/S-ltd/P-no/H-yes
Spanish

Continental breakfast
Sitting room, Jacuzzis,
swimming pool, suites, cable
TV, phone with dataport

This quaint beachfront inn, recently renovated, is a refreshing alternative to traditional high priced and crowded hotels.
✉ info@trespalmasinn.com ◑ www.trespalmasinn.com

VIEQUES ISLAND ─────────────────────────────

Hacienda Tamarindo
4.5 Km, Rt 996 00765
787-741-0420
Burr & Linda Vail

135-335 BB
16 rooms, 16 pb
Most CC, *Rated*, •
C-ltd/S-ltd/P-no/H-yes
Spanish

Full breakfast
Honor bar, picnic lunch
packed in an insulated back
pack, coffee & tea buffet at
6:30 am
Wireless Internet, sitting
room, library, tennis court,
swimming pool, exercise
room, Bio-bay Tours

"Extraordinary small hotel . . . the nicest place to stay on Vieques." Spectacular Caribbean views, 16 charming rooms decorated with art, antiques & collectibles. Gorgeous gardenside pool. Breakfast awarded best for all Puerto Rican small hotels.
✉ hactam@aol.com ◑ www.haciendatamarindo.com

Rhode Island

BLOCK ISLAND

The Atlantic Inn
High St 02807
800-224-7422 401-466-5883
Anne & Brad Marthens

160-435 BB
22 rooms, 22 pb
Visa, MC, Disc, *Rated*
C-yes/S-no/P-no/H-ltd
Limited German, French,
Spanish
Mid Apr. – Mid-late Oct.

Fresh Baked Breakfast Buffet
Candlelit – four course
dinner, tea, bar
Sitting room, tennis, beaches,
nature walks, antiques,
horseback riding

An 1879 Victorian inn set high on a hill overlooking the ocean & harbor. The Atlantic Inn is surrounded by 6 landscaped acres, sloping lawns, numerous gardens & two of six tennis courts on the island. ✉ AtlanticInn@BIRI.com ○ www.atlanticinn.com

The Blue Dory Inn
Dodge St 02807
800-992-7290 401-466-5891
Ann Law

65-375 BB
11 rooms, 11 pb
Most CC, •
C-yes/S-no/P-yes/H-no
May-October

Buffet
Afternoon tea,
complimentary wine & our
famous Blue Dory cookies
Sitting room, cable TV, walk
to beach, Jacuzzi, A/C, ocean
views

The Blue Dory Inn is a 100-year-old Victorian house that sits at the head of the famous Crescent Beach. Short walking distance to the ferry, fine restaurants and island shops. ✉ rundezvous@aol.com ○ www.blockislandinns.com/html/bluedory.html

Gables Inn & II
1319 Dodge St 02807
401-466-2213
Barbara & Stanley Nyzio

55-185 BB
21 rooms, 8 pb
Visa, MC
C-yes/S-no/P-no/H-ltd
Mid May to November

Continental breakfast
Coffee, tea, & cocoa available
anytime
Complimentary beach
supplies, access to
refrigerator, grills & picnic
tables

1880 Victorian inn at the edge of the village, close to beaches and restaurants. Relax in the ambience of ornate tin ceilings and antique furniture in comfortable sitting rooms or on our shaded verandas. ✉ gablesinn@aol.com

The Rose Farm Inn
1005 Roslyn Rd 02807
401-466-2034
Judith B. Rose

159-309 BB
19 rooms, 17 pb
Most CC
C-ltd/S-no/P-no/H-yes
April-October

Continental plus breakfast
Afternoon tea
Bicycle, beach chair and
umbrella rental

The Rose Farm Inn is known for its natural setting, romantic rooms and informal hospitality. This peaceful sea and country setting is only a few minutes walk from the village and beaches. ✉ rosefarm@riconnect.com ○ www.rosefarminn.com

BRISTOL

Point Pleasant Inn & Resort
333 Poppasquash Rd 02809
800-503-0627 401-253-0627
Trish & Gunter Hafer

375-675 BB
7 rooms, 7 pb
Visa, MC, •
C-ltd/S-ltd/P-no/H-ltd
German, Spanish,
Latvian, Portuguese
April-November

Full breakfast
Tea, open bar, snacks,
complimentary wine
Sitting room, library, bikes,
tennis, Jacuzzis, swimming
pool, suites, fireplaces,
landscaped garden

Point Pleasant Inn & Resort is located on Poppasquash Point, a peninsula located in Bristol, Rhode Island. An English country manor house from another era, the Inn offers a rare look at life from the pages of a romance novel. ✉ trishwwi1@aol.com ○ www.pointpleasantinn.com

1900 House, Narragansett, RI

BRISTOL

William's Grant Inn
154 High St 02809
800-596-4222 401-253-4222
Diane & Warren Poehler

109-199 BB
5 rooms, 5 pb
Most CC, *Rated*, •
C-ltd/S-ltd/P-no/H-ltd

Juice, fruit, muffins, entree
Liqueurs and soft drinks,
cookies, bottle of wine
Sitting room, library, wireless
Internet, TV DVD VCR

On a quiet tree-lined street. 1808 Colonial Federal style home filled with family antiques and artist's fine work. Ceiling fans and A/C in all rooms. High speed wireless broadband.
✉ wmgrantinn@earthlink.net ✪ www.wmgrantinn.com

NARRAGANSETT

1900 House
59 Kingstown Rd 02882
401-789-7971
Sandra & Bill Panzeri

95-150 BB
4 rooms, 2 pb
Cash, Checks, *Rated*
C-ltd/S-no/P-no/H-no

Full breakfast
Winter cider, summer tea
Book Swap, antique
postcards, porch, homemade
quilts

Located in the historic village of Narragansett just footsteps away from a favorite Victorian vacation spot. The 1900 House retains the charm and grace of a bygone era, with bright, open rooms filled with antiques.
✉ 1900house@cox.net ✪ www.1900houseri.com

Blueberry Cove Inn
75 Kingstown Rd 02882
800-478-1426 401-792-9865
Seely & David Gerraughty

90-300 BB
9 rooms, 9 pb
Visa, MC
C-ltd/S-no/P-ltd/H-ltd

Full breakfast
"Romantic Roses" and
"Sweetie" packages, all
rooms have robes, hair
dryers, Egyptian cotton
linens

1870's home in quiet neighborhood. Top vacation spot; short walk to town beach & the Towers. Newport, Mystic Village & Block Island nearby. Whirlpool suite; fireplaces, WiFi, apartment for families. Nine golf courses within a 15 minute drive.
✉ innkeeper@blueberrycoveinn.com ✪ www.blueberrycoveinn.com

NARRAGANSETT

The Richards
144 Gibson Ave 02882
401-789-7746
Steven & Nancy Richards

145-230 BB
4 rooms, 4 pb
Checks, *Rated*, •
C-ltd/S-no/P-no/H-ltd

Full gourmet breakfast
Complimentary sherry in
room
Library with fireplace, tennis
courts nearby, fireplaces in
bedrooms, air conditioning,
WiFi

Gracious accommodations in an English country setting. Awaken to the smell of gourmet coffee and freshly baked goods. Water garden with Koi.
✉ therichards144@hotmail.com ◊ www.therichardsbnb.com

NEWPORT

1 Murray House B&B
1 Murray Pl 02840
888-848-2048 401-846-3337
Noreen O'Neil

99-199 BB
2 rooms, 3 pb
Visa, MC, Disc, *Rated*
C-ltd/S-ltd/P-yes/H-no
10 months

Gourmet breakfast
In room tea & coffee
In-ground swimming pool,
hot tub, flower gardens,
TV/VCR, A/C, private patios,
in-room breakfast

Located in the lovely Newport Mansion & Cliff Walk district. 5 minute walk to beach, 4 minutes to downtown Newport. Private baths & patios with room. Swimming pool, hot tub & flower gardens. Gourmet breakfast served to your charming room. Pets welcome.
✉ murrayhousebnb@aol.com ◊ www.murrayhouse.com

1873 Architects Inn –
George Champlin Mason
House
2 Sunnyside Place 02840
877-466-2547 401-845-2547
Nick & Brian

99-369 BB
5 rooms, 5 pb
Visa, MC, *Rated*, •
C-ltd/S-no/P-no/H-no

Full organic gourmet
breakfast
Afternoon refreshments,
evening sherry
Cable TV/VCR, air
conditioning, fireplaces,
parlor, library, wireless
Internet, in-room massages

Romantic and elegant, the 1873 Architects Inn-George C. Mason House was built as the private residence of Mason, a famous Newport "Gilded Age" architect. Lovingly restored into a B&B Inn located in the heart of Newport. Welcoming guests for twelve years.
✉ Reservations@InnBliss.com ◊ www.ArchitectsInn.com

Abigail Stoneman Inn
102 Touro St 02840
800-845-1811 401-847-1811
Suzanne Spinelli

195-595 BB
5 rooms, 5 pb
Visa, MC, AmEx,
Rated, •
C-ltd/S-no/P-no/H-no

Multi-Course Breakfast
Afternoon High Tea,
Connoisseur Collection Tea
Menu, Artisanal Chocolates
Dreamy Night Pillow Menu,
Renewal Bath Bar, Private
Tea For Two Room, Water
Bar, Breakfast In Bed

Experience Newport, Rhode Island's deluxe Bed and Breakfast Inn, intimate and private by design. Enjoy relaxed elegance and warm hospitality, with truly indulgent personal services, the perfect rejuvenating escape or romantic getaway. AAA Four Diamond
✉ win@legendaryinnsofnewport.com ◊ www.abigailstonemaninn.com

Almondy Inn
25 Pelham St 02840
800-478-6155 401-848-7202
Evelyne Valkenberg

145-365 BB
5 rooms, 5 pb
Visa, MC, AmEx,
Rated, •
C-ltd/S-no/P-no/H-no
Dutch, Spanish, French,
German

Full Gourmet Breakfast
In-room coffee service;
afternoon wine & cheese
Off-street parking provided,
Jacuzzis, fireplaces, suites,
wireless Internet access

The Almondy Inn, built in the 1890's is an elegantly restored B&B conveniently located in downtown Newport, RI, just steps from Bannister's Wharf, historic downtown restaurants, shops and galleries and minutes from Newport beaches and Mansions.
✉ info@almondyinn.com ◊ www.almondyinn.com

NEWPORT

Attwater Villa
22 Liberty St 02840
800-392-3717 401-846-7444
Roland Caron

99-350 BB
15 rooms, 15 pb
Most CC
C-yes/S-ltd/P-no/H-no
April 1-Nov. 15

Continental plus breakfast
Afternoon tea
Sitting room, 4 star
restaurant nearby, small
conference room

Elegance with the intimacy of a guesthouse. Master suites, queen rooms & apartment suites in a 1910 "House of the Evening." Located off historic Bellevue Ave. in the heart of Newport.
✉ Innkeeper@attwatervilla.com ○ www.attwatervilla.com

Beech Tree Inn
34 Rhode Island Ave 02840
800-748-6565 401-847-9794
Jim & Cindy Mahood

139-399 BB
8 rooms, 8 pb
Most CC, *Rated*, •
C-ltd/S-ltd/P-yes/H-no
Russian

Biggest breakfast in town
Snacks, complimentary wine
Sitting room, library,
Jacuzzis, suites, fireplaces,
cable TV, soda machine, ice
machine, garden

This charming Victorian home, built in 1887, was lovingly renovated, and offers spacious rooms with private baths, cable TV, air conditioning, lovely gardens and sundecks.
✉ cmquilt13@cox.net ○ www.beechtreeinn.com/bt/btindex.html

Black Duck Inn
29 Pelham St 02840
800-206-5212 401-841-5548
Lisa Foisy

99-314 BB
8 rooms, 7 pb
Most CC, *Rated*, •
C-ltd/S-no/P-no/H-no

Full breakfast
Sitting room, cable, Jacuzzis,
fireplaces, A/C

This large, well-appointed, newly renovated in art deco and traditional design is conveniently located opposite Bowen's Wharf in downtown Newport. Shops, restaurants, historic mansions and sailing are all in walking distance.
✉ innkeeper@blackduckinn.com ○ www.blackduckinn.com

Burbank Rose
111 Memorial Blvd W 02840
888-297-5800 401-849-9457
Brian Cole

78-225 BB
6 rooms, 6 pb
Most CC
C-ltd/S-no/P-ltd/H-no

Continental breakfast
Some of our suites have a full
kitchen that is fully stocked
with juice, milk, teas, coffee,
fruit
Shared sitting rooms, suites
with day bed and trundle
bed

Welcome to Burbank Rose Bed and Breakfast! A convenient downtown location within walking distance to shops, restaurants and clubs. Suites featuring kitchens, private parking, AC, cable TV and wireless Internet, you can't go wrong!
✉ theburbankrose@yahoo.com ○ www.burbankrose.com

Chestnut Inn
99 3rd St 02840
401-846-0173 401-847-6949
Bill, Eileen & Cheryl Nimmo

75-150 BB
2 rooms
•
C-yes/S-yes/P-yes/H-no

Continental breakfast
Sitting room, library, tennis,
suites, cable TV, fishing,
swimming

One block from Narragansett Bay, in Newport's historic "Point" section. A perfect getaway for couples and families. Children and pets welcome.
✉ chstnut99@aol.com ○ www.newportchestnutinn.com

Cliffside Inn
2 Seaview Ave 02840
800-845-1811 401-847-1811
Lynzie Golden

135-595 BB
16 rooms, 16 pb
Visa, MC, AmEx,
Rated, •
C-ltd/S-no/P-no/H-no
Spanish

Multi-Course Breakfast
Internationally acclaimed
afternoon tea, wine bar & in-
room wine service
Evening turndown service,
artisan chocolates & sweets,
getaway packages

Home of Newport artist Beatrice Turner, Cliffside has earned a worldwide reputation as one of New England's most distinguished luxury Inns with whirlpools, fireplaces, grand beds and refined elegance. AAA 4 Diamond. Great Tea Rooms of America.
✉ reservations@legendaryinnsofnewport.com ○ www.cliffsideinn.com

NEWPORT

The Francis Malbone House
392 Thames St 02840
800-846-0392 401-846-0392
Will Dewey

99-475 BB
20 rooms, 20 pb
Most CC, *Rated*, •
C-ltd/S-no/P-no/H-yes
Italian, French,
April through November

Full Gourmet Breakfast
Afternoon tea from 3:00 –
5:00 pm
Professional &
knowledgeable innkeepers,
getaway packages, harbor-
front location

Historic Inn, c. 1760, recently awarded a rating of "Extraordinary" from ZAGAT Survey. Offers a warm and luxurious yet relaxed atmosphere in the heart of Newport on the harborfront.
✉ francismalbone@yahoo.com ✆ www.malbone.com

Ivy Lodge
12 Clay St 02840
800-834-6865 401-849-6865
Daryl & Darlene McKenzie

100-319 BB
8 rooms, 8 pb
Most CC, *Rated*
C-yes/S-ltd/P-no/H-ltd

Full breakfast
Cable TV, A/C, CD/radio,
direct-dial phone w/data
port, VCR or DVD player

Welcome to Ivy Lodge! Located in the heart of Newport's Mansion District, romantic Ivy Lodge provides luxurious family suites with off-street parking and a leisurely breakfast served daily.
✉ innkeepers@ivylodge.com ✆ www.ivylodge.com

Marshall Slocum Inn
29 Kay St 02840
800-372-5120 401-841-5120
Mark & Dana Spring

155-275 BB
5 rooms, 5 pb
Most CC, *Rated*, •
C-ltd/S-no/P-no/H-no

Full breakfast
Brunches by arrangement
Sitting room, library, front
porch with rockers

Meticulously preserved to reflect the charm and beauty of its Victorian heritage. Your ideal escape provides a choice of guestrooms which are tastefully decorated to combine the charm of Newport with all the modern amenities.
✉ info@marshallslocuminn.com ✆ www.marshallslocuminn.com

Melville House Inn
39 Clarke St 02840
800-711-7184 401-847-0640
Bob & Priscilla Peretti

99-285 BB
6 rooms, 6 pb
Visa, MC, AmEx,
Rated, •
C-ltd/S-no/P-no/H-ltd

Full breakfast
Afternoon tea & cookies, soft
beverages, juice and bottled
water
Wireless Internet

A 1750 Colonial Inn in Newport's Historic Hill District, one block from the Thames Street harborfront. The Melville House is on National Register of Historic Places and is like a step into the past.
✉ info@melvillehouse.com ✆ www.melvillehouse.com

Newport Blues Inn
96 Pelham St 02840
800-206-5212 401-847-4400
Lisa Foisy

99-350 BB
12 rooms, 12 pb
Most CC
C-ltd/S-no/P-no/H-no
French, German,
Spanish

Full breakfast
Large porch, garden patio,
parlor, A/C, cable, fridge,
phone with modem jack

The Newport Blues Inn, one of Newport's finest Inns, offers our guests an experience of classic RI charm with a modern day style and appeal. Perfectly situated within walking distance to all that Newport offers.
✉ innkeeper@newportbluesinn.com ✆ www.newportbluesinn.com

Old Beach Inn
19 Old Beach Rd 02840
888-303-5033 401-849-3479
Cyndi & Luke Murray

100-375 BB
7 rooms, 7 pb
Visa, MC, Disc, *Rated*
C-ltd/S-no/P-no/H-no

Continental plus breakfast
Full breakfast Sundays
Gazebo, fish pond, patio,
sitting room, fireplaces,
garden, some A/C & TVs

Elegant Victorian B&B filled with romance, history and charm. Ideal location, lovely gardens, comfortable guestrooms.
✉ info@oldbeachinn.com ✆ www.oldbeachinn.com

NEWPORT

Pilgrim House Inn	90-255 BB	Continental plus breakfast
123 Spring St 02840	11 rooms, 11 pb	Complimentary sherry,
800-525-8373 401-846-0040	Most CC, *Rated*, •	shortbread
Barry & Debbie Fonseca	C-ltd/S-no/P-no/H-no	Deck with view of harbor,
		living room with fireplace,
		cable TV in all rooms, free
		wireless Internet

Elegant Victorian inn two blocks from the harbor in Newport's historic district. Rooftop deck with view of Newport Harbor. Walking distance to shops, dining & sights, Cliff Walk.
✉ Innkeeper@PilgrimHouseInn.com ☼ www.pilgrimhouseinn.com

Samuel Durfee House	110-280 BB	Full breakfast
352 Spring St 02840	5 rooms, 5 pb	Afternoon refreshments &
877-696-2374 401-847-1652	Visa, MC, •	snacks including coffee, tea,
Heather & Michael de Pinho	C-ltd/S-no/P-no/H-no	sodas
		WiFi throughout the inn, TV,
		phone and refrigerator in
		guest sitting room, some
		rooms have TV's

An elegant 1803 Federal period bed and breakfast Inn located downtown, just a block from the harbor and two blocks from Bellevue Avenue. All rooms are spacious and tastefully decorated. Perfect for a romantic getaway.
✉ innkeeper@samueldurfeehouse.com ☼ www.samueldurfeehouse.com

The Victorian Ladies	129-289 BB	Full gourmet breakfast
63 Memorial Blvd 02840	11 rooms, 11 pb	Sitting room, fireplaces,
888-849-9960 401-849-9960	Most CC, *Rated*, •	cable TV, accommodations
Cheryl & Harry Schatmeyer	C-ltd/S-no/P-no/H-no	for business travelers,
	Closed in January	wireless Internet

A Victorian period home with an English cottage feeling, surrounded by beautiful gardens and courtyards. Wonderful gourmet breakfast.
✉ info@victorianladies.com ☼ www.victorianladies.com

PROVIDENCE

C.C. Ledbetter	95-115 BB	Continental plus breakfast
326 Benefit St 02903	5 rooms, 2 pb	Sitting room with fireplace,
401-351-4699	Most CC	cable TV, 3 ultra wedding
C. C. Ledbetter	C-ltd/S-no/P-ltd/H-no	rooms, rose garden
	French, some Italian	

On historic Benefit Street directly across from the John Brown house. Comfortable, charmingly furnished, a half block from Brown University and one block from the Rhode Island School of Design. Higher rates for parents' weekends and graduations.
☼ www.ccledbetter.com

Edgewood Manor & The	129-299 BB	Full gourmet breakfast
Newhall House	18 rooms, 18 pb	Sitting rooms, marble
232 Norwood Ave 02905	Most CC, •	Jacuzzis, 2 bedroom suites,
800-882-3285 401-781-0099	C-ltd/S-no/P-no/H-ltd	fireplaces, cable TV
Joy Generali	French	

Greek Revival Mansion and architectural jewel, c.1905, adorned with leaded and stained glass, fine art and period antiques. Guest rooms and suites luxuriously decorated in Victorian and Empire style.
✉ edgemanor@aol.com ☼ www.providence-lodging.com

Tell your hosts Pamela Lanier sent you.

PROVIDENCE

Jacob Hill Inn
888-336-9165 508-336-9165
Bill & Eleonora Rezek

179-459 BB
12 rooms, 12 pb
Most CC, *Rated*
S-no/P-no/H-ltd
Polish

Full gourmet breakfast
Cheese plate
w/complimentary wine, 24
hour self serve hot/cold
beverages available, cookies
& fruit
Billiard room w/plasma
home theater, pool, tennis,
fireplaces, large Jacuzzi tubs,
spa, meeting room

Located on a peaceful country estate, a 10 minute drive from downtown, the Convention Center, Rhode Island School of Design & Brown University. Recipient of the prestigious AAA 4-diamond award & ZAGAT 2007 Top U.S. Hotels, Resorts & Spas.
✉ host@jacobhill.com 🌐 www.Inn-Providence-RI.com

The Old Court B&B
144 Benefit St 02903
401-751-2002
Max Gallagher

145-215 BB
10 rooms, 10 pb
Most CC, *Rated*, •
C-ltd/S-no/P-no/H-no

Full breakfast
Complimentary tea, assorted
breads
Antiques, cable TV in every
room, Private bath in every
room wet bars in some
rooms, free WiFi

The Old Court B&B was built in 1863, Italianate in design and in ornate details; the B&B combines tradition with contemporary standards of luxury. The Old Court is filled with antique furniture and chandeliers.
✉ reserve@oldcourt.com 🌐 www.oldcourt.com

SOUTH KINGSTOWN

Admiral Dewey Inn
668 Matunuck Beach Rd
02879
800-457-2090 401-783-2090
Joan LeBel

110-160 BB
10 rooms, 8 pb
Visa, MC, *Rated*
C-ltd/S-ltd/P-no/H-no
Polish

Continental plus breakfast
Snacks
Sitting room, bicycles, cable
TV

The past comes alive in this 1898 Victorian, which has been lovingly restored and furnished with antiques in the Victorian style. Listed on the National Historic Register.
🌐 www.admiraldeweyinn.com

WAKEFIELD

Eden Manor
154 Post Rd 02879
877-430-1613 401-792-8234
Lloyd & Bernadette Eden

125-275 BB
12 rooms, 10 pb
Visa, MC
C-yes/S-no/P-yes/H-no

Deluxe breakfast buffet
Fireplaces, gardens, dining
room, porch, sun room,
weddings, reunions &
meetings

Imagine this unique Victorian mansion only a few miles north of the beautiful Atlantic Ocean. Relax with us and step into an era of opulence few travelers have the opportunity to experience.
✉ edenmanor@cs.com 🌐 www.EdenManorBandB.com

Sugar Loaf Hill B&B
607 Main St 02879
401-789-8715
Stephanie & David Osborn

95-169 BB
4 rooms, 3 pb
Visa, MC
C-yes/S-no/P-no/H-ltd
Some Greek & Spanish

Full breakfast
Dining room, living room,
parlor, guest fridge, porch,
fireplaces

Sugar Loaf Hill Bed and Breakfast is nestled on 1½ acres in a charming historic area, peacefully surrounded by stone walls, hollies, rhododendrons, and large shade trees.
✉ sugarloafhill@verizon.net

WESTERLY————————————————————————————

The Villa	125-320 BB	Full breakfast on weekends
190 Shore Rd 02891	8 rooms, 8 pb	Outdoor hot tub, heated
800-722-9240 401-596-1054	Most CC, *Rated*, •	swim pool, 2 fireplaces, 4
Michael & Barbara Cardiff	C-ltd/S-no/P-no/H-ltd	Jacuzzi suites, 1.5 acres

Escape to our Mediterranean style villa. We set the stage for your romantic getaway. You'll fall in love and want to return. Outdoor pool and hot tub. Adjacent to golf course. Private and romantic.
✉ villa@riconnect.com ◐ www.thevillaatwesterly.com

WICKFORD————————————————————————————

Haddie Pierce House	125-150 BB	Full breakfast
146 Boston Neck Rd 02852	5 rooms, 5 pb	Tea, coffee, soft drinks
866-4HADDIE 401-294-7674	Most CC	Double parlor, front porch &
Darya & John Prassl	C-ltd/S-no/P-no/H-no	patio, walk to the beach or
		village

The Haddie Pierce House is a restored Victorian home in historic Wickford Village. Five rooms with private baths. Antiques and period furnishings provide a casual elegance. Walk to the beach or village shops. Listed on the National Historic Register.
✉ info@HaddiePierce.com ◐ www.HaddiePierce.com

Wickford Junction Inn	130-150 BB	Gourmet breakfast
1266 Old Baptist Rd 02852	4 rooms, 3 pb	Afternoon goodies and
401-295-4434	Visa, MC	refreshments
Jackie McCarthy	C-ltd/S-ltd/P-no/H-ltd	Garden, ponds, waterfall,
		sitting area, Jacuzzi, pool,
		beach towels, chairs, etc.,
		family suite

A lovingly restored 1880's Country Victorian houses our charming B&B. We're beautifully situated in a park-like setting at the gateway to historic Wickford. Family suite available.
✉ wickfordjctinn@cox.net ◐ www.wickfordjctinn.com

WOONSOCKET————————————————————————————

Pillsbury House B&B	95-135 BB	Full breakfast
341 Prospect St 02895	4 rooms, 4 pb	Complimentary wine and
800-205-4112 401-766-7983	Most CC	beverages
Roger Bouchard	C-ltd/S-no/P-no/H-no	Sitting room, suite, fireplace,
		accommodate business
		travelers, high speed
		wireless Internet

Built in 1875, The Pillsbury House is tucked away on quiet and historic Prospect Street in Woonsocket's fashionable North End. Close to Boston, Providence and Newport.
✉ rogerwnri@prodigy.net ◐ www.pillsburyhouse.com

WYOMING————————————————————————————

Stagecoach House Inn	100-199 BB	Continental plus breakfast
1136 Main St 02898	12 rooms, 12 pb	Lobby, porch, garden,
888-814-9600 401-539-9600	Visa, MC, AmEx, *Rated*	seasonal fireplaces, Jacuzzi
Bill & Debbie Bokon	C-ltd/S-no/P-no/H-ltd	tubs, massage therapy, free
		WiFi

An historic building located in the village of Wyoming, RI, recently renovated guestrooms and suites. Accompanying the old are many new conveniences, making the Stagecoach House the warm and cozy country inn that it is today.
✉ info@stagecoachhouse.com ◐ www.stagecoachhouse.com

South Carolina

ABBEVILLE——————————————————————————————————————

Hearthside Manor B&B
1304 N Main St 29620
866-710-8311 864-366-6555
Lanie & Richard Reeder

95-129 BB
3 rooms, 3 pb
Visa, MC
C-ltd/S-ltd/P-ltd/H-no
Dutch

Full on weekends,
continental M-F
Complimentary coffee, tea,
non-alcoholic drinks &
snacks
VCR, DVD, movie and book
library, board games,
bicycles, wireless Internet
access

Step into an atmosphere of graceful elegance & cozy ambience in this Historic Victorian Inn located a mile from Abbeville Square. Three beautiful antique furnished bedrooms with private baths, numerous amenities and modern conveniences.
✉ info@hearthsidemanorbedandbreakfast.com ◑ www.hearthsidemanorbedandbreakfast.com

ANDERSON——————————————————————————————————————

Evergreen B&B
1103 S Main St 29621
864-375-9064
Myrna Ryter

108 BB
5 rooms, 5 pb
Visa, MC, AmEx
C-yes/S-ltd/P-no/H-no

Continental breakfast
Living room, kitchen,
Laundry, Day spa services
are available next door.

The B&B is an affordable destination get-away. Day Spa next door. Oldest Historical Mansion of Anderson Romantic, relaxing, for couples or group. Walking distance to downtown fun and sports activities nearby. Tennis, golf, hiking. restaurants, art, shops.
✉ info@spa-it.com ◑ www.spa-it.com

BEAUFORT——————————————————————————————————————

Beaulieu House at Cat Island
3 Sheffield Ct 29907
866-814-7833 843-770-0303
Diann Corsaro

175-225 BB
5 rooms, 5 pb
Most CC
C-yes/S-no/P-yes/H-yes

Full breakfast
Refreshments on the
veranda
Jacuzzi, verandas, private
baths, ceiling fans,
kitchenette

Beaulieu House is the only waterfront B&B in Beaufort . . . Five minutes from the Historic District . . . Adjacent to the Sanctuary at Cat Island & fine dining at the British Open Pub . . . Stay at the Beaulieu House where South Carolina meets Paradise . . .
✉ beaulieubb@aol.com ◑ www.beaulieuhouse.com

TwoSuns Inn
1705 Bay St 29902
800-532-4244 843-522-1122
Henri & Patricia Safran

140-175 BB
6 rooms, 6 pb
Visa, MC, AmEx, *Rated*
C-ltd/S-ltd/P-ltd/H-yes
French

Full gourmet breakfast
Afternoon tea,
complimentary wine
Sitting room, public tennis
courts, computer, fax, cable
TV, WiFi

1917 Certified Historic Building with finest bay view. Gourmet breakfast fare, modern amenities and the personal attention of caring hosts. Mid-way between Charleston and Savannah.
✉ twosuns@islc.net ◑ www.twosunsinn.com

BENNETTSVILLE

Breeden Inn, Cottages, &	120-180 BB	Full breakfast
Retreat on Main	13 rooms, 13 pb	Tea, soda, coffee upon
404 E Main St 29512	Most CC, *Rated*, •	arrival, bedtime chocolates,
888-335-2996 843-479-3665	C-ltd/S-no/P-no/H-no	snack packages in hospitality
Wesley & Bonnie Park		area at each house
		Pool, private phones w/free
		LD, free faxing & high speed
		wireless, TV/VCR/DVD,
		video library, bikes

Comfortable, elegant, romantic & historic stay, midway between NY & FL, near the NC/SC beaches. Four 19th-century houses offer 13 guestrooms, luxurious bedding lush winding garden walks, large in-ground pool, wonderful Southern porches, wireless high speed.
✉ info@breedeninn.com ◐ www.breedeninn.com

CHARLESTON

1807 Phoebe Pember House	140-250 BB	Continental breakfast
26 Society St 29401	6 rooms, 6 pb	Wine reception on Friday
843-722-4186	Visa, MC, AmEx	Business traveler
Anne G. Shue	C-ltd/S-no/P-no/H-no	accommodations, concierge,
		turndown service, yoga
		studio

200 year-old Federal-style Charleston property with carriage and coach houses, with beautiful piazzas overlooking private walled gardens. In the heart of the Historic District with private parking. On-site retreat center and yoga studio.
✉ info@phoebepemberhouse.com ◐ www.phoebepemberhouse.com

1843 Battery Carriage	99-299 BB	Continental breakfast
House Inn	11 rooms, 11 pb	Complimentary wine
20 S Battery 29401	Most CC, *Rated*, •	Free wireless Internet access
800-775-5575 843-727-3100	S-no/P-no/H-no	available in some rooms and
Elizabeth Kilminster		the lobby.

For a truly memorable Charleston experience, stay in the Battery Carriage House Inn, located in the garden of the Stevens-Lathers house, one of the most gracious houses on the city's historic harbor front. Eleven intimate rooms and continental breakfast.
✉ batterych@bellsouth.net ◐ www.batterycarriagehouse.com

21 East Battery Bed &	150-395 BB	Full breakfast
Breakfast	3 rooms, 3 pb	Fresh pastries, fruit, juices
21 E Battery 29401	Most CC, •	Fireplace, antiques, off street
800-543-4774 843-556-0500	C-ltd/S-no/P-no/H-ltd	parking, complimentary
Abigail Martin		admission to Historic
		Museum on property.

This privately owned luxury bed and breakfast is nestled in the Carriage House of Charleston's historic 1825 Edmondston-Alston House, one of the first dwellings constructed along the High Battery facing Charleston Harbor.
✉ info@21eastbattery.com ◐ www.21eastbattery.com

36 Meeting Street	125-200 BB	Continental breakfast
36 Meeting St 29401	3 rooms, 3 pb	Sitting room, kitchenettes,
843-722-1034	Visa, MC, *Rated*	TV, and phones in rooms.
Vic & Anne Brandt	C-ltd/S-ltd/P-no/H-no	

Experience the intimacy of being a resident in the most exclusive part of Charleston's Historic Residential District. Suites have private entrance, elegant furnishings, four poster mahogany rice beds.
✉ info@36meetingstreet.com ◐ www.36meetingstreet.com

CHARLESTON

A B&B at 4 Unity Alley	175-300 BB	Full breakfast
4 Unity Alley 29401	3 rooms, 3 pb	Small garden, cable TV,
843-577-7777 843-577-6660	Visa, MC	telephone, fax machine, off-
Richard Schneider, Don Smith	C-ltd/S-no/P-ltd/H-no	street parking, tennis, golf
	Spanish	and swimming nearby

The only B&B located in the heart of Charleston's French Quarter. Large rooms, antiques, garden. Breakfast served in our formal dining room. Park in our garage and walk everywhere.
✉ unitybb@aol.com ♦ www.unitybb.com

Ashley Inn B&B	119-249 BB	Full breakfast
201 Ashley Ave 29403	7 rooms, 7 pb	Afternoon tea, sandwiches &
800-581-6658 843-723-1848	Visa, MC, •	cookies, complimentary
Barry Carroll	C-ltd/S-ltd/P-no/H-no	sherry
		Sitting room, fireplace,
		complimentary bikes, free
		off-street parking

Sleep until the fragrance of southern cooking lures you to garden breakfast. Featured in Gail Greco's Nationally Televised "Country Inn Cooking." Charleston's Gourmet Breakfast Place.
✉ reservations@ashleyinnbb.com ♦ www.charleston-sc-inns.com/ashley

Barksdale House Inn	119-205 BB	Continental breakfast
27 George St 29401	14 rooms, 14 pb	Afternoon tea or sherry
888-577-4980 843-577-4800	Most CC	Cable TV, in-room coffee
Patti Enloe	C-ltd/S-no/P-ltd/H-no	makers, free WiFi, gas
	Spring & Fall	fireplaces, built-in dry bars,
		antiques

Sample the European opulence of The Barksdale House Inn, Charleston's most elegant yet intimate inn. Luxurious comforts await you in each of the fourteen rooms. A historic home built in 1778 beautifully restored to its original grandeur.
✉ stay@barksdalehouse.com ♦ www.barksdalehouse.com

The Broad Street Guest House	185-250 BB	Full breakfast
133 Broad St 29401	4 rooms, 4 pb	Lunch available.
843-577-5965	Most CC	
Hadassah Rothenberg	C-yes/S-no/P-ltd/H-no	

Welcome to Charleston's first kosher B&B located right in the middle of the historic district. 1800's home is artfully decorated to be warm, comfortable, and accommodating for individuals and families with children.
✉ stay@charlestonkosherbedandbreakfast.com
♦ www.charlestonkosherbedandbreakfast.com/index.php

The Cabell House	165-355 BB	Continental breakfast
8 Church St 29401	4 rooms, 4 pb	Option for a Hot Breakfast
843-723-7551	Visa, MC, AmEx, •	buffet at our sister property
Ms. Randy Cabell	C-ltd/S-no/P-ltd/H-no	next door (Guests make $7.50
	French	contribution.)
		WiFi, flat-screen TV, porch &
		rockers, common living
		room, garden available for
		gatherings/weddings.

The Cabell House puts you in the heart of Charleston, steps away from the High Battery with views of the Harbor and Ft Sumter. We're happy to help you with recommendations & reservations, for restaurants, tours & entertainment. Easy walk to everything!!
✉ info@cabellhouse.com ♦ www.cabellhouse.com

CHARLESTON————————————————————————————————————

Cannonboro Inn B&B
184 Ashley Ave 29403
800-235-8039 843-723-8572
Diane Mott

89-250 BB
6 rooms, 6 pb
Most CC, •
C-ltd/S-no/P-no/H-no

Full breakfast
Afternoon tea, sandwiches,
goodies
Sitting room, garden,
complimentary bikes, free
off-street parking

Antebellum home c.1850 in Charleston's historic district. Breakfast served on a piazza overlooking a country garden. Fireplaces in rooms. A place to be pampered with very special southern hospitality.
✉ reservations@cannonboroinnbb.com 🌐 www.charleston-sc-inns.com/cannonboro

**Charleston Governor's
House**
117 Broad St 29401
800-720-9812 843-720-2070
Mary Kittrell

195-575 BB
11 rooms, 11 pb
Visa, MC, AmEx, *Rated*
C-ltd/S-ltd/P-no/H-ltd
Closed Christmas Day

Continental plus breakfast
Lowcountry Tea of local
recipes and evening sherry
3 living rooms, whirlpools,
wet bars, concierge,
verandah, free parking, free
wireless Internet

The Governor's House Inn is a National Historic Landmark reflecting the Old South's civility and grandeur. Praised by one national publication as "Charleston's most glamorous and sophisticated Inn," the Inn blends historic splendor and romantic elegance.
✉ governorshouse@aol.com 🌐 www.governorshouse.com

Fulton Lane Inn
202 King St 29401
866-720-2940 843-720-2600
Lisa Anderson

165-325 BB
27 rooms, 27 pb
Most CC, *Rated*, •
C-yes/S-no/P-no/H-yes

Full breakfast
Bar service, complimentary
wine
Sitting room, suites available,
babysitters, hot tubs,
conference facility

This Victorian inn on quiet pedestrian lane was built in 1870 by Confederate blockade runner John Rugheimer. Furnished with antiques & historically accurate reproductions.
✉ landerson@charminginns.com 🌐 www.fultonlaneinn.com

The Indigo Inn
8 Cumberland St. 29401
800-845-7639 843-577-5900
Ignatius Nazareth

139-239 BB
40 rooms, 40 pb
Most CC
C-yes/S-ltd/P-ltd/H-ltd

Continental plus breakfast
Late afternoon hors
d'oeuvres and beverages

The Charleston Inn of distinction offers superior accommodations and lodging in the heart of the city's historic district featuring 19th century style with 21st century comfort.
✉ info@indigoinn.com 🌐 www.indigoinn.com

The Jasmine House
64 Hasell St. 29401
800-845-7639 843-577-5900
Ignatius Nazareth

149-316 BB
11 rooms, 11 pb
Most CC
S-no/P-no/H-no

Continental plus breakfast

The Jasmine House offers luxurious accommodations in a Southern Style. Within walking distance to the bustling City Market and surrounded by Charleston's finest restaurants, specialty shops and historic sights.
✉ info@jasminehouseinn.com 🌐 www.jasminehouseinn.com

John Rutledge House
116 Broad St 29401
866-720-2609 843-723-7999
Kathy Leslie

215-405 BB
19 rooms, 19 pb
Most CC, *Rated*, •
C-yes/S-ltd/P-no/H-yes

Continental breakfast
Afternoon iced tea, evening
sherry and brandy
Parlor room, concierge,
turndown service,
babysitters, whirlpools

John Rutledge, a signer of the US Constitution, built this elegant home in 1763. Visit and relive history. Downtown location near shopping & historic sites.
✉ kleslie@chaminginns.com 🌐 www.johnrutledgehouseinn.com

CHARLESTON

King George IV Inn
32 George St 29401
888-723-1667 843-723-9339
Terry & Debra Flowers

89-225 BB
10 rooms, 8 pb
Most CC, *Rated*, •
C-ltd/S-no/P-no/H-ltd

Southern style/stuffed
croissants
Refreshments are available
all day in the Breakfast
Room.
Three levels of porches, off
street parking. Cable TV and
refrigerators in every room.

A four story Federal style home furnished in antiques, originally the 1790's home of a Charleston journalist & Jeffersonian politician, Peter Freneau. All rooms have decorative fireplaces, hardwood floors, high ceilings with moldings.
✉ info@kinggeorgeiv.com ○ www.kinggeorgeiv.com

Kings Courtyard Inn
198 King St 29401
866-720-2949 843-723-7000
Lisa Anderson

150-300 BB
41 rooms, 41 pb
Most CC, *Rated*, •
C-yes/S-ltd/P-no/H-yes

Continental breakfast
Afternoon wine and sherry,
turndown, wine tasting
Sitting room, parking
available, hot tub,
conference room

Located in the heart of the Historic District and surrounded by countless interesting boutiques and antique shops, it is a mere stroll from the famous harbor, historic homes and attractions.
✉ landerson@charminginns.com ○ www.kingscourtyardinn.com

Lavender and Lace
136 Tradd St 29401
843-723-8968
Judy Brown

99-210 BB
3 rooms, 3 pb
Cash, Checks
C-yes/S-no/P-no/H-ltd

Continental plus breakfast
Bicycles available to tour
historic Charleston

Come and be pampered! This 1870 Victorian painted lady has been lovingly restored to create the inviting ambience of past splendor. Fresh baked pastries abound. Located in the true historic district, surrounded by beautiful homes and gardens.
✉ sitpark@aol.com

Palmer Home
5 E Battery 29401
843-853-1574
Francess Palmer

200-425 BB
5 rooms, 5 pb
Visa, MC, AmEx, *Rated*
C-ltd/S-no/P-ltd/H-no

Full breakfast
Thurs Continental breakfast,
Full other days. Wine &
Cheese served in the
afternoon.
Sitting room, piazzas, historic
district, pool, parking, wine
& cheese

Enjoy a room with a view. One of the fifty famous homes in the city; furnished in period antiques; piazzas overlook harbor & Fort Sumter where the Civil War began.
✉ palmerbnb@aol.com ○ www.palmerhomebb.com

Palmer's Pinckney Inn
19 Pinckney St 29401
866-722-1733 843-722-1733
Cindy Brunell

150-250 BB
5 rooms, 5 pb
Visa, MC, AmEx
C-ltd/S-ltd/P-yes/H-ltd

Continental breakfast
Homemade cookies and
muffins, lemonade & soft
drinks are available anytime,
am or pm!
Free off street parking, gas
fireplaces, Jacuzzi tubs,
concierge services

Centrally located in the historic Market area in downtown Charleston, within walking distance to shops and restaurants. Five bedrooms with private baths, two with Jacuzzi tubs, four with fireplaces.
✉ pinckneyinn@comcast.net ○ www.pinckneyinn.com

CHARLESTON

The Thomas Lamboll House B&B
19 King St 29401
888-874-0793 843-723-3212
Marie & Emerson Read

135-195 BB
2 rooms, 2 pb
Visa, MC
C-ltd/S-no/P-no/H-no

Continental plus breakfast
Tennis and golf nearby, off-street parking

Built in 1735 in the historic district of Charleston. Bedrooms have queen size beds, private baths and French doors leading to the piazza.
✉ lamboll@aol.com ◑ www.Lambollhouse.com/home.htm

Two Meeting Street Inn B&B
2 Meeting St 29401
888-723-7322 843-723-7322
Pete & Jean Spell

219-465 BB
9 rooms, 9 pb
Cash, Checks, *Rated*
C-ltd/S-no/P-no/H-no
Closed December 24 – 26

Full breakfast
Low country afternoon tea, evening sherry
Free WiFi, concierge, fireplaces, wrap-around verandah, gardens, waterfront, antiques, private porch

A romantic b&b located in the historic district of Charleston, South Carolina. A full breakfast, afternoon tea and evening sherry are included in each night stay. Gardens, wraparound porches, elegant rooms and view of the water are luxurious.
✉ innkeeper2meetst@bellsouth.net ◑ www.twomeetingstreet.com

Wentworth Mansion
149 Wentworth St 29401
888-466-1886 843-853-1886
Jennifer Morgan

295-720 BB
21 rooms, 21 pb
Most CC, *Rated*, •
C-yes/S-ltd/P-yes/H-yes

European buffet breakfast
Afternoon welcome with wine and sherry
Bar service, sitting room, library, suites, cable TV, fireplaces, conference, wireless Internet, spa

This world-class AAA 5-diamond hotel is furnished with antiques and has original fireplaces and crystal chandeliers. Beautifully renovated, it is located in the heart of downtown Historic District.
✉ jmorgan@charminginns.com ◑ www.wentworthmansion.com

CONWAY

The Cypress Inn
16 Elm St 29526
800-575-5307 843-248-8199
Carol & Hugh Archer, Anne &
George Bullock

130-225 BB
11 rooms, 11 pb
Visa, MC, AmEx,
Rated, •
C-ltd/S-no/P-no/H-yes

Full breakfast
Snacks, bottled water, soda, iced tea, lemonade, wine, and beer.
Jacuzzi, heat/air, plush robes, TV/VCR, phones with dataports & voice mail, WiFi

The Cypress Inn is tucked away in the charming town of Conway, SC, just 12 miles from Myrtle Beach. Near golfing, shopping, beach and great restaurants. Voted the "Most Elegant" on the SC Coast by Arrington's Inn Traveler.
✉ info@acypressinn.com ◑ www.acypressinn.com

The Moore Farm House B&B
3423 Hwy 319 29526
866-MOORE BB 843-365-7479
Harry & Cathy Pinner

95-155 BB
4 rooms, 4 pb
Visa, MC
C-ltd/S-no/P-no/H-no

Full breakfast
Welcome drinks & cookies at check-in, guest fridge with free drinks and snacks
WiFi connection, ceiling fans, TV & DVD, plush terrycloth robes, whirlpool tubs, library, pool table

The Moore Farm House Bed & Breakfast continues a long tradition of warm hospitality in a rural setting, minutes from the charming old river town of Conway & 15 miles from Myrtle Beach.
✉ info@TheMooreFarmHouse.com ◑ www.TheMooreFarmHouse.com

FOLLY BEACH

Water's Edge Inn
79 W 2nd St 29439
800-738-0884 843-588-9800
Paul Lauer

199-279 BB
8 rooms, 8 pb
Visa, MC, AmEx
C-ltd/S-ltd/P-no

Continental breakfast
Complimentary bottled
water and other beverages,
cocktails and light hors
d'oeuvres
Fireplaces, down comforters,
plasma flat screen TV, iPod
ports, wireless telephone &
Internet

Nestled on the scenic marsh and just two short blocks from the pristine beaches of the Atlantic Ocean, Water's Edge offers a truly unique experience like no other in the area. Many extras invite you to relax, unwind and enjoy your surroundings.
info@innatfollybeach.com   www.innatfollybeach.com

GEORGETOWN

Harbor House B&B
15 Cannon St 29440
877-511-0101 843-546-6532
Meg Tarbox

150-185 BB
4 rooms, 4 pb
Visa, MC, *Rated*, •
S-ltd/P-no/H-no

Full South Carolina breakfast
afternoon refreshments of
shrimp or crab dip,
complimentary wine, beer,
soft drinks, and juices
Bicycles, fireplaces, cable
TV, waterfront,
accommodates business
travelers

Harbor House is the only waterfront bed and breakfast in Georgetown, SC. Enjoy the breezes from the harbor on our porch. Stroll through the historic district and dine on the waterfront.
info@harborhousebb.com   www.harborhousebb.com

Mansfield Plantation B&B
1776 Mansfield Rd 29440
866-717-1776 843-546-6961
Kathryn Green

150-200 BB
9 rooms, 9 pb
Most CC, •
C-yes/S-ltd/P-yes/H-no
German

Full breakfast
Dinner by reservation
Sitting room, library, suites,
fireplaces, boat dock, pets
welcome

Historic Antebellum plantation house & guesthouses nestled amid moss-laden oaks, marshes & 900 private acres. Enjoy antique furnishings, paintings, collectibles; hammocks, swings, & bird watching.
mightymansfield@aol.com   www.mansfieldplantation.com

GREENVILLE

Pettigru Place
302 Pettigru St 29601
877-362-4644 864-242-4529
Lori Donaldson

119-199 BB
5 rooms, 5 pb
Most CC, *Rated*, •
C-ltd/S-no/P-no/H-no

Full gourmet breakfast
Snacks, wine and cheese, tea
service
Free wireless high speed
Internet; suites, fireplace,
cable TV, conferences

Voted Greenville's Favorite B&B, one of Nation's Top 3 for Business; in peaceful, tree-lined, Historic District, an easy stroll to 50 restaurants, Theater & Business District. Free wireless Internet.
info@pettigruplace.com   www.pettigruplace.com

GREER

Candleberry Inn & Spa
105 Marshland Ln 29650
864-201-1411
Elaine Kelly Hufstetler

110-160 BB
5 rooms, 5 pb
Most CC, •
C-ltd/S-no/P-ltd/H-yes

Full breakfast
Snacks & refreshments.
Candlelight dinners
available.
Day spa, library, hair salon

Candleberry Inn is a newer Cape Cod-style home on 1.7 landscaped acres east of Greenville, just 3 miles from the airport. Offering a country setting with city conveniences, an ideal location for weddings, retreats, reunions & special events.
info@candleberryinn.us   www.candleberryinn.us

LANDRUM

Country Mouse Inn
120 North Trade Ave 29356
866-339-8701 864-457-4061
Sheri Britt-Rogers & Barbara
Pierce-Britt

95-165 BB
5 rooms, 5 pb
Most CC
C-yes/S-no/P-yes/H-ltd

Full breakfast
Wireless Internet, am/fm
radio alarm clock, business
center, meeting room,
concierge

*Enjoy the beautiful view of Hogback Mountain rocking away on the front porch of our 1857
Antebellum home. A unique B&B offering the pleasures of home to pleasure and business
travelers.*

✉ elchilerojo1@aol.com ○ www.countrymouseinn.com

The Red Horse Inn
45 Winston Chase Court 29356
864-895-4968
Mary Wolters

175-315 BB
12 rooms, 12 pb
Visa, MC, Disc, •
C-ltd/S-ltd/P-ltd/H-ltd

Continental plus breakfast
Each cottage has a kitchen.
Don't want to go out to eat?
Enjoy a pizza brought to your
room!
Dining area, living room,
fireplace, bedroom, bath,
sitting area, TV, A/C

*This romantic couples retreat is great for romantic winery getaways and some of the best
romantic vacations ever. Situated on 190 rolling acres, in the midst of horse country with
extraordinary mountain views.*

✉ theredhorseinn@aol.com ○ www.theredhorseinn.com

LATTA

**Abingdon Manor Inn &
Restaurant**
307 Church St 29565
888-752-5090 843-752-5090
Michael & Patty Griffey

175-210 BB
7 rooms, 7 pb
Most CC, *Rated*, •
C-ltd/S-ltd/P-no/H-no

Full breakfast
Fine dining, full service
liquor, beer & wine. AAA 4
Diamond rating
Sitting rooms, library, suites,
turndown service, cable TV

*Experience the grandeur of Abingdon Manor. The only luxury inn (AAA-4 diamond) with
such close proximity to I-95 in Georgia or the Carolinas (5 miles east). Historic, elegant,
and comfortable.* ✉ abingdon@bellsouth.net ○ www.abingdonmanor.com

LYMAN

Walnut Lane Inn
110 Ridge Rd 29365
800-949-4686 864-949-7230
Hoyt Dottry & David Ades

125-155 BB
6 rooms, 6 pb
Most CC, •
C-ltd/S-ltd/P-ltd/H-ltd

Full breakfast
Complimentary evening
dessert with tea, coffee or
wine upon request. Always a
bottomless cookie jar
FREE wireless Internet,
weddings catering, country
setting, but minutes to
Greenville & Spartanburg

*As you while away the hours of the evening, sit and relax with your favorite beverage or
take tea in the front parlor. A complimentary dessert is always a true delight, especially
when shared over conversation with other guests . . .*

✉ info@walnutlaneinn.com ○ www.walnutlaneinn.com

MT PLEASANT

Old Village Post House
101 Pitt St. 29464
800-549-POST 843-388-8935
Lee Cohen

145-195 BB
6 rooms, 6 pb
Most CC
C-ltd/S-no/P-no/H-ltd

Full breakfast
Full service
Tavern/Restaurant on site.
Wireless high-speed Internet
access, cable TV, telephone,
whirlpool tub, hair dryer,
irons

*Offering travelers gracious and inviting accommodations set in the heart of a quaint,
historic fishing community. Minutes from downtown Charleston or the beaches on Sullivan's Island and the Isle of Palms.*

✉ Lcohen@mavericksouthernkitchens.com
○ www.mavericksouthernkitchens.com/ovph/index.html

MYRTLE BEACH

Serendipity Inn	55-149 BB	Continental plus breakfast
407 N 71st Ave 29572	15 rooms, 15 pb	Pool, hot tub, grill, garden
800-762-3229 843-449-5268	Most CC, *Rated*	room, living room, kitchen,
Kay & Phil Mullins	C-yes/S-no/P-no/H-yes	Internet access

Unique and secluded, this Spanish Mission-style inn offers a totally different approach to beach accommodations.
✉ serendipity-inn@worldnet.att.net ◗ www.serendipityinn.com

PAWLEYS ISLAND

Litchfield Plantation	230-635 BB	Full breakfast
Kings River Rd 29585	32 rooms, 32 pb	Fine dining restaurant on the
800-869-1410 843-237-9121	Most CC, *Rated*, •	premises, access to fully-
Louise Fitzpatrick	C-ltd/S-no/P-no/H-no	equipped kitchen
	German	Pool, concierge service, day-use beach-house, private baths, cable TV, telephones, data port

Litchfield Plantation is an extraordinary retreat on a 1750s coastal rice plantation. Meticulously transformed into a country inn, with some of the most exceptional accommodations you will ever encounter.
✉ vacation@litchfieldplantation.com ◗ www.litchfieldplantation.com

Sea View Inn	190-275 AP	Full breakfast
414 Myrtle Ave 29585	20 rooms, 20 pb	Ask for details on menus for
843-237-4253	Cash, Checks, *Rated*	late afternoon and evening
Sassy & Brian Henry	C-yes/S-no/P-no/H-ltd	meals
		Overhead fan, ocean/marsh views, private hot water beach showers, living rooms, beachfront property

Are you looking for an oceanfront inn? Sea View Inn is on a private beach with the ocean on one side and a pristine salt marsh on the other. Sea View inn offers the ultimate beach vacation that is truly a step back in time. Barefoot freedom at its best!
✉ seaviewinn@sc.rr.com ◗ www.seaviewinn.net/

SUMMERVILLE

Flowertown B&B	100-145 BB	Continental breakfast
710 S Main St 29483	4 rooms, 4 pb	Complimentary drinks
843-851-1058	Visa, MC, AmEx	Sitting room, fireplace, cable
Veronique & Gregory Elam	C-ltd/S-no/P-no/H-no	TV, computer, wireless
	French	Internet access

Historic Victorian house, c. 1889, with beautiful southern porches, bountiful gardens, pond and cottage. Across from beautiful azalea park in historic district. Downtown Charleston 20 minutes away. Beaches, lakes, golf, plantations nearby.
✉ innkeeper@flowertownbandb.com ◗ www.flowertownbandb.com

Kings Inn B&B	159-189 BB	Full breakfast
207 Central Ave 29483	5 rooms, 5 pb	Check-in snacks, afternoon
877-486-0419 843-486-0419	Visa, MC, AmEx	tea, dessert, fruit, non-
Kristan Sagliocco	C-yes/S-ltd/P-ltd/H-ltd	alcoholic beverage, wine & cheese
		Pool, bikes/surrey, bridal suite with whirlpool bath, concierge and turndown available

Gorgeous 1872 Historic Home steps away from downtown Summerville. Only 23 miles to Charleston, SC, minutes from plantations, the airport and attractions! Bridal and 2-bedroom family suites available. Private parties, meetings & intimate weddings welcome.
✉ kristanbb@hotmail.com ◗ www.kingsinnsummerville.com

SUMMERVILLE————————————————————————

| **Linwood Historic Home & Gardens**
200 S Palmetto 29483
843-871-2620
Linda & Peter Shelbourne | 75-175 EP
3 rooms, 3 pb
Visa, MC
C-ltd/S-ltd/P-no/H-ltd | Pool, A/C, some rooms with fireplaces |

Experience Linwood Historic Home and Garden—a sanctuary from the hustle-bustle, cares and concerns of the world.
✉ linwoodbb@aol.com

| **The Pink Dolphin B&B**
301 E Richardson Ave 29483
843-821-0232
Ken & Dianne Thomas | 87-117 BB
3 rooms, 3 pb
Visa, MC
C-ltd/S-ltd/P-ltd/H-ltd | Full Southern Breakfast
Complimentary welcome beverage, coffee/tea service to the room
Jacuzzi baths, luxurious robes, free wireless Internet, in house massage, meditation room |

From the full Southern Breakfast to the Tiptoe Turndown Service in the evening, we strive to make you feel pampered and at home. Just two blocks from Summerville's quaint Main Street, guests have an easy stroll to the Historic district.
✉ seaandbreeze@earthlink.net ○ www.thepinkdolphin.com

| **Price House Cottage B&B**
224 Sumter Ave 29483
843-871-1877
Jennifer & David Price | 165 BB
1 rooms, 1 pb
Visa, MC, AmEx
C-ltd/S-ltd/P-ltd/H-ltd | Full gourmet breakfast on weekends
Kitchen stocked with soft drinks, juice & teas
Tennis court, Jacuzzi, fireplace, cable TV, complimentary high speed Internet access, CD player |

Restored 1812 servants' quarters, gourmet continental breakfast in cottage weekdays, full gourmet breakfast by candlelight chandelier in Main House weekends. Luxurious appointments & decor in Summerville's historic district.
✉ phcbb@knology.net ○ www.pricehousecottage.com

| **Woodlands Resort & Inn**
125 Parsons Rd 29483
800-774-9999 843-875-2600
Marty Wall | 195-850 EP
19 rooms, 19 pb
Most CC, *Rated*, ●
C-yes/S-ltd/P-yes/H-no
German, French, Spanish | Breakfast, lunch and dinner served in the dining room (closed Sunday nights), bar, afternoon tea
24-hr. concierge srvc, day spa, bikes, clay tennis cts, outdoor heated pool, croquet, walking trails |

A step ahead in luxury, and a step back in time. Nestled in the splendor of palmettos, moss-draped oak, and towering magnolias is a place of elegance, comfort, and gracious hospitality.
✉ reservations@woodlandsinn.com ○ www.woodlandsinn.com

WINNSBORO————————————————————————

| **Honeysuckle Acres**
70 Honeysuckle Ln 29180
800-387-1112 803-635-7583
Harold and Patricia Frish | 90-130 BB
3 rooms, 2 pb
Visa, MC, *Rated*
C-ltd/S-no/P-no/H-no
Italian, French | Full breakfast
Epicurean picnic baskets available, complimentary soft drink/wine
Cable TV/VCR/DVD, in-room CD player, library, turndown service, picnic grove with outside fireplace |

Honeysuckle Acres is a massive four-column Colonial home built in 1927. The house is reminiscent of an Antebellum mansion. It is set on seven park-like acres and is complete with the original stables and the original carriage stone in front.
✉ honeysuckleacresbb@yahoo.com

South Dakota

CANOVA

Skoglund Farm B&B
24375 438th Ave 57321
605-247-3445
Alden & Delores Skoglund

40-75 MAP
4 rooms
Rated
C-yes/S-ltd/P-yes/H-no
Swedish

Full breakfast
Family-style homecooked
meals
Sitting room, piano, bicycles,
newspaper, A/C

Enjoy an overnight stay on a real farm on the South Dakota prairie. Return to your childhood—animals, country walking, homecooked meals.
✉ PASkoglund@excite.com ◐ www.SkoglundFarm.com

CUSTER

Custer Mansion
35 Centennial Dr 57730
877-519-4948 605-673-3333
Bob & Pat Meakim

65-130 BB
5 rooms, 5 pb
Visa, MC, *Rated*, •
C-yes/S-no/P-no/H-no

Full breakfast
Afternoon tea, full cookie jar
with refreshments
Library, bikes, tennis,
horseback riding, golf
nearby, year round hot tub,
wireless Internet

Historic 1891 Victorian on 1 acre in heart of beautiful and scenic Black Hills. The area is famous for its breath taking monuments, and Custer mansion is well known for providing Western hospitality, & delicious, homebaked food.
✉ cusmanbb@gwtc.net ◐ www.custermansionbb.com

Strutton Inn B&B
12046 US Hwy 16 57730
605-673-2395
Cary & Denice Strutton

99-149 BB
9 rooms, 9 pb
Visa, MC, *Rated*, •
C-ltd/S-ltd/P-no/H-ltd
May thru October

Full breakfast
Complimentary evening
snacks are available with
coffee, cappuccino, hot
chocolate and lemonade
Jacuzzis, fireplace, satellite
dish, turndown service with
mint on pillow

Elegant romantic hideaway. Country Victorian home on four acres with veranda, gazebo, antiques. Nine rooms, each with private bath, whirlpool tub, king bed.
✉ struttoninn@gwtc.net ◐ www.struttoninn.com

DEADWOOD

Black Hills Hideaway
11744 Hideaway Rd 57732
877-500-4433 605-578-3054
Kathy & Ned Bode

119-189 BB
8 rooms, 8 pb
Visa, MC, Disc, *Rated*,
•
C-ltd/S-ltd/P-no/H-ltd

Full breakfast
Lunch/dinner (fee), snacks,
complimentary wine
Sitting rooms, bikes,
Jacuzzis, fireplaces, decks,
hot tubs, conferences

Mountain inn with cathedral ceiling & wood interior, tucked in National Forest. You'll be pampered on 67 wooded acres with fresh mountain air, the aroma & whispering of pines, peace & solitude.
✉ hideaway@enetis.net ◐ www.enetis.net/~hideaway

GARY

Pleasant Valley Lodge
18278 SD Hwy 22 57237
605-272-5614
Steven & Sharon Maas

55-95 BB
10 rooms, 8 pb
Most CC
C-yes/S-no/P-ltd/H-ltd

Continental breakfast
Sitting room, library,
Jacuzzis, fireplaces, cable
TV, accommodations for
business travel

Lodge and cabins located in beautiful wooded valley. Some rooms with private baths and antiques. Quiet, serene rooms with decks and great views.
✉ sdsteverman@yahoo.com

HILL CITY

Coyote Blues Village B&B
23165 Horsemans Ranch Rd
57745
888-253-4477 605-574-4477
Christine & Hans-Peter Streich

65-155 BB
10 rooms, 10 pb
Most CC, *Rated*, •
C-yes/S-ltd/P-ltd/H-ltd
German, French

Swiss Specialty Breakfast
Espresso, cappuccino, tea,
dinner, vegetarian dining
Satellite TV, wireless
Internet, fridge, private hot
tubs and patios

European styled bed and breakfast, tucked away on 30 wooded acres north of Hill City. Swiss specialty breakfast. Patios and hot tubs. Near Mount Rushmore, Crazy Horse, and Custer State Park. Located in the Black Hills, South Dakota.
✉ coyotebb@wildblue.net 🌐 www.coyotebluesvillage.com

PIERRE

River Place Inn
109 River Pl 57501
605-224-8589
Connie Jacobs

75-125 BB
4 rooms, 3 pb
Visa, MC, *Rated*, •
C-ltd/S-ltd/P-ltd/H-no

Full breakfast
Snacks, sodas
Cable TV, wireless Internet,
accommodate business
travelers

Beautiful three story inn on the Lewis & Clark Trail. Rent a two person kayak from the inn and tour the Missouri River. ✉ cjjacobs@pie.midco.net

RAPID CITY

Abend Haus & Audrie's
23029 Thunderhead Falls
57702
605-342-7788
Audry Kuhnhauser

185-210 BB
7 rooms, 7 pb
Cash, *Rated*
S-no/P-no/H-no
May 1–Nov 1

Full breakfast
Complimentary snacks
Restaurant nearby, trout
fishing, hiking, bicycles, hot
tubs

The ultimate in charm and Old World hospitality. Our spacious cottages are furnished with comfortable European antiques. All feature a private entrance, private bath, patio, hot tub and full Black Hill's style breakfast. 🌐 www.audriesbb.com

Willow Springs Cabins
11515 Sheridan Lake Rd 57702
605-342-3665
Joyce & Russell Payton

145-190 BB
2 rooms, 2 pb
Rated
C-ltd/S-no/P-no/H-no

Full gourmet breakfast
Coffee, tea, hot chocolate,
popcorn, cookies. Outdoor
gas grill provide for your use.
TV/DVD, stereo, fridge,
microwave, outdoor hot
tubs, hiking trails, mountain
stream, itinerary plans

Privacy at its best! Secluded, antique filled, log cabins in the beautiful Black Hills National Forest. Great views, gourmet breakfasts in your cabin, private outdoor hot tubs. A relaxing romantic retreat! Willow Springs requires a minimum two night stay.
✉ wilosprs@rapidnet.com 🌐 www.willowspringscabins.com

SPEARFISH

Yesterday's Inn
735 8th St 57783
866-898-1616 605-644-0210
Bert Oxborrow & Linda
Springer

75-250 BB
7 rooms, 3 pb
Visa, MC
C-ltd/S-no/P-no/H-ltd

Full breakfast
Soft drinks and snacks are
provided
WiFi

A beautifully appointed Victorian home with beautiful grounds, gazebos, fish pond, cable TV, wireless Internet, fireplaces. Breakfasts and desserts are delicious. Complimentary soft drinks and snacks are provided. Open year round.
✉ yesterdaysinn@spe.midco.net 🌐 www.yesterdaysinn.net

WEBSTER

Lakeside Farm
13476 437th Ave 57274
605-486-4430
Glenn & Joy Hagen

60 BB
3 rooms, 2 pb
Rated
C-yes/S-no/P-no/H-no

Full breakfast
Tea or coffee, cookies,
snacks
Sitting room, bicycles,
museum, factory outlet

Sample country life with us. A family-owned farm. Northeastern SD lakes area. Fresh air, open spaces. Fresh milk, homemade cinnamon rolls. ✉ gjhagen@venturecomm.net

Tennessee

The Brentwood B&B
6304 Murray Ln 37027
800-332-4640 615-373-4627
Ly Anne Thorman

145-250 BB
6 rooms, 6 pb
Visa, MC, AmEx, *Rated*
C-ltd/S-no/P-no/H-ltd

Full Gourmet breakfast
Snacks
Parlor, Garden Room, Dining
Room, spas, suites,
fireplaces, cable TV, fax, DSL

The Brentwood is a luxurious country B&B in one of Nashville's finest neighborhoods. This 5 acre estate of casual elegance is convenient to Nashville & Franklin's many attractions while retaining the quiet solitude of the country.
✉ info@brentwoodbandb.com ✪ www.brentwoodbandb.com

Mayor's Mansion Inn
801 Vine St 37403
888-446-6569 423-265-5000
Cindi & Mark Ladd,
Owners/Melanie Walker, GM

160-295 BB
11 rooms, 11 pb
Most CC, *Rated*, •
C-ltd/S-no/P-no/H-yes

Full breakfast
Hors d'oeuvres & late night
desserts on weekends,
cookies, early morning
coffee
Luxurious monogrammed
robes, irons/ironing boards,
TV/VCR, CD alarm clocks

The award-winning Mayor's Mansion Inn is a luxurious Victorian Romanesque mansion, with 11 rooms, originally built by the mayor of Chattanooga in 1889.
✉ info@mayorsmansioninn.com ✪ www.mayorsmansioninn.com

Magnolia House B&B
Luxury Suites
1231 Madison St 37040
931-552-4545
Margaret Welker

119-129 BB
2 rooms, 2 pb
Most CC
C-yes/S-no/P-ltd/H-no

Full breakfast
Wi Fi, fax, copy machine,

Located in the historic district of Clarksville, Tennessee, one mile from downtown. 1940's Georgian style home. Featured in newspaper articles and home tours. Two luxury suites await you! Ft. Campbell is nearby, plus Ft. Donelson Civil War Park.
✉ margaretwelker@aol.com ✪ www.magnoliabb.com

Candlewycke Manor
500 Davis Ln SW 37312
423-339-3232
Wacoe Lineberry; Herschel &
Regenia Collier

95-125 BB
3 rooms, 3 pb
Visa, MC, AmEx
C-yes/S-no/P-no/H-ltd

Bountiful Southern breakfast
Homemade evening desserts
Reading nook, deck, swing,
croquet, horseshoes

Located in Cleveland, TN, Candlewycke's guests enjoy the quiet of the country, and still have the luxury of being a few minutes from town. Quaint and comfortable—it feels like home, without the work!
✉ info@candlewyckemanor.com ✪ www.candlewyckemanor.com

COSBY

Creekwalk Inn at	95-235 BB	Gourmet Breakfast
Whisperwood Farm	9 rooms, 9 pb	Dinner by reservation. Picnic
166 Middle Creek Rd 37722	Most CC, *Rated*, •	lunches by request (extra
800-962-2246 423-487-4000	C-ltd/S-no/P-no/H-ltd	fee).
Janice & Tifton Haynes		Romantic and casual,
		romance packages, massage,
		nature trails

Romantic award winning log home bed and breakfast in the Smoky Mountains of East Tennessee near Gatlinburg. Our Smoky Mountain bed and breakfast serves gourmet food and offers romance packages, whirlpools, fireplaces, and fine dining. Honeymoon packages.
✉ janice@creekwalkinn.com ○ www.creekwalkinn.com

DANDRIDGE

Mountain Harbor Inn	129-599 BB	Bountiful Breakfast Buffet
1199 Hwy 139 37725	15 rooms, 15 pb	Intimate candlelight dessert
877-379-1313 865-397-1313	Most CC	Kitchenette, TV, microwave,
Billy R. Inmon	C-yes/S-ltd/P-yes/H-yes	refrigerator, coffee maker,
		fireplace, hot tub, Wifi

Mountain Harbor Inn Resort on the Lake offers uniquely luxurious, resort accommodations near Gatlinburg and Pigeon Forge Tennessee with a beautiful view of Douglas Lake caressed by the majesty of the Great Smoky Mountains. A perfect romantic getaway.
✉ e-mail@mountainharborinn.com ○ www.mountainharborinn.com

DUCKTOWN

The Company House Inn	89-99 BB	Full breakfast
125 Main St 37326	7 rooms, 7 pb	Soft drinks, tea, coffee &
800-343-2909 423-496-5634	Visa, MC, *Rated*, •	sweets
Margaret Tonkin & Mike	C-ltd/S-ltd/P-ltd/H-no	Deck overlooking water
Fabian		garden, rocking chair front
		porch, selection of books,
		piano, big screen TV

Circa 1850 inn located in the Copper Basin Area of the Southern Appalachian Mountains near the Ocoee River Olympic Whitewater Center. The breakfasts get rave reviews. Enjoy the big screen TV in the parlor or the rocking chair front porch.
✉ companyhouse@etcmail.com ○ www.companyhousebandb.com

ERIN

Five Oaks B&B	75 BB	Full breakfast
51 Averitt Dr 37061	4 rooms	Afternoon tea & snacks,
931-289-5533	Cash, Checks	refreshments included
Margaret Mann	C-ltd/S-ltd/P-no/H-ltd	Cable TV, refrigerator, ceiling
		fan, clock radio, coffeemaker,
		turn-down service, WiFi

Historic lodging, fine dining & a taste of Ireland are all genuinely offered at this 19th-century Victorian home that sits on the hill above the village of Erin.
✉ fiveoaksbandb@peoplestell.net

GATLINBURG

Berry Springs Lodge	149-249 BB	Bountiful Breakfast Served
2149 Seaton Springs Rd 37862	11 rooms, 11 pb	24 hour complimentary
888-760-8297 865-908-7935	Visa, MC, Disc, •	beverages & snacks, nightly
Patrick & Sue Eisert	C-ltd/S-no/P-no/H-yes	signature desserts
		In-room Jacuzzis, turndown
		service, massage service,
		balconies, spectacular
		sunrises and sunsets, TV

Newly built Lodge. Relaxing luxury & first class service. Close to Dollywood; minutes to hiking trails, shopping & horseback riding. Romantic rooms & suites, some with Jacuzzi. Spa services.
✉ stay@berrysprings.com ○ www.berrysprings.com

GATLINBURG————————————————————————————

Buckhorn Inn
2140 Tudor Mtn Rd 37738
866-941-0460 865-436-4668
Lee & John Mellor

115-295 BB
24 rooms, 24 pb
Most CC, *Rated*
C-ltd/S-ltd/P-no/H-yes
Spanish, French, Latin

Full breakfast
Dinner, sack lunches,
afternoon refreshments
Fireplaces, Jacuzzis, Fitness
Center, coffeemakers, nature
trail, library, bathrobes, WiFi

Set on a ridge facing spectacular views of the mountains, Buckhorn Inn is the area's most historic inn and the only inn in the area that serves dinner every evening.
✉ info@buckhorninn.com ◆ www.buckhorninn.com

Eight Gables Inn
219 N Mountain Trl 37738
800-279-5716 865-430-3344
Penelope Binning

140-270 BB
19 rooms, 19 pb
Most CC, *Rated*, •
C-ltd/S-ltd/P-no/H-no

Full breakfast
Afternoon tea, evening
dessert, complimentary
coffee, tea, non-alcoholic
beverages & bottled water
All rooms have cable TV, CD
& video players, bathrobes,
imported soaps, concierge
services & WiFi

Minutes from Gatlinburg and Pigeon Forge; our casual elegance will win you over. Our unique charm, warm hospitality and gracious service are the perfect compliment to your stay here in the mountains. 19 luxurious rooms and suites. AAA 4 Diamond Award.
✉ inquiries@eightgables.com ◆ www.eightgables.com

Four Sisters Inn
425 Stuart Ln 37738
866-914-3687 865-430-8411
Jackie Price

125-220 BB
6 rooms, 6 pb
Most CC
C-yes/S-ltd/P-no/H-yes

Continental breakfast on
request.
Guest rooms phones, Cable
TV with HBO, Cable Internet
and/or WiFi access, free
parking downtown

Come experience the best small inn in town. The Four Sisters' Inn is a luxuriously appointed six-room inn located at the end of a quiet wooded street. Private, quiet, yet close to everything.
✉ jackie@4sistersinn.com ◆ www.4sistersinn.com

The Foxtrot B&B
1520 Garrett Lane 37738
888-436-3033 865-436-3033
Bob & Shirley Price

145-185 BB
4 rooms, 4 pb
Most CC
C-ltd/S-no/P-no/H-ltd
French

3 course gourmet breakfast
Evening desert, 24 hour
gourmet coffee & tea service,
soft drinks & bottled water in
the room
Library with fireplace, on-
site spa services, access to
pool, tennis courts, fitness
center

Nestled in the trees at the crest of the mountain, the Foxtrot Bed and Breakfast offers 2 suites (w/ fireplaces and balconies) and 2 luxurious deluxe king rooms all with private baths (3 w/ Jacuzzi tubs) and spectacular views of the Great Smoky Mountains.
✉ information@thefoxtrot.com ◆ www.thefoxtrot.com

Laurel Springs Lodge B&B
204 Hill St 37738
888-430-9211 865-430-9211
Karen and Dan Berry

119-159 BB
5 rooms, 5 pb
Visa, MC, Disc
C-ltd/S-no/P-no/H-no
January to December

Full breakfast
Snacks
Sitting room, library,
fireplace, hot tub

Authentic 1930s mountain lodge. Nestled on a wooded hillside in Gatlinburg, an easy walk to downtown. Overlooks the Little Pigeon River.
✉ relax@laurelspringslodge.com ◆ www.laurelspringslodge.com

GREENEVILLE

Nolichuckey Bluffs	95-155 BB	Full breakfast
295 Kinser Park Ln 37743	8 rooms, 8 pb	Afternoon tea, snacks
800-842-4690 423-787-7947	Most CC, •	Library, bicycles, Jacuzzis,
Brooke & Patricia Sadler	C-yes/S-no/P-ltd/H-no	fireplaces, disc golf, retreat,
		reunions, groups

Quiet luxury cabins in a country setting. Fireplaces, full kitchens, trails, English garden and spectacular mountain and river views. Disc golf and grist mill on property.
✉ cabins@usit.net ◑ www.tennessee-cabins.com

JACKSON

Highland Place B&B Inn	145-195 BB	Full breakfast
519 N Highland Ave 38301	4 rooms, 4 pb	Gourmet, romantic or
877-614-6305 731-427-1472	Most CC, •	business dinners available
Cindy & Bill Pflaum	C-ltd/S-no/P-ltd/H-ltd	for couples and small groups
		Library, living room,
		fireplaces, high speed IP
		WiFi connection, cable TV,
		VHS players

1911 Colonial Revival mansion full of Southwestern art, handmade furniture, quality arts and crafts. Four guestrooms with queen beds, private baths, cable TV with movies and music, WiFi Internet access. Romantic and business dinners available with notice.
✉ relax@highlandplace.com ◑ www.highlandplace.com

KINGSPORT

Fox Manor Historic B&B Inn	110-150 BB	Full breakfast
1612 Watauga St 37664	6 rooms, 6 pb	Afternoon tea, desserts,
888-200-5879 423-378-3844	Most CC, *Rated*	bottomless cookie jar, fresh
Susan & Walter Halliday	S-no/P-no/H-no	homemade popcorn
		Sitting room, English pub bar,
		parlor, fireplaces, library,
		veranda, dining room,
		gazebo, WiFi, TV/DVD

Upon arrival, you will notice the original carriage steps used by passengers to disembark from their horse-drawn carriages. This is your first clue that you've arrived at a truly unique & historic inn.
✉ shalliday@foxmanor.com ◑ www.foxmanor.com

KINGSTON

Whitestone Country Inn	150-305 BB	Full breakfast
1200 Paint Rock Rd 37763	21 rooms, 21 pb	Dinner (fee)
888-247-2464 865-376-0113	Most CC, *Rated*	Whirlpool tubs, fireplaces,
Paul and Jean Cowell	C-ltd/S-no/P-no/H-yes	DVD players, conference
		center, wedding chapel

Whitestone Country Inn's 360 secluded acres on the shores of Watts Bar Lake. Views of the Smoky Mountains. Luxurious lodging, whirlpool tubs, gourmet dining. Weddings and events.
✉ moreinfo@whitestoneinn.com ◑ www.whitestoneinn.com

KNOXVILLE

Maplehurst Inn	79-249 BB	Full breakfast
800 W Hill Ave 37902	11 rooms, 11 pb	Snacks, juices, cookies, fruit
800-451-1562 865-523-7773	Visa, MC, AmEx, •	Parlour, library, suites,
Sonny & Becky Harben	C-yes/S-no/P-ltd/H-no	conference facilities,
		Penthouse with deck &
		Jacuzzi

Lovely downtown mansion overlooking the Tennessee River in historic Maplehurst Park. Walk to U.T., convention center, riverfront restaurants, museums, etc. Unique accommodations blend 18th century charm with modern amenities.
✉ themaplehurstinn@gmail.com ◑ www.maplehurstinn.com

Edgeworth Inn, Monteagle, TN

MONTEAGLE

Edgeworth Inn
#23 Reppard Ave, MSSA 37356
931-924-4000
Jeannine Clements

100-225 BB
12 rooms, 12 pb
Visa, MC, AmEx,
Rated, •
C-yes/S-no/P-yes/H-ltd
French

Full gourmet breakfast
Award winning restaurant on
site, candlelit dinner
available
Gift shop, library, verandas,
swim, hike, summer
program, family suites

Built in 1896, The Edgeworth Inn is a rambling antique-filled Queen Anne style structure with 12 guestrooms, elegantly appointed and each with its own bath. The oldest continuously operated Inn in the area, with modern conveniences.
✉ edgeworthinn@charter.net ❂ www.edgeworthinn.com

Monteagle Inn
204 W Main St 37356
931-924-3869
Jim Harmon

160-265 BB
13 rooms, 13 pb
Visa, MC, Disc, *Rated*,
•
C-ltd/S-no/P-no/H-yes

Full, hot gourmet breakfast
snacks, cheese & fruit plates
for wine; chocolates with
roses in room
Large living room, patio,
garden with gazebo, front
porch & conference room,
fireplace

Monteagle Inn is a 13-suite B&B situated atop the beautiful Cumberland Plateau in Monteagle, Tennessee. Beautifully appointed interiors, balconies, patios, courtyards, gardens, and a wonderful front porch create a comfortable European atmosphere.
✉ suites@monteagleinn.com ❂ www.monteagleinn.com

MOUNTAIN CITY

Prospect Hill B&B Inn
801 W Main St/ Hwy 67 37683
800-339-5084 423-727-0139
Robert & Judy Hotchkiss

99-240 BB
5 rooms, 5 pb
Most CC, *Rated*, •
C-yes/S-ltd/P-ltd/H-ltd

Full breakfast, always with
fruit
Snacks, chocolates,
complimentary beverages,
bottled water in the room's
snack basket.
Porch/balcony, fireplaces,
a/c, whirlpool tubs, cable TV,
garden, views, fireflies, your
concierge.

Large, comfortable, very private and luxurious rooms. Perfect for a romantic getaway or nature-lover's vacation. Elopements for 2; weddings for 100-New Wedding Room! Perfect tranquility, views. Whirlpools and fireplaces. c.1889 mansion. Relax. Reconnect.
✉ inn@prospect-hill.com ❂ www.prospect-hill.com

NASHVILLE

Daisy Hill Bed & Breakfast
2816 Blair Blvd 37212
800-239-1135 615-297-9795
Darrel, Linda & Bengson

120-175 BB
3 rooms, 3 pb
Visa, MC, AmEx
C-ltd/S-no/P-no/H-ltd

Full breakfast
Beverages & Snacks
available.
Living Room with fireplace,
observatory, library

Classic Tudor Revival Style Home, built in 1925 in Historic Hillsboro Village. Eight minutes to downtown Nashville. Six-block walk to Vanderbilt University.
✉ daisyhil@bellsouth.net ✪ www.daisyhillbedandbreakfast.com

NEWPORT

Christopher Place
1500 Pinnacles Way 37821
800-595-9441 423-623-6555
Marston Price

165-330 BB
8 rooms, 8 pb
Most CC, *Rated*, •
C-ltd/S-no/P-no/H-ltd

Full breakfast
Gourmet 4 course dinner,
picnic lunches & snacks
Swimming, tennis, sauna,
exercise room, videos,
library, fireplaces

On 200 acres near Gatlinburg in the Smoky Mountains. Voted best bed and breakfast in the area. Named one of the 10 most romantic in the country. AAA 4 Diamond. Fine dining. Luxury rooms. Personal service.
✉ stay@christopherplace.com ✪ www.christopherplace.com

ONLY

Chestnut Hill Ranch B&B
3001 Browns Bend Rd 37140
931-729-0153
Cher Boisvert-Tanley &
George Tanley

129-285 BB
3 rooms, 3 pb
Visa, MC, *Rated*
C-ltd/S-no/P-no/H-yes
Spanish, French

Full gourmet-country
breakfast
Evening beverage and
pastries. Specialty dinners,
luncheons, picnic baskets,
available with notice.
Hot tub in gazebo, Great
Room with fireplace. Private
baths, Fireplaces, Event
Center-Group events

Southern hospitality at its absolute finest. Set on 53 acres in the beautiful Duck River Valley the original farmhouse, built around 1908 has undergone recent renovation that blends the character and charm of the period with the modern comforts of today.
✉ chestnuthillranch@earthlink.net ✪ www.chestnuthillranch.com

PIGEON FORGE

Evergreen Cottage Inn
800-962-2246 423-453-4000
Janice Becker

129-189 BB
14 rooms, 14 pb
Most CC
C-ltd/S-ltd/P-ltd/H-ltd

Full breakfast
Fireplace rooms, hiking,
Jacuzzi tubs. On site wedding
chapel.

Evergreen Cottage Inn is just minutes from Dollywood and Patriot Park, city center, and the Old Mill. Bedrooms feature fireplaces and whirlpool tubs and offer unique lodging in the Smoky Mountains of Tennessee.
✉ janice@wildflowermountain.com ✪ www.evergreencottageinn.com

RED BOILING SPRINGS

Armour's Red Boiling Springs Hotel
321 E Main St 37150
615-699-2180
Dennis & Debra Emery

69-129 BB
16 rooms, 16 pb
Most CC
C-yes/S-no/P-no/H-yes

Full breakfast
Dinner available with
advance notice; full country
luncheons and dinners
available for groups of 12+
Mineral Baths, Steam Bath,
Massage by CMT (advance
notice required), Suites,
large Dining Room (80)

National Register 85 year old hotel. 14 rooms & 2 suites, furnished with antiques, & private baths. Porches with rockers on 2 levels overlooking Salt Lick Creek, WiFi, Mineral & Steam Baths available, massages available by CMT's by appointment.
✉ armourshotel@yahoo.com ✪ www.armourshotel.com

SEVIERVILLE

Blue Mountain Mist Country Inn & Cottages	115-189 BB	Full country breakfast
1811 Pullen Rd 37862	20 rooms, 20 pb	Evening desserts, soda, tea,
800-497-2335 865-428-2335	Most CC, *Rated*, •	snacks
Norman & Sarah Ball	C-yes/S-no/P-no/H-ltd	Wrap-around porch & sitting
		rooms, concierge service,
		beautiful grounds

A cozy Bed and Breakfast in the Smokies where Local Heritage, Christian Hospitality and country charm relaxes and consoles the most weary of travelers.
✉ relaxed@bluemountainmist.com ❍ www.bluemountainmist.com

Persephone's Retreat	135 BB	Full breakfast
2279 Hodges Ferry Rd 37862	5 rooms, 5 pb	Music room, living room,
865-428-3904	Visa, MC	porches, movies available,
Victoria & Rod	C-yes/S-no/P-no/H-yes	fishing

Built in 1887, this 120-year-old farmhouse is on the banks of historic French Broad River. Whether its supervised fishing, lounging in the hammock, or a fireside sing-along, families find a lot to do in-between sightseeing and nearby tourist attractions.
✉ vnichols@esper.com ❍ www.bedandbreakfast.cc

TOWNSEND

Dancing Bear Lodge	140-330 BB	Continental plus breakfast
137 Apple Valley Wy 37882	29 rooms, 29 pb	Dining room serving
800-369-0111 865-448-6000	Visa, MC, Disc	breakfast and dinner.
Matt Alexander	C-yes/S-no/P-ltd/H-yes	Featherbeds, outdoor hot
		tub, outdoor fireplace.

Reawaken your spirit by indulging in the rustic luxury of Dancing Bear Lodge and our awe-inspiring panoramas. Whether visiting the Smokies for relaxation, sport, romance or business, we inspire getaways as expansive & free-spirited as the Smokies itself.
✉ info@dancingbearlodge.com ❍ www.dancingbearlodge.com

Gracehill B&B	250-325 BB	3 Course Full Breakfast
1169 Little Round Top Wy	4 rooms, 4 pb	Complimentary stocked
37882	Visa, MC, AmEx,	snack area, coffee, tea, soda,
866-448-3070 865-448-3070	*Rated*, •	fruit drinks, bottled water
Kathleen Janke	C-ltd/S-no/P-no/H-ltd	WiFi, guest computer, Sat
		TV/VCR/DVD, fitness center,
		massage, whirlpool, steam
		shower, fireplaces

Award winning 3 yrs in a row "Best Scenic View from a B&B in the U.S.," Inn Traveler Magazine. Blount County's Bravo Award for Beautiful Gardens. 360-degree view of the Great Smoky Mountains National Park. Near Gatlinburg, Pigeon Forge, Townsend.
✉ bestview@gracehillbandb.com ❍ www.gracehillbandb.com

WARTRACE

Ledford Mill	95-125 BB	Full breakfast
1195 Shipman Creek Rd 37183	3 rooms, 3 pb	Refreshments & snacks
931-455-2546	Visa, MC	available
John & Mildred Spear	C-yes/S-no/P-ltd/H-no	Waterfalls, garden, sitting
		area, video library, antiques

Relax at historic Ledford Mill at the headwaters of Shipman's Creek, an 1884 gristmill listed on the National Register of Historic Places and the Tennessee Heritage Trail. 3 unique rooms with private baths. Waterfalls, gardens, antique shop.
✉ spears_games@msn.com

Texas

**The Sanford House Inn &
Spa**
506 N Center St 76011
877-205-4914 817-861-2129
McBerg, Inc.

179-299 BB
10 rooms, 10 pb
Most CC, *Rated*
C-ltd/S-ltd/P-no/H-yes

Full breakfast
Lunch is served Tues. – Sat.
from 11am-2pm and is open
to the public, private dining
is available
Spa, salon, dining, full bar,
weddings, receptions,
corporate meetings, socials.

Arlington's premier Bed & Breakfast, restaurant, bar, spa and event facility. Luxurious rooms and full breakfast included with your overnight stay. Courtyard weddings & receptions for groups up to 250.
✉ info@thesanfordhouse.com ◐ www.thesanfordhouse.com

1110 Carriage House Inn
1110 W 22½ St 78705
866-472-2333 512-472-2333
Tressie Damron

100-350 BB
8 rooms, 8 pb
Most CC, •
C-ltd/S-no/P-no/H-ltd

Full Breakfast or Continental
Plus
Coffee, tea; delicious treat
upon arrival. Purchase their
delicious homemade
chocolate truffles!
Private entrances, free WiFi,
Cable TV, phones, kitchens,
Jacuzzi, deck/porch, gazebo,
pond, birding

Carriage House Inn was voted one of the Top Ten Breakfasts in the USA. Organic foods are served, and the Inn can accommodate vegans, vegetarians, celiacs, and those of us that just like good food! You'll have your own private table.
✉ dcarriagehouse@aol.com ◐ www.carriagehouseinn.org

Austin Folk House
506 W 22nd St 78705
866-472-6700 512-477-9639
Sylvia Mackey

85-225 BB
9 rooms, 9 pb
Most CC
C-ltd/S-ltd/P-no/H-yes
Spanish

Full breakfast
Afternoon sweets and
evening wine
Cable TV and VCR, private
phone lines and voice mail,
robes, fine toiletries

Beautifully restored in 2001, this B&B offers historic charm without sacrificing modern comfort and convenience. Decorated with antiques and a large collection of folk art. Centrally located.
✉ sylvia@austinfolkhouse.com ◐ www.austinfolkhouse.com

The Bed Rox
5113 Doss Rd 78734
866- 249-8325 512-266-3560
Roxann Johnson

135-225 BB
4 rooms, 4 pb
Visa, MC
C-yes/S-ltd/P-yes/H-no

Continental breakfast
Texas hot tub, Internet, cable
TV, fireplace, spacious decks
& large living area

We sit on five and a half acres on Lake Travis and have three cabins that are very private. Walking paths are provided to each one and on the way you can say hi to two very loving mini donkey's Sancho and Juan. You will love it here . . .
✉ rox@thebedrox.com ◐ www.thebedrox.com

AUSTIN

Brava House B&B
1108 Blanco St 78703
866-892-5726 512-478-5034
Robin Kyle

119-169 BB
5 rooms, 5 pb
Most CC
C-yes/S-ltd/P-yes/H-yes

Continental Plus and Full
breakfast
Tea available each afternoon
Wireless Internet, TV with
cable, private phone,
hairdryers, ironing board

Brava House offers private suites located in central Austin. Minutes to State Capital, 6th Street, Convention Center and University of Texas. Antiques and fireplace suites create character and charm.
✉ robin@bravahouse.com ◔ www.bravahouse.com

Star of Texas Inn
611 W 22nd St 78705
866-472-6700 512-477-9639
Sylvia

95-225 BB
10 rooms, 10 pb
Most CC
C-ltd/S-no/P-ltd/H-ltd

Full breakfast
Wraparound porch, balcony,
high speed wireless Internet,
parlor

Star of Texas Inn is a Victorian mansion built in 1897. A relaxed and comfortable place to stay in central Austin. Near to downtown and the University of Texas.
✉ sylvia@austinfolkhouse.com ◔ www.staroftexasinn.com

BRADY

Shatzie Guest Ranch
Hwy 87 S 76825
888-991-6749 888-991-6749
Charla

350 BB
8 rooms, 6 pb
Most CC
C-yes/S-no/P-no/H-ltd

Continental plus breakfast
Cook on hand; Full Kitchen
with utensils
Family Friendly, Special
Events, BS TV/DVD/VCR,
Patio, BBQ, Fire Pit, Parking,
Laundry Fac., Jacuzzi

Want to live almost Every Texan's Dream? Try this Beautiful Ranch located in the middle of the wonderful Texas Hill Country! You will have the ranch all to yourself on 200 acres located on the San Saba River.
✉ stay@fredericksburg-lodging.com ◔ www.fredericksburg-lodging.com/Shatzie-ranch

BRAZORIA

Roses & the River
2434 Country Rd 506 77422
800-610-1070 979-798-1070
Dick & Mary Jo Hosack

150 BB
3 rooms, 3 pb
Most CC, *Rated*, •
C-ltd/S-ltd/P-no/H-no

Full breakfast
Snacks
Jacuzzis, fireplaces, cable
TV, VCRs in each room with
video library

Beautifully decorated Texas farmhouse on banks of San Bernard River, landscaped with 250 rose bushes. "You deserve a little R&R" is our motto.
✉ rosesandtheriver@yahoo.com ◔ www.rosesandtheriver.com

BRENHAM

Ant Street Inn
107 W Commerce 77833
800-805-2600 979-836-7393
Tommy & Pam Traylor

129-269 BB
15 rooms, 15 pb
Most CC, *Rated*
C-ltd/S-no/P-no/H-yes

Included is your choice from
menu
The Capital Grill located in
the inn offers lunch & dinner
everyday except Wednesday.
Rocking chairs, veranda,
courtyard garden. 2 meeting
rooms, sitting areas, wine &
beer for sale

Relax in rocking chairs on the back balcony overlooking the courtyard. Enjoy some restaurants in the historic Ant Street area or dine in the Inn at the Capital Grill with your favorite beer or wine.
✉ stay@antstreetinn.com ◔ www.antstreetinn.com

BRENHAM

The Brenham House	129-159 BB	Full gourmet breakfast
705 Clinton St 77833	4 rooms, 4 pb	Coffee and tea, sodas,
979-251-9947	Most CC	popcorn, bottled water, &
James and Susan Lopez	C-ltd/S-ltd/P-no/H-no	afternoon refreshments.
		Library, sun porch, living
		room, sitting areas
		throughout the gardens.
		Secure tickets and tee time.

The Brenham House Bed and Breakfast is a premiere Bed and Breakfast establishment. The home is surrounded by cottage gardens and is within walking distance of the Historic downtown where you can find great shopping, restaurants and theatre.
✉ brenhamhouse@sbcglobal.net ○ thebrenhamhouse.com

Far View	95-205 BB	Full breakfast
1804 S Park St 77833	9 rooms, 9 pb	Lighter fare, low fat, low carbo-
888-FAR-VIEW 979-836-1672	Most CC	hydrate & vegetarian meals
Steve & Linda	C-ltd/S-ltd/P-no/H-yes	are available upon request
		A/C, swimming pool, outdoor
		fireplace, 24 hr complimentary
		hot & cold drinks, WiFi

Warm hospitality awaits in this restored 1925 prairie-style home, a Texas Recorded Historical Landmark on a 2-acre retreat. Far View features elegant rooms, dedicated to your comfort. Near Historic Brenham, TX, 70 miles from Houston, 90 from Austin.
✉ stay@farviewbedandbreakfast.com ○ www.farviewbedandbreakfast.com

Ingleside B&B	95-210 BB	Full Gourmet Breakfast
409 E Main St 77833	5 rooms, 5 pb	Weekend treats include wine
979-251-7707	Most CC	& cheese
Connie Hall	C-ltd/S-ltd/P-ltd/H-ltd	Free wireless Internet,
		antiques, cable TV/DVD, air
		purifier, robes, canopy bed,
		fireplace, privacy

Beautifully restored 1923 home, conveniently located just a short stroll from downtown Brenham. Our goal is to provide even the seasoned traveler the unique experience of being surrounded by beauty and the enjoyment of southern hospitality at its best.
✉ connie@inglesidebb.com ○ www.inglesidebb.com

Mariposa Ranch B&B	105-250 BB	Full breakfast
8904 Mariposa Ln 77833	11 rooms, 11 pb	Snack baskets, picnic
877-647-4774 979-836-4737	Visa, MC, AmEx	baskets, dinners available
Johnna & Charles	C-yes/S-ltd/P-no/H-no	Parlor, Library,
Chamberlain	Spanish	TV/VCR/DVD, Video Library,
		Weddings, Business
		Accommodations, Jacuzzi,
		Housekeeping

Private cabins, cottages and suites including an 1860 Texas Plantation home, and an early Texas antique log cabin. All with private baths, some with Jacuzzis-for-two or antique claw foot tubs. Swimming pool, weddings, special occasions are our specialty.
✉ info@mariposaranch.com ○ www.mariposaranch.com

Murski Homestead B&B	120-205 BB	Full Self Serve breakfast
1662 Old Independence Rd	3 rooms, 3 pb	Special order private
77833	Visa, MC, Disc, *Rated*	gourmet dinners &
877-690-0676 979-830-1021	C-ltd/S-ltd/P-no/H-ltd	breakfasts, in room coffee
Pamela Murski		service
		Concierge, spa services,
		local airport pickup

Experience True Texas Hospitality! Original 1896 homestead, gourmet meals, incredible views, cooking classes, wildlife & birding, history, shopping, live theater, relax in the evening on the century old front porch swing, photographers dream!
✉ pmurski@sbcglobal.net ○ www.murskihomesteadbb.com

BURNET

Lakeside Lodge
201 Lakewood Dr 78611
512-756-4935
John & Virginie

85-135 EP
5 rooms, 5 pb
Visa, MC, *Rated*
C-ltd/S-ltd/P-no/H-ltd

Full breakfast
Full breakfast $7.50 per
person
Shady Lakefront patio w/lake
breeze, dock, boat ramp,
small refrigerator, coffee
pot/filters, TV

Lakeside Lodge caters to travelers seeking a peaceful waterfront setting with a B&B atmosphere. Located on the scenic northeast side of Lake Buchanan. Hiking, birding, scenic river cruise, Eagle Eye observatory, antiquing, all nearby.
✉ lakesidelodge@281.com ✪ www.lakesidelodgetx.com

CALVERT

Calvert Inn
406 E Texas St 77837
800-290-1213 979-364-2868
Sandy Hudson

135-145 BB
3 rooms, 3 pb
Most CC, •
S-no/P-no/H-no

Full breakfast
Assorted beverages available
at all times; gourmet dining
for 6 or more by reservation.
Victorian gazebo for
weddings, on-site catering for
receptions

The Calvert Inn positively glows! Listed in the National Register and previously owned by P.C. Gibson, cotton merchant. The Inn gives the distinct feeling of being in the Old South with its park-like manicured lawns on 3 blissful, tree shaded acres. HAT-PAII
✉ stay@calvertinn.com ✪ www.calvertinn.com

CANTON

Redbird Retreat B&B
10025 FM 1255 75103
903-829-9632
Peggy & Jim Cox

95-150 BB
5 rooms, 5 pb
Cash, Checks
S-no/P-no/H-no

Full gourmet or country
breakfast
Coffee bar
TV/VCRs, ceiling fans & A/C
in every room; board games
& videos on site, small
groups

Redbird Retreat is nestled on seven acres of woods adjoining a private lake. Just 10 minutes from Canton's World Famous Trade Days. A fantastic place to hold business meetings, retreats, or other small groups.
✉ reservations@redbirdretreat.com ✪ www.redbirdretreat.com

CANYON LAKE

The Lakehouse B&B
1519 Glenn Drive 78133
866-616-5253 830-899-5099
Justin Robinson

175-235 BB
4 rooms, 4 pb
C-ltd/S-ltd/P-no/H-no

Full breakfast

Nestled near New Braunfels on the south-shore of Canyon Lake, the Lakehouse B&B, a Texas Hill Country bed and breakfast, is conveniently located near several of the area's finest day-trip destinations including Wimberley, Gruene and Boerne.
✉ questions@thelakehousebb.com ✪ www.thelakehousebb.com/index.htm

CAT SPRING

BlissWood B&B at Lehmann Legacy Ranch
13300 Lehmann Legacy Ln
78933
713-301-3235
Carol L. Davis

149-189 BB
9 rooms, 9 pb
Visa, MC
C-yes/S-no/P-ltd/H-ltd
German

Continental plus breakfast
Restaurant, snacks,
complimentary wine
Bicycles, swimming pool,
suites, fireplaces, cable TV,
accommodate business
travel

Peaceful country setting amongst majestic live oaks. Five antique-filled houses to choose from. Horseback riding, catch and release bass fishing, trap shooting. Only 50 miles west of Houston.
✉ carol@blisswood.net ✪ www.blisswood.net

CEDAR CREEK

Blue Heron B&B	99-129 BB	Breakfast from our breakfast
583 Union Chapel Rd 78612	4 rooms, 4 pb	menu
512-789-9597	Visa, MC, AmEx	Tea, coffee, juices, bottled
Janice Mouton	C-yes/S-no/P-no/H-no	water and snacks available. Den with books & videos, workout room, hot tub, patio garden, fish pond, snacks and beverages.

Get a little taste of the country & relax in the comfort of deluxe accommodations at our two story Colonial style home, just 15 minutes from Austin Bergstrom International Airport & 10 minutes from Historic Bastrop.
✉ blueheron@blueheron-bnb.com ◐ www.blueheron-bnb.com

CLEBURNE

The Anglin Rose B&B	70-100 BB	Full breakfast
808 S Anglin 76031	3 rooms, 1 pb	Snacks & beverages
817-641-7433	C-ltd/S-ltd/P-ltd/H-ltd	Complimentary basket upon
Milton & Saundra Williams		departure

Recently restored to its original 1892 elegance and authenticity, this home is encompassed with antiques true to its time. Charming, historic home nestled in centuries old oak trees.
✉ info@anglinrose.com ◐ www.anglinrose.com

COMFORT

Idlewilde Lodge B&B	87-132 BB	Full breakfast
115 Highway 473 78013	2 rooms, 2 pb	Lunch/dinner available,
830-995-3844	Cash, Checks, *Rated*	snacks
Connie Hank & Nicholas Engel	C-yes/S-ltd/P-ltd/H-ltd	Complimentary wine, sitting room, library, tennis court, pool, pavilion

Customized service is our motto and our specialty is a large, full country breakfast complete with table linens, candlelight, fine china, and classical music.
✉ idlewilde@hctc.net

Meyer B&B on Cypress Creek	99-210 BB	Full breakfast
845 High St 78013	28 rooms, 28 pb	Swimming pool, creek,
888-995-6100 830-995-2304	Most CC	Jacuzzi, hot tub, dining
Shane Schleyer	C-yes/S-no/P-no/H-ltd	room, fireplace, WiFi

Meyer Bed & Breakfast offers one of the most scenic, peaceful & romantic getaways in the Texas Hill Country.
✉ info@meyerbedandbreakfast.com ◐ www.meyerbedandbreakfast.com

CONROE

Heather's Glen	150-195 BB	Full breakfast
200 E Phillips 77301	3 rooms, 3 pb	Snacks, soft drinks
800-66-JAMIE 936-441-6611	Visa, MC, Disc, *Rated*,	Color TV in rooms, phones,
Ed & Heather George	•	goosedown comforters
	C-ltd/S-ltd/P-ltd/H-ltd Some Spanish	

Heather's Glen B&B & Carriage House—restored to authentic period look w/out sacrificing modern conveniences. Furnishings reflect grace & elegance of past w/lace curtains & antique glassed windows.
✉ heathersbb@aol.com ◐ www.heathersglen.com

DALLAS

B & G's B&B	55 BB	Full or Continental Plus
15869 Nedra Way 75248	3 rooms, 3 pb	Sitting room, cable TV,
972-386-4323	C-ltd/S-ltd/P-no/H-no	accommodate business
Betty & George Hyde		travelers

Retreat from the city-sounds by escaping into the suburbs in prestigious Far North Dallas, where hosts, Betty and George Hyde, will direct you to the many sights in and around North Texas. ✉ bghyde@sbcglobal.net

DALLAS

Corinthian B&B
4125 Junius St 75246
866-598-9988 214-818-0400
Dan Tucker

95-295 BB
5 rooms, 5 pb
Visa, MC, AmEx
C-ltd/S-no/P-no/H-no

Full plated gourmet breakfast
daily
Afternoon snacks; cookies
and sandwiches, signature
Olde English Toffee
Bathrobe, quality linen,
hairdryer, phone, TV

The Corinthian Bed and Breakfast is a historic home near the heart of Dallas, in the Peak-Suburban Historic District near the Swiss Avenue area of famous homes.
✉ innkeeper@corinthianbandb.com 🌐 www.corinthianbandb.com

Hotel St. Germain
2516 Maple Ave 75201
800-683-2516 214-871-2516
Claire Heymann

290-650 BB
7 rooms, 7 pb
Visa, MC, AmEx,
Rated, •
C-ltd
French, Spanish

Continental plus breakfast
Room service, bar service,
dinner, snacks,
complimentary wine,
restaurant
Concierge, butler service,
turndown, valet parking,
Internet & fax, library,
Jacuzzi, fireplaces

Award-winning boutique hotel. A European oasis in the century-old French Hotel Particulie in uptown Dallas. New Orleans gardened courtyard, Old World style, with New World conveniences and luxury. ✉ genmgrstgermain@aol.com 🌐 www.hotelstgermain.com

DENTON

The Heritage Inns
815 N Locust 76201
888-565-6414 940-565-6414
John & Donna Morris

95-160 BB
12 rooms, 12 pb
Most CC, *Rated*, •
C-yes/S-ltd/P-ltd/H-yes
Some Spanish

Special diets
Complimentary gourmet
coffee, tea, sodas, bottled
water, and popcorn are
available throughout the
inns
Sitting room, library,
Jacuzzis, suites, fireplaces,
satellite TV, wireless Internet,
balconies

The Heritage Inns are three separate houses; The Redbud House, The Magnolia House, and The Pecan House. Each is beautifully restored with its own distinct style and flair. A full gourmet breakfast is served in the Redbud dining room each morning.
✉ innkeeper@theheritageinns.com 🌐 www.theheritageinns.com

FORT DAVIS

Old Schoolhouse B&B
401 N Front St 79734
432-426-2050
Carla & Steve Kennedy

93-101 BB
3 rooms, 1 pb
Visa, MC, Disc
C-ltd/S-no/P-no/H-no
German

Full breakfast
Free sodas, water, tea, coffee
& snacks
Microwave oven, refrigerator,
hairdryers, robes, library

This century old adobe schoolhouse sits in shaded comfort in a pecan orchard in the shadow of Sleeping Lion Mountain. Western hospitality puts each guest's needs first.
✉ kennedys@schoolhousebnb.com 🌐 www.schoolhousebnb.com

FORT WORTH

Lockheart Gables Romantic B&B
5220 Locke Ave 76107
888-224-3278 817-738-5969
David & Marilyn Lewis

189-229 BB
6 rooms, 6 pb
Most CC
S-ltd/P-no/H-ltd

Full breakfast
Cookies, special drinks, complimentary picture
Jacuzzi tubs, fireplaces, wedding accommodations, tea
room, parlor, music room, romance, common area

Lockheart Gables Romantic Bed and Breakfast, located in Fort Worth, Texas, is the choice for couples planning their honeymoon, an anniversary or birthday or just wanting a private, peaceful romantic getaway.
✉ marilynlewis143@yahoo.com 🌐 www.lockheartgables.com

FORT WORTH

MD Resort B&B
601 Old Base Rd 76078
866-489-5150 817-489-5150

109-499 BB
18 rooms, 14 pb
Visa, MC, AmEx,
Rated, •
C-ltd/S-no/P-ltd/H-ltd

Full breakfast
Country picnic baskets for
two, or a romantic dinner for
two in suite
Pool, spa, hay rides, game
room, sitting area, outdoor
sports, carriage rides, pecans

A Texas ranch B&B conveniently located in the Dallas/Fort Worth area. MD Resort offers modern conveniences with an Old West atmosphere. Close to the big city, yet quietly secluded from the bustling workaday world.
✉ customerservice@mdresort.com ◐ www.mdresort.com

The Texas White House
1417 8th Ave 76104
800-279-6491 817-923-3597
Jamie & Grover McMains

125-235 BB
5 rooms, 5 pb
Most CC, *Rated*, •
C-ltd/S-ltd/P-ltd/H-ltd

Full, gourmet breakfast
Snacks and Cold Drinks
Sitting room, porches,
gazebo, garden, business
accommodations, fireplace,
sauna, whirlpool tub

Historically designated, award winning, country-style home has been restored to its original 1910 grandeur with simple yet elegant decor. Centrally located, within 5 minutes of downtown Fort Worth. Two suites, three rooms.
✉ txwhitehou@aol.com ◐ www.texaswhitehouse.com

FREDERICKSBURG

115 Austin Place
115 Austin St 78624
888-991-6749 830-997-0443
Ron Maddux

119-169 BB
2 rooms, 2 pb
Most CC
S-ltd/P-no/H-ltd

Continental breakfast
Coffee & tea bar
Hot tub, patio, authentic
1930's furnishings

Austin Place offers a memorable experience, different from the Victorian or Country Style that so typifies most bed & breakfasts today.
✉ stay@fredricksburg-lodging.com ◐ www.fredericksburg-lodging.com/Austin-place/default.asp

A B&B at Settlers Crossing
104 Settlers Crossing Rd 78624
800-874-1020 830-997-2722
David & Judy Bland

135-195 BB
7 rooms, 7 pb
C-yes/P-ltd

Continental plus delivered to
you

A unique blend of charm and casual elegance rarely offered anywhere. Featuring seven private historic guesthouses with fireplaces and wonderful 18th and 19th century country antiques. "One of America's Top 10"—Travel & Leisure.
◐ www.settlerscrossing.com

A Place in Time
614 S Washington St 78624
877-493-7132 830-997-5110
Jonathan E. Morse

85-150 BB
5 rooms, 4 pb
Most CC
C-ltd/S-ltd/P-no/H-no

Full breakfast
Coffee & tea facilities
Ceiling fans, private
entrance, library, conference
rooms, wireless Internet,
board games

Renew, refresh and revitalize in this romantic 1914 Historic traditional B&B. Just blocks from Main Street, we're "a little country in the city." Gardens and friendly wrap around porch invite family gatherings, anniversaries, girl's weekends, and more.
✉ Info@APlaceInTimeBandB.com ◐ www.aplaceintimebandb.com

A Way of the Wolf Country Inn
458 Wolf Way 78624
888-WAY-WOLF 830-997-0711
Ron & Karen Poidevin

115-145 BB
7 rooms, 5 pb
Rated
C-ltd/S-ltd/P-no/H-no

Full breakfast
Coffee, tea, soft drinks
Living room, kitchen, pool,
screened porches, gas grills,
prayer center, conference
facility

60 acres in Texas Hill Country. Tastefully furnished with antiques. Ideal for a romantic getaway or retreat. Restored Civil War cabin and restored Amish barn with full baths and mini kitchens. ✉ waywolf@ctesc.net ◐ www.wayofthewolf.com

FREDERICKSBURG ─────────────────────────

A.L. Patton Suites on Main
332 W Main St 78624
830-997-0443
Ron Maddux

119-179 BB
2 rooms, 2 pb
Most CC
S-no/P-no/H-no

Continental breakfast
Complimentary cheese,
chocolates & fresh fruit plate,
coffee & tea bar
Fireplace, Jacuzzi, climate
controlled rooms

This historic building was built in 1853 & sits on Main Street, only 2 blocks from the Central shopping district.
✉ stay@fredricksburg-lodging.com ◐ www.fredericksburg-lodging.com/A-I-patton

─────────────────────────

Alte Welt Gasthof
142 E Main St 78624
888-991-6749 830-997-0443
Ron & Donna Maddux

150-159 BB
2 rooms, 2 pb
Most CC, *Rated*, •
C-ltd/S-no/P-no/H-no
German

Continental breakfast
Afternoon tea, snacks,
complimentary wine
Jacuzzis, suites, cable TV,
accommodate business
travelers

Beautiful European and antique decor. Vintage fabrics and fine linens enhance the Old World ambience of this historic inn. It's only a block away from Fredericksburg's historic Marktplatz.
✉ stay@texas-bed-n-breakfast.com ◐ www.texas-bed-n-breakfast.com

─────────────────────────

Blumenthal Farms B&B
9400 E US Hyway 290 78666
877-990-9319 830-997-6327
John & Marilyn Schulz

100-125 BB
4 rooms, 4 pb

Full breakfast

Blumenthal Farms backs up to the meandering Pedernales River. You can stroll down to the river and bird-watch or wade in the cool shallow waters. Come visit the beautiful Hill Country area and relax in a rustic old German-built saloon.
✉ bbblum@beecreek.net ◐ www.blumenthalfarms.com

─────────────────────────

Camp David B&B
830-997-7797
Molly & Bobby Sagebiel

99-149 BB
6 rooms, 6 pb
C-yes/S-ltd/P-no/H-no

Full breakfast
Breakfast delivered to your
door
King beds, whirlpool tubs,
fully equipped kitchens,
fireplaces, Internet

Come enjoy warm, inviting and historic Fredericksburg, Texas at the Camp David Bed and Breakfast, the finest of Fredericksburg Texas bed and breakfasts and cottage rentals.
✉ campdavidbb@austin.rr.com ◐ www.campdavidbb.com

─────────────────────────

Corner Cottage B&B
305 S. Orange St 78624
830-990-8265
Marsha Thompson

89-129 BB
3 rooms, 3 pb
Visa, MC, Disc
C-yes/S-ltd/P-no/H-no

Full Gourmet Breakfast
Free* romantic picnic basket
lunch for two with a three
night stay.
Wireless Internet, old-fashion
bicycles, hammock, porch
swing, ice machine, cable TV
with DVD/VCR library

Full Gourmet Breakfast, Private Entrance, Jacuzzi Tub, Wireless Internet, and Gas Fireplace with each suite. Corner Cottage was featured in Country Decorating Ideas Magazine twice! Come and visit a time where the clock loses importance.
✉ rthompson1134@austin.rr.com ◐ www.fredericksburgcornercottage.com

─────────────────────────

Tell your hosts Pamela Lanier sent you.

FREDERICKSBURG

Magnolia House
101 E Hackberry St 78624
800-880-4374 830-997-0306
Claude & Lisa Saunders

105-165 BB
5 rooms, 5 pb
Most CC, *Rated*, •
C-ltd/S-ltd/P-no/H-ltd

Two course gourmet
breakfast
Fresh baked goodies every
afternoon, complimentary
wine & soft drinks
Two sitting rooms, patio,
waterfall, koi pond, large
front porch

A bed & breakfast known for gracious Southern hospitality and their 2 course gourmet breakfasts. This elegant historic home features 5 guestrooms (2 are suites with fireplaces) tastefully decorated and appointed with guests' comfort in mind.
✉ stay@magnolia-house.com ✪ www.magnolia-house.com

Schandua Suite
205 E Main St 78624
888-990-1415 830-990-1415
Sharla & Jonathan Godfrey

175-300 BB
1 rooms, 1 pb
Visa, MC, Disc, *Rated*
C-ltd/S-ltd/P-no/H-no

Continental plus breakfast
Snacks, complimentary hors-
d'oeuvres upon arrival
Sitting room, library, suites,
cable TV, robes, chocolates,
phone, fine antiques &
family heirlooms

Luxury suite located in the heart of the historic district. Pullman kitchen, quaint shops all within walking distance, private balcony overlooking secluded courtyard.
✉ sharla44@hctc.net ✪ www.schandua.com

Town Creek B&B
304 N Edison 78624
877-777-6848 830-997-6848
Connie & Tim Gikas

149-169 BB
6 rooms, 6 pb
Most CC, *Rated*
C-ltd/S-no/P-no/H-ltd

Full breakfast
Tea and coffee in rooms
Central A/C, Sun Porch,
Great Room

Graciously renovated 1890s farmhouse on an acre of land, adjacent to the Fredericksburg Historical District. Main Street shopping, dining and live music is only two short blocks away. Six suites with private baths and private outside entrances.
✉ towncreekbb@gmail.com ✪ www.fredericksburg-fun.com

GALVESTON

Avenue O B&B
2323 Ave O 77550
866-762-2868 409-762-2868
Connie & Jim Porter

95-170 BB
4 rooms, 3 pb
Most CC
C-yes/S-no/P-ltd/H-no

Full breakfast
Outdoor grill available, tasty
treats delivered to your room
daily
Video library, gardens, patio,
living room, dining room,
Jacuzzi, wireless Internet

Located in the historic Silk Stocking District just blocks from the beach and minutes from the Strand, this 1923 Mediterranean-style Bed and Breakfast exhibits a comfortable elegance throughout.
✉ connie@avenueo.com ✪ www.avenueo.com

Lost Bayou Guesthouse
1607 Ave. L 77550
832-613-5884 409-770-0688
Phil DeMarco

125-175 BB
5 rooms, 3 pb
Most CC
C-ltd/S-no/P-no/H-no

Continental plus breakfast
Breakfast: Croissant,
Kolache, or Breakfast Taco,
cereals, fresh fruits, juices,
sodas, coffee & tea
A/C with remote control, a
bag of ice for the beach,
wireless Internet, massage
by Chito Bernardo

Built in 1890 and a survivor of the great hurricane of 1900 this historical Victorian home is located in the Lost Bayou historic district, in the city of Galveston Texas. With 5 large bedrooms this centrally located historical bed and breakfast.
✉ sales@lostbayou.com ✪ www.lostbayou.com

GLEN ROSE—————————————————————————————

Country Woods Inn | 100-250 BB | Barn breakfast buffet plus
420 Grand Ave 76043 | 13 rooms, 13 pb | Kitchens, cookout patios,
888-849-6637 817-279-3002 | Visa, MC | campfire circles in every unit
Helen Kerwin | C-yes/S-ltd/P-ltd/H-ltd | Campfire circles, swimming
 | | hole, petting barnyard,
 | | horseshoes, porches

Award-winning, family friendly Inn on the Paluxy River. 40 acres surrounded by nature. 13 cabins, century-old guesthouses. Walk to Downtown Square. Minutes to Fossil Rim & Dinosaur State Park.
✉ countrywoodsinn@yahoo.com ◔ www.countrywoodsinn.com

Inn on the River | 139-219 BB | Full breakfast
205 SW Barnard 76043 | 22 rooms, 22 pb | A delicious four-course
800-575-2101 254-897-2929 | Most CC, *Rated* | dinner is served every
Ernest & Shirley Reinke | C-ltd/S-no/P-no/H-yes | Friday and Saturday night.
 | | Mineral pool, bikes, meeting
 | | facilities, wireless Internet

Inn on the River is an extraordinary B&B offering 22 romantic rooms and fine dining. No two rooms are alike, and each is tastefully decorated with an antique armoire, fine European linens, a feather bed and a goose-down comforter.
✉ inn@innontheriver.com ◔ www.innontheriver.com

GONZALES—————————————————————————————

Belle Oaks Inn | 75-175 BB | Full gourmet breakfast
222 St Peter 78629 | 5 rooms, 5 pb | Snacks, sodas, etc.
830-857-8613 | Most CC, *Rated* | Pool, bicycles, TV, VCR,
Richard Tiller & Clint Hille | C-ltd/S-no/P-no/H-ltd | robes, hairdryers, in-room
 | | coffee service

1912 Louisiana Plantation Style mansion transformed into a modern tribute to the Southern charm, hospitality, and grace of a bygone era.
✉ info@belleoaksinn.com ◔ www.belleoaksinn.com

GRAHAM—————————————————————————————

Elm Street B&B | 175-445 EP | Full breakfast
830 Elm St 76450 | 3 rooms, 3 pb | A private guesthouse with all
888-362-4262 940-362-4262 | Visa, MC | the amenities of home.
Karen McMillan | C-yes/S-no/P-no/H-no |

A lavishly furnished 1906 Victorian just two-hours west of Dallas/Fort Worth. The Elm Street Bed & Breakfast is an unhosted guesthouse accommodating up to 8 guests.
✉ info@elmstbandb.com ◔ www.elmstbandb.com

GRANBURY—————————————————————————————

1890 Captain's House B&B | 130-185 BB | Full breakfast delivered to
123 W Doyle 76048 | 4 rooms, 4 pb | room
817-579-6664 | C-ltd/S-ltd/P-no/H-no |
Bob & Liz Hayes | |

Visit the historic Captain's House Bed and Breakfast in Granbury, Texas and you will enjoy a relaxing experience. The Captain's House is a lake front property with fantastic views of Lake Granbury, Texas from our large balcony.
✉ captainshouse123@sbcglobal.net ◔ www.captainshouse.info/

Alfonso's Loft | 110-125 BB | Full breakfast
137 E Pearl 76048 | 1 rooms, 1 pb | Coffee, pastries, bottled
817-573-3308 | Most CC | water & sodas are available
Kay Collerain | C-ltd/S-no/P-no/H-no | in the afternoon

If you are looking for a quiet place to spend the night or maybe a weekend, look no further than Alfonso's Loft B&B overlooking historic Granbury square.
✉ stay@alfonsosloft.com ◔ www.alfonsosloft.com

GRANBURY

American Heritage House B&B	169-349 BB	Multi-Course Gourmet
225 W. Moore Street 76022	9 rooms, 9 pb	Breakfast
866-778-3768 817-578-3768	Most CC, •	Complimentary soft drinks &
Ron & Karen Bleeker	C-ltd/S-ltd/P-ltd/H-ltd	bottled water available day
		and night
		Conference room, business
		center, putting green, music
		& game rooms, on-site
		massage & Jacuzzi

The American Heritage House B&B is located in Granbury, Texas nestled in the lush Brazos River valley of Northern Texas. Delight in yesterday's grandeur with the opulent conveniences of today!
✉ info@americanheritagehouse.com ○ www.americanheritagehouse.com

Arbor House & Angel of the Lake	120-190 BB	Gourmet Breakfast
	10 rooms, 10 pb	Afternoon dessert, soft
530 E Pearl St 76048	Most CC, *Rated*, •	drinks, peanuts, M&M's,
800-641-0073 817-573-0073	C-ltd/S-ltd/P-ltd/H-yes	coffee & tea
John and Judy Maxwell		Corporate/Church Retreats,
		SmallWeddings, Fireplace,
		Gazebo, Jacuzzis, Cable TV,
		InRoom Massages, Internet

Arbor House & Angel of the Lake is a luxury Beachside Inn on beautiful Lake Granbury & is opposite new Granbury Convention Center. Voted one of the top 5 B&B's in North America for "Best Weekend Escape & "Best Breakfast." A new Queen Ann Victorian home.
✉ stay@granbury-bed-and-breakfast.com ○ www.granbury-bed-and-breakfast.com

Inn on Lake Granbury	215-375 BB	Full breakfast
205 W Doyle St 76048	7 rooms, 7 pb	Appetizers & beverages each
877-573-0046 817-573-0046	Most CC, •	afternoon at 5:30pm
Jim Leitch & Cathy Casey	C-ltd/S-no/P-no/H-yes	Weddings & events,
		fireplaces, porches,
		balconies, robes, TV,
		Internet, fire pits, pool

Featuring almost two acres of landscaped gardens, a flagstone pool, and scenic lakefront views. Imagine a romantic walk down winding pathways to Lake Granbury's water's edge.
✉ info@innonlakegranbury.com ○ www.innonlakegranbury.com

The Iron Horse Inn	150-245 BB	Full gourmet breakfast
616 Thorp Spring Rd 76048	8 rooms, 8 pb	Afternoon desserts, drinks,
817-579-5535	Most CC	appetizers served.
Paul & Theresa Martin	C-ltd/S-no/P-no/H-no	Private baths, luxurious
		linens, robes in suites, free
		WiFi Internet, front porch
		and fish ponds

The largest historic bed and breakfast inn(6500 sq.ft.) in Granbury, TX. This gorgeous 1905 Craftsman estate boasts hand-milled wood, leaded glass, and large livingrooms and suites. Eight guestrooms/suites/private baths. Gardens, pond, & retreat center.
✉ info@theironhorseinn.com ○ www.theironhorseinn.com

Nutt House Historic Hotel	89-175 BB	Full breakfast
119 E Bridge St 76048	7 rooms, 7 pb	Private Jacuzzi baths, king
888-678-0813 817-279-1207	Most CC, •	beds, Frette Linens, spa,
Michele Moore	C-ltd/S-no/P-no/H-no	antiques

Beautiful Historic Hotel located on the Square in Granbury, Texas. This landmark hotel is the most well known building in the Lake Granbury area.
✉ stay@nutt-house-hotel.com ○ www.nutt-hotel.com

GRANBURY

Pomegranate House B&B	75-205 BB	Full breakfast
1002 W Pearl St 76048	4 rooms, 4 pb	Snacks, hot teas, and soft
888-503-7659 817-279-7412	Most CC	drinks always available.
Sara & Tom Baker	C-ltd/S-no/P-yes/H-no	Evening dessert.
	April thru December	Custom packages available
		by request.

Romantic bed and breakfast with four private, upscale cottages where you can relax around the waterfall/koi pond in the garden courtyard, or enjoy some of Granbury's wonderful activities. Enjoy your private porch with a good book. Pet Friendly.
✉ pomegranatehousebandb@yahoo.com ✆ www.pomhouse.com

GRAPEVINE

Garden Manor B&B Inn	115-195 BB	Full breakfast
205 E College St 76051	4 rooms, 4 pb	Bottled water, soft drinks,
877-424-9177 817-424-9177	Visa, MC, AmEx	morning coffee service,
Judy & Gunther Dusek	C-ltd/S-no/P-no/H-no	turndown service with
		chocolate truffles
		Wireless cable, wireless
		Internet connections, &
		closet mini-frig with free soft
		drinks/water

Garden Manor B&B Inn is 7 minutes from DFW Int'l Airport and designed for both business and leisure travel. 1 block from Main Street with shops, restaurants, theatre, live music & wine tasting rooms. 3 guestrooms, 1 suite. Weddings and receptions hosted.
✉ info@gardenmanorbandb.com ✆ www.gardenmanorbandb.com

HOUSTON

Lovett Inn	99-250 BB	Continental breakfast
501 Lovett Blvd 77006	12 rooms, 12 pb	Library, pool, hot tub,
800-779-5224 713-522-5224	Most CC	wireless Internet access,
Dan Lueken	C-ltd/S-no/P-ltd/H-no	gazebo

Charming 1920s former mayor's mansion near downtown, museums, convention and medical centers and Galleria. Weddings, receptions and business events hosted.
✉ reservations@lovettinn.com ✆ www.lovettinn.com

Modern B&B	100-250 BB	Full breakfast
4003 Hazard Street 77098	10 rooms, 8 pb	Wine, hot tea and snacks.
800-462-4014 832-279-6367	Most CC, •	Sitting room, tandem bicycle
Lisa Thompson	C-yes/S-ltd/P-ltd/H-ltd	available, workout room,
	German, Spanish	vegan/vegetarian friendly

Beautiful Bed & Breakfast in the heart of Houston, minutes away from downtown, the Galleria, Medical Center and the Museum District. We love to host weddings, receptions and business events. Stay at Modern B&B and escape the traditional!
✉ lisa@modernbb.com ✆ www.modernbb.com

Robin's Nest B&B	130-186 BB	Full breakfast Or Continental
4104 Greeley St 77006	8 rooms, 8 pb	Liquors in the parlor for your
800-622-8343 713-528-5821	Most CC, *Rated*, •	enjoyment. Tea and coffee
Robin Smith & Jessica	C-yes/S-ltd/P-yes/H-ltd	station upstairs.
Whatley	Rusty French/	Parlor & sunroom
	Portuguese & Fluent	downstairs
	Spanish	

Robin's Nest consists of three historical houses setting side by side in Houston's Museum District, also called Montrose: The Victorian, called the Big Nest (c. 1898), a charming Craftsman called The Little Nest (c. 1920), and the Third Nest (c.1938).
✉ robin@therobin.com ✆ www.therobin.com

HOUSTON ——————————————————————————

Sara's Bed & Breakfast Inn	99-165 BB	Full weekends, cont. plus
941 Heights Blvd 77008	12 rooms, 12 pb	weekdays
800-593-1130 713-868-1130	Visa, MC, AmEx, •	Cold drinks, coffee, tea
Bob McCreight	C-ltd/S-no/P-no/H-no	Sitting room, large deck,,
	Spanish	bicycles, parties or
		receptions, suites

A stay at Sara's Bed & Breakfast Inn is comforting, inviting and one you'll to take pleasure in returning to time and time again. This beautiful Queen Anne mansion is located just four miles from downtown Houston, irt the Historic Heights.
✉ stay@saras.com ○ www.saras.com

IRVING ——————————————————————————

Jefferson Street B&B Inn	99-180 BB	Full breakfast
512 S Jefferson St 75060	10 rooms, 10 pb	Breakfast is optional. The
972-253-2000	Most CC, *Rated*	cost is $7 per person per
Lee Lowrie	C-ltd/S-no/P-no/H-yes	meal.
		Cable TV with 160+ channels,
		fiber optic wireless Internet,
		free private off-street parking,

AAA-Approved. Between Dallas & Ft Worth. Charming quiet neighborhood, just 6 miles from DFW and Love Field Airports. Wonderful, clean and fun Texas themed rooms with great Stearns & Foster mattresses, WiFi, cable TV, climate control.
✉ jeffersonstreetbnb@hotmail.com ○ www.jeffersonstreetbnb.com

JASPER ——————————————————————————

Swann Hotel B&B	99-129 BB	Full breakfast
250 N Main 75951	6 rooms, 4 pb	Snacks and soft drinks
877-489-9717 409-489-9010	Visa, MC, AmEx	Parlour, baby grand piano,
Mary & Jerry Silmon	C-ltd/S-no/P-ltd/H-ltd	balconies, porches, massage
		facility nearby

1901 restored Victorian boutique hotel in downtown Jasper. Walk to art galleries, massage therapy, quaint shops, lovely park with a creek and lighted jogging trail. Minutes from Lake Sam Rayburn and Martin Dies Park for golf, bird watching, & canoeing.
✉ swannhotel2005@yahoo.com ○ www.hotelswann.com

JEFFERSON ——————————————————————————

Hale House Inn B&B	90-145 BB	Full breakfast
702 S Line St. 75657	6 rooms, 6 pb	
903-665-9955	Most CC	
Timm & Karen Jackson	C-ltd/S-no/P-ltd/H-no	

The Hale House Inn offers six beautifully appointed guestrooms with private baths, a charming veranda and gazebo where you can choose to have breakfast. This Jefferson Texas bed and breakfast Inn is a delightful setting for an ideal getaway.
✉ mystay@thehalehouseinn.com ○ www.thehalehouseinn.com

The Pride House	99-139 BB	Full on weekends
409 Broadway 75657	9 rooms, 9 pb	
903-665-8845	Visa, MC, Disc	
Jenny Lovelace-Elliot	C-yes/S-no/P-ltd/H-ltd	

The Pride House of Jefferson, is proud to re-open our doors to guests—both old and new—and experience a simpler time and way of life with all the amenities you've come to expect from a quality Bed and Breakfast in Jefferson.
✉ stay@thepridehouse.com ○ www.thepridehouse.com

Shepherd's Pasture	105 BB	Full breakfast
Rt 2 Box 128 75657	Most CC	Snacks, lunch & dinner
903-665-2647	C-yes/S-no/P-no/H-yes	Sitting room, basketball
Romey Kilgore & Jessica		court, volleyball court,
Akers		workout room, game room,
		business service center

We welcome anyone in search of a place to rest, refresh and recharge! Enjoy a time of peace, rest and retreat and support our military community at the same time. 2 separate houses, 6 bedrooms each. ✉ info@unitedweservemil.org ○ www.shepherdspasture.com

MCKINNEY

Dowell House c. 1870 B&B
1104 S Tennessee St 75069
972-562-2456
The Muellers

155 BB
2 rooms, 2 pb
Most CC, •
S-no/P-no/H-no

Full breakfast – 9 AM
Snacks, complimentary
beverage
Hot tub, whirlpool bath,
satellite TV, guest parlor,
desks, free wireless Internet,
business rate

Romantic and elegant, this historic B&B is near the quaint town square in McKinney, Texas, the perfect place to escape from the city. The house was a filming location for the original "Benji" movie.
✉ lookin4ancestrs@sbcglobal.net 𝗖 www.dowellhouse.com

MINEOLA

Munzesheimer Manor
202 N Newsom 75773
888-569-6634 903-569-6634
Bob & Sherry Murray

90-120 BB
7 rooms, 7 pb
Most CC, *Rated*, •
C-ltd/S-ltd/P-no/H-ltd

Full gourmet breakfast
Hot cider, cold lemonade,
fresh baked cookies
Sitting room, fireplaces,
cable TV, accommodate
business travelers

1898 Victorian with wraparound porches. Victorian nightgowns, gourmet breakfasts, and special pampering. Featured in national magazines and named as one of "Best Twelve B&Bs in Texas."
✉ innkeeper@munzesheimer.com 𝗖 www.munzesheimer.com

NEW BRAUNFELS

Acorn Hill B&B
250 School House 78132
800-525-4618 830-907-2597
Pam Thomas

145-170 BB
6 rooms, 6 pb
Most CC, *Rated*, •
C-yes/S-no/P-ltd/H-no

Full breakfast
Dining room, antiques,
organ, porches, pool, hot tub,
garden, weddings

Just five minutes from the Guadalupe River and downtown Gruene, and ten minutes from historic New Braunfels, find an old log Schoolhouse, a 1905 Victorian House and three romantic cottages. Enjoy our beautiful pool, hot tub and country setting.
✉ acornhill@acornhillbb.com 𝗖 www.acornhillbb.com

Antoinette's Cottage
1258 Greune Rd 78130
830-606-6929
Cheryle Fuller

175-245 BB
3 rooms, 3 pb
Visa, MC
C-ltd/S-no/P-ltd/H-no

Home cooked continental
Special dietary needs
accommodated.
A small refrigerator is in each
room. Some pets may be
accepted.

The oldest house in Gruene has four rooms of distinction, beautiful gardens and a lovely porch, claw foot tubs, and ceiling fans. Period antiques and professional decorations, with modern amenities, will make this a memorable stay. Breakfast on the porch!
✉ cfuller007@satx.rr.com 𝗖 www.antoinettescottage.com

Gruene Country Homestead
832 Gruene Rd 78130
800-238-5534 830-606-0216
Ed & Billie Miles

125-210 BB
21 rooms, 21 pb
Visa, MC, *Rated*
C-yes/S-no/P-ltd/H-yes

Continental plus breakfast
Bar service
Spas, pool, suites, cable TV,
tavern with live music,
wireless Internet

A country inn presented as a collection of historic farm houses located on eight acres of an original German homestead. Guests are invited to enjoy the swimming pool, hot tub and beautiful grounds landscaped with native plants.
✉ staff@gruenehomesteadinn.com 𝗖 www.gruenehomesteadinn.com

Gruene Mansion Inn
1275 Gruene Rd 78130
830-629-2641
Cecil & Judi Eager

159-340 BB
31 rooms, 31 pb
Visa, MC, AmEx
C-yes/S-no/P-no/H-ltd

Breakfast buffet
Porch, antiques, clawfoot
tubs, fireplaces

Sitting on the banks of the Guadalupe River, & adjacent to Gruene Hall, the Gruene Mansion Inn offers you the opportunity to enjoy lodging in the most unique Texas style.
✉ frontdesk@gruenemansioninn.com 𝗖 www.gruenemansioninn.com

570 Texas

NEW BRAUNFELS

Hunter Road Stagecoach Stop 5441 FM 1102 78132 830-620-9453 Jeff and Bettina	115-200 BB 4 rooms, 4 pb Most CC, *Rated*, • C-ltd/S-ltd/P-ltd/H-yes	Full gourmet breakfast Sitting room, dog trot, porches, TV, walking and bike trails

Texas landmark constructed 150 years ago by Amish settlers. Authentically restored Fachwerk house & log cabin. All are surrounded by gardens of antique roses and herbs.
✉ stagecoach@satx.rr.com ✆ www.stagecoachbedandbreakfast.com

Kuebler Waldrip Haus B&B 1620 Hueco Springs Loop 78132 800-299-8372 830-625-8300 Margaret K. Waldrip & son, Darrell Waldrip	80-185 BB 11 rooms, 11 pb Most CC, • C-yes/S-no/P-ltd/H-yes Spanish	A 9:30AM full candlelight breakfast Enjoy free complimentary homemade snacks, drinks, and Blue Bell Ice Cream in our common room. Relax, rock on a porch with a cold drink, a book and video library, gift shop (pewter, books, pics).

Relax on 43 acres near Gruene, New Braunfels, San Antonio. Perfect for business, getaways, family reunions, weddings, and corporate retreats. Kuebler Waldrip Haus B&B offers one of the "Best breakfasts in Texas!"
✉ kueblerwaldripinfo@att.net ✆ www.kueblerwaldrip.com

Lamb's Rest Inn 1385 Edwards Blvd 78132 888-609-3932 830-609-3932 Judy & George Rothell	150-225 BB 6 rooms, 6 pb Visa, MC, Disc, • C-ltd/S-ltd/P-no/H-no	Full breakfast Breakfast served Sun/Thurs buffet 9–10:30am. Fri/Sat breakfast is served in dining room at 9am Jacuzzis, pool, hot tub, river access, kitchenette, fireplaces, cable TV/VCR, wireless Internet

Enjoy true Texas hospitality on the Guadalupe River near the historic village of Gruene. A peaceful, romantic atmosphere awaits you in tranquil gardens.
✉ info@lambsrestinn.com ✆ www.lambsrestinn.com

Prince Solms Inn B&B 295 E San Antonio St 78130 800-625-9169 830-625-9169 Al Buttross	125-175 BB 14 rooms, 14 pb Most CC C-ltd/S-no/P-ltd/H-ltd	Full breakfast Welcome snacks and water in room upon arrival Romantic, full service bar, parlor, phone, cable, courtyard

Experience pampered hospitality at Prince Solms Inn, one of Texas' most historic treasures in Hill Country, offering 13 guestrooms, luxurious suites & one cottage, plus scrumptious country breakfasts.
✉ princesolmsinn@msn.com ✆ www.princesolmsinn.com

PITTSBURG

Carson House Inn & Grille 302 Mt Pleasant St 75686 888-302-1878 903-856-2468 Eileen & Clark Jesmore	94-119 BB 8 rooms, 8 pb Most CC, *Rated* C-yes/S-ltd/P-ltd/H-no	Full breakfast Lunch & dinner available, restaurant and bar Sitting room, Jacuzzi, suites, cable TV, accom. bus. travelers

Historic Victorian Inn built in 1878, featuring rare curly pine wainscoting. Restored and operated for 14 years as a Fine Dining restaurant and Inn. Rooms have antique charm and modern amenities. East Texas Piney Woods very attractive, near lakes & parks.
✉ mailus@carsonhouse.com ✆ www.carsonhouse.com

PITTSBURG

Pecan House
212 College St 75686
866-Pecan-55 903-856-5504
Peter Jessop

75-105 BB
6 rooms, 6 pb
Most CC
C-ltd/S-ltd/P-no/H-ltd

Full breakfast
English tea room, Victorian
surroundings, high speed
wireless Internet, cable TV,
free nat'l calls.

Elegant restored Victorian home, a splendid example of craftsmanship from 100 years ago. With all the grace of traditional English & European Service.
✉ pete@pecanhousedesign.com ◐ www.pecanhousebnb.com

SALADO

Brambley Hedge Country Inn
1530 FM 2268 East 76571
800-407-2310 254-947-1914
Billie & Carolanne Hanks

115-125 BB
4 rooms, 4 pb
Most CC
C-ltd/S-no/P-no/H-no
Some Spanish
Closed Christmas, Easter

Full breakfast
Snacks
Sitting room with fireplace

Romantic, peaceful, secluded on 50+ acres, wildlife, private decks outside each room, Christian atmosphere, bountiful breakfasts, European country decor, 2 minutes by car to shops & restaurants.
✉ bandbincountry@aol.com ◐ www.brambleyhedgesalado.com

The Inn at Salado
7 N Main St 76571
800-724-0027 254-947-0027
Rob & Suzanne Petro

75-160 BB
12 rooms, 12 pb
Most CC
C-ltd/S-no/P-no/H-no

Full breakfast
Sitting room, fireplaces,
cable TV, conference,
weddings & receptions

The Inn displays both a Texas Historical Marker & a Nat'l Register listing. Walking distance to shopping & dining. The Inn is a great place for couples to get away & for business retreats.
✉ rooms@inn-at-salado.com ◐ www.inn-at-salado.com

SAN ANTONIO

1908 Ayres Inn
124 W. Woodlawn Ave 78212
210-736-4232
M. Eifler & H. Llanas

99-275 BB
4 rooms, 4 pb
Most CC
C-ltd/S-no/P-no/H-no
Spanish

Continental Breakfast and
Hot Items
Baked Fresh Hot Pepper
Turkey, Feta Cheese and
Spinach stuffed Croissants.
Cinnamon Rolls, Espresso
Wifi, fax, copy machine, and
printer, books, magazines,
games, patio and pond,
gardens

San Antonio Bed and Breakfast. Located in the historic neighborhood of Monte Vista, this two-story neoclassic home built in 1908 by the renowned architect Atlee B. Ayres at 124 West Woodlawn is listed in the National Registry of Historic Places.
✉ sa1908ayresinn@msn.com ◐ www.1908ayresinn.com

A Beckmann Inn & Carriage House
222 E Guenther St 78204
800-945-1449 210-229-1449
Lisa Cantu

109-189 BB
5 rooms, 5 pb
Most CC, *Rated*
C-ltd/S-no/P-no/H-no

Gourmet breakfast with
dessert
Butter cookies, welcome
"tea"
Convenient location, trolley,
porches, refrigerators, TVs,
phones, hairdryers, irons

Set in the beautiful King William historic district, A Beckmann Inn & Carriage House is a "hidden treasure," the perfect location for enjoying San Antonio at its very best, whether for business or leisure travel.
✉ stay@beckmanninn.com ◐ www.beckmanninn.com

SAN ANTONIO

Aaron Pancoast Carriage House – A Noble Inn	159-299 BB	Continental plus breakfast
107 Madison St 78204	9 rooms, 9 pb	Afternoon refreshments,
800-221-4045 210-225-4045	Most CC, *Rated*, •	snacks
Don & Liesl Noble	C-ltd/S-no/P-no/H-yes	Gas fireplaces, outdoor pool,
	Spanish	children welcome, full
		kitchens, cable TV, Internet
		access

Lovingly restored and updated with modern amenities and technology that today's sophisti-cated traveler desires. Three large suite arrangements perfect for private honeymoons, quiet vacations or small reunions.
✉ stay@nobleinns.com ❖ www.nobleinns.com/carriage.html

Arbor House Suites	115-179 BB	Continental breakfast
109 Arciniega 78205	8 rooms, 8 pb	Restaurants nearby,
888-272-6700 210-472-2005	Most CC	refrigerator, microwave,
Ronald R. Stinson	C-yes/S-no/P-yes/H-yes	coffeepot
		Sitting room, Jacuzzi, suites,
		cable TV, business travelers,
		telephones, Internet access

The 4 buildings are clustered around a lush garden with a beautiful fountain, outdoor seating & umbrella tables. Centrally located 1 block from historic La Villita and the River Walk, 2 blocks from Henry B. Gonzales Convention Center.
✉ arborhaus@aol.com ❖ www.arborhouse.com

Beauregard House	129-199 BB	Full Gourmet Breakfast
215 Beauregard St 78204	6 rooms, 6 pb	Picnic lunches available with
888-667-0555 210-222-1198	Most CC, *Rated*	notice
Beauregard House Staff	C-ltd/S-no/P-no/H-ltd	Cable TV, wireless Internet,
	Spanish	free off-street parking,
		concierge services, robes

1905 Victorian located in the quiet elegance of the historic King William District, one block from the Riverwalk & Trolley. Within walking distance of all major downtown attractions. Six unique guestrooms all with private baths.
✉ relax@TheBeauregardHouse.com ❖ www.BeauregardHouse.com

Bonner Garden Bed & Breakfast	115-165 BB	Gourmet Breakfast
145 East Agarita Avenue 78212	6 rooms, 6 pb	Refreshments available at all
800-396-4222 210-733-4222	Most CC, *Rated*, •	times
Margi & Jim Herbold	C-yes/S-ltd/P-no/H-no	Sitting room, library, rooftop
		patio, pool, TV, DVD, VCR,
		phone, broadband Internet

Award-winning Italian villa built in 1910 for Mary Bonner, the internationally known artist. Listed on the National Historic Registry surrounded by lush gardens and overlooks down-town San Antonio.
✉ lanierbb@bonnergarden.com ❖ www.bonnergarden.com

Brackenridge House	125-300 BB	Full breakfast
230 Madison 78204	6 rooms, 6 pb	Snacks, complimentary wine
877-271-3442 210-271-3442	Visa, MC, AmEx,	Bikes, Jacuzzis, suites, cable
Bennie & Sue Blansett	*Rated*, •	TV, VCR, phone, heated
	C-ltd/S-no/P-ltd/H-no	swimming pool, WiFi

Native Texan owners & innkeepers will guide you through your visit from their beautiful Greek Revival home in historic King William.
✉ brackenridgebb@aol.com ❖ www.brackenridgehouse.com

SAN ANTONIO

Christmas House B&B
2307 McCullough 78212
800-268-4187 210-737-2786
Penny & Grant Estes

85-125 BB
4 rooms, 4 pb
Visa, MC, Disc, *Rated*,
•
C-ltd/S-ltd/P-no/H-ltd

Full breakfast
Full breakfast Two
restaurants within walking
distance Tex-Mex and Italian
Sitting room, private/semi
private veranda, private
bathrooms, TV

Christmas House B&B is near San Antonio's famous Alamo and Riverwalk (1.5 miles) with bus service available close to the door. Built in 1908, it is located in the historic Monte Vista District.
✉ christmashsb@earthlink.net ✆ www.christmashousebnb.com

Fiesta Bed and Breakfast
1823 Saunders Ave. 78207
210-226-5548
David Newbern

65-95 BB
2 rooms, 2 pb
Most CC
C-ltd/S-ltd/P-ltd/H-ltd
Spanish

Full breakfast
Complimentary cocktail
upon arrival, private catered
dinner available
Wireless Internet access,
library

A modern Latino ambience style B&B located in the original Mexican historical district of San Antonio, minutes to el Centro. The vivid and festive colors in our home will re-energize and lift your spirits with a unique sense of amistad.
✉ fiestabandb@sbcglobal.net ✆ www.fiestabandb.com

The Inn at Craig Place
117 W Craig Pl 78212
877-427-2447 210-736-1017
Gregg & Kelly Alba

115-205 BB
5 rooms, 5 pb
Most CC, *Rated*
S-ltd/P-no/H-no
French

3 course gourmet breakfast
Hospitality corner with light
snacks, coffee, tea and soft
drinks along with a bedtime
snack
Evening sweet, romance &
celebration packages,
wireless high speed Internet,
fireplaces, Jacuzzis

The Inn sets the scene for romance, comfort & indulgence for your special occasion. The Inn provides the peaceful retreat you've earned for recovery & relaxation following a day of meetings.
✉ stay@craigplace.com ✆ www.craigplace.com

Inn on the Riverwalk
129 Woodward Pl 78204
800-730-0019 210-225-6333
Johanna Gardner & Scott
Kiltoff

99-299 BB
14 rooms, 14 pb
Most CC, *Rated*, •
C-yes/S-no/P-yes/H-ltd
Spanish

Full breakfast
Water, fruit juice, teas &
coffees, snacks
River views from porches,
Free parking, Free WiFi, TV,
A/C, refrigerators, desks, spa
tubs,

Located in the heart of downtown San Antonio, we're situated on the famous San Antonio Riverwalk. We will book your romantic getaway from Champagne and Chocolates on your bed, to reservations for a fabulous dinner on the Riverwalk, to a carriage ride home
✉ innkeeper@innontheriverwalksa.com ✆ www.innontheriverwalksa.com

The OgT Inn Riverwalk
209 Washington St 78204
800-242-2770 210-223-2353
Don & Liesl Noble

189-449 BB
10 rooms, 10 pb
Most CC, *Rated*, •
C-ltd/S-no/P-no/H-no

Full gourmet breakfast
Afternoon refreshments,
evening port & sherry
Sitting room, library, A/C,
cable TV, phone, 1½ acres of
gardens on the Riverwalk
downtown

Elegant, romantic, Antebellum mansion on 1.5 acres on the Riverwalk in the King William Historic District. European antiques, quiet comfort & luxury. Shopping, dining, Alamo & Convention Center, 2 to 4 blocks. Trolley service to all downtown attractions.
✉ stay@nobleinns.com ✆ www.nobleinns.com/oge.html

SANDIA————————————————————————————————

Knolle Farm & Ranch Bed,	145-190 BB	Full breakfast
Barn & Breakfast	9 rooms, 7 pb	Lunch & dinner available,
13016 Farm Rd 70 78383	Visa, MC, AmEx, *Rated*	snacks, complimentary wine
361-547-2546	C-yes/S-no/P-yes/H-yes	Sitting room, library, suites,
Beth Knolle	Spanish	cable TV, accommodate
		business travelers, rec room

An upscale, historic Guest Ranch catering to discriminating outdoor enthusiasts, with world-class hunting and sporting activities. We also specialize in weddings, reunions and retreats.
✉ knollefarm@the-l.net ○ www.knolle.com

SEABROOK————————————————————————————————

Beacon Hill Guest House	135-260 BB	Hot plated breakfast at the
B&B	8 rooms, 8 pb	B&B
3701 Nasa Rd One 77586	Most CC	snacks
281-326-7643	C-yes/S-no/P-ltd/H-yes	WiFi, Cable, Dish, waterfront,
Delaina Hanssen		equipped kitchens, 13'x13'
		outdoor Chess, tall trees &
		manicured lawn

Romance your partner or bring your family for a refreshing getaway. Business meetings and luncheon meetings welcome. We offer 5 houses in 2 locations, all on the water—to serve your needs. Restaurants within walking distance.
✉ hanssen@aol.com ○ www.visitbeaconhill.com

Palm Lodge B&B	149-189 BB	Full breakfast
1010 Milby St 77586	3 rooms, 3 pb	Complimentary snacks &
281-291-7513	Visa, MC, Disc	beverages
Linda Wells Bonnin	C-ltd/S-no/P-no/H-ltd	Dining room, bicycles,
		binoculars

You're invited to open the massive cypress doors to Palm Lodge country bed & breakfast & enter into a home filled with southern hospitality & Texas charm.
✉ info@visitpalmlodge.com ○ www.visitpalmlodge.com

SMITHVILLE————————————————————————————————

9E Ranch B&B	155-225 BB	Full breakfast basket
2158 Highway 304 78957	4 rooms, 4 pb	delivered
512-497-9502	Visa, MC, *Rated*, •	Coffee and tea in cabins.
Joan Bohls	C-yes/S-no/P-yes/H-no	Weekday breakfast of
		muffins and juice left in
		cabin.
		Heat and Air conditioning

Experience the beauty and tranquility of Texas by staying in the Texas Lone Star, Eagles' Nest log cabin, Michelle's Log Cabin or the new 2 bedroom Daisy Cottage on a hill at the 9E Ranch in Lost Pines, Bastrop. Available for weddings.
✉ logcabins@9eranch.com ○ www.9eranch.com

Katy House	95-150 BB	Full country breakfast
201 Ramona St 78957	5 rooms, 5 pb	Most rooms have in-room
800-843-5289 512-237-4262	Most CC, *Rated*, •	mini-fridge, coffee & tea
Sallie & Bruce Blalock	C-ltd/S-no/P-ltd/H-no	available all day, cookies
		baked fresh each day
		Sitting room, queen size
		beds, TV, VCR, ceiling fans,
		fireplace, balcony, free WiFi

Katy House B&B is located in the beautiful, old railroad town of Smithville, Texas. This historic Texas B&B is handsomely decorated in American antiques and railroad memorabilia. All rooms have private baths, TV, cable, WiFi. One block from Main Street.
✉ innkeeper@katyhouse.com ○ www.katyhouse.com

SPICEWOOD

Chanticleer Log Cabin B&B
530 Lost Cove Dr 78669
830-693-4269
LC & Mallonee Mellenger

165 BB
1 rooms, 1 pb
Visa, MC
S-no/P-no/H-no

Continental breakfast
Kitchenette includes,
microwave, refrigerator,
coffee maker.

Restored log cabin on 26 acres with Lake Travis frontage, a screened porch, stone fireplace, line-dried linens, robes & bath gels. Privacy & comfort are paramount. Rates with & without breakfast; all rates include homemade granola & chocolate chip cookies
✉ chanticleer_bb@yahoo.com ◑ www.chanticleerlogcabin.com

STEPHENVILLE

September Song B&B
615 N Clinton St 76401
254-965-6104
Ed & Marlene Dupas

75-85 BB
2 rooms, 2 pb
Visa, MC
C-ltd/S-no/P-no/H-no

Full breakfast

Situated on a historic cobblestone street in the heart of Stephenville, this B&B offers comfortable lodging amenities as well as suggestions of things to do and see.
✉ septembersong@nctv.com

TOLAR

The Windmill Farm B&B
6625 Colony Road 76476
817-279-2217 – Cell 254-835-4168
Chuck & Ruby Rickgauer

125-150 BB
3 rooms, 3 pb
Visa, MC, Disc
C-yes/S-no/P-yes/H-ltd

Full breakfast delivered to
cabin

3 private cabins on 26 country acres with over 40 windmills. We offer a great view of Texas with beautiful sunsets as the porches face west.
✉ crickgauer@itexas.net ◑ www.thewindmillfarm.com/BedBreakfast.htm

TYLER

Rosevine Inn
415 S Vine 75702
903-592-2221
Bert & Rebecca Powell

110-195 BB
7 rooms, 7 pb
Most CC, *Rated*, •
C-ltd/S-no/P-no/H-no
French

Full breakfast
Snacks and refreshments on
arrival; picnic lunch for fee
with notice
Sitting room, library, spa,
outdoor hot tub, courtyard,
game room, WiFi

Experience the old fashioned concept of guest housing at the Rosevine Inn B&B, an excellent alternative to the ordinary hotel routine. The first B&B located in Tyler, Texas, "The Rose Capital of the World."
✉ rosevine@dctexas.net ◑ www.rosevine.com

VICTORIA

Friendly Oaks B&B
210 E. Juan Linn St. 77901
361-575-0000
Bill & CeeBee McLeod

65-90 BB
4 rooms, 4 pb
Most CC, *Rated*
C-ltd/S-no/P-no/H-ltd

Full breakfast

Friendly Oaks B&B is nestled among several huge live oak trees in a quiet preserved historic area. Close to banks, courts, restaurants, antique shops and the new Performing Arts Center. Scrumptious full breakfasts feature Texas produce.
✉ innkprbill@aol.com

WACO

Judge Baylor House
908 Speight Ave 76706
888-522-9567 254-756-0273
Bruce & Dorothy Dyer

77-115 BB
5 rooms, 5 pb
Visa, MC, •
C-yes/S-no/P-no/H-yes

Full breakfast
Afternoon tea, snacks
Sitting room, private
entrance, antiques, stained
glass windows, patio

Decorated with antiques and Texas Hill Country art. Quiet and comfortable bedrooms. Near Baylor University and IH-35. One of Arrington's 25 Best Bed and Breakfasts in the US.
✉ judgebaylor@judgebaylorhouse.com ◑ www.judgebaylorhouse.com

WAXAHACHIE

The BonnyNook Inn
414 W Main St 75165
972-938-7207
Vaughn & Bonnie Franks

125-160 BB
5 rooms, 5 pb
Visa, MC, Disc, *Rated*,
•
C-yes/S-ltd/P-yes/H-ltd

Full breakfast
Dinner by reservation
Snacks, whirlpool tubs in 3
rooms, piano, antiques

1887 Victorian home located near Square, in a historic national district. Each room is a different experience. Plants & fresh flowers, country garden.
✉ vaughn@bonnynook.com ✆ www.bonnynook.com

WEATHERFORD

Angels Nest
1105 Palo Pinto St 76086
817-596-8295 – Cell 817-599-9600
Candice Dyer

89-175 BB
10 rooms, 10 pb
C-ltd/S-no/P-no/H-ltd

Full breakfast
Breakfast-in-bed every
morning with our breakfast
delivery trays outside your
door.
Jacuzzi tubs, antiques, sitting
areas, common room,
private verandahs, gardens,
TV

Welcome to Angel's Nest Bed and Breakfast, located in the beautiful Weatherford, Texas. This unique bed and breakfast will help ease the pain of a stressful week at the office or create a romantic experience you will never forget!
✉ candy@angels-nest.com ✆ angels-nest.com

WIMBERLEY

Bandits Hideaway
2324 Flite Acres Rd. 78676
888-244-7777 512-847-9088
Joyce Grimes

95-120 EP
2 rooms, 2 pb
C-ltd/S-ltd/P-ltd/H-no

Coffee & tea
BBQ grill, air conditioning

Guests have been enjoying life's simple pleasures at the hideaway for over 18 years. This riverside lodging accommodation is named after Bandit the original resident border collie. Rosie, the current resident dog, loves our guests like Bandit did.
✆ www.banditshideaway.com

Blair House
100 Spoke Hill Rd 78676
877-549-5450 512-847-1111
Mike & Vickie Schneider

150-285 BB
11 rooms, 11 pb
Most CC, *Rated*, •
C-ltd/S-no/P-no/H-yes

Full 3 course breakfast
Homemade dessert,
beverages, 5 Course Dinner
offered on Saturdays, picnic
baskets available
Living room, lounge, library,
spa services, sauna,
massage, nature trail,
bicycles, cooking school

This fine Country Inn/Bed and Breakfast is situated on 22 acres of beautiful Texas Hill Country land just 1.5 miles south of the heart of Wimberley. Rated as one of the top 5 B&B's in the area on a consistent basis.
✉ info@blairhouseinn.com ✆ www.blairhouseinn.com

Creekhaven Inn
400 Mill Race Ln 78676
800-827-1913 512-847-9344
Pat & Bill Appleman

150-275 BB
14 rooms, 14 pb
Most CC, •
S-ltd/P-no/H-yes

Breakfast Buffet
Welcome reception for
Friday night arrivals
Massages available, great
room, library, swimming
creek, swing, fire pits, patios,
hot tub

Texas Hill Country elegance is yours at this romantic waterfront haven, lush in its natural setting, exquisite décor and gracious hospitality.
✉ pat@creekhaveninn.com ✆ www.creekhaveninn.com

WIMBERLEY

Prow'd House B&B
304 Rocky Springs Rd 78676
866-720-7666 512-847-1900
Donna & Dave Kyte

100-150 BB
6 rooms, 6 pb
Visa, MC
C-ltd/S-no/P-no/H-no

Full breakfast
Breakfast is served each
morning in the dining area or
on the patio, weather
permitting.
Queen bed, private full
bathroom, TV, DVD player,
Internet access, coffee pot,
hairdryer, private patio

A beautiful example of a "Lindal Cedar Home" with a cedar lined towering cathedral ceiling and huge prow windows that open up a panorama of Hill Country views.
✉ prowdhouse@anvilcom.com ○ www.prowdhouse.com

**Serenity Farmhouse Inn &
Spa**
251 Circle Dr 78676
888-882-8985 512-847-8985
Kathleen Taylor

180-250 BB
7 rooms, 7 pb
P-yes

Full breakfast
Coffee service
Heart-shaped whirlpool
bathtubs for two, fireplaces,
private patios, satellite TV

Serenity Farmhouse Inn, a beautiful luxurious wedding destination on more than 20 picturesque acres. All cottages feature decorator furnishings hand painted furniture with exquisite Hill Country and European decor.
✉ serenity@anvilcom.com ○ www.serenityfarmhouseinn-spa.com

Wimberley Inn
200 Ranch Road 3237 78676
877-447-3750 512-847-3750
Denese & Dan Washam

79-199 BB
21 rooms, 21 pb
Visa, MC, AmEx
C-ltd/S-no/P-no

Continental breakfast
High speed Internet
available, individually
controlled A/C-heating,
select DVD & CD collection

Wimberley Inn provides a tranquil, intimate and quiet stay, surrounded by live oaks and cedars. At the same time the Inn is within walking distance to the galleries, gift shops and restaurants of the Wimberley Square,
✉ wimberley_inn@yahoo.com ○ www.wimberleyinn.com

Utah

CEDAR CITY

A Garden Cottage B&B
16 N 200 W 84720
866-586-4919 435-586-4919
Gary & Diana Simkins

99-139 BB
5 rooms, 5 pb
Most CC, *Rated*, •
C-ltd/S-no/P-no/H-ltd

Yummy full breakfast
Snacks available all day
Free WiFi, parlor w/TV and
VCR-DVD, A/C, fireplace,
gardens, hairdryers,
irons/ironing boards

Cedar City Utah's most charming and romantic B&B. Enchanted English Cottage nestled in an award winning old-fashioned garden. Five romantic, antique-filled bedchambers await your pleasure. Just across from the Utah Shakespearean Festival!
✉ romance@thegardencottagebnb.com ◐ www.thegardencottagebnb.com

Amid Summer's Inn B&B
140 South 100 West 84720
888-586-2601 435-586-2600
Charlene& Gary Elsasser

99-169 BB
8 rooms, 8 pb
Most CC, *Rated*, •
C-ltd/S-ltd/P-no/H-ltd

Full warm gourmet breakfast
Fruit smoothies, home baked
cookies, chocolates, fresh
fruit, assorted beverages &
tea served daily
Nightly turn down service,
daily room service, dinner
reservations, massage by
appointment

Award-winning English Tudor built after the turn of the century in historic, downtown Cedar City, Utah. Voted Best Breakfast 2008–2009 Worldwide! Close to Utah Shakespearean Festival, Cedar Breaks Monument, Zion National Park, Bryce Canyon & ski resorts.
✉ info@amidsummersinn.com ◐ www.amidsummersinn.com

The Anniversary House
133 S 100 W 84720
800-778-5109 435-865-1266
Nan Johnson

89-139 BB
5 rooms, 5 pb
Most CC, *Rated*
C-ltd/S-no/P-ltd/H-yes

Full Gourmet Breakfast
Cake and beverages always
available
Reservations for dining or
spa treatments.
Complementary beverages
and cake 24/7

It's All About You! Set quietly along a tree-covered lane, The Anniversary House Bed and Breakfast is a warm and welcoming arts and crafts style home. All five bedrooms are as different in character as the four seasons. We cater to our guests comfort.
✉ stay@theanniversaryhouse.com ◐ www.theanniversaryhouse.com

Big Yellow Inn B&B
234 S 300 W 84720
435-586-0960
Scott & Barbara Hunt

79-199 BB
17 rooms, 17 pb
Visa, MC, AmEx
C-yes/S-no/P-no/H-yes

Full breakfast
Guest office, library with
video collection

Our Georgian Revival home is located one block from the Utah Shakespearean Festival. We offer 17 air conditioned rooms all with private baths, including our 900 square foot gable suite.
✉ stay@bigyellowinn.com ◐ www.bigyellowinn.com

The Iron Gate Inn B&B
100 N 200 W 84720
800-808-4599 435-867-0603
Susan & CR Wooten

99-159 BB
10 rooms, 10 pb
Most CC, •
C-ltd/S-no/P-ltd/H-yes

Full Breakfast
Afternoon wine, soft drinks
Patio for outdoor dining,
parlor, living room, 2
fireplaces, spacious grounds

A beautiful Victorian B&B, but not cluttered or too frilly! Enjoy spacious, comfortable king/queen rooms with private baths, and a fabulous breakfast! Close to Zion Nat'l Park and Bryce Canyon, 2 blocks from the Utah Shakespearean Festival. Free WiFi.
✉ theirongateinn@msn.com ◐ www.TheIronGateInn.com

CEDAR CITY

Willow Glen Inn
3308 N Bulldog Rd 84720
866-586-3275 435-586-3275
Violet & Phil Carter

59-225 BB
9 rooms, 9 pb
Most CC, *Rated*, •
C-yes/S-no/P-no/H-no

Full breakfast
Catered parties for groups of
20 or more by reservation
Sitting room, suites, fireplace,
conference facilities

Willow Glen has 9 unique rooms on 9 acres of landscaped yards & gardens. The perfect base for trips to 3 national parks, the Utah Shakespearean Festival & winter skiing at Brian Head Resort.
✉ info@willowgleninn.com ◐ www.willowgleninn.com

ESCALANTE

Escalante's Grand Staircase B&B Inn
280 W Main St 84726
866-826-4890 435-826-4890
Linda and Tom Mansell

135-155 BB
8 rooms, 8 pb
Most CC, *Rated*, •
C-ltd/S-no/P-no/H-ltd

Full breakfast
Food allergies
accommodated with 1 week
advanced notice
Spacious rooms with heat &
A/C, DirecTV, cell phones,
Internet in all rooms, sky
lights

Escalante's Grand Staircase is located in the heart of Escalante—home of the Grand Staircase Escalante National Monument. Peaceful, quiet and smoke-free. Serving scrumptious gourmet breakfasts. Highway 12 is our home.
✉ stay@escalantebnb.com ◐ escalantebnb.com

GLENDALE

Historic Smith Hotel B&B
295 N Main St 84729
800-528-3558 435-648-2156
Rochelle & Mike

68-92 BB
7 rooms, 7 pb
Visa, MC, *Rated*, •
C-yes/S-no/P-ltd/H-ltd

Full breakfast
Sitting room, screened
porch, 2 acres to roam,
swing, BBQ & picnic table

Historic 1927 hotel; lovely view of nearby bluffs from guest porch. Located in beautiful Long Valley between Zion and Bryce Canyon National Parks. Two acres to roam.
✉ smith_hotel@email.com ◐ www.historicsmithhotel.com

Windwhisper Cabin B&B
Hwy 89 Mile Marker 92 84729
435-648-2162
Terry & Audrey Behling

89-129 BB
3 rooms, 2 pb
Most CC
C-yes/S-ltd/P-no/H-ltd
Closed winter

Full breakfast
Garden, patio, wildlife,
nature, down comforters,
private entrance, beautiful
flagstone patio, cabin

People are attracted to our inn, offering 2 guestrooms and 1 private cabin, because of our location, between Zion National Park and Bryce Canyon, but are pleasantly surprised to find a peaceful home-away-from-home!
✉ windwhisper@color-country.net ◐ www.windwhisperbb.com

MOAB

Desert Hills B&B
1989 S Desert Hills Ln 84532
435-259-3568
Vic & Anna Bruno

115-145 BB
5 rooms, 5 pb
Most CC, *Rated*, •
C-ltd/S-no/P-no/H-no
Dutch, French, German
March through October

Full breakfast
Afternoon tea and coffee
Sitting room, library, spa,
fireplace, cable TV, A/C, fan,
hair dryer, iron

Oasis of elegance, comfort and tranquility. Dazzling views of colorful rock formations and snow-capped mountain peaks. Secluded location near Moab's scenic golf course. Belgian owners/innkeepers. Just a short 50 miles from Green River.
✉ info@deserthillsbnb.com ◐ www.deserthillsbnb.com

MOAB ───────────────

Sunflower Hill Luxury Inn
185 N 300 E 84532
800-662-2786 435-259-2974
Stucki family

120-225 BB
12 rooms, 12 pb
Most CC, *Rated*, •
C-ltd/S-no/P-no/H-no

Full breakfast
Evening refreshments, 24
hour beverage service and
snacks available.
Outdoor pool, hot tub, A/C,
robes, spa amenities, cd
players, cable TV/VCR

Inviting country retreat adorned with antiques and a most tasteful decor. Serene setting with lush flower gardens, shade trees and a spectacular outdoor pool. Healthy homemade breakfast. Sunflower Hill is Moab's top rated property (1998 to present—AAA).
✉ innkeeper@sunflowerhill.com ♻ www.sunflowerhill.com

MT. CARMEL ───────────────

**Arrowhead Country Inn
and Cabins**
2155 S State St 84755
888-821-1670 435-648-2569
Jane & Jim Jennings

79-179 BB
10 rooms, 10 pb
Most CC, •
C-yes/S-ltd/P-yes/H-yes
Apr 1st through Dec 31st

Farm Fresh Breakfast Feast
Broken Arrow Restaurant:
Upscale Southwestern
Cuisine prepared with fresh
local ingredients
Views, spacious cabins and
suites, farm fresh breakfast
feast, Jacuzzi, swimming
pool, movie library

A charming and intimate B&B in Southern Utah on Scenic Highway 89, near Maynard Dixon's home studio and between Zion, Bryce and the Grand Canyon. The property has 5 luxury cabins and 5 rooms in the main lodge. Incredible views of the nearby White Cliffs.
✉ duelj1@color-country.net ♻ www.arrowheadbb.com

PARK CITY ───────────────

The Blue Church Lodge
424 Park Ave 84060
800-626-5467 435-649-8009
Louise Wismer

150-650 BB
26 rooms, 24 pb
Cash, Checks, *Rated*,
•
C-yes/S-no/P-no/H-no

Continental breakfast
Hot tubs, gameroom,
kitchens, fireplaces, ski
lockers, sitting room

An eleven suite and townhouse property nestled between the Wasatch Mountains and Park City's Historic Main Street. Just steps away from award-winning restaurants, trendy shops, pubs, live theatre and skiing, there's truly something for everyone.
✉ bcl@qwestoffice.net ♻ www.thebluechurchlodge.com

Old Town Guest House
1011 Empire Ave 84060
800-290-6423 #3710 435-649-2642
Deb Lovci

99-250 BB
4 rooms, 4 pb
Visa, MC, AmEx,
Rated, •
C-ltd/S-no/P-no/H-no

Healthy "Park City" breakfast
Afternoon snacks, tea, and
other items depending on
the season.
Hot tub, common room, boot
dryers, ski storage, robes,
business center,
wireless.Eco-friendly Inn

Nestled in the heart of Park City, Old Town Guest House is the perfect place for active skiers, hikers & bikers wishing to enjoy the mountains of Utah. We are Park City's best for comfort, convenience & affordability. You won't find a better deal!!
✉ Dlovci@cs.com ♻ www.oldtownguesthouse.com

Washington School Inn
543 Park Ave 84060
800-824-1672 435-649-3800
Jean Carlan

150-620 BB
15 rooms, 15 pb
Visa, MC, AmEx, *Rated*
S-no/P-no/H-ltd
German, Spanish

Full breakfast
Afternoon wine & appetizers
Spa, sauna, ski lockers,
mezzanine area, dining room

In the heart of Park City, Utah, a most elegant, luxurious & full service bed & breakfast style Inn can be found, the Washington School Inn. It's just a block from Town Lift & Main Street.
✉ info@washingtonschoolinn.com ♻ www.washingtonschoolinn.com

PARK CITY
Woodside Inn
1469 Woodside Ave 84068
888-241-5890 435-649-3494
Bob & Carolyn McCallister

109-349 BB
7 rooms, 7 pb
Most CC, *Rated*, •
C-ltd/S-no/P-no/H-yes

Full breakfast
Snacks, complimentary wine
Sitting room, Jacuzzis, suites,
cable TV, elevator, business
traveler accommodations

The only newly-constructed B&B in Park City! Fully air conditioned with elevator. Woodside Inn is minutes from Park City's restaurants, art galleries, shops and famous Main Street. ✉ info@woodsideinn.com ◑ www.woodsideinn.com

PROVIDENCE
Providence Inn B&B
10 South Main St 84332
800-480-4943 435-752-3432
Karl Seethaler

99-199 BB
17 rooms, 17 pb
Most CC
C-ltd/S-no/P-no/H-ltd

Full hot gourmet breakfast
Two person jetted tubs,
TV/VCR, free high speed
wireless access, dial up
access

The Providence Inn offers the perfect accommodations for any occasion, whether you're traveling for business or pleasure. Listed on the Nat'l Register of Historic Places. Weddings, receptions, luncheons and special celebrations hosted. Onsite church. ✉ stay@ProvidenceInn.com ◑ www.providenceinn.com

SALT LAKE CITY
Ellerbeck Mansion B&B
140 N B St 84103
800-966-8364 801-355-2500
Debbie

119-149 BB
6 rooms, 6 pb
Most CC, *Rated*, •
C-ltd/S-no/P-no/H-ltd

Full breakfast
Water, soft drinks, hot
chocolate and snacks
available
Telephone, TV, turndown
service, sitting room,
fireplace, wireless Internet,
library

Short 5 block walk to Temple Square and downtown Salt Lake City. 20 minutes from ski resorts. Historic 1892 mansion built by Thomas Ellerbeck, chief clerk to Brigham Young. Built in historic avenues neighborhood. ✉ ellerbeckmansion@qwestoffice.net ◑ www.ellerbeckbedandbreakfast.com

Haxton Manor
943 E South Temple 84102
877-930-4646 801-363-4646
Buffi & Douglas King

120-200 BB
7 rooms, 7 pb
Visa, MC, AmEx,
Rated, •
C-ltd/S-no/P-no/H-yes
Spanish

Continental plus breakfast
Tea, snacks
Sitting room, library, Jacuzzi,
fireplace, cable TV,
conferences, Guest laundry
service

Tucked neatly within the heart of the Salt Lake Valley, and minutes away from city center and many world famous canyon ski areas, is historic Haxton Manor. English-style, historic country Inn conveniently located within walking distance of the university. ✉ innkeepers@haxtonmanor.com ◑ www.haxtonmanor.com

Parrish Place B&B
720 E Ashton Ave 84106
801-832-0970
Jeff & Karin Gauvin

89-139 BB
5 rooms, 5 pb
Most CC, *Rated*, •
S-ltd/P-no/H-no
Swedish

Continental plus breakfast
Complimentary beverages
Cable TV/VCR, video library,
free WiFi, hot tub, robes and
guest telephone.

Come and experience the elegance of a hundred plus years of architectural beauty recaptured at the Parrish Place. ✉ info@parrishplace.com ◑ www.parrishplace.com

Silver Fork Lodge
11332 E Big Cottonwood
Canyon 84121
888-649-9551 801-533-9977
Dan Knopp & Rose Rogers

90-200 BB
7 rooms, 7 pb
Most CC
C-yes/S-no/P-no/H-no

Full breakfast
Restaurant, bar service
Sitting room, library, sauna,
outdoor hot tub, cable TV

Rustic log ski lodge nestled in the Wasatch National Forest. Full service restaurant on premises, outdoor Jacuzzi, indoor sauna. The restaurant was voted "best food with a view." ✉ silverforklodge27@sisna.com ◑ www.silverforklodge.com

582   Utah

SALT LAKE CITY ──────────────────────────────

Wildflowers B&B
936 E 1700 S 84105
800-569-0009 801-466-0600
Cill Sparks & Jeri Parker

85-145 BB
5 rooms, 5 pb
Most CC, *Rated*, •
C-ltd/S-no/P-no/H-no
French

Full breakfast
Restaurant nearby
Sitting room, library, deck,
stained glass windows

*National Historic 1891 Victorian offering delights of past and comforts of the present.
Wildflower gardens, close to park, downtown, ski resorts.*
✉ lark2spur@aol.com ○ www.wildflowersbb.com

SANDY ──────────────────────────────

Castle Creek Inn
7391 S Creek Rd 84093
800-571-2669 801-567-9437
Sallie Calder

129-259 BB
10 rooms, 10 pb
Most CC, *Rated*
C-ltd/S-no/P-no/H-yes

Full breakfast
Afternoon tea, snacks
Jacuzzis, fireplaces, cable
TV, accom. bus. travelers,
suites

*An authentic Scottish castle, nestled among tall oak trees, provides ten elegant suites each
uniquely decorated with castle decor.*
✉ salliecal@msn.com ○ www.castleutah.com

ST. GEORGE ──────────────────────────────

**Green Gate Village Historic
Inn**
76 W Tabernacle 84770
800-350-6999 435-628-6999
Lin & Ed Sandstrom

99-259 BB
14 rooms, 14 pb
Most CC, *Rated*, •
C-ltd/S-no/P-no/H-ltd

Full breakfast
Lunch of home-made soups,
sandwiches & sweat treats
available Mon-Sat at Judd's
General Store
Pool, business & reception
centers, meeting rooms,
restaurant, snack bar, gift
shop

*Welcome to the Green Gate Village Historic Inn. Behind our green gates you'll discover 14
unique buildings including nine beautifully restored pioneer homes, nestled in a garden-
like setting around our "Village Green" and swimming pool.*
✉ stay@greengatevillageinn.com ○ www.greengatevillageinn.com

TEASDALE ──────────────────────────────

Muley Twist Inn
249 West 125 St 84773
800-530-1038 435-425-3640
Eric & Penny Kinsman

99-140 BB
5 rooms, 5 pb
Visa, MC, AmEx,
Rated, •
C-yes/S-no/P-no/H-yes
April 1 – Oct 15

Full breakfast
Afternoon tea, snacks
Sitting room, library,
accommodations for
business travelers,
wheelchair accessible

*Distinctive lodging at the edge of the world. Newly built, 5-room B&B with private baths,
delicious breakfasts, gourmet coffee and magnificent views from large porches. Come and
enjoy the quiet!*
✉ muley@rof.net ○ www.muleytwistinn.com

TORREY ──────────────────────────────

SkyRidge Inn B&B
950 E Hwy 24 84775
800-448-6990 435-425-3222
Irene & Kim

89-164 BB
6 rooms, 6 pb
Visa, MC, AmEx, *Rated*
C-ltd/S-ltd/P-no/H-ltd

Full breakfast
Beverages; snacks and hors
d'oeuvres, sangria & tea
served between 5:00–5:30
p.m.
Contemporary art, southwest
gifts, gift gallery, evening turn
down service

*Nationally recognized for its magnificent views & artfully decorated rooms, SkyRidge Bed
& Breakfast Inn offers guests a restful experience with 4-Diamond quality and attention.*
✉ info@skyridgeinn.com ○ www.skyridgeinn.com

Vermont

ARLINGTON ────────────────

Arlington Inn
#3904 Historic Rt 7A 05250
800-443-9442 802-375-6532
Eric & Elizabeth Berger

99-319 BB
17 rooms, 17 pb
Most CC, *Rated*, •
C-yes/S-ltd/P-no/H-yes

Full breakfast
Afternoon Snack & Hot
Mulled Cider, Gourmet
Dining, Full Service Tavern
with Wine List
Victorian Parlor, Country
Gardens, Gazebo, Carriage
Barn, Porches & Patio's,
Jacuzzi's, FP, Internet

Experience elegance and style in this Victorian Inn decorated with beautiful antiques. 17 luxurious rooms, fireplaces, Jacuzzi's, and full breakfast. Editor's Pick Yankee Travel Guide. ✉ stay@arlingtoninn.com ◌ www.arlingtoninn.com

Arlington's West Mountain Inn
144 West Mountain Inn Rd
05250
802-375-6516
The Carlson Family

165-340 MAP
20 rooms, 20 pb
Visa, MC, AmEx,
Rated, •
C-yes/S-ltd/P-no/H-yes
French

Full breakfast
Dinner included, bar
Fruit, chocolates, llamas,
piano, dining room, flowers,
conference room

150-acre hillside estate; hike or ski woodland trails. Fish the Battenkill. Hearthside dining, charming rooms. Relax and enjoy the llamas, goats and rabbits. 2006 "Fodor's Choice" and a Yankee Travel Guide "Editor's Pick" twice in the last five years.
✉ info@westmountaininn.com ◌ www.westmountaininn.com

Country Willows c.1850
332 E Arlington Rd 05250
800-796-2585 802-375-0019
Anne & Ron Weber

146-185 BB
5 rooms, 5 pb
Visa, MC
C-ltd/S-no/P-no/H-no

Award winning, bountiful
breakfasts
Late afternoon light
refreshments, optional
Sitting room with fireplace,
library, suites, in-room
fireplaces, coffee service

Gracious Queen Anne Victorian Inn, c.1850 on the National Register of Historic Places. Intimate, romantic and family-owned! Arlington is a charming and historic village. Ski Bromley or Stratton. Famed BattenKill, "home" river of Orvis headquarters!
✉ cwillows332@myfairpoint.net ◌ www.countrywillows.com

Hill Farm Inn
458 Hill Farm Rd 05250
800-882-2545 802-375-2269
Lisa & Al Gray

110-250 BB
15 rooms, 15 pb
Most CC, *Rated*, •
C-yes/S-no/P-no/H-no

Full country breakfast
Afternoon/evening tea
Walking trails along the river,
farm animals, views,
fireplaces, A/C, cable TV,
weddings

200 year old dairy farm on 50 acres along the Battenkill River, walking trails, farm animals, spectacular views. Full country breakfast. Suites, cabins, fireplaces, kitchens. Families welcome. Minutes to Manchester, VT. Country weddings.
✉ stay@hillfarminn.com ◌ www.hillfarminn.com

BARNARD ────────────────

The Fan House
Rt 12 N 05031
802-234-9096
Sara Widness

160-240 BB
3 rooms, 3 pb
Visa, MC, •
C-ltd/S-no/P-ltd/H-no
Italian, some German

Full breakfast
Beverage, cheese and
crackers
Sitting room, library, garden,
lake within 3 minute walk

Guests visibly relax upon entering the 1840 country kitchen. They're home. They sense they will sleep well, enveloped in understated elegance, sensuous comfort and style.
✉ swidness@aol.com ◌ www.thefanhouse.com

BARNARD———————————————————————————

The Maple Leaf Inn
5890 Vermont Rt 12 05031
800-516-2753 802-234-5342
Nancy & Mike Boyle

160-290 BB
7 rooms, 7 pb
Visa, MC, *Rated*
C-ltd/S-no/P-no/H-yes

Full gourmet breakfast
Afternoon tea, snacks,
complimentary wine
Sitting room, library, tennis
court, Jacuzzis, fireplaces,
satellite TV

A Victorian-style farmhouse nestled snugly within sixteen acres of maple and birch trees is The Maple Leaf Inn. The inn is located in Barnard, VT. A quintessential village with steepled churches, general store, country lanes and back roads.
✉ innkeeper@mapleleafinn.com ◐ www.mapleleafinn.com

BELLOWS FALLS———————————————————————

Readmore Bed, Breakfast & Books
1 Hapgood St 05101
802-463-9415
Stewart & Dorothy Read

150-250 BB
5 rooms, 5 pb
Visa, MC, Disc
C-ltd/S-no/P-no/H-ltd
A little French

Full gourmet breakfast
Afternoon tea on request
Robes, turndown service,
flowers, chocolate on
pillows, fireplaces & Jacuzzi,
gift shop, concierge

Start the day with a full, gourmet breakfast. Come stroll through our gardens, relax in our gazebo or on the front porch. Sample the tea offerings. On chilly days, cuddle up by the fire with a book.
✉ read@sover.net ◐ www.readmoreinn.com

BENNINGTON———————————————————————

Alexandra B&B Inn
916 Orchard Rd 05201
888-207-9386 802-442-5619
Daniel & Amanda Tarquino

105-195 BB
12 rooms, 12 pb
Most CC, *Rated*
C-ltd/S-no/P-no/H-ltd
Spanish

Full Gourmet Breakfast
Afternoon tea; full bar & fine
dining restaurant serving to
guests only.
Cable TV, phones, fireplaces,
A/C, wireless Internet, sitting
room, sun room, terrace,
gardens.

An 1859 Vermont Farm House Inn with splendid views overlooking the Bennington Monument & Green Mountains of Vermont, the Alexandra B&B offers an elegant understated respite for weary business travelers or vacationing adventurers.
✉ alexandr@sover.net ◐ www.alexandrainn.com

Eddington House Inn
21 Main St 05257
800-941-1857 802-442-1511
Patti Eddington

89-159 BB
3 rooms, 3 pb
Most CC
C-ltd/S-no/P-no/H-ltd

Full gourmet breakfast
Afternoon refreshments,
endless desserts, in room
chocolate truffles
Fireplaces, air conditioning,
Wifi, bicycle storage

Elegantly restored Southern Vermont bed and breakfast nestled in the heart of North Bennington Village. Walk to Bennington College, award winning restaurants and waterfalls. Close to Covered Bridges, Green Mountains & Shopping. Great VT Getaway Packages.
✉ edhousevt@comcast.net ◐ www.eddingtonhouseinn.com

Four Chimneys Inn & Restaurant
21 West Rd Rte 9 05201
802-447-3500
Lynn & Pete Green

125-295 BB
11 rooms, 11 pb
Most CC, *Rated*, •
C-ltd/S-no/P-no/H-yes
Polish
Peak: June thru October

Full breakfast
Casual Fine Dining. Full wine
list and cocktails.
Dinner, cocktail lounge,
patios, beautiful grounds, in
room massage, in room high
speed Internet

One of New England's premier inns located on 11 magnificent acres, in historic Old Bennington, VT. 11 uniquely appointed rooms each with private bath, TV, phone & A/C, Internet. Full breakfast. Casual fine dining with full bar. Warm & friendly atmosph
✉ innkeeper@fourchimneys.com ◐ www.fourchimneys.com

BENNINGTON

South Shire Inn	125-250 BB	Full breakfast
124 Elm St 05201	9 rooms, 9 pb	Afternoon tea & homemade
888-201-2250 802-447-3839	Visa, MC, *Rated*	cookies.
George & Joyce Goeke	C-ltd/S-no/P-no/H-no	A/C, telephone, fireplaces, whirlpool bath, TVs with VCR. Wireless Internet. Wake up.

Elegant Victorian Inn offering luxurious accommodations, private baths, A/C and fireplaces. Walk to restaurants, shops and historic sites. Full breakfast served.
✉ relax@southshire.com ◐ www.southshire.com

BOLTON VALLEY

Black Bear Inn	89-350 BB	Full Country Breakfast
4010 Bolton Access Rd 05477	25 rooms, 25 pb	Candlelight dinners, full bar,
800-395-6335 802-434-2126	Visa, MC, Disc, •	extensive, reasonably priced
Brian & Jill Drinkwater	C-yes/S-no/P-yes/H-ltd	wine list
		Free WiFi, parlor, public and private hot tubs, outdoor pool, suites, fireplaces, cable, books

Mountaintop Country Inn, featuring 25 individually decorated rooms and suites. Many with hot tubs and Vermont firestoves. Pet-friendly, family-friendly, the only ski-in/ski-out inn in Vermont! Full Country Breakfasts each day and Gourmet Candlit Dinners.
✉ blkbear@wcvt.com ◐ www.blackbearinn.travel

BRANDON

Churchill House Inn	100-180 BB	Full breakfast
Route 73 E 05733	8 rooms, 8 pb	Complimentary 24-hr
800-320-5828 802-247-3078	Most CC, •	beverage bar; 4-course
Seth & Olya Hopkins	C-ltd/S-no/P-no/H-no	dinner $30, by advance
	Russian	reservation only; trail lunch
	Closed most of April	$6
		Four gracious common rooms; open-hearth stoves; WiFi; computer; CD library; piano; hike/bike tours

Classic country inn welcoming guests since 1872. Experience the serenity of the Green Mountains just outside pleasant Brandon village. Vermont Green Hotel with great New England food (featured by Gourmet), lots of charm. Family reunions are a specialty.
✉ stay@churchillhouseinn.com ◐ www.churchillhouseinn.com

The Lilac Inn	125-320 BB	Full breakfast
53 Park St 05733	9 rooms, 9 pb	private receptions including
800-221-0720 802-247-5463	Visa, MC, AmEx,	business meetings,
Doug & Shelly Sawyer	*Rated*, •	weddings, anniversaries, &
	C-ltd/S-no/P-ltd/H-ltd	special celebrations
	French	Weddings, business meetings, romantic gardens, dining, DVD, cable TV, A/C, private baths

The Lilac Inn is a leading, luxury Vermont Country Inn known for romantic getaway weekends, custom weddings & receptions and special occasions—in any season. The feel throughout is that of a "small luxury hotel with personal service to match."
✉ innkeeper@lilacinn.com ◐ www.lilacinn.com

BRATTLEBORO————————————————————————————————————

1868 Crosby House
175 Western Avenue 05301
800-638-5148 802-257-7145
Lynn Kuralt

110-175 BB
7 rooms, 7 pb
Cash, Checks, •
C-ltd/S-no/P-no/H-no

Full breakfast
Snacks & Afternoon Tea
Sitting room, library,
whirlpool, suites, cable TV,
fireplaces, wireless Internet,
train pickup/drop

Historic home decorated with family heirlooms and collected antiques, luxurious accommodations, elegant gourmet breakfasts. Private baths, fireplaces, whirlpool, wireless Internet, Landscaped gardens, walking trails, close to town shops & restaurants.
✉ lynn@crosbyhouse.com ☼ www.crosbyhouse.com

Forty Putney Road B&B
192 Putney Rd 05301
800-941-2413 802-254-6268
Tim and Amy Brady

159-289 BB
6 rooms, 6 pb
Most CC, *Rated*, •
C-ltd/S-no/P-no/H-ltd

Gourmet Breakfast
Our cozy in-house pub offers
light fare as well as a wide
variety of wines and beers.
Sun rooms, beautiful
gardens, outdoor dining,
library, hiking/bike trails,
TVs, WiFi, A/C

Forty Putney Road is just steps from downtown Brattleboro, VT. Enjoy comfortably elegant lodging in our French Provincial mansion. Stroll our beautiful gardens, enjoy a glass of wine in our cozy fire-lit pub, or relax in our sun room with a good book.
✉ innkeepers@fortyputneyroad.com ☼ www.fortyputneyroad.com

Green River Bridge House
2435 Stage Road 05301
800-528-1868 802-257-5771
Joan Seymour

165-235 BB
3 rooms, 3 pb
Most CC
S-no/P-no

Full breakfast
Afternoon tea and snacks
Spa services, Jacuzzi, game
room

Built in 1830, this charming B&B once housed the Green River Post Office and is nestled against the meandering river that gave it its name. It is luxurious in comfort and sensuous in visual appeal.
✉ grbh@sover.net ☼ www.greenriverbridgehouse.com

Meadowlark Inn B&B
Orchard St 05303
800-616-6359 802-257-4582
Lucia Osiecki & Deborah
Jones

139-239 BB
8 rooms, 8 pb
Visa, MC, AmEx, *Rated*
C-yes/S-no/P-no/H-ltd
Spanish

Full breakfast
Afternoon tea & snacks
Sitting room, library,
fireplaces, cable TV, free
wireless Internet access

Fully restored 1870's Vermont country inn with amenities that will surprise and delight guests! Relaxing & quiet with panoramic views all around. A delicious full breakfast prepared & served by the owners who just happen to be trained chefs.
✉ innkeeper@meadowlarkinnvt.com ☼ www.meadowlarkinnvt.com

BRIDGEWATER CORNERS————————————————————————————

October Country Inn
362 Upper Rd 05035
800-648-8421 802-672-3412
Edie & Chuck Janisse

165-195 BB
10 rooms, 10 pb
Visa, MC, *Rated*, •
C-yes/S-no/P-no/H-ltd
Spanish

Full country breakfast
Coffee, tea, cookies, beer &
wine licensed; Dinner (when
available) is $30.00 per
person.
Pool, gardens, library, games,
hiking, bicycling, skiing,
snowboarding

October Country Inn is loved because guests feel like they're at home here. Experience genuine Vermont hospitality—enjoy the relaxed atmosphere and farmhouse charm surrounded by the scenic splendor of the Green Mountains.
✉ innkeeper@octobercountryinn.com ☼ www.vermontinns.net

BURLINGTON————————————————————————————————

Lang House on Main Street	145-225 BB	Gourmet breakfasts
360 Main St 05401	11 rooms, 11 pb	Afternoon snack of cookies,
877-919-9799 802-652-2500	Most CC	coffee, tea, and or lemonade.
Kim Borsavage	C-yes/S-no/P-no/H-yes	For sale cheese plates, beer
		and wine
		Robes for guest use, in-room
		AC/heat control, alarm
		clocks, off-street parking,
		wireless Internet

Beautifully kept period furnishings & antiques. Soaring ceilings, stained glass windows, & stunning woodwork & plaster detailing, with a rosette pattern repeated throughout the house.   ✉ innkeeper@langhouse.com ◐ www.langhouse.com

CHESTER————————————————————————————————

Fullerton Inn	89-209 BB	Continental plus breakfast
40 The Common 05143	21 rooms, 21 pb	Dinner available, excellent
866-884-8578 802-875-2444	Visa, MC, AmEx	restaurant serving dinner 5–9
Bret & Nancy Rugg	C-ltd/S-no/P-no/H-no	pm Monday through
		Saturday
		Restaurant, bar, sitting room,
		suites, fireplaces, conference
		room, wireless Internet, TV
		in bar

Elegant comfortable inn on the Village Green. Guests will find immaculate rooms & a professional, courteous staff. Casual dining available in our restaurant. Relax in our Tavern with a local brew.
✉ getaway@fullertoninn.com ◐ www.fullertoninn.com

Henry Farm Inn	100-165 BB	Full breakfast
2206 Green Mountain Tpke	9 rooms, 9 pb	Fireplace, sitting room,
05143	Most CC, *Rated*, •	swimming & skating pond,
800-723-8213 802-875-2674	C-yes/S-ltd/P-no/H-ltd	cross-country ski trail
Patricia & Paul Dexter		

1700s Colonial in country setting, 1 mile from Chester Village. Fifty-six acres including pond, meadow, woods & river. Nine spacious guestrooms all with private baths. Children very welcome.
✉ info@henryfarminn.com ◐ www.henryfarminn.com

Hugging Bear Inn & Shoppe	125-185 BB	A delicious country
244 Main St 05143	6 rooms, 6 pb	breakfast
800-325-0519 802-875-2412	Most CC, *Rated*	Afternoon snack of Vermont
Georgette Thomas	C-yes/S-no/P-no/H-no	cheddar cheese, cider, tea
		and coffee
		A/C, 2 living rooms, library,
		computer, Internet, wireless,
		games, toys, gift shop,
		collectibles

Vermont family B&B and teddy bear shop. Elegant Victorian in National Historic District. Largest selection of Steiff, Muffy Vanderbear and Artist bears in New England.
✉ inn@huggingbear.com ◐ www.huggingbear.com

Inn Victoria	115-295 BB	Full gourmet breakfast
321 Main St 05143	7 rooms, 7 pb	Afternoon tea, dinner by
802-875-4288	Visa, MC, *Rated*	prior arrangement
Julie & Jonathan Pierce	C-ltd/S-no/P-no/H-yes	Victorian parlor, cable TV,
	some Spanish	DVD, Jacuzzis, fireplaces,
		A/C, WiFi Internet, hot tub,
		robes

You've found us!! Rated in the Top Ten Bed and Breakfast Inns in the USA. Rated the top B&B in Vermont 2006 2007. Romantic and Luxurious blended with charm and friendly service. The epitome of B&B experience
✉ innkeeper@innvictoria.com ◐ www.innvictoria.com

CHESTER

Park Light Inn
232 Depot St 05143
888-875-4417 802-875-4417
Jo-Ann & Jack

159-289 BB
5 rooms, 5 pb
Visa, MC, AmEx, •
C-yes/S-no/P-no/H-no
Danish

3 Course Gourmet Breakfast
24 hr free tea, coffee, snacks
etc., additional meals (extra
fee) available with 24 hours
notice
Romance, common rooms
and areas, plush robes,
suites, wood burning stoves,
fireplaces, porches/decks

*The Park Light Inn is one of Southern Vermont's most luxurious and romantic destinations.
All of today's modern amenities in a casual but elegant setting, including mountain views,
floral gardens, hot-tub, pool table & much more, all at reasonable rates.*
✉ innkeepers@parklightinn.com ☏ www.parklightinn.com

Quail Hollow Inn
Route 11 05143
888-829-9874 802-875-2794
Peter Stearns & Bob Elklinson

119-199 BB
7 rooms, 7 pb
Visa, MC, AmEx, *Rated*
C-yes/S-no/P-no/H-no

Full breakfast
The Pub Room – enjoy a
wide selection of beer &
wine
Great Room, TV, stereo,
games, DVD, videos,
fireplace, WiFi, Jacuzzi

*The Quail Hollow Inn, built in the mid-1800's, is located in the lovely Victorian town of
Chester, one of the most scenic parts of Vermont. Skiing and championship golf courses are
nearby. We offer scrapbooking retreats. Wireless Internet is available.*
✉ quailinn@vermontel.net ☏ www.quailhollowinn.com

Rose Arbour B&B
55 School St 05143
802-875-4767
Suzanne Nielsen

95-150 BB
3 rooms, 1 pb
Visa, MC, Disc
C-ltd/S-no/P-no/H-no

Full breakfast
Tea room/ tea & lunches
served
Sitting room/library, VCR &
DVD, antiques, down
comforters, gift shop & tea
room

*A visit to Rose Arbour recalls & restores a pace of life from an earlier era, allowing you the
opportunity to slow things down a little. Sip & savor life instead of gulping it down without
ever tasting its pleasures.*
✉ suzy@rosearbour.com ☏ www.rosearbour.com

CHITTENDEÑ

Fox Creek Inn
49 Dam Rd 05737
800-707-0017 802-483-6213
Sandy and Jim Robertson

195-400 MAP
9 rooms, 9 pb
Visa, MC, AmEx,
Rated, •
C-ltd/S-no/P-ltd/H-yes

Full breakfast
Dinner included
Complimentary soft drinks,
tea, coffee, snacks upon
request
Full bar & wine cellar, sitting
room, library and dining
room

*Small sophisticated country inn hidden away in the Green Mountains. Excellent restaurant,
first class wine list, full bar. Wonderfully spacious and comfortable rooms offering peace
and quiet.* ✉ innkeeper@foxcreekinn.com ☏ www.foxcreekinn.com

---

Mountain Top Inn & Resort
195 Mountain Top Rd 05737
800-445-2100 802-483-2311
Khele Sparks

160-575 BB
30 rooms, 30 pb
Visa, MC, AmEx, •
C-yes/S-no/P-yes/H-yes

Full breakfast
Lunch, dinner available;
morning & afternoon snacks
Beach, pontoon boat, flyfish,
trail ride, ice skate, xc ski,
snowshoe, sleigh ride,
snowmobile, kayak

*Classic mountain resort set on 350 acres. Breathtaking lake & mountain views, endless
outdoor adventures. Equestrian & Nordic Ski & Snowshoe Center with 60km of trails.
Creative cuisine, casual bistro fare, or seasonally on the terrace. Great packages.*
✉ stay@mountaintopinn.com ☏ www.mountaintopinn.com

DORSET

Marble West Inn	125-225 BB	Full breakfast
1847 Dorset West Rd 05251	8 rooms, 8 pb	Refreshments, afternoon tea,
800-453-7629 802-867-4155	Visa, MC, AmEx, *Rated*	sitting room, library
Sammi & Rob Lemonik	C-ltd/S-no/P-no/H-no	

Historic 1840 Greek Revival inn. Elegant, quiet, peaceful, off busy main road, with mountain views, gardens & trout ponds. 8 individually decorated guestrooms, all with private baths & A/C. Close to restaurants, shops, museums, designer outlets.
✉ innkeeper@marblewestinn.com ✪ www.marblewestinn.com

Squire House	165-250 BB	Full breakfast
3395 Dorset W Rd 05251	3 rooms, 3 pb	Afternoon tea
802-867-0281	Cash, Checks	Common rooms, fireplaces,
Gay & Roger Squire	C-ltd/S-no/P-no/H-no	antiques, piano, books,
		dining room, wireless
		Internet access

A gracious country estate built in 1918 & carefully renovated, a luxurious B&B on 11 private acres. Elegant, with rich architectural details, yet relaxed & informal.
✉ info@squirehouse.com ✪ www.squirehouse.com

EAST DOVER

Cooper Hill Inn	110-240 BB	Full breakfast
117 Cooper Hill Rd 05341	10 rooms, 10 pb	We provide all meals for
800-783-3229 802-348-6333	Visa, MC	group reunions and catering
Charles & Lee Wheeler	C-yes/S-no/P-no/H-no	for weddings of up to 200
	Mandarin, Spanish	people
	Closed April	Sitting room,
		Jacuzzi/fireplaces in some
		rooms, fireplace, game room,
		satellite TV, wireless Internet

A hilltop inn with one of the most spectacular views in New England. The perfect place for weddings, retreats, or family reunions.
✉ coopinn@sover.net ✪ www.cooperhillinn.com

FAIRLEE

Silver Maple Lodge & Cottages	72-109 BB	Continental breakfast
520 US Rt 5 S 05045	15 rooms, 13 pb	Sitting room, cottages
800-666-1946 802-333-4326	Most CC, •	w/fireplaces, bicycles, canoe
Scott & Sharon Wright	C-yes/S-ltd/P-ltd/H-ltd	rentals, Hot air balloon
		flights arranged

Quaint country inn located in scenic resort area. Convenient to antique shops, fishing, golf, swimming, tennis & winter skiing.
✉ scott@silvermaplelodge.com ✪ www.silvermaplelodge.com

GAYSVILLE

Cobble House Inn	99-140 BB	Please advise of special
1 Cobble House Rd 05746	4 rooms, 4 pb	needs.
802-234-5458	Cash, Checks, •	Afternoon snack, tea &
Tony Caparis	C-yes/S-no/P-ltd/H-ltd	coffee. Lunches and dinners
		are also available with
		advance notice.
		Free WiFi, Laundry, TV,
		Massage, woodstove, large
		porch, library, snowshoes,
		gold pans available

Cobble House Inn is a grand 1860's late-Victorian mansion, set in a hillside on the White River bank. Enjoy swimming, tubing, kayaking, fishing, snowshoeing, X-country skiing. The only bed and breakfast in the Village of Gaysville and Town of Stockbridge.
✉ unwind@cobblehouseinn.com ✪ www.cobblehouseinn.com

GOSHEN

High Meadow B&B
1742 Goshen Ripton Rd 05733
802-247-3820
Patrice Lopatin

110-120 BB
3 rooms, 1 pb
Cash, Checks
C-ltd/S-no/P-ltd/H-no
Some Spanish, French
and Norwegian

Early continental/later full
Available: custom box
lunches & dinners with prior
notice to stay. Guests can
store food as well.
Kitchen use, wild
mushroom/wild edibles
forays, wild apple cider
pressing, kayak rental,
broadband

*High Meadow is a cheerful sunny little 3-bedroom cottage located in The Green Mountain
National Forest area in Goshen Vermont with water and mountain views.*
✉ highmeadowbedandbreakfast@gmail.com ○ www.highmeadowbb.com

GREENSBORO

Highland Lodge
Caspian Lake Rd 05841
802-533-2647
David & Wilhelmina Smith

265-330 MAP
19 rooms, 19 pb
Visa, MC, Disc, •
C-yes/S-ltd/P-no/H-ltd
Dutch, Japanese
5/22-10/12; 12/23-3/15

Full breakfast
Lunch (fee) in dining room;
box lunches available,
cottages have kitchenettes or
refrigerators
Tennis, beach, boats, play
program, 50 KM cross
country ski & snowshoe
trails, family nordic quest

*A most comfortable, extremely clean family resort with elegant homemade meals. Country
inn & cottages with lakeside beach, boats, tennis, 50KM exquisite cross-country ski trails
and views. Ideal for family vacations, reunions, romantic getaways, retreats.*
✉ highland.lodge@verizon.net ○ www.highlandlodge.com

HARDWICK

Kimball House
173 Glenside Ave 05843
802-472-6228
Sue Holmes

89-99 BB
3 rooms
C-ltd/S-no/P-no/H-ltd

Full breakfast
Light supper available with
prior arrangements.
Kitchen, porches, gardens,
dining room

*The house has a warm comfortable feeling and is situated on large well-groomed and
garden filled grounds. There is a timeless beauty that surrounds the house and grounds that
makes leaving difficult.* ✉ holmesue@aol.com ○ www.kimballhouse.com

HINESBURG

The Hidden Gardens B&B
693 Lewis Creek Rd 05461
802-482-2118
Marcia C. Pierce

80-145 BB
2 rooms
Most CC
C-ltd/S-no/P-no/H-no

Full breakfast
Cookies, shortbread, tea,
soda
Living room and sunroom,
pond, DSL wireless Internet,
bicycles, camp, gardens,
private bath option

*Contemporary large-timbered post and beam home with vaulted ceilings, surrounded by 26
acres of woods and gardens. Great getaway for adults visiting Vermont's Champlain Valley
and Green Mountains.*
✉ info@thehiddengardens.com ○ www.thehiddengardens.com

HUNTINGTON

**Sleepy Hollow Inn, Ski &
Bike Center**
1805 Sherman Hollow Rd
05462
866-254-1524 802-434-2283
Molly Peters

105-155 BB
8 rooms, 6 pb
Visa, MC, AmEx
C-yes/S-no/P-no/H-yes

Full breakfast
Swimming pond, wood-fired
sauna, weddings, events,
sitting rooms, fireplaces, trail
passes

*Welcome to Sleepy Hollow, a Vermont Country Inn featuring acclaimed Nordic skiing and
mountain biking, in a beautiful setting. Moose, deer, wild turkey, and other wildlife abound.*
✉ info@skisleepyhollow.com ○ www.skisleepyhollow.com

HYDE PARK ───────────────────────────────

Fitch Hill Inn	100-210 BB	Full breakfast
258 Fitch Hill Rd 05655	6 rooms, 6 pb	Tea, cocoa, cider or
800-639-2903 802-888-3834	Most CC, *Rated*, •	lemonade, and cookies in
Julie & John Rohleder	C-ltd/S-no/P-no/H-no	the afternoon
	German	TVs, video library, board
		games, Internet computer,
		WiFi, CD players, CD library

Quiet retreat on 3 acres overlooking Green Mountains, 10 miles north of Stowe. Beautifully renovated 200 yr-old house with 4 guestrooms & 2 one-room suites with fireplace and whirlpool tub. Full breakfast. ✉ innkeeper@fitchhillinn.com ◐ www.fitchhillinn.com

The Governor's House In	95-265 BB	Full breakfast
Hyde Park	8 rooms, 6 pb	Afternoon tea, snacks,
100 Main St 05655	Visa, MC, AmEx, •	dinner & picnics by request
866-800-6888 802-888-6888	C-yes/S-no/P-no/H-yes	Fireplaces, high-speed
Suzanne Boden	French	Internet, cable/VCR/DVD,
	June- March	movie library, snacks, Ben &
		Jerry's ice cream

Centerpiece of quiet Hyde Park village, Governor's House offers modern comfort with the gracious elegance of an earlier time. Bedroom fireplaces. Afternoon tea. Intimate weddings. Jane Austen weekends. Many specials and the perfect elopement package. ✉ info@OneHundredMain.com ◐ www.OneHundredMain.com

JAMAICA ───────────────────────────────

Three Mountain Inn	165-370 BB	Full breakfast
Main St, Rt 30 05343	15 rooms, 15 pb	AAA 4-Diamond dining room,
800-532-9399 802-874-4140	Most CC, *Rated*, •	fully stocked bar, award
Jennifer & Ed Dorta-Duque	C-ltd/S-no/P-ltd/H-ltd	winning wine list
	Spanish	All rooms have A/C and heat,
		augmented with gas
		fireplaces, wireless Internet
		access in common room

The Three Mountain Inn, located in the unspoiled village of Jamaica, VT, is a perfect choice to spend a few days of rest and relaxation. We invite you to enjoy a warm and comfortable atmosphere, with exceptional food and the finest personal service. ✉ stay@threemtn.com ◐ www.threemountaininn.com

JEFFERSONVILLE ───────────────────────────────

Smuggler's Notch Inn	89-129 BB	$10 gift card for restaurant
55 Church St 05464	11 rooms, 11 pb	Full breakfast, lunch, pub &
866-644-6607 802-644-6607	Visa, MC, AmEx, *Rated*	dinner menus including:
Patrick & Lisa Martin	C-yes/S-no/P-no/H-no	burgers, sandwiches, wings,
		nachos, steak,
		Dining room, tavern, bakery,
		Jacuzzi tubs, fireplaces,
		deck, hot tub, disc. lift
		tickets, Sat.TV

The Smugglers' Notch Inn is a family-friendly, 11-room Inn complete with a 65-seat dining room, full-service bakery & a 60-seat tavern. Our executive chef, Lorri Dunn, has been featured in Gourmet magazine & our inn has been featured in Yankee Magazine. ✉ info@smuggsinn.com ◐ www.smuggsinn.com

JERICHO ───────────────────────────────

1804 Potter House	65-75 BB	Full breakfast
2 Plains Rd 05465	3 rooms	Afternoon tea, snacks
802-899-1276	Most CC, *Rated*, •	Sitting room, fireplaces,
Mike & Bear Mumley	C-ltd/S-no/P-no/H-no	cable TV, accommodates
		business travelers

Historic Colonial Inn used as stagecoach stop & tavern. Wide board floors, antiques, cozy quilts, 4-poster beds. Enjoy a full, homemade breakfast with farm fresh eggs and locally produced sausage. Amos and Andy our black lab mix are waiting to greet you. ✉ Potrhowz@together.net

JERICHO————————————————————————

Homeplace B&B	115-125 BB	Full breakfast
90 Old Pump Rd, Essex Jt.	6 rooms, 4 pb	Common room with puzzles,
05465	Cash, Checks	piano
802-899-4694	C-yes/S-no/P-ltd/H-no	
Mariot Huessy		

A unique Vermont B&B welcoming you with comfortable beds, full country breakfasts, European antiques, Vermont craftwork, and charm. Located halfway between Lake Champlain and Mount Mansfield in Northern Vermont.
✉ mariot@homeplacebandb.com 🌐 www.homeplacebandb.com

Sinclair Inn	120-160 BB	Full breakfast
389 Vermont Rt 15 05465	6 rooms, 6 pb	Complimentary beverages,
800-433-4658 802-899-2234	Visa, MC, *Rated*	coffee, tea, home baked
Don and Elisabeth Huber	C-ltd/S-no/P-no/H-yes	treats, cakes, brownies, pies,
	Some French	cookies, bread pudding
		Parlor with satellite TV,
		telephone, living room with
		fireplace, WiFi throughout
		inn

1895 Queen Anne restored to Victorian splendor. Rooms have private baths, antique furnishings. Extensive perennial gardens w/view. 5 star gourmet restaurants nearby. Rural setting 25 minutes from Burlington. Full gourmet breakfast.
✉ sinclairinn@verizon.net 🌐 www.sinclairinnbb.com

KILLINGTON————————————————————————

Birch Ridge Inn	90-325 BB	Full breakfast
37 Butler Rd 05751	10 rooms, 10 pb	Dinner plans available
800-435-8566 802-422-4293	Most CC, *Rated*, •	Restaurant, fireplace lounge,
Bill Vines & Mary Furlong	C-ltd/S-no/P-no/H-yes	many rooms are air
		conditioned & have
		fireplaces & whirlpool tubs

Experience Vermont in style. 10 rooms surrounded by gardens, nestled in the Green Mountains. Start with a country breakfast, finish with fine dining. Killington Ski and Golf Resort less than 1 mile away. Handicap accessible.
✉ innkeepers@birchridge.com 🌐 www.birchridge.com

Inn at Long Trail	75-235 BB	Full breakfast
Rt 4, Sherburne Pass 05751	19 rooms, 19 pb	Irish pub (lunch/dinner), or
800-325-2540 802-775-7181	Visa, MC, AmEx,	candlelit dining Fall and
Murray & Patty McGrath	*Rated*, •	Winter in main dining room
	C-yes/S-no/P-ltd/H-ltd	Sitting room, hot tub,
	Summer, fall, winter	weekend Irish music

A classic Vermont ski lodge/bed & breakfast offering country bedrooms, whirlpool rooms and fireplace suites. Candlelit dining fall and winter. McGrath's Irish Pub serves food daily, with live Irish music weekends.
✉ ilt@vermontel.net 🌐 www.innatlongtrail.com

Kokopelli Inn	45-245 BB	Continental breakfast
4337 Rt 4 05751	16 rooms, 16 pb	Happy Hour in the lounge
877-422-9888 802-422-9888	Visa, MC, AmEx	Bar & lounge, hot tub, pool
Marty Bursaw	C-yes/S-no/P-ltd/H-no	table, WiFi, living room,
		packages

Enjoy the large living room with a magnificent fireplace & plush sofas. Have a glass of wine at the Rusty Cage lounge & help yourself to the hot tub or a game of pool. Single, double, & Family rooms w/private baths at affordable prices.
✉ stay@kokopelliinnspa.com 🌐 www.kokopelliinnspa.com

KILLINGTON

Snowed Inn
104 Miller Brook Rd 05751
800-311-5406 802-422-3407
Manfred & Jeanne Karlhuber

89-385 BB
20 rooms, 20 pb
Most CC, *Rated*, •
C-yes/S-no/P-no/H-ltd
German
6/15-4/15

Continental plus breakfast
Sitting room, Jacuzzis, suites,
WiFi throughout inn, cable
TV, fireplaces

Distinctive country rooms and suites complimented by a fieldstone fireplace lounge, greenhouse breakfast room, outdoor hot tub overlooking brook.
✉ snowedinn@vermontel.net ◒ www.snowedinn.com

The Vermont Inn
Rt 4 05701
800-541-7795 802-775-0708
Mitchell & Jennifer Duffy

100-255 BB
16 rooms, 16 pb
Most CC, *Rated*
C-yes/S-no/P-no/H-yes
French, Spanish
Memorial Day-April 1

Full country breakfast
Meal plan available, bar,
cider and cookies in the
afternoon
Fitness room, sauna, hot-tub,
suites, family suites, business
services, pool

Mitchell & Jennifer Duffy are pleased to welcome you to the Vermont Inn. Please join us at our circa 1840 small country inn on five acres in the Green Mountains. We offer the charm of a family run inn with excellent New England and Continental cuisine.
✉ relax@vermontinn.com ◒ www.vermontinn.com

LINCOLN

The Old Hotel
233 E River Rd 05443
802-453-2567
Matthew Wood

65-95 BB
7 rooms
Visa, MC
C-yes/S-no/P-yes/H-no

Full breakfast
Pet-friendly, living room,
dining room, game room,
sitting room, office, kitchen,
public bathroom

An old hotel converted into a bed and breakfast, located in a lovely village nestled in the foothills of the Green Mountains. Hiking, biking, skiing, arts & entertainment just minutes away.
✉ theoldhotel@GMATV.net ◒ www.oldhotel.net

LOWER WATERFORD

Rabbit Hill Inn
Lower Waterford Rd 05848
800-76-BUNNY 802-748-5168
Brian & Leslie Mulcahy

199-399 BB
19 rooms, 19 pb
Most CC, *Rated*, •
S-no/P-ltd/H-yes

Full candlelit breakfast
Afternoon tea and pastries,
multi-course dinner available
Pub & game room, candlelit
turndown service, in-room
massage, personalized
concierge, free WiFi.

Stylish country inn established in 1795. We invite you to this tranquil place – an oasis of unparalleled comfort, heartfelt hospitality, soul-inspiring surroundings, and service that anticipates and pampers.
✉ info@rabbithillinn.com ◒ www.rabbithillinn.com

LUDLOW

Andrie Rose Inn
13 Pleasant St 05149
800-223-4846 802-228-4846
Michael & Irene Maston

110-330 BB
15 rooms, 15 pb
Most CC, *Rated*, •
C-yes/S-no/P-yes/H-no

Continental and full breakfast
Dinner Friday and Saturday
by reservation, snacks, Beer,
Fairly priced and well
rounded wine list.
Sitting room, library, Jacuzzi,
suites, fireplace, cable TV
VCR/DVD, outdoor hot tub

Beautiful historic property in elegant c.1829 country village, Okemo Ski Mountain. Romantic whirlpool tub suites; family suites.
✉ innkeepers@andrieroseinn.com ◒ www.andrieroseinn.com

LUDLOW

The Combes Family Inn
953 E Lake Rd 05149
800-822-8799 802-228-8799
Ruth & Bill Combes

86-196 BB
11 rooms, 11 pb
Most CC, •
C-yes/S-no/P-ltd/H-no
French
Closed 4/1-5/1

Full breakfast
Coffee, tea, hot chocolate, cold drinks on demand. Ruth's delicious dinners by reservations. BYOB
TV lounge and quiet reading room, with fire places.Games, piano, library, videos, wireless Internet

The Combes Family Inn is a century-old farmhouse nestled on a quiet country backroad off Vermont's scenic Route 100. 50 acres of woods and meadows for exploring.
✉ billcfi@tds.net ❂ www.combesfamilyinn.com

The Governor's Inn
86 Main St 05149
800-468-3766 802-228-8830
Jim & Cathy Kubec

159-299 BB
8 rooms, 8 pb
Most CC, *Rated*, •
C-ltd/S-no/P-no/H-no
French

Full 3 course breakfast
Afternoon tea, gourmet picnics
Fully air-conditioned, fireplace & cable TV in most rooms, luxurious robes, wireless Internet access

Romantic, 8-room Victorian B&B inn in Ludlow, Vermont, on village green. Full breakfast and afternoon tea. Near Okemo skiing. Walk to shops/restaurants. Luxury rooms, fireplaces, antiques, cable TV, whirlpool tubs. Wireless Internet access.
✉ info@thegovernorsinn.com ❂ www.thegovernorsinn.com

LYNDONVILLE

The Wildflower Inn
2059 Darling Hill Rd 05851
800-627-8310 802-626-8310
Jim & Mary O'Reilly

125-475 BB
24 rooms, 24 pb
Visa, MC, AmEx,
Rated, •
C-yes/S-no/P-yes/H-ltd
Nepali

Full breakfast
Afternoon tea, snacks, dinner available, snack bar, restaurant
Pool, hot tub, sauna, tennis & basketball courts, nature trails, wireless Internet

You're sure to enjoy roaming over the inn's property, discovering the amenities the Wildflower Inn has to offer for the single traveler, family, or group.
✉ info@wildflowerinn.com ❂ www.wildflowerinn.com

MANCHESTER

The Inn at Manchester
3967 Main St 05254
800-273-1793 802-362-1793
Frank & Julie Hanes

155-295 BB
18 rooms, 18 pb
Most CC, *Rated*, •
C-ltd/S-no/P-no/H-no

Full Breakfast
Fully licensed pub.
Sitting rooms, library, fireplaces, pool, porch, A/C, gardens, free Internet access

A Gem in the Green Mountains. Casual elegance & warm hospitality. Charming guestrooms, comfortable & inviting common areas. Beautiful grounds, gardens, pool, patio & fully licensed pub.
✉ innkeepers@innatmanchester.com ❂ www.innatmanchester.com

Reluctant Panther Inn & Restaurant
17-39 West Road 05254
800-822-2331 802-362-2568
Jerry & Liz Lavalley

179-729 BB
20 rooms, 20 pb
Most CC
C-yes/S-no/P-yes/H-yes

Full American Breakfast
Room Service, Dinner, Fine Dining Restaurant, also Panther Pub Restaurant with light fare, Tavern
Fireplaces, 2-person spa, gardens, WiFi, TV/DVD, fitness ctr, massage room, business office

Romantic country inn and restaurant in southern Vermont's historic Manchester Village offers elegant newly refurbished accommodations with in-room fireplaces (some with two), Jacuzzis tubs ß deux and exceptional mountain views. Walk to outlet shopping.
✉ stay@reluctantpanther.com ❂ www.reluctantpanther.com

MANCHESTER CENTER

The Inn at Ormsby Hill
1842 Main St 05255
800-670-2841 802-362-1163
Ted & Chris Sprague

205-535 BB
10 rooms, 10 pb
Visa, MC, AmEx,
Rated, •
C-ltd/S-no/P-no/H-yes

Full gourmet breakfast
Afternoon refreshments;
welcome cookies upon
arrival in room
Sitting room, library, all
rooms have a fireplace &
Jacuzzi for two, flat-screen
TVs

Renowned for comfort, heartfelt hospitality & profound attention to detail. Romantic, luxurious bed chambers with canopies, fireplaces, & air-conditioning.
✉ stay@ormsbyhill.com ◐ www.ormsbyhill.com

MARLBORO

Colonel Williams Inn
111 Staver Rd 05344
802-257-1093
Nancie & John Marinaro

100-210 BB
12 rooms, 12 pb
Visa, MC
C-yes/S-no/P-yes/H-yes
German

Full breakfast
Dinner, afternoon tea,
restaurant, bar service,
tavern
Sitting room, library, spas,
fireplaces, satellite TV, hot
tub room

Historic 1769 country inn with large spring-fed pond and beautiful views of the Green Mountains. Wide-board floors, 9 fireplaces and numerous early antique features create a sensational ambience for our guests. Barn weddings. Pet-friendly carriage house.
✉ info@colonelwilliamsinn.com ◐ www.colonelwilliamsinn.com

MONTGOMERY CENTER

English Rose Inn
195 Vermont Rt 242 05471
888-303-3232 802-326-3232
Gary & Mary Jane Bouchard-Pike

85-165 BB
14 rooms, 14 pb
Visa, MC, Disc
C-yes/S-no/P-ltd/H-ltd

Deluxe Gourmet Breakfast
Fine dining restaurant, award
winning chefs
3 sitting areas w/ wood
burning fireplace, WiFi, cell
phone reception, TV/VCR,
movie channels

Nestled within the gorgeous Vermont Green Mountains, our location provides a beautiful backdrop for any special family or business occasion.
✉ stay@theenglishroseinn.com ◐ www.englishroseinnvermont.com

The Inn on Trout River
241 Main St 05471
800-338-7049 802-326-4391
Lee & Michael Forman

104-184 BB
10 rooms, 10 pb
Most CC, *Rated*, •
C-yes/S-no/P-no/H-no

Full breakfast menu
Sitting room, library,
bicycles, tennis court,
fireplaces

Vermont Historic District, 7 covered bridges, downhill and cross-country skiing, vast snowmobile trails. 10 rooms, private baths, queen beds, down comforters.
✉ info@troutinn.com ◐ www.troutinn.com

Phineas Swann B&B Inn
195 Main St 05471
802-326-4306
John Perkins & Jay Kerch

119-299 BB
8 rooms, 8 pb
Most CC, *Rated*, •
C-ltd/S-no/P-yes/H-ltd
German and some
French

Full gourmet breakfast
Free soda, personal
icemakers in rooms, free
snacks, fabulous "all day"
afternoon tea
Flat screen TVs, private
phones, Internet access +
WiFi, baby grand player
piano

AAA 3 Diamond Rated—one of Vermont's most elegant country inns, right in the heart of a charming New England village. We are just 12 miles from the Canadian border, and very popular with skiers and fall foliage leaf peepers. Come experience the best!
✉ info@phineasswann.com ◐ www.phineasswann.com

MONTPELIER————————————————————————————

Betsy's B&B
74 E State St 05602
802-229-0466
Jon & Betsy Anderson

70-140 BB
12 rooms, 12 pb
Most CC, *Rated*, •
C-yes/S-no/P-ltd/H-no
Some Spanish

Full breakfast
Snacks, fruit
Suites, in-room voice mail &
data ports, wireless Internet
access

Set in a quiet historic district just two blocks from town, Betsy's is both comfortably homey & romantically Victorian. The beds are so comfortable that breakfast just has to be good.
✉ betsysbnb@comcast.net ☼ www.BetsysBnB.com

The Inn at Montpelier
147 Main St 05602
802-223-2727
Rick & Rita Rizza

132-229 BB
19 rooms, 19 pb
Most CC, *Rated*
C-yes/S-no/P-no/H-no

Generous continental plus
breakfast
Full bar, snacks
Sitting room, fireplaces,
cable TV, accommodate
business travelers, free
wireless access

An elegant, historic Inn in the capital city. Each room is furnished with unique antiques, art and fine reproductions. Best porch in Vermont.
✉ innatmontpelier@comcast.net ☼ www.innatmontpelier.com

MORETOWN————————————————————————————

The Belding House
746 Rt 100 05660
802-496-7420
Clif Thompson & Larry
Richichi

149-169 BB
5 rooms, 5 pb
Visa, MC, AmEx, •
C-ltd/S-no/P-no

Gourmet Candle Light
Breakfast
Afternoons Bring Delicious
Hors D'Oeuvres, Wine &
Local Beers. Don't Miss Our
Evening Desserts.
Wedding/Event Barn For
Banquets Up To 80 People.
Secluded Garden Gazebo On
Two Acres Of Lush Lawn.

"The Art of Inn Keeping Redefined" A boutique, intimate and romantic c.1810 Vermont farmhouse featuring crackling fireplaces, featherbeds and down comforters. Gourmet breakfast by candle light and outstanding service. Welcome Home.
✉ info@beldinghouse.com ☼ beldinghouse.com

NEWFANE————————————————————————————

Four Columns Inn on the Green
21 West St 05345
800-787-6633 802-365-7713
Debbie & Bruce Pfander

175-400 BB
15 rooms, 15 pb
Most CC, *Rated*, •
C-yes/S-no/P-ltd/H-ltd

Full breakfast buffet
Afternoon tea, dinner
available, restaurant
Bar service, sitting room,
Jacuzzis, pool, suites,
massage, fireplaces, cable
TV, DVD library

Innkeepers are friendly and hospitable, making the Inn a happy and comfortable place to be. Recently featured in Country Home Magazine, Travel Holiday and Country Inns Magazine. ✉ innkeeper@fourcolumnsinn.com ☼ www.fourcolumnsinn.com

NORTHFIELD————————————————————————————

Northfield Inn
228 Highland Ave 05663
802-485-8558
Aglaia Stalb

119-179 BB
12 rooms, 9 pb
Most CC, *Rated*, •
C-ltd/S-no/P-no/H-no
Greek

Full gourmet breakfast
Pastries, fresh fruit, assorted
hot & cold beverages &
snacks available all day, plus
evening wine.
Guest PC, WiFi, TV, videos,
DVD/VCR, library, Koi pond,
hiking trails, bicycles, Pool &
River nearby

This turn-of-the-century mansion, once occupied by a Royal Princess, has been restored to its original Victorian elegance, tastefully decorated with period furnishings, beautiful gardens, peaceful koi pond, antique apple orchard & surrounded by woodlands.
✉ thenorthfieldinn@aol.com ☼ www.TheNorthfieldInn.com

Casa Bella Inn, Pittsfield, VT

PERKINSVILLE

The Inn at Weathersfield	140-285 BB	Full breakfast
1342 Rt 106 05151	12 rooms, 12 pb	Afternoon refreshments,
802-263-9217	Most CC, *Rated*	dinner & pub menu
Dave & Jane Sandelman	C-ltd/S-no/P-no/H-ltd	21 acres with walking trails, full restaurant & bar, Internet access

Known for its distinctive style of lodging and dining, it is the perfect choice for a quiet getaway in Southern Vermont. The Inn at Weathersfield is more than a simple B&B, it is more like a small European style or boutique hotel.
✉ stay@weathersfieldinn.com ◐ www.weathersfieldinn.com

PERU

Johnny Seesaw's	80-240 BB	Full breakfast
3574 VT Route 11 05152	22 rooms, 22 pb	Dinner every night, full bar
800-424-CSAW 802-824-5533	Visa, MC, Disc, *Rated*	Tennis, swimming pool,
Gary Okun	C-yes/S-yes/P-yes/H-ltd	library, sitting room, formal
	French	dining room, center
	Closed April–May	fireplace, private cottages

Welcome to Johnny Seesaw's! This unique country lodge features cozy rooms, 3 room suites, and cottages with 2 bedrooms, 2 baths and living room with fireplace; restaurant, wine list, Olympic sized pool, tennis court and welcomes children and pets.
✉ jseesaws@sover.net ◐ www.jseesaw.com

PITTSFIELD

Casa Bella Inn	90-135 BB	Full breakfast
Rt 100 05762	8 rooms, 8 pb	Chef owned restaurant/bar
877-746-8943 802-746-8943	Visa, MC, AmEx, *Rated*	service, afternoon
Susan & Franco Cacozza	C-ltd/S-no/P-no/H-no	refreshments
	Italian, German, and	Sitting room with potbelly
	Spanish	stove, mini suites, self-guided tours

Travel to our scenic mountain valley location and enjoy one of Vermont's finest full service inns. Looking for lodging near Killington? Give us a call. Considering a hotel or motel? Try our B&B for personal service in the heart the Green Mountains.
✉ info@casabellainn.com ◐ casabellainn.com

PROCTORSVILLE

Golden Stage Inn
399 Depot St 05153
800-253-8226 802-226-7744
Sandy & Peter Gregg

89-330 BB
10 rooms, 8 pb
Visa, MC, *Rated*, •
C-yes/S-no/P-no/H-yes

Full breakfast
Bottomless cookie jar,
afternoon tea, snacks
Sitting room, pool, fireplace,
TV, A/C, OKEMO Ski
Package, Six Loose Ladies
Coupon, Dining Coupon

The Okemo Ski Resort is only 3 miles away. Near Weston, Woodstock, Coolidge Site, Priory and Chester. 1790 Stage Coach stop and an Underground Railroad link, this historic Colonial B&B Inn offers true Vermont hospitality.
✉ goldenstageinn@tds.net ◐ www.goldenstageinn.com

PUTNEY

Hickory Ridge House
53 Hickory Ridge Rd S 05346
800-380-9218 802-387-5709
Gillian Pettit

150-225 BB
8 rooms, 8 pb
Visa, MC
C-ltd/S-no/P-ltd/H-ltd

Full breakfast
Complimentary tea, coffee,
cold soft drinks & snacks
Sitting rooms, fireplaces,
cable TV, DVD players, WiFi

Located on a quiet country road in Putney, VT, and listed in the National Register of Historic Places, Hickory Ridge House offers modern convenience in a private, rural setting.
✉ mail@hickoryridgehouse.com ◐ www.hickoryridgehouse.com

QUECHEE

Inn at Clearwater Pond
984 Quechee-Hartland Road
05059
888-918-4INN (4466) 802-295-0606
Christine DeLuca

165-295 BB
5 rooms, 5 pb
Cash, Checks
C-yes/S-ltd/P-yes/H-ltd

and Continental/Full
Assorted cookies and sweets
Fruit, Granola Bars, Biscotti,
Tea, Coffee
Hotair ballooning, swimming
pond, massage therapy,
workout room, weddings,
bike/canoe/kayak rentals

A beautiful gentleman's farm and inn catering to the discerning traveler and family. Superb distant views, swimming pond, on-site massage therapy, hot-air ballooning, workout room, weddings and special events.
✉ innatclearwaterpond@gmail.com ◐ www.innatclearwaterpond.com

READING

Bailey's Mills
1347 Bailey's Mills Rd 05062
800-639-3437 802-484-7809
Barbara Thaeder

120-189 BB
3 rooms, 3 pb
•
C-ltd/S-ltd/P-ltd/H-no

Full breakfast
Afternoon tea, refreshments
Sitting room, library,
fireplaces, pond, stream,
walking paths; 50 acres

History-filled country home overlooking "Spite Cemetery." Colorful breakfast in Colonial dining room, solarium or on the front porch.
✉ info1@baileysmills.com ◐ www.baileysmills.com

RICHMOND

The Richmond Victorian Inn
191 E Main St 05477
888-242-3362 802-434-4410
Frank & Joyce Stewart

119-169 BB
5 rooms, 5 pb
Visa, MC, Disc, *Rated*
C-ltd/S-no/P-no/H-no
French (limited)

Full gourmet breakfast
British-style afternoon teas
served Sundays, Sept-May.
Private Dinners-See website
for more info.
Free WiFi, books, magazines,
TV/VCR, good conversation,
dinner reservations,
discount ski passes

Lovely, restored 1850s Queen Anne Victorian, 12 miles from Burlington. Private bathrooms, comfortable antique furnishings, full gourmet breakfasts. Historic Round Church, shops, excellent restaurants within walking distance. Convenient to many activities.
✉ innkeeper@richmondvictorianinn.com ◐ www.richmondvictorianinn.com

ROCHESTER

Liberty Hill Farm
511 Liberty Hill 05767
802-767-3926
Bob & Beth Kennett

75-220 MAP
7 rooms
Cash, Checks
C-yes/S-no/P-no/H-no

Full breakfast
Full dinner is served at 6 pm
with farm fresh local
ingredients, maple syrup,
cheese, local fruits
Sitting rooms, library, river
tubes, cribs and high chairs;
snowshoes, mt bikes, XC ski
rental

There is always a warm welcome at Liberty Hill Farm. This working dairy farm, nestled between the White River and the Green Mountains, provides excellent meals and family activities year round.
✉ beth@libertyhillfarm.com 🌐 www.libertyhillfarm.com

RUTLAND

The Inn at Rutland
70 N Main St 05701
800-808-0575 802-773-0575
Leslie & Steven Brenner

119-229 BB
8 rooms, 8 pb
Most CC, *Rated*, •
C-yes/S-no/P-no/H-no

3 course gourmet breakfast
Afternoon tea & home baked
cookies
A/C, TV & phone in rooms,
library, parlor with wood
burning fireplace

The Inn at Rutland is a stately Victorian Mansion built by William F. Burditt for his family in 1889 and located within a few miles of Killington, Vermont. Fronted by a large wraparound porch, the Inn affords breathtaking views of the Green Mountains.
✉ stay@innatrutland.com 🌐 www.innatrutland.com

SANDGATE

Green River Inn
3402 Sandgate Rd 05250
888-648-2212 802-375-2272
Bob & Carol Potozney

124-243 BB
16 rooms, 16 pb
Visa, MC, AmEx
C-yes/S-no/P-yes/H-ltd

Full breakfast
Tea, snacks, bar
Fireplace, Jacuzzi, spa
services, pet friendly
accommodations, television,
cottage, retreats

We invite all who seek to relax, rejuvenate and explore the natural harmony of the mountains, the soothing sounds of the river, the magnificent star-filled skies and the beautiful surrounding valley.
✉ stay@greenriverinn.com 🌐 www.greenriverinn.com

SAXTONS RIVER

The Inn at Saxtons River
27 Main St 05154
802-869-2110
Debi Tabb

99-189 BB
16 rooms, 16 pb
Most CC
C-yes/S-no/P-yes/H-no

Continental breakfast
Pub and restaurant on the
premises.
Wireless Internet,
housekeeping, room service,
car service

Charming, historic 16 room inn with restaurant and pub situated in the heart of Saxtons River. Conveniently located within a half hour drive to many Southern Vermont's finest attractions.
✉ innatsr@vermontel.net 🌐 www.saxtonsriverinn.com

SHELBURNE

Heart of the Village Inn
5347 Shelburne Rd 05482
877-808-1834 802-985-2800
Geoff & Maureen Conrad

150-270 BB
9 rooms, 9 pb
Visa, MC, AmEx, •
C-yes/S-no/P-ltd/H-yes

Full Vermont Breakfast
Complimentary afternoon
tea & cookies, wine & beer
from our list, box lunches on
request
TV, telephone, air
conditioning, high speed
Internet access

Casually elegant Queen Anne Victorian in a historic Vermont village. Perfect for Vermont leisure & business travel, small conferences, retreats & weddings.
✉ innkeeper@heartofthevillage.com 🌐 www.heartofthevillage.com

SHREWSBURY———————————————————————————

Crisanver House	140-375 BB	Gourmet country breakfast
1434 Crown Point Rd 05738	8 rooms, 8 pb	Afternoon Tea, Dinner by
800-492-8089 802-492-3589	Visa, MC, AmEx,	reservation
Michael & Carol Calotta	*Rated*, •	Conservatory, Library,
	C-ltd/S-no/P-no/H-no	Jacuzzi, Heated Pool, Tennis,
	Italian	Snowshoeing, Wireless
	Closed in April and Nov.	Internet, Skiing, Porch

Escape to a cherished experience with gracious hospitality, marvelous accommodations, great food, wonderful service, magnificent views/surroundings and blissful setting. Be relaxed, revived, refreshed and rekindled in spirit-all as described by our guests
✉ info@crisanver.com ◊ www.crisanver.com

Maple Crest Farm	60-100 BB	Full breakfast
2512 Lincoln Hill Rd 05738	9 rooms, 2 pb	Afternoon tea, snacks
802-492-3367	Most CC, *Rated*	Sitting room, library, suites,
William & Donna Smith	C-ltd/S-no/P-no/H-yes	fireplaces
	February-December	

1808 Federal style, 27 room home, high in the Green Mountains, lovingly preserved for 7 generations. 320 acres to hike/walk. Furnished with antiques, 10 miles south of Rutland, 12 miles to Ludlow.
✉ maplecrestbnb@vermontel.net ◊ www.smithmaplecrestfarm.com/Bed_and_Breakfast.html

SOUTH LONDONDERRY———————————————————————

Londonderry Inn	99-336 BB	Full breakfast
Rte 100 05155	24 rooms, 24 pb	Afternoon cookies & tea;
800-644-5226 802-824-5226	Most CC, *Rated*	wine & beer, soda, ice cream
Chrisman & Maya Kearn	C-yes/S-no/P-no/H-ltd	Fireplaces, billiards, movie
		room, pool

Historic Vermont Family Lodge overlooking the West River. Relaxed hospitality, fireplaces, family suites, children welcome, hot buffet breakfast, fresh-baked cookies, spring-fed pool, sledding hill.
◊ www.londonderryinn.com

STOWE———————————————————————————————

Auberge de Stowe	69-119 BB	Continental plus breakfast
692 S Main St 05672	6 rooms, 6 pb	Sitting room, Jacuzzis,
800-387-8789 802-253-7787	Most CC	swimming pool, fireplaces
Chantal & Shawn Kerivan	C-yes/S-no/P-no/H-no	
	French, German	

A 6 room country inn. Relax by the fireplace or hot tub in the winter, cool down in the swimming pool or river in the summer, all in the company of your host family.
✉ info@aubergedestowe.com ◊ aubergedestowe.com

Brass Lantern Inn	99-199 BB	Full country breakfast
717 Maple St 05672	9 rooms, 9 pb	Tea with fresh baked cookies
800-729-2980 802-253-2229	Visa, MC, AmEx,	& pastries are available
Nancy Beres	*Rated*, •	every afternoon.
	C-ltd/S-no/P-no/H-no	Fireplaces, whirlpool, patio,
		wireless Internet access,
		cable TV upon request,
		individual heat & A/C

An Authentic B&B Inn in the quaint village of Stowe Vermont. Award winning breakfast. Charming and romantic bed and breakfast with country quilts and antique furniture. Outdoor hot tub. fireplaces with whirlpool tubs and magnificent mountain view
✉ info@brasslanterninn.com ◊ www.brasslanterninn.com

STOWE————————————————————————————

The Gables Inn	80-250 BB	Full breakfast
1457 Mountain Rd 05672	18 rooms, 18 pb	Complimentary apres ski in
800-GABLES-1 802-253-7730	Most CC, *Rated*, •	winter
Annette Monachelli & Randy	C-yes/S-no/P-ltd/H-ltd	Sitting room, fireplace,
Stern		swimming pool (summer),
		hot tub, ping pong, A/C

Stowe's classic Vermont country inn. Antiques, wood floors, nice views. Rooms range from cozy inn rooms to luxury accommodations with Jacuzzis and fireplaces. Our breakfast is legendary.
✉ info@gablesinn.com ○ www.gablesinn.com

Green Mountain Inn	119-749 EP	Continental & Full Buffet
18 Main St 05672	107 rooms, 107 pb	options
800-253-7302 802-253-7301	Most CC, *Rated*, •	Complimentary afternoon
Patti Clark	C-yes/S-no/P-no/H-ltd	tea & cookies; Weekly winter
		wine & cheese parties;
		restaurant on site.
		Unique shops, heated
		outdoor pool, health club,
		massage, library, WiFi,
		conference/banquet facility

Beautifully restored 1833 resort in the heart of Stowe village. The Inn offers the perfect blend of country elegance & modern comfort, in antique-furnished rooms, luxury suites & village townhouses.
✉ info@gminn.com ○ www.greenmountaininn.com

Honeywood Inn	89-179 BB	Full breakfast
4583 Mountain Rd 05672	10 rooms, 10 pb	Afternoon tea during regular
800-821-7891 802-253-4846	Most CC, *Rated*, •	and high season
Carolyn & Bill Cook	C-ltd/S-no/P-no/H-no	Large living room, satellite
		TV room, heated pool
		(summer), 2 hot tubs

Warm hospitality awaits you in our cozy 3 diamond awarded B&B, nestled at the base of Mount Mansfired the highest mountain in Vermont. Babbling brook, waterfall, wooded walking trail on our 9 beautiful acres. Full breakfast, afternoon tea, free WiFi.
✉ honeywd@aol.com ○ www.honeywoodinn.com

Ski Inn	45-185 MAP	Continental breakfast
5037 Mountain Rd 05672	10 rooms, 6 pb	Full breakfast in winter,
802-253-4050	Visa, MC, AmEx, *Rated*	dinner (optional)
Mrs. Harriet Heyer	C-ltd/S-no/P-ltd/H-no	Private baths, skiing, golf &
	Some French	tennis nearby, shuttle to ski
		areas

Guests will find friendliness and personal attention at Ski Inn. Best of all are the very reasonable rates, attesting to a successful family-run operation with over a half-century commitment to value and style!
✉ harriet.1@ski-inn.com ○ ski-inn.com/pl

Stowe Inn	89-319 BB	Continental Breakfast in
123 Mountain Rd 05672	35 rooms, 35 pb	season
800-546-4030 802-253-4030	Most CC, •	Dinner at the Stowe Inn
Jed & Annika Lipsky	C-yes/S-no/P-ltd/H-ltd	Tavern
		Sitting rooms, hot tub,
		swimming pool(summer
		only), game room

Beautiful 1820 Stowe Inn & Tavern, perfectly located in the Village of Stowe. A cozy country inn with 16 rooms in the Main Inn or 20 economy motel rooms in a separate building, all with private bath & cable TV.
✉ hello@stoweinn.com ○ www.stoweinn.com

STOWE

Timberholm Inn
452 Cottage Club Rd 05672
800-753-7603 802-253-7603
Tom & Susan Barnes

94-218 BB
10 rooms, 10 pb
Visa, MC, *Rated*, •
S-no/P-no/H-no

Full breakfast
Afternoon treats: locally
blended teas and homemade
cookies
Weddings, civil unions, cable
TV, small refrigerator,
microwave, hot tub

*Tucked into a wooded hillside in Stowe, Vermont, The Timberholm Inn is a country inn
with the ambience of a bygone era and the warm interior of rich knotty pine. Built in 1949,
it remains one of the most popular year round lodging properties to this day.*
✉ info@timberholm.com ◐ www.timberholm.com

WAITSFIELD

1824 House Inn
2150 Main St 05673
800-426-3986 802-496-7555
John Lumbra

99-173 BB
8 rooms, 8 pb
Visa, MC, AmEx,
Rated, •
S-no/P-no/H-ltd

Full breakfast
Dinner by candlelight
available by reservation;
afternoon tea, treats
Living room, dining room,
antiques, art, garden, patio,
Jacuzzi, WiFi, in-room
phones, data ports

*A small, intimate country inn in the picturesque Mad River Valley. Features comfortable
rooms with private baths and superb dining. You will be treated as our special guests, but
will leave here our friends.*
✉ stay@1824house.com ◐ www.1824house.com

The Inn at Round Barn Farm
1661 E Warren Rd 05673
802-496-2276
Anne Marie DeFreest & Tim
Piper

165-315 BB
12 rooms, 12 pb
Visa, MC, AmEx,
Rated, •
C-ltd/S-no/P-no/H-ltd

Full breakfast
Afternoon cookies and
evening hors d'oeuvres
Sitting room, library,
Jacuzzis, swimming pool,
fireplace, cable TV

*Vermont's premiere B&B has been a landmark in the Sugarbush Mad River Valley for over
15 years. A hospitable staff, wonderful food, well-decorated guestrooms and a beautiful
setting on 245 acres await you.*
✉ Info@InnattheRoundBarn.com ◐ www.theroundbarn.com

Mad River Inn
243 Tremblay Rd 05673
800-832-8278 802-496-7900
Luc Maranda

115-175 BB
9 rooms, 9 pb
Visa, MC, AmEx, •
C-yes/S-no/P-no/H-no
French

Full breakfast
Afternoon tea
Cable TV, business traveler
accommodations, Hot Spring
outdoor hot tub

*From the moment you enter the sunny front room or our Inn, with white wicker furniture
and pastel floral prints, the flower-bedecked back porch overlooking the gazebo, and lush
gardens in open fields, you will know you have arrived in heavenly Vermont.*
✉ madriverinn@madriver.com ◐ www.madriverinn.com

Millbrook Inn & Restaurant
Route 17 05673
800-477-2809 802-496-2405
Joan & Thom Gorman

110-190 BB
7 rooms, 7 pb
Visa, MC, AmEx, *Rated*
C-ltd/S-no/P-ltd/H-no
Some French
Closed April-May & Nov.

Full cooked-to-order
breakfast
Full dinner from restaurant
Complimentary
refreshments, 3 sitting
rooms, vegetarian dining
menu

*Charming hand-stenciled guestrooms with handmade quilts, country gourmet dining, vege-
tarian choices, in our small candlelit restaurant. Chef-owned and operated since 1979.
Large, landscaped back yard for relaxing.*
✉ gorman@millbrookinn.com ◐ www.millbrookinn.com

WAITSFIELD————————————————————————————

Mountain View Inn
1912 Mill Brook Rd 05673
802-496-2426 ,
Fred & Susan Spencer

100-135 BB
7 rooms, 7 pb
Most CC
C-yes/S-no/P-no/H-no

Full breakfast

An 1826 farmhouse made into a comfortable inn with private baths and family heirlooms. Comfortable accommodations in the country just minutes from the quaint shops in Waitsfield or the hiking trails and ski slopes at Sugarbush and Mad River Glen.
✉ info@vtmountainviewinn.com ✆ www.vtmountainviewinn.com

The Waitsfield Inn
5267 Main St 05673
800-758-3801 802-496-3979
Ronda & Mike Kelley

124-179 BB
14 rooms, 14 pb
Most CC
C-ltd/S-no/P-no/H-no
French and some
German

Full breakfast
Common rooms, games, TV,
VCR, fireplaces, free WiFi,
walk to shops & restaurants,
shuttle to slopes

The Waitsfield Inn is a historical 1825 Vermont Farmhouse in the center of Waitsfield Village. All our rooms have private baths and most have A/C. This Bed and Breakfast is home to both Sugarbush and Mad River Ski Resorts and many outdoor activities.
✉ lodging@waitsfieldinn.com ✆ www.waitsfieldinn.com

Weathertop Mountain Inn
755 Mill Brook Rd, Rt 17 05673
800-800-3625 802-496-4909
Lisa & Michael Lang

99-279 BB
9 rooms, 9 pb
Most CC
C-ltd/S-no/P-ltd/H-no
Spanish

Full prepared-to-order
breakfast
Evening dining, Southeast
Asian specialties, local
microbrews, fine wine &
quality sake available
Hot tub, sauna, game room,
exercise room, great room
with fireplace, wireless DSL,
evening dining

Not your typical country inn . . . . .Asian antiques & art, eclectic evening cuisine & thoughtful amenities to enhance your visit to Vermont's Mad River Valley. Visit us to discover why Weathertop Mountain Inn is not your typical country inn.
✉ stay@weathertopmountaininn.com ✆ www.weathertopmountaininn.com

Wilder Farm Inn
1460 Main St 05673
800-496-8878 802-496-9935
Luke & Linda Iannuzzi

110-165 BB
8 rooms, 8 pb
Visa, MC, AmEx, •
C-ltd/S-no/P-no/H-no

Country Gourmet breakfast
Fresh baked afternoon
snacks, evening cordials,
fireside s'mores. Veg/vegan
breakfast available.
Library, 2 fireplaces, WiFi,
cable TV, swim hole & Mad
Path, lovely grounds, on-site
pottery studio

Come and relax at the Wilder Farm Inn (c. 1860) with spectacular views no matter what season. Surrounded by the Green Mountains, the Mad River Valley boasts beauty beyond belief, true country living at its best. Come as Guests . . . Leave as Friends
✉ info@wilderfarminn.com ✆ wilderfarminn.com

Yellow Farmhouse Inn
550 Old County Rd 05673
877-257-5767 802-496-4263
Mike & Sandra Anastos

119-239 BB
8 rooms, 8 pb
Visa, MC
C-ltd/S-no/P-no/H-yes

Full gourmet breakfast
Morning coffee/tea &
afternoon snacks
Vermont Castings stoves,
Jacuzzis, whirlpool tubs, air
conditioners, WiFi Internet

Romantic and secluded, the Yellow Farmhouse Inn is nestled on 10 acres just minutes from Sugarbush Ski Resort, Mad River Glen Ski Area, restaurants, shopping, nightlife & all the Mad River Valley has to offer.
✉ innkeeper@yellowfarmhouseinn.com ✆ www.yellowfarmhouseinn.com

WALLINGFORD

White Rocks Inn
1774 US 7 S 05773
866-446-2077 802-446-2077
Rita & Malcolm Swogger

120-300 BB
7 rooms, 7 pb
Visa, MC, AmEx
C-ltd/S-no/P-ltd/H-no

3-course candlelight breakfast
Afternoon snacks and beverages
Library, porch, parlor, dining room, bicycles, hiking & snowshoe trails, picnic table, pond, gazebo

This is a Vermont Bed and Breakfast at its best, the way you always dreamed it would be—an elegant, romantic, peaceful country retreat. The farm beckons with the architecture of its Greek Revival farmhouse and landmark Gothic barn.
✉ info@whiterocksinn.com 🌐 www.whiterocksinn.com

WARREN

Beaver Pond Farm Bed & Breakfast
1225 Golf Course Rd 05674
800-685-8285 802-583-2861
Kim and Bob Sexton

99-200 BB
4 rooms, 4 pb
Visa, MC, AmEx, •
C-ltd/S-no/P-no/H-no

Full Gourmet Breakfast
Coffee, tea, afternoon treat; wine & beer extra
Fireplace, hot tub, wireless Internet, TV/DVDs, coffee bar, beer & wine bar, sleds, snowshoes

Rejuvenate your spirit at our distinctive and intimate Vermont farmhouse. Pamper yourself with gourmet breakfasts and treats, glorious views and a soothing hot tub. Stroll or snowshoe our 5 rolling acres.
✉ innkeeper@beaverpondfarminn.com 🌐 www.beaverpondfarminn.com

Sugar Lodge
2197 Sugarbush Access Rd 05674
800-982-3465 802-583-3300
Susan & Robert Cummiskey

79-189 BB
22 rooms, 22 pb
Visa, MC, AmEx
C-yes/S-no/P-no/H-yes

Continental breakfast
Homemade cookies, beer & wine bar
Hot tub, outdoor pool, central A/C, fireplaces, wine & beer bar, laundry facilities, ice machine

A classic mountain lodge next to the Sugarbush Resort. Nestled in the Green Mountains & within an hour of Burlington, Montpelier & all of Vermont's most popular attractions.
✉ mail@sugarlodge.com 🌐 www.sugarlodge.com

West Hill House B&B
1496 West Hill Rd 05674
800-898-1427 802-496-7162
Peter & Susan MacLaren

140-235 BB
8 rooms, 8 pb
Most CC, *Rated*, •
C-ltd/S-no/P-no/H-ltd

Award-winning full breakfast
Coffee, tea, snacks, accessible cookie jar, cash bar. Dinner by advance arrangement.
Wine cellar, library, TVs & movies, in-room fireplaces, Jacuzzis, phones, WiFi/DSL, snowshoes.

Comfortable, well-appointed 1850 home on quiet lane near Sugarbush Resort. Gardens, ponds, gazebo. Near fine restaurants, quaint villages. Guestrooms have fireplaces & whirlpool or steam shower. A lovely spot to relax, romance, refresh.
✉ innkeepers@westhillbb.com 🌐 www.westhillbb.com

WATERBURY

Grunberg Haus B&B Inn & Cabins
Route 100 S 05676
800-800-7760 802-244-7726
Jeff & Linda Connor

95-185 BB
14 rooms, 8 pb
Visa, MC, Disc, •
C-yes/S-no/P-ltd/H-no

Full cooked breakfast
Refreshments, snacks in self-serve pub/gameroom
Forest trails, deck, balconies, self-serve pub/gameroom with woodstove, living room fireplace

Austrian chalet offering romantic guestrooms with balconies, antiques, quilts and summer cabins. Rural, casual, quiet . . . Often described by guests as "cozy, relaxing, hospitable."
✉ info@grunberghaus.com 🌐 www.grunberghaus.com

WATERBURY

Old Stagecoach Inn
18 N Main St 05676
800-262-2206 802-244-5056
John Barwick

75-180 BB
11 rooms, 8 pb
Most CC, *Rated*
C-yes/S-no/P-ltd/H-no
German

Full breakfast
Bar service
Sitting room, library, bar,
family/group travel, A/C,
parlor, antiques, WiFi, wood
burning fireplace

Meticulously restored village Inn on the National Register of Historic Places. Located in the heart of the Green Mountains on scenic Route 100, right between the resort areas of Stowe and Sugarbush.
✉ lodging@oldstagecoach.com ◔ www.oldstagecoach.com

WEST DOVER

Deerfield Valley Inn
120 Rt 100 05356
800-639-3588 802-464-6333
Doreen Cooney

99-175 BB
9 rooms, 9 pb
Most CC, *Rated*
C-yes/S-no/P-no/H-no

Full breakfast
Afternoon tea, snacks
Sitting room, fireplace, cable
TV, conference facilities

Charming country inn built in 1885. All guestrooms are individually decorated, some with woodburning fireplaces, all with private bathrooms & TVs.
✉ deerinn@vermontel.com ◔ www.deerfieldvalleyinn.com

The Inn at Mount Snow
401 Route 100 05356
866-587-7669 802-464-8388
Glenda Belicove

109-309 BB
14 rooms, 14 pb
Visa, MC, AmEx
C-yes/S-no/P-no/H-no

Hot country breakfast
Restaurant for Dinner on
premises
Wireless Internet, in-room
massage available

Located at the base of the Mount Snow Resort in West Dover, Vermont, The Inn at Mount Snow is your home away from home when visiting southern Vermont. The first officially designated Green Hotel in the area.
✉ info@theinnatmountsnow.com ◔ www.innatmountsnow.com

Inn at Sawmill Farm
7 Crosstown Rd 05356
800-493-1133 802-464-8131
Brill Williams

325-475 MAP
21 rooms, 21 pb
Visa, MC, AmEx, •
C-yes/P-yes/H-yes
May 23 until March 29

Full Country Breakfast
Rates include 5-course
dinner, restaurant, afternoon
tea
Air-jetted tubs, balcony,
fireplaces, pool, tennis,
fitness room, ponds,
weddings, fly fishing

The Inn is noted for its warmth and courtesy, which is extended to guests when you arrive. Immediately feel at home in this re-creation of an old Vermont barn, where the interior was discreetly altered, keeping some reminders of an earlier life.
✉ sawmill@sover.net ◔ www.theinnatsawmillfarm.com

Red Oak Inn
45 Route 100 05356
866-573-3625 802-464-8817
Robert & Debra Buehler

69-259 BB
24 rooms, 24 pb
Most CC, *Rated*, •
C-yes/S-ltd/P-yes/H-ltd

Full breakfast
Snack & soda machines
available
Outdoor pool, hot tub, suites,
2 fireplace lounges, cable TV,
exercise room, game room,
BYOB tavern

Fall in love with our impeccably landscaped, 4 season country inn. You'll enjoy a New England vacation in the picture postcard setting you've always dreamed of.
✉ info@redoakinn.com ◔ www.redoakinn.com

606   Vermont

WEST DOVER

The Snow Goose Inn
Rt 100 05356
888-604-7964 802-464-3984
Cyndee & Ron Frere

125-375 BB
13 rooms, 13 pb
Most CC, *Rated*, •
C-yes/S-no/P-yes/H-yes

Full country breakfast
Complimentary wines &
snacks in early evening
Fireplaces, gardens, Jacuzzis,
wireless Internet access,
guest computer, full
housekeeping, fax

Ideal for a romantic getaway from the hassle of city life. Comfort & charm amid 3 wooded acres, pond & natural gardens. Most of our antique filled rooms have wood fireplaces & 2 person Jacuzzis.
stay@snowgooseinn.com www.snowgooseinn.com

WEST GLOVER

Rodgers Country Inn
582 Rodgers Rd 05875
800-729-1704 802-525-6677
Nancy Rodgers

50-70 BB
5 rooms
Visa, MC, AmEx
C-yes/S-no/P-no/H-no

Full breakfast
Dinner is offered for guests.
Sitting room, TV/VCR, lake,
country cooking

Peace, quiet and a friendly atmosphere. Located in the Northeast Kingdom of Vermont. Dinner is also offered to our guests. Family operated for over 40 years.
jnrodger@together.net www.rodgerscountryinn.com

WEST WARDSBORO

Edelweiss at Snow Mountain Farms
758 Sheldon Hill Road 05360
877-EDLWEIS 802-896-6530
Mary Lyn Bourque

115-240 BB
3 rooms, 3 pb
Visa, MC, •
C-ltd/S-no/P-no/H-ltd
late May through mid-Oct

Candlelight Vermont
Breakfast
Afternoon tea or happy hour
refreshments each day
(included). Dinner available
with advance reserv.
Wood Fireplace,
TV/VCR/DVD, 24-hour
coffee/snacks, concierge,
small business services,
WiFi.

The Inn is located on one of the most scenic roads in America in southern Vermont. Nearby are many of the top Vermont attractions, including the majestic Green Mountains, many outdoor recreational activities, music, art and unending shopping and antiquing
edelweissbandb@att.net www.edelweissbandb.com

WESTMINSTER

Blue Haven Christian B&B
6963 US Rt 5 05158
888-879-9008 802-463-9008
Helene

99-200 BB
5 rooms, 4 pb
Most CC, *Rated*, •
C-ltd/S-no/P-no/H-no
French

Continental plus breakfast
Afternoon tea, snacks,
complimentary wine, let us
make dinner arrangements
for you
Sitting room, library, suites,
fireplaces, TV

1830 schoolhouse boasts charming period settings, fireplaced common rooms, sumptuous breakfast by the woodstove, slumber in goosedown, amid handpainted treasures by artist innkeeper Helene.
blue.haven58@gmail.com bluehavenvt.com

WESTMORE

WilloughVale Inn
793 VT Route 5A South 05860
800-594-9102 802-525-4123
Dana Wehe

103-325 BB
18 rooms, 18 pb
Most CC, *Rated*, •
C-yes/S-no/P-yes/H-yes

Continental plus breakfast
Breakfast for Inn room guests
only
Bicycles, 1 double kayak, 1
single kayak, 2 canoes and 1
rowboat for rent

The perfect getaway in Vermont's Northeast Kingdom, with lakeside accommodations and stunning mountain views. The Inn offers 10 unique guestrooms and 8 fully-equipped lakefront cottages.
info@willoughvale.com www.willoughvale.com

WESTON

The Inn at Weston
630 Main St. 05161
802-824-6789
Bob & Linda Aldrich

185-325 BB
13 rooms, 13 pb
Visa, MC
C-ltd/S-no/P-yes/H-ltd

Full breakfast
Restaurant, fine dining on site, afternoon refreshments
A/C, TV, CD & VCR players, fireplaces, orchid greenhouse, whirlpool tubs, decks, weddings, reunions

An 1848 farmhouse on 7 acres, nestled in a quintessential southern Vermont village offers warm, friendly service. Most of the rooms have Jacuzzi tubs, fireplaces, feather beds & some offer private decks. The dining room serves locally harvested cuisine.
✉ theinnatweston@comcast.net ○ www.innweston.com

WILLISTON

Catamount B&B
592 Governor Chittenden Rd 05495
888-680-1011 802-878-2180
Jim & Lucy McCullough

85-125 BB
3 rooms, 1 pb
Visa, MC, Disc
C-yes/S-no/P-no/H-ltd

Continental plus breakfast
Sitting room, bikes, fireplace, suites, accommodate business travelers, WiFi, activity rental

This beautiful 1796 historic home in the country is located just minutes from Lake Champlain, Burlington shops, restaurants and area attractions. Trail side activities include mountain biking, trail running/walking, cross country skiing, and snowshoeing.
✉ bandb@catamountoutdoor.com ○ www.catamountoutdoor.com/bedandbreakfast.html

WILMINGTON

Nutmeg Country Inn
153 Rt 9 W 05363
800-277-5402 802-464-7400
Gerry & Susan Goodman

89-299 BB
14 rooms, 14 pb
Most CC, *Rated*
C-yes/S-no/P-no/H-ltd
Spanish

Full breakfast from menu
Afternoon tea, on-site restaurant open to the public, The SteakHouse Grill
Sitting room, TVs, rooms & suites with woodburning fireplace, A/C, whirlpool, gardens

"Charming & cozy" early American farmhouse, with refined country comfort. Luxurious & romantic suites. ✉ nutmegcountryinn@hotmail.com ○ www.nutmeginn.com

WINDSOR

Juniper Hill Inn
153 Pembroke Rd 05089
800-359-2541 802-674-5273
Ari Nikki & Robert Dean

145-350 BB
17 rooms, 17 pb
Most CC, *Rated*, •
C-ltd/S-no/P-ltd/H-ltd
Finnish

Full breakfast
Dinner by reservation Thurs-Monday, tea, snacks
Restaurant, bar, sitting room, library, swimming pool, fireplace, walking nature trails

Luxurious and romantic historic Colonial mansion with unsurpassed location featuring richly appointed guestrooms, working fireplaces, four poster beds, canopies & numerous amenities. Woodstock and Dartmouth nearby. Surrounded by nature. Select Registry.
✉ Innkeeper@juniperhillinn.com ○ www.juniperhillinn.com

WOODSTOCK

Apple Hill Inn
2301 Hartwood Way (via Happy Valley Rd) 05073
802-457-9135
Andrew & Beverlee Cook

135-225 BB
3 rooms, 3 pb
Most CC
C-yes/S-no/P-yes/H-no

Hearty, healthy buffet breakfast
Catered afternoon teas, brunches, receptions, small dinners by arrangement
Tea Room, solarium, deck, views, free Wireless Internet, facility for weddings, special events

Apple Hill Inn offers its guests the ultimate in hospitality. From the time you arrive until the time you depart your experience is Vermont at its very best. Located high on a hill in the Green Mountains, overlooking the Ottaquechee River and waterfalls.
✉ applehill1@aol.com ○ www.applehillinn.com

WOODSTOCK

Applebutter Inn
7511 Happy Valley Rd 05091
800-486-1734 802-457-4158
Barbara Barry & Michael
Pacht

80-225 BB
6 rooms, 6 pb
Visa, MC, *Rated*
C-ltd/S-no/P-no/H-ltd

Full gourmet breakfast
Homemade cookies and
complimentary teas in the
afternoon. Vegetarian and
vegan meals on request.
WiFi throughout, library,
cable TV, fireplace sitting
room, Music Room with
grand piano

*Authentic luxurious 1854 country home with six gorgeous air conditioned guestrooms (4
with fireplace/stove), centrally located between the villages of Woodstock & Quechee.*
✉ aplbtrn@comcast.net ◐ www.applebutterinn.com

Ardmore Inn
23 Pleasant St 05091
800-497-9652 802-457-3887
Charlotte & Cary
Hollingsworth

135-225 BB
5 rooms, 5 pb
Most CC, *Rated*, •
C-ltd/S-no/P-no/H-no

Full breakfast
Afternoon refreshments
Common areas include a
library with gas fireplace, an
indoor porch and lawn
garden

*1867 Greek Revival style townhome in the Historic Village. Walk to shops, galleries,
antiquing, and restaurants. Hiking, bike riding and golf are nearby as well as cross country
and downhill skiing. Something to do in any of Vermont's beautiful seasons.*
✉ ardmoreinn@aol.com ◐ www.ardmoreinn.com

Canterbury House
43 Pleasant St 05091
800-390-3077 802-457-3077
Bob & Sue Frost

135-200 BB
7 rooms, 7 pb
Visa, MC, *Rated*
C-ltd/S-no/P-no/H-no

Gourmet full plated breakfast
Sitting room, WiFi, Internet
Access, TVs, patio, fishing,
golf, skiing, Hiking

*An 1880 Victorian townhouse restored to offer modern comfort & historic authenticity. All
7 rooms have private baths and summer A/C. Within walking distance of the Village Green.*
✉ stay@thecanterburyhouse.com ◐ www.thecanterburyhouse.com

**Carriage House of
Woodstock**
Route 4 West 05091
800-791-8045 802-457-4322
Debbie & Mark Stanglin

100-195 BB
9 rooms, 9 pb
Most CC
C-ltd/S-no/P-no/H-ltd

Full breakfast
Afternoon snack
Parlor with fireplace, wraparound porch, private
parking lot

*1865 Victorian B&B located just one mile west of the village of Woodstock. Nine uniquely
decorated rooms, all with private baths—one with fireplace. Several with TV & whirlpool
tub. The Carriage House is on the Vermont Register of Historic Places.*
✉ stanglin@sover.net ◐ www.carriagehousewoodstock.com

Deer Brook Inn
535 Woodstock Rd 05091
802-672-3713
David Kanal

115-185 BB
5 rooms, 5 pb
Visa, MC, AmEx, *Rated*
C-ltd/S-no/P-no/H-no

Full breakfast
Afternoon tea
Sitting room, suite, fireplace,
A/C, cable TV, in-room music
systems, WiFi, porch, lawns
& gardens

*Indulge yourself in our historic inn set on 5 acres of lawns, gardens, and wooded areas.
Spacious, romantic accommodations with private baths, music systems and wireless Internet. Includes a 3 course breakfast in the dining room or on the terrace.*
✉ deerbrook@vermontel.net ◐ www.deerbrookinn.com

**The Lincoln Inn at the
Covered Bridge**
Rte 4 W 05091
802-457-3312
Amy Martsolf

125-175 BB
6 rooms, 6 pb
Visa, MC, AmEx
C-ltd/S-no/P-no/H-no

Full breakfast
Restaurant, bar service,
biking, sitting room, library

*The Lincoln Inn in Woodstock is a warm, cozy country inn located 2.5 miles west of the
Woodstock Village Green. Far enough from the village of Woodstock to be quiet, yet close
enough to go to town in a few short minutes.*
✉ lincolninfo@comcast.net ◐ www.lincolninn.com

WOODSTOCK

The Village Inn of	150-320 BB	Full breakfast
Woodstock	8 rooms, 8 pb	Victorian parlor & tavern on
41 Pleasant St 05091	Visa, MC, *Rated*	premises, sitting room,
800-722-4571 802-457-1255	C-ltd/S-no/P-no/H-no	perennial shaded garden
Evelyn & David Brey	German	

Eight elegant, romantic rooms with period antiques, private baths, A/C & cable TV await in our restored Victorian gem in the Village. Rates include a 3 course breakfast with pastries made in-house. It's your time away, let us help you make the most of it!
✉ stay@villageinnofwoodstock.com ◐ www.villageinnofwoodstock.com

Woodbridge Inn of	99-199 BB	Full breakfast
Woodstock	6 rooms, 6 pb	Late afternoon refreshments
546 Woodstock Road 05091	Most CC, *Rated*, •	Guest lounge area with Large
866-Woodbridge 802-672-1800	C-ltd/S-ltd/P-no/H-no	Screen TV, outdoor deck,
Amy Audsley		Ottaquechee River

CIRCA 1870. Located only minutes away from the Village Green, the Woodbridge Inn of Woodstock VT is a beautiful Four Season Bed and Breakfast which sits atop the banks of the historic Ottauquechee River and is surrounded by the beautiful Green Mountains.
✉ woodbridgeinn@comcast.net ◐ www.woodbridgeinnofwoodstock.com

The Woodstocker Inn	110-340 BB	Hot cooked to order full
61 River St 05091	9 rooms, 9 pb	breakfast
866-662-1439 802-457-3896	Visa, MC, AmEx, *Rated*	European breakfasts
Dora Foschi, David Livesley	S-no/P-no/H-no	including British specialties
	Italian	such as boiled eggs &
		soldiers, beans on toast
		WiFi, ample car parking,
		sitting room, library, mainly
		organic supplies, recycled
		paper goods

Award winning 1830's village Cape home. Organic food, recycled paper goods, eclectic European boutique style, indulgent bathrooms. Accredited Green inn.
✉ innkeeper@woodstockervt.com ◐ www.woodstockervt.com

Virgin Islands

CHARLOTTE AMALIE

At Home In The Tropics Bed	175-230 BB	Full breakfast
& Breakfast Inn	4 rooms, 4 pb	honor bar
1690 (25) Dronningens Gade	Visa, MC, AmEx	pool, a/c, in-room safes, high
00804-6877	C-ltd/S-no/P-no/H-no	speed Internet, cable TV
340-777-9857		
Pam Eckstein		

Bright and airy restored c 1803 St Thomas courtyard property located on Government House steps on Blackbeard's Hill. Swimming pool and water views from every room and deck. Easy walk down old Danish steps to historic harbor, restaurants, yachts & ferries.
✉ athomeinthetropics@earthlink.net ◑ www.athomeinthetropics.com

Bellavista B&B	150-245 BB	Full breakfast
2713 Murphy Gade 12-14 00802	4 rooms, 4 pb	Complimentary bottled
888-333-3063 340-714-5706	Most CC	water and fresh fruit
Wendy Snodgrass	C-ltd/S-ltd/P-no/H-no	Concierge, turndown
		service, flowers in room,
		swimming pool, tropical
		garden

A delightfully inviting estate overlooking the harbor at Charlotte Amalie. Experience the personalized service and quality amenities of a traditional B&B with distinctive Caribbean style.
✉ mail@bellavista-bnb.com ◑ www.bellavista-bnb.com

Bunker Hill Hotel	98-129 BB	Full breakfast
7A Commandant Gade 00802	15 rooms, 15 pb	Restaurant, lunch & dinner
340-774-8056	Visa, MC, AmEx, •	available
Angela Rawlins	C-yes/S-ltd/P-no/H-no	Swimming pool, suites, cable
		TV, accommodates business
		travelers

A small, unique, clean, & comfortable B&B Inn, conveniently located in the historic district area of Charlotte Amalie, just a few minutes walking distance to many points of interest.
✉ info@bunkerhillhotel.com ◑ www.bunkerhillhotel.com

Magens Valley Inn	165-195 BB	Full breakfast
6399 Estate Wintberg 00802	1 rooms, 1 pb	Optional gourmet "Dinners
340-714-4405	Visa, MC	on the Deck," and "Welcome
Steve & Leslie Rockstein	C-ltd/S-no/P-no/H-no	Dinners" available,
		vegetarian diets honored
		3 room apartment, private
		entrance, airport pickup,
		discount car rental, wedding
		photography

Nestled on the lush north side of St. Thomas, with stunning ocean views, Magens Valley Inn is your private getaway. Our one-acre of peaceful Caribbean paradise is perfect for honeymoons, private retreats or just getting away from it all.
✉ info@magensvalleyinn.com ◑ www.magensvalleyinn.com

CHARLOTTE AMALIE

Miller Manor Hotel & Guesthouse
2527 Prindcesse Gade 00804
888-229-0762 340-774-1535
Marj and Harry

89-160 EP
8 rooms, 7 pb
Most CC, •
C-yes/S-ltd/P-no/H-no

Enjoy complimentary coffee
or tea from 7:00 – 10:00 a.m
Breakfast is available during
high season.
Satellite TV, microwave,
small fridge A/C, wireless
Internet, Fax service,
laundry facilities

Charming and historic Danish Manor house built in the 1800's with a wonderful view of St. Thomas harbor. Close to the airport, and within walking distance to shopping and ferries to nearby islands. Amenities include AC, wireless Internet and satellite TV.
✉ info@millermanor.com ❂ www.millermanor.com

CHRISTIANSTED

Villa Greenleaf
11 Estate Montepellier 00821
888-282-1001 340-719-1958
Jeff Teel

205-365 BB
5 rooms, 5 pb
Most CC, •
C-ltd/S-no/P-no/H-no

Full breakfast
Tropical drinks and hors
d'oeuvres at sunset
Private terraces, living room,
pool and Jacuzzi, concierge,
car rental included in the
nightly rate

Where the annual temperature is 82 degrees, with cool breezes and breathtaking sunsets, we welcome you to Villa Greenleaf on St. Croix. Come join us in the most relaxed atmosphere that the Caribbean has to offer.
✉ info@villagreenleaf.com ❂ www.villagreenleaf.com

CRUZ BAY

The Hillcrest Guest House
#157 Enighed 00831
340-776-6774
Phyllis Hall

155-195 BB
4 rooms, 4 pb
Most CC, •
C-yes/S-no/P-no/H-no

Breakfast items are placed in
Suite
Tea, coffee, snacks, drinks &
liquor
Kitchenette w/microwave,
food, coffee & tea makers, air
conditioner, TV Cable, Free
WiFi, DVD movie

Vacation rental suites with view of Cruz Bay. Sunsets and cool breezes. Turquoise water & white sandy beaches. Suites have a kitchen, private bath & are air conditioned. Complimentary menu includes food and drinks.
✉ hillcrestguesthouse@yahoo.com ❂ www.HillcrestStJohn.com

ST. CROIX

Carringtons Inn St. Croix
56 Estate Herman Hill 00820
877-658-0508 340-713-0508
Claudia & Roger Carrington

100-165 BB
5 rooms, 5 pb
Visa, MC, AmEx,
Rated, •
S-no/P-no/H-no

Full breakfast
Snacks
Sitting room, swimming pool,
cable TV, accommodate
business travelers

Welcome to Carrington's Inn—your home in the Caribbean. Five spacious and beautifully decorated rooms surround the pool and patio. Personalized service is our trademark.
✉ info@carringtonsinn.com ❂ www.carringtonsinn.com

Virginia

AMHERST

Crump's Mountain Cottage 69-130 BB Continental plus breakfast
2150 Indian Creek Rd 24521 2 rooms, 1 pb Tea, coffee and popcorn
866-868-4118 434-277-5563 Cash, Checks, *Rated*, Stocked fishing pond, hiking
Carolyn & Curtis Crump • trails, games, music, movie
  C-yes/S-no/P-yes/H-no videos, cards, puzzles &
  guided nature tour

Solitary Cottage nestled in Blue Ridge Mountains, on 103 wooded acres, panoramic views from deck. Refresh your spirit with nature's sights & sounds. Enjoy the quiet & solitude. Hike on the property or in nearby G.W. National Forest. Guided tours offered
✉ crumpmtcottage@pngusa.net ◷ www.crumpmtncottage.com

ARLINGTON

Captain McGuire's House 115-345 BB Continental plus breakfast
Prince Street 22202 2 rooms, 2 pb Restaurant
888-549-3415 703-549-3415 Visa, MC, Disc, • Sitting room, library,
Linda Egerton S-no/P-no/H-no Jacuzzis, fireplaces, suites,
  cable TV

Historic, charming, authentic 1816 townhouse in middle of Old Town Alexandria. Hospitable hostess. Delightful atmosphere. Guests keep returning!
✉ bbinfo@aabbn.com

ASHLAND

The Henry Clay Inn 95-195 BB Continental buffet breakfast
114 N Railroad Ave 23005 14 rooms, 14 pb Parlor, large porches, Jacuzzi
804-798-3100 Most CC, *Rated* in suites, fireplaces in
Ann-Carol M. Houston C-yes/S-no/P-ltd/H-yes common areas, small town
  pleasures, WiFi

Southern charm with fireplaces, a large front porch with rocking chairs, 14 period furnished rooms, a gallery featuring local artists and a Parlor that opens onto a balcony overlooking the old Ashland train station.
✉ information@henryclayinn.com ◷ www.henryclayinn.com

BASYE

Sky Chalet Mountain Lodge 69-155 BB Continental breakfast
259 Sky Chalet Lane, Rt 263 6 rooms, 6 pb Mountain views, stone
22810 Visa, MC, Disc, • fireplaces, kitchens,
877-867-8439 540-856-2147 C-yes/S-yes/P-yes/H-no kitchenettes, decks, sitting
Ken & Mona Seay rooms, Jacuzzi for two

Renovated mountaintop Bed and Breakfast Lodge in the Shenandoah Valley with spectacular mountain and valley views. Private baths, private decks, fireplaces, kitchens, kitchenettes, Jacuzzi for two. The Mountain Lovers' paradise in the Shenandoah Valley!
✉ skychalet@skychalet.com ◷ www.skychalet.com

BOSTON

The Inn on Thistle Hill
5541 Sperryville Pike 22713
540-987-9357
Seane Malone

145-215 BB
4 rooms, 4 pb
Visa, MC, Disc, •
C-ltd/S-no/P-no/H-ltd

Fabulous cooked to order breakfast
Completely candle-lit (about 75 candles!), gourmet 5-course dinner by advance reservation.
Raindrop Aromatherapy Massage, Aquachi Foot Spa, Consults, Energy Balancing, Aromatherapy Classes

The Inn on Thistle Hill nestles against the hillside of its ten acres of both wooded & open land in the foothills of the Blue Ridge Mountains. Visit wineries, go antiquing, hike Old Rag Mountain or simply relax in the garden or ramble through our woods.
✉ theinnonthistlehill@earthlink.net ✪ www.theinnonthistlehill.com/welcome.htm

BOWLING GREEN

ColumnWood B&B
233 N Main St 22427
866-633-9314 804-633-5606
Patrick DeCrane & Michael Thomas

100-140 BB
4 rooms, 4 pb
Most CC, *Rated*
C-ltd/S-no/P-ltd/H-no

Full breakfast
Guest refrigerator is stocked with sodas, ice tea, cookies; lunch/dinner available with notice
Dining area, whirlpool tubs, European showers, European parlor stoves, TV, stereo, maid service, CD

With over 5,000 sq ft of hardwood floors, ColumnWood is one of Bowling Green's largest historic homes. In addition to high ceilings and pocket doors, it is blessed with many large windows, which still have their original "wavy" glass. Small dogs welcome.
✉ patmike@bealenet.com ✪ www.columnwood.com

BRIDGEWATER

Bridgewater Inn & Cottage
104 W College St 22812
540-828-4619
Mary Stevens Ayers

105-170 BB
3 rooms, 2 pb
Visa, MC, *Rated*
C-yes/S-no/P-yes/H-no

Full breakfast
Snacks, complimentary wine
Library, tennis, pool, fireplace, cable, bus. traveler accommodations, hot tub, sun room on site

Bridgewater Inn and Cottage has two suites that offer ultimate comfort and each detail has been carefully considered for our guests. Romance, elegance, tranquility, and privacy describe the ambience of Bridgewater Inn and Cottage.
✉ bridgewaterinn_cottage@msn.com ✪ www.bridgewaterinnandcottage.com

CAPE CHARLES

Cape Charles House B&B
645 Tazwell Ave 23310
757-331-4920
Bruce & Carol Evans

120-200 BB
5 rooms, 5 pb
Most CC, *Rated*, •
C-ltd/S-ltd/P-no/H-no

Full gourmet breakfast
Complimentary tea and sweets, wine and cheese, special dietary needs by arrangement
Parlors, formal dining room, antiques, wrap-around porch, wireless Internet, Jacuzzis, cable TV

Cape Charles House received the Governor's Award for Virginia Hospitality. A comfortably elegant, romantic getaway in 1912 Colonial Revival. Oriental rugs, antiques and collections are incorporated into the beautifully decorated, lovingly restored home.
✉ stay@capecharleshouse.com ✪ www.capecharleshouse.com

CHARLES CITY————————————————————————

Edgewood Plantation
4800 John Tyler Hwy 23030
800-296-EDGE 804-829-2962
Julian & Dot Boulware

130-200 BB
8 rooms, 8 pb
Visa, MC, *Rated*, •
C-ltd/S-no/P-ltd/H-no

Full breakfast
Complimentary
refreshments, special
holiday dinners & teas
Tea room, shops, fireplaces,
formal gardens, gazebos,
pool, fishing, TV/VCR

Circa 1849, historical, 7,000 square foot, 4-story mansion. 10 working fireplaces. Double spiral staircase. Incredible furnishings and antiques; well appointed. Registered State and National Landmark.
✉ reservations@edgewoodplantation.com ✪ www.EdgewoodPlantation.com

North Bend Plantation
12200 Weyanoke Rd 23030
804-829-5176
George & Ridgely Copland

135-175 BB
4 rooms, 4 pb
Visa, MC
C-ltd/S-yes/P-no/H-ltd

Full breakfast
Early coffee & tea, Afternoon
Tea
Bicycles, pool, library, parlor
games, fireplace, croquet,
volleyball, direct TV, WiFi

Historic Landmark 1819 Federal style manor. Spacious, elegant rooms, private baths, original antiques, hammocks, three porches, lush grounds, pool on site. National Register property.
✉ ridgely37@aol.com ✪ www.northbendplantation.com

CHARLOTTESVILLE————————————————————

200 South Street Inn
200 South St W 22902
800-964-7008 434-979-0200
Brendan Clancy

130-270 BB
20 rooms, 20 pb
Visa, MC, AmEx, •
C-yes/S-no/P-no/H-yes
French

Continental plus breakfast
Lunch, Monday-Friday,
dinner weekends,
complimentary wine,
restaurant
Sitting room, fireplaces,
library, whirlpool tubs, TV

A relaxing, comfortable home-style atmosphere with all the conveniences of an elegant hotel. The South Street Inn offers old-world ambience in the middle of Charlottesville's lively downtown.
✉ southst@cstone.net ✪ www.southstreetinn.com

Dinsmore House Inn
1211 W Main St 22903
877-882-7829 434-974-4663
Ryan & Denise Hubbard

109-259 BB
8 rooms, 8 pb
C-ltd/S-no/P-no/H-ltd

Full breakfast
Refreshments
Pool, hot tub, fitness center,
beautiful brick courtyard,
wrap-around windows,
atmosphere.

The Dinsmore House Bed & Breakfast combines a perfect location with luxurious comfort, creating a unique Charlottesville experience.
✉ info@dinsmorehouse.com ✪ www.dinsmorehouse.com

The Foxfield Inn
2280 Garth Rd 22901
866-FOX-FLDN 434-923-8892
Mary Pat & John Hulburt

185-280 BB
5 rooms, 5 pb
Visa, MC
S-no/P-no/H-yes

Full breakfast
Homemade cookies, fine
Virginia wine, tea and more
Gathering room, in-room
Jacuzzi, fireplace, canopy
beds, Bose radios in rooms,
outside heated spa

A luxury country Inn only minutes from Monticello and UVA, featuring rooms with Jacuzzi, fireplace, handcrafted canopy queen size bed. Outside heated spa and restful teahouse. Rated #1 in 2004, 2005, 2006, 2007, 2008 for Charlottesville.
✉ stay@foxfield-inn.com ✪ www.foxfield-inn.com

CHARLOTTESVILLE

Inn at Monticello
Hwy 20 S 22902
877-735-2982 434-979-3593
Carolyn Patterson & Bob Goss

155-245 BB
5 rooms, 5 pb
Visa, MC, AmEx, *Rated*
C-ltd/S-no/P-no/H-no
Some French
Closed Christmas

Full gourmet breakfast
Complimentary local beer &
wine
Sitting room, large front
porch, secure wireless
access

19th century manor, perfectly located 2 miles from Thomas Jefferson's beloved "Monticello." The Inn at Monticello is an upscale and award winning Charlottesville bed and breakfast.
✉ stay@innatmonticello.com ◓ www.innatmonticello.com

Inn at the Crossroads
866-809-2136 434-979-6452
Jim & Janet Stern

119-219 BB
6 rooms, 6 pb
Most CC, *Rated*, •
C-ltd/S-ltd/P-no/H-ltd

Full breakfast
Tree and porch swings,
gazebo, bike and jog directly
from the property

National Historic Register Inn with panoramic mountain views. 10 to 15 minutes from the University of Virginia, Charlottesville, Monticello, Skyline Drive and Blue Ridge Parkway.
✉ info@crossroadsinn.com ◓ www.crossroadsinn.com

**Prospect Hill Plantation Inn
& Restaurant**
2887 Poindexter Rd 22906
800-277-0844 540-967-0844
The Sheehan Family since
1977

195-350 BB
13 rooms, 13 pb
Most CC, *Rated*, •
C-ltd/S-ltd/P-no/H-ltd

Full brkfast-in-bed or Dining
Rm
Elegant dining Sun-Thur 7pm,
Fri-Sat 8pm, w/comp. wine
reception½hr. prior, snacks
in rm on arr.
Jacuzzis in 8 rms, all with
fireplaces, 40+ acres of
manicured grounds,
bicycles, honeymoon
packages

Historic plantation manor on 50 ac with 13 romantic rooms & cottages just 15 mi East of C'ville, VA. Working fireplaces in all rooms, 8 w/Jacuzzis, outdoor pool. B&B rates from $195 prie-fixe dinner at $49pp or all-inclusive package rates avail.
✉ innkeeper@prospecthill.com ◓ www.prospecthill.com

CHINCOTEAGUE

Cedar Gables Seaside Inn
6095 Hopkins Ln 23336
888-491-2944 757-336-6860
Claudia Kesseler

155-190 BB
4 rooms, 4 pb
Visa, MC, Disc, *Rated*
C-ltd/S-no/P-no/H-no

Full gourmet breakfast
A surprise or two will be
offered from time to time in
the afternoon
All suites have Jacuzzis,
fireplaces, TV/VCR, CD,
upscale decor, waterview,
decks, central heat/A/C

Waterfront inn overlooking Little Oyster Bay. All rooms have fireplaces, Jacuzzi baths. Open to waterfront decks with breathtaking views of Assateague Island. Upscale establishment with many amenities, including pool & hot tub overlooking the water.
✉ cdrgbl@intercom.net ◓ www.cedargable.com

Channel Bass Inn
6228 Church St 23336
800-249-0818 757-336-6148
David & Barbara Wiedenheft

115-195 BB
6 rooms, 6 pb
Most CC, *Rated*, •
C-yes/S-no/P-yes/H-no
French, Dutch, German,
Spanish
Late March – November

Full breakfast
Inn guests enjoy a proper
English afternoon tea at a
special rate of $9.00 per
person.
Sitting room, piano, library,
bikes, beach paraphernalia,
TV, Tea Room, gardens,
meals on the porch

A world of peaceful elegance surrounds you when you enter the Channel Bass Inn. Originally built as a private home in 1892, the Inn was converted to a small hotel in the 1920s. Today it offers a wonderful respite to travelers from all over the world.
✉ barbara@channelbassinn.com ◓ www.channelbassinn.com

616   Virginia

CHINCOTEAGUE

Miss Molly's Inn
4141 Main St 23336
800-221-5620 757-336-6686
Sam & Lin Mazza

120-185 BB
7 rooms, 5 pb
Most CC, *Rated*, •
C-ltd/S-no/P-ltd/H-no

Gourmet breakfast
Afternoon refreshments and
vegetarian breakfast
available
Sitting room, bicycles, beach
items, library and garden

Miss Molly's Inn sits on the bay and has five wonderful porches with plenty of rocking chairs and a large deck on the second floor that overlooks the bay. We also have a beautiful screened-in porch full of flowers.
✉ missmollysinn@verizon.net ✪ www.missmollys-inn.com

CHURCHVILLE

Buckhorn Inn & Restaurant
2487 Hankey Mountain Hwy
24421
877-337-8660 540-337-8660
Garlan & Sylvia Yoder

110-135 BB
5 rooms, 5 pb
Visa, MC, *Rated*
C-yes/S-no/P-ltd/H-ltd
Spanish, limited German
Closed January

Full breakfast
Country & Seafood Buffet
Restaurant – Thursday,
Friday & Saturday dinner,
snacks, coffee, tea, soda
Suite with fireplace, satellite
TV in rooms, guest lounge,
banquet ; party facilities

A 200 year-old stage coach stop in the scenic Shenandoah Valley that still has much of it original character and construction. A 5 room B&B with a restaurant known for excellent country and seafood buffets. Great place for weddings, meetings and parties.
✉ garlan@thebuckhorninn.net ✪ www.thebuckhorninn.com

COPPER HILL

Bent Mountain Lodge
9039 Mountain View Dr 24079
540-651-2500
Bonnie & Jesse Lawrence

90-120 BB
10 rooms, 10 pb
Visa, MC
C-yes/S-no/P-yes/H-yes
Portuguese

Continental breakfast
Tea any time
Decks, 5 Jacuzzi tubs,
gazebo, wedding facilities,
kitchen, fireplaces, new sun
rooms, TV, Internet

15000 Sq. Ft. with 10 suites, king or queen with private bath, many with private decks or porches and great views at 3200 Ft. overlooking Blue Ridge Parkway 15 miles south of Roanoke, VA. Excellent location for weddings. Handicap suites and ramps.
✉ mscmom74@swva.net ✪ www.bentmountainlodgebedandbreakfast.com

CROZET

The Inn at Sugar Hollow Farm
6051 Sugar Hollow Rd 22932
866-566-7388 434-823-7086
Dick & Hayden Cabell

140-250 BB
9 rooms, 9 pb
Visa, MC, AmEx, *Rated*
C-ltd/S-no/P-no/H-no

Full breakfast
Beverages, butlers' pantries
Fireplaces, double whirlpool
tubs, several common
rooms, 2 terraces, WiFi, TV
Den, gardens

Serene, romantic country retreat, mountain streams near Shenandoah Park, Blue Ridge Mountains and wineries. Fireplaces, double whirlpool tubs, hiking, biking, near Monticello and University of Virginia.
✉ Innkeeper@sugarhollow.com ✪ www.sugarhollow.com

CULPEPER

Fountain Hall
609 S East St 22701
800-29-VISIT 540-825-8200
Steve & Kathi Walker

125-175 BB
6 rooms, 6 pb
Most CC, *Rated*, •
C-yes/S-no/P-no/H-yes

Continental plus breakfast
Complimentary beverages,
fresh fruits
Common rooms, books,
fireplaces, movies, porches,
golf nearby, hiking, rooms
with whirlpool, history

Gracious accommodations for business & leisure. Centrally located in historic Culpeper, between Washington D.C., Charlottesville & Skyline Drive.
✉ visit@fountainhall.com ✪ www.fountainhall.com

DUBLIN

Rockwood Manor
5189 Rockwood Rd 24084
540-674-1328
Frank Drummund

120-170 BB
8 rooms, 6 pb
Most CC
C-ltd/S-ltd/P-no/H-ltd

Full breakfast
Historic grand staircase,
fireplace, sitting area,
weddings, receptions, grand
patio, bright decor

Welcome to The Rockwood Manor in beautiful Dublin, Virginia! Experience the romantic elegance and superb tranquility of an incomparable Virginia gem. Located near many attractions and even the home of President Thomas Jefferson.
✉ info@rockwood-manor.com ♦ www.rockwood-manor.com

DYKE

Cottages at Chesley Creek Farm
2369 Brokenback Mountain Rd 22935
866-709-9292 434-985-7129
Chuck Swinney & Stu White

175-200 EP
4 rooms, 4 pb
Cash, Checks
S-no/P-no/H-no

No meals provided
BBQ grill
Jacuzzi, fireplace, solitude,
fully equipped kitchen,
dishes towels and linens
provided, pool

Four secluded cottages in the Blue Ridge Mountains of VA, completely furnished with exception of food. To ensure your privacy there is no TV or phone. There is a stereo & lots of books, gas fireplace, Jacuzzi & queen bed. Enjoy trails & mountain views.
✉ info@chesleycreekfarm.com ♦ www.chesleycreekfarm.com

FREDERICKSBURG

La Vista Plantation
4420 Guinea Station Rd 22408
800-529-2823 540-898-8444
Michele & Edward Schiesser

145-165 BB
2 rooms, 2 pb
Visa, MC, Disc, •
C-yes/S-no/P-no/H-no

Fresh brown eggs/our hens
Complimentary soft drinks,
bottled water, ice, fresh
brown eggs from resident
hens
Sitting room, fridge, library,
A/C, S.TV/VCR/CD player,
fishing, gardens, radio,
fireplaces, video library

Lovely 1838 National Register listed Classical Revival country home on 10 acres outside historic Fredericksburg, VA. Antiques, working fireplaces, gardens & old trees. Stocked pond with dock & row boat. Formal room or 2 bedroom apartment perfect for families.
✉ info@lavistaplantation.com ♦ www.lavistaplantation.com

Richard Johnston Inn
711 Caroline St 22401
877-557-0770 540-899-7606
Bonnie De Lelys

105-210 BB
9 rooms, 9 pb
Visa, MC, AmEx,
Rated, •
C-yes/S-no/P-yes/H-ltd

Full breakfast on weekends
Concierge & reservations
services available, video
library, wireless high speed
Internet

The Richard Johnston Inn makes an ideal get away for a vacation, weekend retreat, business trip or conference and still reflects the charm and grace of a past era, while providing all of the amenities of today for the comfort of our guests.
✉ rjohnstoninn@staffnet.com ♦ www.therichardjohnstoninn.com

FRONT ROYAL

Killahevlin B&B
1401 N Royal Ave 22630
800-847-6132 540-636-7335
Tom & Kathy Conkey

155-255 BB
6 rooms, 6 pb
Most CC, *Rated*
C-ltd/S-no/P-no/H-no

Full breakfast
Complimentary snacks, beer
& wine
Scenic, sitting room,
whirlpools, gazebos,
screened porch, private Irish
pub

Historic Edwardian mansion. Civil War encampment hill. Mountain views, working fireplaces, whirlpool tubs, antiques. Prepare to be pampered.
✉ kllhvln@comcast.net ♦ www.vairish.com

GLOUCESTER

The North River Inn
8777 Toddsbury Lane 23061
877-248-3030 804-693-1616
Breck & Mary Montague

155-245 BB
6 rooms, 6 pb
Visa, MC
C-ltd/S-no/P-no/H-no

Full breakfast
coffee, tea, cereal, juice, ice
laundry facilities at Cottage
and Creek House, canoes
available

The North River Inn spreads graciously across one-hundred waterfront acres in Virginia's historic Tidewater region off the Chesapeake Bay. A National Register Landmark and Virginia Historic Landmark, the Inn is located on the North River.
✉ innkeeper@northriverinn.com 🌐 www.northriverinn.com

GORDONSVILLE

Sleepy Hollow Farm B&B
16280 Blue Ridge Turnpike
22942
800-215-4804 540-832-5555
Beverley Allison & Dorsey
Allison-Comer

80-175 BB
5 rooms, 5 pb
Visa, MC, *Rated*
C-yes/S-no/P-yes/H-no
Spanish, French

Full breakfast
Freshly baked cake, cookies,
beverages
Baby Grand piano,
conference room, croquet,
gazebo, pond fishing

Sleepy Hollow Farm is a family farmhouse and cottage that sits in a natural hollow, surrounded by woods and farmland. An ideal setting for weddings, family reunions or retreats.
✉ thehollow@sleepyhollowfarmbnb.com 🌐 www.sleepyhollowfarmbnb.com

Wolftrap Farm
17379 Wolftrap Dr 22942
540-832-1803
Keith Cuthrell

110-250 BB
5 rooms, 4 pb
Most CC
C-yes/S-no/P-ltd/H-ltd
French

Full breakfast
Hot tub, ponds, horse
stables, patio, porch, kitchen,
trails

On a 584-acre horse and cattle farm, with mountain views, miles of forest trails, rolling pastures, abundant creeks and brooks, nine ponds, and easy access to all the attractions of Charlottesville and the Central Virginia area.
✉ wolftrapfarm@yahoo.com 🌐 www.thewolftrapfarm.com

GOSHEN

Hummingbird Inn
30 Wood Ln 24439
800-397-3214 540-997-9065
Dan & Patty Harrison

140-175 BB
5 rooms, 5 pb
Visa, MC, AmEx, •
C-ltd/S-ltd/P-ltd/H-no

Full breakfast
Beverages & snacks, dinners
with reservations
Comfy rooms, whirlpool
tubs, double shower,
fireplaces, verandas,
computer w/free Internet
access

Unique Carpenter Gothic house offering an acre of grounds, deck next to the stream, accommodations w/comfortable furnishings, modern amenities & warm hospitality await you. Want to relax, perfect place. . watch the hundreds of hummingbirds visiting us!
✉ stay@hummingbirdinn.com 🌐 www.hummingbirdinn.com

HAMPTON

Magnolia House B&B
232 S Armistead Ave 23669
757-722-2888
Lankford & Joyce Blair

145-240 BB
3 rooms, 3 pb
Most CC
C-ltd/S-no/P-no/H-ltd

Full breakfast
Luxury linens, robes and
slippers for use, WiFi access,
massage available on
request.

Offering luxury accommodations, great breakfasts, delicious snacks, lots of music from jazz to classical in a Queen Anne Victorian home with eclectic decor. Located in the Chesapeake Bay city of Hampton.
✉ stay@maghousehampton.com 🌐 www.maghousehampton.com

HARRISONBURG

By the Side of the Road B&B
491 Garbers Church Rd 22801
866-274-4887 540-801-0430
Janice & Dennis Fitzgerald

169-289 BB
7 rooms, 7 pb
Visa, MC, •
C-yes/S-ltd/P-no/H-yes

Gourmet Breakfast
We provide an assortment of
snacks to Cottage guests;
homebaked sweets to Main
House guests
Help with tee times, dining,
bike/hiking, outdoor
recreation, tours, massage,
TV, CD, whirlpool tubs

*By the Side of the Road B&B offers a unique combination of the pleasures of a peaceful
country retreat and the convenience of being within minutes of all the amenities and
entertainment of the thriving city of Harrisonburg.*
✉ stay@bythesideoftheroad.com ◔ www.bythesideoftheroad.com

Stonewall Jackson Inn B&B
547 E Market St 22801
800-445-5330 540-433-8233
Dr. Wayne Engel

99-179 BB
10 rooms, 10 pb
Most CC, *Rated*
C-ltd/S-no/P-ltd/H-ltd
Afrikaans and Dutch

Full Gourmet Quality
Breakfast
Homemade treats, in-room
snacks, chocolates, etc. We
accommodate vegan and
special dietary requests.
Superb Amenities: Concierge
Service, Free WiFi,
Individually Climate
Controlled Rooms, Patio
Dining

*"A Night's Delight–A Breakfast to Remember"... is our mission, and succinctly describes the
legendary Award Winning "Stonewall Jackson Experience"! We are a Certified Virginia
Green, 3-Diamond Inn.*
✉ info@stonewalljacksoninn.com ◔ www.StonewallJacksonInn.com

HOT SPRINGS

Vine Cottage Inn
7402 Sam Snead Highway
24445
800-410-9755 540-839-2422
Jo & Jonah Windham

75-130 BB
14 rooms, 8 pb
Most CC
C-yes/S-ltd/P-no/H-no

Full breakfast
Porch, garden, spa nearby,
private & shared baths,
convenient location

*Our room configurations include family style lodging and romantic rooms for two. All
rooms include a full fixed menu breakfast.*
✉ innkeeper@vinecottageinn.com ◔ www.vinecottageinn.com

IRVINGTON

The Hope and Glory Inn
65 Tavern Rd 22480
800-497-8228 804-438-6053
Peggy & Dudley Patteson

175-430 BB
35 rooms, 35 pb
Visa, MC, AmEx, *Rated*
C-yes/S-no/P-ltd/H-no

Full breakfast
Catered events
Sitting room, massages,
bikes, tennis court, croquet
& bocce on premises, pool

*Travel & Leisure ranks us one of this country's Great Inns. Frommer's Travel Guide—three
stars—its highest rating! Historic schoolhouse, quaint cottages, lush gardens, waterfront
village.*
✉ inquiries@hopeandglory.com ◔ www.hopeandglory.com

KILMARNOCK

Kilmarnock Inn
34 East Church St 22482
804-435-0034
Nancy Travers

150-250 BB
16 rooms, 16 pb
Most CC
C-yes/S-ltd/P-ltd/H-yes

Full breakfast
Full on-site catering available
Gathering room,
spa/wellness room, onsite
massage, bicycles, full
service bar & lounge

*Kilmarnock Inn, celebrating our Presidential Heritage with each of our cottages and our
main house named for the 8 Virginia Presidents. The Main House was built circa 1884 &
the cottages were designed to replicate the facades of the president's homes.*
✉ nancytravers@kilmarnockinn.com ◔ kilmarnockinn.com

LEXINGTON————————————————————————————————

1868 Magnolia House Inn
501 S Main St 24450
540-463-2567
Tim & Jan Decker

139-189 BB
5 rooms, 5 pb
Most CC, *Rated*
C-ltd/S-no/P-no/H-no

Full breakfast
Soft drinks, bottled water,
crackers, homemade cookies
Parlor with library &
fireplace, porches, garden

A short walk from downtown restaurants, museums, and boutiques, this 1868 Shenandoah Victorian style Inn, with its high ceilings, tall windows, porches and fireplaces, offers a comfortable mix of antiques, Oriental rugs, and traditional furnishings.
✉ magnolia@rockbridge.net ✆ www.magnoliahouseinn.com

A B&B at Llewellyn Lodge
603 S Main St 24450
800-882-1145 540-463-3235
John & Ellen Roberts

85-179 BB
6 rooms, 6 pb
Most CC, *Rated*, •
C-ltd/S-no/P-no/H-no

Order from a menu
Afternoon tea, seasonal
refreshments, snacks
Large screen High Definition
TVs in most rooms, guest
fridge, Free WiFi, guest
computer, Fax, copier

Great in-town Lexington location, walk to all the historic sites and restaurants. Blue-ribbon, full breakfasts. Experienced advice on hiking, canoeing, golf, guided fly fishing trips. Your host John is a Lexington native.
✉ stay@llodge.com ✆ www.llodge.com

A Cabin at The Highlands
C/O 521 South Main Street
24450
540-463-2593
Antonia Albano & Barney
Brown

135-198 EP
5 rooms, 5 pb
Most CC
C-ltd/S-no/P-ltd/H-no
Spanish, some French

Wine
Hiking trails; books &
magazines; two rivers.
Cabins are well supplied.
High quality bedding

Choose from one of five historic, rustic, authentic log cabins, tastefully restored with modern amenities. Each cabin is unique with walnut, cherry, oak and chestnut logs, heating & AC, custom kitchens, bathrooms, often with claw-foot tubs and shower.
✉ innkeepers@southriverhighlands.com ✆ www.southriverhighlands.com

---

Applewood Inn & Llama Trekking
Buffalo Bend Rd 24450
800-463-1902 540-463-1962
Linda & Chris Best

110-150 BB
4 rooms, 4 pb
Visa, MC, AmEx
C-ltd/S-no/P-yes/H-ltd
German

Full breakfast
Hot cider, beverages, fridge,
pantry; Limited dinner
availability (please inquire)
Fireplaces, sitting room,
library, porches, pool, hiking,
llama treks (with optional
picnic lunch).

Spectacular passive solar home on 35 acres. Mountain views. Close to historic Lexington and Natural Bridge. Miles of trails for hiking and llama treks. Full in-ground swimming pool. Heart healthy breakfasts. For nature lovers.
✉ inn@applewoodbb.com ✆ www.applewoodbb.com

Auberge de la Ville
408 S Main St 24450
866-288-4715 540-463-4715
Natalie Boldurian

140-225 BB
5 rooms, 5 pb
Visa, MC, AmEx
C-ltd/S-no/P-no/H-no

Full breakfast
Internet access, movies,
guest phone, library

Enticing, Eclectic and Elegant—Featuring only the finest in furnishings, and what we hope you will find to be the most luxurious sleeping chambers in all of Rockbridge County.
✉ innatlexington@yahoo.com ✆ aubergedelaville.com

Brierley Hill
985 Borden Rd 24450
800-422-4925 540-464-8421
Ken & Joyce Hawkins – Diana
Mercik, Asst Innkeeper

120-295 BB
6 rooms, 6 pb
Visa, MC, AmEx, *Rated*
C-ltd/S-ltd/P-no/H-yes

Full breakfast
Afternoon refreshments
Hiking, canoeing, horseback
riding, free high-speed
Internet

English country house atmosphere. Magnificent views of Blue Ridge Mountains & Shenandoah Valley. Experience the relaxed elegance — just five minutes from downtown.
✉ relax@brierleyhill.com ✆ www.brierleyhill.com

LEXINGTON

House Mountain Inn
455 Lonesome Dove Tr 24450
540-464-4004
Jeff & Jamie Irvine

138-365 MAP
9 rooms, 9 pb
Visa, MC, AmEx
C-ltd/S-ltd/P-ltd/H-yes

Hearty gourmet breakfast
Wine and cheese reception
every afternoon at 4:00;
Dinner available for extra
fee.
On-site trails, 2 fishing ponds,
horse stalls, pub, massage;
Cabin also available;
Conferences.

Secluded on a private mountain near Lexington, Virginia, the House Mountain Inn offers gracious bed and breakfast hospitality and rustic lodging elegance in a breathtakingly beautiful Shenandoah Valley location.
✉ housemtninn@hughes.net ○ www.housemountaininn.com

Stoneridge B&B
246 Stoneridge Ln 24450
800-491-2930 540-463-4090
Jim, Evelyn, John & Sandy
Stallard

90-150 BB
5 rooms, 5 pb
Most CC, *Rated*
C-ltd/S-no/P-ltd/H-no
German, French

Full gourmet breakfast
Afternoon refreshments,
four-course candlelit dinner
available nightly by prior
arrangement
Sitting room, library,
whirlpools, suite, fireplaces,
Direct TV

A touch of elegance in an historic setting. Once the center of a 400 acre Shenandoah Valley farm, Stoneridge offers a glimpse of Antebellum life. The original house was built in 1829 with bricks made on the property.
✉ stoneridge@ntelos.net ○ www.stoneridge-inn.com

LURAY

Spring Farm Retreat
13 Wallace Ave 22835
866-780-7827 540-843-0606
Carlos Ruiz

195-250 EP
5 rooms, 3 pb
Most CC
C-yes/S-no/P-yes/H-no
Spanish

Includes a fully equipped
kitchen for you to prepare all
your own favorite meals.
Patio w/ BBQ grill
Wood burning and gas
fireplace, outdoor hot tub,
cable TV/VCR/DVD, stereo,
10 private acres

Sleeps 2–12 comfortably. Allstar Lodging offers Spring Farm Retreat as a historic Colonial vacation rental, built in 1795 with over 200 years of history. Secluded on 10 acres with a natural spring, 5 bdrm /3 bths includes separate cottage, outdoor hot tub
✉ allstar@allstarlodging.com

LYNCHBURG

Federal Crest Inn B&B
1101 Federal St 24504
800-818-6155 434-845-6155
Ann & Phil Ripley

145-185 BB
5 rooms, 4 pb
Most CC, *Rated*, •
C-ltd/S-no/P-no/H-no

Full breakfast
Afternoon beverages &
snacks
Sitting room, library, '50s
cafe, A/C, 60" TV, Jacuzzi,
antiques, conference room,
WiFi

Romantic and elegant! This unique and spacious 1909 mansion with seven fireplaces and antiques offers charm, comfort and modern conveniences. Theater with 60 inch TV on the 3rd floor. Conference center available.
✉ info@federalcrest.com ○ www.federalcrest.com

LYNCHBURG

Ivy Creek Farm	149-199 BB	Full gourmet breakfast
2812 Link Rd 24503	3 rooms, 3 pb	Afternoon wine, tea &
800-689-7404 434-384-3802	Visa, MC, AmEx	refreshments
Marilyn & Lynn Brooks	C-ltd/S-no/P-no/H-ltd	Turn-down with chocolates,
		library, laundry facilities,
		central A/C, Direct TV, DVD,
		WiFi, pool, spa

Welcome to Ivy Creek Farm, the quintessential Virginia bed and breakfast with memorable, gourmet breakfasts and luxurious accommodations. Casually elegant three-bedroom B&B, standing on ten private wooded acres in the city of Lynchburg.
✉ info@ivycreekfarm.com ○ www.ivycreekfarm.com

MADISON

Ebenezer House B&B	80-120 BB	Full breakfast
122 Seville Rd 22738	3 rooms, 2 pb	
888-948-3695	Visa, MC	
Doris Webb	C-yes/S-no/P-ltd/H-yes	

Family friendly country chalet. A home away from home. Seven miles south of Madison, 500 ft off US 29. Close to all historical sites, restaurants, local vineyards, UVA, and the beautiful Blue Ridge Mtns. Full country breakfast with friendly conversation.
✉ dmwebb@hughes.net ○ www.theebenezerhousebb.com

MIDDLEBURG

Briar Patch B&B	95-270 BB	Full weekends, continental
23130 Briar Patch Ln 20117	9 rooms, 3 pb	weekdays
866-327-5911 703-327-5911	Most CC	Continental breakfast on
Ellen Goldberg & Dan	C-yes/S-ltd/P-yes/H-ltd	weekdays, free snacks &
Haendel		drinks
		Free high speed wireless
		Internet, pool, hot tub, suites,
		fireplaces, accommodates
		business traveler

Historic farm (c. 1805) on 47 rolling acres in the heart of Virginia horse, antiques & wine country. Large pool, hot tub, mountain views, & grazing horses. We host weddings, business meetings, and other social & business events.
✉ info@briarpatchbandb.com ○ www.briarpatchbandb.com

MT. JACKSON

Strathmore House on the Shenandoah	135-175 BB	Three course breakfast
658 Wissler Rd 22842	4 rooms, 4 pb	Afternoon treats and snacks
888-921-6139 540-477-4141	Cash, Checks, *Rated*	Parlor, library, accom.
Kay & Jim Payne	S-no/P-no/H-no	business travelers,
	Spanish	wraparound porch, four
		acres of land

Occupying the Shenandoah Valley's most spectacular location, overlooking an historic covered bridge & Shenandoah River, this elegant 1892 Victorian offers four romantic bedrooms, private baths, wraparound porches, landscaped gardens and gourmet breakfast
✉ strath@shentel.net ○ www.StrathmoreHouse.com

Widow Kip's Country Inn	110-135 BB	Family style breakfast
355 Orchard Dr 22842	7 rooms, 7 pb	Courtyard, original
800-478-8714 540-477-2400	Visa, MC, ●	fireplaces, pool, bicycles,
Betty & Bob Luse	C-yes/S-no/P-yes	WiFi available

Your hosts welcome you to their 1830 restored Victorian homestead. It is nestled on 7 rural acres that offer a birds-eye view of the Shenandoah River—just 50 yards away.
✉ widokips@shentel.net ○ www.widowkips.com

NEW CHURCH

Garden and Sea Inn	85-225 BB	Full breakfast
4188 Nelson Road 23415	9 rooms, 9 pb	Snacks, Cookies, Soft drinks,
800-824-0672 757-824-0672	Most CC, *Rated*, •	Sherry
Dorothee and Thomas Renn	C-yes/S-no/P-yes/H-yes	Pool, sitting room, library,
	German, French	Jacuzzis, suites, fireplaces,
	January thru November	TV/DVD, refrigerators,
		coffeemakers

Romantic Victorian B&B near Chincoteague and Assateague Islands, yet perfectly located for those visiting the Eastern Shores quaint towns and marinas. Large rooms, heated pool, TV/DVD, A/C, refrigerators, gardens, full gourmet breakfast, Pets welcome!
✉ innkeeper@gardenandseainn.com ✆ www.gardenandseainn.com

NEWPORT NEWS

Boxwood Inn	105-135 BB	Full breakfast
10 Elmhurst St 23603	4 rooms, 4 pb	Dinner packages available.
757-888-8854	Visa, MC, *Rated*	on-site catering
Kathy Hulick	C-ltd/S-no/P-no/H-ltd	Antiques, weddings, catering

We invite you to stay in this gracious & charming circa 1896 Inn featuring 4 antique-filled rooms. Complimentary breakfast in the "Blue Willow" Tea Room. Enjoy the old world style and ambience.
✉ bnb@boxwood-inn.com ✆ www.Boxwood-Inn.com

ORANGE

Greenock House Inn	145-245 BB	Elegant Gourmet Breakfast
249 Caroline St 22960	5 rooms, 5 pb	Evening hors d'oeuvres and
800-841-1253 540-672-3625	Most CC, *Rated*	wine by request. Dinner
Lill & Rich Shearer	S-no/P-no/H-ltd	available.
		Parlor, library, whirlpool
		tubs, A/C, fireplaces, cable TV.

Stay in a restful, relaxing setting. Enjoy genteel company and gourmet meals including evening hors d'oeuvres. In the morning, indulge in a gourmet breakfast before enjoying your day exploring Orange! Convenient to D.C. and Richmond.
✉ reservations@greenockhouse.com ✆ www.greenockhouse.com

Holladay House	125-235 BB	Full breakfast
155 W Main St 22960	6 rooms, 6 pb	Beverages, homemade
800-358-4422 540-672-4893	Most CC	cookies, and refreshments
Sam & Sharon Elswick	C-yes/S-ltd/P-ltd/H-ltd	included in the room price.
		In-room massage, fireplaces,
		Jacuzzi, TV/DVD, alarm
		clock/CD, robes, wireless
		Internet, PC

This Federal style B&B (ca. 1830) is located in the heart of Orange, a quintessential historic Virginia town. Enjoy an elegant breakfast, curl up by the nineteenth-century marble fireplace, grab a homemade cookie, or relax in a luxurious whirlpool tub.
✉ innkeeper@holladayhousebandb.com ✆ www.holladayhousebandb.com

Inn on Poplar Hill	139-199 BB	Gourmet country breakfast
278 Caroline St 22960	6 rooms, 6 pb	Afternoon refreshments,
866-767-5274 540-672-6840	Visa, MC, •	stocked cookie jar
Victoria & Marty Tourville	C-ltd/S-no/P-ltd/H-no	Garden weddings, murder
		mystery dinners, wildflower
		trails, fishing pond, antiques,
		billiards

A casually elegant Queen Anne Victorian built in the 1890's by the great granddaughter of Thomas Jefferson. The Inn overlooks the historic town of Orange, VA. Surrounded by 28 acres with an abundance of wildflowers, walking trails and country charm.
✉ stay@innonpoplarhill.com ✆ www.innonpoplarhill.com

ORANGE

Mayhurst Inn
12460 Mayhurst Ln 22960
888-672-5597 540-672-5597
Jack & Pat North

165-245 BB
8 rooms, 8 pb
Visa, MC, AmEx, *Rated*
C-yes/S-no/P-yes/H-yes

Full, 3-course breakfast
Evening refreshments, with
selected Virginia wines,
crackers & gourmet cheeses,
cookies & sweets
In-room massages, fireplaces,
double whirlpools tubs,
luxury linens, extensive
amenities on 37 acres

We invite you to relax in the grandeur of history when Southern life was slower and more gracious. This marvelously preserved and restored plantation home c. 1859 can transport you to a romantic time far away from today's stresses. The perfect getaway.
✉ mayhurstbandb@aol.com ✆ www.mayhurstinn.com

THE PLAINS

Grey Horse Inn
4350 Fauquier Ave 20198
877-253-7020 540-253-7000
John & Ellen Hearty

112-225 BB
6 rooms, 6 pb
Most CC, *Rated*, •
C-yes/S-no/P-ltd/H-yes
French, Spanish, Arabic

Full breakfast
Hunt country upgrade –
wine & cheese plate
Jacuzzi, private balcony,
queen/king beds, antiques,
gardens, TV/video, A/C

Grey Horse Inn is in The Plains, VA near Middleburg & Warrenton & close to Washington. Minutes from the Blue Ridge Mountains, Civil War sites, Great Meadow & wineries. Fine dining is nearby. ✉ innkeeper@greyhorseinn.com ✆ www.greyhorseinn.com

PURCELLVILLE

Middle Grove Inn
37175 Jeb Stuart Rd 20132
866-338-1802 540-338-0918
Bob & Vicki Moore

75-110 BB
5 rooms, 3 pb
Visa, MC, AmEx, •
S-no/P-no/H-no

Full breakfast
Afternoon tea for parties of 6
or more
Sitting room, library, pool,
Jacuzzi, fireplace, TV, billiard
table, exercise room, groups,
retreats

Want to escape life's hectic pace? Renew your mind, body & spirit? Plan your own or participate in an organized retreat.
✉ Middlegroveinn@comcast.net ✆ www.middlegroveinn.com

RICHMOND

Grace Manor Inn
1853 W Grace St 23220
804-353-4334
Dawn & Albert Schick

175-215 BB
4 rooms, 4 pb
Most CC
S-ltd/P-no/H-no

Gourmet, 3-Course Breakfast
Complimentary bottle of wine
& cheese plate upon arrival
Concierge, reservations, sight
seeing & dinner recommendations & driving directions

'Let us pamper you' is their motto, and Grace Manor Inn will do just that. Step back in time as you enter this historical mansion decorated in period pieces. Enjoy complimentary wine and cheese in your suite. Leave feeling relaxed and rejuvenated.
✉ innkeeper@thegracemanorinn.com ✆ www.thegracemanorinn.com

SALEM

Brugh's Inn of Salem
1226 Lynchburg Turnpike
24153
800-756-4991 540-375-2978
Phillis Brugh

90-160 BB
3 rooms, 3 pb
Visa, MC, AmEx
C-yes/S-no/P-ltd/H-no

Full breakfast
Afternoon snacks offered
daily. Coffee, teas, and
bottled water available all
day!
Luxurious linens, flat screen
TVs, gas fireplaces

Offering the character and warmth of yesteryear combined with today's technologies and comforts. Renovated with your comfort in mind, each room has a private bath, flat screen TV, gas log fireplace and a Queen size bed.
✉ brughsinn@yahoo.com ✆ www.brughsinn.com

SALEM

Inn At Burwell Place
601 W Main St 24153
540-387-0250
Cindi Lou MacMackin

115-175 BB
4 rooms, 4 pb
Visa, MC, AmEx, *Rated*
C-ltd/S-no/P-no/H-no

Continental breakfast
Snacks, freshly baked sweet
items, complimentary soda
& wine
Sitting room, Jacuzzis, suites,
fireplaces, cable TV,
business travelers

A gracious mansion, that once welcomed dignitaries and chief executives, is renovated and restored for those wanting to retreat into the walls of a historic Southern mansion. Originally built in 1907 with magnificent views of the Blue Ridge Mountains.
✉ burwellplace@yahoo.com 🌐 www.burwellplace.com

SMITHFIELD

The Church Street Inn
1607 S Church St 23430
757-357-3176
Peter & Angie Lowry

109-179 BB
12 rooms, 12 pb
Most CC, *Rated*, •
C-yes/S-no/P-no/H-ltd

Continental Plus
Complimentary tea & coffee,
wine tasting some evenings
Walking tour, shopping, golf,
fishing nearby

A 12 bedroom Guest Inn located in historic Smithfield, VA. Under new ownership & recently renovated. Come & enjoy some Southern hospitality with a British accent.
✉ plowry@charterinternet.com 🌐 www.smithfieldchurchstreetinn.com

SPERRYVILLE

Hopkins Ordinary
47 Main St 22740
540-987-3383
Sherri Fickel, Kevin Kraditor

130-285 BB
6 rooms, 6 pb
Visa, MC
C-ltd/S-no/P-ltd/H-ltd
Spanish

Full breakfast
Beverages are offered in the
afternoon. Port, cookies or
other sweets are available in
the evening.
Fireplaces, wrap-around
porches, high-speed wireless
access, private balconies,
gardens, dining room

Hopkins Ordinary is a bed and breakfast inn located in the historic village of Sperryville, Virginia in the foothills of the Blue Ridge Mountains near Shenandoah National Park. Surrounded by wineries and farms in Rappahannock County, Virginia.
✉ innkeeper@hopkinsordinary.com 🌐 www.hopkinsordinary.com

STANARDSVILLE

Blue Ridge Mountain Inn
3625 Spotswood Trail 22973
434-566-2555
Heather Tusing

129-199 BB
10 rooms, 10 pb
Most CC
S-ltd/P-no/H-ltd

Continental breakfast
Hand-made truffles, home
baked cookies,
complimentary room
beverages, evening
chocolates
Satellite TV, deck side hot
tub, in-room fridge, CD
player, wireless Internet
access

A modern and elegant inn located in the heart of Virginia's Blue Ridge Mountains. The sweeping mountain views will delight you and the personal service invites you to slow down and be pampered!
✉ innkeeper@blueridgemountaininn.com 🌐 www.blueridgemountaininn.com

STANARDSVILLE

The Lafayette Inn
146 E Main St 22973
434-985-6345
Alan & Kaye Pyles

105-195 BB
7 rooms, 7 pb
Most CC, *Rated*
C-yes/S-ltd/P-no/H-no

Full breakfast
Tavern, dinner available.
Private Chef's tasting for two
under candlelight! Full
catering service.
Gas fireplaces, gazebo, cable
TV, wireless Internet.
Concierges service-wine
tours, in room massage.

As in the past, The Lafayette offers the best of Virginia; a nineteenth century setting with fine foods, comfort and hospitality. We will have your gas fireplace blazing and lights set romantically. ✉ alan@thelafayette.com ✆ www.thelafayette.com

South River Country Inn
3003 South River Rd 22973
877-874-4473 434-985-2901
Judy & Cliff Braun

110-159 BB
4 rooms, 4 pb
Visa, MC, AmEx,
Rated, •
C-ltd/S-no/P-no/H-no

Full breakfast
Snacks
Fish in our stocked ponds or
trout stream (license
required), business services

Escape to the country! We're situated on a working farm in the midst of over 1,000 acres of open, rural landscape with panoramic views of the Blue Ridge Mountains. South River Country Inn – a destination, not a stopover!
✉ southrivercountryinn@earthlink.net ✆ www.southrivercountryinn.com

STANLEY

Milton House B&B Inn
113 W Main Street 22191
540-778-2495
John Carria

115-195 BB
5 rooms, 5 pb
Visa, MC, *Rated*
S-no/P-no/H-no

Full/Continental delivered to
you
Afternoon teas, specialty
trays en suite, vegan &
vegetarian cuisine upon
prior request
Cable TV, DVD/VCR, In-room
coffee/tea, alarm clocks,
Jacuzzis, in room
refrigerators, fireplaces

This unique 1913 historic Southern Colonial home was ordered from the Sears Roebuck catalogue. Located in the bucolic town of Stanley, 7 miles south of Luray in the Shenandoah River Valley near the famous Luray Caverns and Skyline Drive.
✉ miltonhouseinn@yahoo.com ✆ www.miltonhouseinn.com

White Fence B&B
275 Chapel Rd 22851
800-211-9885 540-778-4680
Mike & Sally Dixon

145-165 BB
4 rooms, 4 pb
Visa, MC, Disc, *Rated*,
•
C-ltd/S-no/P-no/H-no
French

Full breakfast
Snacks, soft drinks, breakfast
baskets
Jacuzzi, fireplace,
microwave, cable TV

Lovely 1845 Victorian on 3 beautiful acres in the Shenandoah Valley near Luray & Shenandoah National Park. Luxury accommodations include cottage, carriage house & suites in the house. We offer a Virginia Elopement Package & other special romantic packages
✉ whitefencebb@aol.com ✆ www.whitefencebb.com

STAUNTON

Frederick House
28 N New St 24401
800-334-5575 540-885-4220
Denny Eister & Karen
Cooksey

99-273 BB
23 rooms, 23 pb
Most CC, *Rated*, •
C-yes/S-no/P-no/H-no

Full hot homemade breakfast
Guests may arrange for
Special Items to be awaiting
their arrival.
Five historic residences offer
sitting rooms, library,
conference facilities

Frederick House's five beautifully restored 19th century residences offer 23 spacious rooms and suites in award winning buildings. In the heart of historic downtown Staunton, a culturally rich district with theatre, dining, and shopping.
✉ stay@frederickhouse.com ✆ www.frederickhouse.com

STAUNTON

The Staunton Choral Gardens B&B
216 W Frederick St 24401
540-885-6556
Carolyn Avalos

85-200 BB
5 rooms, 5 pb
Visa, MC, Disc
C-ltd/S-no/P-yes/H-no

Multi-course b'fast. incl. dessert
Snacks available all the time. Guest microwaves & refrigerators, also.
TV lounge, front parlor, frpl in 3 rooms, several gardens & courtyard with water garden.

Elegant & restful B&B located in historic downtown Staunton. Free high-speed wireless Internet service. All rooms have private baths. Central AC throughout + several gardens. Multi-course gourmet breakfasts, catering to guests' requests—incl. dessert!
✉ reservations@stauntonbedandbreakfast.com ○ www.StauntonBedandBreakfast.com

STEELES TAVERN

Alpine Hideaway Cottages
8400 N. Lee Hwy 24476
800-895-6121 540-377-9261
Eileen Hoernlein

185-235 EP
3 rooms, 3 pb
Visa, MC, Disc
C-ltd/S-no/P-no/H-ltd

Breakfast basket available for a fee.
Hot tub, deck, satellite TV/VCR, CD player, high speed Internet, fireplace, kitchen, skylight

Let our romantic cottages atop the Blue Ridge Mountains seduce you with their 80 mile panorama of the blue-green mountains. The cottages have all the latest amenities including hot tubs, and many attractions are minutes away.
✉ stay@alpinehideaway.com ○ www.alpinehideaway.com

Sugar Tree Inn
145 Lodge Trail, Hwy 56 24483
800-377-2197 540-377-2197
Jeff & Becky Chanter

148-248 BB
13 rooms, 13 pb
Visa, MC, *Rated*
C-ltd/S-no/P-no/H-ltd
February – December

Full breakfast
Three course gourmet dinner by reservation on weekends. Casual fare dinner most weekdays.
Woodburning fireplaces, whirlpool tubs, ceiling fans, VCRs/video tapes

Less than a mile from the Blue Ridge Parkway, & located on 28 acres at 2,800 feet, the Inn is a place of rustic elegance, peace & tranquility. All of our rooms feature woodburning fireplaces. ✉ innkeeper@sugartreeinn.com ○ www.sugartreeinn.com

STRASBURG

Hotel Strasburg
213 S Holliday St 22657
800-348-8327 540-465-9191
Gary & Carol Rutherford,
Renee Yates

89-190 BB
29 rooms, 29 pb
Most CC, *Rated*, •
C-yes/S-yes/P-no/H-no

Continental breakfast
Restaurant, bar service, full breakfast available on weekends for an additional charge
Snacks, meeting rooms, sitting room, near beach, Jacuzzi in some rooms

Charming 1902 Victorian restoration rooms with period antiques, some Jacuzzi suites and gracious Southern hospitality. AAA 3 Diamond rated restaurant.
✉ thehotel@shentel.net ○ www.hotelstrasburg.com

URBANNA

Atherston Hall B&B
250 Prince George St 23175-0757
804-758-2809
Bill & Judith Dickinson

105-175 BB
4 rooms, 4 pb
Visa, MC
C-yes/S-no/P-yes/H-ltd

Full breakfast
Dinner by arrangement Sun – Wed in winter, Afternoon Tea by arrangement
English toiletries, wireless Internet , 2 sitting rooms, 1 w/TV/DVD; small dogs OK by arrangement

Nestled one block away from the main street and the harbor, Atherston Hall is just around the corner from all Urbanna has to offer.The elegance of English country living in the heart of historic Urbanna. Wonderfully restored. Great hospitality.
✉ judith@atherstonhall.com ○ www.atherstonhall.com

Barclay Cottage B&B, Virginia Beach, VA

VIRGINIA BEACH

Barclay Cottage B&B	95-250 BB	Full multi-course breakfast
400 16th St 23451	5 rooms, 3 pb	Breakfast sunrise picnic by
866-INN-1895 757-422-1956	Most CC, *Rated*, •	prior request,
Stephen & Marie-Louise	S-no/P-no/H-no	complimentary hot & cold
LaFond	French	beverages & snacks 24/7
		Broadband WiFi, extensive
		library of books, DVDs, VHS
		videos, games, ABC license,
		gift shop

This award-winning historic Inn, only 2 minutes walk to the beach, welcomes you with open arms from the moment you arrive. Antiques, handmade quilts, high-quality bedding, thirsty towels, luxurious robes, & sweet surprises await you in each room.
✉ innkeepers@barclaycottage.com 🌐 www.barclaycottage.com

Beach Spa Bed and	95-265 BB	Full breakfast
Breakfast	8 rooms, 8 pb	Internet hook ups, WiFi,
2420 Arctic Ave 23451	Visa, MC, AmEx	heated spa pool
888-422-2630 757-422-2621	C-yes/S-no/P-no/H-yes	
Greg & Yvonne		

Centrally located 2 blocks from the Virginia Beach Resort. Majestic porches, butterfly bushes and a cascading waterfall welcome guests into the enchanting retreat. A great alternative to hotel accommodations and perfect for a romantic getaway.
✉ greg@beachspabednbreakfast.com 🌐 www.beachspabednbreakfast.com

Country Villa B&B Inn and	179-350 BB	3 course gourmet breakfast
Day Spa	2 rooms, 2 pb	Complimentary wine,
2252 Indian River Rd 23456	Visa, MC, *Rated*	homemade cookies, sodas,
757-721-3844	S-no/P-no/H-no	bottled water, tea, coffee, hot
Teresa & Phil Bonifant	Some French	chocolate, gourmet candy
		SPA Services, Wireless
		Internet, Beach Supplies,
		Picnic basket, Specialty
		cakes, Pool & Hot Tub.

Minutes from beach, 3 course gourmet, breakfast, customized per individual. Flex mealtimes, private dining, pool, hot tub, in-room Jacuzzi, refrigerator, fireplace, massages/facials, complimentary wine, refreshments. Winery tours. Outdoor Pool & Hot Tub.
✉ innkeeper@countryvillainn.com 🌐 www.countryvillainn.com

WARM SPRINGS

The Inn at Gristmill Square	95-160 BB	Continental breakfast
Rte 645 24484	17 rooms, 17 pb	Dinner, bar
540-839-2231	Visa, MC, Disc, *Rated*,	Sauna, swimming pool,
The McWilliams Family	•	tennis courts
	C-yes/S-yes/P-no/H-ltd	

Casual country hideaway, historic original mill site dating from 1800's. Each room individually decorated.
✉ grist@tds.net ✪ www.gristmillsquare.com

WARRENTON

Black Horse Inn	155-325 BB	Full breakfast
8393 Meetze Rd 20187	9 rooms, 9 pb	Afternoon Hunt Country tea
540-349-4020	Most CC, *Rated*, •	offers wine, sherry, port,
Lynn Pirozzoli	C-ltd/S-ltd/P-no/H-yes	hors d'oeuvres and cookies
		Complimentary wine, bar
		service, sitting room, library,
		fishing, rooms with Jacuzzis

Historic Southern plantation style mansion with nine guestrooms, in the heart of hunt country. Elegant new reception facility seats 200. Stone fireplaces. Grand ballroom, gazebo, manicured gardens.
✉ relax@blackhorseinn.com ✪ www.blackhorseinn.com

WASHINGTON

Fairlea Farm Bed and	155-205 BB	Hearty full country breakfast
Breakfast	4 rooms, 4 pb	Afternoon refreshments,
636 Mt Salem Ave 22747	Cash, Checks, *Rated*,	including tea, fresh local
866-FAIRLEA 540-675-3679	•	cider or lemonade and
Susan & Walt Longyear	C-ltd/S-no/P-no/H-no	homemade baked items
	French	Parlor fireplace, views,
		terrace, gazebo, gardens,
		cattle, sheep, miniature
		donkeys, national park

Our guests enjoy our spectacular Blue Ridge Mountain views, lush pasture land, perennial gardens and a five-minute stroll to the historic village of Little Washington and its famous restaurant, The Inn at Little Washington.
✉ longyear@shentel.net ✪ www.fairleafarm.com

Foster Harris House	195-335 BB	4-course lavish breakfast
189 Main St 22747	5 rooms, 5 pb	Evening wine or beer
800-874-1152 540-675-3757	Visa, MC, AmEx, *Rated*	Luxury linens, spa robes,
Diane & John MacPherson	C-ltd/S-no/P-no/H-ltd	bicycle rentals, breathtaking
		views, 2 blocks to Inn at
		Little Washington

Nestled in the foothills of the Blue Ridge Mountains, minutes from Shenandoah National Park & steps from the world-renowned Inn at Little Washington, the Foster Harris House offers comfortable, refined accommodations in an enchanting country setting.
✉ stay@fosterharris.com ✪ www.fosterharris.com

Gay Street Inn	165-255 BB	Early continental + full
160 Gay St 22747	4 rooms, 4 pb	breakfast
540-675-3288	Most CC, *Rated*	Bar service, complimentary
Jay Brown & Kevin Adams	C-ltd/S-no/P-ltd/H-no	wine
	German	Library with fireplace,
		outdoor seating, free
		wireless Internet service,
		nearby bicycle rentals.

Nestled against the Blue Ridge Mountains. Steps from renowned restaurants. Within minutes of Shenandoah National Park, wineries, antique stores, horseback riding. The best part of a visit to Gay Street Inn may simply be sitting on our front porch!
✉ innkeeper@gaystreetinn.com ✪ www.gaystreetinn.com

WASHINGTON

Middleton Inn
176 Main St 22747
800-816-8157 540-675-2020
Mary Ann Kuhn

275-575 BB
7 rooms, 7 pb
Visa, MC, AmEx,
Rated, •
C-ltd/S-no/P-ltd/H-no

Full breakfast
Afternoon wine & cheese,
tea, evening port
Nightly turndown service,
twice daily maid service,
massages, fireplaces,
complimentary newspapers

An historic country estate, Middleton Inn has received the prestigious Four Diamond AAA Award for excellence in accommodations & service in an elegant atmosphere for eight years now. Nine fireplaces, mountain views, marble baths. Select Registry member.
✉ innkeeper@middletoninn.com ✪ www.middletoninn.com

WHITE POST

L'Auberge Provencale
13630 Lord Fairfax Hwy 22620
800-638-1702 540-837-1375
Alain & Celeste Borel

155-325 BB
14 rooms, 14 pb
Most CC, *Rated*, •
C-ltd/S-ltd/P-no/H-ltd
French

Full gourmet breakfast
Dinner, restaurant, bar
service, picnic, wine, cheese
& fruit plate, chocolate
strawberries
Luxury accommodations,
refreshments, flowers, sitting
room, gardens

Executive Chef from France presents nationally acclaimed cuisine. Extensive wine list. Elegant accommodations with fireplaces, aromatherapy steam showers for two, Jacuzzi tubs for two and private entrances.
✉ info@laubergeprovencale.com ✪ www.laubergeprovencale.com

WILLIAMSBURG

A Primrose Cottage
706 Richmond Rd 23185
800-522-1901 804-829-5441
Inge Curtis

199-250 EP
2 rooms, 1 pb
Visa, MC, *Rated*, •
C-ltd/S-no/P-no/H-no
German

Water access, minutes to
boat rental and launching
ramp

A Williamsburg, self-catering cottage on the Chickahominy River. A peaceful hideaway just 15 short minutes from Williamsburg.
✉ ingecurtis@aol.com ✪ www.primrose-cottage.com

Applewood Colonial B&B
605 Richmond Rd 23185
757-903-4306
Monty & Denise Fleck

135-165 BB
2 rooms, 2 pb
Visa, MC, *Rated*, •
C-yes/S-no/P-no/H-no

Full breakfast
Coffee & tea available all day,
please let us know of any
dislikes or allergies prior to
arrival

The perfect location to enjoy all the historic sites, or just relax in one of our elegant, romantic and thoughtfully appointed suites, with TVs, phone and wireless Internet.
✉ info@williamsburgbandb.com ✪ www.williamsburgbandb.com

Bentley Manor Inn
720 College Terrace 23185
877-334-0641 757-253-0202
Fred & Jane Garland

125-185 BB
4 rooms, 4 pb
Visa, MC
C-ltd/S-no/P-no/H-no

Full country breakfast
Sitting room, suites, cable TV,
free wireless Internet access,
business traveler
accommodations

Charming classic brick Colonial in the heart of historic Williamsburg, VA, adjacent to William and Mary College, a leisurely stroll to Colonial Williamsburg, a short drive to Jamestown and Yorktown . . . Capture the timeless essence of Colonial Williamsburg.
✉ info@bentleymanorinn.com ✪ www.bentleymanorinn.com

WILLIAMSBURG

Colonial Gardens B&B	145-185 BB	Full Gourmet Breakfast
1109 Jamestown Rd 23185	4 rooms, 4 pb	Wine & Cheese hour, snacks
800-886-9715 757-220-8087	Most CC, *Rated*, •	& drinks available 24 hours
Karen & Ron Watkins	C-ltd/S-ltd/P-no/H-ltd	in stocked guest refrigerator
		Concierge service for dining
		reservations, golf, fax, copier,
		pilot-friendly!

Colonial Gardens is an enchanting escape into old world European romance and elegance. With its silks and satins, fine Italian linens, richly ornate furniture, and the allure of over an acre of gardens.
✉ Colonialgardensbandb@verizon.net ♻ www.colonial-gardens.com

Fife & Drum Inn	165-285 BB	Full breakfast
441 Prince George St 23185	9 rooms, 9 pb	Snacks
888-838-1783 757-345-1776	Most CC, *Rated*, •	Cable TV, VCRs, individual
Billy & Sharon Scruggs	C-ltd/S-no/P-no/H-ltd	phone lines, free WiFi, soft
		bathrobes, many other
		amenities

Historic Williamsburg's only downtown lodging. Located adjacent to The College of William & Mary, Merchants Square, & Colonial Williamsburg. For guests seeking their own private address the Drummers Cottage is offered.
✉ bscruggs@FifeAndDrumInn.com ♻ www.FifeAndDrumInn.com

Governor's Trace	150-175 BB	Full breakfast
303 Capitol Landing Rd 23185	3 rooms, 3 pb	Antiques, fireplaces,
800-303-7552 757-229-7552	Visa, MC, Disc, •	porches, common area,
Dick & Sue Lake	S-no/P-no/H-no	library, free wireless Internet

Closest B&B to historic Colonial Williamsburg. "...vies for the most romantic (in Williamsburg)" —Washington Post. Candlelit breakfast served in your room. One room has wood-burning fireplace. Two rooms have private screened-in porches.
✉ govtrace@cavtel.net ♻ www.governorstrace.com

Inn at 802	145-175 BB	Gourmet breakfast
802 Jamestown Rd 23185	4 rooms, 4 pb	Guest kitchen with snacks &
888-757-3316 757-345-3316	Most CC, *Rated*	beverages, wine, special
Cathy & Joe Bradley	C-ltd/S-no/P-no/H-no	meals upon request
		Free WiFi, computer, printer,
		library, TV, DVD, movies,
		bathrobes, hairdryer,
		complimentary beverage

Walk to Colonial Williamsburg and the College of William and Mary. Enjoy period-style antiques and reproductions, tranquil courtyard with exquisite gardens, guest kitchen and complimentary beverages.
✉ cathy@innat802.com ♻ www.innat802.com

Magnolia Manor Inn	155-215 BB	Full breakfast
700 Richmond Rd 23185	4 rooms, 4 pb	Coffee, tea, muffins &
800-462-6667 757-220-9600	Visa, MC, AmEx	cookies
Scott & Jennifer Carter	C-ltd/S-no/P-no/H-no	Suites, fireplaces, fresh
		flowers, whirlpool tubs, turn-
		down service, living room

At Magnolia Manor experience Colonial Williamsburg history and hospitality. Each morning begins with a gourmet breakfast in the lovely dining room by the fireplace. It is the perfect setting for a romantic getaway or a relaxing retreat.
✉ magnoliamanorinn@yahoo.com ♻ www.magnoliamanorwmbg.com

Newport House B&B, Williamsburg, VA

WILLIAMSBURG

Mulberry Garden Manor	145-165 BB	Full breakfast
800 Jamestown Rd 23185	3 rooms, 3 pb	Central air & heat, Egyptian
877-258-7795 757-258-7799	Visa, MC	cotton sheets and towels,
Micki & Jeff Jacobsen	C-ltd/S-no/P-no/H-no	European down pillows and
		comforters

This Colonial two story bed and breakfast situated behind a white picket fence is newly decorated with a French & English Flair. Each of the spacious rooms exudes the traditions of Colonial architecture with modern appointments and convenience.
✉ micki@mulberrygardenmanor.com 🌐 www.mulberrygardenmanor.com

Newport House B&B	175-185 BB	Full breakfast
710 S Henry St 23185	2 rooms, 2 pb	Sitting room, Library,
877-565-1775 757-229-1775	*Rated*, •	harpsichord, Ballroom for
John & Cathy Millar	C-yes/S-no/P-no/H-no	receptions
	French	

Designed in 1756. Completely furnished in period. 5-minute walk from historic area. Colonial dancing every Tuesday evening.
✉ info@newporthousebb.com 🌐 www.newporthousebb.com

Piney Grove at Southall's	130-260 BB	Full Plantation Breakfast
Plantation	5 rooms, 5 pb	Snacks, complimentary wine
16920 Southall Plantation	Most CC, *Rated*, •	Sitting room, library,
23187	C-yes/S-no/P-no/H-no	swimming pool, reception
804-829-2480	Some German	areas
The Gordineer Family		

Two centuries ago Furneau Southall welcomed guests to his plantation . . . Today the Gordineer family welcomes you to relive Virginia's Golden Age in Williamsburg's James River Plantation country. ✉ lodging@pineygrove.com 🌐 www.pineygrove.com

Williamsburg Manor	99-199 BB	Full Regional Breakfast
600 Richmond Rd 23185	5 rooms, 5 pb	Freshly Baked Cookies,
800-422-8011 757-220-8011	Most CC, •	Coffee, Hot Chocolate,
Laura Reeves	C-yes/S-no/P-ltd/H-ltd	Lemonade and Soft Drinks
		are always available
		Catering services, wedding
		packages, gift certificates,
		fax/internet, and cable

Welcome to the Williamsburg Manor, where our guests enjoy gracious Southern hospitality in a French and eclectic setting!The interior spaces and gardens of the Mano have recently been updated to combine the spirit of downtown with the most modern amenities
✉ williamsburgoccasions@gmail.com 🌐 www.williamsburg-manor.com

WILLIAMSBURG

Williamsburg Sampler B&B Inn
922 Jamestown Rd 23185
800-722-1169 757-253-0398
Ike Sisane

160-215 BB
4 rooms, 4 pb
Visa, MC, *Rated*, •
C-ltd/S-no/P-no/H-no

Full breakfast
Wet bar & fridge in suites,
complimentary sodas
18th century carriage house,
antiques, pewter, samplers,
suites, fireplaces

Williamsburg's finest plantation style Colonial home. Richly furnished. Guests have included descendants of John Quincy Adams, Capt. John Smith and Charles Dickens.

✉ info@williamsburgsampler.com ◐ www.williamsburgsampler.com

WOODSTOCK

Candlewick Inn
127 N Church St 22664
540-459-8008
Sharon & Dennis Pike

130-180 BB
4 rooms, 4 pb
Visa, MC
S-no/P-no/H-no

Full breakfast
Five o'clock tea, lemonade or
hot cider
A/C, Parlor player piano,
Jacuzzi in suite, sitting areas
in all rooms

The Candlewick Inn is a beautifully restored pre-Civil War home located in picturesque Shenandoah County, Virginia. The Inn is on the National Historic Registry.

✉ candlewickinnllc@hotmail.com

Inn at Narrow Passage
US 11 and Chapman Landing
Rd 22664
800-459-8002 540-459-8000
Ellen & Ed Markel

120-175 BB
12 rooms, 12 pb
Most CC, *Rated*, •
C-yes/S-ltd/P-no/H-yes

Full breakfast
Colonial tea, lemonade, iced
tea, soft drinks & snacks
Two common rooms, dining
room with fireplace, small
meetings, free WiFi, lawn
overlooking river

Historic 1740s inn with 5 acres on the Shenandoah River, I-81 Exit 283, two miles south of Woodstock, VA, on Rt 11. Full fireside breakfast in the Colonial dining room. Fishing, hiking, antiques, vineyards, battlefields, great restaurants nearby.

✉ innkeeper@narrowpassage.com ◐ www.narrowpassage.com

Washington

ABERDEEN ─────────────────────────────

A Harbor View Inn
111 W 11th St 98520
877-533-7996 360-533-7996
Cindy Lonn

149-225 BB
5 rooms, 5 pb
Visa, MC, AmEx,
Rated, •
C-ltd/S-no/P-no/H-ltd
Little Spanish & German

Full Country Breakfast and
snack
Huge selection of Afternoon
tea, organic snacks and
coffee.
Sitting room, tennis court,
suites, fireplace, cable TV,
accommodates business
travelers

*Historic Colonial Revival home, antiques, every room with waterview, located in a historic
district, walking homes tour included with your stay and breakfast in the sunroom overlooking the harbor.*
✉ info@aharborview.com ◐ www.aharborview.com

ANDERSON ISLAND ─────────────────────

The Inn at Burg's Landing
8808 Villa Beach Rd 98303
253-884-9185
Ken & Annie Burg

90-140 BB
4 rooms, 2 pb
C-yes/S-no/P-no/H-no

Full breakfast
Weddings, reunions, special
events, birthday parties

*A beautiful B&B situated along the peaceful shores of Anderson Island overlooking the
magnificent Puget Sound. A short distance from The Anderson Island Historical Society
Museum and offers spectacular views of Puget Sound, and a deck with a hot tub.*
✉ burgslanding@yahoo.com ◐ www.burgslandingbb.com

ASHFORD ──────────────────────────────

**Alexander's Country Inn,
Restaurant & Day Spa**
37515 State Rd 706 E 98304
800-654-7615 360-569-2300
Bernadette Ronan

99-175 BB
12 rooms, 12 pb
Visa, MC, *Rated*, •
C-yes/S-no/P-no/H-ltd

Full breakfast
Complimentary wine &
seasonal fresh fruits,
acclaimed restaurant
Day Spa offering massage,
parlor with fireplace, hot tub,
Media Room w/big screen
TV/DVDs, WiFi

*One mile from Mount Rainier National Park. Retains its historic charm and character while
still providing modern amenities. Full breakfast, evening wine, use of the media room and
hot tub are included in the daily rate. Two self-catered vacation cabins.*
✉ info@alexanderscountryinn.com ◐ www.alexanderscountryinn.com

BAINBRIDGE ISLAND ───────────────────

Holly Lane Gardens
9432 Holly Farm Ln 98110
206-842-8959
Patti Dusbabek

90-135 BB
5 rooms, 4 pb
Most CC
C-yes/S-no/P-yes/H-ltd

Full breakfast
Beverages, homemade
international desserts
Reading, entertainment
center, libraries, hot tub, 8.6
acres

*Olympic Mountain views, flowers, woodlands. Cottage and Suite offer bedroom, front
room, kitchen and bath. Clerestory Room on the 2nd floor of the house, has a spectacular
mountain & garden view.*
✉ patti.dusbabek@comcast.net ◐ www.hollylanegardens.com

BELFAIR

Selah Inn on Hood Canal
130 NE Dulalip Landing 98528
877-232-7941 360-275-0916
Bonnie & Pat McCullough

95-200 BB
4 rooms, 4 pb
Visa, MC, *Rated*, •
C-ltd/S-no/P-no/H-ltd

Full breakfast
Lunch & dinner available
Bar service, sitting room,
library, Jacuzzi, fireplaces,
cable TV, ensuite massage,
deck hot tub.

An elegant NW lodge with a majestic view of the Hood Canal. Breakfast of Eggs Benedict. Access to the beach for digging clams; we'll steam them for your first of five courses at dinner. Business travelers are welcome. ✉ innkeeper@selahinn.com ✆ www.selahinn.com

BELLEVUE

A Cascade View
13425 NE 27th St 98005
888-883-7078 425-883-7078
Marianne & Bill Bundren

130-150 BB
2 rooms, 2 pb
Visa, MC, AmEx, *Rated*
C-yes/S-ltd/P-no/H-no

Full breakfast
Afternoon tea if requested
Sitting room, library,
fireplaces, cable TV,
accommodate business
travelers, wireless Internet

Panoramic views of the Cascade Mountains with extensive colorful and fragrant gardens. 2 beautiful rooms with private baths and extra amenities, fireplace, TV/VCR, sitting room, full breakfasts. The perfect location for the tourist or business traveler.
✉ innkeepers@acascadeview.com ✆ www.acascadeview.com

BELLINGHAM

Anderson Creek Lodge
5602 Mission Rd 98226
360-966-0598
Dwight & Tara Lucky

110-160 BB
5 rooms, 5 pb
Most CC
C-yes/S-no/P-no/H-no

Full cooked breakfast
Complimentary bottled
water, assorted black, green
and herbal teas, coffee and
sodas.
Hot tub with full back
massage jets, walking trails,
wireless DSL, cable TV, 200+
video library

Anderson Creek Lodge is a bed and breakfast and meeting center that offers you a wonderfully relaxed and comfortable atmosphere. Our traditional Northwest lodge features a huge, two-story stone fireplace and extensive use of local wood.
✉ andersoncreek@msn.com ✆ www.andersoncreek.com

CAMANO ISLAND

Camano Blossom
1462 Larkspur Ln 98282
866-629-6784 360-629-6784
Melissa Hsu

108-138 BB
4 rooms, 4 pb
Most CC, *Rated*
C-ltd/S-no/P-ltd/H-no
Mandarin, Taiwanese

Full gourmet breakfast
Gourmet Chinese dinner
service, reservations
requested; snacks, wine
Sitting room, space for
overnight parking of trailer
boats or RVs

A weekend getaway, an ideal place to reward that special employee, out of the ordinary location for your small wedding, our goal is to pamper you and help you to experience the beauty and comfort that attracted us to this island property.
✉ reservations@camanoblossombandb.com ✆ www.camanoblossombandb.com

Inn at Barnum Point
464 S Barnum Rd 98282
800-910-2256 360-387-2256
Carolin Barnum

125-225 BB
3 rooms, 3 pb
Visa, MC, Disc, *Rated*,
•
C-yes/S-no/P-no/H-no

Full breakfast brunch
Complimentary beverages
Sitting room, library,
sidewalks, landscaping,
outside lighting, waterfront
views from every window!

All rooms have spectacular water and mountain views. Enjoy our spacious 900 sq ft suite. A Cape Cod house on a bluff overlooking Port Susan Bay and the Cascade Mountains. Private bath and fireplaces. A tranquil place to relax, beachcomb, enjoy the birds.
✉ innkeeper@innatbarnumpoint.com ✆ www.innatbarnumpoint.com

636 Washington

CATHLAMET

Bradley House Inn
61 Main St 98612
360-795-3030
Dennis & Audi Belcher

79-99 EP
4 rooms, 2 pb
Visa, MC
C-ltd/S-no/P-no/H-no

Breakfast is available at
9:00am for an additional
charge.
Mansion is available for
small weddings, family &
class reunions business
functions & showers

*We are the only lodging in Cathlamet and we are on the Lewis & Clark Trail. Escape to
yesteryear. Built in 1907, this elegant home sits on a knoll overlooking the historic town of
Cathlamet, Puget Island & the Columbia River.*
✉ bradleyhouse@centurytel.net ♦ www.bradleyhousebb.com

The Villa at Little Cape Horn
48 Little Cape Horn Rd 98612
360-578-9100
Joan Chester

175-299 BB
4 rooms, 4 pb
Visa, MC, •
C-ltd/S-no/P-ltd/H-ltd

Full breakfast

*Perched 80 feet above the famous Columbia River this Tuscany inspired villa offers a
secluded setting and uninterrupted views of the river and wildlife. Your room is appointed
with all the comforts of home.*
✉ villacapehorn@aol.com ♦ www.villalittlecapehorn.com

COLVILLE

Lazy Bee B&B
3651 Deep Lake Boundary Rd
99114
509-732-8917
Bud Budinger & Joann
Bender

129 BB
2 rooms
Visa, MC
C-ltd/S-ltd/P-ltd/H-ltd

Continental breakfast
Lunch, dinner, afternoon tea,
snacks
Library, bicycles, fireplaces,
accommodate business
travelers New! Outdoor
romantic bedroom

*The Lazy Bee is a rustic lodge nestled at the base of Red Mountain with a view of Stone
Mountain near the Canadian border. We've deliberately slowed the pace of life in order to
give guests less stress and a sense of tranquility.*
✉ budinger.bender@plix.com ♦ www.travelguides.com/home/Lazy_Bee/

COUPEVILLE

Anchorage Inn
807 N Main St 98239
877-230-1313 360-678-5581
Dave & Dianne Binder

89-149 BB
7 rooms, 7 pb
Visa, MC, *Rated*, •
C-ltd/S-ltd/P-ltd/H-ltd

Full breakfast
Cookies, popcorn, coffee,
tea, cider, hot chocolate and
cold beverages
WiFi, cable TV, VCR, DVD,
telephone, dinner
reservations, porch and
patio, maps, umbrellas.

*The Anchorage Inn Bed and Breakfast is a Victorian Inn located on beautiful Whidbey
Island near Puget Sound, in the historic town of Coupeville, Washington. Perfect for privacy, group retreats, wedding, anniversary, and engagements. An Escape for lovers.*
✉ crowsnest@anchorage-inn.com ♦ www.anchorage-inn.com

The Blue Goose Inn
702 N Main St 98239
877-678-4284 360-678-4284
Sue & Marty

119-149 BB
6 rooms, 6 pb
Most CC, *Rated*
C-ltd/S-no/P-no/H-no

Scrumptious full breakfast
Fresh baked cookies, hot
beverages all day. Cheese
platters, wine & champagne
available on request.
Cable TV, WiFi, hair dryers,
bath amenities, fireplaces,
ceiling fans, views, walk to
shops & dining

*History and contemporary comforts are graciously combined in neighboring Victorian
homes. Large rooms, private baths, scrumptious breakfast, water and mountain views,
friendly personalized service. Walking distance to shops, dining, and beaches.*
✉ stay@bluegooseinn.com ♦ www.bluegooseinn.com

COUPEVILLE

Captain Whidbey Inn
2072 W Capt. Whidbey 98239
800-366-4097 360-678-4097

85-230 BB
29 rooms, 17 pb
Most CC, *Rated*, •
C-ltd/S-no/P-no/H-no

Full breakfast
All meals available, bar
Sitting room, bicycles,
library, sailboats & rowboats

The Captain Whidbey Inn, located in the heart of Ebey's Landing National Historic Reserve is surrounded by forest and hugs the shore of Whidbey Island's Penn Cove.
✉ info@captainwhidbey.com ✆ www.captainwhidbey.com

Compass Rose
508 S Main St 98239
800-237-3881 360-678-5318
Jan & Marshall Bronson

115 BB
2 rooms, 2 pb
Cash, Checks
S-no/P-no/H-no

Candlelight Breakfast
Coffee or tea upon arrival
Antiques

This fine 1890 Queen Anne Victorian home, on the National Register of Historic Places, is now an elegant two room bed and breakfast, furnished with antiques and glorious things from around the globe by the hosts, Captain and Mrs. Marshall Bronson.
✆ www.compassrosebandb.com

Garden Isle Guest Cottages
207 NW Coveland 98239
877-881-1203 360-678-5641
Dan & Darrellyn Currier

130-250 BB
5 rooms, 1 pb
Visa, MC
C-yes/S-no/P-no/H-yes

Continental breakfast
Hot tub, gas fireplace, living
room, laundry area, kitchen,
TV

Located on picturesque Whidbey Island, in the charming 1853 town of Coupeville. Two peaceful, lovely and delightful country garden cottages with hot tub, and a wonderful vacation home with views of Mt. Baker and Penn Cove.
✉ stay@gardenislecottages.com ✆ www.gardenislecottages.com

DES MOINES

Elsie's Bay Manor
27615 10th Ave S. 98198
253-839-5237
Elsie

95 BB
2 rooms, 2 pb
Cash, Checks
C-ltd/S-ltd/P-no/H-no

Continental plus breakfast
Coffee & tea facilities, cold
beverages, guest fridge and
microwave
Deck, sitting area, views,
airport pick-up available,
concierge services

Bay Manor, is a handsome, turn of the century, three story red brick house. It stands in an acre of land, and has stunning views of the snow capped Olympic Mountains and the Puget Sound.
✉ elsietravel@qwest.net ✆ www.elsiesbaymanor.com

EASTSOUND

**Kangaroo House B&B on
Orcas Island**
1459 North Beach Rd 98245
888-371-2175 360-376-2175
Charles Toxey & Jill Johnson

100-190 BB
5 rooms, 5 pb
Most CC, *Rated*, •
C-ltd/S-no/P-no/H-no

Full breakfast
Special diets on request,
fireplace, sitting room, hot
tub in garden

1907 Craftsman B&B near Eastsound on beautiful Orcas Island in WA State's San Juan Islands, offering a friendly alternative to hotel or motel stays with its home-like atmosphere, and the added value of a delicious full breakfast.
✉ innkeeper@KangarooHouse.com ✆ www.KangarooHouse.com

FREELAND

Bay Breeze B&B Cottages
5660 S Double Bluff Rd 98249
888-547-4179 360-321-4277
Janice & David de Wolf

129-149 BB
2 rooms, 2 pb
Visa, MC, *Rated*, •
C-yes/S-no/P-no/H-no

Continental breakfast mid-week
Homemade cookies, coffee, teas, cocoa, bottled water, bottled orange juice, popcorn, etc.
Fireplaces, 2-person Jacuzzi tubs, private deck, TV/VCR/DVD, mini kitchenettes, shower in bathroom.

Welcoming island getaway. B&B cottages with 2-person romantic Jacuzzis, fireplaces, great breakfast, pastoral and water views, nearby beach to stroll. Guests pampered Whidbey Island style.
✉ stay@baybreezecottages.com ◐ www.baybreezecottages.com

FRIDAY HARBOR

Bird Rock Hotel
35 First St 98250
800-352-2632 360-378-5848
Adam & Laura Saccio

59-345 BB
15 rooms, 11 pb
Visa, MC, *Rated*, •
C-yes/S-no/P-no/H-yes
Spanish, French, German, Dutch, Japanese

Gourmet breakfast delivered you
Afternoon snacks and refreshments
Rooms have ipod-docking radio, beach cruiser bikes for use, free WiFi, flat-panel HDTV

An exquisitely crafted, eco-intelligent collection of stylishly modern rooms ranging from simple, European-style sleeping rooms rooms to deluxe, harbor-view suites.
✉ stay@birdrockhotel.com ◐ www.birdrockhotel.com

Harrison House Suites B&B
235 C St 98250
800-407-7933 360-378-3587
Anna Maria de Freitas, David Pass, Michael Buckle

125-375 BB
5 rooms, 5 pb
Visa, MC, AmEx,
Rated, •
C-yes/S-ltd/P-yes/H-ltd

Full breakfast
On-site catering in our Garden Cafe. Homemade cookies delivered to your suite each afternoon
Use of bikes/kayaks, laundry facilities, off-street parking, reading and video library

A hillside retreat conveniently located 1½ blocks from the ferry terminal and historic downtown Friday Harbor. Old world charm combined with contemporary conveniences offer one of a kind accommodations in this historic residence.
✉ innkeeper@harrisonhousesuites.com ◐ www.harrisonhousesuites.com

GIG HARBOR

Bear's Lair B&B
13706 92nd Ave Ct NW 98329
877-855-9768 253-857-8877
Giulio & Jenny Santori

105-205 BB
4 rooms, 4 pb
Visa, MC, *Rated*
C-ltd/S-no/P-no/H-yes
Spanish, Italian

Full breakfast
Homemade baked goods throughout the day; common room self-service coffee & tea, etc. 24 hours
Upscale accommodations, private cottage, gardens, suites, fireplaces

Luxurious 5 acre country estate-style B&B. Private carriage house perfect for that romantic getaway. Three luxurious rooms in the main house. Breathtaking gardens, island gazebo with duck pond.
✉ bearslairbb@aol.com ◐ www.bearslairbb.com

Tell your hosts Pamela Lanier sent you.

GIG HARBOR

Gig Harbor Lodge	125-200 BB	Gourmet Breakfast
3202 96th St NW 98332	3 rooms, 1 pb	Complimentary snacks &
253-853-4279	Visa, MC	beverages are served during
Gloria Haines	C-ltd/S-no/P-no/H-no	hospitality hour
		Clean & spacious, special
		hospitality hour, plush robes
		& towels, quality bedding,
		views, grounds

Relax in casual elegance! Gig Harbor Lodge is a warm and inviting experience with spacious rooms and suites in a smoke-free environment. We serve a hearty breakfast and afternoon snacks. Our goal is to provide you with a relaxing memorable vacation.
✉ gloriahaines@comcast.com ◑ www.gigharborlodge.com

Waterfront Inn	140-229 BB	Continental plus breakfast
9017 N Harborview Dr 98332	7 rooms, 7 pb	Complimentary tea, hot
253-857-0770	Visa, MC	chocolate & popcorn to go
Steve & Janis Denton	C-ltd/S-no/P-no/H-ltd	with free DVDs
	Spanish	Huge over-the-water sitting
		pier, complimentary kayak
		use, lovely garden

Located at the head of Gig Harbor Bay, the Waterfront Inn offers private, luxurious rooms in a beautiful historic home. Each room has a private entrance, a large bath with Jacuzzi tub, & many rooms have a fireplace with a sitting area & awesome views.
✉ info@waterfront-inn.com ◑ www.waterfront-inn.com

GREENBANK

Guest House Log Cottages	130-350 BB	Full self-serve breakfast
24371 SR 525 98253	6 rooms, 6 pb	TV/DVD/VCR, CD Player,
800-997-3115 360-678-3115	Visa, MC, Disc, *Rated*	exercise room, pool, spa,
Peggy Walker	C-ltd/S-no/P-no/H-ltd	retreat & honeymoon spot

Spark and rekindle your romance at Guest House Log Cottages B&B, a place where your pleasure and comfort are a priority. These beautifully furnished, cozy cottages are scattered on 25 acres of forest on Whidbey Island in Puget Sound.
✉ stay@guesthouselogcottages.com ◑ www.guesthouselogcottages.com

ILWACO

China Beach Retreat Inn	199-299 BB	Full sumptuous gourmet
222 Robert Gray Dr 98624	4 rooms, 4 pb	breakfast
800-INN-1896 360-642-5660	Visa, MC, AmEx	Coffee & tea service
David Campiche & Laurie	C-ltd/S-no/P-no/H-ltd	available all day
Anderson		Group retreats, weddings,
		views, spa tubs

China Beach Retreat is a nest of delights, where your senses receive all that they can demand of nature. This B&B retreat in is elegantly and comfortably furnished in antiques. The decor is an eclectic enhancement of the beautiful views.
✉ innkeeper@chinabeachretreat.com ◑ www.chinabeachretreat.com

Inn at Harbour Village B&B	85-165 BB	Continental plus breakfast
120 Williams Ave NE 98264	10 rooms, 10 pb	Complimentary glass of wine
888-642-0087 360-642-0087	Most CC, *Rated*, •	or sparkling cider in the
Peter and Janis Bale	C-ltd/S-no/P-no/H-no	evening
	some French	An elegant parlor, 1928'
		chapel/auditorium with
		seating for 120, a spacious
		banquet/conference room.

Enjoy the unique experience that is the Inn at Harbour Village, an historic church turned B&B. The Inn offers 9 charming guestrooms with private bathrooms, and an elegant suite with king bed and a private entrance, TV and wireless Internet connection.
✉ innkeeper@innatharbourvillage.com ◑ www.innatharbourvillage.com

LA CONNER

The Heron Inn &
Watergrass Day Spa
117 Maple Ave 98257
877-883-8899 360-466-4626
Martha & George McCarthy

100-200 BB
11 rooms, 11 pb
Visa, MC, *Rated*
C-ltd/S-no/P-no/H-no

European Continental
24 hour coffee & tea service;
award winning cookies at
night
On-site Day Spa, therapeutic
garden hot tub, walking
distance to downtown, new
guesthouse now avail

The Heron Inn, La Conner's award winning country inn & day spa, is a perfect retreat for your relaxing getaway. Some rooms offers Jacuzzis &/or fireplaces and we have 2 new spa rooms.
✉ info@theheron.com ◐ www.theheron.com

Queen of the Valley Inn
12757 Chilberg Rd 98257
888-999-1404 360-466-4578
Shelly Davis

109-229 BB
6 rooms, 6 pb
Most CC, *Rated*
C-ltd/S-ltd/P-ltd/H-no

Full breakfast
Coffee, tea, afternoon snacks
Free sodas and bottled water
24-hour tea station
Library, satellite TV, porches,
wireless Internet, courtyard
garden, weddings/events,
spa service,

Quiet, warm, romantic and luxurious lodging in the Pacific Northwest. The perfect base for exploring the islands, as well as Seattle, WA and Vancouver, B.C., both just an hour away. Whether for a short getaway or an extended stay, the queen welcomes you.
✉ innkeeper@queenofthevalleyinn.com ◐ www.queenofthevalleyinn.com

The Wild Iris Inn
121 Maple Avenue 98257
800-477-1400 360-466-1400
Steve & Lori Farnell

119-209 BB
18 rooms, 18 pb
Visa, MC, AmEx,
Rated, •
C-ltd/S-no/P-no/H-yes

Full breakfast
All rooms have flat panel tvs,
DVD players, cd players,
plush robes and free
wireless Internet.

Relax in one of the Northwest's most charming and romantic country inns. Twelve of the inn's beautifully appointed rooms feature large jetted spa tubs, fireplaces and private decks or balconies with pastoral and Cascade Mountain Views.
✉ fdesk@wildiris.com ◐ www.wildiris.com

LANGLEY

Ashingdon Manor Inn &
Cottages
5023 Langley Rd 98260
866-456-5006 360-221-2334
Daniel & Bay Ginder

109-179 BB
6 rooms, 6 pb
Visa, MC, *Rated*, •
C-ltd/S-no/P-no/H-ltd
Mid Feb. to mid Dec.

Full breakfast
Complimentary tea & wine,
dinner available, English Pub
Sitting room, library, bikes,
suites, fireplaces

Traditional country manor decorated with furnishings and object d'art from around the world.
✉ stay@ashingdonmanor.com ◐ www.ashingdonmanor.com

Country Cottage of Langley
215 6th St 98260
800-713-3860 360-221-8709
Jacki Stewart

139-189 BB
5 rooms, 5 pb
Visa, MC, AmEx,
Rated, •
C-yes/S-no/P-ltd/H-ltd

Full gourmet breakfast
Full, hot breakfast served in
room, on your deck, or in
our Four Seasons dining
room
Scenic dining room, view
deck, living room in main
house, gardens, gazebo,
croquet & bocce ball

A classic 1920 farmhouse with 5 romantic & distinctly designed cottages with private decks on 2 acres of beautiful gardens. Amazing view of Puget Sound, 2-person Jacuzzis, fireplace, gourmet breakfast delivered to your Cottage, short walk to our Village.
✉ stay@acountrycottage.com ◐ www.acountrycottage.com

LANGLEY

Eagles Nest Inn	125-175 BB	Healthy Northwest Gourmet
4680 Saratoga Rd 98260	4 rooms, 4 pb	Hospitality counter
800-243-5536 360-221-5331	Visa, MC, Disc, *Rated*,	(bottomless cookie jar), tea,
Joanne & Jerry Lechner	•	coffee, hot chocolate, cider,
	S-no/P-no/H-no	microwave
		Library, sitting room, cable
		TV, DVD, CD, WiFi Internet,
		fireplace, video library, hot
		tub

Panoramic water views with Northwest ambience & art. A destination B&B on Whidbey Island, next to a 600 acre wildlife preserve. Birding, hiking & mountain bike trails. One mile to Langley restaurants, galleries & shops. Relax & escape everyday life.
✉ eaglnest@whidbey.com ◔ www.eaglesnestinn.com

Saratoga Inn	165-325 BB	Full breakfast
201 Cascade Ave 98260	16 rooms, 16 pb	Afternoon wine, tea & hors
800-698-2910 360-221-5801	Most CC, *Rated*, •	d' oeuvres, freshly-baked
Kayce Nakamura	C-yes/S-no/P-no/H-yes	cookies, drinks available
		throughout the day
		Porch with rocking chairs,
		bicycles to borrow, sitting
		room, conference room

The stunning beauty of Puget Sound and its many islands is the setting for the Saratoga Inn. Your journey begins with a scenic, 20 minute, car-ferry ride from the mainland to Whidbey Island.
✉ saratogainn@whidbey.net ◔ www.saratogainnwhidbeyisland.com

LEAVENWORTH

Abendblume Pension	145-269 BB	Full breakfast
12570 Ranger Rd 98826	7 rooms, 7 pb	Fireplaces, down comforters,
800-669-7634 509-548-4059	Most CC, *Rated*, •	balconies, whirlpool tubs
Randy & Renee Sexauer	S-no/P-no/H-ltd	

Inspired by fine European country inns, Abendblume is one of Leavenworth's finest award winning bed and breakfasts.
✉ info@abendblume.com ◔ www.abendblume.com

All Seasons River Inn	165-230 BB	Full breakfast
8751 Icicle Rd 98826	6 rooms, 6 pb	Snacks and desserts
800-254-0555 509-548-1425	Visa, MC, *Rated*	Game table area, TV room,
Susan and Dale Wells	C-ltd/S-no/P-no/H-yes	bicycles, Jacuzzis, suites,
		fireplaces, refrigerators,
		wireless Internet

Set on a quiet wooded riverbank, this gracious inn offers spacious riverview suites with jetted tubs, private bath, comfortable riverview seating; decks, and fireplace. And oh, what a breakfast!
✉ info@allseasonsriverinn.com ◔ www.allseasonsriverinn.com

Alpenrose Inn	110-210 BB	Full Breakfast
500 Alpine Pl. 98826	15 rooms, 15 pb	Evening dessert. Coffee or
800-582-2474 509-548-3000	Most CC	tea delivered to your room in
Cindy Hassinger	C-ltd/S-no/P-no/H-yes	the morning.
		Wireless Internet, spa on
		premises, pool, hot tub
		under the stars, leisure room

A romantic European Inn located in the Bavarian Village of Leavenworth Washington. Amenities of a B&B with the privacy of a small hotel including fireplaces, outdoor heated pool, outdoor hot tub and in-room spas.
✉ alpenroseinn@yahoo.com ◔ www.alpenroseinn.com

LEAVENWORTH

Autumn Pond B&B
10388 Titus Rd 98826
800-222-9661 509-548-4482
John & Jennifer Lorenz

119-169 BB
5 rooms, 5 pb
Visa, MC, AmEx, *Rated*
C-ltd/S-no/P-no/H-no

Full breakfast

Autumn Pond rests on three quiet country acres, surrounded by panoramic views of the majestic Cascades.
✉ info@autumnpond.com ◐ www.autumnpond.com

Beecher Hill House
9991 Beecher Hill Rd 98847
866-414-0559 509-548-0559
Susie Cochran

150-200 BB
4 rooms, 4 pb
Visa, MC
S-no/P-no/H-no

Full breakfast
Complimentary wine & hors
d'oevres
Spa robes, silk duvets,
hairdryers, TV-DVD-VCR,
phones, queen canopy beds,
turndown service

The historic manor was recently restored and renovated, evolving into an intimate Guest Inn. The ambience and attention to every detail promises a haven for your senses.
✉ info@beecherhill.com ◐ www.beecherhill.com

Enchanted River Inn
9700 E Leavenworth Rd 98826
877-548-9797 509-548-9797
Bill & Kathy Lynn

230-250 BB
3 rooms, 3 pb
Visa, MC, AmEx
S-no/P-no

3 course gourmet breakfast
Pillow top king beds,
binoculars for watching the
area wild life or river
features, guest robes

Situated on the Wenatchee River on a bank 30 feet away from and above the river. Offering extraordinary views from every suite, our kitchen and dining room.
✉ river.inn@verizon.net ◐ www.enchantedriverinn.com

Haus Rohrbach Pension
12882 Ranger Rd 98826
800-548-4477 509-548-7024
Carol & Mike Wentink

95-190 BB
10 rooms, 8 pb
Most CC
C-yes/S-no/P-no/H-ltd

Full country breakfast!
Seasonal pool and year-
round spa, and incredible
gardens

A European-style Country Inn overlooking the beautiful Leavenworth Valley celebrating 34 years of service in 2008. Where hospitality, recreation and relaxation are a tradition.
✉ info@hausrohrbach.com ◐ www.hausrohrbach.com

Inn Vienna Woods
12842 Prowell Rd 98826
888-548-7843 509-548-7843
Barry & Leah Moats

120-175 BB
5 rooms, 3 pb
Most CC
C-ltd/S-no/P-no/H-yes

Fresh, Bountiful, Healthful,
Hot!!
Tea, coffee, cider, cocoa,
wine setups on request
Fireplace Room, Grand
Piano, Jacuzzi, 360° Views,
Gardens, Woods, Free
Parking, Wireless Internet

A warm, elegant inn awaits you in Leavenworths beautiful Icicle Valley.
✉ ivwinfo@charter.net ◐ www.innviennawoods.com

Mountain Home Lodge
8201 Mountain Home Rd
98826
800-414-2378 509-548-7077
Kathy & Brad Schmidt

130-530 BB
12 rooms, 12 pb
Visa, MC, Disc, *Rated*,
●
C-ltd/S-no/P-no/H-ltd
Spanish

Full breakfast
Four course dinner, gourmet
breakfast & lunch included
in price in winter
Fireplace, Jacuzzi, robes,
stereo systems, heated pool,
hot tub, tennis court,
weddings, plasma TVs

On a secluded 20 acre meadow overlooking the Cascades, & surrounded by forest, our luxurious 12 guestroom lodge & cabins combine superb cuisine, year-round variety of outdoor activities, & total pampered relaxation.
✉ info@mthome.com ◐ www.mthome.com

LEAVENWORTH

Pine River Ranch B&B
19668 Hwy 207 98826
800-669-3877 509-763-3959
Tim and Bunnie Gellatly

195-205 BB
6 rooms, 6 pb
Visa, MC, *Rated*, •
S-no/P-no/H-ltd

Full breakfast delivered to you!
Hand Dipped Chocolate Strawberries, Deluxe Fruit, Cheese & Cracker tray
Snowshoes, wireless Internet, discount ski tickets, cross country on property

Pine River Ranch is an all-suite bed and breakfast; the most private in Leavenworth, WA. 6 modern suites with whirlpool Jacuzzi tubs, fireplaces, kitchenettes and breakfast delivered. Perfect for a romantic honeymoon. Ski or snowshoe from your door.
✉ info@prranch.com ◯ www.prranch.com

River Haus in the Pines
9690 E Leavenworth Rd 98826
509-548-9690
Mike & Cindy Hendricks

189-250 BB
3 rooms, 3 pb
Visa, MC
C-ltd/S-no/P-no/H-ltd

Full breakfast
River & mountain views, fireplace, private decks, private bathrooms with soaking tub, TV/DVD/CD

River Haus in the Pines Bed and Breakfast is a craftsman style home beautifully situated on the Wenatchee River with seasonal shoreline access.
✉ info@riverhausinthepines.com ◯ www.riverhausinthepines.com

Run of the River
9308 E Leavenworth Rd 98826
800-288-6491 509-548-7171
Monty & Karen Turner

220-255 BB
6 rooms, 6 pb
Visa, MC, Disc, *Rated*
S-no/P-no/H-yes
Spanish

Hearty, healthy and fresh!
Afternoon tea, treats
Complimentary tandem, mountain bikes & snowshoes, expert tips on discovering the magic of the Valley

As Washington's only 4-star inn rated by NW Best Places, Run of the River has earned its distinction for peaceful romance and luxury surroundings. The six suites offer a haven of privacy, with fireplaces, Jacuzzi tubs and decks to view the refuge.
✉ info@runoftheriver.com ◯ www.runoftheriver.com

LONG BEACH

A Rendezvous Place B&B
1610 California Ave S 98631
866-642-8877 360-642-8877
Peggy Miller & Sheila Wells

129-219 BB
5 rooms, 6 pb
Visa, MC, Disc, *Rated*,
•
C-ltd/S-no/P-no/H-ltd
Russian

Full 3 course breakfast
Coffee, tea, snacks & cookies. Goodie & gift baskets on request. On/off sight catering for 1–40
Library, parlor, piano, table games, DVD/VHS, WiFi, garden & house weddings, gift baskets & catering

This romantic and quiet getaway has comfortable rooms, luxury beds, and beautiful gardens. Homemade cookies in the dining room. Just a short walk to the ocean and the Long Beach peninsula activities. Come, enjoy & discover it all.
✉ relax@rendezvousplace.com ◯ www.rendezvousplace.com

Boreas B&B Inn
607 N Ocean Beach Blvd
98631
888-642-8069 360-642-8069
Susie Goldsmith & Bill Verner

179-199 BB
5 rooms, 5 pb
Most CC, *Rated*, •
C-ltd/S-no/P-no/H-no
Some Spanish

Full gourmet breakfast
Endless triple chocolate brownies, organic Boreas coffee, large tea selection, pistachios, chocolate
Full concierge service, two living rooms with fireplaces, glorious ocean views, very private hot tub

If you love three-course gourmet breakfasts created from local delicacies, glorious ocean vistas, beautiful surroundings, and award-winning gracious service, Boreas Inn is your getaway. The ambience at Boreas entices you to never go home again!
✉ info@boreasinn.com ◯ www.boreasinn.com

LOPEZ ISLAND

Edenwild Inn	170-195 BB	Self serve breakfast
132 Lopez Rd 98261	8 rooms, 8 pb	Patio, living room, dining
800-606-0662 360-468-3238	Visa, MC, *Rated*	room, unique decor,
Kris Weinshilboum	C-ltd/S-no/P-no/H-yes	comfortable
		accommodations, marina
		views, fireplaces

Experience friendly service and the warm atmosphere of Lopez Island from our premium accommodations, nestled in the heart of Lopez Village.
✉ edenwild@rockisland.com ◊ www.edenwildinn.com

LUMMI ISLAND

Full Bloom Farm	120-150 BB	Self-catered full breakfast
2330 Tuttle Ln 98262	2 rooms, 2 pb	Food may be ordered for any
360-758-7173	C-ltd/S-no/P-ltd/H-yes	and all meals prepared in
Elisabeth Marshall		cottage; let us do the
		shopping
		Deck, full kitchen, fireplaces,
		bicycles, award-winning
		gardens, cottage and
		apartment rentals

At Full Bloom Farm, enjoy the relaxing ambience of our lovely cottage and apartment in our beautiful, award-winning garden setting. We raise herbaceous and intersectional peonies—in Spring, the fields are a stunning sight in full bloom.
✉ info@fullbloomfarmpeonies.com ◊ www.fullbloomfarmpeonies.com/vacation/index.html

West Shore Farm B&B	90 BB	Full breakfast
2781 W Shore Dr 98262	2 rooms, 2 pb	Dinner by reservation, tea,
360-758-2600	Visa, MC, AmEx, •	snacks & wine
Polly & Carl Hanson	C-yes/S-no/P-no/H-ltd	Sweeping views from deck of
		the islands, beach,
		mountains, eagles

Guests stay in a unique octagonal home, designed & hand-built by your hosts. A yellow cedar driftwood log from our beach serves as a center pole, enhancing the cozy, all-wood interior.
✉ westshorefarm@msn.com

MT. BAKER

Mt. Baker Lodging, Inc.	109-509 EP	Fully equipped kitchens with
7463 Mt Baker Hwy 98244	95 rooms, 95 pb	cookware. Catering available
800-709-SNOW (7669) 360-599-	Most CC, *Rated*, •	upon request!
2453	C-yes/S-ltd/P-ltd/H-ltd	All bed & bath linens
Guest Services		provided

A delightful alternative to the traditional Mt. Baker area bed & breakfast or inn, Mt. Baker Lodging proudly offers private, self-catered, fully equipped vacation home rentals, located in Glacier and Maple Falls at the gateway to Mount Baker, Washington.
✉ mtbakercabins@msn.com ◊ www.mtbakerlodging.com

MUKILTEO

Hogland House B&B	85-125 BB	Full breakfast or "On Your
917 Webster St 98275	2 rooms, 2 pb	Own"
888-681-5101 425-742-7639	Visa, MC	Hot tub, porches, sitting
Kay Scheller	P-yes/H-no	room, TV/VCR, wireless
		Internet, in-room coffee

A National Historic Register waterfront home with Old World finishes, overlooking Puget Sound in Old Mukilteo. Includes a hot tub, collectibles, wooded trails on five acres on a dead end road.
✉ romance@hoglandhouse.com ◊ www.hoglandhouse.com

Charles Nelson Guest House, Ocean Park, WA

NORDLAND

Beach Cottages on Marrowstone
10 Beach Dr 98358
800-871-3077 360-385-3077
Allison & Stephen Willing

85-240 EP
7 rooms, 7 pb
Visa, MC, *Rated*
C-yes/S-ltd/P-no/H-ltd
German

Full kitchen in each cabin
3 miles of undeveloped
beach, mountains, wildlife,
solitude

This 10 acre property features a naturalized landscape to harmonize with the adjoining 50 acre salt marsh, with access to 2 miles of beach. 1930s Puget Sound beach hideaway, upgraded to modern basics. Island living, island pace of life.
◐ www.beachcottagegetaway.com

NORTH BEND

Roaring River B&B
46715 SE 129th St 98045
877-627-4647 425-888-4834
Herschel & Peggy Backues

109-195 BB
5 rooms, 5 pb
Most CC, *Rated*, •
C-ltd/S-no/P-no/H-no

Full breakfast
Warm breakfast baskets will
be delivered to the door
each morning
Jacuzzis, suites, fireplaces,
cable TV, business travelers,
private entrances, sitting
areas, decks

Choose a hot tub, sauna, or Jacuzzi room. Very romantic, very private, wonderful restaurants, and incredible views of mountains, rivers, forests, and occasional wildlife.
✉ roaringriver@comcast.net ◐ www.theroaringriver.com

OCEAN PARK

Charles Nelson Guest House
26205 Sandridge Rd 98640
888-862-9756 360-665-3016
Ginger Bish

160-180 BB
3 rooms, 3 pb
Most CC
S-no/P-yes/H-no

Full breakfast
Sunroom, fireplace,
hammocks

On the edge of Ocean Park and just within the boundaries of Nachotta, our inn overlooks Willapa Bay and the Wildlife Refuge of Long Island.
✉ cnbandb@charlesnelsonbandb.com ◐ www.charlesnelsonbandb.com

George Johnson House B&B
26301 'N' Place 98640
866-665-6993 360-665-6993
Nancy Craig

125-165 BB
3 rooms, 3 pb
Visa, MC
C-ltd/S-no/P-no

Full Country Breakfast
Antique accessories, high-
speed wireless Internet,
wraparound porch, library
and perennial gardens.

Experience the Peninsula's historic spirit in this beautiful 1913 Craftsman home. Nestled on a quiet street, it's just a short walk to the ocean beach or to the nearby attractions. Each of the three bedrooms offer private bathrooms and wireless Internet.
✉ stay@georgejohnsonhouse.com ◐ www.georgejohnsonhouse.com

PORT ANGELES

Colette's B&B
339 Finn Hall Rd 98362
877-457-9777 360-457-9197
Peter & Lynda Clark

195-395 BB
5 rooms, 5 pb
Visa, MC, *Rated*
S-no/P-no/H-ltd

Multi-Course Gourmet
Breakfast
Afternoon Tea / Evening
Wine / Hors d'oeuvres
Romantic Getaways/Spa &
Concierge Services/Outdoor
Fireplace & Stone
Patio/Movie & Music Library

Fodor's—"Top Choice." Best Places to Kiss-"4 Kisses" Highest Rating. Breathtaking 10-acre oceanfront estate, nestled between the Olympic Range and the Strait of Juan de Fuca. Luxury king suites with Jacuzzi spas for two, fireplaces and oceanfront views.
✉ colettes@colettes.com ○ www.colettes.com

Domaine Madeleine
146 Wildflower Ln 98362
888-811-8376 360-457-4174
Jeri Weinhold

140-310 BB
5 rooms, 5 pb
Most CC, *Rated*
C-ltd/S-ltd/P-no/H-no

Full breakfast
24 hour coffee, tea, hot
chocolate, cookies
Sitting room, library, Jacuzzi,
games, fireplaces, cable TV,
DVDs, maps, guidebooks

Serene, romantic, contemporary estate with panoramic mountain and waterviews. Exquisite gardens, Monet garden replica, European/Asian antiques, fireplace, Jacuzzi, private entrance, renowned 5-course breakfast.
✉ stay@domainemadeleine.com ○ www.domainemadeleine.com

Eden by the Sea
1027 Finn Hall Rd. 98362
360-452-6021
David & Evelyn Brown

135-185 BB
3 rooms, 3 pb
Visa, MC
C-ltd/S-no/P-no/H-ltd

Multiple course gourmet
breakfast
Afternoon Tea, lemonade &
cookies, fruit, fresh veggies,
crackers, chips, nuts.
Great room & library downstairs, large conversation
room with TV upstairs.

A unique Eden by the Sea experience awaits you, secluded on the Olympic Peninsula, in the land of the Great Northwest. This waterfront property will provide you with a peaceful rest in rooms with private baths and views of the water and mountains.
✉ info@edenbythesea.net ○ www.edenbythesea.net/index.html

Five SeaSuns B&B
1006 S Lincoln St 98362
800-708-0777 360-452-8248
Bob & Jan Harbick

105-165 BB
5 rooms, 5 pb
Most CC, *Rated*, •
C-ltd/S-no/P-no/H-ltd

Full breakfast
Bob's famous fresh-baked
cookies!
Free ferry shuttle

Historic B&B surrounded by award winning gardens situated just minutes from Olympic Nat'l. Park and ferries to Victoria, B.C.   ✉ info@seasuns.com ○ www.seasuns.com

Inn at Rooster Hill
112 Reservoir Rd 98363
877-221-0837 360-452-4933
Peggy Frehner

119-189 BB
5 rooms, 5 pb
Most CC
C-ltd/P-yes

Full breakfast
Double jetted Jacuzzi tub,
antique beds, luxury towels
and robes, TV/DVD/CD and
down comforters

Inn at Rooster Hill is a quiet, French-country bed and breakfast set on a 2 + acre piece of wooded property in Port Angeles, Washington. All of our rooms have great amenities and with all new, high-quality bedding, you are assured of a good night's sleep!
✉ info@innatroosterhill.com ○ www.innatroosterhill.com

La Place Sur La Mer
2026 Place Road 98362
888-248-1277 360-565-8029
Lyndee Lapin

159-250 EP
5 rooms, 5 pb
Visa, MC
C-yes/S-no/P-ltd/H-yes

Private hot tub, swimming
pool, sauna, outdoor grill,
full kitchen, satellite TV/WiFi

Welcome to La Place Sur La Mer! We are a beach-side "Bed and Breakfast Inn" and Concierge Vacation Rental located on the breath-taking shores of the Strait of Juan de Fuca offering the only direct walk to the beach in the county!
✉ lyndee@magicalbeach.com ○ www.magicalbeach.com/index.html

Five SeaSuns B&B, Port Angeles, WA

Tudor Inn B&B	135-160 BB	Full Gourmet Breakfast
1108 S Oak 98362	5 rooms, 5 pb	Afternoon refreshment at
866-286-2224 360-452-3138	Most CC, *Rated*	check-in may include hot/cold
Betsy Reed Schultz	C-ltd/S-no/P-no/H-no	beverage and sweets, fruit or
		cheese/crackers
		Fireplace in parlor/library,
		piano, sitting room, outdoor
		deck/front sitting porch, lovely
		gardens

The Tudor Inn is an historic B&B in Port Angeles, on Washington State's beautiful Olympic Peninsula. The Inn has been tastefully restored to retain the rustic charm of the Tudor era. Innkeeper known for hospitality and gourmet breakfasts.
✉ info@tudorinn.com ✆ www.tudorinn.com

PORT ORCHARD

Reflections – A B&B	65-110 BB	Full breakfast
3878 Reflection Ln, E 98366	4 rooms, 2 pb	welcoming libation
360-871-5582	Visa, MC, *Rated*	TV/VCR, fireplace, ceiling
Cathy Hall	C-ltd/S-no/P-no/H-ltd	fans, meeting rooms,
		washer/dryer, library,

Just a short distance from downtown Port Orchard, Reflections Bed & Breakfast Inn is a perfect place for an overnight or weekend stay.
✉ jimreflect@wavecable.com ✆ www.reflectionsbnb.com

PORT TOWNSEND

At Huber's Inn	135-195 $US BB	Special Continental Breakfast
1421 Landes St 98368	3 rooms, 1 pb	All around Wi-Fi/Inside
360-385-3904	Most CC, •	reading sitting rooms/Table
Leticia & Robert Huber	C-ltd/S-no/P-ltd/H-ltd	games Garden terrace/Sitting
	Spanish, French, Italian	corridor with view

Huber's Inn is an elegant cozy & warm personal experience, when renting the rooms or suites at the Inn. As a Vacation Rental for a small group, Huber's Inn Port Townsend offers a gracious, well located, spacious and very memorable, getaway
✉ info@loshuber.com ✆ www.loshuber.com

Bishop Victorian Guest	99-225 $US BB	Continental breakfast
Suites	16 rooms, 16 pb	Coffee, tea, catering
714 Washington St 98368	Most CC, *Rated*, •	Internet access, parking,
800-824-4738 360-385-6122	C-yes/S-no/P-ltd/H-no	conference facilities,
Joe & Cindy Finnie		kitchenettes

Downtown Victorian-era hotel; beautifully restored. Gracious suites. Mountain and water views. Walk to Port Townsend.
✉ joe@rainshadowproperties.com ✆ www.bishopvictorian.com

PORT TOWNSEND

Blue Gull Inn B&B	95-140 $US BB	Full country style breakfast
1310 Clay St 98368	6 rooms, 6 pb	Cookies & treats available in
888-700-0205 360-379-3241	Most CC	the afternoon
John & Renee Eissinger	C-ltd/S-no/P-no/H-no	Whirlpool tubs, beautiful
		gardens, close to downtown

Welcome to warm, county charm in a Victorian setting. This historic uptown B&B was built in 1868, and features six beautifully decorated guestrooms with private baths, some with whirlpool tubs. Full breakfast each day. Close to restaurants and shopping!
✉ bluegull@olypen.com ✆ www.bluegullinn.com

Commander's Beach House	99-225 $US BB	Full breakfast
400 Hudson St 98368	4 rooms, 3 pb	Gourmet hot chocolate, teas,
888-385-1778 360-385-1778	Visa, MC	coffee, and spiced cider
Gail Dionne Oldroyd	C-ltd/S-no/P-no/H-ltd	along with biscottis for
		dunking are available
		Ocean views, living room,
		fireplaces, verandah,
		weddings

This quiet and relaxing Cape Cod style beach house offers the best of both worlds. We are located on the water with miles of beach to explore And.. just three blocks from the excitement of the downtown shops and restaurants. "Come relax and solve nothing"
✉ stay@commandersbeachhouse.com ✆ www.commandersbeachhouse.com

Holly Hill House B&B	94-175 $US BB	Full 3 course breakfast
611 Polk Street 98368	5 rooms, 5 pb	Tea, cocoa, homemade
800-435-1454 360-385-5619	Visa, MC, *Rated*	marshmallows, snacks, wine
Nina & Greg Dortch	C-ltd/S-ltd/P-no/H-no	Gentlemen's parlor with TV,
		DVD & video

Holly Hill House is an 1872 Victorian B&B in the historic uptown district. Providing comfortable & relaxing accommodations that pamper our guests.
✉ info@hollyhillhouse.com ✆ www.hollyhillhouse.com

The James House	135-250 $US BB	Full breakfast
1238 Washington St 98368	12 rooms, 12 pb	Complimentary fresh baked
800-385-1238 360-385-1238	Visa, MC, Cash, Checks,	cookies available daily
Carol McGough	*Rated*, •	Outstanding water &
	C-ltd/S-no/P-no/H-ltd	mountain views, fireplaces,
		wireless Internet, perennial
		gardens.

Port Townsend's premiere inn! This elegant mansion sits on the bluff with sweeping water & mountain views. Each guestroom is beautifully maintained, rich in history & charm with amenities for the discerning traveler. Elegant, comfortable, & romantic!
✉ info@jameshouse.com ✆ www.jameshouse.com

Old Consulate Inn	99-210 $US BB	Full – Seven Dish/Three
313 Walker at Washington	8 rooms, 8 pb	Course
98368	Visa, MC, *Rated*	Coffee, tea, cookies, evening
800-300-6753 360-385-6753	C-ltd/S-no/P-no/H-no	desserts, complimentary
Michael & Sue DeLong		port & sherry
		Sitting room, library, tennis,
		hot tub, billiard, game room,
		parlor, grand piano,
		Victorian antiques

Experience the gracious hospitality of the Victorian past in this beautifully restored Queen Anne masterpiece. This award winning Painted Lady is one of the most photographed and artistically depicted Victorian mansions in the Pacific Northwest.
✉ mike@oldconsulateinn.com ✆ www.oldconsulateinn.com

PORT TOWNSEND

The Swan Hotel
216 Monroe St 98368
800-824-4738 360-385-6122
Don Dobby

99-525 $US EP
13 rooms, 13 pb
Most CC, *Rated*, •
C-ltd/S-no/P-ltd/H-ltd

Coffee & tea service
Small meeting facilities, high
speed Internet access,
catering

A waterfront hotel overlooking Point Hudson Marina, 8 studio rooms, 2 story penthouse that can accommodate up to 8 guests, and 4 garden cottages.
✉ info@rainshadowproperties.com ◑ www.theswanhotel.com

PUYALLUP

Hedman House
502 9th St SW 98371
866-433-6267 253-848-2248
Neil & Normajean Hedman

95-135 $US BB
2 rooms
Visa, MC, Cash, Checks
C-ltd/S-no/P-no/H-no

Sit down breakfast
Covered porch, courtyard,
spa, fireplace, wireless
Internet, central air

Hedman House, a B&B, located in Puyallup, Washington, is a comfortable and romantic lodging alternative to the big hotels and discount motels in Seattle and Tacoma. Perfect for romantic weekend getaways, antiquing, the Fair or business.
✉ contact@hedmanhouse.com ◑ www.hedmanhouse.com

Tayberry Victorian Cottage
7406 80th St E 98371
253-445-1991 253-848-4594
Terry & Vicki Chissus

105-125 $US BB
3 rooms, 3 pb
Most CC
C-yes/S-ltd/P-no/H-no

Full breakfast
Movie snacks & beverages,
in-room coffee service
Hairdryer, TV/VCR/tapes,
piano, computer modem,
iron & board, hot tub, A/C

Warm, comfortable accommodations, delightful decoration, quiet, peaceful surroundings and the most competitive of rates make this the perfect weekend getaway or vacation headquarters.
✉ tayberry@wwdb.org ◑

REDMOND

A Cottage Creek Inn
12525 Avondale Rd NE 98052
425-881-5606
Steve & Jeanette Wynecoop

110-140 $US BB
4 rooms, 4 pb
Visa, MC, AmEx, *Rated*
C-ltd/S-ltd/P-no/H-no
Very little German

Full breakfast
Afternoon tea on request
Sitting room, Jacuzzis, suites,
hot tub, pond, creek,
conference facilities, wireless
DSL, phones

Romantic English Tudor in beautiful, tranquil garden setting. Four lovely rooms/suites with private baths & TV. Many fine wineries & restaurants nearby. Phones & DSL broadband are complimentary. Private nature trail, Hot Tub, Full Breakfast included.
✉ innkeepers@cottagecreekinn.com ◑ www.cottagecreekinn.com

SEATTLE

11th Avenue Inn
121 11th Avenue E 98102
800-720-7161 206-720-7161
Beverly Hawkins

69-169 $US BB
8 rooms, 6 pb
Most CC, *Rated*
C-ltd/S-no/P-no

Full breakfast
50 restaurants within a 15
minute walk.
Free parking, free WiFi and
guest Internet computers,
TV/VCR/Cable, livingroom,
den, front porch.

Walk to the downtown attractions from this charming 8-room inn on a tree-lined side street. Dozens of neighborhood restaurants are nearby, free on-site parking, queen beds, private bathrooms, WiFi, full breakfast, and one block to the park and bus stops.
✉ info@11thavenueinn.com ◑ www.11thavenueinn.com

SEATTLE————————————————————————————————————

An Olympic View B&B Cottage
2705 SW 164th Pl 98166
206-243-6900
Dave & Eileen Schmidt

165-220 $US BB
1 rooms, 1 pb
Visa, MC, *Rated*
C-yes/S-ltd/P-no/H-yes

Full breakfast
Soda's, snacks, fresh fruit,
Afternoon tea. Requests are
taken for special meals
inside cottage.
Private cottage & hot tub,
king bed, wireless Internet,
laundry facilities, Cable TV,
CD/DVD, videos

Awarded "Most Scenic View" & "Best Kept Secret." Private cottage w/ Jacuzzi hot tub overlooking spectacular water/Mtn views. Full kitchen, full breakfast, king bed, living area, TV, DVD, stereo, private bath, walk to beach, close to Seattle attractions.
✉ innkeeper@olympicviewbb.com ✪ olympicviewbb.com

Bacon Mansion B&B
959 Broadway E 98102
800-240-1864 206-329-1864
Daryl J. King

99-234 $US BB
11 rooms, 9 pb
Most CC, *Rated*
C-ltd/S-no/P-ltd/H-ltd

Continental plus breakfast
Tea and cookies out by 4 PM.
Sitting room, library,
conference room, cable TV,
hairdryer, private telephone,
bathrobe, WiFi access

Stay in Seattle's leading Bed and Breakfast and enjoy the charm and comfort of yesterday, with all the convenience of today. One of Capitol Hill's gracious mansions c. 1909.
✉ info@baconmansion.com ✪ www.baconmansion.com

Capitol Hill Guest House
1808 E Denny Way 98122
206-412-REST 206-412-REST
Shannon Seth

95-155 $US BB
5 rooms, 1 pb
Most CC
C-ltd/S-no/P-ltd/H-ltd

Continental plus breakfast
Wireless Internet, access to
gourmet kitchen and laundry
facility, off-street parking,
bike rentals.

An Urban Inn for the savvy traveler. Located just 10 blocks from downtown Seattle. 10 minute bus ride to Space Needle and Waterfront. Your home away from home.
✉ Sleep@CapitolHillGuestHouse.com ✪ www.capitolhillguesthouse.com

Chambered Nautilus Bed and Breakfast Inn
5005 22nd Ave NE 98105
800-545-8459 206-522-2536
Joyce Schulte

104-204 $US BB
10 rooms, 10 pb
Visa, MC, AmEx, *Rated*
C-ltd/S-no/P-ltd/H-no
French

Full 3-course breakfast
Tea, coffee, fruit & cookies
Fireplaces, porches, A/C,
private baths, robes, TV,
hairdryer, in room WiFi,
guest computer

An elegant Inn near the University of Washington campus. Minutes from downtown. Features spacious, quiet and comfortable rooms with Amazing Breakfasts and homemade cookies! Fireplaces in winter, gardens for spring and summer. WiFi throughout.
✉ stay@chamberednautilus.com ✪ www.chamberednautilus.com

Gaslight Inn
1727 15th Ave 98122
206-325-3654
Stephen Bennett

98-158 $US BB
8 rooms, 6 pb
Visa, MC, AmEx, *Rated*
C-ltd/S-no/P-no/H-ltd

Seasonal Continental
breakfast
A wet bar, microwave and
under counter refrigerator
are the only food
storage/preparation facilities
Heated pool, sun deck, living
room, fireplace, library

In restoring Gaslight Inn, we have brought out this bed and breakfast's original turn-of-the-century ambience and warmth, while keeping in mind the additional conveniences and contemporary style needed by today's travelers.
✉ innkeepr@gaslight-inn.com ✪ www.gaslight-inn.com

Salisbury House, Seattle, WA

SEATTLE

Inn at Harbor Steps
1221 First Ave 98101
888-728-8910 206-748-0973
David Huynh

200-275 $US BB
28 rooms, 28 pb
Most CC
C-yes/S-no/P-no/H-yes

Full breakfast
Afternoon wine, tea & hors
d' oeuvres, freshly-baked
cookies, drinks available
throughout the day
Garden views, fireplace,
meeting facilities, indoor
pool

Nestled in the heart of Seattle's sleek arts and business district and crowned by the glamorous Harbor Steps Park, the Inn at Harbor Steps is perfectly located to the best Seattle has to offer.
✉ innatharborsteps@foursisters.com 🌐 www.innatharborsteps.com

Mildred's
1202 15th Ave E 98112
800-327-9692 206-325-6072
Melodee Sarver

125-225 $US BB
4 rooms, 4 pb
Visa, MC, AmEx, Cash,
Checks, *Rated*
C-yes/S-ltd/P-no/H-no

Full breakfast
Afternoon tea or coffee,
homemade cookies
Sitting room, fireplace,
library, veranda, grand
piano, queen beds, front
yard putting green

1890 Victorian. Wraparound verandah, lace curtains, red carpets. City location near bus, electric trolley, park, art museum, flower conservatory.
✉ innkeeper@mildredsbnb.com 🌐 www.mildredsbnb.com

Salisbury House B&B
750 16th Ave E 98112
206-328-8682
Cathryn Wiese

135-189 $US BB
5 rooms, 5 pb
Visa, MC, AmEx, Cash,
Checks, *Rated*
C-ltd/S-no/P-no/H-no

Full breakfast
Complimentary tea/coffee 24
hours
Phones w/voice mail in each
room, free high-speed
wireless Internet access

Elegant Capitol Hill Inn. Ideal location for business or pleasure. Take advantage of Seattle's excellent transit system. Well-appointed rooms with private baths, full breakfasts, two friendly housecats. Highly recommended.
✉ sleep@salisburyhouse.com 🌐 www.salisburyhouse.com

SEATTLE────────────────────────────────────

Shafer Baillie Mansion	139-219 $US BB	Full breakfast
907 14th Ave E 98112	5 rooms, 5 pb	Sitting room, fireplaces.
800-985-4654 206-322-4654	Most CC	Weddings hosted.
Mark Mayhle & Ana Lena	C-yes/S-no/P-no/H-no	
Melka		

*Magnificent 1914 Tudor Revival 14,000 sq ft mansion on Seattle's original Millionaires'
Row. Capitol Hill location, central to all major attractions and amenities: downtown,
waterfront, Pike Place Market, Seattle Center, Washington Convention Center.*
✉ sbmansion@gmail.com ○ www.sbmansion.com

Three Tree Point	150-250 $US BB	Full breakfast
17026 33rd Ave SW 98166	2 rooms, 2 pb	Snacks
888-369-7696 206-669-7646	Visa, MC, AmEx, Cash,	A/C, terry robes & slippers,
Penny & Doug Whisler	Checks	stereo w/CD player, in-room
	C-yes/S-ltd/P-yes/H-ltd	cable TV/VCR, morning
		paper

*Escape to one of Seattle's most enjoyable Bed and Breakfast getaways. Located on a quiet
hillside overlooking Puget Sound and Three Tree Point, this is a true Northwest retreat.*
✉ whisler@3treepointbnb.com ○ www.3treepointbnb.com

Villa Heidelberg B&B	100-285 $US BB	Full breakfast
4845 45th Ave SW 98116	6 rooms, 2 pb	Cable TV, WiFi & fax access,
800-671-2942 206-938-3658	Visa, MC, AmEx,	each bathroom has Noevir
Judy Burbrink	*Rated*, •	products, a hairdryer &
	C-ltd/S-no/P-no/H-no	bathrobes in each room

*1909 Craftsman home, just minutes from the airport & downtown Seattle. Two blocks to
shops, bus & a variety of ethnic restaurants. Great view of Puget Sound and Olympic
Mountains with marvelous sunsets. Close to Lincoln Park and Alki Beach.*
✉ info@villaheidelberg.com ○ www.villaheidelberg.com

SEAVIEW────────────────────────────────────

Shelburne Inn	135-195 $US BB	Full country breakfast
4415 Pacific Way 98644	15 rooms, 15 pb	Freshly baked cookies upon
800-INN-1896 360-642-2442	Visa, MC, AmEx, Cash,	arrival. Restaurant, pub.
Laurie Anderson & David	*Rated*, •	Lobby with fireplace, 2 suites
Campiche	C-yes/S-no/P-no/H-no	
	French, German,	
	Portuguese	

*The oldest surviving Victorian hotel in Washington state, with the time-honored tradition of
superb service, decor and distinguished cuisine. Can accommodate small meetings of up to
30.*
✉ innkeeper@theshelburneinn.com ○ www.theshelburneinn.com

SEDRO-WOOLLEY────────────────────────────────

South Bay Bed & Breakfast	155-185 $US BB	Continental and Full
4095 South Bay Dr 98284	6 rooms, 6 pb	Breakfast
877-595-2086 360-595-2086	Most CC, *Rated*	Guest Pantry feature
Kate Malmgren	C-ltd/S-no/P-yes/H-ltd	microwave popcorn, other
	Feb.- December	snacks, soft drinks, bottled
		water, Cookies
		Oversized jetted tubs,
		fireplaces, patios, 24hr
		coffee-tea, HiSpeed WiFi,
		lake access, dogs OK (fee)

*A stone's throw from Bellingham WA, offering 6 lakeview rooms with private baths,
oversized jetted tubs, fireplaces, private patios, comfortable furnishings, plush down comforters & luxurious linens. Award winning luxury lodging overlooking Lake Whatcom.*
✉ info@southbaybb.com ○ www.southbaybb.com

SEQUIM

Groveland Cottage B&B
4861 Sequim-Dungeness Way
98382
800-879-8859 360-683-3565
Simone Nichols

110-155 $US BB
5 rooms, 5 pb
Most CC
C-ltd/S-no/P-ltd/H-no

Full breakfast
Snacks in the afternoon.
Breakfast to go if early
departure is needed
High speed Internet and lush
gardens

Our Inn is located in the Sequim-Dungeness Valley along the Strait of Juan de Fuca on Washington's beautiful North Olympic Peninsula. Sequim offers convenient access to Olympic National Park, Dungeness Spit National Wildlife Refuge, and the ferry.
✉ simone@olypen.com ◐ www.grovelandcottage.com

Juan de Fuca Cottages
182 Marine Dr 98382
866-683-4433 360-683-4433
Missy & Tom Rief

120-305 $US EP
9 rooms, 9 pb
Visa, MC, Disc, Cash,
Checks, *Rated*
C-yes/S-no/P-ltd/H-ltd

Self serve- purchase own
food
Complimentary coffee &
popcorn
Whirlpool tubs,
CTV/VCR/CD, robes,
slippers, 2 fireplace suites,
kayak rentals, 200 classic
movies

Charming, completely equipped cottages and suites perched on a 50-foot bluff overlooking Dungeness Spit. We have our own private beach on Dungeness Bay. Prepare your own breakfast in cozy kitchens.
✉ juandefuca@olypen.com ◐ www.juandefuca.com

Lost Mountain Lodge
303 Sunny View Dr 98382
888-683-2431 360-683-2431
Dwight & Lisa Hostvedt

235-495 $US BB
5 rooms, 5 pb
Visa, MC, Cash, *Rated*
C-ltd/S-no/P-no/H-ltd
French

Full breakfast
Complimentary lattes &
espresso, welcome tray of
wine & hors d'oeuvres,
chocolates & cookies
Full concierge services,
hydrotherapy spa, 250+
movie collection, hiking
guidebooks, trail maps

Best Places Northwest. Award-winning, idyllic getaway. Private, sunny 9+ acres of mountain views, ponds, waterfalls, wildlife & cottage gardens. Luxury king fireplace suites, lavish linens & superb amenities. Gourmet breakfast, lattes, hydrotherapy spa.
✉ getaway@lostmountainlodge.com ◐ www.lostmountainlodge.com

SNOHOMISH

Pillows & Platters B&B
502 Avenue C 98290
800-214-1305 360-862-8944
Shirley & Dennis Brindle

90-100 $US BB
3 rooms, 2 pb
Visa, MC
C-ltd/S-no/P-no/H-ltd

Full breakfast

Welcome to this cheery house, built in 1892 as the original Methodist Parsonage for the city of Snohomish. Three intriguing rooms available, one with private bath, friendly hosts, and a romantic and relaxing atmosphere. Enjoy your trip!
✉ pillowsandplatters@gmail.com ◐ www.pillowsandplatters.com

SUNNYSIDE

Sunnyside Inn B&B
804 E Edison Ave 98944
800-221-4195 509-839-5557
Karen & Don Vlieger

79-149 $US BB
12 rooms, 12 pb
Visa, MC, AmEx, Cash, •
C-yes/S-no/P-ltd/H-no
French

Full breakfast
Snacks, popcorn, fountain
soda, ice cream, tea
Sitting room, Jacuzzi tubs,
video library, WiFi, near
tennis, golf, & over 40
wineries

Our twelve rooms all have private baths, eight with an in-room double spa tub. This historic 1919 Inn is in the heart of Washington wine country. Modest rates and a family friendly atmosphere will make Sunnyside Inn your home base in the Yakima Valley.
✉ sunnyside@sunnysideinn.com ◐ www.sunnysideinn.com

TACOMA———————————————————————

Branch Colonial House
2420 N 21st St 98406
877-752-3565 253-752-3565
Robin Korobkin

135-209 $US BB
6 rooms, 6 pb
Visa, MC, AmEx, Cash,
Rated, •
C-yes/S-no/P-no/H-no

Full or continental breakfast
Sitting room, jetted tubs,
fireplace, cable TV, Bose
Wave radio/CD, DVD players,
wireless Internet

Nestled above Tacoma's historical Old Town district and over looking Commencement Bay, the Branch Colonial House offers romantic views, antique furnishings, and easy access to all of Puget Sound area dinning and attractions.
✉ stay@branchcolonialhouse.com ☼ www.branchcolonialhouse.com

Chinaberry Hill
302 Tacoma Ave N 98403
253-272-1282
Cecil & Yarrow Wayman

115-245 $US BB
5 rooms, 5 pb
Visa, MC, AmEx, Cash,
Checks, *Rated*, •
C-ltd/S-ltd/P-no/H-no

Hearty breakfasts & serious
coffee
Guest kitchen with
complimentary refreshments
(cookies, sodas, water, teas,
popcorn, hot chocolate).
Bright, spacious suites,
estate gardens, guest cottage,
wraparound porch, high
speed wireless.

1889 Grand Victorian Inn with bay views, fireplaces, private Jacuzzis. Downtown shops & theatres, Antique Row and waterfront dining are all within a few blocks of this remarkable garden retreat.
✉ chinaberry@wa.net ☼ www.chinaberryhill.com

Plum Duff House
619 North K St 98403
888-627-1920 253-627-6916
Peter & Robin Stevens

90-150 $US BB
4 rooms, 4 pb
Visa, MC, AmEx, *Rated*
C-ltd/S-no/P-ltd/H-no

Full breakfast
Tea, coffee, hot chocolate,
cookies, cold drinks, fruit
Gardens, sitting room, sun
room, Jacuzzi, fireplaces, wifi, cable tv/videos, local
phones

Built in 1901 and listed on the Tacoma Historic Register, this unique, charming home has high ceilings, arches, and lovely gardens.
✉ plumduffhouse@gmail.com ☼ www.plumduff.com

Rose Cottage Guest House
1929 Austin Rd NE 98422
866-767-3268 253-927-9437
Myrna & Bill Casey

187-300 $US BB
2 rooms, 2 pb
Visa, MC, Cash, Checks,
Rated
S-no/P-no/H-ltd

Full or continental breakfast
Tea, coffee, soft drinks,
cookies
Privacy, luxury
Jacuzzi/shower queen &
twin beds, wireless Internet,
TV/DVD/VCR, porch, free
parking

Retreat & refresh for a few days to a month in a private guesthouse located between Seattle & Tacoma, within walking distance to the waters of Puget Sound at Dash Point State Park. This whimsical cottage is charming, luxurious & can sleep up to 4 adults.
✉ info@rosecottageguesthouse.com ☼ www.rosecottageguesthouse.com

The Villa
705 N 5th St 98403
888-572-1157 253-572-1157
Kristy & Aaron House

135-235 $US BB
5 rooms, 5 pb
Visa, MC, AmEx, Cash,
Checks, *Rated*, •
C-ltd/S-no/P-ltd/H-yes

Full breakfast
Complimentary snacks, soda
& bottled water
Sitting room, library,
Jacuzzis, suites, fireplaces,
cable TV

Only B&B in the Seattle/Tacoma area to be accepted into "Unique New Inns," based on the beauty, cleanliness, and amenities offered. So authentic-looking is this Mediterranean-style villa that you can imagine it being air-lifted from old Italy.
✉ innkeeper@villabb.com ☼ www.villabb.com

THORP

Country View Guest House
1281 Goodwin Road 98946
866-448-9462 509-964-9251
Holly & Paul Hutchinson

175-195 $US BB
3 rooms, 1 pb
Most CC
C-yes/S-no/P-ltd/H-no

Self-catering breakfast
Muffin & scone basket. Eggs,
bacon/sausage, bread, juice,
milk, coffee and tea. Kitchen
amenities.
Air Conditioning,
dishwasher, washer, dryer,
microwave, telephone and
television with DVD/VCR.

*Enjoy peace and quiet and get a taste of the country life in this private three-bedroom
farmhouse. Located on a fifty-seven acre farm, the house sits on top of a hill with sweeping
views of the Mount Stuart Range, Ellensburg and Thorp.*
✉ countryview@fairpoint.net ✪ www.countryviewguesthouse.com

VASHON ISLAND

Artist's Studio Loft B&B
16529 91st Ave SW 98070
206-463-2583
Jacqueline Clayton

119-215 $US BB
5 rooms, 5 pb
Most CC, *Rated*
C-ltd/S-no/P-no/H-no

Full or expanded continental
Bicycles, Jacuzzis, suites,
fireplace, conference
facilities, kitchenette

*Enchanting & romantic getaway nestled on five acres with flower gardens and hot tub, on
beautiful Vashon Island, minutes from Seattle. Cottages with fireplaces & Jacuzzis. Healing, serene atmosphere, private entrances/baths. Rated 3 diamonds by AAA.*
✉ info@vashonbedandbreakfast.com ✪ www.vashonbedandbreakfast.com

**Swallow's Nest Guest
Cottages**
6030 SW 248th St 98070
800-269-6378 206-463-2646
Bob Keller

105-145 $US EP
7 rooms, 7 pb
Most CC, *Rated*, •
C-yes/S-no/P-ltd/H-ltd

Cottages with kitchens;
coffee, tea, cocoa
Some hot tubs/fireplaces,
golf, boating nearby

*The Swallow's Nest affords travelers the opportunity to sojourn to a private country retreat
on Vashon Island. There are 7 charming cottages in 3 separate locations each furnished in
a comfortable & warm manner, some with views.*
✉ anynest@vashonislandcottages.com ✪ www.vashonislandcottages.com

WALLA WALLA

Inn at Blackberry Creek
1126 Pleasant St 99362
877-522-5233 509-522-5233
Barbara Knudson

125-206 $US BB
3 rooms, 3 pb
Most CC, *Rated*
C-ltd/S-no/P-no/H-ltd

Full breakfast
Cookies, tea, coffee, hot
chocolate, hot cider
Sitting room, library, bikes,
fireplaces, cable TV, DSL
lines

*Quiet country retreat in the middle of town. Victorian charm abounds in this 1906 home.
The antique furnishings provide the charm of 1906, with all the modern amenities to make
your stay enjoyable.*
✉ bknud@hscis.net ✪ www.innatblackberrycreek.com

WENATCHEE

Apple Country B&B
524 Okanogan Ave 98801
509-664-0400
Jerry & Sandi Anderson

85-120 $US BB
6 rooms, 4 pb
Most CC
C-ltd/S-no/P-ltd/H-no

Full breakfast
Sitting room, bicycles, cable
TV, accommodate business
travelers

*Charming 1920 Craftsman home. Gourmet breakfast served daily. Close to downtown,
Convention Center, riverfront and skiing. 18 miles from Leavenworth, WA. Five guestrooms, separate Carriage House.*
✉ innkeepers@applecountryinn.com ✪ www.applecountryinn.com

Tell your hosts Pamela Lanier sent you.

YAKIMA————————————————————————————————

A Touch of Europe	125-137 $US BB	Full breakfast
220 N 16th Ave 98902	2 rooms, 2 pb	Afternoon high tea, fine
888-438-7073 509-454-9775	Most CC, *Rated*, •	dining onsite with prior
Chef Erika & James A. Cenci	C-ltd/S-no/P-no/H-no	arrangement for multi-course
	German	luncheons & dinners

Nearby tennis court & pool, library, museums, wineries, farmers market, farms, orchards

Your destination getaway to our historic Queen Anne Victorian home. Enjoy luxurious surroundings and candlelight dinner—your menu is personalized—just for you. Chef owned B&B and author of 3 cookbooks totaling over 900 pages.

✉ atoeurope@msn.com 🌐 www.winesnw.com/toucheuropeb&b.htm

West Virginia

BERKELEY SPRINGS

Highlawn Inn
171 Market St 25411
888-290-4163 304-258-5700
Sandra M. Kauffman

95-210 $US BB
12 rooms, 12 pb
Visa, MC
C-ltd/S-ltd/P-no

Full gourmet breakfast
Delectable snacks and
springwater-based beverages
are always available
Wrap-around veranda,
gardens, A/C, color TV, some
whirlpools & fireplace

The flavor of a more gracious time saturates this elaborate Victorian bride's house, with its wrap around veranda overlooking the historic spa town of Berkeley Springs, West Virginia.
info@highlawninn.com www.highlawninn.com

CABINS

North Fork Mountain Inn
Smoke Hole Rd 26855
304-257-1108
Ed & Carol Fischer

130-245 $US BB
9 rooms, 9 pb
Visa, MC, *Rated*
C-ltd/S-ltd/P-ltd/H-no

Full breakfast
Dinner available on most
evenings for an additional fee
Sitting room, hot tub,
billiards, video and music
library, Jacuzzis, fireplaces

An outpost of luxury in the wilderness. Secluded, non-resort getaway located on the North Fork Mt. within Monongahela National Forest. Wraparound porches, breathtaking views. Hiking and caverns nearby.
nfmi@wildblue.net www.northforkmtninn.com

CHARLES TOWN

Carriage Inn B&B
417 E Washington St 25414
800-867-9830 304-728-8003
Donn & Marie Davis

105-250 $US BB
7 rooms, 7 pb
Most CC, *Rated*
C-ltd/S-ltd/P-no/H-ltd

Full Gourmet Breakfast
Complimentary afternoon
snack, sodas, tea & coffee
during the day
Civil war memorabilia, A/C,
cable TV/VCR, fireplaces,
Free Wireless Internet,
Special Package,

The Carriage Inn is an 1836 Federal style home in Charles Town's historic district. Romantic Jacuzzi Suites await you. Staying at The Carriage Inn will become a memory that longs to be enjoyed again. Listed in the National Register of Historic Places.
StayAtTheCarriageInn@comcast.net www.carriageinn.com

The Cottonwood Inn
199 Mill Lane 25414
800-868-1188 304-725-3371
Joe & Barbara Sobol

95-135 $US BB
5 rooms, 5 pb
Most CC, *Rated*
C-ltd/S-no/P-no/H-no
Some French

Full breakfast
Sitting room, library,
fireplace, large porch with
rockers and swing, grand
piano

Escape . . . to the quiet! Gracious B&B on 6 acres of sylvan land near many historic and recreational attractions.
barbara@italysource.com www.mydestination.com

Gilbert House of Middleway
Middleway Nat'l Historic
District 25414
304-725-0637
Bernie Heiler

70-140 $US BB
3 rooms, 3 pb
Visa, MC, •
C-ltd/S-ltd/P-no/H-ltd
German, Spanish

Full gourmet breakfast
Complimentary drinks,
snacks, special dietary meals
available on request
Fireplaces, piano, living
room, etc.

Near Harper's Ferry. HABS listed, 18th-century stone house on original settlers' trail into Shenandoah Valley.
gilberthousebb@yahoo.com www.gilberthouse.com

CHARLES TOWN

Hillbrook Inn
4490 Summit Point Rd 25414
800-304-4223 304-725-4223
Carissa & Christopher Zanella

200-325 $US BB
9 rooms, 9 pb
Visa, MC, AmEx, Cash,
Checks, *Rated*
C-yes/S-no/P-ltd/H-ltd
Open Thu-Sun

Two-course Gourmet
breakfast
A sumptuous 7-course
dinner accompanied with
wine, 3-course luncheons or
5 course high tea
Restaurant, sitting room,
library, antiques, art
collection, gardens, weekend
weddings, quilting

Elegant B&B accommodations in an award-winning European style inn. Romantic 7-course dinner. Extensive grounds and gardens with a stream, ponds, and a terrace with a fountain. Eclectic art, antiques and books in beautiful, old-world surroundings.
✉ info@hillbrookinn.com ✪ www.hillbrookinn.com

ELKINS

Tunnel Mountain B&B
Old Rt 33 26241
888-211-9123 304-636-1684
Anne & Paul Beardslee

89-99 $US BB
3 rooms, 3 pb
Rated
C-ltd/S-no/P-no/H-no

Full breakfast
Restaurant nearby
Sitting room with fireplace,
patio, wooded paths, A/C,
scenic views, cable TV

Romantic country fieldstone B&B nestled in scenic West Virginia. Mountains next to National Forest and recreational areas. Also, a vacation cottage available along the river next to national forest. Sleeps up to six people, large deck, private setting.
✪

GLEN DALE

Bonnie Dwaine
505 Wheeling Ave 26038
888-507-4569 304-845-7250
Bonnie & Sidney Grisell

89-125 $US BB
5 rooms, 5 pb
Most CC, *Rated*, •
C-ltd/S-ltd/P-no/H-no

Full or continental plus
breakfast
Complimentary snacks, soft
drinks, ice machine
Great room, living room,
library, fireplaces, A/C,
spacious, high speed
Internet in each room

Victorian warmth, style & elegance with the convenience of modern amenities. This beautiful home displays many antiques. Five guestrooms, each with fireplace private ensuite bath, whirlpool tub & shower and more. Candlelight gourmet breakfast on weekends.
✉ Bonnie@Bonnie-Dwaine.com ✪ www.Bonnie-Dwaine.com

HARPERS FERRY

Harpers Ferry Guest House
800 Washington St 25425
304-535-6955
Al & Alison Alsdorf

90-125 $US BB
3 rooms, 3 pb
Visa, MC, Cash, Checks,
Rated
C-ltd/S-no/P-no/H-ltd

Full breakfast
Snacks, cold drinks
Sitting room, cable TV, mini
theater, free wireless, frame
shop, off-street parking

A wonderfully friendly B&B located right in Historic Harpers Ferry, WV. Walk to shops, restaurants, and Harpers Ferry National Park.
✉ hfgh@comcast.net ✪ www.harpersferryguesthouse.com

Laurel Lodge
844 East Ridge St 25425
304-535-2886
Chris Craig

95-150 $US BB
3 rooms, 2 pb
Visa, MC, AmEx, Cash
C-ltd/S-no/P-no/H-no

Full breakfast
Wired and wireless high-
speed Internet; televisions
available upon request

Relax in our 1915 stone bungalow overlooking the Potomac River gorge in historic Harper's Ferry. Immerse yourself in the history of the area or enjoy the spectacular natural beauty while hiking, biking, or floating down the Shenandoah or Potomac Rivers.
✉ innkeeper@laurellodge.com ✪ www.laurellodge.com

LEWISBURG

General Lewis Inn
301 E Washington St 24901
800-628-4454 304-645-2600
Jim & Mary Noel Morgan

110-155 $US EP
25 rooms, 25 pb
Most CC, *Rated*, •
C-yes/S-no/P-no/H-yes

Breakfast, lunch & dinner are
not included in the rate but
are served in our dining
room
A/C, phones, TV, private
baths, garden

*The General Lewis Inn & Restaurant is a unique blend of the old & new, created &
operated by the same family since 1928.*
✉ info@generallewisinn.com ✪ www.generallewisinn.com

MARTINSBURG

Aspen Hall Inn
405 Boyd Ave 25401
304-260-1750
Charles Connolly & Rebecca
Frye

100-140 $US BB
4 rooms, 4 pb
Visa, MC, Cash, Checks
C-ltd/S-no/P-no/H-no

Continental plus breakfast
Microwave and refrigerator
available for guest use
Breakfast room, cable TV,
wireless Internet access,
grounds, creek, gazebo, A/C,
massage therapy

*Hospitality meets history in this magnificent 250-year-old inn. At the gateway to the Shenan-
doah Valley, 80 mi from Washington, DC. and at the hub of a wide variety of activities and
historic sites. Special weekly & monthly rates for extended stay guests.*
✉ aspenhallinn@verizon.net ✪

ROMNEY

Hampshire House 1884
165 North Grafton St 26757
888-806-1131 304-822-7171
Dana Monopoli

110-425 $US BB
5 rooms, 5 pb
Most CC, *Rated*
C-ltd/S-ltd/P-ltd/H-ltd

Full breakfast
Available upon request:
dinner, lunch, afternoon tea,
wine & cheese, appetizers, &
more
Central A/C, cable TV,
Internet Access (including
wireless), and sound
proofing

*We invite you to stay with us at Hampshire House 1884, located in the beautiful Potomac
Highlands of West Virginia. You will enjoy the charm of the 1800's in this completely
restored period Inn.*
✉ HH1884@aol.com ✪ www.HampshireHouse1884.com

SHEPHERDSTOWN

Thomas Shepherd Inn
300 W German St 25443
888-889-8952 304-876-3715
Jim Ford & Jeanne Muir

115-190 $US BB
6 rooms, 6 pb
Most CC, *Rated*
C-ltd/S-no/P-no/H-no

Full breakfast
Coffee and tea service, with
homemade biscotti, is
available for early risers
Large indoor & outdoor
guest common areas,
wireless Internet, gracious
hospitality, TV/DVD/VCR

*Nestled in the beautiful lower Shenandoah Valley, we offer guests comfortably elegant
accommodations & gracious hospitality in a historic setting within a few blocks of fine
dining & shopping.*
✉ info@thomasshepherdinn.com ✪ www.thomasshepherdinn.com

Wisconsin

ASHLAND

The Inn at Timber Cove	85-135 $US BB	Full breakfast
1319 Sanborn Ave 54806	5 rooms, 5 pb	Evening dessert and tea
715-682-9600	Visa, MC	served in your cottage or
Brian & Tina Miller	C-ltd/S-no/P-no	suite.
	Portuguese	Fireplace room, tea room,
		porches, refrigerator, air
		conditioning, bicycles

A 20-acre northern Wisconsin estate and a name that conjures up images of peaceful seclusion, of quiet and cozy reflection. These are the things we desire all our guests to experience.
✉ timbercove@mailstation.com ☯ www.innattimbercove.com

Second Wind Country Inn	89-159 $US BB	Full breakfast
B&B	3 rooms, 3 pb	Gathering room with board
30475 Carlson Road 54806	Visa, MC, Cash, Checks	games, outdoor bonfire,
715-682-1000	C-ltd/S-no/P-no/H-yes	breakfast on the deck or in
Mark and Kelly Illick		your room, library

Second Wind hosts a beautiful view of Lake Superior's Chequamegon Bay area. Our name, Second Wind, reflects just what we want for you, our guests, to experience.
✉ catchyourbreath@secondwindcountryinn.com ☯ www.secondwindcountryinn.com

BARABOO

Inn at Wawanissee Point	199-299 $US BB	Full Gourmet Breakfast
E 13609 Tower Rd 53913	4 rooms, 4 pb	Evening wine & cheese,
608-355-9899	Most CC, •	complimentary bottled
Trudy & Dave Holdener	S-no/P-no/H-yes	water, tea & snacks
	German	Gardens, fitness area, sauna,
		shiatsu massage, outdoor
		spa, robes, lounge, elevator,
		DVD library

This romantic bed & breakfast hideaway, with its magnificent blend of luxurious accommodations & captivating views is on a secluded 42 acre wooded estate in the majestic Baraboo Bluffs. Next to Devil's Lake State Park & near Wisconsin Dells attractions.
✉ info@innatwawanisseepoint.com ☯ www.innatwawanisseepoint.com

Pinehaven B&B	99-145 $US BB	Full breakfast
E 13083 Hwy 33 53913	4 rooms, 4 pb	Fishing, whirlpool, gazebo,
608-356-3489	Visa, MC, *Rated*	rowboat and paddleboat
Lyle & Marge Getschman	C-ltd/S-ltd/P-no/H-no	

Beautiful view of bluffs, small private lake. Tranquil setting. Take a stroll, fish, admire the Belgian draft horses. Relax. Acres to roam. No smoking indoors.
☯ www.pinehavenbnb.com

BELLEVILLE

Cameo Rose Victorian	159-249 $US BB	Full breakfast
Country Inn	5 rooms, 5 pb	Snacks during check-in, 4–6
1090 Severson Rd 53508-9728	Visa, MC, Disc, Cash,	PM
866-424-6340 608-424-6340	Checks, *Rated*	120 scenic acres, gardens,
Dawn & Gary Bahr	C-ltd/S-no/P-no/H-ltd	views, pond, waterfalls,
		woodland, trails, suites,
		whirlpools, fireplaces

What a difference a night makes at a genuine Madison Wisconsin bed and breakfast getaway on 120 scenic acres near vibrant Madison, University of Wisconsin, New Glarus – Little Switzerland and Mount Horeb – Little Norway. "Best breakfast in Midwest" Award.
✉ innkeeper@cameorose.com ☯ www.cameorose.com

BURLINGTON

Hillcrest Inn & Carriage House
540 Storle Ave 53105
800-313-9030 262-763-4706
Mike & Gayle Hohner

120-240 $US BB
6 rooms, 6 pb
Visa, MC, Cash, Checks
C-ltd/S-ltd/P-no/H-no

Full breakfast
Warm & cold beverages, chocolate snack, chocolate lovers package, "Chocolate in every breakfast."
Scenic porch views, fireplaces & whirlpools, historic estate, romance baskets, packages.

Romantic, luxurious & private. Wooded four acre estate with magnificent view. English flower gardens & walking paths. Stately 1908 Edwardian home with elegant Carriage House. Our image is "Chocolate In Every Breakfast" and we love to fulfill desires.
✉ hillcrest@thehillcrestinn.com ✪ www.thehillcrestinn.com

CAMP DOUGLAS

Sunnyfield Farm
N6692 Batko Rd 54618
888-839-0232 608-427-3686
John & Susanne Soltvedt

80-120 $US BB
4 rooms, 2 pb
Rated
C-yes/S-no/P-yes/H-no

Full breakfast
Tea, coffee, snacks
Sitting room, porch, cat & dog on the premises(for those with pet allergies)

Nature lover's paradise. Choose from three bedrooms on second floor or a third floor studio. Aroma of coffee and fresh baked rolls start the day. 160 acres to hike, or snooze on the porch.
✉ info@sunnyfield.net ✪ www.sunnyfield.net

CEDARBURG

Stagecoach Inn B&B
W61 N520 Washington Ave 53012
888-375-0208 262-375-0208
Brook & Liz Brown

85-150 $US BB
12 rooms, 12 pb
Most CC, *Rated*, ●
C-ltd/S-no/P-no/H-no

Continental plus breakfast
Afternoon wine and root beer social; coffee & teas available all day in the Pub area
Wireless Internet, Pub sitting area, outdoor deck, gardens, whirlpools, VCR's in TVs & VCR library

Restored 1853 stone Inn furnished with antiques. Whirlpool and fireplace suites. Convenient location within Historic Cedarburg district, walking distance to shops and restaurants.
✉ innfo@stagecoach-inn-wi.com ✪ www.stagecoach-inn-wi.com

DE PERE

James Street Inn
201 James St 54115
800-897-8483 920-337-0111
Kevin Flatley & Joan Hentges

89-249 $US BB
36 rooms, 36 pb
Most CC, ●
C-yes/S-yes/P-no/H-yes

Continental plus breakfast
Coffee & tea are always available, wine and cheese are served every afternoon
Bar service, fireplaces, private decks, whirlpool, complimentary pass to nearby fitness club

A country inn hidden just outside of Green Bay. Built on the foundation of a c.1858 mill; the river literally flows beneath it. The James Street Inn offers distinctive accommodations in a historic and beautiful setting.
✉ jamesst@netnet.net ✪ www.jamesstreetinn.com

EAU CLAIRE

Otter Creek Inn
2536 Hwy 12 54702
866-832-2945 715-832-2945
Shelley & Randy Hansen

110-210 $US BB
6 rooms, 6 pb
Most CC, *Rated*
S-no/P-no/H-no

Full breakfast
Beverages during check-in times
Rooms have TVs/VCRs, video library for your use

Each guestroom has a whirlpool for 2! Many with fireplaces. Choice of breakfast entree, serving time, breakfast in bed. Spacious 3-story English Tudor, antiques, in-ground pool. Many restaurants nearby. ✉ info@ottercreekinn.com ✪ www.ottercreekinn.com

EPHRAIM

Eagle Harbor Inn
9914 Water St 54211
800-324-5427 920-854-2121
Nedd & Natalie Neddersen

98-256 $US BB
9 rooms, 9 pb
Visa, MC, Disc, *Rated*
C-yes/S-no/P-no/H-yes

Continental Plus Breakfast
Homemade afternoon treats
Pool with current, sauna,
fitness room, croquet,
gardens, playground, grills,
beach, golf nearby

An intimate, New England-style country inn. Filled with antiques, period wallpapers, warm hospitality, books & a fireplace room. An excellent breakfast served garden side in summer! Close to boating, beaches, golf, antiquing, galleries and more.
✉ nedd@eagleharbor.com ◑ www.EagleHarborInn.com

FISH CREEK

Thorp House Inn & Cottages
4135 Bluff Ln 54212
920-868-2444
Christine & Sverre Falck-
Pedersen

115-225 $US BB
11 rooms, 11 pb
Cash, Checks, *Rated*
C-ltd/S-no/P-ltd/H-no
Norwegian

Continental plus breakfast
Restaurants nearby
Sitting room with fireplace,
some guestrooms and
cottages with fireplace, some
with whirlpool

Antique-filled, historic home backed by wooded bluff, overlooking bay. 5 guestrooms with fireplace, 4 with whirlpool. 6 kid-friendly cottages. On National Register.
✉ innkeeper@thorphouseinn.com ◑ www.thorphouseinn.com

GREEN BAY

The Astor House
637 S Monroe Ave 54301
888-303-6370 920-432-3585
Greg & Barbara Robinson

120-159 $US BB
5 rooms, 5 pb
Most CC, *Rated*, •
C-ltd/S-no/P-no/H-no

Continental plus breakfast
Complimentary wine
Double whirlpools, gas
fireplaces, phone, TV, stereo,
VCR, DVD players

Luxurious and romantic, close to all of Green Bay's major attractions. Our five uniquely styled guestrooms indulge our guests in comfort with amenities that include; private baths, double whirlpool tubs, fireplaces, TV with VCR and DVD, and WiFi.
✉ astor@execpc.com ◑ www.astorhouse.com

HARTLAND

Monches Mill House
W301 N9430 Hwy E 53029
262-966-7546
Elaine Taylor

50-85 $US BB
4 rooms, 2 pb
C-yes/S-no/P-yes/H-yes
French

Continental plus breakfast
Lunch in summer by
reservation, fixed menu with
set price
Sitting room, hot tub, bikes,
tennis, canoeing, hiking

House built in 1842, located on the bank of the mill pond. Furnished in antiques, choice of patio, porch or gallery for breakfast enjoyment. Jacuzzi, barn, pond, Oconomowoc River and pond canoeing, tennis court, hiking on Ice Age trail.
◑

HAZEL GREEN

Wisconsin House
2105 E Main St 53811
877-854-2233 608-854-2233
Ken & Pat Disch

80-140 $US BB
8 rooms, 6 pb
Most CC, *Rated*, •
C-yes/S-no/P-no/H-no

Hearty Full Breakfast
Complimentary soft drinks,
beverages & delicious
cookies always available
Library with piano, garden,
gazebo, porches,

An historic, comfortably furnished bed and breakfast, we're located just 10 miles north of Galena, Illinois, 13 miles west of Dubuque, Iowa, and 15 miles south of Platteville, Wisconsin. So close, so different! Stay with us and enjoy each of them.
✉ wishouse@mhtc.net ◑ www.wisconsinhouse.com

HUDSON

Phipps Inn	139-219 $US BB	Full breakfast
1005 3rd St 54016	6 rooms, 6 pb	Complimentary sodas &
888-865-9388 715-386-0800	Visa, MC, AmEx	bottled water available at all
Mary Ellen & Rich Cox	C-ltd/S-no/P-no/H-no	times. Lots of chocolate
		snacks, too!
		Billiards room, whirlpool
		tubs, gas fireplaces, antique
		furnishings, curtained bed

Described as the "Grande Dame" of Queen Anne houses in the St. Croix Valley, the Phipps Inn is a luxurious 1884 Victorian mansion nestled in the charming setting of Hudson's historic Third Street.
✉ mrcox@presenter.com ✪ www.phippsinn.com

LA FARGE

Trillium Cottage	95-110 $US BB	No meats offered
E10596 East Salem Ridge Rd	2 rooms, 2 pb	Homemade breads &
54639	C-yes/S-ltd/P-no/H-no	cookies, jams & jellies, apple
608-625-4492		cider, teas, coffees,
Rosanne Boyett		lemonade in warm weather
		Furnished kitchen, books,
		magazines 85 acres of
		organic fields, woods, tree-
		lined brook

Trillium Country Cottage is a family farm featuring two cozy, private cottages tucked into the hills of the Kickapoo Valley in southwestern Wisconsin. A working farm with cattle, sheep, geese, chickens, friendly farm cats and organic gardens.
✉ info@trilliumcottage.com ✪ www.trilliumcottage.com

LAKE GENEVA

Case's Turn of the Century	95-195 $US BB	Full country breakfast
1599 N Hillside Rd 53147	4 rooms, 4 pb	Cheese & cracker tray, fruit,
262-248-4989	Most CC, *Rated*, •	wine, fresh-baked cookies
Brenda & Bob Case	C-ltd/S-ltd/P-no/H-no	Sitting room, parlor, picture
		gallery, library, TV/VCR,
		whirlpools, boat parking

This Victorian Estate is furnished with a collection of antiques and near antiques. A visit to Case's B&B is like a trip back in time to the gracious era of the 19th century. Lavish flower gardens and trees surround the home.
✉ Reservations@casesbnb.com ✪ www.casesbnb.com

Eleven Gables Inn on Lake	149-330 $US BB	Continental Plus breakfast
Geneva	8 rooms, 8 pb	Private pier, swim, fish, hike,
493 Wrigley Dr 53147	Most CC, *Rated*, •	bike rental, courtesy phone,
262-248-8393	C-yes/S-no/P-yes/H-ltd	fax
Annabelle		

Lakeside historic inn. Romantic bedrooms, bridal chamber, and now with country cottage and family coach house. Fireplaces, down quilts, wet bars, TVs, balconies.
✉ egi@lkgeneva.com ✪ www.lkgeneva.com

French Country Inn	155-295 $US BB	Full breakfast
W 4190 West End Rd 53147	33 rooms, 33 pb	Award-winning Kirsch's
262-245-5220	Visa, MC, Disc, Cash	Restaurant is located on the
Mary Haggermaker	C-yes/S-ltd/P-no/H-ltd	premises
		Dining room, parlour,
		fireplaces, armoires,
		whirlpools, balconies, pool

Our B&B is located in the heart of Wisconsin's famous Geneva Lakes area on the south shore of Lake Como. The Lake Geneva area is both romantic and picturesque with its lazy winding country roads filled with many fine old homes and mansions.
✉ innkeeper@frenchcountryinn.com ✪ www.frenchcountryinn.com

664   Wisconsin

LAKE GENEVA

General Boyd's B&B
W2915 So Lake Shore Dr 53147
888-248-3543 262-248-3543
Robert & Susan Morton

105-155 $US BB
4 rooms, 4 pb
Most CC, *Rated*, •
C-ltd/S-no/P-yes/H-ltd

Full breakfast
Afternoon tea and snacks
and maybe a sip of wine
before dinner, or after?
Available:Highspeed
Wireless Internet & FAX. For
special occasions, your
choice of flowers or wine.

Rolling hills surround this lovely historic home & the classic timber-pegged barns. The five acres are shrouded with greenery dominated by native white oaks.
✉ genlboydsbb@sbcglobal.net ۞ www.generalboydsbb.com

Golden Oaks Mansion
421 Baker St 53147
800-823-2921 262-248-9711
Nancy Golden Bell & Chef
David Bell

145-295 $US BB
7 rooms, 7 pb
Most CC, *Rated*, •
C-ltd/S-no/P-ltd/H-no

Five Course Served Breakfast
Rooms include gourmet
served breakfast for two,
wine, bottled water,
chocolates, & flowers
Drawing room, dining room,
clubroom, breakfast porch,
verandah

Solitude will be found as you succumb to the charm and tranquility of this Lake Geneva Mansion. Our relaxed atmosphere is the perfect setting in which to revitalize your body, mind, and spirit.
✉ info@goldenoaksmansion.com ۞ www.goldenoaksmansion.com

Lazy Cloud Lodge
W4033 Hwy 50 53147
262-275-3322
Keith and Carol Tiffany

130-230 $US BB
19 rooms, 19 pb
Most CC
S-no/P-no/H-yes

Continental plus breakfast
Picnic basket dinner,
complimentary wine &
snacks
Double whirlpool, fireplace,
fridge, microwave, private
entrance, candles

"Lazy Cloud caters to hopeless romantics . . . with double whirlpool baths & cozy fireplaces in each suite . . . A magical place to fall in love all over again."
✉ love@lazycloud.com ۞ www.lazycloud.com

Roses B&B
429 South Lake Shore Dr 53147
262-248-4344
Ruth Ann Bae

140-165 $US BB
4 rooms, 4 pb
Visa, MC, Cash, Checks
S-no/P-no/H-no
May 1 – Nov 15

Two-course Gourmet
Breakfast
complimentary wine, snacks
(in room)
Glassed in porch, deck,
sitting room, books &
magazines, fireplaces in all
rooms, TV/VCR

Comfortable casual elegance one block from Geneva Lake and a short stroll to downtown Lake Geneva. Large comfortable rooms, three with king size beds and private baths, full three-course breakfast served in glassed in porch. Complimentary wine and snacks.
✉ rooms@rosesbnb.com ۞ www.rosesbnb.com

MADISON

Annie's Garden
2117 Sheridan Drive 53704
608-244-2224
Annie & Larry Stuart

179-229 $US BB
1 rooms, 1 pb
Most CC, *Rated*
C-ltd/S-no/P-no/H-no

Full breakfast
Snacks
Library, tennis court, Jacuzzi,
beach, bicycle storage,
fireplaces, suites

Beautiful garden B&B with views all seasons in a 300 acre park. Walk the lake shore, meadows, or woods. One 2-bedroom suite with private bath. Six minutes to downtown and campus.
✉ innkeeper@anniesinmadison.com ۞ www.anniesinmadison.com

MADISON

Arbor House, An Environmental Inn 3402 Monroe St 53711 608-238-2981 John & Cathie Imes	110-230 $US BB 8 rooms, 8 pb Visa, MC, AmEx, *Rated* C-yes/S-no/P-no/H-yes	Full breakfast on weekends Continental breakfast weekdays Cable, massage available, cross-country skiing, 5 fireplaces

Historic landmark across from UW Arboretum has an environmental emphasis. Minutes from the Capitol & UW campus. Corporate rates.
🌐 www.arbor-house.com

The Parsonage B&B 5508 Broadhead Street 53558 877-517-9869 608-838-7383 Craig & Cathy	79-125 $US BB 6 rooms, 4 pb Visa, MC, Cash, Checks C-yes/S-no/P-no/H-no	Full breakfast Jacuzzi available, CD, sitting areas, some views

We pride ourselves on being a convenient and economical Madison, Wisconsin B&B, where a clean room, a gourmet breakfast, a warm environment and a friendly stay are provided to all who pass through our doors. Come experience the best that we have to offer!
✉ Parsonage@chorus.net 🌐 www.parsonagebandb.com

NEWBURG

Welcome Home B&B 4260 W Hawthorne Dr (Hwy Y) 53060 262-675-2525 Diane Miller	65-75 $US BB 2 rooms, 2 pb Cash, Checks C-ltd/S-no/P-ltd/H-yes	Self serve continental + breakfast Dried fruits and nuts, WI cheese, candy dish, coffee, tea, cocoa, popcorn Kitchenette, sitting room, fireplace, screen porch, whirlpool tubs, trails, cableTV/VCR/DVD campfire

Acres of rural silence surround our country home set on a hillside where trees sing in a breeze. Sit on the screen porch to view woodland & prairie, a BIG sky, wildlife. Build a bonfire. Soak in a whirlpool tub. Snuggle under a quilt. Take a hike. Relax!
✉ welcomehome@hnet.net 🌐 www.welcomehomebb.com

OSCEOLA

Pleasant Lake B&B 2238 60th Ave 54020 800-294-2545 715-294-2545 Richard & Charlene Berg	109-159 $US BB 3 rooms, 3 pb Visa, MC, Cash, Checks, *Rated* C-ltd/S-no/P-no/H-no	Full breakfast Snacks Jacuzzis, fireplaces, use of canoe & paddleboat

Nestled on 12 wooded acres overlooking quiet, semi-private Pleasant Lake. Three guestrooms offer queen beds, double whirlpool tubs, lake views & crackling campfires with the stars reflecting on the moonlit lake.
✉ pllakebb@centurytel.net 🌐 www.pleasantlake.com

St. Croix River Inn 305 River St 54020 800-645-8820 715-294-4248 Ben & Jennifer Bruno, Cheryl Conarty	125-250 $US BB 7 rooms, 7 pb Visa, MC C-ltd/S-no/P-no/H-ltd	Full gourmet breakfast Complimentary coffee, tea, snacks, and fresh baked sweet treats! River views, fitness rm, wireless Internet, central heat/air, movies, cds, games, turndown service.

Stay in one of our luxurious suites and enjoy breathtaking panoramic riverviews, turndown service, and a delicious gourmet breakfast served to your room. Experience timeless luxury on the river.
✉ innkeeper@stcroixriverinn.com 🌐 www.stcroixriverinn.com

PRESCOTT

Arbor Inn
434 North Court St 54021
888-262-1090 715-262-2222
John & Deb Sherman

119-199 $US BB
4 rooms, 4 pb
Most CC, *Rated*
C-ltd/S-ltd/P-ltd/H-no
Spanish

Four Course Gourmet
Afternoon tea, snacks, wine, beer
In-house massage, Cable TV, VCR's, DVD's, Choice: in-room breakfast, Lrg Jacuzzi tubs, in-room fridges

Located in the scenic St. Croix River Valley, only 30 minutes south of Minneapolis/St Paul, this 1902 inn is reminiscent of an English country cottage. Vines, porches, and 4 antique filled rooms set the scene for relaxation and romance year round.
✉ relax@thearborinn.com ◐ www.thearborinn.com

REEDSBURG

Parkview B&B
211 N Park St 53959
608-524-4333
Tom & Donna Hofmann

80-98 $US BB
4 rooms, 2 pb
Visa, MC, AmEx, Cash,
Rated, •
C-ltd/S-no/P-no/H-no

Full breakfast
Snacks, wake-up coffee
Sitting room, bicycle storage, park across the street, wi-fi, can accommodate special diets

1895 Victorian home with comfortable antiques, across from City Park. Central to Wisconsin Dells, Baraboo, Spring Green, bike trails. Located in the Park Street Historic District, one block from Main Street.
✉ info@parkviewbb.com ◐ www.parkviewbb.com

Pine Grove Park B&B Guest House
S2720 Hwy V 53959
866-524-0071 608-524-0071
Jean & Kurt Johansen

130-185 $US BB
4 rooms, 4 pb
Most CC
S-no/P-no/H-ltd

Gourmet Country Breakfast
High speed Internet, Walking Trails, Snowshoeing, Large Pond, Whirlpool tubs, fireplace

Enjoy a private romantic getaway in one of our guesthouses with covered porch surrounded by woodlands, wetlands, and native wildflowers, a perfect travel destination for your Wisconsin honeymoon or romantic vacation.
✉ info@pinegroveparkbb.com ◐ www.pinegroveparkbb.com

STEVENS POINT

A Victorian Swan on Water
1716 Water St 54481
800-454-9886 715-345-0595
Joan Ouellette

75-145 $US BB
4 rooms, 4 pb
Most CC, *Rated*, •
C-ltd/S-no/P-no/H-no

Full breakfast
Snacks, complimentary wine
Sitting room, library, garden, TV room, free wireless Internet access, in-house massages

Enjoy award winning breakfast, beautiful gardens, a secret room and whirlpool or a sauna in this 1889 Victorian home. Central Wisconsin location.
✉ victorianswan@charter.net ◐ www.victorianswan.com

Dreams of Yesteryear
1100 Brawley St 54481
715-341-4525
Bonnie & Bill Maher

75-160 $US BB
6 rooms, 4 pb
Most CC, *Rated*
C-ltd/S-ltd/P-no/H-no

Full breakfast
Afternoon tea, snacks
Sitting room, library, tennis court, hot tub, bike trail map, pool, 2 3-room suites

Three story antique embellished National Historic Register Victorian Queen Anne. Only B&B within designated Historic Downtown Main Street Business District. Conveniently located, still Dreams is set in a quiet historic neighborhood surrounded by gardens.
✉ bonnie@dreamsofyesteryear.com ◐ www.dreamsofyesteryear.com

STURGEON BAY

Black Walnut Guest House
454 N 7th Ave 54235
877-255-9568 920-743-8892
Geri Ballard & Mike Shatusky

110-160 $US BB
4 rooms, 4 pb
Visa, MC, Disc, Cash,
Checks
C-ltd/S-no/P-no/H-no

Continental plus breakfast
Private bath, queen bed,
whirlpool tub, antiques, in-
room refrigerator, fireplace,
balcony, TV/DVD

The Black Walnut Guest House features 4 uniquely individual guestrooms, detailed with charm & romance. Sumptuous surroundings, a whirlpool tub, a fireplace and a delicious breakfast served to your room each morning set the mood for your romantic getaway.
✉ stay@blackwalnut-gh.com ⊙ www.blackwalnut-gh.com

Chanticleer Guest House
4072 Cherry Rd 54235
866-682-0384 920-746-0334
Bryon Groeschl & Darrin Day

120-350 $US BB
12 rooms, 12 pb
Most CC
S-no/P-no/H-yes

Continental plus breakfast
Snacks
Jacuzzis, swimming pool,
suites, fireplaces

Nestled among the orchards of Door County, comfort, relaxation and romance were fore-most on the owners' minds when they created Chanticleer Guest House. Get the best of both words – rustic charm and the pampered feel of a Bed and Breakfast.
✉ information@chanticleerguesthouse.com ⊙ www.chanticleerguesthouse.com

---

Garden Gate B&B
434 N Third Ave 54235
877-743-9618 920-743-9618
Robin Vallow

100-145 $US BB
4 rooms, 4 pb
Visa, MC, Cash, Checks
C-ltd/S-no/P-no/H-no

Elegant Breakfast
Whirlpool bath for two,
fireplace A/C, ceiling fans,
TV, VCR, CD/DVD players

Experience romantic elegance in our charming 1890 Victorian home. A choice of comfort-able rooms with well appointed baths assure you of a relaxing visit. And remember . . . breakfast is our signature.
✉ stay@doorcountybb.com ⊙ doorcountybb.com

Inn at Cedar Crossing
336 Louisiana St 54235
920-743-4200
Steve & Kelly Hellmann

75-195 $US BB
9 rooms, 9 pb
Visa, MC, Disc, *Rated*
C-ltd/S-no/P-no/H-no

Full hot breakfast with
choices
Complimentary afternoon
tea, coffee, lemonade & fresh
baked cookies each day
Restaurant & pub on site
offering casual & fine dining,
as well as happy hour
specials

Elegant 1884 inn situated in historic district near shops, restaurants, and museums. Nine romantic rooms feature antique decor, fireplaces, whirlpools, and all the modern ameni-ties. Full hot breakfast with entree choices and afternoon cookies included.
✉ innkeeper@innatcedarcrossing.com ⊙ www.innatcedarcrossing.com

---

Reynolds House B&B
111 S 7th Ave 54235
877-269-7401 920-746-9771
Heather Hall

60-200 $US BB
5 rooms, 5 pb
Visa, MC, AmEx, Cash,
Rated, •
C-ltd/S-no/P-no/H-no

Full breakfast
Afternoon tea, snacks
Sitting room, library,
Jacuzzis, suites, fireplaces,
cable TV

This architecturally significant Queen Anne Home built in 1900 is located within walking distance of downtown Sturgeon Bay. Romantic setting, luxurious accommodations.
✉ hahull@reynoldshousebandb.com ⊙ www.reynoldshousebandb.com

Scofield House
908 Michigan St 54235
888-463-0204 920-743-7727
Dan & Vicki Klein

80-220 $US BB
6 rooms, 6 pb
Visa, MC, Disc, Cash,
Checks
S-no/P-no/H-no

Full breakfast
Complimentary snacks in the
p.m.
A guest phone, refrigerator,
and library of
complimentary video
movies. Wi-fi access.

Luxury and comfort are yours to enjoy, when you surround yourself in the ambience of the Scofield House.
✉ scofldhs@charterinternet.net ⊙ www.scofieldhouse.com

STURGEON BAY

White Lace Inn	70-235 $US BB	Full breakfast
16 N 5th Ave 54235	18 rooms, 18 pb	Complimentary cookies,
877-948-5223 920-743-1105	Most CC, *Rated*	beverages
Dennis & Bonnie Statz	C-ltd/S-no/P-no/H-ltd	Sitting room, gazebo, gardens, fireplaces, whirlpools, TV/VCRs, Wi-Fi

The White Lace Inn's four historic homes are nestled in a friendly old neighborhood, bordered by a white picket fence, surrounded by gardens. We have 18 rooms and suites—15 have a fireplace—12 have a whirlpool—9 have both a fireplace and whirlpool
✉ Romance@WhiteLaceInn.com ◐ www.whitelaceinn.com

VIROQUA

Viroqua Heritage Inn B&B	70-125 $US BB	Full breakfast
220 E Jefferson St 54665	8 rooms, 6 pb	Porches, fireplace,
888-4-HERINN 608-637-3306	Most CC	woodwork, dining room,
Nancy L. Rhodes	C-yes/S-no/P-ltd/H-no	balcony, garden, pond

Located in Wisconsin's Hidden Valley Region, these two elegant Victorian-era B&Bs offer a unique and memorable opportunity to simply relax or enjoy the many activities available around Vernon County.
✉ rhodsent@mwt.net ◐ www.herinn.com

WAUSAU

Rosenberry Inn	90-150 $US BB	Full breakfast
511 Franklin St 54403	8 rooms, 8 pb	We can accommodate most
800-336-3799 715-842-5733	Visa, MC	special diets.
Barry & Linda Brehmer	C-yes/S-no/P-no/H-no	Antiques, refrigerators, coffee makers, CD players, free wireless Internet, fireplaces, TV, library.

The historic-home-turned-B&B features beautiful stained-glass windows, wide halls, a carved oak stairway that leads to the second floor, and a sweeping front porch overlooking Franklin Street – making it the ideal lodging accommodations for you.
✉ innkeeper@rosenberryinn.com ◐ www.rosenberryinn.com

WISCONSIN DELLS

Bowman's Oak Hill B&B	85-175 $US BB	Full breakfast
4169 St Hwy 13 53965	4 rooms, 4 pb	Afternoon and evening
888-253-5631 608-253-5638	Most CC	snacks.
David & Nancy Bowman	C-ltd/S-no/P-no/H-no some Spanish	Robes, spa showers, TV/VCR, video library, large deck with fire pit, sitting room & sun porch.

"Where comfort comes with your key." We are only minutes from all of the Dells area attractions. It is our goal to help you have a fun filled restful vacation or weekend getaway.
✉ bowmansoakhillbb@aol.com ◐ www.bowmansoakhillbedandbreakfast.com

Wyoming

CHEYENNE

Nagle Warren Mansion
222 E 17th St 82001
800-811-2610 307-637-3333
Jim Osterfoss

138-195 $US BB
12 rooms, 12 pb
Visa, MC, AmEx, Cash,
Rated, •
C-yes/S-no/P-ltd/H-yes
Spanish, German

Full breakfast
Afternoon tea; full bar;
luncheons, dinners &
reception. Poor Richards &
Capitol Grill for dinners.
Hot tub, fireplaces, TV,
phone, Wireless, bicycles,
parlour, garden

Ideally situated, the mansion offers all of today's needs in a comfortable & elegant ambience. Let us spoil you while you explore the original West.
✉ jim@nwmbb.com ✺ www.naglewarrenmansion.com

CODY

K3 Guest Ranch
30 Nielsen Trail 82414
888-587-2080 307-587-2080
Jerry Kinkade

159-199 $US BB
4 rooms, 4 pb
Visa, MC, Disc, Cash,
Rated, •
C-yes/S-ltd/P-ltd/H-ltd

Full Western-Style Breakfast
Our breakfast is cooked over
an open fire and served
outdoors in the true Western
way
TV, refrigerator, soft drinks,
hair dryers, irons, toiletries,
books, games, movies,
fishing gear

Welcome to the K3 Guest Ranch Bed and Breakfast located just outside Buffalo Bill's Old West town of Cody, WY. The cowboy and Indian motif will allow you to step back in time for a first hand experience of the real "Wild West." Eat breakfast outdoors.
✉ stay@k3guestranch.com ✺ www.k3guestranchbedandbreakfast.com

DEVILS TOWER

Devils Tower Lodge
#37 State Road 110 82714
888-314-5267 307-467-5267
Frank Sanders

140-225 $US BB
4 rooms, 4 pb
Visa, MC, *Rated*
C-yes/S-no/P-no/H-ltd

Full breakfast
Dinner served on request for
a small fee
Outdoor spa, living room,
piano, indoor climbing wall,
exercise room

Our unique B&B is nestled on 21 acres of prairie and pine, at the base of Devils Tower. Each room has dramatic Tower vistas, queen beds, open-air view decks and private baths. A full country breakfast is served.
✉ frank@devilstowerlodge.com ✺ www.devilstowerlodge.com

Lytle Creek Inn B&B
289 Lytle Creek Rd 82714
307-467-5599
Peter Kim & Dee Carroll

95-125 $US BB
3 rooms, 2 pb
Visa, MC, AmEx, Cash,
Checks
C-ltd/S-no/P-no/H-ltd

Full breakfast
Fresh baked goods always
available for your pleasure.
Free wireless Internet, over
sized decks for your viewing
and relaxing pleasure.

Lytle Creek Inn B&B is nestled at the edge of the western Black Hills in northeastern Wyoming among the oaks and pines that line Lytle Creek Valley. With rural landscapes, and the creek running past our back door, we have something for everyone.
✉ info@lytlecreekinn.com ✺ www.lytlecreekinn.com

FOUR CORNERS ───────────────────────────────

Four Corners Country Inn B&B 24695 US Hwy 85 – PMB 177 82715 307-746-4776 Hazel & Lori Johnson	25-45 $US MAP 7 rooms, 1 pb Visa, MC C-yes/S-no/P-ltd/H-ltd	Full Breakfast Dinner included Sitting room, business traveler accommodations, full RV hookups

The Four Corners Country Inn and B&B is an awesome, quiet, clean, peaceful place, perfect for that special country living experience. Located in the beautiful Black Hills of Wyoming.
✉ 4cornerscountryinn@rtconnect.net www.rtconnect.net/~4cornerscountryinn

JACKSON ───────────────────────────────

A Teton Tree House 6175 Heck of a Hill Rd 83014 307-733-3233 Denny & Sally Becker	195-455 $US BB 6 rooms, 6 pb Visa, MC, Disc, *Rated*, • C-ltd/S-no/P-no/H-no A little Spanish	"Healthy Heart"—no eggs or meat Juices, coffee, teas, beer and wine are available A Grand room with games and books galore

Tucked away, and yet close to two national parks and the town of Jackson, this B&B offers a quiet retreat amidst the trees with unique, comfortable rooms and a warm, friendly atmosphere.
✉ atetontreehouse@aol.com www.cruising-america.com/tetontreehouse

Bentwood B&B 4250 Raven Haven Rd 83001 307-739-1411 Peter & Jennifer Tignor	215-365 $US BB 5 rooms, 5 pb Most CC, *Rated* C-yes/S-no/P-no/H-yes	"Hearty & Sumptuous" Full brkfst Afternoon tea, hors d'oeuvres, evening wine & cheese, personal chef prepared meals available Great Room w/ 3-story river rock fireplace, library, deep Jacuzzi bathtubs, private fireplace & deck

Award-winning "architectural marvel" (Frommer's 2003), a 6,000 sq. ft. log inn with five guest suites, constructed using massive 200 year old logs brought in from Yellowstone Nat'l Park after the great fire of 1988, on 3 old growth acres.
✉ info@bentwoodinn.com www.bentwoodinn.com

Teton View B&B 2136 Coyote Loop 83014 866-504-7954 307-733-7954 Carol and Franz Kessler	189-289 $US BB 3 rooms, 3 pb Visa, MC, Disc C-yes/S-no/P-yes/H-no German Summer and Fall	Guests love our breakfasts Afternoon treat Hot tub, whirlpool tub

Experience the grandeur of the Grand Tetons in our family environment, blending Western hospitality with a European flair. A visit to Teton View B&B in Jackson Hole, neighbor to Yellowstone and Grand Teton National Parks, will bring you back!
✉ info@tetonview.com www.TetonView.com

The Wildflower Inn 3725 N Teton Village Rd 83002 307-733-4710 Ken & Sherrie Jern	250-400 $US BB 5 rooms, 5 pb Visa, MC, *Rated*, • C-yes/S-no/P-no/H-no	Fantastic breakfast A casual afternoon beverage and snack . . . .homemade lemonades, teas, lovely wines, fresh cookies Wireless access, trekking poles, bikes, day packs, great advice on things to see and do in the area

Named "Best of the West" by Sunset Magazine and featured in "Cooking with Paula Deen" the Wildflower Inn is a beautiful log inn on 3 gorgeous acres complete with mountain views. Famous for fantastic food, luxurious rooms and wonderful attention to detail
✉ jhwildflowerinn@cs.com www.jacksonholewildflower.com

LARAMIE

Vee Bar Guest Ranch
2091 State Hwy 130 82070
800-483-3227 307-745-7036
Jim Lefty & Carla Cole

120-150 $US BB
9 rooms, 9 pb
Most CC
C-yes/S-ltd/P-no/H-ltd

Hot food, fruits, breads
Dinners offered Friday &
Saturday nights, steaks &
seafood, served in a warm &
cozy atmosphere
Hot tub; workout room;
saloon w/pool table, board
games & juke box; private
fishing; horses

The Vee Bar located near Laramie, Wyoming just 2½ hours north of Denver, Colorado is a world-renown family guest and dude ranch with a relaxed atmosphere sure to feel like home to your entire family.
✉ veebar@veebar.com 🌐 www.veebar.com

MOOSE

Lost Creek Ranch
Highway 89 83012
307-733-3435
The Halpin Family

$US AP
13 rooms, 13 pb
Visa, MC, Cash
C-yes/S-no/P-no/H-yes
May – October

Price includes all meals
Special requests or dietary
needs can be accommodated
through prior arrangement,
all meals included.
Horses, full spa, skeet,
hiking, airport shuttle, cardio
equip, hot tub, pool, Kid's
Club

Privately owned ranch between Grand Teton Nat'l Park and Bridger-Teton Nat'l Forest. All the excitement of a traditional ranch + luxurious comforts of a full-service spa in the region's most spectacular location. Weekly stays only. Inquire about rates.
✉ ranch@lostcreek.com 🌐 www.lostcreek.com

SARATOGA

Wolf Hotel
101 E Bridge St 82331
307-326-5525
Doug & Kathleen Campbell

67-110 $US EP
10 rooms, 10 pb
Visa, MC, AmEx, Cash
C-yes/S-no/P-no/H-no

No breakfast available.
Lunch: 11:30–2, Mon-Sat.
Dinner: 6–9 (9:30 summer),
Mon-Thu, 6–9:30, Fri–Sat (10
summer), Sun Closed
Five Suites, semi-private
room for meetings and
private parties, porch, pool
table, restaurant, bar.

Built in 1893 as a stage coach stop and listed in the National Register, the Hotel is noted for its fine food and convivial atmosphere. The Hotel anchors Saratoga, one of America's top ten small towns. No stop lights, but a warm, friendly town.
✉ kcampbell@union-tel.com 🌐 www.wolfhotel.com

TETON VILLAGE

Alpenhof Lodge
3255 W Village Dr 83025
800-732-3244 307-733-3242
Mark Johnson

129-509 $US BB
43 rooms, 43 pb
Most CC, *Rated*, •
C-yes/S-no/P-ltd/H-no
German
Winter, Spring, Summer

Full buffet breakfast
Lunch, dinner, restaurant,
bar service, apres ski
Spas, swimming pool,
fireplaces, balconies

European style lodging and dining at the base of the Jackson Hole Mountain Resort, located 1 mile from Grand Teton National Park. Warm hospitality, friendly service, cozy rooms and hearty food.
✉ res@alpenhoflodge.com 🌐 www.alpenhoflodge.com

Tell your hosts Pamela Lanier sent you.

WILSON————————————————————————————

Sassy Moose Inn
3895 W Miles Road 83014
800-356-1277 307-413-2995
Craig Kelley

79-229 $US BB
5 rooms, 5 pb
Most CC
C-yes/S-no/P-yes/H-no

Full breakfast
Wireless Internet & cable TV,
hot tub, firepit, daily
housekeeping, fireplaces

Each of our five guestrooms has its own charm in our comfortable 4800 square foot western-style log home and petit spa. Perfect for a romantic getaway or the ideal family vacation. You can even Rent-The-Inn for your family reunions, or business retreats.

✉ craigerwy@aol.com ⊕ www.sassymoose.com

Canada

Alberta

CALGARY

11th Street Lodging B&B
1307 11th St SW T2R 1G5
403-209-1800
John & Peter

65-200 $CAN BB
3 rooms, 2 pb
Visa, MC
C-ltd/S-no/P-no/H-no

Continental breakfast
Sun porch, garden, cable
television, telephone and
high speed wireless

*Built in 1912, our home has offered guesthouse accommodation since the end of the last
world war. Extensive renovations have graced the building since. All rooms have cable
television, telephone and high speed wireless and ADSL ports.*
✉ bedandbreakfast@11street.com ♦ www.11street.com

**1910 Elbow River Manor
B&B**
2511 Fifth St SW T2S 2C2
866-802-0798 403-802-0799
Sharon

155-210 $CAN BB
3 rooms, 3 pb
Visa, MC, AmEx
C-ltd/S-no/P-no/H-no

Full breakfast
Snacks and beverages
Fitness equipment, spa
services, Internet access,
gardens, laundry services.

*Built in 1910, Elbow River Manor is a luxury bed and breakfast which offers a unique &
unforgettable experience for our guests. The fully restored 4000 square foot arts & craft
style vintage inn features multiple guest common areas, patios and gardens.*
✉ reservations@elbowrivermanor.com ♦ www.elbowrivermanor.com

A Good Knight B&B
1728 7 Ave NW T2N 0Z4
800-261-4954 403-270-7628
Kathryn Knight

95-175 $CAN BB
3 rooms, 3 pb
Visa, MC
C-ltd/S-no/P-no/H-no

Full breakfast
Coffee and tea
Computer and wireless
Internet available, cable
television, deck & garden

*A Good Knight B&B provides lodging in a newly-built, Victorian-styled home, set amongst
the peacefulness and charm of one of Calgary's oldest neighborhoods. The B&B features
gorgeous rooms, all with private baths.*
✉ stay@agoodknight.com ♦ www.agoodknight.com/home.html

Along River Ridge
1919 52 Street NW T3B 1C3
888-434-9555 403-247-1330
Dianne Haskell

85-114 $CAN BB
2 rooms, 2 pb
Visa, MC, AmEx, *Rated*
C-ltd/S-no/P-no/H-ltd

Full breakfast
Afternoon tea, snacks, lunch
& dinner available, beverage
station
Solarium, library, Jacuzzis,
fireplaces, cable TV, VCR,
DVD, large screen TV,
wireless Internet

*Experience 'A Touch of Country in the City,' with the Bow River at your doorstep, city
center less than 15 minutes away, and the majestic Rocky Mountains less than one hour
away. Canada Select 4 star restful, romantic "all seasons" retreat.*
✉ haskell@alongriverridgebb.com ♦ www.alongriverridgebb.com

**Calgary Historic B&B at
Twin Gables**
611-25 Ave SW T2S 0L7
866-271-7754 403-271-7754
Henry & Deirdre Brost

89-225 $CAN BB
3 rooms, 3 pb
Visa, MC, AmEx,
Rated, •
C-ltd/S-no/P-no/H-no

Full breakfast
24 hour beverage center
Parlor, living room, solarium,
computers, Internet access &
business center

*Your private entrance to gracious suites; tastefully decorated. Walk to downtown, Conven-
tion Center, Stampede park. 1 block away from the Elbow River, restaurants, shopping.
Free parking. Computer in rooms. Canada Selects 5 Stars.*
✉ stay@twingables.ca ♦ www.twingables.ca/

CALGARY————————————————————————————————

Calgary Westways Guesthouse	89-169 $CAN BB	Full breakfast
216 25th Ave SW T2S 0L1	5 rooms, 5 pb	Romantic dinner for two
866-846-7038 403-229-1758	Visa, MC, AmEx,	Sitting room, Jacuzzis,
Jonathon Lloyd & Graham	*Rated*, •	fireplaces, cable TV,
McKay	C-ltd/S-no/P-yes/H-no	computer station work
	French	station, bicycles

1912 Arts & Craft style Heritage Home, 20 min walk to downtown Calgary. All rooms have ensuite or private bath, modern amenities. The only 3 Diamond AAA/CAA rated B&B in Calgary. Ask about our Rolls Royce pickup service!
✉ westways@shaw.ca ❂ www.westways.ab.ca/calgary.html

Harvest Lake	95-150 $CAN BB	Full or Continental Breakfast
60 Harvest Lake Crecent NE	3 rooms, 3 pb	Complimentary coffee bar,
T3K 3Y7	Visa, MC	tea, hot chocolate
877-226-3025 403-226-3025	C-yes/S-no/P-no/H-no	Garden, sunroom, WiFi
David & Kathi Hamilton	French	Internet access, sitting room
		with fireplace, TV/DVD/VCR
		and VHS library

Situated on a peaceful and picturesque waterfront setting, this Bed & Breakfast is just minutes away from Calgary's International Airport.
✉ info@harvestlakebnb.com ❂ www.harvestlakebnb.com

Hughes House B&B	65-140 $CAN BB	Continental breakfast
315 11th Ave NE T2E 0Z2	3 rooms, 3 pb	Beverages and snacks
403-804-4431	Cash, Checks	Dining room and piano
Kelly Smith	C-yes/S-no/P-no/H-no	

Hughes House is an elegantly renovated 1914 Victorian home. From the moment you enter the foyer you'll feel the difference. As the 21st century begins, Hughes House provides a welcoming warm atmosphere in an early 1900's setting.
✉ info@hugheshouse.ca ❂ www.hugheshouse.ca

Kensington Riverside Inn	259-459 $CAN BB	Full breakfast
1126 Memorial Dr NW T2N 3E3	19 rooms, 19 pb	Coffee tray & newspaper left
	Most CC	at your door, bedside
403-228-4442	C-ltd/S-no/P-ltd/H-yes	chocolates
Denis Barghshoon		Fireplace, library, patio,
		balcony, view or Jacuzzi,
		Aveda bath amenities, turn
		down service

Offering unmatched river, city and garden views, Kensington Riverside Inn features 19 distinctive rooms and suites that drape guests in sophisticated luxury. Dine at Chef's Table, renowned for sumptuous 5-course tasting menus and eclectic wines.
✉ info@kensingtonrivresideinn.com ❂ www.kensingtonriversideinn.com

Springcreek B&B	100-125 $CAN BB	Full breakfast
256 43 Ave NW T2K 0H6	2 rooms, 2 pb	Tea, hot chocolate, apple
403-803-6235	Visa	cider, etc.
Ken & Betty Jane Janzen	C-yes/S-no/P-no/H-no	Jacuzzi in Sunset Room,
		Internet, sitting room/library
		television and fridge

The Springcreek B&B is located in Calgary, Alberta, Canada in a quiet neighbourhood of Highland Park near Highland Golf Course, downtown, Deerfoot Trail and the airport.
✉ kenandbj@spring-creek.ca ❂ www.spring-creek.ca

COCHRANE

Mountview Cottage
27 Mount View Est T4C 2B2
877-433 8193 403-932-4586
Neil & Marilyn Degraw

95-125 $CAN BB
2 rooms, 1 pb
Visa, MC, *Rated*, •
C-ltd/S-no/P-no/H-yes
April 1 to December 30

Full breakfast
Evening tea or coffee or hot
chocolate with home-baked
pastries
Sitting area with frig,
fireplace, library, pool table,
deck, barbeque, horse
shoes, corral for horse

Valley view with Rocky Mountains 180 degrees on the horizon. Beautiful park-like gardens with fish pond & benches to relax on 4 acres in the foot hills. Enjoy a stroll through wild flowers, tumbleweed & prairie wool. Experience howling coyotes.
✉ degraw@nucleus.com

HINTON

Mountain Vista
1217 Mountainview Estates
T7V 1X3
780-865-2470
Livi & Trent Waller

99-125 $CAN BB
1 rooms, 1 pb
Visa, MC
S-no/P-no

Full breakfast
Cold beverages
Fireplace, satellite TV, pool
table, darts, kitchenette,
wrap around deck

Nestled in the foothills of the Alberta Rocky Mountains, on an acreage setting. Wildlife and scenic beauty is abundant from the moment you arrive. There are many natural wonders only a short drive or walk from our house.
✉ mtn.vista@moradnet.ca ◑ www.mountainvistabb.com

JASPER EAST

Overlander Mountain Lodge
Hwy 16 T7V 1X5
877-866-2330 780-866-2330
Garth & Kathy Griffiths

145-475 $CAN BB
27 rooms, 27 pb
Visa, MC, AmEx,
Rated, •
C-yes/S-no/P-no/H-ltd
French, Spanish

Continental breakfast
Breakfast included mid-
October to mid-June.
Seasonal lunch menu.
Dinner service starts at 5:30
pm.
Lounge, seasonal patio,
library, fireplaces,
conference & wedding
facilities

Beautiful, romantic lodge overlooking Jasper National Park & the Canadian Rockies. Spectacular views & casual fine dining. Weddings, horseback riding, mountain biking/hiking trails, special packages.
✉ overland@telusplanet.net ◑ www.overlandermountainlodge.com

RED DEER

Dutchess Manor Retreat
4813 54 St T4N 2G5
403-346-7776
Susan Uiterwijk

80-100 $CAN BB
3 rooms, 2 pb
Visa, *Rated*
S-no/P-no

Full breakfast
Spa facilities & treatments,
patio, porch, living room

We invite you to experience the most relaxing and indulgent time of your life. We provide delicious home cooked food and with our full service spa on premises, all your cares and woes will disappear.
✉ dmanor@telusplanet.net ◑ www.dmanorretreat.com

British Columbia

ANMORE

The Silver Door
1075 Thomson Rd V3H 4X9
604-949-1322
Reesa Devlin

150-195 $CAN BB
2 rooms, 2 pb
Visa, MC, *Rated*, •
C-ltd/S-no/P-no/H-no

Full breakfast
Snacks, fridge for personal
items, refreshments, bed
snacks, fruit basket, tea,
juices coffee
Heated in-ground pool, hot
tub, steam room, exercise
room, pool table, private
home theater, library

A retreat where the mountains touch the stars, where the deer roam and the black bear comes to call. This is our home. The color silver denotes an air of sophistication and excellence and defines the exemplary service and amenities that you will find.
✉ rdevlin@thesilverdoor.ca 🜚 www.thesilverdoor.ca

BRENTWOOD BAY

Benvenuto B&B
1130 Benvenuto Ave. V8M 1J6
888-544-1088 250-544-1088
Carrie & Clint Coleman

90-165 $CAN BB
3 rooms, 3 pb
Visa, MC
C-yes/S-no/P-ltd/H-no

Full breakfast
Coffee, variety of teas, hot
chocolate, water, etc.
Private balcony, free wireless
Internet, laundry and ironing
facilities.

Benvenuto Bed and Breakfast near Victoria, is a three room (suites) enchanting B&B. We are perfect for vacation accommodation and romantic getaways. Situated in the country-side, all B&B guestrooms have private entrances.
✉ reservations@benvenutobandb.com 🜚 www.benvenutobandb.com

The Boathouse B&B
746 Sea Dr, RR 1 V8M 1B1
866-654-9370 250-652-9370
Harvey Jean Merritt

215-250 $CAN BB
1 rooms, 1 pb
Visa, MC, AmEx
C-ltd/S-no/P-no/H-no
German
April 1 to September 30

Continental breakfast
Ask about our limited self-
catering option (rates reflect
breakfast option choice)
9-ft. rowing dinghy, private
dock

A unique ocean-front cottage offering seclusion, privacy and the luxury of quiet time for two non-smoking adults. Dock your boat or seaplane. Row in our dinghy to Butchart Gardens or a picnic spot. There is off-street parking in our yard.
✉ boathouse@shaw.ca 🜚 www.members.shaw.ca/boathouse

Brentwood Bay B&B
7247 W Saanich Rd V8M 1H4
250-652-2012
Evelyn Hardy

75-215 $CAN BB
3 rooms, 3 pb
Cash, Checks
C-ltd/S-ltd/P-no/H-ltd

Full breakfast
Facilities for weddings,
celebrations and corporate
events.

Brentwood Bay Heritage House, located only minutes from the famous Butchart Gardens. This charming B&B complete with antiqued stained glass windows, hardwood floor, with Persian carpets and offers every amenity to make your stay restful.
✉ info@bcheritagehouse.com 🜚 www.bcheritagehouse.com

BRENTWOOD BAY

Brentwood Lighthouse B&B	135-175 $CAN BB	Full breakfast
759 Sea Dr V8M 1B1	2 rooms, 2 pb	Afternoon refreshments
250-652-9733	Visa, MC	served on our deck. Picnic
Nancy & Allan Adams	C-ltd/S-no/P-ltd/H-no	Baskets prepared upon
		request(additional cost)
		Small library of books and
		DVDs, wireless Internet,
		fireplaces

Brentwood Lighthouse is a west coast contemporary home; custom built for privacy and comfort.Butchart Gardens is a short walk from us. Serenity is our keynote but we are just twenty minutes from downtown Victoria and the Ferry and Airport Terminal
✉ info@brentwoodlighthousebb.com ◑ www.brentwoodlighthousebb.com

BURNABY

Albert View Cottage	130-150 $CAN EP	Complimentary tea and
4840 Albert St. V5C 2H3	3 rooms	coffee. Self catered kitchen.
604-299-4549	Most CC	washer and dryer facilities,
Martin & Ellen O'Reilly	C-yes/S-ltd/P-no/H-no	T.V. with DVD player,
		Internet, telephone with free
		local calling

Albert View Cottage offers a luxurious 3 bedroom home setting in magnificent Burnaby, British Columbia. Relax in front of the TV, wake up in beautiful Vancouver, and go to bed after watching beautiful sunsets on our fully furnished 300sq ft patio.
✉ jackeen@telus.net ◑ www.albertviewcottage.com/index.html

Haddon House B&B	125-195 $CAN BB	Full breakfast
5558 Buckingham Ave V5E	3 rooms, 3 pb	Complimentary cold
2A1	Visa, MC, *Rated*	beverages, coffee maker/tea,
888-522-2363 604-522-2363	C-ltd/S-ltd/P-ltd/H-no	small kitchenette with
Johannes & Marie-Louise	German	microwave
Stolz		Office center, wireless
		Internet, 2 bikes, DVD and
		book library, piano, radio,
		telephone, gas BBQ

This Dutch Colonial Heritage home is situated amidst the natural beauty of Deer Lake, in the heart of Burnaby's cultural district. Newly renovated with modern amenities and classic elegance. Only 15 mins from downtown Vancouver. Check website for rates.
✉ info@haddonhouse.ca ◑ www.haddonhouse.ca

CHEMAINUS

Chemainus Tudor Inn	100-165 $CAN BB	Full breakfast from menu
10050 Panorama Ridge Rd	3 rooms, 3 pb	Coffee & tea
V0R 1K0	Visa, MC, *Rated*, •	Ocean views, quiet &
877-246-2393 250-246-2393	C-yes/S-no/P-no/H-no	spacious rooms, private
Alan & Linda Donohue		baths, lounge, satellite TV,
		Internet access, computer

The Chemainus Tudor Inn is everything you look for in a B&B. Quiet and spacious rooms, stunning ocean and mountain views, delicious breakfasts, and convenient access to area attractions.
✉ reservations@chemainustudorinn.com ◑ www.chemainustudorinn.com

---

Tell your hosts Pamela Lanier sent you.

Cobble House B&B, Cobble Hill, BC

CLINTON

Poolside Paradise B&B
405 Spruce Ave V0K 1K0
250-459-7990
Lorne & Luan Bernhardt

85-100 $CAN BB
3 rooms, 3 pb
Cash
C-yes/S-ltd/P-no/H-ltd
American Sign
Language, some simple
Spanish

Full Gourmet breakfast
Cocoa, teas, herbal teas,
coffee, specialty coffees,
popcorn and snacks are
always available
Indoor pool, hot tub, BBQ,
guest den, in-room
VCRs/TVs, kitchen, library,
guest dining room, gardens

Three theme bedrooms, queen beds, private baths, lg. indoor pool, hot tub, garden, solarium, guest dining room & den, TV, videos. Historic Clinton, Gold Rush Trail, Hwy 97, hike, ski, fish, hunt, snowmobile, lakes, wildlife, birds. Romantic, quiet, private
✉ info@poolsideparadisebb.com ◐ www.poolsideparadisebb.com

COBBLE HILL

Cobble House B&B
3105 Cameron-Taggart Rd V0R
1L6
866-743-2672 250-743-2672
Ingrid & Simon Vermegen

105-115 $CAN BB
3 rooms, 3 pb
Visa, MC, •
C-yes/S-ltd/P-no/H-ltd
Dutch, German

Full breakfast
Complimentary tea or coffee
Wireless Internet, sitting
room, Jacuzzi, cable TV, bar
fridge in each room,
individual heat control

Cobble House is a peaceful haven in the heart of Vancouver Island's growing wine and culinary region in the Cowichan Valley. Centrally located on a forested acreage, we are still only 45 minutes north of Victoria. ✉ cobblehouse@shaw.ca ◐ www.cobble-house.com

GIBSONS

Beachside Cottage Rentals
484 Marine Dr V0N 1V0
604-987-2591
Marie and Jim Bensley

100-300 $CAN EP
5 rooms, 2 pb
Cash, Checks
C-yes/S-ltd/P-ltd/H-ltd

Self-contained full kitchen
swim float and boat ramp,
pool table in big house,
barbecue, laundry facilities
and deck

Beachside Cottage Rentals offers two waterfront accommodations for 2–15 people with spectacular views located in beautiful Gibsons, British Columbia.
✉ jimbensley@shaw.ca

GIBSONS——————————————————————————————

Bonniebrook Lodge
1532 Oceanbeach Esplanade
V0N 1V5
877-290-9916 604-886-2887 .
Lina Jakobs

179-299 $CAN BB
7 rooms, 7 pb
Visa, MC, AmEx, *Rated*
C-yes/S-no/P-yes/H-ltd

Full Canada select breakfast
Room service from onsite
fine dining restaurant
"chasters," bar fridge
stocked.
Ocean view suites, private
Jacuzzi, LCD/TV, pure cotton
linens, feather bedding,
sunset views.

Well-appointed oceanfront inn. Seven Suites with Jacuzzi for two, fireplace, TV/ VCR, complimentary movies, CD player, fridge, complimentary coffee, King beds, private sundecks, ocean view steps from beach, full breakfast included.
✉ info@bonniebrook.com ◐ www.bonniebrook.com

Caprice B&B
866-886-4270 604-886-4270
Lois Choksy & Jeanette
Panagapka

125-165 $CAN BB
3 rooms, 3 pb
Visa, MC
S-no/P-yes/H-ltd

Full breakfast
swimming pool, hot tub, and
terrace

Enjoy this pet friendly, spacious, oceanview home surrounded by majestic cedars and gardens. Luxurious rooms, ensuite baths, private entrances, kitchenettes, hot tub and swimming pool. Recommended by the Lonely Planet Guide for British Columbia.
✉ stay@capricebb.com ◐ www.capricebb.com

HALFMOON BAY————————————————————————

Granite Ridge B&B
604-885-9233
Anne & Marty

140-170 $CAN BB
2 rooms, 2 pb
Visa, MC
S-no/P-no/H-ltd
Estonian
May 1 – Oct 31

Continental breakfast
Complimentary Port or
Sherry
Hot tub, gardens, patios and
decks

Granite Ridge B&B offers four of life's most important R's: Rest, Relaxation, Rejuvenation and Romance. Our adult oriented non-smoking waterfront B&B and Cottage is located on the Sunshine Coast in British Columbia, Canada.
✉ graniteridge@dccnet.com ◐ www.graniteridgebb.com

Halfmoon Bay Cabin
8617 Redrooffs Rd V0N 1Y1
866-333-2468 604-885-0764
Dr. John Richmond

199-269 $CAN EP
Visa, MC
C-yes/S-no/P-no/H-ltd

Full equipped kitchen, chef
available for meals, outdoor
shower, Jacuzzi, spa
services, BBQ

This rustic, yet luxurious 1300 sq. ft. cabin, sky lit throughout, provides complete privacy with a spectacular ocean view. Situated on a hill surrounded by an English country garden, the cabin is just steps from the waterfront and has its own beach.
✉ stay@halfmoonbaycabin.com ◐ www.halfmoonbaycabin.com

Loghouse at Halfmoon Bay
5635 Mintie Rd V0N 1Y2
604-885-4771
Charles & Vanessa

115-140 $CAN BB
2 rooms, 2 pb
Visa, MC, *Rated*
C-yes/S-no/P-no/H-ltd

self catered with full supplies
Fruit juice, Coffee/Tea.Fresh
fruit Supplies restocked
daily.
Wireless Internet,
TV/DVD/VCR. HotTub on
main deck, BBQ on patio.

Welcome to The Loghouse at Halfmoon Bay, a unique West Coast bed & breakfast located on British Columbia's beautiful Sunshine Coast. Enjoy the warmth and charm of staying in a loghome only a stone's throw from the beach.
✉ info@loghouse-halfmoonbay.com ◐ www.loghouse-halfmoonbay.com

682   British Columbia

s

HALFMOON BAY

Rockwater Secret Cove Resort
Ole's Cove Rd V0N 1Y0
877-296-4593 604-885-7038
Kevin Toth

119-399 $CAN
38 rooms, 38 pb
Most CC
C-yes/S-no/P-ltd/H-yes

Continental except June 21-Sept. 15
Cocktail bar, restaurant
Patio, games room, outdoor heated pool, massage

The best kept secret among Sunshine Coast Accommodations is Rockwater Secret Cove Resort. What was once the Lord Jim's Resort Hotel, this magical oasis has been transformed into a private paradise for distinguished guests.
✉ reservations@rockwatersecretcoveresort.com ◐ www.rockwatersecretcoveresort.com

KELOWNA

A Lakeview Heights B&B
3626 Royal Gala Dr V4T 2N9
800-967-1319 250-707-1234
Anne & Mike Murphy

85-145 $CAN BB
3 rooms, 3 pb
Visa, MC, *Rated*
C-ltd/S-no/P-no/H-ltd
French, some German & Italian.

Extensive gourmet breakfast
Vegetarian or special diets by advance request, welcoming beverage on arrival, in-room tea/coffee
Guest living room, view patio with outdoor furniture, local area touring assistance & reservations

Imagine . . . a Canada Select 4-star B&B with spectacular lake, mountain & vineyard views, where you can enjoy luxury accommodations with private bathrooms, warm hospitality and gourmet breakfasts at an affordable price . . . that's A Lakeview Heights B&B.
✉ info@mountainsideaccommodations.com
◐ www.mountainsideaccommodations.com/lakeview/

Aaron's Pool & Spa B&B
2160 Wilkinson St V1Y 3Z8
250-860-6814
Rick & Marie Gruenke

95-150 $CAN BB
2 rooms, 2 pb
Visa, *Rated*
C-yes/S-no/P-no/H-ltd

Continental plus breakfast
In-room coffee and fridge
In-ground swimming pool, spa-suite, TV/DVD Movies and cable Internet in rooms, pampering inclusions

We are tucked into a nice, quiet residential area, conveniently located close to the lake, shopping and downtown Kelowna. Enjoy breakfast in the privacy of your own suite or when weather permits, on the pool patio.
✉ info@kelownabb.com ◐ www.kelownabb.com

Accounting for Taste B&B
1108 Menu Rd V1Z 2J5
866-769-2836 250-769-2836
Rosemary & Michael Botner

90-120 $CAN BB
3 rooms, 3 pb
Visa, MC, AmEx
C-ltd/S-no/P-no/H-no
French

continental /optional cooked dish
Coffee, tea, juice
2 Night Minimum Deck, sunroom, lounge, cable TV, Hot tub, high speed Internet, Wine Tours, wine library

On Mount Boucherie in British Columbia's Okanagan Valley, with views of the lake and vineyards. Just minutes from downtown Kelowna for shopping, theatres, museums, galleries, spas, fine dining and historic sites.
✉ rosemary@accountingfortaste.ca ◐ www.accountingfortaste.ca

KIMBERLEY

House Alpenglow B&B
3 Alpenglow Ct V1A 3E3
877-257-3645 250-427-0273
Merna & Darrell Abel

80-150 $CAN BB
3 rooms, 3 pb
Cash, Checks, •
C-ltd/S-no/P-no/H-ltd

Full breakfast
Tea, coffee, juice
Hot tub, cozy down duvets, antiques, handcrafted furniture, free wireless Internet

Enjoy spectacular mountain scenery from this authentic, uniquely designed Bavarian 'Haus.' Private, spacious wood adorned rooms, handcrafted king & queen beds, down duvets, private baths.
✉ alpenglo@telus.net

LADNER

Canoe Pass Inn
3383 River Road West V4K 3N2
604-946-6780
Jackie & Colin Smith

130-150 $CAN BB
2 rooms, 2 pb
Cash, Checks
C-ltd/S-no/P-ltd/H-no

Full breakfast
Colins smoked salmon lox and fresh salmon when in season for the BBQ at wholesale prices.
hot tub, barbeque and fire pit

Our unique floating home bed and breakfast is located at the mouth of the Fraser River in an historically rich area of Ladner known as Canoe Pass. Enjoy the experience of spending a night on a floating home with an uninterrupted view of the river.
✉ canoepassinn@dccnet.com ○ www.canoepassinn.com

LUND

Sevilla Island Resort
604-414-6880
Ian Hobbs and Donna Kaye Hobbs

145-185 $CAN BB
4 rooms, 4 pb
Visa, MC
C-ltd/S-ltd/P-no/H-ltd

Full breakfast
Full meal plan available which includes lunch, dinner and snacks for $50 per person
oceanside hot tub, exercise room

At Sevilla Island Resort we focus on providing both relaxing oceanside vacations and memorable eco-adventures to guests of all ages. We offer oceanfront accommodations, exquisite meals, and a wide range of eco-adventure activities.
✉ info@sevillaislandresort.ca ○ www.sevillaislandresort.ca

MADEIRA PARK

Ruby Lake
Site 20, Comp 25, RR#1 V0N-2H0
800-717-6611 604-883-2269
The Cogrossi Family

80-220 $CAN EP
21 rooms, 11 pb
Visa, MC
C-yes/S-no/P-ltd/H-yes

Dinner available in award winning authentic Italian "Trattoria" restaurant
Therapeutic massage, private hiking & mountain biking trails, canoe rentals

Surrounded by a bountifully rich natural environment and an inspiring cultural landscape. Savor each and every moment. Enjoy our discrete lakeside accommodation, dine on our outstanding Italian cuisine, relax in our beautiful landscaped gardens.
✉ info@rubylakeresort.com ○ rubylakeresort.com

MALAHAT

Prancing Horse Retreat
573 Ebedora Ln V0R 2L0
877-887-8834 250-743-9378
Elaine & Allan Dillabaugh

175-375 $CAN BB
7 rooms, 7 pb
Visa, MC, AmEx,
Rated, •
C-ltd/S-no/P-no/H-ltd

Full breakfast
Restaurant
Tennis, Jacuzzis, pool, suites, fireplace, cable TV, accommodations for business travelers

Our Victorian Villa is located just 20 minutes north of Victoria, overlooking the ocean and snow-capped Olympic mountain range. Our luxury suites offer double tubs and fireplaces.
✉ stay@prancinghorse.com ○ www.prancinghorse.com

NORTH VANCOUVER

Beachview Retreat
611 Beachview Dr V7G 1P8
604-782-5999
Julie & Eric Startup

155-195 $CAN BB
3 rooms, 3 pb
Visa, MC, *Rated*
C-ltd/S-no/P-no/H-no

4–5 course breakfast
Afternoon tea
Billiard and entertainment room, sun soaked front porch, sitting room with fireplace and garden

Our home, with beautiful ocean and mountain views offers you a retreat within minutes of Vancouver City and many world class outdoor recreational opportunities. Come and be pampered by the food, the location and the hospitality.
✉ julie@beachviewretreat.com ○ www.beachviewretreat.com

NORTH VANCOUVER

Crystal's View
420 Tempe Crescent V7N 1E6
604-987-3952
Crystal Davis

115-265 $CAN BB
3 rooms, 3 pb
Visa, MC, •
C-ltd/S-no/P-no/H-no

Full breakfast
Tea, coffee, cookies,
refreshments
Panoramic views, double
Jacuzzi-Thermomasseur,
chromatherapy, sundeck,
fireplace

*Outstanding panoramic views from every room from this luxurious Bed and Breakfast.
Experience modern comforts and Canadian hospitality. Centrally located in a quiet neighborhood. Canada Select 4½ Stars!*
✉ Crysview@shaw.ca ◐ www.bc-bedandbreakfast.com

Lockhaven Waterfront B&B
2136 Lockehaven Rd V7G 1X6
604-928-8225
Denise and Noulan Bowker

165-339 $CAN BB
2 rooms, 2 pb
Visa, MC, AmEx,
Rated, •
S-no/P-no/H-no

Full breakfast
In-suite kitchenettes
Self-serve use of shared
laundry, in-suite computers,
wireless Internet & phones,
free long distance

*Lockehaven is a true waterfront property with stunning ocean and mountain views, only
25 minutes to downtown Vancouver. Large suites with king beds, expansive decks, kitchenettes, computers w/WiFi and outdoor hot tubs. See our website for photos & video*
✉ hosts@lockehaven.ca ◐ www.lockehaven.ca

Ocean Breeze Executive
462 E 1st St V7L 1B7
800-567-5171 604-988-0546
Margaret Gradowska

129-195 $CAN BB
5 rooms, 5 pb
Visa, MC, AmEx, •
C-ltd/S-no/P-ltd/H-no
Polish, Italian, German

Full breakfast
Complimentary purified
water daily in each room.
Dietary/low fat option upon
request. Fresh fruits.
Wireless Internet,
kitchenettes in some rooms,
patios with view of
Vancouver, daily newspaper

*This Vancouver B&B is perfect alternative to Vancouver hotels; well appointed rooms with
fridges for cold drinks/medications, coffee makers, private bathrooms, TVs, wireless Internet, ocean views. Centrally located to all attractions. Walk to waterfront.*
✉ info@oceanbreezevancouver.com ◐ www.oceanbreezevancouver.com

---

ThistleDown House
3910 Capilano Rd V7R 4J2
888-633-7173 604-986-7173
Rex Davidson

95-295 $CAN BB
6 rooms, 6 pb
Visa, MC, *Rated*, •
C-ltd/S-no/P-no/H-no
German
February to November

Full Gourmet Breakfast
Afternoon tea of homemade
pies, cakes or pastries
served in the lounge or the
garden; sherry & port
Goose down or silk-filled
duvets, antiques, fireplaces,
library, gardens, WiFi, full
concierge

*Internationally acclaimed, ThistleDown is a 1920 Craftsman-style, heritage-listed home,
restored with great care & filled with antiques, handcrafted furnishings & works of art from
around the world. Breakfast is deliciously gourmet, service is impeccable.*
✉ info@thistle-down.com ◐ www.thistle-down.com

PEMBERTON

Greenwood Country Inn
1371 Greenwood St V0N 2L0
877-977-5607 604-894-5607
Margit de Haan

95-150 $CAN BB
3 rooms, 3 pb
Visa, MC
C-yes/S-no/P-ltd/H-ltd
German

Full breakfast
Home-cooked dinners by
request
Kitchenette, small weddings,
local art, decks, fireplace,
lounge

Nestled on a bluff high above the village of Pemberton, British Columbia, offering unparalleled views from every direction. Take your breath away beauty!
✉ reserve@greenwoodcountryinn.com ◐ www.greenwoodcountryinn.com

PENDER ISLAND

Oceanside Inn
4230 Armadale Rd V0N 2M0
800-601-3284 250-629-6691
Bill & Maggie Rumford

159-239 $CAN BB
3 rooms, 3 pb
Visa, MC
S-no/P-no/H-no
May thru October

Full breakfast
Complimentary beverages in room
Sitting room, library, private hot tubs/deck, suites, fireplaces, restaurants nearby

Oceanside is nestled on 3 acres of oceanfront, with beach access where our guests can retreat from the rapid pace of city life. Privacy is characteristic of life at Oceanside. Private outdoor hot tubs for all rooms.
✉ oceanside@penderisland.com ✪ www.penderisland.com

POWELL RIVER

SunCatcher Bed and Breakfast
877 487-1087 604-487-1087
Yvonne and Len Johnson

95-110 $CAN BB
2 rooms, 2 pb
Cash, Checks, *Rated*
C-ltd/S-ltd/P-yes/H-no

Full breakfast
Fresh baked goods served at 4pm, fruit bowl, coffee and tea
Fire pit, gardens, patio, local history books, guest lounge, fridge, microwave, coffee, tea.

Sun Catcher B&B offers delightful Bed and Breakfast accommodations nestled into a beautiful, tranquil seaside garden in Powell River on BC's famed Sunshine Coast. Come, discover the vast array of pleasures that oceanfront living can provide!
✉ suncatcherbb@shaw.ca ✪ www.suncatcherbb.ca/

PRINCE RUPERT

Eagle Bluff Lighthouse B&B
201 Cow Bay Rd V8J 1A2
800-833-1550 250-627-4955
Mary Allen & Bryan Cox

70-110 $CAN BB
7 rooms, 5 pb
Visa, MC
C-yes/S-no/P-no/H-ltd

Full breakfast
Tea, coffee & kitchen facilities, common area
Full decks and sitting room, phone/fax and Internet

Experience Prince Rupert's waterfront. Fully renovated heritage home in historic Cow Bay.
✉ eaglebed@citytel.net ✪ www.citytel.net/eaglebluff

RICHMOND

Doorknocker B&B
13211 Steveston Hwy V6W 1A5
866-877-8714 604-277-8714
Jeanette & Chris

99-149 $CAN BB
3 rooms, 3 pb
Visa, MC, AmEx, •
C-ltd/S-no/P-no/H-no
German

Full breakfast
Coffee, assorted teas, filtered water, cookies
Library, free wireless Internet, gardens, gazebo, heated indoor pool, sauna, fitness equip, art gallery

The Doorknocker B&B is a Tudor-style Manor on an estate surrounded by gardens and mountain views. Central to everything in Vancouver, a luxurious country getaway in the city. The largest collection of doorknockers you'll ever see cover the front doors!
✉ thedoorknocker@shaw.ca ✪ www.thedoorknocker.com

SAANICHTON

Wintercott Country House
1950 Nicholas Rd V8M 1X8
800-708-4344 250-652-2117
Peter & Diana Caleb

95-125 $CAN BB
3 rooms, 3 pb
Visa, *Rated*
C-yes/S-no/P-ltd/H-no

Full breakfast
Garden, sitting room, TV, DVD/ video player, fireplace, extra pillows, duvet, blanket, robes

Just 15 minutes from Victoria, through idyllic scenes of sheep and horses, colourful vegetables and flower farm roadside markets is Wintercott Country House. A peaceful setting with an English style country garden surrounded by Douglas Fir trees.
✉ wintercott@shaw.ca ✪ www.wintercott.com

SALT SPRING ISLAND

Absolutely Salt Spring
120 Forest Hill Place V8K 1J9
866-279-0472 250-538-0196
Cornelia Krikke

125-180 $CAN BB
3 rooms, 2 pb
Visa, MC, *Rated*, •
C-yes/S-no/P-no/H-no

Continental plus breakfast.
Private entrances & patio,
Internet, TV/DVD, CD, Yoga
classes, studio space, Green
accommodations

Spacious self contained 1 br Lake-view apartment can expand to 3 br. Or beautiful 1 or 2 br Garden Suite—both with patios and private entrances!—accommodates up to 6. Weekly or multi-day rates. Enjoy the west coast's natural beauty—relax.

✉ info@absolutelysaltspring.com ◎ www.absolutelysaltspring.com

Always Welcome
529 Fulford Ganges Rd V8K 2K1
888-537-0785 250-537-0785
Tanya & David Macdonald

125-145 $CAN BB
2 rooms, 2 pb
Visa, MC
C-ltd/S-ltd/P-no/H-no

with local & organic choices
Coffee, teas & cocoa stocked
daily
Patios, terrace, sitting room,
book nook, wood-burning
stove

Wonderful antiques and modern amenities surround you as you sip your coffee on the deck or patio overlooking our 5 acres of meadow and forest to view Ganges Harbor and the surrounding islands.

✉ macdon74@telus.net ◎ www.alwayswelcome.ca

Armand Heights B&B
221 Armand Way V8K 2B6
800-427-0241 250-653-0077
Irina & Juergen Floercke

145-200 $CAN BB
3 rooms, 3 pb
Visa, MC
C-ltd/S-no/P-no/H-ltd

Full breakfast
Island-made chocolate
Balconies, private entrances,
private fridge, robes,
hairdryers, fireplaces, hot
tub, trails

Armand Heights B&B offers three beautifully romantic rooms, each with their own private entrance and balcony overlooking a magnificent view of the southern Gulf Islands, the mainland and mountains in the distance.

✉ bookings@armandheights.com ◎ www.armandheights.com

Blue Heron
1160 North Beach Road V8K 1B3
877-537-1373 250-537-1373
Elizabeth Anne Turner

199-225 $CAN BB
2 rooms, 2 pb
Visa, MC
S-no/P-no/H-ltd

Continental plus breakfast
Fireplaces, soaker tubs, In
suite kitchenettes and
private patios

The Blue Heron Oceanfront Bed and Breakfast on Salt Spring Island offers accommodations with two private suites featuring patios, fireplaces and soaker tubs where distance to the beach is measured in footsteps.

✉ eturner@blueheronbb.ca ◎ www.blueheronbb.ca

Ganges Hill B&B
212 Fulford Ganges Rd V8K 2K7
250-537-4701
Ted & Debra Olson

95-140 $CAN BB
2 rooms, 2 pb
Visa, MC
C-yes/S-no/P-ltd/H-ltd

Basket with fresh baked
items
Kitchen stocked with coffees,
teas, milk, cream and eggs

Welcome! to Ganges Hill Bed and Breakfast—this special 3 acre property is a 100 year old farmstead that is just a 3 minute walk to Ganges Village, with a view of the Southern Gulf Islands and San Juan Islands.

✉ debolson@telus.net ◎ www.gangeshillbandb.com

The Greenbrier on Park
173 Park Drive V8K 2R7
250-537-6905
Jackie Berry

120-190 $CAN BB
3 rooms, 3 pb
Visa, MC
C-yes/S-ltd/P-no/H-ltd

Full arrival breakfast
Coffee, tea and staples
Garden Suite – Fully
equipped kitchen, patio and
BBQ. Loft Suite – Mini-
kitchen, patio and BBQ

The Greenbrier on Park offers a large spacious two bedroom Garden Suite and a fabulous Loft Suite in the Heart of Ganges, walking distance to the Saturday Market, marinas, shops and dining.

✉ grbrier@telus.net ◎ www.thegreenbrier.ca/index.html

SALT SPRING ISLAND

Sky Valley Inn
421 Sky Valley Rd V8K 2C3
866-537-1028 250-537-9800
Richard Slosky

170-220 $CAN BB
3 rooms, 3 pb
Rated
C-ltd/S-no/P-no/H-ltd

Gourmet breakfast
Gardens, pool, fireplace,
fresh cut flowers, a
complimentary decanter of
sipping Sherry, robes

Sky Valley is a Salt Spring Island Bed and Breakfast and the island's only luxury French country retreat, on eleven acres of natural beauty.
✉ info@skyvalleyinn.com ◐ www.skyvalleyinn.com

Wisteria Guest House
268 Park Dr., RR3 C8 V8K 2S1
888-537-5899 250- 537-5899
Len & Beverly Brown

99-169 $CAN BB
9 rooms, 5 pb
Visa, MC, AmEx
C-ltd/S-no/P-ltd/H-no

Full breakfast
Coffee and tea
A lounge with books, cable
TV and VCR

Come and enjoy the relaxed atmosphere of the Wisteria Guest House B&B on beautiful Salt Spring Island, British Columbia. The Wisteria Guest House offers a variety of accommodations with 6 bed and breakfast rooms, a garden cottage and 2 studio rooms.
✉ info@wisteriaguesthouse.com ◐ www.wisteriaguesthouse.com/index.html

SAVONA

Lakeside Country Inn
7001 Savona Access Road V0K 2J0
800-909-7434 250-373-2528
Donn & Margaret Sherman

80-185 $CAN BB
9 rooms, 9 pb
Most CC, *Rated*, •
C-yes/S-ltd/P-no/H-no
German

Bed & Breakfast or Room
Only Rates
Complimentary in room tea
and coffee, snacks can be
purchased from bar fridge
and snack basket
Cable TV, high-speed
Internet, phones,
coffeemaker, bar, fridge,
private entrance & balcony,
bikes

A delightful Bed and Breakfast Inn on Kamloops Lake, near Kamloops. Choose from lake view rooms with a queen bed and balcony or larger kitchen suites with patios. Private beach, fragrant flower gardens and shaded lawns. Room only rates also available.
✉ info@lakesidecountryinn.com ◐ www.kamloops-accommodations.com

SECHELT

A Place by the Sea BB & Spa
5810 Marine Way V0N 3A6
866-885-2746 604-885-2745
Nancy and Shay

199-329 $CAN BB
3 rooms, 3 pb
Visa, MC, *Rated*
C-ltd/S-ltd/P-no/H-no

2 course breakfast served in
suite
Ocean view hot tub,
beachfront sauna, sea
kayaking, fishing & private
cruises, in-Suite Spa Services

A Place by the Sea is a luxury, adult oriented deluxe waterfront Sunshine Coast accommodation destination, located in Sechelt, British Columbia. This Sunshine Coast bed and breakfast accommodation features spacious, luxurious theme suites with amenities.
✉ info@aplacebythesea.com ◐ www.aplacebythesea.com

The Tuwanek Hotel
7545 Islet Place V0N 3A4
800-665-2311 604-885-3442
Chris and Krista Cutlan

199-279 $CAN BB
5 rooms, 5 pb
Most CC, *Rated*, •
C-yes/S-no/P-no/H-yes

2 course served in-suite
Snack bar with wide variety
of snacks and soft drinks
Day Spa , Movie Theater,
Games Room, Pool Table,
Business Centre, Wireless
Internet, BBQ area, snacks

Welcome to the Tuwanek Hotel, a Luxury Boutique Bed and Breakfast located on the Sunshine Coast of British Columbia, Canada. This 5 Star Luxury Waterfront Destination is located just a short 45 minute ferry ride from Vancouver, BC.
✉ info@tuwanekhotel.com ◐ www.tuwanekhotel.com/index2.html

688 British Columbia

SHAWNIGAN LAKE

Marifield Manor B&B
2039 Merrifield Lane V9L 3Y1
888-748-6015 250-743-9766
John & Bridgett Shelagh

115-250 $CAN BB
6 rooms, 6 pb
Most CC
C-yes/S-no/P-no/H-no

Full breakfast
Tea
TV/VCR available for rooms,
computer/Internet access
and garden

*On a hilltop overlooking Shawnigan Lake, just beyond the breathtakingly beautiful Mala-
hat Drive, sits the grand Edwardian mansion called Marifield Manor offering 6 rooms with
private baths.* ✉ mariman@pacificcoast.net ◐ www.marifieldmanor.com

SIDNEY

Beacon Inn at Sidney
9724 Third St V8L 3A2
877-420-5499 250-655-3288
Denise Peat

119-259 $CAN BB
9 rooms, 9 pb
Visa, MC, *Rated*, ●
C-ltd/S-no/P-no/H-no
French

Full gourmet breakfast
Coffee/tea tray outside your
door before breakfast.
Common area guest fridge &
coffee/tea station.
Cozy Guest Lounge with
fireplace newspapers,
magazines and
complimentary afternoon
Sherry.

*The Area's only 5-Star property. Near Victoria, Butchart Gardens, ferries & airport. Luxuri-
ous guestrooms, spa-like ensuite bathrooms with soaker or jetted tub, A/C, F/P's, WiFi, CD
player/clock/radios. Stroll to local shops, restaurants & waterfront.*
✉ info@beaconinns.com ◐ www.thebeaconinn.com

Orchard House
9646 6th St V8L 2W2
888-656-9194 250-656-9194
Gerry & Gaye Martin

89-99 $CAN BB
2 rooms, 2 pb
MC, *Rated*
C-ltd/S-no/P-no/H-no

Full breakfast
wireless Internet, refrigerator
in Rose Room, common
room . . . also vacation
rentals in other areas.

*Your hosts, Gerry and Gaye, invite you to enjoy this romantic, heritage, arts & crafts 1914
home in quiet, friendly "Sidney-By-The-Sea," just minutes from Victoria. Experience the
casual elegance of an earlier era . . .* ✉ oldorchardhouse@shaw.ca ◐ www.orchardhouse.ca

SOOKE

Markham House
1775 Connie Road V9Z 1C8
888-256-6888 250-642-7542
Lyall & Sally Markham

105-250 $CAN BB
4 rooms, 4 pb
Most CC, *Rated*, ●
C-ltd/S-no/P-ltd/H-no
French

Full breakfast
Afternoon tea, snacks, guest
pantry
Cable TV, VCR, DVD stereo &
telephone in all rooms, WiFi
available, terry robes, turn
down service

*10 acre countryside hideaway in the hills of Sooke. British and Oriental antiques, 30
minutes to Victoria, near beaches and hiking trails. Peace and quiet, 4 fully equipped units,
suite with luxurious amenities, private cottage with wood stove and hot tub*
✉ mail@markhamhouse.com ◐ www.markhamhouse.com

Moonlit Cove B&B
5219 Sooke Rd V0S 1N0
250-642-2278
Christine

160-240 $CAN BB
4 rooms, 3 pb
Cash, *Rated*
C-ltd/S-ltd/P-no/H-yes
German

Full Breakfast delivered to
you
Tea, coffee, snack foods in
cottages, special dietary
needs accommodated with
notice
Spa services available with
advance appointment,
Video/Book library, hot tub,
private deck

*Enjoy the majestic, unspoiled wilderness of Canada's West Coast, with 180 degree views of
forest and ocean with the Olympic Mountains in the distance. Only 35 km from the City of
Victoria! We are located on the world famous Galloping Goose Trail.*
✉ chrishoffman@shaw.ca

SOOKE

Ocean Wilderness Inn
9171 West Coast Road V0S 1N0
800-323-2116 250-646-2116
Lori LeCount

130-210 $CAN BB
7 rooms, 7 pb
Visa, MC, AmEx, •
C-ltd/S-no/P-ltd/H-ltd

Full breakfast
Coffee and Tea available 24 hours.
Refrigerator, sitting room, hot tub, wireless Internet and guest computer.

Our oceanside seven room inn is a perfect getaway distance. Only 30 miles west of Victoria. Rainforest trail to remote beach. Hot tub. Exquisite gardens. Full breakfast featuring local and organic ingredients. Award winning local restaurants.
✉ stay@oceanwildernessinn.com ○ www.oceanwildernessinn.com

Richview House By The Sea
7031 Richview Dr V9Z 0T3
866-276-2480 250-642-5520
Francois & Joan Gething

195-250 $CAN BB
3 rooms, 3 pb
Visa, MC, *Rated*
C-ltd/S-no/P-no/H-no
French

Full breakfast
Guest kitchen with teas, coffee, refrigerator, ice, cutlery & plates, ironing board & iron
Sitting room, wood fireplaces, private hot tubs, steam room, room service breakfast available

Located on an 80' cliff viewing the Olympic Mtns. and the Strait of Juan de Fuca! Quiet location, gorgeous gardens. 3 rooms with private entrances, private Jacuzzis, wood fireplaces, steam room. Owner crafted furniture and woodwork.
✉ richview@bnbsooke.com ○ www.richviewhouse.com

Seascape Inn
6435 Sooke Rd V9Z 0A8
888-516-8811 250-642-7677
Sandy Bohn

110-225 $CAN BB
3 rooms, 3 pb
Visa, MC, AmEx, •
C-yes/S-ltd/P-no/H-no
German

Full breakfast
Hot tubs, bbqs, daily housekeeping, tourist information.

Waterfront property overlooking Sooke Harbour. Unique romantic "cottage," studio cabin and inn-house suite. Exceptional views.
✉ seascape@sookebandb.com ○ www.sookenet.com/seascape

Sooke Harbour House
RR #4 V9Z 0T4
800-889-9688 250-642-3421
Sinclair & Frederique Philip

289-640 $CAN BB
28 rooms, 28 pb
Visa, MC, *Rated*, •
C-yes/S-no/P-yes/H-yes
French

Full or continental breakfast
Dinner, restaurant
Wet bars , fireplaces, sitting room, piano, steam showers, Jacuzzi, infared sauna, library, bikes, cooking

Romantic little inn right on the water, located 45 minutes southwest of Victoria on Vancouver Island, BC. Wonderful attention to detail in every area of the inn.
✉ info@sookeharbourhouse.com ○ www.sookeharbourhouse.com

Tir Na Nog Irish Musical B&B
1523 Winslow Dr V9Z 1A9
250-642-1897
Patrick & Patricia

140-185 $CAN BB
2 rooms, 2 pb
Visa
C-ltd/S-no/P-ltd/H-ltd

Full breakfast
Wedding location, wedding photography, wedding music, wedding coordination and consulting, flowers

Tir Na Nog offers wonderful ocean views, gourmet food, live Celtic music nightly with harp and classical guitar, fresh cut flowers, the perfect location for romantic getaways, and garden weddings. East Sooke park just steps away, 35 minutes from Victoria.
✉ pat-pat@shaw.ca ○ www.victoriabed-breakfast.com

SPENCES BRIDGE

The Inn at Spences Bridge
3649 Hwy #8 V0K 2LO
877-354-1997 250-458-2311
Ray & Lynne Nigalis

68-125 $CAN BB
12 rooms, 5 pb
Visa, MC, AmEx,
Rated, •
C-yes/S-ltd/P-ltd/H-yes
Limited French

Continental breakfast
Restaurant open 11am – 9pm,
full menu, vegetarian
Lounge, riverside dining, gift
shop, library, hiking, bicycles

A beautiful country inn and B&B on the scenic Thompson River. Comfortable lodging &
fine vegetarian dining in BC's oldest operating hotel, just 3.5 hrs NE of Vancouver through
the Fraser Canyon.
✉ theinn@spencesbridge.ca 🌐 www.spencesbridge.ca

SURREY

B&B on the Ridge
5741 146th St V3S 2Z5
888-697-4111 604-591-6065
Dale & Mary Fennell

80-140 $CAN BB
3 rooms, 3 pb
Cash, Checks, *Rated*
C-ltd/S-ltd/P-no/H-no
Hungarian

Full breakfast
Snacks, refreshments upon
arrival, nightly goodies,
coffee & tea making facilities
Sundeck, cable TV/VCR,
wireless Internet access,
tourist info, free local calls,
parking

Escape from the city to a delightful, tastefully decorated B&B situated on ½ acre, with a
quiet country atmosphere. This comfortable escape from the city is conveniently located to
everything the Greater Vancouver area has to offer.
✉ stay@bbridgesurrey.com 🌐 www.bbridgesurrey.com

The Daly Bed & Bread Guest
House
13152 Marine Dr V4A 1E7
877-523-1399 604-531-2531
John & Susan Howard

100-165 $CAN BB
3 rooms, 3 pb
Most CC, *Rated*, •
C-yes/S-ltd/P-ltd/H-ltd
Some French & German

Full breakfast
Snacks; tea & coffee in suites;
accommodate special diets
& allergies, home made jams
Sitting rooms, beach chairs &
umbrellas, beach towels, free
long distance phone calls

Elegant oceanview inn conveniently located near Vancouver Int'l Airport, Gulf Island
Ferries and 10 minutes from the International Border. Pick-up service. Wildlife viewing,
Burns Bog and Boundary Bay.
✉ reservations@dalybedandbread.com 🌐 www.dalybedandbread.com

TSAWWASSEN

Beach Grove Guest House
1580 Gillespie Rd V4L 1W1
888-887-2201 604-943-1664
June Stacey

95-150 $CAN BB
3 rooms, 1 pb
Visa
C-yes/S-no/P-yes/H-no

Full breakfast
Wood burning fireplace in
living room, Internet access
in rooms, cozy terry cloth
robes

Welcome to Beach Grove Guest House, a bed & breakfast located in sunny Tsawwassen,
one of the most peaceful and beautiful areas in the Lower Mainland of British Columbia,
notably the area with the most sunshine.
✉ info@beachgroveguesthouse.com 🌐 www.beachgroveguesthouse.com

UCLUELET

A Snug Harbour Inn
460 Marine Dr V0R 3A0
888-936-5222 250-726-2686
Susan Brown & Drew Fesar

190-355 $CAN BB
6 rooms, 6 pb
Visa, MC, *Rated*
S-no/P-yes/H-yes

Full breakfast
Fresh baked goods available
throughout the day
Sitting room, hot tubs,
fireplaces, private beach &
decks, incredible views

One of Canada's finest Inns. Exceptional privacy, romance & incredible cliffside oceanfront
setting. Private decks, fireplaces, luxury robes & heated floors. Handicapped & pet friendly
rooms.
✉ drew@awesomeview.net 🌐 www.awesomeview.com

VANCOUVER

A Harbourview Retreat B&B
4675 W 4th Ave V6R 1R6
866-221-7273 604-221-7273
Penny Crosby

170-240 $CAN BB
2 rooms, 2 pb
Visa, MC
C-ltd/S-no/P-no/H-no

Full breakfast
Hot tub, luxurious bed
linens, towels, and
bathrobes, high speed
Internet

A Harbourview Retreat Bed and Breakfast is a newly restored and renovated 1914 Crafts-man style heritage home, combining modern convenience with character and beauty.
✉ penny@ahvr.com ◔ www.aharbourviewretreat.com

A Tree House B&B
2490 W 49th Ave V6M 2V3
877-266-2960 604-266-2962
Barb & Bob Selvage

109-199 $CAN BB
4 rooms, 2 pb
Visa, MC, *Rated*, •
C-ltd/S-ltd/P-no/H-no

Full gourmet breakfast
Courtesy beverage for
celebrations, chocolates on
the pillow, in room tea,
coffee, filtered water
Sitting room, high speed
wireless Internet, TV/videos,
DVDs, on-street parking,
decks, laundry service

"Bauhaus Mood, Zen Spirit": modern metropolitan home featuring contemporary art, warm hospitality, personalized service, and substantial, gourmet breakfasts. A TreeHouse offers refined simplicity in a beautiful, exclusive neighborhood.
✉ bb@treehousebb.com ◔ www.treehousebb.com

AAA Catherine's B&B
668 E 29 Ave V5V 2R9
800-463-9933 604-875-8968
Catherine Vong

69-149 $CAN BB
12 rooms, 10 pb
Visa, MC, AmEx, •
C-yes/S-no/P-no/H-no
most Asian languages

Full breakfast
Internet, VCR/cable in guest
lounge, discounted local tour
rates and car rental

We offer year round, affordable bed and breakfast accommodations with spectacular views near all major Vancouver tourist attractions, transportation, parks and recreation.
✉ bnbvancouver@gmail.com ◔ www.aaabedandbreakfast.com

Barclay House
1351 Barclay St V6E 1H6
800-971-1351 604-605-1351
JJ Kalns

155-295 $CAN BB
6 rooms, 6 pb
Visa, MC, AmEx,
Rated, •
C-ltd/S-no/P-no/H-no

Full 3-course gourmet
breakfast
Assorted pastries and fruit
Wifi, cable, DVD, alarm,
fridge, coffee/tea, robes,
hairdryers, safes, free
parking & local calls

Downtown! Voted best hotel in Vancouver two years running! AAA 3 Diamonds. From-mer's favorite! Fodors Pick! Seattle Times favourite!
✉ info@barclayhouse.com ◔ www.barclayhouse.com

Camelot Inn
2212 Larch St V6J 3P7
604-739-6941
Inara Austrinz

120-179 $CAN BB
5 rooms, 5 pb
Visa, *Rated*, •
C-ltd/S-no/P-no/H-no

Full breakfast
Breakfast available for $11
per person. Afternoon tea,
snacks
Sitting room, library,
fireplaces, cable TV, videos,
full kitchen in suites

Romantic, friendly, peaceful & convenient, adjacent to downtown. Restored 1912 Edward-ian home, 2 blocks from sandy beaches and next to Granville Island public market.
✉ stay@camelotinnvancouver.com ◔ www.camelotinnvancouver.com

VANCOUVER————————————————————————————————

English Bay Inn
1968 Comox St V6G 1R4
866-683-8002 604-683-8002
Boban Vuckovic

149-299 $CAN BB
6 rooms, 6 pb
Most CC, *Rated*, •
C-ltd/S-no/P-no/H-no
Spanish, Korean, Malay,
Serbian, Italian etc.

Full breakfast
Tea, coffee, port, sherry
Sitting rooms, library,
fireplace, laundry, concierge,
restaurant reservations etc.

Tucked away between high-rise apartments in a quiet corner of Vancouver's Downtown West End offering an unexpected hideaway in the heart of the city. Walk to Stanley Park, English Bay Beach, and downtown.
✉ stay@englishbayinn.com 🌐 www.englishbayinn.com

House on Dunbar B & B
3926 20 Ave West V6S 1G4
604-224-6355
Joanne Renwick

110-150 $CAN BB
3 rooms, 3 pb
Visa, MC, AmEx
C-ltd/S-ltd/P-no/H-no

Healthy Heart breakfast
selection
Kitchen for guest use. Tea,
coffee, soft drinks available.
Fresh fruit and snacks.
Computer with high speed
Internet. Daily maid service.
Complete linen change every
3 days.

Central location to many of the Vancouver sights, but remains in a quiet neighborhood. All suites have private bathrooms.
✉ houseondunbar@gmail.com 🌐 houseondunbarbandb.com

**Kenya Court Ocean Front
Guest House**
2230 Cornwall Ave V6K 1B5
604-738-7085
Dr. & Mrs. H.R. Williams

110-130 $CAN BB
7 rooms, 7 pb
Cash, Checks, *Rated*
C-ltd/S-no/P-no/H-no
Italian, French, German

Full buffet breakfast
Complimentary tea/coffee
Downtown on Kitsilano Bay,
spacious and elegant suites
with stunning views

Oceanfront heritage guesthouse overlooking Kitsilano Beach, mountains, English Bay. Gourmet breakfast served in rooftop solarium with stunning views of the ocean & city. In operation since 1986.
✉ h&dwilliams@telus.net

Kings Corner B&B
4006 Glen Dr V5V 4T3
604-879-7997
Anne & Christopher King

70-105 $CAN BB
2 rooms, 2 pb
Cash
C-yes/S-no/P-ltd/H-no

Full breakfast
Wireless Internet and hot tub

You'll always receive a warm welcome at King's Corner 1912 heritage Vancouver bed and breakfast home. With our central location in a quiet residential neighborhood it is the perfect place to stay!
✉ talkischeap@shaw.ca 🌐 www.kingscornerbb.com

Manor Guest House
345 West 13th Ave V5Y 1W2
604-876-8494
Brenda Yablon

90-240 $CAN BB
10 rooms, 6 pb
Visa, MC, *Rated*
C-ltd/S-no/P-no/H-no
French, German

Full gourmet vegetarian
breakfast
Guest kitchen use, dinner by
prior arrangement
Conference facilities for up to
25, parlor & music room,
English garden, decks

An Edwardian mansion on the southeastern edge of downtown Vancouver, in a safe & elegant neighborhood. Spacious rooms, private baths, free parking. Top-floor suite sleeps six. Close to shopping, restaurants & public transit.
✉ info@manorguesthouse.com 🌐 www.manorguesthouse.com

VANCOUVER

Nelson House
977 Broughton St V6G 2A4
866-684-9793 604-684-9793
David Ritchie

88-198 $CAN BB
6 rooms, 4 pb
Visa, MC
C-ltd/S-ltd/P-no/H-no
French
Closed 12/24, 25, 31 &
1/1

Full Canadian Breakfast
Mini-refrigerators & filtered
water in some rooms. Tea &
coffee in the Shangri-La
Suite.
Off-street parking, garden,
fireplaces, library, wireless
Internet, 3 decks, en-suite
Jacuzzi

Downtown, where you want to be! West End location only steps to the best of Vancouver, near Stanley Park and Robson Street shopping. Character, comfort, convenience for business and vacation.
✉ info@downtownbandb.com 🌐 www.downtownbandb.com

O Canada House B&B
1114 Barclay St V6E 1H1
877-688-1114 604-688-0555
Susanne Munro-Condon

135-285 $CAN BB
7 rooms, 7 pb
Visa, MC, *Rated*, •
C-ltd/S-no/P-no/H-no

Full gourmet breakfast
Complimentary guest pantry
and sherry
Sitting room, video library,
parlor, fireplace, wrap-
around porch, English
garden, Queen Anne decor

Beautifully restored Historic Victorian house in quiet downtown location. Furnished in late Victorian style, home of the Buchan version of the Canadian National Anthem, first sung here in 1909.
✉ info@ocanadahouse.com 🌐 www.ocanadahouse.com

Stanley Park Inn
1030 Chilco St V6G 4R6
604-683-8063
Bob Chapin

250-350 $CAN BB
3 rooms, 3 pb
AmEx
C-yes/S-no/P-no/H-ltd

Full breakfast
Sherry and port in the
afternoon and evening
Parlour, library, high-speed
wireless

Experience the elegance of bygone eras and Vancouver's natural appeal. Exquisite 18th and 19th century English and French antiques in a restored 1930s Tudor-style home, 1 block from Stanley Park, English Bay. Three guestrooms with private baths
✉ chapinr@telus.net 🌐 www.stanleyparkinn.com

Star Stay Experiences
1419 Pendrell St V6G 1S3
604-609-2770
Boyd McConnelly

300 $CAN EP
6 rooms, 6 pb
Most CC
C-yes/S-ltd/P-yes/H-no

Tea and coffee. Full kitchen
in suites.
24 hour room service,
movies on demand, laptop
rentals, Internet access

For the ultimate Hollywood North Experience, stay in one of our three bedroom suites, all of which have been in TV or movie productions and/or been the "home" of Hollywood actors while shooting in Vancouver.
✉ Boyd@vanmovietours.com 🌐 www.vanmovietours.com/includes/ss1.php

The West End Guest House
1362 Haro St V6E 1G2
888-546-3327 604-681-2889
Evan Penner & Ron Cadarette

145-265 $CAN BB
7 rooms, 7 pb
Most CC, *Rated*, •
C-ltd/S-no/P-no/H-no
French

Full breakfast
In summer, iced tea is served
after 4pm on the sun deck.
Sherry in the
parlour.(5–7pm)
Sundeck for summer
relaxation, homey parlour,
guestroom phones, bikes,
Internet and guest computer.

Walk to Stanley Park, beaches; enjoy quiet ambience of comfortable historic inn. Popular with romantic couples. Fireplace, antiques, robes. Top floor skylit romantic room with fireplace, sleighbed and slipper bathtub.
✉ info@westendguesthouse.com 🌐 www.westendguesthouse.com

VERNON

Lakeside Illahee Inn
15010 Tamarack Dr V1B 2E1
888-260-7896 250-260-7896
Peter & Debbie Dooling

119-359 $CAN BB
5 rooms, 5 pb
Visa, MC, *Rated*, •
C-ltd/S-no/P-no/H-ltd
German

Full gourmet breakfast
Waterfront sunset dining
offered May to September,
events, meetings
Lounges, fireplaces, jet &
soaker baths, heated tile
floors, coffee bar, kayaks &
firepit, WiFi

One of British Columbia's superlative Waterfront Country Inns. Awarded the "6th Best on the Waterfront" B&B, Country Inn throughout North America. Well known as "the Jewel of the Okanagan" for fine accommodations and hospitality.
✉ info@illahee.com ❂ www.illahee.com

VICTORIA

Abbeymoore Manor
1470 Rockland Ave V8S 1W2
888-801-1811 250-370-1470
Anne Mosher & Ian MacPhee

119-249 $CAN BB
7 rooms, 7 pb
Visa, MC, *Rated*, •
C-ltd/S-no/P-ltd/H-no

Gourmet Breakfast
Tea and coffee station, guest
refrigerator with
complimentary soft drinks,
fresh fruit and snacks
High speed Internet access,
library, 2 daily newspapers,
Aveda beauty products in
every room

We offer B&B rooms or self-contained suites at ground level and a penthouse suite with ocean and mountain views. Across the street from the Governors mansion, near Craigdarroch Castle and the Art Gallery. A 5 minute drive to all downtown attractions.
✉ innkeeper@abbeymoore.com ❂ www.abbeymoore.com

Abigail's Hotel
906 McClure St V8V 3E7
800-561-6565 250-388-5363
Wes Wong

189-420 $CAN BB
23 rooms, 23 pb
Visa, MC, AmEx,
Rated, •
C-yes/S-no/P-ltd/H-no
German, Spanish,
Portuguese

Full gourmet breakfast
Evening appetizers
Social hour, fireside library,
Spa Treatment Room, Gift
Shop, Garden Patio

Intimate . . . Elegant . . . Exclusive . . . Experience the charm of our unique 5 star bed & breakfast boutique hotel, 3 blocks from downtown. Guests enjoy our gourmet breakfast, evening appetizers and "The Pearl" spa treatment room. Free parking.
✉ innkeeper@abigailshotel.com ❂ www.abigailshotel.com

Albion Manor
224 Superior St. V8V 1T3
877-389-0012 250-389-0012
Don Halton & Fernando
Garcia

99-199 $CAN BB
8 rooms, 8 pb
Visa, MC, *Rated*
C-ltd/S-ltd/P-ltd/H-ltd
Spanish, Italian

Full gourmet breakfast
Gardens, patios, balconies,
fireplaces, Jacuzzis, special
packages & surprises
available

Our gracious 1892 Heritage Home is located on a peaceful oak-tree lined street in the historic James Bay district, a 5 minute walk from the US ferry terminal, the ocean, shopping & Victoria's major venues. The crowning touch to your Victoria visit.
✉ info@albionmanor.com ❂ www.albionmanor.com

Amethyst Inn at Regents Park
1501 Fort St V8S 1Z6
888-265-6499 250-595-2053
Abel

119-399 $CAN BB
13 rooms, 13 pb
Most CC, *Rated*, •
C-ltd/S-no/P-no/H-no
Japanese, Mandarin

Full Gourmet Breakfast
Bottled water & soft drinks,
evening sherry, tea, coffee &
cookies in the parlour
High speed wireless Internet,
telephone, cable TV, DVD,
CD player in all rooms

Built in 1885, Amethyst Inn authentically reflects the Victorian era. Victoria's exceptionally romantic inn, awarded "Best Breakfast in Canada," Inn Traveler, 2005.
✉ innkeeper@amethyst-inn.com ❂ www.amethyst-inn.com

VICTORIA

Amore by the Sea B&B and Seaside Spa	125-245 $CAN BB	Complimentary 3-course breakfast
246 Delgada Rd V9C 3W2	3 rooms, 3 pb	Breakfast served in the
888-82-VIEWS 250-474-5505	Visa, MC, *Rated*	dining room with
	C-ltd/S-no/P-no/H-no	outstanding views; mini-
	French	fridges, wet bar, hot drinks
		Spa, hot tub overlooking
		West Coast beach (views),
		seaside spa services, beach
		front

Voted 'Most Romantic Hideaway!' Outstanding beach front property! Offering the best seaside location in Victoria. The only B&B in Victoria offering unobstructed views in all guestrooms! The best rates for an ocean front location!
✉ Stay@AmoreByTheSea.com ✆ www.AmoreByTheSea.com

Ashcroft House B&B	119-199 $CAN BB	Full breakfast
670 Battery St V8V 1E5	5 rooms, 5 pb	Coffee, tea, bottled water,
866-385-4632 250-385-4632	Most CC	fresh fruit
Paulanne & David	C-ltd/S-ltd/P-no/H-no	TV, VCR, electric fireplace,
		kitchenette, WiFi, guest
		computer, laundry facilities,
		bike storage

Our little touches & attention to the details at our Victoria bed and breakfast will leave you wishing you had more time! At Ashcroft House B&B, we know you will enjoy it's unmistakable sense of comfort and peace, with all those sunny windows!
✉ Paulanne@AshcroftHouseBandB.com ✆ www.AshcroftHouseBandB.com

Binners'...A Contemporary Oasis	139-275 $CAN BB	Full breakfast
58 Linden Ave V8V 4C8	3 rooms, 3 pb	In-room bar fridge with soft
888-409-5800 250-383-5442	Most CC, *Rated*, ●	drinks, spring water; in-room
Binners & Edward Davidson	C-ltd/S-ltd/P-no/H-ltd	coffee, teas
	Some French	WiFi, Computer loan, e-mail,
		concierge services, in-room
		phones

4.5 star boutique-style with elegant, comfortable suites & rooms. Fireplaces, Jacuzzis, gourmet 3-course breakfast. Just 3 minutes from downtown and + block to stunning ocean & mountain views & walkways. Concierge & spa services.
✉ hosts@binners.com ✆ www.BinnersVictoria.com

Birds of a Feather Oceanfront B&B	140-185 $CAN BB	Full breakfast
206 Portsmouth Dr V9C 1R9	3 rooms, 3 pb	Afternoon tea, snacks
800-730-4790 250-391-8889	Visa, MC, *Rated*, ●	Sitting room, bicycles,
Annette Moen & Dieter Gerhard	C-yes/S-no/P-no/H-no	kayaks, canoe, private dock,
	German	WiFi, guest computer,
		fireplaces, kitchenettes

Affordable luxury at nature's doorstep is just 15 minutes from downtown Victoria. Warm hospitality and unique amenities at this romantic, West Coast destination. Nestled on the shores of a wildlife bird sanctuary with a private dock on the lagoon.
✉ frontdesk@victorialodging.com ✆ www.victorialodging.com

Cottage Pirouette B&B	95-145 $CAN BB	Continental breakfast
401 Lampson St V9A 5Y9	6 rooms, 4 pb	Japanese breakfast is also
877-386-2166 250-386-2166	Most CC	available. At check-in, a hot
Lorraine Nygaard-Ishizaki	C-yes/S-no/P-no/H-no	pot of tea and cookies
	Japanese	refresh you.
		Two dining rooms, living
		room, bicycle storage, hot
		tub, robes, koi pond, patio,
		piano, harp, guitar

Our Bed & Breakfast in Victoria BC is situated within minutes of downtown Victoria and the beautiful Inner Harbour, the centre of tourist activities in Victoria British Columbia.
✉ info@cottagepirouette.com ✆ www.cottagepirouette.com

VICTORIA——————————————————————————————————————

Cougar's Crag
1155 Woodley Ghyll Dr V9C
4H9
888-808-2724 250-478-8993
Steve Schweighofer & Michel
Wagner

185-235 $CAN BB
2 rooms, 2 pb
Visa, MC, *Rated*
C-yes/S-no/P-yes/H-no
French

Full breakfast
Small fridge & microwave in
room; complimentary coffee,
soft drinks, bottled water.
Laundry service, dog care,
Internet, fireplace, library &
coffee maker

*The Crag is on 15 acres situated on a forested ridge overlooking the Strait of Juan de Fuca
and the Olympic Mountains—30 minutes from downtown Victoria. We are one of the most
exclusive and pet-friendly B&Bs on Vancouver Island.*
✉ info@cougarscrag.com ❂ www.cougarscrag.com

Culinary Acres
394 Wray Ave V9E 2H6
250-294-2848
Dorothee Tilly & Ullrich
Geissler-Tilly

119-149 $CAN BB
2 rooms, 2 pb
Visa
C-yes/S-no/P-no/H-no

Full breakfast
Packed picnic available
Cooking classes available,
deck

*Welcome and enjoy your stay in our elegant country B&B or vacation rental on a quiet
organic acreage in Victoria, BC, Canada. Only minutes from world famous Butchart Gardens and a short drive to the Inner Harbor, Empress hotel and parliament buildings.*
✉ stay@culinaryacres.com ❂ www.culinaryacres.com

Cycle Inn B&B
3158 Anders Rd V9B 4C4
800-506-3396 250-478-6821
Joanne Cowan

75-125 $CAN BB
3 rooms, 2 pb
Cash
C-yes/S-ltd/P-ltd/H-ltd
French, German,
Spanish,

Delicious breakfast
Drinks on the deck, or
English style tea
Rec room fridge, sauna, VCR,
library, games, bicycle lock
up, maps, swings, BBQ, deck,
boats, quiet.

*A lovely waterfront residence located on the famous Galloping Goose Trail. Whether you
have come to see your child safely into the new school, you are on a golfing holiday, or in
business meetings, by evening this is a must stay!*
✉ stay@cycleinn.com ❂ www.cycleinn.com

**Dashwood Manor Seaside
Heritage B&B**
1 Cook St V8V 3W6
800-667-5517 250-385-5517
Dave & Sharon Layzell

125-285 $CAN BB
11 rooms, 11 pb
Visa, MC, *Rated*, •
C-ltd/S-no/P-no/H-no
French

Full breakfast
Knowledgeable and
experienced owners give
valuable assistance with trip
planning and reservations.

*Best ocean views in Victoria! Dashwood Manor is Victoria's only seaside heritage B&B in
walking distance to downtown. Breathtaking views of the ocean and snow-capped mountains of Washington's Olympic Peninsula from each guestroom.*
✉ info@dashwoodmanor.com ❂ www.dashwoodmanor.com

Denniston by the Sea B&B
430 Grafton St V9A 6S3
888-796-2699 250-385-1962
Rosemary Denniston

135-200 $CAN BB
3 rooms, 3 pb
Visa, MC, •
C-ltd/S-no/P-no/H-no
seasonal

Delicious full breakfast
Coffee/tea, beverage self-
service is available in
guestrooms as well as fresh
fruit and goodies
Fireplaces, microwave,
refrigerator, phone,
TV/VCR/DVD, WiFi, Jacuzzi,
guest living room, books

*Located oceanfront in Victoria, British Columbia. Early 1900's Tudor-style home on the
Pacific Northwest Coast with stupendous views of the Olympic Mountains across the Strait
of Juan de Fuca.*
✉ info@dennistonbythesea.com ❂ www.dennistonbythesea.com

VICTORIA ———————————————————————————————

Emerald Forest B&B
1006 Rocky Glen Rd V9C 3X7
877-735-2422 250-391-9154
Zarine & Martin Vogel

110-150 $CAN BB
3 rooms, 3 pb
Cash, Checks
C-ltd/S-no/P-ltd/H-no
German

Full breakfast
Internet and fax services
available, living room with
fireplace

Welcome to our home nestled in the deep embrace of nature in Victoria, BC. A place of quiet reflection or energizing conversations where people from all walks of life share a memorable experience and leave, we hope, feeling that much richer.
✉ stay@emeraldforest.ca ◑ www.emeraldforest.ca

End of the Mile
2945 Humpback Rd V9B 5X1
250-294-5733
Cinda & Richard

125 $CAN BB
2 rooms
Visa, MC
C-ltd/S-no/P-yes/H-no

Full breakfast
Cool refreshments and
snacks upon arrival
Pellet fireplace, pool table,
wireless Internet, horseshoe
pit and hot tub

Located just outside the wonderful city of Victoria, End of the Mile Bed & Breakfast offers a pet and biker friendly, serene and quaint setting with outstanding hospitality for a relaxing and memorable stay. Pet sitting while you enjoy the sites.
✉ endofthemile@shaw.ca ◑ endofthemile.com

Fisher House Victoria
333 Simcoe St V8V 4C8
877-386-6252 250-386-6252
Harriet Fisher

125-150 $CAN BB
3 rooms, 3 pb
Visa, MC
C-ltd/S-no/P-no/H-no
May – September

Continental plus breakfast
Complementary coffee, tea
and cookies available all day
Dining room, garden, patio,
parlor, cable TV, robes, guest
fridge, wireless Internet

Close to downtown and Victoria's spectacular inner harbour, Fisher House Bed and Breakfast offers very comfortable accommodation and warm hospitality for both the vacation or business traveler. Walk from the Seattle Clipper & Blackball ferries.
✉ info@fisherhousevictoria.com ◑ www.fisherhousevictoria.com

Gazebo Bed & Breakfast
5460 Old W Saanich Rd V9E
2A7
877-211-2288 250-727-2420
Linda & Martin Vernon

155-220 $CAN BB
3 rooms, 3 pb
Visa, MC, *Rated*, •
C-ltd/S-no/P-no/H-ltd

Full breakfast
Complimentary beverages
Wireless Internet, guest
computer, sauna, massages,
double Jacuzzis, fireplaces,
glorious garden

Relax at a Victoria manor house bed and breakfast near the Butchart Gardens in a quiet central location. Stay in a secluded cottage or elegant rooms surrounded by lovely gardens. Sauna and massage services. WiFi. Canada Select 5 Stars at 4 star prices
✉ stay@gazebo-victoria.com ◑ www.gazebo-victoria.com

Humboldt House B&B Inn
867 Humboldt St V8V 2Z6
888-383-0327 250-383-0152
David & Vlasta Booth

129-295 $CAN BB
6 rooms, 6 pb
Visa, MC, AmEx,
Rated, •
C-ltd/S-no/P-no/H-no
Czech, German, French

Full Gourmet breakfast
Afternoon tea,
complimentary sparkling
wine, truffles
Sitting room, library,
Jacuzzis, suites, fireplaces,
cable TV

Victoria's most romantic and private B&B. Relax by firelight in your Jacuzzi; feast on a gourmet breakfast in the privacy of your room. Large windows offer a peaceful view of neighbouring St. Ann's Academy and its apple orchard.
✉ rooms@humboldthouse.com ◑ www.humboldthouse.com

698   British Columbia

VICTORIA

Oak Bay Guest House	89-190 $CAN BB	Three course cooked
1052 Newport Ave V8S 5E3	11 rooms, 11 pb	breakfast
800-575-3812 250-598-3812	Visa, MC, *Rated*, •	Complimentary tea, coffee &
Egle Vair	C-ltd/S-no/P-no/H-no	hot chocolate
	German, SwissGerman,	Sitting room with TV/VCR,
	Dutch	library, hairdryers, ironing
		board

The Oak Bay Guest House is a charming Tudor-style Victorian historic home welcoming travelers since 1922. Furnished with antiques, surrounded by beautiful gardens, in an elegant neighborhood with access to scenic walks, beaches and golf.
✉ stay@oakbayguesthouse.com ❂ www.oakbayguesthouse.com

Selkirk Guest House	100-135 $CAN EP	Breakfast not included but
934 Selkirk Ave V9A 2V1	6 rooms, 3 pb	available for $7.00 per person
800-974-6638 250-389-1213	Visa, MC, *Rated*	for full breakfast
Lyn & Norman Jackson	C-yes/S-no/P-yes/H-ltd	Library, Jacuzzi, suite,
		fireplace, cable TV, accom.
		bus. travelers, boats

Selkirk Guest House is a historic waterfront guesthouse offering bed and breakfast accommodation in beautiful Victoria, British Columbia, Canada. Unique Vancouver Island setting on the Gorge Waterway. Casual atmosphere, ideal for families.
✉ info@selkirkguesthouse.com ❂ www.SelkirkGuestHouse.com

Spinnakers Brewpub &	129-249 $CAN BB	Basket of baked goods sent
Guest House	11 rooms, 11 pb	to room
308 Catherine St V9A 3S8	Visa, MC, AmEx,	Lunch served from 11am to
877-838-2739 250-386-2739	*Rated*, •	4pm, dinner from 4pm to
Paul Hadfield	C-yes/S-no/P-yes/H-ltd	10:30pm; farm fresh local &
		organic ingredients
		Restaurant, bar, laundry, dial
		up Internet access in room,
		water & truffles delivered in
		afternoon

Canada's first in-house Brewpub offers heritage & contemporary accommodations in luxurious rooms with queen beds, deluxe bedding, Jacuzzi tubs, wood or gas fireplaces, original art & breakfast.
✉ spinnakers@spinnakers.com ❂ www.spinnakers.com

WEST VANCOUVER

Creekside B&B	149-249 $CAN BB	Full gourmet, ranch breakfast
1515 Palmerston Ave V7V 4S9	2 rooms, 2 pb	Complimentary wine,
604-926-2599	Visa, MC, •	snacks, tea, coffee, juices
Donna Hawrelko	C-ltd/S-ltd/P-ltd/H-no	TV, fireplace, 2-person
	Ukrainian	Jacuzzi tubs, stocked
		refrigerators in rooms

Private, quiet, woodsy, creekside hideaway. Close to parks, skiing, mountains, beaches & ocean. Large bright rooms with balconies. Discount coupons for dining & activities. 2 day minimum stay.
✉ donna.hawrelko@telus.net

WESTBANK

Alexandria House B&B	99-120 $CAN BB	Full breakfast
2462 Alexandria Way V4T 1T6	3 rooms, 3 pb	Monogrammed bath robes,
877-291-0817 250-768-4226	Visa, MC	TV, VCR, DVD, Wireless
Suzanne Stickler	C-ltd/S-ltd/P-no/H-ltd	Internet, and sun deck.
	May-October	

Located in the wine country of Okanagan Valley. We offer our guests warm hospitality in our cozy and elegant home. Step out on the large deck to a park-like garden with an abundance of trees and beautiful flowers.
✉ alexandriahouse@shaw.ca ❂ www.alexandriahousebandb.com

WHISTLER—————————————————————————

Alpine Chalet Whistler Inn
Bed & Breakfast
3012 Alpine Crescent V0N 1B3
800-736-9967 604-935-3003
Cynthia & Fritz Feldmann

139-399 $CAN BB
8 rooms, 8 pb
Visa, MC, *Rated*
C-ltd/S-no/P-no/H-yes
Swiss, German

Gourmet Full breakfast
Free parking & local calling,
outdoor Jacuzzi, indoor
steam room & WiFi, coffee or
tea & smiles!

Eight stylish guestrooms, each with in-floor heated ensuite, some with Jacuzzi and fireplaces. Only 2 kms to Village shopping, dining, entertainment and to ski lifts. Free parking. Gourmet breakfast by our Swiss Chef. We look forward to welcoming you!
✉ stay@whistlerinn.com ♻ www.whistlerinn.com

Bear Trail Inn
7422 Ambassador Cresent
V0N 1B0
604-938-1617
Pam Thompson

67-290 $CAN BB
4 rooms, 4 pb
Visa, MC
C-yes/S-no/P-ltd/H-no

Full & Continental Available
Hot-tub, sauna, fireplaces,
on-site professional
masseuse, TV, cable, DVD,
CD

Our Inn is one of the closest B&B's to Whistler Village. Located in White Gold Estates, with Lost Lake Park in your backyard, it is an easy 10 minute walk to the Village. We feature a large outdoor hot tub, beautiful views and a scrumptious breakfast.
✉ rooms@telus.net ♻ www.whistlerdreams.com/beartrail.html

Cedar Springs B&B Lodge
8106 Cedar Springs Rd V0N
1B8
800-727-7547 604-938-8007
Joern & Jackie Rohde

99-299 $CAN BB
8 rooms, 6 pb
Visa, MC, AmEx, •
C-yes/S-no/P-no/H-ltd
German and Australian

Full breakfast
Home baked snacks for
afternoon tea & iced tea in
the summer
Guest lounge with
TV/DVD/VCR, wet bar,
sauna, hot tub, decks,
gardens, bike rentals, free
Internet

Casual Canadian hospitality and comfort. Sumptuous breakfasts, seasonal afternoon teas and dinners; fireside living and dining room. Comfortable rooms; sauna, hot tub. Canada Select 3+ Star Rating.
✉ info@whistlerinns.com ♻ www.whistlerbb.com

Golden Dreams
6412 Easy St V0N 1B6
800-668-7055 604-932-2667
Ann & Terry Spence

115-185 $CAN BB
3 rooms, 1 pb
Visa, MC, •
C-ltd/S-ltd/P-ltd/H-no
German, French

Homecooked nutritious
breakfast
Will cater to
vegetarian/special diets,
complimentary snacks for
apres ski, welcome drink in
summer
Free wireless Internet. Daily
housekeeping. Eco-friendly
B&B, recycling, composting,
chemical-free!

Serving great B&B memories since 1987! Be surrounded by mountain beauty, choose one of our unique theme rooms and awaken to a wholesome breakfast. "Arrive as strangers, leave as friends."
✉ ann@goldendreamswhistler.com ♻ www.goldendreamswhistler.com

WHITE ROCK—————————————————————————

Apple Creek B&B
14686 32nd Ave V4P 2J7
604-760-7077
Beverley Olafson

100-175 $CAN BB
3 rooms
Visa, MC, •
C-yes/S-no/P-ltd/H-no

Full home cooked breakfast
Tea, coffee, beverages & light
evening snacks
Gardens, ponds, trails,
indoor swimming pool,
sauna, fireplace, billiard
table, family room, squash

Regarded as one of the premier homes in the Vancouver region, on five landscaped acres. Furnished with a world class collection of Canadian antiques, fireplaces, squash court & indoor pool. Beach & golf nearby. A luxury private or corporate retreat stay.
✉ info@applecreekbb.com ♻ www.applecreekbb.com

WHITE ROCK ─────────────────────────

Beachside Sausalito	89-179 $CAN BB	Continental breakfast
B&B/Guest Suites	8 rooms, 8 pb	Double Jacuzzi, deck, BBQ
1185 Oxford St V4B 3P5	Visa, MC, •	fireplace, hot tubs
604-538-3237	C-yes/S-no/P-yes/H-yes	
Robert Yearsley		

Steps to the beach, pier & restaurants, Beachside Sausalito B&B/Suites is surrounded by a 3 mile crescent of sun drenched sandy beaches, San Juan & Gulf Islands. White Rock is BC's Riviera. Romantic, family, friends, corporate? We have it all!
✉ info@sausalitobb.com ◑ www.sausalitobb.com

Manitoba

WINNIPEG ─────────────────────────

River Gate Inn	89-129 $CAN BB	Full breakfast
186 West Gate R3C 2E1	6 rooms, 4 pb	Complimentary coffee, tea,
866-397-3345 204-474-2761	Visa, MC, AmEx, *Rated*	biscuits/cake and fruit.
Keith & Michelle Sanheim	C-ltd/S-no/P-no/H-no	Water, a small fridge and a
	A little French, German,	microwave also.
	Italian	Heated pool, parlor,
		fireplace, library, sunporch,
		Jacuzzi tub, formal dining
		room, billiard table

Welcome to the River Gate Inn, a tastefully restored 18th century style building in the heart of Winnipeg. This stately home is set on spacious grounds with many mature elms & other trees. Come pamper yourself! Canada Select 4½ Star rating!
✉ info@rivergateinn.com ◑ www.rivergateinn.com

New Brunswick

COCAGNE ─────────────────────────

Cocagne Bay B&B	$US BB	Full breakfast
2515 Rte 535 E4R 1N6		A/C, walk to beach, central
888-576-6301 506-576-6301		TV, hot tub, off street parking
Albert & Cecile Leger		

Rejuvenate yourself in the fresh and invigorating ocean air, relax on the exterior patio overlooking Cocagne Bay. You can experience the rustic beauty and serenity of Cocagne, or simply stop off here on your way to nearby tourist attractions.
✉ info@cocagnebb.ca ◑ www.cocagnebb.ca

Marshlands Inn, Sackville, NB

GRAND FALLS

Cote's B&B Inn
575 Broadway Blvd W E3Z 2L2
877-444-2683 506-473-1415
Norma Cote

105-175 $CAN BB
5 rooms, 5 pb
Visa, MC, AmEx,
Rated, •
C-ltd/S-no/P-no/H-no
French

Gourmet Breakfast
5 course candlelight dinner;
picnics, fruit, vegetable, or
cheese trays for 2 with
advance notice
Fireplace, whirlpools, patio,
hot tub, high speed Internet,
massage, video library

At Cotes B&B Inn find the warmth and sense of well-being you have been looking for. Relax in the quiet and comfortable surroundings, and appreciate the special touches of elegance and tranquility in the luxurious rooms.
✉ stay@cotebb-inn.com 🌐 www.cotebb-inn.com

LAKEVILLE

Auberge Wild Rose Inn
17 Baseline Rd E1H 1N5
888-389-7673 506-383-9751
Fred & Dianne Logan

125-250 $CAN BB
16 rooms, 16 pb
Visa, MC, AmEx,
Rated, •
C-ltd/S-no/P-no/H-no
French

Full breakfast
The inn provides dinner by
reservation only from 5:30 to
8:00 in the evening
Sitting room, whirlpools,
suites, fireplaces, cable TV,
business travelers, wireless
Internet

Cozy, comfortable inn exudes romance from the warm fireplaces to the quaint antiques. This, coupled with a gourmet breakfast makes for a memorable stay.
✉ wildroseinn@hotmail.com 🌐 www.wildroseinn.com

SACKVILLE

Marshlands Inn
55 Bridge St E4L 3N8
800-561-1266 506-536-0170
Lucy & Barry Dane

99-205 $CAN BB
18 rooms, 18 pb
Visa, MC
C-yes/S-no/P-ltd/H-ltd
Spanish, Italian

Continental plus breakfast
Licensed fine dining
Parlours, fireplaces, gardens,
verandas, antique store

The Marshlands Inn is one of Canada's best known country inns. This pre-Confederation home, operating as an inn for over 60 years, has been the stopping place for many of Canada's notables and visiting celebrities. Even the Queen of England has stayed.
✉ marshlds@nbnet.nb.ca 🌐 www.marshlands.nb.ca

SAINT JOHN

Homeport Historic Inn c 1858
80 Douglas Ave E2K 1E4
888-678-7678 506-672-7255
Ralph & Karen Holyoke

95-175 $CAN BB
10 rooms, 10 pb
Visa, MC, AmEx,
Rated, •
C-yes/S-no/P-yes/H-ltd
French and some
German

Full gourmet breakfast
Complimentary afternoon tea
& refreshments, fully stocked
bar
5 star luxury & service is our
motto; all rms have TV, phone,
data port, & A/C in season.

High on a hill, with a commanding view of the Bay of Fundy, the historic port & city skyline of Saint John, the Homeport provides the perfect setting to relax & enjoy the gracious ambience of Canada's oldest incorporated city. Affordable luxury awaits.
✉ stay@homeport.nb.ca 🌐 www.homeport.nb.ca

Inn On The Cove & Spa
1371 Sand Cove Rd. E2M 4Z9
877-257-8080 506-672-7799
Ross & Willa Mavis

125-225 $CAN BB
8 rooms, 8 pb
Visa, MC, AmEx
C-yes/S-no/P-ltd/H-no

Full breakfast
Spa treatments, high speed
Internet, private decks

Enjoy the warmth, charm and friendly environment of Inn on the Cove & Spa on the edge of the majestic Bay of Fundy. Experience exemplary hospitality, fine dining and the unparalleled path to relaxation, wellness and beauty in our Spa.
✉ spa@innonthecove.com 🌐 www.innonthecove.com

SHEDIAC

Auberge Maison Vienneau Inn
426 Main St E4P 2G4
866-532-5412 506-532-5412
Marie & Norbert Vienneau

79-98 $CAN BB
5 rooms, 5 pb
Most CC, *Rated*, •
C-ltd/S-no/P-no/H-no
French

Full breakfast
Antiques, Grand Salon,
fireplace, bicycles,

A charming B&B that will offer you a taste good, wholesome maritime hospitality and together with the Shediac region, will offer cultural and sport activities that will fulfill your stay. Ideal as a romantic escape, business trip or family reunion.
✉ info@maisonvienneau.com 🌐 www.maisonvienneau.com

ST. MARTINS

The Quaco Inn
16 Beach St. E5R 1C7
888-833-4772 506-833-4772
Rudy Kath Zinn

99-200 $CAN BB
15 rooms, 15 pb
Visa, MC
C-yes/S-no/P-no/H-ltd
French
April – November

Full breakfast
No meals are included in
price, however a full meal
plan option is available
Balcony overlooking the bay,
skylight and fireplace

In the small, serene fishing village of St. Martins stands the luxurious Quaco Inn just 150 feet from the beaches of the Bay of Fundy where the highest tides in the world sweep in and out each day at our doorstep. ✉ quacoinn@nb.sympatico.ca 🌐 www.quacoinn.com

The Weslan Inn
45 Main St. E5R 1B4
506-833-2351
Sue & Chris

122-135 $CAN BB
3 rooms, 3 pb
Most CC
C-yes/S-no/P-no/H-no
1 April – 30 November

Full breakfast
Jacuzzi, views,

Come experience a gracious and fully restored sea captain's home situated in the heart of St. Martin's. Relax in this private and intimate environment. Enjoy a Jacuzzi in the privacy of your spacious bath and wake to the breathtaking view of the Bay.
✉ views@weslaninn.com 🌐 www.weslaninn.com/info.html#bottom

TITUSVILLE

Klinker Jim's B&B
266 Titusville Rd E5N 8A4
877-424-7700 506-832-7740
Janet Kilpatrick

90 $CAN BB
2 rooms, 2 pb
Cash, Checks
C-yes/S-no/P-ltd/H-no

Full breakfast

Klinker Jim's B&B 200 acre farm has a country atmosphere with meadows and gardens to stroll. Visit a giant's grave or feed rainbow trout and enjoy walking trails or cross-country skiing and snow-shoeing in season.
✉ jkilpatr@nb.sympatico.ca 🌐 www.klinkerjims.netfirms.com

Newfoundland

L'ANSE AUX MEADOWS

Viking Village B&B	72-78 $CAN BB	Full breakfast
877-858-2238 709-623-2238	5 rooms, 5 pb	Dinner available,
Thelma Hedderson	Visa, MC, *Rated*, •	complimentary snack
	C-yes/S-no/P-ltd/H-no	Sitting room, cable TV,
		accommodate business
		travelers, suites

Viking Nest B&B serves a full breakfast every day. Complimentary evening snack also available, and we will recommend our favorite restaurants. Single rates available.
✉ vikingnest@nf.aibn.com ◯ www.vikingvillage.ca

PORT BLANDFORD

Terra Nova Hospitality	65-125 $CAN BB	Full breakfast
Home & Cottages	21 rooms, 21 pb	Lunch, dinner, afternoon tea,
888-267-2373 709-543-2260	Visa, MC, AmEx, •	snacks, restaurant, bar
Rhoda Parsons	C-yes/S-no/P-no/H-yes	service
		Sitting room, library,
		Jacuzzis, suites, fireplaces,
		cable

Terra Nova offers a full breakfast with homemade jams and bread. The property overlooks the ocean and is a spacious and luxurious home with cottages offered as well.
✉ terranova@nf.aibn.com ◯ www.terranova.nfld.net

ST. JOHN'S

A Gower Street House	69-225 $CAN BB	Full breakfast
180 Gower St A1C 1P9	4 rooms, 3 pb	Air conditioning during
800-754-0058 709-754-0058	Most CC, *Rated*, •	summer season, center of
Leonard Clarke	C-yes/S-no/P-ltd/H-ltd	downtown, free, private off-
	Russian, Ukrainian	street parking

Center of St. John's Newfoundland downtown historic properties area, 5 minute walking radius of all tourist attractions. Victorian townhouse, cozy rooms, quiet, well-lit street next to cathedrals, museum, fine restaurants and even Ches's fish and chips.
✉ gowerhouse@abbainn.com

Nova Scotia

ANNAPOLIS ROYAL

Hillsdale House Inn	79-149 $CAN BB	Full breakfast
519 St. George B0S 1A0	13 rooms, 13 pb	Offering spirits, beer and
877-839-2821 902-532-2345	Visa, MC, AmEx,	featuring wines from Nova
Paul Stackhouse & Val	*Rated*, •	Scotia. Picnic lunches, snack
Peterson	C-yes/S-no/P-yes/H-ltd	items available.
	April – Nov	Wireless Internet, 3 spacious
		parlours, laundry service
		available, indoor games,
		outdoor activities

Located in historic Annapolis Royal one of Nova Scotia's finest inns, the Hillsdale House inn allows you to reconnect with nature, discover history and experience early French Acadian culture, lulling you back to a slower gentler time.
✉ info@hillsdalehouseinn.ca ◯ www.hillsdalehouseinn.ca

ANNAPOLIS ROYAL

Queen Anne Inn
494 St. George St B0S 1A0
877-536-0403 902-532-7850
Greg Pyle

99-229 $CAN BB
12 rooms, 12 pb
Visa, MC, *Rated*, •
C-yes/S-no/P-ltd/H-yes
May 1 – November 30

Full breakfast
Serving dinners in our
restaurant Tues, Wed, Thurs,
Fri & Sat.
Featherbeds, color TVs,
bathrobes, CD clock radios,
hairdryers, A/C throughout
the Inn

Top 10 accommodations in the Maritimes, this Victorian home c.1865. Gracious guestrooms delightfully furnished with antiques & paintings. 3-course breakfast. Historic sites nearby. Manicured gardens, and path leading to Ducks Unlimited nature trail.
✉ queenanne@queenanneinn.ns.ca ◔ www.queenanneinn.ns.ca

CALEDONIA

Aunt Nettie's B&B
9865 Hwy #8 B0T 1B0
888-628-8383
Pat & Chuck Groocock

75-99 $CAN BB
3 rooms, 2 pb
Visa, MC
C-yes/S-ltd/P-no/H-yes

Full breakfast
Cable TV, air conditioning,
guest lounge and Internet
access

Welcome to our B&B and home in Caledonia Nova Scotia. Come and enjoy country hospitality in our circa 1890 home nestled amidst stately pines, maples and country gardens, providing a perfect place to stay for your short break or vacation.
✉ auntnettiesbb@hotmail.com ◔ www.auntnetties.ca/

CANNING

The Farmhouse Inn
9757 Main St B0P 1H0
800-928-4346 902-582-7900
Julie & Andrea Kelly

89-160 $CAN BB
6 rooms, 6 pb
Visa, MC, AmEx,
Rated, •
C-yes/S-no/P-no/H-ltd

Full breakfast
Afternoon tea
A/C, guest parlor, 2-person
whirlpool tubs, fireplaces,
cable TV, VCR

Charming country getaway in a historic village. Cozy renovated 1860 farmhouse close to wineries, hiking & highest tides. Queen, king or 2 twin bedrooms, A/C, wireless Internet, TV/VCR, ensuite washroom. Suites have 2-person Jacuzzi &/or fireplace.
✉ farmhous@ns.sympatico.ca ◔ www.farmhouseinn.ca

CENTREVILLE

Delft Haus
1942 Hwy 359 B0P 1J0
866-851-4333 902-678-4333
Ray & Debra Ridley

115-145 $CAN BB
4 rooms, 4 pb
Visa, MC, AmEx,
Rated, •
C-yes/S-no/P-no/H-ltd
French and German

Full breakfast
Complimentary tea & coffee
available throughout your
stay
Aveda Spa services, free
vacation guide online,
library, bikes, wireless
Internet

A luxurious classic Victorian B&B that now incorporates onsite Aveda Spa services for that special relaxing getaway or romantic vacation. We can help you plan your perfect holiday in Nova Scotia so that you see everything and miss nothing.
✉ info@delfthaus.com ◔ www.delfthaus.com

GUYSBOROUGH

DesBarres Manor Inn
90 Church Street B0H 1N0
902-533-2099
Audrey Firth

149-259 $CAN BB
10 rooms, 10 pb
Visa, MC, AmEx, *Rated*
C-yes/S-no/P-no/H-no

Full breakfast
Chef's complimentary Taste
of Nova Scotia reception.
Afternoon tea service.
Gourmet evening dining.
High Speed WiFi, phone,
cable TV, four-piece baths,
hair dryers, robes, Gilchrist
& Soames spa toiletries

"The crowning jewel of a fabulous trip to Nova Scotia," DesBarres Manor blends the elegance of the past with modern luxury. Nestled in the charming seaside village of Guysborough, stately 1837 inn pampers with luxury accommodations and gourmet dining.
✉ reservations@desbarresmanor.com ◔ www.desbarresmanor.com

HALIFAX

Garden View B&B
6052 Williams St B3K 1E9
888-737-0778 902-423-2943
Joe Bowlby-Lalonde & Carol
Bowlby Sifton

70-130 $CAN BB
3 rooms, 1 pb
Visa, MC
C-yes/S-no/P-no/H-ltd

Gourmet breakfast
Whirlpool tub, living room,
fireplace, cable TV, gardens,
wireless Internet, in-room
safes

"Rest and relaxation in the heart of Halifax." Victorian style home, and garden complete with antiques and original art to share with our guests. We are in a very quiet residential neighbourhood close to downtown and many attractions.
✉ carol.sifton@ns.sympatico.ca ❂ www.novascotiabedandbreakfast.ca/

The Halliburton
5184 Morris St B3J 1B3
888-512-3344 902-420-0658
Robert Pretty

155-325 $CAN BB
29 rooms, 29 pb
Most CC, *Rated*, •
C-yes/S-no/P-no/H-no

Continental plus breakfast
Dinner nightly, cocktails in
library or courtyard,
restaurant, bar
Suites, fireplace, cable, LCD
TV, garden, courtyard,
unique decor, wireless
Internet access

Halifax's historic boutique hotel with fine dining and gracious lodging. The Halliburton offers accommodations and Maritime hospitality in a trio of heritage townhouses. 29 guestrooms and suites with private baths.
✉ rpretty@thehalliburton.com ❂ www.thehalliburton.com

Heritage Hideaway B&B
36 Rutledge St B4A 1W9
902-835-3605
Diane Gillis

115-139 $CAN BB
2 rooms, 2 pb
Visa, MC
C-yes/S-no/P-no/H-no

Full breakfast

Welcome to Heritage Hideaway, one of Halifax's most romantic B&Bs. Relax and unwind in our circa 1870 Victorian home and experience tranquil ambience and gracious hospitality; making for a memorable Nova Scotia stay.
✉ info@heritagehideaway.com ❂ www.heritagehideaway.com

The Pepperberry Inn B&B
2688 Joseph Howe Drive B3L
4E4
877-246-3244 902-479-1700
Mike & Karen Kinley

130-215 $CAN BB
5 rooms, 5 pb
Visa, MC, AmEx, *Rated*
C-yes/S-no/P-no/H-no
German

Three-course gourmet
breakfast
Guest fridge with
complimentary bottled water
and fruit juices and a
tea/coffee making facility
Lounge, study, film/book
library, cable TV, wireless
Internet, large gardens and
rear deck

Relax and enjoy the age-old charm of this beautiful 1915 heritage home situated on over an acre of park-like grounds only minutes from the downtown area. Easy access to the airport and a great base for exploring the south shore and the Annapolis Valley.
✉ information@pepperberryinn.com ❂ www.pepperberryinn.com

HUBBARDS

Pleasant View B&B
9301 St. Margaret's Bay Rd B0J
1T0
902-857-1201
Marian & Gene Foster

115-135 $CAN BB
6 rooms, 6 pb
Cash, Checks, •
C-yes/S-no/P-yes/H-ltd

Full breakfast
Breakfast included in Main
House only
Lounge, decks, patio, shared
kitchen in Guest House

Pleasant View Guest House and Bed & Breakfast is centrally located in the heart of Nova Scotia's scenic Lighthouse Route, Hwy. #3, on the South Shore.
✉ thefosters@pleasantviewbandb.com ❂ www.pleasantviewbandb.com

LUNENBURG

1826 Maplebird House	85-110 $CAN BB	Full breakfast
36 Pelham St B0J 2C0	4 rooms, 4 pb	Pool, Internet, wood burning
888 -395-3863 902-634-3863	Visa, MC, *Rated*	stove, TV/DVD/CD, piano,
Susie Scott & Barry Chappell	C-ltd/S-no/P-no/H-no	patio, books, games and
		family room.

A restored heritage home (circa 1826) once used as a dairy farm, this year celebrating its 182nd birthday and 17 years as a bed and breakfast. Enjoy a relaxed atmosphere in our home, catching sunrises and sunsets on the verandah.
✉ barry.susie@maplebirdhouse.ca ◐ www.maplebirdhouse.ca

Atlantic Sojourn	80-105 $CAN BB	Full breakfast
56 Victoria Rd B0J 2C0	4 rooms, 4 pb	Complimentary coffee, tea &
800-550-4824 902-634-3151	Visa, MC	cookies
Sebelle Deese & Susan Budd	C-yes/S-no/P-no/H-no	Living room with cable TV,
	May 1 – November 1	VCR, DVD, games, movies,
		magazines, parlour, deck,
		garden with koi pond

Enjoy a stay in one of four rooms with ensuite bath and full breakfast. Let Lunenburg be your hub for day trips along the South Shore, Halifax, Peggy's Cove, Annapolis Royal, or Bay of Fundy. Off street parking, wireless Internet, secure bike storage.
✉ atlanticsojourn@eastlink.ca ◐ www.atlanticsojourn.com

Kaulbach House Historic Inn	99-169 $CAN BB	Full breakfast
75 Pelham St B0J 2C0	6 rooms, 6 pb	Wireless Internet.
800-568-8818 902-634-8818	Visa, MC, AmEx,	Refrigerator available and
David and Jenny Hook	*Rated*, ●	dinner reservations
	C-yes/S-no/P-no/H-no	organized. Daily newspapers.

Overlooking the waterfront, the Kaulbach House Historic Inn offers elegant accommodation in a gracious Victorian atmosphere in Lunenburg, a UNESCO World Heritage Site. The ideal place to unwind, relax and enjoy this beautiful area.
✉ info@kaulbachhouse.com ◐ www.kaulbachhouse.com

Lunenburg Inn	89-199 $CAN BB	Full breakfast
26 Dufferin St B0J 2C0	7 rooms, 7 pb	Complimentary
800-565-3963 902-634-3963	Visa, MC, *Rated*, ●	refreshments during your
Donna & Deryl Rideout	C-yes/S-no/P-no/H-ltd	stay and fresh baked cookies
	April 1 to November 30	in the afternoon
		Sun deck, verandah, sitting
		room, whirlpool tubs,
		TV/VCR, Internet, licensed
		bar for guests only

We hope you'll feel at home in our beautifully restored, classic Victorian-style Inn located on the edge of the World Heritage Site of Old Town Lunenburg. We take great pride in our service and the attention to detail.
✉ innkeepers@lunenburginn.com ◐ www.lunenburginn.com

Rum Runner Inn	79-179 $CAN BB	Continental breakfast
66-70 Montague St B0J 2C0	13 rooms, 13 pb	Restaurant with international
888-778 6786 902-634-9200	Visa, MC, *Rated*	cuisine on site
Eva Ziegler	C-yes/S-no/P-no/H-ltd	Glassed in veranda with
	German	outstanding view
		overlooking Lunenburg's
		harbour & golf course

The Rum Runner Inn, located in the historic town of Lunenburg, can take you back to days gone by, when rum-running was a favorite backhaul for Lunenburg captains taking salt cod to the Caribbean.
✉ info@rumrunnerinn.com ◐ www.rumrunnerinn.com

LUNENBURG————————————————————————————————

Smugglers Cove Inn
139 Montague St B0J 2C0
888-777-8606 902-634-7500
Eva Ziegler

89-179 $CAN BB
20 rooms, 20 pb
Visa, MC, *Rated*, •
C-yes/S-no/P-ltd/H-ltd
German
May – October

Continental breakfast
Lunch & dinner in our
Restaurant "Spanish
Galleon"

Our tastefully decorated Inn in the heart of the Historic District offers you the ultimate impression of Lunenburg's charm. You will experience a comfortable & pleasant stay with a fantastic waterview. We now have free Wireless High Speed Internet access.
✉ info@smugglerscoveinn.ca ❂ www.smugglerscoveinn.ca

WOLFVILLE————————————————————————————————

In Wolfville Luxury B&B
56 Main Street B4P 1B7
888-542-0400 902-542-0400
Bailey & Tim Sousa

99-160 $CAN BB
4 rooms, 4 pb
Visa, MC, AmEx,
Rated, •
C-ltd/S-ltd/P-no/H-ltd
Ukrainian

Full gourmet breakfast
Guest refrigerator with
complimentary bottled
water, coffee makers with
complimentary tea and
coffee
Cable TV, DVD & VCRs,
Internet, fax machine
available, robes & slippers,
iron and ironing board

They say, there is no place like the Annapolis Valley. Lush greenery, vast orchards, pristine vineyards and peaceful ambience are sure to please all who discover it. When you are visiting Wolfville, at the heart of the valley, come and stay in luxury!
✉ inwolfville@ns.sympatico.ca ❂ www.inwolfville.ns.ca

Ontario

ANCASTER————————————————————————————————

Tranquility Base
110 Abbey Close L9G 4K7
877-649-9290 905-648-1506
Shirley & Larry Woods

85-95 $CAN BB
3 rooms, 2 pb
Visa, MC, AmEx, *Rated*
C-ltd/S-no/P-no/H-no

Full breakfast
Refreshments & dinner on
request
Family room, library. Robes,
slippers, hair dryer, fridge,
coffee maker, juice for your
convenience

Our home has lovely Victorian dolls, art, and other antiques. We enjoy history, antiques traveling and meeting people.
✉ tranquilitybnb@cogeco.ca ❂ www.tranquilitybase.on.ca/

BOURGET————————————————————————————————

The Bourget Inn & Spa
4105 Bouvier Rd K0A 1E0
866-487-3277 613-487-3277
Sandra & Peter Blais

99-242 $CAN BB
9 rooms, 9 pb
Visa, MC, *Rated*, •
C-ltd/S-no/P-no/H-no
French

Full breakfast
On-site gourmet dining.
Lunch and dinner by
reservation.
Full service spa, hot tub,
pool, sauna and steam bath.
Activities on-site. Bordering
the forest.

Escape the city for a relaxing spa retreat to The Bourget Inn & Spa. Ottawa's perfect spa getaway is only 25 minutes away. The nine room Inn is quiet and personal giving you the warm feel of a B&B and all the benefits of large spa hotel.
✉ info@bourgetspa.com ❂ www.bourgetspa.com

BOWMANVILLE

Willow Pond Country	99-235 $CAN BB	Full breakfast
2460 Concession Rd #7 L1C	3 rooms, 3 pb	Coffee/tea, milk/cream, fresh
3K2	Visa, MC, AmEx, •	fruit; Dinner available (MAP
866-261-7494 905-263-2405	C-yes/S-ltd/P-ltd/H-ltd	rates)
Lynn & Randy Morrison		Heated pool, spa treatments,
		large pond & creek, Wedding
		ceremonies, tent Receptions,
		meetings

Peace, tranquility & a touch of luxury await you. Spot the Great Blue Heron & Canadian Geese around our natural pond & creek. Relax in your private suite with DVD surround sound or stay in a cozy room. Bring your horse with you—stalls available.
✉ lynn@willowpondbedandbreakfast.ca ◐ www.willowpondbedandbreakfast.ca

CHELTENHAM

The Top of the Hill B&B	80-95 $CAN BB	Full breakfast
14318 Creditview Rd L0P 1C0	3 rooms, 1 pb	Dinners by special request
905-838-3790	Visa, MC	Air conditioning, cable TV,
Shelley & Steve Craig	C-yes/S-no/P-no/H-no	hot tub, guest refrigerator

The Top of the Hill is an historic home located on two lush acres of the Niagara Escarpment. It offers all the charm of days gone by and the modern amenities guests would expect today. Voted Best Breakfast in Canada 2006 by Arrington's Inn Traveler.
✉ thetopofthehill@rogers.com

DELTA

Denaut Mansion Country	155-175 $CAN BB	Full breakfast
Inn	5 rooms, 5 pb	dinners served on request
5 Mathew St K0E 1G0	Visa, MC, •	for guests, local and fresh
877-788-0388 613-928-2588	C-ltd/S-no/P-no/H-no	ingredients
Mariska & Theo Kriebel	French, German, Dutch	heated pool, gardens, guest
	April 1st – October 31st	canoes at our dock, hiking,
		cycle tours, silence, wide
		variety of books

Luxury, romantic, historic inn feature. All rooms are uniquely decorated, Aveda amenities. Restored heritage stone mansion built in 1849 on 11 acres in an historic village in the Rideau Lakes/1000 Islands
✉ goodtimes@denautmansion.com ◐ www.denautmansion.com

DORSET

The Nordic Inn	110-250 $CAN BB	Full breakfast
1019 Nordic Inn Rd L0R 2C0	12 rooms, 12 pb	Lunch available, snacks
705-766-2343	Visa, MC, AmEx, •	Fire pits, playground, llamas,
Jane & Andre Tieman	C-yes/S-no/P-yes/H-ltd	20 miles of trails,
	Dutch, French	snowmobiling, canoeing,
		hiking

Family outdoor adventures in Muskoka—Haliburton—Algonquin—Lake of Bays. Excellent value for modern, clean, cozy accommodations located high on a hill overlooking the quaint hamlet of Dorset.
✉ info@thenordicinn.com ◐ www.thenordicinn.com

ELORA

Drew House	110-225 $CAN BB	Full breakfast
120 Mill St E N0B 1S0	11 rooms, 7 pb	Gardens, whirlpools,
519-846-2226	S-no/P-no/H-no	fireplace, weddings,
Kathleen Stanley & Roger		antiques, cooking classes
Dufau		

Nestled in the Village of Elora, Drew House offers a magical retreat from the pressures of everyday life. The childhood home of Ontario Premier George Drew, this enchanting 1½-acre estate has been "re-created" for your enjoyment.
✉ rdufau@drewhouse.com ◐ www.drewhouse.com

GANANOQUE

Trinity House Inn	99-250 $CAN BB	Country Buffet
90 Stone St S K7G 1Z8	8 rooms, 8 pb	Dinner, restaurant, bar
800-265-4871 613-382-8383	Visa, MC, *Rated*	service
J. O'Shea	C-ltd/S-no/P-ltd/H-yes	Sitting room, suites, cable TV,
	Closed January	waterfall gardens, rocking
		chair veranda

Trinity House Inn is for those who appreciate Old World charm & hospitality, together with genuine beauty & the comfort it brings. Eight guestrooms, award-winning Victorian waterfall gardens, fine dining and a terraced patio.
✉ info@trinityinn.com ✆ www.trinityinn.com

GRIMSBY

Vinifera, The Inn on Winery Row	145-169 $CAN BB	Full breakfast
245 Main St E L3M 1P5	4 rooms, 4 pb	Chef's Dinners for your
905-309-8873	Visa, MC	group of 8 people arranged
Barbara & Ron	C-ltd/S-no/P-no/H-no	with 30 days notice. Call for
		details.
		Pool, pool table, library with
		gas fireplace

Welcome to our 1846 Italianate Inn, set on 1½ acres on the wine route in Grimsby, Ontario. Step back in time for a relaxing, memorable stay where the hospitality is topped only by the delectable treats that the Viticulture of this area can provide.
✉ barbatviniferainn@yahoo.ca ✆ www.viniferainn.ca

GUELPH

Wakefield House B&B	70-110 $CAN BB	Full breakfast/dietary
11 Graham St N1G 2B6	5 rooms, 3 pb	requirements
519-822-1479	Cash, Checks	Complimentary beverages
Suzanne Wakefield	C-yes/S-no/P-ltd/H-ltd	and snacks
		Wireless high speed Internet,
		guest fridge, fireplace, living
		room, gardens, ample
		parking

Enjoy our lush gardens, relax in the classic comfort of the living room, or snuggle into any one of the three tastefully appointed guest bedrooms on a quiet tree-lined street in the Old University Area of Guelph, Canada's Royal City.
✉ suzanne@wakefieldhouse.ca ✆ www.wakefieldhouse.ca

Willow Manor	100-110 $CAN BB	Full breakfast
408 Willow Rd N1H 6S5	5 rooms, 5 pb	Specialty diets can be
866-763-3574 519-763-3574	C-ltd/S-no/P-ltd/H-no	accommodated by prior
Donna Cooper		arrangement at time of
		reservation.
		Fireplace, antique baby
		grand piano, Oriental rugs,
		gardens, pool & patio

Willow Manor is a premier, award-winning bed & breakfast in Guelph. Proven performance over 16 years and an international reputation for quality. An outdoor swimming pool and landscaped gardens on 2½ acres. Business and tourist guests welcome!
✉ willowmanor1@on.aibn.com ✆ www.willowmanorbb.com

HAMILTON

Rutherford House B&B	115-115 $CAN BB	Full breakfast
293 Park St S L8P 3G5	2 rooms, 2 pb	Sitting room, central A/C,
905-525-2422	Visa, MC, AmEx, *Rated*	parking, wireless, TV/VCR,
David & Janis Topp	C-ltd/S-no/P-no/H-no	fridges, coffeemakers, secret
		garden

Late Victorian home, downtown Hamilton Heritage District. B&B luxury and comfort-ensuite baths, down duvets, breakfast to spoil you, dining/sitting room with fireplace. Easy walk to everything downtown offers. 65km drive to Niagara Falls.
✉ david.janis.topp@sympatico.ca ✆ www.rutherfordbb.com

KINGSTON

Rosemount Inn
46 Sydenham St K7L 3H1
888-871-8844 613-531-8844
Holly Doughty

169-275 $CAN BB
11 rooms, 11 pb
Visa, MC, •
S-no/P-no/H-no

Gourmet breakfast
Afternoon refreshments
Spa, phone, high speed
Internet, fireplace, A/C,
Vinotherapy Spa

1850 Tuscan Villa in Kingston. 3 blocks from shops, museums, restaurants, 1000 Islands Cruises and the University. Enjoy a haunted walk—stories of hauntings, hangings and history, stopping at the inn! D'Vine Spa experience with aromatherapy.
✉ rosemt@kingston.net ◐ www.rosemountinn.com

NEW HAMBURG

Waterlot Restaurant & Inn
17 Huron St N N3A IKI
519-662-2020
Leslie Elkeer

90-120 $CAN BB
3 rooms, 1 pb
Visa, MC, AmEx
C-ltd/S-ltd/P-yes/H-ltd

Continental breakfast
Lunch & dinner available,
bar, fine dining restaurant,
snacks, hors d'oeuvres,
evening wine tasting
Library, TV/VCR, sitting
room, large deck/porch,
flower garden, fireplace, fine
antiques

Nestled along a millpond, in the quaint village of New Hamburg, stands the Waterlot Restaurant and Inn. Built as a stately, private residence in 1847, the Waterlot has been a culinary landmark in the region since 1974.
✉ waterlot@waterlot.com ◐ www.waterlot.com

NIAGARA FALLS

Kilpatrick Manor B&B
4601 Second Ave L2E 4H3
866-976-2667 905-321-8581
Kevin & Nance Kilpatrick

109-199 $CAN BB
3 rooms, 3 pb
Visa, MC, *Rated*, •
S-no/P-no/H-no

Two course Chef prepared
breakfast
Indulge with a unique and
delicious candlelight dinner
prepared and served by Chef
Kevin Kilpatrick.
In-room massages, Breakfast-
in-bed, Dinner, Movie library,
Awesome packages.

Romantic, luxurious & delicious. The Kilpatrick Manor is a beautiful 1891 Victorian home with 3 guestrooms all with ensuite bathrooms, fireplace & seating area, TV & DVD, bathrobe, slippers and fresh flowers. Chef Kevin creates scrumptious breakfasts.
✉ stay@kilpatrickmanor.com ◐ www.kilpatrickmanor.com

Lion's Head
5239 River Rd L2E 3G9
905-374-1681
Helena Harrington

100-225 $CAN BB
5 rooms, 5 pb
Visa, MC, AmEx
S-ltd/P-no/H-no

Full "French" gourmet
breakfast
Common sitting room and
reading room overlooking
Niagara Gorge

Welcome to historic Lion's Head, an award winning, luxurious bed and breakfast with a fabulous location overlooking the Niagara Gorge. A 10 minute walk to the Falls. Full gourmet breakfast served.
✉ lionshead@idirect.com ◐ www.lionsheadbb.com

NIAGARA ON THE LAKE

6 Oak Haven
6 Oak Dr L0S 1J0
866-818-1195 905-468-7361
Christine Rizzuto

110-150 $CAN BB
3 rooms, 3 pb
Visa, MC
C-ltd/S-ltd/P-no/H-ltd

Gourmet food
Tea, snacks & coffee
Garden oasis, pond, gazebo,
great room, fridge, spa
services, fireplaces, bikes,
wireless Internet

Welcome to 6 Oak Haven, where our motto is "There are no strangers here, only friends we have not yet met!" Located in a quiet area of Niagara on the Lake, 6 Oak Haven is a 5 minute walk to the Lake, amazing sunsets & 15 minute walk to the Old Town.
✉ info@oakhavenbb.com ◐ www.niagaraonthelakeoakhaven.com

NIAGARA ON THE LAKE

Ben Brae on-the-Park
22 Park Ct L0S 1J0
866-468-7224 905-468-7224
Lynda & David Hancock

138-188 $CAN BB
3 rooms, 3 pb
Cash, Checks, *Rated*,
•
C-ltd/S-no/P-no/H-ltd

Full breakfast
Patio/deck, sitting room,
attractive garden setting,
fireplace, Jacuzzi

A lovely custom home built specifically to host the weary traveler. Situated on a mature 1/3 acre vista complete with wildlife, features three tastefully appointed guestrooms, all with private bathrooms. Walk to Shaw, bike/hiking trail, wineries, shops.
✉ benbrae@aol.com 🌐 www.benbrae.com

Brockamour Manor
433 King St. L0S 1J0
905-468-5527
Rick Jorgensen & Colleen
Cone

145-250 $CAN BB
6 rooms, 6 pb
Visa, MC, AmEx
C-ltd/S-ltd/P-no/H-no

Full breakfast
Games room with billiards
table & wood burning
fireplace. covered front
porch

Our Niagara-on-the-Lake Bed and Breakfast is a perfect location for a romantic getaway or to escape the everyday; to enjoy theatre, restaurants, quaint shops and wineries! Or, simply relax amongst the trees on an acre of designated heritage property.
✉ info@brockamour.com 🌐 www.brockamour.com

Downhome B&B
93 William St L0S 1J0
888-223-6433 905-468-3173
James Down

165-195 $CAN BB
3 rooms, 3 pb
Visa, MC, AmEx
S-no/P-no/H-no
Russian, Ukrainian

Full three course gourmet
breakfast
Coffee, tea, cookies and
sweets available 24/7
Garden sitting areas , mini-
fridge in rooms, Jacuzzi, gas
fireplace, lounge sitting room

Our Georgian home is situated in a quiet area of the Olde Towne, only four blocks from shops, theatres, & fine restaurants. Enjoy a good night's sleep in our 15" pillow top mattress queen size beds and wake to the aroma of a three course gourmet breakfast
✉ info@downhomeniagara.ca 🌐 www.downhomeniagara.ca

Grand Victorian
15618 Niagara Parkway L0S
1J0
905-468-0997
Eva Kessel

170-225 $CAN BB
6 rooms, 6 pb
Visa, MC
C-ltd/S-no/P-no/H-ltd

Full breakfast

Whispers of time gone by. This historic circa 1870s mansion has grandiose interiors with fireplaces, 4 poster beds and antiques. Wrap around verandah. A parkland setting with tennis, surrounded by Reif Estates Vineyards. Across from Niagara River.
✉ Eva@grandvictorian.com 🌐 www.grandvictorian.ca

The Grange at Stag Hollow
50 Firelane 11A RR3 L0S 1J0
905-938-0698
Philip Thornber & Bibi Adams

230-290 $CAN BB
3 rooms, 3 pb
Visa, MC, *Rated*
S-no/P-no/H-ltd
French

Gourmet Breakfast
Patios, fireplaces, whirlpool
tubs, balconies, TV lounge,
fridge, ice maker, free
Internet

A private, vintage, 2 acre lakefront estate located amidst the vineyards, restaurants, theaters and sights of Historic Niagara-on-the-Lake, Ontario, Canada: the only B&B on Lake Ontario. Luxury and gourmet breakfasts combine with a cozy lakeside setting.
✉ thegrange@staghollow.ca 🌐 www.staghollow.ca

Graystone B&B
612 Victoria St L0S 1J0
888-414-0099 905-468-2733
Nicky & Ben Sadoon

120-150 $CAN BB
3 rooms, 3 pb
Visa, MC
C-yes/S-ltd/P-no/H-ltd

Gourmet Breakfast
Always a tea or coffee pot on
Jacuzzi, TV, hairdryers, clock
radio, wireless Internet &
daily "turn down" service on
request

Voted the 6th best overall Bed & Breakfast in North America and the only one in Canada. We promise to captivate you with truly gracious hospitality!
✉ GraystoneBandB@aol.com 🌐 www.graystonebb.com

NIAGARA ON THE LAKE

**Historic Inns of Niagara –
Post House**
95 Johnson St L0S 1J0
877-349-POST 905-468-9991
Barbara Ganim

199-379 $CAN BB
11 rooms, 11 pb
Visa, MC, AmEx, •
C-yes/S-no/P-no/H-ltd

Full Epicurean Breakfast
Homebaked coffee cakes,
muffins with local fresh
fruits, early coffee; will assist
with diet needs
"Amenities of a Five Star
Hotel in a bed & breakfast
setting"; romantic packages
offering privacy

*This home is one of a collection of three fine historic homes in the Heritage District,
offering a 2 minute stroll to Main Street. Amenities of a Five Star hotel in a bed & breakfast
setting. Our home has been completely restored with in-room baths.*
✉ post@posthouseinn.com ◐ www.historicinnsofniagara.com

John's Gate Gourmet B&B
155 John St W L0S 1J0
866-566-4283 905-468-4882
Meheroo Jamshedji

95-150 $CAN BB
3 rooms, 3 pb
Visa, MC, *Rated*, •
C-yes/S-no/P-no/H-no
Hindi

Full gourmet breakfast
Juice, soft drinks, 24-hour
tea/coffee station.
Wireless Internet, fax,
computer facilities, will help
with other travel and dinner
arrangement

*Pre-Victorian style home, custom-built with private entrance, living and dining rooms for
guests. Centrally located just off the main road into Niagara-on-the-Lake and to the Niagara
Parkway. We are 1 km to the downtown Queen Street shopping strip.*
✉ info@johnsgate.com ◐ www.johnsgate.com

Schoolmaster's House B&B
307 Mississiaugua St L0S 1J0
866-863-3303 905-468-1299
Jane & Steven Vasil

125-175 $CAN BB
3 rooms, 3 pb
Visa, MC, AmEx
S-no/P-no/H-yes

Full breakfast
7:30 am coffee & tea service
to your door with a copy of
the day's newspaper
Computer, fax machine,
Internet access, library,
telephone

*Early 19th c. Heritage B&B in the heart of Niagara Wine Country, a short stroll to theatres,
shops and fine dining. Enchanting accommodations, sumptuous breakfasts. Wake well
rested and feeling refreshed; walk, hike, bike or drive the scenic lake front.*
✉ info@schoolmastershouse.com ◐ www.schoolmastershouse.com

Simcoe Manor
242 Simcoe St L0S 1J0
866-468-4886 905-468-4886
John Gartner

199-300 $CAN BB
5 rooms, 5 pb
Visa, MC
C-ltd/S-ltd/P-no/H-ltd

Full gourmet breakfast
Complimentary tea, coffee
and water.
Guest parlour with fireplace,
reading materials, heated
swimming pool, cable TV

*Stately "Old Town" home graciously harmonizes tradition, ambience & friendliness with
modern comfort. Park setting, steps from attractions, theatre, dining, shopping, golf. A/C,
fireplaces, porch.*
✉ stay@simcoemanor.com ◐ simcoemanor.com

Victorian Suites Inn
1391 Niagara Stone Road L0S
1J0
888-717-6600 905-468-8777
Kathy Poursanidis

199-399 $CAN BB
6 rooms, 6 pb
Visa, MC, AmEx
C-yes/S-no/P-no/H-yes

Bedside Continental
Breakfast
In room treats, picnics
available by prior
arrangement; evening tea
service; popcorn on request
Turndown and concierge
service, DVD library,
umbrellas

*Luxurious new Colonial style Inn on Niagara's famous Wine Route. Beautifully appointed
guestrooms with fireplaces, Mirolin Hydrotherapy Air Tubs, sitting areas, some with private
patios. Non-smoking. AAA and CAA 3 Diamond rating.*
✉ info@victoriansuitesinn.com ◐ www.victoriansuitesinn.com

NIAGARA ON THE LAKE

Wishing Well Historical Cottage Rental
156 Mary St L0S 1J0
866-226-4730 905-980-0346
Maria Rekrut

150-250 $CAN BB
2 rooms, 2 pb
Cash, Checks, *Rated*, •
C-yes/S-no/P-no/H-ltd
Italian, Spanish, French

Continental plus breakfast
Gourmet coffees, teas and juices, full use of kitchen with ingredients, oils, herbs and spices,
Spa Services, spa bath amenities, robes, slippers, Fireplaces, Wireless Internet/phone, central A/C.

Circa 1871 historic summer cottage of the Canadian Soprano Maria Rekrut. This "Museum within a Cottage" is filled with antiques. A Welcome Gift Basket awaits you upon Arrival!! Your in home kitchen is fully stocked with an upscale continental breakfast.
✉ info@celebritybb.com ◐ www.niagaracottageandspa.com

OAKVILLE

Alex & Sheila's Haslemere House
46 Cameo St L6J 5Y1
905-337-3085
Alex & Sheila Roche

94-200 $CAN BB
2 rooms, 2 pb
Visa, MC, AmEx
C-ltd/S-no/P-no/H-no
Some French

Full breakfast
Tea, coffee and cookies, candies
Patio gardens, library, conservatory, swimming pool, piano, wireless Internet for laptop users

Visit historic Haslemere House Bed and Breakfast, an English Arts & Crafts manor with attractive garden and pool near Lake Ontario in lovely south east Oakville, 5 mins to downtown Oakville. King/queen/twin beds, ensuite bathrooms, TV, wireless Internet
✉ bbhouse@mac.com ◐ www.haslemerehouse.com

OTTAWA

Albert House Inn
478 Albert St K1R 5B5
800-267-1982 613-236-4479
Cathy & John Delroy; Tammy, Manager

108-178 $CAN BB
17 rooms, 17 pb
Visa, MC, AmEx, *Rated*, •
C-ltd/S-no/P-ltd/H-no

Full breakfast
Complimentary beverages & room service menu
Lounge with fireplace, complimentary guest Internet desk and WiFi, fax/photocopier, guest laundry.

Downtown Victorian inn where guests can walk to Parliament, Canadian War Museum, National Archives Library, shopping, dining, entertainment and business meetings. Fabulous breakfasts, free wireless & Internet desk. Parking available. CAA/AAA approved.
✉ contact@albertinn.com ◐ www.albertinn.com

Alexander House B&B
542 Besserer St K1N 6C7
613-797-5355 613-789-6520
Sandra & Stephen Hartman

85-125 $CAN BB
3 rooms, 3 pb
Visa, MC
C-ltd/S-no/P-no/H-no
French

Full breakfast
Jacuzzi, central A/C, cable TV, garden, ceiling fans, off street parking, free Wifi

Charming Arts and Crafts Bed and Breakfast in the heart of Canada's Capitol: Ottawa. Our home was built in 1933 and features stained glass windows and oak woodwork.
✉ alechouse@hotmail.com ◐ www.ottawabandb.com

Auberge McGee's Inn
185 Daly Ave K1N 6E8
800-262-4337 613-237-6089
Jason, Judy, Sarah & Ken Armstrong

90-198 $CAN BB
14 rooms, 14 pb
Visa, MC, •
C-yes/S-no/P-no/H-ltd
French, Spanish

Full breakfast
Free local calls, Jacuzzi tubs, cable TV, fireplaces, voicemail, wireless Internet, free parking

Located downtown, this award winning 1886 historic Victorian inn is on the east side of the Rideau Canal in Sandy Hill. Walking distance to Parliament Hill, museums, theatre, bike paths & the ByWard Market. Please join us! You will not be disappointed.
✉ contact@mcgeesinn.com ◐ www.mcgeesinn.com

OTTAWA

Gasthaus Switzerland Inn
89 Daly Ave K1N 6E6
888-663-0000 613-237-0335
Sabina & Josef Sauter

118-288 $CAN BB
22 rooms, 22 pb
Visa, MC, AmEx, *Rated*
C-ltd/S-no/P-no/H-no
French, Swiss-German,
German, Spanish

Full Swiss breakfast buffet
Garden, A/C, Meeting &
Conference Room,
Weddings, free WiFi, Internet
access

A cozy family-run small hotel offers historic charm with modern comfort. Free WiFi-wireless Internet access. Downtown, next to the Byward Market, University of Ottawa, Congress Centre, Conference Centre, USA Embassy, National Gallery and the Rideau Canal
✉ info@ottawainn.com 🌐 www.ottawainn.com

OWEN SOUND

The Highland Manor Inn
Grand Victorian B&B
867 4th Ave A West N4K 6L5
877-372-2699 519-372-2699
Linda Bradford, Paul Neville

120-160 $CAN BB
4 rooms, 4 pb
Visa, MC
C-ltd/S-no/P-no/H-no

Full gourmet breakfast
Library, sitting room with
grand piano, guest
refrigerator and phone, Free
High Speed Wireless Access

Historic 7500 sq. ft. 1872 Victorian Mansion—queen rooms with fireplace and en suite bath. Ideal location for a romantic getaway, peaceful business retreat, girls' weekend or wedding. Close to Bruce Trail, museums and galleries. Wraparound verandah.
✉ info@highlandmanor.ca 🌐 www.highlandmanor.ca

STRATFORD

Avon & John B&B
72 Avon St N5A 5N4
877-275-2954 519-275-2954
Ray & Leonora Hopkins

120-125 $CAN BB
3 rooms, 3 pb
Visa, MC, AmEx,
Rated, •
C-ltd/S-no/P-no/H-no
Dutch, French, German

Full English breakfast
We are happy to
accommodate special diets
provided prior notice is
given.
Sitting room, library,
Jacuzzis, fireplaces, cable
TV, accommodate business
travelers

The warm hospitality & comfort of our beautiful century home, our magnificent full English breakfast, the wonderful award winning gardens; all of this along with our reasonable rates provides exceptional value and a memorable Stratford experience.
✉ avonjohn@cyg.net 🌐 www.cyg.net/~avonjohn

Stewart House Inn
62 John St N N5A 6K7
866-826-7772 519-271-4576
Marc Armstrong

175-350 $CAN BB
6 rooms, 6 pb
Visa, MC, AmEx,
Rated, •
C-ltd/S-no/P-no/H-no

Full gourmet breakfast
In-room early am coffee/tea
service; 24-hr complimentary
cappuccino/espresso
machine, pm treats
Sitting room, library, salt
water pool, fireplaces, cable
TV, wireless Internet access

This magnificent 1870 Victorian mansion is situated on an acre of beautiful residential woodlands, overlooking the tranquil Avon River parklands, and is a short two-block stroll to the Theatre District and Downtown Stratford. Seasonal saltwater pool.
✉ reservations@stewarthouseinn.com 🌐 www.stewarthouseinn.com

Stone Maiden Inn
123 Church St N5A 2R3
866-612-3385 519-271-7129
Jim & Elaine Spencer

165-260 $CAN BB
14 rooms, 14 pb
Visa, MC, *Rated*
C-yes/S-no/P-no/H-ltd

Full breakfast
Light afternoon tea included
in rates, complimentary
coffee or tea & paper outside
room in morning
A/C, telephones, cable TV,
some fireplaces, VCRs,
whirlpool tubs, bar fridge,
piano

We offer quiet Victorian elegance in a residential area, with superior accommodation, and the utmost in personal service. AAA/CAA Three Diamond rated.
✉ smaiden@execulink.com 🌐 www.StoneMaidenInn.com

TORONTO

312 Seaton – A Toronto B&B
312 Seaton St M5A 2T7
866-968-0775 416-968-0775
Ted Bates & Nick Franjic

95-185 $CAN BB
5 rooms, 3 pb
Visa, MC, AmEx, *Rated*
C-ltd/S-no/P-no/H-ltd

Full breakfast
Bottled water, tea, coffee,
fresh fruit & yogurt available
at all times
High speed Internet, wireless
& hard wire, computer, A/C,
TV, mini-fridge

A detached Victorian home on a quiet tree-lined street, in downtown Toronto's historical "Cabbagetown." Four guestrooms, 2 with private baths, and one fully furnished apartment. Parties and meetings hosted.
✉ info@312seaton.com ✪ www.312seaton.com

Banting House Inn
73 Homewood Ave M4Y 2K1
800-823-8856 416-924-1458
Paul Hyde

85-155 $CAN BB
7 rooms, 1 pb
Visa, MC, AmEx,
Rated, ●
C-ltd/S-no/P-ltd/H-no
French

Full breakfast
Sitting room, library, suites,
fireplace, cable TV, parking

An elegant Edwardian home offering a peaceful respite to the hustle and bustle of downtown Toronto.
✉ bantinghs@aol.com ✪ www.bantinghouse.com

By The Park B&B
92 Indian Grove M6R 2Y4
416-520-6102 416-761-9778
Margo & Ziggy Rygier

80-215 $CAN BB
8 rooms, 8 pb
Visa, MC, AmEx
C-yes/S-no/P-no/H-ltd

Full Vegetarian Breakfast
Private kitchen in one-
bedroom suite or shared
kitchenettes with some
suites.
Living room, wood-burning
fireplace, cable TV, garden,
fountain, porch, parking,
wireless Internet

Selected as top 5% "The Best Places to Bed and Breakfast in Ontario" by Janette Higgins We offer various accommodation: traditional B&B with full vegetarian breakfast, self-contained one-bedroom suite and bedrooms with ensuite bathrooms/shared kitchen.
✉ bytherparkbb@rogers.com ✪ www.bythepark.ca

The French Connection
102 Burnside Dr M6G 2M8
800-313-3993 416-537-7741
Diane Richard

150-240 $CAN BB
5 rooms, 3 pb
Visa, MC
C-yes/S-ltd/P-no/H-no
French
Closed Dec 23 -Jan 3

Elegant & imaginative
breakfast
Make tea and use the
microwave oven anytime
Formal living room, grand
piano, reading room,
TV/VCR/DVD, free WiFi
Internet, microwave, kettle

Nestled among lush trees on top of a hill among some of the finest homes in the older part of the City. Five minutes from the City's famous castle (Casa Loma) and near the St. Clair West subway station.
✉ info@thefrenchconnection.com ✪ www.thefrenchconnection.com

Pimbletts Guest House B&B
242 Gerrard St E M5A 2G2
416-921-6898
Geoffrey Pimblett

105-125 $CAN BB
12 rooms, 12 pb
Visa, MC, AmEx, *Rated*
C-yes/S-no/P-no/H-no

Full breakfast
Wireless Internet, parking,
telephone, fax machine,
copier, deck

Pimblett's B&B—another illustrious house of repute. Charles Dickens and Oscar Wilde would most certainly have stayed here. An Englishman's home in the heart of downtown Toronto. Free parking, close to public transport, private bathrooms.
✉ pimbletts@sympatico.ca ✪ www.pimblett.ca

Prince Edward Island

CHARLOTTETOWN

Elmwood Heritage Inn
121 North River Rd C1A 3K7
877-933-3310 902-368-3310
Jay & Carol Macdonald

110-259 $CAN BB
7 rooms, 7 pb
Visa, MC, AmEx,
Rated, •
C-yes/S-no/P-no/H-no

Full fresh gourmet breakf
Complimentary coffee, te
service, pop & juice, bub
and bedside chocolates f
celebrations
Informed, personalized
Concierge service, 8
fireplaces, whirlpools, A/
TV/VCR, irons/boards, W

*5 Star Elmwood Heritage Inn is on a secluded acre estate in historic Charlottetown
Quiet Victorian elegance, modern amenities(WiFi), gourmet breakfasts(veg and c*
available)and friendly informative concierge service for planning daily excursions
✉ elmwood@pei.sympatico.ca ✪ www.elmwoodinn.pe.ca/

**Fairholm National Historic
Inn**
888-573-5022 902-892-5022
Terry O'Malley

125-285 $CAN BB
7 rooms, 7 pb
Visa, MC, AmEx
C-yes/S-no/P-no/H-yes

Full breakfast
concierge service, free
wireless Internet, gardens
"furnished" for your rela>
pleasure

Fairholm boasts large rooms with inlaid hardwood floors, fine stained glass wind
imported wallpaper and superb architecture. All rooms have air conditioning, TV/L
fireplaces, sitting areas, full baths, some with whirlpool tubs and furnished gardens.
✉ stay@fairholminn.com ✪ www.Fairholminn.com

**Heritage Harbour House
Inn**
9 Grafton St C1A 1K3
800-405-0066 902-892-6633
Arie & Jinny van der Gaag

90-210 $CAN BB
21 rooms, 21 pb
Visa, MC, AmEx, •
C-yes/S-no/P-no/H-yes
Spanish, Japanese,
French

Full breakfast with all hor
baking
Off-street parking, bike
storage, laundry facilities
wireless Internet, public
computer, A/C

The elegance and character of a stately old family dwelling, combined with today's mo
amenities. Our inn's twenty one rooms and suites all have different decor and are
nished in a warm, home style atmosphere.
✉ reservations@hhhouse.net ✪ www.hhhouse.net

The Snapdragon B&B Inn
177 Fitzroy Street C1A153
866-235-7164 902-368-8070
Nadell Hebert

85-185 $CAN BB
6 rooms, 6 pb
Visa, MC, AmEx,
Rated, •
C-yes/S-no/P-no

Fresh fruit and Full Hot
Breakfast
Wired and wireless Interr
cable TV, VCR, phones in
rooms. Fax, courier &
printing available

A garden in the heart of an Island. Combine a 4½ star owner operated B&B with a w
class destination and you have a recipe for a great vacation. The Snapdragon is the pe
place to enjoy one of Canada's great treasures — Prince Edward Island!
✉ relax@thesnapdragon.com ✪ www.thesnapdragon.com

Tell your hosts Pamela Lanier sent you.

GEORGETOWN

Georgetown Inn
62 Richmond St C0A 1L0
877-641-2414 902-652-2511
Arlene Smith & Don Taylor

79-149 $CAN BB
8 rooms, 8 pb
Visa, MC, AmEx,
Rated, •
C-ltd/S-ltd/P-no/H-ltd

Full breakfast
Dinner by request, afternoon
tea; guest kitchen available at
all hours
Sitting room, cable TV,
accommodations for
business travelers, Internet &
email

Totally remodeled 1840's heritage home, one block from historic Georgetown Harbour. Warm hospitality, excellent breakfasts and outstanding dining room.
✉ gtowninn@pei.sympatico.ca ♦ www.georgetownhistoricinn.com

MARSHFIELD

Woodmere B&B
98 Linden Rd C1A 7J7
800-747-1783 902-628-1783
Wallace & Doris Wood

85-110 $CAN BB
4 rooms, 4 pb
Visa, MC
C-yes/S-no/P-no

Full breakfast
Rose gardens & standard
bred horses, separate guest
entrance

We invite you to enjoy our Colonial home where our guests' comfort is our priority. Our inn offers a pristine setting enriched with rose gardens & standard bred horses.
✉ woodmere@pei.sympatico.ca

Quebec

ANJOU

CafT-Couette Moka B&B
6544 Terrasse Val d'Anjou
H1M 1T1
514-863-2701
Daniel Beaudoin

75-90 $CAN BB
1 rooms, 1 pb
C-yes/S-no/P-no/H-no
French, a little bit of
Spanish

Full breakfast
Dinner is available on
request
Tour guide and driver is
available on request

A comfortable and peaceful lodging arranged to accommodate 1 or 2 people or a small family up to 5 people. Near restaurants, bus and metro stops Radisson and HonorT-Beauregard. Great deal for business travelers, 20 minutes from Dorval Airport.
✉ moka-bb@hotmail.com

AYER'S CLIFF

Auberge Ripplecove Inn
700 Ripplecove Rd J0B 1C0
800-668-4296 819-838-4296
Jeffrey Stafford

266-710 $CAN MAP
34 rooms, 34 pb
Visa, MC, AmEx,
Rated, •
C-ltd/S-no/P-no/H-ltd
French

Full breakfast and Dinner
Four diamond restaurant on
site. International and
French cuisine with Award
winning wine cellar.
Spa, conference/event
facilities, fireplaces,
whirlpools, private
balconies, tennis, beach,
boating

On a peninsula overlooking the sparkling waters of Lake Massawippi in Quebec's Eastern Townships, the Ripplecove Inn shines like the rarest of gems. Regardless of which room you choose, all of the rooms offer a charming and luxurious country ambience.
✉ info@ripplecove.com ♦ www.ripplecove.com

CHATEAU RICHER

Auberge Baker
8790 Royale G0A 1N0
866-824-4478 418-824-4478
Gaston Cloutier

75-135 $CAN BB
7 rooms, 7 pb
Most CC, *Rated*, •
C-yes/S-no/P-no/H-ltd
French

Full breakfast
Fine dining restaurant is
located on ground level,
MAP also available
Sitting room, bar terrace, fine
cuisine dining room, free
parking lot, WiFi Internet
access

*In 1935, Alvin A. Baker converted the LeFrancois home, built in 1840, into a country inn.
Restored with great attention, each room of the old house has a private bathroom as well
as antique furniture.*
✉ gcloutier@auberge-baker.qc.ca 🌐 www.auberge-baker.qc.ca/introang.html

LASALLE

**Hebergement Touristique Le
Pole des Rapides**
8091 Simonne H8P 3M5
514-363-4779
Cynthia Habib

115-150 $CAN BB
2 rooms, 1 pb
Most CC, *Rated*
C-yes/S-no/P-no/H-ltd
French

Continental breakfast
Map & Touristic Info,
Internet, Baby/Child's Bed,
Boardgames, Storage for:
Bikes, Skis or Kayak

*Comfortable Montreal Apartment Suite with Full Kitchen, Breakfast, TV, Computer, Free
High Speed Internet and Parking. Ideal for travelers seeking the Comforts and Privacy of
their own home. Close to everything. Call to Guarantee Availability*
✉ hebergement_touristique_lpdr@videotron.ca 🌐 pages.videotron.com/tourlpdr/welcome.html

LEVIS

Au Gre du Vent B&B
2 rue Fraser G6V 3R5
866-838-9070 418-838-9020
Michele Fournier & John
L'Heureux

115-145 $CAN BB
5 rooms, 5 pb
Visa, MC, AmEx,
Rated, •
C-yes/S-no/P-ltd/H-no
French

Full breakfast
Breakfast made with local
products
Central air, sitting room, pool
& patio, bicycle storage
facilities, free parking

*Highest Quebec Province classification "5 Stars." Only 5 minutes from Hwy 20 and within
walking distance to the ferry leading you to the heart of Old Quebec City (crossing time: 10
minutes). An authentic & charming B&B facing Old Quebec City.*
✉ augreduvent@msn.com 🌐 www.au-gre-du-vent.com

Au Petit Chateau
664 St Joseph St G6V 1J4
877-833-2798 418-655-1938
Helene & Richard Daignault

105-185 $CAN BB
4 rooms, 2 pb
Visa, MC, •
C-yes/S-no/P-no/H-no
French, Spanish,
Portuguese

5 Star Gourmet Breakfast
Air conditioning, hairdryer,
radio-alarm clock, toiletries
and more

*Au Petit Chateau is a 1914, mansion-like, 3-story, Scottish-brick, Victorian house located on
a 25,000 square foot property, overlooking the St-Lawrence River, and just minutes away
from Old Quebec City!*
✉ auchateau@videotron.ca 🌐 www.aupetitchateau.com

MAGOG

À Tout Venant
20 rue Bellevue J1X 3H2
888-611-5577 819-868-0419
Luc & Vicky B. St-Jacques

75-105 $CAN BB
5 rooms, 5 pb
Visa, MC, AmEx,
Rated, •
C-yes/S-no/P-no/H-no
French

Gourmet International
Breakfast
Tea, coffee & herbal tea
Full kitchen, TV, VCR DVD,
stereo and fireplace.
Massage therapy onsite.
Wireless Internet.

*À Tout Venant B&B will fulfill all desires, with 5 rooms with private baths, hearty break-
fasts, free WiFi, a massage therapy room with 2 tables, a peaceful garden, getaway packages and great location.*
✉ info@atoutvenant.com 🌐 www.atoutvenant.com

MAGOG

La Maison Drew
206 rue des Pins J1X 2H9
888-639 9941 819-843-8480
David & Brigitte

85-110 $CAN BB
4 rooms, 4 pb
Visa, MC, *Rated*
C-yes/S-no/P-no/H-no
French

Full breakfast
Sitting room, library, cable
TV, DVD, A/C, fireplace,
kitchen, fireplace, wireless
Internet

Spacious rooms, kitchen with fridge, microwave oven at your disposal, steps away from the town center, lake & restaurants, and near all cultural & outdoor activities.
✉ lamaisondrew@sympatico.ca ◐ www.maisondrew.com

La Maison Hatley
558 Hatley St W J1X 3G4
888-995-6606 819-868-6606
Christiane & Vincent Arena

85-115 $CAN BB
4 rooms, 4 pb
Cash, *Rated*, •
C-ltd/S-no/P-no/H-no
French, Italian

Full breakfast
Tea or coffee
Air conditioning, exterior hot
tub open year around

La Maison Hatley B&B offers comfortable lodging, in a quaint, ancestral home built in 1875. Come and enjoy the outdoor hot tub, open all year around.
✉ lamaisonhatley@cgocable.ca ◐ www.lamaisonhatley.com

MONTREAL

Accueil Chez Francois
4031 Papineau H2K 4K2
514-239-4638
Francois Baillergeau

90-145 $CAN BB
5 rooms, 3 pb
Visa, MC, AmEx, *Rated*
C-yes/S-no/P-no/H-no
French

Hearty breakfast
Coffee, hot chocolate, herbal
tea, juices
Wireless Internet access,
A/C, television, non-allergic
quilts, hairdryer, slippers

In the heart of Montreal, we are located in the Plateau Mont-Royal where restaurants, lively bars, fashion designers & well-known theatres are all waiting for your enjoyment.
✉ chezfrancois@videotron.ca ◐ www.chezfrancois.ca

Armor Manoir Sherbrooke
157 Sherbrooke E St H2X 1C7
800-203-5485 514-285-0895
Annick Legall

99-139 $CAN BB
22 rooms, 22 pb
Visa, MC, •
C-yes/S-yes/P-no/H-no
French

Continental breakfast
Complimentary coffee
3 rooms with whirlpool,
Jacuzzis, lake swimming,
bicycles

A century-old home transformed into an exquisite and charming hotel, located near Saint-Denis and Saint-Laurent streets, renowned for their fine restaurants, boutiques and bistros. Newly remodeled.
✉ info@armormanoir.com ◐ armormanoir.com

Auberge De La Fontaine
1301 Rachel E St H2J 2K1
800-597-0597 514-597-0166
Connie

129-250 $CAN BB
21 rooms, 21 pb
Visa, MC, AmEx,
Rated, •
C-yes/S-ltd/P-no/H-ltd
French

Full healthy buffet breakfast
Free access to the kitchen for
a snacks, coffee and juice;
bar service
Terrace, complimentary
WiFi, dry-cleaning service
(fee), meeting room, guest
computer available.

Facing a magnificent park and ideally located in the heart of the Plateau Mont-Royal district. Our delightful, elegant rooms and suites will charm you. The Auberge de La Fontaine is a three star, 3 diamond hotel with over sixteen years of experience.
✉ info@aubergedelafontaine.com ◐ www.aubergedelafontaine.com/site/montreal-hotel/index.cfm

L'Auberge de la Place Royale
115 rue de la Commune W
H2Y 2C7
514-287-0522
Fouli Tsatoumas & Christina
Tsatoumas

155-450 $CAN BB
12 rooms, 12 pb
Visa, MC, AmEx, *Rated*
C-yes/S-no/P-no/H-no
French & Greek
April till December

Full breakfast
Babysitting, fax & copier,
laundry service, concierge,
whirlpool tubs, A/C

L'Auberge de la Place Royale is a charming, small hotel, located in the heart of the picturesque Old Port of Montreal.
✉ info@aubergeplaceroyale.com ◐ www.aubergeplaceroyale.com

MONTREAL————————————————————————————————

Le Cartier
1219 Rue Cartier H2K 4C4
877-524-0495 514-917-1829
Richard Lemmetti

60-125 $CAN BB
7 rooms, 4 pb
Visa, MC, AmEx,
Rated, •
C-yes/S-no/P-no/H-no
French

Continental breakfast
Kitchen facilities (except NO
cooking), microwave,
refrigerator, etc . . . are
available
Laundry service (extra cost),
A/C, cable TV, HS wireless
Internet. Airport shuttle at
discount.

Beautiful Montreal Downtown (Village) Bed and Breakfast—Private studio-suite style with nice back yard. 1 min from subway. Walking distance to all city attractions.
✉ bb_le_cartier@hotmail.com 🌐 www.bblecartier.com

Manoir Ambrose
3422 Stanley St H3A 1R8
888-688-6922 514-288-6922
Claude Jouhannet

75-190 $CAN BB
22 rooms, 18 pb
Visa, MC, AmEx,
Rated, •
C-yes/S-no/P-no/H-no
French

Continental breakfast
Complimentary coffee or tea
in the afternoon
Phone, cable TV, sitting
room, air conditioning,
wireless Internet access,
laundry

Victorian-style lodge in downtown Montreal on the slope of Mount Royal, close to Peel Metro station, McGill University Museum, restaurants, Montreal underground shopping. Quiet surroundings & friendly atmosphere. Personality, comfort & affordable prices.
✉ claude@manoirambrose.com 🌐 www.manoirambrose.com

Montreal Oasis
3000 de Breslay H3Y 2G7
514-935-2312
Lena Blondel

70-135 $CAN BB
3 rooms, 1 pb
Cash, Checks, *Rated*
C-ltd/S-ltd/P-no/H-no
Swedish, French,
German, Spanish

Full gourmet breakfast
Sitting room, lake swimming,
bicycles

Spacious downtown house with garden. Close to the Fine Arts Museum and Crescent Street. Gourmet 3-course breakfast, world-traveled hostess, Swedish, African, and Asia art.
✉ BB@aei.ca

PERCE————————————————————————————————

Fleur de Lys B&B
248, route 132 G0C 2L0
800-399-5380 418-782-5380
Kenneth Cahill

69-109 $CAN BB
4 rooms, 4 pb
Most CC, •
C-yes/S-no/P-no/H-ltd
French

Continental plus breakfast
Sitting room, magazines,
booking services for boat
and city tours

Right at the core of Percé, we offer you a fabulous stay in our newly decorated rooms. Whether for a week or a night, you will always remember your stay in Percé. Don't miss it!
✉ fleurdelys@globetrotter.net 🌐 www.gaspesie.com/fleurdelys

QUEBEC CITY————————————————————————————

Hotel Le Clos Saint-Louis
69 rue St-Louis G1R 3Z2
800-461-1311 418-694-1311
Ghyslaine Donais

165-255 $CAN BB
18 rooms, 18 pb
Visa, MC, AmEx,
Rated, •
S-no/P-no/H-no

Continental plus breakfast
Tea set service
Queen size beds, down
comforters, A/C, wireless
Internet, CD player,
concierge service

Expert in the art of romantic vacation experiences, discover our beautiful dream like escape for two in a place that provides intimacy, peacefulness and a perfect backdrop for romantic evenings in Old Quebec City.
✉ info@clossaintlouis.com 🌐 www.clossaintlouis.com

ST. PETRONILLE

Auberge La Goeliche
22 Chemin du Quai G0A 4C0
888-511-2248 418-828-2248
Marie Andree

128-283 $CAN BB
19 rooms, 19 pb
Most CC, *Rated*
C-yes/S-no/P-no/H-ltd
French, Spanish

Full breakfast
French cuisine
Sitting room, art shop,
outdoor swimming pool, bar
service

Overhanging the St. Lawrence River, this castle-like inn offers a breathtaking view of Quebec City, a 15-minute drive away. It is also close to famous Mt. Ste. Anne Ski Center.
✉ infos@goeliche.ca ☯ www.goeliche.ca

SUTTON

Le Domaine Tomali-Maniatyn
377 Chemin Maple J0E 2K0
450-538-6605
Alicja Bedkowska

125-200 $CAN BB
5 rooms, 5 pb
Visa, MC, *Rated*
C-ltd/S-no/P-no/H-ltd
French, Polish

Continental breakfast
Garden, reading room,
conference room,
indoor/outdoor swimming
pool, sat. TV, WiFi, weddings

In Sutton (QC), our B&B is a 5 suns "Certified B&B and Country Inn," Quebec Tourism's highest rating. Amenities include: 5 cozy antique furnished suites with a panoramic view, a tropical indoor swimming pool, on-site access to skiing, biking and hiking.
✉ info@maniatyn.com ☯ www.maniatyn.com

Saskatchewan

ANNAHEIM

Backroads Bed and Breakfast
Main Street S0K 0G0
306-598-2141
Shirl and Les Kunz

60-200 $CAN BB
5 rooms
MC
C-yes/S-no/P-ltd/H-no

Full breakfast
Deck, movie library

Affordable, comfortable accommodations for the traveler, vacationer or people who want to escape to a place of solitude with good service. We also have a guesthouse with all the amenities of home. Deck and firepit in the backyard.
✉ lskunz@bogend.ca ☯ www.backroadsbb.ca

PRINCE ALBERT

Hillcrest Inn B&B
133 – 20th St W S6V 4G1
866-763-4113 306-763-4113
Morris & Dalelene Yelland

79-94 $CAN BB
5 rooms, 3 pb
Visa, MC
C-ltd/S-no/P-no/H-ltd

Full breakfast
Bottled spring water and
sodas, fresh homemade
snack, fruit, chocolates
Sun deck, balcony, original
artwork gallery, flower
garden with paths

Hillcrest Inn, built in 1890, is among the oldest residences in Prince Albert. Recently renovated character home with modern amenities, open all seasons. Located 3 blocks from Prince Albert city centre.
✉ info@hillcrestinn.ca ☯ www.hillcrestinn.ca

Yukon Territory

WHITEHORSE

Fox Creek Wilderness B&B
Fox Creek Rd Y1A 6P9
867-668-2220
Joe Campana & Linda
Lamarche

135-135 $CAN BB
3 rooms, 3 pb
Visa, MC, •
C-ltd/S-no/P-no/H-yes
French & Italian

Full breakfast
We can also prepare,
individualized breakfasts
and multiple course Special
Occasion Meals, and wine
Small library, BBQ, full
kitchen, sundeck, garden,
airport pick-up can be
arranged, laundry facility

You find Fox Creek Wilderness B&B north of Whitehorse, Yukon, on the historic North Klondike Highway.It is a spacious log house in the midst of wilderness, wildlife, lakes, and mountains. You may also view the Aurora Borealis from the house, unobstructed.
✉ joelinda@foxcreekwild.com ◐ www.foxcreekwild.com

Worldwide

Asia

China

BEIJING────────────────────────────

China Beijing Hutong Courtyard B&B	45 – 85 $US BB	Traditional Chinese

**China Beijing Hutong
Courtyard B&B**
28 Maoer Hutong
+44 (0) 1189-706-846
Sally Roese

45 – 85 $US BB
4 rooms, 3 pb
C-yes/S-no/P-no/H-no
Chinese, English
All year

Traditional Chinese
Breakfast
Complimentary tea & coffee,
lunch & dinner for fee
TV, DVD Player, A/C, heating,
safe in each room, guest
fridge, microwave, washing
machine, common living
room, dining room, free
Internet, free local phone
calls

A typical Beijing traditional Hutong courtyard house in historic residential area in central Beijing. Traditional carved Chinese furniture in every room. Walking distance to several main tourist attractions. The house and area are full of characters
🌐 www.bb-china.com/book-online/html_pages/pid8_english.html

India

JAIPUR────────────────────────────

**Umaid Bhawan (Heritage
Home)**
Behari Marg
+91-141-2201276
Ranvijay

2,400 – 3,500 ¤ INR BB
28 rooms, 28 pb
Visa, MC
C-ltd/S-no/P-no/H-ltd
English, Hindi
All year

Continental breakfast
Delectable range of Indian
cuisine offered.
A/C, TV, alarm clock,
hairdryer, wake up service,
pool, business center,
Internet cafe, laundry
service, private balconies,
folk dance/puppet show,
library, BBQ grill

Built on traditional Rajput style, the balconies are intricately carved, there are many courtyards, terraces, a beautiful garden and the rooms are furnished with antiques. An exotic attraction of traditional Rajasthani ambience and modern luxuries.
✉ info@umaidbhawan.com 🌐 www.umaidbhawan.com

Thailand

HUA HIN────────────────────────────

The Bee & B
226/32 Petchakasem Road
+1-954-688-4743
Supensri "Bee" Wagner

35 – 60 € BB
4 rooms, 4 pb
Visa, MC, AmEx
C-yes/S-ltd/P-ltd/H-ltd
Thai, English
All year

Gourmet Breakfast
Heated Jacuzzi, cocktail bar,
WiFi, airport pickup, tour
services, in-room massage,
32" LCD TV, DVD, library of
free movies, teak wood bath
tubs, therapeutic showers

Located in Hua Hin, Thailand, we offer plush, romantic rooms with 32" LCD TV/DVD player, teak wood soaking bathtubs, mood lighting, unique spa-style showers, heated Jacuzzi, cocktail bar, full gourmet breakfasts, and free WiFi Internet. Central location!
✉ info@beeandb.com 🌐 www.beeandb.com

Australia-S. Pacific

Australia

APOLLO BAY————————————————————————

Claerwen Retreat	110 – 360 ¤ AUD BB	Full breakfast
480 Tuxion Road	8 rooms, 8 pb	Cheese platter and wine for a
+61-3-5237-7064	Visa, MC, AmEx,	light supper.
Cornelia Elbrecht	*Rated*, •	Pool, tennis court, spa,
	C-yes/S-no/P-no/H-yes	beach, massage, 2 night
	English, German, French	minimum on weekends
	All year	

Exclusively situated on top of the highest hill overlooking the Great Ocean Road coastline with panoramic views. Claerwen Retreat provides an elegant stay within easy reach to the surrounding national parks.
✉ cornelia_elbrecht@claerwen.com.au 🌐 www.claerwen.com.au

CAIRNS————————————————————————

Galvin's Edge Hill	95 – 125 ¤ AUD BB	Continental plus breakfast
61 Walsh Street	2 rooms, 1 pb	Weekly fresh market for local
+61-7-4032-1308	*Rated*	Cairns produce.
Jesse & Julie Low	C-yes/S-ltd/P-no/H-no	Private entrance, patio,
	English	lounge w/TV/VCR, extensive
	All year	library, pool, lush tropical
		gardens, telephone, laundry
		facilities, luggage storage

Located in quiet, leafy Edge Hill; five minutes drive to downtown and airport; luxurious two-bedroom private apartment, magnificent swimming pool and gardens; walk to Edge Hill village restaurants, shops, Botanic Gardens, rainforest walks.
✉ info@galvinsonedge.com.au 🌐 www.galvinsonedge.com.au

EAST MELBOURNE————————————————————————

Magnolia Court Boutique	120-288 ¤ AUD BB	Full breakfast
Hotel	26 rooms, 26 pb	Tea & coffee facilities
101 Powlett St.	Most CC	TV, A/C, direct dial phone,
+61-3-9419-4222	C-yes/S-no/P-no/H-no	Internet access, fridge,
Lou & Demi Cataldi	English	hairdryer, in room safe,
	All year	period furnishings, en suite
		baths, recently renovated

Elegance and charm tucked away in gracious, East Melbourne. Set amidst prestigious and leafy historic houses a few minutes walk from Fitzroy Gardens reflecting the grand old streets from the days of the lucky strikes in the Goldfields.
✉ info@magnolia-court.com.au 🌐 www.magnolia-court.com.au/

KALORAMA————————————————————————

Holly Gate House	160 – 225 ¤ AUD BB	Full or continental breakfast
1308 Mt Dandenong Tourist Rd	3 rooms, 3 pb	Special dietary requirements
+61-3-9728-3218 +61-3-9728-3218	Visa, MC, *Rated*, •	catered for.
Loraine & Bob Potter	C-no/S-no/P-no/H-no	Log Fire in Guest's living
	English	room, Outside Pool, BBQ, air
	All year, except	conditioned, centrally
	Christmas & Boxing Day	heated, onsite parking. Gift
		Vouchers available.

Luxury Bed & Breakfast accommodation in the beautiful Dandenong Ranges, Kalorama, Victoria, Australia. There's something for everyone . . . bushland walks and picnics, cool-country gardens, birds and wildlife, wineries, galleries and lots more.
✉ reception@hollygatehouse.com.au 🌐 www.hollygatehouse.com.au

MELBOURNE

Fountain Terrace Bed and Breakfast	165 – 245 ¤ AUD BB	Full breakfast
28 Mary St, St. Kilda	7 rooms, 7 pb	Tea and coffee, glass of wine
+61-3-9593-8123	Most CC, *Rated*, •	Guest sitting room, close to
Heikki & Penny Minkkinen	C-ltd/S-no/P-no/H-ltd	beach and restaurants
	English, Finnish, German	
	All year	

Europe Fountain Terrace provides excellent accommodation with the grandeur and elegance of a small, private hotel. Close to all facilities, a perfect place to stay while in Melbourne, Australia.
✉ info@fountainterrace.com.au 🌐 www.fountainterrace.com.au

OLINDA

Candlelight Cottages	210 – 300 AUD ¤BB	Continental breakfast
7-9 Monash Ave	4 rooms, 4 pb	Full available upon request
+61-3-0055-3011 +61-3-9751-2464	Visa, MC, AmEx, •	Kitchen with microwave,
Peta & Laurie Rolls	C-yes/S-no/P-ltd/H-no	Early Cooker stove, fridge,
	English	VCR/DVD player, tapes &
	All year	DVDs, stereo and CDs, log
		burning open fire, spa baths
		with glass ceilings above

Three beautiful individual Cottages 1 hour from Melbourne. Candlelight c1890 is a little "house" with a veranda; french doors, lead lights in windows, brick and polished floors, a delightful private garden with a waterfall and lovely outdoor sitting area.
✉ stay@candlelightcottages.com.au 🌐 www.candlelightcottages.com.au

SYDNEY

Bet's B&B	140 AUD ¤BB	Self-catered
176 Johnston St., Annandale	1 rooms, 1 pb	Breakfast ingredients
+61-2-9660-8265	Visa, MC	provided in the kitchenette
Bet Dalton	C-no/S-no/P-no/H-no	Queen beds, modern
	English, Filipino	bathroom & laundry, fully
	All year	equipped kitchen, dining
		table, lounge area w/sofa,
		armchairs, coffee table,
		TV/DVD, writing desk,
		private entrance

Just 2 miles from the heart of Sydney, Bet's B&B is a modern, fully self-contained artist-style studio, beautifully designed and furnished, with a modern kitchen, spotless bathroom and laundry. Secure private entrance. 15 minutes by bus or train to city.
✉ stay@betsbandb.com.au 🌐 www.betsbandb.com.au

WILLIAMSTOWN

B&B at Stephanie's	175 – 275 ¤ AUD BB	Full breakfast
154 Ferguson St	7 rooms, 7 pb	Biscuits & cheese,
+61-3-9397-5587	Most CC, *Rated*, •	complimentary port &
Stephanie Merifield	C-ltd/S-no/P-no/H-ltd	chocolates.
	English	Sitting room, Private
	All year	courtyards

Luxury accommodation in the Historic Seaport of Williamstown, 10 mins by car, 25 mins by train or 45 mins by Ferry to CBD of Melbourne. Historic & Romantic get-a-way that is just a short 150m walk to the extensive Melbourne rail & tram network.
✉ info@stephanies.biz 🌐 www.stephanies.biz

Tell your hosts Pamela Lanier sent you.

Fiji

MATEI————————————————————————————————

Maravu Plantation Resort	260 – 650 $US BB	Full breakfast
Taveuni Island	21 rooms, 21 pb	Full board, half board,
888-FIJI-NOW +679-332-4303	Visa, MC, AmEx,	afternoon tea/coffee
Jochen Kiess	*Rated*, •	Gym, spa, mountain bikes,
	C-yes/S-yes/P-no/H-yes	kayaks, horseback riding,
	English, German	swimming pool, white sandy
	All year	beach, bar, restaurant, tour
		desk, guided tours,
		snorkeling, boat tours,
		adventure

Maravu's beautiful tropical setting with well-appointed cottages offers easy access to fascinating jungles and hikes. It is a perfect hideaway for adventure, relaxation, culture and unique experiences. ✉ maravu@connect.com.fj ✪ www.maravu.net

New Zealand

ACACIA BAY————————————————————————————————

Paeroa Lakeside Lodge	250 – 400 ¤ NZD BB	Full breakfast
21 Te Kopua St	3 rooms, 3 pb	Generous continental and
+64-7-378-8449	Visa, MC, *Rated*, •	full, cooked breakfasts.
Barbara & John Bibby	C-ltd/S-no/P-no/H-no	Email, fax, tea, coffee,
	English, Spanish,	toiletries, library, sitting
	German	room, beach swimming,,
	All year	massage

Experience tranquility at Paeroa Lakeside Homestay with an abundance of bird life in our spacious established garden that gently descends to our private beach. Paeroa Lakeside Homestay has a 5 Star rating with Boutique Lodges and Qualmark Status.
✉ bibbys@taupohomestay.com ✪ www.taupohomestay.com

CHRISTCHURCH————————————————————————————————

Dyers House B&B	320 ¤ NZD BB	Continental plus breakfast
85 Dyers Pass Rd	3 rooms, 3 pb	Tea, coffee, snacks, wine &
+64-3-337-1675	Visa, MC, AmEx,	soda. Cafe is nearby.
Angela & Barry Hawkins	*Rated*, •	Spectacular views, indoor
	C-ltd/S-no/P-no/H-no	pool, TV/DVD, under-floor
	English	heating, laundry facilities,
	All year	broadband Internet,
		library/TV room, sitting
		room, toiletries, hairdryer

Relax in one of Cashmere's oldest homes. Recently renovated rooms provide all the modern conveniences and are decorated with warmth and charm. Great views throughout the house no matter what the season.
✉ barry.hawkins@paradise.net.nz ✪ www.dyershouse.co.nz

Tell your hosts Pamela Lanier sent you.

GREYMOUTH

Oak Lodge Homestay
286 State Hwy 6, Coal Creek
+64-3-768-6832
Shirley & Alastair Inman

160 – 280 ¤ NZD BB
5 rooms, 5 pb
Visa, MC
C-ltd/S-no/P-no/H-ltd
English
All year

Full breakfast
Dinner available @ $60nzd
per head. Pre booked.
Tennis court, hot tub,
swimming pool, sauna,
billiards room, extensive
gardens, guest lounge with
tea and coffee making
facilities

This quality Bed and Breakfast, is set in rural surroundings 3 km north of Greymouth. Centrally situated to visit Paparoa National Park. Great fishing rivers, and walks nearby. A great place to relax and enjoy the essence of New Zealand
✉ relax@oaklodge.co.nz ✪ www.oaklodge.co.nz

Rosewood B&B
20 High St
+800 185 748 +64-3-768-4674
Rhonda & Stephan Palten

175 – 220 ¤ NZD BB
5 rooms, 4 pb
Visa, MC, *Rated*, •
C-yes/S-ltd/P-no/H-yes
English, German
All year

Full breakfast
Tea, coffee, home-made
biscuits
Separate guest lounge,
Wireless Internet, courtesy
pick-up from Trans-Alpine
train

Rosewood is one of Greymouth's finest old character homes, restored and situated a few minutes walk from the town center and restaurants. A relaxed friendly atmosphere to be spoiled in.
✉ stay@rosewoodnz.co.nz ✪ www.rosewoodnz.co.nz

NELSON

Boutique Hotel Warwick House
64 Brougham St
0800-022233 in NZ
+64-3-548-3164
Nick Ferrier

185 – 395 ¤ NZD BB
5 rooms, 5 pb
Visa, MC, *Rated*, •
C-yes/S-ltd/P-yes/H-yes
English, German
All year. High Season –
Dec. to March.

Full breakfast
Home made foods, dinner for
groups may be arranged
Luxury accommodation, en-
suite lounges, library,
clawfoot baths, Grand
Ballroom. Massage and
Aroma therapy on site Local
info.

Warwick House offers luxurious, boutique B&B accommodation in Nelson's well-known, turreted castle. Intriguing history, impressive architectural features and graceful ambience in one of Nelson's most fascinating buildings.
✉ enquiries@warwickhouse.co.nz ✪ www.warwickhouse.co.nz

The Wheelhouse Inn
41 Whitby Rd
+64-3-546-8391
Ralph Hetzel

140 – 220 ¤ NZD EP
8 rooms, 5 pb
•
C-yes/S-no/P-no/H-no
English, basic Spanish
All year

Tea, coffee, snacks, breakfast
on request.
Spectacular sea views, bikes,
TV, DVD, CD, & stereo, high
speed Internet, private
barbecue area, binoculars

Spectacular sea views can be enjoyed from all 5 of our affordable, luxurious accommodations. Set in a private, native bush setting yet only minutes away from the beach, waterfront, central Nelson and the Abel Tasman National park.
✉ wheelhouse@ts.co.nz ✪ www.wheelhouse.nelson.co.nz

Tell your hosts Pamela Lanier sent you.

QUEENSTOWN————————————————————————

Coronet View Deluxe B&B	165 – 250 ¤ NZD BB	Continental breakfast
30 Huff St	20 rooms, 18 pb	Tea, coffee, wine and snacks.
0800-89-6766 +64-3-442-6766	Visa, MC, *Rated*, •	Dinners on request.
Neil & Karen	C-yes/S-ltd/P-no/H-ltd	Jacuzzi, barbecue, lounges,
	English, Japanese	pool, spa, $20 airport pickup
	All year	and drop offs, wireless
		Internet (fee), no smoking
		environment

Elevated spacious houses with spectacular views over Queenstown, Coronet Peak, Remarkable Mountains & Lake Wakatipu, the exclusive Coronet View B&B.
✉ Stay@coronetview.com 🌐 www.coronetview.com

Pencarrow B&B	595 NZD ¤BB	Four course breakfast
678 Frankton Rd	4 rooms, 4 pb	Complimentary drink,
+64-3-442-8938	Most CC, *Rated*, •	afternoon sweet
Bill & Kari Moers	C-ltd/S-ltd/P-no/H-ltd	Sitting room, writing desk,
	English	library, tea/coffee facilities,
	All year	fresh flowers, laundry, bar
		services, cell phones,
		Internet laptop, turn down
		service with gift

Pencarrow offers luxury accommodations with magnificent views of Lake Wakatipu and the Remarkables Ranges. Luxury suites with lavish baths. Located on four acres, private, and quiet with Spa.
✉ info@pencarrow.net 🌐 www.pencarrow.net

WANAKA————————————————————————

Riversong B&B	150 – 170 ¤ NZD BB	Continental plus breakfast
5 Wicklow Terrace, RD2	3 rooms, 2 pb	Evening meal $55 per person
+64-3-443-8567	Visa, MC, *Rated*, •	by arrangement
Ann & Ian Horrax	C-yes/S-no/P-yes/H-no	Tea & coffee facilities,
	English	balconies, SKY TV, WiFi,
	All year	fishing guidance, tourist
		information, on-site parking,
		historic riverside setting,
		library, outstanding views

On the banks of the Clutha River, one of the most historic areas of Central Otago, Riversong offers the ultimate in a relaxed, friendly, satisfying and scenic B&B home stay.
✉ info@riversongwanaka.co.nz 🌐 www.riversongwanaka.co.nz

Caribbean

Antigua / Barbuda

ST. JOHN'S————————————————————————

Long Bay Resort Inn	300 – 600 $US MAP	Full breakfast
Long Bay #442	25 rooms, 25 pb	Lunch, Dinner, Restaurant,
800-291-2005 268-463-2005	Visa, MC, AmEx, •	Cocktail Bar Service
Christian J. Lafaurie	C-yes/S-yes/P-no/H-no	Beach resort, water sports,
	English	tennis, billiards, library,
	All year	games room, rooms &
		cottages

A Caribbean Beach Resort that is peaceful, friendly and family oriented. Offering tennis, water sports, a library and a games room. Owner operated Since 1966, now guided by the 2nd generation.
✉ info@longbayhotel.com 🌐 www.longbayhotel.com

Bahamas

ANDROS

Small Hope Bay Lodge	418 – 485 $US AP	Full breakfast
Fresh Creek	21 rooms, 21 pb	Includes 3 meals, bar drinks
800-223-6961 242-368-2013	Most CC	& beverages
General Manager	C-yes/S-yes/P-yes/H-yes	Ceiling fans, private baths,
	English	A/C (in some rooms), hot
	All year	tub, scuba & snorkeling
		packages, bicycles, kayaks,
		private beach, solarium,
		lodge, patio

Small Hope Bay Lodge, has been hosting scuba divers, nature lovers & friends in the Bahamas since 1960. Unspoiled & virtually undiscovered, Andros Island is the most established dive resort in the Caribbean. It is peaceful, secluded, and a great getaway.
✉ shbinfo@smallhope.com 🌐 www.smallhope.com

FREEPORT

Dundee Bay Villas	74 – 199 $US EP	Fully-equipped kitchens
20 Dundee Bay Drive	10 rooms, 10 pb	A/C, cable TV (2/unit),
866-771-7778 242-352-8038	Visa, MC	stove/oven, fridge,
Stacy Knowles	C-yes/S-no/P-no/H-no	dishwashers in most units,
	English	microwaves, coffee makers,
	All year	toasters, dishes/flatware,
		patio, balcony, pool, jet tubs

Come enjoy the 'feel like family' atmosphere created especially for guests at Dundee Bay Villas in tropical Freeport. Relax in the natural beauty of brilliant sunrises, golden sunsets, swaying palms, miles of beaches and turquoise waters.
✉ dundeebayvillas@hotmail.com 🌐 www.dundeebayvillas.com

NASSAU

Arawak Inn	75 – 125 $US EP	Complimentary tea selection
West Bay Street	5 rooms, 5 pb	in your room
242-322-2638	Visa, MC, •	Microwave, refrigerator,
Lloyd & Elizabeth Ann Gay	C-ltd/S-no/P-no/H-no	cable TV, A/C, private
	English	bathroom, daily maid
	All year	service, cabana, gift shop,
		book exchange

Enjoy a family island experience at our cozy little inn situated within easy reach of downtown Nassau. Surrounded by gardens with hummingbirds and butterflies, and just around the corner from the local zoo, historic sites and the famous Fish Fry.
✉ arawakinn@gmail.com 🌐 www.expressionsbyann.com

Orchard Garden Hotel	80 – 110 $US EP	A/C, pool, tropical gardens,
Village Road	42 rooms, 42 pb	cable TV, balcony, patio,
242-393-1297	Visa, MC, •	microwaves, fridges,
John Knowles	C-yes/S-yes/P-no/H-no	kitchenette, staff on duty 24
	English	hours, daily housekeeping
	All Seasons	

The Orchard Garden Hotel & Suites is a small, charming discount hotel in Nassau, Bahamas, with air-conditioned rooms, studio-efficiencies, and swimming pool, amidst a two-acre tropical garden of flowering vines and shrubs and century-old silk cotton trees
✉ info@orchardbahamas.com 🌐 www.orchardbahamas.com

SANDY POINT ─────────────────────────────

Oeisha's Resort
Queens Highway
314-664-4106 242-366-4139
Michelle Engelbrecht

110 – 170 $US BB
8 rooms, 8 pb
●
C-yes/S-yes/P-yes/H-yes
English
All year

Full breakfast
We offer several meal plans
to accommodate guests.
Beautiful ocean front, bar,
restaurant, mini fridge, SAT-
TV, WiFi, ceiling fan, A/C,
safe, CD AM/FM clock radio,
fresh Island fruit, coffee & tea

Oeisha's Resort offers 8 newly renovated rooms with private baths, sitting areas & luxurious bedding. All of the conveniences of home & the sweet life of the Bahamas may be found here. Relax and enjoy this remote & friendly settlement of Sandy Point.
✉ islandlife@oeishasresort.com ◐ www.oeishasresort.com

Barbados

CHRIST CHURCH ─────────────────────────

Little Bay Hotel
St. Lawrence Gap
246-420-7587
General Manager

118 – 194 $US EP
10 rooms, 10 pb
Visa, MC, AmEx
C-yes/S-yes/P-yes/H-yes
English
All year

Restaurant, Bar, Lounge
Conference Center, bar &
restaurant, business
services, beach front,
horseback riding, tour desk

The Little Bay Hotel offers ocean view rooms and a charming location on Barbados. Barbados is an island with beautiful beaches, friendly people, much to see and do and a serene atmosphere. It is as the saying goes 'Just beyond your imagination.'
✉ little_bay@caribsurf.com ◐ littlebayhotelbarbados.com

Meridian Inn
St. Lawrence Gap
246-420-6495
Gordon Keenan

69 – 99 $US EP
16 rooms, 16 pb
Visa, MC
C-ltd/S-ltd/P-no/H-no
English
All year

Restaurant nearby,
beverages for sale
A/C, balcony, microwave, TV,
kitchenette, daily maid
service, ceiling fans

This sixteen room apartment hotel is situated at the quiet end of St. Lawrence Gap, on the south coast of the island, close to nightlife, dining, water sports and activities.
✉ meridianinn@sunbeach.net ◐ meridianinn.com

ST. JAMES ──────────────────────────────

Treasure Beach Hotel
Payne's Bay – James Bay
800-223-6510 246-432-1346
Hamish Watson

180 -1,860 $US EP
35 rooms, 35 pb
Visa, MC, AmEx, ●
C-yes/S-ltd/P-no/H-yes
English
All year

BP and MAP available for
fee.
All suite hotel, AC bedrooms,
entertainment, fresh water
pool, water sports, baby-
sitting, business services,
beach, award winning
restaurant, complimentary
WiFi Internet

The premier boutique hotel in Barbados, overlooking the beautiful white-sand beach at Paynes Bay on the west coast. Thirty-five (35) air conditioned suites all recently renovated. Treasure Beach features a freshwater pool and an award winning restaurant.
✉ reservations@treasurebeachhotel.com ◐ www.treasurebeachhotel.com

ST. MICHAEL

Sweetfield Manor
Brittons New Road
888-744-4310 246-429-8356
George & Ann Clarke

195 – 575 $US BB
7 rooms, 5 pb
Most CC, •
C-ltd/S-ltd/P-no/H-no
English, German
Open year round!

Full Gourmet Breakfast
Welcome drinks, Ice Tea and
fresh baked goods.
A/C in all Guest Rooms,
Swimming Pool with
Waterfall & Spa, full access to
all main rooms, pool and
gardens. Minutes form
beaches, shopping,
restaurants, sights and Port.

TOP CARIBBEAN PICK of ISLANDS Magazine 2008 An Authentic 100 yr old Plantation Great House fully restored and offering just 7 exclusive private fully air conditioned guest-rooms. A gorgeous tropical lagoon styled pool & spa, close to everything!
✉ clarke@sweetfieldmanor.com 🌐 www.sweetfieldmanor.com

Cayman Islands

GRAND CAYMAN

Shangri-La B&B
1 Sticky Toffee Lane
345-526-1170
Eileen Davidson

119 – 189 $US BB
6 rooms, 6 pb
Most CC
C-ltd/S-no/P-no/H-ltd
English
All year

Full breakfast
Guests may use the kitchen
for snacks
TV, hairdryers, pool, Jacuzzi,
A/C, in–Room safes, phone,
iron & laundry services, bicycles, beach chairs & towels

Shangri-La B&B is a tropical lakeside retreat, with six Caribbean style, en suite bedrooms, an exotic pool and Jacuzzi offering dreamy scenery and a lush garden.
✉ info@shangrilabandb.com 🌐 www.shangrilabandb.com

Dominica

PORTSMOUTH

Picard Beach Cottages
Ross Boulevard, Prince
Rupert Bay
767-445-5131
Janice Armour

80 – 220 $US BB
18 rooms, 18 pb
Visa, MC, AmEx, •
C-yes/S-yes/P-no/H-no
English
All year

Continental breakfast
Lunch, Dinner, Snacks (fee)
Laundromat, childcare,
security, tour desk,
restaurant, bar,
entertainment, afternoon tea,
sitting room, pool, fridge,
phone, room service, A/C,
balcony, wake-up calls

Explore the glorious natural aspects of Dominica staying in luxury and comfort at Picard Beach Cottages. Wooden cottages with traditional Dominican 18th Century architecture and furnishings, cottages are spacious and feature many modern amenities.
✉ picardbeach@cwdom.dm 🌐 www.avirtualdominica.com/picard.htm

ROSEAU

Anchorage Hotel
Castle Comfort
767-448-2638
Janice Armour

69 – 118 $US BB
32 rooms, 32 pb
Visa, MC, AmEx, •
C-yes/S-yes/P-no/H-ltd
English
All year

Full American Breakfast
Restaurant, lunch, dinner,
afternoon tea
Sitting room, bar service,
snacks, swimming pool, dive
center, TV, A/C, telephone,
Internet access,

The Anchorage is an informal, elegant hotel. The lounge, pool, terrace and restaurant open out to a wide expanse of the Caribbean Sea and brilliant sunsets.
✉ anchorage@cwdom.dm 🌐 www.anchoragehotel.dm

ROSEAU

Portsmouth Beach Hotel	60 – 120 $US BB	Continental breakfast
on a Golden Sand Beach	80 rooms, 80 pb	Lunch, dinner, afternoon tea,
767-445-5142	Visa, •	snack available
Janice Armour	C-yes/S-yes/P-no/H-yes	Sitting room, bar service,
	English	swimming pool, A/C, cable
	All year	TV, telephone, wireless
		Internet, refrigerator access

Portsmouth Beach Hotel is located on a golden sand beach on the north-west coast of Dominica, just half a mile from Portsmouth. Set in a tropical garden are eighty rooms, each with a private bathroom, and veranda.
✉ pbh@cwdom.dm ✪ www.avirtualdominica.com/pbh.htm

Jamaica

KINGSTON

Anchorage Jamaica	80 – 125 $US BB	Continental Jamaican
2 Gwendon Park Avenue	7 rooms, 6 pb	Breakfast
876-925-1067	C-no/S-no/P-no/H-no	Jamaican Breakfast $10 extra
Jennifer Tame	English	for apartment guests
	All year	Fans, A/C, TV, coffee & tea
		Facility, WiFi connection
		available

The Anchorage Bed & Breakfast property is set in the beautiful residential foothills on the outskirts of Kingston, Jamaica's commercial and cultural capital, just ten minutes away from New Kingston.
✉ anchorage@flowja.com ✪ www.anchoragejamaica.com

Knolford Polo Ranch	100 $US BB	Continental breakfast
Riverside	15 rooms, 15 pb	Jamiacan style cuisine
876-929-5462	C-yes/S-ltd/P-no/H-no	Orchards, tennis, polo, pool,
Mark Harris	English	Polo Bar, All Inclusive
	All Season	

The Knolford Polo & Tennis Ranch is Jamaica's polo and tennis paradise. It is located in a snugly secluded, lush tropical valley outside Riversdale, St. Catherine, Jamaica in the center of the Island.
✉ knolford@yahoo.com ✪ www.knolford.com

LITTLE BAY

Coral Cove Resort	250 $US AP	Full breakfast
#2 Old Hope Rd.,	15 rooms, 15 pb	All meals and drinks
217-548-2452	Most CC, •	included Fresh baked
Steve Zindars	C-yes/S-ltd/P-no/H-ltd	deserts
	English, Spanish, French	Room service, Internet
	All year	access, bicycles, bar/lounge,
		library, snorkeling gear &
		instruction, laundry service,
		child care, meeting &
		banquet facilities, wedding
		coordinator

Coral Cove Resort is a place that holds everything that is magical about the island of Jamaica. A secluded, All-Inclusive Beach Resort perfect for weddings and gatherings of family and friends. A little piece of paradise for relaxation, fun and romance.
✉ cclbayj@yahoo.com ✪ www.coralcovejamaica.com

NEGRIL

SeaSand Eco Villas
Norman Manley Blvd
876-892-6935
Debra Boyle

160 – 370 $US BB	Breakfast (incl. first day only)
11 rooms, 11 pb	Welcome beverage, rum, beer
Visa, MC, •	& soda
C-yes/S-yes/P-no/H-ltd	Cable TV, DVD player, library,
English, Jamaican Patois	games, A/C, housekeeper,
All year	chef, groundskeepers, purified water

Exclusive beach front complex of four elegant houses in lush tropical gardens on a private beach. Spacious rooms, exceptionally private and relaxing atmosphere, accompanied by a personal housekeeper and cook.
✉ debraboyle_greenisland@yahoo.com ◯ www.seasandecovillas.com

Xtabi B&B
Lighthouse Road, Westend
876-957-0524 876-957-0121
David Prebble

55 – 225 $US EP	Restaurant serves breakfast,
24 rooms, 24 pb	lunch and dinner.
Most CC, •	Pool, lagoon, diving
C-yes/S-yes/P-no/H-no	packages & tours, cable TV,
English	A/C, kitchenettes in some
All year	rooms, all rooms and cottages have private baths with a veranda or deck

Xtabi, meeting place of the gods, the name as exotic as the quaint cottages and octagon shaped bungalows lying across the land and on rocky terraces above a turquoise sea. In Negril tourism is not set apart from Jamaican life because everyone is family.
✉ xtabiresort@cwjamaica.com ◯ www.xtabi-negril.com

OCHO RIOS

The Blue House
White River Estates, White River
876-994-1367
Elise Yap

120 – 240 $US BB	Full breakfast
5 rooms, 5 pb	Dinner plans available, beer &
Visa, MC, •	wine
C-yes/S-ltd/P-no/H-no	Large airy rooms, A/C in bed-
English	rooms, private bathrooms,
All year	ceiling fans, cable TV. Wireless Internet and computer for guest use. In-room safes, irons and ironing board.

Ocho Rios, Jamaica luxury bed and breakfast inn/boutique hotel. The Blue House, an award winning Caribbean villa with private Cozy Cottage, offers 5 bedroom vacation accommodations, nestled in lush gardens, minutes from the beach. Romantic getaway.
✉ elise@thebluehousejamaica.com ◯ www.thebluehousejamaica.com

Hibiscus Lodge Hotel
83 Main Street
876-974-2676
Michelle Doswald

128 – 140 $US BB	Full breakfast
26 rooms, 26 pb	Restaurant, bar, lunch,
Most CC, •	dinner
C-yes/S-yes/P-no/H-yes	AC, pool, tennis, hot tub, TV
English	room, laundry service,
All year	gardens

Set amid 3 acres of lush gardens on a cliff overlooking the ocean. Centrally located in the heart of Ocho Rios. Where your vacation can be as relaxing, or active as you want it to be!
✉ mdoswald@cwjamaica.com ◯ www.hibiscusjamaica.com

ST. ANN'S BAY

High Hope Estate
16 Top Road
876-972-2277
Ludovica & Dennis

110 – 185 $US EP	Ala Carte Menu changes daily
5 rooms, 5 pb	Complimentary afternoon tea
Visa, MC, *Rated*, •	Pool, private beach club, na-
C-ltd/S-ltd/P-no/H-no	ture trails, massages, facials,
English, Italian, and	in-room coffee, turn down ser-
some German	vice, golf, tennis, sailing and
All year	diving . . . .all nearby

Especially for special people . . . Five beautifully furnished guestrooms located on 40 acres of botanical gardens. Highly acclaimed restaurant featuring Jamaican and Italian specialty dishes. High Hope offers guests peace, tranquility, and natural beauty.
✉ dr@highhopeestate.com ◯ www.highhopeestate.com

TREASURE BEACH

Button Bay Beach Getaway
Button Bay
876-815-9029
Gladys Finlason

119 $US BB	Full breakfast
12 rooms, 12 pb	All meals are freshly cooked
Rated	by our staff.
C-yes/S-yes/P-yes/H-no	A/C, parking, patio, beach
English	chairs/towels, Internet,
Parrot Villa and 9 double	housekeeping service,
rooms all year	private pool, CD/library,
	hairdryer, coffee maker,
	DVD, VCR, mini-fridge,
	washer

Button Bay Beach Getaway offers 9 theme rooms set in a natural paradise and the very private Parrot Villa is a 3 bedroom retreat. The private restaurant serves fresh seafood and authentic Jamaican cuisine.
✉ buttonbay@comcast.net ◎ www.buttonbayjamaica.com

Panama

LAS CUMBRES

Pequeno Paraiso B&B
594 Calle 12
+507-6691-6254
Anita & Rick

75 – 90 $US BB	Full breakfast
3 rooms, 1 pb	We also cater to guests with
•	special dietary needs
C-ltd/S-no/P-ltd/H-no	Swimming pool, sun bathing
English, Spanish, French,	terrace w/lounge chairs &
Italian	tables, Jacuzzi, common
All year	living areas, WiFi, A/C,
	bathrobes, hairdryer,
	unlimited free long distance
	to Canada & USA

Pequeno Paraiso B&B is located in Las Cumbres, Panama a very picturesque suburb of Panama City that is surrounded by mountains, fresh air and lush tropical fauna.
✉ anita2013@gmail.com ◎ www.pequenoparaiso.net

St. Lucia

SOUFRIERE

La Haut Plantation
La Haut Plantation
758-459-7008
Stephanie Allain

100 -375 $US BB	Full breakfast
15 rooms, 15 pb	Tea, coffee & fresh fruit in
Visa, MC, Disc, *Rated*,	season in room daily
•	Outdoor pool, gardens,
C-ltd/S-ltd/P-no/H-no	lounge with snooker table &
English & Patois	piano, library with books &
All year	magazines, free shuttle to
	town and beach at fixed
	times, beach towels

Step back in time when life was simple. Enjoy Caribbean country plantation life, panoramic Pitons view, friendly staff, tasty and healthy local food, two pools, bird/whale/dolphin watch, rum punch & cocoa tea. Come embrace the magic of La Haut.
✉ lahaut@candw.lc ◎ www.lahaut.com

St. Vincent / Grenadines

BEQUIA

Bequia Beachfront Villas Road Town 800-367-8455 284-495-4467 Anita Cottoy	159 – 2330 $US BB 8 rooms, 8 pb Visa, MC, AmEx, *Rated*, • C-yes/S-ltd/P-no/H-yes English All year	Breakfast starter Supply in Villa. Breakfast starter supplies in refrigerator. All villas have AC, TV, fully-equipped kitchens, porch or balcony, daily maid service, WiFi access, beach, laundry service.

Bequia Beachfront Villas are situated on a pristine mile long beach called Friendship Bay. Cooling trade winds and gentle breezes create a pleasant & relaxing environment. Villas are unique and comfortable with spectacular views and upscale amenities.
✉ ftrhotel@surfbvi.com ✆ www.fortrecovery.com/bequia/

Tortola BVI

ROAD TOWN/TORTOLA

Sebastian's On The Beach Hotel Little Apple Bay 800-336-4870 284-495-4212 Ursla Miloleiczik	75 -375 $US EP 35 rooms, 35 pb Most CC, • C-yes/S-no/P-yes/H-no English, German All year	Full breakfast Breakfast, lunch and dinner available for a fee. Bar service, gift store, commissary, water sports, beach, WiFi, Internet desk in reception, A/C, refrigerator, hot/cold water, two units with whirlpool

Turn off the phone, the fax, the cable TV . . . and lose yourself at the British Virgin Islands' best kept secret . . . Sebastian's On the Beach Hotel & Restaurant, located on a luxurious, white sand beach in Little Apple Bay on Tortola's North Shore.
✉ sebhotel@surfbvi.com ✆ www.sebastiansbvi.com

WEST END

Fort Recovery Beachfront Villas The Towers 800-367-8455 284-495-4467 Anita Cottoy	185 – 360 $US BB 32 rooms, 32 pb Visa, MC, AmEx, *Rated*, • C-yes/S-ltd/P-no/H-yes English, Spanish All year	Coffee, tea, breads, jams Full American breakfast offered and dinner daily. Sitting room, library, swimming pool, private beach, mini spa, WiFi, historic Fort, restaurant

Fort Recovery Resort is Located on the calm, Caribbean side of the island where cooling trade winds give us constant breezes. This unique, Villa-Style resort provides an intimate and fantastic Caribbean vacation experience, with resort conveniences.
✉ ftrhotel@surfbvi.com ✆ www.fortrecovery.com/tortola/index.html

Trinidad / Tobago

MARAVAL

Monique's Guest House
114/116 Saddle Road
868-628-2351 868-628-3334
Monica Charbonne

75 – 90 $US EP	Guesthouse Restaurant
20 rooms, 20 pb	onsite
Visa, MC, *Rated*, •	Breakfast, lunch, restaurant,
C-yes/S-yes/P-no/H-yes	snacks, bar
English	Internet, bar service, sitting
All year	room, laundry, iron/board,
	microwave in all kitchenette
	rooms, kettle with
	coffee/tea/sugar milk/fridge
	in std rooms.

Though small, our accommodation compares with multinational hotels, combined with personalized attention, and a homey atmosphere.
✉ info@moniquestrinidad.com 🌐 www.moniquestrinidad.com

Central-S. America

Argentina

BUENOS AIRES

B&B Olleros 3000
Olleros 3000, Colegiales
+54-11-4554-7269
Claudine & Juan

62 – 86 $US BB	Continental breakfast
3 rooms, 2 pb	Tea, beer, mineral water
•	Sitting/music room,
C-ltd/S-no/P-no/H-no	gymnasium, newspapers,
Spanish, French, English,	fax, computer, WiFi, fridge,
Italian	hairdryer, laundry, travel
All year	advice & information

Stylish guesthouse in a central and quiet neighborhood within walking distance of trendy Palermo in Buenos Aires. Sophisticated & comfortable accommodations hosted by Claudine, a professional in hospitality, and Juan, an architect & art historian.
✉ info@olleros3000.com.ar 🌐 www.claudinehomes-buenosaires.com

Belize

AMBERGRIS CAYE

Coral Bay Villas
PO Box 1, San Pedro
+501-226-3003
Herman & Linda Penland

105 – 165 $US EP	Short walk to near by
6 rooms, 6 pb	restaurants and shops.
Most CC	Private beach, lounges &
C-yes/S-no/P-no/H-yes	hammocks, maid service,
Spanish, English	bicycles, kayaks, cable TV,
All year	A/C, golf cart rentals,
	assistance with tours &
	reservations, fully-equipped
	kitchens

Coral Bay Villas offers luxurious, beach front accommodations with a spectacular view of the Caribbean Sea and the Barrier Reef. Six deluxe condos are situated on a white sandy beach, shaded by palm trees, with large terraces to catch the sea breeze.
✉ cbayvillas@btl.net 🌐 www.coralbaybelize.com

AMBERGRIS CAYE

SunBreeze Suites	165-205 $US EP	Private Ocean Front Balcony,
San Pedro Town	21 rooms, 21 pb	Equipped Kitchen, A/C,
800-820-1631 011-501-226-4675	C-yes/S-ltd/P-no/H-no	Cable TV, Phone, Hairdryer,
Julia Edwards	Spanish, English	Iron/Board, Clock Radio,
	All Seasons	Daily
		Maid/Dive/Tour/Laundry
		Service, Pool, Safety Deposit

SunBreeze Suites is situated on a Caribbean Island in Belize, a fast growing vacation destination, allowing for the perfect balance between modern amenities mixed with the charm of a small Island.
✉ sunbreezesuites@sunbreezesuites.com ✪ www.sunbreezesuites.com

BELIZE CITY

Coningsby Inn	55 – 60 $US EP	On request
76 Regent St	10 rooms, 10 pb	Air conditioning, TV, laundry
+501-227-1566	Most CC	service, snack & gift shop,
Jeanette Neal	C-yes/S-ltd/P-ltd/H-yes	wireless Internet
	English	
	All year	

Coningsby Inn is near the end of Regent Street in a quiet setting just½block from the sea and close to downtown. The Inn is an ideal spot to feel at home while still being in the city. The rooms are large and pleasantly-furnished .
✉ coningsby_inn@btl.net ✪ www.coningsby-inn.com

The Great House Inn	100 – 150 $US EP	In house Smoky Mermaid
#13 Cork Street	16 rooms, 16 pb	Restaurant & Bar, 6am-10pm
+501-223-3400	Most CC, *Rated*, •	Cable TV, hair dryers,
Steve Maestre	C-yes/S-yes/P-no/H-no	telephone, fax, desk, safety
	English, Spanish	deposit boxes, air
	All year	conditioning, coffee makers,
		Iron boards, bottle water,
		cookies & coffee daily,
		wireless Internet

The look and feel of yesterday with today's modern conveniences make The Great House, Belize's most desirable "outpost" away from home. Meticulously appointed, spacious rooms with all the amenities for your comfort and convenience.
✉ greathouse@btl.net ✪ www.greathousebelize.com

CAYE CAULKER

Iguana Reef Inn	110 – 165 $US BB	Continental breakfast
PO Box 31	13 rooms, 13 pb	Many local restaurants in
+501-226-0213	Visa, MC, Disc, •	walking distance
Mario Guizar & Jim	C-ltd/S-ltd/P-no/H-no	A/C, ceiling fans, in-room
Dombrowski	English, Spanish	refrigerator, safety box,
	All year	swimming pool, bar

Discover the Iguana Reef Inn on Caye Caulker – a resort that blends casual elegance with barefoot informality. Located on the water's edge, the Inn offers decidedly upscale accommodations in a secluded location in the heart of a charming fishing village.
✉ iguanareef@btl.net ✪ www.iguanareefinn.com

Lazy Iguana	95 -145 $US BB	Continental breakfast
Caye Caulker	4 rooms, 4 pb	Free Bottled Water
361-723-0455 +501-226-0350	Visa, MC, AmEx	AC, Ceiling Fans, WiFi, Sitting
Mo & Irene Miller	C-no/S-ltd/P-no/H-no	Room, Cable TV, Garden,
	Spanish, English	Rooftop Palapa
	All year	

The Lazy Iguana Bed and Breakfast on the island of Caye Caulker, Belize is more than a hotel! The Lazy Iguana Bed and Breakfast is a charming and exclusive private resort surrounded by lush tropical gardens, and we offer a great breakfast!
✉ lazyiguanabb@aol.com ✪ www.lazyiguana.net

CAYE CAULKER

Morgan's Inn	25 – 45 $US EP	No food is offered.
Beach-front	3 rooms, 3 pb	Stove available upon
+501-226-0178	Visa, MC	request. Butane is guest's
Ellen McRae	C-yes/S-ltd/P-ltd/H-ltd	responsibility. Refrigerator.
	English	
	All year	

Morgan's Inn has 3 Belizean-style cabins available. All cabins are beach-front, with plenty of coconut trees on the land. All have hot/cold showers and large covered porches for relaxing. Marine biologist guide on-site. $25.00 rate for longer stays.
✉ sbf@btl.net

COROZAL

Serenity Sands Bed and	75 – 115 $US BB	Full breakfast
Breakfast	4 rooms, 4 pb	Alarm clock, BBQ grill, board
Mile 4, Consejo Road	Visa, MC	games, DVD player, Internet
+501-649-2391	C-ltd/S-ltd/P-no/H-no	access, library,
Penny & Don Lebrun, Jill &	English	satellite/cable TV, telephone,
Phyl Mason	All Seasons	washer/dryer, A/C, ceiling
		fans, private entrance

Serenity Sands Bed and Breakfast is a comfortable, environmentally friendly Bed and Breakfast where travelers can come for stunning scenery, beautiful sunrises and the peace and tranquility of a secluded beach.
✉ info@serenitysands.com ۞ www.serenitysands.com

CROOKED TREE VILLAGE

Bird's Eye View Lodge	70 – 100 $US BB	Continental Breakfast
Belize City	20 rooms, 20 pb	Belizean & International food
+501-203-2040	Visa, MC, AmEx, •	also available.
Verna & Denver Gillett	C-yes/S-ltd/P-no/H-yes	A/C, bar, restaurant, laundry
	English & Creole	service, TV, bicycle, tour
	All year	guides, souvenir shop, tours,
		transfer services, boat
		cruises, bird watching from
		patio, crocodile safaris

Bird's Eye View Lodge is a Belizean family owned 20 room eco-lodge situated in the heart of the Crooked Tree Sanctuary. The top neotropical birding site in Belize is Crooked Tree and the Bird's Eye View Lodge is the place to stay.
✉ birdseye@btl.net ۞ www.birdseyeviewbelize.com

SAN IGNACIO

The Lodge at Chaa Creek	300 – 575 $US BB	Full breakfast
Macal River	23 rooms, 23 pb	Wine
877-709-8708 +501-824-2037	Most CC, •	Full service spa, in-room
Michael & Lucy Fleming	C-yes/S-yes/P-ltd/H-no	safe, coffee service,
	English and Spanish	restaurant & bar, office
	All year	services, Internet, mountain
		bikes, concierge services

Live the adventure! Canoe on pristine rivers, hike, bike, and horseback-ride through jungle trails, explore Maya caves & temples, and enjoy charming accommodations, excellent dining and exotic spa treatments in a private 365-acre Nature Reserve.
✉ reservations@chaacreek.com ۞ www.chaacreek.com

Tell your hosts Pamela Lanier sent you.

SAN PEDRO TOWN————————————————————————

Ak'Bol Yoga Retreat & Eco Resort
North of the Bridge
+501-226-2073
Milio and Kirsten

35 – 150 $US EP
37 rooms, 7 pb
Visa, MC
C-yes/S-ltd/P-no/H-no
Spanish, English
All Seasons

On-Site Restaurant: Meals
$0.25 – $7.50
Bamboo Open-Air Rain
Shower, Two Yoga Studios,
On-Site Restaurant, Private
Cabanas, Carved mahogany
sinks w/conch shell faucets,
house keeping, airport pick
up free, Pool

Welcome to life unplugged at Ak'bol, Maya for Heart of the Village, Belize's first Yoga Retreat and Family Eco Resort. We welcome you to this beachfront sanctuary, located on the tranquil North side of Belize's largest island, Ambergris Caye.
✉ info@akbol.com 🌐 www.akbol.com

Mata Rocks Resort
47 Coconut Drive
888-628-2757 +501-226-2336
Terry Anderson & Liz Cechini

110 – 231 $US BB
17 rooms, 17 pb
Visa, MC, AmEx, •
C-yes/S-ltd/P-no/H-yes
English/Spanish
All year

Continental Breakfast
Snacks, beachfront bar
serves casual lunches
Free Wireless,
complimentary bicycles, free
taxi transport, beachfront,
pool

The soft sandy beach just outside your door at Mata Rocks Resort beckons you to enjoy our sparkling blue Caribbean Sea. Whether you want privacy or access to adventure, our peaceful and serene beachfront hotel invites you to Ambergris Caye in Belize.
✉ reservations@matarocks.com 🌐 www.MataRocks.com

The Palms
Oceanfront
+501-226-3322
Chris Beaumont

148 – 265 $US EP
13 rooms, 13 pb
Most CC
C-yes/S-no/P-no/H-yes
Spanish, English
All year

"First Day" coffee & gallon of
fresh cool water
Refrigerator, stove,
microwave, blender,
coffeemaker, toaster, pans,
dishes, silverware, TV's, A/C,
ceiling fans, phone, Hi-Speed
DSL ($25 USD/Wk), private
verandas

The Palms Oceanfront Suites are truly a paradise found. Come soak in the sun and frolic in the azure waters without compromising on the quality of your accommodations. Strike out from San Pedro town and discover the natural wonderland of Belize.
✉ thepalms@belizepalms.com 🌐 www.belizepalms.com

SunBreeze Hotel
Ambergris Caye
800-688-0191
+501-226-2191/2345
Julia Edwards

115 -178 $US EP
43 rooms, 43 pb
Visa, MC, AmEx,
Rated, •
C-yes/S-no/P-no/H-ltd
English and Spanish
All year

Meal plan available
Fresh Water Pool,
Pool/Beach Towels, Bike
Rental, Volley Ball, Baby
Sitting, Safe Deposit Boxes,
Tour Desk, TV, Hairdryer,
Iron/Board available upon
request

SunBreeze Hotel is a great value vacation getaway spot. Ideal for all age groups looking for that home away from home feeling.
✉ sunbreezehotel@sunbreeze.net 🌐 www.sunbreeze.net

Bolivia

COPACABANA

Hotel Rosario del Lago
Rigoberto Paredes St.
Costanera s/n
+591-2244-1756
Claudio Vera Loza

39 – 52 $US BB
30 rooms, 30 pb
Visa, MC, *Rated*, •
C-yes/S-yes/P-yes/H-no
Spanish, English, French
All year

American Buffet Breakfast
Fresh lake trout, pasta,
International menu
Internet WiFi, restaurant with
lake view, TV, safe deposit
boxes, bottled water

The hotel is a Colonial style building. Spectacular views of Lake Titicaca from the guest-rooms and outdoor balcony in the sitting area. The hotel is only a block from the lake front.
✉ reservaslago@hotelrosario.com 🌐 www.hotelrosario.com/lago/

LA PAZ

Hotel Rosario
Avenida Illampu 704
+591-2245-1658
Eduardo Zeballos

43 -85 $US BB
42 rooms, 42 pb
Visa, MC, *Rated*, •
C-yes/S-ltd/P-no/H-no
Spanish, English
All year

Buffet breakfast
Restaurant serves dinner, tea
& coca mate, bar
Sitting room, travel agency,
free Internet access, luggage
deposit, cable TV/64
channels, heater, safe
deposit boxes, hairdryers,
toiletries

A beautifully restored Colonial building with a sunny courtyard. The décor features many motifs from the Aymara and Quechua cultures. Hotel Rosario is centrally located near the colorful, crafts markets of La Paz.
✉ reservas@hotelrosario.com 🌐 www.hotelrosario.com

Costa Rica

ALAJUELA

Orquideas Inn
Central Valley
+506-2433-7128
Liseth Alean

59 – 160 $US BB
26 rooms, 26 pb
Visa, MC
C-yes/S-ltd/P-no/H-ltd
Spanish, English
All year

Full breakfast
Lunch & dinner available in
the restaurant.
Friendly English speaking
staff, pool, secluded outdoor
Jacuzzi, TV, phone, coffee
maker, hairdryer, safe, A/C,
bar, spa, gift shop, laundry
service, luggage storage

The Inn is nestled on over 10 acres of lush natural tropical gardens teeming with exotic tropical fruits, flowers, birds and butterflies. From the minute you arrive, your cares melt away as you take a dip in the pool or relax in the outdoor Jacuzzi.
✉ info@orquideasinn.com 🌐 www.orquideasinn.com

Pura Vida Wellness Retreat & Spa
A Mountain Resort in Costa Rica
888-767-7375 770-483-0238

77 – 1,370 $US AP
50 rooms, 30 pb
Visa, MC
C-yes/S-no/P-no/H-no
English, Spanish
All year

Continental breakfast
Wholesome, delicious meals
included, 5 night rate
Pool, Jacuzzi, indoor and
outdoor Meditation sites,
gardens, coffee makers

Welcome to Wellness & Yoga in Costa Rica. We look forward to being your host at this beautiful resort. Pura Vida Retreat and Spa is considered by some as the Wellness & Yoga destination of choice outside the United States.
✉ reservations@puravidaspa.com 🌐 www.puravidaspa.com

BIRRI

La Catalina Hotel & Suites
Beside Cetal La Catalina
866-436-9399 866-771-7778
Pia Kocchiu

45 -199 $US BB
22 rooms, 22 pb
Most CC, *Rated*, •
C-yes/S-yes/P-no/H-yes
English
All year

Full breakfast
Internet, phone, TV, 2 heated
pools, tennis court, private
gym, gardens, fabulous
valley views

La Catalina Hotel & Suites is a majestic, private resort, located a few miles just outside the Capital City of San Jose. Set on six lush acres surrounded by tropical flowers, trees & ponds with many gracious amenities.
✉ info@lacatalinasuites.com 🌐 www.lacatalinasuites.com

DOMINICAL

Cascadas Farallas Villas
Baru-Dominical
+506-8882-7717
Fateh Kaur Bolivar

120 – 350 $US BB
6 rooms, 6 pb
Visa, MC, •
C-ltd/S-no/P-no/H-no
English, Spanish,
German, Italian
All year

Organic Gourmet Breakfast
Private chef for lunch/dinner
+Detox menu & vega
Yoga & meditation, Nature
tour and private waterfalls
incl. beach 5 minutes
transport free daily, Detox
packages w/ Javanese Jamu,
Jaguar massage!

Private Waterfalls! Balconies hang right over the top of the waterfalls. Luxury Balinese style Waterfall Villas in an exceptionally beautiful tropical rainforest. Cascadas Farallas has naturally rock carved 5 cascading waterfalls like a Stairway to Heaven
✉ info@farallas.com 🌐 www.waterfallvillas.com

DRAKES BAY

El Mirador Lodge
On a Hill
877-769-8747 +506-2223-4060
Jamie Umana

90 $US AP
12 rooms, 12 pb
Visa, MC, *Rated*
C-yes/S-yes/P-yes/H-no
English, Spanish
All year

Full breakfast
All meals, natural juices &
coffee break
Private bathrooms, there are
rooms with electricity &
rooms without, some have
an ocean view, tours,
restaurant & transportation
available

El Mirador Lodge has one of the most spectacular views in Drake's Bay. The lodge, is located on the hill just 200 meters from the ocean. Fall asleep to the sound of the ocean waves crashing on the shore and awaken to a cool morning breeze.
✉ info@mirador.co.cr 🌐 www.mirador.co.cr

ESCAZU

Out of Bounds Lodge and B&B
1km West from Commercial
Paco Ol
+506-2288-6762
Meranda Glesby & Matteo
Brancacci Soto

70 – 120 $US BB
5 rooms, 5 pb
Most CC, •
C-yes/S-ltd/P-no/H-yes
English
All year

Full breakfast
Fresh fruit drink or coffee on
arrival
BBQ grill, fax, photo copier,
DVD/CD, Sony Play Station,
washer/dryer, books,
magazines, games, operating
tour company, bikes, snorkel
gear, surf boards, non-
smoking

We proudly announce the opening of our beautiful new Hotel B&B with amazing views overlooking the Central Valley, located on the Old Road to Santa Ana in the suburb of San Rafael Escazu. The rooms are hotel style rooms, not the typical B&B.
✉ mermatt@racsa.co.cr 🌐 www.bedandbreakfastcr.com

ESCAZU———————————————————————————

Posada El Quijote Country Inn
Apartado 528-1260
+506-2289-8401
Dick & Claudia Furlong

85 – 105 $US BB
8 rooms, 8 pb
C-yes/S-ltd/P-no/H-no
Spanish, English
All year

Full American Breakfast
Made to Order!
Direct phone line, cable TV, laundry facilities, closed porch and balcony, sitting area, fully equipped kitchen, fully tiled european bath, sleeping area

Charming, with many luxuries, in a lush tropical setting, this charming and elegant country inn offers spectacular views of the Central Valley & exquisitely decorated rooms with ultra-modern bathrooms, at very comfortable rates, including full breakfast.
✉ quijote@quijote.co.cr ✪ www.quijote.co.cr

HEREDIA———————————————————————————

The Cariari Bed & Breakfast
Avenida de la Marina, 12
Ciudad de Cariari
866-224-8339 +506-2239-2585
Laurie Blizzard

65 – 90 $US BB
3 rooms, 2 pb
●
C-yes/S-no/P-yes/H-yes
Spanish, English
All year

Full Breakfast Menu
Fresh fruit always available. Beverage & bocas
WiFi, computer, TV, refrigerators, ceiling fans, deck – for meetings and friends, laundry facilities, spanish classes, tour information, reservations, auto rentals

This beautiful Spanish style home in a safe residential area, has lovely grounds with patio and a warm friendly atmosphere. Our huge roof-deck is available for meditation, yoga, reading, bird watching or just plain relaxing.
✉ laurie@cariaribb.com ✪ www.cariaribb.com

JACO BEACH———————————————————————————

Sonidos del Mar
Calle Hidalgo
+506-2643-3924
Laurie & Howard Koseff

250 – 300 $US BB
4 rooms, 4 pb
C-yes/S-no/P-no/H-no
English
All Seasons

Continental breakfast
AC, pool, outside shower, DVD player, beautiful gardens, laundry service, gas grill, SAT-TV, parking, housekeeping, fully equipped kitchen, furnished deck, hot tub

Steps from the beach alongside a river in a secluded tropical paradise, this new contemporary designed vacation home/ B and B will bring out the Zen in you. This stunning setting is alive with a diversity of exotic wildlife, birds and plants.
✉ dosbaldeagles@hotmail.com ✪ www.sonidosdelmar.com

MANUEL ANTONIO———————————————————————————

La Colina Hotel and Sunset Terrace
Edge of the rainforest
800-686-4711 +506-2777-0231
Chef Michael McDermott

39 – 95 $US BB
13 rooms, 13 pb
Most CC, ●
C-yes/S-yes/P-yes/H-no
English, Spanish
All year

Full breakfast
Culinary seafood dishes and American style steaks.
WiFi, Internet & business services, TV, balconies, ceiling fans, A/C, room safe, laundry, pool, beach mat rentals, some suites with coffee maker, cooking facilities

With one of the most visually stunning backdrops in the country, La Colina Hotel and Sunset Terrace in Manuel Antonio offers travelers comfort and easy access to one of the most lush places in Costa Rica.
✉ lacolina07@gmail.com ✪ www.lacolina.com

MANUEL ANTONIO

Villas Lirio
Quepos/Manuel Antonio area
+506-2520-1900
Robert Bogdanovich

135 – 195 $US EP
23 rooms, 23 pb
C-yes/S-yes/P-no/H-ltd
English, Spanish
All year

Self-catered kitchen in the rooms
Laundry service, secure parking, smoking permitted, 2 pools, ocean view balcony, BBQ, ceiling fans, A/C, kitchen, stove, microwave, fridge, phone, TV

Casa Roland's Villas Lirio is located in the Quepos/Manuel Antonio area on the central Pacific Coast of Costa Rica. This secluded hotel is decorated with fine furnishings and unique art created by local artists, including renowned painter Deirdre Hyde.
✉ reservations@rolandhotels.com 🌐 www.villaslirio.com

MONTEVERDE

Arco Iris Lodge
Santa Elena de Monteverde
+506-2645-5067
Susanna Stoiber

70 – 180 $US EP
20 rooms, 20 pb
Visa, MC
C-yes/S-no/P-no/H-ltd
English, Deutsch, Espanol
All year

Buffet style breakfast
Optional Breakfast is $7.00, hot & cold drinks
Tour desk, library, laundry service, in room safe, parking, private transport, jeep/boat/taxi to La Fortuna, free Internet, hot water, balcony or terrace

Well cared for German owned mountain lodge in easy walking distance to the village. Tropical gardens, birds and butterflies, delicious breakfast, Cloud Forest Excursions, horses, organic garden, reliable tours and transfers, reasonable rates.
✉ arcoiris@racsa.co.cr 🌐 www.arcoirislodge.com

La Colina Lodge
Apartdo #56-5655
+506-2645-5009
Kevin

38 – 45 $US BB
11 rooms, 7 pb
Visa, MC
C-yes/S-ltd/P-yes/H-ltd
Spanish, English
All year

Full breakfast
Refreshments, large group meal plans lunch/dinner
Sat-TV, DVD, books, Queen beds, warm woven fabrics, Guatemalan furniture, balconies. Camping $5.00 per person

La Colina Lodge, formerly known as the Flor Mar, is nestled in the tranquil mountains of Costa Rica. Surrounded by Cloud Forest and the Quaker community, away from the noise and bustle of the town.
✉ lacolinalodge@hotmail.com 🌐 www.lacolinalodge.com

MONTEZUMA

Nature Lodge Finca Los Caballos
4 km south from Cobano
+506-2642-0124
Christian Klien

81 – 183 $US BB
12 rooms, 12 pb
Visa, MC
C-yes/S-ltd/P-no/H-ltd
English
All year

Full breakfast
Dinner under the stars with exquisite food & wine
Open air showers, large private decks & terraces, jungle views, unique grotto style bathrooms, restaurant, horses, guided tours, wellness

Welcome to our charming hotel and restaurant inspired by the natural beauty around Montezuma. Our small lodge is perched on a hill, somewhere between heaven and the sea, with views of the jungle and the ocean. Come, get in touch with nature.
✉ naturelc@racsa.co.cr 🌐 www.naturelodge.net

Tell your hosts Pamela Lanier sent you.

PUERTO JIMENEZ

Lookout Inn	115 – 175 $US AP	Breakfast, lunch & dinner
Carate	9 rooms, 7 pb	Drinks are separate
815-955-1520 757-644-5967	Visa, ●	Pool, hot tub, beach, private
Terry Conroy	C-yes/S-yes/P-yes/H-no	baths, hiking, kayaking,
	English, Spanish	lounge, library, observation
	All year	deck & bar, extensive
		gardens, WiFi

The Lookout Inn is a beautifully designed inn, nestled on the hillside of a Costa Rican rain forest, along the coast overlooking the Pacific Ocean and Corcovado National Park.
✉ reservations@lookout-inn.com 🌐 www.lookout-inn.com

PUNTARENAS

Villa Cabomar	75 – 85 $US BB	Full breakfast
Barrio El Carmen	3 rooms, 3 pb	A variety of restaurants
703-481-0241	C-yes/S-no/P-no/H-yes	within walking distance.
Martha Cropper	English	Patio, spa, kitchen, WiFi,
	All year	laundry, phone service
		available, (pre-paid
		telephone cards for
		international calls), pool
		with water cascade and jets,
		atrium, gate

Located in an established residential neighborhood, Villa Cabomar features all the comforts of home with a spectacular volcanic sand beach a block away in the Pacific port town of Puntarenas.
✉ the_cropper_family@msn.com 🌐 www.rent-cabomar.com

ROSARIO DE NARANJO

Vista del Valle Plantation Inn	100 – 175 $US BB	Full breakfast
Calle Indio	12 rooms, 12 pb	Full Service Restaurant &
+506-2450-0900 +506-2450-0800	Visa, MC, AmEx, ●	Bar
Elisa	C-ltd/S-ltd/P-no/H-yes	Private villas, fine dining,
	English & Spanish	pool, Jacuzzi, Internet hot
	All year	spot, spa services, nature
		trails, horse riding, weddings
		& small meetings, travel
		assistance

A very special place awaits the traveler in search for the perfect destination to experience the beauty of Costa Rica. At Vista del Valle, our goal is to create a worry-free haven of quiet and natural beauty for our guests. Only 20 minutes from Airport.
✉ frontdesk@vistadelvalle.com 🌐 www.vistadelvalle.com

SAN JOSE

Adventure Inn Hotel	65 – 107 $US BB	Full breakfast
50m este de la entrada de los	34 rooms, 34 pb	Delicious lunches and
Arcas Ciudad Cariari	Visa, MC, AmEx,	dinners at reasonable rates
+506-2239-2633	*Rated*, ●	Mayan waterfall Jacuzzi,
Eric & Mike Robinson	C-yes/S-ltd/P-ltd/H-yes	WiFi, Internet, guest
	Spanish, English	computers, fully equipped
	All year	gym, rain forest & volcano
		tours, car and 4WD rentals,
		A/C, free airport transfer,
		safe area

Value-priced smoke-free hotel/B&B between San Jose and airport, huge rooms with A/C, cable, WiFi, full American breakfast, 4 guest computers, sports bar, gym, Mayan waterfall Jacuzzi, tour rain forests, volcanoes, car rentals, outstanding guest comments.
✉ lanier@adventure-inn.com 🌐 www.adventure-inn.com

Casa El Dorado	135 – 185 $US BB	Full Gourmet Breakfast
San Antonio	5 rooms, 5 pb	Complimentary afternoon cof-
866-612-0348 +506-8318-7517	Visa, MC, AmEx	fee & tea, appetizers
Axel & Pamela Ruehlemann	C-yes/S-no/P-no/H-no	WiFi, cable TV, DVD, free calls
	English, Spanish,	to USA, mini-bar, safe deposit
	German	box, king beds, private veran-
	All year	da & roof top access, Jacuzzi

The Casa El Dorado is a small exclusive boutique hotel nestled in the green mountains of Escazu, Costa Rica overlooking the capital city of San Jose. We offer our guests luxurious accommodations in a Spanish Colonial Villa with breathtaking views.
✉ axel@casaeldorado.com 🌐 www.casaeldorado.com

Casa Lima B&B	55 – 95 $US BB	Continental plus breakfast
Del Colegio Humbolt 175 nort	23 rooms, 23 pb	On-site restaurant offers
50 oeste case #23	Most CC	local, Int. & Cuban food
786-758-7885	C-yes/S-ltd/P-ltd/H-ltd	WiFi Internet access, cable
Nelson Ruiz	English, Spanish	TV, DVD player, comfortable
	All Season	beds, private full bathroom
		with accessories.

"Un pequeño paraiso" is what we often hear from our guests . . . "A small-paradise." Casa Lima is an exclusive bed and breakfast nestled in one of Costa Rica's most unique and privileged neighborhoods, Rohomoser.
✉ info@casalimacr.com 🌐 www.casalimacr.com

Dunn Inn B&B	59 – 99 $US EP	Restaurant, coffee free all
Calle 5, Avenida 11, Barrio	26 rooms, 26 pb	day at the Cafe
Amón	Visa, MC, AmEx, •	Mini bars, mini gym, sitting
800-360-9521 +506-2222-3232	C-yes/S-ltd/P-yes/H-yes	room, exchange, safe deposit
Isabel de Esteban	Spanish, English	boxes, parking, quality
	All year	linens, cable w/60 channels,
		direct phone, WiFi, Internet,
		hairdryer, and much more

Whether you are traveling for business or pleasure, the Hotel Dunn Inn is a perfect choice for a memorable stay. This charming 1929 mansion was renovated in 1989 and known for providing exceptionally friendly service and is a favorite among many locals.
✉ dunninn@racsa.co.cr 🌐 www.hoteldunninn.com

Hotel Casa Roland	95 – 200 $US BB	Full breakfast
Rohrmoser	20 rooms, 20 pb	Restaurant & bar
+506-2290-5462 +506-2231-6571	C-yes/S-yes/P-yes/H-yes	Maid service, concierge
Robert Bogdanovich	English, Spanish	services, cable TV, fine art
	All year	by local artists, private
		baths, mini-refrigerator, A/C,
		Internet and computer
		access, fully-equipped suites

A friendly staff awaits you at Casa Roland, an elegant B&B in the quiet Embassy District of San Jose. With 20 guestrooms in the main house or 2 suites in the adjacent 3 bedroom houses, guests will find accommodations suiting the most discerning traveler.
✉ reservations@rolandhotels.com 🌐 www.casa-roland.com

Hotel Hemingway	30 – 65 $US BB	Tropical buffet breakfast
Calle 9 y Avenida 9, Barrio	17 rooms, 17 pb	Snack bar, room service
Amón	Visa, MC, AmEx,	available
+506-2221-1804	*Rated*, •	Jacuzzi, book-trade library,
Joshua Wroniewicz	C-yes/S-ltd/P-ltd/H-no	computer, WiFi connection,
	English, Spanish,	tours to the rain forests,
	German	volcanoes, rafting, rental
	All year	Cars Available

Close to nightlife, museums, dining & shopping. Warm ambience with jungle surroundings are accented with Mayan statues & Costa Rican art, setting your mood to venture out & discover Costa Rica. ✉ hemingway@hemingwayinn.com 🌐 www.hemingwayinn.com

Mexico

AJIJIC ──────────────────────────────────────

Casa de las Flores	80 – 125 $US BB	Full breakfast
38 Zaragoza Pte St.	5 rooms, 5 pb	Complimentary bottle of
206-274-5740 +52-376-766-1164	Visa, MC, AmEx	wine (on arrival)
Steve Cross & Fernando	C-yes/S-ltd/P-ltd/H-ltd	Pool, fridge, microwave,
Gomez	Spanish, English	coffee maker, hairdryer,
	All year	ceiling fan, patio area, flat
		screen TV, SKY TV, DVD
		player, gym, bicycle,
		treadmill, universal machine

One of Ajijic's true Mexican gems, nestled on a cobblestone street just 2½ blocks from the town's main plaza. Casa Flores is one of the Lake Chapala areas outstanding rental B&B properties.
✉ stevieblake2@hotmail.com ❂ www.casafloresajijic.com

Casa Del Sol Bed &	80 – 100 $US BB	Full breakfast
Breakfast Inn	8 rooms, 8 pb	Purified water, mini kitchen
Javier Mina #7	C-yes/S-ltd/P-no/H-yes	TV/DVD, free phone, ceiling
866-403-9275 +52-376-766-0050	Spanish, English	fans, two units w/fireplace,
Cathy Roberts	All year	most w/balconies, cozy bar,
		heated pool, purified-
		pressurized Water, smoke-
		free environment, guest mini
		kitchen

Welcome to the comfort and hospitality of Casa del Sol, a beautiful small Inn located in the heart of the 16th century village of Ajijic, Mexico.
✉ info@casadelsolinn.com ❂ www.casadelsolinn.com

Los Artistas B&B	69 – 89 $US BB	Full Gourmet Breakfast
Constitucion 105	6 rooms, 6 pb	Beverages; No Breakfast on
+52-376-766-1027	*Rated*, ●	Sunday
Linda Brown & Kent Edwards	C-ltd/S-ltd/P-ltd/H-no	Pool, private bath, secure
	Spanish, English	park, lush gardens/grounds,
	All year	guest refrigerator, daily
		paper, reading area, sun
		room, porch

Our six guestrooms, each with a unique decor and private bath, provide views of the tranquil gardens, swimming pool, the fountains and fishpond.
✉ artistas@laguna.com.mx ❂ www.losartistas.com

Villa Eucaliptos	70 – 90 $US BB	Full breakfast
16 de Septiembre #127	5 rooms, 5 pb	Pool, Jacuzzi, cable TV in
+52-376-766-1400	Most CC, *Rated*	rooms, tea & coffee facilities,
Ralph Moniz	C-yes/S-yes/P-ltd/H-ltd	refrigerator, guest computer,
	English, Spanish	WiFi, library
	All year	

Villa Eucaliptos is a beautiful private Mexican Villa located one block from Lake Chapala in the heart of Ajijic. Enter into a private world all of your own, set in Colonial Spanish architecture with magnificent 15 foot ceilings and arches.
✉ villaeucaliptos@gmail.com ❂ www.villaeucaliptos.com

Tell your hosts Pamela Lanier sent you.

ALAMOS

Casa De Maria Felix
Galeana #41
+52-647-428-0929
Lynda Morris

45 – 65 $US BB
6 rooms, 6 pb
Visa, MC
C-ltd/S-no/P-no/H-no
English, Spanish
All year

Self-Catered
Fully-equipped kitchenettes
Private sitting & dining areas,
kitchens, garden, pool, A/C,
some rooms have a Jacuzzi
or fireplace, new gym,
central location

Casa de Maria Felix offers new and elegant accommodations in a beautifully landscaped environment. It was built from ruins of the original homestead of Maria Felix, a legendary movie actress. Go back in time to old Mexico in the town of Alamos.
✉ casamariafelix@hotmail.com ◐ www.casademariafelix.com

BUCERIAS

Casa Cielito Lindo
Calle Fibba #12
705-447-1104
Sandi & Brian Barkwell

100 -150 $US BB
3 rooms, 3 pb
•
C-ltd/S-ltd/P-no/H-no
English
October – May

Full Hot Breakfast
Meals are available on
request.
Egyptian cotton bedding,
private baths, maid service
daily, safes, street parking,
private pool and terraces.

Casa Cielito Lindo situated on the north shore of the Bay of Banderas on the longest most beautiful stretch of Pacific Coast beach. The hand crafted Cherub fountain inside our gated yard, the gleaming marble floors, the attention to detail are delightful.
✉ info@waterfrontdreamvacations.com ◐ www.waterfrontdreamvacations.com

Casa Loma Bonita
Nicolas Bravo #26
415-310-5435
David Pantoja

125 – 235 $US BB
4 rooms, 4 pb
C-yes/S-ltd/P-no/H-no
English, Spanish
All year

Full breakfast
On site restaurant with
authentic Mexican cuisine.
Luxurious king size bed,
comfortable sitting area,
refreshing swimming pool,
large private bathroom, rich
marble floors, stunning
balcony views, relaxing
porch & patios

Casa Loma Bonita is just minutes North of Puerto Vallarta in Bucerias. This is a unique villa property overlooking Bahia de Banderas, close to championship golf courses, white sand beaches, one-of-a-kind shops and a variety of dining experiences.
✉ dpantoja@hotmail.com ◐ www.casalomabonita.com

CABO SAN LUCAS

Cabo Inn Hotel
20 De Noviembre Y Leona
Vicario
+52-624-143-0819
Stanley & Maria Patenaude

58 – 120 $US EP
20 rooms, 20 pb
Visa, MC
C-ltd/S-ltd/P-no/H-no
English, Spanish
All year

Free coffee in the morning.
Free drinking water.
A/C, fridges (1st floor units),
community kitchen, social
whirlpool, library, sun deck,
beach, mall, night clubs,
restaurants, discounts on
activities

Come and enjoy Los Cabos' best budget accommodation. The inn is located in a beautiful setting in the warmth of the tropics and will cater to gatherings of all kinds of large groups, weddings, reunions, etc, with a range of activities for every guest.
✉ info@caboinnhotel.com ◐ www.caboinnhotel.com

Tell your hosts Pamela Lanier sent you.

CABO SAN LUCAS

Casa Bella Boutique Hotel	160 – 50 $US BB	Continental breakfast
Hidaldo #10 Colonia Centro	14 rooms, 14 pb	Pool, terraces, A/C, SAT-TV,
+52-624-143-6400	Visa, MC, AmEx	Internet access, laundry
Sra. Barbara Ungson	C-ltd/S-no/P-no/H-no	facilities
	Spanish, English	
	All year	

Casa Bella Boutique Hotel is a Colonial hacienda located on the main plaza in the heart of Cabo San Lucas, Mexico. Casa Bella Boutique Hotel is a unique and memorable experience to make your trip to Los Cabos complete.
✉ barbara@casabellahotel.com 🌐 www.casabellahotel.com

Casa Pablito Bed &	80 – 110 $US BB	Continental breakfast
Breakfast & Hotel	14 rooms, 14 pb	Queen or two twin beds,
Hidalgo Street #1906	Visa, MC, *Rated*, •	cooking facilities,
866-444-1139 +52-624-143-1971	C-no/S-no/P-no/H-no	refrigerator, A/C, Cable TV
Daniel Uribe	English, Spanish	w/RC, privacy drapes,
	All year	private bedroom w/shower,
		Jacuzzi, pool and parking
		area

Casa Pablito offers a breakfast area with Mexican decor under a beautiful and colorful Palapa, an intimate and warm atmosphere, a perfect place to start your day.
✉ reserv@casapablitoloscabos.com 🌐 www.casapablitoloscabos.com

The Los Nido Inn	89 – 149 $US BB	Continental breakfast
Lomas Del Tule @ KM 17.5	6 rooms, 6 pb	Meal & catering services
877-417-9658 619-819-8212	Most CC	available.
Karl Klaesson	C-ltd/S-ltd/P-no/H-yes	WiFi, direct US phone,
	Spanish, English	waterfall, pool, palapa bar,
	All year	maid service 6 days/wk, A/C,
		BBQ area, prepaid LD calling
		available

Within short walking distance of The Sea Of Cortez lies two suites and four rooms, nestled around a magnificent waterfall, swimming pool, Palapa Bar, and lush tropical gardens. Call +52-624-144-0588   ✉ karl@losnidos.com 🌐 www.losnidos.com

CANCUN

B&B Quinta Bianca	25 – 60 $US BB	Mexican or Fitness Breakfast
Justo Sierra Nr. 38	8 rooms, 3 pb	Our signature dish is
423-373-0740 +52-988-482-096	C-yes/S-ltd/P-no/H-ltd	Mexican Breakfast or Fitness
Lilia & Blanca Basauri; Bianca	English, German,	Double futon bed, make-up
Buchel	Spanish	area, A/C, Ceiling Fans,
	All year	nicely decorated rooms,
		additional Water closet in
		each house, daily
		housekeeping, Phone for
		Local Calls

Located in a safe residential area of Cancun, Quinta Bianca offers 8 bedrooms split in 3 Houses. Each house has 3 bedrooms and 1 of them with a large private bathroom, the other 2 guestrooms share a big bath.
✉ quintabianca@hotmail.com 🌐 www.bedandbreakfast.com/quintana-roo-cancun-bbquintabianca.html

Maria De Lourdes Hotel	55 – 65 $US BB	Continental breakfast
Ave. Yaxchilan #80	57 rooms, 57 pb	Full service restaurant and
+52-998-884-4744	Visa, MC, •	bar.
Patricio Millet	C-yes/S-yes/P-no/H-no	Swimming pool, snacks,
	Spanish, English	laundry, travel agency, car
	All year	rental, snorkeling, baby-
		sitting

Looking for a nice budget hotel in downtown Cancun, close to entertainment, markets, restaurants, bars and services. The Hotel Maria De Lourdes is the place to stay.
✉ hotelmariadelourdes@hotelmariadelourdes.com 🌐 www.hotelmariadelourdes.com

CELESTUN

Hotel Eco Paraiso Xixim
Km 10 del viejo camino a Si,
Municipio de Celestún
800-400-3333 +52-988-916-2100
Verena Gerber

152 – 240 $US MAP
15 rooms, 15 pb
Visa, MC, AmEx, •
C-yes/S-yes/P-yes/H-no
English, Spanish
All year

Full breakfast
Breakfast only or half-board
rates also available
Swimming pool, beach,
library, lounge, videos,
games, restaurant, bar,
private baths, safe deposit
boxes, maid service, kayaks,
bicycles, museums & tour
assistance

Nestled on a 3-mile stretch of virgin beach, Eco Paraiso offers 15 spacious bungalows, each overlooking the emerald green Gulf of Mexico. Designed to meet strict ecological standards while providing a unique experience with nature, a perfect getaway!
✉ info@ecoparaiso.com 🌐 www.ecoparaiso.com

CHAPALA

Quinta Quetzalcoatl
Calle Zaragoza #307
+52-376-765-3653
Rob Cracknell

75 – 150 $US BB
9 rooms, 9 pb
C-no/S-ltd/P-no/H-no
English, Spanish
All year

Full breakfast
Many restaurant selections &
shops near by
Swimming pool & private
sunning areas, BBQ, outside
tables & chairs, parking,
private car rental, tours &
chauffeur services, an honor
bar, fax, Internet access

Totally restored & decorated, this villa has become a fine, romantic small Inn featuring 5 Suites and 3 Casitas. Located on the north shore of beautiful Lake Chapala, Mexico, QQ is "the" place to indulge yourself in peace and relaxation.
✉ qqinnchapala@yahoo.com 🌐 www.accommodationslakechapala.com

CHELEM

Sand Castle Inn
Calle 13 #250 Poligono lll
+52-969-035-4275
Katie

75 – 130 $US BB
4 rooms, 4 pb
Visa, MC, *Rated*, •
C-yes/S-ltd/P-no/H-no
Spanish, English
All year

Full breakfast
Bottled Water in rooms, beer
& wine
WiFi, palapa bar, parking,
room service, outdoor
Jacuzzi, massages by
appointment, free Merida
airport pickup, fridge,
microwave, coffee maker,
DVD player & library

Eclectic beach front B&B on the sunny Gulf of Mexico. See for yourself why this area of the Yucatan has been a well kept secret for years. Make your reservation today at the Sand Castle Inn.
✉ sandcastleinn@aol.com 🌐 sandcastleinnmexico.com

COZUMEL

Summer Place Inn
10 Avenida Sur #1199
+52-987-872-6300
Henny Watts

65 – 155 $US BB
7 rooms, 7 pb
Most CC, •
C-ltd/S-ltd/P-no/H-ltd
English, Spanish, Danish
All year

Self-help 24 hours a day
Full kitchen stocked with
breakfast foods.
TV, DVD player, bicycles, full
kitchen, stocked fridge, A/C,
laundry, Internet phone,
wireless Internet, wave
boards, library, beach
towels, coolers

Conveniently located downtown in Cozumel, the Summer Place Inn offers private units and a charming condo. Competitively priced, the accommodations can be booked nightly, weekly or monthly.
✉ info@cozumelinn.com 🌐 www.cozumelinn.com

GUADALAJARA————————————————————————————

Villa Ganz Hoteles
1739 Lopez Cotilla
+52-333-120-1416
Sally Rangel

200 – 280 $US BB
9 rooms, 9 pb
Visa, MC, AmEx
C-ltd/S-ltd/P-no/H-ltd
English, Spanish
All year

Continental breakfast
Welcome Cocktail
Phone, cable TV, WiFi, A/C,
established garden, terrace
w/fireplace for meetings and
romantic dinners, honor-
system bar, parking

A boutique hotel now in Guadalajara. Villa Ganz offers 9 stylish suites in the elegant ambience of a restored 1930's residence, consisting of three Grand Master, five Master, and one junior suite, our residence provides a warm welcome.
✉ info@villaganz.com 🌐 www.villaganz.com

GUANAJUATO————————————————————————————

**Casa Estrella de la
Valenciana**
Callejon Jalisco 10
866-983-8844 +52-473-732-1784
Sharon Schaap Mendez

185 – 265 $US BB
6 rooms, 6 pb
Most CC
C-ltd/S-no/P-ltd/H-ltd
Spanish, English
All year

Full breakfast served from 9
to 10
Other meals available with
advance request.
Luxury linens, Sat-TV,
DVD/VHS player, CD/clock
radio, hairdryer, bathrobes,
iron/board

Perched on a hillside, with spectacular panoramic city and mountain views, Casa Estrella de la Valenciana welcomes you to experience Colonial Mexico and its treasures.
✉ info@mexicaninns.com 🌐 www.mexicaninns.com

HECELCHAKAN————————————————————————————

Hacienda Blanca Flor
y 88kms de la Ciudad de
Merida
800-639-9512 +52-999-258-042
Ricardo Casillas Mendieta

135 – 160 $US BB
18 rooms, 18 pb
C-yes/S-ltd/P-no/H-no
Spanish, English
All year

Continental plus breakfast
Restaurant with regional &
international cuisine
Conference room, swimming
pool, horses, bicycles,
tropical gardens

Hotel Hacienda Blanca Flor is located in the heart of the Mayan World, in the State of Campeche not far from Yucatan State. A former Hacienda restored and transformed into a Hotel.
✉ hblancaf@prodigy.net.mx 🌐 blancaflor.com.mx/

HUATULCO————————————————————————————

Agua Azul la Villa B&B
AP25, Lote 18, Manzana 6,
Residencial Conejos
+52-958-581-0265
Richard Gazer

109 -129 $US BB
6 rooms, 6 pb
Visa, MC
C-no/S-no/P-no/H-no
English, Spanish
All year

Continental plus breakfast
Honor Bar, bottled drinking
water
Cascade swimming pool,
large terrazas, library,
gardens, private ocean view
terrace, A/C, fans, phone

With stunningly beautiful ocean views & spacious private terraces off of every guestroom, Agua Azul la Villa offers a tranquil vacation destination in a tropical paradise for adults. Your Canadian host will be glad to orient you to the area.
✉ gaurei@hotmail.com 🌐 www.bbaguaazul.com

Tell your hosts Pamela Lanier sent you.

HUATULCO

Huatulco B&B
Sierra de Miahuatlan 109
866-505-5581 +52-958-583-4132
Curtis Morrow & Imelda
Alvarez

50 – 80 $US BB
6 rooms, 6 pb
C-ltd/S-no/P-no/H-no
Spanish, English
All year

Full breakfast
Any meal on request,
extended breakfast items
also
Satellite TV, VCR, water pik
shower heads, make-up
lighting, hairdryer, cookware,
appliances, dishes, parking

*Huatulco B&B is luxuriously appointed and is a Mexican Cantera Fountain Courtyard Style
Home. There are three spacious Master Suites upstairs that have all the amenities of a
modern American home.*
✉ huatulcobandb@aol.com 🌐 www.huatulcobedandbreakfast.com

LA PAZ

El Angel Azul
Independencia No 518
+52-612-125-5130
Esther Ammann

100 – 195 $US BB
10 rooms, 10 pb
Visa, MC, *Rated*
C-ltd/S-ltd/P-no/H-no
Spanish, English,
German
All year

Full breakfast
Afternoon Tea and the Bar is
open until 7pm.
Bar & lounge, Internet & free
wireless, garden, cable TV
for guests in lounge, en suite
showers, A/C, radios, tour
arrangements, afternoon tea
early bird coffee, library

*El Angel Azul is a fascinating place that recaptures the spirit and culture of old La Paz.
Located in the heart of La Paz, the building was formerly the town's courthouse. Completely renovated and redesigned as a B&B inn, it is an historic landmark.*
✉ hotel@elangelazul.com 🌐 www.elangelazul.com

MANZANILLO

Pepe's Hideaway
Apartado Postal 77, La Punta
+52-314-333-0616
Pepe Telarana

200 – 250 $US AP
6 rooms, 6 pb
Visa, MC, *Rated*, •
C-no/S-yes/P-no/H-no
Spanish, English
All year

Full breakfast
An all inclusive gourmet
experience!
Swimming pool, Jacuzzi, bar,
restaurant, private baths,
ceiling fans, Mini Bar,
hammock on private
veranda, massage Service,
Internet & telephone access

*A private nature reserve in Manzanillo, Mexico. Accommodations in luxury thatched-roof
bungalows with spectacular views and awesome sunsets. Pepes Hideaway is a handmade
paradise.*
✉ pepeshideaway1@mac.com 🌐 www.pepeshideaway.com

MAZATLAN

**Casa De Leyendas of
Mazatlan**
Venustiano Carranza #4
602-445-6192 +52-669-981-6180
Glenn & Sharon Sorrie

79 – 115 $US BB
6 rooms, 6 pb
Visa, MC, *Rated*, •
C-ltd/S-ltd/P-ltd/H-no
English/Spanish
All year

Full or Continental Breakfast
Fruits, juices, breads, coffee
& tea always available.
Pool/spa, maid service,
laundry service, A/C, safes,
WiFi, free calls to U.S. &
Canada, concierge service,
purified water throughout

*A wonderful 2-story, 8,000 square foot home. Each of its 6 bedrooms has its own private
bath and a unique view of the Arte de Museum, the Pacific Ocean or the Courtyard area.*
✉ info@CasaDeLeyendas.com 🌐 www.casadeleyendas.com

MAZATLAN

Mazatlan Ocean Front Inn
127 Paseo Claussen
925-608-8350 925-608-8350
Jim & Candace Penn

65 – 95 $US BB
6 rooms, 6 pb
Most CC, •
C-ltd/S-ltd/P-ltd/H-no
Spanish, English
Open all year

Continental plus breakfast
Beer, soft drinks & snacks
are complimentary
A/C, DSL, WiFi, ceiling fans,
assisted planning/booking
activities, BBQ, beach
chairs/towels, bicycles,
security gate, maid service,
laundry service, SAT-TV,
DVD

The Mazatlan Ocean Front Inn is a unique water front property located just a short walk to the famous Olas Altas Beach and Mazatlan's Old Historic District. The Inn has unobstructed views of the Pacific Ocean, the Gold Zone and Mazatlans three islands
✉ candacepenn@hotmail.com ✆ www.mazatlanoceanfrontinn.com

Meson De Cynthia
Sixto Osuna #408
775-636-8686
Cynthia Romero

65 – 95 $US BB
7 rooms, 7 pb
Visa, MC
C-ltd/S-no/P-no/H-ltd
Spanish, English
All year

Continental breakfast
Mexican snacks and dinners,
by arrangement.
A/C, microwave, cable TV,
coffee maker, Internet, maid
service, laundry service,
special accommodation
requests, patio w/view

Located in the heart of Mazatlan in the Historic District, the recently restored, historic building, the Meson De Cynthia, is a five room, two suite B&B, embedded amidst continuous cultural and traditional events.
✉ elmesondecynthia@hotmail.com ✆ www.mesondecynthia.com

Olas Altas Bed & Breakfast
Dr. Hector Gonzalez Guevara
#3
702-505-4144 +52-668-4395
Bill McGrady

125 and up $US BB
6 rooms, 6 pb
Most CC
C-ltd/S-ltd/P-no/H-ltd
Spanish, English
All year

Full breakfast
In room refrigerators filled
with refreshments.
Pool, pressurized/purified
water system, sunny/shaded
dining and repose areas,
formal dining for 12, full
service pool bar,
international phone, laundry,
a/c, cable TV

Come and enjoy a very unique and exclusive bed and breakfast . . . featuring all the amenities of a first-class boutique hotel . . . sitting just steps away from the famous Olas Altas (high waves) beach known for its great surfing, fishing, and hospitality.
✉ wwmcgrady@charter.net ✆ olasaltasmaz.com

MERIDA

Casa Ana B&B
Calle 52 #469, between 51 & 53
+52-999-181-6655
+52-999-924-0005
Ana Ilano

40 – 50 $US BB
5 rooms, 5 pb
C-yes/S-ltd/P-ltd/H-ltd
Spanish, English
All year

Continental breakfast
Home-cooked meal on
request.
Tropical garden, natural
rock, swimming pool, palapa,
A/C, ceiling fans, hammocks,
daily maid service

Five immaculate spacious rooms, each with a private bath and air conditioning, offering peace and tranquility a heartbeat from the Plaza Principal in El Centro. Casa Ana is in the White City, as Merida is known, centrally located with great rates.
✉ info@casaana.com ✆ www.casaana.com

MERIDA————————————————————————

Casa Del Balam
Calle 60 No. 488 x 57 Centro
800-624-8451 +52- 999-924-2150
Gricell Moreno

75 – 120 $US BB
51 rooms, 51 pb
Visa, MC, AmEx,
Rated, •
C-yes/S-ltd/P-no/H-ltd
Spanish, English
All year

Continental breakfast
Las Palomas Restaurant &
Bar
Pool, elevators, boutique,
silver shop, parking service,
safe, access to golf club, fee
services include massages,
babysitter, crib, room
service, laundry, WiFi cards

Welcome to Hotel Casa del Balam, one of the oldest, most distinguished hotels in Merida on the Yucatan Peninsula. One of the few original Mexican Art Deco buildings left in this Colonial City. The hotel is newly renovated with modern conveniences.
✉ info@casadelbalam.com ✪ www.hotelcasadelbalam.com

Casa Mexilio
Calle 68 no. 495, x59, y57
877-639-4546 +52-999-928-2505

60 – 120 $US BB
11 rooms, 11 pb
Visa, MC, AmEx
C-no/S-no/P-no/H-no
English, Spanish
All year

Cooked to order or
Continental
Breakfast is our gift to you.
A/C, TV, tropical pool, lush
tropical gardens, wrap-
around terraces, roof-top
terraces, patio, bar, lounge,
steam bath, vintage Mayan
art

Welcome to a small historic hotel that still strikes a dominant chord in Yucatan's cultural, political, and artistic life, as it has in past centuries. Casa Mexilio is a rich mix of memories and themes of the lives of those who have inhabited its rooms.
✉ casamexilio@earthlink.net ✪ www.casamexilio.com

Cascadas de Merida
Calle 57 #593-C, x 74A y 76
305-978-5855 +52-999-923-8484
Ellyne & Chucho Basto

83 – 96 $US BB
4 rooms, 4 pb
Rated
C-ltd/S-ltd/P-no/H-no
English, Spanish
All year

Full breakfast
Bottled water,
Spacious living & dining
areas, spa services, library,
kitchen, individual casitas,
WiFi, cable TV, pool,
waterfall, secure parking,
A/C

An oasis in the midst of the city, filled with water & light, combining traditional and modern design, materials, technology and amenities we have created the perfect blend of comfort and culture.
✉ info@cascadasdemerida.com ✪ www.cascadasdemerida.com

Hacienda San Pedro Nohpat
San Pedro Nohpat
+52-999-988-0542
Iona Chamberlin & Erwin
Beug

75 – 195 $US BB
10 rooms, 10 pb
Visa, MC
C-yes/S-ltd/P-yes/H-yes
English, Spanish
All year

Intn'l Continental + Cook to
Order
Dinner served in restaurant.
Lunch on request.
En suite baths, pool, Jacuzzi,
massage, gardens, lounges,
patios, A/C, TV, VCR, sitting
areas, concierge service,
restaurant, Internet access,
phone, on-site childcare

With the new millennium came new Canadian owners to the Hacienda San Pedro Nohpat in the Yucatan. An historic 16th century hacienda has been transformed with a mix of Old Spanish Colonial décor and modern amenities into a quaint boutique hotel.
✉ haciendaholidays@hotmail.com ✪ www.haciendaholidays.com

MERIDA———————————————

Hotel Casa San Angel
Montejo #1 x 49 Centro
+52-999-928-1800
Alberto Banuet

130 – 180 $US EP
15 rooms, 15 pb
Visa, MC, AmEx, •
C-no/S-no/P-no/H-yes
English, French, Spanish
All year

Optional Delicious breakfast.
Private parking, WiFi,
beautiful setting, A/C, ceiling
fans, TV, hammocks, safe
deposit box, two world class
boutiques exclusive in the
Yucatan

*Welcome to Hotel Casa San Angel, a family owned boutique hotel in the heart of Merida,
Yucatan, Mexico. The historical building has been restored with love and care with beautiful murals in the interior, while still conserving the original architecture.*
✉ info@hotelcasasanangel.com ◯ www.hotelcasasanangel.com

Hotel Marionetas
Calle 49 #516 x 62 and 64
+52-999-928-3377
Sofi & Dan Bosco

95 – 115 $US BB
8 rooms, 8 pb
Visa, MC
C-ltd/S-ltd/P-no/H-ltd
Spanish, English
All year

Delicious Gourmet Breakfast
Pool, A/C, TV, phone, safe
deposit box, small fridge,
hairdryer, secured parking,
laundry Service, wake-up
calls, tour Booking,
multilingual staff, 24hr
Doctor, cafe

*Hotel Marionetas is a small, luxury boutique hotel in Merida set in a colorful garden. Enjoy
the charm of this fully complimented, Colonial home without giving up the conveniences of
modern life.*
✉ info@hotelmarionetas.com ◯ www.hotelmarionetas.com

**In Ka'an Bed & Breakfast &
Other Accommodations**
Calle 15, No. 527, x24 y26
+52-999-943-4156
Bonnie Wrenshall

90 $US BB
3 rooms, 3 pb
C-yes/S-ltd/P-yes/H-ltd
English
All year

Full breakfast
Lunch served with prior
notice
Large swimming pool, 22m
lap pool, extensive library,
videos, DVD

*"In Ka'an," is a happy blending of Mexican architecture and ambience with Canadi-
an/American standards of comfort. Enjoy your breakfast on the terrace overlooking the
pool. For those who prefer their own space, we offer fully furnished guesthouses.*
✉ bonnie@inkaan.com ◯ www.inkaan.com

Tolok-Nah Bed & Breakfast
Calle 4-A No. 78 por 1-A y 1-B
+52-999-944-7841
Alfonso Cetina Belmonte

55 – 90 $US BB
3 rooms, 3 pb
Visa, MC
C-yes/S-ltd/P-ltd/H-no
Spanish, English
All year

Full breakfast
Coffee, ice tea, purified water
Pool, terrace, A/C, ceiling
fans, safe, cable TV, hydro-
massage tub, transportation
to/from airport, garage, daily
room cleaning service, wake
up calls, laundry

*Tolok-Nah is a very beautiful house that offers bed and breakfast services, this is a perfect
place for national and international travelers to enjoy the peace and comfort which only
the Yucatan land can provide.*
✉ info@tolok-nah.com ◯ www.tolok-nah.com/english/index.php

**Villa Maria Hotel &
Restaurant**
Colonia Centro
+52-999-923-3357
Octavio Monsalve Uribie

100 – 160 $US EP
11 rooms, 11 pb
C-no/S-no/P-no/H-no
Spanish, English
All year

Outdoor patio or air-
conditioned dining room.
Luxury rooms, A/C, mini bar,
TV, room service, secure
parking at hotel, spa services
by appointment

*Hotel Villa Maria occupies a seventeenth century mansion, sensitively restored and with a
very romantic atmosphere. In the midst of the city, Hotel Villa Maria provides a quiet and
elegant retreat with eleven luxury rooms.*
✉ hotelesvillamaria@yahoo.com.mx ◯ www.villamariamerida.com/index.htm

MORELIA

Hotel Virrey de Mendoza
310 Avenida Madero, Pte.
Centro Historico
800-450-2000 +52-443-312-0633
Alberto Lemus

2,100 – 4,100 Pesos ¤ BB
35 rooms, 35 pb
Visa, MC, AmEx, •
C-yes/S-ltd/P-yes/H-ltd
English, Spanish
All year

Full American breakfast
Lunch, Dinner in restaurant,
bottled water in room
Safe deposit boxes, currency
exchange, fax, Internet,
bilingual staff, laundry, dry
cleaning, covered parking,
valet, 24hr medical Service,
baby sitter on request

Hotel Virrey de Mendoza is strategically located in the historic center of Morelia, one of the most beautiful Colonial cities of Mexico, designated by Unesco and Patrimonio de la Humanidad.
✉ hvirrey@prodigy.net.mx ☯ www.hotelvirrey.com

OAXACA

Casa Colonial
Apdo 640, Calle Miguel
Negrete 105
800-758-1697 +52-951-516-5280
Jane & Thornton Robison

95 $US BB
15 rooms, 12 pb
Visa, MC
C-yes/S-yes/P-yes/H-yes
Spanish, English
All year

Full breakfast
Lunch, Dinner (fee)
Sitting room, library,
verandas, tropical gardens,
limited secure parking,
phone, fax, Internet service,
including WiFi.

An inn that is run very much as a country manor. The extensive library, friendly Oaxacan staff, lush gardens, personal service, excursion arrangements and superior food have made Casa Colonial a destination in itself for 30 years!
✉ reservations@casa-colonial.com ☯ www.casa-colonial.com

Casa Machaya
Hillside
+52-951-132-8203
Alvin & Arlene Starkman

475 couple/week $US BB
2 rooms, 1 pb
C-yes/S-yes/P-no/H-no
English, Spanish
All Year

Full breakfast
Cereal, eggs, coffee,
bread/rolls, fruit, jam, etc
Bed sitting room, fully
equipped, private eat-in
kitchen includes (fridge,
stove, microwave, coffee
maker & juicer) patio,
optional extra bedroom,
Internet, cable

Our Oaxaca B&B provides a spacious, hillside home with panoramic vistas and complete privacy. We're both child and senior friendly. We offer guests your own kitchen with dining table and chairs, a sitting room, patio, full bath & optional extra bedroom.
✉ oaxacadream@hotmail.com ☯ www.oaxacadream.com

Casa Sagrada
M. Alcala #203, Centro
310-455-6085 +52-951-516-4275
Mary Jane Gagnier

105 – 165 $US MAP
12 rooms, 6 pb
Visa, MC, AmEx
C-yes/S-ltd/P-no/H-ltd
Spanish, English
All year

Full Breakfast and Dinner
included
Lunches available.
Vegetarian meals upon
request.
We specialize in guided
horseback riding from
beginners to advanced,
hiking excursions, cooking
classes and the traditional
healing arts including
massage and temascal.

With only twelve guestrooms and a home-style atmosphere, Casa Sagrada is the perfect place to retreat from your busy life. Immerse yourself in a traditional Zapotec village surrounded by ancient culture and stunning panoramic views.
✉ info@casasagrada.com ☯ www.casasagrada.com

OAXACA

Hacienda Los Laureles-Spa
Hidalgo 21
+52-951-501-5300
Peter Kaiser

198 – 389 $US BB
23 rooms, 23 pb
Visa, MC, AmEx,
Rated, •
C-yes/S-yes/P-no/H-yes
Spanish, English,
German
All year

Special Oaxacan (Full)
Breakfast
Full-service restaurant, bar &
room service.
Welcome cocktail, fruit &
flowers on arrival, turn down
& laundry service, mini-
fridge, en suite baths,
telephones, Internet, spa,
swimming pool, massage,
gardens

Hacienda Los Laureles-SPA in a quiet area of Oaxaca is a completely renovated hacienda for guests who want to enjoy a unique locale & a relaxing stay in a 5-star, 4 diamond luxury boutique hotel enhanced by traditional architecture & a personable staff.
✉ bookings@hotelhaciendaloslaureles.com ☻ www.hotelhaciendaloslaureles.com

La Casa de Mis Recuerdos
Pino Suarez #508
877-234-4706 +52-951-515-8483
William & Nora Gutierrez

50 – 120 $US BB
10 rooms, 8 pb
Visa, MC, •
C-no/S-no/P-no/H-no
Spanish, English
All year

Two course Oaxaquenian
breakfast
Special dietary meals with
advance notice.
Cool refreshments on arrival,
Non-Smoking, WiFi, Daily
Housekeeping, Low-Cost LD
Calls, Purified Bottled Water,
optional Cooking Classes,
Private Dinner Parties

Nestled in the emerald hills of Mexico's state of Oaxaca, lies a romantic gem of a city by the same name. This charming Colonial town is one of Mexico's national treasures, a show-case of the real Mexico, an authentic Mexican experience.
✉ misrecue@hotmail.com ☻ www.misrecuerdos.net

PATZCUARO

Hotel Mansion Iturbe
Portal Morelos 59, Plaza Don
Vasco
866-678-6102 +52-434-342-0368
Margarita Arriaga & Sons

99 – 160 $US BB
12 rooms, 12 pb
Visa, MC, AmEx, *Rated*
C-yes/S-ltd/P-no/H-no
Spanish, French, English
All year

You can choose from our
Menu
Lunch & dinner, snacks,
cocktails, coffee & tea
Sitting room, bar service,
snacks, library, bikes,
cooking courses, solarium,
gift shop, tours &
transportation assistance,
WiFi, I-Net, room safe, hair
dryer

Located right in front of the stunning Plaza Vasco de Quiroga. Close to everything. This historic B&B Hotel offers 12 individually decorated rooms. The majority of the rooms have private balconies. Complete gourmet breakfast & complimentary cocktail hour.
✉ mansioniturbe@yahoo.com ☻ www.mansioniturbe.com

La Casa Encantada
Dr.Coss No. 15
619-819-8398 +52-434-342-3492
Victoria Ryan

90 – 135 $US BB
12 rooms, 12 pb
C-ltd/S-ltd/P-ltd/H-ltd
English, Spanish
All year

Full breakfast
Many nearby restaurants
offer discounts to guests
Computer, wireless Internet,
daily maid service, garden
patios, living room, piano,
fireplace, cable TV, tour
arrangements &
transportation, massage

La Casa Encantada is an idyllic place to get away from it all. Inside the adobe walls there is an abundance of color in the lush gardens, patios and portals. The setting is tranquil. The house is a masterpiece of Colonial architecture.
✉ cynbthia01@lacasaencantada.com ☻ www.lacasaencantada.com

PUERTO MORELOS

Rancho Sak Ol Libertad Super Manzana 3, Calle en Proyecto +52-998-871-0181 Valente Quintana	55 – 130 $US BB 14 rooms, 14 pb Visa, MC, Disc, • C-ltd/S-yes/P-yes/H-ltd English, Spanish All year	Continental plus breakfast Fruits & juice cereal yogurt eggs bread coffee/tea Large common room, fans, AC, common kitchen, massage, bikes, snorkel equipment, hammocks, thatched roofs

A true vacation away from the fast pace. A place to set your own pace, enjoy, play, explore, or just relax in the hammocks. A place to reflect and renew.
✉ reservations@ranchosakol.com 🌐 www.ranchosakol.com

PUERTO VALLARTA

Arco Iris Paseo de los Delfines #115 310-943-6366 +52-322-221-5527 Thom & Ran	155 – 255 $US BB 3 rooms, 4 pb Visa, MC C-ltd/S-ltd/P-ltd/H-no Spanish, English All Seasons	Full breakfast Guests are greeted with a welcome drink and tour. Ocean view rooms, Chef Thom's epicurean delights, maid/turn down service, LD calling, theater room, A/C, laptop, Hi-Def TV, WiFi, sound deck, Jacuzzi, beach towels

Welcome to Arco Iris! Reopened in its spectacular new location, Arco Iris now offers superior comfort, sumptuous breakfasts and even better views! Don't wait to return to Puerto Vallarta's preferred gay and lesbian accommodation. All are welcome.
✉ pvviews@yahoo.com 🌐 www.gaybnb.com

Casa Amorita Calle Iturbide #309 at Calle Matamoros +52-322-222-4926 Rita Love	100 – 185 $US BB 4 rooms, 4 pb C-no/S-yes/P-no/H-no Spanish, English All year	Full breakfast Roof top terrace, sun decks, balcony, garden, pool

Casa Amorita is in the heart of Puerto Vallarta with an incredible view of Banderas Bay, the Cathedral Guadalupe and the Sierra Madre Mountains.
✉ ritalove@hotmail.com 🌐 www.casaamorita.com

Casa Corazon Ampas #326 866-648-6893 George T. Tune	55 – 100 $US BB 42 rooms, 42 pb C-yes/S-ltd/P-no/H-no Spanish, English All year	Full breakfast Sliding door w/terrace, private entry bath, maid service, some rooms with TV, A/C, and mini fridges, 9 person elevator, kitchenettes include table, fridge & stove

Welcome to Casa Corazon Hotel, "House of Hearts," a quaint B&B that has grown into a small family hotel on the beach in beautiful Puerto Vallarta, Mexico. Casa Corazon Hotel sits on a hillside overlooking beautiful Bandera Bay.
✉ casacorazon1@yahoo.com 🌐 www.casacorazonvallarta.com

Casa del Angel Col. Alta Visa 720-204-2070 +52-322-222-4469 Robin Spencer	100 – 200 $US BB 2 rooms, 2 pb C-yes/S-ltd/P-no/H-ltd Spanish, English All Seasons	Full breakfast A chef can be provided for a private meal service. Pool, free long distance calls to U.S. & Canada, high speed Internet. Owner a lot of knowledge of best places and things to do.

Casa del Angel is a luxury B&B, the unique setting of the villa offers complete privacy while affording a magnificent panoramic view of the ocean, jungle and the heart of Vallarta.
✉ robinsworld05@msn.com 🌐 www.freewebs.com/casadelangel/index.htm

PUERTO VALLARTA

Casa Helga – Cresencia
Amapas Hillside, Banderas Bay
800-418-3322 203-372-3111
Helga Farrill

1,000 – 2,500 $US EP
5 rooms, 5 pb
C-no/S-no/P-no/H-no
English, Spanish
All year

Private baths, A/C, heated infinity pool, en suite Jacuzzi, sat-TV, VCR, CD, DVD, phone, Internet, private coach house

Perched high on a cliff overlooking the wide expanse of Puerto Vallarta's spectacular Bay of Banderas in the Conchas Chinas "Golden Zone," this luxury home is one of the largest villas in Puerto Vallarta.
✉ casahelga@aol.com ◐ www.casahelga.com/puerto-vallarta/villas/crescencia

Casa Helga – Profundo
Mismaloya Shore, Banderas Bay
800-418-3322 203-372-3111
Helga Farrill

660 – 2000 $US EP
4 rooms, 4 pb
C-ltd/S-ltd/P-no/H-ltd
Spanish, English
All year

A/C, heated Infinity pool, Jacuzzi, TV/CD/DVD, Internet, attentive staff

Along Mismaloya's shoreline within a short walk to Mismaloya beach, this majestic private villa is tucked into the rocky, shoreline across the bay from the islands of Los Arcos.
✉ casahelga@aol.com ◐ www.casahelga.com/puerto-vallarta/villas/profundo

Casa Helga Carmelita
Conchas Chinas Hillside
800-418-3322 203-372-3111
Helga Farrill

1070 – 2300 $US EP
5 rooms, 7 pb
C-ltd/S-ltd/P-no/H-ltd
Spanish, English
All year

A/C; private terrace, Jacuzzi, SAT-TV/DVD, stereo, private cook, horseman and maid; fabulous art work

This spectacular five bedroom villa is set on the hillside in upper Conchas Chinas within five minutes of downtown and walking distance to the beach. Offering the best in comfort, sophisticated decor, fabulous artwork, spacious terraces and unique spaces.
✉ casahelga@aol.com ◐ www.casahelga.com/puerto-vallarta/villas/carmelita

Casa Tres Vidas
126 Calle Sagitario
888-640-8100
Margaret & Ruth

500 – 850 $US EP
10 rooms, 10 pb
Visa, MC, AmEx
C-yes/S-no/P-no/H-no
Spanish, English
All year

Cost of food extra
Chef will prepare 2 meals a day for a fee.
Private pool, heated Jacuzzi, cable TV, CD/DVD players, maid service

Casa Tres Vides is located directly on the beach of Playa Conchas Chinas just minutes south of charming downtown Puerto Vallarta, Mexico. Luxury 3 or 4 bedroom beach front villas that when combined create a 6, 7 or 10 bedroom private villa.
✉ info@villasinvallarta.com ◐ www.casatresvidas.com

Los Cuatro Vientos Hotel
Matamoros 520
+52-322-222-0161
Gloria Whiting

Inquire $US BB
15 rooms, 15 pb
Visa, MC
C-yes/S-yes/P-no/H-no
English & Spanish
All year

Continental breakfast
Meals available at Chez Elena, on-site restaurant
Refreshingly cool deep pool, the town's best-loved venue for super sized margaritas, spectacular sunsets, three scenic levels with stair access, roof top bar, restaurant

Established in 1956, and tucked away on a hillside in a tropical paradise amidst a profusion of flowers, Los Cuatro Vientos (The Four Winds), is a small hotel that continues to be a favorite with guests seeking a traditional Mexican setting.
✉ fourwinds@cuatrovientos.com ◐ www.cuatrovientos.com

SAN FRANCISCO

Casa Obelisco	225 $US BB	Full breakfast
Calle Palmas	4 rooms, 4 pb	Soft drinks, beer, wine,
415-233-4252 +52-311-258-4315/6	Visa, MC	cocktails, snacks, lunch
Judi & John Levens, Barbara	C-no/S-no/P-no/H-no	Pool, pool bar, sun decks,
& Bill Kirkwood	English, Spanish,	roof top lounge area, beach,
	German	horseback riding, snorkeling,
	10/1 – 5/31	hiking

Romantic, exotic get away you've been dreaming about. Exquisite two story oceanfront home in Mediterranean style overlooking a deserted white sand half moon beach with tropical palms in a quaint little village -great restaurants in the new Riviera Nayarit
✉ reservations@casaobelisco.com 🌐 www.casaobelisco.com

SAN JOSE DEL CABO

Boca De Los Palmas	150 – 325 $US BB	Full breakfast
Nuevas San Luis	2 rooms, 2 pb	Daily maid
866-781-8159 503-922-0465	C-yes/S-no/P-no/H-no	service/caretaker, full suites,
Marti & Lloyd Miesen	English	Sat-TV, Internet, DVD, CD,
	All year	A/C, Egyptian cotton linens,
		walled/gated residence,
		pool, spa, BBQ,
		washer/dryer

You will know you've found paradise when you escape the crowds to this beautiful beach front home, just steps from the spectacular Sea of Cortez, landscaped with palm trees, varieties of cactus, flowers, and an aviary full of sweet singing birds.
✉ marti@martimiesen.com 🌐 www.martimiesen.com

El Encanto Inn	95 – 240 $US EP	Complimentary coffee &
Calle Morelos #133	26 rooms, 26 pb	bottled water
+52-624-142-0388	Visa, MC, AmEx	A/C, Direct TV, fountain,
Blanca	C-yes/S-no/P-no/H-ltd	pool, lush tropical gardens,
	Spanish, English	some rooms w/mini bar, CD
	All year	

The gracious El Encanto Inn, is a small hotel with an intimate ambience and located in the heart of San José del Cabo with its charming narrow streets, historic buildings and tree shaded boulevards.
✉ info@elencantoinn.com 🌐 www.elencantoinn.com

Villa del Faro	140 – 525 $US BB	Full breakfast
65 Camino Costero	5 rooms, 6 pb	Full bar and wine list.
Devora Wise	Most CC	Gourmet dinner on request.
	C-yes/S-ltd/P-no/H-ltd	Pool, terrace, fountains,
	Spanish, English, French	custom rugs, private
	Open October to August	balcony, Sat-TV, private
		beach, canopy king bed,
		kitchen, fireplaces, outdoor
		shower

Exquisitely off the grid! An eco-hotel, Villa del Faro is a unique oasis nestled on a deserted beach. It was created as a labor of love by artisans and architects. One hour north of the Los Cabos Airport, but a world away in seclusion and serenity.
✉ rental@villadelfaro.net 🌐 www.villadelfaro.net

SAN MIGUEL DE ALLENDE

Antigua Capilla Bed and Breakfast
Callejon de Chepito 16, Int 1,.
Zona Centro
972-346-8245
Antonieta and Francisco

150 $US BB
8 rooms, 8 pb
Visa, MC
C-ltd/S-no/P-ltd/H-ltd
Spanish, English
All Seasons

Full breakfast
We also offer you a well stocked Honor Bar.
Gas Fireplace, Flat Screen Cable TV, DVD, CD, MP3, Radio, Apple TV w/movie library, Stocked Honor Bar, Maid Service, IPod Dock, Hi-Speed Wire & WiFi, King/Queen Beds

Antigua Capilla Bed and Breakfast in San Miguel offers you world-class hospitality, comfort and elegance. Come enjoy the fantastic views of the Parroquia and the city center from Antigua Capilla's outdoor living area and rooftop terrace.
✉ info@antiguacapilla.com 🌐 www.antiguacapilla.com

Arcos del Atascadero
Callejon Atascadero #5B
301-591-4129 301-591-4129
Patricia Merrill Marquez

70 – 110 $US BB
7 rooms, 5 pb
Most CC
C-ltd/S-no/P-no/H-no
English, Spanish
All year

No Breakfast Served Sundays
Fruit & juices, hot dish, breads, coffee, teas
Pool, DirecTV, WiFi Internet, massage, guest PC, airport pickup, laundry, gourmet Mexican meals by prior request, heated pool, game room, free US phone calls, kitchen

Enjoy your vacation in San Miguel Allende by staying at our beautiful Bed & Breakfast! So much more intimate and snug than an average hotel, we strive and take pleasure in making your stay at our Bed & Breakfast an occasion worth repeating.
✉ arqpatty@gmail.com 🌐 www.bedandbreakfastinmexico.com

Hacienda de las Flores
Hospicio 16
+52-415-152-1859
+52-415-152-1808
A. Franyutti, C. Finkelstein

96 – 185 $US BB
16 rooms, 16 pb
Visa, MC, *Rated*, •
C-yes/S-yes/P-yes/H-no
English, French, Spanish
All year

Full breakfast
Catering on request for weddings, 2–100 people.
Bar, garden, pool, 2 conference rooms, executive meetings, accommodations for business travelers, wireless Internet, catering for weddings, parties, out door pool.

Hacienda de las Flores is an exclusive, tranquil and casual hotel which is a stimulus to modern life. It has beautiful gardens in the heart of town that are reminders of a serene way of life of yesteryear.
✉ info@haciendadelasflores.com 🌐 www.haciendadelasflores.com

La Mansion Del Bosque
Aldama 65, Apdo. 206
+52-415-152-0277
Ruth Hyba

90 – 145 $US MAP
22 rooms, 22 pb
C-yes/S-ltd/P-yes/H-ltd
Spanish, English
All year

Complete breakfast
2 meals breakfast 8–10am evening meal at 7:30am
Sitting room, library, hot mineral pools nearby, spas nearby, fitness, massage, fireplaces, tiled tubs, laundry service available

Colonial style with terraces, balconies, patios filled with flowers and tropical greenery. Rooms are colorfully decorated using many antiques and Mexican crafts. A unique oasis where you are surrounded by a profusion of flowers and shrubs.
✉ manruth@unisono.net.mx 🌐 www.infosma.com/mansion

SAN MIGUEL DE ALLENDE

Villa Mirasol	80 -150 $US BB	Complete Breakfast w/
Pila Seca #35	12 rooms, 12 pb	longer stays
+52-415-152-8057	Most CC, *Rated*, •	Tea Time (Merienda), lunch
Amparo Rivas & Carmen	C-ltd/S-ltd/P-no/H-ltd	service, wine
Avery	English, Spanish	Sitting room, library, golf,
	All year	Internet

Villa Mirasol is located only five minutes from the center, Jardin our main square and a very short distance to Bellas Artes, The Angela Peralta Theatre and Instituto Allende (Arts School).
✉ amparo@villamirasolhotel.com 🌐 www.villamirasolhotel.com

SAYULITA

Tia Adriana's	46 – 160 $US BB	Full breakfast
#7 Calle Delfines	9 rooms, 9 pb	Breakfast not included July
888-221-9247 +52-329-291-3029	C-yes/S-no/P-yes/H-yes	to October.
Adrienne Adams	English, Spanish	Private baths, kitchenettes,
	All year	apartments, views,
		waterfront, beach towels,
		snorkeling, boogie boards,
		sitting areas, tour
		arrangements

Tia Adriana's B&B is only 100 steps to the water's edge, nestled in the little fishing village of Sayulita just 30 miles from Puerto Vallarta. Sayulita's friendly atmosphere, spectacular beaches, fresh seafood and gorgeous views will capture your heart.
✉ stayinsayu@yahoo.com 🌐 www.tiaadrianas.com

TLAQUEPAQUE

Casa de las Flores	95 – 105 $US BB	Continental plus breakfast
Santos Degollado 175	7 rooms, 7 pb	Inquire about other meals
888-582-4896 +52-333-659-3186	Visa, MC, *Rated*	offered
Stan Singleton & Jose	C-ltd/S-ltd/P-no/H-ltd	Shopping or sightseeing
Gutierrez	Spanish, English	trips, translating, available
	All year	for small events

This B&B is just 15 minutes away from the center of Guadalajara and just three blocks from the famous historic center of Tlaquepaque one of the largest crafts and arts capitals of Mexico.
✉ info@casadelasflores.com 🌐 www.casadelasflores.com

Casa del Retoño B&B	75 – 85 $US BB	Continental breakfast buffet
Matamoros #182, Col. Centro	8 rooms, 8 pb	Meals can be arranged for
+52-333-635-7636	Visa, MC, AmEx, *Rated*	special occasions.
Eslye Berenice Panduro	C-yes/S-ltd/P-yes/H-no	Terrace with books &
Gonzalez	English, Spanish	magazines, garden with lawn,
	All year	flowers & fruit trees, TV,
		radio alarm clock, fan,
		telephone, fax, computer
		with DSL Internet, WiFi
		Internet & printer

Enjoy the comfort, tranquility & warmth of a Mexican family house, built with typical Mexican materials, which guarantee you an unforgettable stay. Two blocks away from downtown Tlaquepaque.
✉ info@lacasadelretono.com.mx 🌐 www.lacasadelretono.com.mx

TLAQUEPAQUE

La Villa del Ensueño	95 – 125 $US BB	Full breakfast
Florida 305	20 rooms, 20 pb	Bar with snacks, coffee, tea,
800-220-8689 +52-333-635-8792	Visa, MC, AmEx,	fruit basket
Felix Vidales & Vicente Garcia	*Rated*, •	Restaurant, bar, laundry, dry
	C-yes/S-ltd/P-no/H-ltd	cleaning, A/C,
	Spanish and English	manicure/pedicure,
	All year	masseuse service on site,
		phone, fax, free WiFi and
		LAN, cable TV, free parking,
		2 pools, outdoor Jacuzzi

A 4 star Inn preferred by Frommers, AAA, Best Places to Stay, etc. & the only local members of the Professional Association of Innkeepers International. Member Historic Haciendas of Jalisco. Extensively renovated. The first boutique hotel in the area.
✉ aldez@pacbell.net ◐ www.villadelensueno.com

Quinta Don Jose Boutique Hotel	85 – 150 $US BB	Full a la carte is also
Reforma #139	18 rooms, 18 pb	available
866-629-3753 +52-333-635-7522	Visa, MC, AmEx,	Light lunch menu available.
Arturo & Estela Magana	*Rated*, •	Gourmet avail @ 5:00pm
	C-yes/S-ltd/P-ltd/H-ltd	Courtesy airport pick-up, fine
	Spanish, French	dining at our restaurant
	All year	"TlaquePasta," area tours,
		intimate bar, pool, tree
		shaded patio, free WiFi,
		guest computer desk

An oasis in the heart of Tlaquepaque, the decorative arts and crafts capital of Mexico in the greater Guadalajara area. We are a boutique hotel that specializes in personal service to our guests while sharing our local traditions, food, people and Fiesta!
✉ info@quintadonjose.com ◐ www.quintadonjose.com

Panama

PANAMA CITY

The Balboa Inn	65 – 95 $US BB	Full breakfast
Calle Cruces 2311a	7 rooms, 7 pb	Vegetarian breakfast
+507-314-1520	Visa, MC, *Rated*, •	Private bathrooms, WiFi,
Saskia Swartz	C-yes/S-ltd/P-yes/H-no	Direct TV, air conditioning,
	English	ceiling fans, big covered
	All year	terrace, gardens, airport
		pickup, taxi service or a
		trusted private driver.

Rated # 3 in listings of B&B's, the Balboa Inn is a small Bed & Breakfast at the foot of Panama's landmark, Ancon Hill. Conveniently located between downtown, Amador Causeway & just minutes away from the domestic airport & Panama Canal
✉ reservations@thebalboainn.com ◐ www.thebalboainn.com

Casa Las Americas	65 – 75 $US BB	Full breakfast
Cangrejo District	3 rooms, 1 pb	Free soft drinks available all
866-573-8588 +507-399-7783	Visa, MC, AmEx	day.
Ron Griffith	C-yes/S-ltd/P-no/H-ltd	A/C, cable TV, WiFi, phone
	English, Spanish	calls to US/Canada, two
	All Seasons	sitting Rooms with TV/DVD,
		safe, child care services
		available, free parking

Minutes from exciting casinos, restaurants, and business districts, our inn is economical but ideal for tourists, business travelers and retirees.
✉ mail@casalasamericas.com ◐ www.casalasamericas.com

PANAMA CITY

El Litoral
Lot 12 Punta Prieta
514-332-6416 +507-6658-1143
Anne-Marie & RenÃ©

75 – 90 $US BB
4 rooms, 3 pb
Visa, MC
C-yes/S-no/P-no/H-no
French, English, Spanish
All year

Full breakfast
Swimming pool, wireless
Internet, beaches, parking,
spa, tennis, golf, horseback
riding

We are offering peaceful atmosphere in a great decor were you can really enjoy your vacations. Quality, comfort and great hosts is the best recipe for your stay in Panama.
✉ lenaicke@gmail.com 🌐 www.litoralpanama.com

La Dulce Colmena Bed & Breakfast
Altos de Betania
+507-6799-1375
Earl & Enna

55 – 65 $US BB
3 rooms, 2 pb
C-yes/S-no/P-no/H-no
English, Spanish
All Seasons

Full breakfast
Dinner on request
WiFi, water wise
establishment, safe, covered
parking, cellular phone for
hire, baggage storage
available, A/C, fan on
request, mini-bar, Cable TV,
hairdryer on request

La Dulce Colmena "the sweet beehive" warmly welcomes you and we appreciate your valued visit. Our B&B is situated in Altos de Betania, a beautiful residential suburb 15 minutes away from Panama City Center.
✉ info@ladulcecolmena.com 🌐 www.ladulcecolmena.com

Peru

CUZCO

Del Prado Inn
Uriel Gracia #310
+518-422-4442
Diana

65 – 145 $US BB
18 rooms, 18 pb
Most CC, •
C-yes/S-yes/P-no/H-ltd
Spanish, English, Italian
All year

Full breakfast
Lunch, Dinner & Room
Service
Non-smoking rooms, free
Internet access, safe deposit
box, close circuit TV in
common areas, central
heating, electric locks,
telephones

Hotel Del Prado Inn is at the historical center of the city of Cuzco, archaeological capital of South America. While visiting Machu Picchu and Cuzco, Hotel Del Prado Inn offers a pleasant stay with high quality service and customized attention.
✉ admin@delpradoinn.com 🌐 www.delpradoinn.com

Picoaga Hotel
Calle Santa Teresa 344
+511-242-8488
Roxana Ferreccio B. Gerente
de Ventas

135 – 188 $US BB
72 rooms, 72 pb
Visa, MC, AmEx, •
C-yes/S-ltd/P-no/H-ltd
Spanish, English, French
All year

Buffet Breakfast
Two restaurants,
International & Peruvian
cuisine
Fridge bar, cable TV, safe
deposit box, A/C, central
heating, phones, telemusic,
alarm clock, hair dryer

Picoaga Hotel is a first class hotel, originally the mansion of Spanish Noble, Marquis de Picoaga, now converted into comfortable and modern accommodations.
✉ reservas@picoagahotel.com 🌐 www.picoagahotel.com

LIMA

Bella Park B&B	37 – 55 $US BB	Continental breakfast
Jose Gabriel Aguilar 750,	7 rooms, 7 pb	Lunch and dinners from
Maranga-San Miguel	Visa, MC, AmEx, •	$7.00 – $10.00
+511-264-2057	C-yes/S-ltd/P-no/H-ltd	Private bathrooms, WiFi,
Susana Sanchez	Spanish, English	cable TV, clock radio, DVD
	All Season	players available, wake-up
		call, laundry service
		available, 24hr reception

Bella Park B&B is located in the town of San Miguel, 8 minutes away from the Jorge Chavez International airport in Lima, Perú. The B&B was recently renovated.
✉ bellaparkperu@msn.com ○ www.bellaparkperu.com

Europe

Austria

INNSBRUCK

Hotel Weisses Kreuz	35 – 64 € BB	Breakfast Buffet
Herzog-Friedrich-Str. 31	40 rooms, 31 pb	Direct dial telephone, radio,
+43-5125-94790	Visa, MC, AmEx,	cable TV, Internet access &
Dr. Josef Ortner	*Rated*, •	WiFi, wonderful views, city
	C-yes/S-ltd/P-yes/H-ltd	centre
	English, French, Italian,	
	German	
	All year	

A traditional Austrian inn open since 1465, situated in Innsbruck's Gothic old town. There is a cozy, familiar atmosphere, wooden ceilings, antique furniture and friendly service. Mozart stayed here in 1769. All major sights within easy walking distance.
✉ hotel@weisseskreuz.at ○ www.weisseskreuz.at

OBERALM BEI HALLEIN

Schloss Haunsperg	135 – 210 € BB	Full breakfast
Hammerstr. 51	8 rooms, 8 pb	Snacks, complimentary wine
+43-6245-80662	Most CC, •	Sitting room, library,
Family Von Gernerth	C-yes/S-yes/P-yes/H-no	bicycles, baroque chapel,
	English, Italian, German	gardens & private clay tennis
	All year	court, golf, horseback riding,
		squash & winter sports all
		close by

Schloss Haunsperg is a 14th century, country manor house offering elegantly appointed rooms and suites with period furniture. Surrounded by secluded gardens with a friendly, family-owned atmosphere, it is just 15 minutes from Salzburg.
✉ info@schlosshaunsperg.com ○ www.schlosshaunsperg.com

SALZBURG

Altstadthotel Amadeus	88 – 180 € BB	Large breakfast buffet
Linzer Gasse 43 – 45	25 rooms, 25 pb	Free afternoon coffee & Tea
+43-6628-71401	Most CC, *Rated*, •	Cable TV, safe, telephone
Eric Walketseder	C-yes/S-yes/P-yes/H-ltd	
	German, French, Italian	
	All year	

The Hotel Amadeus is a small, exclusive hotel with charming and fully equipped rooms in the heart of Salzburg. The Amadeus is a family run, traditional hotel. A large breakfast buffet is included.
✉ salzburg@hotelamadeus.at ○ www.hotelamadeus.at

SALZBURG

Hotel Walkner
Seeham am Obertrumer See
+43-6217-5550
Hilda Haberl

39 – 59 € BB
22 rooms, 22 pb
Visa, MC, AmEx,
Rated, •
C-yes/S-yes/P-yes/H-ltd
English, French, German
All year

Full breakfast
Lunch, afternoon tea,
complimentary wine, snacks
Restaurant, bar, heated
swimming pool, sauna, game
room, bikes, safe deposit
box, chapel/shrine,
WiFi/wireless LAN, child
care services, laundry

The province of Salzburg is very special with its mountains, hills, meadows, lakes, nature in all forms, and, of course, the cultured, unspoiled Salzburg way of life. Hotel Walkner is situated in the middle of all this perfection – welcome to our hotel!
✉ hotel.walkner@eunet.at ✪ www.hotel-walkner.at

Sallerhof Hotel Bed & Breakfast
Hauptstrasse 9
+43-6246-72521
Schnoell-Reichl Klaus

80 – 104 € BB
26 rooms, 26 pb
Visa, MC, AmEx, *Rated*
C-yes/S-no/P-no/H-ltd
English, German, Italian
All year

Extensive buffet breakfast
Many restaurants are nearby,
just a 3 minute walk
Non-smoking rooms, modern
furnishings & all the features
needed, bathroom with
shower & hairdryer, WC. A
bright, comfortable &
welcoming ambience, free
Internet

Visit the original "Sound of Music" Scenery in Austria. The four star hotel is just 4 miles from the old town of Salzburg, 1 mile from the motorway (highway) exit Salzburg Sued 7 miles from the airport Salzburg and 5 miles from Salzburg's railway station
✉ office@sallerhof.com ✪ www.sallerhof.com

VIENNA

Apartments Rothensteiner
Neustiftgasse 66
+43-1523-9643
Bernd Rothensteiner

85 – 225 € BB
18 rooms, 18 pb
Visa, MC
C-yes/S-yes/P-yes/H-yes
English, German, Italian
All year

Full breakfast
Full-service restaurant on
the premises.
Completely furnished
apartments, TV, telephone,
private baths, free Internet
access, room safes & safe
deposit boxes, rooftop
terrace, parking

Apartments Rothensteiner is a traditional Viennese property meeting the highest standards of excellent accommodation. The studio and family apartments are decorated in beautiful, classic furnishings. Within walking distance to Vienna's city center.
✉ rothensteiner@netland.at ✪ www.rothensteiner.com

Central Apartments & Vacation Rentals Vienna
Muehlgasse 6
+43-6991-1406-665
Mr. Daryoush Voshmgir

110 – 130 € EP
7 rooms, 7 pb
Visa, MC, *Rated*
C-yes/S-ltd/P-ltd/H-no
English, German, Italian,
Farsi
All year

Fully equipped modern
kitchens, cable TV, DVD &
CD player, telephone, fax,
answering machine, PC with
Internet access, Stereo HIFI,
ironing board, hair dryer

Four-star self-catering apartments in prime location in the city center in Vienna – Austria: Family friendly, modern and fully furnished business and vacation apartments suitable for short-term or long-term accommodation in the center of Vienna.
✉ apartments.vienna@eunet.at ✪ www.central-apartments-vienna.com

VIENNA

Hotel Kugel	80 – 130 € BB	Buffet Breakfast
Siebensterngasse 43	31 rooms, 26 pb	Beer, wine, soft drinks, tea,
+43-1523-3355	•	coffee
Johannes Roller	C-yes/S-ltd/P-no/H-no	Garage, bar service, library,
	German, English, Italian,	free baby cot, mini-bar,
	French, Spanish, Polish	hairdryer, TV
	All year	

Situated in an historic part of Vienna between St. Stephen's Cathedral and Schönbrunn Palace, Hotel Kugel offers its guests a traditional, relaxed Viennese atmosphere. Romantic canopy bedrooms and budget rooms are moderately priced.
✉ office@hotelkugel.at ✪ www.hotelkugel.at

Belgium

BRUGGE

Alegria B&B	80 – 100 € BB	Full breakfast
St. Jakobsstraat 34B-C	6 rooms, 6 pb	Tea or coffee on request
+32-5033-0937	Visa, MC, *Rated*, •	Garden, beauty treatments,
Veronique De Muynck	C-yes/S-ltd/P-no/H-no	shop, parking garage, close
	Italian, French, Dutch,	to Market Square
	German	
	All year	

Alegria B&B is a tastefully renovated Manor House with a beautiful inner garden and coach house. Alegria is just steps away from the historical Market Square in Brugge.
✉ alegriabb@skynet.be ✪ users.skynet.be/alegriabb/

Anselmus Hotel Brugge	100 – 140 € BB	Continental breakfast
Riddersstraat 15	16 rooms, 16 pb	Free tea & coffee making
+32-5034-1374	Visa, MC, AmEx, *Rated*	facilities, bar service
Magda Maenhoudt	C-yes/S-no/P-no/H-no	Multi-lingual reception, wake-
	French, Dutch, English,	up calls, lounge, private
	German, Spanish	bath, phone, radio, TV,
	All year	computer, Free WiFi, garden,
		safety deposit box, private
		parking, valet service

One of the most beautiful family run hotels in Bruges. Built in an old mansion house where Anselmus Boetius de Boodt once lived in the 16th century. Located in the old city center.
✉ info@anselmus.be ✪ www.anselmus.be

Hotel Heritage	152 – 416 € EP	Room service, hot & cold
Niklaas Desparsstraat 11	24 rooms, 24 pb	buffet breakfast 15 €
+32-5044-4444	Visa, MC, AmEx,	Health Center w/Sauna &
Mr & Mrs Johan Creytens	*Rated*, •	Turkish Steam Bath, sun bed
	C-ltd/S-no/P-no/H-no	(fee), sun deck, fitness room
	English, French,	w/cardio systems, baggage
	German, Dutch	room, parking, WiFi,
	All year	babysitting, Stroller, high
		chair

A 19th century mansion house, recently renovated into a small luxurious family run hotel, 20 rooms and 4 suites, with modern facilities and personal service, in the historic city center.
✉ info@hotel-heritage.com ✪ www.hotel-heritage.com

BRUGGE

Hotel Prinsenhof
Ontvangersstraat 9
+32-5034-2690
Katrien & Thierry Lemahieu

155 – 335 € EP
19 rooms, 19 pb
Visa, MC, AmEx,
Rated, •
C-yes/S-no/P-yes/H-ltd
Flemish/Dutch, French,
German, English
All year

Hot and Cold Buffet Breakfast
17€
A/C, TV, DVD, CD, mini bar,
trouser press, safe, bathrobe,
hairdryer, WiFi, reception,
cozy lounge, breakfast room,
baggage room, private
parking or fee

A family run hotel with a warm ambience and a feeling that all guests are important. All bedrooms are peaceful, beautifully furnished in a traditional style and elegance.
✉ info@prinsenhof.com ♻ www.prinsenhof.com

WIJNENDALE-TORHOUT

Woodside Bed & Breakfast
Mosselstraat 26
+32-5022-3777
Luc & Stacey Van de Velde

75 € BB
3 rooms, 3 pb
C-yes/S-ltd/P-no/H-no
English, French,
German, Dutch
All year

Continental breakfast
Free coffee and tea, baby cot,
books & games, Internet, fax,
private parking.

Flemish/English couple offers you a beautiful bed and breakfast near Bruges. 3 modern and comfortable rooms with private bathroom, seating area, Internet and TV-DVD. Free private parking area. Many possibilities for day trips and activities !
✉ info@woodside.be ♻ www.woodside.be/english.html

Czech Republic

PRAGUE

Betlem Club Hotel
9 Betlemske Namesti
+420-2-2222-1574
Pavel Kika

40 -120 € BB
23 rooms, 23 pb
Visa, MC, *Rated*, •
C-yes/S-ltd/P-yes/H-ltd
Czech, English, German,
Italian, French
All year

Full Breakfast
Bar Service
lobby bar, laundry, exchange
office, baby sitting, safe,
lounge rentals in Gothic
Cellar, transport from
anywhere in the Czech
Republic to the hotel, free
Internet

The Betlem Club a 13th Century Gothic House with its original Gothic Cellar, is located in the historical center of Prague, just opposite the Bethlehem Chapel, where Master Jan Hus, one of the greatest theological reformers once worked.
✉ betlem.club@login.cz ♻ www.betlemclub.cz/

England, U.K.

BATH

Bath Paradise House Hotel
86-88 Holloway
+44-1225-317-723
General Manager

65 – 170 £ BB
11 rooms, 11 pb
Visa, MC, AmEx, *Rated*
C-yes/S-no/P-no/H-ltd
English
All year

Full breakfast
Complimentary tea, coffee &
biscuits in room.
Sitting room, walled gardens,
TV/DVD, radio, Hospitality
Tray, WiFi Internet, Molton
Brown products

Behind the classic and dignified exterior, Paradise House conceals more than half an acre of splendid walled gardens. Panoramic views overlook the City of Bath, Royal Crescent and the Abbey below. ✉ info@paradise-house.co.uk ♻ www.paradise-house.co.uk

BATH————————————————————

Dorian House
One Upper Oldfield Park
+44-1225-426-336
Kathryn Hugh

80 -165 £ BB
11 rooms, 11 pb
Most CC, *Rated*, •
C-yes/S-no/P-no/H-no
English
All year

Full English & Buffet
Breakfast
Near to spa, drawing room,
garden, small bar, car park,
Free WiFi

Enter an atmosphere of period charm in Dorian House. Panoramic views overlooking Bath. Five diamond rating by AA/RAC/ETC. Licensed. Off-street parking. Ten minute walk to Roman Baths/City center. ✉ info@dorianhouse.co.uk ❂ www.dorianhouse.co.uk

Marlborough House
1 Marlborough Ln
+44-1225-318-175
Peter Moore

95 – 130 £ BB
6 rooms, 6 pb
Visa, MC, *Rated*, •
C-yes/S-no/P-ltd/H-no
English
Closed Christmas Eve
and Christmas Day

Abundant vegetarian
breakfast
Marlborough House
specializes in organic foods.
Fabulous hosts, antiques,
history, tours, walks, music,
theater, advice

An enchanting warm and friendly Victorian house close to the Royal Crescent, Assembly Room, Guild Hall, Jane Austen Centre, Roman Baths and Thermal Spas. We are renowned for our relaxed atmosphere, excellent breakfasts and easy conversations.
✉ mars@manque.dircon.co.uk ❂ www.marlborough-house.net

Oldfields Hotel
102 Wells Rd
+44-1225-317-984
General Manager

65 – 155 £ BB
16 rooms, 16 pb
Visa, MC, AmEx, *Rated*
C-yes/S-no/P-no/H-no
English
All year

Full breakfast
Smoked salmon, English &
Vegetarian breakfast
Drawing room, garden, car
park, Jacuzzi tub, TV, DVD,
telephones, Wireless
Internet, Air-con

An elegant & traditional B&B with panoramic views of Bath & only 10 minutes walk to Bath city center. Magnificent drawing room & dining room with spectacular views of Bath.
✉ info@oldfields.co.uk ❂ www.oldfields.co.uk

Villa Magdala
Henrietta Rd
+44-1225-466-329
Roy & Lois Thwaites

95 -165 £ BB
18 rooms, 18 pb
Visa, MC, *Rated*
C-yes/S-no/P-no/H-ltd
English, Italian, Spanish,
German
All year

Full breakfast
refreshment trays in all
rooms
Lounge, refreshment trays,
TV, radio, direct dial phones,
four poster beds, smoke free
environment, private
parking, Complimentary
wireless Internet access.

Villa Magdala is peacefully located in a quiet residential area and overlooks Henrietta Park, one of Bath's most beautiful parks. It is only a 3 minutes level walk to the Roman Baths, city center, shops and restaurants.
✉ enquiries@villamagdala.co.uk ❂ www.villamagdala.co.uk

KIRKBY STEPHEN————————————————————

Augill Castle
South Stainmore
+44-1768-341-937
Simon & Wendy Bennett

160 £€ BB
11 rooms, 11 pb
Most CC
C-yes/S-yes/P-yes/H-no
English
All year

Full breakfast
Dinner, wine, packed lunch
available.
Showers, Big Baths, Molton
Brown Toiletries, Four Poster
Beds, Piano, Duck Pond,
Video Library, DVDs, Games
Room, Baby Listening,
Interconnecting Rooms,
Weddings, Parties

When John Bagot Pearson, a gentleman of leisure and considerable means, commissioned the castle in 1837, his vision was of a weekend retreat where he could entertain his friends in a style reminiscent of a medieval banquet.
✉ enquiries@stayinacastle.com ❂ www.stayinacastle.com

LONDON

22 Jermyn Street
22 Jermyn St
800-682-7808 +44-2077-342-353
Henry Togna, Laurie Smith

220 – 450 $¤EP
18 rooms, 18 pb
Most CC, *Rated*, •
C-yes/S-ltd/P-yes/H-yes
English, French, Italian,
Spanish, Arabic
All year

Room service only
Lunch, dinner (fee), 24 hour
room service
Membership to
Health/Sports Club with
sauna, solarium, wireless
Internet access from all
rooms, guest computer,
hairdryers, mini bar, DVD
library

Luxurious award winning townhouse in the heart of London, ideal for theater goers. Let Henry and Laurie take care of you! Complimentary wine and snacks. Most of the rooms are suites.
✉ office@22jermyn.com ○ www.22jermyn.com

Barry House
12 Sussex Place
+44-2077-237-340
Bobby Bhasin

80 – 105 £ BB
17 rooms, 15 pb
Visa, MC, AmEx,
Rated, •
C-yes/S-no/P-no/H-no
English
All year

English breakfast
Tea/coffee making facilities
en suite
TV, phone, hair dryer, tea &
coffee making facilities, free
wireless Internet access in all
rooms

The Barry House offers family friendly accommodations in central London. It is close to Hyde Park, Marble Arch and many of London's famous sights. A recommended hotel with a 3 star guest rating by Visit Britain.
✉ hotel@barryhouse.co.uk ○ www.barryhouse.co.uk/

Lincoln House Hotel
33 Gloucester Place, Marble
Arch
+44-2074-867-630
Joseph Sheriff

89 – 139 £ BB
23 rooms, 23 pb
Visa, MC, AmEx
C-yes/S-yes/P-no/H-yes
English, Deutch,
Francois
All year

Full Breakfast
Choice of full, vegetarian,
continental or in-room
Wireless Internet, en-suite
bathrooms, mini fridge,
trouser press, unlimited tea
& coffee, satellite TV,
telephone, hair dryer, close
to lots of restaurants

A delightfully charming and affordable Georgian B&B hotel, located in the heart of London's West End. Near to all the diverse scenes and activities London has to offer, ideal for shopping, leisure and business trips. Includes a superb English breakfast.
✉ reservations@centrallondonbandb.co.uk ○ www.centrallondonbandb.co.uk

---

Vicarage Hotel
10 Vicarage Gate, Kensington
+44-2072-294-030
Eileen & Martin Diviney

42 – 140 £ BB
17 rooms, 8 pb
Visa, MC, AmEx, *Rated*
C-yes/S-no/P-no/H-no
English, Spanish
All year

Full breakfast
Hot drinks
Sitting room, dining room,
antiques, centrally heated
rooms

A charming Victorian house, on a quiet residential garden square, in an upscale area of Kensington, only a stroll from Kensington Palace and Gardens and the exciting shops on Kensington High Street.
✉ vicaragehotel@btconnect.com ○ www.londonvicaragehotel.com

Windsor House Hotel
12 Penywern Rd Earls Ct
+44-2073-739-087
Jan Wardle

44 – 65 £ BB
25 rooms, 25 pb
Visa, MC, *Rated*
C-yes/S-yes/P-yes/H-yes
English
All year

Full breakfast
Free use of the hotel kitchen
for preparing food
Sunny, safe garden patio

This family run hotel is in a beautiful Victorian building that has many of the original features. The Windsor prides itself on it's spotless environment. All you need for a comfortable and inexpensive stay in London. Feel at home away from home.
✉ bookings@windsor-house-hotel.com ○ www.windsor-house-hotel.com

OXFORD

Nanford Guest House
137 Iffley Rd
+44-1865-244-743
Bartholomew Cronin

40 £ BB
10 rooms, 10 pb
Most CC, •
C-yes/S-yes/P-no/H-yes
English, French, Spanish
All year

Full English breakfast
Private secure parking,
ground floor rooms

Period guesthouse located 5 minutes on foot from the University of Oxford. All rooms have private en suite baths, color TV and tea sets.
✉ b.cronin@btinternet.com 🌐 www.nanfordguesthouse.com

STRATFORD-UPON-AVON

Victoria Spa Lodge
Bishopton Lane, Warwickshire
+44-1789-267-985
Paul & Dreen Tozer

65 – 70 £ BB
7 rooms, 7 pb
Visa
C-yes/S-no/P-no/H-no
English
All year

Full breakfast
Vegetarian breakfast
available
Country setting by canal,
central heating, hairdryers,
hot beverage stations, TV,
radio-alarms, historic
accommodation, Wireless
Internet Connection for guest
use.

Set in the country overlooking Stratford canal, all rooms have modern conveniences. An attractive and very comfortable home. Enjoy walks along tow-paths to Stratford and other villages.
✉ ptozer@victoriaspalodge.demon.co.uk 🌐 www.victoriaspa.co.uk/

WINDERMERE

Linthwaite House Hotel
Crook Rd
+44-1539-488-600
Mike Bevans

180 – 359 £ BB
27 rooms, 27 pb
Most CC, *Rated*, •
C-yes/S-no/P-ltd/H-yes
French, Spanish,
German
All year

Full English breakfast
Lunch, dinner, restaurant,
English afternoon tea
Bar service, sitting room,
pool, sauna, hot tubs, tennis
courts, bicycles, in-room
massage and beauty
treatments

Excellent modern British cuisine using local produce, extensive worldwide wine list and attentive staff. Linthwaite House Hotel, located in the heart of England's beautiful Lake District, has a sublime hilltop setting overlooking Lake Windermere and area.
✉ market@linthwaite.com 🌐 www.linthwaite.com

France

AMBOISE

La Prairie B&B and Gites
La Maison Neuve
+33-2-4153-0496
Samantha Acres

90 – 120 € BB
5 rooms, 5 pb
Visa, MC, •
C-yes/S-no/P-no/H-ltd
French, English
All year

Continental plus breakfast
Evening meals and French
cookery lessons!
Heated swimming pool, 2
lakes for fishing, horses to
ride, bicycles

La Prairie offers quality Gites, self-catering cottages and B &B accommodations within easy driving distance of the chateau and vineyards of the Loire Valley. Ride horses, fish in two lakes, swim in the swimming pool or relax in the gardens.
✉ samacres@aol.com 🌐 www.laprairie-loire.com

BAYEUX

Clos de Bellefontaine
6, Rue de Bellefontaine
+33-6-8142-2481 +33-6-8142-2481
Carole & Jerome Mallet

95 – 150 € BB
2 rooms, 2 pb
Rated, •
C-yes/S-no/P-ltd/H-no
English, French
All year

Fruits, home made cakes
Sitting room, garden &
terrace, gated parking

Located within the Historic Bayeux, also within walking distance from the Historical Center, near the D.day Beaches, one and a half hour drive from Honfleur or Le Mont-Saint-Michel. In a quiet garden enclosed by walls.
✉ clos.bellefontaine@wanadoo.fr ◑ clos.bellefontaine.monsite.wanadoo.fr/

La Ferme du Pressoir B&B
Le Haut St Louet
+33-2-4153-0496
Odile & Jacques Delalande

80 – 135 € BB
5 rooms, 5 pb
Visa, MC, •
C-yes/S-no/P-no/H-no
French
All year

Continental plus breakfast
Evening meals by
arrangement
Kitchen for guest use, private
cottage

La Ferme du Pressoir offers quality accommodations in a stone farmhouse dating from circa 1650. The farm has remained in the same family since it was built! A charming and unique guesthouse in Normandy with gracious hospitality.
✉ samacres@aol.com ◑ www.bandbnormandie.com

La Foulerie
14240 Cahangnes
+33-2-3177-7953
Jean Luc & Irene Tallec

65 € BB
3 rooms, 3 pb
Visa, MC, *Rated*
C-yes/S-no/P-no/H-yes
French, English
All year

Continental breakfast
Billiard room, TV/DVD,
fireplace, garden

La Foulerie is one of a group of old farmhouses & is over 250 years old. It has been lovingly & artistically restored to maintain its original architecture.
✉ jean.tallec@wanadoo.fr ◑ www.lafoulerie.net

Manoir Les Equerres
Monceaux en Bessin
+33-2-3192-0341
Didier Chambry

75 € BB
4 rooms, 4 pb
C-ltd/S-no/P-no/H-no
French
All year

Continental breakfast
Wooded park, parking,
billiards room, TV, verandas
with beautiful views

You will be enchanted by this handsome, welcoming Norman Manor House, close to Bayeux, it has been in the family for six generations. Enjoy breakfast on the veranda or take invigorating strolls through the attractive 2-hectare tree-lined park.
✉ didier.chambry@wanadoo.fr ◑ monsite.wanadoo.fr/manoirchambresdhotes

BEUVRON EN AUGE

Le Pave d'Hotes
Le Bourge
+33-2-3139-3910
Jerome Bansard

80 – 110 € EP
4 rooms, 4 pb
C-ltd/S-no/P-yes/H-yes
French, English
All year

Continental Plus Breakfast
available for 15 Euro.
Private terrace, SAT-TV, WiFi,
phone, mini-bar, safe, private
parking

Le Pave d'Hotes offers an authentic Normand House blended with old world charm and contemporary comfort. The rooms offer a view of the Caimpaign, a calming that will give you a recuperative rest.
✉ info@pavedauge.com ◑ www.pavedauge.com

BIRON

Le Prieure' at Chateau Biron
Le Bourg
+33-9-6047-4607
Elisabeth Vedier

120 – 180 € BB
5 rooms, 5 pb
Visa, MC, •
C-ltd/S-no/P-no/H-no
French, English,
German, some Spanish
April thru mid-
November

Continental breakfast
Evening aperitifs, dinner
with wine (on request)
Jacuzzi, bathrobes,
hairdryers, fine bed linens,
fans, tea & coffee facilities,
Internet access, sitting room,
terrace & stunning views, all
beds are twin, Queen or King

A Luxury B&B in Dordogne, South West France, just below the Château de Biron, Le Prieuré is a beautiful historic 16th C. building, elegantly furnished and restored to the highest modern standards.
✉ leprieurebiron@yahoo.com ◐ www.leprieurebiron.com

CAUNES-MINERVOIS

L'Ancienne Boulangerie
Rue St. Genes
+33-4-6878-0132
Roy Compton & Gareth
Armstrong

65 -85 € BB
6 rooms, 5 pb
C-yes/S-no/P-yes/H-no
English, a little French
All year

Continental breakfast
Traditional restaurants
abound in the area.
Sitting Room, library,
bicycles, terrace

Comfortable, renovated bakery with pleasant terrace more than three centuries old in the heart of a medieval village with a 1,200-year-old abbey; surrounded by vineyards and communal forest.
✉ ancienne.boulangerie@free.fr ◐ www.ancienneboulangerie.com

DRAGEY-RONTHON

Domaine de Belleville
11 Route de St Marc
+33-2-3348-9396
Florence & Olivier Brasme

76 € BB
2 rooms, 2 pb
Visa, MC, *Rated*
C-yes/S-no/P-no/H-no
French, English
All year

Continental breakfast
WiFi in each room on
request.

In the Normandy region and the Mont St. Michel bay area, enjoy your stay at a B&B filled with character and charm in a XVIIth century house. Private cottages are available to rent with a privileged view of Mont-Saint-Michel.
✉ belleville@mt-st-michel.net ◐ www.mt-st-michel.net

LABRUGUIÈRE

Les Marronniers
Place de la Mairie
+33-4-6672-8477
John Karavias & Michel
Comas

105 -120 € BB
4 rooms, 4 pb
Rated, •
C-no/S-no/P-no/H-no
French, English
All year

Continental breakfast
Dinner. 49euro 4-courses,
Aperitifs wine included.
Heated pool from May until
the end of September.
Central heating during cooler
months. TV, VCR, CD player,
coffee and tea making
facilities in each bedroom.
Free Wireless

Les Marronniers is a small haven in Provence in the charming village of La Bruguiere. A fully restored mansion built in 1812 with a front courtyard, shaded by chestnut trees where guests often dine. At the back of the house is a heated pool and garden.
✉ info@lesmarronniers.biz ◐ www.lesmarronniers.biz

Tell your hosts Pamela Lanier sent you.

LONGUEVILLE

Le Roulage
Le Roulage
+33-2-3122-0349
Janine & Daniel Leroyer

65 € BB
2 rooms, 2 pb
C-ltd/S-no/P-no/H-no
French, English
All year

Continental breakfast
Private baths, sitting room,
library, gardens

Le Roulage is a guesthouse with great character surrounded by lovely gardens. There are 2 very comfortable upstairs bedrooms in the residence with a private guest entrance. The rooms feature period furnishings & are decorated in warm & harmonious colors.
✉ dan.leroyer@wanadoo.fr 🌐 perso.wanadoo.fr/leroulage

PARIS

Eiffel Tower Apartment
4 Boulevard Pasteur
212-313-9425
Nicole Vincent

125 – 205 € EP
3 rooms, 1 pb
Visa, MC, AmEx
C-yes/S-no/P-no/H-no
English, French, Russian,
German
All year

Two level apartment,
laundry facilities, hair dryer,
shutters, microwave, coffee
maker, bath + w/c, stereo
w/CD, Cable TV, dresser,
bookshelves, phone, WiFi
Internet incl

Imagine leaving your apartment and before your eyes, the splendor of the Invalid's Dome and the grandeur of the Eiffel Tower. The views from this unit with six windows establishes your presence in Paris.
✉ info@france-paris.fr 🌐 www.paris-rental.fr

Hotel Britannique
20 Ave Victoria
+33-1-4233-7459
J.F. Danjou

140 – 271 € EP
39 rooms, 39 pb
Visa, MC, AmEx,
Rated, •
C-yes/S-no/P-no/H-no
English, Spanish, French
All year

Complimentary Afternoon
Tea, Breakfast Buffet
Sound proof rooms, bar
service, sitting room, A/C,
WiFi, direct dial phone, safe,
hairdryer, cribs

An authentic, charming hotel located in the historical center of Paris. Ideal for walking the oldest districts such as the Louvre, les Halles, le Marais, Saint Germain des Pres & the Latin Quarter.
✉ danjou@hotel-britannique.fr 🌐 www.hotel-britannique.fr

La Ferme du Chateau
5 Route de Boissy
+33-1-3486-5394
Denis & Corinne Lavenant

80 – 140 € BB
4 rooms, 4 pb
C-yes/S-no/P-no/H-no
French /English
All year

French breakfast
Each room has a television &
Internet access, 2 bicycles at
your disposal, maps, guide
books, parlors & games,
covered patio & private
parking

Corinne & Denis will make you feel welcome in this restored 17th Century old farmhouse, our family's birthplace for 8 generations. Our charming abode is located in the countryside 39 km West of Paris.
✉ info@la-ferme-du-chateau.com 🌐 www.la-ferme-du-chateau.com

Le Clos Medicis
56 Rue Monsieur le Prince
+33-1-4329-1080
Olivier Meallet

140 – 295 € EP
38 rooms, 38 pb
Visa, MC, AmEx,
Rated, •
C-yes/S-yes/P-no/H-yes
English, Italian, Spanish,
French, Portuguese
All year

Buffet Breakfast 13 €.
Afternoon tea.
A/C, phone, safe, hairdryer,
bar service, sitting room,
bathrobes, fireplace, garden,
complimentary WiFi, non-
smoking rooms available

Hotel Clos Médicis is a charming, boutique hotel (3 stars) located in Paris on the Left Bank in Saint Germain des Prés. Once a private residence dating back to 1860, it has been tastefully renovated with all the modern comforts and conveniences.
✉ message@hotelclosmedicisparis.com 🌐 www.hotelclosmedicisparis.com

PARIS

Le Relais du Louvre
19 rue des Pretres-Saint-
Germain-l'Auxerrois
+33-1-4041-9642
Sophie Aulnette

165 – 430 € EP
21 rooms, 21 pb
Most CC, *Rated*, •
C-yes/S-ltd/P-yes/H-no
French German, Italian
All year

Room service on request
from 6pm to 3am
Courtyard, A/C, mini bar,
safe deposit box, hairdryer,
phone, free WiFi, SAT-TV,
laundry service, parking
space on request, concierge
service

*Situated between the Louvre and Notre-Dame, the Relais du Louvre is in the historic heart
of Paris. Within the walls of an 18th century building, the charm of yesteryear is recreated
in this small hotel with restful color schemes and period furnishings.*
✉ contact@relaisdulouvre.com ✪ www.relaisdulouvre.com

Louvre Apartment
58 Rue des Lombards
212-313-9425
Chantal France

125 – 185 € EP
2 rooms, 1 pb
Visa, MC, AmEx
C-yes/S-no/P-no/H-no
English, French, Russian,
German
All year

Wine, water, cold drinks in
the fridge
Pickup-service from Paris
airport to the apartment
available, bike rental, fully
equipped kitchen, free WiFi
Internet, free calls to US and
Canada

*Located in the heart of Paris. Close to the Seine, Louvre and Notre Dame. We offer fully
furnished apartments designed for elegant living in the center of Paris. From four nights to
several weeks.*
✉ info@france-paris.fr ✪ www.paris-rental.fr

PUTANGES-PONT-ECREPIN

Le Bosquet
10 Rue Mont Roussel
+33-2-3367-4070
Richard & Magda Green

60 – 105 € BB
5 rooms, 5 pb
C-ltd/S-no/P-ltd/H-no
English and French
All year

Continental breakfast
We offer supper or dinner
with wine by arrangement
Tea & coffee making
facilities, hairdryers, use of
iron and ironing board,
petanque, picnic grounds,
barbecue

*A warm welcome awaits you at this elegant manor set on two acres of walled grounds
overlooking a picturesque riverside village. Le Bosquet offers 5 individually decorated, en-
suite rooms and is ideally situated to explore Normandy.*
✉ pamelalanier@explorenormandy.co.uk ✪ www.explorenormandy.co.uk

RIEUX-MINERVOIS

**Le Domaine Aux Quat'
Saisons**
26 Avenue Georges
Clemenceau
+33-4-6824-4973
David Coles

120 – 140 € BB
6 rooms, 6 pb
Visa, MC
C-no/S-no/P-no/H-ltd
French, English
All year

Continental plus breakfast
Dinner served 3x Weekly:
Monday, Wednesday, Friday
CD/radio, art deco, marble
fireplaces, antique furniture,
2 guest salons, TV-DVD, WiFi,
luxury baths, pool, parking,
restaurant, library, 2-acre
landscaped garden

*Welcome to Hotel le Domaine aux Quat'Saisons, a hotel bed and breakfast offering six en
suite luxury rooms, and a fine restaurant, all near the historic city of Carcassonne and
within 45 minutes of Mediterranean beaches and 90 minutes to Spain.*
✉ info@southoffrancehotel.com ✪ www.southoffrancehotel.com

Tell your hosts Pamela Lanier sent you.

SARLAT-LA CANEDA

Les Cordeliers	69 -99 € BB	Continental breakfast
51 Rue Des Coreliers	7 rooms, 7 pb	Tea & coffee facilities
+33-5-5331-9466	Visa, MC, AmEx	Air conditioning, luxury king-
Chris Johnson	C-ltd/S-no/P-no/H-no	size beds, WiFi, free parking
	French, English	close by
	All year	

Les Cordeliers is a luxury bed and breakfast overlooking the beautiful memorial square of the Petite Regaudie in the center of the famous medieval town of Sarlat-la-Canéda. It is the best B&B accommodation in the Dordogne.
✉ info@hotelsarlat.com 🌐 www.hotelsarlat.com

ST-SATURNIN-LÈS-APT

Le Mas Perreal	100 -130 € BB	Full breakfast
Quartier La Fortune	5 rooms, 5 pb	Special dietary
+33-4-9075-4631	Visa, MC	requirements, just let us
Elisabeth & Kevin Widrow	C-yes/S-no/P-no/H-yes	know.
	French, English, Spanish,	Bikes, French lessons, pool,
	Portuguese, touch of	gardens, private terraces, en
	Provencal	suite bathrooms, panoramic
	All year	views

Le Mas Perreal is set amidst 17 acres of vineyards and cherry orchard in the heart of Provence. The luxurious room decorations are inspired by the colors of Provence.
✉ elisabeth-kevin@masperreal.com 🌐 www.masperreal.com

ST. LO

Le Haut Quesnay	55 € BB	Continental plus breakfast
Le Dezert	2 rooms, 2 pb	A meal on night of arrival
+33-2-3355-4168	C-yes/S-no/P-ltd/H-no	may be provided
Helen Taylor	English, French	Tea & coffee making
	All year	facilities, hairdryer, A/C,
		views over the meadows,
		ample wardrobe space

Le Haut Quesnay is a beautiful stone house built during the 16th century, set amongst 9 acres of meadows in a secluded place away from the road, it offers a peaceful location with excellent accommodation.
✉ jwallace939@hotmail.com 🌐 www.lehautquesnay.com

ST. SEURIN D'UZET

Blue Sturgeon	95 € BB	Continental plus breakfast
3 rue de la cave	5 rooms, 5 pb	Local caviar, oysters, fresh
+33-5-2674-1718	*Rated*	fish and shell fish
Robert Stansfield	C-ltd/S-no/P-no/H-no	Bar, lounge and dining area
	French, English,	with log burning stove,
	All Seasons	garden, large park with lake
		and a pool backing onto
		sunflowers fields

Unique B&B built in 1740 by the Prince of Chenac. Once a wine store, a small port in "the village of caviar" on the Girond Estuary, 1 hour from Bordeaux. Completely renovated, luxurious chic style with modern interiors and original contemporary paintings.
✉ bluesturgeon@gmail.com 🌐 www.bluesturgeon.com

VILLENNES SUR SEINE

Dormouse House
34 Rue de Medan
+33-1-3975-9573
Lisa Kuhn (Quinn)

120 – 140 € BB
3 rooms, 2 pb
Rated
C-yes/S-no/P-yes/H-no
English, French, Spanish,
some Italian
All year

Cereals, yogurt, breads, fruit,
etc
3 course dinners 25E/13E
under 10's; wine 10–15
Jacuzzi, library, living room,
fireplace, den, winter garden,
room, deck, antiques/art,
WiFi, free calls, bikes, fax,
heated towels (winter),
garden, free coffee/tea

Dormouse House is a luxury B&B in a garden setting. Amenities include a Jacuzzi, fireplace, onsite parking and a view of the Seine Valley. Located in a charming village 23 minutes by direct train to Paris. Please call to confirm reservations.
✉ lisa.dormousehouse@gmail.com ❂ www.dormousehouse.com

Germany

MARKT EINERSHEIM

Old Doctors House Bed & Breakfast
Nuernberger Strasse 5
+49-9326-99983/84
Dr. Wolfram Braun

60 -78 € BB
3 rooms, 3 pb
Rated
C-yes/S-ltd/P-ltd/H-no
German, English
All Seasons

Breakfast buffet
Variety of beverages, free tea
and coffee, cakes
hairdryers, cosmetic mirrors,
toiletries, iron/board, shoe
cleaning and sewing
supplies, books, information
materials, patio, gazebo,
large garden, rental bicycles,
grill

The Old Doctor's House is a lovingly restored property originally built in 1792. Experience the coziness of this historic house with lots of charm and comfort. Feel at home in our spacious, quiet guestrooms which are comfortably furnished with antiques.
✉ travelangel@t-online.de ❂ www.travelangel.de

Ireland

CARLOW

Barrowville Town House
Kilkenny Road
+353-599-143324
Anna & Dermot Smyth

50 – 65 € BB
7 rooms, 7 pb
Visa, MC, AmEx,
Rated, •
C-yes/S-ltd/P-no/H-no
English.
All year

Traditional Breakfast
Several restaurants within
walking distance.
Sitting room, car park,
gardens, direct dial phone,
TV, hairdryer, non-smoking

The Barrowville Town House is a premier quality guesthouse, a three Star Georgian listed property. Antique furnishings throughout, traditional breakfast served in the conservatory overlooking gardens.
✉ barrowvilletownhouse@eircom.net ❂ www.barrowville.com

COUNTY GALWAY

Cashel House Hotel
Cashel
+353-953-1001
McEvilly Family

190 – 390 € BB
32 rooms, 32 pb
Visa, MC, AmEx,
Rated, •
C-yes/S-ltd/P-ltd/H-ltd
English, French, German
All year

Full breakfast
Lunch, dinner, afternoon tea,
snacks, restaurant
Bar service, sitting room,
library, bicycles, tennis
court, horseback riding,
small beach, television,
hairdryers

Cashel House Hotel is an elegant country manor set in a beautiful garden by the sea. Connemara pony breeding & horseback riding on site. Near a huge wilderness touring area. There are 19 rooms & 13 suites with a fine dining restaurant on the premises.
✉ res@cashel-house-hotel.com 🌐 www.cashel-house-hotel.com

GALWAY

Delphi Lodge
Leenane
+353-954-2222
Peter Mantle

200 – 266 € BB
12 rooms, 12 pb
Visa, MC, •
C-no/S-ltd/P-ltd/H-yes
French, English
All year

Full breakfast
Lunch, dinner, afternoon tea
Sitting room, library, salmon
fly fishing, spas nearby,
Peter's amazing wine cellar
featuring 300 wines

If you want to stay in a beautiful and delightful 1830's Country House, in one of the most spectacular settings in Ireland, come stay with us at the Delphi Lodge in Connemara.
✉ stay@delphilodge.ie 🌐 www.delphilodge.ie

INISTIOGE

Cullintra House
The Rower
+353-514-23614
Patricia Cantlon

35 – 55 € BB
6 rooms, 3 pb
C-ltd/S-ltd/P-ltd/H-ltd
English
All year

Full breakfast
Dinner @ 9:00 p.m., € 35–40
extra. Wine Lic.
Fishing, nature walks,
conferences, art
studio/garden room, a cat
lovers paradise

If you like romantic candlelit dinners, this is the perfect place for you. Set on 230 acres, nature walks are a must. The farm is an animal & bird sanctuary & a nature paradise.
✉ info@cullintrahouse.com 🌐 www.cullintrahouse.com

KENMARE

Davitts B&B
Henry St
+353-644-2741
Mary Cremin

40 – 50 € BB
11 rooms, 11 pb
Visa, MC, AmEx, *Rated*
C-yes/S-yes/P-no/H-yes
English
All year

Large buffet & hot breakfast
menu
Full Bar/Restaurant serving
all day
Bar Bistro & Restaurant
downstairs, SAT-TV, direct
dial phones – CPU
compatible, sitting room and
dining room, hairdryers,
parking

Situated on the Ring of Kerry and ideally located for exploring the Beara and Dingle peninsulas. We are situated in the center of the town convenient to all restaurants & shopping.
✉ info@davitts-kenmare.com 🌐 www.davitts-kenmare.com

KILLARNEY

Kathleens Country House
Tralee Rd, County Kerry
+353-643-2810
Kathleen O'Regan-Sheppard

57.50 € and up ¤BB
17 rooms, 17 pb
Visa, MC, AmEx,
Rated, •
C-yes/S-no/P-ltd/H-yes
English
12th April until 12th
October

Full breakfast
Fresh local produce also
superb restaurants nearby
Large bathtubs, high
pressure showers,
orthopedic beds, TV,
hairdryers, telephone, tea &
coffee making facilities.
Massage and beauty
treatments by appointment
nearby.

Traditional hospitality combined with courteous, personal attention are the way of life here in Kathleens. This luxury 4 star residence is a tranquil oasis on 3 acres of beautiful gardens with a private car park. Only one mile to Killarney Town.
📧 info@kathleens.net 🌐 www.kathleens.net

MOUNTRATH

Roundwood House
Laois
+353-578-732120
Frank & Rosemarie Kennan

75 – 85 € BB
10 rooms, 10 pb
Most CC, •
C-yes/S-ltd/P-ltd/H-no
English, Spanish, French
All year except 25
December

Full breakfast
Dinner available
Drawing room, bar service,
library, gardens, croquet,
Boule

Beautiful Palladian villa surrounded by its own woods. A piece of warm & welcoming history. We aim to create a special place where personal service comes naturally and life is taken at a relaxed pace.
📧 roundwood@eircom.net 🌐 www.roundwoodhouse.com

SHANAGARRY

Ballymaloe House
County Cork
+353-214-652531
Mrs. Myrtle Allen, Mrs. Hazle
Allen

220 – 320 € BB
33 rooms, 33 pb
Most CC, *Rated*, •
C-yes/S-no/P-yes/H-yes
English
All year

Full breakfast
Lunch & Dinner served
daily, Children's Tea
Drawing room with small
library, summer swimming
pool, bicycles, croquet lawn,
children's play area, 5 hole
golf course, craft & gift shop

Ballymaloe is a grand country house on a large family farm, east of Cork City, Ireland. Guests enjoy comfortable accommodations and an award winning restaurant in pleasant rural surroundings.
📧 res@ballymaloe.ie 🌐 www.ballymaloe.ie

WESTPORT

The Garden Gates B&B
Rinnaseer, Islandeady
+353-949-023110
Martina Sammon

80 – 130 € BB
4 rooms, 4 pb
Visa, MC
C-yes/S-ltd/P-no/H-yes
English,
All year

Full breakfast
Coffee & tea facilities
Rooms serviced daily,
towels, tea & coffee facilities,
iron/board, Children's cot,
high chair, hair dryers and
TV

Welcome to the Garden Gates, a country bed & breakfast offering tranquil accommodation, positioned in a wonderful location, ideal for exploring the West Coast of Ireland and all its beautiful panoramas and sites.
📧 info@westportgardengates.com 🌐 www.westportgardengates.com

Italy

ASCIANO————————————————————————————

Podere Finerri
Loc. Finerri, 7
+39-0577-704475
Daniela Di Cesare

100 – 140 € EP
11 rooms, 9 pb
C-yes/S-ltd/P-yes/H-ltd
Italian, English
All year

Full Breakfast available for 12
Euros.
Linen/towels, daily cleaning,
laundry, child care, dog
sitting, private dinners and
chef

*Podere Finerri is a 1700's farmhouse with breathtaking views over the Siena hills, totally
surrounded by fields of wheat, vineyards and olive groves. Finerri Olive Grove produces
organic olive oil.*
✉ malayres@yahoo.com ✪ www.thelazyolive.com

ASSISI————————————————————————————

Malvarina B&B
Vie Pieve de Sant 'Appolinare
32
+39-0758-064280
Claudio Fabrizi

52 – 140 € BB
12 rooms, 12 pb
Visa, MC
C-yes/S-no/P-no/H-ltd
Italian, English
All year

Full breakfast
Cooking lessons, wine and
oil tasting.
Cooking classes, hiking,
horseback riding nearby,
swimming pool, fireplace

*The delightful Malvarina Farm with its charming, country-style accommodations, excellent
local cuisine, warm and congenial host family, and ideal location.*
✉ info@malvarina.it ✪ www.malvarina.it

BUONCONVENTO————————————————————————

Podere Salicotto
Loc. Salicotti 73, Strada Prov. le
Pieve a Salti
+39-0577-809087
Silvia Forni

140 – 220 € BB
7 rooms, 7 pb
Visa, MC, •
C-ltd/S-no/P-no/H-no
Italian, English, German
All year

Continental breakfast
In room coffee & tea
Plush linens, tea/coffee &
tisanes, private safe,
Hairdryer, A/C, Heating,
bathrobes, pool towels, daily
cleaning, BBQ, salt water
pool, bicycles, WiFi

*Podere Salicotto features panoramic views of the rolling Tuscan hills, magnificent sunrises
and sunsets, intimate ambience and located near Montalcino and Siena. A warm welcome
to Podere Salicotto, from Silvia & Paolo, its owners and hosts.*
✉ info@poderesalicotto.com ✪ www.poderesalicotto.com

CALCI————————————————————————————

Bellosguardo di Calci B&B
Via Di Pari 4
+39-0509-34101
Signora Lisa Young

65 – 110 € BB
3 rooms, 1 pb
Visa, MC
C-yes/S-no/P-yes/H-no
Italian, English
All year

Full breakfast
Sitting room, terrace, hearth,
good hiking and biking
routes, nearby outdoor pool

*Located outside the town of Calci, at an altitude of 190M, we offer 3 double rooms, all with
panoramic views. Bellosguardo B&B is a 150 year old farmhouse surrounded by 1.4
hectares of terraced olive groves in Monte Pisano.*
✉ lisa@bellosguardo.pi.it ✪ www.bellosguardo.pi.it

CANNOBIO

Hotel Pironi
Via Marconi, #35
+39-0323-70624
Mr. Massimo Albertella

140 – 170 € BB
12 rooms, 12 pb
Visa, MC, AmEx, •
C-ltd/S-ltd/P-no/H-no
Italian, German, French,
English
Open from March to
November

Full breakfast
Mini Bar, Safe Deposit Box,
Hairdryer, Satellite TV,
Private Car Park, Garage,
WiFi connection

This small charming hotel is situated in a 15th century palace, once a Franciscan monastery, in Cannobio, a village on the shores of Lake Maggiore. Stylishly elegant, the rooms all feature antique furniture combined with the modern comforts guests expect.
✉ info@pironihotel.it 🌐 www.pironihotel.it

CASTELFRANCO EMILIA

Villa Gaidello
Via Gaidello 18-20
+39-0599-26806
Paola Giovanna Bini

86 – 126 € BB
8 rooms, 8 pb
Visa, MC, AmEx,
Rated, •
C-yes/S-no/P-no/H-no
Italian, English
From September 1st to
July 31st.

Continental breakfast
3 acres of lovely grounds,
swimming pool – 10km away,
tennis court – 1km away.

Villa Gaidello is a large farm and estate of recently renovated farmhouses dating back to the 1700–1800s, surrounded by lush grounds and trees. Villa Gaidello with its many charming characteristics is an oasis out of time.
✉ info@gaidello.com 🌐 www.gaidello.com

CASTELLINA IN CHIANTI

Tenuta Di Ricavo
Localita Ricavo, 4
+39-0577-740221
Christina Lobrano-Scotoni

185 – 400 € BB
23 rooms, 23 pb
Visa, MC, •
C-yes/S-no/P-no/H-no
English, Italian, German,
French
April 11 – November

Breakfast Buffet
Restaurant open for dinner,
closed Sunday
Bar, sitting room with
fireplace, library, gym, chess
& table games, snooker,
outdoor sitting area, 2 pools,
garden, walking paths,
Internet at reception, WiFi
room

Tenuta di Ricavo is where history, natural beauty & hospitality meet . . . A medieval hamlet in the heart of Chianti offers 23 comfortable rooms & suites with modern amenities. Centrally located, Tuscany's best is in quick & easy reach.
✉ ricavo@ricavo.com 🌐 www.ricavo.com

CASTIGLIONE D'ORCIA

Castello di Ripa d'Orcia
Via della Contea 1/16
+39-0577-897376
The Aluffi Rossi Family

110 – 160 € BB
13 rooms, 13 pb
Visa, MC, •
C-ltd/S-ltd/P-no/H-no
English, French, Italian
All year

Continental breakfast
Dinner – upon reservation
Rustic Tuscan furniture,
pool, terrace, restaurant,
fireplace, wedding chapel,
meeting room, tasting room –
Orcia Wines & Extra Virgin
Olive Oil, bikes on request,
phone

The castle of Ripa d'Orcia dates back to and is set in a 12th Century Medieval Hamlet. Restored to a comfortable country residence bed & breakfast which offers hospitality along with the discovery of its fine wines and Extra Virgin Olive Oil production.
✉ info@castelloripadorcia.com 🌐 www.ripadorcia.it

CETONA ──

La Frateria Di Padre Eligio	240 – 300 € BB	Full breakfast
Convento San Francesco	7 rooms, 7 pb	Lunch and dinner in our
+39-0578-238261	Visa, MC, AmEx	elegant restaurant.
Maria Grazia Daolio	C-yes/S-ltd/P-no/H-no	Lounge, gardens, woods,
	Italian, English, French	restaurant, period antiques,
	All year	privacy, peaceful, authentic
		atmosphere, mystic aura, No
		TV

Padre Eligio's "La Frateria" has been created in one of the most beautiful monuments made by man, the convent of Saint Francis, founded by the Saint in 1212, an example of late middle ages convent life, still intact.
✉ info@lafrateria.it ❂ www.lafrateria.it/

CORTINA D'AMPEZZO ────────────────────────────────

Hotel Menardi	53 – 140 € BB	Continental plus breakfast
Via Majon No. 110	51 rooms, 51 pb	Lunch, Dinner (fee),
+39-0436-2400	Visa, MC, •	Afternoon Tea
The Menardi Family	C-yes/S-ltd/P-no/H-no	Wellness Center, sauna,
	English, German,	steam bath, whirlpool,
	French, Italian	massage, bar, restaurant,
	All year	complimentary wine, sitting
		room, library

At the turn of century it was an ancient family house, an inn with a stable and a bar, a post-house on the route connecting the Habsburg Empire to the Kingdom of Italy.
✉ info@hotelmenardi.it ❂ www.hotelmenardi.it

CORTONA ──

Casa Bellavista B&B	120 – 140 € BB	Sumptuous Buffet Breakfast
Loc. Creti C.S. 40	4 rooms, 4 pb	Traditional Tuscan dinners
+39-0575-610311	Visa, MC, •	may be arranged.
Simonetta Demarchi	C-yes/S-yes/P-yes/H-no	The Sitting Room offers
	Italian and English	comfort to enjoy music, read
	All year	or plan your next day's
		travels. Relax in one of our
		hammocks or enjoy a swim
		in our pool. Free Vespa use
		for guests.

Nestled on a hilltop in the Val di Chiana, amid fields of sunflowers, olive groves and vineyards Casa Bellavista is your Tuscan dream. Experience Tuscan country life while you enjoy views of the Abbazia di Farneta, Montepulciano, Lucignano and Cortona.
✉ info@casabellavista.it ❂ www.casabellavista.it

──

Casa Portagioia	140 – 170 € BB	Continental plus breakfast
Pieve di Chio, 56	7 rooms, 7 pb	Lunch, Dinner (twice a
+39-0575-650154	Most CC, *Rated*, •	week)
Terry & Marcello	C-yes/S-no/P-no/H-no	Bicycles, heated pool,
	Italian, English	library, sitting room, bar
	March to November 5	

Award Winning B&B in Tuscany. Highly rated, boutique hotel and B&B in Tuscany. A small estate situated near the historic town of Cortona. Perfect location for touring the many beautiful towns of Tuscany and Umbria.
✉ lanier@tuscanbreaks.com ❂ www.tuscanbreaks.com

CORTONA

Poggio San't Angelo	99 – 250 € BB	Continental breakfast
Farneta di Cortona, 42	6 rooms, 6 pb	Tuscan dishes and healthy
+39-0575-610365	C-yes/S-yes/P-yes/H-yes	ingredients.
Donato Torresi	Italian, English	Satellite TV, bathroom
	All Season	w/shower, restaurant – fine
		dining, wellness spa with
		various massage offerings

The country house Poggio Sant'Angelo, located near the Abbey of Farneta, one of Tuscany's most charming abbeys, offers its guests a unique chance to experience the atmosphere and the enchantment of an ancient Leopoldine-age country-home.
✉ info@poggiosantangelo.it 🌐 www.poggiosantangelo.it/

FLORENCE

A Teatro B&B	70 – 140 € BB	Continental plus breakfast
Via Verdi 12	6 rooms, 6 pb	Fresh fruit, croissant, yogurt,
+39-5526-38242	Visa, MC, AmEx,	cheese, cereals . . .
Daniela Baldassini	*Rated*, •	Elevators, breakfast lounge,
	C-yes/S-ltd/P-ltd/H-no	luggage room, A/C, parking
	Italian, English	on request, babysitting,
	All year	event booking, TV, mini bar,
		city maps, multilingual staff

A Teatro B&B is a small, friendly, and welcoming B&B situated in the heart of renaissance Florence, Piazza Santa Croce, one of the oldest districts of the city. We are located in a renovated flat, which offers delightful, individually decorated rooms.
✉ info@a-teatro.com 🌐 www.a-teatro.com

Albergo Torre Di	290 – 390 € EP	American breakfast € 25.00
Bellosguardo	16 rooms, 16 pb	Afternoon tea, bar service,
Via Roti Michelozzi, 2	Most CC	simple dinner if req.
+39-5522-98145	C-yes/S-yes/P-yes/H-no	Pool, parking, library, sitting
Giovanni Amerigo Franchetti	Italian, English, French,	room, hot tub, sauna, Jacuzzi
	German, Spanish,	
	Portuguese	
	All year	

The Tower is the guardian of Bellosguardo's landscape of soft hills with olive groves and cypresses. This 14th-century tower and renaissance villa, the Hotel Torre di Bellosguardo offers rich hospitality in a unique atmosphere.
✉ info@torrebellosguardo.com 🌐 www.torrebellosguardo.com

Antica Posta B&B	65 – 99 € BB	Continental breakfast
Viale Belfiore 50	6 rooms, 5 pb	Tuscan cooking classes
+39-0553-245068	Visa, MC, AmEx, •	available on request.
Matteo Pelacani	C-yes/S-ltd/P-ltd/H-ltd	Hair dryer, color TV, mini-
	Italian	bar, air conditioning,
	All year	

The B&B Antica Posta is situated at the first floor of a palace, just in the heart of Florence. Our guests will be able to enjoy this marvelous city in our comfortable and unique Bed & Breakfast.
✉ dante@anticaposta.net 🌐 www.anticaposta.net

B&B Villa La Sosta	94 – 130 € BB	Continental breakfast
via Bolognese #83	5 rooms, 5 pb	We serve healthy breakfasts.
+39-3358-349992 +39-0554-	Visa, MC, •	Billiard room, panoramic
95073	C-yes/S-no/P-no/H-ltd	windowed attic, private
Antonio & Giuseppina Fantoni	Italian, English, Spanish	parking WiFi, Internet, daily
	All year	cleaning, provision of tourist
		information material, TV

A charming and elegant B&B situated in one of Florence's most exclusive residential areas. Only 10 minutes walking distance from the historic city center.
✉ info@villalasosta.com 🌐 www.villalasosta.com

FLORENCE

Casa Rovai
Via Fiesolana 1
+39-3474-852643 +39-0552-469856
Anna Maria Meo

90 – 200 € BB
6 rooms, 6 pb
Visa, MC, AmEx, *Rated*
C-yes/S-no/P-no/H-ltd
Italian, English, French,
German, Spanish,
Portuguese
All year

Buffet Breakfast
Mineral water, tea & coffee,
healthy food
Free Internet corner in
breakfast room, private baths
(inside the room or just
outside), A/C, TV – SAT, free
Internet connection, safe

Renovated in 2005, and tastefully decorated with original 18th and 20th century furniture, the property has been under this family's ownership since the turn of the 1900's. 6 elegant guestrooms with painted ceilings and walls. Only steps from the Uffizi.
✉ info@casarovai.com ✆ www.casarovai.com

Dei Mori
Via Dante Alighieri, 12
+39-0552-11438
Suzanne, Peter and Danny

70 – 120 € BB
5 rooms, 5 pb
Visa, MC, •
C-yes/S-no/P-ltd/H-no
Italian, English, French
All year

Continental plus breakfast
ADSL, WiFi, CD player &
library, concierge service,
flowers, fridge, iron/board,
luggage storage, public
parking, ticket reservation
service wake up calls

The Dei Mori is a lovely 5-room B&B in a 19th century building, offering warm, clean and inviting accommodations with superb hospitality. Friendly and reasonably priced. A wonderful location in the Historical Center of Florence. ✉ deimori@bnb.it ✆ www.deimori.it/

Hotel Casci
Via Cavour 13
+39-0552-11686
Paolo Lombardi

90 -230 € BB
24 rooms, 24 pb
Visa, MC, AmEx, *Rated*
C-yes/S-ltd/P-ltd/H-yes
English, French,
German, Spanish
All year

Buffet style breakfast
Bar/coffee shop in lobby,
Breakfast in Fresco Room
A/C, fridge, direct dial phone,
TV, radio, hairdryer, safe box,
WiFi, Internet in lobby, tour &
car rental desk, concierge res-
ervations, laundry service

Situated in a 15th century palace in central Florence, originally the home and property of the infamous composer, G. Rossini, this small, welcoming hotel, run by the Lombardi Family, is perfect for the individual traveler, families and small groups alike.
✉ info@hotelcasci.com ✆ www.hotelcasci.com

Hotel Morandi Alla Crocetta
Via Laura 50
+39-0552-344747
Paolo Antuono

80 – 220 € EP
10 rooms, 10 pb
Visa, MC, AmEx,
Rated, •
C-yes/S-yes/P-yes/H-no
English, French, Italian,
German
All year

Continental plus breakfast
Tea & Bar Service,
Continental Brkfst 12.00
€/pers
Sitting room, library, garage,
antiques, A/C, WiFi and
Internet access

Following an ancient tradition of hospitality the Hotel Morandi Alla Crocetta offers a quiet comfortable and distinguished atmosphere in the former convent of the Crocetta. It is today a place where one can enjoy a pleasant and relaxed stay in Florence.
✉ welcome@hotelmorandi.it ✆ www.hotelmorandi.it

In Piazza della Signoria
Via dei Magazzini 2
+39-0552-399546
Sonia & Alessandro Pini

220 – 280 € BB
10 rooms, 10 pb
Visa, MC, AmEx
C-yes/S-no/P-no/H-no
Italian, English, German,
French

Full breakfast
Restaurant reservation
service available.
Safe, hairdryer, LCD
television with satellite,
Internet, air conditioning

The In Piazzadella Signoria is a warm and lovely bed and breakfast open to all the friends in the world. Each of our rooms are decorated and designed for your comfort. We are close to many churches and restaurants for your convenience.
✉ info@inpiazzadellasignoria.com ✆ www.inpiazzadellasignoria.it

FLORENCE

Residenza Giulia	79 – 99 € BB	Continental breakfast
Via Porte Nuova 19	5 rooms, 5 pb	TV, fridge bar, ceiling fans,
+39-0553-216646	Visa, MC, AmEx	bus service, taxi service,
David Torrini	C-yes/S-no/P-yes/H-no	elevator, small fee for gym,
	Italian, English	parking, childcare
	All year	

Located only 5 minutes from the Duomo and the central station Santa Maria Novella, Residenza Giulia is in the heart of Florence, convenient to all of its museums and churches, with a sauna, massage treatments and off street parking.
✉ anna@residenzagiulia.com ◑ www.residenzagiulia.com

Residenza La Torricella	100 – 130 € BB	Buffet breakfast
Via Vecchia de Pozzolatico 25	8 rooms, 8 pb	Milk, coffee, tea, home made
+39-0552-321808	Visa, MC, •	cake, ham, eggs . . .
Marialisa Manetti	C-yes/S-ltd/P-yes/H-no	A/C, mini bar, safe, phone,
	Italian, English	hairdryer, SAT-TV, WiFi,
	All year	sitting room, pool, garden,
		bicycles, solarium, bar,
		parking

La Torricella, set in a rural Renaissance dwelling nestled in the hills surrounding the city of Florence, a few minutes away from the Historic Center, is the ideal place for anyone who wishes to enjoy the beauty and serenity of the Tuscan countryside.
✉ info@farmholidaylatorricella.it ◑ www.farmholidaylatorricella.it

Tuscany Farm Holidays	90 – 110 € BB	Continental plus breakfast
Estate Savernano	8 rooms, 8 pb	Chianti Wine, Extra Virgin
50066 Vaggio	Visa, MC	Olive Oil as farmed
+39-0558-656946	C-yes/S-ltd/P-yes/H-no	A/C, SAT-TV, Fridge, Phone,
David Panoni	Italian, English, German,	Safe Box, Covered Parking,
	French	Pool in Garden amongst
	All year	Olive Trees (Towels incl.),
		Wide Terraces, Farm Product
		Tasting

Savernano is at the center of the triangle between three of the most beautiful towns – Florence – Siena – Arezzo. Comfortable suites with private baths. Amazing views of a beautiful panorama—the Tuscan hillsides.
✉ info@agriturismosavernano.com ◑ www.agriturismosavernano.com

Villa Antea	100 – 180 € BB	Large Buffet Breakfast
Via Puccinotti 46	6 rooms, 6 pb	Special meals with prior
+39-0554-84106	Most CC, •	notice
Serena Lenzi	C-yes/S-no/P-yes/H-yes	free WiFi Internet
	Italian, English, French	connection, A/C, LCD TV,
	All Season	mini bar, personal safety box

The charming Villa Antea is an intimate and romantic Relais in the city of Florence. Surrounded by antiques, precious tapestries and 21st centuries amenities, this is a truly unique place to spend a delightful holiday in a friendly and warm atmosphere.
✉ info@villaantea.com ◑ www.villaantea.com

GAIOLE IN CHIANTI

Borgo Argenina B&B	170 – 240 € BB	Buffet breakfast
Gaiole in Chianti (Siena)	12 rooms, 10 pb	Villa rental available
+39-0577-747117	Most CC, *Rated*, •	Hairdryer, telephone,
Elena Nappa	C-yes/S-no/P-no/H-no	stocked mini bar, free private
	English, Italian French	parking, Internet access
	January to November	

Borgo Argenina is in a medieval hamlet that took six years to restore to it's present splendor, in a flower-filled setting. The work was performed by the best artisans in the area. Guests will enjoy the Tuscan traditions & country side.
✉ info@borgoargenina.it ◑ www.borgoargenina.it

GARGAGNAGO

Villa Monteleone	75 – 85 € BB	Continental plus breakfast
via Monteleone 12	3 rooms, 3 pb	Free tours of the cellar and
+39-0457-704974	Visa, MC	guided wine tastings
Lucia D. Raimondi	C-yes/S-ltd/P-no/H-ltd	San Vito Suite has a full bath
	Italian, Spanish, English	& sauna, the Santa Lena
	March to November	Suite has a splendid terrace,
		and just added the San Paolo
		Suite

*Villa Monteleone is set in a 17th century villa surrounded by vineyards and a beautiful park
that has been designated a national monument.*
✉ bedandbreakfast@villamonteleone.com 🌐 www.villamonteleone.com

LEVANTO

Hotel Garden	80 – 130 € BB	Breakfast Buffet
Corso Italia 6	17 rooms, 17 pb	Library, free WiFi, organized
+39-0187-808173	Most CC, •	boat excursion to Cinque
Damiano Cassola	C-yes/S-ltd/P-ltd/H-no	Terre, free private parking (5
	Italian, English, German	minutes walk from hotel)
	All year	

*Quality of service & friendship are the Daneri – Cassola family values and for all our guests
who wish for a pleasant stay in Levanto at the Hotel Garden, an oasis of cordiality.*
✉ info@nuovogarden.com 🌐 www.nuovogarden.com

Hotel Nazionale	100 – 148 € BB	Buffet breakfast
Via Jacopo Da Levanto 20	38 rooms, 38 pb	includes local Ligurian
+39-0187-808102	Most CC, *Rated*, •	focaccia.
Angela Lagomarsino	C-yes/S-ltd/P-yes/H-no	Bar service, garden,
	English, German, French	panoramic roof terrace,
	open from 28.03 to 02.11	sitting room, parking, suites,
		phone, hair dryer, room safe,
		TV, minibar, A/C, WiFi, air
		conditioning, lift

*Friendly family-run hotel, conveniently situated close to town, the beach, train, boats &
"Cinque Terre." The Hotel Nazionale has been a symbol of the resort town of Levanto's
hospitality for more than a century.*
✉ hotel@nazionale.it 🌐 www.nazionale.it

LUCCA

Alla Corte degli Angeli	130 – 200 € BB	Buffet Breakfast
Via delgli Angeli n23	13 rooms, 13 pb	Breakfast included
+39-0583-469204	Visa, MC, *Rated*, •	Mini-Bar, shower or Jacuzzi
Pietro Bonino	C-yes/S-no/P-yes/H-yes	tub, save box, TV, dial direct
	Italian, French, , English,	telephone, A/C, wake up call,
	spanish	iron, bathrobe, iPod, slipper,
	All year	WiFi.

*La Corte Degli Angeli stands cupped within the encircling walls of Lucca, crowned with its
sheltering trees. It is the size of a jewel-box both intimate yet spacious and is full of charm
and fascinating attractions.*
✉ info@allacortedegliangeli.com 🌐 www.allacortedegliangeli.com

Da Elisa alle Sette Arti	45 – 70 € EP	Breakfast available for
Via Elisa, 25	10 rooms, 4 pb	additional cost
+39-0583-494539	Visa, MC, AmEx	Guest kitchen – Bike Rental –
Andrea Mencaroni	C-yes/S-ltd/P-yes/H-no	Free Wireless in the rooms –
	Italian, English	Fax Service – Maps and
	All year	Magazines – Massages – Free
		luggage storage – Call Taxi.

*We provide a relaxing holiday within the walls of Lucca, in harmony with the medieval
spirit of the town. "Da Elisa" offers fine art-deco styled accommodations with a lovely guest
kitchen.*
✉ info@daelisa.com 🌐 www.daelisa.com

LUCCA

Villa Romantica
Via N. Barbantini, 246
+39-0583-496872
Emanuele Favilla

70 -170 € BB
6 rooms, 6 pb
Most CC, *Rated*
C-yes/S-ltd/P-no/H-no
English, French, Italian
All year

Full breakfast
Fridge, Jacuzzi, hairdryer,
satellite TV, direct dial
telephone, pool, Internet
access, gardens, bicycles

Villa Romantica is situated a short two minute walk to the city walls & a five minute walk from the center of Lucca. We offer six guestrooms, with all the modern comforts.
✉ info@villaromantica.it ◑ www.villaromantica.it

MARATEA

Romantik Hotel Villa Cheta Elite
Acquafredda
+39-9738-78134
Stefania Aquadro

136 – 260 € BB
20 rooms, 20 pb
Most CC,
C-yes/S-yes/P-yes/H-yes
German, English, Italian
All year

Full breakfast
Restaurant, bar service
Sitting room, tennis court in
the vicinity, massages, tours,
yoga, sailing

The Romantik Hotel Villa Cheta Elite is a small Art Nouveau villa with a dreamy view of the Mediterranean Sea. Nestled in an exquisite garden, it is an oasis of relaxation.
✉ info@villacheta.it ◑ www.villacheta.it

MERANO

Hotel Castel Fragsburg Relais & Chateaux
Via Fragsburg 3
+39-0473-244071
Alexander Ortner

192 – 700 € MAP
20 rooms, 20 pb
Visa, MC, AmEx,
Rated, •
C-yes/S-no/P-no/H-yes
Italian, German, French,
English
April – November

Full breakfast buffet
à la carte Restaurant for
lunch and dinner
Spa, sauna, heated outdoor
pool, library, smoking
lounge, terrace with
panoramic view, W-Lan
access in the whole hotel,
private park

The old hunting lodge Relais & Chateaux Castel Fragsburg is located in a fantastic position above Merano surrounded by gorgeous nature and spectacular mountains. Enjoy the cuisine and relaxing Spa of the smallest First-Class-Hotel in the Dolomites
✉ info@fragsburg.com ◑ www.fragsburg.com

MONTEBELLUNA

Villa Serena
via Cal di Mezzo, #107
+39-4233-00210
Serena

87 – 90 € BB
22 rooms, 22 pb
Most CC
C-yes/S-no/P-no/H-yes
Italian, English
All Season

Buffet Breakfast
A/C, private bathrooms –
some w/Jacuzzi, mini bar,
TV, ISDN, ADSL, WiFi, all
rooms are non-smoking,
wheelchair accessible rooms
available

The soft profile of the Costa d'Oro hills of Montello, is the natural back drop of Villa Serena: an elegant country mansion, in eighteenth's century style. Surrounded by the green Treviso country, Villa Serena is situated in Montebelluna, a dynamic city.
✉ info@villaserenaonline.com ◑ www.villaserenaonline.com

NAPLES

B&B Il Giardino Segreto
Via Foria 216
+39-0814-44304
Mario Uggiano

45 -120 € BB
3 rooms, 3 pb
C-yes/S-no/P-no/H-no
English, French, Dutch,
Italian
All year

Continental breakfast
Weather permitting breakfast
is served in garden.
Private walled 18th century
garden, fine linens, daily
cleaning, heating, concierge,
tourist guides/map, Internet,
fax, luggage storage, garage

Spacious rooms with balconies on the Royal Botanical Gardens, private baths, continental breakfast, secret garden, tips and tricks to fully enjoy a spectacular city.
✉ mario@ilgiardinosegreto.org ◑ www.ilgiardinosegreto.org

PALERMO

Casa Giuditta Palermo
Via Savona 10, Piazza Kalsa
+39-3282-250788
Salvatore Gallo

78 – 98 € BB
4 rooms, 4 pb
Visa, MC, AmEx,
Rated, •
C-yes/S-yes/P-yes/H-yes
English, Italian, Russian
All year

Italian Breakfast
Coffee and tea maker
A/C, SAT-TV, cradle if
required, personal driver
(upon request),
washer/dryer, dishwasher,
nearby restaurants, bar,
stores & supermarket

Casa Giuditta offers travelers beautiful Air-Con 17th century apartments in the center of the city, near the sea in Sicily, Italy, in the town of Palermo. The fully furnished apartments may be rented by the day or week and can accommodate 1 to 6 people.
✉ casagiuditta@yahoo.com ✆ www.casagiuditta.com

PERUGIA

Le Torri di Bagnara
Strada della Bruna, 8
+39-0755-792001
Countess Zenaide Giulia
Giunta

130 -215 € BB
7 rooms, 7 pb
Visa, MC, AmEx, •
C-yes/S-no/P-no/H-yes
English, French, Italian
February 27 to January 6

Huge Continental plus
breakfast
Delicious & genuine local
cuisine.
1500 acre estate with small
lakes, hunting reserve, farm
livestock, three Medieval
Castles, panoramic pool,
bikes, Botanic Gardens, Farm
Estate, WiFi, Children's
playground

Secluded but at the center of Umbria, experience a close encounter with history and nature. Le Torri di Bagnara is made of Medieval Historic Residences, a luxury Abbey and a Tower residence, each lavishly furnished, in the center of a 1500 acre estate.
✉ info@letorridibagnara.it ✆ www.letorridibagnara.it

PETTENASCO

Hotel Giardinetto
Via Provinciale 1
+39-0323-89118
Ezio & Caterina Primatesta

85 – 150 € BB
59 rooms, 59 pb
Visa, MC, AmEx,
Rated, •
C-yes/S-no/P-yes/H-yes
Italian, English, German,
French
From 1st April to 20th
Ocotber

Continental breakfast
Lunch, dinner, afternoon tea,
restaurant
Sitting room, bicycles,
swimming pool, bar service,
private beach, boat rental,
water ski, landing stage

Giardinetto, known for its renowned cooking has an enchanting restaurant with veranda. Beautifully located directly on the lake front, the Terrace Restaurant offers excellent meals inside or outside by candlelight.
✉ hotelgiardinetto@tin.it ✆ www.lagodortahotels.com

ROME

66 Imperial Inn Deluxe B&B
Via del Viminale 66
+39-0648-25648
Mingardi Anna Rita

70 – 140 € BB
12 rooms, 12 pb
Visa, MC, •
C-yes/S-no/P-no/H-ltd
English, Italian
All year

Full breakfast
Guest fridge in the breakfast
area with water, etc
Shower massage, hairdryer,
A/C, WiFi , mini fridge, safe
deposit box, Cable-TV, daily
cleaning service, towel and
linen change every 3 days,
tax included

66 Imperial Inn DeLuxe B&B offers you the opportunity to stay in the old town center near the Opera Theatre, The Basilica of Santa Maria Maggiore, the Colosseum and the Fori Imperiali. The relais de charmes one of more famous Bed and Breakfast in Rome.
✉ info@66imperialinn.com ✆ www.66imperialinn.com

ROME————————————————————————————————

Alex's B&B Care	64 – 74 € BB	Full Italian Breakfast
Via Germanico, 55	9 rooms, 7 pb	En-suite baths, TV, air
+39-3393-532924	Visa, MC	conditioning, inside
Alessandro Care	C-yes/S-ltd/P-yes/H-no	courtyard and garden
	English, French, Spanish	
	All year	

A completely renovated, early 19th Century Casa Carè furnished with new quality furniture, is centrally located in Rome close to Saint Peter's Basilica.
✉ carealex@yahoo.com ◐ www.abbcare.com

B&B The Center of Rome	75 – 150 € BB	Full breakfast
Via Cola di Rienzo 212	5 rooms, 5 pb	Breakfast served in your
+39-0645-478019	Visa, MC, AmEx	room
Giorgio Primavera	C-yes/S-yes/P-yes/H-yes	Tastefully furnished, bed &
	Italian, English, Spanish,	bath linen, hairdryer, A/C,
	French, German	TV, tea/coffee facilities,
	All year	elevator

The Center of Rome, a very comfortable Bed and Breakfast, is located in via Cola di Rienzo, a street famous for shopping in fashion, near and suited to visit St. Peter's Square and the Vatican City.
✉ giorgioprimavera@fastwebnet.it ◐ www.thecenterofromebeb.it

B&B Evergreen	40 – 120 € BB	Continental plus breakfast
Via Milazzo 23	6 rooms, 6 pb	Central heating & A/C, SAT-
+39-0644-363186	Most CC	TV, direct phone, hairdryer,
Fiori Laura	C-no/S-no/P-no/H-yes	toiletries, safe box, luggage
	Italian, English	storage, elevator, tour
	All year	bookings, 24 hour reception,
		special taxi rate

If you are seeking complete comfort with a complement of services, room designs precise in detail, in the heart of Historical Rome, then the Evergreen, a family managed, meticulously maintained Bed & Breakfast is definitely the lodging for you.
✉ info@evergreenrome.com ◐ www.evergreenrome.com

B&B Maggiore	65 – 130 € BB	Continental breakfast
Piazza Santa Maria Maggiore	7 rooms, 7 pb	Restaurants & cafes nearby
12	Visa, MC	Mini bar, desk, TV, hairdryer,
+39-3897-895869	C-yes/S-no/P-yes/H-no	heating, WiFi, Internet, fax,
Giuliano Foriere	Italian, English	newspapers, tour assistance
	All year	& information

At B&B Maggiore the windows look over the center of Rome and guests are given an unforgettable memory of the ancient city. Ideal for discerning guests who would like more than just a place to sleep. Perfect for families, business travelers & small groups.
✉ bandbmaggiore@hotmail.it ◐ www.bbmaggiore.com

Casa Franci Bed & Breakfast	70 – 120 € BB .	Continental breakfast
Via della Stazione di San	3 rooms, 3 pb	Tea & coffee, cappuccino,
Pietro 22	Visa, MC, •	espresso, cereals, fruit
+39-3934-191484	C-yes/S-ltd/P-no/H-no	TV, DVD, movies, PC for
Francesca	English, Italian, Spanish,	small fee, balcony, wake-up
	French	call, non-smoking rooms, cot,
	All year	coffee maker, mini-bar,
		central heating, hairdryer

If you are looking for a quiet, centrally-located, yet affordable place in Rome's Tourist center, come and enjoy breakfast with a view of St.Peter's Dome from our cozy Bed and Breakfast in Rome, Italy.
✉ hellotomymail-casafranci@yahoo.com ◐ www.casafrancibedandbreakfast.com

ROME—

Giornate Romane B&B
Viale Guglielmo Marconi, 810
+39-0670-11525
Marco Narciso

45 – 120 € BB
3 rooms, 1 pb
Visa
C-yes/S-yes/P-yes/H-no
Italian, English
All Seasons

Full Mediterranean Breakfast
A/C, SAT-TV, in-room safe,
alarm clock, bath amenities,
hairdryer, cooking &
washing facilities, shuttle
service, 24/7 reception

Can you imagine yourself in the timeless realm of the Eternal City? For more than a 1000 years, the capital of the Roman Empire has been the center of the world hidden by a peaceful garden, you can find your private space in history in our themed rooms.
✉ info@giornateromane.it 🌐 www.giornateromane.it

Hotel Modigliani
Via della Purificazione, 42
+39-0642-815226
Marco & Giulia Di Tillo

100 – 200 € BB
24 rooms, 24 pb
Most CC
C-yes/S-no/P-no/H-ltd
English, German,
French, Italian, Spanish
All year

Continental breakfast
Espresso, cappuccino, tea,
chocolate, cakes
Garden, view from top floor
suites, sitting room, library,
art, copier, fax, mini bar, Sat-
TV, safe, A/C, hairdryer

A charming 3 Star hotel in the center of Rome, near The Spanish Steps and Via Veneto, with inner garden, luxury salon, a view from superior rooms on the top floor, including independent apartments, and family rooms.
✉ info@hotelmodigliani.com 🌐 www.hotelmodigliani.com

Hotel Piazza Di Spagna
Via Mario de'Fiori, 61
+39-0667-93061
Elisabetta Giocondi

180 -350 € BB
17 rooms, 17 pb
Visa, MC, AmEx
C-yes/S-ltd/P-no/H-no
English, French, German
All year

Continental plus breakfast
Afternoon tea
Sitting room, cable TV,
hairdryer, fully-stocked mini-
bar, choice of Jacuzzi tub or
Teuco-shower Rooms,
Internet, phone, recently
refurbished, roof garden,
tours

Situated on a charming street between Via Condotti e Via delle Croce, only two minutes walk from the Spanish Steps, the location is ideal for sightseeing, shopping, visiting museums and restaurants.
✉ info@hotelpiazzadispagna.it 🌐 www.hotelpiazzadispagna.it

Hotel Villa Del Parco
110 Via Nomentana
+39-0644-237773
Alessandro Bernardini

165 € BB
29 rooms, 29 pb
Visa, MC, AmEx, •
C-yes/S-yes/P-yes/H-yes
English, French, Spanish
All year

Continental plus breakfast
Snacks, bar service
Mini bar, A/C, Satellite TV,
radio, direct phone, ADSL,
safe, sitting room, parking
facility, garden, small
weddings

Villa del Parco is a lovely late 19th Century Villa in art nouveau style, surrounded by the greenery of a tranquil residential neighborhood, close to the historic center of Rome.
✉ info@hotelvilladelparco.it 🌐 www.hotelvilladelparco.it

Mirko B&B
Viale Spartaco 68
+39-0658-11544
Mirko Bucci

70 – 100 € BB
3 rooms, 2 pb
Visa, MC
C-yes/S-yes/P-yes/H-yes
Italian, English, German
All year

Continental plus breakfast
Assorted mini-bar drinks
available for Euro €1.50
TV, A/C, refrigerator, mini
bar with a variety of drinks,
spacious kitchen, second
floor lift

Our B&B in Rome is situated in the Tuscolana Cinecittà Area, near the public garden "Acquedotti Park" ("Parco degli Acquedotti"), surrounded by greenery and near the ruins of the Ancient Roman Aqueducts.
✉ info@mirkobeb.com 🌐 www.mirkobeb.com

RUSSI

Hotel Villa Roncuzzi
Via Marino Silvestroni 6
+39-0544-534776
Partizia Poggi

160 € BB
22 rooms, 22 pb
Visa, MC, AmEx, •
C-yes/S-no/P-yes/H-yes
Italian, English
All Seasons

Continental breakfast
Room service, A/C, phone,
hair-dryer, TV LCD, SAT &
SKY TV, mini bar, wireless
Internet, parking, free
bicycles, shuttle service
from/to Russi's and Forli'
Railway

Villa Roncuzzi hotel is an early 20th century country residence, recently renovated in absolute observance of original design. Set on splendid grounds with age-old linden and box-trees, a pool, and a spacious courtyard graced by an art nouveau fountain.
✉ info@villaroncuzzi.it ✪ www.villaroncuzzi.it

SARTEANO

Agriturismo La Sovana
via di Chiusi 37
+39-0756-00197
Olivi Giuseppe

134 – 192 € BB
15 rooms, 15 pb
Visa, MC, AmEx,
Rated, •
C-yes/S-ltd/P-no/H-yes
Italian, English
All year

Continental plus breakfast
Snacks & dinner –
Restaurant for guests only
Pool, Jacuzzi, tennis courts,
lake, fishing, football pitch,
bicycles, promenades

La Sovana is a charming group of old stone houses nestled among the green hills of Tuscany. Located in the south of Siena, La Sovana is an unforgettable setting for a romantic holiday.
✉ info@lasovana.com ✪ www.lasovana.com

SICILY

Hotel Villa Schuler
Via Roma, Taormina
+39-0942-23481
Gerhard Schuler

102 – 240 € BB
27 rooms, 27 pb
Most CC, *Rated*
C-yes/S-no/P-no/H-no
Italian, English, German,
French, Spanish, Dutch
All year

Continental plus served a la
carte
Sicilian ice cream specialties
Large subtropical gardens,
palm-terrace pavilion, winter
garden, sun roof, small
library, piano, 24-hr bar &
room service, shuttle to
beaches, WiFi & Internet
access

Family owned Villa Schuler was converted from a Sicilian villa into a hotel in 1905. In recent years the hotel has been extensively refurbished emphasizing its original elegance, charm and atmosphere. Superbly situated high above the Ionian Sea.
✉ info@hotelvillaschuler.com ✪ www.hotelvillaschuler.com/en/

SIENA

Bosco della Spina
via della tinaia 13, Lupompesi
Murlo
+39-0577-814605
Brigida Meoni

150 – 230 € BB
14 rooms, 14 pb
Most CC, •
C-yes/S-yes/P-yes/H-yes
Italian, English, French
All year

Buffet
Restaurant & Pizzeria open
all day, lunch & dinner
Library, bicycles, massages,
pool, wine tasting

This beautifully renovated, ancient medieval farm is located in an historic Italian town. There are 14 apartments, each one decorated with great care, offering a panoramic view of the Tuscany hills.
✉ bsturist@boscodellaspina.com ✪ www.boscodellaspina.com

Tell your hosts Pamela Lanier sent you.

SIRACUSA

Giuggiulena Villa
via Pitagora da Reggio, 35
+39-0931-468142
Sabrina Perasole

100-115 € BB
6 rooms, 6 pb
Most CC, *Rated*, •
C-yes/S-yes/P-ltd/H-yes
Italian, English
2009

Continental breakfast
A rich buffet breakfast
including local specialties.
Air conditioning, heating,
satellite TV, mini-bar and
WiFi. Daily room cleaning
and change of towels. Last
but not least, our beautiful
terrace and access to the sea.

The Giuggiulena Hotel, ranked as a "bed and breakfast" in the tourist literature, is a shelter carved into a cliff overlooking a bay off of the ocean on the east coast of Sicily.
✉ info@giuggiulena.it ✪ www.giuggiulena.it

Palazzo del Sale
Via Sannta Teresa 25
+39-0931-65958
Sabrina Perasole

90 – 120 € BB
7 rooms, 7 pb
C-ltd/S-ltd/P-no/H-no
Italian, English
All year

Continental breakfast
Sat-TV, A/C-heating, mini bar,
fridges, communal cooking
space, Internet, bicycles, sun
terrace

Palazzo del Sale known as the Salt or White Gold building, has high ceilings and walls of stone embedded with details in a unique and pleasant style, gives an authentic feel to the place. All seven rooms furnished with beautiful original appointments.
✉ info@palazzodelsale.it ✪ www.palazzodelsale.it

TAORMINA

Hotel Villa Carlotta
Via Pirandello 81
+39-0942-626058
Andrea & Rosaria Quartucci

130 – 450 € BB
23 rooms, 23 pb
Most CC, *Rated*, •
C-yes/S-no/P-no/H-yes
English, Italian, French,
German
All year

Breakfast Buffet
Fresh pasta, salads, pool
service, wine bar
24 hour room service,
complimentary WiFi Internet
access, lounge bar, pool,
concierge services, valet
parking.

Our property is considered a very special hotel in Taormina featuring exceptional classy accommodations in harmony with local culture.
✉ info@villacarlotta.net ✪ www.hotelvillacarlottataormina.com

Hotel Villa Ducale
Via Leonardo da Vinci, 60
+39-0942-28153
Andrea & Rosaria Quartucci

120 – 450 € BB
17 rooms, 17 pb
Most CC, *Rated*, •
C-yes/S-no/P-no/H-yes
English, French,
German.
All year

Buffet breakfast
Wide choice of fresh pasta
salads & hot snacks
Wine & spirits bar service,
library, sitting room, hot
tubs, spa, free shuttle to
beach & town center, free
Internet access and PC use

Small luxury hotel in a authentic Sicilian villa featuring individually decorated antique style rooms and suites plus a unique view of the Mediterranean sea and volcano Etna.
✉ info@villaducale.com ✪ www.villaducale.com

La Pensione Svizzera
Via L. Pirandello, 26
+39-9422-3790
Pancrazio Vinciguerra

80 – 110 € BB
22 rooms, 22.pb
Visa, MC, AmEx, •
C-yes/S-no/P-yes/H-no
Italian, English, German,
French
All year

Breakfast Buffet
Our bar is open from
10.00a.m. until 1.00a.m.
Child care, bar, WiFi, hair
dryer, safe, 24hr front desk,
attraction & reservation
assistance, SAT-TV, A/C,
garden, laundry service,
balcony, ocean/sea views

The hotel is a perfect example of a small and charming hotel. Located on Via Pirandello, one of the most beautiful panoramic roads of Taormina, it is a short walk to the town center.
✉ info@pensionesvizzera.com ✪ www.pensionesvizzera.com

VENICE

B&B Sandra
Cannaregio 2452
+39-0417-20957
Alessandra Soldi

85 – 130 € BB
2 rooms, 2 pb
Rated
C-yes/S-no/P-no/H-ltd
English, French, Italian
All year

Continental breakfast
Kettle and cups are available
in the room.
Terrace, A/C, very quiet and
romantic.

B&B Sandra stands along-side one of the main canals in the Old City Center, close to the most important sites in Venice.
✉ info@bbalessandra.com 🌐 www.bbalessandra.com

BBvenezia B&B
calle Bainsizza 3 Sant'Elena
+39-0415-200529
Roberto Bacci

50 -130 € BB
3 rooms, 3 pb
C-yes/S-no/P-no/H-no
Italian, English, French,
Spanish
Open All year

Continental breakfast
Snacks, cereals, yogurt,
chocolate, fruits, etc
Terrace roof, garden, TV,
WiFi, A/C, heating, ensuite
bathrooms, complimentary
computer in common area

BBvenezia offers accommodations in a modern, comfortable building located in Sant'Elena, a very peaceful residential district of Venice, just a 20 minute walk away from San Marco Square. Ensuite bathrooms, A/C, WiFi, TV, heating in all rooms.
✉ info@bbvenezia.com 🌐 www.bbvenezia.com

Ca Centopietre
Dorsoduro 1198, Campiello
Centopietre
+39-0412-960838
Carlo Palmisano

80 – 180 € BB
5 rooms, 5 pb
Visa, MC, AmEx,
Rated, •
C-yes/S-no/P-no/H-no
English, French,
German, Italian
All year

Continental Breakfast Buffet
Private bathrooms, two
rooms w/Jacuzzi bath, A/C &
heating control, hairdryer,
safe, phone, Internet, satellite
TV, mini bar, all rooms WiFi
equipped

Ca' Centopietre, a Venetian Residence recently renovated is situated a few steps from the Accademia Bridge and from the Galleria of the Fine Arts, in the exclusive district of Dorsoduro, near St. Mark's Square and near major points of interest.
✉ info@centopietre.net 🌐 www.centopietre-venice.com

Ca' Arco Antico
San Polo 1451
+39-0412-411227
Marco Angelini

80 – 240 € BB   ·
8 rooms, 8 pb
Visa, MC, AmEx,
Rated, •
C-yes/S-no/P-no/H-no
English, Spanish, French,
German
All year

Continental breakfast
Safe deposit box, hairdryer,
alarm clock, mini bar,
refrigerator, WiFi Internet,
TV, A/C, heat

Boasting traditional floors "alla Veneziana" and typical local lead-latticed windows – created by Murano glass masters – the guesthouse offers a complete array of modern services provided in the best guesthouses in Venice.
✉ info@arcoanticovenice.com 🌐 www.arcoanticovenice.com

Casanova ai Tolentini
Fondamenta del Gafaro 3515
+39-3498-782995
Alberto & Monica

70 – 400 € BB
19 rooms, 19 pb
Visa, MC, *Rated*
C-yes/S-no/P-yes/H-no
Italian, English, french,
spanish
All Seasons

Buffet Breakfast
Half board service upon
request
A/C, heating, safe, WiFi,
Internet, flat screen SAT TV,
courtesy kit, hairdryers,
luggage storage, private
baths, laundry service on
request, partner restaurant

The Venice of Your Dreams is welcoming and accessible at the B&B Casanova ai Tolentini, just two minutes from the Piazzale Rome car park, near the direct boat line for San Marco and Rialto.
✉ info@casanovaaitolentini.com 🌐 www.casanovaaitolentini.com/en/index.htm

VENICE

Corte Di Villa Colloredo
via Brusaura 24, San Bruson di
Dolo
+39-3482-102337
Sara Frison

59 – 110 € EP
4 rooms, 4 pb
C-yes/S-no/P-no/H-ltd
Italian, German, French,
English
All year

Breakfast available at 5–10
Euro dependent on menu
Bed linens, towels, fireplace

Just 15 minutes from Venice-Venezia, Italy, The Villa Colloredo offers a melding of both ancient with contemporary with this bed & breakfast accommodation and vacation lodging in a peaceful, architecturally and agriculturally rich countryside atmosphere.
info@villacolloredo.com ◐ www.villacolloredo.com

Hotel Bernardi Semenzato
SS. Apostoli, Cannaregio 4363-
66
+39-0415-227257
Maria Teresa Pepoli

60 – 90 € BB
25 rooms, 18 pb
Most CC, •
C-yes/S-ltd/P-yes/H-no
Italian, English, French,
German Spanish
All year

Continental breakfast
Snacks
Sitting room, hot tub, terrace
on the roof, exchange, A/C,
Sat-TV, in room tea/coffee
stations, free Internet access
WiFi connection

Welcome to the Hotel Bernardi Semenzato, a delightful hotel, situated in the heart of the old city, in a safe and quiet area, close to all major attractions and shopping sites. Completely renovated rooms, some with views, private baths & antiques.
info@hotelbernardi.com ◐ www.hotelbernardi.com

Residenza Cà Dario
Santa Croce 642
+39-0415-242719
Monica & Susanna

80-130 € BB
6 rooms, 2 pb
Visa, MC, AmEx,
Rated, •
C-yes/S-no/P-no/H-no
English Italian
All year

Continental breakfast
Coffee & tea making facilities.
Breakfast basket.
All rooms are air-conditioned
and overlooking the
waterway. Some rooms are
shared bathroom, others
with private bathroom. Cable
TV available only in en-suite
rooms.

Residenza Cà Dario is located in the historical center of Venice in a quiet private courtyard. All rooms are modern, comfortably furnished, non-smoking and air-conditioned. Most rooms have a view over a nearby waterway or on the private courtyard.
info@residenzacadario.it ◐ www.residenzacadario.it

VICO EQUENSE

Astoria Hotel
Corso Filangieri 23, Sorrento
Coast
+39-0818-015700
Domenico Balsamo

55 – 150 € BB
23 rooms, 23 pb
Visa, MC, Disc, •
C-yes/S-no/P-yes/H-no
Italian, English, German,
French, Spanish
All year

Buffet Breakfast
Bar & lounge, sandwiches
and snacks available
Children's Zone, childcare,
24hr front desk, airport P/U,
bar/lounge, bicycle/boat
rental, laundry/valet service,
safe deposit box, A/C,
balconies, bidets, hairdryer,
WiFi

Uniquely situated in the enchanting scenery of the Gulf of Naples, the setting for the Hotel Astoria offering guests, a warm family atmosphere close to the Sea.
info@astoriavico.com ◐ www.astoriavico.com

796   Europe

Netherlands

AMSTERDAM

Amsterdam B&B Barangay
Droogbak 15
+31-62-504-5432
GD Yosalina-Bouman

68 – 148 € BB
4 rooms, 2 pb
Visa, MC, AmEx
C-ltd/S-ltd/P-ltd/H-no
Dutch, German, Filipino,
Visayan, English
All year

Full breakfast
Private bathroom, fridge, TV,
radio-alarm, VHS, DVD, CD,
cell phone on request

Your friendly, tropical hide-away in the center of Amsterdam, just three minutes walk from the Central Station and all attractions are literally just around the corner.
✉ rooms@barangay.nl ◐ www.barangay.nl

B&B Amsterdam
Sloterkade 65-1
+31-20-679-2753
Paul & Karen Galdermans

80 – 120 € BB
3 rooms, 2 pb
C-ltd/S-no/P-no/H-no
English, Dutch, German,
French, Spanish
All year

Cereals & fresh milk
Coffee & tea making facilities
Canal side location. Rates
based on length of stay.

Romantic rooms on a lovely canal opposite the Vondelpark. Convenient location, reasonable prices & recommended by various guide books. Some rooms with private baths. Easygoing hospitality make this a charming place to stay in Amsterdam.
✉ pgaldermans@chello.nl ◐ www.bedandbreakfastamsterdam.net

Hotel Aadam Wilhelmina
Koninginneweg 169
+31-20-662-5467

75 – 125 € BB
24 rooms, 24 pb
Visa, MC, AmEx,
Rated, •
C-yes/S-no/P-no/H-no
Dutch, English
All year

Continental plus breakfast
Cable TV, direct dial phone,
apartment, fully-equipped
kitchen, large rooms

Hotel Wilhelmina is a pleasant and charming, superior hotel that is open all year round and offers attractive room rates, especially during the high-value season from October through March.
✉ bookhotel@euronet.nl ◐ www.hotel-aadam-wilhelmina.nl

Hotel Piet Hein
Vossiusstraat 53
+31-20-662-7205
Mr. C. Breider

120 – 325 € BB
80 rooms, 80 pb
Visa, Most CC, •
C-yes/S-yes/P-no/H-no
Dutch, English, French,
German
All year

Dutch Breakfast Buffet
Bar service
Phone w/laptop connection,
cable TV with in-house
movie system, safe, A/C,
hairdryer, lounge bar,
breakfast room

Welcome to Hotel Piet Hein offering guests a pleasant, nautical atmosphere and located at the Vondelpark in the heart of Amsterdam. Whether you are here to experience the rich culture, nightlife, or shopping, it is an ideal location to appreciate it all.
✉ info@hotelpiethein.nl ◐ www.hotelpiethein.nl/

Kamer 01
Derde Weteringdwarsstraat 44
+31-65-477-6151
Peter & Wolter

190 – 250 € BB
2 rooms, 2 pb
Visa, MC
C-ltd/S-no/P-no/H-no
Dutch, English
All year

Full breakfast
We invite you for a
complimentary pre-dinner
drink
A/C, flat screen TV, DVD
player, in room Mac
computer with Internet
access, I-Tunes with library

In the heart of Amsterdam you will find "Kamer 01" a B&B designed with a philosophy of style and personal service. A beautiful 17th century historic building where guests will come to appreciate the authentic feel of Amsterdam.
✉ kamer01@xs4all.nl ◐ www.kamer01.nl

AMSTERDAM ————————————————————————————————

King Hotel
Leidsekade 85-86 / 1017 PN
+31-20-624-9603

115 – 195 € BB
26 rooms, 26 pb
Most CC
C-yes/S-no/P-no/H-no
Dutch, English
All

Dutch Continental Buffet
Numerous bars, restaurants
and bistros nearby.
LCD TV, phone, safe,
hairdryer, tea/coffee
facilities, Internet available
on request

King Hotel is a classic, intimate hotel, full of atmosphere. Fully renovated in 2007 and transformed into a chic, modern family run hotel. Ideally located in the heart of the city by the side of one of the most picturesque canals in Amsterdam.
✉ booking@x54all.nl 🌐 www.hotel-king.nl

Logement Hanna Penso
Nieuwe Keizersgracht 24 A
+31-20-626-3163
Beatrijs Stemerding

110 € BB
3 rooms, 3 pb
Visa, MC
C-ltd/S-no/P-no/H-no
English, Dutch, German,
French
All year

Guests may make own
breakfast
Ingredients for self serve
included in price
Kitchenette, TV & Internet
connection

Hanna Penso is located in an 18th century canal-side property. Three ground-floor rooms, including a romantic garden house. Close to many major tourist attractions. Very attractive and quiet surroundings.
✉ info@hannapenso.nl 🌐 www.hannapenso.nl

Maes B&B
Herestraat 26hs
+31-20-427-5165
K. B. Harrison

105 – 195 € BB
2 rooms, 2 pb
Visa, MC, AmEx
C-ltd/S-no/P-no/H-no
English, Dutch, Russian,
some French and
German
All year

Continental plus breakfast
Tea & coffee available all
times in guest kitchen
Private baths

In the center of Amsterdam, only minutes away from the museums and within walking distance from all major sights and nightlife spots, yet in a quiet residential area.
✉ maesinfo@xs4all.nl 🌐 www.bedandbreakfastamsterdam.com

Marcel's Creative Exchange
Leidsestraat 87
+31-20-622-9834
Marcel Van Woerkom

140 – 160 € EP
4 rooms, 3 pb
Visa
C-ltd/S-ltd/P-no/H-no
Dutch, English, French,
Italian
All year

TV in most rooms & stereo in
all rooms.

Immaculate rooms with contemporary designer furniture in a beautifully restored home in Amsterdam's City Center, an Official City Landmark, originally built in the 1600's and lovingly restored in the late 1800's.
✉ info@marcelamsterdam.nl 🌐 www.marcelamsterdam.com

Palace Bed & Breakfast Amsterdam
Spuistraat 224
+31-64-260-8847
Rudy Kouwenberg

109 – 149 € BB
2 rooms, 2 pb
C-yes/S-no/P-no/H-no
Dutch, English
All year

Continental breakfast
Coffee & tea facilities, fridge,
toaster, microwave, TV
w/International channels,
DVD, alarm clocks, WiFi, hair
studio, indoor garden

Palace B&B is one of the most convenient and accessible B&Bs in Amsterdam, making it very attractive to visitors of this beautiful city. The building dates back to 1794 and is quite beautiful with all the details.
✉ info@palace-bb.nl 🌐 www.palace-bb.nl

AMSTERDAM ──────────────────────────────────────

Parkview Bed & Breakfast
van Ostadestraat 197
+31-65-568-9769
M. Stam

40 – 195 € EP
2 rooms, 2 pb
C-yes/S-ltd/P-no/H-no
Netherlands, English
All year

Afternoon Tea, coffee, cake
Well equipped kitchen,
laundry room, parking
spaces for extra fee

Nestled in the middle of Amsterdam, at one of the most beautiful places, with a view of the famous Sarphatiepark, we offer one of the nicest rooms for a great stay in Amsterdam, where you can have a great time in a great city.
✉ info@bedandbreakfastparkview.com ◯ www.bedandbreakfastparkview.com

──

Prinsenhuis B&B
Prinsengracht 967
+31-20-521-0610
Brick & Elena Ogden

275 – 285 € BB
3 rooms, 3 pb
Visa, MC
C-yes/S-ltd/P-no/H-no
Netherlands, English,
French, Italian, Spanish,
German, Russian
All year

Fruit jams, cheese, fresh
bread
Ingredients for self serve
included in price.
Shampoo, Conditioner and
Body Wash products; fully-
equipped Italian kitchens
from Valcucine; plasma-TVs
w/DVD, washing mc, ADSL,
Fax/Printer, Rooms stock for
several days

Prinsenhuis is a newly renovated 18th century monument canal house, and home to some of the most beautiful and exclusive apartments in Amsterdam. The location is the famous Prinsengracht, situated in the heart of the old city centre.
✉ info@prinsenhuis.nl ◯ www.prinsenhuis.nl

Norway

ULVIK ──

Uppheim Farm
Ovragardsvegen
+47-5652-6293
Helen Uppheim

900 ¤ NOK BB
3 rooms, 1 pb
Visa, MC
C-no/S-no/P-no/H-ltd
English, Norwegian,
some German
April 1 – September 30

Typical Norwegian Breakfast
Packed lunches can made
available on request.
En-suite bathroom, fully
equipped kitchen, dining area,
private entrance, private
garden, BBQ, TV, WiFi

Uppheim Farm at Ulvik, Norway can offer up to 6 guests a private apartment with a garden situated in a beautiful 18th century Norwegian farmhouse overlooking the spectacular fjord and mountains. ✉ helen@uppheim-farm.com ◯ www.uppheim-farm.com

Poland

KRAKOW ───────────────────────────────────────

Krakow 1st B&B
POD Wawelem
(Straszewskiego St.)
+516-883-6113
Marian and Kristine

79 – 89 $US BB
15 rooms, 15 pb
Visa, MC, AmEx, ●
C-yes/S-ltd/P-no/H-ltd
Polish, English
All year

Continental breakfast
Breakfast is self-served
continental in your room.
High ceiling with fans,
satellite TV/radio, no
smoking, phone w/deposit,

Best location in the city center. A 10 minute walk to Main Square and other city attractions. Next to the Royal Castle Wawel. Friendly and secure enviroment. Clean and comfortable accommodation. You will feel like home or better.
✉ mak42351@aol.com ◯ www.krakowbedandbreakfast.com

Portugal

CASCAIS────────────────────────────────

Casa da Pergola
Avenida de Valbom, N 13
+351-21-484-0040
Patricia Goncalves

92-144 € BB
10 rooms, 10 pb
C-yes/S-ltd/P-no/H-ltd
Portuguese, English and
French
All year

English Breakfast
Wardrobe, central heating,
oil heater, A/C, table Fan,
hair dryer, phone, some
w/private balcony

The Pergola House, which owes it name to the Mediterranean structure of solar protection found in the garden, has preserved its XIXth century mansion features. This and the neighboring house have been in Patricia's family since the early XXth century.
✉ pergolahouse@netc.pt ✪ www.pergolahouse.com

OUREM────────────────────────────────

Casa Alta Royal Lodge
Castelo de Ourem
+351-24-954-3515
Fr. Guilbert Mariani

175 – 215 € BB
2 rooms, 2 pb
●
C-yes/S-yes/P-no/H-ltd
English, Portuguese
All year

Full English Breakfast
Lunch/Dinner: Full €30 or
Light €20, with wine
Fireplaces, transportation,
spiritual services,
garden/roof-top terraces,
tower seating, chapel, library,
pool

Casa Alta Royal Lodge is a former royal lodge located in the Castle of Ourem, 12 minutes by car to the famous Fatima Shrine. Unsurpassed in the region for comfort, decoration, intimacy, attention to detail and service, guests enjoy the best of two worlds.
✉ casa.alta@gmail.com ✪ www.casaaltaroyallodge.com

PORTO────────────────────────────────

Guest House Douro
Rua Fonte Taurina 99-101
+351-22-201-5135
Carmen and Joao

110 – 140 € BB
8 rooms, 8 pb
Most CC
C-ltd/S-no/P-no/H-no
Portugues, English,
Spanish, French,
German
All Seasons

Continental plus breakfast
A/C, safe deposit box, LCD
TV, direct dial phone,
wireless Internet access, Fax,
Copy Service, room service,
wood floors

Nestled in the heart of historical Oporto, set on the city's Ferdinand wall, the Guest House Douro offers a unique, warm, personal experience, the first and only guesthouse on the Riviera waterfront, the city's most fascinating and romantic neighborhood
✉ guesthousedouro@sapo.pt ✪ www.guesthousedouro.com

REDONDO────────────────────────────────

Agua d'Alte
Aldeia da Serra 14
+351-26-698-9170
Victor & Alexandra Fernandes

85 – 180 € BB
10 rooms, 10 pb
Most CC, *Rated*, ●
C-yes/S-yes/P-yes/H-yes
French, Spanish,
Portuguese, understand
Italian
All year

Buffet breakfast
Dinner at request at 25
Euros, drinks extra
Air conditioning, fireplaces,
TV, bicycles, games, minibar,
swimming pool and
amenities from L'Occitane in
every bathroom

At Agua d'Alte you can enjoy the fantastic sky and landscapes, the splendid food and warm reception; here you can "hear the silence," you can "feel" nature, and you can reduce your heart-beats.
✉ herdade@aguadalte.com ✪ www.wonderfulland.com/aguadalte

SINTRA

Casa Miradouro	85 – 135 € BB	Breakfast Buffet
Rua Sotto Mayor, 55	8 rooms, 8 pb	Afternoon snacks &
+351-21-910-7100	Visa, MC, *Rated*, •	beverages, restaurants near
Charlotte Lambregts	C-yes/S-no/P-no/H-no	by
	English, Portuguese,	Sitting room, gardens, TV,
	French, German	library, touring assistance
	Closed 13 Jan 09 – 12 Feb	
	09(remodeling)	

Casa Miradouro has fantastic views towards the ocean and over Sintra up to the Pena Palace and Moorish Castle. Providing comfort and superb hospitality since 1994, it is beautifully situated and within walking distance to the charming town of Sintra.
✉ mail@casa-miradouro.com ✪ www.casa-miradouro.com

Quinta Da Capela	140 – 190 € BB	Full breakfast
Rua Barbosa Bogace	9 rooms, 9 pb	Dinner, tea, snacks, wine
+351-21-929-0170	Visa, MC, AmEx,	Bar service, library, sitting
Arthur Da Silva Pereira	*Rated*, •	room, sauna, swimming
	C-ltd/S-no/P-no/H-ltd	pool, gardens
	English, German,	
	French, Spanish	
	All year	

A 16th century Manor, transformed into one of Europe's most charming and picturesque Inns. Beauty and peace surrounds you, just 30 minutes from Lisbon and steps away from the Atlantic Coast.
✉ quintadacapela@hotmail.com ✪ www.quintadacapela.com

VIANA DO CASTELO

Casa Santa Filomena	50 – 60 € BB	Continental breakfast
Estrada de Cabanas	5 rooms, 4 pb	Beverages & snacks
+351-25-898-1619 +351-22-617-	C-yes/S-yes/P-no/H-no	Sitting room, lounge, Sat-TV,
4161	Portuguese	A/C, bar, gardens, parking
Mary Kendall	All year	

A grand entrance gate beckons you at the Casa Santa Filomena, a solid, stonewalled building, a renovated farmhouse that was built in the 1920s, tucked away into a quiet corner of an already quiet village between the hills and seaside.
✉ soc.com.smiths@mail.telepac.pt

Scotland, U.K.

ARGYLL

Taychreggan Hotel	105 – 262 £ BB	Full breakfast
Kilchrenan, by Taynuilt	18 rooms, 18 pb	Five course table d'hotel
+44-186-683-3211	Visa, MC, AmEx, •	dinner/room service
Fiona Sutherland	C-no/S-no/P-no/H-no	Games room, lounge, loch
	English, French	fishing, bar, free parking
	All year	

Top Scottish country house hotel. Beautifully situated amid the mountains and forests of Argyll on the shores of Loch Awe. Stylish and comfortable accommodations with hospitality including fine dining and a superb wine list.
✉ info@taychregganhotel.co.uk ✪ www.taychregganhotel.co.uk

EDINBURGH

Southside Guest House	120 – 260 £ BB	Full breakfast
8 Newington Rd	8 rooms, 8 pb	Vegetarian and vegan meals
+44-131-668-4422	Visa, MC, AmEx,	also available
Franco & Lynne Galgani	*Rated*, •	Library featuring Edinburgh,
	C-ltd/S-no/P-no/H-no	DVD library, TV/DVD, WiFi,
	Italian, French, English,	direct phones, non-smoking,
	German, Spanish	fireplaces, hairdryer
	All year	

Southside Guest House has eight, elegant en-suite bedrooms providing stylish bed and breakfast accommodations in the center of Edinburgh, close to the Historical Old Town.
✉ info@southsideguesthouse.co.uk ❂ www.southsideguesthouse.co.uk

Spain

BARCELONA

Aparthotel Silver Barcelona	59 – 130 € EP	Continental breakfast extra
Breton de los Herreros, 265	49 rooms, 49 pb	Wide range of restaurants of
+34-93-218-9100	Visa, MC, AmEx,	all types nearby.
Ignasi Junyent	*Rated*, •	Heating, A/C, direct phone,
	C-yes/S-ltd/P-no/H-yes	TV, safe, Café & Bar, private
	Spanish, English, Italian,	garden, room service,
	French	laundry service, parking,
	All year	Internet, 24hr reception,
		some rooms w/balcony

Aparthotel Silver is one of the most highly recommended Barcelona hotels, with 49 well appointed rooms. Guests enjoy a pleasant stay thanks to constant improvements and the fact that we offer a range of hospitality, comforts and services.
✉ reservations@hotelsilver.com ❂ www.hotelsilver.com

Barcelona Las Ramblas	25 – 35 € EP	Breakfast is available and not
Apartments	10 rooms, 10 pb	included in price
Las Ramblas 42	Most CC, *Rated*, •	Living room, private balcony,
+34-69-509-7612	C-yes/S-ltd/P-no/H-no	free use of kitchen, bed
Paul Bosch	English, Svenska	linens & towels, VAT incl.
	All year	

Cozy apartment located in the heart of Eixample, the center of Barcelona near Rambla Catalunya and Passeig de Gracia.
✉ barcelonaguesthouse@yahoo.com

Barcino 147 Bed and	85 – 220 € BB	Continental breakfast
Breakfast	6 rooms, 3 pb	TV, DVD, Ipod audio system,
Gran Via de las Corts 662	Visa, MC, *Rated*, •	laundry, secure building
+34-69-958-6100	C-yes/S-no/P-no/H-no	with porter, use of kitchen,
Ferran	English, Spanish, Catalan	coffee, expresso, tours, hair
	All Year	dryer, iron, wireless Internet,
		air conditioning

Come and enjoy Barcelona in the comfort of our classically stylish bed and breakfast. Located in the heart of the city, our spacious apartment has been beautifully renovated and furnished with local art and antiques..
✉ barcino147@yahoo.com ❂ www.barcino147.com/index.php

BARCELONA

Gothic Garden House
Carrer De Sant Pere Mes alt
+34-93-268-4135
Patricia Miguel

60 – 75 € EP
3 rooms, 0 pb
C-yes/S-no/P-no/H-ltd
Spanish, English, Catalan
All year

Kitchen use, breakfast for €5
available
Shared baths, private
balconies, living room with
TV, self-service refrigerator &
microwave, washer/dryer,
many nearby restaurant
choices, convenient location

The Gothic Garden House is a small accommodation offering guests an opportunity to experience the authentic atmosphere of the historic Gothic Quarter at the center of the city of Barcelona. ✉ gothicgarden@spainbb.com ✪ www.spainbb.com

---

Marina View B&B
Paseo de Colon
+34-60-920-6493
Jose Maria Torruella

113 – 130 € BB
5 rooms, 5 pb
Visa, MC
C-ltd/S-ltd/P-no/H-no
English
All Season

Continental breakfast
Complimentary coffee and
tea
A/C, Satellite TV, mini-bar,
desk with Internet access,
safe box

Welcome to Marina View B&B in Barcelona, Spain. Located on the seafront promenade and flanked by two of the city's major arteries Via Layetana and Las Ramblas. Our elegant residence offers you the privilege of a Mediterranean view.
✉ info@marinaviewbcn.com ✪ www.marinaviewbcn.com

Petit Hotel
C. Laforja 67, 1-2
+34-93-202-3663
Leo & Rosa

66 – 130 € EP
4 rooms, 4 pb
Visa, MC, AmEx, •
C-yes/S-no/P-no/H-no
Spanish, English,
German, French, Italian
All season

Continental breakfast
A continental breakfast for
3,90 Euros per guest.
TV, mini-bar, A/C and
heating, hairdryer, cradle,
laundry service, luggage
storage, safety box, Internet
access, phone, fax, elevator,
parking nearby

Feel at home away from home! Stay at Petit Hotel, the first official B&B in Barcelona. Reserve a comfortable, cozy and well-furnished room located in one of Barcelona's most affluent and secure neighborhoods: Sarriá-St. Gervasi.
✉ info@petit-hotel.net ✪ www.petit-hotel.net

CAZALLA DE LA SIERRA

Las Navezuelas
Caretera A- 432 Km 43,5. Ap.
Correo nº 14
+34-95-488-4764
Luca Cicorella & Marilo
Martin

65 – 150 € BB
32 rooms, 16 pb
C-yes/S-yes/P-yes/H-yes
Spanish, English
All year

Full breakfast
Kitchens, dining rooms
Pool, a variety of stay options
including apartments,
balconies, views

The Cicorella-Tena Family Welcomes you and wishes you a happy stay in Las Navezuelas, a peaceful corner of the Sierra Norte De Sevilla, an area of exceptional ecological richness which is now a biosphere conservation area.
✉ navezuela@arrakis.es ✪ www.lasnavezuelas.com

CUENCA

Posada De San Jose
Julian Romero 4
+34-96-921-1300
Antonio & Jennifer Cortinas

68 – 157 € EP
31 rooms, 22 pb
Most CC, •
C-yes/S-yes/P-yes/H-no
English, French, Spanish
All year

Cold Continental Buffet
Home made tapas and
regional dishes in the
evening
Bar service, sitting room,
terrace & garden, afternoon
coffee, regional tapas, light
suppers available

The Posada de San Jose is situated in the heart of the old historic quarter of Cuenca, in a 17th Century Building. Its old portal invites you to admire the views. Enjoy the advantage of being within a stone's throw of all major monuments, galleries, etc.
✉ info@posadasanjose.com ✪ www.posadasanjose.com

GRANADA

Bed & Breakfast Granada Homestay
Constitucion, 11 – 4º Derecha
+34-95-820-0817
Victor Ovies

49 – 64 € BB
4 rooms, 2 pb
Visa, MC
C-ltd/S-no/P-no/H-ltd
Spanish, French,
Portuguese, Italian,
English
Closed 08/Jan/2009 to
13/Mar/2009

Continental plus breakfast
Help yourself to a cup of tea
in the evenings.
Tea, coffee, WiFi access in
rooms, computer use &
Internet access in the
common area

Whether you are a student of Spanish, a business person, a tourist or just a two day visitor, stay at Victor's Bed & Breakfast in Granada and feel at home. The rooms are quiet, bright, cozy and spacious.
mail@victorovies.net ◯ www.granadahomestay.com

Carmen del Cobertizo
Calle Cobertizo de Santa Inés
6
+34-95-822-7652
Lorena Padilla Torres

145 – 280 € EP
5 rooms, 5 pb
Visa, MC, AmEx, •
C-yes/S-ltd/P-no/H-ltd
Spanish, English, French
All year

Full breakfast 15€
Romantic lunch and dinner
in the garden or salon
Central heating, hairdryer,
toiletries, Internet WiFi,
views of Alhambra, Arabic
style pool, sun beds, garden

Built on ruins of a 16th Century dwelling, the Carmen del Cobertizo, is a typical blend of a garden & orchard setting found in Granada, and remains the oldest Cobertizo in Eastern Andalucia.
info@carmendelcobertizo.com ◯ www.carmendelcobertizo.com

El Numero 8 – Traveler House
Almez 8
+34-95-822-0682
Rafael Kotcherha

50 – 65 € EP
4 rooms, 4 pb
Visa, MC
C-ltd/S-ltd/P-ltd/H-no
Spanish, English
All year

Honesty bar in patio area
Laundry facilities, private
kitchens, rooftop terrace,
honesty bar, self-catered
units

Individual apartments in the historical Albayzin neighborhood of Granada. Great prices for the quality. This area of Granada has narrow winding cobblestone streets and is very peaceful as no cars are allowed.
casaocho@gmail.com ◯ www.elnumero8.com

IZNAJAR

Casa Rural El Olivar
Calle Cierzos y Cabreras 6
+34-95-753-4928
Christian & Kathleen Van
Calster

75 – 85 € BB
5 rooms, 5 pb
Visa, MC
C-yes/S-no/P-no/H-yes
Spanish, Dutch, German,
French, English
All year

Continental plus breakfast
Guest kitchen & barbecue
are at your disposal
Living room, TV, kitchen,
barbecue, swimming pool,
large terrace with sun beds,
equipped playground, ping-
pong, petanque, mini-golf,
terrace under palm trees

Casa Rural El Olivar, a rural paradise amongst Andalusian olive groves, with stunning views over the hills and the quiet blue of the dramatically shaped lake of Iznajar. An ideal base for exploring the attractive cultures of Malaga, Granada, and Cordoba.
info@casaruralelolivar.com ◯ www.casaruralelolivar.com

Tell your hosts Pamela Lanier sent you.

PADUL

Ithaca B&B
Villa Ithaca, C/C1-22 El Puntal
+34-95-877-4008
Jeremy Colwell

50 – 100 € BB	Full breakfast
4 rooms, 4 pb	Dinner by prior
C-yes/S-no/P-no/H-ltd	arrangement, coffee, tea &
English, Spanish, French	goodies
All year	Pool, garden, lounge, library, TV, DVD, film collection, table tennis & table football, Internet access, private baths, sun loungers, balcony

Ithaca B&B in the village of Padul (just 15 minutes from Granada) offers a high standard of accommodation in a very clean, relaxed and informal setting. Sitting at the edge of the Parque Natural de Sierra Nevada, it is surrounded by natural beauty.
✉ info@villaithaca.com ◓ www.villaithaca.com

PINOS DEL VALLE

Casa Aire de Lecrin
Calle Aire No. 2
+34-95-879-3937
Ane-Muriel Bazin

40 – 60 € BB	Continental breakfast
6 rooms, 6 pb	Dinners and picnic baskets
Most CC	by prior arrangement
C-ltd/S-ltd/P-yes/H-yes	Daily room cleaning,
Spanish, French, English	fireplaces, wood stove,
All Seasons	balconies, TV, games, roof terrace, pool

In the heart of the wonderful Lecrin Valley in the picturesque village of Pinos del Valle, we have now opened a rare old house which offers accommodation and breakfast.
✉ contact@casa-aire-de-lecrin.com ◓ www.casa-aire-de-lecrin.com

PRIEGO DE CORDOBA

Casa de Suenos Guesthouse
La Cubertilla 5, Fuente Tojar
+34-95-772-0820
Moira & John Smyuth

46 – 66 € BB	Continental breakfast
3 rooms, 0 pb	English Cooked Breakfast
C-yes/S-no/P-yes/H-no	additional at 4€ pp
English	Each room has en suite
All year	facilities, BBQ, microwave, fridge, coffee & tea facilities, guest lounge, sun terrace, enclosed courtyard, pleasant & relaxing surroundings

See the real Spain! Enjoy the tranquility offered by a traditional Spanish Cortijo situated in the beautiful countryside. Casa de Suenos is surrounded by olive groves and picturesque hillside settlements and Cordoba and Granada are close by.
✉ casa-de-suenos@hotmail.com ◓ www.suenos-es.com

SITGES

Antonio's Guesthouse
Passeig de Vilanova, 58 –
Sitges
+34-93-894-9207
Antonio Esquerra

80 – 120 € BB	Continental breakfast
6 rooms, 6 pb	few minutes walk to many
Visa	restaurants.
C-ltd/S-yes/P-ltd/H-no	Terrace, mini bar, TV, WiFi,
Spanish, English	ceiling fan, heating, safe
All year	deposit box

A Mediterranean house surrounded by a beautiful garden with 6 luxury bedrooms each with a private en-suite bath. An idyllic setting in Sitges, minutes from beaches & nightlife, only 30 minutes from Barcelona. ✉ info@antoniossitges.com ◓ www.antoniossitges.com

La Masia Casanova
Pasaje Casanova 8
+34-93-818-8058
Gene & Simon

100 – 160 € BB	Continental breakfast
6 rooms, 6 pb	Three course dinner in the
Visa, MC	evening is available.
C-no/S-ltd/P-ltd/H-no	Pool, mini-bar, TV, DVD,
Spanish, English	library, WiFi Internet, safe,
All Season	turkish bath, sauna, Jacuzzi

Once a beautiful vineyard and winery, built in 1842 La Masia Casanova is a luxurious guesthouse, spectacularly situated against a mountainside in the middle of the Penedès wine region. The inn radiates the rustic and restful ambience of yesteryear.
✉ info@masiacasanova.com ◓ www.masiacasanova.comindex.html

SIURANA D'EMPORDA

El Moli	70 - 85 € BB	Full breakfast
Mas Moli	6 rooms, 6 pb	Evening meal offered for
+34-97-252-5139	Visa, MC	added cost
Maria Pages	C-ltd/S-no/P-ltd/H-no	Private baths, balconies,
	Spanish, English, French	living area, terrace, dinner
	All Year	served nightly, farm stay,
		spacious with comfortable
		king sized beds

This Catalan B&B is situated in the center of Alt Empordà , in the Girona province, (Spain) set in a rural atmosphere and close to Costa Brava and Cap de Creus. The house is surrounded by a large garden, full of trees, on the banks of the Siurana Brook.
✉ casaelmoli@hotmail.com ✪ www.elmolidesiurana.com

Switzerland

ADELBODEN

Boutique Hotel Beau-Site	100 – 250 € BB	Breakfast Buffet
Fitness & Spa	35 rooms, 35 pb	Two restaurants offering
Dorfstrasse 5	Visa, MC, *Rated*, •	snacks to fine dining.
+41-33-673-2222	C-yes/S-ltd/P-ltd/H-ltd	Bath or shower, WC, most
Markus Luder	German, English,	with balcony, hairdryer, cable TV, radio,
	French, Italian	phone/wake-up/modem,
	All year	mini bar, tea & coffee-maker, sauna/steam bath, fitness studio

Located just 40 minutes from Interlaken. The Hotel Beau-Site in the Bernese Highlands provides a rare opportunity to enjoy life to the fullest. A special hotel in a special setting which is breath taking and beautiful all year round.
✉ info@hotelbeausite.ch ✪ www.hotelbeausite.ch/

INTERLAKEN

Hotel Rugenpark-B&B	53 – 85 € BB	Hearty Swiss breakfast buffet
Interlaken	21 rooms, 10 pb	Free coffee & tea, self-service
Rugenparkstrasse 19	Visa, MC	guest kitchen
+41-33-822-3661	C-yes/S-no/P-yes/H-no	Free Wireless, Internet
Ursula Grossniklaus & Chris	German, French,	Station, booking office for
Ewald	Spanish, English	excursions and adventure
	All year	activities, guest kitchen, English book exchange, lovely garden, free parking, guest laundry

Interlaken Switzerland's top rated B&B accommodation with free Internet, free wireless lan, guest kitchen, laundry facilities, excellent personal service, clean and cozy rooms, lovely garden, a huge breakfast buffet and all at low budget hostel rates.
✉ info@rugenpark.ch ✪ www.rugenpark.ch

INTERLAKEN

Swiss-Inn Apartments	80 – 165 $US EP	Complimentary coffee & tea
General Guisanstrasse 23	9 rooms, 9 pb	in room
+41-33-822-3626	Visa, MC, AmEx	TV, balconies, wireless
J. P. & Veronica Mueller	C-yes/S-yes/P-no/H-no	Internet, laundromat, A/C in
	English	Apartments, fireplace, free
	All year	parking, relaxing garden,
		children's playground

Located in a quiet residential area, owned and operated by the Family Müller-Lohner, just a three minute walk to the train station, and the center of town. The Swiss Inn has been renovated several times and now offers 5 apartments and 4 rooms.
✉ info@swiss-inn.ch ❂ www.swiss-inn.ch/

LES PLEIADES

Les Sapins Hotel Restaurant	80 – 90 $US BB	Continental breakfast
Lally sur Blonay – Route des	16 rooms, 5 pb	Halfboard or a la carte
Monts	Visa, MC, •	dinner or/and lunch
+41-21-943-1395	C-yes/S-no/P-ltd/H-yes	Jacuzzi & sauna, snowshoe
Agnes Stutz	French, English,	rentals, safe, TV, telephone
	German, Spanish	
	All year	

Les Sapins at Lally offers wonderful views from its beautiful setting nestled on mountain-side. High up in the alpine meadowlands above Lake Geneva, this hotel and restaurant offers the best of Swiss hospitality and cuisine at reasonable prices.
✉ info@les-sapins.ch ❂ www.les-sapins.ch

REGENSBERG

Rote Rose	220 – 410 ¤ CHF BB	Continental breakfast
Oberburg 17	8 rooms, 8 pb	Afternoon tea, snacks
+41-44-853-1013	MC, •	Kitchens & sitting rooms, en-
Christina Schaefer	C-ltd/S-no/P-no/H-no	suites, rose gardens, art
	English, German,	gallery, swimming pool
	French, Italian	
	All year	

The Rote Rose is an elegant country inn set in a fully restored ancient building. The spacious, antique-filled suites with superb views and a beautiful rose garden are located in the unspoiled medieval village of Regensberg.
✉ info@rote-rose.com ❂ www.rote-rose.com

RICHTERSWIL

Villa Magnolia Richterswil	130 – 190 ¤ CHF BB	Continental Breakfast Buffet
Chruezweg 18	4 rooms, 4 pb	On advance order: Brunch,
+41-44-784-3964	*Rated*	Five OClock Tea
Lonny Jeszenszky	C-yes/S-no/P-yes/H-no	Living room, small guest
	German, English,	library, tea kitchen, non-
	French, Italian	smoking house, quiet rooms,
	April through November	garden/gazebo, high-speed
	15th	Internet, bathrobes,
		hairdryer, sauna, radio,
		TV/DVD, bicycles

"Your charming home at Lake Zurich." Situated in the green heart of Richterswil, surround-ed by a garden of Mediterranean flair, the "Villa Magnolia" makes you feel as though you have been invited to a gentry mansion. We breed beautiful Great Danes!
✉ villa-magnolia-richterswil@bluewin.ch ❂ villa-magnolia.ch/index

ZURICH

Claridge Hotel Zurich	220 – 450 ¤ CHF EP	Breakfast buffet 29 CHF
Steinwiesstrasse 8-10	31 rooms, 31 pb	Market fresh local &
+41-44-267-8787	Visa, MC, AmEx,	Mediterranean cuisine
Mr. Beat R. Blumer	*Rated*, •	Trendy Lounge & Bar,
	C-yes/S-ltd/P-yes/H-no	terrace, parking, computer
	English, French,	workstation in every room
	German, Spanish, Italian,	with free high-speed Internet,
	Chinese	TV, radio, coffee & tea
	All year, expect	facilities, WLan
	Christmas/New Year	

The Claridge Hotel Zurich is perfectly located right in the city center, yet very quiet, near theaters & the museum of fine art. Within walking distance to lake Zurich and all of the city's main attractions, shopping & business districts, and hospitals
✉ info@claridge.ch ◐ www.claridge.ch

Palais Kraft	330 – 490 ¤ CHF BB	Continental breakfast buffet
Kraftstrasse 33 (at Toblerplatz)	3 rooms, 3 pb	Complimentary veggie
+41-44-388- 8485	Visa, MC, AmEx,	snacks and soft drinks
Martin Frank	*Rated*, •	Coffee maker, express
	C-ltd/S-no/P-ltd/H-yes	checkout, local calls,
	German, English, French	parking, hairdryers,
	All year	laundry/valet services, mini
		bar, room service, safe
		deposit box, sauna, Internet,
		voice mail

Zurich's most prestigious residential building, the Palais Kraft, designed by architect Christoph Schweinfurth, and built 1994–97. The Palais Kraft contains luxurious guestrooms, suites, family apartments, penthouses and offices, most with high ceilings.
✉ welcome@palaiskraft.com ◐ www.palaiskraft.com

VOTE

FOR YOUR CHOICE OF
INN OF THE YEAR

Did you find your stay at a Bed & Breakfast, Inn or Guesthouse listed in this Guide particularly enjoyable? Use the form below, or just drop us a note, and we'll add your vote for the "Inn of the Year." The winning entry will be featured in the next edition of **The Complete Guide to Bed & Breakfasts, Inns and Guesthouses in the U.S., Canada, and Worldwide.**

Please base your decision on:

- Helpfulness of Innkeeper   • Quality of Service
- Cleanliness   • Amenities   • Decor   • Food

Look for the winning Inn in the next Updated & Revised edition of **The Complete Guide to Bed & Breakfasts, Inns and Guesthouses in the U.S., Canada, and Worldwide.**

To the editors of **The Complete Guide to Bed & Breakfasts**:

I cast my vote for "Inn of the Year" for:

Name of Inn _____

Address _____

_____

Phone _____

Reasons _____

_____

I would also like to (please check one)

___ Comment ___ Critique ___ Suggest

Your Name: _____

Address: _____

_____

E-mail: _____

Comment _____

_____

_____

Please send your entries to:
The Complete Guide to Bed & Breakfast Inns
PO Box D
Petaluma, CA 94953
or E-mail: lanier@TravelGuideS.com